Test Booklet No. 3947251

Test Booklet Code CH1

MEDACE

NEET (UG)

SELF ASSESSMENT KIT

Solutions

Topics Covered

Expression of Concentration of Solution

Vapour Pressure, Henry's Law and Raoult's Law

Colligative Properties, Abnormal Molecular Mass and van't Hoff Factor

Important Instructions

- This Booklet Contains – 3 Topic Tests and One Test on Complete Chapter.
- Each question carries 4 marks.
- For each correct response the candidate will get 4 marks and for every incorrect response, 1 mark will be additionally deducted from the total score.
- Use **Blue/Black** point pen only for filling the OMR.
- Rough work is to be done in the space provided for this purpose in the test booklet only.

Name of the Candidate (In Capitals) ______________________

____

Candidate's Signature ______________

Invigilator's Signature ______________

Facsimile signature stamp of center superintendent______________

Do not open this Booklet until you start attempting the Test

Topical Follow Thru

Test 1

Syllabus Different Methods For Expressing the Concentration of Solution : Molarity, Molality, Mole Fraction, Percentage (by Volume and Mass Both).

For deeper insight **Scan the QR Code**

Important Instructions

- The test is of 30 minutes duration and contains 15 multiple choice questions (Four options with a single correct answer).
- Choose the correct option and fill the OMR given on the last page of test accordingly.
- At some instances, you may find more than 1 option may be correct. In such circumstances, you have to judge the most appropriate answer as per the conditions given in the question.

1. What will be the mass percentage of a solvent in the mixture obtained by mixing 300 g of a 25% and 400 g of 40% solution by mass?

(a) 66.43% (b) 55.21%
(c) 72.12% (d) 58.37%

2. Given below are two statements, one is labelled as Assertion (A) and the other is labelled as Reason (R).

Assertion (A) Molarity of a solution in liquid state changes with temperature.

Reason (R) The volume of a solution changes with change in temperature.

In the light of the above statements, choose the correct answer from the options given below.

(a) Both (A) and (R) are true and (R) is the correct explanation of (A).
(b) Both (A) and (R) are true but (R) is not the correct explanation of (A).
(c) (A) is true but (R) is false.
(d) (A) is false but (R) is true.

3. The mole fraction of ethylene glycol ($C_2H_6O_2$) in an aqueous solution containing 40% of $C_2H_6O_2$ by mass is

(a) 0.680 (b) 0.162
(c) 0.932 (d) 0.093

4. With the increase of temperature, the quantity that will change is

(a) molality
(b) weight fraction of solute
(c) fraction of solute present in 1L water
(d) mole fraction

5. A molal solution is one that contains one mole of the solute in

(a) 1000 g of the solvent
(b) 22.4 litre of the solvent
(c) one litre of the solvent
(d) 100 mL of the solution

6. Given below are two statements.

Statement I Mixture of camphor in nitrogen is an example of solid in gaseous solvent.

Statement II In a solution, the component present in largest quantity is called solute.

In the light of the above statements, choose the correct answer from the options given below.

(a) Both Statement I and Statement II are incorrect.
(b) Statement I is correct but Statement II is incorrect.
(c) Statement I is incorrect but Statement II is correct.
(d) Both Statement I and Statement II are correct.

7. Select the correct statements from the following.

(A) Molarity is equal to number of moles of solute dissolved in 1 L solvent.
(B) For sodium carbonate, molarity and normality are equal.
(C) Molality is equal to number of moles of solute dissolved in 1 L of solution.

(D) Ratio of mole fraction of solute and solvent is equal to the ratio of their moles.

(E) Mass by volume percentage is defined as the mass of solute dissolved in 100 mL of the solution.

Choose the correct answer from the options given below.

(a) A, B and D (b) D and E
(c) B, C and D (d) A, D and E

8. If mole fraction of methanol is 0.02 in an aqueous solution and density of solution is 0.994 g/cm^3. Then its molality will be

(a) 1.13 m (b) 11.3 m
(c) 2.26 m (d) 3.47 m

9. In a solution, moles of each *A, B* and *C* are 0.2 moles. Sum of mole fraction is

(a) 0.1 (b) 0.3
(c) 1.0 (d) $\frac{1}{3}$

10. 5 g of CH_3COOH is dissolved in one litre of ethanol and surprisingly there is no reaction between them. If the density of ethanol is 0.789 g/mL, then the molality of resulting solution is

(a) 0.0256 m (b) 0.1056 m
(c) 0.1288 m (d) 0.4476 m

11. Given below are two statements.

Statement I When a solution is saturated, a thermodynamic equilibrium exists between the undissolved solute and dissolved solute.

Statement II Molality gives the more accurate reading than molarity.

In the light of the above statements, choose the correct answer from the options given below.

(a) Both Statement I and Statement II are incorrect.
(b) Statement I is correct but Statement II is incorrect.
(c) Statement I is incorrect but Statement II is correct.
(d) Both Statement I and Statement II are correct.

12. A certain aqueous solution of $FeCl_3$ (formula mass = 162) has a density of 1.1 g/mL and contains 40% $FeCl_3$. Molar concentration of this solution is

(a) 0.02 M (b) 0.16 M
(c) 2.72 M (d) 1.47 M

13. When 2.04 g $BaCl_2$ is dissolved in water to have 10^6 g of solution, concentration of the solution is

(a) 10.4 ppm (b) 0.05 ppm
(c) 0.5 ppm (d) 2.04 ppm

14. A solution weighing '*a*' g has molality '*b*'. The molecular mass of solute, if the mass of solute is '*c*' g, will be

(a) $\frac{c}{b} \times \frac{1000}{(a-c)}$ (b) $\frac{b}{a} \times \frac{1000}{(a-b)}$
(c) $\frac{b}{c} \times \frac{1000}{(a-c)}$ (d) $\frac{c}{a} \times \frac{1000}{(b-a)}$

15. The mole fraction of nitrogen in a mixture containing 70 grams nitrogen, 140 grams of oxygen and 44 grams of carbon dioxide is

(a) 0.361 (b) 0.317
(c) 0.292 (d) 5.021

Response Index

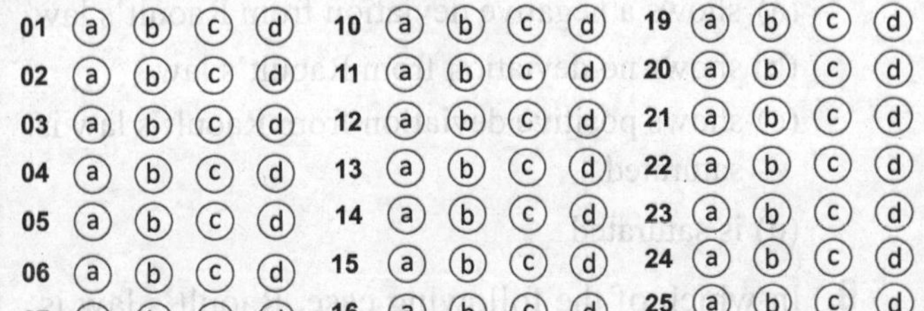

Performance Scanner

> 90% Excellent ! You have mastered these topics. The concepts of these topics are at your fingertips. Move on to the next test and maintain this momentum.

76-90% Very Good ! You have a good command over these topics. Revise these topics again after a few days and enhance your performance.

60-75% Good ! You have a wide scope to learn for these topics. Revise these topics again.

<60 Not Satisfactory! You have a long way ahead of you to master these topics. Revise it thoroughly.

Test 2

Syllabus The Vapour Pressure of Solutions and Raoult's Law-Ideal and Non-Ideal Solutions, Vapour Pressure-Composition Plots For Ideal and Non-Ideal Solutions.

For deeper insight **Scan the QR Code**

Important Instructions

- The test is of 30 minutes duration and contains 15 multiple choice questions (Four options with a single correct answer).
- Choose the correct option and fill the OMR given on the last page of test accordingly.
- At some instances, you may find more than 1 option may be correct. In such circumstances, you have to judge the most appropriate answer as per the conditions given in the question.

1. At room temperature vapour pressure of pure water is 23.8 mm of Hg. Mole fraction of sucrose in its aqueous solution is 0.1, then vapour pressure of solution will be

(a) 23.92 mm Hg (b) 24.21 mm Hg
(c) 21.42 mm Hg (d) 31.44 mm Hg

2. In which case, Raoult's law is used to determine molecular weight?

(a) Dilute solution of electrolyte.
(b) Concentrated solution of electrolyte.
(c) Dilute solution of non-electrolyte.
(d) Concentrated solution of non-electrolyte.

3. A solution was prepared by mixing 30 mL chloroform and 50 mL acetone. The volume of mixture will be

(a) > 80 mL (b) < 80 mL
(c) = 80 mL (d) > 80 L

4. Which of the following liquid pairs shows a positive deviation from Raoult's law?

(a) Water-nitric acid
(b) Benzene-methanol
(c) Water-hydrochloric acid
(d) Acetone-chloroform

5. Which of the following is not correct for ideal solution ?

(a) $\Delta S_{\text{mix}} = 0$
(b) $\Delta H_{\text{mix}} = 0$
(c) It obeys Raoult's law.
(d) $\Delta V_{\text{mix}} = 0$

6. When acetone is added to chloroform, then hydrogen bond is formed between them. These liquids show

(a) positive deviation from Raoult's law
(b) negative deviation from Raoult's law
(c) no deviation from Raoult's law
(d) volume is slightly increased

7. Given below are two statements.

Statement I Solubility of gas in liquid decreases with increasing temperature.
Statement II Solubility of gas in liquid does not depend on pressure.
In the light of the above statements, choose the correct answer from the options given below.

(a) Both Statement I and Statement II are incorrect.
(b) Statement I is correct but Statement II is incorrect.
(c) Statement I is incorrect but Statement II is correct.
(d) Both Statement I and Statement II are correct.

8. An azeotropic solution of two liquids has boiling point lower than either when it

(a) shows a negative deviation from Raoult's law
(b) shows no deviation from Raoult's law
(c) shows positive deviation from Raoult's law is saturated
(d) is saturated

9. In which of the following case, Raoult's law is not applicable?

(a) 1M NaCl (b) 1 M Urea
(c) 1 M Glucose (d) 1 M Sucrose

10. Which of the following statement is correct about Raoult's law obeyed by a binary liquid solution?

(a) The forces of attraction between like molecules are greater than those between unlike molecules.

(b) The forces of attraction between like molecules are smaller than those between unlike molecules.

(c) The force of attractions between like molecules are more or less identical with those between unlike molecules.

(d) The volume occupied by unlike molecules are different.

11. K_H values for carbon dioxide, formaldehyde and vinyl chloride are 1.67, 1.83×10^{-5}, 0.611 kbar respectively. Then the decreasing order of solubility will be

(a) formaldehyde > carbon dioxide > vinyl chloride

(b) carbon dioxide > vinyl chloride > formaldehyde

(c) formaldehyde > vinyl chloride > carbon dioxide

(d) vinyl chloride > carbon dioxide > formaldehyde

12. For which of the following gases, Dalton's law of partial pressure is not applicable?

(a) H_2 and He (b) NH_3 and HCl

(c) N_2 and H_2 (d) N_2 and O_2

13. Two liquids A and B have vapour pressure in the ratio $p_A^\circ : p_B^\circ = 1:4$ at a certain temperature. Suppose that we have an ideal solution of A and B in the mole fraction ratio $A:B = 1:4$, the mole fraction of A in the vapour in equilibrium with the solution at the given temperature is

(a) 0.25

(b) 0.06

(c) 0.50

(d) 0.33

14. An azeotropic mixture of chloroform and diethyl ether possesses boiling point higher than either that of chloroform or diethyl ether. The mixture shows

(a) negative deviation from Raoult's law

(b) positive deviation from Raoult's law

(c) no deviation from ideal behaviour

(d) that the solution is saturated

15. The vapour pressure of pure benzene and toluene are 180 and 100 torr respectively. The mole fraction of toluene in vapour phase in contact with equimolar solution of benzene and toluene is

(a) 0.50

(b) 0.16

(c) 0.27

(d) 0.36

Response Index

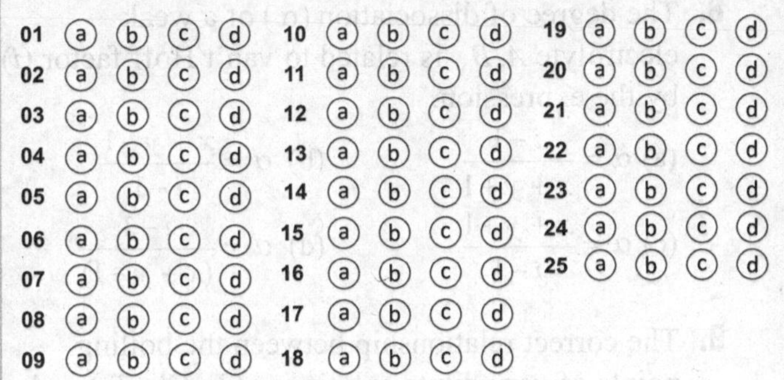

Performance Scanner

> 90% Excellent !	You have mastered these topics. The concepts of these topics are at your fingertips. Move on to the next test and maintain this momentum.
76-90% Very Good !	You have a good command over these topics. Revise these topics again after a few days and enhance your performance.
60-75% Good !	You have a wide scope to learn for these topics. Revise these topics again.
<60 Not Satisfactory!	You have a long way ahead of you to master these topics. Revise it thoroughly.

Test 3

Syllabus Colligative Properties of Dilute Solutions : Relative Lowering of Vapour Pressure, Depression of Freezing Point, Elevation of Boiling Point and Osmotic Pressure, Determination of Molecular Mass Using Colligative Properties, Abnormal Value of Molar Mass, van't Hoff Factor and Its Significance.

For deeper insight **Scan the QR Code**

Important Instructions

- The test is of 30 minutes duration and contains 25 multiple choice questions (Four options with a single correct answer).
- Choose the correct option and fill the OMR given on the last page of test accordingly.
- At some instances, you may find more than 1 option may be correct. In such circumstances, you have to judge the most appropriate answer as per conditions given in the question.

1. The molal freezing point constant for water is 1.86° C/molal. Therefore, the freezing point of 0.1 m NaCl solution in water is expected to be

(a) – 1.86°C (b) – 0.186°C
(c) –0.372°C (d) 3.72°C

2. The molal elevation constant of water =0.52° C/molal. The boiling point of 1.0 molal aqueous KCl solution (assuming complete dissociation of KCl), therefore should be

(a) 100.52°C (b) 101.04°C
(c) 99.48°C (d) 38.96°C

3. Urea solution is 20% by weight of solution. Then, what will be its boiling point. When water boils at 1 atm pressure and 1 molal glucose solution boils at 100.52°C.

(a) 102.17°C (b) 104.21°C
(c) 101.73°C (d) 103.21°C

4. Osmotic pressure of a solution containing 0.1 mole of solute per litre at 273 K is

(a) $(0.1/1) \times 0.082 \times 273$ atm
(b) $0.1 \times 2 \times 0.082 \times 273$ atm
(c) $(1/0.1) \times 0.082 \times 273$ atm
(d) $(0.1/1) \times 273/0.082$ atm

5. Which one of the following salt would have the same value of van't Hoff factor as that of $K_3[Fe(CN)_6]$?

(a) $Al_2(SO_4)_3$ (b) NaCl
(c) Na_2SO_4 (d) $Al(NO_3)_3$

6. In which of the following case, van't Hoff factor is maximum?

(a) 30% ionised $FeCl_3$
(b) 40% ionised K_2SO_4
(c) 20% ionised $SnCl_4$
(d) 50% ionised KCl

7. Which of the following statement is correct for the boiling point of solvent containing a dissolved solid substance ?

(a) Boiling point of the liquid is depressed.
(b) Boiling point of the liquid is elevated.
(c) There is no effect on the boiling point.
(d) The change depends upon the polarity of liquid.

8. The degree of dissociation (α) of a weak electrolyte A_xB_y is related to van't Hoff factor (i) by the expression.

(a) $\alpha = \dfrac{i-1}{x+y+1}$ (b) $\alpha = \dfrac{x+y-1}{i-1}$
(c) $\alpha = \dfrac{x+y+1}{i-1}$ (d) $\alpha = \dfrac{i-1}{(x+y-1)}$

9. The correct relationship between the boiling points of very dilute solutions of $BaCl_2(T_1)$ and KCl (T_2), having the same molarity.

(a) $T_1 = T_2$
(b) $T_1 > T_2$
(c) $T_2 > T_1$
(d) relation between T_1 and T_2 cannot be predicted

10. The freezing point of a solution prepared from 1.25 g of non-electrolyte and 20g of water is –1.1°C. If molar depression constant is 1.86 K kg mol^{-1} then molar mass of the solute will be

(a) 105.7 g/mol (b) 106.7 g/mol
(c) 115.3 g/mol (d) 93.9 g/mol

11. Given below are two statements, one is labelled as Assertion (A) and the other is labelled as Reason (R).

Assertion (A) 1 M glucose and 1 M fructose solution are isotonic solutions.

Reason (R) The given solution have same osmotic pressure.

In the light of the above statements, choose the correct answer from the options given below.

(a) Both (A) and (R) are true and (R) is the correct explanation of (A).
(b) Both (A) and (R) are true but (R) is not the correct explanation of (A).
(c) (A) is true but (R) is false.
(d) (A) is false but (R) is true.

12. A solution of two miscible liquids showing negative deviation from Raoult's law will have

(a) increased vapour pressure, increased boiling point
(b) increased vapour pressure, decreased boiling point
(c) decreased vapour pressure, increased boiling point
(d) decreased vapour pressure, decreased boiling point

13. Which of the following is not a colligative property?

(a) Osmotic pressure
(b) Elevation in boiling point
(c) Vapour pressure
(d) Depression in freezing point

14. Which of the following statement is correct?

(a) Lowering of vapour pressure takes place only in ideal solution.
(b) Lowering of vapour pressure does not depend upon the solvent at a given concentration of solute.
(c) Solvents with higher boiling points have higher vapour pressure.
(d) Relative lowering of vapour pressure does not depend upon the solvent at a given concentration of the solute.

15. For which of the following, van't Hoff factor cannot be greater than unity?

(a) $K_4[Fe(CN)_6]$ (b) $AlCl_3$
(c) NH_2CONH_2 (d) KNO_3

16. What will be the freezing point of an aqueous solute containing 20% by mass of glucose, 10% by mass of urea and 1% by mass of KCl? $K_f(H_2O) = 1.86$ K kg mol^{-1})

(a) –225°C (b) 0°C
(c) – 8.22°C (d) – 4.63°C

17. The order of increasing freezing point of C_2H_5OH, $Ba_3(PO_4)_2$, Na_2SO_4, KCl and Li_3PO_4 in aqueous solution is

(a) $Ba_3(PO_4)_2 < Na_2SO_4 < Li_3PO_4 < C_2H_5OH < KCl$
(b) $Ba_3(PO_4)_2 < C_2H_5OH < Li_3PO_4 < Na_2SO_4 < KCl$
(c) $C_2H_5OH < KCl < Na_2SO_4 < Ba_3(PO_4)_2 < Li_3PO_4$
(d) $Ba_3(PO_4)_2 < Li_3PO_4 < Na_2SO_4 < KCl < C_2H_5OH$

18. Which of the following 0.10 m aqueous solution will have the highest depression in freezing point?

(a) $Al_2(SO_4)_3$
(b) $C_5H_{10}O_5$
(c) KI
(d) $C_{12}H_{22}O_{11}$

19. The decreasing order of osmotic pressures of 50 g glucose (p_1), 50 g urea (p_2) and 50 g sucrose (p_3) at 273 K when dissolved in 250 mL of water separately is

(a) $p_1 > p_2 > p_3$
(b) $p_2 > p_3 > p_1$
(c) $p_2 > p_1 > p_3$
(d) $p_3 > p_2 > p_1$

20. The values of observed and calculated molecular weight of silver nitrate are 92.64 g/mol and 170 g/mol respectively. The degree of dissociation of silver nitrate will be

(a) 60% (b) 83.5%
(c) 46.7% (d) 60.23%

21. Osmotic pressure of 0.1 M aqueous solution of $MgCl_2$ at 300 K is 4.92 atm. What will be the percentage ionisation of the salt?

(a) 50% (b) 60%
(c) 80% (d) 70%

22. The temperature at which 10% aqueous solution (w/V) of glucose will exhibit the osmotic pressure of 16.4 atm is
($R = 0.082\,L\ atm\ mol^{-1}\ K^{-1}$)

(a) 364.4 K (b) 30 K
(c) 394.5 K (d) 90 K

23. Given below are two statements.

Statement I Reverse osmosis is used in the desalination of sea-water.

Statement II Cellulose acetate is permeable to water but impermeable to impurities and ions present in sea water.

In the light of the above statements, choose the correct answer from the options given below.

(a) Both Statement I and Statement II are incorrect.
(b) Statement I is correct but Statement II is incorrect.
(c) Statement I is incorrect but Statement II is correct.
(d) Both Statement I and Statement II are correct.

24. Which of the following statement is correct?

(a) The relative lowering of vapour pressure of a solution is equal to the mole fraction of the solute present in the solution.
(b) Passage of solute molecules towards solution side through semipermeable membrane is osmosis.
(c) The boiling point of a solution is always lower than the solvent.
(d) The boiling point of a liquid is the temperature at which its vapour pressure becomes equal to 260 mm Hg.

25. The molal freezing point constant for water is $1.86°C\ kg\ mol^{-1}$. If 342 g of cane sugar is dissolved in 1000g of water, then what will be the temperature at which the solution will freeze?

(a) −2.43°C (b) 2.43°C
(c) −1.86°C (d) 1.86°C

Response Index

01	a	b	c	d	10	a	b	c	d	19	a	b	c	d
02	a	b	c	d	11	a	b	c	d	20	a	b	c	d
03	a	b	c	d	12	a	b	c	d	21	a	b	c	d
04	a	b	c	d	13	a	b	c	d	22	a	b	c	d
05	a	b	c	d	14	a	b	c	d	23	a	b	c	d
06	a	b	c	d	15	a	b	c	d	24	a	b	c	d
07	a	b	c	d	16	a	b	c	d	25	a	b	c	d
08	a	b	c	d	17	a	b	c	d					
09	a	b	c	d	18	a	b	c	d					

Performance Scanner

> 90% Excellent !	You have mastered these topics. The concepts of these topics are at your fingertips. Move on to the chapter test and maintain this momentum.
76-90% Very Good !	You have a good command over these topics. Revise these topics again after a few days and enhance your performance.
60-75% Good !	You have a wide scope to learn for these topics. Revise these topics again.
<60 Not Satisfactory!	You have a long way ahead of you to master these topics. Revise it thoroughly.

Chapter Break Thru

Syllabus			
Syllabus	Different Methods For Expressing the Concentration of Solution : Molarity, Molality, Mole Fraction, Percentage (by Volume and Mass Both).	The Vapour Pressure of Solutions and Raoult's Law-Ideal and Non-Ideal Solutions, Vapour Pressure-Composition Plots For Ideal and Non-Ideal Solutions.	Colligative Properties of Dilute Solutions : Relative Lowering of Vapour Pressure, Depression of Freezing Point, Elevation of Boiling Point and Osmotic Pressure, Determination of Molecular Mass Using Colligative Properties, Abnormal Value of Molar Mass, van't Hoff Factor and its Significance.

Important Instructions

- The test is of 1 hour duration and contains 50 multiple choice questions (Four options with a single correct answer).
- Choose the correct option and fill the OMR given on the last page of test accordingly.
- At some instances, you may find more than 1 option may be correct. In such circumstances, you have to judge the most appropriate answer as per the conditions given in the question.

1. Which of the following solution will have the highest boiling point ?

(a) 0.1 M $FeCl_3$

(b) 0.1 M $BaCl_2$

(c) 0.1 M NaCl

(d) 0.1 M Urea (NH_2CONH_2)

2. Match List-I with List-II.

	List-I	List-II
A.	Ideal solution	I. K_f
B.	Henry's constant	II. $\Delta S_{mix} > 0$
C.	Ebullioscopic constant	III. K_H
D.	Cryoscopic constant	IV. K_b

Choose the correct answer from the options given below.

(a) A-II, B-III, C-IV, D-I

(b) A-II, B-IV, C-III, D-I

(c) A-I, B-II, C-III, D-IV

(d) A-IV, B-II, C-III, D-I

3. A compound X undergoes complete tetramerisation in a given organic solvent. The van't Hoff factor i is

(a) 4.0 (b) 0.25 (c) 0.125 (d) 2.0

4. Choose the incorrect statement from the following.

(a) Solubility of solid in a liquid increases with increase in temperature for endothermic reaction.

(b) Solubility of gas in liquids increases with increase of pressure.

(c) Solubility of gases in liquids increases with increase of temperature.

(d) Pressure have no significant effect on solubility of solid on liquid.

5. Which one of the following statement is incorrect?

(a) Greater the lowering of vapour pressure, greater is the boiling point of the solution.

(b) Greater the lowering of vapour pressure, greater is the freezing point of the solution.

(c) At the freezing point, the solute and the solvent have same vapour pressure.

(d) The unit of molal depression constant are Km^{-1}.

6. Molality of a sulphuric acid solution having mole fraction of 0.14 is

(a) 4 m (b) 6 m

(c) 9 m (d) 2 m

7. Consider the statement given below regarding the osmotic pressure.

I. Directly proportional to molar concentration of the solution.

II. Inversely proportional to the molecular weight of the solute.

III. Inversely proportional to the temperature.

IV. Directly proportional to the volume of the solute.

V. It is defined as the pressure that just stops the flow of solvent.

Total number of correct statement for osmotic pressure of a solution is ....

(a) 1 (b) 3

(c) 4 (d) 2

8. Two solutions *A* and *B* are separated by a semipermeable membrane. As a result of osmosis the level of solution *A* is found to rise. It implies that

(a) solution *A* is more concentrated than solution *B*.

(b) solution *B* is more concentrated than solution *A*.

(c) the solute molecules of *A* are smaller than those of *B*.

(d) the solute molecules of *B* are smaller than those of *A*.

9. Given below are two statements, one is labelled as Assertion (A) and the other is labelled as Reason (R).

Assertion (A) ΔH_{mixing} and ΔV_{mixing} for non-ideal solution with positive deviation is zero.

Reason (R) $A—B$ interaction is less than that between $A—A$ and $B—B$ components.

In the light of the above statements, choose the correct answer from the options given below.

(a) Both (A) and (R) are true and (R) is the correct explanation of (A).

(b) Both (A) and (R) are true but (R) is not the correct explanation of A.

(c) (A) is true but (R) is false.

(d) (A) is false but (R) is true.

10. When the depression in the freezing point is carried out then equilibrium exist between

(a) liquid solvent and solid solvent

(b) liquid solute and solid solvent

(c) liquid solute and solid solute

(d) liquid solvent and solid solute

11. When 20 g of naphthoic acid ($C_{11}H_8O_2$) is dissolved in 50 g of benzene ($K_f = 1.72$ K kg mol^{-1}), freezing point depression of 2K is observed. The van't Hoff factor (i) is

(a) 0.5 (b) 1

(c) 2 (d) 3

12. Which of the following solutions will have the maximum lowering of vapour pressure at 300 K?

(a) 1 M NaCl

(b) 1 M $BaCl_2$

(c) 1 M Sucrose

(d) 1 M Phenol

13. Dissolving 120 g of urea (molar mass = 60 g mol^{-1}) in 1000 g of water gave a solution of density 1.15 g/mL. The molarity of the solution is

(a) 1.78 M (b) 2.00 M

(c) 2.05 M (d) 2.22 M

14. A 5.2 molal aqueous solution of methyl alcohol CH_3OH is supplied. What is the mole fraction of methyl alcohol in the solution?

(a) 0.190 (b) 0.086

(c) 0.050 (d) 0.100

15. The number of pairs of solution among the following showing positive deviation from Raoult's law.

I. *n*-hexane and *n*-heptane II. Acetone and ethanol

III. Phenol and aniline IV. HNO_3 and H_2O

V. CCl_4 and acetone

(a) 1 (b) 3

(c) 4 (d) 5

16. The molarity of a solution obtained by mixing 750 mL of 0.5 M HCl with 250 mL of 2 M HCl will be

(a) 1.75 M (b) 0.975 M

(c) 0.875 M (d) 1.00 M

17. Molar solubility of He, N_2 and O_2 are plotted against partial pressure of the gas at constant temperature.

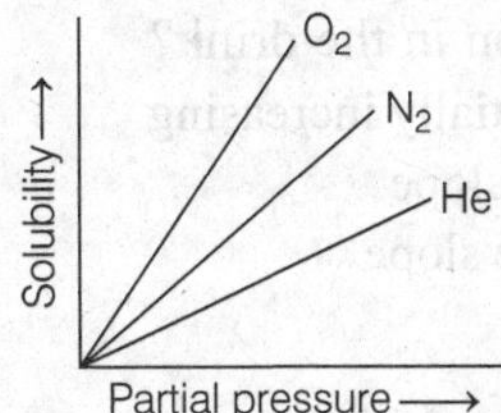

Henry's law constant for these gases will lie in the sequence as

(a) $O_2 > N_2 > He$ (b) $O_2 < N_2 < He$
(c) $O_2 = N_2 = He$ (d) $O_2 > N_2 < He$

18. The vapour pressure of a non-volatile solid in a liquid solution in a closed container depends upon

(a) nature of liquid
(b) surface area of the container
(c) temperature
(d) Both (a) and (b)

19. The density (in g mL^{-1}) of 3.60 M sulphuric acid solution that is 29% H_2SO_4 (Molar mass = 98 g mol^{-1}) by mass will be

(a) 1.45 (b) 1.64 (c) 1.88 (d) 1.22

20. The concentration of a solution obtained by mixing 300 g of 25% solution of NH_4NO_3 with 150 g of a 40% solution of NH_4NO_3 is

(a) 30% (b) 35% (c) 38% (d) 40%

21. The molar fraction of a gas dissolved in a solvent is given by Henry's law. If the Henry's law constant for a gas in water at 298 K is 5.55×10^7 torr and the partial pressure of the gas is 200 torr, then what is the amount of the gas dissolved in 1.0 kg of water?

(a) 2.0×10^{-4} mol (b) 2.5×10^{-5} mol
(c) 3.7×10^{-6} mol (d) 1.2×10^{-3} mol

22. 5 mL of non-volatile solute is mixed with 100 mL of H_2O. The vapour pressure of water above the solution is

(a) equal to the vapour pressure of pure water
(b) equal to the vapour pressure of the solution
(c) less than the vapour pressure of pure water
(d) more than the vapour pressure of pure water

23. Given below are two statements.

Statement I One molar aqueous solution has always higher concentration than one molal.

Statement II The molality of a solution depends upon the density of the solution whereas molarity does not.

In the light of the above statements, choose the correct answer from the options given below.

(a) Both Statement I and Statement II are incorrect.
(b) Statement I is correct but Statement II is incorrect.
(c) Statement I is incorrect but Statement II is correct.
(d) Both Statement I and Statement II are correct.

24. 12 g of urea is dissolved in 1 L of water and 68.4 g of sucrose is dissolved in 1 L of water. The lowering of vapour pressure of first solution is

(a) equal to second solution
(b) triple than second solution
(c) less than second solution
(d) double than that of second solution

25. Which one of the following statement given below concerning properties of solution describe a colligative effect ?

(a) Boiling point of pure water decreases by the addition of ethanol.
(b) Vapour pressure of pure water decrease by the addition of nitric acid.
(c) Vapour pressure of pure benzene decrease on addition of naphthalene.
(d) Boiling point of pure benzene increasing by the addition of toluene.

26. The phase diagram for the pure solvent (solid lines), and the solution (non-stable solute dashed lines) are recorded below. The quantity indicated by L in the figure is

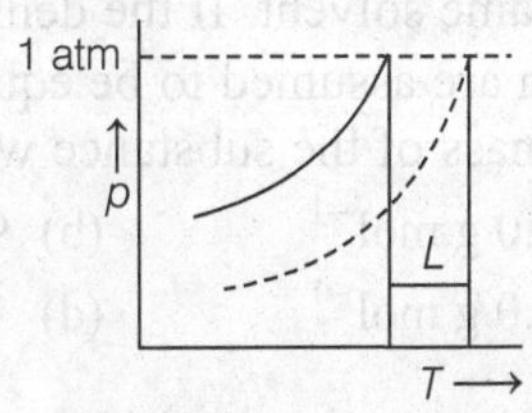

(a) Δp (b) ΔT_f
(c) $K_f m$ (d) $K_b m$

27. Given below are two statements.

Statement I 0.1 M solution of glucose has higher depression in freezing point than 0.1 M solution of urea.

Statement II Molar mass of glucose is greater than that of urea.

In the light of the above statements, choose the correct answer from the options given below.

(a) Both Statement I and Statement II are incorrect.
(b) Statement I is correct but Statement II is incorrect.
(c) Statement I is incorrect but Statement II is correct.
(d) Both Statement I and Statement II are correct.

28. Which of the following azeotropic solution has the boiling point less than boiling points of the constituents *A* and *B*?

(a) $CHCl_3$ and CH_3COCH_3
(b) CS_2 and CH_3COCH_3
(c) CH_3CH_2OH and CH_3COCH_3
(d) CH_3CHO and CS_2

29. An aqueous solution is 1.0 molal in KI. What change will cause the vapour pressure of the solution to increase?

(a) Addition of water
(b) Addition of NaCl
(c) Addition of Na_2SO_4
(d) Addition of 1.00 molal KI

30. At 25°C, the total pressure of an ideal solution obtained by mixing 3 moles of *A* and 2 moles of *B* is 184 torr. What is the vapour pressure (in torr) of pure *B* at the same temperature? (Vapour pressure of pure *A*, at 25°C, is 200 torr)

(a) 180 (b) 160
(c) 16 (d) 100

31. A 5.25% solution of a substance is isotonic with 1.5% solution of urea (molar mass = 60 g mol^{-1}) in the same solvent. If the densities of both the solution are assumed to be equal to 1.0 g cm^{-3} molar mass of the substance will be

(a) 210.0 g mol^{-1} (b) 90.0 g mol^{-1}
(c) 115.0 g mol^{-1} (d) 105.0 g mol^{-1}

32. When CO_2 is introduced into aerated drinks and sealed, then what will be the nature of the graph between partial pressure of CO_2 and its concentration in the drink?

(a) Exponentially increasing
(b) Positive slope
(c) Negative slope
(d) Constant

33. An aqueous solution freezes at −0.186°C ($K_f = 1.86$ K kg mol^{-1}, $K_b = 0.512$ K kg mol^{-1}) what is the elevation in boiling point?

(a) 0.186 K
(b) 0.512 K
(c) 0.86 K
(d) 0.0512 K

34. If the degree of dissociation of aqueous solution of a weak monobasic acid is determined to be 0.3, then the observed freezing point will be what percentage higher than the expected/theoretical freezing point?

(a) 30% (b) 40%
(c) 60% (d) 50%

35. In countries near to polar region, the roads are sprinkled with $CaCl_2$. This is

(a) to minimize the snow formation
(b) to minimize pollution
(c) to minimize the accumulation of dust on the road
(d) to minimize wear and tear of the roads

36. Which of the following graph represents correctly about the changes in thermodynamic parameters during the formation of 1 mole of an ideal binary solution?

(a) 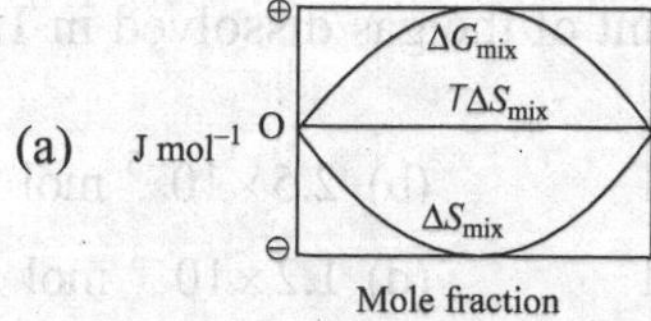

(b) 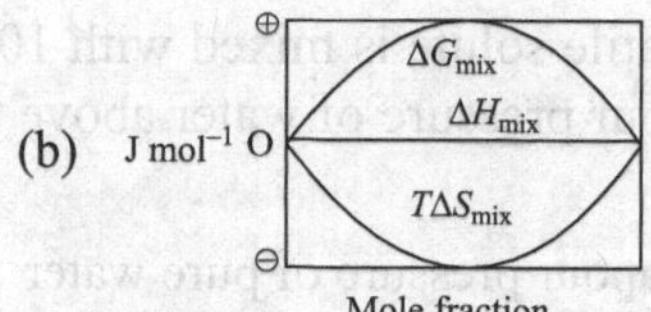

(c) 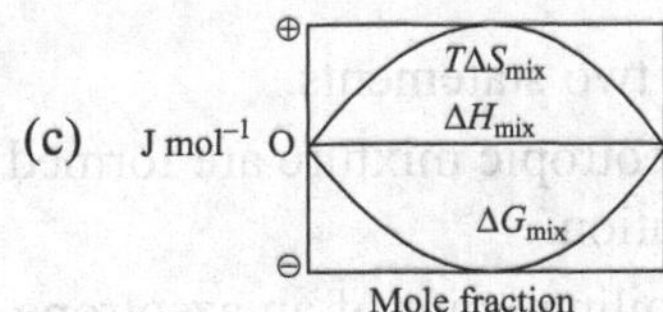

(d) 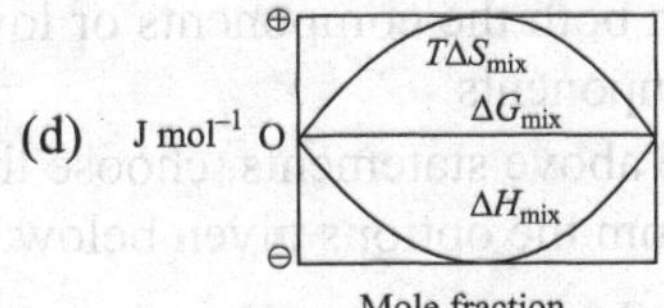

37. Which of the following solution will have the highest boiling point?

(a) 10% solution of glucose in water.

(b) 10% solution of sucrose in water.

(c) 10% solution of sodium chloride in water.

(d) 10% solution of calcium chloride in water.

38. What is the freezing point of a solution containing 8.1 g HBr in 100 g water, assuming the acid to be 90% ionised (K_f for water $= 1.86\,\text{K kg mol}^{-1}$) ?

(a) 0.85°C (b) −3.53°C

(c) 0°C (d) −0.35°C

39. If osmotic pressure of 1 M urea is π, then what will be the osmotic pressure for 0.1 M NaCl?

(a) π (b) $0.1\,\pi$ (c) 2π (d) $0.2\,\pi$

40. According to William Henry's, law, the solubility of a gas in liquid depends on the pressure of the gas. If '*m*' is the molality of the gas and '*p*' is its pressure, then which of the following plot is in accordance with the law.

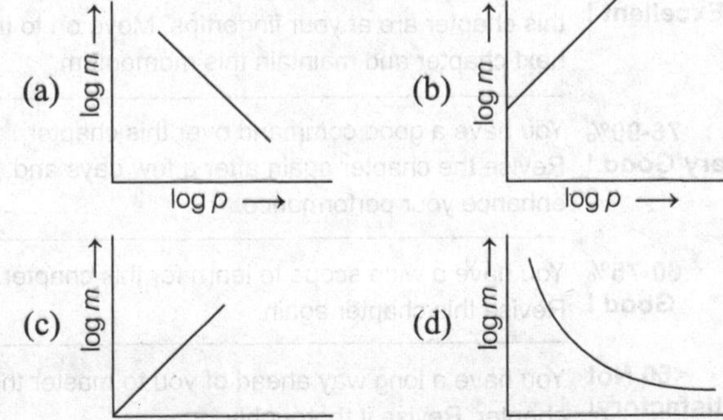

41. Phenol dimerises in benzene having van't Hoff factor 0.54. What is the degree of association?

(a) 0.46 (b) 0.27

(c) 0.54 (d) 0.92

42. Four solutions of K_2SO_4 with the concentration 0.1 m, 0.01 m, 0.001 m and 0.0001 m are available. The maximum value of van't Hoff factor, *i* corresponds to

(a) 0.0001 m solution

(b) 0.001 m solution

(c) 0.01 m solution

(d) 0.1 m solution

43. According to Henry's law, the partial pressure of gas (p_{gas}) is directly proportional to mole fraction of gas in liquid solution, $p_{gas} = K_H x_{gas}$, where K_H is Henry's constant. Which of the following are correct?

I. K_H is characteristic constant for a given gas solvent system at given temperature.

II. Higher is the value of K_H, lower is solubility of gas for a given partial pressure of gas.

III. K_H has temperature dependence.

IV. K_H decreases with increase of temperature.

V. K_H increases with temperature.

Choose the most appropriate answer from the options given below.

(a) I, II and V (b) II, III, IV and V

(c) I, II, III and V (d) I, III, IV and V

44. The vapour pressure curves of the same solute in the same solvent are shown below. The curves do not intersect with each other.

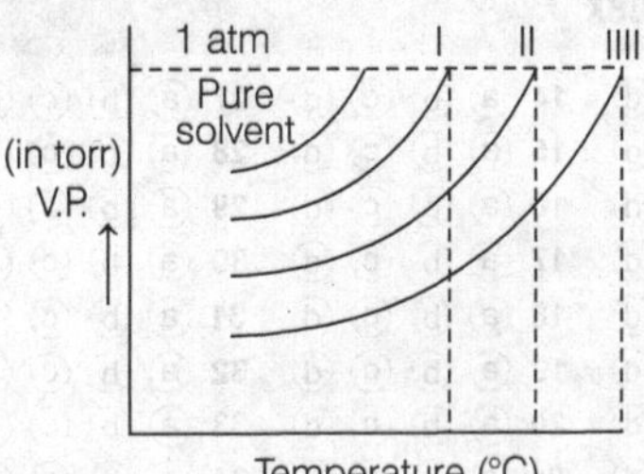

The concentration of solution are in order of

(a) I < II < III (b) I = II = III

(c) I > II > III (d) I > III > II

45. Which of the following statements is incorrect ?

I. The solution which show a large positive deviation from Raoult's law will form minimum boiling azeotropes at specific compositions.

II. Azeotropic mixture are binary mixture having same composition in liquid and vapour phase.

III. The solutions which show a large negative deviation from Raoult's law form a maximum boiling azeotropes.

IV. Chloroform and methyl acetate show positive deviation from Raoult's law.

V. A mixture of water and hydrochloric acid forms a solution with negative deviation from Raoult's law.

Choose the most appropriate answer from the options given below.

(a) I and III (b) Only IV
(c) II and IV (d) III and V

46. A molal solution of sodium chloride has a density of 1.21 g mL^{-1}. The molarity of this solution is

(a) 4.153 M (b) 1.143 M
(c) 2.950 M (d) 3.152 M

47. Heptane and octane form an ideal solution. At 313 K, the vapour pressure of the two liquids are 105.0 kPa and 46.0 kPa respectively. What will be the vapour pressure of the mixture of 25 g of heptane and 35 g of octane?

(a) 76.55 kPa (b) 72.32 kPa
(c) 69.5 kPa (d) 80.5 kPa

48. Given below are two statements.

Statement I Azeotropic mixture are formed only by non-ideal solution.

Statement II Boiling point of an azeotrope is either higher than both the components or lower than both the components.

In the light of the above statements, choose the correct answer from the options given below.

(a) Both Statement I and Statement II are incorrect.
(b) Statement I is correct but Statement II is incorrect.
(c) Statement I is incorrect but Statement II is correct.
(d) Both Statement I and Statement II are correct.

49. Which of the following has minimum osmotic pressure?

(a) 200 mL of 2M NaCl solution.
(b) 200 mL of 1M glucose solution.
(c) 200 mL of 2M urea solution.
(d) All have same osmotic pressure.

50. van't Hoff factor of aqueous solution of X, Y and Z are 2.8, 1.8 and 3.5 respectively, which of the following match is correct?

(a) Boiling point of solution $\Rightarrow X < Y < Z$
(b) Freezing point of solution $\Rightarrow Z < X < Y$
(c) Osmotic pressure $\Rightarrow X = Y = Z$
(d) Vapour pressure of solution $\Rightarrow Y < X < Z$

Response Index

01 ⓐ ⓑ ⓒ ⓓ	14 ⓐ ⓑ ⓒ ⓓ	27 ⓐ ⓑ ⓒ ⓓ	40 ⓐ ⓑ ⓒ ⓓ
02 ⓐ ⓑ ⓒ ⓓ	15 ⓐ ⓑ ⓒ ⓓ	28 ⓐ ⓑ ⓒ ⓓ	41 ⓐ ⓑ ⓒ ⓓ
03 ⓐ ⓑ ⓒ ⓓ	16 ⓐ ⓑ ⓒ ⓓ	29 ⓐ ⓑ ⓒ ⓓ	42 ⓐ ⓑ ⓒ ⓓ
04 ⓐ ⓑ ⓒ ⓓ	17 ⓐ ⓑ ⓒ ⓓ	30 ⓐ ⓑ ⓒ ⓓ	43 ⓐ ⓑ ⓒ ⓓ
05 ⓐ ⓑ ⓒ ⓓ	18 ⓐ ⓑ ⓒ ⓓ	31 ⓐ ⓑ ⓒ ⓓ	44 ⓐ ⓑ ⓒ ⓓ
06 ⓐ ⓑ ⓒ ⓓ	19 ⓐ ⓑ ⓒ ⓓ	32 ⓐ ⓑ ⓒ ⓓ	45 ⓐ ⓑ ⓒ ⓓ
07 ⓐ ⓑ ⓒ ⓓ	20 ⓐ ⓑ ⓒ ⓓ	33 ⓐ ⓑ ⓒ ⓓ	46 ⓐ ⓑ ⓒ ⓓ
08 ⓐ ⓑ ⓒ ⓓ	21 ⓐ ⓑ ⓒ ⓓ	34 ⓐ ⓑ ⓒ ⓓ	47 ⓐ ⓑ ⓒ ⓓ
09 ⓐ ⓑ ⓒ ⓓ	22 ⓐ ⓑ ⓒ ⓓ	35 ⓐ ⓑ ⓒ ⓓ	48 ⓐ ⓑ ⓒ ⓓ
10 ⓐ ⓑ ⓒ ⓓ	23 ⓐ ⓑ ⓒ ⓓ	36 ⓐ ⓑ ⓒ ⓓ	49 ⓐ ⓑ ⓒ ⓓ
11 ⓐ ⓑ ⓒ ⓓ	24 ⓐ ⓑ ⓒ ⓓ	37 ⓐ ⓑ ⓒ ⓓ	50 ⓐ ⓑ ⓒ ⓓ
12 ⓐ ⓑ ⓒ ⓓ	25 ⓐ ⓑ ⓒ ⓓ	38 ⓐ ⓑ ⓒ ⓓ	
13 ⓐ ⓑ ⓒ ⓓ	26 ⓐ ⓑ ⓒ ⓓ	39 ⓐ ⓑ ⓒ ⓓ	

Performance Scanner

> 90% Excellent !	You have mastered this chapter. The concepts of this chapter are at your fingertips. Move on to the next chapter and maintain this momentum.
76-90% Very Good !	You have a good command over this chapter. Revise the chapter again after a few days and enhance your performance.
60-75% Good !	You have a wide scope to learn for this chapter. Revise this chapter again.
<60 Not Satisfactory!	You have a long way ahead of you to master this chapter. Revise it thoroughly.

Scan for Online Chapter Test

Scan for Online Unit Test

Space for Rough Work

Space for Rough Work

Test Booklet No. **3947252**

Test Booklet Code **CH2**

MEDACE

NEET (UG)

SELF ASSESSMENT KIT

Electrochemistry

Topics Covered

Electrochemical Cells and Nernst Equation

Conductance and Electrolysis

Batteries and Fuel Cells

Important Instructions

- This Booklet Contains – 3 Topic Tests and One Test on Complete Chapter.
- Each question carries 4 marks.
- For each correct response the candidate will get 4 marks and for every incorrect response, 1 mark will be additionally deducted from the total score.
- Use **Blue/Black** point pen only for filling the OMR.
- Rough work is to be done in the space provided for this purpose in the test booklet only.

Name of the Candidate (In Capitals)

____

____

Candidate's Signature ______________

Invigilator's Signature ______________

Facsimile signature stamp of center superintendent______________

Do not open this Booklet until you start attempting the Test

Topical Follow Thru

Test 1

Syllabus Electrochemical Cell, Electrolytic and Galvanic Cells, Different Types of Electrodes, Electrode Potentials Including Standard Electrode Potential, Half-Cell and Cell Reactions, E.M.F. of a Galvanic Cell, Nernst Equations and its Applications, Cell Potential and Gibb's Free Energy Change.

For deeper insight **Scan the QR Code**

Important Instructions

- The test is of 30 minutes duration and contains 15 multiple choice questions (Four options with a single correct answer).
- Choose the correct option and fill the OMR given on the last page of test accordingly.
- At some instances, you may find more than 1 option may be correct. In such circumstances, you have to judge the most appropriate answer as per the conditions given in the question.

1. The reaction is spontaneous if the cell potential is

(a) positive (b) negative
(c) zero (d) infinite

2. In the electrochemical cell, $Zn|Zn^{2+}||Cu^{2+}|Cu$ the negative electrode is

(a) Cu (b) Cu^{+2} (c) Zn (d) Zn^{+2}

3. Match List-I with List-II.

List-I	List-II
A. Electrolytic cell	I. Concentration cell
B. Diffusion of ions	II. Unit of electrical charge
C. $E_{cell} = \frac{0.059}{n} \log \frac{C_{cathode}}{C_{anode}}$	III. Converts electrochemical energy into chemical energy
D. Faraday	IV. Salt-bridge

Choose the correct answer from the options given below.

(a) A-III, B-IV, C-I, D-II
(b) A-III, B-I, C-II, D-IV
(c) A-II, B-I, C-III, D-IV
(d) A-II, B-IV, C-I, D-III

4. The standard oxidation potential of zinc and silver in water at 268 K are

$$Zn(s) \longrightarrow Zn^{2+} + 2e^-;\ E° = 0.76\ V$$
$$Ag(s) \longrightarrow Ag^{2+} + 2e^-;\ E° = -0.80\ V$$

Which of the following reactions actually takes place?

(a) $Zn(s) + 2Ag^+(aq) \longrightarrow Zn^{2+}(aq) + 2Ag(s)$
(b) $Zn^{2+}(aq) + 2Ag(s) \longrightarrow 2Ag^+(aq) + Zn(s)$
(c) $Zn(s) + Ag(s) \longrightarrow Zn^{2+}(aq) + Ag^+(aq)$
(d) $Zn^{2+}(aq) + Ag^+(aq) \longrightarrow Zn(s) + Ag(s)$

5. For a spontaneous reaction, ΔG, equilibrium constant (K) and E°_{cell} will be respectively

(a) –ve, > 1, +ve
(b) +ve, > 1, –ve
(c) –ve, < 1, –ve
(d) –ve, > 1, –ve

6. The standard reduction potential for Li^+/Li, Zn^{2+}/Zn, H^+/H_2 and Ag^+/Ag is –3.05, –0.762, 0.00 and +0.80 V respectively. Which of the following has highest reducing capacity?

(a) Ag (b) H_2
(c) Zn (d) Li

7. $E°$ value of Mg^{2+}/Mg is –2.37 V, of Zn^{2+}/Zn is –0.76 V and Fe^{2+}/Fe is –0.44 V. Which of the following statement is correct?

(a) Zn will reduce Fe^{2+}.
(b) Zn will reduce Mg^{2+}.
(c) Mg oxidises Fe.
(d) Zn oxidises Fe.

8. EMF of a cell whose half-cell reactions are given below is

$Mg^{2+} + 2e^- \longrightarrow Mg(s);\ E° = -2.37\ V$

$Cu^{2+} + 2e^- \longrightarrow Cu(s);\ E° = +0.33\ V$

(a) –2.03 V (b) 1.36 V
(c) 2.7 V (d) 2.03 V

9. Standard electrode potential of Ag^+ / Ag and Cu^{2+}/Cu is +0.80 V and +0.34 V respectively. These electrodes are joined together by salt-bridge and if

(a) copper electrode work like cathode, then $E°_{cell}$ is 0.46 V.
(b) silver electrode work like anode, then $E°_{cell}$ is –0.34 V.
(c) copper electrode work like anode, then $E°_{cell}$ is 0.46 V.
(d) silver electrode work like cathode, then $E°_{cell}$ is –0.34 V.

10. NaCl, $MgCl_2$ and $CaSO_4$ are known as

(a) 1-1, 2-1 and 2-2 types electrolyte respectively.
(b) strong, weak and strong electrolytes respectively.
(c) electrolytes with different value of *A* (strength of the electrolyte).
(d) electrolytes with same molar conductivity.

11. $E°_{cell}$ for the reaction, $2H_2O \rightleftharpoons H_3O^+ + OH^-$ at 25°C is –0.8277 V.

The equilibrium constant for the reaction is
(a) 10^{-14} (b) 10^{-23} (c) 10^{-7} (d) 10^{-21}

12. The relation between standard reduction potential of a cell and equilibrium constant is shown by

(a) $E°_{cell} = \frac{n}{0.0591} \log K_C$
(b) $E°_{cell} = \frac{0.0591}{n} \log K_C$
(c) $E°_{cell} = 0.0591 n \log K_C$
(d) $E°_{cell} = \frac{\log K_C}{n}$

13. Which of the following energy changes in galvanic cell ?

(a) Electrical energy → Chemical energy
(b) Chemical energy → Electrical energy
(c) Chemical energy → Internal energy
(d) Internal energy → Electrical energy

14. If a salt-bridge is not used between two half- cells, voltage

(a) drops to zero.
(b) does not change.
(c) increases gradually.
(d) increases rapidly

15. Which is not true for a standard hydrogen electrode ?

(a) The hydrogen ion concentration is 1 M.
(b) Temperature is 25 °C.
(c) Pressure of hydrogen is 1 atm.
(d) It contains a metallic conductor which does not absorb hydrogen.

Response Index

01	ⓐ	ⓑ	ⓒ	ⓓ	10	ⓐ	ⓑ	ⓒ	ⓓ	19	ⓐ	ⓑ	ⓒ	ⓓ
02	ⓐ	ⓑ	ⓒ	ⓓ	11	ⓐ	ⓑ	ⓒ	ⓓ	20	ⓐ	ⓑ	ⓒ	ⓓ
03	ⓐ	ⓑ	ⓒ	ⓓ	12	ⓐ	ⓑ	ⓒ	ⓓ	21	ⓐ	ⓑ	ⓒ	ⓓ
04	ⓐ	ⓑ	ⓒ	ⓓ	13	ⓐ	ⓑ	ⓒ	ⓓ	22	ⓐ	ⓑ	ⓒ	ⓓ
05	ⓐ	ⓑ	ⓒ	ⓓ	14	ⓐ	ⓑ	ⓒ	ⓓ	23	ⓐ	ⓑ	ⓒ	ⓓ
06	ⓐ	ⓑ	ⓒ	ⓓ	15	ⓐ	ⓑ	ⓒ	ⓓ	24	ⓐ	ⓑ	ⓒ	ⓓ
07	ⓐ	ⓑ	ⓒ	ⓓ	16	ⓐ	ⓑ	ⓒ	ⓓ	25	ⓐ	ⓑ	ⓒ	ⓓ
08	ⓐ	ⓑ	ⓒ	ⓓ	17	ⓐ	ⓑ	ⓒ	ⓓ					
09	ⓐ	ⓑ	ⓒ	ⓓ	18	ⓐ	ⓑ	ⓒ	ⓓ					

Performance Scanner

> 90% Excellent !	You have mastered these topics. The concepts of these topics are at your fingertips. Move on to the next test and maintain this momentum.
76-90% Very Good !	You have a good command over these topics. Revise these topics again after a few days and enhance your performance.
60-75% Good !	You have a wide scope to learn for these topics. Revise these topics again.
<60 Not Satisfactory!	You have a long way ahead of you to master these topics. Revise it thoroughly.

Topical Follow Thru

Test 2

Syllabus Electrolytic and Metallic Conduction, Conductance in Electrolytic Solution, Molar Conductivities and their Variations with Concentration : Kohlrausch's Law and its Applications.

For deeper insight **Scan the QR Code**

Important Instructions

- The test is of 30 minutes duration and contains 15 multiple choice questions (Four options with a single correct answer).
- Choose the correct option and fill the OMR given on the last page of test accordingly.
- At some instances, you may find more than 1 option may be correct. In such circumstances, you have to judge the most appropriate answer as per the conditions given in the question.

1. Which of the following solutions cannot conduct electricity?

(a) Sugar in water (b) NaCl in water

(c) $MgCl_2$ in water (d) KCl in water

2. Electrolytes when dissolved in water dissociates into ions. It is because

(a) they are unstable

(b) the water dissolves it

(c) the forces of repulsion increase

(d) the forces of electrostatic attraction are broken down by water

3. How much current should be passed through acidified water for 100 s to liberate 0.224 litre of H_2?

(a) 22.4 A (b) 19.3 A

(c) 9.65 A (d) 1 A

4. Which of the following is a correct match?

(a) Conductance = Sm^{-1}

(b) Conductivity = $\Omega^{-1}\ m^{-1}$

(c) Molar conductivity = $m^2s^{-1}V^{-1}$

(d) Ionic conductivity = Sm^2

5. On passing 96500 coulomb of charge through a solution of $CuSO_4$, the amount of copper liberated is

(a) 64 g (b) 32 g (c) 32 kg (d) 64 kg

6. Match List-I with List-II.

	List-I (Term)		List-II (Formula)
A.	Kohlrausch's law	I.	$\Lambda^\circ_{eq} = \Lambda^\circ_c + \Lambda^\circ_a$
B.	Molar conductivity	II.	$\Lambda^\circ_m = \dfrac{\kappa \times 1000}{\text{Molarity}}$
C.	Degree of dissociation	III.	$\alpha = \dfrac{\Lambda^c_m}{\Lambda^\infty_m}$
D.	Dissociation constant	IV.	$K_\alpha = \dfrac{c\alpha^2}{(1-\alpha)}$

Choose the correct answer from the options given below.

(a) A-III, B-IV, C-I, D-II

(b) A-I, B-II C-III, D-IV

(c) A-IV, B-II, C-I, D-III

(d) A-II, B-III, C-IV, D-I

7. Given below are two statements.

Statement I The molar conductivity of strong electrolyte does not change with dilution at all.

Statement II At high concentration of electrolyte, the ions of opposite charge influence the speed of each other besides the viscosity of medium.

In the light of the above statements, choose the correct answer from the options given below.

(a) Both Statement I and Statement II are incorrect.
(b) Statement I is correct but Statement II is incorrect.
(c) Statement I is incorrect but Statement II is correct.
(d) Both Statement I and Statement II are correct.

8. The mass of a substance liberated at an electrode is proportional to

(a) q (b) $\frac{1}{q}$ (c) q^2 (d) $\frac{1}{q^2}$

9. Which of the following is a poor conductor of electricity ?

(a) CH_3COONa (b) C_2H_5OH
(c) NaCl (d) KOH

10. Units of the properties measured are given below, which of the properties have not been matched correctly ?

(a) Molar conductivity = Sm^2mol^{-1}
(b) Cell constant = m^{-1}
(c) Specific conductance = Sm^2
(d) Equivalent conductance = Sm^2eq^{-1}

11. During the electrolysis of fused NaCl, which reaction occurs at anode?

(a) Chloride ions are reduced.
(b) Sodium ions are reduced.
(c) Chloride ions are oxidised.
(d) Sodium ions are oxidised.

12. In electrolysis, if the duration of the passage of current doubled, the mass liberated is

(a) doubled
(b) halved
(c) increased four times
(d) remains the same

13. According to Faraday's law of electrolysis, the amount of decomposition is proportional to

(a) $\frac{1}{\text{time for which current passes}}$
(b) electrochemical equivalent of the element
(c) $\frac{1}{\text{current}}$
(d) $\frac{1}{\text{electrochemical equivalent}}$

14. The amount of substance liberated at electrodes during electrolysis, when 1 coulomb of electricity is passed is called

(a) chemical equivalent
(b) electrochemical equivalent
(c) equivalent weight
(d) one mole

15. The specific conductance of a 0.1 N KCl solution at 23°C is 0.012 $ohm^{-1}cm^{-1}$. The resistance of cell containing the solution at the same temperature was found to be 55 ohm. The cell constant will be

(a) 0.142 cm^{-1} (b) 0.66 cm^{-1}
(c) 0.918 cm^{-1} (d) 1.12 cm^{-1}

Response Index

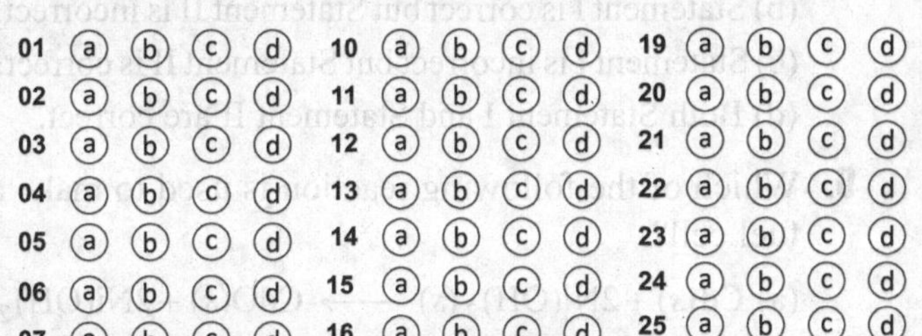

Performance Scanner

> 90% Excellent !	You have mastered these topics. The concepts of these topics are at your fingertips. Move on to the next test and maintain this momentum.
76-90% Very Good !	You have a good command over these topics. Revise these topics again after a few days and enhance your performance.
60-75% Good !	You have a wide scope to learn for these topics. Revise these topics again.
<60 Not Satisfactory!	You have a long way ahead of you to master these topics. Revise it thoroughly.

Test 3

Syllabus Dry Cell and Lead Accumulator, Fuel Cells

For deeper insight **Scan the QR Code** 

Important Instructions

- The test is of 30 minutes duration and contains 15 multiple choice questions (Four options with a single correct answer).
- Choose the correct option and fill the OMR given on the last page of test accordingly.
- At some instances, you may find more than 1 option may be correct. In such circumstances, you have to judge the most appropriate answer as per the conditions given in the question.

1. Which of the following statement is correct regarding a primary cell?

(a) The electrode reactions can be reversed.
(b) It can be recharged.
(c) An example of a primary cell is a mercury cell.
(d) Nickel-cadmium storage cell is a primary cell.

2. When lead storage battery is charged,

(a) PbO_2 is dissolved.
(b) $PbSO_4$ is deposited on lead electrode.
(c) H_2SO_4 is regenerated.
(d) Lead is deposited on lead electrode.

3. Which of the following statement is incorrect about fuel cells?

(a) They are less efficient.
(b) They are free from pollution.
(c) They run till reactants are active.
(d) They are used in automobiles.

4. Lithium is generally used as an electrode in high energy density batteries. This is because lithium

(a) is the lightest element
(b) is reactive
(c) does not corrode easily
(d) has negative reduction potential

5. The overall reaction of a hydrogen-oxygen fuel cell is

(a) $2H_2(g) + O_2(g) \longrightarrow 2H_2O(l)$
(b) $2H_2(g) + 4OH^-(aq) \longrightarrow 4H_2O + 4e^-$
(c) $O_2(g) + 2H_2O(l) + 4e^- \longrightarrow 4OH^-(aq)$
(d) $4OH^-(aq) + 4e^- \longrightarrow 2H_2O(l)$

6. In dry cell, which of the following will act as cathode?

(a) Zn (b) Carbon rod
(c) $Zn + NH_4Cl$ (d) $C + MnO_2$

7. The efficiency of a fuel cell is given by

(a) $\frac{\Delta H}{\Delta G}$ (b) $\frac{\Delta G}{\Delta S}$
(c) $\frac{\Delta G}{\Delta H}$ (d) $\frac{\Delta S}{\Delta G}$

8. Given below are two statements.

Statement I Lead storage battery does not require salt-bridge.

Statement II The solid nature of each oxidising agent and reducing agent prevent direct contact.

In the light of the above statements, choose the correct answer from the options given below.

(a) Both Statement I and Statement II are incorrect.
(b) Statement I is correct but Statement II is incorrect.
(c) Statement I is incorrect but Statement II is correct.
(d) Both Statement I and Statement II are correct.

9. Which of the following reaction is used to make a fuel cell?

(a) $Cd(s) + 2Ni(OH)_3(s) \longrightarrow CdO(s) + 2Ni(OH)_2 + H_2O(l)$
(b) $Pb(s) + PbO_2(s) + 2H_2SO_4 \longrightarrow 2PbSO_4(s) + 2H_2O(l)$
(c) $2H_2(g) + O_2(g) \longrightarrow 2H_2O(l)$
(d) $2Fe(s) + O_2(g) + 4H^+(aq) \longrightarrow 2Fe^{2+}(aq) + 2H_2O(l)$

10. Which of the following statement is incorrect ?

(a) Electrochemical reaction are energy efficient and less polluting.

(b) Fuel cells converts chemical energy into electrical energy.

(c) Hydrogen can be used as a renewable and non-polluting source of energy.

(d) Mercury cell can be used as a secondary cell.

11. Select the incorrect option when a lead storage battery is discharged.

(a) SO_2 is evolved.

(b) Lead sulphate is produced to both electrodes.

(c) Sulphuric acid is consumed.

(d) Water is formed.

12. Manganese dioxide in a dry cell acts as

(a) an electrolyte

(b) a cathode

(c) as an anode

(d) a depolariser

13. Which of the following species are used as oxidants in a fuel cell ?

A. O_2 B. H_2O_2 C. HNO_3

D. NO_2 E. NO

Choose the most appropriate answer from the options given below.

(a) Only A (b) A, B and D

(c) A, B and C (d) B, D and E

14. Given below are two statements.

Statement I The cell potential of mercury cell is 1.35 V which remains constant.

Statement II In mercury cell, the electrolyte is a paste of KOH and ZnO.

In the light of the above statements, choose the correct answer from the options given below.

(a) Both Statement I and Statement II are incorrect.

(b) Statement I is correct but Statement II is incorrect.

(c) Statement I is incorrect but Statement II is correct.

(d) Both Statement I and Statement II are correct.

15. The device that is used to convert energy of combustion of fuels like hydrogen and methane, directly into electrical energy is known as

(a) fuel cell

(b) electrolytic cell

(c) dynamo

(d) Ni-Cd cell

Response Index

01	a b c d	10	a b c d
02	a b c d	11	a b c d

01 (a) (b) (c) (d) 10 (a) (b) (c) (d) 19 (a) (b) (c) (d)

02 (a) (b) (c) (d) 11 (a) (b) (c) (d) 20 (a) (b) (c) (d)

03 (a) (b) (c) (d) 12 (a) (b) (c) (d) 21 (a) (b) (c) (d)

04 (a) (b) (c) (d) 13 (a) (b) (c) (d) 22 (a) (b) (c) (d)

05 (a) (b) (c) (d) 14 (a) (b) (c) (d) 23 (a) (b) (c) (d)

06 (a) (b) (c) (d) 15 (a) (b) (c) (d) 24 (a) (b) (c) (d)

07 (a) (b) (c) (d) 16 (a) (b) (c) (d) 25 (a) (b) (c) (d)

08 (a) (b) (c) (d) 17 (a) (b) (c) (d)

09 (a) (b) (c) (d) 18 (a) (b) (c) (d)

Performance Scanner

> 90% Excellent !	You have mastered these topics. The concepts of these topics are at your fingertips. Move on to the chapter test and maintain this momentum.
76-90% Very Good !	You have a good command over these topics. Revise these topics again after a few days and enhance your performance.
60-75% Good !	You have a wide scope to learn for these topics. Revise these topics again.
<60 Not Satisfactory!	You have a long way ahead of you to master these topics. Revise it thoroughly.

Chapter Break Thru

Syllabus	Electrochemical Cell, Electrolytic and Galvanic Cells, Different Types of Electrodes, Electrode Potentials Including Standard Electrode Potential, Half-Cell and Cell Reactions, E.M.F. of a Galvanic Cell, Nernst Equations and its Applications, Cell Potential and Gibbs Free Energy Change.	Electrolytic and Metallic Conduction, Conductance in Electrolytic Solution, Molar Conductivities and their Variations with Concentration : Kohlrausch's Law and its Applications.	Dry Cell and Lead Accumulator, Fuel Cells

Important Instructions

- The test is of 1 hour duration and contains 50 multiple choice questions (Four options with a single correct answer).
- Choose the correct option and fill the OMR given on the last page of test accordingly.
- At some instances, you may find more than 1 option may be correct. In such circumstances, you have to judge the most appropriate answer as per the conditions given in the question.

1. Which of the following is responsible for electrical conduction of molten sodium chloride?

(a) Free ions
(b) Free electrons
(c) Free molecules
(d) Atoms of sodium and chlorine

2. Which of the following statement is correct ?

(a) Cathode is –ve terminal in both, galvanic and electrolytic cells.
(b) Anode is +ve terminal in both, galvanic and electrolytic cells.
(c) Cathode and anode are –ve terminal in both electrolytic and galvanic cell.
(d) Cathode and anode are +ve terminal in both electrolytic and galvanic cell.

3. How many atoms of calcium will be deposited from a solution of $CaCl_2$ by a current of 25 milliamperes flowing for 60 seconds?

(a) 4.68×10^{18}
(b) 4.68×10^{15}
(c) 4.68×10^{12}
(d) 4.68×10^{9}

4. When 96500 coulomb of electricity is passed through copper sulphate solution, the amount of copper deposited will be

(a) 0.25 mol (b) 0.50 mol
(c) 1 mol (d) 2 mol

5. A cell reaction would be spontaneous if the cell potential and $\Delta_r G$ are respectively

(a) positive and negative
(b) negative and negative
(c) zero and zero
(d) positive and zero

6. Which of the following statement is incorrect?

(a) Ag^+ ion oxidises Cu but $H^{\oplus}$ ion cannot oxidise Cu.
(b) $AgNO_3$ solution cannot be stored in a copper container.
(c) Hydrogen gas cannot reduce zinc ion (Zn^{+2}).
(d) $F^{\ominus}$ ion is weakest reducing agent.

7. The EMF of a galvanic cell is determined by using a

(a) voltmeter (b) ammeter
(c) spectrometer (d) coulometer

8. If the solution of $CuSO_4$ in which copper rod is immersed is diluted to 10 times, then electrode potential

(a) increases by 0.295 V
(b) increases by 0.059 V
(c) decreases by 0.0295 V
(d) decreases by 0.059 V

9. The quantity of electricity needed to liberate 0.5 gram equivalent of an element is

(a) 48250 Faradays
(b) 48250 Coulombs
(c) 193000 Faradays
(d) 193000 Coulombs

10. Given below are two statements, one is labelled as Assertion (A) and the other is labelled as Reason (R).

Assertion (A) The cell potential of mercury cell is 1.35 V, which remains constant.

Reason (R) In mercury cell, the electrolyte does not involve any ion in solution.

In the light of the above statements, choose the correct answer from the options given below.

(a) Both (A) and (R) are true and (R) is the correct explanation of (A).
(b) Both (A) and (R) are true but (R) is not the correct explanation of (A).
(c) (A) is true but (R) is false.
(d) (A) is false but (R) is true.

11. Which of the following statement is incorrect for a galvanic cell when expressed in an abbreviated format ?

(a) Right hand electrode is a positive terminal.
(b) Right hand electrode acts as cathode.
(c) Electrons are released from the anode into the external circuit.
(d) Electrons are released from the cathode into the external circuit.

12. For which of the following species, standard oxidation potential and standard reduction potential is equal ?

(a) SHE (Standard Hydrogen Electrode)
(b) Magnesium electrode
(c) Copper electrode
(d) Nickel electrode

13. $HNO_3(aq)$ is titrated with NaOH(aq) conductometrically, graphical representation of the titration is

(a) 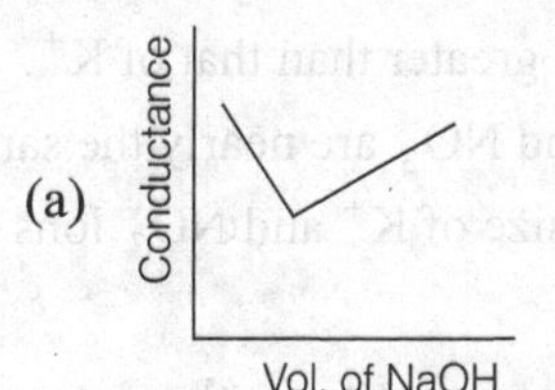

(b) 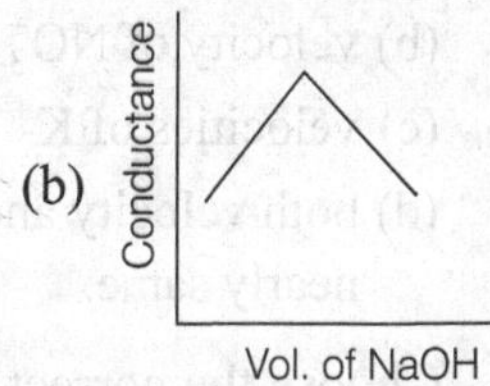

(c) 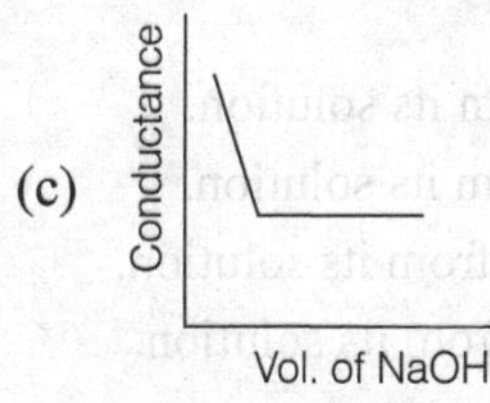

(d) 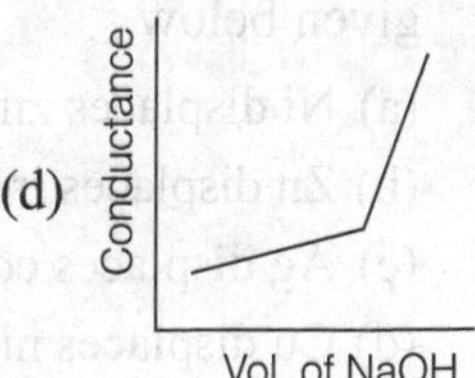

14. Which of the following occurs at cathode in electrolytic cell?

(a) $Ag \longrightarrow Ag^+ + e^-$
(b) $2OH^- \longrightarrow H_2O + \frac{1}{2}O_2 + 2e^-$
(c) $Fe^{2+} \longrightarrow Fe^{3+} + e^-$
(d) $Cu^{2+} + 2e^- \longrightarrow Cu$

15. During electrolysis of NaCl solution, part of the reaction is $Na^+ + e^- \longrightarrow Na$. This is termed as

(a) oxidation (b) reduction
(c) deposition (d) cathode reaction

16. Which of the following is not generally used as an electrolyte in the salt-bridges in an electrochemical cell?

(a) NaCl (b) KNO_3
(c) KCl (d) $ZnSO_4$

17. X g of silver is plated out on a serving tray by electrolysis of a solution containing silver in +1 oxidation state for a period of 8.0 h at a current of 8.46 A. What is the area of the tray if the thickness of silver plating is 0.00254 cm? [Given, density of silver = 10.5 g cm^{-3}]

(a) $10.7 \times 10^4 \text{ cm}^2$ (b) $1.02 \times 10^4 \text{ cm}^2$
(c) $4.1 \times 10^3 \text{ cm}^2$ (d) $102 \times 10^4 \text{ cm}^2$

18. On passing 3 ampere of electricity for 50 minutes, 1.8 gram metal deposits. The equivalent mass of metal is

(a) 2.05 (b) 25.8 (c) 19.3 (d) 30.7

19. Saturated solution of KNO_3 with *agar-agar* is used to make 'salt-bridge' because

(a) size of K^+ is greater than of NO_3^-.

(b) velocity of NO_3^- is greater than that of K^+.

(c) velocities of K^+ and NO_3^- are nearly the same.

(d) both velocity and size of K^+ and NO_3^- ions are nearly same.

20. Choose the correct statement from the options given below.

(a) Ni displaces zinc from its solution.

(b) Zn displaces iron from its solution.

(c) Ag displaces copper from its solution.

(d) Cu displaces nickel from its solution.

21. Match List-I and List-II.

	List-I (Electrode)	List-II (Expression)
A.	Electrode reversible with respect to cation.	I. $Pt/Fe^{2+}/Fe^{3+}$
B.	Electrode reversible with respect to anion	II. $\underset{(1\text{ bar})}{Pt\ /H_2}\mid \underset{(a=1)}{H^+}$
C.	Redox electrode	III. $Ag\mid AgCl(s), HCl(aq)$
D.	Reference electrode	IV. $Ag\mid AgNO_3$

Choose the correct answer from the options given below.

(a) A-III, B-IV, C-II, D-I

(b) A-IV, B-III, C-I, D-II

(c) A-I, B-II, C-III, D-IV

(d) A-II, B-III, C-I, D-IV

22. The standard reduction potentials at 298 K for the following half reaction are given against each.

$$Zn^{2+}(aq)+2e^- \rightleftharpoons Zn(s);\ -0.762$$

$$Cr^{3+}(aq)+3e^- \rightleftharpoons Cr(s);\ -0.740$$

$$2H^+(aq)+2e^- \rightleftharpoons H_2(g);\ 0.00$$

$$Fe^{3+}(aq)+e^- \rightleftharpoons Fe^{2+}(aq);\ 0.770$$

Which of the following is strongest reducing agent?

(a) $Zn(s)$ (b) $Cr(s)$

(c) $H_2(g)$ (d) $Fe^{2+}(aq)$

23. Which of the following metal does not react with the solution of copper sulphate?

(a) Mg (b) Fe

(c) Zn (d) Ag

24. When a concentrated solution of an electrolyte is diluted,

(a) its specific conductance increases.

(b) its equivalent conductance decreases.

(c) its specific conductance decreases and equivalent conductance increases.

(d) both specific and equivalent conductance increase.

25. The relation among conductance (G), specific conductance (κ) and cell constant $\left(\frac{l}{A}\right)$ is

(a) $G=\kappa\frac{l}{A}$ (b) $G=\kappa\frac{A}{l}$

(c) $G\kappa=\frac{l}{A}$ (d) $G=\kappa Al$

26. Given below are two statements, one is labelled as Assertion (A) and the other is labelled as Reason (R).

Assertion (A) If $\overset{\circ}{\lambda}_{Na^+}$ and $\overset{\circ}{\lambda}_{Cl^-}$ are molar limiting conductivity of sodium and chloride ion respectively, then the limiting molar conductivity for sodium chloride is given by the equation :

$$\overset{\circ}{\lambda}_{NaCl}=\overset{\circ}{\lambda}_{Na^+}+\overset{\circ}{\lambda}_{Cl^-}$$

Reason (R) This is according to Kohlrausch law of independent migration of ions.

In the light of the above statements, choose the correct answer from the options given below.

(a) Both (A) and (R) are true and (R) is the correct explanation of (A).

(b) Both (A) and (R) are true but (R) is not the correct explanation of (A).

(c) (A) is true but (R) is false.

(d) (A) is false but (R) is true.

27. The standard reduction potential at 25°C for the following half reaction is given:

$$Zn^{2+}+2e^- \longrightarrow Zn;\quad E°=-0.762\text{ V}$$

$$Mg^{2+}+2e^- \longrightarrow Mg;\quad E°=-2.37\text{ V}$$

When zinc dust is added to the solution of $MgCl_2$ then
(a) $ZnCl_2$ is formed
(b) Mg is precipitated
(c) Zn dissolved in the solution
(d) no reaction takes place

28. Which of the following expression is correct?
(a) $\Delta G° = -nFE°_{cell}$
(b) $\Delta G° = +nFE°_{cell}$
(c) $\Delta G° = 2.303\,RT \log K_{eq}$
(d) $\Delta G° = -nF \log K_C$

29. The standard electrode potentials : $E°_{(I_2/I^-)}$, $E°_{(Br^-/Br_2)}$ and $E°_{(Fe/Fe^{+2})}$ are respectively +0.54 V, –1.09 V and 0.44 V. On the basis of above data which of the following process is non-spontaneous?
(a) $Br_2 + 2I^- \longrightarrow 2Br^- + I_2$
(b) $Fe + Br_2 \longrightarrow Fe^{2+} + 2Br^-$
(c) $Fe + I_2 \longrightarrow Fe^{2+} + 2I^-$
(d) $I_2 + 2Br^- \longrightarrow 2I^- + Br_2$

30. Based on the following information arrange four metals *A*, *B*, *C* and *D* in order of decreasing ability to act as reducing agent.
I. Only *A*, *B* and *C* react with 1 M HCl to give $H_2(g)$.
II. When *C* is added to solution to the other metal ions, metallic *B* and *D* are formed.
III. Metal *C* does not reduce A^{+n}.
(a) $C > A > B > D$
(b) $C > A > D > B$
(c) $A > C > D > B$
(d) $A > C > B > D$

31. Match List-I with List-II.

List-I (Reduction process)	List-II (Charge required)
A. 1 mole of MnO_4^- to Mn^{+2}	I. 193000 C
B. 1 mole of $Cr_2O_7^{-2}$ to Cr^{+3}	II. 283500 C
C. 1 mole of Sn^{+4} to Sn^{+2}	III. 482500 C
D. 1 mole of Al^{+3} to Al	IV. 579000 C

Choose the correct answer from the options given below.
(a) A-I, B-III, C-II, D-IV
(b) A-III, B-IV, C-II, D-I
(c) A-IV, B-II, C-I, D-III
(d) A-III, B-IV, C-I, D-II

32. Given : $E°_{Ag^+/Ag} = 0.80\,V$, $E°_{Mg^{+2}/Mg} = -2.37\,V$, $E°_{Cu^{+2}/Cu} = 0.34\,V$, $E°_{Hg^{+2}/Hg} = 0.79\,V$
Which of the following statement is correct ?
(a) $AgNO_3$ can be stored in copper vessel.
(b) $Mg(NO_3)_2$ can not be stored in copper vessel.
(c) $CuCl_2$ can be stored in silver vessel.
(d) $HgCl_2$ can be stored in copper vessel.

33. The resistance of 0.5 M solution of an electrolyte in a cell was found to be 50 Ω. If the electrodes in the cell are 2.2 cm apart and have an area of 4.4 cm^2 then the molar conductivity (in Sm^2mol^{-1}) of the solution is
(a) 0.2 (b) 0.02 (c) 0.002 (d) 0.001

34. In the cell reaction,
$Cu(s) + 2Ag^+(aq) \longrightarrow Cu^{2+}(aq) + 2Ag(s)$,
$E°_{cell} = 0.46\,V$ by doubling the concentration of Cu^{2+}, E_{cell} is
(a) doubled
(b) halved
(c) increased but less than double
(d) decreased by a small fraction

35. Given below are two statements, one is labelled as Assertion (A) and the other is labelled as Reason (R).
Assertion (A) If an aqueous solution of NaCl is electrolysed, the product obtained at the cathode is H_2 gas and not Na.
Reason (R) Gases are liberated faster than the metals.
In the light of the above statements, choose the correct answer from the options given below.
(a) Both (A) and (R) are true and (R) is the correct explanation of (A).
(b) Both (A) and (R) are true but (R) is not the correct explanation of (A).
(c) (A) is true but (R) is false.
(d) (A) is false but (R) is true.

36. Pair of compounds that can exist together is

(A) $HgCl_2$, $SnCl_2$ (B) $FeCl_2$, $SnCl_2$
(C) $FeCl_3$, KI (D) $FeCl_3$, $SnCl_2$
(E) $HgCl_2$, $FeCl_2$

(a) Only B (b) C and D
(c) A, C and E (d) B, D and E

37. Consider the following relations.

(i) $E_{cell} = \frac{0.0591}{n} \log K_C$
(ii) $-\Delta G° = -nFE°$
(iii) Cell constant $= \frac{\text{Conductivity}}{\text{Conductance}}$
(iv) First law of electrolysis $= W \propto Q$
(v) $\alpha = \frac{\Lambda^{\circ}_m}{\Lambda_m}$

Number of correct relationship among the following is ....

(a) 3 (b) 2 (c) 4 (d) 1

38. The current flowing in a copper voltmeter is 1.6 A. The number of Cu^{2+} ions deposited at the cathode per minute are

(a) 1.5×10^{20} (b) 3×10^{20}
(c) 6×10^{20} (d) 1×10^{19}.

39. Select the correct statement for the weak electrolyte.

(a) They have higher degree of dissociation at higher concentration.
(b) The change in Λ_m with dilution is due to decrease in the degree of dissociation and number of ions in the solution that contains electrolyte.
(c) Λ_m increase steeply on dilution near high concentration.
(d) At infinite dilution, electrolyte dissociate completely but at such low concentration, the conductivity of solution is low and cannot be measured accurately.

40. Which of the following statement is wrong ?

(a) Specific conductance is the conductance of 1 cm^3 electrolyte solution.
(b) Specific conductance increase while equivalent conductance decrease on increasing dilution.
(c) The maximum value of equivalent conductance of weak electrolyte cannot be determined by extrapolation of curve between Λ_{eq} and $\sqrt{C}$.
(d) The conductivity of metal is due to mobility of electrons.

41. Select the incorrect statement from the following.

(a) E_{cell} is an intensive parameter.
(b) A negative $E°$ means that the redox couple is a stronger reducing agent than the H^+/H_2 couple.
(c) The amount of electricity required for oxidation or reduction depends on the stoichiometry of the electrode reaction.
(d) The amount of chemical reaction which occur at any electrode during electrolysis by a current is proportional to the rate of electricity passed through the electrolyte.

42. Given below are two statements, one is labelled as Assertion (A) and the other is labelled as Reason (R).

Assertion (A) Molar conductivity of a weak electrolyte at infinite dilution can not be determined experimentally.

Reason (R) Kohlrausch law help to find the molar conductivity of a weak electrolyte at infinite dilution.

In the light of the above statements, choose the correct answer from the options given below.

(a) Both (A) and (R) are true and (R) is the correct explanation of (A).
(b) Both (A) and (R) are true but (R) is not the correct explanation of (A).
(c) (A) is true but (R) is false.
(d) (A) is false but (R) is true.

43. Which of the following metal pair will couple to give maximum emf for a voltaic cell?

$$E^{\circ}_{Ca} = -2.87\,V, E^{\circ}_{Cu} = 0.34\,V$$
$$E^{\circ}_{Au} = -1.50\,V, E^{\circ}_{Pb} = -0.13\,V$$

(a) Fe and Cu (b) Pb and Cu
(c) Cu and Au (d) Ca and Cu

44. Choose the incorrect statement from the following.

(a) Mercury cell is a primary cell providing a constant potential.
(b) In the electrolytic cell, reduction occurs at anode and in galvanic cell, oxidation takes place at anode.
(c) Galvanised iron does not rust.
(d) During recharging, lead storage cell works as electrolytic cell.

45. A factory produces 40 kg of calcium in 2 hours by electrolysis. How much aluminium can be produced by same current in 2 hours if current efficiency is 50 % ?

(a) 22 kg (b) 18 kg
(c) 9 kg (d) 20 kg

46. What is the charge on tin if 7.42 g of metallic tin is deposited by passage of 24125 C charge through a solution containing the ion? [Atomic weight of Sn = 118 amu]

(a) +1 (b) +3
(c) +2 (d) +4

47. EMF of hydrogen electrode in terms of pH is (at 1 atm pressure)

(a) $E_{H^+/H_2} = \frac{RT}{F}$ pH

(b) $E_{H^+/H_2} = \frac{RT}{F} \times \frac{1}{pH}$

(c) $E_{H^+/H_2} = \frac{2.303RT}{F} \times pH$

(d) $E_{H^+/H_2} = -0.0591 \times pH$

48. Deduce from the following $E°$ values of half-cells. What combination of two half-cells would result in a galvanic cell with the largest potential?

I. $A \longrightarrow A^+ + e^-$; $E° = -0.24$ V
II. $B^+ + e^- \longrightarrow B$; $E° = -2.1$ V
III. $C \longrightarrow C^{+2} + 2e^-$; $E° = -0.38$ V
IV. $D^{2-} \longrightarrow D^- + e^-$; $E° = -0.59$ V
V. $P \longrightarrow P^{+2} + 2e^-$; $E° = -0.47$ V

Choose the correct answer from the options given below.

(a) II and III (b) I and V
(c) III, II, and IV (d) I and II

49. The reason for increase in electrical conduction of a weak electrolyte with increase in temperature.

(a) Increase in the number of ions.
(b) Increase in the speed of ions.
(c) Increase in the degree of dissociation of electrolytes.
(d) All of the above

50. Pure water does not conduct electricity because it is

A. neutral
B. readily decomposed
C. completely ionised
D. almost unionised
E. the concentration of (H^+ and OH^-) ions extremely high.

(a) Only A (b) Only D
(c) B and E (d) B, C and E

Response Index

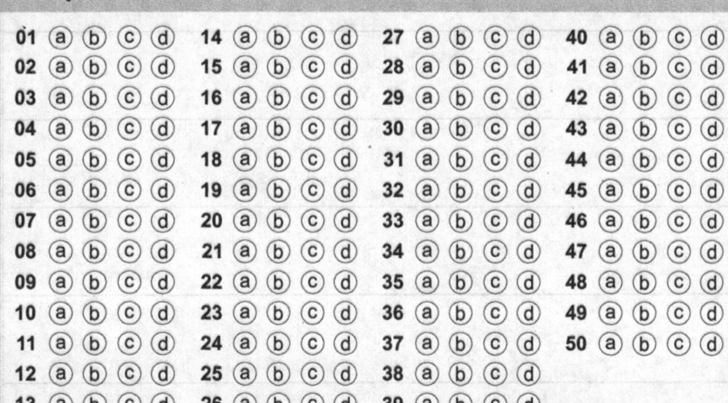

01 ⓐ ⓑ ⓒ ⓓ	14 ⓐ ⓑ ⓒ ⓓ	27 ⓐ ⓑ ⓒ ⓓ	40 ⓐ ⓑ ⓒ ⓓ
02 ⓐ ⓑ ⓒ ⓓ	15 ⓐ ⓑ ⓒ ⓓ	28 ⓐ ⓑ ⓒ ⓓ	41 ⓐ ⓑ ⓒ ⓓ
03 ⓐ ⓑ ⓒ ⓓ	16 ⓐ ⓑ ⓒ ⓓ	29 ⓐ ⓑ ⓒ ⓓ	42 ⓐ ⓑ ⓒ ⓓ
04 ⓐ ⓑ ⓒ ⓓ	17 ⓐ ⓑ ⓒ ⓓ	30 ⓐ ⓑ ⓒ ⓓ	43 ⓐ ⓑ ⓒ ⓓ
05 ⓐ ⓑ ⓒ ⓓ	18 ⓐ ⓑ ⓒ ⓓ	31 ⓐ ⓑ ⓒ ⓓ	44 ⓐ ⓑ ⓒ ⓓ
06 ⓐ ⓑ ⓒ ⓓ	19 ⓐ ⓑ ⓒ ⓓ	32 ⓐ ⓑ ⓒ ⓓ	45 ⓐ ⓑ ⓒ ⓓ
07 ⓐ ⓑ ⓒ ⓓ	20 ⓐ ⓑ ⓒ ⓓ	33 ⓐ ⓑ ⓒ ⓓ	46 ⓐ ⓑ ⓒ ⓓ
08 ⓐ ⓑ ⓒ ⓓ	21 ⓐ ⓑ ⓒ ⓓ	34 ⓐ ⓑ ⓒ ⓓ	47 ⓐ ⓑ ⓒ ⓓ
09 ⓐ ⓑ ⓒ ⓓ	22 ⓐ ⓑ ⓒ ⓓ	35 ⓐ ⓑ ⓒ ⓓ	48 ⓐ ⓑ ⓒ ⓓ
10 ⓐ ⓑ ⓒ ⓓ	23 ⓐ ⓑ ⓒ ⓓ	36 ⓐ ⓑ ⓒ ⓓ	49 ⓐ ⓑ ⓒ ⓓ
11 ⓐ ⓑ ⓒ ⓓ	24 ⓐ ⓑ ⓒ ⓓ	37 ⓐ ⓑ ⓒ ⓓ	50 ⓐ ⓑ ⓒ ⓓ
12 ⓐ ⓑ ⓒ ⓓ	25 ⓐ ⓑ ⓒ ⓓ	38 ⓐ ⓑ ⓒ ⓓ	
13 ⓐ ⓑ ⓒ ⓓ	26 ⓐ ⓑ ⓒ ⓓ	39 ⓐ ⓑ ⓒ ⓓ	

Performance Scanner

> 90% Excellent !	You have mastered this chapter. The concepts of this chapter are at your fingertips. Move on to the next chapter and maintain this momentum.
76-90% Very Good !	You have a good command over this chapter. Revise the chapter again after a few days and enhance your performance.
60-75% Good !	You have a wide scope to learn for this chapter. Revise this chapter again.
<60 Not Satisfactory!	You have a long way ahead of you to master this chapter. Revise it thoroughly.

Scan for Online Chapter Test

Scan for Online Unit Test

Space for Rough Work

Space for Rough Work

Space for Rough Work

Test Booklet No. **3947253**

Test Booklet Code **CH3**

MEDACE
NEET (UG)
SELF ASSESSMENT KIT

Chemical Kinetics

Topics Covered

- Rate of Chemical Reaction and Rate Expression
- Order, Molecularity and Half-Life Period
- Arrhenius Theory, Activation Energy, Collision and Related Theories

Important Instructions

- This Booklet Contains – 3 Topic Tests and One Test on Complete Chapter.
- Each question carries 4 marks.
- For each correct response the candidate will get 4 marks and for every incorrect response, 1 mark will be additionally deducted from the total score.
- Use **Blue/Black** point pen only for filling the OMR.
- Rough work is to be done in the space provided for this purpose in the test booklet only.

Name of the Candidate (In Capitals) ________________

____

Candidate's Signature ________

Invigilator's Signature ________

Facsimile signature stamp of center superintendent________

Do not open this Booklet until you start attempting the Test

Topical Follow Thru

Test 1

Syllabus Rate of a Chemical Reaction, Factors Affecting the Rate of Reaction, Elementary and Complex Reactions

For deeper insight **Scan the QR Code**

Important Instructions

- The test is of 30 minutes duration and contains 15 multiple choice questions (Four options with a single correct answer).
- Choose the correct option and fill the OMR given on the last page of test accordingly.
- At some instances, you may find more than 1 option may be correct. In such circumstances, you have to judge the most appropriate answer as per the conditions given in the question.

1. The rate of chemical reaction at constant temperature is proportional to

(a) the amount of products formed
(b) the product of masses of the reactants
(c) the product of the molar concentration of the reactants
(d) the mean free path of the reaction

2. The rate law for reaction between the substances A and B is given by rate $= k[A]^n [B]^m$.

On doubling the concentration of A and halving the concentration of B, the ratio of the new rate to the initial rate of reaction will be

(a) $(m+n)$ (b) $(n-m)$
(c) $2^{(n-m)}$ (d) $2^{\frac{1}{m+n}}$

3. The rate at which a substance reacts depends on its

(a) atomic mass (b) equivalent mass
(c) molecular mass (d) active mass

4. The chemical reaction, $2O_3 \longrightarrow 3O_2$ proceeds as follows

(i) $O_3 \rightleftharpoons O_2 + O$ ...(Fast)
(ii) $O + O_3 \rightleftharpoons 2O_2$ ...(Slow)

The rate law expression for given process should be

(a) $r = k'[O_3]^2$ (b) $r = k'[O_3]^2[O_2]^{-1}$
(c) $r = k'[O_3][O_2]$ (d) $r = k'[O_3]^3[O_2]^2$

5. For the reaction

$2H_2(g) + 2NO(g) \rightleftharpoons N_2(g) + 2H_2O(g)$ the observed rate expression is, rate $= k_f[NO]^2[H_2]$.

The rate expression for the reverse reaction is

(a) $k_b[NO][H_2O]^2$
(b) $\frac{k_b[N_2][H_2O]^2}{[NO]}$
(c) $k_b[N_2][H_2O]$
(d) $\frac{k_b[N_2][H_2O]^2}{[H_2]}$

6. In the synthesis of ammonia from nitrogen and hydrogen gases, if 1.8×10^{-2} moles of hydrogen disappears in 10 minutes, the number of moles of ammonia formed in 0.4 minutes is

(a) 1.8×10^{-3} (b) 4.8×10^{-4}
(c) 4×10^{-2} (d) 3.6×10^{-2}

7. The rate of a reaction is expressed in different ways as follows

$$+\frac{1}{2}\frac{d[C]}{dt} = -\frac{1}{3}\frac{d[D]}{dt} = +\frac{1}{4}\frac{d[A]}{dt} = -\frac{d[B]}{dt}$$

The reaction is

(a) $4A + B \longrightarrow 2C + 3D$
(b) $B + 3D \longrightarrow 4A + 2C$
(c) $A + B \longrightarrow C + D$
(d) $B + D \longrightarrow A + C$

8. For a reaction,

$$xA + yB \longrightarrow zC$$

$$\frac{-d[A]}{dt} = \frac{-d[B]}{dt} = \frac{+1.5d[C]}{dt}$$

then x, y and z are

(a) 1, 1, 1 (b) 3, 2, 3
(c) 3, 2, 2 (d) 2, 2, 3

9. For the reaction
$2N_2O_5(g) \longrightarrow 4NO_2(g) + O_2(g)$, the ratio of the rate of decomposition of N_2O_5 to rate of formation of NO_2 is

(a) 4:1 (b) 1:4
(c) 2:1 (d) 1:2

10. For a reaction $A + B \longrightarrow$ Products, it is observed that doubling the concentration of B causes the reaction rate to increase eight times, but doubling the concentration of A has no effect on the rate of reaction. The rate equation is therefore

(a) rate $= k[A]^2$ (b) rate $= k[B]^3$
(c) rate $= k[A][B]$ (d) rate $= k[A]$

11. The rate of a reaction that does not involve gases is not dependent on

(a) pressure (b) temperature
(c) concentration (d) catalyst

12. For reaction $2A + B \longrightarrow$ Product, the active mass of B is kept constant and that of A is doubled. The rate of reaction will then

(a) increase 2 times (b) increase 4 times
(c) decrease 2 times (d) decrease 4 times

13. Nitrogen tetraoxide (N_2O_4) decomposes as

$$N_2O_4(g) \longrightarrow 2NO_2(g)$$

If the pressure of N_2O_4 falls from 0.50 atm to 0.46 atm in 30 minutes, the rate of appearance of $NO_2(g)$ is

(a) 0.006 atm min^{-1} (b) 0.003 atm min^{-1}
(c) 0.012 atm min^{-1} (d) 0.0026 atm min^{-1}

14. For the reaction $N_2 + 3H_2 \rightleftharpoons 2NH_3$, if $\frac{\Delta[NH_3]}{\Delta t} = 2 \times 10^{-4}$ mol L^{-1} s^{-1}, the value of $\frac{-\Delta[H_2]}{\Delta t}$ would be

(a) 1×10^{-4} mol L^{-1} s^{-1} (b) 3×10^{-4} mol L^{-1} s^{-1}
(c) 4×10^{-4} mol L^{-1} s^{-1} (d) 6×10^{-4} mol $L^{-1}s^{-1}$

15. The rate of disappearance of SO_2 in the reaction $2SO_2 + O_2 \longrightarrow 2SO_3$ is 1.28×10^{-3} mol L^{-1} s^{-1} than the rate of formation of SO_3 is

(a) 0.64×10^{-3} mol L^{-1} s^{-1}
(b) 0.80×10^{-3} mol L^{-1} s^{-1}
(c) 1.28×10^{-3} mol L^{-1} s^{-1}
(d) 1.60×10^{-3} mol L^{-1} s^{-1}

Response Index

01	a	b	c	d	10	a	b	c	d	19	a	b	c	d
02	a	b	c	d	11	a	b	c	d	20	a	b	c	d
03	a	b	c	d	12	a	b	c	d	21	a	b	c	d
04	a	b	c	d	13	a	b	c	d	22	a	b	c	d
05	a	b	c	d	14	a	b	c	d	23	a	b	c	d
06	a	b	c	d	15	a	b	c	d	24	a	b	c	d
07	a	b	c	d	16	a	b	c	d	25	a	b	c	d
08	a	b	c	d	17	a	b	c	d					
09	a	b	c	d	18	a	b	c	d					

Performance Scanner

> 90% Excellent !	You have mastered these topics. The concepts of these topics are at your fingertips. Move on to the next test and maintain this momentum.
76-90% Very Good !	You have a good command over these topics. Revise these topics again after a few days and enhance your performance.
60-75% Good !	You have a wide scope to learn for these topics. Revise these topics again.
<60 Not Satisfactory!	You have a long way ahead of you to master these topics. Revise it thoroughly.

Test 2

Syllabus Order and Molecularity of Reaction, Rate Law, Rate Constant and its Units, Differential and Integral Forms of Zero and First Order Reactions and their Half-Lives.

For deeper insight **Scan the QR Code**

Important Instructions

- The test is of 30 minutes duration and contains 15 multiple choice questions (Four options with a single correct answer).
- Choose the correct option and fill the OMR given on the last page of test accordingly.
- At some instances, you may find more than 1 option may be correct. In such circumstances, you have to judge the most appropriate answer as per the conditions given in the question.

1. Which of the following statement is incorrect about molecularity of a reaction?

(a) Molecularity of an elementary reaction is the number of molecules of the reactants present in the balanced equation.

(b) Molecularity of a reaction is the number of molecules in the slowest step.

(c) It is always a whole number.

(d) Order of reaction is always less than molecularity of a reaction.

2. Half-life period of a first order reaction is 1400 seconds. The specific rate constant of the reaction is

(a) $0.5\times 10^{-2}\ s^{-1}$ (b) $4.9\times 10^{-4}\ s^{-1}$

(c) $5.0\times 10^{-2}\ s^{-1}$ (d) $5.0\times 10^{-3}\ s^{-1}$

3. The time for half life period of a certain reaction $A\rightarrow$ Products is 1 hour. When the initial concentration of the reactant A is 2.0 mol L^{-1}, how much time does it take for its concentration to become from 0.50 to 0.25 mol L^{-1} if it is a zero order reaction?

(a) 1 hr (b) 4hr

(c) 0.5 hr (d) 0.25 hr

4. A reaction is 50% complete in 2 hours and 75% complete in 4 hours, the order of reaction is

(a) 0 (b) 1

(c) 2 (d) 3

5. The half-life period of a first order chemical reaction is 6.93 min. The time required for the completion of 99% of the chemical reaction will be

(a) 230.3 min (b) 23.03 min

(c) 46.06 min (d) 460.6 min

6. Consider the following data for reaction, $A\rightarrow$ product and find the order of reaction.

$[A]$ (mol/L)	d[Product]/dt (mol/L/s)
0.003	45.0×10^{-5}
0.009	5.0×10^{-5}
0.012	2.5×10^{-5}

(a) 1 (b) –2 (c) –1 (d) 2

7. The inversion of cane sugar is represented by

$$C_{12}H_{22}O_{11} + H_2O \longrightarrow C_6H_{12}O_6 + C_6H_{12}O_6$$

The above reaction is an example of

(a) second order reaction

(b) unimolecular reaction

(c) pseudo-unimolecular reaction

(d) zero order reaction

8. 87.5% of the substance disintegrated in 45 minutes (first order reaction). What is its half-life?

(a) 15 min (b) 30 min

(c) 45 min (d) 60 min

9. Half-life of a reaction is found to be inversely proportional to the cube of initial concentration. The order of reaction is

(a) 4 (b) 3 (c) 5 (d) 2

10. Which of the following statement is correct about zero order reaction?

(a) The graph between $[A]$ *versus* time is a straight line with positive slope (where $[A]$ is concentration of reactant)

(b) Rate of reaction is independent of concentration.

(c) Unit of rate constant is concentration^{-1}.

(d) Unit of rate constant is concentration^{-1} time^{-1}.

11. Select the incorrect statement.
(a) Inversion of cane sugar is an example of pseudo first order reaction.
(b) Molecularity of a reaction may be zero or fractional
(c) For a first order reaction $t_{1/2} = \frac{0.693}{k}$
(d) Rate of zero order reaction is independent of initial concentration of reactant.

12. Which of the following is an example of pseudo unimolecular reaction?
(a) $CH_3COOCH_3 + H_2O \xrightarrow{H^+} CH_3COOH + CH_3OH$
(b) $2N_2O_5 \longrightarrow 4NO_2 + O_2$
(c) $2FeCl_3 + SnCl_2 \longrightarrow SnCl_4 + 2FeCl_2$
(d) $NaOH + HCl \longrightarrow NaCl + H_2O$

13. Select the incorrect statement regarding first order reaction.
(a) Time for half-life change $t_{1/2}$ is independent of initial concentration.
(b) Change in the concentration unit does not change the rate constant (k).
(c) Time for half-change X rate constant = 0.693.
(d) The unit of k is mole^{-1} min^{-1}.

14. 75% of a first order reaction is completed in 60 minute. What will be the time required for completion of 93.75% of the reaction (in minutes)?
(a) 30 min (b) 60 min
(c) 90 min (d) 120 min

15. Consider the following statements.
Statement I Acid catalysed hydrolysis of ethyl acetate is a pseudo first order reaction.
Statement II Water does not take part in the above reaction.
In the light of the above statements, choose the most appropriate answer from the options given below.
(a) Both Statement I and Statement II are incorrect.
(b) Statement I is correct but Statement II is incorrect.
(c) Statement I is incorrect but Statement II is correct.
(d) Both Statement I and Statement II are correct.

Response Index

01	a	b	c	d	10	a	b	c	d	19	a	b	c	d
02	a	b	c	d	11	a	b	c	d	20	a	b	c	d
03	a	b	c	d	12	a	b	c	d	21	a	b	c	d
04	a	b	c	d	13	a	b	c	d	22	a	b	c	d
05	a	b	c	d	14	a	b	c	d	23	a	b	c	d
06	a	b	c	d	15	a	b	c	d	24	a	b	c	d
07	a	b	c	d	16	a	b	c	d	25	a	b	c	d
08	a	b	c	d	17	a	b	c	d					
09	a	b	c	d	18	a	b	c	d					

Performance Scanner

> 90% Excellent !	You have mastered these topics. The concepts of these topics are at your fingertips. Move on to the next test and maintain this momentum.
76-90% Very Good !	You have a good command over these topics. Revise these topics again after a few days and enhance your performance.
60-75% Good !	You have a wide scope to learn for these topics. Revise these topics again.
<60 Not Satisfactory!	You have a long way ahead of you to master these topics. Revise it thoroughly.

Test 3

Syllabus Arrhenius Theory, Activation Energy and its Calculation, Collision Theory of Bimolecular Gaseous Reaction, The Effect of Temperature on the Rate of Reactions

For deeper insight **Scan the QR Code**

Important Instructions

- The test is of 30 minutes duration and contains 25 multiple choice questions (Four options with a single correct answer).
- Choose the correct option and fill the OMR given on the last page of test accordingly.
- At some instances, you may find more than 1 option may be correct. In such circumstances, you have to judge the most appropriate answer as per the conditions given in the question.

1. The activation energy of a reaction at a given temperature is found to be 2.303 RT J mol^{-3}. The ratio of rate constant to the Arrhenius factor is

(a) 0.01 (b) 0.1
(c) 0.02 (d) 0.001

2. Which of the following statements is correct?

(a) The temperature coefficient of a reaction is the ratio of the rate constants at two temperatures that differ by 10°C.
(b) The temperature coefficient of a reaction is the ratio of the rate constants at 298 K and 308 K.
(c) The temperature coefficient of most of the reactions lies between 2 and 3.
(d) In an endothermic reaction, activation energy of reactants is more than that of the products.

3. What is the energy of activation of a reaction if its ratio doubles when the temperature is raised from 260 K to 300 K?

(a) 2.7 kcal
(b) 41 kcal
(c) 13.8 kcal
(d) 52 kcal

4. Which of the following statements is correct about collision theory?

(a) Every collision between reactants leads to chemical reaction.
(b) Rate of reaction is proportional to velocity of molecules.
(c) All reactions which occur in gaseous phase are zero order reactions.
(d) Rate of reaction is directly proportional to collision frequency of reactants.

5. Which of the following plots is in accordance with the Arrhenius equation?

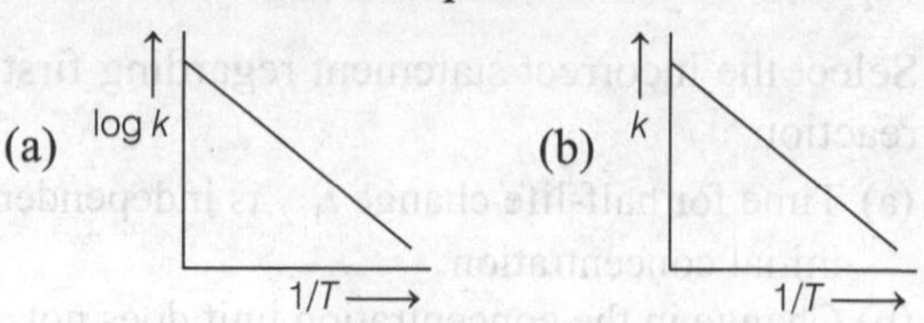

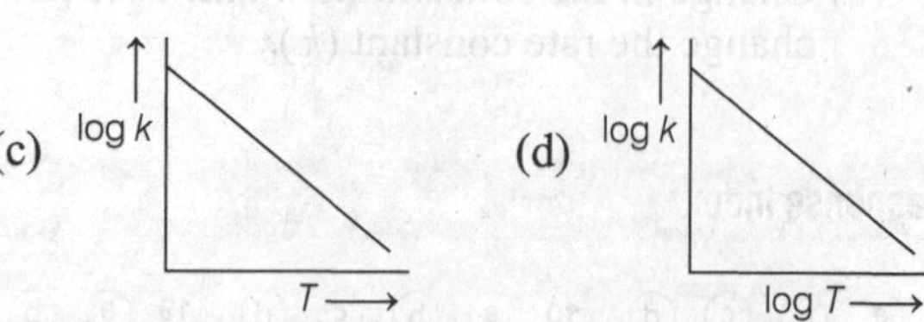

6. If for a first order reaction, the values of A and E_a are 4×10^{13} s^{-1} and 98.6 kJ/mol respectively, then at what temperature will its half-life period be 10 minutes?

(a) 330 K (b) 300 K
(c) 330.95 K (d) 311.45 K

7. Consider the following statements regarding catalyst.

I. Inhibitor reduces the rate of reaction.
II. Catalyst participate in a chemical reaction by forming temporary bonds with reactants.
III. It does not alter Gibbs energy.
IV. It catalyse spontaneous reactions but does not catalyse non-spontaneous reaction.
V. It change the equilibrium constant of a reaction.

Choose the correct statement(s) and mark the option accordingly.

(a) Only I (b) II and V
(c) III and IV (d) I, II, III and IV

8. The activation energy of a reaction can be determined from the slope of which of the following graph?

(a) $\ln k$ vs $\frac{1}{T}$ (b) $\frac{T}{\ln k}$ vs $\frac{1}{T}$

(c) $\ln k$ vs T (d) $\frac{\ln k}{T}$ vs T

9. Which of the following statements is incorrect?

(a) The catalyst does not affect the equilibrium of a reaction.

(b) Reaction with higher activation energy has higher rate constant.

(c) In an exothermic reaction, the activation energy of the reverse reaction is higher than that of the forward reaction.

(d) Half-life period of a first order reaction is independent of initial concentration.

10. The rate constant (k') of one of the reaction is found to be double that of the rate constant (k'') of another reaction. Then, the relationship between the corresponding activation energies of the two reactions (E_a' and E_a'') can be represented as

(a) $E_a' > E_a''$ (b) $E_a' < E_a''$

(c) $E_a' = E_a''$ (d) $E_a' = 4E_a''$

11. The correct reaction profile diagram for a positive catalyst reaction is

(a)

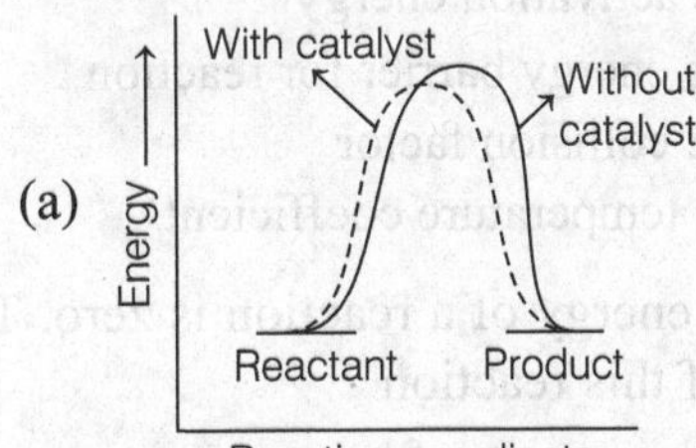

(b)

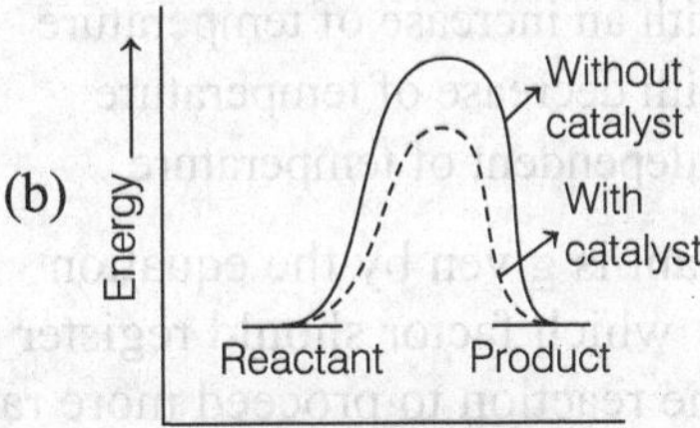

(c)

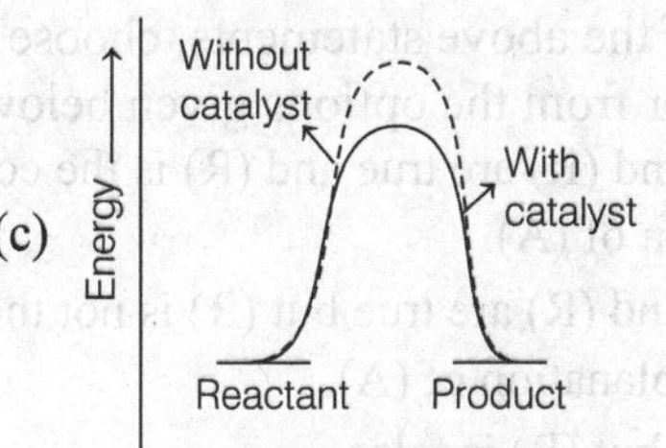

(d)

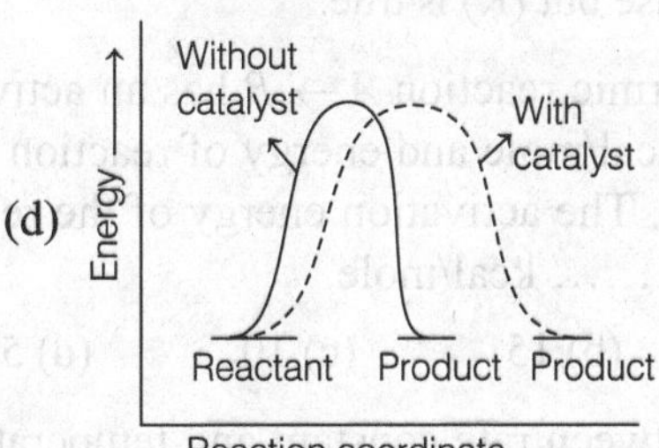

12. The rate constant is doubled when temperature increase from 27°C to 37°C. Activation energy in kJ is

(a) 34 (b) 54 (c) 100 (d) 50

13. With respect to the equation $k = Ae^{-E_a/RT}$ in chemical kinetics, which one of the following statement is correct?

(a) k is equilibrium constant.

(b) A is adsorption factor.

(c) E_a is energy of activation.

(d) R is Rydberg's constant.

14. For a reaction, activation energy $(E_a) = 0$ and rate constant $(k) = 3.2 \times 10^6 \text{ s}^{-1}$ at 300 K. What is the value of the rate constant at 300 K?

(a) $3.2 \times 10^{-12} \text{ s}^{-1}$ (b) $3.2 \times 10^{6} \text{ s}^{-1}$

(c) $6.4 \times 10^{12} \text{ s}^{-1}$ (d) $6.4 \times 10^{6} \text{ s}^{-1}$

15. Given below are two statements, one is labelled as Assertion (A) and the other is labelled as Reason (R).

Assertion (A) Rate of chemical reaction is directly proportional to the frequency of successful collision between reactant molecules.

Reason (R) More collisions means opportunities for the reactant molecules to reacts with each other, which increases the rate of reaction.

In the light of the above statements, choose the correct answer from the options given below.

(a) Both (A) and (R) are true and (R) is the correct explanation of (A).

(b) Both (A) and (R) are true but (R) is not the correct explanation of (A).

(c) (A) is true but (R) is false.

(d) (A) is false but (R) is true.

16. An endothermic reaction $A \rightarrow B$ has an activation energy 15 kcal/mole and energy of reaction 5 kcal/mole. The activation energy of the reaction $B \rightarrow A$ is .... kcal/mole.

(a) 20 (b) 15 (c) 10 (d) 5

17. Relation between rate constant and temperature by Arrhenius equation is

(a) $\log_e A = \log_e k - \frac{E_a}{RT}$

(b) $\log k = A \frac{E_a}{RT}$

(c) $\log_e k = \log_e A - \frac{E_a}{RT^2}$

(d) $\log A = RT \ln E_a - \ln k$

18. The reason for almost doubling the rate of reaction on increasing the temperature of the reaction system by 10°C is

(a) increase in the value of threshold energy

(b) increase in collision frequency

(c) increase in the fraction of the molecules having energy equal to threshold energy or more

(d) decrease in activation energy

19. Given below are two statements, one is labelled as Assertion (A) and the other is labelled as Reason (R).

Assertion (A) The value ΔG increases when a catalyst is added to it.

Reason (R) Gibbs free energy is a state function.

In the light of the above statements, choose the correct answer from the options given below.

(a) Both (A) and (R) are true and (R) is the correct explanation of (A).

(b) Both (A) and (R) are true but (R) is not the correct explanation of (A).

(c) (A) is true but (R) is false.

(d) (A) is false but (R) is true.

20. The rate of a reaction is doubled for every 10° rise in temperature. The increase in reaction rate as a result of temperature rise from 10° to 100° is

(a) 112 (b) 512

(c) 400 (d) 614

21. Match List-I with List-II.

List-I (Characteristic)	List-II (Reason)
A. Catalyst alters the rate of reaction.	I. By lowering the activation energy.
B. Energetically favourable reactions are sometimes slow.	II. By increasing the concentration of the reactant.
C. Area under the Maxwell-Boltzmann curve is constant.	III. Proper orientation is not always there.
D. Frequency of successful collisions is increased.	IV. Total probability is one.

Choose the correct answer from the options given below.

(a) A-I, B-III, C-IV, D-II

(b) A-II, B-III, C-IV, D-I

(c) A-III, B-IV, C-I, D-II

(d) A-III, B-II, C-IV, D-I

22. A catalyst increase the rate of reaction because it

(a) increase the activation energy

(b) decrease the energy barrier for reaction

(c) decrease the collision factor

(d) increase the temperature coefficient

23. The activation energy of a reaction is zero. The rate constant of this reaction

(a) increase with increase of temperature

(b) decrease with an increase of temperature

(c) decrease with decrease of temperature

(d) is nearly independent of temperature

24. The rate constant is given by the equation $k = pZe^{-E_a/RT}$ which factor should register a decrease for the reaction to proceed more rapidly.

(a) T (b) Z

(c) E_a (d) p

25. Consider the following statements.

Statement I The number of collision per second per unit volume of the reaction mixture is called collision frequency.

Statement II The proper orientation of reactant molecules lead to bond formation whereas improper orientation makes them simply bounce back and no products are formed.

In the light of the above statements, choose the most appropriate answer from the options given below.

(a) Both Statement I and Statement II are incorrect.

(b) Statement I is correct but Statement II is incorrect.

(c) Statement I is incorrect but Statement II is correct.

(d) Both Statement I and Statement II are correct.

Response Index

01	a	b	c	d	10	a	b	c	d	19	a	b	c	d
02	a	b	c	d	11	a	b	c	d	20	a	b	c	d
03	a	b	c	d	12	a	b	c	d	21	a	b	c	d
04	a	b	c	d	13	a	b	c	d	22	a	b	c	d
05	a	b	c	d	14	a	b	c	d	23	a	b	c	d
06	a	b	c	d	15	a	b	c	d	24	a	b	c	d
07	a	b	c	d	16	a	b	c	d	25	a	b	c	d
08	a	b	c	d	17	a	b	c	d					
09	a	b	c	d	18	a	b	c	d					

Performance Scanner

> 90% Excellent !	You have mastered these topics. The concepts of these topics are at your fingertips. Move on to the chapter test and maintain this momentum.
76-90% Very Good !	You have a good command over these topics. Revise these topics again after a few days and enhance your performance.
60-75% Good !	You have a wide scope to learn for these topics. Revise these topics again.
<60 Not Satisfactory!	You have a long way ahead of you to master these topics. Revise it thoroughly.

Chapter Break Thru

Syllabus	Rate of a Chemical Reaction, Factors Affecting the Rate of Reaction, Elementary and Complex Reactions.	Order and Molecularity of Reaction, Rate Law, Rate Constant and its Units, Differential and Integral Forms of Zero and First Order Reactions and their Half-Lives.	Arrhenius Theory, Activation Energy and its Calculation, Collision Theory of Bimolecular Gaseous Reaction, The Effect of Temperature on the Rate of Reactions.

Important Instructions

- The test is of 1 hour duration and contains 50 multiple choice questions (Four options with a single correct answer).
- Choose the correct option and fill the OMR given on the last page of test accordingly.
- At some instances, you may find more than 1 option may be correct. In such circumstances, you have to judge the most appropriate answer as per the conditions given in the question.

1. In the following reaction, how is the rate of appearance of the underlined product related to the rate of disappearance of the underlined reactant?

$$BrO_3^-(aq) + \underline{5Br^-}(aq) + 6H^+(aq) \longrightarrow \underline{3Br_2}(l) + 3H_2O(l)$$

(a) $\frac{d[Br_2]}{dt} = -\frac{5}{3}\frac{d[Br^-]}{dt}$

(b) $\frac{d[Br_2]}{dt} = -\frac{d[Br^-]}{dt}$

(c) $\frac{d[Br_2]}{dt} = -\frac{d[Br^-]}{dt}$

(d) $\frac{d[Br_2]}{dt} = -\frac{3}{5}\frac{d[Br^-]}{dt}$

2. Choose the incorrect option for following reaction, ammonia and oxygen react at high temperature as

$$4NH_3(g) + 5O_2(g) \longrightarrow 4NO(g) + 6H_2O(g)$$

In an experiment, the rate of formation of NO is 3.6×10^{-3} mol L^{-1} s^{-1}.

	List-I (Reaction)	List-II (Properties)
(a)	$-\frac{1}{4}\frac{d[NH_3]}{dt} = -\frac{1}{5}\frac{[dO_2]}{dt} = \frac{1}{4}\frac{d[NO]}{dt} = \frac{1}{6}\frac{d[H_2O]}{dt}$	Rate of reaction
(b)	3.6×10^{-3} mol/L/s	Rate of disappearance of NH_3
(c)	4.5×10^{-3} mol/L/s	Rate of formation of O_2
(d)	1.4×10^{-3} mol/L/s	Rate of formation of H_2O

3. Select the incorrect statement about the rate of reaction.

(a) The rate of reaction decreases with decrease in temperature.
(b) The rate of reaction is uniform in zero order reaction.
(c) The rate of reaction depends upon the surface area of the solid reactant.
(d) Average and instantaneous rate of reaction is defined for micro and macroscopic time interval respectively.

4. Given below are two statements.

Statement I The order of reaction is always equal to the sum of the stoichiometic coefficient of reactant in the balanced chemical equation of a reaction.

Statement II The order of a reaction can be fractional number.

In the light of the above statements, choose the correct answer from the options given below.

(a) Both Statement I and Statement II are incorrect.
(b) Statement I is correct but Statement II is incorrect.

(c) Statement I is incorrect but Statement II is correct.
(d) Both Statement I and Statement II are correct.

5. Match the List-I with List-II.

List-I (Reaction)	List-II (Unit)
A. Zero order reaction	I. s^{-1}
B. First order reaction	II. mol/L/s
C. Second order reaction	III. $mol^{-2}L^2s^{-1}$
D. Third order reaction	IV. $mol^{-1}Ls^{-1}$

Choose the correct answer from the options given below.
(a) A-II, B-I, C-IV, D-III
(b) A-II, B-I, C-III, D-IV
(c) A-I, B-II, C-IV, D-III
(d) A-IV, B-I, C-II, D-III

6. For a reaction $3A \longrightarrow$ product, the rate of reaction doubles if the concentration of A is increased by four times. The order of reaction is
(a) 1 (b) 2
(c) 0.5 (d) 2.5

7. The rate of reaction, $2NO(g) + Cl_2(g) \longrightarrow 2NOCl(g)$, becomes doubled when the concentration of Cl_2 is doubled. However, when the concentration of both the reactants are doubled, the rate becomes eight times. The order with respect to NO and Cl_2 and overall order of reaction is

	w.r.t NO	w.r.t. Cl_2	Overall
(a)	1	0	2
(b)	1	2	3
(c)	3	2	1
(d)	2	1	3

8. The rate of disappearance of the MnO_4^- ion in the following reaction is $536 \times 10^{-3}\ Ms^{-1}$. Then the rate of appearance of I_2 is

$$2MnO_4^- + 10I^- + 16H^+ \longrightarrow 2Mn^{2+} + 5I_2 + 8H_2O$$

(a) $9.8 \times 10^{-3}\ Ms^{-1}$
(b) $13.4 \times 10^{-3}\ Ms^{-1}$
(c) $18.3 \times 10^{-2}\ Ms^{-1}$
(d) $21.3 \times 10^{-2}\ Ms^{-1}$

9. Given below are two statements, one is labelled as Assertion (A) and the other is labelled as Reason (R).

Assertion (A) The rate of reaction increases by increasing the temperature.

Reason (R) By increasing the temperature of reaction the number of activated molecules having energy greater than threshold energy increases.

In the light of the above statements, choose the correct answer from the options given below.
(a) Both (A) and (R) are true and (R) is the correct explanation of (A).
(b) Both (A) and (R) are true, but (R) is not the correct explanation of (A).
(c) (A) is true but (R) is false.
(d) (A) is false but (R) is true.

10. For a reaction $2NO(g) + Cl_2(g) \rightleftharpoons 2NOCl(g)$. When concentration of Cl_2 is doubled, the rate of reaction becomes two times of the original. When the concentration of NO is doubled the rate becomes four times. What is the order of the reaction?
(a) 1 (b) 3
(c) 4 (d) 2

11. The rate constant of reaction with a virus is $3.3 \times 10^{-4}s^{-1}$. Time required for the virus to becomes 75% inactivated is
(a) 35 min (b) 70 min
(c) 105 min (d) 17.5 min

12. For a first order reaction, the ratio of time taken to complete $\frac{3}{4}$ of the reaction and time taken to complete half of the reaction is
(a) 2 (b) 1
(c) 3.5 (d) 4.5

13. The half-life of a first order reaction is 60 min. How long will it take to consume 90% of the reactant?
(a) 50 min (b) 100 min
(c) 150 min (d) 200 min

14. If decomposition reaction $A(g) \longrightarrow B(g)$ follows first order kinetics, then the graph of rate of formation (R) of B against time t will be

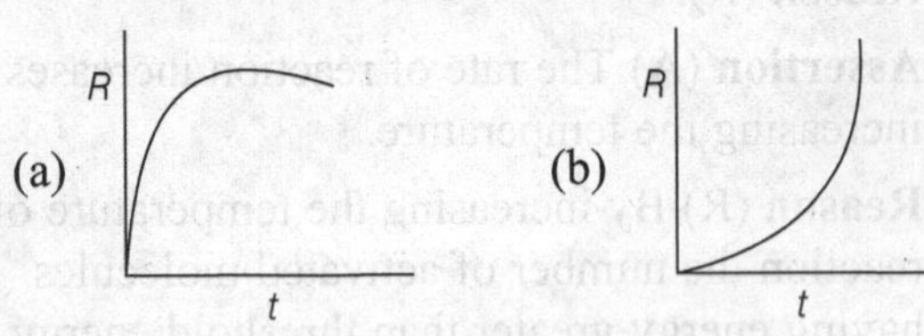

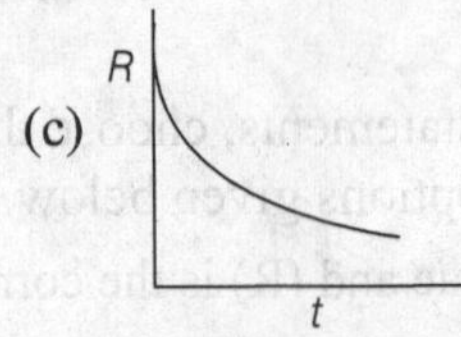

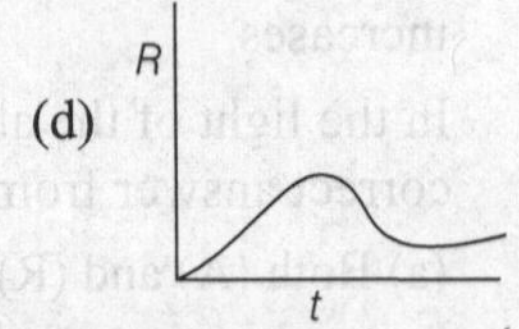

15. Match the List-I with List-II.

List-I	List-II
A. Order of a complex reaction is determined by	I. Order of slowest step
B. Mathematical expression for rate of reaction	II. Rate of reaction
C. Rate of reaction for zero order of reaction is equal to	III. Rate law
D. Units of rate constant for zero order reaction is same as that of	IV. Rate constant

Choose the correct answer from the options given below.

(a) A-I, B-III, C-IV, D-II
(b) A-II, B-III, C-I, D-III
(c) A-III, B-II, C-I, D-IV
(d) A-IV, B-I, C-II, D-III

16. Azoisopropane decomposes according to the following reaction,

$$(CH_3)_2CHN{=}NCH(CH_3)_2(g) \xrightarrow{250\text{-}290°C} N_2(g) + C_6H_{14}(g)$$

It is found to be a first order reaction. If the initial pressure is p_0 and pressure of the mixture at time t is p_t. Then the rate constant (k) would be

(a) $k = \dfrac{2303}{t}\log\dfrac{p_0}{2p_0 - p_t}$

(b) $k = \dfrac{2303}{t}\log\dfrac{p_0 - p_t}{p_0}$

(c) $k = \dfrac{2303}{t}\log\dfrac{p_0}{p_0 - p_t}$

(d) $k = \dfrac{2303}{t}\log\dfrac{2p_0}{2p_0 - p_t}$

17. Following data were obtained during the thermal decomposition of sulphuryl dichloride (SO_2Cl_2) at constant volume and 285°C. [$\log 1.55 = 0.19$; $\log 3.10 = 0.49$]

Time (s)	0	240	600
Pressure (torr)	180	244	302

Rate constant is

(a) $0.0182\ s^{-1}$
(b) $0.0282\ s^{-1}$
(c) $0.00182\ s^{-1}$
(d) $0.00282\ s^{-1}$

18. Which of the following statement is correct for zero order reaction?

(a) The rate constant is dimensionless.
(b) Amount of reactant remains the same throughout the reaction.
(c) $t_{1/2} \propto \dfrac{1}{\text{initial concentration of the reactant}}$
(d) A plot of concentration of reactant *vs* time is straight line with slope equal to $-k$.

19. The reaction $A(g) \longrightarrow B(g) + 2C(g)$ is a first order reaction with rate constant $2.772 \times 10^{-3} s^{-1}$. Starting with 0.1 mole of A in 2 L vessel, the concentration of A after 250 s when the reaction is allowed to take place at constant pressure and at 300 K temperature is

(a) Antilog (−1.001)
(b) Antilog (−1.601)
(c) Antilog (−1.001)
(d) Antilog (1.601)

20. For the first order reaction, $A \longrightarrow B + C$, carried out at 27°C. If 3.8×10^{-16}% of the reactant molecules exists in the activated state, the E_a (activation energy) of the reaction is

Given, $\log 3.8 = 0.58$

(a) 12 kJ mol^{-1}
(b) 831.4 kJ mol^{-1}
(c) 100 kJ mol^{-1}
(d) 88.57 kJ/mol^{-1}

21. Given below are two statements.

Statement I The half-life of zero order reaction is $t_{1/2} = \frac{[A_0]}{2k}$.

Statement II The half-life of zero order reaction is directly proportional to initial concentration.

In the light of the above statements, choose the correct answer from the options given below.

(a) Both Statement I and Statement II are incorrect.
(b) Statement I is correct but Statement II is incorrect.
(c) Statement I is incorrect but Statement II is correct.
(d) Both Statement I and Statement II are correct.

22. If a catalyst drops the activation energy of a reaction at 25°C from 80 kJ to 40 kJ. The magnitude of the affect on the forward reaction rate and backward rate is

(a) decreases by 10^7 times
(b) increases by 10^7 times
(c) decreases by 10^5 times
(d) decreases by 10^5 times

23. The rate of a reaction is tripled, when temperature changes from 20°C to 50°C. The energy of activation for the reaction ($R = 8.314$ J/K/mol) is

(a) 20.8 kJ/mol
(b) 23.8 kJ/mol
(c) 24.8 kJ/mol
(d) 28.8 kJ/mol

24. The Arrhenius equation for the rate constant of decomposition of methyl nitrite and ethyl nitrite are as follows

$$k_1(\text{s}^{-1}) = 10^{13}\exp\left(-\frac{152300}{RT}\right)\text{J/mol}$$

and $k_2\ (\text{s}^{-1}) = 10^{14}\exp\left(-\frac{157700}{RT}\right)$ J/mol

The temperature at which the rate constants are equal is

(a) 273 K
(b) 282 K
(c) 382 K
(d) 308 K

25. The distribution of molecular kinetic energy at two temperatures is as shown in the following graph

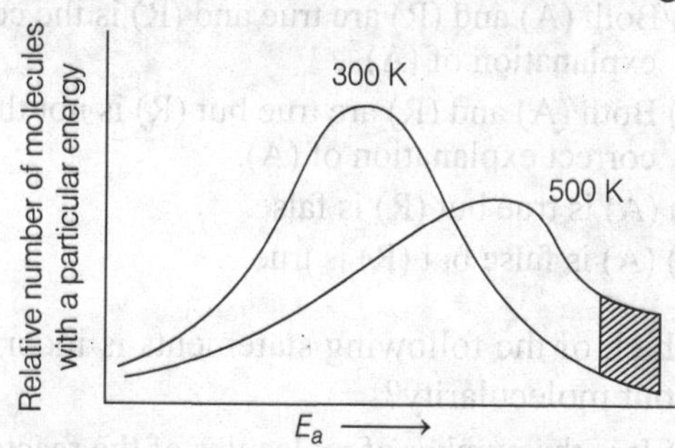

Which of the following conclusions is/are correct?

I. The number of molecules with energy E_a or greater is proportional to the shaded area for each temperature.
II. The number of molecules with energy E_a or less is proportional to the shaded area for each temperature.
III. Increasing the temperature of the substances decreases the fraction of molecules which collide with energies greater than E_a.
IV. The graph follows the Maxwell-Boltzmann energy distribution law.
V. The peak of the curve corresponds to the most probable kinetic energy.

Choose the correct answer from the options given below.

(a) IV and V
(b) I and III
(c) I, IV and V
(d) II and IV

26. Which factor has no major effect on the rate of reaction?

(a) Molecularity
(b) Temperature
(c) Concentration of reactant
(d) Nature of reactant

27. Given below are two statements, one is labelled as Assertion (A) and the other is labelled as Reason (R).

Assertion (A) Order and molecularity are same for a complex reaction.

Reason (R) Order is determined experimentally and in general molecularity is the sum of the stoichiometric coefficient of rate determining elementary step.

In the light of the above statements, choose the correct answer from the options given below.
(a) Both (A) and (R) are true and (R) is the correct explanation of (A).
(b) Both (A) and (R) are true but (R) is not the correct explanation of (A).
(c) (A) is true but (R) is false.
(d) (A) is false but (R) is true.

28. Which of the following statements is incorrect about molecularity?
(a) It is the number of molecules of the reactants taking part in a single step chemical reaction.
(b) It is calculated from the reaction mechanism.
(c) It may be either a whole number or fractional.
(d) It depends on the rate determining step in the reaction.

29. For a reaction, $2N_2O_5 \longrightarrow 4NO_2 + O_2$, if the value of rate and rate constant are 1.02×10^{-4} mol L^{-1} s^{-1} and 3.4×10^{-5} s^{-1} respectively then the concentration of N_2O_5 at that time will be
(a) 1.732 mol L^{-1}
(b) 3 mol L^{-1}
(c) 1.02×10^{-4} mol L^{-1}
(d) 3.2×10^{5} mol L^{-1}

30. According to collision theory, most molecular collision do not lead to reaction. Which of the following is the best appropriate necessary condition for collisions to successfully lead to reaction?
(a) Colliding molecule must have energy less than activation energy.
(b) A catalysts must be present at the collision.
(c) The colliding particles must be properly oriented in space when they collide and a catalyst must be present at the collision.
(d) Colliding molecule must have energy greater than activation energy and proper orientation of the molecules together.

31. Given below are two statements, one is labelled as Assertion (A) and the other is labelled as Reason (R).
Assertion (A) $R = Ae^{-E_a/RT}$, the Arrhenius equation represents the dependence of rate constant with temperature.
Reason (R) Plot of log k against $\frac{1}{T}$ is linear and the activation energy can be calculated with this plot.
In the light of the above statements, choose the correct answer from the options given below.
(a) Both (A) and (R) are true and (R) is the correct explanation of (A).
(b) Both (A) and (R) are true but (R) is not the correct explanation of (A).
(c) (A) is true but (R) is false.
(d) (A) is false but (R) is true.

32. Which of the following relations appears to be first order reaction?
$2N_2O_5(CCl_4) \longrightarrow 4NO_2(CCl_4) + O_2(g)$
I. $\frac{-d[N_2O_5]}{dt} = k[N_2O_5]$
II. $t_{50} = \frac{\log_e 2}{k}$
III. $[N_2O_5] = -kt + [N_2O_5]_0$
IV. $\frac{-d[N_2O_5]}{dt} = k[N_2O_5]^2$
V. $\log_e [N_2O_5] = -kt + \log_e [N_2O_5]_0$
Choose the correct answer from the options given below
(a) I, II and V (b) I, II and IV
(c) II and V (d) I, II and III

33. If in the fermentation of sugar in an enzymatic solution that is 0.12 M, the concentration of sugar is reduced to 0.06 M in 10 hr and 0.03 M in 20 hr. Thus, order of the reaction is
(a) 3 (b) 2 (c) 1 (d) 0

34. For a zero order reaction, the plot of concentration *vs* time is linear with
(a) positive slope and zero intercept
(b) negative slope and zero intercept
(c) positive slope and non-zero intercept
(d) negative slope and non-zero intercept

35. If initial concentration of reactants in certain reaction is doubled, the half-life period of the reaction doubles then the order of the reaction is
(a) zero (b) first
(c) second (d) third

36. Rate of a reaction can be expressed by Arrhenius equation as, $k = Ae^{-E_a/RT}$. In this equation, E_a represent

(a) the energy above which all the colliding molecules does react.

(b) the energy below which colliding molecules does not react.

(c) the total energy of the reacting molecules at a temperature, T.

(d) the fraction of molecules with energy greater than the activation energy of the reaction.

37. If a reaction $A + B \rightarrow C$, is exothermic to the extent of 50 kJ/mol and the forward reaction has an activation energy of 349 kJ/mol, the activation energy for reverse reaction in kJ/mol is

(a) 324 (b) 399
(c) 40 (d) 100

38. Given below are two statements.

Statement I Rate of zero order reaction is constant at constant temperature.

Statement II For zero order reaction $A \rightarrow B$, successive half-life of reaction decreases with the progress of the reaction.

In the light of the above statements, choose the correct answer from the options given below.

(a) Both Statement I and Statement II are incorrect.
(b) Statement I is correct but Statement II is incorrect.
(c) Statement I is incorrect but Statement II is correct.
(d) Both Statement I and Statement II are correct.

39. Select the incorrect statement about collision theory of reaction rate.

(a) It explains the effect of temperature on the rate of reaction.

(b) It assumes that the reactants must be in correct orientation to react.

(c) It predicts that rate does not depend on the frequency at which reactants collide.

(d) The collisions which have higher than the threshold value will give successful reaction.

40. For the zero order reaction $A \rightarrow B + C$; initial concentration of A is 0.1 M. If $A = 0.08$ M after 10 minutes, then its half-life and completion time are respectively

(a) 10 min ; 20 min
(b) 2×10^{-3} min, 4×10^{-3} min
(c) 25 min, 50 min
(d) 250 min, 500 min

41. The half-life period of a first order reaction is 15 minutes. The amount of substance left after one hour will be

(a) $\frac{1}{4}$ of the original amount

(b) $\frac{1}{8}$ of the original amount

(c) $\frac{1}{16}$ of the original amount

(d) $\frac{1}{32}$ of the original amount

42. According to the Arrhenius theory, the speed of the reaction increases because

(a) adsorption produces heat which increases the speed of the reaction.

(b) catalyst lowers the activation energy of the reaction.

(c) the concentration of reactant molecules at the active centres of the catalyst becomes high due to adsorption.

(d) in the process of adsorption, the activation energy of the molecules very large.

43. For given zero order reaction $A \rightarrow B + C$. If initial concentration of A is 2 M and rate of reaction is 2×10^{-2} M / sec, then half-life of reaction is

(a) 25 sec (b) 50 sec
(c) 100 sec (d) 60 min

44. The activation energy of a reaction is zero. Then the rate constant of the reaction is

(a) increases with increase of temperature
(b) decreases with decrease of temperature
(c) decreases with increase of temperature
(d) independent of temperature

45. The plot of a concentration of the reactant *vs* time for a reaction is a straight line with a negative slope. The reaction follows a

(a) first order (b) zero order
(c) second order (d) pseudo first order

46. In a first-order reaction $A \rightarrow B$, if k is rate constant and initial concentration of the reactant A is 0.6 M, then the half-life is

(a) $\frac{\log 2}{k}$ (b) $\frac{\log 2}{k\sqrt{0.6}}$

(c) $\frac{\ln 2}{k}$ (d) $\frac{0.0693}{0.6\,k}$

47. For the non-stoichiometric reaction, $2A + B \longrightarrow C + D$, the following kinetic data were obtained in three separate experiments, all at 298 K.

Initial concentration of A	Initial concentration of B	Initial rate of formation of C
0.1 M	0.1 M	1.3×10^{-3}
0.1 M	0.2 M	1.3×10^{-3}
0.2 M	0.1 M	2.6×10^{-3}

(a) $\frac{dC}{dt} = k[A][B]$ (b) $\frac{dC}{dt} = k[A]^2[B]$

(c) $\frac{dC}{dt} = k[A][B]^2$ (d) $\frac{dC}{dt} = k[A]$

48. The rate of the reaction $A + 2B \longrightarrow 3C$ gets increased by 72 times when the concentation of A is tripled and that of B is doubled. The order of the reaction with respect to A and B are

(a) 1, 2 (b) 2, 3

(c) 3, 2 (d) 2, 2

49. The data given below are for the reaction of NO and Cl_2 to form NOCl at 295 K.

$[Cl_2]$	[NO]	Initial rate $\times 10^{-3}$ (mol L^{-1} s^{-1})
0.05	0.05	1
0.15	0.05	3
0.05	0.15	9

Which of the following is the order with respect to NO and Cl_2 in the reaction?

(a) 1, 2 (b) 2, 1 (c) 3, 1 (d) 1, 3

50. Two reactants take part in a chemical reaction. The rate of reaction is directly proportional to the concentration of one of them and inversely proportional to the concentration of the other. The order of reaction is

(a) zero (b) 1 (c) 2 (d) 4

Response Index

01	ⓐ ⓑ ⓒ ⓓ	14	ⓐ ⓑ ⓒ ⓓ	27	ⓐ ⓑ ⓒ ⓓ	40	ⓐ ⓑ ⓒ ⓓ
02	ⓐ ⓑ ⓒ ⓓ	15	ⓐ ⓑ ⓒ ⓓ	28	ⓐ ⓑ ⓒ ⓓ	41	ⓐ ⓑ ⓒ ⓓ
03	ⓐ ⓑ ⓒ ⓓ	16	ⓐ ⓑ ⓒ ⓓ	29	ⓐ ⓑ ⓒ ⓓ	42	ⓐ ⓑ ⓒ ⓓ
04	ⓐ ⓑ ⓒ ⓓ	17	ⓐ ⓑ ⓒ ⓓ	30	ⓐ ⓑ ⓒ ⓓ	43	ⓐ ⓑ ⓒ ⓓ
05	ⓐ ⓑ ⓒ ⓓ	18	ⓐ ⓑ ⓒ ⓓ	31	ⓐ ⓑ ⓒ ⓓ	44	ⓐ ⓑ ⓒ ⓓ
06	ⓐ ⓑ ⓒ ⓓ	19	ⓐ ⓑ ⓒ ⓓ	32	ⓐ ⓑ ⓒ ⓓ	45	ⓐ ⓑ ⓒ ⓓ
07	ⓐ ⓑ ⓒ ⓓ	20	ⓐ ⓑ ⓒ ⓓ	33	ⓐ ⓑ ⓒ ⓓ	46	ⓐ ⓑ ⓒ ⓓ
08	ⓐ ⓑ ⓒ ⓓ	21	ⓐ ⓑ ⓒ ⓓ	34	ⓐ ⓑ ⓒ ⓓ	47	ⓐ ⓑ ⓒ ⓓ
09	ⓐ ⓑ ⓒ ⓓ	22	ⓐ ⓑ ⓒ ⓓ	35	ⓐ ⓑ ⓒ ⓓ	48	ⓐ ⓑ ⓒ ⓓ
10	ⓐ ⓑ ⓒ ⓓ	23	ⓐ ⓑ ⓒ ⓓ	36	ⓐ ⓑ ⓒ ⓓ	49	ⓐ ⓑ ⓒ ⓓ
11	ⓐ ⓑ ⓒ ⓓ	24	ⓐ ⓑ ⓒ ⓓ	37	ⓐ ⓑ ⓒ ⓓ	50	ⓐ ⓑ ⓒ ⓓ
12	ⓐ ⓑ ⓒ ⓓ	25	ⓐ ⓑ ⓒ ⓓ	38	ⓐ ⓑ ⓒ ⓓ		
13	ⓐ ⓑ ⓒ ⓓ	26	ⓐ ⓑ ⓒ ⓓ	39	ⓐ ⓑ ⓒ ⓓ		

Performance Scanner

> 90% Excellent !	You have mastered this chapter. The concepts of this chapter are at your fingertips. Move on to the next chapter and maintain this momentum.
76-90% Very Good !	You have a good command over this chapter. Revise the chapter again after a few days and enhance your performance.
60-75% Good !	You have a wide scope to learn for this chapter. Revise this chapter again.
<60 Not Satisfactory!	You have a long way ahead of you to master this chapter. Revise it thoroughly.

Scan for Online Chapter Test

Scan for Online Unit Test

Test Booklet No. **3947254**

Test Booklet Code **CH4**

MEDACE
NEET (UG)
SELF ASSESSMENT KIT

p-Block Element-II

Topics Covered

Group 15 Elements

Group 16 Elements

Group 17 Elements

Group 18 Elements

Important Instructions

- This Booklet Contains – 4 Topic Tests and One Test on Complete Chapter.
- Each question carries 4 marks.
- For each correct response the candidate will get 4 marks and for every incorrect response, 1 mark will be additionally deducted from the total score.
- Use **Blue/Black** point pen only for filling the OMR.
- Rough work is to be done in the space provided for this purpose in the test booklet only.

Name of the Candidate (In Capitals) ____________________

____

Candidate's Signature ____________________

Invigilator's Signature ____________________

Facsimile signature stamp of center superintendent ____________________

Do not open this Booklet until you start attempting the Test

Topical Follow Thru

Test 1

Syllabus General Introduction, Electronic Configuration, General Trends in Physical and Chemical Properties of Elements of Across the Periods and Down the Groups, Unique Behaviour of 1st Elements

For deeper insight **Scan the QR Code** 

Important Instructions

- The test is of 30 minutes duration and contains 25 multiple choice questions (Four options with a single correct answer).
- Choose the correct option and fill the OMR given on the last page of test accordingly.
- At some instances, you may find more than 1 option may be correct. In such circumstances, you have to judge the most appropriate answer as per the conditions given in the question.

1. Which of the following is an incorrect statement?

(a) N_2 is less reactive at room temperature.
(b) The covalency of nitrogen is 2 in N_2O_5.
(c) Single N—N bond is weaker than single P—P bond.
(d) N_2 is used in cryosurgery.

2. Select the correct statements.

I. Bond angle in PH_4^+ is higher than that in PH_3.
II. $R_3P=O$ exist but $R_3N=O$ does not (R = alkyl group).
III. All the bonds of PCl_5 are equivalent.
IV. NH_3 and PH_3 both form hydrogen bonding.
V. NH_3 forms bubbles when passed slowly in water but PH_3 dissolves.

Choose the correct answer from the options given below.

(a) I, III and IV
(b) III, IV and V
(c) I, IV and V
(d) I and II

3. Choose the correct statement about H_3PO_4.

(a) It has 3 P—OH bonds.
(b) On heating it gives pyrophosphorus acid.
(c) Its basicity is two.
(d) It does not act as oxidising agent.

4. Match the List-I with List-II.

	List-I (Compound)		List-II (Oxidation state of nitrogen)
A.	Dinitrogen monoxide	I.	+5
B.	Dinitrogen trioxide	II.	+1
C.	Dinitrogen tetroxide	III.	+3
D.	Dinitrogen pentoxide	IV.	+4

Choose the correct answer from the options given below.

(a) A-I, B-II, C-IV, D-III (b) A-II, B-III, C-IV, D-I
(c) A-III, B-I, C-II, D-IV (d) A-I, B-III, C-II, D-IV

5. Which of the following is the correct order for reducing character?

(a) $NH_3 > PH_3 > AsH_3 > SbH_3 > BiH_3$
(b) $PH_3 > NH_3 > AsH_3 > SbH_3 > BiH_3$
(c) $PH_3 > NH_3 > AsH_3 > BiH_3 > SbH_3$
(d) $BiH_3 > SbH_3 > AsH_3 > PH_3 > NH_3$

6. Select the incorrect statement about phosphorus and its compounds.

(a) White phosphorus is poisonous, insoluble in water.
(b) β-black phosphorus is formed when red phosphorus is heated in a sealed tube at 803 K.
(c) Phosphene is used in Holme's signals.
(d) On large scale nitric acid is produced by the process named Ostwald's process.

7. Which of the following statements is incorrect about ammonia?
(a) On large scale it is manufacture by Haber's process.
(b) It has trigonal pyramidal structure.
(c) It has higher melting and boiling points than expected.
(d) It is sp^2 hybridised.

8. Given below are two statements, one is labelled as Assertion (A) and the other is labelled as Reason (R).
Assertion (A) BiH_3 is the strongest reducing agent amongst all the hydrides of group 15 elements.
Reason (R) The Bi—H bond dissociation enthalpy is the lowest as compared to other hydrides of group 15 elements.
In the light of the above statements, choose the correct answer from the options given below.
(a) Both (A) and (R) are true and (R) is the correct explanation of (A).
(b) Both (A) and (R) are true, but (R) is not the correct explanation of (A).
(c) (A) is true but (R) is false.
(d) (A) is false but (R) is true.

9. Given below are two statements.
Statement I PCl_5 is more covalent than PCl_3.
Statement II When PCl_5 is heated, PCl_3 is formed.
In the light of the above statements, choose the most appropriate answer from the options given below.
(a) Both Statement I and Statement II are incorrect.
(b) Statement I is correct but Statement II is incorrect.
(c) Statement I is incorrect but Statement II is correct.
(d) Both Statement I and Statement II are correct.

10. Match List-I with List-II.

	List-I	List-II
A.	Orthophosphorus acid	I. $(HPO_3)_3$
B.	Cyclometaphosphoric acid	II. H_3PO_2
C.	Hypophosphorus acid	III. $H_4P_2O_7$
D.	Pyrophosphoric acid	IV. H_3PO_3

Choose the correct answer from the options given below.
(a) A-IV, B-I, C-II, D-III (b) A-I, B-IV, C-III, D-II
(c) A-II, B-III, C-IV, D-I (d) A-IV, B-I, C-III, D-II

11. Which of the following compound has the highest boiling point?
(a) NH_3 (b) PH_3
(c) AsH_3 (d) SbH_3

12. PCl_5 exists but NCl_5 does not because
(a) nitrogen has no vacant 2*d*-orbitals
(b) NCl_5 is unstable
(c) nitrogen atom is much smaller than P
(d) nitrogen is highly insert

13. Given below are two statements, one is labelled as Assertion (A) and the other is labelled as Reason (R).
Assertion (A) PH_3 has lower boiling point than NH_3.
Reason (R) In liquid state PH_3 molecules are associated through van der Waals' forces, but NH_3 molecules are associated through hydrogen bonding.
In the light of the above statements, choose the correct answer from the options given below.
(a) Both (A) and (R) are true and (R) is the correct explanation of (A).
(b) Both (A) and (R) are true, but (R) is not the correct explanation of (A).
(c) (A) is true but (R) is false.
(d) (A) is false but (R) is true.

14. Match List-I with List-II.

	List I (Oxide)	List II (Type of bond)
A.	N_2O_4	I. 1 N=O bond
B.	NO_2	II. 1 N—O—N bond
C.	N_2O_5	III. 1 N—N bond
D.	N_2O	IV. 1 N=N/N≡N bond

Choose the correct answer from the option given below.
(a) A-II, B-IV, C-III, D-I
(b) A-II, B-I, C-III, D-IV
(c) A-III, B-I, C-IV, D-II
(d) A-III, B-I, C-II, D-IV

15. Dilute nitric acid on reaction with Ag liberates
(a) NO gas (b) NO_2 gas
(c) N_2 gas (d) O_2 gas

16. Which one of the following combines with Fe (II) ions to form a brown complex?

(a) N_2O (b) NO
(c) N_2O_3 (d) N_2O_5

17. Which of the following is a tetrabasic acid?

(a) Orthophosphorus acid
(b) Orthophosphoric acid
(c) Metaphosphoric acid
(d) Pyrophosphoric acid

18. Ammonium dichromate on heating gives

(a) chromium oxide and ammonia
(b) chromic acid and nitrogen
(c) chromium oxide and nitrogen
(d) chromic acid and ammonia

19. Conc. HNO_3 can be stored in container of

(a) Al (b) Sn (c) Cu (d) Zn

20. Which is used as catalyst in the Haber process for the manufacture of NH_3?

(a) Pt (b) Fe + Mo
(c) CuO (d) Al_2O_3

21. There is very little difference in acid strength in the series H_3PO_4, H_3PO_3 and H_3PO_2 because

(a) phosphorus in these acids exists in different oxidation states
(b) the hydrogen in these acids are not all bounded to the phosphorus
(c) phosphorus is not a highly electronegative element
(d) phosphorus oxides are less basic

22. Which of the following element of group VA does not show allotropy?

(a) N (b) Bi (c) P (d) As

23. Number of 'P—OH bond' is same for which of the following oxoacids.

A. Hypophosphorus B. Orthophosphorus
C. Pyrophosphorus D. Hypohosphoric
E. Orthophosphoric

Choose the most appropriate answer from the options given below.

(a) B and D only
(b) B and C only
(c) A and E only
(d) A, B and E only

24. Identify the incorrect statement about group 15 element.

A. Dinitrogen is a diatomic gas which acts like an inert gas at room temperature.
B. The common oxidation state of these element are −3, +3 and +5.
C. Nitrogen has unique ability to form $p\pi$- $p\pi$ multiple bonds.
D. The stability of its oxidation state increase down the group.
E. Nitrogen show a maximum covalency of 6.

Choose the correct answer from the options given below.

(a) A, B, D only (b) A, C, E only
(c) B, D, E only (d) D and E only

25. Concentrated nitric acid react with P_4 gives

(a) $H_3P_2O_5$, NO and H_2O
(b) H_3PO_4 NO_2 and H_2O
(c) H_3PO_3, NO_2 and H_2O
(d) H_3PO_2, NO and H_2O

Response Index

01	a	b	c	d	10	a	b	c	d	19	a	b	c	d
02	a	b	c	d	11	a	b	c	d	20	a	b	c	d
03	a	b	c	d	12	a	b	c	d	21	a	b	c	d
04	a	b	c	d	13	a	b	c	d	22	a	b	c	d
05	a	b	c	d	14	a	b	c	d	23	a	b	c	d
06	a	b	c	d	15	a	b	c	d	24	a	b	c	d
07	a	b	c	d	16	a	b	c	d	25	a	b	c	d
08	a	b	c	d	17	a	b	c	d					
09	a	b	c	d	18	a	b	c	d					

Performance Scanner

> 90% Excellent !	You have mastered these topics. The concepts of these topics are at your fingertips. Move on to the next test and maintain this momentum.
76-90% Very Good !	You have a good command over these topics. Revise these topics again after a few days and enhance your performance.
60-75% Good !	You have a wide scope to learn for these topics. Revise these topics again.
<60 Not Satisfactory!	You have a long way ahead of you to master these topics. Revise it thoroughly.

Test 2

Syllabus General Introduction, Electronic Configuration, General Trends in Physical and Chemical Properties of Elements Across the Periods and Down the Groups, Unique Behaviour of 1st Element

For deeper insight Scan the QR Code

Important Instructions

- The test is of 30 minutes duration and contains 15 multiple choice questions (Four options with a single correct answer).
- Choose the correct option and fill the OMR given on the last page of test accordingly.
- At some instances, you may find more than 1 option may be correct. In such circumstances, you have to judge the most appropriate answer as per the conditions given in the question.

1. The nature of oxide SeO_2 and TeO_2 is indexed as 'X' and 'Y' type respectively. The correct set of X and Y is

(a) X = Basic; Y = Amphoteric
(b) X = Acidic; Y = Acidic
(c) X = Acidic; Y = Amphoteric
(d) X = Amphoteric; Y = Basic

2. Which of the following is the correct order for the acidic character?

(a) $H_2Se < H_2O < H_2S < H_2Te$
(b) $H_2O < H_2S < H_2Se < H_2Te$
(c) $H_2O < H_2Se < H_2S < H_2Te$
(d) $H_2Te < H_2Se < H_2S < H_2O$

3. Consider the following statements about oxygen.

I. It has three isotopic form.
II. It is paramagnetic in nature.
III. It shows covalency of 4 only.
IV. It shows –2 oxidation state.
V. It is used in oxyacetylene welding.

Choose the correct statement and mark the correct option given below.

(a) I and III (b) II, III, IV and V
(c) III, IV and V (d) I, II, IV and V

4. Given below are two statements, one is labelled as Assertion (A) and the other is labelled as Reason (R).

Assertion (A) The electron gain enthalpy with negative sign is less for oxygen than that of sulphur.

Reason (R) Oxygen has small size thus its electron density is less.

In the light of the above statements, choose the correct answer from the options given below.

(a) Both (A) and (R) are true and (R) is the correct explanation of (A).
(b) Both (A) and (R) are true, but (R) is not the correct explanation of (A).
(c) (A) is true but (R) is false.
(d) (A) is false but (R) is true.

5. Choose the incorrect statement.

(a) Sulphur is mainly extracted by Frasch process.
(b) Monoclinic sulphur is the stable form of sulphur.
(c) Rhombic sulphur transforms to monoclinic sulphur when heated above 369 K.
(d) Rhombic sulphur is also known as α-sulphur.

6. Which of the following statements is not correct about ozone?

(a) It is an allotropic form of oxygen.
(b) Its molecule is angular in shape.
(c) Its O—O—O bond angle is 117°.
(d) Its O—O bond length is identical with that of molecular oxygen.

7. Sulphuric acid on reaction with PCl_5 gives product X of phosphorus. The oxidation state of P in the product X is

(a) +5 (b) +6
(c) +3 (d) +2

8. Given below are two statements.

Statement I H_2O is liquid while H_2S is gas.

Statement II SF_6 is known but SCl_6 is not.

In the light of the above statements, choose the most appropriate answer from the options given below.
(a) Both Statement I and Statement II are incorrect.
(b) Statement I is correct but Statement II is incorrect.
(c) Statement I is incorrect but Statement II is correct.
(d) Both Statement I and Statement II are correct.

9. Which of the following statements is correct about peroxodisulphuric acid?
(a) It contains O—O bond.
(b) It has six OH groups.
(c) It has two S = O bonds.
(d) Its formula is $H_2S_2O_7$.

10. Which of the following statement is true about ozone?
(a) It is harmful because ozone is dangerous to living organism.
(b) It is beneficial because oxidation reaction can proceed faster in the presence of ozone.
(c) It is beneficial because ozone cuts out the ultraviolet radiation of the sun.
(d) It is harmful because ozone cuts out the important radiation of the sun which are vital for photosynthesis.

11. Given below are two statements.
Statement I α and β forms of sulphur can change reversibly between themselves with slow heating or slow cooling.
Statement II At room temperature the stable crystalline form of sulphur is monoclinic sulphur.
In the light of the above statement, choose the correct answer from the option given below.
(a) Both Statement I and Statement II are incorrect.
(b) Statement I is correct but Statement II is incorrect.
(c) Statement I is incorrect but Statement II is correct.
(d) Both Statement I and Statement II are correct.

12. The correct order of electron gain enthalpy is
(a) S > Se > Te > O
(b) Te > Se > S > O
(c) O > S > Se > Te
(d) S > O > Se > Te

13. The total no. of acidic oxides from the following list is
$$SO_2, N_2O, TeO_2, NO, CO, SO_3, SeO_2$$
(a) 3 (b) 4 (c) 5 (d) 6

14. For OF_2 molecule consider the following.
A. Number of lone pairs on oxygen is 2.
B. FOF angle is less than 104.5°.
C. Oxidation state of O is –2.
D. Molecule is bent 'V' shaped.
E. Molecular geometry is linear.
Choose the correct statements from the options given below.
(a) C, D, E only (b) B, E, A only
(c) A, C, D only (d) A, B, D only

15. Which of the elements of group 16 has the maximum tendency of catenation?
(a) Oxygen (b) Sulphur
(c) Selenium (d) Tellurium

Response Index

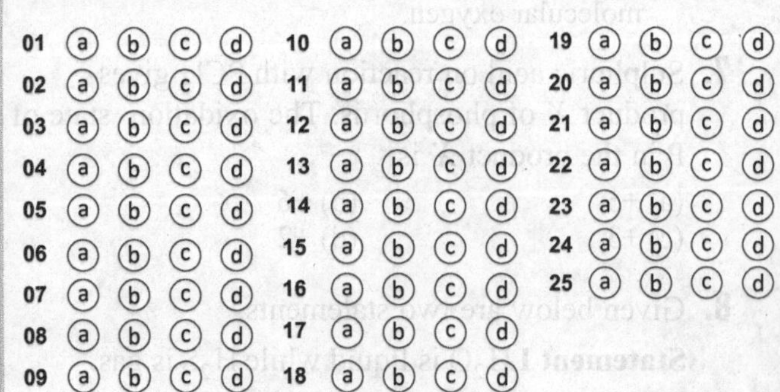

Performance Scanner

> 90% Excellent ! You have mastered these topics. The concepts of these topics are at your fingertips. Move on to the next test and maintain this momentum.

76-90% Very Good ! You have a good command over these topics. Revise these topics again after a few days and enhance your performance.

60-75% Good ! You have a wide scope to learn for these topics. Revise these topics again.

<60 Not Satisfactory! You have a long way ahead of you to master these topics. Revise it thoroughly.

Test 3

Syllabus General Introduction, Electronic Configuration, General Trends in Physical and Chemical Properties of Elements Across the Periods and Down the Groups, Unique Behaviour of 1st Element

For deeper insight **Scan the QR Code**

Important Instructions

- The test is of 30 minutes duration and contains 15 multiple choice questions (Four options with a single correct answer).
- Choose the correct option and fill the OMR given on the last page of test accordingly.
- At some instances, you may find more than 1 option may be correct. In such circumstances, you have to judge the most appropriate answer as per the conditions given in the question.

1. Which of the following is the covalent oxide of iodine?

(a) I_2O_9 and I_2O_4
(b) I_2O_7 and I_2O_9
(c) Only I_2O_5
(d) I_2O_4 and I_2O_7

2. When chlorine reacts with concentrated NaOH under hot condition, the oxidation state of chlorine changes from zero to

(a) −1 and +5
(b) +1 and +4
(c) +5 and +3
(d) −1 and +1

3. Which of the following product is formed when chlorine is reacted with excess of ammonia?

(a) NCl_3 and HCl
(b) N_2 and HCl
(c) NH_4Cl and NCl_3
(d) NH_4Cl and N_2

4. Match List-I with List-II.

	List-I (Compounds)	List-II (Structure)
A.	ClF_3	I. Pentagonal bipyramidal
B.	IF_5	II. Bent T-shaped
C.	IF_7	III. Square pyramidal
D.	I_3^-	IV. Linear

Choose the correct answer from the options given below.

(a) A-III, B-II, C-I, D-IV
(b) A-II, B-III, C-I, D-IV
(c) A-IV, B-III, C-II, D-I
(d) A-I, B-II, C-IV, D-III

5. The increasing order of oxidising power of oxoacids of chlorine is

(a) $HClO_4 < HClO_3 < HClO_2 < HClO$
(b) $HClO < HClO_2 < HClO_3 < HClO_4$
(c) $HClO_2 < HClO < HClO_4 < HClO_3$
(d) $HClO_2 < HClO < HClO_3 < HClO_4$

6. Which of the following is the incorrect use of chlorine?

(a) Used for bleaching wood pulp, cotton etc.
(b) In the preparation of phosgene, tear gas and mustard gas.
(c) In the extraction of gold and platinum.
(d) It is used for arc welding.

7. Choose the incorrect statement.

(a) Bromine and iodine are highly soluble in organic solvent.
(b) Fluorine has smaller bond dissociation enthalpy than chlorine.
(c) Fluorine forms number of stable oxoacids.
(d) I_2O_5 is used in the estimation of carbon monoxide.

8. Hydrofluoric acid is not preserved in glass bottles because

(a) It reacts with the visible part of light.
(b) It reacts with the sodium oxide of the glass composition.
(c) It reacts with the aluminium oxide of the glass composition.
(d) It reacts with the silicon dioxide of glass.

9. Fluorine reacts with water and may give
(a) HF and O_2
(b) HF and OF_2
(c) HF and O_3
(d) HF, O_2 and O_3

10. The increasing order of reactivity of halogen is
(a) $I_2 < Br_2 < Cl_2 < F_2$
(b) $Cl_2 < F_2 < Br_2 < I_2$
(c) $Cl_2 < Br_2 < I_2 < F_2$
(d) $I_2 < Cl_2 < Br_2 < F_2$

11. The correct order of stability of oxoacids of chlorine is
(a) $HClO_4 > HClO_3 > HClO_2 > HClO$
(b) $HClO > HClO_3 > HClO_2 > HClO_4$
(c) $HClO_3 > HClO_4 > HClO_2 > HClO$
(d) $HClO_4 > HClO_2 > HClO_3 > HClO$

12. Super halogen is
(a) F_2 (b) Cl_2
(c) Br_2 (d) I_2

13. The van der Waals' forces in halogens decrease in the order
(a) $F_2 > Cl_2 > Br_2 > I_2$
(b) $I_2 > Br_2 > Cl_2 > F_2$
(c) $Br_2 > Cl_2 > F_2 > I_2$
(d) $Cl_2 > Br_2 > I_2 > F_2$

14. Match List-I with List-II.

	List-I	List-II
A.	F_2O	I. sp^2-hybridisation
B.	ClO_2	II. sp^3-hybridisation
C.	BrF_3	III. sp^3d^2-hybridisation
D.	IF_5	IV. sp^3d-hybridisation

Choose the correct answer from the options given below.
(a) A-III, B-II, C-I, D-IV
(b) A-IV, B-III, C-II, D-I
(c) A-I, B-II, C-III, D-IV
(d) A-II, B-I, C-IV, D-III

15. Given below are two statements, one is labelled as Assertion (A) and the other is labelled as Reason (R).
Assertion (A) Iodine forms heptafluoride.
Reason (R) Because 5*d*-orbital are available for valence shell expansion.
In the light of the above statements, choose the correct answer from the options given below.
(a) Both (A) and (R) are true and (R) is the correct explanation of (A).
(b) Both (A) and (R) are true, but (R) is not the correct explanation of (A).
(c) (A) is true but (R) is false.
(d) (A) is false but (R) is true.

Response Index

01 ⓐ ⓑ ⓒ ⓓ	10 ⓐ ⓑ ⓒ ⓓ	19 ⓐ ⓑ ⓒ ⓓ
02 ⓐ ⓑ ⓒ ⓓ	11 ⓐ ⓑ ⓒ ⓓ	20 ⓐ ⓑ ⓒ ⓓ
03 ⓐ ⓑ ⓒ ⓓ	12 ⓐ ⓑ ⓒ ⓓ	21 ⓐ ⓑ ⓒ ⓓ
04 ⓐ ⓑ ⓒ ⓓ	13 ⓐ ⓑ ⓒ ⓓ	22 ⓐ ⓑ ⓒ ⓓ
05 ⓐ ⓑ ⓒ ⓓ	14 ⓐ ⓑ ⓒ ⓓ	23 ⓐ ⓑ ⓒ ⓓ
06 ⓐ ⓑ ⓒ ⓓ	15 ⓐ ⓑ ⓒ ⓓ	24 ⓐ ⓑ ⓒ ⓓ
07 ⓐ ⓑ ⓒ ⓓ	16 ⓐ ⓑ ⓒ ⓓ	25 ⓐ ⓑ ⓒ ⓓ
08 ⓐ ⓑ ⓒ ⓓ	17 ⓐ ⓑ ⓒ ⓓ	
09 ⓐ ⓑ ⓒ ⓓ	18 ⓐ ⓑ ⓒ ⓓ	

Performance Scanner

> 90% Excellent !	You have mastered these topics. The concepts of these topics are at your fingertips. Move on to the next test and maintain this momentum.
76-90% Very Good !	You have a good command over these topics. Revise these topics again after a few days and enhance your performance.
60-75% Good !	You have a wide scope to learn for these topics. Revise these topics again.
<60 Not Satisfactory!	You have a long way ahead of you to master these topics. Revise it thoroughly.

Test 4

Syllabus General Introduction, Electronic Configuration, General Trends in Physical and Chemical Properties of Elements Across the Periods and Down the Groups, Unique Behaviour of 1st Element

For deeper insight **Scan the QR Code**

Important Instructions

- The test is of 30 minutes duration and contains 15 multiple choice questions (Four options with a single correct answer).
- Choose the correct option and fill the OMR given on the last page of test accordingly.
- At some instances, you may find more than 1 option may be correct. In such circumstances, you have to judge the most appropriate answer as per the conditions given in the question.

1. Which of the following is incorrect about noble gases?

(a) They have very low boiling point.
(b) It been difficult to study the chemistry of radon.
(c) Helium is used in diving apparatus.
(d) XeF_3 and XeF_5 are examples of xenon fluorides.

2. Select the incorrect reaction.

(a) $XeF_2 + SbF_5 \longrightarrow [XeF_3]^+ [SbF_6]^-$
(b) $XeF_2 + PF_5 \longrightarrow [XeF]^+ [PF_6]^-$
(c) $XeF_4 + O_2F_2 \xrightarrow{143\text{ K}} XeF_6 + O_2$
(d) $2XeOF_4 + SiO_2 \longrightarrow 2XeF_2 + SiF_4 + 2O_2$

3. The hybridisation of XeF_4 and XeF_6 respectively are

(a) sp^3d^2 and sp^3d^3 (b) sp^3d and sp^3d^2
(c) sp^3 and sp^3d^2 (d) sp^3d^1 and sp^3d^3

4. Which of the following inert gas liquifies easily?

(a) Kr (b) He (c) Ne (d) Ar

5. Which element out He, Ar, Kr and Xe forms least number of compound?

(a) He (b) Ar (c) Kr (d) Xe

6. In $XeF_2, XeF_4, XeFe_6$ the number of lone pairs on Xe is respectively.

(a) 2, 3, 1 (b) 1, 2, 3
(c) 4, 1, 2 (d) 3, 2, 1

7. The correct order of solubility in water for He, Ne, Ar, Kr, Xe is

(a) Xe > Kr > Ar > Ne > He
(b) He > Ne > Ar > Kr > Xe
(c) Ar > Ne > He > Kr > Xe
(d) Ne > Ar > Kr > He > Xe

8. Compound X reacts with silica and forms $XeOF_4$ and SiF_4. What will be the hybridisation and geometry of compound X?

(a) sp^3d^2 and octahedral
(b) sp^3d^3 and distorted octahedral
(c) sp^3d and square planar
(d) sp^3d and tetrahedral

9. Which of the following statements is not correct for a noble gas?

(a) Ar is used in electric bulbs.
(b) Kr is obtained during radioactive disintegration.
(c) Half-life of Rn is only 3.8 days.
(d) He is used to producing very low temperature.

10. Which one of the following noble gases is not found in the atmosphere?

(a) Rn (b) Kr
(c) Ne (d) Ar

11. XeF_4 on partial hydrolysis produces

(a) XeF_2 (b) $XeOF_2$
(c) $XeOF_4$ (d) XeO_3

12. The shape of XeF_2 molecule is

(a) square planar
(b) trigonal bipyramidal
(c) trigonal planar
(d) linear

13. Which of the following fluorides of xenon is impossible?

(a) XeF_6 (b) XeF_4
(c) XeF_3 (d) XeF_2

14. The noble gas which forms maximum number of compound is

(a) Ar (b) He
(c) Xe (d) Ne

15. Which one of the following statements regarding helium is incorrect?

(a) It is used to produce and sustain powerful superconducting magnet.
(b) It is used as a cryogenic agent for carrying out experiments at low temperature.
(c) It is used to fill gas balloons instead of hydrogen because it is lighter and flammable.
(d) It is used in gas-cooled nuclear reactors.

Response Index

No.	Options	No.	Options	No.	Options
01	(a) (b) (c) (d)	10	(a) (b) (c) (d)	19	(a) (b) (c) (d)
02	(a) (b) (c) (d)	11	(a) (b) (c) (d)	20	(a) (b) (c) (d)
03	(a) (b) (c) (d)	12	(a) (b) (c) (d)	21	(a) (b) (c) (d)
04	(a) (b) (c) (d)	13	(a) (b) (c) (d)	22	(a) (b) (c) (d)
05	(a) (b) (c) (d)	14	(a) (b) (c) (d)	23	(a) (b) (c) (d)
06	(a) (b) (c) (d)	15	(a) (b) (c) (d)	24	(a) (b) (c) (d)
07	(a) (b) (c) (d)	16	(a) (b) (c) (d)	25	(a) (b) (c) (d)
08	(a) (b) (c) (d)	17	(a) (b) (c) (d)		
09	(a) (b) (c) (d)	18	(a) (b) (c) (d)		

Performance Scanner

> 90% Excellent !	You have mastered these topics. The concepts of these topics are at your fingertips. Move on to the chapter test and maintain this momentum.
76-90% Very Good !	You have a good command over these topics. Revise these topics again after a few days and enhance your performance.
60-75% Good !	You have a wide scope to learn for these topics. Revise these topics again.
<60 Not Satisfactory!	You have a long way ahead of you to master these topics. Revise it thoroughly.

Chapter Break Thru

Syllabus	General Introduction, Electronic Configuration, General Trends in Physical and Chemical Properties of Elements Across the Periods and Down the Groups, Unique Behaviour of 1st Element	General Introduction, Electronic Configuration, General Trends in Physical and Chemical Properties of Elements Across the Periods and Down the Groups, Unique Behaviour of 1st Element	General Introduction, Electronic Configuration, General Trends in Physical and Chemical Properties of Elements Across the Periods and Down the Groups, Unique Behaviour of 1st Element	General Introduction, Electronic Configuration, General Trends in Physical and Chemical Properties of Elements Across the Periods and Down the Groups, Unique Behaviour of 1st Element

Important Instructions

- The test is of 1 hour duration and contains 50 multiple choice questions (Four options with a single correct answer).
- Choose the correct option and fill the OMR given on the last page of test accordingly.
- At some instances, you may find more than 1 option may be correct. In such circumstances, you have to judge the most appropriate answer as per the conditions given in the question.

1. Which of the following form of sulphur show paramagnetic behaviour?

(a) S_2 (b) S_8
(c) S_6 (d) S_4

2. Select the incorrect match from the following option.

(a)	$p\pi$- $p\pi$ bond formation	$\rightarrow$	O_2 molecule
(b)	Puckered ring	$\rightarrow$	S_8
(c)	Rhombic (α) allotropes	$\rightarrow$	Sulphur
(d)	Monoclinic (β) allotropes	$\rightarrow$	Oxygen

3. Given below are two statements.

Statement I Ozone is poisonous in nature yet it is used in water purification.

Statement II Ozone is thermodynamically unstable than oxygen.

In the light of the above statements, choose the correct answer from the options given below.

(a) Both Statement I and Statement II are incorrect.
(b) Statement I is correct but Statement II is incorrect.
(c) Statement I is incorrect but Statement II is correct.
(d) Both Statement I and Statement II are correct.

4. Select the incorrect match of the order with the property mention in the bracket.

(a) $F^- > Cl^- > Br^- > I^-$ (Stability of halide ion of group 16 elements)
(b) $H_2S < H_2Se < H_2Te$ (Reducing character)
(c) $H_2Te < H_2Se < H_2S < H_2O$ (H—*B*—H bond angle)
(d) $H_2O < H_2S < H_2Se < H_2Te < H_2Po$ (Thermal stability

5. Select the acidic and amphoteric oxide from the given oxides.

I. P_4O_{10} II. Al_2O_3 III. SnO_2
IV. CaO V. N_2O_5 VI. Na_2O VII. SO_3

Choose the correct answer from the options given below.

	Acidic oxide	Amphoteric oxide
(a)	I and II	II and IV
(b)	I, V and VII	II and III
(c)	I, III and VII	II, III and IV
(d)	II, III and IV	I, V, VI and VII

6. Which of the following does not react with oxygen directly?

(a) Zn (b) Ti (c) Pt (d) Fe

7. Given below are two statements.

Statement I Rhombic sulphur is most stable allotrope and is called as α-sulphur.

Statement II Plastic sulphur contains long inverted *zig-zag* chain and these chains are formed by opening of S_8 rings.

In the light of the above statements, choose the correct answer from the options given below.

(a) Both Statement I and Statement II are incorrect.
(b) Statement I is correct but Statement II is incorrect.
(c) Statement I is incorrect but Statement II is correct.
(d) Both Statement I and Statement II are correct.

8. Match the List-I with List-II.

	List-I (Name of oxoacid of sulphur)	List-II (Formula)
A.	Marshall's acid	I. H_2SO_5
B.	Oleum	II. $H_2S_2O_8$
C.	Caro's acid	III. $H_2S_2O_7$
D.	Dithionic acid	IV. $H_2S_2O_6$

Choose the correct answer from the options given below.

(a) A-II, B-III, C-I, D-IV
(b) A-I, B-II, C-III, D-IV
(c) A-III, B-II, C-I, D-IV
(d) A-IV, B-III, C-II, D-I

9. Select the incorrect match of the order, and the properties given in bracket.

(a) $F_2 < Cl_2 < Br_2 < I_2$ (Melting point)
(b) $I_2 < F_2 < Br_2 < Cl_2$ (Bond dissociation enthalpy)
(c) $I_2 < Br_2 < Cl_2 < F_2$ (Oxidising nature)
(d) I < Br < Cl < F (Negative electron gain enthalpy)

10. Select the correct statement for halogens.

I. Fluorine show –1 oxidation state only whereas other elements of this group show –1, +1, +3, +5, and +7.
II. All the halogens have high value of ionisation energy and exhibit non-metallic character.
III. The ionic character of metal halide increases on going down the group as *M*F< *M*Cl< *M*Br< *MI* (where, *M* is a monovalent metal)
IV. Cl_2 is more reactive than ClF.
V. On hydrolysis ClF forms HOCl and HF.

Choose the correct answer from the options given below.

(a) I, II and V (b) II and III
(c) I, II and III (d) I and III

11. Choose the incorrect match of the order with respect to the property mention in the bracket.

(a) HF < HCl < HBr < HI (Acidic nature)
(b) HI < HBr < HCl < HF (Thermal stability)
(c) HF < HCl < HBr < HI (Reducing character)
(d) HF < HBr < HI < HCl (Boiling point)

12. Which of the following analogies is incorrect?

(a) Oxidising agent : $F_2 > Cl_2$: : Electron gain enthalpy (with negative sign) : $F_2 < Cl_2$
(b) $HOCl_3$: Chloric acid : : $HOBrO_2$: Perbromic acid
(c) BrF_3 : Trigonal bipyramidal :: ClF_5 : Square pyramidal
(d) ClF_3 : Used for the production of UF_6 : : SO_2 : Used in bleaching of wool and silk

13. Select the correct statement about chlorine.

I. Horn silver and carnalite are major source of chlorine.
II. In Deacon process, Cl_2 is obtained by heating of HCl and O_2 at 723K in presence of $CuCl_2$ catalyst.
III. $Cl_2 + H_2O$ used as permanent bleaching action.
IV. When excess Cl_2 is added into NH_3 then NCl_3 is obtained while excess of ammonia with Cl_2 gives ammonium chloride.
V. Electronegativity of nitrogen is less than that of chlorine.

Choose the correct answer from the options given below.

(a) I, II and III (b) II, III and IV
(c) I, II, III and IV (d) I, III and V

14. Which of the following gases is not prepared by using chlorine gas?

(a) Phosgene gas (b) Tear gas
(c) Mustard gas (d) *Syn* gas

15. Which of the following reaction does not give precipitate with HCl?

(a) $AgNO_3 + HCl \longrightarrow AgCl + HNO_3$
(b) $Pb(NO_3)_2 + 2HCl \longrightarrow PbCl_2 + 2HNO_3$
(c) $Hg_2(NO_3)_2 + 2HCl \longrightarrow Hg_2Cl_2 + 2HNO_3$
(d) $NH_3 + HCl \longrightarrow NH_4Cl$

16. Correct order of acidic nature of oxo acid of chlorine is

(a) $HOCl < HClO_2 < HClO_3 < HClO_4$
(b) $HOCl < HClO_2 < HClO_4 < HClO_3$
(c) $HClO_4 < HClO_3 < HClO_2 < HOCl$
(d) $HClO_4 < HClO_3 < HClO < HClO_2$

17. In contact process,

$$2SO_2 + O_2 \underset{}{\overset{V_2O_5}{\rightleftharpoons}} 2SO_3(g)$$

Favourable condition for the preparation of more yield of SO_3 is/are

(a) at low temperature (720 K) and high pressure with V_2O_5 catalyst.
(b) at high pressure and high temperature with V_2O_5 catalyst.
(c) at low temperature and low temperature with alumina catalyst.
(d) at low temperature (720 K) and high pressure with alumina catalyst.

18. Select the correct statement about ozone.

(a) It turns filter paper soaked in alcoholic solution of benzidine to blue colour.
(b) It causes mercury to stick to the side of the glass tube.
(c) It turns moist starch iodide paper into red colour.
(d) It decolourises $KMnO_4$ or $K_2Cr_2O_7$.

19. Select the incorrect statement about physical properties of inert gas.

(a) These are sparingly soluble in water and solubility decreases with increase in atomic number.
(b) Ionisation enthalpy of these gases are very high due to stable electronic configuration.
(c) In general, the enthalpies of fusion and vaporisation of these elements are very low and increases down the group.
(d) Due to stable configuration, noble gases have no tendency to accept additional electrons.

20. Match the List-I with List-II.

	List-I (Xenon compounds)	List-II (Shape)
A.	$XeOF_2$	I. Pyramidal
B.	$XeOF_4$	II. T-shape
C.	XeO_3	III. Square pyramidal
D.	XeF_4	IV. Square planar

Choose the correct answer from the options given below.

(a) A-I, B-II, C-IV, D-III
(b) A-II, B-III, C-I, D-IV
(c) A-III, B-II, C-IV, D-I
(d) A-I, B-II, C-III, D-IV

21. Which of the following statements regarding the noble gas is incorrect?

(a) The boiling point increases from He to Xe.
(b) Radon is found in atmosphere.
(c) The correct atomic radius order for noble gases is He < Ne < Ar < Kr < Xe.
(d) Xenon does not form XeF_5.

22. Given below are two statements, one is labelled as Assertion (A) and the other is labelled as Reason (R).

Assertion (A) Dioxygen is a gas, while sulphur is a solid at room temperature.

Reason (R) O_2 molecules are held together by van der Waals' forces, while sulphur shows catenation and form S—S bonds.

In the light of the above statements, choose the correct answer from the options given below.

(a) Both (A) and (R) are true and (R) is the correct explanation of (A).
(b) Both (A) and (R) are true but (R) is not the correct explanation of (A).
(c) (A) is true but (R) is false.
(d) (A) is false but (R) is true.

23. Correct order of decreasing number of π-bonds in H_2SO_4, H_2SO_5 and $H_2S_2O_6$ is

(a) $H_2SO_5 > H_2SO_4 > H_2SO_6$
(b) $H_2SO_6 > H_2SO_5 > H_2SO_4$
(c) $H_2SO_6 > H_2SO_4 > H_2SO_5$
(d) $H_2SO_6 > H_2SO_5 = H_2SO_4$

24. In XeO_3F_2, the number of bond pair(s), π-bond(s) and lone pair(s) on Xe atom respectively are

(a) 5, 3, 0 (b) 5, 2, 0
(c) 4, 2, 2 (d) 4, 4, 0

25. Which of the following option contain all chalcogen elements?

(a) Se, Te and Po (b) O, Ti and Po
(c) S, Te and Pm (d) Se, Te and Pu

26. How will the boiling point of H_2S relate with H_2O, if the boiling point of H_2O is 373 K?
(a) It is less than 300 K.
(b) It equal to 300 K.
(c) It more than 373 K.
(d) It greater than 300 K but less than 373 K.

27. Which of the following hydrides does not have reducing property?
(a) H_2O (b) H_2S
(c) H_2Se (d) H_2Te

28. Consider the following reactions.

$$Zn + \underset{\text{(dil.)}}{HNO_3} \longrightarrow Zn(NO_3)_2 + H_2O + X$$

$$Zn + \underset{\text{(conc.)}}{HNO_3} \longrightarrow Zn(NO_3)_2 + H_2O + Y$$

The oxidation state of N in *X* and *Y* are respectively.
(a) +1 and +4 (b) +2 and +4
(c) +4 and +2 (d) +2 and +1

29. Consider the following statements about group 15 elements.

I. Bi (V) is a stronger oxidising agent than Sb (V).
II. Nitrogen show catenation properties more than phosphorus.
III. N—N single bond is weaker than P—P bond.
IV. Electronegativity of N is the third highest in the periodic table.
V. All the elements of this group are polyatomic.

Select the correct statement and choose the correct statement and mark the option accordingly.
(a) I, III and V
(b) I, III, IV and V
(c) II, III and IV
(d) III, IV and V

30. All the element of group 15 show allotropy except
(a) nitrogen (b) phosphorus
(c) arsenic (d) antimony

31. Nitrous acid HNO_2 undergoes disproportionation reaction in acidic medium giving *X*, *Y* and H_2O as products. During this reaction the oxidation state of N changes from +3 to
(a) +5 and +2 (b) +1 and +2
(c) +2 and +3 (d) +4 and +3

32. Given below are two statements, one is labelled as Assertion (A) and the other is labelled as Reason (R).

Asserton (A) The H—*M*—H bond angle of 15 group hydrides decreases on moving down the group.

Reason (R) The electronegativity of central atom decreases and atomic size increases on moving down the group.

In the light of the above statements, choose the correct answer from the options given below.
(a) Both (A) and (R) are true and (R) is the correct explanation of (A).
(b) Both (A) and (R) are true but (R) is not the correct explanation of (A).
(c) (A) is true but (R) is false.
(d) (A) is false but (R) is true.

33. Given below are two statements.

Statement I PCl_5 cannot act as Lewis base.
Statement II BiH_3 is a stronger reducing agent.

In the light of the above statements, choose the correct answer from the options given below.
(a) Both Statement I and Statement II are incorrect.
(b) Statement I is correct but Statement II is incorrect.
(c) Statement I is incorrect but Statement II is correct.
(d) Both Statement I and Statement II are correct.

34. Very pure nitrogen can be prepared by the thermal decomposition of
(a) $Ba(N_3)_2$ (b) $(NH_4)_2Cr_2O_7$
(c) NH_4NO_2 (d) $(NH_4)_2SO_4$

35. Find *A*, *B* and *C* in the following reactions

$$NO + N_2O_4 \xrightarrow{250\text{ K}} A$$

$$Pb(NO_3)_2 \xrightarrow{673\text{ K}} B + PbO + O_2$$

$$HNO_3 + P_2O_5 \longrightarrow HPO_3 + C$$

	A	*B*	*C*
(a)	N_2O_3	NO_2	N_2O_5
(b)	NO_2	N_2O_3	N_2O_5
(c)	NO	NO_2	N_2O_5
(d)	N_2O_3	NO	N_2O_4

36. The oxide(s) in which one nitrogen is directly bonded with other nitrogen atom is/are
(a) N_2O, N_2O_5
(b) N_2O_4 and N_2O_3
(c) N_2O_4 only
(c) Only N_2O_5

37. Select the by-products formed during the recovery of NH_3 from Solvay process?
(a) $CaCl_2$ and H_2O
(b) $Ca(OH)_2$ and Na_2SO_4
(c) $NaHCO_3$ and $CaCl_2$
(d) NH_4Cl and $CaCl_2$

38. A xenon compound 'A' upon partial hydrolysis gives $XeOF_4$. The number of lone pair of electrons present in compound A is
(a) one (b) two
(c) zero (d) three

39. Consider the following statements about PCl_5.
I. In this molecule, orbitals of phosphorus are assumed to undergo sp^3d-hybridisation.
II. The geometry of PCl_5 is trigonal bipyramidal.
III. PCl_5 has two axial bonds which are stronger than three equatorial bonds.
IV. The three equatorial bonds of PCl_5 lie in a plane.
V. In solid state it exists as $[PCl_4]^+$ $[PCl_6]^-$.

Choose the incorrect statement and mark the option accordingly.
(a) I, II, III and V
(b) II, III, IV and V
(c) III, IV and V
(d) I, II, IV and V

40. The number of P—OH bond present in $H_4P_2O_6$, $H_4P_2O_7$ and H_3PO_3 are respectively
(a) 4, 4 and 2
(b) 4, 2 and 1
(c) 2, 4 and 1
(d) 4, 1 and 1

41. Among $H_4P_2O_6$, $H_4P_2O_7$, $H_4P_2O_5$ and $(HPO_3)_n$ the one which can create silver mirror from $AgNO_3$ solution is
(a) $H_4P_2O_6$ (b) $H_4P_2O_7$
(c) $(HPO_3)_n$ (d) $H_4P_2O_5$

42. The interhalogen compound formed from the reaction of bromine with excess of fluorine is a
(a) hypohalite (b) halate
(c) perhalate (d) halite

43. Reaction of thionyl chloride with white phosphorus forms a compound $[A]$, which on hydrolysis gives $[B]$, a tribasic acid. $[A]$ and $[B]$ are respectively
(a) PCl_3 and H_3PO_3
(b) PCl_5 and H_3PO_4
(c) $POCl_3$ and H_3PO_4
(d) P_4O_6 and H_3PO_3

44. The number of Cl=O bond(s) in perchloric acid is
(a) 0 (b) 3 (c) 2 (d) 1

45. Which of the following statements correctly describe the electrons configuration and properties of noble gases?
(a) All noble gases have general formula $[Ar]4s^2 4p^6$ leading to their high reactivity.
(b) Noble gases have complete outer electron shells with configuration ns^2 and ns^2np^6.
(c) Noble gases have unfilled p-orbitals in their outermost electron shells.
(d) Noble gases exhibit a variety of oxidation states due to their partially filled p-orbitals.

46. The correct bond dissociation enthalpy of halogen is
(a) $Cl_2 > F_2 > Br_2 > I_2$
(b) $I_2 > Br_2 > Cl_2 > F_2$
(c) $F_2 > Cl_2 > Br_2 > I_2$
(d) $Cl_2 > Br_2 > F_2 > I_2$

47. Which of the following is the correct order of decreasing oxidising power of perhalates?
(a) $ClO_4^- > BrO_4^- > IO_4^-$
(b) $BrO_4^- > ClO_4^- > IO_4^-$
(c) $IO_4^- > BrO_4^- > ClO_4^-$
(d) $BrO_4^- > IO_4^- > ClO_4^-$

48. Which of the following interhalogen compounds does not exist?
(a) IF_7 (b) ClF_3
(c) ICl (d) $BrCl_7$

49. Match the compound give in Column I with the hybridisation and shape given in Column II and mark the correct option.

	Column I	Column II
A.	XeF_6	I. Distorted octahedral
B.	NH_3	II. Square planar
C.	$XeOF_4$	III. Pyramidal
D.	XeF_4	IV. Square pyramidal

(a) A-I, B-III, C-IV, D-II
(b) A-I, B-II, C-IV, D-III
(c) A-IV, B-III, C-I, D-II
(d) A-IV, B-I, C-II, D-III

50. The correct order of electron gain enthalpy (negative value) of halogens is

(a) F > Cl > Br > I
(b) Cl > Br > F > I
(c) Cl > F > Br > I
(d) I > Br > Cl > F

Response Index

01 ⓐ ⓑ ⓒ ⓓ	14 ⓐ ⓑ ⓒ ⓓ	27 ⓐ ⓑ ⓒ ⓓ	40 ⓐ ⓑ ⓒ ⓓ
02 ⓐ ⓑ ⓒ ⓓ	15 ⓐ ⓑ ⓒ ⓓ	28 ⓐ ⓑ ⓒ ⓓ	41 ⓐ ⓑ ⓒ ⓓ
03 ⓐ ⓑ ⓒ ⓓ	16 ⓐ ⓑ ⓒ ⓓ	29 ⓐ ⓑ ⓒ ⓓ	42 ⓐ ⓑ ⓒ ⓓ
04 ⓐ ⓑ ⓒ ⓓ	17 ⓐ ⓑ ⓒ ⓓ	30 ⓐ ⓑ ⓒ ⓓ	43 ⓐ ⓑ ⓒ ⓓ
05 ⓐ ⓑ ⓒ ⓓ	18 ⓐ ⓑ ⓒ ⓓ	31 ⓐ ⓑ ⓒ ⓓ	44 ⓐ ⓑ ⓒ ⓓ
06 ⓐ ⓑ ⓒ ⓓ	19 ⓐ ⓑ ⓒ ⓓ	32 ⓐ ⓑ ⓒ ⓓ	45 ⓐ ⓑ ⓒ ⓓ
07 ⓐ ⓑ ⓒ ⓓ	20 ⓐ ⓑ ⓒ ⓓ	33 ⓐ ⓑ ⓒ ⓓ	46 ⓐ ⓑ ⓒ ⓓ
08 ⓐ ⓑ ⓒ ⓓ	21 ⓐ ⓑ ⓒ ⓓ	34 ⓐ ⓑ ⓒ ⓓ	47 ⓐ ⓑ ⓒ ⓓ
09 ⓐ ⓑ ⓒ ⓓ	22 ⓐ ⓑ ⓒ ⓓ	35 ⓐ ⓑ ⓒ ⓓ	48 ⓐ ⓑ ⓒ ⓓ
10 ⓐ ⓑ ⓒ ⓓ	23 ⓐ ⓑ ⓒ ⓓ	36 ⓐ ⓑ ⓒ ⓓ	49 ⓐ ⓑ ⓒ ⓓ
11 ⓐ ⓑ ⓒ ⓓ	24 ⓐ ⓑ ⓒ ⓓ	37 ⓐ ⓑ ⓒ ⓓ	50 ⓐ ⓑ ⓒ ⓓ
12 ⓐ ⓑ ⓒ ⓓ	25 ⓐ ⓑ ⓒ ⓓ	38 ⓐ ⓑ ⓒ ⓓ	
13 ⓐ ⓑ ⓒ ⓓ	26 ⓐ ⓑ ⓒ ⓓ	39 ⓐ ⓑ ⓒ ⓓ	

Performance Scanner

> 90% Excellent !	You have mastered this chapter. The concepts of this chapter are at your fingertips. Move on to the next chapter and maintain this momentum.
76-90% Very Good !	You have a good command over this chapter. Revise the chapter again after a few days and enhance your performance.
60-75% Good !	You have a wide scope to learn for this chapter. Revise this chapter again.
<60 Not Satisfactory!	You have a long way ahead of you to master this chapter. Revise it thoroughly.

Scan for Online Chapter Test

Scan for Online Unit Test

Test Booklet No. **3947255**

Test Booklet Code **CH5**

MEDACE
NEET (UG)
SELF ASSESSMENT KIT

d and *f*-Block Elements

Topics Covered
Properties of Transition Elements

Important Compounds of Transition Elements

Inner Transition Elements

Important Instructions

- This Booklet Contains – 3 Topic Tests and One Test on Complete Chapter.
- Each question carries 4 marks.
- For each correct response the candidate will get 4 marks and for every incorrect response, 1 mark will be additionally deducted from the total score.
- Use **Blue/Black** point pen only for filling the OMR.
- Rough work is to be done in the space provided for this purpose in the test booklet only.

Name of the Candidate (In Capitals) ______________________

____

Candidate's Signature ______________________

Invigilator's Signature ______________________

Facsimile signature stamp of center superintendent ______________________

Do not open this Booklet until you start attempting the Test

Topical Follow Thru

Test 1

Syllabus

Transition Elements General Introduction, Electronic Configuration, Occurrence and Characteristics, General Trends in Properties of the First-Row Transition Elements, Physical Properties, Ionisation Enthalpy, Oxidation States, Atomic Radii, Colour, Catalytic Behaviour, Magnetic Properties, Complex Formation, Interstitial Compounds, Alloy Formation.

For deeper insight **Scan the QR Code**

Important Instructions

- The test is of 30 minutes duration and contains 15 multiple choice questions (Four options with a single correct answer).
- Choose the correct option and fill the OMR given on the last page of test accordingly.
- At some instances, you may find more than 1 option may be correct. In such circumstances, you have to judge the most appropriate answer as per the conditions given in the question.

1. All the following statement about the transition elements are true except

(a) All of the transition elements are predominantly metallic.

(b) In aqueous solution many of their simple ions are coloured.

(c) Most of the transition elements show pronounced catalytic activity.

(d) Most of the transition elements show only one oxidation state.

2. The first ionisation enthalpy of zirconium (Zr) is lower than that of hafnium (Hf) despite Hf having a greater atomic number. This anomaly is primarily due to

(a) the presence of f-electrons in Hf

(b) greater relativistic effects in Hf

(c) lanthanoid contraction in Hf

(d) stronger metallic bonding in Zr

3. Which of the following 3d-transition elements exhibits an unexpected increase in atomic radius compared to its preceding element?

(a) Chromium (Cr)

(b) Manganese (Mn)

(c) Iron (Fe)

(d) Cobalt (Co)

4. Which of the following ions has the least magnetic moment?

(a) Cu^{+2} (b) Ni^{+2} (c) Co^{+2} (d) Fe^{+2}

5. Which of the following statement is incorrect about d-block elements?

(a) Elements have partially filled d-orbitals.

(b) Zn, Cd, Hg do not exhibit characteristic properties of transition elements.

(c) The general electronic configuration of transition elements is $(n-1)d^{1-10}ns^{1-2}$.

(d) First element of second transition series is hafnium.

6. Consider the following graph between $\Delta_a H°$ (kJ/mol) and atomic number for first three transition series.

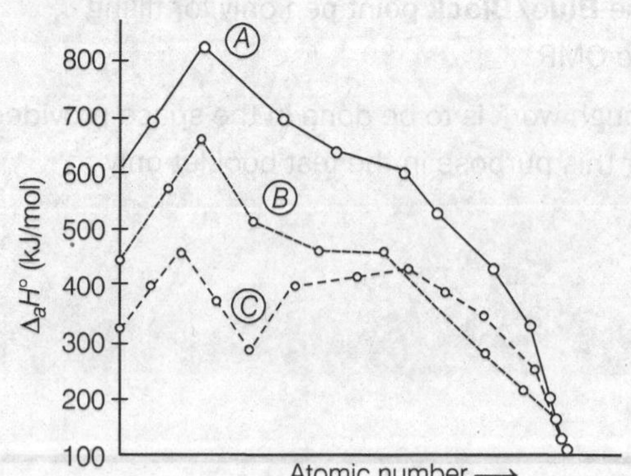

A, *B* and *C* refer for elemental series. Determine the name of transition metals for *A*, *B* and *C*.

	A	*B*	*C*
(a)	I series	II series	III series
(b)	II series	I series	III series
(c)	III series	I series	II series
(d)	III series	II series	I series

7. In the following transition elements, the lowest melting point and boiling point is exhibited by
(a) Cr
(b) Hg
(c) Cu
(d) Au

8. Choose the incorrect statement about atomic and ionic radii of transition elements.
(a) Both radii of transition elements are smaller than those of *s*-block elements and larger than *p*-block elements.
(b) As the atomic number increase, atomic radii first decrease, till the middle, after that it becomes almost constant then increases toward the end of the periods.
(c) When the increased nuclear charge and increased screening effect balance each other, the atomic radii become almost constant.
(d) Due to lanthanoid contraction atomic radii increases.

9. Many transition metals form interstitial compounds. Which of the following is not the characteristic of these interstitial compounds?
(a) They have high melting points.
(b) They are very hard.
(c) They retain metallic conductivity.
(d) They are chemically more reactive than the pure metals.

10. Cuprous ion is colourless while cupric ion is coloured because
(a) both have fully-filled *p* and *d*-orbitals.
(b) cuprous ion and cupric ion both have completely filled *d*-orbital.
(c) both have unpaired electrons in the *d*-orbitals.
(d) cuprous ion has completely filled *d*-orbitals while cupric ion has incompletely filled *d*-orbitals.

11. Which of the following ion has highest ionic radii?
(a) Cr^{3+}
(b) Mn^{3+}
(c) Sc^{3+}
(d) Co^{3+}

12. Match List-I with List-II.

	List-I (Metal ion)		List-II (Magnetic moment)
A.	Co^{3+}	I.	$\sqrt{8}$ BM
B.	Cr^{3+}	II.	$\sqrt{35}$ BM
C.	Fe^{3+}	III.	$\sqrt{15}$ BM
D.	Ni^{2+}	IV.	$\sqrt{24}$ BM

Choose the correct answer from the options given below.
(a) A-IV, B-III, C-II, D-I
(b) A-III, B-II, C-I, D-IV
(c) A-IV, B-I, C-II, D-III
(d) A-III, B-I, C-IV, D-II

13. Choose the incorrect statement from the following about interstitial compounds.
(a) They are formed when small atoms are trapped inside the crystal lattices of metals.
(b) They are non-stoichiometric.
(c) They are chemically reactive.
(d) They retain metallic conductivity.

14. Which of the following metal ion has magnetic moment $\mu = 3.87$ BM ?
(a) V^{3+}
(b) Fe^{2+}
(c) Cr^{3+}
(d) Ti^{3+}

15. Consider the given statements.

Statement I Low oxidation states are found when a complex compound has ligands capable of π-acceptor character in addition to the σ-bonding.

Statement II In $Ni(CO)_4$ and $Fe(CO)_5$, the oxidation state of nickel and iron is +1.

In the light of the above statements, choose the most appropriate answer from the options given below.

(a) Both Statement I and Statement II are incorrect.
(b) Statement I is correct but Statement II is incorrect.
(c) Statement I is incorrect but Statement II is correct.
(d) Both Statement I and Statement II are correct.

Response Index

01	a	b	c	d	10	a	b	c	d	19	a	b	c	d
02	a	b	c	d	11	a	b	c	d	20	a	b	c	d
03	a	b	c	d	12	a	b	c	d	21	a	b	c	d
04	a	b	c	d	13	a	b	c	d	22	a	b	c	d
05	a	b	c	d	14	a	b	c	d	23	a	b	c	d
06	a	b	c	d	15	a	b	c	d	24	a	b	c	d
07	a	b	c	d	16	a	b	c	d	25	a	b	c	d
08	a	b	c	d	17	a	b	c	d					
09	a	b	c	d	18	a	b	c	d					

Performance Scanner

> 90% Excellent !	You have mastered these topics. The concepts of these topics are at your fingertips. Move on to the next test and maintain this momentum.
76-90% Very Good !	You have a good command over these topics. Revise these topics again after a few days and enhance your performance.
60-75% Good !	You have a wide scope to learn for these topics. Revise these topics again.
<60 Not Satisfactory!	You have a long way ahead of you to master these topics. Revise it thoroughly.

Topical Follow Thru

Test 2

Syllabus Preparation, Properties and Uses of $K_2Cr_2O_7$ and $KMnO_4$

For deeper insight **Scan the QR Code**

Important Instructions

- The test is of 30 minutes duration and contains 15 multiple choice questions (Four options with a single correct answer).
- Choose the correct option and fill the OMR given on the last page of test accordingly.
- At some instances, you may find more than 1 option may be correct. In such circumstances, you have to judge the most appropriate answer as per the conditions given in the question.

1. Consider the following reaction.

$$K_2Cr_2O_7 \xrightarrow{\Delta} A + B + C;$$

B is green coloured compound then it would be

(a) K_2CrO_4 (b) Cr_2O_3
(c) CrO_3 (d) O_2

2. Which of the following decreasing order of basic character is correct for the following species?

(a) CrO > VO > FeO > TiO
(b) TiO > FeO > VO > CrO
(c) TiO > VO > CrO > FeO
(d) VO > CrO > TiO > FeO

3. In the neutral or faintly alkaline medium, $KMnO_4$ oxidises iodide into iodate. The change in oxidation state of manganese in this reaction is from

(a) −5 (b) 4 (c) 5 (d) −3

4. $KMnO_4$ (acidified) $+ HCl \longrightarrow H_2O + X(g)$; X is a

(a) red liquid
(b) violet gas
(c) greenish yellow gas
(d) yellow-brown gas

5. On heating pyrollusite with KOH in presence of air, we get

(a) $KMnO_4$ (b) K_2MnO_4
(c) $Mn(OH)_2$ (d) Mn_3O_4

6. The colour of $K_2Cr_2O_7$ changing from red orange to lemon yellow on treatment with aqueous KOH is because of the

(a) reduction of $\overset{VI}{Cr}$ to $\overset{III}{Cr}$
(b) formation of chromium hydroxide
(c) conversion of dichromate to chromate
(d) oxidation of potassium hydroxide to potassium peroxide

7. In which compound chromium has +6 oxidation state

(a) $K_2Cr_2O_7$
(b) $CrCl_3$
(c) $Cr_2(SO_4)_3$
(d) CrO_2

8. The product of oxidation of I^- ion by MnO_4^- in alkaline medium is

(a) I_2 (b) IO_3^-
(c) IO_4^- (d) I_3^-

9. When $KMnO_4$ is reduced with oxalic acid in acidic solution, the oxidation number of Mn changes from

(a) +7 to +4
(b) +6 to +4
(c) +7 to +2
(d) +4 to +2

10. When MnO_2 is fused with KOH, a coloured compound is formed. The product and its colours is

(a) K_2MnO_4, green
(b) $KMnO_4$, purple
(c) Mn_2O_3, brown
(d) Mn_3O_4, black

11. The colour of $KMnO_4$ is due to

(a) $L \rightarrow M$ charge transfer transition
(b) $\sigma - \sigma$ * transition
(c) $M \rightarrow L$ charge transfer transition
(d) $d - d$ transition

12. x, y and z are respectively,

$$MnO_4^- + xe^- \xrightarrow{\text{(Alkaline medium)}} A$$

$$MnO_4^- + ye^- \xrightarrow{\text{(Acidic medium)}} B$$

$$MnO_4^- + ze^- \xrightarrow{\text{(Neutral medium)}} C$$

(a) 1, 2, 3 (b) 1, 5, 3
(c) 1, 3, 5 (d) 5, 3, 1

13. Potassium dichromate ($K_2Cr_2O_7$) is a well-known oxidising agent in acidic medium. Which of the following statement is incorrect regarding its reactions?

(a) It oxidises ferrous ion (Fe^{2+}) to ferric ion (Fe^{3+}).
(b) It oxidises iodide ion (I^-) to iodine (I_2).
(c) It oxidises sulphur dioxide (SO_2) to sulphate ion (SO_4^{2-}).
(d) It oxidises hydrogen peroxide (H_2O_2) to water (H_2O) and O_2.

14. Consider the statements given below.

Statement I Potassium permanganate is prepared by fusion of MnO_2 with an alkali metal hydroxide and an oxidising agent like KNO_3.

Statement II Commercially, $KMnO_4$ is prepared by alkaline oxidative fusion of MnO_2 followed by electrolytic oxidation of mangnate (VI).

In the light of the above statements, choose the most appropriate answer from the options given below.

(a) Both Statement I and Statement II are incorrect.
(b) Statement I is correct but Statement II is incorrect.
(c) Statement I is incorrect but Statement II is correct.
(d) Both Statement I and Statement II are correct.

15. Which of the following statement is incorrect?

(a) The chromate ion is tetrahedral whereas the dichromate ion consist of two tetrahedral sharing one corner with Cr—O—Cr bond angle of 126°.
(b) Sodium and potassium dichromates are strong oxidising agents.
(c) Potassium dichromate is used as secondary standard in volumetric analysis.
(d) Acidified potassium dichromate oxidises iodide to iodine.

Response Index

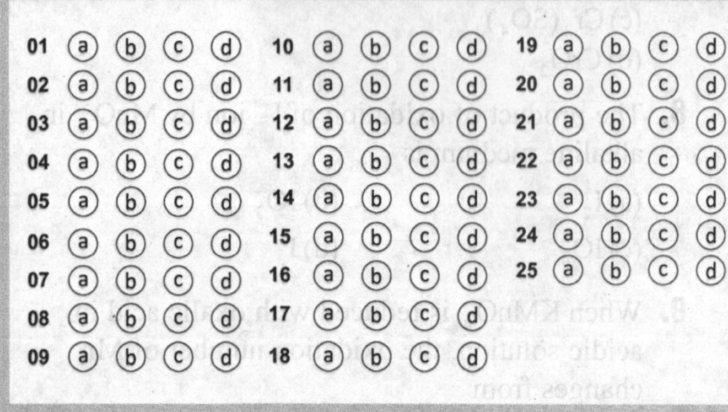

01	a	b	c	d	10	a	b	c	d	19	a	b	c	d
02	a	b	c	d	11	a	b	c	d	20	a	b	c	d
03	a	b	c	d	12	a	b	c	d	21	a	b	c	d
04	a	b	c	d	13	a	b	c	d	22	a	b	c	d
05	a	b	c	d	14	a	b	c	d	23	a	b	c	d
06	a	b	c	d	15	a	b	c	d	24	a	b	c	d
07	a	b	c	d	16	a	b	c	d	25	a	b	c	d
08	a	b	c	d	17	a	b	c	d					
09	a	b	c	d	18	a	b	c	d					

Performance Scanner

> 90% Excellent !	You have mastered these topics. The concepts of these topics are at your fingertips. Move on to the next test and maintain this momentum.
76-90% Very Good !	You have a good command over these topics. Revise these topics again after a few days and enhance your performance.
60-75% Good !	You have a wide scope to learn for these topics. Revise these topics again.
<60 Not Satisfactory!	You have a long way ahead of you to master these topics. Revise it thoroughly.

Topical Follow Thru

Test 3

Syllabus

Inner Transition Elements

Lanthanoids : Electronic Configuration, Oxidation States and Lanthanoid Contraction.

Actinoids : Electronic Configuration and Oxidation States.

For deeper insight **Scan the QR Code**

Important Instructions

- The test is of 30 minutes duration and contains 15 multiple choice questions (Four options with a single correct answer).
- Choose the correct option and fill the OMR given on the last page of test accordingly.
- At some instances, you may find more than 1 option may be correct. In such circumstances, you have to judge the most appropriate answer as per the conditions given in the question.

1. Which of the following statement about cerium is incorrect?

(a) The common oxidation state of cerium are +3 and +4.

(b) Cerium (IV) acts as an oxidising agent.

(c) The +4 oxidation state of cerium is more stable than +3 oxidation state in solution.

(d) Its electronic configuration is $[Xe]4f^1 5d^1 6s^2$.

2. Number of electrons present in $4f$ orbital of Ho^{3+} ion is ....

(Given, atomic number of Ho = 67)

(a) 10 (b) 15

(c) 20 (d) 36

3. The electronic configurations of bivalent europium and trivalent cerium are

(Atomic number : Xe = 54, Ce = 58, Eu = 63)

(a) $[Xe]4f^4$ and $[Xe]4f^9$

(b) $[Xe]4f^7$ and $[Xe]4f^1$

(c) $[Xe]4f^7 6s^2$ and $[Xe]4f^2 6s^2$

(d) $[Xe]4f^2$ and $[Xe]4f^7$

4. The radius of La^{+3} (At. no. of La = 57) is 1.06 Å. Which one of the following given values will be closest of the radius of Lu^{+3} (At. no. of Lu = 71)?

(a) 1.40 Å

(b) 1.06 Å

(c) 0.85 Å

(d) 1.60 Å

5. Consider the following statements.

I. $La(OH)_3$ is the least basic among hydroxides of lanthanoids.

II. Zr^{4+} and Hf^{4+} possess almost the same ionic radii.

III. Ce^{4+} can act as an oxidising agent.

IV. Most common oxidation state of lanthanoid is +2.

V. Lanthanoid contraction occurs due to poor shielding by electrons in f-orbitals.

Choose the correct answer from the given options below.

(a) I, III and V (b) II, III and V

(c) I, II and IV (d) I, II and III

6. Consider the following statements regarding CeO_2.

I. It is a diamagnetic in nature.

II. It is a good oxidising agent.

III. It is soluble in water.

IV. Ce have +2 oxidation state in CeO_2.

V. It is a pale-yellow white compound.

Choose the correct answer from the options given below.

(a) I, II and IV (b) I, II and V

(c) II and III (d) I, II and III

7. The reason for the stability of Gd^{3+} ion is,

(a) $4f$ subshell half-filled.

(b) $4f$ subshell completely filled.

(c) possesses the general electronic configuration of noble gas

(d) decrease

8. Across the lanthanoid series, the basicity of the lanthanoid hydroxides.
(a) Increase
(b) First increase and then decrease
(c) First decrease and then increase
(d) Decrease

9. Arrange Ce^{+3}, La^{+3}, Pm^{+3} and Yb^{+3} in increasing order of their ionic radii.
(a) $Yb^{3+} < Pm^{3+} < Ce^{3+} < La^{3+}$
(b) $Ce^{3+} < Yb^{3+} < Pm^{3+} < La^{3+}$
(c) $Yb^{3+} < Pm^{3+} < La^{3+} < Ce^{3+}$
(d) $Pm^{3+} < La^{3+} < Ce^{3+} < Yb^{3+}$

10. The maximum oxidation state exhibited by actinoid ions is
(a) +5 (b) +4
(c) +7 (d) +8

11. Which one of the following is radioactive lanthanoids ?
(a) Pu (b) Lu
(c) Eu (d) Pm

12. Which of the following metal ions show paramagnetism ?
(a) La^{3+} (b) Ce^{4+}
(c) Lu^{3+} (d) Yb^{3+}

13. Consider the statements given below.
Statement I In general, actinoids show +3 oxidation state.
Statement II The maximum oxidation state increases from +4 in Th to +5, +6 and +7 respectively in Pa, U and Np but decreases in succeeding elements.
In the light of the above statements, choose the most appropriate answer from the options given below.
(a) Both Statement I and Statement II are incorrect.
(b) Statement I is correct but Statement II is incorrect.
(c) Statement I is incorrect but Statement II is correct.
(d) Both Statement I and Statement II are correct.

14. Which of the following statement is incorrect?
(a) In the lanthanoids, La (II) and Ln (III) compounds are predominant species.
(b) The formation of Ce^{IV} is favoured by its noble gas configuration.
(c) Eu^{2+} is a strong oxidising agent.
(d) Yb^{2+} which has f^{14} configuration is a reductant.

15. Consider the species given below.
No, Lr, Am, Cm, Bk
The species that have completely filled f-orbital is
(a) No, Lr (b) Am, No
(c) Cm, Bk (d) Lr, Bk

Response Index

01	a	b	c	d	10	a	b	c	d	19	a	b	c	d
02	a	b	c	d	11	a	b	c	d	20	a	b	c	d
03	a	b	c	d	12	a	b	c	d	21	a	b	c	d
04	a	b	c	d	13	a	b	c	d	22	a	b	c	d
05	a	b	c	d	14	a	b	c	d	23	a	b	c	d
06	a	b	c	d	15	a	b	c	d	24	a	b	c	d
07	a	b	c	d	16	a	b	c	d	25	a	b	c	d
08	a	b	c	d	17	a	b	c	d					
09	a	b	c	d	18	a	b	c	d					

Performance Scanner

> 90% Excellent !	You have mastered these topics. The concepts of these topics are at your fingertips. Move on to the chapter test and maintain this momentum.
76-90% Very Good !	You have a good command over these topics. Revise these topics again after a few days and enhance your performance.
60-75% Good !	You have a wide scope to learn for these topics. Revise these topics again.
<60 Not Satisfactory!	You have a long way ahead of you to master these topics. Revise it thoroughly.

Chapter Break Thru

Syllabus	Transition Elements : General Introduction, Electronic Configuration, Occurrence and Characteristics, General Trends in Properties of the First-Row Transition Elements, Physical Properties, Ionisation Enthalpy, Oxidation States, Atomic Radii, Colour, Catalytic Behaviour, Magnetic Properties, Complex Formation, Interstitial Compounds, Alloy Formation.	Preparation, Properties and Uses of $K_2Cr_2O_7$ and $KMnO_4$	Inner Transition Elements **Lanthanoids** : Electronic Configuration, Oxidation States and Lanthanoid Contraction. **Actinoids** : Electronic Configuration and Oxidation States.

Important Instructions

- The test is of 1 hour duration and contains 50 multiple choice questions (Four options with a single correct answer).
- Choose the correct option and fill the OMR given on the last page of test accordingly.
- At some instances, you may find more than 1 option may be correct. In such circumstances, you have to judge the most appropriate answer as per the conditions given in the question.

1. Number of unpaired electron in Mn^{2+} is

(a) 3 (b) 5 (c) 4 (d) 1

2. The atomic radii of the elements are almost same of which series.

(a) Fe, Co, Ni (b) Na, K, Rb
(c) F, Cl, Br (d) Li, Be, B

3. The correct increasing order of spin onlymagnetic moment (in BM) for Mn^{2+}, Cr^{2+} and Ti^{2+} ions is

(a) $Ti^{2+} < Cr^{2+} < Mn^{2+}$
(b) $Cr^{2+} < Mn^{2+} < Ti^{2+}$
(c) $Mn^{2+} < Ti^{2+} < Cr^{2+}$
(d) $Ti < Mn^{2+} < Cr^{2+}$

4. Choose the incorrect statement from the following.

(a) Ti < V < Cr < Mn (Increasing number of oxidation states)
(b) $Ti^{3+} < V^{3+} < Cr^{3+} < Mn^{3+}$ (Increasing magnetic moment)
(c) Ti > V > Cr > Mn (Decreasing melting points)
(d) Ti < V < Mn < Cr (Increasing 2nd ionisation enthalpy)

5. Which one of the following oxides is ionic in nature?

(a) MnO (b) Mn_2O_7
(c) CrO_3 (d) P_2O_5

6. Which is not correct statement about the chemistry of 3*d* and 4*d*-series elements?

(a) 3*d*-elements show more oxidation states than 4*f*-series elements.
(b) The energy difference between 3*d* and 4*s*-orbitals is very little.
(c) Eu (II) is more stable than Ce (II).
(d) The paramagnetic character in 3*d*-series element increases from scandium to copper.

7. The actinoids exhibit more number of oxidation state in general than the lanthanoids. This is because

(a) the 5*f*-orbitals extend further from the nucleus than the 4*f* orbitals.
(b) the 5*f*-orbitals are more buried than the 4*f*-orbitals.
(c) there is similarity between 4*f* and 5*f*-orbitals in their angular part of the wave function.
(d) the actinoids are more reactive than the lanthanoids.

8. Identify the incorrect statement among the following.

(a) 4*f* and 5*f*-orbitals are equally shielded.
(b) *d*-block elements show irregular and erratic chemical properties among themselves.
(c) La and Lu have partially filled *d*-orbitals and no other partially filled orbitals.
(d) The chemistry of various lanthanoids is very similar.

9. Lanthanoid contraction is caused due to the
(a) same effective nuclear charge from Ce to Lu.
(b) imperfect shielding on outer electrons by $4f$-electron from the nuclear charge.
(c) appreciable shielding on outer electrons by $4f$-electrons from the nuclear charge.
(d) appreciable shielding on outer electrons by $5d$-electrons from the nuclear charge.

10. Which of the following statement is not true?
(a) Colourless compounds of transition elements are paramagnetic.
(b) Coloured compounds of transition element are paramagnetic.
(c) Colourless compounds of transition element are diamagnetic.
(d) Transition elements form the complex compound.

11. Given below are two statements, one is labelled as Assertion (A) and the other is labelled as Reason (R).
Assertion (A) $5d$-transition elements possess higher ionisation enthalpies than $3d$ and $4d$-transition elements.
Reason (R) Due to greater effective nuclear charge ionisation enthalpy of $5d$-elements is greater than $3d$ and $4d$-elements.
In the light of the above statements, choose the correct answer from the options given below.
(a) Both (A) and (R) are true and (R) is the correct explanation of (A).
(b) Both (A) and (R) are true but (R) is not the correct explanation of (A).
(c) (A) is true but (R) is false.
(d) (A) is false but (R) is true.

12. $K_2Cr_2O_7$ on heating with aqueous NaOH gives
(a) CrO_4^{2-} (b) $Cr(OH)_3$
(c) $Cr_2O_7^{2-}$ (d) $Cr(OH)_2$

13. Which oxide of manganese is amphoteric?
(a) MnO_2 (b) Mn_2O_3
(c) Mn_2O_7 (d) MnO

14. The electronic configurations of Eu (Atomic no. 63), Gd (Atomic no. 64) and Tb (Atomic no. 65) are
(a) $[Xe]4f^7 6s^2$, $[Xe]4f^8 6s^2$ and $[Xe]4f^8 5d^1 6s^2$
(b) $[Xe]4f^3 5d^1 6s^2$, $[Xe]4f^7 5d^1 6s^2$ and $[Xe]4f^9 6s^2$
(c) $[Xe]4f^6 5d^1 6s^2$, $[Xe]4f^7 5d^1 6s^2$ and $[Xe]4f^8 5d^1 6s^2$
(d) $[Xe]4f^7 6s^2$, $[Xe]4f^7 5d^1 6s^2$ and $[Xe]4f^9 6s^2$

15. Consider the following statements.
$E^\circ_{(M^{2+}/M)}$ value for copper is positive (+0.34 V).
Which of the following is the correct reason for this statement ?
(a) Cu^{2+} ion stable.
(b) It is due to absence of vacant d-orbitals.
(c) It is due to sum of high $\Delta_i H_{(I)}$ and $\Delta_i H_{(II)}$ enthalpies.
(d) It is due to atomisation enthalpy.

16. Which of the following elements have half-filled f-orbitals in their ground state?
(Given, atomic number Sm = 62, Eu = 63, Tb = 65, Gd = 64, Pm = 61)
A. Sm B. Eu C. Tb D. Gd E. Pm
Choose the correct answer from the options givem below.
(a) B and D only (b) A and E only
(c) A and B only (d) C and D only

17. Which of the following is paramagnetic?
(a) Ni^{2+} (b) Cu^{+}
(c) Zn^{2+} (d) Sc^{3+}

18. Given below are two statements.
Statement I MnO_4^{2-} and MnO_4^- ions are tetrahedral in shape.
Statement II MnO_4^{2-} ion is diamagnetic but the MnO_4^- is paramagnetic.
In the light of the above statements, choose the correct answer from the options given below.
(a) Both Statement I and Statement II are incorrect.
(b) Statement I is correct but Statement II is incorrect.
(c) Statement I is incorrect but Statement II is correct.
(d) Both Statement I and Statement II are correct.

19. Which of the following pair of metal has/have approximately similar radii?
I. Y, La II. Sc, Ti
III. Zr, Hf IV. Nb, Ta
V. Cr, Mn
(a) I, II and V (b) I, II and III
(c) III and IV (d) II, III and IV

20. Which of the following is the correct sequence of atomic weights of given elements ?

(a) Fe > Co > Ni (b) Ni > Co > Fe
(c) Co > Ni > Fe (d) Fe > Ni > Co

21. Which of the following element has maximum first ionisation potential?

(a) V (b) Ti
(c) Cr (d) Mn

22. Which of the following transition metals show acidic nature in their oxides?

I. CrO_3 II. Mn_2O_7 III. NiO
IV. CaO V. FeO

(a) I and III (b) I and II
(c) III and IV (d) III, IV and V

23. Which of the following statement(s) is/are correct?

I. The structure of dichromate ion consist two tetrahedral structure sharing an oxygen atom.
II. $Cr_2O_7^{2-}$ and CrO_4^{2-} (chromate ion) exist in equilibrium with each other at a pH = 4.
III. The shape of CrO_4^{2-} ion is tetrahedral.
IV. Dichromate ion, on addition of alkali, change into chromate ion.
V. Nessler's reagents contains $[HgI_4]^{2-}$.

(a) I and II (b) I, II, III and V
(c) II, III and IV (d) I, II, III, IV and V

24. Given below are two statements, one is labelled as Assertion (A) and the other is labelled as Reason (R).

Assertion (A) Europium (II) is more stable than cerium (II).
Reason (R) Cerium salts are used as catalyst in petroleum cracking.
In the light of the above statements, choose the correct answer from the options given below.

(a) Both (A) and (R) are true and (R) is the correct explanation of (A).
(b) Both (A) and (R) are true but (R) is not the correct explanation of (A).
(c) (A) is true but (R) is false.
(d) (A) is false but (R) is true.

25. Least reactive metal is

(a) Fe (b) Os
(c) Ni (d) Pt

26. Which of the following general configuration of outermost shell represent chromium element [Cr atomic no. =24]?

(a) d^5s^1 (b) d^6s^0
(c) d^4s^2 (d) d^3s^2

27. Which of the following alloys contain only Cu and Zn?

(a) Bronze (b) Brass
(c) Gun metal (d) Bell metal

28. Zinc forms two important alloys, (i) Brass and (ii) German silver. Metals present in them mainly are

(a) in (i) zinc and tin; and in (ii) zinc, silver and nickel.
(b) in (i) zinc and iron; and in (ii) zinc, nickel and cobalt.
(c) in (i) zinc and copper; and in (ii) zinc, copper and nickel.
(d) in (i) zinc and aluminium; and in (ii) zinc, nickel and aluminium.

29. Given below are two statements, one is labelled as Assertion (A) and the other is labelled as Reason (R).

Assertion (A) Transition metals are good catalysts.
Reason (R) V_2O_5 or Pt is used in the preparation of H_2SO_4 by contact process.
In the light of the above statements, choose the correct answer from the options given below.

(a) Both (A) and (R) are true and (R) is the correct explanation of (A).
(b) Both (A) and (R) are true but (R) is not the correct explanation of (A).
(c) (A) is true but (R) is false.
(d) (A) is false but (R) is true.

30. Which of the following metal forms an amphoteric oxide?

(a) Ca (b) Fe
(c) Cu (d) Zn

31. Match List-I and List-II.

List-I (Reactant)	List-II (Product)
A. $I^- + 2MnO_4^- + H_2O \xrightarrow{\text{Neutral medium}}$	I. $MnO_2 + H^+$
B. $MnO_4^- + 2H_2O + Mn^{2+} \longrightarrow$	II. $Mn^{2+} + SO_4^{2-} + H_2O$
C. $SO_3^{2-} + MnO_4^- + H^+ \longrightarrow$	III. $IO_3^- + MnO_2$
D. $I^- + MnO_4^- + H^+ \longrightarrow$	IV. $Mn^{2+} + I_2 + H_2O$

Choose the correct answer from the options given below.

(a) A-III, B-I, C-II, D-IV
(b) A-III, B-IV, C-I, D-II
(c) A-IV, B-I, C-II, D-III
(d) A-IV, B-I, C-III, D-II

32. Which of the following is not a use of *d*-block elements?

(a) MnO_2 is used in the manufacture of dry battery cells. Ni and Cd are used in rechargeable batteries.
(b) Zinc is used in the galvanisation of iron.
(c) $TiCl_4$ with $Al(CH_3)_3$ or $Al(C_2H_5)_3$ is used as oxidising reagent in the reaction of alkene.
(d) Iron catalysts used in the preparation of ammonia from nitrogen and hydrogen.

33. Which of the following set of atomic numbers of the atom belong to the same periods of periodic table ?

I. 58, 63, 71 II. 91, 99, 103
III. 52, 71, 41 IV. 71, 74, 54

(a) I and II (b) II and III
(c) III and IV (d) I and IV

34. Given below are two statements.

Statement I Highest oxidation state of transition metals are found in their compounds with fluorine and oxygen.

Statement II The common oxidation states of Ti are +3 and +4.

In the light of the above statements, choose the correct answer from the options given below.

(a) Both Statement I and Statement II are incorrect.
(b) Statement I is correct but Statement II is incorrect.
(c) Statement I is incorrect but Statement II is correct.
(d) Both Statement I and Statement II are correct.

35. Choose the correct option for following reactions.

I. $Cr_2O_7^{2-} + H_2S + H^+ \longrightarrow Cr^{3+} + \text{Major product } (A) + H_2O$

II. $Cr_2O_7^{2-} + 6I^- + H^+ \longrightarrow Cr^{3+} + H_2O + \text{Major product } (B)$

A and *B* are

	(*A*)	(*B*)
(a)	S	I^-
(b)	S_2	I_2
(c)	S	I_2
(d)	H_2S_2	HI

36. Determine *A*, *B* and *C* in the following reactions.

$Fe_2CrO_4 + NaOH + O_2 \longrightarrow A + Fe_2O_3 + H_2O$

$A \xrightarrow{H_2SO_4} B + H_2O + Na_2SO_4$

$B \xrightarrow{KCl} C$ (major)

Choose the correct option.

	A	*B*	*C*
(a)	$Na_2Cr_2O_3$	$Na_2Cr_2O_7$	$K_2Cr_2O_7$
(b)	$Na_2Cr_2O_7$	$Na_2Cr_2O_3$	$K_2Cr_2O_7$
(c)	Na_2CrO_4	$Na_2Cr_2O_5$	$K_2Cr_2O_7$
(d)	Na_2CrO_4	$Na_2Cr_2O_7$	$K_2Cr_2O_7$

37. $\mu = \sqrt{15}$ is true for the pair.

(a) Co^{+2}, Cr^{+3} (b) Fe^{+2}, Cr^{+3}
(c) Fe^{+3}, Fe^{+2} (d) Mn^{+2}, Fe^{+2}

38. The transition element have a characteristic electronic configuration which can be represented as

(a) $(n-2)\,s^2p^6d^{1-10}\,(n-1)\,s^2p^6ns^2$
(b) $(n-2)\,s^2p^6d^{1-10}\,(n-1)\,s^1p^6d^1$ or d^1ns^1
(c) $(n-1)\,s^1p^6d^{10}ns^2p^6nd^{1-10}$
(d) $(n-1)\,s^2p^6d^{1-10}\,ns^{1-2}$

39. The atomic number of vanadium (V), chromium (Cr), manganese (Mn) and iron (Fe) are respectively 23, 24, 25 and 26. Which one of these may be expected to have the highest second ionisation enthalpy?

(a) V (b) Cr
(c) Mn (d) Fe

40. Which of the following statement is not correct about the electronic configuration of gaseous chromium atom?
(a) It has 5 electron in 3*d* and one electron in 4*s*-orbitals.
(b) The principal quantum numbers of its valence electron is 4.
(c) It has 6 electrons in 3*d*-orbital.
(d) Its valence electrons have quantum no. 4, 0 and 0.

41. Iron exhibits +2 and +3 oxidation states. Which of the following statement about iron is incorrect?
(a) Ferrous oxide is more basic in nature than the ferric oxide.
(b) Ferrous compounds are relatively more ionic than the corresponding ferric compounds.
(c) Ferrous compounds are less volatile than the corresponding ferric compounds.
(d) Ferrous compounds are more easily hydrolysed than the corresponding ferric compounds.

42. Most powerful oxidising property of manganese is shown by which of the following oxidation state ?
(a) Mn (+7) (b) Mn (+2)
(c) Mn (+4) (d) Mn (+5)

43. $N_2(g) + 3H_2(g) \xrightarrow{Fe + Mo} 2NH_3(g)$; In Haber's process, Mo is used as
(a) a catalyst
(b) a catalytic promoter
(c) an oxidising agent
(d) as a catalytic poison

44. Complete the following.

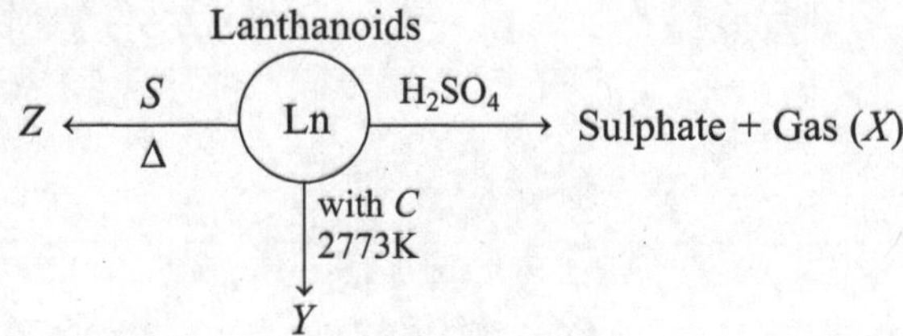

X, Y, Z are

	X	*Y*	*Z*
(a)	O_2	LnC	LnS
(b)	H_2	LnC	Ln_2S_2
(c)	H_2	LnC_2	Ln_2S_3
(d)	O_2	LnC_2	LnS

45. Cu (I) ion is not stable in aqueous solution. Which of the following is the correct reason?
(a) It gives disproportionation reaction.
(b) It gives displacement reaction in aqueous solution.
(c) Smaller size of Cu^+ ion.
(d) Larger size of Cu^+ ion.

46. Consider the following statements.
A. Paramagnetic susceptibility of the order of $10^{-6} cm^3 mol^{-1}$ observed for $KMnO_4$ is due to temperature independent pramagnetism.
B. Chromite ore on fusion with sodium carbonate gives Na_2CrO_4 and Fe_2O_3.
C. The reaction of $FeCl_3 \cdot 6H_2O$ with $SOCl_2$ yields $FeCl_3$, SO_2 and hydrochloric gas.
D. The oxidation states of chromium in CrO_4^{2-} and $Cr_2O_7^{2-}$ are same.
E. Interstitial compounds have high melting points, higher than those of pure metals.

Choose the correct option from the given options below.
(a) A and E (b) B, C, D and E
(c) A, B and E (d) A, B, C, D and E

47. Which of the following statements are correct ?
I. Manganese exhibits +7 oxidation state in its oxide.
II. Ruthenium and osmium exhibit +8 oxidation in their oxides.
III. Sc shows +4 oxidation state which is oxidising in nature.
IV. Cr shows oxidising nature in +6 oxidation state.
V. MnO_4 shows intense pink colour when Mn is in its highest oxidation state.
(a) II and III
(b) I, II, IV and V
(c) I and III
(d) II, III and IV

48. Match the catalysts to the correct processes.

Catalyst	Process
A. $TiCl_4$	I. Wacker process
B. $PdCl_2$	II. Zeigler-Natta polymerisation
C. $CuCl_2$	III. Contact process
D. V_2O_5	IV. Deacon's process

Choose the correct answer from the options given below.
(a) A-II, B-III, C-IV, D-I
(b) A-III B-I, C-II, D-IV
(c) A-III, B-II, C-IV, D-I
(d) A-II, B-I, C-IV, D-III

49. Which of the following species is expected to show the highest magnetic moment? (At. no. Cr = 24, Mn = 25, Co = 27, Ni = 28, Cu = 29)
(a) Cr^{2+} (b) Mn^{2+}
(c) Cu^{2+} (d) Co^{2+}

50. Reason of lanthanoid contraction is
(a) negligible screening effect of '4*f*' orbitals
(b) negligible screening effect of '5*f*' orbital
(c) decreasing nuclear charge
(d) increasing screening effect

Response Index

01	ⓐ	ⓑ	ⓒ	ⓓ	14	ⓐ	ⓑ	ⓒ	ⓓ	27	ⓐ	ⓑ	ⓒ	ⓓ	40	ⓐ	ⓑ	ⓒ	ⓓ
02	ⓐ	ⓑ	ⓒ	ⓓ	15	ⓐ	ⓑ	ⓒ	ⓓ	28	ⓐ	ⓑ	ⓒ	ⓓ	41	ⓐ	ⓑ	ⓒ	ⓓ
03	ⓐ	ⓑ	ⓒ	ⓓ	16	ⓐ	ⓑ	ⓒ	ⓓ	29	ⓐ	ⓑ	ⓒ	ⓓ	42	ⓐ	ⓑ	ⓒ	ⓓ
04	ⓐ	ⓑ	ⓒ	ⓓ	17	ⓐ	ⓑ	ⓒ	ⓓ	30	ⓐ	ⓑ	ⓒ	ⓓ	43	ⓐ	ⓑ	ⓒ	ⓓ
05	ⓐ	ⓑ	ⓒ	ⓓ	18	ⓐ	ⓑ	ⓒ	ⓓ	31	ⓐ	ⓑ	ⓒ	ⓓ	44	ⓐ	ⓑ	ⓒ	ⓓ
06	ⓐ	ⓑ	ⓒ	ⓓ	19	ⓐ	ⓑ	ⓒ	ⓓ	32	ⓐ	ⓑ	ⓒ	ⓓ	45	ⓐ	ⓑ	ⓒ	ⓓ
07	ⓐ	ⓑ	ⓒ	ⓓ	20	ⓐ	ⓑ	ⓒ	ⓓ	33	ⓐ	ⓑ	ⓒ	ⓓ	46	ⓐ	ⓑ	ⓒ	ⓓ
08	ⓐ	ⓑ	ⓒ	ⓓ	21	ⓐ	ⓑ	ⓒ	ⓓ	34	ⓐ	ⓑ	ⓒ	ⓓ	47	ⓐ	ⓑ	ⓒ	ⓓ
09	ⓐ	ⓑ	ⓒ	ⓓ	22	ⓐ	ⓑ	ⓒ	ⓓ	35	ⓐ	ⓑ	ⓒ	ⓓ	48	ⓐ	ⓑ	ⓒ	ⓓ
10	ⓐ	ⓑ	ⓒ	ⓓ	23	ⓐ	ⓑ	ⓒ	ⓓ	36	ⓐ	ⓑ	ⓒ	ⓓ	49	ⓐ	ⓑ	ⓒ	ⓓ
11	ⓐ	ⓑ	ⓒ	ⓓ	24	ⓐ	ⓑ	ⓒ	ⓓ	37	ⓐ	ⓑ	ⓒ	ⓓ	50	ⓐ	ⓑ	ⓒ	ⓓ
12	ⓐ	ⓑ	ⓒ	ⓓ	25	ⓐ	ⓑ	ⓒ	ⓓ	38	ⓐ	ⓑ	ⓒ	ⓓ					
13	ⓐ	ⓑ	ⓒ	ⓓ	26	ⓐ	ⓑ	ⓒ	ⓓ	39	ⓐ	ⓑ	ⓒ	ⓓ					

Performance Scanner

> 90% Excellent !	You have mastered this chapter. The concepts of this chapter are at your fingertips. Move on to the next chapter and maintain this momentum.
76-90% Very Good !	You have a good command over this chapter. Revise the chapter again after a few days and enhance your performance.
60-75% Good !	You have a wide scope to learn for this chapter. Revise this chapter again.
<60 Not Satisfactory!	You have a long way ahead of you to master this chapter. Revise it thoroughly.

Scan for Online Chapter Test

Scan for Online Unit Test

Space for Rough Work

Space for Rough Work

Test Booklet No. **3947256**

Test Booklet Code **CH6**

MEDACE
NEET (UG)
SELF ASSESSMENT KIT

Coordination Compounds

Topics Covered

Coordination Number, Nomenclature and Isomerism of Coordination Compounds

Valence Bond Theory and Crystal Field Theory

Bonding in Organometallic Compounds and Applications of Coordination Compounds

Important Instructions

- This Booklet Contains – 3 Topic Tests and One Test on Complete Chapter.
- Each question carries 4 marks.
- For each correct response the candidate will get 4 marks and for every incorrect response, 1 mark will be additionally deducted from the total score.
- Use **Blue/Black** point pen only for filling the OMR.
- Rough work is to be done in the space provided for this purpose in the test booklet only.

Name of the Candidate (In Capitals) ______________

____

____

Candidate's Signature ______________

Invigilator's Signature ______________

Facsimile signature stamp of center superintendent ______________

Do not open this Booklet until you start attempting the Test

Topical Follow Thru

Test 1

Syllabus Introduction to Coordination Compounds, Werner's Theory, Ligands, Coordination Number, Denticity, Chelation, IUPAC Nomenclature of Mononuclear Coordination Compounds, Isomerism.

For deeper insight **Scan the QR Code** 

Important Instructions

- The test is of 30 minutes duration and contains 15 multiple choice questions (Four options with a single correct answer).
- Choose the correct option and fill the OMR given on the last page of test accordingly.
- At some instances, you may find more than 1 option may be correct. In such circumstances, you have to judge the most appropriate answer as per the conditions given in the question.

1. The IUPAC name of complex $K_3[Fe(CN)_6]$ is

(a) potassium hexacyanoiron (II)
(b) tripotassium hexacyanoiron (II)
(c) potassium hexacyanoferrate (II)
(d) potassium hexacyanoferrate (III)

2. The coordination number of the element E in the complex $[E(en)_2(C_2O_4)]NO_2$ is

(a) 6 (b) 4 (c) 5 (d) 3

3. For the complexes,
(A) $[Ni(H_2O)_5NH_3]^{2+}$, (B) $[Ni(H_2O)_4(NH_3)_2]^{2+}$ and (C) $[Ni(H_2O)_3(NH_3)_3]^{2+}$.
The correct statement is

(a) (A) and (B) show only geometrical isomerism.
(b) (A) and (B) show geometrical and optical isomerism.
(c) (B) and (C) show geometrical and optical isomerism.
(d) (B) and (C) show only geometrical isomerism.

4. Which one of the following is expected to exhibit optical isomerism? (en = ethylenediamine)

(a) *cis*-$[Pt(NH_3)_2Cl_2]$
(b) *trans*-$[Pt(NH_3)_2Cl_2]$
(c) *cis*-$[Co(en)_2Cl_2]$
(d) *trans*-$[Co(en)_2Cl_2]$

5. The maximum number of isomers is given by

(a) $[Ni(C_2O_4)(en)_2]^{2-}$
(b) $[Ni(en)(NH_3)_4]^{2+}$
(c) $[Cr(SCN)_2(NH_3)_4]^{+}$
(d) $[Co(NH_3)_4Cl_2]$

6. The following ligand is

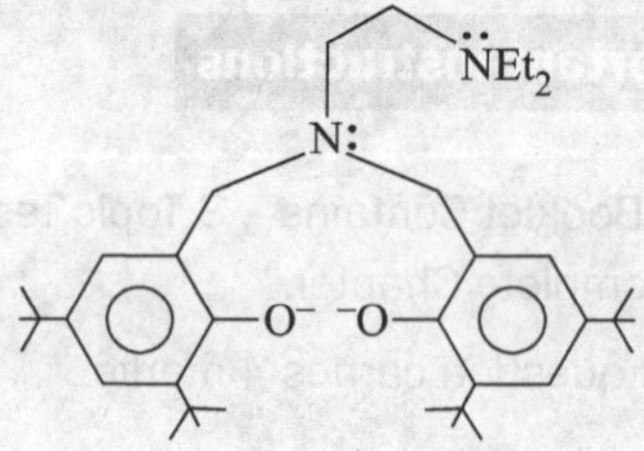

(a) tridentate
(b) tetradentate
(c) hexadentate
(d) bidentate

7. Which of the following types of octahedral complexes will exhibit geometrical isomerism (where, M = metal, a, b = achiral ligand)?

(a) $[Ma_6]$
(b) $[Ma_5b]$
(c) $[Ma_4b_2]$
(d) $[M(aa)_3]$

8. Match List-I with List-II.

List-I (Complexes)		List-II (Oxidation number)	
A.	$[Cr(H_2O)_6]Cl_3$	I.	+1
B.	$[Cr(C_6H_6)_2]$	II.	+3
C.	$K_2[Cr(CN)_2(O)_2(O_2)(NH_3)]$	III.	0
D.	$[Mn(CN)_6]^{5-}$	IV.	+6

Choose the correct answer from the options given below.
(a) A-II, B-III, C-IV, D-I
(b) A-III, B-IV, C-II, D-I
(c) A-I, B-II, C-III, D-IV
(d) A-IV, B-I, C-II, D-III

9. For the reaction given below.
$CoCl_3.xNH_3 + AgNO_3(aq) \longrightarrow$
If two equivalents of AgCl precipitate out, then the value of x will be
(a) 2 (b) 3
(c) 4 (d) 5

10. Given below are two statements.
Statement I The coordination number of a central metal atom in complex is determined by the number of ligands around a metal ion bonded by sigma and pi-bonds both.
Statement II The coordination number of a central metal atom in complex is determined by the number of ligands around a metal ion bonded by pi-bonds.

In the light of the above statements, choose the correct answer from the options given below.
(a) Both Statement I and Statement II are incorrect.
(b) Statement I is correct but Statement II is incorrect.
(c) Statement I is incorrect but Statement II is correct.
(d) Both Statement I and Statement II are correct.

11. $[Co(NH_3)_5NO_2]Cl_2$ and $[Co(NH_3)_5(ONO)]Cl_2$ are related to each other as
(a) geometrical isomers
(b) optical isomers
(c) linkage isomers
(d) coordination isomers

12. The possible number of optical isomers in $[Co(en)_2Cl_2]^+$ are
(a) 2 (b) 3 (c) 4 (d) 6

13. Which of the following doesn't have optical isomer?
(a) $[Co(NH_3)_3Cl_3]$
(b) $[Co(en)_3]Cl_3$
(c) $[Co(en)_2Cl_2]Cl$
(d) $[Co(en)(NH_3)_2Cl_2]Cl$

14. The number of donor sites in dimethyl glyoxime, glycinato, diethylenetriamine and EDTA are respectively
(a) 2, 2, 3 and 4 (b) 2, 2, 3 and 6
(c) 2, 2, 2 and 6 (d) 2, 3, 3 and 6

15. The oxidation state of central atom in the complex $[Co(NH_3)_4ClNO_2]$ is
(a) +2 (b) −2
(c) +3 (d) −3

Response Index

01	a	b	c	d	10	a	b	c	d	19	a	b	c	d
02	a	b	c	d	11	a	b	c	d	20	a	b	c	d
03	a	b	c	d	12	a	b	c	d	21	a	b	c	d
04	a	b	c	d	13	a	b	c	d	22	a	b	c	d
05	a	b	c	d	14	a	b	c	d	23	a	b	c	d
06	a	b	c	d	15	a	b	c	d	24	a	b	c	d
07	a	b	c	d	16	a	b	c	d	25	a	b	c	d
08	a	b	c	d	17	a	b	c	d					
09	a	b	c	d	18	a	b	c	d					

Performance Scanner

> 90% Excellent !	You have mastered these topics. The concepts of these topics are at your fingertips. Move on to the next test and maintain this momentum.
76-90% Very Good !	You have a good command over these topics. Revise these topics again after a few days and enhance your performance.
60-75% Good !	You have a wide scope to learn for these topics. Revise these topics again.
<60 Not Satisfactory!	You have a long way ahead of you to master these topics. Revise it thoroughly.

Test 2

Syllabus Bonding-Valence Bond Approach, Basic Idea of Crystal Field Theory, Colour and Magnetic Properties.

For deeper insight **Scan the QR Code**

Important Instructions

- The test is of 30 minutes duration and contains 15 multiple choice questions (Four options with a single correct answer).
- Choose the correct option and fill the OMR given on the last page of test accordingly.
- At some instances, you may find more than 1 option may be correct. In such circumstances, you have to judge the most appropriate answer as per the conditions given in the question.

1. The pair of compounds having the same hybridisation for the central atom is

(a) $[Cu(NH_3)_4]^{2+}$ and $[Ni(NH_3)_4]^{2+}$
(b) $[Cu(NH_3)_4]^{2+}$ and $[Zn(NH_3)_4]^{2+}$
(c) $[Co(NH_3)_6]^{3+}$ and $[Co(H_2O)_6]^{3+}$
(d) $[NiCl_4]^{2-}$ and $[PtCl_4]^{2-}$

2. The total number of unpaired electrons present in the complex $K_3[Cr(ox)_3]$ is

(a) 3 (b) 2
(c) 1 (d) 0

3. The spin only magnetic moment value for the complex $[Co(CN)_6]^{4-}$ is

(a) 3 (b) 2
(c) 4 (d) 5

4. Given below are two statements.

Statement I The type of hybridisation and magnetic property of the complex $[MnCl_6]^{3-}$ respectively are sp^3d^2 and paramagnetic.

Statement II $[Fe(H_2O)_6]^{3+}$ responds to an external magnetic field.

In the light of the above statements, choose the correct answer from the options given below.

(a) Both Statement I and Statement II are incorrect.
(b) Statement I is correct but Statement II is incorrect.
(c) Statement I is incorrect but Statement II is correct.
(d) Both Statement I and Statement II are correct.

5. Match List-I with List-II.

List-I (Complex)		List-II (Hybridisation)	
A.	$[CoF_6]^{3-}$	I.	sp^3d^2
B.	$[NiCl_4]^{2-}$	II.	d^2sp^3
C.	$[Ni(CN)_4]^{2-}$	III.	sp^3
D.	$[Co(CN)_6]^{3-}$	IV.	dsp^2

Choose the correct answer from the options given below.

(a) A-III, B-IV, C-II, D-I
(b) A-I, B-III, C-IV, D-II
(c) A-II, B-IV, C-III, D-I
(d) A-III, B-IV, C-I, D-II

6. For octahedral complex Mn(II) and tetrahedral complex Ni(II) complexes, consider the following statements.

I. Both the complexes can be high spin.
II. Ni(II) complex can very rarely be low spin.
III. With strong field ligands, Mn(II) complexes can be low spin.
IV. Aqueous solution of Mn(II) ions is pink in colour.
V. Ni(II) complex can very rarely be high spin.

The correct statements are

(a) I, II, III and IV
(b) I, III, IV and V
(c) I, III and IV only
(d) II, III and IV only

7. The increasing order of wavelength of absorption for the complex ions

I. $[Cr(NH_3)_6]^{3+}$ II. $[CrCl_6]^{3-}$ III. $[Cr(H_2O)_6]^{3+}$

IV. $[Cr(CN)_6]^{3-}$ is

(a) IV < II < III < I
(b) IV < III < II < I
(c) IV < I < III < II
(d) II < III < I < IV

8. Which of the following is the correct order for the value of crystal field splitting (Δ_o) of the given complexes ?

(a) $[Cr(H_2O)_6]^{3+} < [Os(H_2O)_6]^{3+} < [Mo(H_2O)_6]^{3+}$
(b) $[Os(H_2O)_6]^{3+} < [Cr(H_2O)_6]^{3+} < [Mo(H_2O)_6]^{3+}$
(c) $[Os(H_2O)_6]^{3+} < [Mo(H_2O)_6]^{3+} < [Cr(H_2O)_6]^{3+}$
(d) $[Cr(H_2O)_6]^{3+} < [Mo(H_2O)_6]^{3+} < [Os(H_2O)_6]^{3+}$

9. Consider the following statements regarding valence bond theory.

I. It cannot explain the colour exhibited by transition metal complexes.
II. It can predict quantitatively the magnetic properties of transition metal complexes.
III. It cannot distinguish ligand as weak and strong field one.
IV. It can give a quantitative interpretation of the thermodynamic or kinetic stabilities of coordination compound.
V. It can make exact predictions regarding the tetrahedral and square planar structures of 4-coordinate complexes.

Choose the correct statements and mark the option accordingly.

(a) I and III
(b) I, II and IV
(c) II, III and IV
(d) III, IV and V

10. The correct order of the spin only magnetic moment of metal ions (in low spin complexes) is

(a) $[Cr(NH_3)_6]^{2+} > [Ru(NH_3)_6]^{3+} > [Fe(CN)_6]^{4-} > [V(CN)_6]^{4-}$
(b) $[V(CN)_6]^{4-} > [Cr(NH_3)_6]^{2+} > [Ru(NH_3)_6]^{3+} > [Fe(CN)_6]^{4-}$
(c) $[V(CN)_6]^{4-} > [Ru(NH_3)_6]^{3+} > [Cr(NH_3)_6]^{2+} > [Fe(CN)_6]^{4-}$
(d) $[Cr(NH_3)_6]^{2+} > [V(CN)_6]^{4-} > [Ru(NH_3)_6]^{3+} > [Fe(CN)_6]^{4-}$

11. Given below are two statements, one is labelled as Assertion (A) and the other is labelled as Reason (R).

Assertion (A) All octahedral complexes of Ni^{2+} are outer orbital.

Reason (R) In Ni^{2+}, only sp^3d^2 hybridisation is possible.

(a) Both (A) and (R) are true and (R) is the correct explanation of (A).
(b) Both (A) and (R) are true but (R) is not the correct explanation of (A).
(c) (A) is false but (R) is true.
(d) (A) is true but (R) is false.

12. Which one of the cyano complexes would exhibit the lowest value of paramagnetic behaviour? (Atomic number Cr = 24, Mn = 25, Fe = 26, Co = 27)

(a) $[Co(CN)_6]^{3-}$
(b) $[Fe(CN)_6]^{3-}$
(c) $[Mn(CN)_6]^{3-}$
(d) $[Cr(CN)_6]^{3-}$

13. Which of the following complex is paramagnetic and inner orbital complex?

(a) $[Fe(CN)_6]^{4-}$
(b) $[Cr(NH_3)_6]^{3+}$
(c) $[Co(NH_3)_6]^{3+}$
(d) $[Fe(NO_2)_6]^{4-}$

14. Select the incorrect statement from the following.

(a) For the complex, $[CoF_6]^{3-}$, F^- is a weak-field ligand, so that $\Delta_o < P$ (electron-pairing energy) and is thus high spin complex.
(b) For the complex, $[Co(NH_3)_6]^{3+}$, NH_3 is a strong-field ligand, so that $\Delta_o > P$ and thus low spin complex.
(c) Stability order $[Co(H_2O)_6]^{3+} > [Rh(H_2O)_6]^{3+}$
(d) Greater the ionic charge on the central metal ion, the greater the value of Δ (CFSE).

15. Match List-I with List-II.

List-I (Complexes)	List-II (Geometry and magnetic moment)
A. $[Ag(CN)_2]^-$	I. Square planar and 1.73 B.M.
B. $[Cu(CN)_4]^{3-}$	II. Linear and zero
C. $[Cu(CN)_6]^{4-}$	III. Octahedral and 1.73 B.M.
D. $[Cu(NH_3)_4]^{2+}$	IV. Tetrahedral and zero

Choose the correct answer from the options given below.

(a) A-II, B-IV, C-III, D-I
(b) A-III, B-IV, C-I, D-II
(c) A-I, B-III, C-IV, D-II
(d) A-IV, B-III, C-II, D-I

Response Index

01	a	b	c	d	10	a	b	c	d	19	a	b	c	d
02	a	b	c	d	11	a	b	c	d	20	a	b	c	d
03	a	b	c	d	12	a	b	c	d	21	a	b	c	d
04	a	b	c	d	13	a	b	c	d	22	a	b	c	d
05	a	b	c	d	14	a	b	c	d	23	a	b	c	d
06	a	b	c	d	15	a	b	c	d	24	a	b	c	d
07	a	b	c	d	16	a	b	c	d	25	a	b	c	d
08	a	b	c	d	17	a	b	c	d					
09	a	b	c	d	18	a	b	c	d					

Performance Scanner

> 90% Excellent !	You have mastered these topics. The concepts of these topics are at your fingertips. Move on to the next test and maintain this momentum.
76-90% Very Good !	You have a good command over these topics. Revise these topics again after a few days and enhance your performance.
60-75% Good !	You have a wide scope to learn for these topics. Revise these topics again.
<60 Not Satisfactory!	You have a long way ahead of you to master these topics. Revise it thoroughly.

Test 3

Syllabus Importance of Coordination Compounds. (In Qualitative Analysis, Extraction of Metals and in Biological Systems)

For deeper insight **Scan the QR Code**

Important Instructions

- The test is of 30 minutes duration and contains 15 multiple choice questions (Four options with a single correct answer).
- Choose the correct option and fill the OMR given on the last page of test accordingly.
- At some instances, you may find more than 1 option may be correct. In such circumstances, you have to judge the most appropriate answer as per the conditions given in the question.

1. The compound formed by dissolving gold and platinum in *aqua-regia* is

(a) $[AuCl_4]^{3-}$ and $[PtCl_6]^{2-}$

(b) $[AuCl_4]^-$ and $[PtCl_6]^{4-}$

(c) $[AuCl_4]^-$ and $[PtCl_6]^{2-}$

(d) $[AuCl_4]^-$ and $[PtCl_4]^{2-}$

2. Among the following, which is not the π-bonded organometallic compound?

(a) $(CH_3)_4Sn$

(b) $K[PtCl_3(\eta^2-C_2H_4)]$

(c) $Fe(\eta^5-C_5H_5)_2$

(d) $Cr(\eta^6-C_6H_5)_2$

3. Which of the following biomolecules contain a non-transition metal ion?

(a) Vitamin B-12 (b) Chlorophyll

(c) Haemoglobin (d) Insulin

4. In black and white photography, the developed film is fixed by washing with hypo solution which dissolves the undecomposed AgBr to form

(a) $[Ag(S_2O_3)_2]^{3-}$ complex ion

(b) $[Ag(SO_4)_2]^{3-}$ complex ion

(c) $[Ag(SO_3)_2]^{3-}$ complex ion

(d) None of the above

5. Which of the following is incorrect?

(a) Chlorophyll is the coordination compound of Mg.

(b) Haemoglobin is the coordination compound of Fe.

(c) Cyanocobalamine is the coordination compound of Cu.

(d) Wilkinson catalyst is the coordination compound of Rh.

6. The structure of $[Mn_2(CO)_{10}]$ compound displays

(a) one Mn—Mn bond, four terminal CO and six bridging CO

(b) one Mn—Mn bond, ten terminal CO and zero bridging

(c) no Mn—Mn bond, six terminal CO and four bridging

(d) no —Mn—Mn bond, eight terminal CO and two bridging

7. $[Co_2(CO)_8]$ is an organometallic compound due to the presence of

(a) Co—C bond (b) Co—Co bond

(c) Co—O bond (d) C—O bond

8. In which of the following metal carbonyls CO forms a bridge between metal atoms?

(a) $[Co_2(CO)_8]$

(b) $[Mn_2(CO)_{10}]$

(c) $[Os_3(CO)_{12}]$

(d) $[Ru_3(CO)_{12}]$

9. The number of complexes which will exhibit synergic bonding amongst $Ni(CO)_4$, $Fe(CO)_5$, $[Cr(CO)_6]$, $[Co_2(CO)_8]$ and $[V(CO)_6]^-$ is

(a) 3 (b) 4

(c) 2 (d) 5

10. Today, there is growing interest in the use of chelate therapy in medicinal chemistry. Like excess of copper and iron are removed by the chelating ligands *A* and *B* *via* the formation of coordination compounds. Here, *A* and *B*, respectively are

(a) D-penicillamine and desferrioxime B
(b) D-penicillamine and desferrioxime X
(c) desferrioxime B and D-penicillamine
(d) desferrioxime X and B-penicillamine

11. Match List-I with List-II.

List-I (Substances)	List-II (Element present)
A. Zeiglar-Natta catalyst	I. Rhodium
B. Blood pigment	II. Cobalt
C. Wilkinson catalyst	III. Iron
D. Vitamin B_{12}	IV. Titanium

Choose the correct answer from the options given below.

(a) A-II, B-IV, C-I, D-III
(b) A-II, B-III, C-IV, D-I
(c) A-III, B-II, C-IV, D-I
(d) A-IV, B-III, C-I, D-II

12. Which of the following compound is σ and π bonded?

(a) $Fe(CH_3)_3$
(b) $[Fe(\eta^5 - C_5H_5)_2]$
(c) $[Co(CO)_5NH_3]^{2+}$
(d) $K[PtCl_3(\eta^2 - C_2H_4)]$

13. Which of the following doesn't have a metal carbon bond?

(a) $K[Pt(C_2H_4)Cl_3]$
(b) $Ni(CO)_4$
(c) $Al(OC_2H_5)_3$
(d) C_2H_5MgBr

14. Wilkinson's catalyst is used in

(a) polymerisation
(b) condensation
(c) halogenation
(d) hydrogenation

15. The complex used as an anti-cancer agent is

(a) *trans*-$[Co(NH_3)_3Cl_3]$
(b) *cis*-$[PtCl_2(NH_3)_2]$
(c) *cis*-$K_2[PtCl_2Br_2]$
(d) Na_2CO_3

Response Index

01	a	b	c	d	10	a	b	c	d	19	a	b	c	d
02	a	b	c	d	11	a	b	c	d	20	a	b	c	d
03	a	b	c	d	12	a	b	c	d	21	a	b	c	d
04	a	b	c	d	13	a	b	c	d	22	a	b	c	d
05	a	b	c	d	14	a	b	c	d	23	a	b	c	d
06	a	b	c	d	15	a	b	c	d	24	a	b	c	d
07	a	b	c	d	16	a	b	c	d	25	a	b	c	d
08	a	b	c	d	17	a	b	c	d					
09	a	b	c	d	18	a	b	c	d					

Performance Scanner

> 90% Excellent !	You have mastered these topics. The concepts of these topics are at your fingertips. Move on to the chapter test and maintain this momentum.
76-90% Very Good !	You have a good command over these topics. Revise these topics again after a few days and enhance your performance.
60-75% Good !	You have a wide scope to learn for these topics. Revise these topics again.
<60 Not Satisfactory!	You have a long way ahead of you to master these topics. Revise it thoroughly.

Chapter Break Thru

Syllabus	Introduction to Coordination Compounds, Werner's Theory, Ligands, Coordination Number, Denticity, Chelation, IUPAC Nomenclature of Mononuclear Coordination Compounds, Isomerism.	Bonding-Valence Bond Approach, Basic Idea of Crystal Field Theory, Colour and Magnetic Properties.	Importance of Coordination Compounds. (In Qualitative Analysis, Extraction of Metals and in Biological Systems)

Important Instructions

- The test is of 1 hour duration and contains 50 multiple choice questions (Four options with a single correct answer).
- Choose the correct option and fill the OMR given on the last page of test accordingly.
- At some instances, you may find more than 1 option may be correct. In such circumstances, you have to judge the most appropriate answer as per the conditions given in the question.

1. Which would exhibit ionisation isomerism?

(a) $[Cr(NH_3)_6]Cl_3$
(b) $[Co(NH_3)_5Br]SO_4$
(c) $[Cr(en)_2Cl_2]$
(d) $[Cr(en)_3Cl_3]$

2. Predict the order of Δ_o for the following compounds.

(I) $[Fe(H_2O)_6]^{+2}$
(II) $[Fe(CN)_2(H_2O)_4]$
(III) $[Fe(CN)_4(H_2O)_2]^{-2}$

(a) $\Delta_o(I) < \Delta_o(II) < \Delta_o(III)$
(b) $\Delta_o(II) < \Delta_o(I) < \Delta_o(III)$
(c) $\Delta_o(III) < \Delta_o(II) < \Delta_o(I)$
(d) $\Delta_o(II) < \Delta_o(III) < \Delta_o(I)$

3. If $\Delta_o < P$, the correct electronic configuration for d^4 system will be

(a) $t_{2g}^4 e_g^0$ (b) $t_{2g}^3 e_g^1$
(c) $t_{2g}^0 e_g^4$ (d) $t_{2g}^2 e_g^2$

4. Which of the following complex has a possibility to exist as a meridional isomer?

(a) $[Co(NH_3)_3(NO_2)_3]$
(b) $[Co(en)_3]$
(c) $[Co(en)_2Cl_2]$
(d) $[Pt(NH_3)_2Cl_2]$

5. Number of complex which show optical isomerism among the following is ....

cis-$[Cr(ox)_2Cl_2]^{-3}$, $[Co(en)_3]^{+3}$
cis-$[Pt(en)_2Cl_2]^{+2}$, *cis*-$[Co(en)_2Cl_2]^+$
trans-$[Pt(en)_2Cl_2]^{+2}$

(a) 4 (b) 5
(c) 6 (d) 4

6. The number of geometrical isomers of $[Co(NH_3)_3(NO_2)_3]$ are

(a) 0 (b) 2
(c) 3 (d) 4

7. The magnetic moment of complexes given below are in the order

I. $Ni(CO)_4$ II. $[Mn(CN)_6]^{-4}$
III. $[Cr(NH_3)_6]^{+3}$ IV. $[CoF_6]^{-3}$

(a) I > II > III > IV (b) I < II < III < IV
(c) IV > II > I > III (d) IV < II < I < III

8. Which of the following is not an organometallic compound?

(a) Ethyl magnesium bromide
(b) Tetraethyl lead
(c) Sodium ethoxide
(d) Trimethyl aluminium

9. Select the most stable ion among the following options.
(a) $[Fe(OH)_6]^{3-}$ (b) $[FeCl_6]^{3-}$
(c) $[Fe(CN)_6]^{3-}$ (d) $[Fe(H_2O)_6]^{3+}$

10. The magnetic moment of $[Cu(NH_3)_4]^{+2}$ was found to be 1.73 BM. The number of unpaired electron in the complex is
(a) 0 (b) 1 (c) 2 (d) 3

11. Which of the following is σ and π bonded organometallic compound?
(a) $[Fe(\eta^5-C_5H_5)_2]$ (b) $[Co(CO)_5(NH_3)]^{2+}$
(c) $[Al(CH_3)_3]+TiCl_4$ (d) $[RhCl(PPh_3)_3]$

12. Select the option with correct property.
(a) $[Ni(CO)_4]$ and $[NiCl_4]^{2-}$ both diamagnetic.
(b) $[Ni(CO)_4]$ and $[NiCl_4]^{2-}$ both paramagnetic.
(c) $[NiCl_4]^{2-}$ diamagnetic, $[Ni(CO)_4]$ paramagnetic.
(d) $[Ni(CO)_4]$ diamagnetic, $[NiCl_4]^{2-}$ is paramagnetic.

13. Given below are two statements, one is labelled as Assertion (A) and the other is labelled as Reason (R).
Assertion (A) Low spin complexes have lesser number of unpaired electrons.
Reason (R) $[FeF_6]^{3-}$ is a low spin complex.
(a) Both (A) and (R) are true and (R) is the correct explanation of (A).
(b) Both (A) and (R) are true but (R) is not the correct explanation of (A).
(c) (A) is true but (R) is false.
(d) (A) is false but (R) is true.

14. The coordination number of cobalt in $[Co(en)_2Br_2]Cl_2$ is
(a) 2 (b) 4 (c) 6 (d) 8

15. Out of TiF_6^{2-}, CoF_6^{3-}, Cu_2Cl_2 and $NiCl_4^{2-}$ (Z of Ti = 22, Co = 27, Cu = 29, Ni = 28) the colourless species are
(a) Cu_2Cl_2 and $NiCl_4^{2-}$
(b) TiF_6^{2-} and Cu_2Cl_2
(c) CoF_6^{3-} and $NiCl_4^{2-}$
(d) TiF_6^{2-} and CoF_6^{3-}

16. Which of the following complex ion is expected to absorb light in visible region?
(a) $[Ti(en)_2(NH_3)_2]^{4+}$
(b) $[Sc(NH_3)_4(H_2O)_2]^{3+}$
(c) $[Cr(NH_3)_6]^{3+}$
(d) $[Zn(CN)_4]^{2-}$

17. Given below are two statements, one is labelled as Assertion (A) and the other is labelled as Reason (R).
Assertion (A) A chelating ligand must possess two or more lone pairs at such a distance that it may form suitable strain free rings at the metal ion.
Reason (R) $H_2N—NH_2$ is a chelating ligand.
(a) Both (A) and (R) are true and (R) is the correct explanation of (A).
(b) Both (A) and (R) are true but (R) is not the correct explanation of (A).
(c) (A) is true but (R) is false.
(d) (A) is false but (R) is true.

18. Which among the following will not give an organometallic compound?
(a) $RX + Mg \xrightarrow{\text{Dry ether}}$
(b) $Na + CH_3CH_2OH \longrightarrow$
(c) $CH_3MgI + SnCl_4 \longrightarrow$
(d) $TiCl_4 + (CH_3CH_2)_3Al \longrightarrow$

19. Which of the following is incorrectly matched?

	Complex	Number of unpaired electrons
(a)	$[FeF_6]^{3-}$	5
(b)	$[Cr(en)_3]^{2+}$	2
(c)	$[Co(NH_3)_6]^{3+}$	0
(d)	$[Mn(H_2O)_6]^{2+}$	5

20. Consider the following complex,
$$[Co(NH_3)_5(CO_3)]ClO_4$$
The coordination number, oxidation number, number of *d*-electrons and number of unpaired *d*-electrons on the metals are respectively.
(a) 6, 2, 7, 3 (b) 7, 2, 7, 1
(c) 5, 3, 6, 4 (d) 6, 3, 6, 4

21. Given below are two statements.

Statement I Most metal ions exhibit more than one coordination number.

Statement II For most cation, the coordination number depends on the size and charge of the cation.

In the light of above statements, choose the most appropriate answer from the options given below.

(a) Both Statement I and Statement II are incorrect.
(b) Statement I is correct but Statement II is incorrect.
(c) Statement I is incorrect but Statement II is correct.
(d) Both Statement I and Statement II are correct.

22. Which of the following is optically inactive?

(a) $[Co(en)_3]^{3+}$
(b) $[Co(ox)_3]^{3+}$
(c) *cis*-$[CoCl_2(en)_2]^{2+}$
(d) *trans*-$[CoCl_2(en)_2]^+$

23. The correct order of energies of *d*-orbitals of metal ion in square planar complex is

(a) $d_{xy} = d_{yz} = d_{zx} > d_{x^2-y^2} = d_{z^2}$
(b) $d_{x^2-y^2} = d_{z^2} > d_{xy} = d_{yz} = d_{zx}$
(c) $d_{x^2-y^2} > d_{z^2} > d_{xy} = d_{yz} = d_{zx}$
(d) $d_{x^2-y^2} > d_{xy} > d_{z^2} > d_{zx} = d_{yz}$

24. *fac* and *mer*-isomer is associated with which of the following general formula?

(a) $[M(AA)_2]$ (b) $[M(AA)_3]$
(c) $[MABCD]$ (d) $[MA_3B_3]$

25. Which of the following IUPAC name is correct?

(a) $[Cu(H_2O)(NH_3)Br_2]$
Ammineaquadibromo copper (I)
(b) $Na_3[Al(C_2O_4)_3]$
Trisodiumtrioxalato aluminate (III)
(c) $Na_2[Ni(EDTA)]$
Disodium ethylenediamminetetraacetatonickel(II)
(d) $[Co(NH_3)_5ONO]SO_4$
Pentaamminenitro cobalt (III) sulphate

26. Consider the following statements.

I. Hardness of water is estimated by simple titration with Na_2EDTA.
II. The formula of Wilkinson catalyst is $[(Ph_3P)_2RhCl_2]$.
III. Cyanocobalamin is B_{12} and contains cobalt.
IV. Carboxypeptidase-A is an enzyme and contain magnesium.
V. Haemoglobin is the red pigment of blood and contains iron.

Choose the incorrect statements and mark the option accordingly.

(a) I, II and V
(b) II and IV
(c) III, IV and V
(d) I, II and III

27. What will be the oxidation number of Pt in $[Pt(C_2H_4)Cl_3]^-$?

(a) +2 (b) +1
(c) +4 (d) +3

28. Among the following species, the one which causes the highest CFSE, Δ_o as a ligand is

(a) Cl^- (b) en
(c) CN^- (d) NCS^-

29. The correct structure of $Fe(CO)_5$ is

(a) octahedral
(b) tetrahedral
(c) square pyramidal
(d) trigonal bipyramidal

30. Choose the correct statement from the following for metal carbonyls?

(a) π-back bonding weakness M — C bond order as well as CO bond order.
(b) π-back bonding weakness M — C bond order but strengthens CO bond order.
(c) π-back bonding strengthens M — C bond order as well as CO bond order.
(d) π-back bonding strengthens M — C bond order and weakens CO bond order.

31. Select the compound which is not an organometallic compound?

(a) Tetraethyl lead (TEL)
(b) Lithium diethylcuprate (I)
(c) Lithium aluminium tertiarybutoxide hydride
(d) *p*-chloro-*m*-methoxyphenyl magnesium chloride

32. In $Fe(CO)_5$, the Fe—C bond possesses
(a) π-character only
(b) both σ and π characters
(c) ionic character
(d) σ-character only

33. Which ligand is useful for removal of the toxic effect of lead metal in body in chelate therapy treatment?
(a) COO^- | COO^-
(b) CH_3COO^-
(c) Ethylene diamminetetraacetate $(EDTA)^{4-}$
(d) AsO_4^{3-}

34. Given below are two statements, one is labelled as Assertion (A) and the other is labelled as Reason (R).
Assertion (A) CO and CN are referred as π acid ligands.
Reason (R) In CO and CN, occupied π type orbitals are present.
(a) Both (A) and (R) are true and (R) is the correct explanation of (A).
(b) Both (A) and (R) are true but (R) is not the correct explanation of (A).
(c) (A) is false but (R) is true.
(d) (A) is true but (R) is false.

35. Zeiglar-Natta catalyst is an organometallic compound. Which of the following metal is present in it?
(a) Iron (b) Titanium
(c) Rhodium (d) Zirconium

36. Which of the following is diamagnetic in nature?
(a) $K_3[Cu(CN)_4]$
(b) $K_2[Cu(CN)_4]$
(c) $K_3[Fe(CN)_6]$
(d) $K_4[FeCl_6]$

37. Which of the following has the highest magnetic moment?
(a) $[FeF_6]^{3-}$ (b) $[Fe(CN)_6]^{3-}$
(c) $[MnCl_6]^{3-}$ (d) $[Mn(CN)_6]^{3-}$

38. Consider the following statement regarding $[Cr(NH_3)_6]Cl_3$
I. The complex involves d^2sp^3 hybridisation and is octahedral in shape.
II. The complex is paramagnetic.
III. The complex is an outer orbital complex.
IV. The complex gives white precipitate with silver nitrate solution.
V. The number of unpaired electrons are 3.
Choose the correct statements and mark accordingly.
(a) I, II, IV and V (b) I, III and IV
(c) III, IV and V (d) IV and V

39. Which one of the following complexes is less likely to absorb visible light?
(A) $[Sc(H_2O)_6]^{3+}$ (B) $[Ti(NH_3)_6]^{4+}$
(C) $[V(NH_3)_6]^{3+}$ (D) $[Zn(NH_3)_6]^{2+}$
(E) $[Co(NH_3)_6]^{3+}$
Choose the correct option.
(a) A, B, D and E (b) A, B, C and E
(c) B, C and D (d) C, D and E

40. If the number of unpaired electrons present in $[Co(NH_3)_6]Cl_2$ and $[Co(NH_3)_6]Cl_3$ are x and y respectively. Thus, the sum of the value of x and y is
(a) 2 (b) 1 (c) 3 (d) 4

41. The compound that shows optical isomerism is
(a) $[Co(CN)_6]^{3-}$ (b) $[Cr(C_2O_4)_3]^{3-}$
(c) $[ZnCl_4]^{2-}$ (d) $[Cu(NH_3)_4]^{2+}$

42. Match List-I with List-II.

	List-I (Complex)	List-II (Isomerism type)
A.	$[Pd(PPh_3)_2(SCN)_2]$	I. Ionisation isomerism
B.	$[Co(NH_3)_5(NO_3)]SO_4$	II. Linkage isomerism
C.	$[Cr(H_2O)_5Cl]Cl_2.H_2O$	III. Coordination isomerism
D.	$[Cu(NH_3)_4][Pt(CN)_4]$	IV. Hydrate isomerism

Choose the correct option from the following.
(a) A-I, B-IV, C-II, D-III
(b) A-II, B-I, C-IV, D-III
(c) A-IV, B-II, C-I, D-III
(d) A-II, B-I, C-II, D-IV

43. The complex ion that has geometrical isomers is

(a) $[Co(en)_3]^{3+}$ (b) $[Ni(NH_3)_5Br]^+$
(c) $[Co(NH_3)_2(en)_2]^{3+}$ (d) $[Cr(NH_3)_4(en)]^{3+}$

44. The sum of oxidation states of two silver ions in $[Ag(NH_3)_2][Ag(CN)_2]$ complex is

(a) 3 (b) 2 (c) 4 (d) 1

45. The coordination number of cobalt in $Na[Co(bpy)Cl_4]$ is

(a) 6 (b) 5 (c) 8 (d) 7

46. The IUPAC name for the complex $[Co(NO_2)(NH_3)_5]Cl_2$ is

(a) nitro-N-pentaammine cobalt (III) chloride
(b) nitro-N-pentaammine cobalt (III) chloride
(c) pentaammine nitrito-N-cobalt (III) chloride
(d) pentaammine nitrito-N-cobalt (II) chloride

47. Which of the following pair will show linkage isomers?

(a) $[PtCl_2(NH_3)_4]Br_2$ and $[PtBr_2(NH_3)_4]Cl_2$
(b) $[Co(NH_3)_5]NO_3SO_4$ and $[Co(NH_3)_5SO_4]NO_3$
(c) $[Pd(PPh_3)_2(NCS)_2]$ and $[Pd(PPh_3)_2(SCN)_2]$
(d) $[Cu(NH_3)_4][PtCl_4]$ and $[Pt(NH_3)_4][CuCl_4]$

48. Consider the following complexes.

I. $[Pt(NH_3)_3Cl]^+$
II. $[Pt(NH_3)Cl_5]^-$
III. $[Pt(NH_3)_2Cl(NO_2)]$
IV. $[Pt(NH_3)_4ClBr]^{2+}$
V. $[Co(H_2O)Cl(en)_2]Cl$

Among I to V, the complexes that can display geometrical isomerism are

(a) I, III and V (b) III, IV and V
(c) II, IV and V (d) II, III and V

49. Which of the following is an example of homoleptic complex?

(a) $[Co(NH_3)_6]Cl_3$
(b) $[Co(NH_3)_5Cl]Cl_2$
(c) $[Co(NH_3)_4Cl_2]$
(d) $[Co(NH_3)_5Cl]Cl_2$

50. The number of the species which can be considered to be anti-cancer species among the following :

(i) 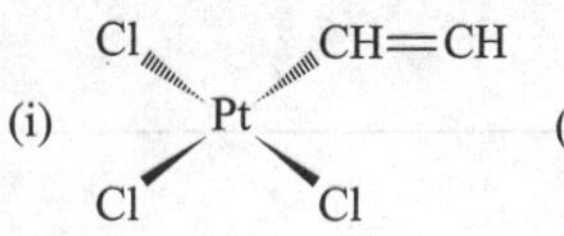

(ii) 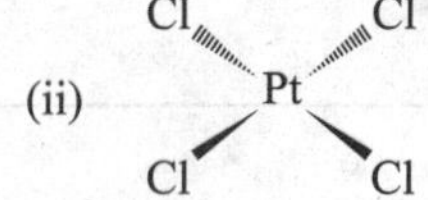

(iii) 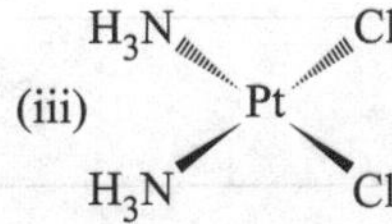

(iv) 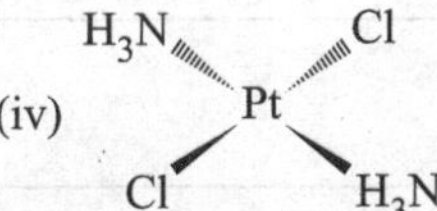

(v) 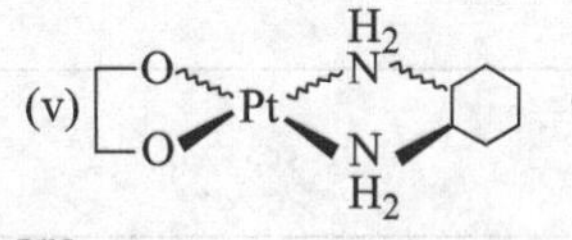

(vi) H₃N, Pt, O, H₃N, O

are

(a) 1 (b) 2
(c) 3 (d) 4

Response Index

01 (a) (b) (c) (d)	14 (a) (b) (c) (d)	27 (a) (b) (c) (d)	40 (a) (b) (c) (d)
02 (a) (b) (c) (d)	15 (a) (b) (c) (d)	28 (a) (b) (c) (d)	41 (a) (b) (c) (d)
03 (a) (b) (c) (d)	16 (a) (b) (c) (d)	29 (a) (b) (c) (d)	42 (a) (b) (c) (d)
04 (a) (b) (c) (d)	17 (a) (b) (c) (d)	30 (a) (b) (c) (d)	43 (a) (b) (c) (d)
05 (a) (b) (c) (d)	18 (a) (b) (c) (d)	31 (a) (b) (c) (d)	44 (a) (b) (c) (d)
06 (a) (b) (c) (d)	19 (a) (b) (c) (d)	32 (a) (b) (c) (d)	45 (a) (b) (c) (d)
07 (a) (b) (c) (d)	20 (a) (b) (c) (d)	33 (a) (b) (c) (d)	46 (a) (b) (c) (d)
08 (a) (b) (c) (d)	21 (a) (b) (c) (d)	34 (a) (b) (c) (d)	47 (a) (b) (c) (d)
09 (a) (b) (c) (d)	22 (a) (b) (c) (d)	35 (a) (b) (c) (d)	48 (a) (b) (c) (d)
10 (a) (b) (c) (d)	23 (a) (b) (c) (d)	36 (a) (b) (c) (d)	49 (a) (b) (c) (d)
11 (a) (b) (c) (d)	24 (a) (b) (c) (d)	37 (a) (b) (c) (d)	50 (a) (b) (c) (d)
12 (a) (b) (c) (d)	25 (a) (b) (c) (d)	38 (a) (b) (c) (d)	
13 (a) (b) (c) (d)	26 (a) (b) (c) (d)	39 (a) (b) (c) (d)	

Performance Scanner

> 90% Excellent !	You have mastered this chapter. The concepts of this chapter are at your fingertips. Move on to the next chapter and maintain this momentum.
76-90% Very Good !	You have a good command over this chapter. Revise the chapter again after a few days and enhance your performance.
60-75% Good !	You have a wide scope to learn for this chapter. Revise this chapter again.
<60 Not Satisfactory!	You have a long way ahead of you to master this chapter. Revise it thoroughly.

Scan for Online **Chapter Test** 

Scan for Online **Unit Test** 

Space for Rough Work

Space for Rough Work

Space for Rough Work

Test Booklet No. **3947257**

Test Booklet Code **CH7**

MEDACE
NEET (UG)
SELF ASSESSMENT KIT

Haloalkanes and Haloarenes

Topics Covered

- Haloalkanes
- Haloarenes
- Some Important Polyhalogen Compounds

Important Instructions

- This Booklet Contains – 3 Topic Tests and One Test on Complete Chapter.
- Each question carries 4 marks.
- For each correct response the candidate will get 4 marks and for every incorrect response, 1 mark will be additionally deducted from the total score.
- Use **Blue/Black** point pen only for filling the OMR.
- Rough work is to be done in the space provided for this purpose in the test booklet only.

Name of the Candidate (In Capitals) ____________________

____

Candidate's Signature ____________________

Invigilator's Signature ____________________

Facsimile signature stamp of center superintendent ____________________

Do not open this Booklet until you start attempting the Test

Topical Follow Thru

Test 1

Syllabus **Haloalkanes** : General Methods of Preparation, Properties and Reactions, Nature of C—*X* Bond, Mechanism of Substitution Reactions.

For deeper insight **Scan the QR Code**

Important Instructions

- The test is of 30 minutes duration and contains 15 multiple choice questions (Four options with a single correct answer).
- Choose the correct option and fill the OMR given on the last page of test accordingly.
- At some instances, you may find more than 1 option may be correct. In such circumstances, you have to judge the most appropriate answer as per the conditions given in the question.

1. Consider the reaction given below.

$$CH_3CH{=}CH_2 \xrightarrow{\text{HI / Peroxide}} P$$

The product P formed is

(a) CH_3CHICH_3
(b) $CH_3CH_2CH_2I$
(c) $ICH_2CH{=}CH_2$
(d) CH_3CH_2I

2. For the conversion,

$$BrCH_2CH_2Br \longrightarrow H—C{\equiv}C—H$$

the reagents used is/are

(a) Zn/CH_3OH
(b) aqueous KOH followed by $NaNH_2$
(c) alcoholic KOH followed by $NaNH_2$
(d) alcoholic KOH

3. The bromoalkane and alkyne that are used for the synthesis of 3-octyne by using sodium amide are respectively

(a) $BrCH_2CH_2CH_2CH_3$ and $CH_3CH_2C{\equiv}CH$
(b) $BrCH_2CH_2CH_2CH_2CH_3$ and $CH_3C{\equiv}CH$
(c) $BrCH_2CH_2CH_3$ and $CH_3CH_2CH_2C{\equiv}CH$
(d) $BrCH_2CH_2CH_2CH_2CH_3$ and $CH_3CH_2C{\equiv}CH$

4. Consider the following reaction.

$$CH_3—\overset{\overset{CH_3}{|}}{\underset{\underset{H}{|}}{C}}—CH_2Br \xrightarrow[CH_3OH]{CH_3O^-}$$

The major product formed in reaction is

(a) $CH_3—\underset{\underset{CH_3}{|}}{CH}—CH_2OCH_3$

(b) $CH_3—\underset{\underset{OCH_3}{|}}{CH}—CH_2CH_3$

(c) $CH_3—\overset{\overset{CH_3}{|}}{C}{=}CH_2$

(d) $CH_3—\overset{\overset{CH_3}{|}}{\underset{\underset{OCH_3}{|}}{C}}—CH_3$

5. For the following bromides,

$$\underset{(A)}{Me\diagup\!\diagdown\!\diagup Br} \qquad \underset{(B)}{CH_2{=}CH—CH(Br)—Me} \qquad \underset{(C)}{Me—CH_2—CH(Br)—Me}$$

The correct order of S_N1 reactivity is
(a) $A > B > C$ (b) $B > A > C$
(c) $B > C > A$ (d) $C > B > A$

6. Arrange the compound $CH_3CH_2CH_2Cl$ (I), $CH_3CH_2CHClCH_3$ (II), $(CH_3)_2CHCH_2Cl$ (III) and $(CH_3)_3C—Cl$ (IV) in order of decreasing tendency towards S_N2 reactions.
(a) IV > III > II > I
(b) III > IV > II > I
(c) I > III > II > IV
(d) II > I > III > IV

7. Which of the following compounds will give racemic mixture on nucleophilic substitution by OH^- ion?

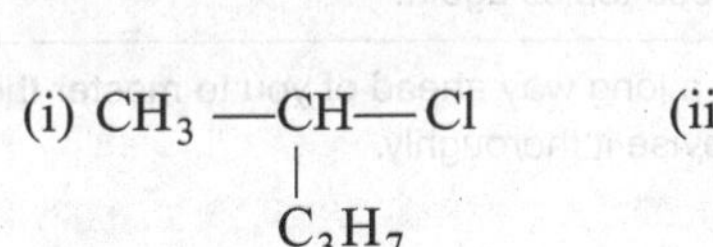

(ii) $CH_3—C(Cl)(C_3H_7)—CH_3$

(iii) $CH_3—CH(C_3H_7)—CH_2Cl$

(a) Only (i)
(b) (i), (ii) and (iii)
(c) Both (ii) and (iii)
(d) Both (i) and (iii)

8. Which of the following product will be formed when ethylidene dibromide is warmed with metallic sodium?
(a) Butane
(b) But-1-ene
(c) But-2-ene
(d) 1, 4-dibromo-2-butene

9. Which of the following are correctly arranged in the decreasing order of dipole moment?
(a) CH_3Cl, CH_3Br, CH_3F
(b) CH_3Cl, CH_3F, CH_3Br
(c) CH_3Br, CH_3Cl, CH_3F
(d) CH_3Br, CH_3F, CH_3Cl

10. For the given reaction,

$$R—Cl + NaI \xrightarrow{\text{Acetone}} R—I + NaCl$$

Which alkyl chloride will give maximum yield?
(a) $CH_3—C(CH_3)_2—Cl$
(b) $CH_3—CH_2—CH_2—Cl$
(c) $C_6H_5—CH(CH_3)—Cl$
(d) $C_6H_5—C(CH_3)_2—Cl$

11. Consider the following reaction,

$$CH_2{=}CHCH_2CH{=}CH_2 \xrightarrow{\text{NBS}} A.$$

The major product A is
(a) $CH_2{=}CHCH(Br)CH{=}CH_2$
(b) $CH_2{=}CHCH{=}CHCH_2Br$
(c) $CH{=}CHCH_2CN{=}CHBr$
(d) $CH_2{=}CHCH_2C(Br){=}CH_2$

12. Which of the following is tertiary alkyl halide?
(a) 2-chloro-2-methylbutane
(b) 1-chloropropane
(c) 2-chloropropane
(d) Cyclohexyl chloride

13. Which of the following statement is incorrect?
(a) C_2H_5Br reacts with alc. KOH to form C_2H_5OH.
(b) C_2H_5Br when treated with metallic sodium give ethane.
(c) C_2H_5Br when treated with sodium ethoxide form diethyl ether.
(d) Both (a) and (b)

14. What is the main product of the reaction between 2-methylpropene with HBr?
(a) 1-bromobutane
(b) 1-bromo-2-methylpropane
(c) 2-bromobutane
(d) 2-bromo-2-methylpropane

15. The metal which is used in Wurtz synthesis is
(a) Ba
(b) Al
(c) Na
(d) Fe

Response Index

01	a	b	c	d	10	a	b	c	d	19	a	b	c	d
02	a	b	c	d	11	a	b	c	d	20	a	b	c	d
03	a	b	c	d	12	a	b	c	d	21	a	b	c	d
04	a	b	c	d	13	a	b	c	d	22	a	b	c	d
05	a	b	c	d	14	a	b	c	d	23	a	b	c	d
06	a	b	c	d	15	a	b	c	d	24	a	b	c	d
07	a	b	c	d	16	a	b	c	d	25	a	b	c	d
08	a	b	c	d	17	a	b	c	d					
09	a	b	c	d	18	a	b	c	d					

Performance Scanner

> 90% Excellent !	You have mastered these topics. The concepts of these topics are at your fingertips. Move on to the next test and maintain this momentum.
76-90% Very Good !	You have a good command over these topics. Revise these topics again after a few days and enhance your performance.
60-75% Good !	You have a wide scope to learn for these topics. Revise these topics again.
<60 Not Satisfactory!	You have a long way ahead of you to master these topics. Revise it thoroughly.

Test 2

Syllabus **Haloarenes** : General Methods of Preparation, Properties and Reactions, Nature of C—X Bond, Mechanism of Substitution Reactions.

For deeper insight **Scan the QR Code**

Important Instructions

- The test is of 30 minutes duration and contains 15 multiple choice questions (Four options with a single correct answer).
- Choose the correct option and fill the OMR given on the last page of test accordingly.
- At some instances, you may find more than 1 option may be correct. In such circumstances, you have to judge the most appropriate answer as per the conditions given in the question.

1. Consider the following reaction.

$$X \xleftarrow{Cl_2/h\nu} C_6H_5CH_3 \xrightarrow{Cl_2/FeCl_3} \underset{\text{(Major)}}{Y}$$

Here, Y and X respectively are,

(a) benzyl chloride, *m*-chlorotoluene
(b) benzal chloride, *o*-chlorotoluene
(c) *m*-chlorotoluene, *p*-chlorotoluene
(d) *p*-chlorotoluene, trichloromethylbenzene

2. Given below are two statements, one is labelled as Assertion (A) and the other is labelled as Reason (R).

Assertion (A) Out of $C_6H_5CHClC_6H_5$ (I) and $C_6H_5CH_2Cl$ (II), II gets hydrolysed more easily than I by *aq.* KOH.

Reason (R) In S_N1 reactions, stability of carbocations is responsible for the reactivity.

In the light of the above statements, choose the correct answer from the options given below.

(a) Both (A) and (R) are true and (R) is the correct explanation of (A).
(b) Both (A) and (R) are true but (R) is not the correct explanation of (A).
(c) (A) is true but (R) is false.
(d) (A) is false but (R) is true.

3. Given below are two statements.

Statement I Presence of nitro group decreases the nucleophilic substitution reactions in aryl halides.

Statement II The intermediate carbocation destabilised due to the presence of nitro group.

In the light of the above statements, choose the correct answer from the options given below.

(a) Both Statement I and Statement II are incorrect.
(b) Statement I is correct but Statement II is incorrect.
(c) Statement I is incorrect but Statement II is correct.
(d) Both Statement I and Statement II are correct.

4. The raw material for Raschig process and Dow's process respectively are

(a) benzene and chlorobenzene
(b) chlorobenzene and phenol
(c) anisole and diazobenzene
(d) phenol and chlorobenzene

5. Among the following reactions, the example of Wurtz-Fittig reaction is

(a) $C_6H_5I + 2Na + CH_3I \longrightarrow C_6H_5CH_3 + 2NaI$
(b) $2C_6H_5I + 2Na \longrightarrow C_6H_5C_6H_5 + 2NaI$
(c) $2CH_3CH_2I + 2Na \longrightarrow CH_3CH_2CH_2CH_3 + 2NaI$
(d) $CH_3Br + AgF \longrightarrow CH_3F + AgBr$

6. In the given reaction sequence,

$$C_8H_{10} \xrightarrow[H_2SO_4]{HNO_3} A \xrightarrow[\Delta]{Br_2} B$$

the major product B is

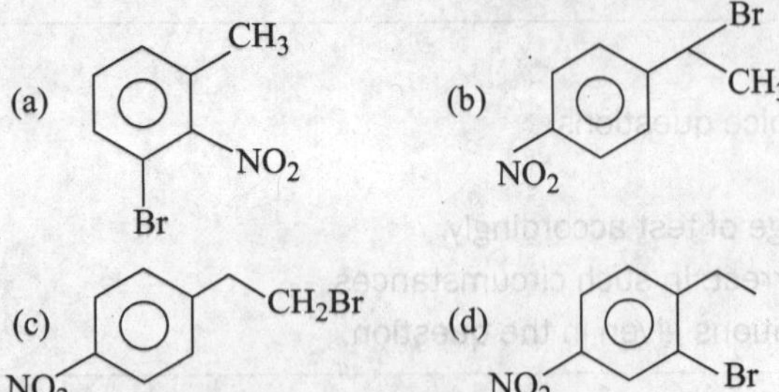

7. The C—Cl bond length in chlorobenzene is less than the C—Cl bond length in chloromethane because of the ....

(a) resonance effect in haloarenes
(b) instability of phenyl cation
(c) difference in hybridisation of carbon in C—Cl bond
(d) possible repulsion between nucleophile and chlorobenzene

8. Given below are two statements, one is labelled as Assertion (A) and the other is labelled as Reason (R).

Assertion (A) 2-chloronitrobenzene is more reactive as compared to chlorobenzene for nucleophilic substitution reaction.

Reason (R) Due to presence of electron withdrawing effect of the nitro group.

In the light of the above statements, choose the correct answer from the options given below.

(a) Both (A) and (R) are true and (R) is the correct explanation of (A).
(b) Both (A) and (R) are true but (R) is not the correct explanation of (A).
(c) (A) is true but (R) is false.
(d) (A) is false but (R) is true.

9. Identify the compound X in the following reaction.

$$C_6H_5NH_2 \xrightarrow[273\text{-}278K]{NaNO_2+HCl} C_6H_5\overset{+}{N_2}\overset{-}{Cl} \xrightarrow{Cu_2Cl_2} X + N_2$$

(a) C_6H_5Cl (b) C_6H_6
(c) $C_6H_4Cl_2$ (d) C_6Cl_6

10. Which of the following reaction is incorrect?

(a) Bromobenzene $\xrightarrow[\text{DMF, 470 K}]{CuCN}$ Benzonitrile (C₆H₅CN)

(b) Chlorobenzene $\xrightarrow[Cu_2O,\ 475\ K,\ 60\ atm]{2NH_3}$ Aniline (C₆H₅NH₂)

(c) Iodobenzene $\xrightarrow[\text{Sealed tube}]{Cu}$ C₆H₅CuI

(d) Chlorobenzene $\xrightarrow[CH_3-Cl]{\text{Na, ether}}$ Toluene (C₆H₅CH₃)

11. Identify the major product in the following reaction.

$$C_6H_5Cl + CH_3-\underset{H}{\overset{CH_3}{C}}-CH_2Br \xrightarrow{\text{Anhyd. } AlCl_3} \underset{(Major)}{Product}$$

(a) p-$ClC_6H_4-CH_2-CH(CH_3)-CH_3$

(b) o-$ClC_6H_4-CH_2-CH(CH_3)_2$

(c) $C_6H_5-CH_2-CH(CH_3)_2$

(d) p-$ClC_6H_4-C(CH_3)_2-CH_3$

12. Product of the following reaction is

F-benzene-NO_2 (para) $\xrightarrow{NaOCH_3}$ Product

(a) OCH_3 / NO_2 (para)
(b) F / OCH_3 (para)
(c) F, OCH_3 (ortho), NO_2 (para)
(d) F, OCH_3 (meta), NO_2 (para)

13. Consider the following compounds.

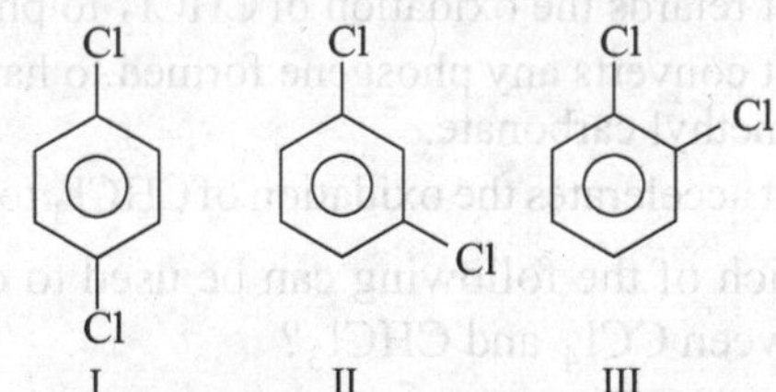

The correct order of melting point of dichlorobenzene is

(a) I > II > III (b) III > II > I
(c) I > III > II (d) II > I > III

14. Which of the following is not the correct match?

(a) Chlorobenzene + 2Na ⟶ Biphenyl ⇒ Fittig reaction

(b) $C_6H_5N_2^+Cl^-$ $\xrightarrow{Cu_2Cl_2}$ $C_6H_5Cl + N_2$ ⇒ Sandmeyer's reaction

(c) $C_2H_5Cl + NaI \longrightarrow C_2H_5I + NaCl$ ⇒ Swarts reaction

(d) Chlorobenzene + CH_3COCl $\xrightarrow{\text{Anhy. } AlCl_3}$ 4-chloroacetophenone (Cl, $COCH_3$) ⇒ Friedel-Crafts reaction

15. The compound (*A*) formed in the following reaction is

Benzene $\xrightarrow{Cl_2, Fe}$ (*A*)

(a) benzyl alcohol
(b) chlorobenzene
(c) 2-chlorotoluene
(c) 4-chlorotoluene

Response Index

01	(a) (b) (c) (d)		10	(a) (b) (c) (d)		19	(a) (b) (c) (d)							
02	(a) (b) (c) (d)		11	(a) (b) (c) (d)		20	(a) (b) (c) (d)							
03	(a) (b) (c) (d)		12	(a) (b) (c) (d)		21	(a) (b) (c) (d)							
04	(a) (b) (c) (d)		13	(a) (b) (c) (d)		22	(a) (b) (c) (d)							
05	(a) (b) (c) (d)		14	(a) (b) (c) (d)		23	(a) (b) (c) (d)							
06	(a) (b) (c) (d)		15	(a) (b) (c) (d)		24	(a) (b) (c) (d)							
07	(a) (b) (c) (d)		16	(a) (b) (c) (d)		25	(a) (b) (c) (d)							
08	(a) (b) (c) (d)		17	(a) (b) (c) (d)										
09	(a) (b) (c) (d)		18	(a) (b) (c) (d)										

Performance Scanner

> 90% Excellent !	You have mastered these topics. The concepts of these topics are at your fingertips. Move on to the next test and maintain this momentum.
76-90% Very Good !	You have a good command over these topics. Revise these topics again after a few days and enhance your performance.
60-75% Good !	You have a wide scope to learn for these topics. Revise these topics again.
<60 Not Satisfactory!	You have a long way ahead of you to master these topics. Revise it thoroughly.

Test 3

Syllabus Uses, Environmental Effects of Chloroform, Iodoform, Freons and DDT.

For deeper insight **Scan the QR Code**

Important Instructions

- The test is of 30 minutes duration and contains 15 multiple choice questions (Four options with a single correct answer).
- Choose the correct option and fill the OMR given on the last page of test accordingly.
- At some instances, you may find more than 1 option may be correct. In such circumstances, you have to judge the most appropriate answer as per the conditions given in the question.

1. Given below are two statements.

Statement I $CHCl_3$ is stored in closed transparent bottle.

Statement II Chloroform is slowly oxidised by air in the presence of light to carbonyl chloride.

In the light of the above statements, choose the correct answer from the options given below.

(a) Both Statement I and Statement II are incorrect.
(b) Statement I is correct but Statement II is incorrect.
(c) Statement I is incorrect but Statement II is correct.
(d) Both Statement I and Statement II are correct.

2. Iodoform gives a precipitate with $AgNO_3$ on heating but chloroform does not. Which of the following is the correct reason for this statement?

(a) C—I bond in iodoform is weak and C—Cl bond in chloroform is strong.
(b) Chloroform is covalent.
(c) Iodoform is ionic.
(d) $AgNO_3$ does not react with chloroform.

3. Chloroform when treated with benzene in presence of anhydrous $AlCl_3$, the product formed is X. The product X is

(a) chlorobenzene
(b) toluene
(c) mixture of *ortho-* and *para-*chlorotoluene
(d) triphenyl methane

4. Which of the following is the correct reason that a small amount of alcohol is usually added to $CHCl_3$ bottles?

(a) It retards the anaesthetic property of $CHCl_3$.
(b) It retards the oxidation of $CHCl_3$ to phosgene.
(c) It converts any phosgene formed to harmless methyl carbonate.
(d) It accelerates the oxidation of $CHCl_3$ to phosgene.

5. Which of the following can be used to distinguish between CCl_4 and $CHCl_3$?

(a) RNH_2 + KOH (alc.)
(b) RCN + KOH (alc.)
(c) Hydrolysis
(d) Burning in air

6. Benzene hexachloride is used as

(a) dye and insecticide
(b) antimalarial drug and antibiotic
(c) antibiotic and dye
(d) insecticide

7. Which of the following product is formed when chloroform is reacted with acetone?

(a) Insecticide
(b) Hypnotic drug
(c) Analgesic
(d) Isocyanide

8. A sample of chloroform before being used as an anaesthetic agent is tested by

(a) ammoniacal cuprous chloride
(b) Fehling's solution
(c) silver nitrate solution after boiling with alcoholic KOH
(d) silver nitrate solution in the cold

9. Which of the following statements are correct regarding freons?

I. Freon-14 is CF_4, Freon-13 is CF_3Cl, Freon-12 is CF_2Cl_2 and Freon-11 is $CFCl_3$.
II. Freons are chlorofluorocarbons.
III. Freons are used as refrigerants.
IV. Freon is manufactured from tetrachloromethane by Finkelstein reaction.
V. Freons are highly reactive.

Choose the correct answer from the options given below.

(a) I and II (b) III, IV and V
(c) I, II and III (d) Only V

10. Chloropicrin is obtained by the reaction of

(a) chlorine on picric acid
(b) nitric acid on chloroform
(c) steam on carbon tetrachloride
(d) nitric acid on chlorobenzene

11. Which of the following are responsible for depletion of the ozone layer?

(a) Freons (b) Polyhalogens
(c) Ferrocene (d) Fullerenes

12. When $CHCl_3$ is boiled with NaOH, it gives

(a) formic acid
(b) trihydroxy methane
(c) acetylene
(d) sodium formate

13. Chloroform is used in testing the presence of

(a) primary amines
(b) secondary amines
(c) tertiary amines
(d) nitro compounds

14. The organic compound X on heating with CuO produces CO_2 but not water. The compound X is

(a) chloroform
(b) methane
(c) ethyl iodide
(d) carbon tetrachloride

15. Given below are two statements, one is labelled as Assertion (A) and the other is labelled as Reason (R).

Assertion (A) CCl_4 is well known fire extinguisher. However, after using it to extinguisher fire, the room should be well ventilated.

Reason (R) CCl_4 produces phosgene by reaction with water vapour at high temperature.

In the light of the above statements, choose the correct answer from the options given below.

(a) Both (A) and (R) are true and (R) is the correct explanation of (A).
(b) Both (A) and (R) are true but (R) is not the correct explanation of (A).
(c) (A) is true but (R) is false.
(d) (A) is false but (R) is true.

Response Index

01	a	b	c	d	10	a	b	c	d	19	a	b	c	d
02	a	b	c	d	11	a	b	c	d	20	a	b	c	d
03	a	b	c	d	12	a	b	c	d	21	a	b	c	d
04	a	b	c	d	13	a	b	c	d	22	a	b	c	d
05	a	b	c	d	14	a	b	c	d	23	a	b	c	d
06	a	b	c	d	15	a	b	c	d	24	a	b	c	d
07	a	b	c	d	16	a	b	c	d	25	a	b	c	d
08	a	b	c	d	17	a	b	c	d					
09	a	b	c	d	18	a	b	c	d					

Performance Scanner

> 90% Excellent !	You have mastered these topics. The concepts of these topics are at your fingertips. Move on to the chapter test and maintain this momentum.
76-90% Very Good !	You have a good command over these topics. Revise these topics again after a few days and enhance your performance.
60-75% Good !	You have a wide scope to learn for these topics. Revise these topics again.
<60 Not Satisfactory!	You have a long way ahead of you to master these topics. Revise it thoroughly.

Chapter Break Thru

Syllabus	**Haloalkanes** : General Methods of Preparation, Properties and Reactions, Nature of C—*X* Bond, Mechanisms of Substitution Reactions.	**Haloarenes** : General Methods of Preparation, Properties and Reactions, Nature of C—*X* Bond, Mechanism of Substitution Reactions.	Uses, Environmental Effects of Chloroform, Iodoform, Freons, and DDT.

Important Instructions

- The test is of 1 hour duration and contains 50 multiple choice questions (Four options with a single correct answer).
- Choose the correct option and fill the OMR given on the last page of test accordingly.
- At some instances, you may find more than 1 option may be correct. In such circumstances, you have to judge the most appropriate answer as per the conditions given in the question.

1. $CH_3—\underset{\underset{OH}{|}}{\overset{\overset{CH_3}{|}}{C}}—CH_3 \xrightarrow[\text{Room temp.}]{\text{Conc. HCl}} \text{Product } (P)$

tert-butyl alcohol

Product of the above reaction is

(a) 1-chloro-2-methylpropane

(b) 2-chloro-2-methylpropane

(c) 1, 2-dichloro-2-methyl propane

(d) 1, 3-dichloro-2-methyl propane

2. The correct IUPAC name of the given compound is

$(CH_3)(H)C{=}C(CH_3)—CH(Br)(CH_3)$

(a) 1-bromo-2-methylbut-2-ene

(b) 3-bromo-2-methylbut-1-ene

(c) 4-bromo-3-methylpent-2-ene

(d) 2-bromo-3-methylpent-3-ene

3. Product of the following reaction is

$CH_3—CH_2—\overset{\overset{C_2H_5}{|}}{C}{=}CH—CH_3 + HBr \xrightarrow{H_2O_2} ?$

(a) $CH_3—CH_2—\underset{\underset{Br}{|}}{\overset{\overset{C_2H_5}{|}}{C}}—CH_2—CH_3$

(b) $CH_3—CH_2—\underset{\underset{H}{|}}{\overset{\overset{C_2H_5}{|}}{C}}—\underset{\underset{Br}{|}}{CH}—CH_3$

(c) $CH_3—CH_2—\underset{\underset{H}{|}}{\overset{\overset{C_2H_5}{|}}{C}}—CH_2—CH_2—Br$

(d) $CH_3\overset{\overset{Br}{|}}{CH}—\overset{\overset{OH}{|}}{CH}—C_2H_5$

4. Consider the reactions given below.

I. 1-bromo-1-methylcyclohexane $\xrightarrow{\text{Alc. KOH}}$ methylenecyclohexane (Minor) + 1-methylcyclohexene (Major)

II. 1,2-dichlorocyclohexane $\xrightarrow[\Delta]{\text{Zn dust}}$ benzene

III. 1-chloropropane $\xrightarrow[\text{Acetone}]{\text{NaI}}$ 1-iodopropane

IV. 1-chloropropane $\xrightarrow{\text{Alc. KOH}}$ propene

V. 1,1-dichloropropane $\xrightarrow[\Delta]{NaNH_2 \text{ (excess)}}$ propyne

The number of correct reactions are

(a) 1 (b) 2 (c) 3 (d) 4

5. Correct order of following alkyl halides in the decreasing order of S_N1 reactivity is

I. CH_3CH_2Cl
II. $CH_2=CHCH(Cl)CH_3$
III. $CH_3CH_2CH(Cl)CH_3$

(a) I > II > III (b) II > I > III
(c) II > III > I (d) III > II > I

6. The compounds *A* and *B* formed in the following reaction is

$$CH_3COOH + Ag_2CO_3 \longrightarrow A \xrightarrow[CCl_4]{Br_2} B$$

	A	*B*
(a)	CH_3COOAg	CH_3Br
(b)	CH_3COOAg	CH_3COOCH_3
(c)	CH_3COOAg	CH_3CH_3
(d)	CH_4	$CH_3—Br$

7. Correct order of boiling point of the following compounds.

I. $CH_3CH_2CH_2CH_2—Cl$
II. $CH_3—CH(Cl)—CH_2—CH_3$
III. $CH_3—CH(CH_3)—CH_2—Cl$
IV. $(CH_3)_3C—Cl$

Choose the correct answer from the options given below.

(a) I > II > III > IV (b) II > I > III > IV
(c) III > II > I > IV (d) IV > III > II > I

8. Which of the following statement is incorrect about S_N1 reaction?

(a) The rate of reaction depends only on the concentration of alkyl halide.
(b) Order of reactivity toward S_N1 reaction is 1° > 2° > 3° of alkyl halide.
(c) Allylic and benzylic halides show greater reactivity towards S_N1 reaction.
(d) In this reaction, racemic mixture is obtained.

9. Choose the incorrect statement about S_N2 reaction.

(a) S_N2 reaction depends on concentration of reactant as well as concentration of nucleophile.
(b) Optically active alkyl halide gives complete inversion through S_N2 reaction.
(c) Weaker nucleophile favours S_N2 reaction, whereas stronger nucleophile favours, S_N1 reaction.
(d) Minimum steric hindrance favours S_N2 reaction.

10. Given below are two statements.

Statement I Reaction between alcohols and H*X* follows S_N1 mechanism.

Statement II In S_N1 mechanism, transition state formation takes place.

In the light of the above statements, choose the correct answer from the options given below.

(a) Both Statement I and Statement II are incorrect.
(b) Statement I is correct but Statement II is incorrect.
(c) Statement I is incorrect but Statement II is correct.
(d) Both Statement I and Statement II are correct.

11. Which of the following statement is not responsible for *neo*-pentyl bromide to undergo nucleophilic substitution reaction very slowly?

(a) It is primary alkyl halide so, slow rate towards S_N1 reaction is obtained.
(b) It is sterically hindered halide which reacts slowly through S_N2 mechanism.
(c) Due to larger sphere of alkyl group, it will give more steric hindrance and decrease reactivity toward S_N2 reaction.
(d) Clevage of the C—Br bond produces a secondary carbocation.

12. Consider some alkyl halides.

I. I   II. F
III. Cl   IV. Br

Choose the correct order towards S_N2 reaction.

(a) II < III < IV < I
(b) II < I < III < IV
(c) IV < III < II < I
(d) I < II < III < IV

13. Given below are two statements, one is labelled as Assertion (A) and the other is labelled as Reason (R).

Assertion (A) In comparison to C_2H_5Br, it is difficult to carry out S_N1 reaction on vinyl bromide.

Reason (R) Vinyl group is an electron donating group in vinyl bromide.

In the light of the above statements, choose the correct answer from the options given below.

(a) Both (A) and (R) are true and (R) is the correct explanation of (A).
(b) Both (A) and (R) are true but (R) is not the correct explanation of (A).
(c) (A) is true but (R) is false.
(d) (A) is false but (R) is true.

14. Choose the correct order of density of following alkyl halides.

I. $CHCl_3$ II. CH_2Cl_2
III. CCl_4 IV. CH_3Cl

Choose the correct option.

(a) I < II < III < IV
(b) IV < II < I < III
(c) IV < III < II < I
(d) IV < I < III < II

15. Match List-I with List-II.

	List-I (Reaction)	List-II (Mechanism)
A.	(alkenyl chloride, Cl) $\xrightarrow[\text{CH}_3\text{COOH Solvent}]{\text{CH}_3\text{COO}^-}$	I. E_{1CB}
B.	(alkenyl chloride, Cl) + CH_3OH $\xrightarrow{\text{Ethanol Solvent}}$	II. E_2
C.	$O{=}S(CH_3)$–CH(CH₃)… with OPh $\xrightarrow{\text{EtO}^-}$	III. S_N2
D.	Ph–CH₂CH₂CH₂–Br and Ph–C(D)(D)–CH₂–Br $\xrightarrow{\text{Alc. KOH}}$	IV. S_N1

Choose the correct answer from the options given below.

(a) A-III, B-IV, C-I, D-II
(b) A-II, B-I, C-IV, D-III
(c) A-II, B-I, C-III, D-IV
(d) A-III, B-IV, C-II, D-I

16. Given below are two statements.

Statement I Chlorobenzene reacts with NaOH and forms phenol.

Statement II Alkyl halide on reaction with $LiAlH_4$ will give alcohol.

In the light of the above statements, choose the correct answer from the options given below.

(a) Both Statement I and Statement II are incorrect.
(b) Statement I is correct but Statement II is incorrect.
(c) Statement I is incorrect but Statement II is correct.
(d) Both Statement I and Statement II are correct.

17. Find the final product of the reaction,

$$C_6H_5Cl \xrightarrow[Cu_2O]{NH_3} X \xrightarrow{NaNO_2 + HCl} Y \xrightarrow[\text{Warm}]{KI} \underset{\text{(Final product)}}{Z}$$

(a) Benzene
(b) Iodobenzene
(c) Biphenyl
(d) 1, 4-dichlorobenzene

18. Which of the following reagent is suitable for the conversion of iodoform to ethyne?

(a) Ag/powder + Δ
(b) $AgNO_3$/Δ
(c) Air, moisture/Heat
(d) Red P

19. In the reaction,

$$A \xrightarrow[\text{Pyridine}]{SOCl_2} C_6H_5{-}CH_2{-}Cl \xrightarrow{KCN} B \xrightarrow{H_2O/H^+} C$$

A and *C* are respectively

	A	*C*
(a)	benzene	benzaldehyde
(b)	phenyl methanol	2-phenyl ethanoic acid
(c)	phenol	2-phenyl ethanol
(d)	benzene	benzoic acid

20. Arrange the following compounds in increasing order of reactivity towards nucleophilic substitution?

I. Cl (chlorobenzene) II. Cl, NO_2 III. Cl, NO_2, NO_2 IV. Cl, NO_2, NO_2, NO_2

Select the correct answer from the options given below.

(a) I < II < III < IV (b) I < II < IV < III

(c) IV < III < II < I (d) IV < III < I < II

21. Which of the following product is formed when HBr reacts with $CH_2=CH-OCH_3$ under anhydrous conditions at room temperature?

(a) CH_3CHO and CH_3Br

(b) $BrCH_2CHO$ and CH_3OH

(c) $BrCH_2-CH_2-OCH_3$

(d) $H_3C-CHBr-OCH_3$

22. Which of the following method(s) used for the allylic halogen substitution?

I. Halogenation at high temperature.

II. NBS in sunlight.

III. Reaction with sulphonyl chloride in sunlight.

IV. Reaction with NH_3.

V. Reaction with *aq.* KOH.

Choose the correct answer from the options given below.

(a) I, II and III (b) II and IV

(c) IV and V (d) I and III

23. The final product formed in the reaction.

$$C_7H_8 \xrightarrow{3Cl_2/\Delta} A \xrightarrow{Br_2/Fe} B \xrightarrow{Zn/HCl} C; \text{ is}$$

(a) *o*-bromotoluene

(b) *m*-bromotoluene

(c) 3-bromo-2, 2, 6-trichlorotoluene

(d) *p*-bromotoluene

24. H, C, CH_3, CH_3, CH_3 $\xrightarrow[hv]{Cl_2}$?

The compound which represents the major monochlorination isomer formed in the above reaction is

(a) CH, CH_3, CH_3, H_3C, Cl (b) Cl, C, CH_3, CH_3, CH_3

(c) CH_3, CH, CH_3, CH_3, Cl (d) CH_3, Cl, $CH(CH_3)_2$

25. Which of the following pairs have both compounds with net non-zero dipole moment?

(a) 1, 4-dichlorobenzene, 1,3-dichlorobenzene

(b) CH_2Cl_2, $CHCl_3$

(c) Benzene, anisole

(d) *cis*-butene, *trans*-butene

26. The compound which has the shortest C—Cl bond is

(a) H_3C-Cl (b) Cl, CH, ‖, CH_2

(c) H_3C, $H_3C-C-Cl$, CH_3 (d) HC, Cl, ‖, CH_2

27. Consider the following compounds.

I: $CH_3CH_2CH_2CH_2Br$

II: $CH_3-C(CH_3)_2-Br$

III: $CH_3-CH_2-CH(CH_3)-Br$

The correct decreasing order of boiling point is

(a) I > III > II

(b) II > I > III

(c) I > II > III

(d) III > I > II

28. On the reaction,

NO_2-benzene $\xrightarrow{Br_2/Fe} P \xrightarrow{Sn/HCl} Q$

The formed products P and Q are

	P	Q
(a)	p-bromonitrobenzene	p-bromoaniline
(b)	o-bromonitrobenzene	o-bromoaniline
(c)	o, p-dibromonitrobenzene	o, p-dibromoaniline
(d)	m-bromonitrobenzene	m-bromoaniline

29. The increasing order of reactivity of the following bromides in S_N1 reaction is

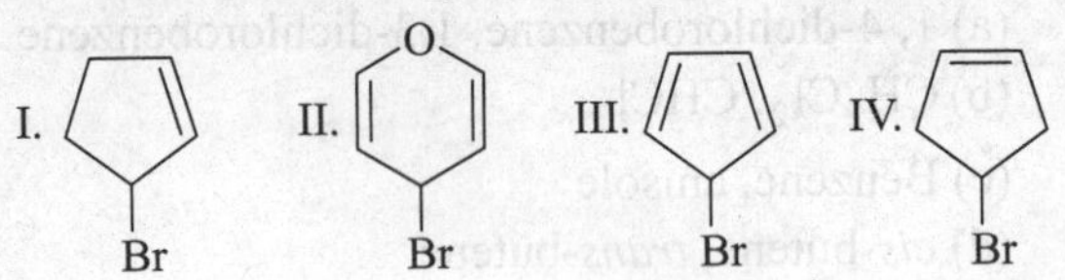

(a) III > I > II > IV
(b) III > II > I > IV
(c) II > III > I > IV
(d) II > I > IV > III

30. A Grignard's reagent may be made by reacting magnesium with

(a) methyl amine
(b) diethyl ether
(c) ethyl iodide
(d) ethyl alcohol

31. The general formula for alkyl halides is

(a) $C_nH_{2n+1}X$
(b) $C_nH_{2n+2}X$
(c) $C_nH_{n+1}X$
(d) $C_nH_{2n}X$

32. Among the following, the molecule with the highest dipole moment is

(a) CH_3Cl
(b) CH_2Cl_2
(c) $CHCl_3$
(d) CCl_4

33. The main product will be

Ph_2CH–C_6H_4–$CH_3 \xrightarrow{\text{Excess } Cl_2/h\nu}$ Product

(a) $(C_6H_5)_2C(H)$–C_6H_4–CCl_3

(b) $(C_6H_5)Cl_2C$–C_6H_4–CH_2–Cl (Cl on benzene ring)

(c) $(C_6H_5)_2C(Cl)$–C_6H_4–CCl_3

(d) $(C_6H_5)_2C(Cl)$–C_6H_4–$CHCl_2$

34. The reaction of toluene with Cl_2 in the presence of $FeCl_3$ gives X and in presence of light gives Y. Thus, X and Y are

(a) X = benzyl chloride, Y = m-chlorotoluene
(b) X = benzal chloride, Y = o-chlorotoluene
(c) X = m-chlorotoluene, Y = p-chlorotoluene
(d) X = o- and p-chlorotoluene, Y = trichloromethyl benzene

35. Order of reactivity towards nucleophilic substitution reaction of the compound.

I. p-NMe_2–C_6H_4–Cl
II. p-NO_2–C_6H_4–Cl
III. 1-Cl-2,4-$(NO_2)_2C_6H_3$
IV. 1-Cl-2,4,6-$(NO_2)_3C_6H_2$

(a) I > II > III > IV
(b) II > I > III > IV
(c) IV > III > II > I
(d) III > IV > II > I

36. Consider the following statements.

I. Grignard reagents should be prepared under anhydrous conditions.
II. Haloalkanes are more reactive towards nucleophilic substitution reaction than haloarenes.
III. 2-chlorobutane is a chiral molecule.
IV. Phenol on reacting with NaBr and H_2SO_4 gives *ortho*-bromophenol.
V. Alkyl halides are polar in nature, thus they are soluble in water.

Choose the incorrect statement and mark the option accordingly.

(a) I, IV and V
(b) II, IV and V
(c) I, II and III
(d) II and III

37. Given below are two statements, one is labelled as Assertion (A) and the other is labelled as Reason (R).

Assertion (A) Aryl iodides are prepared in the presence of an oxidising agent such as HNO_3.
Reason (R) Reactions of arenes with iodines are reversible in nature.

In the light of the above statements, choose the correct answer from the options given below.

(a) Both (A) and (R) are true and (R) is the correct explanation of (A).
(b) Both (A) and (R) are true but (R) is not the correct explanation of (A).
(c) (A) is true but (R) is false.
(d) (A) is false but (R) is true.

38. Identify *A* and predict the type of reaction,

$$\text{3-bromoanisole} \xrightarrow{NaNH_2} A$$

(a) *m*-anisidine and substitution reaction
(b) *o*-anisidine and elimination addition reaction
(c) 2-bromoanisole and cine substitution reaction
(d) anisole and cine substitution reaction

39. Compound *A* on reaction with aqueous KOH will give acetaldehyde. Here, compound *A* is

(a) 1,2-dichloroethane
(b) 1,1-dichloroethane
(c) chloroacetic acid
(d) ethyl chloride

40. Which of the following is the main compound obtained when chlorobenzene is heated with chloral in presence of concentrated H_2SO_4?

(a) DDT (b) TNT
(c) BHC (d) PCC

41. Consider the following reaction.

$$C_6H_5Cl + NaOH \longrightarrow C_6H_5O^-Na^+$$

The reaction conditions required in the above reaction is

(a) 573 K, Cu, 300 atm
(b) 643 K, Cu, 300 atm
(c) 573 K, 300 atm
(d) 623 K, 300 atm

42. Under basic conditions which of the following undergo elimination most readily?

(a) $(CH_3)_3CCl$
(b) $CH_3CH_2—CH_2—CH_2Cl$
(c) $CH_3CH_2CH_2—CH_2—Cl$
(d) $(CH_3)_2CH—CH_2Cl$

43. Which of the following reactant(s) will be used to prepare a pure sample of *n*-hexane using sodium metal as one reactant?

(a) Ethyl chloride and *n*-butyl chloride
(b) Ethyl chloride and *n*-butyl bromide
(c) *n*-propyl bromide
(d) Methyl bromide and *n*-pentyl chloride

44. *m*-substituted product with respect to methyl group is formed by the halogenation of

(a) 3-methylbenzaldehyde (CH_3, CHO)
(b) 2-nitrotoluene (CH_3, NO_2)
(c) 2-methylphenol (CH_3, OH)
(d) 3-nitrotoluene (CH_3, NO_2)

45. Consider the following reaction.

$$\text{Naphthalene} \xrightarrow[\text{(ii) EtOH}]{\text{(i) } Br_2/CCl_4}$$

The major product formed in the above reaction is

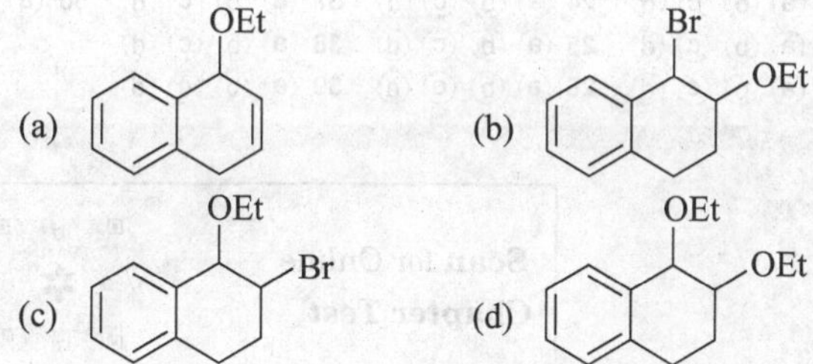

46. Consider the following statements.

I. Methylene chloride is used as refrigerant and dewaxing agent.
II. Triiodomethane is used as an antiseptic.
III. Exposure to CCl_4 causes liver cancer in humans.
IV. In stratosphere, freon is able to initiate chain reactions.
V. The full form of DDT is *o, p*-dichlorodiphenyl trichloroethane.

Choose the correct statements and mark the option accordingly.

(a) I, III and V (b) III, IV and V
(c) I, II, III and IV (d) I, II, III and V

47. Which of the following represents nucleophilic aromatic substitution reaction?

(a) Reaction of benzene with Cl_2 in sunlight.
(b) Hydrolysis of benzyl bromide.
(c) Reaction of NaOH with dinitrochlorobenzene.
(d) Sulphonation of benzene.

48. Which of the following statement is incorrect regarding benzyl chloride?

(a) It gives white precipitate with alcoholic $AgNO_3$.
(b) It is an aromatic compound with substitution in the side chain.
(c) It undergoes nucleophilic substitution reaction.
(d) It is less reactive than vinyl chloride.

49. Among the following, the one which reacts most readily with ethanol is

(a) *p*-nitrobenzyl bromide
(b) *p*-chlorobenzyl bromide
(c) *p*-methoxybenzyl bromide
(d) *p*-methyl benzyl bromide

50. Benzene $\xrightarrow[\text{(ii) Conc. } HNO_3]{\text{(i) } Cl_2/\text{Anhyd. } AlCl_3}$ Product

(a) Cl, NO_2 or Cl, NO_2
(b) Cl, NO_2 or Cl, NO_2
(c) Cl, NO_2
(d) Cl, NO_2 or Cl, NO_2

Response Index

01 ⓐ ⓑ ⓒ ⓓ	14 ⓐ ⓑ ⓒ ⓓ	27 ⓐ ⓑ ⓒ ⓓ	40 ⓐ ⓑ ⓒ ⓓ
02 ⓐ ⓑ ⓒ ⓓ	15 ⓐ ⓑ ⓒ ⓓ	28 ⓐ ⓑ ⓒ ⓓ	41 ⓐ ⓑ ⓒ ⓓ
03 ⓐ ⓑ ⓒ ⓓ	16 ⓐ ⓑ ⓒ ⓓ	29 ⓐ ⓑ ⓒ ⓓ	42 ⓐ ⓑ ⓒ ⓓ
04 ⓐ ⓑ ⓒ ⓓ	17 ⓐ ⓑ ⓒ ⓓ	30 ⓐ ⓑ ⓒ ⓓ	43 ⓐ ⓑ ⓒ ⓓ
05 ⓐ ⓑ ⓒ ⓓ	18 ⓐ ⓑ ⓒ ⓓ	31 ⓐ ⓑ ⓒ ⓓ	44 ⓐ ⓑ ⓒ ⓓ
06 ⓐ ⓑ ⓒ ⓓ	19 ⓐ ⓑ ⓒ ⓓ	32 ⓐ ⓑ ⓒ ⓓ	45 ⓐ ⓑ ⓒ ⓓ
07 ⓐ ⓑ ⓒ ⓓ	20 ⓐ ⓑ ⓒ ⓓ	33 ⓐ ⓑ ⓒ ⓓ	46 ⓐ ⓑ ⓒ ⓓ
08 ⓐ ⓑ ⓒ ⓓ	21 ⓐ ⓑ ⓒ ⓓ	34 ⓐ ⓑ ⓒ ⓓ	47 ⓐ ⓑ ⓒ ⓓ
09 ⓐ ⓑ ⓒ ⓓ	22 ⓐ ⓑ ⓒ ⓓ	35 ⓐ ⓑ ⓒ ⓓ	48 ⓐ ⓑ ⓒ ⓓ
10 ⓐ ⓑ ⓒ ⓓ	23 ⓐ ⓑ ⓒ ⓓ	36 ⓐ ⓑ ⓒ ⓓ	49 ⓐ ⓑ ⓒ ⓓ
11 ⓐ ⓑ ⓒ ⓓ	24 ⓐ ⓑ ⓒ ⓓ	37 ⓐ ⓑ ⓒ ⓓ	50 ⓐ ⓑ ⓒ ⓓ
12 ⓐ ⓑ ⓒ ⓓ	25 ⓐ ⓑ ⓒ ⓓ	38 ⓐ ⓑ ⓒ ⓓ	
13 ⓐ ⓑ ⓒ ⓓ	26 ⓐ ⓑ ⓒ ⓓ	39 ⓐ ⓑ ⓒ ⓓ	

Performance Scanner

> 90% Excellent !	You have mastered this chapter. The concepts of this chapter are at your fingertips. Move on to the next chapter and maintain this momentum.
76-90% Very Good !	You have a good command over this chapter. Revise the chapter again after a few days and enhance your performance.
60-75% Good !	You have a wide scope to learn for this chapter. Revise this chapter again.
<60 Not Satisfactory!	You have a long way ahead of you to master this chapter. Revise it thoroughly.

Scan for Online Chapter Test

Scan for Online Unit Test

Test Booklet No. **3947258**

Test Booklet Code **CH8**

MEDACE

NEET (UG)

SELF ASSESSMENT KIT

Alcohols, Phenols and Ethers

Important Instructions

- This Booklet Contains – 3 Topic Tests and One Test on Complete Chapter.
- Each question carries 4 marks.
- For each correct response the candidate will get 4 marks and for every incorrect response, 1 mark will be additionally deducted from the total score.
- Use **Blue/Black** point pen only for filling the OMR.
- Rough work is to be done in the space provided for this purpose in the test booklet only.

Topics Covered

Preparation, Properties and Uses of Alcohols

Preparation, Properties and Uses of Phenols

Preparation, Properties and Uses of Ethers

Name of the Candidate (In Capitals)

____

____

Candidate's Signature ________

Invigilator's Signature ________

Facsimile signature stamp of center superintendent________

Do not open this Booklet until you start attempting the Test

Topical Follow Thru

Test 1

Syllabus

Alcohols : General Methods of Preparation, Properties, Reaction and Uses, Identification of Primary, Secondary and Tertiary Alcohols, Mechanism of Dehydration.

For deeper insight **Scan the QR Code**

Important Instructions

- The test is of 30 minutes duration and contains 15 multiple choice questions (Four options with a single correct answer).
- Choose the correct option and fill the OMR given on the last page of test accordingly.
- At some instances, you may find more than 1 option may be correct. In such circumstances, you have to judge the most appropriate answer as per the conditions given in the question.

1. Which of the following statement about alcohols is correct?

(a) Lower members are insoluble in water.

(b) Solubility of alcohols in water decreases with increase in molecular masses.

(c) Higher members have a pleasant smell and have burning taste, lower members are colourless and tasteless.

(d) The boiling points of alcohol decreases with increase in number of C-atoms.

2. Given below are two statements.

Statement I The bond angle in alcohol is slightly less than the tetrahedral angle.

Statement II Variation in bond angle of alcohol is due to the repulsion between the unshared electron pairs of oxygen.

In the light of the above statements, choose the correct answer from the options given below.

(a) Both Statement I and Statement II are incorrect.

(b) Statement I is correct but Statement II is incorrect.

(c) Statement I is incorrect but Statement II is correct.

(d) Both Statement I and Statement II are correct.

3. Match List-I with List-II.

List-I (Compound)	List-II (IUPAC name)
A. $HOCH_2—CH(OH)—CH_2OH$	I. Cyclopentanol
B. $CH_3—C(CH_3)_2—OH$	II. Hydroxyquinol
C. OH on cyclopentane ring	III. 2-methylpropan-2-ol
D. benzene ring with OH, OH, OH	IV. Propan-1,2,3-triol

Choose the correct match from the options given below.

(a) A-II, B-III, C-I, D-IV

(b) A-III, B-II, C-IV, D-I

(c) A-IV B-III, C-I, D-II

(d) A-IV, B-I, C-III, D-II

4. Given below are two statements, one is labelled as Assertion (A) and the other is labelled as Reason (R).

Assertion (A) Alcohols act as Lewis bases.

Reason (R) It is due to the presence of unshared electron pairs on oxygen.

In the light of the above statements, choose the most appropriate answer from the options given below.

(a) Both (A) and (R) are true and (R) is the correct explanation of (A).

(b) Both (A) and (R) are true, but (R) is not the correct explanation of (A).

(c) (A) is true but (R) is false.

(d) (A) is false but (R) is true.

5. Choose the incorrect statement.

(a) PCC is the complex of chromium trioxide with pyridine and HCl.

(b) Denaturation of alcohol is the mixing of $CuSO_4$ and pyridine to make the commercial alcohol for drinking.

(c) Methanol is known as wood spirit.

(d) Vinylic alcohol contains —OH group bonded to a carbon-carbon double bond.

6. Select the correct order of boiling point of given alcohol.

(a) $CH_3-C(CH_3)_2-OH > CH_3-CH(CH_3)-CH_2OH > CH_3CH_2CH_2CH_2OH$

(b) $CH_3CH_2CH_2CH_2OH > CH_3-C(CH_3)_2-OH > CH_3-CH(CH_3)-CH_2OH$

(c) $CH_3-C(CH_3)_2-OH < CH_3-CH(CH_3)-CH_2OH < CH_3CH_2CH_2CH_2OH$

(d) $CH_3-C(CH_3)_2-OH < CH_3CH_2CH_2CH_2OH < CH_3-CH(CH_3)-CH_2OH$

7. Which of the following statement is incorrect regarding preparation of alcohols?

(a) Aldehydes and ketones on catalytic reduction by hydrogenation give primary alcohol and secondary alcohol respectively.

(b) Alkyl halides on reaction with alcoholic potash gives alcohol.

(c) Aldehydes on reaction with Grignard's reagent gives primary or secondary alcohol.

(d) Carboxylic acids are reduced to primary alcohols by lithium aluminium hydride.

8. Choose the incorrect statement.

(a) Solubility of alcohol decreases with increase in size of alkyl/aryl groups.

(b) Alcohols react with active metals like Na, K etc., to produce corresponding alkoxides or phenoxides.

(c) Alcohols act as Bronsted acid in the presence of strong acid.

(d) Alcohols react with both nucleophiles and electrophiles.

9. Which of the following is the correct order of reactivity of HCl, HBr and HI with alcohols?

(a) HI > HBr > HCl

(b) HI > HCl > HBr

(c) HCl > HBr > HI

(d) HBr > HCl > HI

10. Given below are two statements.

Statement I In alcohols, the boiling point decreases with increase in the branching of the carbon chain.

Statement II There is an increase in van der Waals' forces between the number of carbon atoms with decrease in the surface area in alcohols.

In the light of the above statements, choose the correct answer from the options given below.
(a) Both Statement I and Statement II are incorrect.
(b) Statement I is correct but Statement II is incorrect.
(c) Statement I is incorrect but Statement II is correct.
(d) Both Statement I and Statement II are correct.

11. Number of possible product formed in the given reaction is

OH (structure) $\xrightarrow{\text{Conc. } H_2SO_4/\Delta}$?

(a) 2 (b) 3
(c) 4 (d) 5

12. What will be the major product of given reaction?

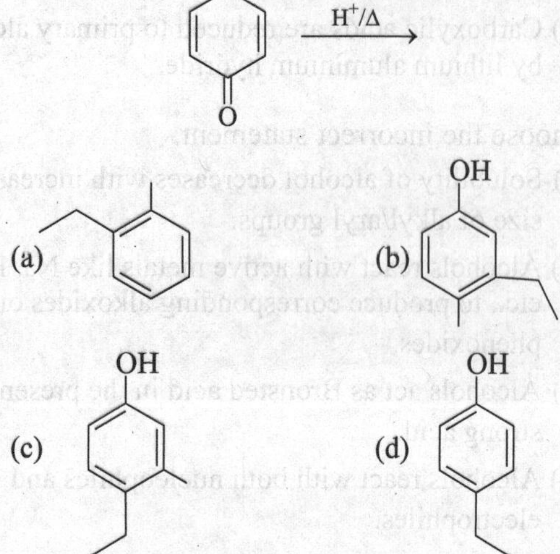

13. Which of the following product will not be formed when reaction of C_2H_5OH with H_2SO_4 at different conditions takes place?
(a) Ethylene
(b) Diethyl ether
(c) Acetylene
(d) Ethyl hydrogen sulphate

14. Given below are two statements.
Statement I The acidic character of alcohols is due to the polar nature of O—H bond.
Statement II An electron releasing group ($-CH_3$, $-C_2H_5$) increases the electron density on oxygen tending to decrease the polarity of O—H bond.
In the light of the above statements, choose the correct answer from the options given below.
(a) Both Statement I and Statement II are incorrect.
(b) Statement I is correct but Statement II is incorrect.
(c) Statement I is incorrect but Statement II is correct.
(d) Both Statement I and Statement II are correct.

15. Choose the incorrect statement from the following.
(a) Alcohols are soluble in Lucas reagent while their halides are immiscible.
(b) Primary alcohols do not produce turbidity at room temperature with Lucas reagent.
(c) Alcohols on dehydration to form alkenes on treating with a protic acid, i.e. H_2SO_4, H_3PO_4
(d) Oxidation of alcohols involves the formation of carbon-oxygen double bond with cleavage of O—H bonds only.

Response Index

01	a	b	c	d	10	a	b	c	d	19	a	b	c	d
02	a	b	c	d	11	a	b	c	d	20	a	b	c	d
03	a	b	c	d	12	a	b	c	d	21	a	b	c	d
04	a	b	c	d	13	a	b	c	d	22	a	b	c	d
05	a	b	c	d	14	a	b	c	d	23	a	b	c	d
06	a	b	c	d	15	a	b	c	d	24	a	b	c	d
07	a	b	c	d	16	a	b	c	d	25	a	b	c	d
08	a	b	c	d	17	a	b	c	d					
09	a	b	c	d	18	a	b	c	d					

Performance Scanner

> 90% Excellent !	You have mastered these topics. The concepts of these topics are at your fingertips. Move on to the next test and maintain this momentum.
76-90% Very Good !	You have a good command over these topics. Revise these topics again after a few days and enhance your performance.
60-75% Good !	You have a wide scope to learn for these topics. Revise these topics again.
<60 Not Satisfactory!	You have a long way ahead of you to master these topics. Revise it thoroughly.

Test 2

Syllabus

Phenols : General Methods of Preparation, Properties, Acidic Nature, Electrophilic Substitution Reaction, Halogenation, Nitration, Sulphonation, Reimer-Tiemann Reaction.

For deeper insight **Scan the QR Code**

Important Instructions

- The test is of 30 minutes duration and contains 15 multiple choice questions (Four options with a single correct answer).
- Choose the correct option and fill the OMR given on the last page of test accordingly.
- At some instances, you may find more than 1 option may be correct. In such circumstances, you have to judge the most appropriate answer as per the conditions given in the question.

1. Choose the incorrect statement.

(a) The hydroxyl group in phenol is directly attached to sp^2-hybridised carbon of benzene ring.

(b) The charge distribution in phenol causes the oxygen of —OH group to be positive.

(c) The reactions of phenol with metals and sodium hydroxide indicate its basic nature.

(d) In alkoxide ion, the negative charge is localised on oxygen, while in phenoxide ion the charge is delocalised.

2. Complete the following reaction

o-Cresol (benzene ring with CH_3 and OH) $\xrightarrow[\text{(ii) } CH_3I]{\text{(i) } aq.\ NaOH}$?

(a) Ring with CH_3, OH, CH_3 (2,6-dimethylphenol)

(b) Ring with CH_3, OH, and CH_3 para to OH

(c) Ring with CH_3 and OCH_3

(d) Ring with CH_3, OH, and CH_3 at the bottom

3. Given below are two statements.

Statement I Bromination of phenol takes place even in the absence of Lewis acid.

Statement II In phenol, —OH group attached to benzene ring has highly deactivating effect.

In the light of the above statements, choose the correct answer from the options given below.

(a) Both Statement I and Statement II are incorrect.

(b) Statement I is correct but Statement II is incorrect.

(c) Statement I is incorrect but Statement II is correct.

(d) Both Statement I and Statement II are correct.

4. Select the product formed in the given reaction.

Phenol (OH) $\xrightarrow[\text{Conc. } H_2SO_4]{\text{Conc. } HNO_3}$?

(a) Phenol with O_2N, NO_2 at both ortho positions and NO_2 at para position

(b) Phenol with NO_2 at ortho position

(c) Phenol with NO_2 at meta position

(d) CH_3-substituted ring with NO_2 para

5. Given below are two statements, one is labelled as Assertion (A) and the other is labelled as Reason (R).

Assertion (A) *o*-nitrophenol is more volatile than *p*-nitrophenol.

Reason (R) There occurs intramolecular hydrogen bonding in *o*-nitrophenol and intermolecular hydrogen bonding in *p*-nitrophenol.

In the light of the above statements, choose the correct answer from the options given below.

(a) Both (A) and (R) are true and (R) is the correct explanation of (A).
(b) Both (A) and (R) are true but (R) is not the correct explanation of (A).
(c) (A) is true but (R) is false.
(d) (A) is false but (R) is true.

6. Match List-I with List-II.

List-I (Reactant)	List-II (Product)
A. OH + Zn ⟶	I. Sodium phenoxide
B. OH $\xrightarrow[H_2SO_4]{Na_2Cr_2O_7}$	II. Benzene
C. OH (i) $CHCl_3$ + *Aq.* NaOH (ii) NaOH (iii) $H^{\oplus}$ ⟶	III. Salicylaldehyde
D. 2 OH + 2Na ⟶	IV. Benzoquinone

Choose the correct match from the options given below.

(a) A-III, B-II, C-IV, D-I
(b) A-II, B-IV, C-III, D-I
(c) A-I, B-II, C-III, D-IV
(d) A-IV, B-II, C-III, D-I

7. Given below are two statements.

Statement I Dipole moment of phenol is smaller than that of methanol.

Statement II In phenol C—O bond is less polar, whereas in methanol, C—O bond is more polar.

In the light of the above statements, choose the correct answer from the options given below.

(a) Both Statement I and Statement II are incorrect.
(b) Statement I is correct but Statement II is incorrect.
(c) Statement I is incorrect but Statement II is correct.
(d) Both Statement I and Statement II are correct.

8. Which of the following is the correct order of acidic nature of phenol?

(a) OH/NO_2 (para) > OH/CH_3 (para) > OH > OH/NO_2 (ortho)

(b) OH/NO_2 (para) > OH/NO_2 (ortho) > OH/CH_3 (para) > OH

(c) OH > OH/CH_3 (para) > OH/NO_2 (ortho) > OH/NO_2 (para)

(d) OH/NO_2 (para) > OH/NO_2 (ortho) > OH > OH/CH_3 (para)

9. Which of the following compound is more acidic?

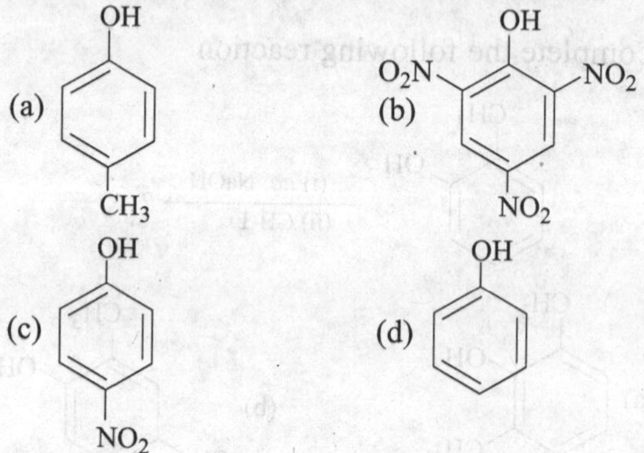

10. Given below are two statements, one is labelled as Assertion (A) and the other is labelled as Reason (R).

Assertion (A) Phenol reacts with CH_3I in the presence of NaOH to form methoxybenzene.

Reason (R) Phenoxide ion is a better electrophile than phenol.

In the light of the above statements, choose the correct answer from the options given below.

(a) Both (A) and (R) are true and (R) is the correct explanation of (A).
(b) Both (A) and (R) are true but (R) is not the correct explanation of (A).
(c) (A) is true but (R) is false.
(d) (A) is false but (R) is true.

11. The major product in the following reaction is

$$HOCH_2-C_6H_4-OH\ (p) + HCl \xrightarrow{Heat}$$

(a) $ClCH_2-C_6H_4-OH$ (p)
(b) $ClCH_2-C_6H_4-Cl$ (p)
(c) $HOCH_2-C_6H_3(Cl)-OH$ (Cl ortho to OH)
(d) $HOCH_2-C_6H_4-Cl$ (p)

12. Phenol $\xrightarrow[H^+]{CHCl_3/NaOH}$ Salicylaldehyde

The above reaction is known as

(a) Riemer-Tiemann reaction
(b) Bucherer reaction
(c) Gattermann synthesis
(d) Perkin reaction

13. Given below are two statements.

Statement I Phenols are weakly acidic.

Statement II Phenols are freely soluble in NaOH solution and are weaker acids than alcohols and water.

In the light of the above statements, choose the correct answer from the options given below.

(a) Both Statement I and Statement II are incorrect.
(b) Statement I is correct but Statement II is incorrect.
(c) Statement I is incorrect but Statement II is correct.
(d) Both Statement I and Statement II are correct.

14. The structure of intermediate A in the following reaction is

$$C_6H_5-CH(CH_3)-CH_3 \xrightarrow{O_2} A \xrightarrow[H_2O]{H^+} C_6H_5OH + H_3C-CO-CH_3$$

(a) $C_6H_5-O-CH(CH_3)-CH_3$
(b) $C_6H_5-C(CH_3)(CH_3)-O-O-H$
(c) $C_6H_5-O-O-CH(CH_3)-CH_3$
(d) $C_6H_5-CH(CH_3)-CH_2-O-O-OH$

15. Given below are two statements, one is labelled as Assertion (A) and the other is labelled as Reason (R).

Assertion (A) Phenol is more reactive than benzene towards electrophilic substitution reaction.

Reason (R) In case of phenol, the intermediate carbocation is more resonance stabilised.

In the light of the above statements, choose the correct answer from the options given below.

(a) Both (A) and (R) are true and (R) is the correct explanation of (A).
(b) Both (A) and (R) are true, but (R) is not the correct explanation of (A).
(c) (A) is true but (R) is false.
(d) (A) is false but (R) is true.

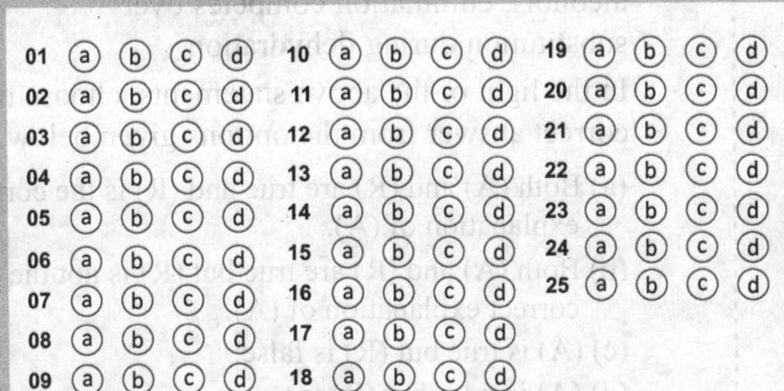

Performance Scanner

> 90% Excellent !	You have mastered these topics. The concepts of these topics are at your fingertips. Move on to the next test and maintain this momentum.
76-90% Very Good !	You have a good command over these topics. Revise these topics again after a few days and enhance your performance.
60-75% Good !	You have a wide scope to learn for these topics. Revise these topics again.
<60 Not Satisfactory!	You have a long way ahead of you to master these topics. Revise it thoroughly.

Test 3

Syllabus **Ethers** : General Methods of Preparation, Structure, Properties, Reactions and Uses.

For deeper insight **Scan the QR Code**

Important Instructions

- The test is of 30 minutes duration and contains 15 multiple choice questions. (Four options with a single correct answer).
- Choose the correct option and fill the OMR given on the last page of test accordingly.
- At some instances, you may find more than 1 option may be correct. In such circumstances, you have to judge the most appropriate answer as per the conditions given in the question.

1. Choose the incorrect statements.

(a) Ethers form peroxides by free radical oxidation.
(b) Ethers are used as industrial solvents for oils, resins, guns etc.
(c) An ether oxygen can only be found within an acyclic carbon chain.
(d) The lower ethers are highly volatile and flammable.

2. Given below are two statements.

Statement I The cleavage of C—O bond in ethers take place under drastic condition with excess of hydrogen halides.

Statement II Ethers are the least reactive among all the functional groups.

In the light of the above statements, choose the correct answer from the options given below.

(a) Both Statement I and Statement II are incorrect.
(b) Statement I is correct but Statement II is incorrect.
(c) Statement I is incorrect but Statement II is correct.
(d) Both Statement I and Statement II are correct.

3. Select the incorrect match of IUPAC name for given ethers.

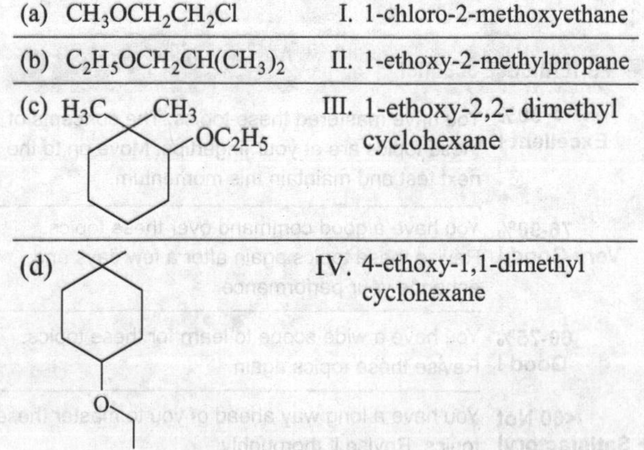

(a) $CH_3OCH_2CH_2Cl$	I. 1-chloro-2-methoxyethane
(b) $C_2H_5OCH_2CH(CH_3)_2$	II. 1-ethoxy-2-methylpropane
(c) H_3C, CH_3, OC_2H_5 (cyclohexane ring)	III. 1-ethoxy-2,2- dimethyl cyclohexane
(d) (cyclohexane ring with O-ethyl)	IV. 4-ethoxy-1,1-dimethyl cyclohexane

4. Determine the product of the following reaction.

$$CH_3-\overset{CH_3}{\overset{|}{C}H}-CH_2-O-CH_2-CH_3+HI \longrightarrow \text{Product}$$

(a) $CH_3-\overset{CH_3}{\overset{|}{C}H}-CH_2-I+CH_3-CH_2OH$

(b) $CH_3-\overset{CH_3}{\overset{|}{C}H}-CH_2-OH+CH_3-CH_2I$

(c) $CH_3-\overset{CH_3}{\overset{|}{C}H}-CH_3+CH_3-CH_2OH$

(d) $CH_3-\overset{CH_3}{\overset{|}{C}H}-CH_2-OH+CH_3-CH_3$

5. Given below are two statements, one is labelled as Assertion (A) and the other is labelled as Reason (R).

Assertion (A) Ethers are obtained during the dehydration of secondary and tertiary alcohols.

Reason (R) In the secondary and tertiary alcohols, elimination competes over substitution during dehydration.

In the light of the above statements, choose the correct answer from the options given below.

(a) Both (A) and (R) are true and (R) is the correct explanation of (A).
(b) Both (A) and (R) are true but (R) is not the correct explanation of (A).
(c) (A) is true but (R) is false.
(d) (A) is false but (R) is true.

6. Consider the following reaction.

$$H_3C-CH_2-CH_2-OC(CH_3)_3 \xrightarrow{\text{Excess HI}} A+B$$

Choose the correct option.

	A	*B*
(a)	$H_3C-CH_2-CH_2OH$	$I-C(CH_3)_3$
(b)	$H_3C-CH_2-CH_2I$	$HO-C(CH_3)_3$
(c)	$H_3C-CH_2-CH_2OH$	$HO-C(CH_3)_3$
(d)	$H_3C-CH_2-CH_2I$	$I-C(CH_3)_3$

7. Given below are two statements.

Statement I The C—O bond length (141 pm) of ether is almost same as in alcohols.

Statement II The bond angle in ether is slightly greater than the tetrahedral angle due to repulsive interaction between the two bulky (*R*) groups.

In the light of the above statements, choose the correct answer from the options given below.

(a) Both Statement I and Statement II are incorrect.
(b) Statement I is correct but Statement II is incorrect.
(c) Statement I is incorrect but Statement II is correct.
(d) Both Statement I and Statement II are correct.

8. Consider the following reaction.

1-bromo-2-methylcyclohexane (cyclohexane ring with CH_3 and Br) $+ CH_3OH \longrightarrow$ Product

(a) cyclohexane ring with CH_3 and OCH_3 on the same carbon
(b) cyclohexane ring with CH_3 and OCH_3 on adjacent carbons
(c) cyclohexane ring with OCH_3 and OCH_3 on adjacent carbons
(d) cyclohexane ring with CH_3

9. Given below are two statements, one is labelled as Assertion (A) and the other is labelled as Reason (R).

Assertion (A) *tert*-butyl methyl ether react with HBr to form *tert*-butyl bromide and methanol.

Reason (R) It follows S_N2 mechanism.

In the light of the above statements, choose the correct answer from the options given below.

(a) Both (A) and (R) are true and (R) is the correct explanation of (A).
(b) Both (A) and (R) are true but (R) is not the correct explanation of (A).
(c) (A) is true but (R) is false.
(d) (A) is false but (R) is true.

10. The reaction given below is known as

$$CH_3-\underset{CH_3}{\overset{CH_3}{C}}-\bar{O}Na^+ + CH_3CH_2Cl \xrightarrow[-NaCl]{} CH_3-\underset{CH_3}{\overset{CH_3}{C}}-O-CH_2-CH_3$$

(a) Kolbe's synthesis
(b) Wurtz synthesis
(c) Williamson synthesis
(d) Williamson continuous esterification process

11. Which of the following reaction doesn't yield an ether?

(a) Sodium methoxide reacts with dimethyl sulphate.
(b) Sodium ethoxide reacts with ethyl bromide.
(c) Sodium ethoxide reacts with bromocyclopentane.
(d) Ethanol reacts with CH_2N_2 in presence of HBF_4OH.

12. The product *Y* formed from the given reaction is

$$\text{Phenol (}C_6H_5OH\text{)} + C_2H_5I \xrightarrow[\text{Anhyd. } C_2H_5OH]{^-OC_2H_5} Y$$

(a) $C_6H_5OC_2H_5$
(b) $C_2H_5OC_2H_5$
(c) $C_6H_5OC_6H_5$
(d) C_6H_5I

13. Which of the following reactions will not result in formation of anisole?

(a) Phenol + dimethyl sulphate in presence of a base.
(b) Sodium phenoxide is treated with methyl iodide.
(c) Reaction of diazomethane with phenol.
(d) Reaction of methyl magnesium iodide with phenol.

14. Given below are two statements, one is labelled as Assertion (A) and the other is labelled as Reason (R).

Assertion (A) Anisole undergoes electrophilic substitution at *o*- and *p*-position.

Reason (R) Anisole is less reactive than phenol towards electrophilic substitution reaction.

In the light of the above statements, choose the correct answer from the options given below.

(a) Both (A) and (R) are true and (R) is the correct explanation of (A).

(b) Both (A) and (R) are true but (R) is not the correct explanation of (A).

(c) (A) is true but (R) is false.

(d) (A) is false but (R) is true.

15. When diethyl ether is treated with excess of Cl_2 in the presence of sunlight, then the product formed is

(a) $CH_3CHCl—O—CH_2CH_3$

(b) $CH_3CHCl—O—CHClCH_3$

(c) $CCl_3—CCl_2—O—CCl_2—CCl_3$

(d) $CH_3CCl_2—O—CHClCH_3$

Response Index

01	a	b	c	d	10	a	b	c	d	19	a	b	c	d
02	a	b	c	d	11	a	b	c	d	20	a	b	c	d
03	a	b	c	d	12	a	b	c	d	21	a	b	c	d
04	a	b	c	d	13	a	b	c	d	22	a	b	c	d
05	a	b	c	d	14	a	b	c	d	23	a	b	c	d
06	a	b	c	d	15	a	b	c	d	24	a	b	c	d
07	a	b	c	d	16	a	b	c	d	25	a	b	c	d
08	a	b	c	d	17	a	b	c	d					
09	a	b	c	d	18	a	b	c	d					

Performance Scanner

> 90% Excellent !	You have mastered these topics. The concepts of these topics are at your fingertips. Move on to the chapter test and maintain this momentum.
76-90% Very Good !	You have a good command over these topics. Revise these topics again after a few days and enhance your performance.
60-75% Good !	You have a wide scope to learn for these topics. Revise these topics again.
<60 Not Satisfactory!	You have a long way ahead of you to master these topics. Revise it thoroughly.

Chapter Break Thru

Syllabus	**Alcohols** : General Methods of Preparation, Properties, Reaction and Uses, Identification of Primary, Secondary and Tertiary Alcohols, Mechanism of Dehydration.	**Phenols** : General Methods of Preparation, Properties, Acidic Nature, Electrophilic Substitution Reaction, Halogenation, Nitration, Sulphonation, Reimer-Tiemann Reaction.	**Ethers** : General Methods of Preparation, Structure, Properties, Reactions and Uses.

Important Instructions

- The test is of 1 hour duration and contains 50 multiple choice questions (Four options with a single correct answer).
- Choose the correct option and fill the OMR given on the last page of test accordingly.
- At some instances, you may find more than 1 option may be correct. In such circumstances, you have to judge the most appropriate answer as per the conditions given in the question.

1. Primary and secondary alcohols on action of reduced copper give

(a) aldehydes and ketones respectively
(b) ketones and aldehydes respectively
(c) only aldehydes
(d) only ketones

2. Which one of the following reactions would produce secondary alcohol?

(a) $C_6H_5\overset{O}{\overset{\|}{C}}CH_3 \xrightarrow[\text{(ii) } H^+]{\text{(i) } CH_3MgBr}$

(b) $C_6H_5\overset{O}{\overset{\|}{C}}CH_3 \xrightarrow[\text{(ii) } H^+]{\text{(i) } LiAlH_4}$

(c) $CH_3CHO \xrightarrow[\text{(ii) } H^+]{\text{(i) } LiAlH_4}$

(d) $CH_3\overset{O}{\overset{\|}{C}}CH_3 \xrightarrow[\text{(ii) } Br_2]{\text{(i) } OH^-}$

3. The compound that will give a positive result with $FeCl_3$ is

(a) ethanol (b) methanol
(c) phenol (d) anisole

4. X, Y, Z reaction are respectively.

CH=CH$_2$; X → CH$_2$—CH$_2$—OH ; Y → OH ; Z → OH

(a) Hydration reaction
(b) Hydroboration oxidation, hydration and oxymercuration demercuration
(c) Hydroboration oxidation, oxymercuration demercuration and hydration
(d) Oxymercuration demercuration, hydroboration oxidation and hydration

5. Given below are two statements, one is labelled as Assertion (A) and the other is labelled as Reason (R).

Assertion (A) Phenol is a stronger acid than ethanol.
Reason (R) Groups with $+M$ effect decreases the acidity at p-position.

In the light of the above statements, choose the correct answer from the options given below.

(a) Both (A) and (R) are true and (R) is the correct explanation of (A).
(b) Both (A) and (R) are true but (R) is not the correct explanation of (A).
(c) (A) is true but (R) is false.
(d) (A) is false but (R) is true.

6. Anisole on treatment with HNO_3 and conc. H_2SO_4 gives

(a) phenol (b) nitrobenzene
(c) o- and p-nitroanisole (d) o-nitroanisole

7. Which of the following is the major product for the following reaction?

OH ; $\xrightarrow[\text{(0-5°C)}]{NaNO_2 + HCl}$ Product

(a) p-nitrosobenzenediazonium chloride ($N_2^+Cl^-$, NO) (b) OH, NO (meta) (c) OH, NO (para) (d) NO, NO

(c) OH, SO_3H, Br (d) OH, Br

8. Electrophilic substitution reaction in phenol takes place at which position?

(a) *p*-position only (b) *m*-position only
(c) *o*-position only (d) *o*- and *p*-position

9. Which of the following statement is correct for phenol?

(a) It is insoluble in water.
(b) It has lower melting point compared to aromatic hydrocarbons of comparable molecular weight.
(c) It has higher boiling point than toluene.
(d) It doesn't show acidic property.

10. Given below are two statements.

Statement I *p*-nitrophenol is more acidic than *m*-nitrophenol and *o*-nitrophenol.

Statement II Ethanol will give immediate turbidity with Lucas reagent.

In the light of the above statements, choose the correct answer from the options given below.

(a) Both Statement I and Statement II are incorrect.
(b) Statement I is correct but Statement II is incorrect.
(c) Statement I is incorrect but Statement II is correct.
(d) Both Statement I and Statement II are correct.

11. Identify the end product (Y) of the following sequence of reaction.

$$\text{Phenol} \xrightarrow[100°C]{\text{Conc. } H_2SO_4} X \xrightarrow{Br_2/H_2O} Y$$

(a) OH, Br, Br, SO_3H (b) OH, Br, Br, Br

12. Match List-I with List-II.

	List-I (Compound)		List-II (pK_a)
A.	Ethanol	I.	10.0
B.	Phenol	II.	15.9
C.	*m*-nitrophenol	III.	7.2
D.	*p*-nitrophenol	IV.	8.4

Choose the correct match from the option given below.

(a) A-I, B-II, C-III, D-IV (b) A-IV, B-I, C-II, D-III
(c) A-III, B-IV, C-I, D-II (d) A-II, B-I, C-IV, D-III

13. Which of the following statement is correct regarding Kolbe's reaction?

(a) It gives anisole from phenol.
(b) It gives salicylaldehyde from phenol and CHI_3.
(c) It gives salicylic acid from phenol in presence of CO_2 and NaOH.
(d) It gives salicylic acid from phenol and CO_2.

14. Given below are two statements, one is labelled as Assertion (A) and the other is labelled as Reason (R).

Assertion (A) Reimer-Tiemann reaction of phenol with $CHCl_3$ in NaOH at 340 K followed by acidification gives salicylaldehyde as the major product.

Reason (R) The reaction occurs through intermediate formation of dichloro carbene.

In the light of the above statements, choose the correct answer from the options given below.

(a) Both (A) and (R) are true and (R) is the correct explanation of (A).
(b) Both (A) and (R) are true but (R) is not the correct explanation of (A).
(c) (A) is true but (R) is false.
(d) (A) is false but (R) is true.

15. The compound which will readily couple with benzene diazonium chloride is
(a) benzoic acid
(b) phenol
(c) benzene
(d) benzaldehyde

16. Which of the following is phenolic?
(a) Phthalic acid
(b) Benzyl alcohol
(c) Picric acid
(d) Phenyl acetic acid

17. In the reaction

$$CH_3-\underset{|}{\overset{CH_3}{\overset{|}{C}}}H-CH_2-O-CH_2-CH_3+HI \xrightarrow{\Delta} \ldots$$

Which of the following compounds will be formed?

(a) $CH_3-\overset{CH_3}{\overset{|}{C}H}-CH_2OH+CH_3CH_2-I$

(b) $CH_3-\overset{CH_3}{\overset{|}{C}H}-CH_2I+CH_3CH_2OH$

(c) $CH_3-\underset{CH_3}{\underset{|}{C}H}-CH_3+CH_3CH_2OH$

(d) $CH_3-\underset{CH_3}{\underset{|}{C}H}-CH_2OH+CH_3CH_3$

18. Given below are two statements, one is labelled as Assertion (A) and the other is labelled as Reason (R).
Assertion (A) CH_3OH is a nucleophile.
Reason (R) CH_3OH forms sodium methoxide on reaction with NaH.
In the light of the above statements, choose the correct answer from the options given below.
(a) Both (A) and (R) are true and (R) is the correct explanation of (A).
(b) Both (A) and (R) are true but (R) is not the correct explanation of (A).
(c) (A) is true but (R) is false.
(d) (A) is false but (R) is true.

19. Match List-I with List-II.

List-I (Reactants)	List-II (Products)
A. Phenol, Zn/Δ	I. Salicylaldehyde
B. Phenol, $CHCl_3$, NaOH, HCl	II. Salicylic acid
C. Phenol, CO_2, NaOH, HCl	III. Benzene
D. Phenol, conc. HNO_3	IV. Picric acid

Choose the correct match from the options given below :
(a) A-IV, B-II, C-I, D-III
(b) A-IV, B-I, C-II, D-III
(c) A-III, B-I, C-II, D-IV
(d) A-III, B-IV, C-I, D-II

20. Commercially methanol is prepared by
(a) reduction of CO in presence of $ZnO-Cr_2O_3$
(b) reaction of methane with water vapours at 900°C in presence of Ni catalyst.
(c) reduction of HCHO by $LiAlH_4$
(d) reduction of HCHO by aqueous NaOH

21. On reaction with hot conc. H_2SO_4, which one of the following compounds loses a molecule of water?
(c) CH_3COCH_3 (b) CH_3COOH
(c) CH_3OCH_3 (d) CH_3CH_2OH

22. The reaction between an alcohol and an acid with the elimination of water molecule is called
(a) esterification (b) saponification
(c) etherification (d) elimination

23. At room temperature the alcohol that does not reacts with Lucas reagent is
(a) benzyl alcohol
(b) 2-butanol
(c) tertiary butyl alcohol
(d) benzyl alcohol

24. Boiling point of alcohol is comparatively higher than corresponding alkane due to
(a) intermolecular hydrogen bonding
(b) intramolecular hydrogen bonding
(c) volatile nature
(d) both inter and intramolecular hydrogen bonding

25. The order of acidic strength of X, Y and Z is

Phenol (OH) —Dil. HNO_3→ X (o-isomer) + Y (p-isomer)

Phenol —Conc. HNO_3+H_2SO_4→ (Z) Major

(a) $X > Y > Z$ (b) $Z > X > Y$
(c) $Y > Z > X$ (d) $Z > Y > X$

26. The alcohol that produces turbidity immediately with $ZnCl_2$ + conc. HCl at room temperature.

(a) 1-hydroxybutane (b) 2-hydroxybutane
(c) 2-hydroxy-2-methyl propane
(d) 1-hydroxy-2-methyl propane

27. Choose the correct order of dehydration rate of S_N1 reaction of following alcohols?

I. (cyclohexanol, OH) II. (cyclohex-2-en-1-ol, OH) III. (benzene ring with CH(OH) ring, OH) IV. (cyclohexadienol, OH)

(a) I > II > III > IV (b) III > IV > II > I
(c) IV > III > II > I (d) I > III > IV > II

28. Given below are two statements, one is labelled as Assertion (A) and the other is labelled as Reason (R).

Assertion (A) Resorcinol turns $FeCl_3$ solution purple.
Reason (R) Resorcinol have phenolic group.

In the light of the above statements, choose the correct answer from the options given below.

(a) Both (A) and (R) are true and (R) is the correct explanation of (A).
(b) Both (A) and (R) are true but (R) is not the correct explanation of (A).
(c) (A) is true but (R) is false.
(d) (A) is false but (R) is true.

29. Alcohol can be prepared from alkene by which of the following reactions?

(a) Elimination (b) Substitution
(c) Reduction (d) Oxidation

30. The product of the reaction is

(1-methylcyclohexene oxide, CH_3, O) + HBr ⟶

(a) (cyclohexane with CH_3, OH on C-1 and Br on C-2) (b) (cyclohexane with CH_3, Br on C-1 and OH on C-2)
(c) (1-methylcyclohexene, CH_3) (d) (cyclohexene with CH_3 and Br)

31. To prepare ethyl *tert*-butyl ether by Williamson's synthesis, the reactants needed are

(a) sodium ethoxide and sodium *tert*-butoxide
(b) sodium ethoxide and *tert*-butyl bromide
(c) sodium *tert*-butoxide and ethyl bromide
(d) ethyl alcohol and *tert*-butyl alcohol

32. Which of the following is not true in case of reaction with heated copper at 300°C?

(a) Phenol → Benzyl alcohol
(b) Primary alcohol → Aldehyde
(c) Secondary alcohol → Ketone
(d) Tertiary alcohol → Olefin

33. Propanal can be converted into 1-propanol by using which of the following reagents?

(a) $KMnO_4/H^{\oplus}/\Delta$
(b) $KMnO_4/\overset{\ominus}{O}H/\Delta$
(c) $NH_2—NH_2/\overset{\ominus}{O}H/\Delta$
(d) $NaBH_4$

34. Ether is formed when ethyl alcohol is heated with conc. H_2SO_4. The conditions is excess of

(a) H_2SO_4 at 170°C (b) C_2H_5OH at 140°C
(c) C_2H_5OH at 180°C (d) H_2SO_4 at 100°C

35. Phenol and benzoic acid is distinguished by

(a) NaOH (b) $NaHCO_3$
(c) Na_2CO_3 (d) H_2SO_4

36. Consider the statement given below.

A. A secondary alcohol on oxidation gives a ketone.
B. Ethanol reacts with conc. H_2SO_4 at 180°C to yield ethylene.
C. Methanol reacts with iodine and sodium hydroxide to give a yellow precipitate of iodoform.
D. Hydrogen gas is liberated when sodium is added to alcohol.
E. Alcohol can be prepared from alkene by hydration.

Total number of correct statement are

(a) 2 (b) 4
(c) 5 (d) 1

37. $A \xleftarrow[\Delta]{Cu} CH_3CH_2OH \xrightarrow[\Delta]{Al_2O_3} B$

A and *B* respectively are

(a) alkene, alkanal
(b) alkyne, alkanal
(c) alkanal, alkene
(d) alkene, alkyne

38. Given below are two statements, one is labelled as Assertion (A) and the other is labelled as Reason (R).

Assertion (A) *p*-nitrophenol is a stronger acid than *o*-nitrophenol.

Reason (R) Intramolecular H-bonding makes *o*-isomer weaker than *p*-isomer.

In the light of the above statements, choose the correct answer from the options given below.

(a) Both (A) and (R) are true and (R) is the correct explanation of (A).
(b) Both (A) and (R) are true but (R) is not the correct explanation of (A).
(c) (A) is true but (R) is false.
(d) (A) is false but (R) is true.

39. Phenol (OH) $\xrightarrow{Y}$ o-bromophenol (OH, Br) + p-bromophenol (OH, Br)

The reagent *Y* is

(a) $Br_2/FeBr_3$
(b) Br_2/CS_2
(c) Both (a) and (b)
(d) Br_2 water

40. 1-phenylethanol can be prepared by the reaction of benzaldehyde with

(a) methyl bromide
(b) ethyl magnesium iodide
(c) methyl magnesium iodide
(d) methyl bromide and aluminium bromide

41. Phenol (OH) $+ CHCl_3 + NaOH \longrightarrow$ (O^-Na^+, CHO)

The electrophile involved in the above reaction is

(a) trichloromethyl carbanion ($\overset{\ominus}{C}Cl_3$)
(b) formyl carbocation ($\overset{\oplus}{C}HO$)
(c) dichloromethyl carbocation ($\overset{\oplus}{C}HCl_2$)
(d) dichlorocarbene ($:CCl_2$)

42. $A \xleftarrow{Br_2, H_2O}$ p-cresol (OH, CH_3) $\xrightarrow{Br_2, CS_2} B$ (Major)

'*A*' and '*B*' are respectively

(a) 2,6-dibromo-4-methylphenol (OH, Br, Br, CH_3) and 2-bromo-4-methylphenol (OH, Br, CH_3)
(b) 2,4,6-tribromophenol (OH, Br, Br, Br) and 3-bromo-4-methylphenol (OH, Br, CH_3)
(c) 2,6-dibromo-4-methylphenol (OH, Br, Br, CH_3) and 3-bromo-4-methylphenol (OH, Br, CH_3)
(d) 2,4,6-tribromophenol (OH, Br, Br, Br) and 2-bromo-4-methylphenol (OH, Br, CH_3)

43. Which of the following is not a characteristic of alcohols?

(a) They are lighter than water.
(b) Their boiling points rise fairly uniform with increasing molecular weight.
(c) Lower member are insoluble in water and organic solvent but solubility regularly increase with molecular weight.
(d) Lower member have pleasant smell and burning taste while higher member are odourless and tasteless.

44. The dehydration of 2-methyl butanol with conc. H_2SO_4 give

(a) 3-methyl butene
(b) pentene
(c) 2-methyl but-2-ene
(d) 2-methyl pent-2-ene

45. The alcohol which easily reacts with conc. HCl is

(a) $CH_3—CHOH—CH_2—CH_3$
(b) $(CH_3)_3—C—OH$
(c) $CH_3—CH_2—CH_2—CH_2—OH$
(d) $(CH_3)_3—CH—CH_2OH$

46. Given below are two statements, one is labelled as Assertion (A) and the other is labelled as Reason (R).

Assertion (A) The acidity of alcohols follows the order 1° > 2° > 3°.

Reason (R) +*I*-effect of the additional alkyl group favours the cleavage of O—H.

In the light of the above statements, choose the correct answer from the options given below.

(a) Both (A) and (R) are true and (R) is the correct explanation of (A).
(b) Both (A) and (R) are true but (R) is not the correct explanation of (A).
(c) (A) is true but (R) is false.
(d) (A) is false but (R) is true.

47. OH

$\xrightarrow[\Delta]{\text{Conc. } H_2SO_4}$ Major product

(a)
(b)
(c)
(d) SO_3H

48. The product '*P*' is

$CH_3CH{=}CH$— —OH $\xrightarrow{HBr}$ *P*

(a) $CH_3CHBrCH_3$— —OH
(b) CH_3CH_2CHBr— —OH
(c) $CH_3CHBrCH_2$— —Br
(d) CH_3CH_2CHBr— —Br

49. Consider the following reaction.

$$\underset{(A)}{CH_3—CH_2—O—H} + \underset{(B)}{CH_3—\overset{O}{\overset{\|}{C}}—OH} \xrightarrow{H^{\oplus}} CH_3—CH_2—O—\overset{O}{\overset{\|}{C}}—CH_3 + HOH$$

In the above reaction, ester formation takes place by

(a) breaking of O—H bond of (*A*) and O—H bond of (*B*)
(b) breaking of C—O bond of (*A*) and C—O bond of (*B*)
(c) breaking of O—H bond of (*A*) and C—O bond of (*B*)"
(d) breaking of C—O bond of (*A*) and O—H bond of (*B*)

50. Which of the following compounds is most acidic?

(a) Phenol
(b) Aniline
(c) 1-butanol
(d) 2-methylphenol

Response Index

01 ⓐ ⓑ ⓒ ⓓ	14 ⓐ ⓑ ⓒ ⓓ	27 ⓐ ⓑ ⓒ ⓓ	40 ⓐ ⓑ ⓒ ⓓ
02 ⓐ ⓑ ⓒ ⓓ	15 ⓐ ⓑ ⓒ ⓓ	28 ⓐ ⓑ ⓒ ⓓ	41 ⓐ ⓑ ⓒ ⓓ
03 ⓐ ⓑ ⓒ ⓓ	16 ⓐ ⓑ ⓒ ⓓ	29 ⓐ ⓑ ⓒ ⓓ	42 ⓐ ⓑ ⓒ ⓓ
04 ⓐ ⓑ ⓒ ⓓ	17 ⓐ ⓑ ⓒ ⓓ	30 ⓐ ⓑ ⓒ ⓓ	43 ⓐ ⓑ ⓒ ⓓ
05 ⓐ ⓑ ⓒ ⓓ	18 ⓐ ⓑ ⓒ ⓓ	31 ⓐ ⓑ ⓒ ⓓ	44 ⓐ ⓑ ⓒ ⓓ
06 ⓐ ⓑ ⓒ ⓓ	19 ⓐ ⓑ ⓒ ⓓ	32 ⓐ ⓑ ⓒ ⓓ	45 ⓐ ⓑ ⓒ ⓓ
07 ⓐ ⓑ ⓒ ⓓ	20 ⓐ ⓑ ⓒ ⓓ	33 ⓐ ⓑ ⓒ ⓓ	46 ⓐ ⓑ ⓒ ⓓ
08 ⓐ ⓑ ⓒ ⓓ	21 ⓐ ⓑ ⓒ ⓓ	34 ⓐ ⓑ ⓒ ⓓ	47 ⓐ ⓑ ⓒ ⓓ
09 ⓐ ⓑ ⓒ ⓓ	22 ⓐ ⓑ ⓒ ⓓ	35 ⓐ ⓑ ⓒ ⓓ	48 ⓐ ⓑ ⓒ ⓓ
10 ⓐ ⓑ ⓒ ⓓ	23 ⓐ ⓑ ⓒ ⓓ	36 ⓐ ⓑ ⓒ ⓓ	49 ⓐ ⓑ ⓒ ⓓ
11 ⓐ ⓑ ⓒ ⓓ	24 ⓐ ⓑ ⓒ ⓓ	37 ⓐ ⓑ ⓒ ⓓ	50 ⓐ ⓑ ⓒ ⓓ
12 ⓐ ⓑ ⓒ ⓓ	25 ⓐ ⓑ ⓒ ⓓ	38 ⓐ ⓑ ⓒ ⓓ	
13 ⓐ ⓑ ⓒ ⓓ	26 ⓐ ⓑ ⓒ ⓓ	39 ⓐ ⓑ ⓒ ⓓ	

Performance Scanner

> 90% Excellent !	You have mastered this chapter. The concepts of this chapter are at your fingertips. Move on to the next chapter and maintain this momentum.
76-90% Very Good !	You have a good command over this chapter. Revise the chapter again after a few days and enhance your performance.
60-75% Good !	You have a wide scope to learn for this chapter. Revise this chapter again.
<60 Not Satisfactory!	You have a long way ahead of you to master this chapter. Revise it thoroughly.

Scan for Online Chapter Test

Scan for Online Unit Test

Test Booklet No. 3947259

Test Booklet Code CH9

MEDACE
NEET (UG)
SELF ASSESSMENT KIT

Aldehydes, Ketones and Carboxylic Acids

Topics Covered

- Preparation, Properties and Uses of Aldehydes
- Preparation, Properties and Uses of Ketones
- Preparation, Properties and Uses of Carboxylic Acids

Important Instructions

- This Booklet Contains – 3 Topic Tests and One Test on Complete Chapter.
- Each question carries 4 marks.
- For each correct response the candidate will get 4 marks and for every incorrect response, 1 mark will be additionally deducted from the total score.
- Use **Blue/Black** point pen only for filling the OMR.
- Rough work is to be done in the space provided for this purpose in the test booklet only.

Name of the Candidate (In Capitals) ____________

____

Candidate's Signature ____________

Invigilator's Signature ____________

Facsimile signature stamp of center superintendent____________

Do not open this Booklet until you start attempting the Test

Topical Follow Thru

Test 1

Syllabus General Method of Preparation, Properties and Uses, Nature of Carbonyl Group, Nucleophilic Addition to $>C=O$ Group, Nucleophilic Addition Reaction, Grignard Reagent, Oxidation, Reduction, Aldol Condensation, Cannizzaro Reaction.

For deeper insight **Scan the QR Code**

Important Instructions

- The test is of 30 minutes duration and contains 15 multiple choice questions (Four options with a single correct answer).
- Choose the correct option and fill the OMR given on the last page of test accordingly.
- At some instances, you may find more than 1 option may be correct. In such circumstances, you have to judge the most appropriate answer as per the conditions given in the question.

1. Choose the incorrect statement from the following.

(a) Carbonyl compounds are attacked by nucleophiles.
(b) An aldehyde has a greater partial positive charge on its carbonyl carbon.
(c) Hydration of CCl_3CHO is more than that of CH_3CHO.
(d) Protonation of a carbonyl compound decreases electrophilic nature and thus, nucleophilic attack is retarded.

2. Given below are two statements, one is labelled as Assertion (A) and the other is labelled as Reason (R).

Assertion (A) The carbonyl carbon is an electrophilic centre and the carbonyl oxygen is a nucleophilic centre.

Reason (R) The carbon oxygen double bond is polarised due to higher electronegativity of oxygen relative to carbon.

In the light of the above statements, choose the most appropriate answer from the options given below.

(a) Both (A) and (R) are true and (R) is the correct explanation of (A).
(b) Both (A) and (R) are true but (R) is not the correct explanation of (A).
(c) (A) is true but (R) is false.
(d) (A) is false but (R) is true.

3. Which of the following method cannot produce aldehydes?

(a) Dehydrogenation of secondary alcohols.
(b) Oxidation of primary alcohols.
(c) Hydration of ethyne with acid.
(d) Ozonolysis of alkenes.

4. Given below are two statements.

Statement I Benzaldehyde is less reactive in nucleophilic addition reactions than propanal.

Statement II Benzaldehyde can be obtained from the hydrolysis of the product formed during side chain chlorination of toluene.

In the light of the above statements, choose the correct answer from the options given below.

(a) Both Statement I and Statement II are incorrect.
(b) Statement I is correct but Statement II is incorrect.
(c) Statement I is incorrect but Statement II is correct.
(d) Both Statement I and Statement II are correct.

5. Benzaldehyde on reaction with acetophenone in the presence of sodium hydroxide solution gives

(a) $C_6H_5CH=CHCOC_6H_5$
(b) $C_6H_5COCH_2C_6H_5$
(c) $C_6H_5CH=CHC_6H_5$
(d) $C_6H_5CH(OH)COC_6H_5$

6. Consider the following reaction.

(3-chlorobenzaldehyde: benzene ring with CHO and Cl) $\xrightarrow{50\%KOH}$ Product (P)

The product P is

(a) (benzene ring with CH_2OH and OH) + (benzene ring with CH_2COO^- and Cl)

(b) (benzene ring with CH_2OH and Cl) + (benzene ring with COO^-K^+ and Cl)

(c) (benzene ring with CH_2OH and OH) + (benzene ring with OH and OH)

(d) (benzene ring with CH_2OH and OH) + (benzene ring with COO^- and OH)

7. Given below are two statements, one is labelled as Assertion (A) and the other is labelled as Reason (R).

Assertion (A) Formaldehyde cannot be prepared by the Rosenmund reduction.

Reason (R) Formyl chloride is unstable at room temperature.

In the light of the above statements, choose the most appropriate answer from the options given below.

(a) Both (A) and (R) are true and (R) is the correct explanation of (A).

(b) Both (A) and (R) are true but (R) is not the correct explanation of (A).

(c) (A) is true but (R) is false.

(d) (A) is false but (R) is true.

8. Consider the following reaction.

$$CH\equiv CH + H_2O \xrightarrow[H_2SO_4]{HgSO_4} \text{Product } (P)$$

Product P is

(a) acetaldehyde (b) benzaldehyde

(c) ethanoic acid (d) ethanol

9. The aldol condensation of acetaldehyde results in the formation of

(a) $CH_3CH(OH)CH_2CH(=O)$

(b) $CH_3CH_2CH(OH)CH(=O)$

(c) $CH_3C(=O)CH(OH)CH_3$

(d) $CH_3CH_2OH + CH_3COOH$

10. Which of the following is an example of Aldol condensation?

(a) $HCHO \xrightarrow{\text{Dil. NaOH}} CH_3OH$

(b) $2CH_3CHO \xrightarrow{\text{Dil. NaOH}} CH_3CH(OH)CH_2CHO$

(c) $C_6H_5CHO + HCHO \xrightarrow{\text{Dil. NaOH}} C_6H_5CH_2OH$

(d) $2CH_3COCH_3 \xrightarrow{\text{Dil. NaOH}}$ $CH_3C(OH)(CH_3)CH_2COCH_3$

11. Formaldehyde when treated with KOH gives methanol and potassium formate. The reaction is known as

(a) Perkin reaction

(b) Claisen reaction

(c) Cannizzaro reaction

(d) Cross-aldol condensation reaction

12. In which of the following reduction method, $SnCl_2/HCl$ is used as a catalyst?

(a) Stephen's reduction

(b) Cannizzaro reduction

(c) Clemmensen's reduction

(d) Rosenmund's reduction

13. When acetaldehyde reacts with PCl_5, the resulting compound is

(a) ethyl chloride (b) ethylene chloride

(c) ethylidene chloride (d) trichloro acetaldehyde

14. $CH_3CHO + CH_3MgBr \longrightarrow B \xrightarrow{H_2O} A$

The product A in the given reaction is

(a) primary alcohol (b) secondary alcohol

(c) tertiary alcohol (d) ketone

15. In ozonolysis reaction, alkene gives

$$\text{Alkene} \xrightarrow[H_2O/Zn]{O_3} \text{Butanal}$$

Suitable alkene for preparation of butanal is

(a) 2-methyl-2-butene

(b) 1-pentene

(c) 2-pentene

(d) 2, 3-dimethyl but-2-ene

Response Index

01	a	b	c	d	10	a	b	c	d	19	a	b	c	d
02	a	b	c	d	11	a	b	c	d	20	a	b	c	d
03	a	b	c	d	12	a	b	c	d	21	a	b	c	d
04	a	b	c	d	13	a	b	c	d	22	a	b	c	d
05	a	b	c	d	14	a	b	c	d	23	a	b	c	d
06	a	b	c	d	15	a	b	c	d	24	a	b	c	d
07	a	b	c	d	16	a	b	c	d	25	a	b	c	d
08	a	b	c	d	17	a	b	c	d					
09	a	b	c	d	18	a	b	c	d					

Performance Scanner

> 90% Excellent !	You have mastered these topics. The concepts of these topics are at your fingertips. Move on to the next test and maintain this momentum.
76-90% Very Good !	You have a good command over these topics. Revise these topics again after a few days and enhance your performance.
60-75% Good !	You have a wide scope to learn for these topics. Revise these topics again.
<60 Not Satisfactory!	You have a long way ahead of you to master these topics. Revise it thoroughly.

Test 2

Syllabus General Methods of Preparation, Properties, Reaction and Uses, Reduction, Aldol Condensation, Haloform Reaction, Chemical Tests to Distinguish Between Aldehydes and Ketones

For deeper insight **Scan the QR Code**

Important Instructions

- The test is of 30 minutes duration and contains 15 multiple choice questions (Four options with a single correct answer).
- Choose the correct option and fill the OMR given on the last page of test accordingly.
- At some instances, you may find more than 1 option may be correct. In such circumstances, you have to judge the most appropriate answer as per the conditions given in the question.

1. Which of the following reaction can produce ketones?

(a) Oxidation of primary alcohols.
(b) Oxidation of secondary alcohols.
(c) Dehydrogenation of tertiary alcohols.
(d) Dehydrogenation of primary alcohols.

2. Predict the product (C) in the following reaction.

$$HC\equiv CH \longrightarrow A \xrightarrow{CH_3MgX} B \xrightarrow{[O]} C$$

(a) Ethanol (b) Propanone
(c) Acetone (d) Acetophenone

3. Which one of the following compound is prepared in the laboratory from benzene by a substitution reaction?

(a) Acetophenone (b) Hydrazone
(c) Cyclohexane (d) Oxime

4. Which of the following compound gives acetone on ozonolysis?

(a) $(CH_3)_2C{=}C(CH_3)_2$
(b) $CH_3CH{=}CH_2$
(c) $C_6H_5CH{=}CH_2$
(d) $CH_3{-}CH{=}CH{-}CH_3$

5. Which of the following reaction is not shown by ketones?

(a) Reaction with Fehling solution.
(b) Reaction with HCN.
(c) Reaction with 2, 4-dinitrophenyl hydrazine.
(d) Reaction with $NaHSO_3$.

6. Which of the following statement is incorrect about chemical properties of acetophenone?

(a) It is reduced to methyl phenyl carbinol by sodium and ethanol.
(b) It is oxidised to benzoic acid with acidified $KMnO_4$.
(c) It undergoes electrophilic substitution reactions.
(d) It does not undergo iodoform reaction with iodine and alkali.

7. Consider the following reaction.

$$CH_3{-}C\equiv CH \xrightarrow{\text{Reagent}} CH_3{-}\overset{\overset{O}{\|}}{C}{-}CH_3$$

Which of the following reagent is used for above conversion?

(a) CrO_3 (b) $H_2O, H_2SO_4/Hg^{+2}$
(c) $NaBH_4$ (d) $LiAlH_4$

8. Given below are two statements.

Statement I Ketones are soluble in water but its solubility decreases with an increase in the length of the chain.

Statement II The formation of cyanohydrin from a ketone is an example of nucleophilic addition.

In the light of the above statements, choose the correct answer from the options given below.

(a) Both Statement I and Statement II are incorrect.
(b) Statement I is correct but Statement II is incorrect.
(c) Statement I is incorrect but Statement II is correct.
(d) Both Statement I and Statement II are correct.

9. Consider the following reaction.

$$(H)(H_3C)C{=}C(CH_3){-}\overset{\overset{O}{\|}}{C}{-}CH_3 + NaOCl \longrightarrow \text{Product } (P)$$

The product (*P*) is

(a) $CH_3CH=C(CH_3)COOH + NaCl$

(b) $CH_3CH_2-CH(CH_3)COONa + CHCl_3$

(c) $CH_3CH=C(CH_3)COONa + CHCl_3$

(d) $CH_3CH_2-CH(CH_3)COOH + NaCl$

10. Given below are two statements, one is labelled as Assertion (A) and the other is labelled as Reason (R).

Assertion (A) The solubility of ketones in water decreases with increase of size of the alkyl group.

Reason (R) Ketones undergo intermolecular association due to dipole-dipole interactions.

In the light of the above statements, choose the correct answer from the options given below.

(a) Both (A) and (R) are true and (R) is the correct explanation of (A).

(b) Both (A) and (R) are true but (R) is not the correct explanation of (A).

(c) (A) is true but (R) is false.

(d) (A) is false but (R) is true.

11. Acetophenone is prepared from benzene by using which of the following method?

(a) Rosenmund reaction (b) Sandmeyer reaction
(c) Wurtz reaction (d) Friedel-Craft reaction

12. The most appropriate reagent for the conversion of 2-pentanone into acetic acid is

(a) chromic acid (b) dilute $KMnO_4$
(c) alkaline $KMnO_4$,Δ (d) sodium hypochlorite

13. Select the correct reagent for the following transformation.

HO–(cyclopentyl)–C(=O)–CH_3 ⟶ HO–(cyclopentyl)–CH_2CH_3

(a) Zn(Hg), HCl (b) NH_2NH_2, OH^-
(c) H_2/Ni (d) $NaBH_4$

14. Which of the following statements regarding chemical properties of acetophenone are incorrect?

I. It is reduced to 3° alcohol by Grignard reagent.
II. It is oxidised to benzoic acid with acidified $KMnO_4$.
III. It doesn't undergo electrophilic substitution like nitration at *meta*-position.
IV. It doesn't undergo iodoform reaction with iodine and alkali.

Choose the most appropriate answer from the options given below.

(a) I and II only (b) II and IV only
(c) III and IV only (d) I and III only

15. In the given reaction

Cyclohexanone $\xrightarrow{HCN} A \xrightarrow[H_2O]{LiAlH_4} B$

A and *B* will respectively be

(a) Cyclohexane(OH)(CN) and Cyclohexane(OH)(CHO)

(b) Cyclohexane(OH)(CN) and Cyclohexane(OH)(CH_2NH_2)

(c) Cyclohexane(OH)(CN) and Cyclohexyl–CH_2–NH_2

(d) Cyclohexyl–CN and Cyclohexyl–CH_2–NH_2

Response Index

01	a	b	c	d	10	a	b	c	d	19	a	b	c	d
02	a	b	c	d	11	a	b	c	d	20	a	b	c	d
03	a	b	c	d	12	a	b	c	d	21	a	b	c	d
04	a	b	c	d	13	a	b	c	d	22	a	b	c	d
05	a	b	c	d	14	a	b	c	d	23	a	b	c	d
06	a	b	c	d	15	a	b	c	d	24	a	b	c	d
07	a	b	c	d	16	a	b	c	d	25	a	b	c	d
08	a	b	c	d	17	a	b	c	d					
09	a	b	c	d	18	a	b	c	d					

Performance Scanner

> 90% Excellent !	You have mastered these topics. The concepts of these topics are at your fingertips. Move on to the next test and maintain this momentum.
76-90% Very Good !	You have a good command over these topics. Revise these topics again after a few days and enhance your performance.
60-75% Good !	You have a wide scope to learn for these topics. Revise these topics again.
<60 Not Satisfactory!	You have a long way ahead of you to master these topics. Revise it thoroughly.

Test 3

Syllabus General Method of Preparation, Properties, Reaction and Uses, Acidic Strength and Factors Affecting it.

For deeper insight **Scan the QR Code**

Important Instructions

- The test is of 30 minutes duration and contains 15 multiple choice questions (Four options with a single correct answer).
- Choose the correct option and fill the OMR given on the last page of test accordingly.
- At some instances, you may find more than 1 option may be correct. In such circumstances, you have to judge the most appropriate answer as per the conditions given in the question.

1. Which of the following reagent is used for the conversion of ethanoic acid to ethanoic anhydride?

(a) $SOCl_2, \Delta$ (b) P_2O_5, Δ (c) PCl_3, Δ (d) CrO_3, Δ

2. Which of the following is the correct increasing order of acidity for given carboxylic acid?

COOH (*p*-OCH_3), COOH, COOH (*p*-NO_2)

(a) COOH (*p*-OCH_3) < COOH < COOH (*p*-NO_2)

(b) COOH (*p*-OCH_3) > COOH < COOH (*p*-NO_2)

(c) COOH (*p*-OCH_3) < COOH < COOH (*p*-NO_2)

(d) COOH (*p*-OCH_3) < COOH (*p*-NO_2) < COOH

3. Consider the following reaction.

COOH (benzene) $\xrightarrow[\text{Conc. } H_2SO_4]{\text{Conc. } HNO_3}$ Product

Major product formed in above reaction is

(a) COOH, *o*-NO_2 (b) COOH, *m*-NO_2

(c) COOH, *p*-NO_2 (d) COOH, *p*-NH_2

4. Given below are two statements.

Statement I Carboxylic acids are resonance hybrids.

Statement II Carboxylic acids can be reduced to alcohols by treatment with $LiAlH_4$.

In the light of the above statements, choose the correct answer from the options given below.

(a) Both Statement I and Statement II are incorrect.

(b) Statement I is correct but Statement II is incorrect.

(c) Statement I is incorrect but Statement II is correct.

(d) Both Statement I and Statement II are correct.

5. Complete the following reaction.

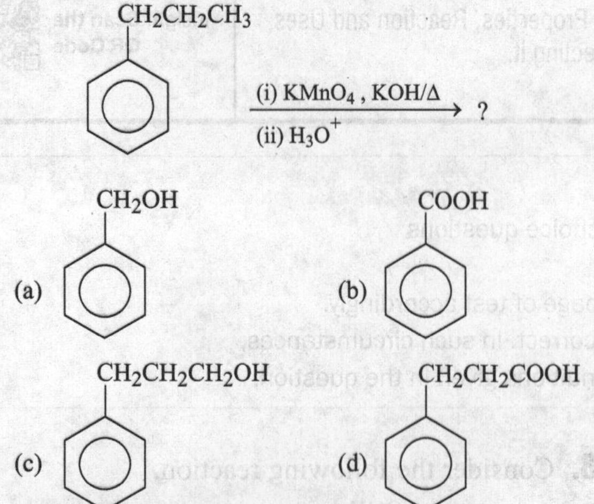

6. Select the incorrect statements.

(a) The conjugate base of carboxylic acid, a carboxylate ion, is stabilised by three equivalent resonance structures.

(b) Carboxylate ion is more stabilised than phenoxide ion.

(c) Carboxylic acids have higher boiling points than aldehydes, ketones and alcohols.

(d) Aromatic carboxylic acid do not undergo Friedel-Craft's reaction.

7. Which of the following acid can not be prepared by Grignard reagent?

(a) Acetic acid

(b) Succinic acid

(c) Formic acid

(d) Ethanoic acid

8. Identify the product from the following reaction.

(Benzoic acid, COOH) $\xrightarrow{Br_2/FeBr_3}$ Product

(a) COOH with Br, Br (3,5-dibromobenzoic acid)

(b) COOH with Br (meta)

(c) CH_2OH with Br (meta)

(d) COOH with Br (ortho)

9. Given below are two statements, one is labelled as Assertion (A) and the other is labelled as Reason (R).

Assertion (A) Cl—CH_2COOH is a stronger acid than CH_3COOH.

Reason (R) —Cl group exhibits – *I* effect.

In the light of the above statements, choose the correct answer from the options given below.

(a) Both (A) and (R) are true and (R) is the correct explanation of (A).

(b) Both (A) and (R) are true, but (R) is not the correct explanation of (A).

(c) (A) is true but (R) is false.

(d) (A) is false but (R) is true.

10. Which one of the following compounds will give HVZ reaction?

(a) Benzoic acid

(b) Formic acid

(c) 2, 2-dimethyl propanoic acid

(d) 2-methylpropanoic acid

11. The compound given below has an odour of banana.

$$CH_3COOCH_2\underset{\substack{|\\CH_3}}{CH}—CH_2CH_3$$

Which pair of reactant can be used to produce this ester under suitable conditions?

(a) $CH_3CH_2\underset{\substack{|\\CH_3}}{CH}CH_2COOH + CH_3OH$

(b) $CH_3CH_2\underset{\substack{|\\CH_3}}{CH}CH_2COOH + CH_3CH_2OH$

(c) $CH_3CH_2\underset{\substack{|\\CH_3}}{CH}CH_2OH + CH_3COOH$

(d) $CH_3\underset{\substack{|\\CH_3}}{CH}CH_2CH_2CH_2OH + CH_3COOH$

12. The products *A* and *B* formed respectively in the given reaction is

$$R—Mg—X + CO_2 \xrightarrow{\text{Dry ether}} A \xrightarrow{H_3O^+} B$$

(a) $RCOO^-MgX^+$, $RCOOH$

(b) (Benzoic acid, COOH), NH_3

(c) $RCOOH$, $RCOO^-MgX^+$

(d) RCN, $RCOOH$

13. Select the incorrect statement from the following.

(a) Acidic hydrolysis of esters gives directly carboxylic acid.

(b) Basic hydrolysis of esters gives carboxylates.

(c) Nitriles are hydrolysed to carboxylic acid and then to amides in the presence of H^+ or OH^- as a catalyst.

(d) Grignard reagent reacts with CO_2 to form salts of carboxylic acids.

14. Product of the following reaction is

$$CH_3-\underset{\underset{O}{\parallel}}{C}-\overset{\overset{O}{\parallel}}{C}-H \xrightarrow{HO^-} \text{Product}$$

(a) CH_3COOH

(b) $CH_3-\underset{\underset{OH}{|}}{CH}-\underset{\underset{O}{\parallel}}{C}-H$

(c) $CH_3-\underset{\underset{O}{\parallel}}{C}-COOH$

(d) $CH_3-\underset{\underset{OH}{|}}{CH}-COOH$

15. Given below are two statements.

Statement I pK_a value of 4-nitrobenzoic acid is lower than benzoic acid.

Statement II Due to presence of NO_2 (strong electron withdrawing group), it stabilise carboxylate anion.

In the light of the above statements, choose the correct answer from the options given below.

(a) Both Statement I and Statement II are incorrect.

(b) Statement I is correct but Statement II is incorrect.

(c) Statement I is incorrect but Statement II is correct.

(d) Both Statement I and Statement II are correct.

Response Index

01	a	b	c	d	10	a	b	c	d	19	a	b	c	d
02	a	b	c	d	11	a	b	c	d	20	a	b	c	d
03	a	b	c	d	12	a	b	c	d	21	a	b	c	d
04	a	b	c	d	13	a	b	c	d	22	a	b	c	d
05	a	b	c	d	14	a	b	c	d	23	a	b	c	d
06	a	b	c	d	15	a	b	c	d	24	a	b	c	d
07	a	b	c	d	16	a	b	c	d	25	a	b	c	d
08	a	b	c	d	17	a	b	c	d					
09	a	b	c	d	18	a	b	c	d					

Performance Scanner

> 90% Excellent !	You have mastered these topics. The concepts of these topics are at your fingertips. Move on to the chapter test and maintain this momentum.
76-90% Very Good !	You have a good command over these topics. Revise these topics again after a few days and enhance your performance.
60-75% Good !	You have a wide scope to learn for these topics. Revise these topics again.
<60 Not Satisfactory!	You have a long way ahead of you to master these topics. Revise it thoroughly.

Chapter Break Thru

Syllabus	General Method of Preparation, Properties and Uses, Nature of Carbonyl Group, Nucleophilic Addition to >C=O Group, Nucleophilic Addition Reaction, Grignard Reagent, Oxidation, Reduction, Aldol Condensation, Cannizzaro Reaction.	General Methods of Preparation, Properties, Reaction and Uses, Reduction, Aldol Condensation, Haloform Reaction, Chemical Tests to Distinguish Between Aldehydes and Ketones	General Method of Preparation, Properties, Reaction and Uses, Acidic Strength and Factors Affecting it.

Important Instructions

- The test is of 1 hour duration and contains 50 multiple choice questions (Four options with a single correct answer).
- Choose the correct option and fill the OMR given on the last page of test accordingly.
- At some instances, you may find more than 1 option may be correct. In such circumstances, you have to judge the most appropriate answer as per the conditions given in the question.

1. In the given reaction

O, CH_3 $\xrightarrow{SeO_2}$ X

Product X is

(a) O, CHO (b) O, O, CH_3

(c) O, CH_3, O (b) O, CH_3, O

2. Select the incorrect statement about carbonyl compound.

(a) Carbonyl compounds are polar compounds.

(b) Carbon atom of carbonyl compound is sp^2-hybridised.

(c) Carbonyl compounds are planar.

(d) π-electron cloud shifted towards carbon atom of carbonyl compound.

3. Consider the following reaction,

OH $\xrightarrow{\text{Reagent}}$ O, H

Which of the following reagents is not suitable for above conversion?

(a) CrO_3/H_2SO_4

(b) H_2SO_4

(c) $(C_5H_5N)_2CrO_3/CH_2Cl_2$

(d) $(CH_3COO)_4Pb$

4. In oxo process,

$$CH_2{=}CH_2 \xrightarrow[HCo(CO)_4,\ \Delta,\ atm]{CO/H_2} \text{Product}$$

What will be the major product of the reaction ?

(a) CH_3—CHO (b) CH_3—C(=O)—CH_3

(c) CH_3—CH_2—CHO (d) CH_3—COOH

5. Consider the following reaction.

CH_3 (toluene) $\xrightarrow[\text{(ii) } H_3O^+/373K]{\text{(i) } CrO_3[O],\ (CH_3CO)_2O}$ Product (P)

The main product P is
(a) benzaldehyde
(b) benzoic acid
(c) *p*-hydroxy benzaldehyde
(d) *p*-hydroxy acetophenone

6. Arrange the following compounds in order of reactivity towards nucleophilic addition reaction.

I. $(C_6H_5)(H)C{=}O$ II. $(C_6H_5)(CH_3)C{=}O$

III. $(H)(H)C{=}O$ IV. $(CH_3)(H)C{=}O$

Choose the correct answer from the options given below.
(a) II < I < IV < III (b) II < I < III < IV
(c) IV < III < I < II (d) IV < III < II < I

7. Product of the following reaction is

$(R)(H)C{=}O + \text{Semicarbazide} \longrightarrow ?$

(a) $(R)(H)C{=}N{-}\overset{O}{\overset{\|}{C}}{-}NH{-}NH_2$

(b) $(R)(H)C{=}N{-}NH{-}\overset{O}{\overset{\|}{C}}{-}NH_2$

(c) $(R)(H)C{=}C(NH_2)(NH{-}NH_2)$

(d) $(R)(H)C{=}NNHC_6H_5$

8. Which of the following reaction is incorrect?

(a) $R{-}\overset{O}{\overset{\|}{C}}{-}CH_3 + 3NaOI \longrightarrow CHI_3 + RCOONa$

(b) $CH_3{-}\overset{O}{\overset{\|}{C}}{-}CH_2{-}CH_2{-}\overset{O}{\overset{\|}{C}}{+}SeO_2 \xrightarrow{\Delta}$
$\qquad CH_3$
$CH_3{-}\overset{O}{\overset{\|}{C}}{-}\overset{O}{\overset{\|}{C}}{-}CH_2{-}C(=O){-}CH_3$

(c) $2HCHO + H_2 \xrightarrow[+H_2]{Ni/Pt/Pd} CH_3OH$

(d) $CH_3COCH_3 + NaBH_4 \longrightarrow CH_3{-}\underset{OH}{\underset{|}{CH}}{-}CH_3$

9. Which of the following statement is incorrect?
(a) Ketones are reduced into alcohol in presence of aluminium *iso*-propoxide.
(b) In presence of Zn-Hg/HCl, $>C{=}O$ group of carbonyl compounds reduces to alkane.
(c) Benzaldehyde reduces into toluene in presence of hydrazine and potassium *tert*-butoxide in glycol.
(d) Acetaldehyde reduces into alcohol in presence of red P and HI at 425 K.

10. Given below are two statements, one is labelled as Assertion (A) and the other is labelled as Reason (R).

Assertion (A) Carboxylic acid is stronger acid than phenol.
Reason (R) Carboxylate ion is relatively less stable as compared to the phenoxide ion.
In the light of the above statements, choose the correct answer from the options given below.
(a) Both (A) and (R) are true and (R) is the correct explanation of (A).
(b) Both (A) and (R) are true but (R) is not the correct explanation of (A).
(c) (A) is true but (R) is false.
(d) (A) is false but (R) is true.

11. Match the List-I with List-II.

	List-I (Carbonyl compound with different reagents)	List-II (Product)
A.	Semicarbazide	I. Hydrazone
B.	2, 4-DNP	II. 2, 4-dinitrophenyl hydrazone
C.	Hydrazine	III. Oxime
D.	Hydroxylamine	IV. Semicarbazone

Choose the correct answer from the options given below.
(a) A-IV, B-II, C-I, D-III
(b) A-I, B-II, C-III, D-IV
(c) A-II, B-IV, C-I, D-III
(d) A-III, B-IV, C-II, D-I

12. In the following given reaction,

$$C_6H_5\text{—}CH{=}CH_2 \xrightarrow{KMnO_4/KOH} A \xrightarrow{H_3O^+} B$$

Products *A* and *B* are

(a) $C_6H_5\text{—}CH_2\text{—}CH_2\text{—}\overset{-}{CO}\overset{+}{OK}$, $C_6H_5\text{—}CH_2CH_2COOH$

(b) $C_6H_5\text{—}CO\overset{-}{O}\overset{+}{K}$, $C_6H_5\text{—}COOH$

(c) $C_6H_5\text{—}CH_2\text{—}CO\overset{-}{O}\overset{+}{K}$, $C_6H_5\text{—}CH_2CHO$

(d) $C_6H_5\text{—}CH_2\text{—}CH_2\,CO\overset{-}{O}\overset{+}{K}$, $C_6H_5\text{—}CH_2CH_2\text{—}CHO$

13. In the following reaction,

$$CH_3\text{—}COOH \xrightarrow[PCl_3]{Cl_2} A \xrightarrow{Aq.\ KOH} B$$

Here, products *A* and *B* respectively are

(a) $CH_2(Cl)\text{—}COOH$ and CH_4

(b) $CH_2(Cl)\text{—}COOH$ and $CH_2(OH)\text{—}COOH$

(c) CCl_3COOH and $COOH\text{—}CHO$

(d) $CH_2(Cl)\text{—}COOH$ and $CH_3\text{—}OH$

14. Arrange the following carboxylic acids in decreasing order of acidic strength.

$HC{\equiv}C\text{—}COOH$, C_6H_5COOH, $CH_2{=}CH\text{—}COOH$, CH_3COOH

Choose the correct answer from the options given below.

(a) $C_6H_5COOH > CH_2 = CH\text{—}COOH > CH_3COOH > HC{\equiv}C\text{—}COOH$

(b) $HC{\equiv}C\text{—}COOH > C_6H_5COOH > CH_2 = CH\text{—}COOH > CH_3COOH$

(c) $CH_2{=}CH\text{—}COOH > CH_3COOH > HC{\equiv}C\text{—}COOH > C_6H_5COOH$

(d) $HC{\equiv}C\text{—}COOH > CH_2{=}CH\text{—}COOH > C_6H_5COOH > CH_3COOH$

15. Given below are two statements.

Statement I Fatty acids that are essential to human beings are made up of carboxylic acids.

Statement II Ethylene diamine tetraacetic acid is widely used as a chelating agent.

In the light of the above statements, choose the correct answer from the options given below.

(a) Both Statement I and Statement II are incorrect.
(b) Statement I is correct but Statement II is incorrect.
(c) Statement I is incorrect but Statement II is correct.
(d) Both Statement I and Statement II are correct.

16. Which of the following reaction does not give benzaldehyde?

(a) $C_6H_5CH_3$ + CrO_2Cl_2 and CS_2 followed by H_3O^+

(b) C_6H_5COCl + H_2 in presence of Pd-$BaSO_4$

(c) C_6H_6 + CO + HCl in presence of anhy. $AlCl_3$

(d) C_6H_5COOH + Zn/Hg and conc. HCl

17. Which of the following statement(s) is/are correct?

I. Aldol condensation occurs in aldehydes having α-hydrogen with a dilute base.
II. Methanal is a gas at room temperature while ethanal is a volatile liquid.
III. Aldehydes are less reactive towards nucleophilic addition reactions than ketones.

IV. Lower aldehydes have sharp pungent odours.
V. Aldehydes are easily oxidised to carboxylic acids containing the different number of carbon atom.

Choose the most appropriate answer from the options given below.

(a) I, III and IV (b) II, III and V
(c) I, II and IV (d) I, III and V

18. Match the List-I with List-II.

List-I (Reaction)	List-II (Product)
A. $CH_3—C(=O)—CH_3 \xrightarrow[\text{Conc. HCl}]{\text{Zn—Hg}}$	I. $HO—CH_2—CH_2—CHO$
B. $CH_3—C(=O)—H \xrightarrow[\text{(ii) } H_2O/H^+]{\text{(i) HCN}}$	II. CHI_3
C. $CH_3—C(=O)—H \xrightarrow{\text{NaOI}}$	III. $CH_3—CH(OH)—COOH$
D. $CH_3CHO \xrightarrow[\text{Dil. NaOH}]{CH_2O}$	IV. $CH_3CH_2CH_3$

Choose the correct answer from the options given below.

(a) A-IV, B-II, C-III, D-I
(b) A-IV, B-III, C-II, D-I
(c) A-I, B-II, C-III, D-IV
(d) A-I, B-III, C-II, D-IV

19. Which of the following compound forms in Friedel-Crafts benzoylation of benzene?

(a) Acetophenone (b) Benzophenone
(c) Propanone (d) Butanone

20. Which of the following aldehydes is most soluble in water?

(a) Formaldehyde (b) Acetaldehyde
(c) Phthaldehyde (d) Benzaldehyde

21. Given below are two statements, one is labelled as Assertion (A) and the other is labelled as Reason (R).

Assertion (A) Anhydrides are less reactive than esters for nucleophilic substitution.

Reason (R) $RCOO^-$ is a better leaving group than $R—O^-$.

In the light of the above statements, choose the correct answer from the options given below.

(a) Both (A) and (R) are true and (R) is the correct explanation of (A).
(b) Both (A) and (R) are true but (R) is not the correct explanation of (A).
(c) (A) is true but (R) is false.
(d) (A) is false but (R) is true.

22. Which one of the following compound reacts with HCN and Tollen's reagent, but is not oxidised by Fehling's solutions?

(a) Methanol (b) Ethanal
(c) Benzaldehyde (d) Acetone

23. Identify A and B in the given reactions.

$$2RCOOH + 2Na \longrightarrow 2RCOO^-Na^+ + A$$

$$RCOOH + NaHCO_3 \longrightarrow RCOO^-Na^+ + H_2O + B$$

	A	B
(a)	H_2	CO_2
(b)	H_2O	CO_2
(c)	H_2	CO
(d)	H_2O	CO

24. Given below are two statements.

Statement I Benzoic acid is a stronger acid than acrylic acid.

Statement II The presence of CF_3 group in an acid gives higher acidic strength compared to the presence of NO_2.

In the light of the above statements, choose the correct answer from the options given below.

(a) Both Statement I and Statement II are incorrect.
(b) Statement I is correct but Statement II is incorrect.
(c) Statement I is incorrect but Statement II is correct.
(d) Both Statement I and Statement II are correct.

25. Choose the incorrect statement.

(a) Simple aliphatic carboxylic acids upto C_4 are soluble in water.

(b) Monocarboxylic acid have higher boiling point as compared to the alcohols.

(c) Aliphatic carboxylic acids upto C_7 are colourless liquids at room temperature.

(d) Carboxylic acids are soluble in less polar organic solvents.

26. Consider the following reactions.

CH_2CH_3 (on benzene ring) $\xrightarrow[\text{(ii) } H_3O^+]{\text{(i) Alkaline } KMnO_4}$ Product

Major product formed in above reaction is

(a) $COOH$ (on benzene ring)   (b) CH_2CHO (on benzene ring)

(c) CH_2OH (on benzene ring)   (d) CH_2CH_2COOH (on benzene ring)

27. Predict the product (*D*) in the following reaction.

CH_2CH_3 (on benzene ring) $\xrightarrow[KOH]{KMnO_4} B \xrightarrow{Br_2} C \longrightarrow$

(a) $CH_2—CH—COOC_2H_5$ with Br on CH; ring bearing NO_2

(b) COOH; Br (on benzene ring)

(c) Br; Br; $CH_2COOC_2H_5$ (on benzene ring)

(d) $COOC_2H_5$; Br (on benzene ring)

28. Which of the following compound gives benzoic acid on oxidation?

(a) Chlorophenol (b) Benzyl chloride

(c) Benzophenone (d) Naphthalene

29. Which of the following is incorrect about benzaldehyde?

(a) On oxidation it yields benzoic acid.

(b) On reduction it yields phenol.

(c) It is an aromatic aldehyde.

(d) It is a colourless liquid with an odour of almond oil.

30. Which of the following reagent is used in the reduction of aldehydes to hydrocarbon?

(a) Zn amalgam and HCl acid

(b) $Pd/BaSO_4$

(c) Anhydrous $AlCl_3$

(d) Ni/Pt

31. Given below are two statements.

Statement I Acetaldehyde is largely used for the production of acetic acid and pyridine derivatives.

Statement II When reacted with phenol, formaldehyde forms bakelite, which is used in plastics.

In the light of the above statements, choose the correct answer from the options given below.

(a) Both Statement I and Statement II are incorrect.

(b) Statement I is correct but Statement II is incorrect.

(c) Statement I is incorrect but Statement II is correct.

(d) Both Statement I and Statement II are correct.

32. Given below are two statements, one is labelled as Assertion (A) and the other is labelled as Reason (R).

Assertion (A) Oxidation of aldehyde is easier than ketone.

Reason (R) C—C bond of ketones is stronger than C—H bond of aldehydes.

In the light of the above statements, choose the correct answer from the options given below.

(a) Both (A) and (R) are true and (R) is the correct explanation of (A).

(b) Both (A) and (R) are true but (R) is not the correct explanation of (A).

(c) (A) is true but (R) is false.

(d) (A) is false but (R) is true.

33. Which of the following reagent is used for the preparation of benzaldehyde by oxidation of toluene?
(a) Acidic $KMnO_4$ (b) CrO_2Cl_2
(c) $K_2Cr_2O_7$ (d) Basic $KMnO_4$

34. Consider the following reaction.

$$CH_3-COCH_3 \xrightarrow[H_2O]{Mg/C_6H_6} \text{Product } (P)$$

The product (P) is
(a) *iso*-propyl alcohol (b) glycol
(c) pinacol (d) diacetone alcohol

35. Which reaction is used for the preparation of α-bromoacetic acid?
(a) Kolbe's reaction
(b) Reimer-Tiemann reaction
(c) Hell-Volhard Zelinsky reaction
(d) Perkin's reaction

36. Identify the name of reaction where benzaldehyde changes into benzyl alcohol.
(a) Friedel Craft's reaction
(b) Kolbe's reaction
(c) Wurtz reaction
(d) Cannizzaro reaction

37. Which of the following is strongest acid?
(a) $HCOOH$ ($pK_a = 3.77$)
(b) C_6H_5COOH ($pK_a = 4.22$)
(c) CH_3COOH ($pK_a = 4.71$)
(d) CH_3CH_2COOH ($pK_a = 4.88$)

38. Which of the following compound would undergo aldol condensation?
(a) CCl_3CHO (b) $H_3C-C(CH_3)_2-CHO$
(c) CH_3CH_2CHO (d) $HCHO$

39. In the Rosenmund's reduction, $BaSO_4$ taken with catalyst Pd acts as
(a) promotor (b) catalytic poison
(c) cooperator (d) absorber

40. The reagent with which both aldehyde and acetone react easily is
(a) Fehling's reagent (b) Grignard reagent
(c) Schiff's reagent (d) Tollen's reagent

41. Match List-I with List-II.

	List-I		List-II
A.	$C_6H_5CHO + HCHO \xrightarrow{OH^{\oplus}} C_6H_5CH_2OH + HCOO^{\ominus}$	I.	Cannizzaro reaction
B.	$C_6H_5-H + CH_3COCl \xrightarrow{\text{Anhyd. } AlCl_3} C_6H_5-CO-CH_3$	II.	Friedel-Craft's reaction
C.	$C_6H_6 + CO + HCl \xrightarrow[Cu_2Cl_2]{\text{Anhy. } ZnCl_2} C_6H_5-CHO$	III.	Reimer-Tiemann reaction
D.	Phenol (OH) $\xrightarrow[\text{(ii) } H^+]{\text{(i) } CHCl_3/\text{Alk. } KMnO_4}$ salicylic acid (OH, COOH)	IV.	Gattermann-Koch reaction

Choose the correct answer from the options given below.
(a) A-II, B-I, C-III, D-IV
(b) A-I, B-II, C-IV, D-III
(c) A-IV, B-III, C-I, D-II
(d) A-III, B-II, C-I, D-IV

42. Choose the wrong statement from the following.
(a) Salicylic acid's a monobasic acid.
(b) Methyl salicylate is an ester.
(c) Salicylic acid gives violet colour with neutral ferric chloride as well as brisk effervescence with sodium bicarbonate.
(d) Methyl salicylate does not occur in natural oils.

43. Given below are two statements, one is labelled as Assertion (A) and the other is labelled as Reason (R).
Assertion (A) Carboxylic acid contain a carbonyl group but do not give characteristic reaction of the carbonyl group.
Reason (R) The electrophilicity of the carbonyl carbon is more in carboxylic acid than in aldehydes and ketones.
In the light of the above statements, choose the correct answer from the options given below.
(a) Both (A) and (R) are true and (R) is the correct explanation of (A).

(b) Both (A) and (R) are true but (R) is not the correct explanation of (A).
(c) (A) is true but (R) is false.
(d) (A) is false but (R) is true.

44. Which of the following is a mixed ketone?

(a) Pentanone (b) Acetophenone
(c) Benzophenone (d) Butanone

45. Which of the following reaction is not correctly match with product?

(a) $CH_3-COOH \xrightarrow[Cl_2]{\text{Red P}} CH_3COCl$

(b) 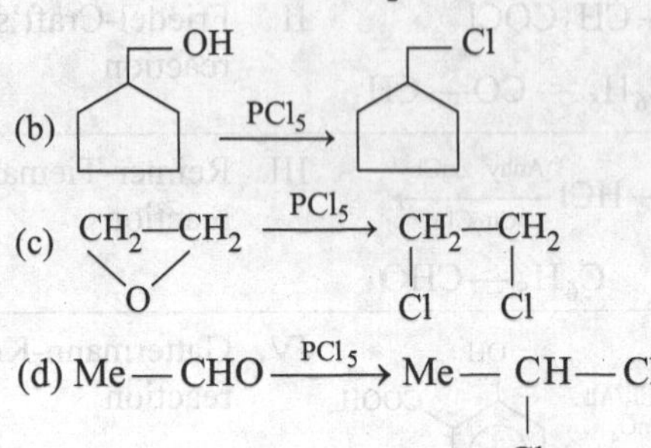

(c) CH_2-CH_2 (with O bridging) $\xrightarrow{PCl_5}$ $CH_2(Cl)-CH_2(Cl)$

(d) $Me-CHO \xrightarrow{PCl_5} Me-CHCl_2$

46. Given below are two statements, one is labelled as Assertion (A) and the other is labelled as Reason (R).

Assertion (A) Benzoic acid is a stronger acid than phenol.

Reason (R) Benzoic acid decomposes NaOH to evolve CO_2 but phenol does not.

In the light of the above statements, choose the correct answer from the options given below.

(a) Both (A) and (R) are true and (R) is the correct explanation of (A).
(b) Both (A) and (R) are true but (R) is not the correct explanation of (A).
(c) (A) is true but (R) is false.
(d) (A) is false but (R) is true.

47. Which one of the following pairs is not correctly matched?

(a) $>C=O \xrightarrow{\text{Clemmensen's reduction}} >CH_2$

(b) $>C=O \xrightarrow{\text{Wolff-Kishner reduction}} H-\overset{|}{\underset{|}{C}}-OH$

(c) $-COCl \xrightarrow{\text{Rosenmund's reduction}} -CHO$

(d) $-C\equiv N \xrightarrow{\text{Stephen reduction}} -CHO$

48. Action of hydrazine on aldehydes and ketones gives compound of the general structure.

(a) $>C=N-NH_2$
(b) $>C=N-OH$
(c) $>C=N-NH-CONH_2$
(d) $>C=N-NH-C_6H_5$

49. Catalyst used in Rosenmund reduction is

(a) $Pd/BaSO_4$ (b) Zn-Hg couple
(c) $LiAlH_4$ (d) Ni/H_2

50. In Wolff-Kishner reduction, the carbonyl group of aldehydes and ketones is converted into

(a) $>CH_2$ group (b) $>CH_3$ group
(c) $-CH_2OH$ group (d) $>CHOH$ group

Response Index

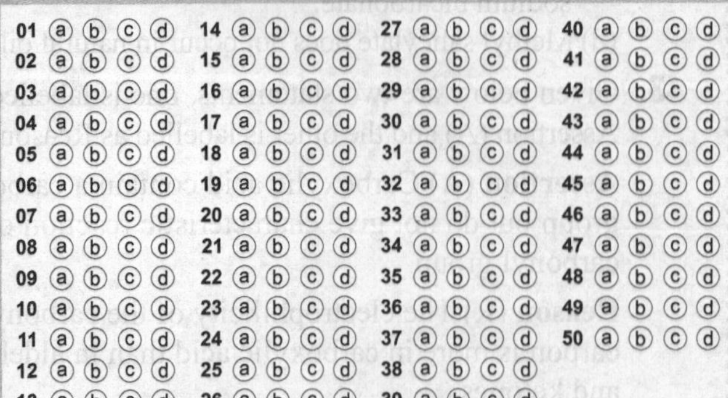

01 ⓐ ⓑ ⓒ ⓓ	14 ⓐ ⓑ ⓒ ⓓ	27 ⓐ ⓑ ⓒ ⓓ	40 ⓐ ⓑ ⓒ ⓓ
02 ⓐ ⓑ ⓒ ⓓ	15 ⓐ ⓑ ⓒ ⓓ	28 ⓐ ⓑ ⓒ ⓓ	41 ⓐ ⓑ ⓒ ⓓ
03 ⓐ ⓑ ⓒ ⓓ	16 ⓐ ⓑ ⓒ ⓓ	29 ⓐ ⓑ ⓒ ⓓ	42 ⓐ ⓑ ⓒ ⓓ
04 ⓐ ⓑ ⓒ ⓓ	17 ⓐ ⓑ ⓒ ⓓ	30 ⓐ ⓑ ⓒ ⓓ	43 ⓐ ⓑ ⓒ ⓓ
05 ⓐ ⓑ ⓒ ⓓ	18 ⓐ ⓑ ⓒ ⓓ	31 ⓐ ⓑ ⓒ ⓓ	44 ⓐ ⓑ ⓒ ⓓ
06 ⓐ ⓑ ⓒ ⓓ	19 ⓐ ⓑ ⓒ ⓓ	32 ⓐ ⓑ ⓒ ⓓ	45 ⓐ ⓑ ⓒ ⓓ
07 ⓐ ⓑ ⓒ ⓓ	20 ⓐ ⓑ ⓒ ⓓ	33 ⓐ ⓑ ⓒ ⓓ	46 ⓐ ⓑ ⓒ ⓓ
08 ⓐ ⓑ ⓒ ⓓ	21 ⓐ ⓑ ⓒ ⓓ	34 ⓐ ⓑ ⓒ ⓓ	47 ⓐ ⓑ ⓒ ⓓ
09 ⓐ ⓑ ⓒ ⓓ	22 ⓐ ⓑ ⓒ ⓓ	35 ⓐ ⓑ ⓒ ⓓ	48 ⓐ ⓑ ⓒ ⓓ
10 ⓐ ⓑ ⓒ ⓓ	23 ⓐ ⓑ ⓒ ⓓ	36 ⓐ ⓑ ⓒ ⓓ	49 ⓐ ⓑ ⓒ ⓓ
11 ⓐ ⓑ ⓒ ⓓ	24 ⓐ ⓑ ⓒ ⓓ	37 ⓐ ⓑ ⓒ ⓓ	50 ⓐ ⓑ ⓒ ⓓ
12 ⓐ ⓑ ⓒ ⓓ	25 ⓐ ⓑ ⓒ ⓓ	38 ⓐ ⓑ ⓒ ⓓ	
13 ⓐ ⓑ ⓒ ⓓ	26 ⓐ ⓑ ⓒ ⓓ	39 ⓐ ⓑ ⓒ ⓓ	

Performance Scanner

> 90% Excellent !	You have mastered this chapter. The concepts of this chapter are at your fingertips. Move on to the next chapter and maintain this momentum.
76-90% Very Good !	You have a good command over this chapter. Revise the chapter again after a few days and enhance your performance.
60-75% Good !	You have a wide scope to learn for this chapter. Revise this chapter again.
<60 Not Satisfactory!	You have a long way ahead of you to master this chapter. Revise it thoroughly.

Scan for Online Chapter Test 

Scan for Online Unit Test 

Test Booklet No. **3947260**

Test Booklet Code **CH10**

Amines

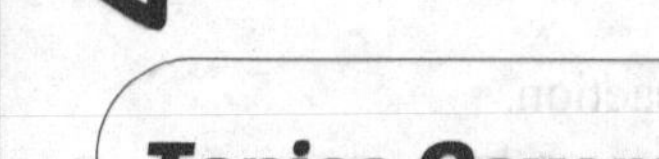

Topics Covered

Aliphatic Amines

Aromatic Amines

Diazonium Salts and Nitrogen Containing Compounds

Important Instructions

- This Booklet Contains – 3 Topic Tests and One Test on Complete Chapter.
- Each question carries 4 marks.
- For each correct response the candidate will get 4 marks and for every incorrect response, 1 mark will be additionally deducted from the total score.
- Use **Blue/Black** point pen only for filling the OMR.
- Rough work is to be done in the space provided for this purpose in the test booklet only.

Name of the Candidate (In Capitals) ____________

____

Candidate's Signature ____________

Invigilator's Signature ____________

Facsimile signature stamp of center superintendent ____________

Do not open this Booklet until you start attempting the Test

Topical Follow Thru

Test 1

Syllabus

Aliphatic Amines : Nomenclature, Classification, Structure, Basic Character, General Methods of Preparation, Properties, Reactions and Uses.

For deeper insight **Scan the QR Code**

Important Instructions

- The test is of 30 minutes duration and contains 15 multiple choice questions (Four options with a single correct answer).
- Choose the correct option and fill the OMR given on the last page of test accordingly.
- At some instances, you may find more than 1 option may be correct. In such circumstances, you have to judge the most appropriate answer as per the conditions given in the question.

1. In the following reaction,

$$C_2H_5—NH_2 + (CH_3CO)_2O \longrightarrow A + B$$

Identify A and B.

(a) $C_2H_5NHCH_3, CH_3COOH$
(b) $C_2H_5NHCH_3, CH_3COOH$
(c) $C_2H_5—NHCOCH_3, CH_3COOH$
(d) $C_2H_5NHCOCH_3$, HCOOH

2. Ethyl amine undergoes oxidation in the presence of $KMnO_4$ to form

(a) an acid
(b) an alcohol
(c) an aldehyde
(d) a nitrogen oxide

3. In the given reaction, the reagent X can be

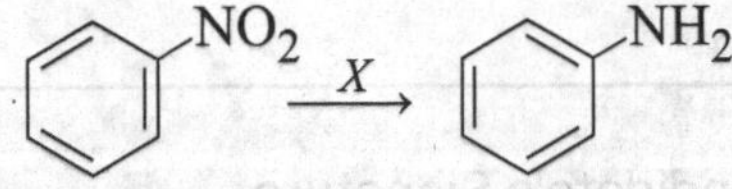

(a) H_2/Pd (b) Fe + HCl
(c) $LiAlH_4$ (d) Ethanol

4. The correct order of basicity of amines in water is

(a) $(CH_3)_2NH > (CH_3)_3N > CH_3NH_2$
(b) $CH_3NH_2 > (CH_3)_2NH > (CH_3)_3N$
(c) $(CH_3)_3N > (CH_3)_2NH > CH_3NH_2$
(d) $(CH_3)_3N > CH_3NH_2 > (CH_3)_2NH$

5. Which of the following amine reacts with aldehyde or ketone to form schiff base?

(a) $R—NH_2$ (b) R_2NH
(c) R_3N (d) None of these

6. Which of the following is an aliphatic primary amine?

(a) $C_6H_5—NH_2$
(b) $CH_3—NH—C_6H_5$
(c) $C_6H_5—CH_2—NH_2$
(d) $C_6H_5—NH—C_6H_5$ (NH bonded to C_6H_5 below)

7. Acetamide is treated separately with the following reagent then which of the given option will give methyl amine?

(a) PCl_5
(b) $NaOH + Br_2$
(c) Sodalime
(d) Hot conc. H_2SO_4

8. In Gabriel synthesis, halide may be

(a) benzyl halide
(b) allyl halide
(c) both (a) and (b)
(d) tertiary alkyl halide

9. Which is the correct IUPAC name for the following compound?

CH_3—(cyclohexane ring)—$\underset{\large CH_3}{\underset{|}{N}}$—$CH_3$

(a) N-methyl-4-methyl-cyclohexanamine
(b) N-(4-methylcyclohexyl)-N-methyl-methanamine
(c) N,N-dimethyl-4-methylcyclohexanamine
(d) N,N-dimethylcyclohexylamine

10. Which one of the following is not a base?

(a) N_2H_4 (b) NH_2OH
(c) $(CH_3)_3N$ (d) N_3H

11. Major product *A* formed in the following reaction is

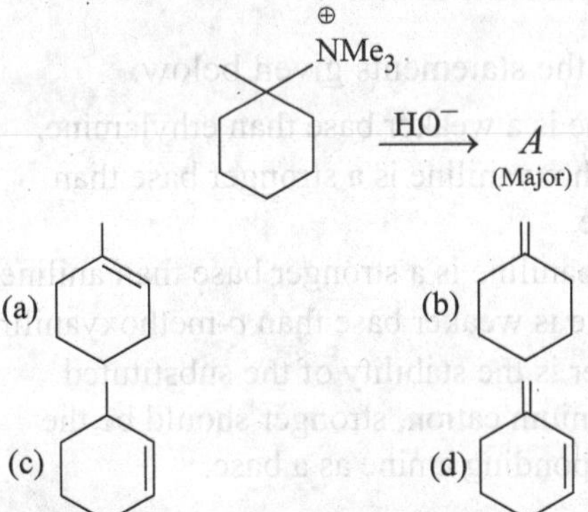

12. The number of reagents used to distinguish between primary, secondary and tertiary amines is

I. Schiff reagent
II. benzene sulphonyl chloride
III. *p*-toluene sulphonyl chloride
IV. Tollen's reagent
V. Fehling's reagent

(a) 1 (b) 2 (c) 3 (d) 4

13. What is the name of following reaction?

$$CH_3—NH_2 + CHCl_3 + KOH \xrightarrow{\Delta} CH_3N \overset{\rightarrow}{=} C + KCl + H_2O$$

(a) Carbylamine reaction
(b) Curtius reaction
(c) Hinsberg's test
(d) Hofmann's test

14. Determine the (*A*) in the following reaction.

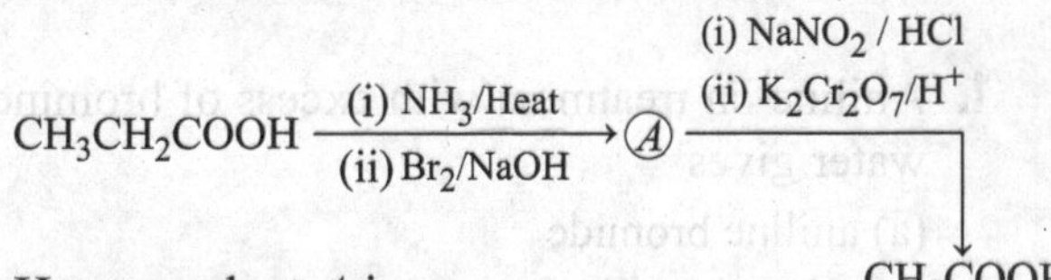

Here, product *A* is

(a) $CH_3—NH_2$
(b) $CH_3—CH_2—NH_2$
(c) $CH_3—CH_2—NH—OH$
(d) $CH_3—CH_2—NH—Br$

15. Final product of the following reaction is

$$CH_3—NH_2 \xrightarrow[\substack{\text{(ii) } PCl_5 \\ \text{(iii) } KCN/C_2H_5OH \\ \text{(iv) } H_2/Pt}]{\text{(i) } NaNO_2/HCl}$$

(a) $CH_3—NC$
(b) $CH_3—CH_2—NH_2$
(c) $CH_3—CH_2—CN$
(d) $CH_3—CH_2—NC$

Response Index

01	a	b	c	d	10	a	b	c	d	19	a	b	c	d
02	a	b	c	d	11	a	b	c	d	20	a	b	c	d
03	a	b	c	d	12	a	b	c	d	21	a	b	c	d
04	a	b	c	d	13	a	b	c	d	22	a	b	c	d
05	a	b	c	d	14	a	b	c	d	23	a	b	c	d
06	a	b	c	d	15	a	b	c	d	24	a	b	c	d
07	a	b	c	d	16	a	b	c	d	25	a	b	c	d
08	a	b	c	d	17	a	b	c	d					
09	a	b	c	d	18	a	b	c	d					

Performance Scanner

> 90% Excellent !	You have mastered these topics. The concepts of these topics are at your fingertips. Move on to the next test and maintain this momentum.
76-90% Very Good !	You have a good command over these topics. Revise these topics again after a few days and enhance your performance.
60-75% Good !	You have a wide scope to learn for these topics. Revise these topics again.
<60 Not Satisfactory!	You have a long way ahead of you to master these topics. Revise it thoroughly.

Test 2

Syllabus

Aromatic Amines : Nomenclature, Classification, Basic Character, General Methods of Preparation, Properties, Reactions and Uses, Identification of Primary, Secondary and Tertiary Amines.

For deeper insight **Scan the QR Code**

Important Instructions

- The test is of 30 minutes duration and contains 15 multiple choice questions (Four options with a single correct answer).
- Choose the correct option and fill the OMR given on the last page of test accordingly.
- At some instances, you may find more than 1 option may be correct. In such circumstances, you have to judge the most appropriate answer as per the conditions given in the question.

1. Aniline on treatment with excess of bromine water gives

(a) aniline bromide

(b) *o*-bromoaniline

(c) *p*-bromoaniline

(d) 2, 4, 6-tribromoaniline

2. Which of the following reaction is correctly matched with its name?

(a) $C_6H_6 + CO + HCl \xrightarrow{AlCl_3}$ Sandmeyer reaction

(b) $C_6H_5NH_2 + Cl_2/H_2O \longrightarrow$ Schotten Baumann reaction

(c) $C_6H_5CONH_2 \xrightarrow{Br_2 + KOH}$ Hofmann Bromamide reaction

(d) $C_6H_5N_2^+Cl^- \xrightarrow{CuCl/HCl}$ Gattermann Koch reaction

3. Consider the following compounds,

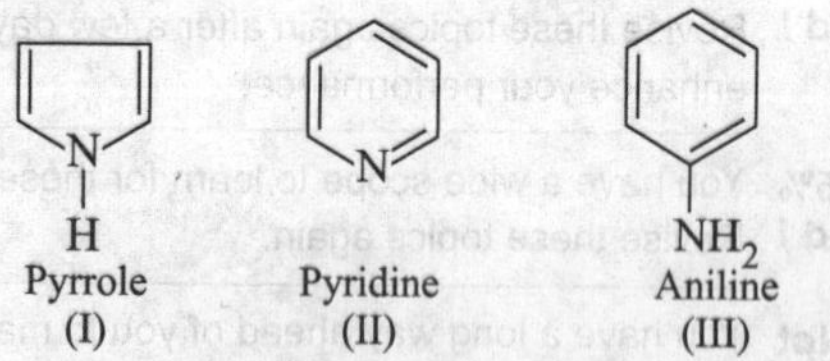

Pyrrole (I) Pyridine (II) Aniline (III)

Which of the following statement is correct?

(a) I is more basic than II.

(b) II is more basic than I and III.

(c) III is more basic than II.

(d) III is less basic than I.

4. Consider the statements given below.

I. Aniline is a weaker base than ethylamine.

II. *p*-methoxyaniline is a stronger base than aniline.

III. *p*-nitroaniline is a stronger base than aniline.

IV. Aniline is weaker base than *o*-methoxyaniline.

V. Greater is the stability of the substituted ammonium cation, stronger should be the corresponding amine as a base.

Total number of correct statements are ....

(a) 1 (b) 3

(c) 2 (d) 5

5. Examine the following two structures for the anilinium ion and choose the correct statement from the ones given below.

$\overset{+}{N}H_3$ (I) $\longleftrightarrow$ NH_3 (II)

(a) Structure II is not an acceptable canonical structure because carbonium ions are less stable then ammonium ions.

(b) Structure II is not an acceptable canonical structure because it is non-aromatic.

(c) Structure II is not an acceptable canonical structure because the nitrogen has 10 valence electrons.

(d) Structure II is an acceptable canonical structure.

6. In the following reaction sequence, predict the compounds X and Y.

$$\text{(4-methylaniline)} \xrightarrow{\text{Excess } Br_2} X \xrightarrow[\text{(ii) } H_3PO_2]{\text{(i) } NaNO_2/HCl} Y$$

(a) 2-bromo-4-methylaniline and 2-bromotoluene (NH_2, Br, CH_3 and Br, CH_3)

(b) 2,6-dibromo-4-methylaniline and 3,5-dibromotoluene (NH_2, Br, Br, CH_3 and Br, Br, CH_3)

(c) 2,4,6-tribromoaniline and 1,3,5-tribromobenzene (NH_2, Br, Br, Br and Br, Br, Br)

(d) 2-bromo-4-methylaniline and 3-bromotoluene (NH_2, Br, CH_3 and Br, CH_3)

7. Given below are two statements, one is labelled as Assertion (A) and the other is labelled as Reason (R).

Assertion (A) When aniline reacts with acetyl chloride (in pyridine) and Br_2/CH_3COOH, followed by hydrolysis formed *p*-bromoaniline as major product.

Reason (R) Acylation increases the activating power of NH_2.

In the light of the above statements, choose the correct answer from the options given below.

(a) Both (A) and (R) are true and (R) is the correct explanation of (A).
(b) Both (A) and (R) are true but (R) is not the correct explanation of (A).
(c) (A) is true but (R) is false.
(d) (A) is false but (R) is true.

8. In the chemical reaction,

$$\underset{\text{Aniline}}{C_6H_5NH_2} \xrightarrow[\text{HCl, 278K}]{NaNO_2} A \xrightarrow[\Delta]{CuCN} B$$

the compounds A and B respectively are
(a) fluorobenzene and phenol
(b) benzene diazonium chloride and benzonitrile
(c) nitrobenzene and chlorobenzene
(d) phenol and bromobenzene

9. Given below are two statements.

Statement I Aniline does not undergo Friedel-Crafts reaction due to salt formation.

Statement II During sulphonation of aniline *p*-aminobenzene sulphonic acid is obtained as the major product.

In the light of the above statements, choose the correct answer from the options given below.
(a) Both Statement I and Statement II are incorrect.
(b) Statement I is correct but Statement II is incorrect.
(c) Statement I is incorrect but Statement II is correct.
(d) Both Statement I and Statement II are correct.

10. Consider the following reaction sequence.

$$\text{(4-methylaniline)} \xrightarrow{Ac_2O} A \xrightarrow[CH_3COOH]{Br_2} B \xrightarrow[H^+]{H_2O} C$$

C would be

(a) NH_2, $COCH_3$, CH_3 (2-acetyl-4-methylaniline)
(b) $COCH_3$, Br, CH_3
(c) NH_2, Br, CH_3 (2-bromo-4-methylaniline)
(d) $NHCOCH_3$, Br, CH_3

11. Given below are two statements, one is labelled as Assertion (A) and the other is labelled as Reason (R).

Assertion (A) Aniline hydrogen sulphate, on heating, forms *p*-aminosulphonic acid.

Reason (R) The sulphonic acid group is electron withdrawing.

In the light of the above statements, choose the correct answer from the options given below.

(a) Both (A) and (R) are true and (R) is the correct explanation of (A).
(b) Both (A) and (R) are true but (R) is not the correct explanation of (A).
(c) (A) is true but (R) is false.
(d) (A) is false but (R) is true.

12. The missing reagent is

$C_6H_5NH_2 \xrightarrow{?} C_6H_5NO_2$

(a) CF_3CO_3H (b) H_2SO_4
(c) LAH (d) $NaBH_4$

13. In the given reaction,

$C_6H_5NH_2 + CHCl_3 + KOH \longrightarrow Y$

The compound Y is
(a) phenyl isocyanide (b) benzyl amine
(c) benzyl chloride (d) sulphanilic acid

14. The IUPAC name of Et–C_6H_3(–CH_3)–NH_2 is

(a) 2-methyl-4-ethyl-phenylamine
(b) 4-ethyl-2-methyl-phenylamine
(c) 1-amino-2-methyl-4-ethylbenzene
(d) 1-ethyl-4-amino-3-methylbenzene

15. How many of the transformation given below would result in aromatic amines?

(i) $C_6H_5CONH_2 + Br_2 + NaOH \longrightarrow$

(ii) Phthalimide potassium (NK) + m-chloro-substituted benzyl halide $\longrightarrow$

(iii) $C_6H_5NO_2 \xrightarrow{H_2,\ Pd/C}$

(iv) $C_6H_5NHCOCH_3 \xrightarrow[(b)\ \text{Alkaline hydrolysis}]{(a)\ HNO_3,\ H_2SO_4}$

(v) $C_6H_5N_2^+Cl^- \xrightarrow{H_2O}$

(a) 2 (b) 3 (c) 4 (d) 5

Response Index

01	a	b	c	d	10	a	b	c	d	19	a	b	c	d
02	a	b	c	d	11	a	b	c	d	20	a	b	c	d
03	a	b	c	d	12	a	b	c	d	21	a	b	c	d
04	a	b	c	d	13	a	b	c	d	22	a	b	c	d
05	a	b	c	d	14	a	b	c	d	23	a	b	c	d
06	a	b	c	d	15	a	b	c	d	24	a	b	c	d
07	a	b	c	d	16	a	b	c	d	25	a	b	c	d
08	a	b	c	d	17	a	b	c	d					
09	a	b	c	d	18	a	b	c	d					

Performance Scanner

> 90% Excellent !	You have mastered these topics. The concepts of these topics are at your fingertips. Move on to the next test and maintain this momentum.
76-90% Very Good !	You have a good command over these topics. Revise these topics again after a few days and enhance your performance.
60-75% Good !	You have a wide scope to learn for these topics. Revise these topics again.
<60 Not Satisfactory!	You have a long way ahead of you to master these topics. Revise it thoroughly.

Test 3

Syllabus **Diazonium Salts** : General Methods of Preparation, Properties, Reactions and Uses. Importance in Synthetic Organic Chemistry.

For deeper insight **Scan the QR Code**

Important Instructions

- The test is of 30 minutes duration and contains 15 multiple choice questions (Four options with a single correct answer).
- Choose the correct option and fill the OMR given on the last page of test accordingly.
- At some instances, you may find more than 1 option may be correct. In such circumstances, you have to judge the most appropriate answer as per the conditions given in the question.

1. Given below are two statements.

Statement I The diazonium salts have general formula $RN_2^+X^-$.

Statement II Secondary aromatic amines form arene diazonium salts which are stable for a long time in solution at low temperature.

In the light of the above statements, choose the correct answer from the options given below.

(a) Both Statement I and Statement II are incorrect.

(b) Statement I is correct but Statement II is incorrect.

(c) Statement I is incorrect but Statement II is correct.

(d) Both Statement I and Statement II are correct.

2. Consider the following route map.

$$(A) \xleftarrow[NaNO_2/Cu]{HBF_4} C_6H_5N_2^+Cl^- \xrightarrow{KI} (B)$$

Here, products *A* and *B* are

	A	*B*
(a)	C_6H_5F	$C_6H_5N_2^+I^-$
(b)	C_6H_5F	$C_6H_5N_2^+I^-$
(c)	$C_6H_5NO_2$	C_6H_5I
(d)	$C_6H_5NO_2$	C_6H_6

3. What type of reagent is required in the following reaction?

$$C_6H_5N_2^+Cl^- + \beta\text{-naphthol} \xrightarrow[?]{?} \text{Orange dye } (C_6H_5-N=N-C_{10}H_6OH)$$

(a) Dil. $C_2H_5OH+ pH(3-4)$

(b) Dil. $NaOH+ pH(9-10)$

(c) Dil. $KOH+ pH(14)$

(d) Dil. $NaOH+ pH(1-2)$

4. In Balz Schiemann reaction,

$$ArNH_2 \xrightarrow[HNO_2]{HBF_4} A \xrightarrow{Heat} B$$

A and *B* are

(a) $ArN_2^+Cl^-BF_3$, Ar—H

(b) $ArN_2^+Cl^-F^-$, Ar—F

(c) $ArN_2^+Cl^-BF_4^-$, Ar—H

(d) $ArN_2^+BF_4^-$, Ar—F

5. Which of the following is a Coupling reaction?

(a) $C_6H_5-N_2Cl + H-C_6H_4-NH_2 \xrightarrow{(pH=4-5)} C_6H_5-N=N-C_6H_4-NH_2$

(b) $R—X + NH_3 \longrightarrow R—NH_2 + HX$

(c) $R—\overset{O}{\overset{||}{C}}—Cl + R—NH_2 \longrightarrow HCl + R—\underset{O}{\underset{||}{C}}—NH—R$

(d) $C_6H_5—NH_2 + NaNO_2 + HCl \xrightarrow{0-5°C} C_6H_5—\overset{+}{N_2}Cl^-$

6. Consider the following reaction.

$C_6H_5NO_2 \xrightarrow{Sn/HCl} X \xrightarrow{C_6H_5COCl} Y + HCl$

What is Y?

(a) Acetanilide (b) Benzanilide
(c) Azobenzene (d) Hydrazobenzene

7. Consider the following reaction.

2, 4-dinitroaniline $\xrightarrow[5°C]{NaNO_2/HCl}$ (A) $\xrightarrow{\text{Anisole}}$ (B)

The product B is

(a) $NO_2—C_6H_3(NO_2)—N{=}N—C_6H_4—OCH_3$

(b) $C_6H_4(NO_2)—N{=}N—C_6H_4—CH_3$

(c) $NO_2—C_6H_4—N{=}N—C_6H_4—OCH_3$

(d) Both (a) and (c)

8. Find the product of the following reactions I and II.

A. $R—CN \xrightarrow{H_2O/OH^{\ominus}} I$

B. $R—NC \xrightarrow{H_2O/H^+} II$

Choose the correct option given below.

	I	II
(a)	$R—COOH$	$RNH_2 + HCOOH$
(b)	$R—\underset{O}{\underset{\|\|}{C}}—NH_2$	$RNH_2 + HCOOH$
(c)	$R—CH_2—NH_2$	$R—NHCH_3 + HCOOH$
(d)	$R—CH_2NHOH$	$R—NHCl_3 + H_2O + CO$

9. Consider the following reaction,

$C_6H_5N_2Cl \xrightarrow{Cu_2Cl_2/HCl} X + \underset{(Y)}{N_2}$

The name of the reaction and product X is

(a) Etard reaction, C_6H_5Cl
(b) Sandmeyer's reaction, C_6H_5Cl
(c) Wurtz Fittig reaction, $C_6H_4Cl_2$
(d) Perkin's reaction, C_2H_2

10. Consider the following reaction.

$C_6H_5NO_2 \xrightarrow[?]{?} C_6H_5COOH$

What type of reagent required for above conversion?

(a) $NaBH_4$; $NaNO_2$ / HCl; CuCN/KCN; H_3O^+. (273-278 K)
(b) Sn+ HCl; $NaNO_2$ + HCl; CuCN/KCN; H_3O^+ (273-278 K)
(c) Sn+ HCl; $AgNO_2$; CuCN/KCN; H_3O^+
(d) Sn+ HCl; $NaNO_2$ + HCl; AgCN; H_3O^+ (273 - 278 K)

11. Nitroethane and nitrobenzene are reduced separately by $LiAlH_4$ in ether. The product formed respectively are

(a) ethanamine, benzenamine
(b) ethanamine, phenylhydroxylamine
(c) ethanamide, azobenzene
(d) ethanamine, azobenzene

12. Predict the product of the reaction.

Naphthalene $\xrightarrow[298\ K]{\text{Fuming } HNO_3}$

(a) 1-nitronaphthalene (NO_2 at position 1)
(b) 1,8-dinitronaphthalene (NO_2, NO_2)
(c) 2-nitronaphthalene (NO_2 at position 2)
(d) 1,2-dinitronaphthalene (NO_2, NO_2)

13. Given below are two statements.

Statements I Azo dye is prepared by the coupling of phenol and *ortho*-nitro aniline.

Statement II *p*-hydroxyazobenzene is a yellow colour dye.

In the light of the above statements, choose the correct answer from the options given below.

(a) Both Statement I and Statement II are incorrect.
(b) Statement I is correct but Statement II is incorrect.
(c) Statement I is incorrect but Statement II is correct.
(d) Both Statement I and Statement II are correct.

14. Product (*P*) of the given reaction is

m-dinitrobenzene (NO_2, NO_2) $\xrightarrow[\text{(ii) Partial reduction}]{\text{(i) } (NH_4)_2S}$ (*A*) $\xrightarrow[\text{(ii) CuCl/HCl}]{\text{(i) NaNO}_2\text{/Dil. HCl}}$ (*P*)

(a) m-dichlorobenzene (Cl, Cl)
(b) m-chloronitrobenzene (NO_2, Cl)
(c) NHOH, Cl (m-substituted)
(d) 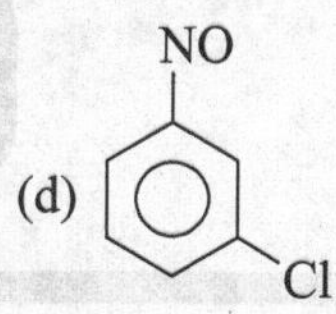

15. Match the List-I with List-II.

List-I	List-II
A. $ArN_2^+Cl^- \xrightarrow{H_2O}$	I. $Ar—C_6H_5$
B. $ArN_2^+Cl^- \xrightarrow[Cu^+]{H_3PO_2}$	II. $Ar—OH$
C. $ArN_2^+Cl^- \xrightarrow{CH_3CH_2OH}$	III. $Ar—H + H_3PO_3 + N_2$
D. $ArN_2^+Cl^- \xrightarrow{C_6H_6}$	IV. $Ar—H$

Choose the correct answer from the options given below.

(a) A-IV, B-III, C-II, D-I
(b) A-III, B-I, C-IV, D-II
(c) A-II, B-IV, C-III, D-I
(d) A-II, B-III, C-IV, D-I

Response Index

01	a	b	c	d	10	a	b	c	d	19	a	b	c	d
02	a	b	c	d	11	a	b	c	d	20	a	b	c	d
03	a	b	c	d	12	a	b	c	d	21	a	b	c	d
04	a	b	c	d	13	a	b	c	d	22	a	b	c	d
05	a	b	c	d	14	a	b	c	d	23	a	b	c	d
06	a	b	c	d	15	a	b	c	d	24	a	b	c	d
07	a	b	c	d	16	a	b	c	d	25	a	b	c	d
08	a	b	c	d	17	a	b	c	d					
09	a	b	c	d	18	a	b	c	d					

Performance Scanner

> 90% Excellent !	You have mastered these topics. The concepts of these topics are at your fingertips. Move on to the chapter test and maintain this momentum.
76-90% Very Good !	You have a good command over these topics. Revise these topics again after a few days and enhance your performance.
60-75% Good !	You have a wide scope to learn for these topics. Revise these topics again.
<60 Not Satisfactory!	You have a long way ahead of you to master these topics. Revise it thoroughly.

Chapter Break Thru

Syllabus	**Aliphatic Amines** : Nomenclature, Classification, Structure, General Methods of Preparation, Properties, Reactions and Uses.	**Aromatic Amines** Nomenclature, Classification, Basic Character, General Methods of Preparation, Properties, Reactions and Uses. Identification of Primary, Secondary and Tertiary Amines.	**Diazonium Salts** : General Methods of Preparation, Properties, Reaction and Uses. Importance in Synthetic Organic Chemistry.

Important Instructions

- The test is of 1 hour duration and contains 50 multiple choice questions (Four options with a single correct answer).
- Choose the correct option and fill the OMR given on the last page of test accordingly.
- At some instances, you may find more than 1 option may be correct. In such circumstances, you have to judge the most appropriate answer as per the conditions given in the question.

1. Number of isomeric primary amines obtained from $C_4H_{11}N$ are

(a) 3 (b) 4 (c) 5 (d) 6

2. Consider the following compounds.

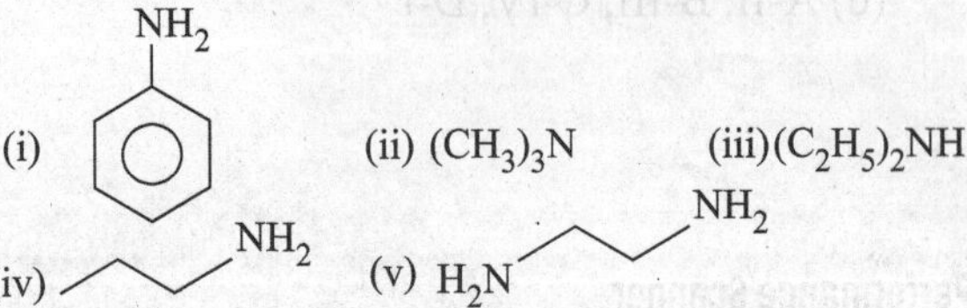

Number of compounds which reacts with Hinsberg's reagent is ....

(a) 2 (b) 4 (c) 5 (d) 3

3. Choose correct order of basic nature of aromatic amines.

(a) Aniline > *m*-nitroaniline > *p*-nitroaniline > *o*-nitroaniline

(b) Aniline > *p*-nitroaniline > *m*-nitroaniline > *o*-nitroaniline

(c) *p*-nitroaniline > aniline > *m*-nitroaniline > *o*-nitroaniline

(d) Aniline > *o*-nitroaniline > *m*-nitroaniline > *p*-nitroaniline

4. Given below are two statements, one is labelled as Assertion (A) and the other is labelled as Reason (R).

Assertion (A) Pyrrole is a weaker base than its hydrogenated product pyrrolidine.

Reason (R) Lone pair of electron on nitrogen atom in pyrrole is delocalised in the π-conjugated system.

In the light of the above statements, choose the correct answer from the options given below.

(a) Both (A) and (R) are true and (R) is the correct explanation of (A).

(b) Both (A) and (R) are true but (R) is not the correct explanation of (A).

(c) (A) is true but (R) is false.

(d) (A) is false but (R) is true.

5. With primary amines, Hinsberg's reagent forms

(a) N-alkylbenzene sulphonamide which is soluble in KOH

(b) N-alkylbenzene sulphonamide which is insoluble in KOH

(c) N, N-dialkylbenzene sulphonamide which is soluble in KOH

(d) N, N-dialkylbenzene sulphonamide which is insoluble in KOH

6. The optically active compound (X)

$$CH_3(C_6H_5)\overset{*}{C}H{-}NH_2$$

On treatment with $NaNO_2/HCl$ give

(a) 1° alcohol with retention of configuration

(b) 2° alcohol with inversion of configuration

(c) racemic mixture of 2° alcohols

(d) racemic mixture of 1° alcohols

7. The major product formed on nitration of N, N-dimethyl aniline with conc. H_2SO_4 and HNO_3 mixture is

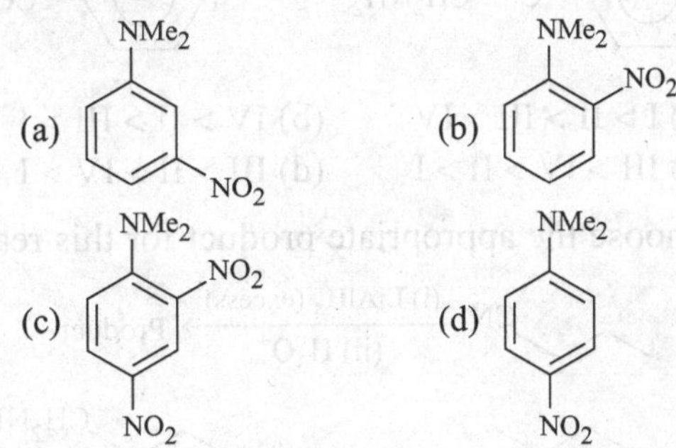

8. Correct statement about the given chemical reaction is

Aniline (NH_2) $\xrightarrow[288\ K]{HNO_2 + H_2SO_4}$ p-nitroaniline (*A*) 2% + m-nitroaniline (*B*) 47% + o-nitroaniline (*C*) 51%

(a) —NH_2 group is *ortho* and *para* directive, so product (*B*) is not possible.
(b) Reaction is possible and compound (*B*) will be the major product.
(c) The reaction will form sulphonated product instead of nitration.
(d) Reaction is possible and compound (*A*) will be major product.

9. RNH_2 reacts with $C_6H_5SO_2Cl$ in *aq.* KOH to give a clear solution. On acidification, a precipitate is obtained which is due to the formation of

(a) $R-\overset{H}{\underset{H}{N^+}}-SO_2C_6H_5OH^-$
(b) $R-N^-SO_2C_6H_5K^+$
(c) $C_6H_5SO_2NH_2$
(d) $R-NH-SO_2-C_6H_5$

10. In the following reaction the reason why *meta*-nitro product also formed is

Aniline (NH_2) $\xrightarrow[\text{Conc. } H_2SO_4,\ 288\ K]{\text{Conc. } HNO_3}$ p-nitroaniline (*A*) 51% + m-nitroaniline (*B*) 47% + o-nitroaniline (*C*) 2%

(a) low temperature
(b) —NH_2 group is highly *meta*-directive
(c) formation of anilinium ion
(d) —NO_2 substitution always takes place at *meta*-position

11. Given below are two statements.

Statement I An alkyl or benzyl halide on reaction with an ethanolic solution of ammonia undergoes nucleophilic substitution reaction.

Statement II The process of cleavage of the C—*X* bond by ammonia molecule is called as ammonolysis.

In the light of the above statements, choose the correct answer from the options given below.

(a) Both Statement I and Statement II are incorrect.
(b) Statement I is correct but Statement II is incorrect.
(c) Statement I is incorrect but Statement II is correct.
(d) Both Statement I and Statement II are correct.

12. Identify *A* and *B* in the following reaction sequence.

Aniline (NH_2) + $CH_3-\underset{O}{\underset{\|}{C}}-Cl \longrightarrow A \xrightarrow[H_2O]{Br_2} B$

(a) $C_6H_5NHCOCH_3$, 2,4-dibromoaniline (NH_2, Br, Br)
(b) 2,4,6-tribromoacetanilide ($NHCOCH_3$, Br, Br, Br), 1,3,5-tribromobenzene (Br, Br, Br)
(c) $C_6H_5NHCOCH_3$, p-bromoaniline (NH_2, Br)
(d) p-aminoacetophenone (NH_2, $COCH_3$), p-aminophenol (NH_2, OH)

13. In the given reaction, the total number of different type(s) of $[X]$ that will undergo given below conversion is ......

$$X \xrightarrow[\text{(b) } H_2O]{\text{(a) LiAlH}_4} \text{Primary amine}$$

(i) $R—NO_2$ (ii) $R—CH{=}N—R$
(iii) $R—C{\equiv}N$ (iv) $RCONH_2$
(v) RNC (vi) RN_3 (vii) $R—M{=}C{=}O$

(a) 3 (b) 4 (c) 5 (d) 6

14. Given below are two statements, one is labelled as Assertion (A) and the other is labelled as Reason (R).

Assertion (A) In strongly acidic solution, aniline become less reactive towards electrophilic reagents.

Reason (R) The amino group being completely protonated in strongly acidic solution, the lone pair of electrons on the nitrogen is no longer available for resonance.

In the light of the above statements, choose the correct answer from the options given below.

(a) Both (A) and (R) are true and (R) is the correct explanation of (A).
(b) Both (A) and (R) are true but (R) is not the correct explanation of (A).
(c) (A) is true but (R) is false.
(d) (A) is false but (R) is true.

15. The following sequence of reaction on 'A' gives

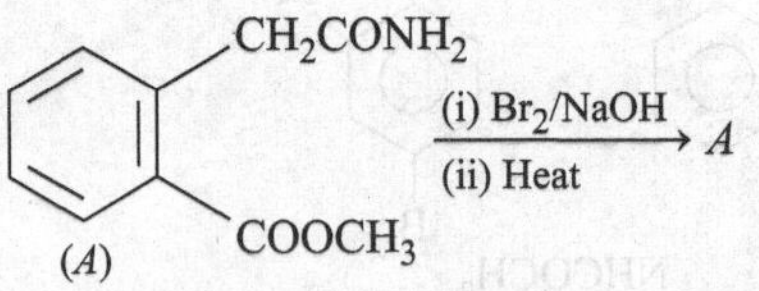

(Benzene ring with CH_2CONH_2 and $COOCH_3$ ortho) (A) $\xrightarrow[\text{(ii) Heat}]{\text{(i) Br}_2\text{/NaOH}} A$

(a) 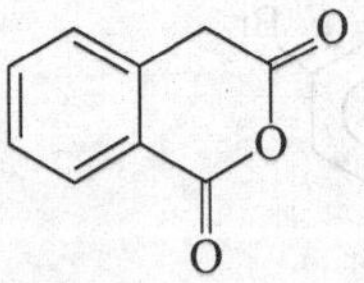 (b) 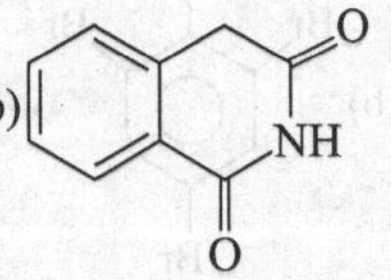 (c) 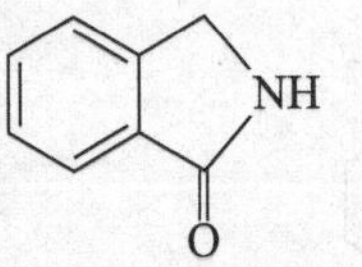 NH (d)

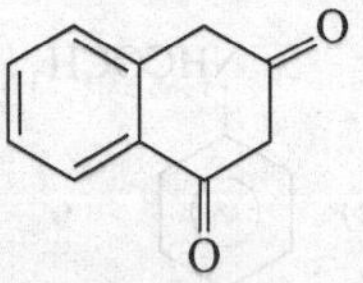

16. The correct order of basic strength of the following compounds is

I. 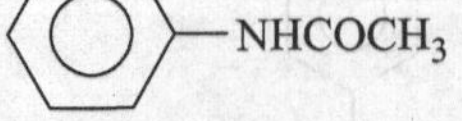 C_6H_5–$NHCOCH_3$ II. 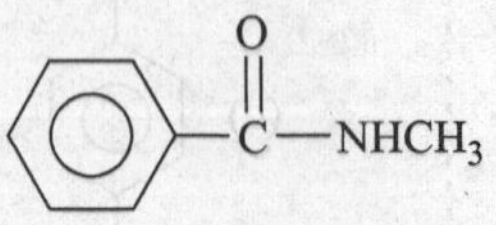 C_6H_5–$\overset{O}{\overset{\|}{C}}$–$NHCH_3$ III. 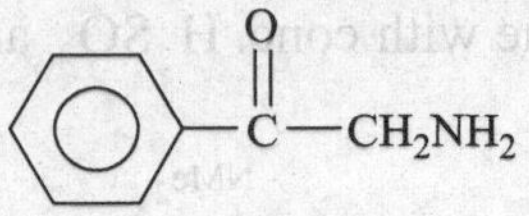 C_6H_5–$\overset{O}{\overset{\|}{C}}$–$CH_2NH_2$ IV. 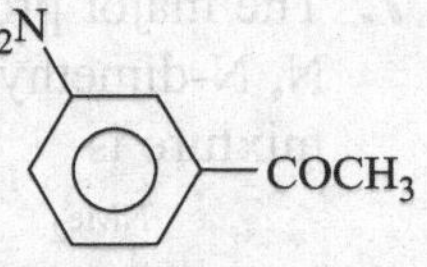 (H_2N, $COCH_3$ substituted benzene)

(a) I > II > III > IV (b) IV > II > III > I
(c) III > IV > II > I (d) III > II > IV > I

17. Choose the appropriate product for this reaction.

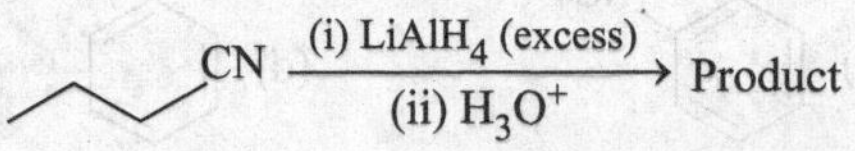

$$\text{(butyl)}–CN \xrightarrow[\text{(ii) } H_3O^+]{\text{(i) LiAlH}_4 \text{ (excess)}} \text{Product}$$

(a) 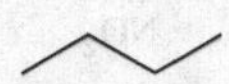 (b) 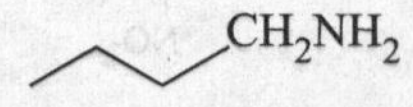 CH_2NH_2 (c) 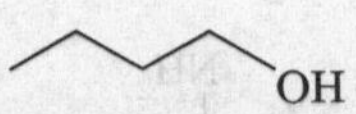 OH (d) 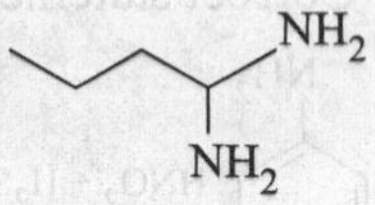 NH_2, NH_2

18. On heating acetamide in presence of P_2O_5, which of the following is formed as a product?

(a) Ammonium acetate
(b) Acetonitrile
(c) NH_3
(d) Methylamine

19. In the following reaction, X is

$$X \xrightarrow{\text{Bromination}} Y \xrightarrow{NaNO_2 + HCl} Z \xrightarrow[C_2H_5OH]{\text{Boiling}} \text{Tribromobenzene}$$

(a) Benzoic acid (b) Salicylic acid
(c) Phenol (d) Aniline

20. Consider the reaction sequence given below, the product 'C' is

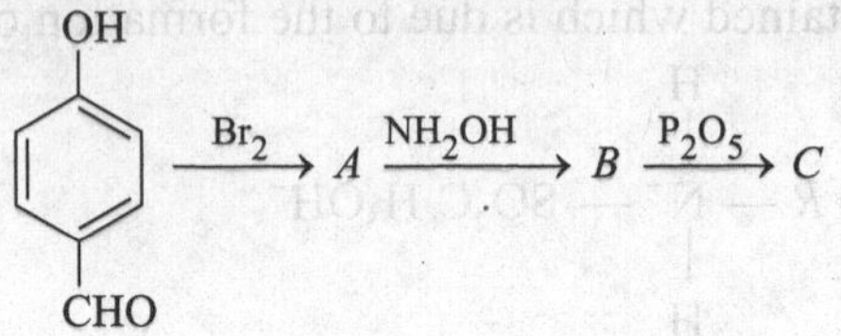

(4-hydroxybenzaldehyde: OH, CHO) $\xrightarrow{Br_2} A \xrightarrow{NH_2OH} B \xrightarrow{P_2O_5} C$

(a) Br, Br, CN (b) HO, Br, Br, CHO
(c) Br, Br, CHO (d) 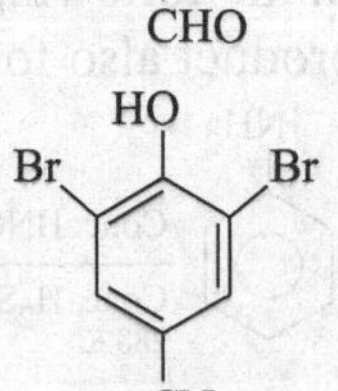 HO, Br, Br, CN

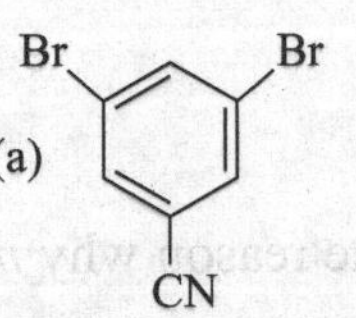

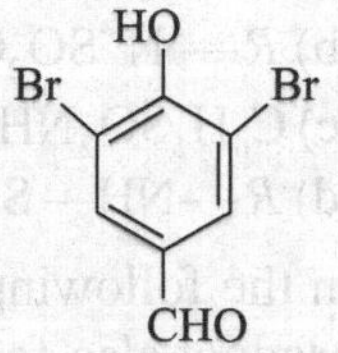

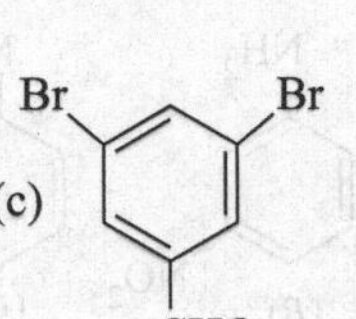

21. In the Gabriel's phthalimide synthesis, phthalimide is treated first with
(a) ethanolic KOH
(b) ethanolic Na
(c) ethanol and H_2SO_4
(d) ether and $LiAlH_4$

22. Product (B) of this reaction is

$$p\text{-}CH_3C_6H_4NH_2 \xrightarrow{NaNO_2/HCl} (A) \xrightarrow[\text{(mild basic medium)}]{\text{Phenol}} (B)$$

(a) CH_3–C_6H_4–N=N–Ph (p-methyl)
(b) HO–C_6H_4–N=N–C_6H_4–CH_3
(c) HO–C_6H_4–Ph
(d) HO–C_6H_4–N=N–C_6H_4–CH_3

23. Consider the following statements.
A. Amines form hydrogen bond.
B. Ethyl amine has higher boiling point than propane.
C. Methyl amine is more basic than ammonia.
D. Dimethyl amine is less basic than methyl amine.
E. The order of basicity in gaseous phase follows the order $3° > 2° > 1° > NH_3$

Choose the option containing all the correct statements.
(a) A, B, C and D
(b) B, C, D and E
(c) B, C and E only
(d) A, B, C and E

24. In given reaction, the reactant X is

$$X \xrightarrow[0\text{-}5°C]{NaNO_2\text{-}HCl} A \xrightarrow[KCN]{CuCN} B \xrightarrow{H_2O/H^+} C_6H_5COOH$$

(a) $C_6H_5CH_2NH_2$
(b) $C_6H_5NH_2$
(c) C_6H_5OH
(d) C_6H_5CN

25. Select the incorrect statement about analysis of amines.
(a) Carbylamine test identify primary amines, aliphatic as well as aromatic. In this test, the compound is warmed with $CHCl_3$ in the presence of alcoholic solution of KOH.
(b) Azo dye test helps to distinguish 1° aromatic amine from 1° aliphatic amine.
(c) Hinsberg test is only given by aromatic primary amines.
(d) Arylamines are less basic than alkylamines.

26. Match the List-I with List-II.

	List-I (Reactant/Reagent)		List-II (Product)
A.	Aniline $\xrightarrow{Conc.\ H_2SO_4, \Delta}$	I.	*p*-nitroaniline
B.	Aniline $\xrightarrow[Conc.\ H_2SO_4]{HNO_3}$	II.	*p*-nitroaniline, *o*-nitroaniline, *m*-nitroaniline
C.	Aniline $\xrightarrow[CH_3COCl\ +\ H_3O^+]{HNO_3}$	III.	Zwitter ion
D.	Aniline $\xrightarrow[CH_3COCl/H_2O]{Br_2}$	IV.	*p*-bromoaniline

Choose the correct answer from the options given below.
(a) A-IV, B-II, C-I, D-III
(b) A-I, B-III, C-II, D-IV
(c) A-III, B-II, C-I, D-IV
(d) A-IV, B-III, C-II, D-I

27. Which of the following will not give Hofmann bromamide reaction ?
(a) $CH_3-\overset{O}{\overset{\|}{C}}-NH_2$
(b) m-Br–C_6H_4–$\overset{O}{\overset{\|}{C}}-NH_2$
(c) $C_6H_5-\overset{O}{\overset{\|}{C}}-NH_2$
(d) $C_6H_5-\overset{O}{\overset{\|}{C}}-NH-CH_3$

28. In the series of reaction,

$$C_6H_5NH_2 \xrightarrow[0-5°C]{NaNO_2/HCl} X \xrightarrow[H_2O]{HNO_2} Y + N_2 + HCl$$

X and Y respectively are

(a) $C_6H_5-N{=}N-C_6H_5, C_6H_5N_2^{\oplus}Cl^{\ominus}$

(b) $C_6H_5N_2^{\oplus}Cl^{\ominus}, C_6H_5-N{=}N-C_6H_5$

(c) $C_6H_5N_2^{\oplus}Cl^{\ominus}, C_6H_5NO_2$

(d) $C_6H_5NO_2, C_6H_6$

29. The correct sequential order to the reagents for the given reaction is

(p-nitroaniline: benzene ring with NO_2 and NH_2) ⟶ (p-iodophenol: benzene ring with OH and I)

(a) HNO_2, Fe/H^+, HNO_2, H_2O/H^+

(b) HNO_2, KI, Fe/H^+, HNO_2, H_2O/ warm

(c) HNO_2KI, HNO_2, Fe/H^+, H_2O/H^+

(d) HNO_2, Fe/H^+, KI, HNO_2, H_2O/ warm

30. In the given reaction,

Cyclopentyl–C(=O)–NH_2 $\xrightarrow[\Delta]{P_2O_5}$ A, the product A is

(a) Cyclopentyl–CH(OH)–NH_2

(b) Cyclopentyl–C≡N

(c) Cyclopentyl–CH_2-NH_2

(d) Cyclopentyl–NH_2

31. Consider the following reaction.

$$R-CH_2-X \xrightarrow[\text{(ii) } K_2Cr_2O_7/H_2SO_4 \quad \text{(iii) } NH_3/\text{Heat} \quad \text{(iv) } Br_2/NaOH]{\text{(i) } Ag_2O/H_2O/NH_3} (P)$$

In this reaction, product (P) formed is

(a) $R-C(=O)-NH_2$ (b) $R-NH_2$

(c) $R-COOH$ (d) $R-C(=O)-NH_4^+$

32. Match List-I with List-II.

List-I (Reaction)	List-II (Products)
I. Aniline $\xrightarrow[\text{(ii) } H_2O\text{, warm}]{\text{(i) } NaNO_2 + HCl}$	P. Salicylaldehyde
II. Phenol $\xrightarrow[\text{(ii) } OH^-]{\text{(i) } C_6H_5N_2Cl}$	Q. Phenol
III. Phenol $\xrightarrow[\text{(ii) } H^+]{\text{(i) } CHCl_3 + aq.\ NaOH}$	R. Salicylic acid
IV. Phenol $\xrightarrow[\text{(ii) } CO_2 \text{ (iii) } H^+]{\text{(i) } NaOH}$	S. *p*-hydroxyazobenzene

Choose the correct answer from the options given below.

(a) I-R, II-Q, III-P, IV-S

(b) I-S, II-Q, III-R, IV-P

(c) I-P, II-S, III-Q, IV-R

(d) I-Q, II-S, III-P, IV-R

33. Major product (R) of the following reaction is :

Aniline $\xrightarrow[\text{Pyridine}]{CH_3COCl} P \xrightarrow[CH_3COOH]{Br_2} Q \xrightarrow{H_3O^+} R$

(a) 2-bromoaniline (NH_2 and Br ortho)

(b) 2,4,6-tribromoaniline

(c) 4-bromoaniline (NH_2 and Br para)

(d) 3-bromoaniline (NH_2 and Br meta)

34. When ethyl amine is heated with chloroform and alcoholic KOH, a compound with offensive smell is obtained. This compound is

(a) a secondary amine

(b) an isocyanide

(c) a cyanide

(d) an acid

35. In the Hofmann bromamide degradation reaction, the number of moles of NaOH and Br_2 used per mole of amine produced are
(a) two moles of NaOH and two moles of Br_2.
(b) four moles of NaOH and one mole of Br_2.
(c) one mole of NaOH and one mole of Br_2.
(d) four moles of NaOH and two moles of Br_2.

36. Consider the following compounds.

NH_2 ; CH_3, N ; NH_2, CH_3 ; Ph, CH_3 ;

Ph, NH_2, CH_3 ; $-CH_2-NH_2$; N, H

The number of amine(s) that can participate in Hofmann's mustard oil reaction is
(a) 7 (b) 5 (c) 4 (d) 2

37. The colour of *p*-amino azobenzene is
(a) orange (b) congo red
(c) bismark brown (d) yellow

38. Positive carbylamine test is given by

$\ddot{N}H_2$ (A) ; $\ddot{N}$–H (B) ; NH_2 (C)

$\ddot{N}$, CH_3 (D) ; Ph, H_3C, NH_2, H (E) ; Ph, $\ddot{N}$, H, CH_3 (F)

Choose the correct answer from the options given below.
(a) A, C and E (b) B, D and A
(c) A, E and D (d) B, D and E

39. Identify the product in following order.

3, 4, 5-tribromoaniline $\xrightarrow[\text{(ii) } H_3PO_2]{\text{(i) Diazotisation}}$?

(a) 3, 4, 5-tribromobenzene
(b) 1, 2, 3-tribromobenzene
(c) 2, 4, 6-tribromobenzene
(d) 3, 4, 5-tribromonitrobenzene

40. Given below are two statements.
Statement I Hofmann bromamide degradation reaction is used for the preparation of tertiary amines.
Statement II In this degradation reaction, migration of an alkyl or aryl group takes place from carbonyl carbon of the amide to the nitrogen atom.
In the light of the above statements, choose the correct answer from the options given below.
(a) Both Statement I and Statement II are incorrect.
(b) Statement I is correct but Statement II is incorrect.
(c) Statement I is incorrect but Statement II is correct.
(d) Both Statement I and Statement II are correct.

41. The major product formed in the reaction given below is

NH_2 $\xrightarrow[0°\text{-}5°C]{NaNO_2/aq.\ HCl}$

(a) 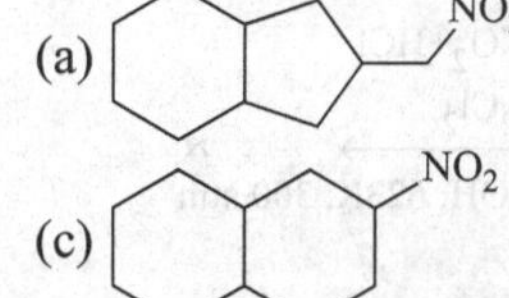

(b) 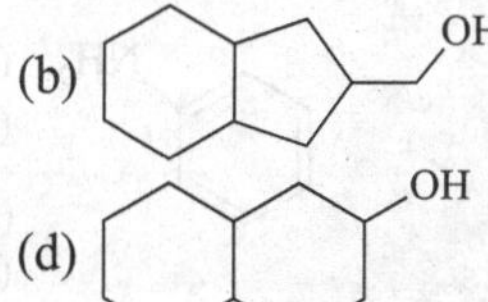

(c) NO_2 (d) OH

42. Aniline reacts with alkyl halide to give
(a) amino compound
(b) tertiary compound
(c) quaternary ammonium compound
(d) azomethane

43. Which reaction sequence would be best to prepare 3-chloroaniline from benzene?
(a) Chlorination, nitration, reduction
(b) Nitration, chlorination, reduction
(c) Nitration, reduction, chlorination
(d) Nitration, reduction, acetylation, chlorination, hydrolysis

44. The product formed when benzene is nitrated by fuming nitric acid is
(a) *m*-dinitrobenzene
(b) nitrobenzene
(c) *sym*-trinitrobenzene
(d) *p*-nitrobenzene

45. Chloropicrin is manufactured by the reaction between Cl_2, NaOH and

(a) nitromethane (b) nitroethane
(c) nitrophenol (d) nitrostyrene

46. $\overset{+}{N_2}BF_4^-$ (on benzene ring) $\xrightarrow{\Delta}$ '*A*'

In the above reaction, product *A* is

(a) fluorobenzene
(b) benzene
(c) 1, 4-difluorobenzene
(d) 1, 3-difluorobenzene

47. Which one of the following compound gives a secondary amine on reduction?

(a) Nitromethane (b) Nitrobenzene
(c) Methyl isocyanide (d) Methyl cyanide

48. Identify the product (*A*) in the following reaction.

NH_2 (aniline) (i) $NaNO_2$+HCl, (ii) Cu_2Cl_2, (iii) NaOH, 623K, 300 atm, (iv) H^+ → *A*

(a) 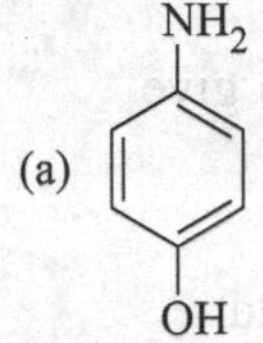

(b) OH (phenol)

(c) NH_2 / Cl (p-chloroaniline) (d) Cl / OH (p-chlorophenol)

49. Given below are two statements, one is labelled as Assertion (A) and the other is labelled as Reason (R).

Assertion (A) Ammonolysis of alkyl halides involves the reaction between alkyl halides and alcoholic ammonia.

Reason (R) Ammonolysis of alkyl halides can be used to prepare only 2° amines.

In the light of the above statements, choose the correct answer from the options given below.

(a) Both (A) and (R) are true and (R) is the correct explanation of (A).
(b) Both (A) and (R) are true but (R) is not the correct explanation of (A).
(c) (A) is true but (R) is false.
(d) (A) is false but (R) is true.

50. Which of the following amines would undergo diazotisation?

(a) Primary aliphatic amines
(b) Primary aromatic amines
(c) Secondary aliphatic amines
(d) Secondary aromatic amines

■ Response Index

01 ⓐ ⓑ ⓒ ⓓ	14 ⓐ ⓑ ⓒ ⓓ	27 ⓐ ⓑ ⓒ ⓓ	40 ⓐ ⓑ ⓒ ⓓ
02 ⓐ ⓑ ⓒ ⓓ	15 ⓐ ⓑ ⓒ ⓓ	28 ⓐ ⓑ ⓒ ⓓ	41 ⓐ ⓑ ⓒ ⓓ
03 ⓐ ⓑ ⓒ ⓓ	16 ⓐ ⓑ ⓒ ⓓ	29 ⓐ ⓑ ⓒ ⓓ	42 ⓐ ⓑ ⓒ ⓓ
04 ⓐ ⓑ ⓒ ⓓ	17 ⓐ ⓑ ⓒ ⓓ	30 ⓐ ⓑ ⓒ ⓓ	43 ⓐ ⓑ ⓒ ⓓ
05 ⓐ ⓑ ⓒ ⓓ	18 ⓐ ⓑ ⓒ ⓓ	31 ⓐ ⓑ ⓒ ⓓ	44 ⓐ ⓑ ⓒ ⓓ
06 ⓐ ⓑ ⓒ ⓓ	19 ⓐ ⓑ ⓒ ⓓ	32 ⓐ ⓑ ⓒ ⓓ	45 ⓐ ⓑ ⓒ ⓓ
07 ⓐ ⓑ ⓒ ⓓ	20 ⓐ ⓑ ⓒ ⓓ	33 ⓐ ⓑ ⓒ ⓓ	46 ⓐ ⓑ ⓒ ⓓ
08 ⓐ ⓑ ⓒ ⓓ	21 ⓐ ⓑ ⓒ ⓓ	34 ⓐ ⓑ ⓒ ⓓ	47 ⓐ ⓑ ⓒ ⓓ
09 ⓐ ⓑ ⓒ ⓓ	22 ⓐ ⓑ ⓒ ⓓ	35 ⓐ ⓑ ⓒ ⓓ	48 ⓐ ⓑ ⓒ ⓓ
10 ⓐ ⓑ ⓒ ⓓ	23 ⓐ ⓑ ⓒ ⓓ	36 ⓐ ⓑ ⓒ ⓓ	49 ⓐ ⓑ ⓒ ⓓ
11 ⓐ ⓑ ⓒ ⓓ	24 ⓐ ⓑ ⓒ ⓓ	37 ⓐ ⓑ ⓒ ⓓ	50 ⓐ ⓑ ⓒ ⓓ
12 ⓐ ⓑ ⓒ ⓓ	25 ⓐ ⓑ ⓒ ⓓ	38 ⓐ ⓑ ⓒ ⓓ	
13 ⓐ ⓑ ⓒ ⓓ	26 ⓐ ⓑ ⓒ ⓓ	39 ⓐ ⓑ ⓒ ⓓ	

■ Performance Scanner

> 90% Excellent !	You have mastered this chapter. The concepts of this chapter are at your fingertips. Move on to the next chapter and maintain this momentum.
76-90% Very Good !	You have a good command over this chapter. Revise the chapter again after a few days and enhance your performance.
60-75% Good !	You have a wide scope to learn for this chapter. Revise this chapter again.
<60 Not Satisfactory!	You have a long way ahead of you to master this chapter. Revise it thoroughly.

Scan for Online Chapter Test 

Scan for Online Unit Test 

Test Booklet No. 3947261

Test Booklet Code CH11

MEDACE

NEET (UG)

SELF ASSESSMENT KIT

Biomolecules

Topics Covered

Carbohydrates

Proteins and Enzymes

Vitamins, Nucleic Acids and Hormones

Important Instructions

- This Booklet Contains – 3 Topic Tests and One Test on Complete Chapter.
- Each question carries 4 marks.
- For each correct response the candidate will get 4 marks and for every incorrect response, 1 mark will be additionally deducted from the total score.
- Use **Blue/Black** point pen only for filling the OMR.
- Rough work is to be done in the space provided for this purpose in the test booklet only.

Name of the Candidate (In Capitals)

____

____

Candidate's Signature __________

Invigilator's Signature __________

Facsimile signature stamp of center superintendent__________

Do not open this Booklet until you start attempting the Test

Topical Follow Thru

Test 1

Syllabus

General Introduction and Importance of Carbohydrates
Carbohydrates : Classification, Aldose and Ketoses; Monosaccharides (Glucose and Fructose) and Constituent Monosaccharides of Oligosaccharides (Sucrose, Lactose and Maltose).

For deeper insight **Scan the QR Code**

Important Instructions

- The test is of 30 minutes duration and contains 25 multiple choice questions (Four options with a single correct answer).
- Choose the correct option and fill the OMR given on the last page of test accordingly.
- At some instances, you may find more than 1 option may be correct. In such circumstances, you have to judge the most appropriate answer as per the conditions given in the question.

1. Choose the incorrect statement with respect to carbohydrate.

(a) These are optically active polyhydroxy aldehyde or polyhydroxy ketones or the compound which can be hydrolysed to them.
(b) Monosaccharides are simple carbohydrates which cannot be hydrolysed to simpler carbohydrates.
(c) Disaccharides give two units of monosaccharide on hydrolysis.
(d) Polysaccharides are sweet in taste, hence they are called as sugars.

2. Consider the reaction given below.

$$\begin{array}{c} CHO \\ | \\ (CHOH)_4 \\ | \\ CH_2OH \end{array} \xrightarrow{Br_2 \text{ water}} X$$

The product X formed in the above reaction is
(a) *n*-hexane
(b) gluconic acid
(c) saccharic acid
(d) glycoaldehyde

3. Select the incorrect statement about dextrose sugar.

(a) Glucose occurs in nature in free state as well as in combined state.
(b) In free state, glucose occurs in sweet fruits and honey.
(c) Hydrolysis of cane sugar gives 1 mole of glucose and 1 mole of fructose.
(d) On hydrolysis of starch, fructose is obtained.

4. Match the List-I with List-II.

	List-I (Carbohydrate structure)		List-II (Specific characteristics)
A.	Glucose	I.	Stereoisomers
B.	Fructose	II.	Stereocentre in cyclic form
C.	Anomeric carbon	III.	Pyranose
D.	Glucose and galactose	IV.	Furanose

Choose the correct answer from the options given below.
(a) A-III, B-IV, C-I, D-II
(b) A-III, B-IV, C-II, D-I
(c) A-IV, B-III, C-I, D-II
(d) A-I, B-II, C-III, D-IV

5. Given below are two statements.

Statement I Glucose gives positive result in 2,4-DNP test.

Statement II Pentaacetate of glucose does not react with hydroxylamine.

In the light of the above statements, choose the correct answer from the options given below.

(a) Both Statement I and Statement II are incorrect.
(b) Statement I is correct but Statement II is incorrect.
(c) Statement I is incorrect but Statement II is correct.
(d) Both Statement I and Statement II are correct.

6. Which of the following compound does not show any reducing test of aldehyde ?
(a) Sucrose (b) Fructose
(c) Maltose (d) Lactose

7. Consider the following reaction.

$$HOCH_2—(CHOH)_4—CHO \xrightarrow{Ni/H_2} Y$$

Product Y formed of the above reaction is
(a) sorbitol (b) phenitol
(c) anisole (d) hexane

8. Identify the structure of β-D-fructofuranose.

(a) [Furanose ring: CH_2OH, O, CH_2OH; H, H, OH, OH; OH, H]
(b) [Furanose ring: CH_2OH, O, OH; H, H, H, CH_2OH; OH, H]
(c) [Furanose ring: CH_2OH, O, OH; H, H, HO, CH_2OH; OH, H]
(d) [Furanose ring: CH_2OH, O, CH_2OH; H, H, H, OH; H, OH]

9. Given below are two statements, one is labelled as Assertion (A) and the other is labelled as Reason (R).

Assertion (A) Glucose gives a reddish brown precipitate with Fehling's solution.

Reason (R) Reaction of glucose with Fehling's solution gives cupric oxide (CuO) and gluconic acid.

In the light of the above statements, choose the correct answer from the options given below.
(a) Both (A) and (R) are true and (R) is the correct explanation of (A).
(b) Both (A) and (R) are true but (R) is not the correct explanation of (A).
(c) (A) is true but (R) is false.
(d) (A) is false but (R) is true.

10. Which of the following statement about sucrose is incorrect?
(a) Sucrose is disaccharide and found in photosynthetic plants.
(b) Aqueous solution of sucrose is dextrorotatory with specific rotation + 66.5°.
(c) Hydrolysis of dilute acid or invertase enzyme with 1 mole of sucrose gives 1 mole of D-glucose and 1 mole of D-fructose.
(d) Sucrose is reducing sugar and show Tollen's test.

11. In open chain structure of D-glucose, —OH group is present on left hand side of carbon atom number
(a) 2 (b) 3
(c) 4 (d) 5

12. The specific rotation of equilibrium mixture of α-D-glucose and β-D-glucose, is ……..
(a) +19 (b) +112
(c) +52 (d) +100

13. Given below are two statements.

Statement I There is a relationship between the ability of a sugar to mutarotate and reduce Tollen's reagent.

Statement II The reduction of Tollen's reagent and mutarotation both depend on the presence of free carbonyl form.

In the light of the above statements, choose the correct answer from the options given below.
(a) Both Statement I and Statement II are incorrect.
(b) Statement I is correct, but Statement II is incorrect.
(c) Statement I is incorrect, but Statement II is correct.
(d) Both Statement I and Statement II are correct.

14. Glucose and fructose form
(a) same osazone
(b) same acid on oxidation
(c) same alcohol when reduced
(d) different osazone

15. Which of the following is the correct structure of L-galactose?

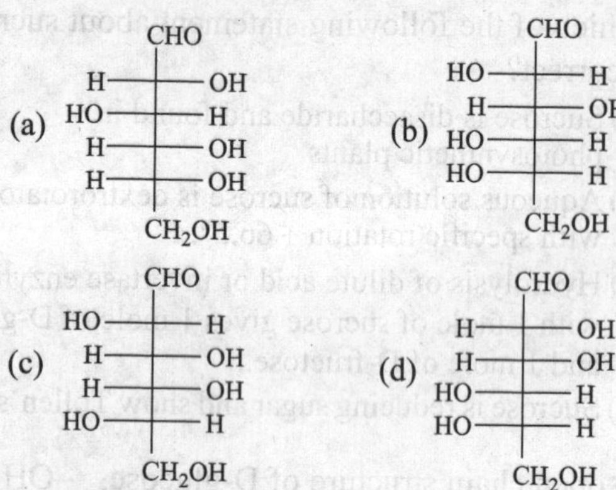

16. Identify the saccharide from the Haworth objection shown below.

CH₂OH, HO, H, O, OH, H, H, H, OH, O, CH₂OH, H, O, OH, H, OH, H, H, H, OH

(a) Lactose (b) Maltose

(c) Fructose (d) Sucrose

17. Complete the following reaction,

$$(C_6H_{10}O_5)_n \xrightarrow[+H_2O]{\text{Diastase}} A \xrightarrow{\Delta} B$$

Products A and B in the reaction above given are

	A	B
(a)	Sucrose	Fructose
(b)	Maltose	Fructose
(c)	Sucrose	Glucose
(d)	Maltose	Glucose

18. Which of the following is a carbohydrate ?

(a) Leucine (b) Albumin

(c) Inulin (d) Maltase

19. Given below are two statements, one is labelled as Assertion (A) and the other is labelled as Reason (R).

Assertion (A) β-glycosidic linkage is present in maltose.

Reason (R) Maltose is composed of two glucose units in which C-1 of one glucose unit is linked to C-4 of another glucose unit.

In the light of the above statements, choose the correct answer from the options given below.

(a) Both (A) and (R) are true and (R) is the correct explanation of (A).

(b) Both (A) and (R) are true but (R) is not the correct explanation of (A).

(c) (A) is true but (R) is false.

(d) (A) is false but (R) is true.

20. Compound A, $C_5H_{10}O_5$ gives a tetraacetate with Ac_2O and oxidation of 'A' with Br_2/H_2O gives an acid, $C_5H_{10}O_6$. Reduction of 'A' with HI gives *iso*-pentane. What is the possible structure of A?

(a) COOH, HO—C—CH₂OH, CHOH, CH₂OH

(b) CHO, HO—C—CH₂OH, CHOH, CH₂OH

(c) CHO, HO—C—H, $(CHOH)_2$, CH₂OH

(d) HO—C=O, HO—C—CH₂OH, CHOH, CH₂OH

21. The term invert sugar refers to an equimolar mixture of

(a) D-glucose and D-galactose

(b) D-glucose and D-fructose

(c) D-glucose and D-mannose

(d) D-glucose and D-ribose

22. The linkage between the two monosaccharide units in lactose is

(a) C_1 of β-D-glucose and C_4 of β-D-galactose

(b) C_1 of β-D-galactose and C_4 of β-D-glucose

(c) C_1 of α-D-galactose and C_4 of β-D-glucose

(d) C_1 of β-D-galactose and C_4 of α-D-glucose

23. The major products A and B in the following reaction sequences are

CHO; H—OH; H—OH; H—OH; CH₂OH

$A \leftarrow$ (i) Br_2/H_2O (ii) $Ca(OH)_2$ (iii) H_2O_2, $Fe_2(SO_4)_3$

$\rightarrow B$ (i) KCN, HCN (ii) H_2, Pd/BaSO$_4$ (iii) H^+/H_2O

(a) A = D-threose, B = D-glucose
(b) A = D-erythrose, B = D-glucose + D-mannose
(c) A = D-threose, B = D-glucose + D-mannose
(d) A = D-tartaric acid, B = D-glucose

24. Choose the incorrect statement from the following.

(a) The pentaacetate of glucose does not react with hydroxylamine indicating the absence of free —CHO group.
(b) Glucose exists in two different crystalline form named as α and β.
(c) Glucose does not give Schiff's test.
(d) The two cyclic hemiacetals of glucose differ only in the configuration of the hydroxyl group at C_2 called anomeric carbon.

25. Consider the following sequence of the reaction.

$$\text{Glucose} \xrightarrow[\text{(Excess)}]{\text{PhNH—NH}_2} (A) \xrightarrow[\text{Heat}]{\text{H}_3\text{O}^\oplus} (B) \xrightarrow{\text{Zn / AcOH}} (C)$$

The product (C) formed is

(a) arabinose (b) fructose
(c) sorbitol (d) mannose

Response Index

01	a	b	c	d	10	a	b	c	d	19	a	b	c	d
02	a	b	c	d	11	a	b	c	d	20	a	b	c	d
03	a	b	c	d	12	a	b	c	d	21	a	b	c	d
04	a	b	c	d	13	a	b	c	d	22	a	b	c	d
05	a	b	c	d	14	a	b	c	d	23	a	b	c	d
06	a	b	c	d	15	a	b	c	d	24	a	b	c	d
07	a	b	c	d	16	a	b	c	d	25	a	b	c	d
08	a	b	c	d	17	a	b	c	d					
09	a	b	c	d	18	a	b	c	d					

Performance Scanner

> 90% Excellent !	You have mastered these topics. The concepts of these topics are at your fingertips. Move on to the next test and maintain this momentum.
76-90% Very Good !	You have a good command over these topics. Revise these topics again after a few days and enhance your performance.
60-75% Good !	You have a wide scope to learn for these topics. Revise these topics again.
<60 Not Satisfactory!	You have a long way ahead of you to master these topics. Revise it thoroughly.

Test 2

Syllabus

Proteins Elementary Idea of α-Amino Acids, Peptide Bond, Polypeptides, Primary, Secondary, Tertiary and Quaternary Structure, Denaturation of Proteins, Enzymes.

For deeper insight **Scan the QR Code**

Important Instructions

- The test is of 30 minutes duration and contains 15 multiple choice questions (Four options with a single correct answer).
- Choose the correct option and fill the OMR given on the last page of test accordingly.
- At some instances, you may find more than 1 option may be correct. In such circumstances, you have to judge the most appropriate answer as per the conditions given in the question.

1. Given below are two statements.

Statement I The amino acids which can not be synethesised in the body are called essential amino acids.

Statement II Glycine and alanine are the examples of the essential amino acids.

In the light of the above statements, choose the correct answer from the options given below.

(a) Both Statement I and Statement II are incorrect.

(b) Statement I is correct, but Statement II is incorrect.

(c) Statement I is incorrect, but Statement II is correct.

(d) Both Statement I and Statement II are correct.

2. In which one of the following enzymes, copper is necessarily associated as an activator?

(a) Carbonic anhydrase

(b) Lactic dehydrogenase

(c) Tryptophanase

(d) Tyrosinase

3. Which of the following is not a classification of proteins?

(a) Enzymes

(b) Antibodies

(c) Antigens

(d) Hormones

4. α-amino acids show optical activity. It is due to

(a) L - NH_2, —C(COOH)(R)—H group

(b) glyceraldehyd

(c) presence of carboxylic acid

(d) presence of amino group

5. What type of bonds is not present in tertiary proteins?

(a) Ionic or salt-bridge

(b) Hydrogen bonds

(c) van der Waals' interactions

(d) Peroxide (O—O) bonds

6. Which of the following is not observed in denaturation of proteins?

(a) Helix structure get uncoiled

(b) Protein loses its biological activity

(c) Protein cannot be coagulated

(d) Due to addition of acid or water, hydrogen bonds are disturbed.

7. Identify the correct statement.

(a) A protein is made of only one type of amino acid.

(b) Peptide bond is formed by the loss of water molecule.

(c) Dipeptides consist of different amino acids.

(d) Glycylalanine is a tripeptide.

8. Which one of the following pairs is incorrectly matched regarding the uses of enzymes with respect to given substances?

(a) Detergent	–	Lipase
(b) Alcohol	–	Nitrogenase
(c) Fruit juice	–	Pectinase
(d) Textile	–	Amylase

9. Consider the following amino acids. The total number of sulphur (S) containing amino acid is ....

I. isoleucine II. cysteine III. lysine
IV. methionine V. glutamic acid

(a) 2 (b) 3
(c) 4 (d) 5

10. Which compound can exist in a dipolar (Zwitter ion) state?
(a) $C_6H_5CH_2CHCN{=}(H_2)COOH$
(b) $(CH_3)_2CH\cdot CH(NH_2)COOH$
(c) $C_6H_5CONHCH_2COOH$
(d) $HOOC\cdot CH_2CH_2COCOOH$

11. Among the following, which of the following compound does not contain ring in its structure?
(a) Furan (b) Thiophene
(c) Pyrrole (d) Cysteine

12. Given below are two statements, one is labelled as Assertion (A) and the other is labelled as Reason (R).

Assertion (A) All naturally occurring α-amino acids except glycine are optically inactive.

Reason (R) Most naturally occurring amino acids have L-configuration.

In the light of the above statements, choose the correct answer from the options given below.
(a) Both (A) and (R) are true and (R) is the correct explanation of (A).
(b) Both (A) and (R) are true but (R) is not the correct explanation of (A).
(c) (A) is true but (R) is false.
(d) (A) is false but (R) is true.

13. Choose the incorrect statement from the following.
(a) α-carbon of α-amino acid is asymmetric.
(b) All proteins are found in L-form.
(c) Human body can synthesise all proteins they need.
(d) At pH = 7, both amino acid and carboxylic groups exist in ionised form.

14. The secondary structure of a protein refers to
(a) α-helical backbone.
(b) hydrophobic interaction.
(c) sequence of α-amino acids.
(d) fixed configuration of the polypeptide back bone.

15. Following amino acid has been found in protein prothrombin but remained undetected due to formation of another common acid (*A*)

$H_3\overset{\oplus}{N}{-}CH{-}COO^{\ominus}$ with $CH_2{-}CH(COO^{\ominus})_2$ $\longrightarrow$ (*A*)

Identify '*A*'.

(a) $H_3\overset{\oplus}{N}{-}CH(COO^{\ominus}){-}CH_2{-}CH_2{-}COO^{\ominus}$

(b) $H_3\overset{\oplus}{N}{-}CH(COO^{\ominus}){-}CH(COO^{\ominus})_2$

(c) $H_2N{-}CH(COO^{\ominus}){-}CH_2COOH$

(d) $H_2N{-}CH(COOH){-}CH(COO^{\ominus})_2$

Response Index

01	(a) (b) (c) (d)	10	(a) (b) (c) (d)	19	(a) (b) (c) (d)
02	(a) (b) (c) (d)	11	(a) (b) (c) (d)	20	(a) (b) (c) (d)
03	(a) (b) (c) (d)	12	(a) (b) (c) (d)	21	(a) (b) (c) (d)
04	(a) (b) (c) (d)	13	(a) (b) (c) (d)	22	(a) (b) (c) (d)
05	(a) (b) (c) (d)	14	(a) (b) (c) (d)	23	(a) (b) (c) (d)
06	(a) (b) (c) (d)	15	(a) (b) (c) (d)	24	(a) (b) (c) (d)
07	(a) (b) (c) (d)	16	(a) (b) (c) (d)	25	(a) (b) (c) (d)
08	(a) (b) (c) (d)	17	(a) (b) (c) (d)		
09	(a) (b) (c) (d)	18	(a) (b) (c) (d)		

Performance Scanner

> 90% Excellent !	You have mastered these topics. The concepts of these topics are at your fingertips. Move on to the next test and maintain this momentum.
76-90% Very Good !	You have a good command over these topics. Revise these topics again after a few days and enhance your performance.
60-75% Good !	You have a wide scope to learn for these topics. Revise these topics again.
<60 Not Satisfactory!	You have a long way ahead of you to master these topics. Revise it thoroughly.

Test 3

Syllabus

Vitamins : Classification and Functions
Nucleic Acids : Chemical Constitution of DNA and RNA, Biological Functions of Nucleic Acids; Hormones (General Introduction).

For deeper insight **Scan the QR Code**

Important Instructions

- The test is of 30 minutes duration and contains 15 multiple choice questions (Four options with a single correct answer).
- Choose the correct option and fill the OMR given on the last page of test accordingly.
- At some instances, you may find more than 1 option may be correct. In such circumstances, you have to judge the most appropriate answer as per the conditions given in the question.

1. Which of the following protein acts as a messenger in living system?

(a) Hormone
(b) Enzyme
(c) Protective protein
(d) Transport protein

2. Which do the following vitamin has isoprene units in its structure?

(a) Vitamin A (b) Vitamin C
(c) Vitamin B_2 (d) Vitamin D

3. Among the following, the incorrect statement is

(a) guanine and uracil are purine nucleobase.
(b) glycine and proline are achiral and chiral amino acids respectively.
(c) DNA contains glycosidic bonds and pentose sugars.
(d) cytosine and thymine are pyrimidine nucleobase

4. The first hormone chemically synthesised in the laboratory is

(a) cortisone (b) insuline
(c) adrenaline (d) estrogen

5. Match List-I with List-II

	List I (Vitamin)		List II (Deficiency disease)
A.	Vitamin A	I.	Beri-Beri
B.	Thiamine	II.	Cheilosis
C.	Ascorbic acid	III.	Xeropthalmia
D.	Riboflavin	IV.	Scurvy

Choose the correct answer from the option given below.

(a) A-IV, B-II, C-III, D-I
(b) A-III, B-II, C-IV, D-I
(c) A-IV, B-I, C-III, D-II
(d) A-III, B-I, C-IV, D-II

6. Which of the following is responsible for heredity character?

(a) DNA (b) RNA
(c) Protein (d) Hormones

7. Which of the following statement about the assembly of nucleotides in a molecule of deoxyribose nucleic acid (DNA) is correct?

(a) A pentose of one unit connects to a pentose of another.
(b) A pentose of one unit connects to the base of another.
(c) A phosphate of one unit connects to a pentose of another.
(d) A phosphate of one unit connects to the base of another.

8. Match the List-I with List-II.

List-I (Compound)	List-II (Characteristic properties)
A. *r*-RNA	I. Carrier of amino acid.
B. *m*-RNA	II. Forms the site for protein synthesis
C. *t*-RNA	III. Carries the genetic information from DNA to ribosomes where protein is synthesised.
D. *Sn*-RNA	IV. Catalyses splicing of pre *m*-RNA

Choose the correct answer from the options given below.

(a) A-I, B-III, C-IV, D-II
(b) A-III, B-I, C-II, D-IV
(c) A-I, B-II, C-IV, D-III
(d) A-II, B-III, C-I, D-IV

9. Which of the following is not a steroid hormones?

(a) Testosterone (b) Estradiol
(c) Progesterone (d) Peptide hormone

10. RNA on hydrolysis does not yield which of the following?

(a) Pentose sugar (b) Phosphoric acid
(c) Amino acid (d) Nitrogen base

11. Which of the following vitamin is soluble in oil and fats but insoluble in water?

(a) Vitamin A (b) Vitamin B_1
(c) Vitamin B_2 (d) Vitamin B_{12}

12. From the vitamin A, B_1, B_{12}, C, D, E and K, the number of vitamins that can be stored in our body is

(a) 5 (b) 6 (c) 7 (d) 4

13. The tripeptide hormone present in most of the living cell is

(a) glutathione (b) glutamine
(c) oxytocine (d) ptyalin

14. The backbone of a nucleic acid molecule consists of

(a) alternating sugar and phosphate groups linked by phosphate ester bonds.
(b) alternating sugar and nitrogen base groups linked by amide bonds.
(c) alternating nitrogen bases and phosphate groups linked by amide bonds and strengthened by hydrogen bonds.
(d) sugar molecules bonded from the C-3 of one molecule to the C-5 of the other by glycosidic linkages.

15. If one strand of DNA has the sequence ATCGTATG, the sequence in the complementary strand would be

(a) TAGCTTAC (b) TCACATAC
(c) TAGCATAC (d) TACGATAC

Response Index

01	a	b	c	d	10	a	b	c	d	19	a	b	c	d
02	a	b	c	d	11	a	b	c	d	20	a	b	c	d
03	a	b	c	d	12	a	b	c	d	21	a	b	c	d
04	a	b	c	d	13	a	b	c	d	22	a	b	c	d
05	a	b	c	d	14	a	b	c	d	23	a	b	c	d
06	a	b	c	d	15	a	b	c	d	24	a	b	c	d
07	a	b	c	d	16	a	b	c	d	25	a	b	c	d
08	a	b	c	d	17	a	b	c	d					
09	a	b	c	d	18	a	b	c	d					

Performance Scanner

> 90% Excellent !	You have mastered these topics. The concepts of these topics are at your fingertips. Move on to the chapter test and maintain this momentum.
76-90% Very Good !	You have a good command over these topics. Revise these topics again after a few days and enhance your performance.
60-75% Good !	You have a wide scope to learn for these topics. Revise these topics again.
<60 Not Satisfactory!	You have a long way ahead of you to master these topics. Revise it thoroughly.

Chapter Break Thru

Syllabus	General Introduction and Importance of Carbohydrates **Carbohydrates** : Classification, Aldose and Ketoses; Monosaccharides (Glucose and Fructose) and Constituent Monosaccharides of Oligosaccharides (Sucrose, Lactose and Maltose).	**Proteins** Elementary Idea of α-Amino Acids, Peptide Bond, Polypeptides, Primary, Secondary, Tertiary and Quaternary Structure, Denaturation of Proteins, Enzymes.	**Vitamins** : Classification and Functions **Nucleic Acids** : Chemical Constitution of DNA and RNA, Biological Functions of Nucleic Acids; Hormones (General Introduction).

Important Instructions

- The test is of 1 hour duration and contains 50 multiple choice questions (Four options with a single correct answer).
- Choose the correct option and fill the OMR given on the last page of test accordingly.
- At some instances, you may find more than 1 option may be correct. In such circumstances, you have to judge the most appropriate answer as per the conditions given in the question.

1. Optical rotations of some compounds along with their structures are given below. Which of them have D-configuration?

(I): CHO; H—C—OH; CH_2OH — (+) rotation

(II): CHO; H—C—OH; HO—C—H; H—C—OH; H—C—OH; CH_2OH — (+) rotation

(III): CH_2OH; C=O; HO—C—H; H—C—OH; H—C—OH; CH_2OH — (–) rotation

(a) I, II, III (b) II, III
(c) I, II (d) III

2. Glucose when heated with CH_3OH in presence of dry HCl gas gives α and β-methyl glucosides because it contains

(a) an aldehyde group
(b) a CH_2OH group
(c) a ring structure
(d) five hydroxyl groups

3. Among the following, the optically inactive amino acids is

(a) lysine (b) glycine
(c) arginine (d) alanine

4. Which of the following is not a function of proteins?

(a) Nail formation
(b) Skin formation
(c) Muscle formation
(d) Providing energy for metabolism

5. Which carbohydrates has highest abundance in human blood?

(a) D-fructose (b) D-glucose
(c) Sucrose (d) Lactose

6. The number of oxygen atoms present in the structure of maltose is

(a) 6 (b) 10
(c) 11 (d) 12

7. Which among following is the sweetest sugar?

(a) Glucose (b) Fructose
(c) Lactose (d) Sucrose

8. The protein which maintain blood sugar level in the human body.

(a) Haemoglobin (b) Oxytocin
(c) Insulin (d) Ptyalin

9. The relation of the isoelectric point for an amino acid to its solubility in water is
(a) the two are not related.
(b) an amino acid is least soluble at its isoelectric point.
(c) an amino acid has the maximum solubility at the isoelectric point.
(d) solubilities of only some amino acids depend on isoelectric point.

10. Given below are two statements, one is labelled as Assertion (A) and the other is labelled as Reason (R).

Assertion (A) D-glucose does not form addition compound with NH_3 and $NaHSO_3$.

Reason (R) The reaction of NH_3 and $NaHSO_3$ with D-glucose are irreversible.

In the light of the above statements, choose the correct answer from the options given below.
(a) Both (A) and (R) are true and (R) is the correct explanation of (A).
(b) Both (A) and (R) are true but (R) is not the correct explanation of (A).
(c) (A) is true but (R) is false.
(d) (A) is false but (R) is true.

11. The correct name of 'Sucrose' is
(a) α-D-glucopyranosyl-β-D-fructofuranoside
(b) β-D-glucopyranosyl-β-D-fructofuranoside
(c) α-D-glucopyranosyl-α-D-fructofuranoside
(d) β-D-glucopyranosyl-α-D-fructofuranoside

12. Which of the following statement is correct?
(a) All amino acids are optically active.
(b) All amino acids except glycine are optically active.
(c) All amino acids except glutamic acid are optically active.
(d) All amino acid except lysine acid are optically active.

13. Which of the following compounds can be detected by Molisch's test?
(a) Sugars
(b) Amines
(c) Primary alcohols
(d) Nitro compounds

14. Select the incorrect statement about ribose.
(a) It is a polyhydroxy compound.
(b) It is an aldehyde sugar.
(c) It has six carbon atoms.
(d) It exhibits optical activity.

15. Which of the following amino acid has aromatic ring?
(a) Alanine (b) Glycine
(c) Tyrosine (d) Lysine

16. Given below are two statements, one is labelled as Assertion (A) and the other is labelled as Reason (R).

Assertion (A) Vitamin D can be stored in our body.

Reason (R) Vitamin D is water soluble.

In the light of the above statements, choose the correct answer from the options given below.
(a) Both (A) and (R) are true and (R) is the correct explanation of (A).
(b) Both (A) and (R) are true but (R) is not the correct explanation of (A).
(c) (A) is true but (R) is false.
(d) (A) is false but (R) is true.

17. Which of the following statement is not correct about glucose?
(a) It is an aldohexose.
(b) On heating with HI it forms *n*-hexane.
(c) It is present in furanose form.
(d) It does not give 2, 4-DNP test.

18. Given below are two statements.

Statement I Two sugar units are joined by 1, 2-glycosidic bond in sucrose.

Statement II It contains C_1-glucose and C_2-fructose glycosidic bond.

In the light of the above statements, choose the correct answer from the options given below.
(a) Both Statement I and Statement II are incorrect.
(b) Statement I is correct, but Statement II is incorrect.
(c) Statement I is incorrect, but Statement II is correct.
(d) Both Statement I and Statement II are correct.

19. Which of the following amino acids are aromatic in nature?

(a) Methionine (b) Isoleucine
(c) Proline (d) Histidine

20. Which one of the following is not an essential amino acid?

(a) Valine (b) Leucine
(c) Lysine (d) Alanine

21. α-helix structure is found in which of the following?

(a) DNA (b) RNA
(c) Lipid (d) Protein

22. Match the List-I with List-II.

List-I (Enzyme)	List-II (Conversion)
A. Invertase	I. Starch into maltose
B. Zymase	II. Maltose into glucose
C. Diastase	III. Glucose into ethanol
D. Maltase	IV. Cane sugar into glucose

Choose the most appropriate answer from the options given below.

(a) A-III, B-IV, C-II, D-I
(b) A-III, B-II, C-I, D-IV
(c) A-IV, B-III, C-I, D-II
(d) A-IV, B-II, C-III, D-I

23. Glucose and mannose are also known as

(a) epimers (b) anomers
(c) ketohexoses (d) disaccharides

24. Which of the following is not present in nucleic acid?

(a) Uracil
(b) 2-amino pyridine
(c) Thymine
(d) Adenine

25. The enzyme ptyalin used for the digestion of food is present in

(a) saliva (b) blood
(c) intestines (d) adrenal glands

26. α-D-glucose and β-D-glucose differ from each other due to difference in one of the carbons with respect to its

(a) size of hemiacetal ring
(b) number of OH groups
(c) configuration
(d) conformation

27. Which of the following contains the highest percentage of protein?

(a) Groundnut (b) Cow's milk
(c) Egg (d) Wheat

28. Which of the following is an aldohexose?

(a) Cellulose (b) Sucrose
(c) Glucose (d) Raffinose

29. Oxidation of D-glucose with Ag_2O gives

(a) D-gluconic acid
(b) L-glucaric acid
(c) L-gluconic acid
(d) D-glucaric acid

30. The deficiency of Vitamin K causes

(a) haemorrhage
(b) increased time of blood clotting
(c) inflammation of lung
(d) Both (a) and (b)

31. Which of the following statement is incorrect?

(a) Glucose is a disaccharide
(b) Starch is a polysaccharide
(c) Glucose and fructose are not anomers
(d) Invert sugar consists of glucose and fructose

32. Protein can be most easily removed from

(a) alkanes (b) alkenes
(c) alkynes (d) benzene

33. Given below are two statements.

Statement I Oxytocin controls the contraction of the uterus during child birth and helps in the release of milk from mammary glands.

Statement II Progesterone is responsible for the preparation of uterus for implantation of fertilised egg.

In the light of the above statements, choose the correct answer from the options given below.

(a) Both Statement I and Statement II are incorrect.
(b) Statement I is correct, but Statement II is incorrect.
(c) Statement I is incorrect, but Statement II is correct.
(d) Both Statement I and Statement II are correct.

34. The pK_{a_1} and pK_{a_2} of an amino acid are 4.6 and 19.4 respectively. The isoelectric point of the amino acid is

(a) 12.0 (b) 7.4
(c) 18 (d) 3.7

35. Consider the following statements.
A. (+)- lactose, $C_{12}H_{22}O_{11}$ contains 8 —OH groups
B. On hydrolysis (+)-lactose gives equal amount of D-(+) glucose and D-(+) galactose
C. (+)-lactose is a β-glycoside formed by the union of molecule of D-(+)-glucose and a molecule of D-(+)- galactose
D. (+)-lactose is a reducing sugar and does not exhibit mutarotation
E. It is commonly known as milk sugar since this disaccharide is found in milk.

Choose the incorrect statement from the option given below

(a) A and E (b) B, C and D
(c) A, B and E (d) Only D

36. Consider the following amino acids.
A. Methionine B. Tryosine C. Proline
D. Glycine E. Alanine

The number of non-essential amino acids is ....

(a) 4 (b) 5
(c) 3 (d) 1

37. The nitrogen base which is present in RNA and absent in DNA is

(a) 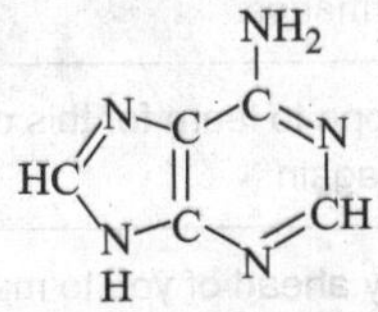 (b)

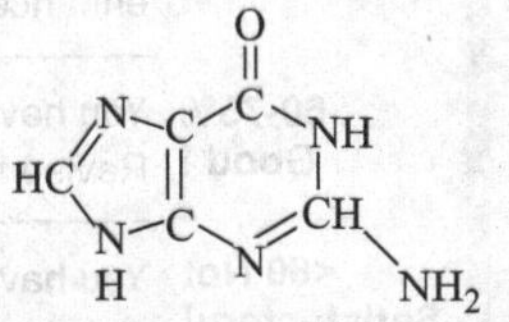

(c) 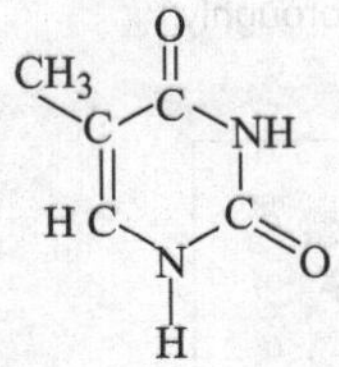 (d)

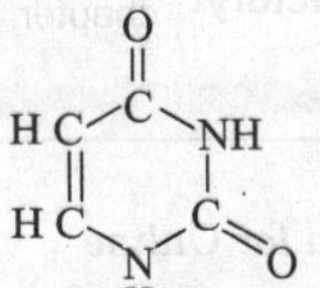

38. Consider the amino acids with their one letter code
I. G → Glycine II. T → Tryptophan
III. V → Valine IV. H → Histidine
V. A → Alanine

The number of correct representation of amino acids with their symbol is

(a) 1 (b) 2
(c) 4 (d) 3

39. Among the following, amino acids which can be synthesised in the body is

(a) lysine
(b) leucine
(c) valine
(d) alanine

40. Given below are two statements.

Statement I Glucose does not give 2, 4-DNP test.

Statement II Glucose exists in cyclic hemiacetal form.

In the light of the above statements, choose the correct answer from the options given below.

(a) Both Statement I and Statement II are incorrect.
(b) Statement I is correct, but Statement II is incorrect.
(c) Statement I is incorrect, but Statement II is correct.
(d) Both Statement I and Statement II are correct.

41. Choose the correct statement regarding α-maltose.

(a) It consists of one α-D-glucopyranose unit and one β-D-glucopyranose unit with 1,2-glycosidic linkage.
(b) It consists of two α-D-glucopyranose units with 1,2-glycosidic linkage.
(c) It consists of two β-D-glucopyranose units with 1,4-glycosidic linkage.
(d) It consists of two α-D-glucopyranose units with 1,4-glycosidic linkage.

42. Denaturation of proteins leads to loss of its biological activity by

(a) formation of amino acids
(b) loss of tertiary structure only
(c) loss of both primary and secondary structures
(d) loss of both secondary and tertiary structures

43. Which one of the following statements is correct for protein synthesis (translation)?
(a) Amino acids are directly recognised by *m*-RNA.
(b) The third base of the codon is less specific.
(c) Only one codon codes for an amino acid.
(d) Every *t*-RNA molecules has more than one amino acid attachments.

44. The hormone that is responsible for the development of secondary sexual character of female is
(a) progesterone (b) oxytocin
(c) estrogen (d) androgen

45. Which of the following bonds, stabilises the helical structure of protein?
(a) Dipeptide bonds
(b) Hydrogen bond
(c) Ether bonds
(d) Peptide bonds

46. Hormone that causes glycogenolysis and gluconeogenesis is
(a) ACTH (b) glucagon
(c) insulin (d) aldosterone

47. Which of the following statements are correct?
I. Sucrose is a non-reducing sugar.
II. Glucose is oxidised by bromine water.
III. Glucose rotates plane polarised light in clockwise direction.
IV. Fructose is oxidised by bromine water.
V. Sucrose is obtained from cane sugar.
Choose the most appropriate answer from the options given below.
(a) I, II, III and V
(b) II, IV only
(c) I, III and IV only
(d) III, IV and V only

48. Glucose gives silver mirror with ammoniacal silver nitrate. It is due to presence of which of the following group?
(a) Aldehydic group
(b) Ester group
(c) Ketone group
(d) Alcoholic group

49. Abnormally low level of thyroxine leads to the disease
(a) hypothyroidism
(b) hypertension
(c) hyperthyrodism
(d) hypoglycemia

50. Which of the following reagent is used to establish the difference between glucose and fructose?
(a) Tollen's reagent
(b) Phenyl hydrazine
(c) P/HI
(d) Conc. HNO_3

■ **Response Index**

01 ⓐ ⓑ ⓒ ⓓ	14 ⓐ ⓑ ⓒ ⓓ	27 ⓐ ⓑ ⓒ ⓓ	40 ⓐ ⓑ ⓒ ⓓ
02 ⓐ ⓑ ⓒ ⓓ	15 ⓐ ⓑ ⓒ ⓓ	28 ⓐ ⓑ ⓒ ⓓ	41 ⓐ ⓑ ⓒ ⓓ
03 ⓐ ⓑ ⓒ ⓓ	16 ⓐ ⓑ ⓒ ⓓ	29 ⓐ ⓑ ⓒ ⓓ	42 ⓐ ⓑ ⓒ ⓓ
04 ⓐ ⓑ ⓒ ⓓ	17 ⓐ ⓑ ⓒ ⓓ	30 ⓐ ⓑ ⓒ ⓓ	43 ⓐ ⓑ ⓒ ⓓ
05 ⓐ ⓑ ⓒ ⓓ	18 ⓐ ⓑ ⓒ ⓓ	31 ⓐ ⓑ ⓒ ⓓ	44 ⓐ ⓑ ⓒ ⓓ
06 ⓐ ⓑ ⓒ ⓓ	19 ⓐ ⓑ ⓒ ⓓ	32 ⓐ ⓑ ⓒ ⓓ	45 ⓐ ⓑ ⓒ ⓓ
07 ⓐ ⓑ ⓒ ⓓ	20 ⓐ ⓑ ⓒ ⓓ	33 ⓐ ⓑ ⓒ ⓓ	46 ⓐ ⓑ ⓒ ⓓ
08 ⓐ ⓑ ⓒ ⓓ	21 ⓐ ⓑ ⓒ ⓓ	34 ⓐ ⓑ ⓒ ⓓ	47 ⓐ ⓑ ⓒ ⓓ
09 ⓐ ⓑ ⓒ ⓓ	22 ⓐ ⓑ ⓒ ⓓ	35 ⓐ ⓑ ⓒ ⓓ	48 ⓐ ⓑ ⓒ ⓓ
10 ⓐ ⓑ ⓒ ⓓ	23 ⓐ ⓑ ⓒ ⓓ	36 ⓐ ⓑ ⓒ ⓓ	49 ⓐ ⓑ ⓒ ⓓ
11 ⓐ ⓑ ⓒ ⓓ	24 ⓐ ⓑ ⓒ ⓓ	37 ⓐ ⓑ ⓒ ⓓ	50 ⓐ ⓑ ⓒ ⓓ
12 ⓐ ⓑ ⓒ ⓓ	25 ⓐ ⓑ ⓒ ⓓ	38 ⓐ ⓑ ⓒ ⓓ	
13 ⓐ ⓑ ⓒ ⓓ	26 ⓐ ⓑ ⓒ ⓓ	39 ⓐ ⓑ ⓒ ⓓ	

■ **Performance Scanner**

> 90% Excellent !	You have mastered this chapter. The concepts of this chapter are at your fingertips. Move on to the next chapter and maintain this momentum.
76-90% Very Good !	You have a good command over this chapter. Revise the chapter again after a few days and enhance your performance.
60-75% Good !	You have a wide scope to learn for this chapter. Revise this chapter again.
<60 Not Satisfactory!	You have a long way ahead of you to master this chapter. Revise it thoroughly.

Scan for Online Chapter Test

Scan for Online Unit Test

Space for Rough Work

Space for Rough Work

Test Booklet No. **3947262**

Test Booklet Code **CH12**

MED ACE
NEET (UG)
SELF ASSESSMENT KIT

Principles Related to Practical Chemistry

Topics Covered

Experiments Involving Physical Chemistry

Analysis of Inorganic Compounds

Analysis of Organic Compounds

Important Instructions

- This Booklet Contains – 3 Topic Tests and One Test on Complete Chapter.
- Each question carries 4 marks.
- For each correct response the candidate will get 4 marks and for every incorrect response, 1 mark will be additionally deducted from the total score.
- Use **Blue/Black** point pen only for filling the OMR.
- Rough work is to be done in the space provided for this purpose in the test booklet only.

Name of the Candidate (In Capitals) __________

Candidate's Signature __________

Invigilator's Signature __________

Facsimile signature stamp of center superintendent __________

Do not open this Booklet until you start attempting the Test

Topical Follow Thru

Test 1

Syllabus

- The Chemistry Involved in the Titrimetric Exercise-Acids, Bases and the Use of Indicators-Oxalic-Acid *vs* $KMnO_4$, Mohr's Salt *vs* $KMnO_4$. Chemical Principles Involved in the Following Experiments.
- Enthalpy of Solution of $CuSO_4$
- Enthalpy of Neutralisation of Strong Acid and Strong Base.
- Preparation of Lyophilic and Lyophobic Sols.
- Kinetic Study of the Reaction of Iodide Ions with Hydrogen Peroxide at Room Temperature.

For deeper insight **Scan the QR Code**

Important Instructions

- The test is of 30 minutes duration and contains 15 multiple choice questions (Four options with a single correct answer).
- Choose the correct option and fill the OMR given on the last page of test accordingly.
- At some instances, you may find more than 1 option may be correct. In such circumstances, you have to judge the most appropriate answer as per the conditions given in the question.

1. For standardising NaOH solution, which of the following is used as a primary standard?
(a) Sodium tetraborate
(b) Ferrous ammonium sulphate
(c) Oxalic acid
(d) Dil. HCl

2. Phenolphthalein does not act as an indicator for the titration between
(a) KOH and H_2SO_4
(b) $Ba(OH)_2$ and HCl
(c) NaOH and acetic acid
(d) oxalic acid and $KMnO_4$

3. The pink colour of phenolphthalein in alkaline medium is
(a) due to negative ion
(b) due to positive form
(c) due to OH^- ions
(d) due to neutral form

4. Which of the following statements is not correct with respect to hydrophilic sols?
(a) The particles are hydrated.
(b) They are quite stable and are not easily coagulated.
(c) They are irreversible.
(d) There are considerable interactions between the dispersed phase and dispersion medium.

5. Gold sol has been prepared by shaking gold chloride ($AuCl_3$) solution with formaldehyde. Which one of the following is true?
(a) $AuCl_3$ has been oxidised by formaldehyde.
(b) $AuCl_3$ has been reduced by formaldehyde.
(c) $AuCl_3$ has been reduced as well as oxidised, i.e. it is a disproportionation reaction.
(d) Reaction between $AuCl_3$ and HCHO is a displacement reaction.

6. Ferric hydroxide sol can be prepared
(a) by shaking $FeCl_3$ solution with dilute NaOH solution
(b) by shaking freshly precipitated $Fe(OH)_3$ with water
(c) by shaking freshly precipitated $Fe(OH)_3$ with sufficient amount of dilute HCl
(d) by shaking $FeCl_3$ with boiling water

7. When mixture of sodium carbonate and sodium hydroxide solution is titrated against HCl, phenolphthalein end point corresponds to
(a) neutralisation of OH^- ions and CO_3^{2-} ions
(b) neutralisation of OH^- ions only
(c) neutralisation of CO_3^{2-} ions only
(d) neutralisation of OH^- ions and half of CO_3^{2-} ions

8. Which one of the following does not involve peptisation?

(a) $Fe(OH)_3$ precipitate shaken with a small amount of dilute HCl.

(b) $Fe(OH)_3$ precipitate shaken with $FeCl_3$ solution.

(c) $AuCl_3$ solution shaken with $SnCl_2$ solution.

(d) $AgNO_3$ solution shaken with KI solution.

9. The sol of egg albumin is prepared

(a) by shaking the white part of the egg with cold water

(b) by shaking the yellow part of the egg with cold water

(c) by shaking the white part of the egg with hot water

(d) by shaking yellow part of the egg with hot water

10. When a colloidal sol is allowed to stand for a couple of days,

(a) colloidal particles will settle at the bottom

(b) colloidal particles will start floating on the surface

(c) either of the above two can happen

(d) colloidal particles will keep on moving within the sol

11. Which one of the following will not scatter light?

(a) Rubber dissolved in benzene.

(b) Sodium chloride shaken with benzene.

(c) Egg albumin shaken with water.

(d) Sulphur dissolved in CS_2.

12. Which one of the following is not suitable in $KMnO_4$ titrations?

(a) Burette with glass stopper

(b) Burette with rubber pinch cock

(c) Glass pipette

(d) Glass titration flask

13. Which of the following is not an indicator?

(a) Phenolphthalein

(b) Methyl orange

(c) Potassium permanganate

(d) Potassium dichromate

14. Change in colour of an indicator during titration does not indicate

(a) completion of reaction

(b) end point in a titration

(c) equivalence point of a titration

(d) exothermic reaction

15. Which one of the following statement is not correct?

(a) NaCl crystals shaken with benzene form a colloidal sol.

(b) A dilute solution of soap is a true solution while concentrated solution forms a colloidal sol.

(c) Colloidal particles can pass through filter paper as well as animal membrane.

(d) Cellulose nitrate shaken with ethanol forms a lyophilic sol.

Response Index

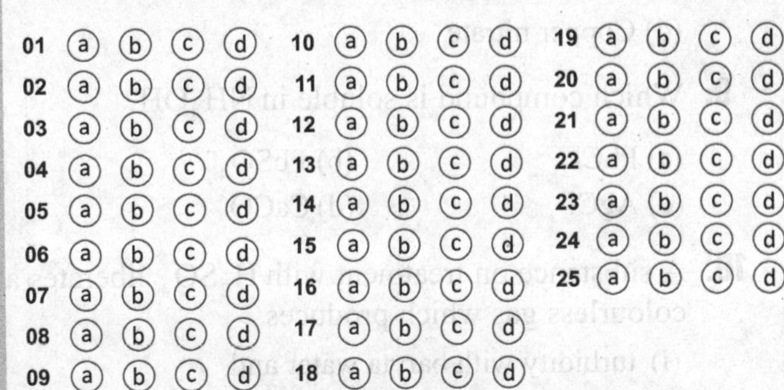

Performance Scanner

> 90% Excellent !	You have mastered these topics. The concepts of these topics are at your fingertips. Move on to the next test and maintain this momentum.
76-90% Very Good !	You have a good command over these topics. Revise these topics again after a few days and enhance your performance.
60-75% Good !	You have a wide scope to learn for these topics. Revise these topics again.
<60 Not Satisfactory!	You have a long way ahead of you to master these topics. Revise it thoroughly.

Test 2

Syllabus

The Chemistry Involved in the Preparation of Mohr's Salt, Potash Alum.
Chemical Principles Involved in the Qualitative Salt Analysis
Cations : Pb^{2+}, Cu^{2+}, Al^{3+}, Fe^{3+}, Zn^{2+}, Ni^{2+}, Ca^{2+}, Ba^{2+}, Mg^{2+}, NH_4^+
Anions : CO_3^{2-}, S^{2-}, SO_4^{2-}, NO_3^-, NO_2^-, Cl^-, Br^-, I^-
(Insoluble Salts Excluded)

For deeper insight **Scan the QR Code**

Important Instructions

- The test is of 30 minutes duration and contains 15 multiple choice questions (Four options with a single correct answer).
- Choose the correct option and fill the OMR given on the last page of test accordingly.
- At some instances, you may find more than 1 option may be correct. In such circumstances, you have to judge the most appropriate answer as per the conditions given in the question.

1. The cation that will not be precipitated by H_2S in the presence of dil. HCl is

(a) Pb^{2+} (b) Cu^{2+}
(c) Co^{2+} (d) As^{3+}

2. Given below are two statements, one is labelled as Assertion (A) and the other is labelled as Reason (R).

Assertion (A) NO_2^- and NO_3^- show brown ring test.

Reason (R) The brown ring test is shown due to formation of $[Fe(NO)(CN)_5]^{2+}$.

In the light of the above statements, choose the correct answer from the options given below.

(a) Both (A) and (R) are true and (R) is the correct explanation of (A).
(b) Both (A) and (R) are true but (R) is not the correct explanation of (A).
(c) (A) is true but (R) is false.
(d) (A) is false but (R) is true.

3. Nessler's reagent is used to detect

(a) CrO_4^{2-} (b) PO_4^{3-}
(c) MnO_4^- (d) NH_4^+

4. Which of the following gives a precipitate with $Pb(NO_3)_2$ but not with $Ba(NO_3)_2$?

(a) Sodium chloride
(b) Sodium acetate
(c) Sodium nitrate
(d) Sodium hydrogen phosphate

5. A blue coloured residue obtained in cobalt nitrate charcoal cavity test is due to

(a) Zn^{2+} (b) Mg^{2+} (c) Sn^{2+} (d) Al^{3+}

6. In the chromyl chloride test, the reagent used is

(a) K_2CrO_4 (b) CrO_3
(c) $K_2Cr_2O_7$ (d) $(NH_4)_2Cr_2O_7$

7. Which of the following will not produce a precipitate with $AgNO_3$ solution?

(a) F^- (b) Br^-
(c) CO_3^{-2} (d) PO_4^{-3}

8. Which of the following gives black precipitate when H_2S gas is passed through its solution?

(a) Acidic $AgNO_3$
(b) $Mg(NO_3)_2$
(c) Ammonical $BaCl_2$
(d) Copper nitrate

9. Which compound is soluble in NH_4OH?

(a) $PbCl_2$ (b) $PbSO_4$
(c) AgCl (d) $CaCO_3$

10. A substance on treatment with H_2SO_4 liberates a colourless gas which produces

(i) turbidity with baryta water and
(ii) turns acidified dichromate solution green

The reaction indicates the presence of

(a) CO_3^{2-} (b) S^{2-}
(c) SO_3^{2-} (d) NO_2^{2-}

11. Which reagent below would enable you to remove sulphate ions from a solutions containing both sulphate and chloride ions?
(a) Sodium hydroxide
(b) Barium hydroxide
(c) Barium sulphate
(d) Potassium hydroxide

12. A solution of a salt in dilute sulphuric acid imparts deep blue colour with starch iodine solution, it confirms the presence of which of the following ions ?
(a) NO_2^- (b) I^-
(c) NO_3^- (d) CH_3COO^-

13. H_2S will precipitate the sulphides of all the metals from the solutions of chlorides of Cu, Zn and Cd if
(a) the solution is aqueous
(b) the solution is acidic
(c) the solution is dilute acidic
(d) any of these solution is present

14. Consider the following species.

$Sr^{2+}, Ba^{2+}, Ca^{2+}, Cu^{2+}, Na^+, K^+, Bi^{3+}$

Number of metal ions characterised by flame test is ....
(a) 3 (b) 5
(c) 6 (d) 7

15. When concentrated H_2SO_4 is added to dry KNO_3 and heated, brown fumes evolve. These fumes are of
(a) SO_3 (b) SO_2
(c) NO_2 (d) NH_3

Response Index

01	a	b	c	d	10	a	b	c	d	19	a	b	c	d
02	a	b	c	d	11	a	b	c	d	20	a	b	c	d
03	a	b	c	d	12	a	b	c	d	21	a	b	c	d
04	a	b	c	d	13	a	b	c	d	22	a	b	c	d
05	a	b	c	d	14	a	b	c	d	23	a	b	c	d
06	a	b	c	d	15	a	b	c	d	24	a	b	c	d
07	a	b	c	d	16	a	b	c	d	25	a	b	c	d
08	a	b	c	d	17	a	b	c	d					
09	a	b	c	d	18	a	b	c	d					

Performance Scanner

> 90% Excellent !	You have mastered these topics. The concepts of these topics are at your fingertips. Move on to the next test and maintain this momentum.
76-90% Very Good !	You have a good command over these topics. Revise these topics again after a few days and enhance your performance.
60-75% Good !	You have a wide scope to learn for these topics. Revise these topics again.
<60 Not Satisfactory!	You have a long way ahead of you to master these topics. Revise it thoroughly.

Test 3

Syllabus

Detection of Extra Elements (Nitrogen, Sulphur, Halogens) in Organic Compounds, Detection of the Following Functional Groups, Hydroxyl (Alcoholic and Phenolic), Carbonyl (Aldehyde and Ketones), Carboxyl and Amino Groups in Organic Compounds.
Organic Compounds : Acetanilide, *p*-nitroacetanilide, Aniline Yellow, Iodoform.

For deeper insight **Scan the QR Code**

Important Instructions

- The test is of 30 minutes duration and contains 15 multiple choice questions (Four options with a single correct answer).
- Choose the correct option and fill the OMR given on the last page of test accordingly.
- At some instances, you may find more than 1 option may be correct. In such circumstances, you have to judge the most appropriate answer as per the conditions given in the question.

1. Sulphanilic acid is fused with sodium metal. The Lassaigne extract may contain
(a) only NaCN
(b) only Na_2S
(c) both NaCN and Na_2S
(d) NaCN, NaCNS and Na_2S

2. Mixture of phenol and benzoic acid can be separated by
(a) NaOH
(b) $NaNH_2$
(c) CH_3OH
(d) $NaHCO_3$

3. A mixture of acetophenone ($C_6H_5—COCH_3$) and benzaldehyde can be separated by
(a) *aq.* NaOH
(b) *aq.* HCl
(c) *aq.* $NaHSO_3$
(d) *aq.* $NaHCO_3$

4. Which of the following statement is not correct regarding preparation of *p*-nitroacetanilide?
(a) Nitration of acetanilide gives a mixture of *o*- and *p*-nitroacetanilide in which the *p*-isomer predominates.
(b) Nitration of acetanilide is carried out with a mixture of conc. HNO_3 + conc. H_2SO_4 to form *p*-nitroacetanilide.
(c) During crystallisation of the crude product, *p*-nitroacetanilide crystallises out leaving *o*-nitroacetanilide in the mother liquor.
(d) *o*-nitroacetanilide is colourless but *p*-nitroacetanilide is yellow coloured.

5. The functional groups present in *m*-nitroaniline are tested by
(a) azo dye test only
(b) Mulliken's test only
(c) both azo dye test and Mulliken's test
(d) both azo dye test and carbylamine test

6. In organic analysis, Brady's reagent is used for the detection of which of the following functional groups?
(a) Alcohol
(b) Carboxylic acid
(c) Aldehyde/Ketones
(d) Secondary amines

7. The best method for separation of naphthalene and benzoic acid from their mixture is
(a) sublimation
(b) chromatography
(c) crystallisation
(d) distillation

8. The Lassaigne's extract is boiled with dil. HNO_3 before testing for halogens because
(a) silver halides are soluble in HNO_3
(b) Na_2S and NaCN are decomposed by HNO_3
(c) Ag_2S is soluble in HNO_3
(d) AgCN is soluble in HNO_3

9. Which of the following process is suitable for the purification of aniline?
(a) Simple distillation
(b) Fractional distillation
(c) Fractional crystallisation
(d) Steam distillation

10. Given below are two statements, one labelled as Assertion (A) and the other is labelled as Reason (R).

Assertion (A) Potassium can be used in Lassaigne test.

Reason (R) Potassium reacts vigorously.

In the light of the above statements, choose the correct answer from the options given below.

(a) Both (A) and (R) are true and (R) is the correct explanation of (A).

(b) Both (A) and (R) are true but (R) is not the correct explanation of (A).

(c) (A) is true but (R) is false.

(d) (A) is false but (R) is true.

11. Which of the following compounds reacts with ferric ions to produce blood red colouration in the Lassaigne's test for detection of extra element in an organic compound?

(a) NaCN (b) Na_2S

(c) NaCNS (d) NaCNO

12. Positive Beilstein test for halogens shows that

(a) a halogen is absent

(b) a halogen is definitely present

(c) a halogen may be present

(d) all the statements are incorrect

13. Which of the following compound does not react with Lucas reagent at room temperature?

(a) 4,4-dimethylpentan-2-ol

(b) 2-methyl-2-propanol

(c) 2-butanol

(d) 4-methyl-1-pentanol

14. Given below are two statements, one is labelled as Assertion (A) and the other is labelled as Reason (R).

Assertion (A) During test for nitrogen with Lassaigne extract on adding $FeCl_3$ solution, sometimes a red precipitate is obtained.

Reason (R) Sulphur is also present.

In the light of the above statements, choose the correct answer from the options given below.

(a) Both (A) and (R) are true and (R) is the correct explanation of (A).

(b) Both (A) and (R) are true but (R) is not the correct explanation of (A).

(c) (A) is true but (R) is false.

(d) (A) is false but (R) is true.

15. Mixture of benzene and aniline can be separated by

(a) sublimation (b) filtration

(c) distillation (d) crystallisation

Response Index

01 ⓐ ⓑ ⓒ ⓓ	10 ⓐ ⓑ ⓒ ⓓ	19 ⓐ ⓑ ⓒ ⓓ
02 ⓐ ⓑ ⓒ ⓓ	11 ⓐ ⓑ ⓒ ⓓ	20 ⓐ ⓑ ⓒ ⓓ
03 ⓐ ⓑ ⓒ ⓓ	12 ⓐ ⓑ ⓒ ⓓ	21 ⓐ ⓑ ⓒ ⓓ
04 ⓐ ⓑ ⓒ ⓓ	13 ⓐ ⓑ ⓒ ⓓ	22 ⓐ ⓑ ⓒ ⓓ
05 ⓐ ⓑ ⓒ ⓓ	14 ⓐ ⓑ ⓒ ⓓ	23 ⓐ ⓑ ⓒ ⓓ
06 ⓐ ⓑ ⓒ ⓓ	15 ⓐ ⓑ ⓒ ⓓ	24 ⓐ ⓑ ⓒ ⓓ
07 ⓐ ⓑ ⓒ ⓓ	16 ⓐ ⓑ ⓒ ⓓ	25 ⓐ ⓑ ⓒ ⓓ
08 ⓐ ⓑ ⓒ ⓓ	17 ⓐ ⓑ ⓒ ⓓ	
09 ⓐ ⓑ ⓒ ⓓ	18 ⓐ ⓑ ⓒ ⓓ	

Performance Scanner

> 90% Excellent !	You have mastered these topics. The concepts of these topics are at your fingertips. Move on to the chapter test and maintain this momentum.
76-90% Very Good !	You have a good command over these topics. Revise these topics again after a few days and enhance your performance.
60-75% Good !	You have a wide scope to learn for these topics. Revise these topics again.
<60 Not Satisfactory!	You have a long way ahead of you to master these topics. Revise it thoroughly.

Chapter Break Thru

Syllabus

- The Chemistry Involved in the Titrimetric Exercises Acids, Bases and the Use of Indicators Oxalic-Acid *vs* $KMnO_4$, Mohr's Salt *vs* $KMnO_4$. Chemical Principles Involved in the Following Experiments.
- Enthalpy of Solution of $CuSO_4$.
- Enthalpy of Neutralisation of Strong Acid and Strong Base.
- Preparation of Lyophilic and Lyophobic Sols.
- Kinetic Study of the Reaction of Iodide Ions with Hydrogen Peroxide at Room Temperature.
- The Chemistry Involved in the Preparation of Mohr's Salt, Potash Alum.
- Chemical Principles involved in the Qualitative Salt Analysis

Cations : Pb^{2+}, Cu^{2+}, Al^{3+}, Fe^{3+}, Zn^{2+}, Ni^{2+}, Ca^{2+}, Ba^{2+}, Mg^{2+}, NH_4^+.

Anions : CO_3^{2-}, S^{2-}, SO_4^{2-}, NO_3^-, NO_2^-, Cl^-, Br^-, I^- (Insoluble Salts Excluded)

Detection of Extra Elements (Nitrogen, Sulphur, Halogens) in Organic Compounds; Detection of the Following Functional Groups, Hydroxyl (Alcoholic and Phenolic), Carbonyl (Aldehyde and Ketones) Carboxyl and Amino Groups in Organic Compounds.

Organic Compounds : Acetanilide, *p*-nitroacetanilide, Aniline Yellow, Iodoform.

Important Instructions

- The test is of 1 hour duration and contains 30 multiple choice questions (Four options with a single correct answer).
- Choose the correct option and fill the OMR given on the last page of test accordingly.
- At some instances, you may find more than 1 option may be correct. In such circumstances, you have to judge the most appropriate answer as per the conditions given in the question.

1. Select the appropriate oxidising agent used in the test for phosphorus.

(a) H_2O_2
(b) KNO_3
(c) Na_2O_2
(d) HNO_3

2. An alkali is titrated against an acid with methyl orange as an indicator. Which of the following is a correct combination?

	Base	Acid	End Point
(a)	Weak	Strong	Colourless to pink
(b)	Strong	Strong	Pinkish red to yellow
(c)	Weak	Strong	Yellow to pinkish red
(d)	Strong	Strong	Pink to colourless

3. Reagent 1-naphthylamine and sulphanilic acid in acetic acid is used for the detection of

(a) N_2O (b) NO_2^-
(c) NO_3^- (d) NO

4. An aqueous solution containing ions such Al^{3+}, Zn^{2+}, Ca^{2+}, Fe^{3+}, Ni^{2+}, Ba^{2+} and Cu^{2+} was treated with conc. HCl followed by H_2S. The total number of cations precipitated during this reaction is ....

(a) 2 (b) 1
(c) 3 (d) 4

5. Which one of the following when dissolved in water gives coloured solution in nitrogen atmosphere?

(a) Cu_2Cl_2 (b) $ZnCl_2$
(c) $CuCl_2$ (d) AgCl

6. Absolute alcohol is prepared from rectified spirit by

(a) fractional distillation
(b) Kolbe's method
(c) azeotropic distillation
(d) vacuum distillation

7. An organic compound X burns with sooty flame. It shows negative test towards Tollen's reagent test and positive for Brady's reagent test. The compound 'X' is

(a) acetophenone (b) acetone
(c) salicylic acid (d) benzaldehyde

8. Match List-I with List-I

List-I (Metal ion)	List-II (Group in qualitative analysis)
A. Al^{3+}	I. Group-V
B. Ca^{2+}	II. Group-IV
C. Ni^{2+}	III. Group-II
D. Cu^{2+}	IV. Group-III

Choose the correct answer from the options given below.

(a) A-III, B-IV, C-II, D-I
(b) A-II, B-IV, C-I, D-III
(c) A-IV, B-III, C-II, D-I
(d) A-IV, B-I, C-II, D-III

9. Sodium nitroprusside, when added to an alkaline solution of sulphide ions, produces purple colour ion due to the formation of

(a) $Na[Fe(H_2O)_5NOS]$
(b) $Na_2[Fe(H_2O)_5NOS]$
(c) $Na_3[Fe(CN)_5NOS]$
(d) $Na_4[Fe(CN)_5NOS]$

10. Small amount of zinc dust is added to reaction mixture during preparation of acetanilide because

(a) zinc catalyses the reaction
(b) zinc helps in crystallisation
(c) zinc protects aniline from oxidation
(d) zinc hydrolysis acetic anhydride

11. A solution of *m*-chloroaniline, *m*-chlorophenol and *m*-chlorobenzoic acid in ethyl acetate was extracted initially with a saturated solution of $NaHCO_3$ to give fraction *A*. The left over organic phase was extracted with dilute NaOH solution to give fraction *B*. The final organic layer was labelled as fraction *C*.

Fraction *A, B* and *C* contain respectively

(a) *m*-chlorobenzoic acid, *m*-chloroaniline and *m*-chlorophenol
(b) *m*-chlorobenzoic acid, *m*-chlorophenol and *m*-chloroaniline
(c) *m*-chlorophenol, *m*-chlorobenzoic acid and *m*-chloroaniline
(d) *m*-chloroaniline, *m*-chlorobenzoic acid and *m*-chlorophenol

12. Given below are two statements.

Statement I Essential oils are purified by steam distillation.

Statement II Essential oils are insoluble in water and are non-volatile in steam.

In the light of the above statements, choose the correct answer from the options given below.

(a) Both Statement I and Statement II are incorrect.
(b) Statement I is correct but Statement II is incorrect.
(c) Statement I is incorrect but Statement II is correct.
(d) Both Statement I and Statement II are correct.

13. Which reagent is used to remove SO_4^{2-} and Cl^- ?

(a) $BaSO_4$
(b) NaOH
(c) $Pb(NO_3)_2$
(d) KOH

14. In steam distillation, the sum of the vapour pressure of the volatile compound and that of water is

(a) equal to atmospheric pressure
(b) less than atmospheric pressure
(c) more than atmospheric pressure
(d) exactly half of the atmospheric pressure

15. A salt gives bright red colour to the flame. This colour indicates the presence of

(a) Ba^{2+}
(b) Sr^{2+}
(c) Ca^{2+}
(d) Cr^{3+}

16. When acetic acid and $K_4[Fe(CN)_6]$ are added to a copper salt, a chocolate precipitate is obtained of the compound.
(a) Copper cyanide
(b) Copper ferrocyanide
(c) Basic copper sulphate
(d) Basic copper cyanide

17. Which of the following does not give a ppt. with silver nitrate solution?
(a) Ethyl bromide
(b) Sodium bromide
(c) Calcium chloride
(d) Sodium chloride

18. Given below are two statements.
Statement I A mixture of salicylaldehyde and *p*-hydroxybenzaldehyde can be separated by fractional distillation.
Statement II Salicylaldehyde is steam volatile but *p*-hydroxybenzaldehyde is not.
In the light of the above statements, choose the correct answer from the options given below.
(a) Both Statement I and Statement II are incorrect.
(b) Statement I is correct but Statement II is incorrect.
(c) Statement I is incorrect but Statement II is correct.
(d) Both Statement I and Statement II are correct.

19. In the flame test of a mixture of salts, a green flame with blue centre was observed. Which one of the following cations may be present?
(a) Cu^{2+} (b) Sr^{2+} (c) Ba^{2+} (d) Ca^{2+}

20. Na_2CO_3 cannot be used to identify
(a) CO_3^{2-} (b) SO_3^{2-} (c) S^{2-} (d) SO_4^{2-}

21. The compound insoluble in acetic acid is
(a) calcium oxide
(b) calcium carbonate
(c) calcium oxalate
(d) calcium hydroxide

22. Reagent used in the qualitative analysis of group IV is
(a) HCl
(b) H_2S (alkaline)
(c) $(NH_4)_2S$
(d) HBr

23. On adding excess of ammonium hydroxide to a copper sulphate solution,
(a) blue precipitate of copper hydroxide is obtained
(b) black precipitate of copper oxide is obtained
(c) a deep blue solution is obtained
(d) no change is observed

24. Which of the following substance are insoluble in concentrated HNO_3?
(a) CdS (b) CuS
(c) PbS (d) $BaSO_4$

25. Which of the following cannot give iodometric titrations?
(a) Fe^{3+} (b) Cu^{2+}
(c) Pb^{2+} (d) Ag^+

26. When H_2S gas is passed through the HCl containing aqueous solutions of $CuCl_2$, $HgCl_2$, $BiCl_3$ and $CoCl_2$, which does not precipitate out?
(a) CuS (b) HgS
(c) Bi_2S_3 (d) CoS

27. A reagent which gives brilliant red precipitate with nickel ions in basic medium is
(a) sodium nitroprusside
(b) neutral $FeCl_3$
(c) *meta*-dinitrobenzene
(d) dimethyl glyoxime

28. The oxidation number of iron in the compound formed during brown ring test for NO_3^- ion is
(a) 2 (b) 1
(c) 5 (d) 3

29. When H_2S is passed through an ammoniacal salt solution *X*, a white precipitate is obtained. *X* can be
(a) cobalt salt (b) nickel salt
(c) manganese salt (d) zinc salt

30. Phenolic group can be identified by a positive
(a) Phthalein dye test
(b) Lucas test
(c) Tollen's test
(d) Carbylamine test

Response Index

01	ⓐ ⓑ ⓒ ⓓ	14	ⓐ ⓑ ⓒ ⓓ	27	ⓐ ⓑ ⓒ ⓓ	40	ⓐ ⓑ ⓒ ⓓ
02	ⓐ ⓑ ⓒ ⓓ	15	ⓐ ⓑ ⓒ ⓓ	28	ⓐ ⓑ ⓒ ⓓ	41	ⓐ ⓑ ⓒ ⓓ
03	ⓐ ⓑ ⓒ ⓓ	16	ⓐ ⓑ ⓒ ⓓ	29	ⓐ ⓑ ⓒ ⓓ	42	ⓐ ⓑ ⓒ ⓓ
04	ⓐ ⓑ ⓒ ⓓ	17	ⓐ ⓑ ⓒ ⓓ	30	ⓐ ⓑ ⓒ ⓓ	43	ⓐ ⓑ ⓒ ⓓ
05	ⓐ ⓑ ⓒ ⓓ	18	ⓐ ⓑ ⓒ ⓓ	31	ⓐ ⓑ ⓒ ⓓ	44	ⓐ ⓑ ⓒ ⓓ
06	ⓐ ⓑ ⓒ ⓓ	19	ⓐ ⓑ ⓒ ⓓ	32	ⓐ ⓑ ⓒ ⓓ	45	ⓐ ⓑ ⓒ ⓓ
07	ⓐ ⓑ ⓒ ⓓ	20	ⓐ ⓑ ⓒ ⓓ	33	ⓐ ⓑ ⓒ ⓓ	46	ⓐ ⓑ ⓒ ⓓ
08	ⓐ ⓑ ⓒ ⓓ	21	ⓐ ⓑ ⓒ ⓓ	34	ⓐ ⓑ ⓒ ⓓ	47	ⓐ ⓑ ⓒ ⓓ
09	ⓐ ⓑ ⓒ ⓓ	22	ⓐ ⓑ ⓒ ⓓ	35	ⓐ ⓑ ⓒ ⓓ	48	ⓐ ⓑ ⓒ ⓓ
10	ⓐ ⓑ ⓒ ⓓ	23	ⓐ ⓑ ⓒ ⓓ	36	ⓐ ⓑ ⓒ ⓓ	49	ⓐ ⓑ ⓒ ⓓ
11	ⓐ ⓑ ⓒ ⓓ	24	ⓐ ⓑ ⓒ ⓓ	37	ⓐ ⓑ ⓒ ⓓ	50	ⓐ ⓑ ⓒ ⓓ
12	ⓐ ⓑ ⓒ ⓓ	25	ⓐ ⓑ ⓒ ⓓ	38	ⓐ ⓑ ⓒ ⓓ		
13	ⓐ ⓑ ⓒ ⓓ	26	ⓐ ⓑ ⓒ ⓓ	39	ⓐ ⓑ ⓒ ⓓ		

Performance Scanner

> 90% Excellent !	You have mastered this chapter. The concepts of this chapter are at your fingertips. Move on to the next chapter and maintain this momentum.
76-90% Very Good !	You have a good command over this chapter. Revise the chapter again after a few days and enhance your performance.
60-75% Good !	You have a wide scope to learn for this chapter. Revise this chapter again.
<60 Not Satisfactory!	You have a long way ahead of you to master this chapter. Revise it thoroughly.

Scan for Online **Chapter Test**

Scan for Online **Unit Test**

Space for Rough Work

Space for Rough Work

Space for Rough Work

Space for Rough Work

Space for Rough Work

Test Booklet No. 3947263

Test Booklet Code SPT1

MEDACE
NEET (UG)
SELF ASSESSMENT KIT

Syllabus Part Thru 1

(Half Syllabus Test)

Chapters Covered

- Solutions
- Electrochemistry
- Chemical Kinetics
- *p*-Block Elements-II
- *d*- and *f*-block Elements
- Coordination Compounds

Important Instructions

- The test is of 45 minutes duration and the Test Booklet contains 45 multiple choice questions (four options with a single correct answer) from Chemistry.
- Candidates are advised to read all questions before they start attempting the question paper.
- Each questions carries 4 marks. For each correct response, the candidate will get 4 marks. For each incorrect response, one mark will be deducted from the total scores.
- In the event of candidate marking more than one option then one mark will be deducted. The maximum marks are 180.
- Use **Blue/Black Point Pen** only for writing particular on this page/marking response on Answer Sheet.

Name of the Candidate (In Capitals) ____________________

Candidate's Signature ____________________

Invigilator's Signature ____________________

Facsimile signature stamp of center superintendent ____________________

Do not open this Booklet until you start attempting the Test

Chemistry (Q. No. 1-45)

1. If the osmotic pressure of cane sugar solution is 4.32 atm at 37°C then, what is the concentration (in mol L^{-1}) of the solution? ($R = 0.0821$ L atm mol^{-1} K^{-1})

(a) 0.180 (b) 0.204
(c) 0.011 (d) 0.170

2. Match List-I with List-II.

List-I (Coordination compounds)		List-II (Central metal atom)	
A.	Chlorophyll	I.	Cobalt
B.	Haemoglobin	II.	Rhodium
C.	Wilkinson catalyst	III.	Iron
D.	Vitamin B_{12}	IV.	Magnesium

Choose the correct answer from the options given below.

(a) A-IV, B-III, C-II, D-I
(b) A-III, B-IV, C-I, D-II
(c) A-III, B-I, C-IV, D-II
(d) A-IV, B-II, C-III, D-I

3. Which of the following compound is least paramagnetic?

(a) $[Zn(H_2O)_6]^{2+}$ (b) $[Cr(H_2O)_6]^{3+}$
(c) $[Fe(H_2O)_6]^{2+}$ (d) $[Cu(H_2O)_6]^{2+}$

4. Consider the statements given below.

Statement I Geometry of any complex depends upon nature of ligands attached.

Statement II $[Ni(CO)_4]$ has square planar geometry while $[Ni(CN)_4]^{2-}$ has tetrahedral geometry.

In the light of the above statements, choose the most appropriate answer from the options given below

(a) Both Statement I and Statement II are incorrect.
(b) Statement I is correct but Statement II is incorrect.
(c) Statement I is incorrect but Statement II is correct.
(d) Both Statement I and Statement II are correct.

5. $KMnO_4$ can be prepared from K_2MnO_4 as per the reaction,

$$3MnO_4^{2-} + 2H_2O \longrightarrow 2MnO_4^- + MnO_2 + 4OH^-$$

The reaction can go to completion by removing OH^- ions by adding

(a) HCl (b) KOH
(c) CO_2 (d) SO_2

6. For an elementary reaction, $2P + Q \longrightarrow P_2Q$. The volume of vessel is quickly reduced to half of its original volume, then rate of reaction will

(a) remains unchanged
(b) decrease four times
(c) increase eight times
(d) decrease eight times

7. Consider the statements given below.

Statement I The presence of a catalyst increases the speed of the forward and backward reaction to the same extent.

Statement II Activation energy for both forward and backward reactions is lowered to different extent.

In the light of the above statements, choose the most appropriate answer from the options given below

(a) Both Statement I and Statement II are incorrect.
(b) Statement I is correct but Statement II is incorrect.
(c) Statement I is incorrect but Statement II is correct.
(d) Both Statement I and Statement II are correct.

8 Select the correct statements from the following.

I. The acidic character increases from H_2O to H_2Te.
II. The thermal stability of hydrides decrease from H_2O to H_2Po.
III. Ozone and sulphur dioxide are gases while selenium dioxide is solid.
IV. Among tetrafluorides, SF_4 is a gas, SeF_4 is a liquid and TeF_4 is a solid.
V. The dissociation constant of hydrides of group 16 elements, decreases down the group.

Choose the correct answer from the options given below.

(a) I, II, III and IV (b) I, IV and V

(c) I, II and III (d) III, IV and V

9. Given below are two statements, one is labelled as Assertion (A) and other is labelled as Reason (R).

Assertion (A) Fe^{2+} ion is paramagnetic in nature.

Reason (R) Fe^{2+} contains three unpaired electrons.

In the light of the above statements, choose the correct answer from the options given below.

(a) Both (A) and (R) are true and (R) is the correct explanation of (A).

(b) Both (A) and (R) are true but (R) is not the correct explanation of (A).

(c) (A) is true but (R) is false.

(d) (A) is false but (R) is true.

10. The elevation in the boiling point of aqueous urea solution is 0.208 K. What is its ΔT_f (in K) value? (For water $K_b = 0.52$ K kg mol^{-1}, $K_f = 1.86$ K kg mol^{-1})

(a) 0.0186 K (b) 0.186 K

(c) 0.744 K (d) 0.0272 K

11. The oxide of *p*-block elements that cannot act as a reducing agent is

(a) SO_2 (b) NO_2

(c) CO_2 (d) ClO_2

12. The time required (in hours) to reduce 3 moles of Fe^{3+} ions to Fe^{2+} ions with 6 amperes of current is ($1 F = 96500 C mol^{-1}$)

(a) 60.4 (b) 40.2

(c) 13.40 (d) 19.2

13. Consider the complexes given below.

$[Mn(CN)_6]^{3-}$, $[Fe(CN)_6]^{3-}$, $[Co(C_2O_4)_3]^{3-}$, $[MnCl_4]^{3-}$, $[Fe(CN)_6]^{4-}$

The total number of inner orbital complexes with diamagnetic nature is

(a) 2 (b) 3 (c) 4 (d) 5

14. The number of unpaired electrons present in the complexes, $[Fe(CN)_6]^{4-}$, $[Fe(H_2O)_6]^{2+}$ and $[Co(H_2O)_6]^{2+}$ respectively is

(a) 3, 4, 1 (b) 0, 4, 3

(c) 0, 2, 1 (d) 3, 1, 2

15. The reaction $A \rightarrow$ products is a first order reaction. In 40 minutes, the concentration of A changes from 1.0 M to 0.25 M. What is the initial rate of reaction when $[A] = 0.4$ M ? ($\log 4 = 2 \times 03010$)

(a) 1.73×10^{-3} mol L^{-1} min^{-1}

(b) 4213×10^{-4} mol L^{-1} min^{-1}

(c) 2.732×10^{-4} mol L^{-1} min^{-1}

(d) 1.386×10^{-2} mol L^{-1} min^{-1}

16. Select the correct statement regarding minimum boiling azeotrope.

(a) A—B molecular interactions are stronger than A—A or B—B interactions.

(b) The total vapour pressure of the mixture is greater than that corresponding to an ideal solution.

(c) There is a slight decrease in volume and pressure when the two components are mixed.

(d) ΔH_{mix} of solution will have a negative value.

17. The rate constant, k for a first order reaction $C_2H_5I(g) \longrightarrow C_2H_4(g) + HI(g)$ is $x\ s^{-1}$ at 800 K and $4x\ s^{-1}$ at 900 K. The energy of activation of the reaction (in kJ mol^{-1}) is ($\log 4 = 0.6$, $R = 8.3\ J K^{-1} mol^{-1}$)

(a) 48.16 (b) 82.57 (c) 38.16 (d) 28.16

18. A solution is formed by the combination of two liquids such as dichloromethane and chloroform. The partial pressures of dichloromethane and chloroform in solution are 571 and 124.8 mm Hg respectively. What is the total pressure of the solution?

(a) 448.3 mm Hg (b) 695.8 mm Hg

(c) 795.8 mm Hg (d) 337.9 mm Hg

19. Consider the statements given below.

Statement I Electronegativity of group 16 element increases down the group from oxygen to tellurium.

Statement II Hydrides of group 16 element show volatility in the order

$$H_2O > H_2S > H_2Se > H_2Te$$

In the light of the above statements, choose the most appropriate answer from the options given below

(a) Both Statement I and Statement II are incorrect.

(b) Statement I is correct but Statement II is incorrect.

(c) Statement I is incorrect but Statement II is correct.

(d) Both Statement I and Statement II are correct.

20. In the following reaction $A \longrightarrow B + C$, rate constant is 0.001 Ms^{-1}. If we start with 1 M of A then concentration of A and B after 10 minutes are respectively.

(a) 0.5 M, 0.8 M (b) 0.6 M, 0.4 M
(c) 0.4 M, 0.6 M (d) 0.8 M, 0.5 M

21. Given below are two statements, one is labelled as Assertion (A) and other is labelled as Reason (R).

Assertion (A) HBr is a weaker acid than HI.
Reason (R) Bond dissociation energy of HI is smaller than that of HBr.

In the light of above statements, choose the correct answer from the options given below.

(a) Both (A) and (R) are true and (R) is the correct explanation of (A).
(b) Both (A) and (R) are true but (R) is not the correct explanation of (A).
(c) (A) is true but (R) is false.
(d) (A) is false but (R) is true.

22. If a solution of urea in water has a boiling point of 100.128°C. Then what will be the freezing point of the same solution. If molal constant of water K_f and K_b are 1.86°C kg mol^{-1} and 0.512°C kg mol^{-1} respectively.

(a) 0.465°C (b) 3.645°C
(c) –3.645°C (d) –0.465°C

23. If the rate constant for a first order reaction is k, then what will be the time required for completion of 40% of the reaction? [Use $\log 6 = 0.8$]

(a) $\frac{4.6}{k}$ (b) $\frac{0.46}{k}$ (c) $\frac{2.3}{k}$ (d) $\frac{0.8}{k}$

24. Choose the incorrect order from the following for group 17 elements.

(a) $I_2 > Br_2 > Cl_2 > F_2$ (Melting point)
(b) $Cl_2 > Br_2 > F_2 > I_2$ (Bond dissociation enthalpy)
(c) HI > HBr > HCl > HI (Bond length)
(d) HF > HCl > HBr > HI (Negative pK_a value)

25. Which of the following is the correct order of the acid strengths of HF, HCl, HBr and HI?

(a) HF < HCl > HBr > HI
(b) HF < HCl < HBr < HI
(c) HF < HCl > HBr > HI
(d) HF > HCl > HBr > HI

26. The product of the reaction of XeF_4 with water is

(a) XeO_3 (b) XeO_4
(c) $XeOF_4$ (d) $XeOF_2$

27. Select the incorrect statement from the following.

(a) For zero order kinetics, $t_{1/2}$ is independent of initial concentration.
(b) For zero order kinetics, equal amount of reactant will decompose in equal amount of time.
(c) For 1st order kinetics, equal percentage of reactant will decompose in equal time.
(d) Rate law expression of reaction may contain concentration of reactants and even concentration of catalyst.

28. Consider the species given below.

(I) Ti^{3+} (II) Cr^{2+} (III) Fe^{2+} (IV) Cu^{2+} (V) Zn^{2+}

The species showing 4.90 BM is

(a) I and IV (b) II and III
(c) IV and V (d) III and IV

29. 2 g of a non-electrolyte solute (Molar mass is 500 g mol^{-1}) was dissolved in 20.4 g of xylene. If the freezing point depression constant K_f of xylene is 8.1 K kg mol^{-1}. Then, the depression in freezing point of xylene is

(a) 57.3 K (b) 1.59 K
(c) 2.30 K (d) 0.002 K

30. Select the incorrect statement from the following.

(a) If an external opposite potential is applied in galvanic cell, and increased slowly, the reaction will stop immediately.
(b) Daniell cell is an example of galvanic cell.
(c) The reduction half reaction of daniel cell is

$$Cu^{2+} + 2e^- \longrightarrow Cu(s)$$

(d) The oxidation half reaction of daniel cell is

$$Zn(s) \longrightarrow Zn^{2+} + 2e^-$$

31. Given below are two statements, one is labelled as Assertion (A) and other is labelled as Reason (R).

Assertion (A) Reverse osmosis is used in the desalination of sea water.

Reason (R) When pressure is applied more than osmotic pressure, pure water is squeezed out of the sea water through the membrane.

In the light of above statements, choose the correct answer from the options given below.

(a) Both (A) and (R) are true and (R) is the correct explanation of (A).

(b) Both (A) and (R) are true but (R) is not the correct explanation of (A).
(c) (A) is true but (R) is false.
(d) (A) is false but (R) is true.

32. Which of the following compound cannot be oxidised by O_3?

(a) $KMnO_4$ (b) $FeSO_4$
(c) K_2MnO_4 (d) KI

33. Match List-I with List-II.

List-I (Element)		List-II (Electronic configuration of Ln^{2+})	
A.	Pr	I.	$4f^5$
B.	Eu	II.	$4f^{11}$
C.	Pm	III.	$4f^3$
D.	Ho	IV.	$4f^7$

Choose the correct answer from the options given below.
(a) A-IV, B-III, C-I, D-II
(b) A-IV, B-I, C-III, D-II
(c) A-III, B-I, C-IV, D-II
(d) A-III, B-IV, C-I, D-II

34. A gas X is dissolved in water at 4 bar pressure, its mole fraction in the solution is 0.04. Find the mole fraction of water in the solution when the pressure of the gas is tripled at the same temperature.

(a) 0.12 (b) 0.36
(c) 0.96 (d) 0.04

35. When a current of 20 A is passed through molten $AlCl_3$ for 3.216 minutes. The mass of Al [Atomic mass of Al = 27 g]

(a) 0.36 g (b) 0.81 g
(c) 0.18 g (d) 0.27 g

36. A 50% solution of cane-sugar (molar mass = 342 g mol^{-1}) is isotonic with 10% solution of a substance A. Find the molecular weight of A.

(a) 0.0324 g/mol
(b) 68.4 g/mol
(c) 32.2 g/mol
(d) 0.0684 g/mol

37. Given below are two statements, one is labelled as Assertion (A) and other is labelled as Reason (R).

Assertion (A) Equivalent conductance of all electrolytes decreases with increasing concentration.

Reason (R) Lesser number of ions are available per gram equivalent at higher concentration.

In the light of above statements, choose the correct answer from the options given below.

(a) Both (A) and (R) are true and (R) is the correct explanation of (A).
(b) Both (A) and (R) are true but (R) is not the correct explanation of (A).
(c) (A) is true but (R) is false.
(d) (A) is false but (R) is true.

38. Cadmium amalgam is prepared by electrolysis of a solution of $CdCl_2$ using a mercury cathode. How long should a current of 8A be passed in order to prepare 10% by wt. Cd in Cd—Hg amalgam on cathode of 4.5 g Hg? (Atomic wt. Cd = 112).

(a) 200 sec (b) 107.7 sec
(c) 215.5 sec (d) 150.3 sec

39. Match List-I with List- II.

List-I	List-II
A. $6XeF_4 + 12H_2O \longrightarrow$	I. $XeO_2F_2 + 4HF$
B. $XeF_6 + 3H_2O \longrightarrow$	II. $XeOF_4 + 2HF$
C. $XeF_6 + H_2O \longrightarrow$	III. $XeO_3 + 6HF$
D. $XeF_6 + 2H_2O \longrightarrow$	IV. $4Xe + 2XeO_3 + 24HF + 3O_2$

Choose the correct answer from the options given below.
(a) A-III, B-IV, C-I, D-II
(b) A-IV, B-III, C-II, D-I
(c) A-II, B-I, C-IV, D-III
(d) A-III, B-I, C-IV, D-II

40. Resistance of a conductivity cell filled with 0.2 mol L^{-1} NaCl is 200 ohm. If the resistance of the same cell when filled with 0.04 mol L^{-1} NaCl solution is 516 ohm, the conductivity of 0.04 mol L^{-1} NaCl solution is (conductivity of 0.2 mol L^{-1} NaCl is 2.58 S m^{-1})

(a) 1.0 S m^{-1} (b) 0.2 S m^{-1}
(c) 2.0 S m^{-1} (d) 0.5 S m^{-1}

41. Cuprous ion is colourless while cupric ion is coloured because

(a) both have half-filled *p* and *d*-orbitals
(b) cuprous ion has incomplete *d*-orbital and cupric ion has a complete *d*-orbital
(c) both have unpaired electrons in the *d*-orbitals
(d) cuprous ion has a completely filled *d*-orbital and cupric ion has an incompletely filled *d*-orbital

42. Which of the following is incorrect order with respect to the property mentioned against it?

(a) MO, M_2O_3, MO_2, M_2O_5 (Decreasing basic nature)
(b) Sc, V, Cr, Mn (Increasing number of oxidation states)
(c) d^5, d^4, d^3, d^1 (Increasing magnetic moment)
(d) Fe^{2+}, Mn^{2+}, Co^{2+}, Cr^{2+} (Decreasing stability)

43. Which of the following statements is not true?

(a) On passing H_2S through acidified $K_2Cr_2O_7$ solution, a milky colour is observed.
(b) $Na_2Cr_2O_7$ is preferred over $K_2Cr_2O_7$ in volumetric analysis.
(c) $K_2Cr_2O_7$ solution in acidic medium is orange.
(d) $K_2Cr_2O_7$ solution becomes yellow on increasing the pH beyond 7.

44. The pair of lanthanoids with highest third ionisation energy is

(a) Sm, Yb (b) Eu, Yb
(c) Dy, Yb (d) Eu, Gd

45. Consider the statements given below.

Statement I If the standard electrode potential of an electrode is greater than zero then its reduced form is more stable as compared to hydrogen gas.

Statement II Fluorine gas has highest tendency to get reduced to fluoride ions.

In the light of the above statements, choose the most appropriate answer from the options given below

(a) Both Statement I and Statement II are incorrect.
(b) Statement I is correct but Statement II is incorrect.
(c) Statement I is incorrect but Statement II is correct.
(d) Both Statement I and Statement II are correct.

Response Index

01 ⓐ ⓑ ⓒ ⓓ	14 ⓐ ⓑ ⓒ ⓓ	27 ⓐ ⓑ ⓒ ⓓ	40 ⓐ ⓑ ⓒ ⓓ
02 ⓐ ⓑ ⓒ ⓓ	15 ⓐ ⓑ ⓒ ⓓ	28 ⓐ ⓑ ⓒ ⓓ	41 ⓐ ⓑ ⓒ ⓓ
03 ⓐ ⓑ ⓒ ⓓ	16 ⓐ ⓑ ⓒ ⓓ	29 ⓐ ⓑ ⓒ ⓓ	42 ⓐ ⓑ ⓒ ⓓ
04 ⓐ ⓑ ⓒ ⓓ	17 ⓐ ⓑ ⓒ ⓓ	30 ⓐ ⓑ ⓒ ⓓ	43 ⓐ ⓑ ⓒ ⓓ
05 ⓐ ⓑ ⓒ ⓓ	18 ⓐ ⓑ ⓒ ⓓ	31 ⓐ ⓑ ⓒ ⓓ	44 ⓐ ⓑ ⓒ ⓓ
06 ⓐ ⓑ ⓒ ⓓ	19 ⓐ ⓑ ⓒ ⓓ	32 ⓐ ⓑ ⓒ ⓓ	45 ⓐ ⓑ ⓒ ⓓ
07 ⓐ ⓑ ⓒ ⓓ	20 ⓐ ⓑ ⓒ ⓓ	33 ⓐ ⓑ ⓒ ⓓ	46 ⓐ ⓑ ⓒ ⓓ
08 ⓐ ⓑ ⓒ ⓓ	21 ⓐ ⓑ ⓒ ⓓ	34 ⓐ ⓑ ⓒ ⓓ	47 ⓐ ⓑ ⓒ ⓓ
09 ⓐ ⓑ ⓒ ⓓ	22 ⓐ ⓑ ⓒ ⓓ	35 ⓐ ⓑ ⓒ ⓓ	48 ⓐ ⓑ ⓒ ⓓ
10 ⓐ ⓑ ⓒ ⓓ	23 ⓐ ⓑ ⓒ ⓓ	36 ⓐ ⓑ ⓒ ⓓ	49 ⓐ ⓑ ⓒ ⓓ
11 ⓐ ⓑ ⓒ ⓓ	24 ⓐ ⓑ ⓒ ⓓ	37 ⓐ ⓑ ⓒ ⓓ	50 ⓐ ⓑ ⓒ ⓓ
12 ⓐ ⓑ ⓒ ⓓ	25 ⓐ ⓑ ⓒ ⓓ	38 ⓐ ⓑ ⓒ ⓓ	
13 ⓐ ⓑ ⓒ ⓓ	26 ⓐ ⓑ ⓒ ⓓ	39 ⓐ ⓑ ⓒ ⓓ	

Performance Scanner

> 90% Excellent !	You have mastered the first half of NEET syllabus (12th). The concepts of this syllabus are on your fingertips. Maintain this momentum.
76-90% Very Good !	You have a good command over the first half of NEET syllabus (12th). Revise it again after a few days and enhance your performance.
60-75% Good !	You have a wide scope to learn for the first half of NEET syllabus (12th). Revise it again.
<60% Not Satisfactory!	You have a long way ahead of you to master the first half of NEET syllabus (12th). Revise it thoroughly.

Scan for Online Part Test

Space for Rough Work

Space for Rough Work

Test Booklet No. 3947264

Test Booklet Code SPT2

MED ACE

NEET (UG)

SELF ASSESSMENT KIT

Syllabus Part Thru 2

(Half Syllabus Test)

Chapters Covered

Haloalkanes and Haloarenes

Alcohols, Phenols and Ethers

Aldehydes, Ketones and Carboxylic Acids

Amines

Biomolecules

Principles Related to Practical Chemistry

Important Instructions

- The test is of 45 minutes duration and the Test Booklet contains 45 multiple choice questions (four options with a single correct answer) from Chemistry.
- Candidates are advised to read all questions before they start attempting the question paper.
- Each questions carries 4 marks. For each correct response, the candidate will get 4 marks. For each incorrect response, one mark will be deducted from the total scores.
- In the event of candidate marking more than one option then one mark will be deducted. The maximum marks are 180.
- Use **Blue/Black Point Pen** only for writing particular on this page/marking response on Answer Sheet.

Name of the Candidate (In Capitals) ____________

____

Candidate's Signature ____________

Invigilator's Signature ____________

Facsimile signature stamp of center superintendent ____________

Do not open this Booklet until you start attempting the Test

Chemistry (Q. No. 1-45)

1. Identify the major product (X) in the following reaction.

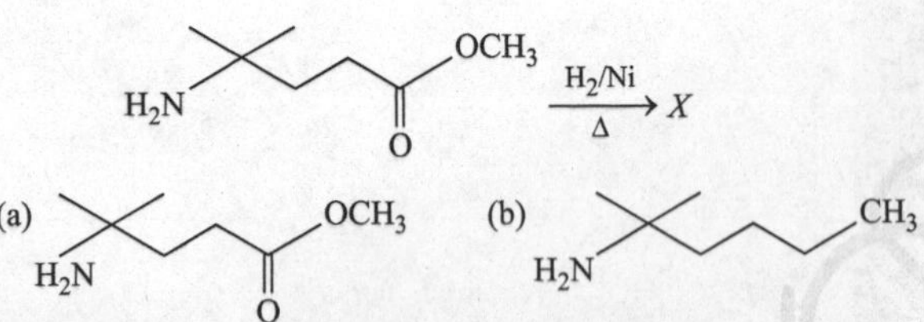

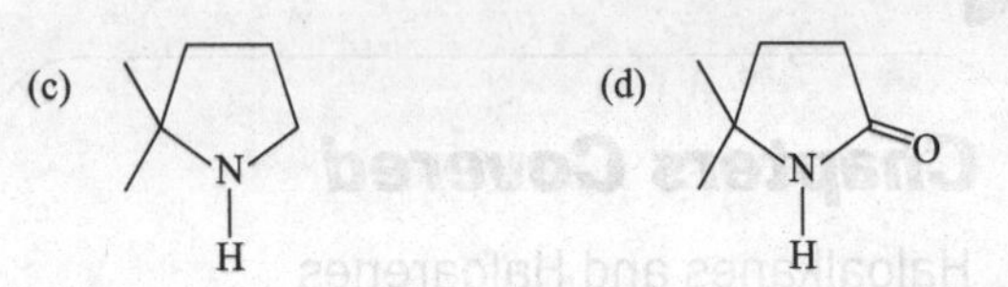

2. Which of the following is formed as a crossed aldol product when propanal acts as an electrophile and butanal as a nucleophile?
(a) 3-hydroxy-2-methyl pentanal
(b) 2-ethyl-3-hydroxypentanal
(c) 3-hydroxy-2-methylbutanal
(d) 2-ethyl-3-hydroxyhexanal

3. Given below are two statements, one is labelled as Assertion (A) and other is labelled as Reason (R).

Assertion (A) Leucine is an essential amino acid.
Reason (R) The amino acids which can be synthesized in our body are called essential amino acids.

In the light of above statements, choose the correct answer from the options given below.
(a) Both (A) and (R) are true and (R) is the correct explanation of (A).
(b) Both (A) and (R) are true but (R) is not the correct explanation of (A).
(c) (A) is true but (R) is false.
(d) (A) is false but (R) is true.

4. The structure of the compound that gives a tribromo derivative on treatment with bromine water is,

(a) CH_3, OH (ortho-cresol)
(b) CH_3, OH (para-cresol)
(c) CH_3, OH (meta-cresol)
(d) CH_2OH (benzyl alcohol)

5. The reaction,

$$2C_2H_5OH \xrightarrow[413\text{ K}]{\text{Conc. } H_2SO_4} (C_2H_5)_2O + H_2O$$ is an example of

(a) electrophilic substitution reaction
(b) nucleophilic substitution S_N1 reaction
(c) E_2 elimination reaction
(d) nucleophilic substitution S_N2 reaction.

6. Which of the following is not a fat soluble vitamin?
(a) Vitamin B complex
(b) Vitamin D
(c) Vitamin E
(d) Vitamin A

7. Ethanol on reaction with alkaline $KMnO_4$ gives X which further reacted with methanol in the presence of an acid gives a sweet compound Y. X and Y respectively are
(a) acetaldehyde and acetone
(b) acetic acid and methyl acetate
(c) formic acid and methyl formate
(d) ethylene and ethyl methyl ether

8. To prepare 3-ethyl-3-pentanol, which of the following pairs of reactants should be used?
(a) $CH_3CH_2COCH_3$ and $CH_3CH_2CH_2MgBr$
(b) $CH_3CH_2COCH_2CH_3$ and CH_3CH_2MgBr
(c) $CH_3CH_2CH_2COCH_2CH_3$ and CH_3MgBr
(d) $CH_3CH_2CH_2COCH_3$ and CH_3CH_2MgBr

9. The solubility in water of $C_6H_5NH_2$(I), $(C_2H_5)_2NH$(II), and $C_2H_5NH_2$(III) increases in the order
(a) II < III < I (b) I < II < III
(c) III < II > I (d) II < I < III

10. Acetic acid reacts separately with the following alcohols. The rate of esterification is highest for
(a) CH_3OH (b) C_2H_5OH
(c) $(CH_3)_2CHOH$ (d) $(CH_3)_3COH$

11. Consider the following sequence of the reaction.

(m-cresol: OH, Me) $\xrightarrow[\text{(ii) } H_3O^+]{\text{(i)}CHCl_3/NaOH, \Delta} X \xrightarrow{Br_2/Fe} Y$

Here, X and Y respectively are

(a) X = (CH₃, Br, OH substituted benzene) Y = (CHO, Me, OH substituted benzene)

(b) X = (Me, OH, CHO substituted benzene) Y = (Me, OH, Br, CHO substituted benzene)

(c) X = (OH, CHO, Me substituted benzene) Y = (H_3C, OH, Br, $CHCl_3$ substituted benzene)

(d) X = (Me, OH, CHO substituted benzene) Y = (Br, Me, OH, CHO substituted benzene)

12. Given below are two statements.

Statement I S_N1 reactions are generally carried out in polar protic solvents like water, alcohol, acetic acid, etc.

Statement II In S_N1 reaction, $C_6H_5CH(C_6H_5)Br$ is less stable than $C_6H_5CH(CH_3)Br$.

In the light of the above statements, choose the most appropriate answer from the options given below.
(a) Both Statement I and Statement II is correct.
(b) Both Statement I and Statement II is incorrect.
(c) Statement I is correct but Statement II is incorrect.
(d) Statement II is incorrect but Statement II is correct.

13. Given below are two statements, one is labelled as Assertion (A) and other is labelled as Reason (R).

Assertion (A) Picric acid is a stronger acid than phenol inspite of absence of carboxylic group.

Reason (R) Three —NO_2 groups in picric acid activate the phenolate ion.

In the light of above statements, choose the correct answer from the options given below.
(a) Both (A) and (R) are true and (R) is the correct explanation of (A).
(b) Both (A) and (R) are true but (R) is not the correct explanation of (A).
(c) (A) is true but (R) is false.
(d) (A) is false but (R) is true.

14. $X \xleftarrow[CH_3OH]{NaBH_4}$ (lactone ring with ketone) $\xrightarrow{LiAlH_4} Y$

The product X and Y respectively are

(a) X = (lactone with OH), Y = (diol with OH, OH, OH)

(b) X = (OH, OH ring compound), Y = (lactone with OH)

(c) Y in both cases
(d) X in both cases

15. The number of compounds that will give a secondary alcohol on reacting with Grignard reagent followed by acid hydrolysis.
I. HCHO II. C_2H_5CHO
III. CH_3COCH_3 IV. $C_2H_5COOC_2H_5$
V. $CH_3COOC_2H_5$
(a) 1 (b) 3 (c) 4 (d) 5

16. Select the incorrect statement about acetophenone?
(a) It gives 2, 4-DNP test.
(b) It does not give Tollen's test.
(c) It gives yellow ppt. with NaOH, Cl_2
(d) It forms $C_7H_6O_2$ in drastic oxidation with $KMnO_4, H^+$.

17. Aniline is treated with a mixture of sodium nitrite and hypophosphorus acid, the product formed is
(a) aniline diazonium hypophosphite
(b) benzene
(c) anilinium hyposphite
(d) aniline diazonium phosphate

18. The linkage between the two monosaccharide units in lactose is
(a) C_1 of β-D-glucose and C_4 of β-D-galactose
(b) C_1 of β-D-galactose and C_4 of β-D-glucose
(c) C_1 of α-D-galactose and C_4 of β-D-glucose
(d) C_1 of α-D-glucose and C_4 of α-D-galactose

19. The major product of dehydration of the following is

Cyclopentyl–C(CH_3)–CH(OH)–CH_3 $\xrightarrow[\Delta]{H_3O^+}$ Product

(a) 1,2-dimethylcyclohexene (CH_3, CH_3)
(b) cyclopentyl–C(CH_3)–CH=CH_2
(c) cyclopentyl–CH=CH_2
(c) cyclopentyl–CH=CH–CH_3

20. Given below are two statements, one is labelled as Assertion (A) and other is labelled as Reason (R).

Assertion (A) The IUPAC name for the compound, $NCCH_2CH_2COOH$ is 3-cyanopropanoic acid.

Reason (R) COOH is considered as substituent group while CN is considered as the principal functional group.

In the light of above statements, choose the correct answer from the options given below.
(a) Both (A) and (R) are true and (R) is the correct explanation of (A).
(b) Both (A) and (R) are true but (R) is not the correct explanation of (A).
(c) (A) is true but (R) is false.
(d) (A) is false but (R) is true.

21. Which of the following pairs form the same osazone?
(a) Glucose and fructose
(b) Glucose and galactose
(c) Glucose and arabinose
(d) Lactose and maltose

22. Which of the following compounds is used to depress the central nervous system?
(a) Iodoform (b) DDT
(c) Freon (d) Chloroform

23. Methyl acetate and ethyl acetate can be distinguished by
(a) hot $KMnO_4$ solution
(b) neutral $FeCl_3$
(c) iodoform test
(d) None of the above

24. Which of the following oxidising agent that used in the test of phosphorus?
(a) Potassium nitrate
(b) Sodium peroxide
(c) Nitric acid
(d) Hydrogen peroxide

25. In the following reaction, the final product M will be

4-chloroaniline (NH_2, Cl) $\xrightarrow[KOH]{CHCl_3}$ (L) $\xrightarrow[300\ K]{HCl}$ M + Methanoic acid

(a) NH_2–C_6H_4–Cl
(b) N≡C–C_6H_4–Cl
(c) C≡N–C_6H_4–Cl
(d) CH_3–NH–C_6H_4–Cl

26. In the given reaction, the final product B will be?

(p-chloronitrobenzene) $\xrightarrow[Fe, \Delta]{Br_2} A \xrightarrow[CH_3OH, \Delta]{CH_3ONa} B$

(a) 2-methoxynitrobenzene (NO_2, OCH_3)
(b) NO_2, OCH_3, Cl substituted benzene
(c) NO_2, Br, OCH_3 substituted benzene
(d) NO_2, OCH_3 (para) substituted benzene

27. 1-nitronaphthalene $\xrightarrow[\Delta]{KMnO_4, H^+}$ Product

The main product is

(a) NO_2, COOH, COOH substituted benzene
(b) benzene-COOH
(c) tetrahydronaphthalene with OH
(d) NO_2, COOH, COOH substituted tetrahydronaphthalene

28. Peptides are composed of amino acids joined by amide bond. Which of the following statements is not correct?

(a) Amide groups are more resistant to hydrolysis than are similar ester groups.
(b) *pπ-pπ* resonance stabilises the amide bond.
(c) Stable conformation of peptides are restricted to those having planar amide groups.
(d) Amide groups do not participate in hydrogen bonding interactions.

29. In the following reaction, A is

$A \xrightarrow{\text{Bromination}} B \xrightarrow{NaNO_2/HCl} C \xrightarrow[C_2H_5OH]{\text{Boiling}}$ *Sym*-tribromobenzene

(a) benzoic acid (b) salicylic acid
(c) phenol (d) aniline

30. Identify the product C in the following given reaction?

$C_2H_5I \xrightarrow{\text{(alc.) KOH}} A \xrightarrow{Br_2} B \xrightarrow{KCN} C$

(a) CH_3CH_2CN
(b) $NCCH_2—CH_2CN$
(c) $BrCH_2—CH_2CN$
(d) $BrCH=CHCN$

31. Which of the following cannot be made by using Williamson's synthesis?

(a) Methoxybenzene
(b) Benzyl-*p*-nitrophenyl ether
(c) *tert*-butyl methyl ether
(d) Di-*tert* butyl ether

32. In the following sequence of reaction, the product (Z) is,

$CH_3CH_2CH_2Br \xrightarrow[\text{(alc)}]{KOH} (X) \xrightarrow{HBr} (Y) \xrightarrow{KOH(aq)} (Z)$

(a) propene
(b) propyne
(c) propan-1-ol
(d) propan-2-1

33. In the following reaction,

p-chloroanisole (OCH_3, Cl) $\xrightarrow{NaNH_2/\text{Liq. Ammonia}} X$

The major product X is

(a) aniline (NH_2)
(b) OCH_3, NH_2 (meta) substituted benzene
(c) OCH_3, Cl (meta) substituted benzene
(d) OCH_3, NH_2 (ortho) substituted benzene

34. X in the given reaction below is,

2 cyclohexanone $\xrightarrow{\text{Dil. NaOH}} A \xrightarrow[HCl]{Zn/Hg} X$

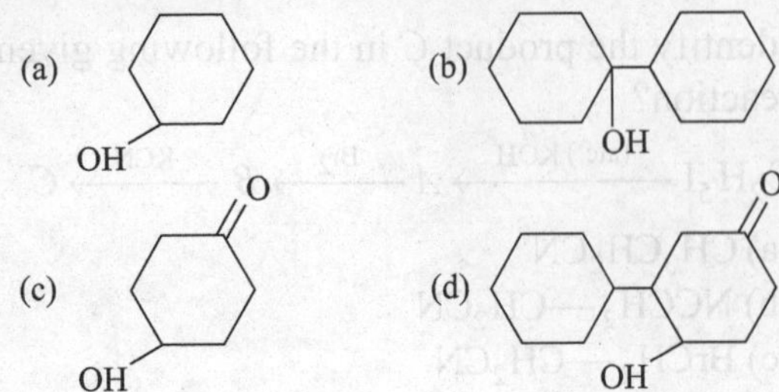

35. Final products of the following reaction are

$$CH_3C \equiv CCH_2CH_3 \xrightarrow[\text{(ii) Hydrolysis} \\ \text{(iii) } H_2O_2]{\text{(i) } O_3}$$

(a) $CH_3COOH + CO_2$
(b) $CH_3COOH + HOOCCH_2CH_3$
(c) $CH_3CHO + CH_3CH_2COOH$
(d) $CH_3COOH + CH_3COCH_3$

36. Match List-I with List-II.

	List-I (Reaction)		List-II (Name of reaction)
A.	$CH_3CH_2CH_2Cl \xrightarrow[\Delta]{\text{NaI, Acetone}} CH_3CH_2CH_2I$	I.	Hunsdiecker reaction
B.	$CH_3CH_2Cl \xrightarrow[\Delta]{Hg_2F_2} CH_3CH_2F$	II.	Fittig reaction
C.	$RCOOAg \xrightarrow[\Delta]{Br_2/CCl_4} RBr$	III.	Finkelstein reaction
D.	$C_6H_5Br \xrightarrow{Na, \Delta} C_6H_5—C_6H_5$	IV.	Swartz reaction

Choose the correct answer from the options given below

(a) A-III, B-IV, C-I, D-II
(b) A-IV, B-III, C-II, D-I
(c) A-I, B-III, C-IV, D-II
(d) A-II, B-III, C-IV, D-I

37. Given below are two statements.

Statement I Fructose does not contain any aldehyde group but still reduces Tollen's reagent.

Statement II In presence of a base, fructose undergoes a rearrangement to form glucose and mannose.

In the light of the above statements, choose the answer from the options given below.

(a) Both Statement I and Statement II is incorrect.
(b) Statement I is correct but Statement II is incorrect.
(c) Statement I is incorrect but Statement II is correct.
(d) Both Statement I and Statement II are correct.

38. An anion 'X' of an aqueous solution of sodium salt gives following results :

$$X \xrightarrow{K_2Cr_2O_7} \text{Green solution}$$

$$X \xrightarrow{Pb(OAc)_2} \text{Black ppt.}$$

Which of the following could be X?

(a) I^- (b) S^{2-}
(c) NO_2^- (d) SO_4^{2-}

39. Which of the following is used to prepare Benzoyl chloride from benzoic acid?

(a) Cl_2, H_2O (b) $SOCl_2$
(c) SO_2, Cl_2 (d) $Cl_2, h\nu$

40. Which of the following is a tautomer of phenol?

(a) (b) OH
(c) OH, O (d) O

41. Consider the following reaction and identify the product Y.

CH_3, O_2N $\xrightarrow[\text{(ii) } CS_2]{\text{(i) } CrO_2Cl_2} [X] \xrightarrow{H_3O^+} Y$

(a) CHO, CHO (b) $\overset{O}{\overset{\|}{C}}—CH_3$
(c) $CH(OC_2H_5)_2$ (d) CHO, NO_2

42. Ethyl amine undergoes oxidation in the presence of $KMnO_4$ to form which compound?

(a) An acid (b) An alcohol

(c) An aldehyde (d) A nitrogen oxide

43. Select the correct statements from the following.

A. Primary aliphatic amines form highly unstable alkyl diazonium salts.

B. Benzene diazonium chloride is prepared by the nitration of aniline with nitrous acid at 273-278 K.

C. Benzene diazonium fluoroborate is water soluble and stable at room temperature.

D. In Sandmeyer reaction, halide ion (Cl^-) can be easily introduced in the benzene ring in the presence of Cu(I) ion.

E. The azo products are often colourless.

Choose the correct answer from the option given below.

(a) A, B, C and D

(b) A, B and D

(c) C and E

(d) B, C, D and E

44. The final product (Y) in the given reaction is

$$F-C_6H_4-NO_2 \xrightarrow[\text{DMF, } \Delta]{(CH_3)_2NH} X \xrightarrow{H_2/Ni}$$

(a) $H_2N-C_6H_4-N(CH_3)_2$

(b) $H_2N-C_6H_4-NH_2$

(c) $O_2N-C_6H_4-NH_2$

(d) $H_2N-C_6H_4-N(CH_3)(NH_2)$

45. Select the incorrect regarding maltose.

(a) It consists of two glucopyranose units.

(b) It is a non-reducing sugar.

(c) Glycosidic bond between C1 of one unit and C4 of the other unit.

(d) It is a disaccharide.

Response Index

01 ⓐ ⓑ ⓒ ⓓ	14 ⓐ ⓑ ⓒ ⓓ	27 ⓐ ⓑ ⓒ ⓓ	40 ⓐ ⓑ ⓒ ⓓ
02 ⓐ ⓑ ⓒ ⓓ	15 ⓐ ⓑ ⓒ ⓓ	28 ⓐ ⓑ ⓒ ⓓ	41 ⓐ ⓑ ⓒ ⓓ
03 ⓐ ⓑ ⓒ ⓓ	16 ⓐ ⓑ ⓒ ⓓ	29 ⓐ ⓑ ⓒ ⓓ	42 ⓐ ⓑ ⓒ ⓓ
04 ⓐ ⓑ ⓒ ⓓ	17 ⓐ ⓑ ⓒ ⓓ	30 ⓐ ⓑ ⓒ ⓓ	43 ⓐ ⓑ ⓒ ⓓ
05 ⓐ ⓑ ⓒ ⓓ	18 ⓐ ⓑ ⓒ ⓓ	31 ⓐ ⓑ ⓒ ⓓ	44 ⓐ ⓑ ⓒ ⓓ
06 ⓐ ⓑ ⓒ ⓓ	19 ⓐ ⓑ ⓒ ⓓ	32 ⓐ ⓑ ⓒ ⓓ	45 ⓐ ⓑ ⓒ ⓓ
07 ⓐ ⓑ ⓒ ⓓ	20 ⓐ ⓑ ⓒ ⓓ	33 ⓐ ⓑ ⓒ ⓓ	46 ⓐ ⓑ ⓒ ⓓ
08 ⓐ ⓑ ⓒ ⓓ	21 ⓐ ⓑ ⓒ ⓓ	34 ⓐ ⓑ ⓒ ⓓ	47 ⓐ ⓑ ⓒ ⓓ
09 ⓐ ⓑ ⓒ ⓓ	22 ⓐ ⓑ ⓒ ⓓ	35 ⓐ ⓑ ⓒ ⓓ	48 ⓐ ⓑ ⓒ ⓓ
10 ⓐ ⓑ ⓒ ⓓ	23 ⓐ ⓑ ⓒ ⓓ	36 ⓐ ⓑ ⓒ ⓓ	49 ⓐ ⓑ ⓒ ⓓ
11 ⓐ ⓑ ⓒ ⓓ	24 ⓐ ⓑ ⓒ ⓓ	37 ⓐ ⓑ ⓒ ⓓ	50 ⓐ ⓑ ⓒ ⓓ
12 ⓐ ⓑ ⓒ ⓓ	25 ⓐ ⓑ ⓒ ⓓ	38 ⓐ ⓑ ⓒ ⓓ	
13 ⓐ ⓑ ⓒ ⓓ	26 ⓐ ⓑ ⓒ ⓓ	39 ⓐ ⓑ ⓒ ⓓ	

Performance Scanner

> 90% Excellent !	You have mastered the second half of NEET syllabus (12th). The concepts of this syllabus are on your fingertips. Maintain this momentum.
76-90% Very Good !	You have a good command over the second half of NEET syllabus (12th). Revise it again after a few days and enhance your performance.
60-75% Good !	You have a wide scope to learn for the second half of NEET syllabus (12th). Revise it again.
<60% Not Satisfactory!	You have a long way ahead of you to master the second half of NEET syllabus (12th). Revise it thoroughly.

Scan for Online
Part Test

Space for Rough Work

Test Booklet No. 3947265

Test Booklet Code NSS1

MED ACE

NEET (UG)

SELF ASSESSMENT KIT

NEET Stepping Stones 1

(Complete Syllabus Test 12th)

Name of the Candidate (In Capitals)

____

____

____

Candidate's Signature ______________

Invigilator's Signature ______________

Facsimile signature stamp of center superintendent______________

Important Instructions

- The test is of 45 minutes duration and the Test Booklet contains 45 multiple choice questions (four options with a single correct answer) from Chemistry.
- Candidates are advised to read all questions before they start attempting the question paper.
- Each questions carries 4 marks. For each correct response, the candidate will get 4 marks. For each incorrect response, one mark will be deducted from the total scores.
- In the event of candidate marking more than one option then one mark will be deducted. The maximum marks are 180.
- Use **Blue/Black Point Pen** only for writing particular on this page/marking response on Answer Sheet.

Do not open this Booklet until you start attempting the Test

Chemistry (Q. No. 1-45)

1. The value of Λ°_{m} of $Al_2(SO_4)_3$ is 858 S $cm^2 mol^{-1}$, while $\Lambda^{\circ}_{SO_4^{2-}}$ is 160 S cm^2/mol. Limiting ionic conductance of Al^{3+} ions is
   (a) 192 S cm^2/mol
   (b) 166 S cm^2/mol
   (c) 189 S cm^2/mol
   (d) 172 S cm^2/mol

2. Given below are two statements.
   Statement I *ortho*-nitrophenol is more acidic than *ortho*-methoxyphenol.
   Statement II $-NO_2$ group is electron withdrawing group, while methoxy group is electron releasing group.
   In the light of the above statements, choose the most appropriate answer from the options given below.
   (a) Both Statement I and Statement II are incorrect.
   (b) Statement I is correct but Statement II is incorrect.
   (c) Statement I is incorrect but Statement II is correct.
   (d) Both Statement I and Statement II are correct.

3. A plot of $\log t_{1/2}$ *versus* $\log C_0$ is given below

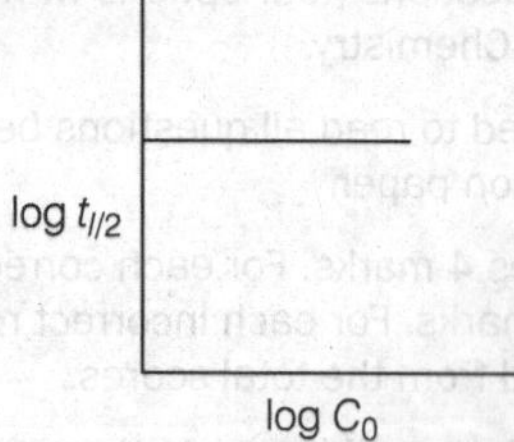

   The conclusion that can be drawn from this graph is
   (a) order = 1, $t_{1/2} = \frac{1}{k_a}$
   (b) order = 1, $t_{1/2} = \frac{2.303}{k}\log 2$
   (c) order = 0, $t_{1/2} = \frac{1}{2k_a}$
   (d) order = 2, $t_{1/2} = \frac{1}{a}$

4. Choose the incorrect statement about sulphur.
   (a) Sulphur exists in S_8 molecule, which have puckered ring structure.
   (b) α-sulphur is more stable than β-form of sulphur.
   (c) S_8 molecule is paramagnetic.
   (d) α and β-form of sulphur both are insoluble in water, but soluble in CS_2.

5. Number of P—O—P bond(s) in one molecule of $H_4P_2O_7$ is
   (a) 1 (b) 2 (c) 3 (d) 4

6. 75.2 g of phenol (C_6H_5OH) is dissolved in 1 kg of solvent of K_f = 14 K $molal^{-1}$. If depression in freezing point is 7K, then the percentage of phenol that dimerises is
   (a) 55% (b) 45%
   (c) 25% (d) 75%

7. Given below are two statements.
   Statement I Dipole moment of chlorobenzene is lower than that of cyclohexyl chloride.
   Statement II sp^2-hybridised carbon in chlorobenzene is more electronegative than sp^3-hybridised carbon in cyclohexyl chloride.
   In the light of the above statements, choose the most appropriate answer from the options given below.
   (a) Both Statement I and Statement II are incorrect.
   (b) Statement I is correct but Statement II is incorrect.
   (c) Statement I is incorrect but Statement II is correct.
   (d) Both Statement I and Statement II are correct.

8. Match the List-I with List-II.

List-I (Term)	List-II (Unit)
A. Conductivity	I. ohm^{-1} cm^2/mol
B. Molar conductance	II. cm^{-1}
C. Equivalent conductance	III. S/cm
D. Cell constant	IV. Ω^{-1} cm^2 $equivalent^{-1}$

Choose the correct answer from the options given below.
(a) A-III, B-I, C-IV, D-II
(b) A-I, B-II, C-III, D-IV
(c) A-III, B-IV, C-II, D-I
(d) A-II, B-III, C-I, D-IV

9. Correct IUPAC name of $[Co(NH_3)_4(NO_2)Cl]NO_3$ is
(a) tetraamminechloridonitro(O)cobalt(III)nitrate
(b) tetraamminechloridonitrito(N)cobalt(III)nitrite
(c) tetraamminechloridonitrito(N)cobalt(III)nitrate
(d) tetraamminechloridonitronitratecobalt(III)nitrate

10. Select the incorrect statement from the following.
(a) $\rangle C{=}O + NaHSO_3$, this reaction can also be used to distinguish methyl ketone from other higher ketones.
(b) Tollen's reagent (ammoniacal solution of silver nitrate) reacts with aldehyde and forms silver mirror.
(c) Ketones are easily oxidised by weak oxidising agent, such as Tollen's reagent or Fehling solution.
(d) Benedict solution is alkaline copper sulphate containing citrate ion as complexing agent. Aldehyde on warming with this solution gives brick red precipitate.

11. Consider the following ions,
I. Cu^{2+} II. Ti^{4+} III. Co^{2+}
IV. Fe^{2+} V. V^{3+}
The coloured ions are
(a) I, II, III and IV
(b) I, III, IV and V
(c) I, IV and V only
(d) II, III and IV

12. The reagent that reacts with nitromethane to form N-methylhydroxyl amine is
(a) Zn/HCl (b) Zn /NH_4Cl
(c) Zn/NaOH (d) Sn/HCl

13. PbO_2 is a powerful oxidising agent when it reacts with acid reagent because
(a) Pb(IV) is in stable oxidation state.
(b) Pb(IV) gets converted into Pb(II).
(c) Pb(IV) gets converted into Pb(0).
(d) Pb(IV) gets converted into Pb(I)

14. Given below are two statements, one is labelled as Assertion (A) and the other is labelled as Reason (R).
Assertion (A) 1° allylic halide are more reactive than 1° *RX* in S_N1 reaction.
Reason (R) Allylic carbocation intermediate is stabilised by resonance.
In the light of the above statements, choose the most appropriate answer from the options given below.
(a) Both (A) and (R) are true and (R) is the correct explanation of (A).
(b) Both (A) and (R) are true but (R) is not the correct explanation of (A).
(c) (A) is true but (R) is false.
(d) (A) is false but (R) is true.

15. Complete the following reaction,

$$C_6H_6 \text{ (benzene)} + O_2 \xrightarrow{V_2O_5,\ 725\ K} \text{Final product } (P)$$

The final product (*P*) is
(a) succinic anhydride
(b) maleic anhydride
(c) maleic acid
(d) succinic acid

16. A galvanic cell is constructed with Ag^+/Ag and Fe^{3+}/Fe^{2+} electrodes. Find the value of $\log[Ag^+]$ at which the emf of the cell is zero at equimolar concentration of Fe^{2+} and Fe^{3+} ions.
$(E^{\ominus}_{Fe^{3+}/Fe^{2+}} = 0.77\ V,\ E^{\ominus}_{Ag^+/Ag} = 0.80\ V)$
(a) +0508 (b) −0.508
(c) −0254 (d) +0254

17. The activation energy for the reaction, $2HI \longrightarrow H_2 + I_2$ is 209.5 kJ/mol at 581 K. The fraction of molecules of reactant having energy equal to or greater than activation energy will be $[10^{-18.83} = 1.48 \times 10^{-19}]$
(a) 1.48×10^{-19}
(b) 1.28×10^{-19}
(c) 428×10^{-19}
(d) 227×10^{-19}

18. Given below are two statements.

Statement I In the first transition series, copper exhibits +1 oxidation state most frequently.

Statement II Cu(I) (gas) has stable electronic configuration.

In the light of the above statements, choose the most appropriate answer from the options given below.

(a) Both Statement I and Statement II are incorrect.
(b) Statement I is correct but Statement II is incorrect.
(c) Statement I is incorrect but Statement II is correct.
(d) Both Statement I and Statement II are correct.

19. A decimolar solution of potassium ferrocyanide at 300 K is 50% dissociated. Osmotic pressure of the solution will be

(a) 1.99 atm (b) 2.98 atm
(c) 7.38 atm (d) 6.62 atm

20. Identify compound [*P*] in the following sequence of reaction.

1-methylnaphthalene (CH_3) $\xrightarrow{Cl_2/h\nu}$ [*P*] $\xrightarrow[373\ K]{H_2O}$ 1-naphthaldehyde (CHO)

(a) Cl (1-chloronaphthalene) (b) CH_2Cl (1-(chloromethyl)naphthalene)
(c) $CHCl_2$ (1-(dichloromethyl)naphthalene) (d) CCl_3 (1-(trichloromethyl)naphthalene)

21. $TiCl_3$ is coloured, while $TiCl_4$ is colourless because

I. Ti^{3+} has one unpaired electron.
II. Ti^{4+} has no unpaired electron.
III. Ti^{3+} shows *d-d* transition.
IV. Ti^{3+} shows charge transfer spectrum.
V. Ti^{4+} shows *d-d* transition.

Choose the correct answer from the options given below.

(a) I and II (b) I, III and V
(c) I, II and III (d) I, II and IV

22. Given below are two statements.

Statement I Alkene changes into aldehyde during oxo reaction.

Statement II Acidity of α-hydrogens of aldehydes and ketones is responsible for aldol reaction.

In the light of the above statements, choose the most appropriate answer from the options given below.

(a) Both Statement I and Statement II are incorrect.
(b) Statement I is correct but Statement II is incorrect.
(c) Statement I is incorrect but Statement II is correct.
(d) Both Statement I and Statement II are correct.

23. Which of the following amino acid is achiral?

(a) Alanine (b) Valine
(c) Histidine (d) Glycine

24. Product of the reaction,

$$CH_2{=}CH_2 + CO + H_2 \xrightarrow[\text{(High temperature)}]{[Co(CO)_4)_2]} A \xrightarrow{H_2/Ni} B$$

A and *B* are respectively

(a) $CH_3—\underset{\overset{\|}{O}}{C}—CH_3$, $CH_3—\underset{\underset{OH}{|}}{CH}—CH_3$
(b) $CH_3—CH_2—CHO$, $CH_3—CH_2—CH_2—OH$
(c) $CH_3—CH_3$, $CH_3—CH_2—OH$
(d) $CH{\equiv}CH$, $CH_3—CH_2—OH$

25. Match the List-I with List-II.

	List-I (Complex)		List-II (Isomerism)
A.	$[CoCl_2(en)_2]^+$	I.	Shows geometrical isomerism only
B.	$[Cr(ox)_3]^{3-}$	II.	Shows optical isomerism only
C.	$[RhCl_3(py)_3]$	III.	Shows geometrical as well as optical isomerism
D.	$[ZnCl_3(NH_3)]$	IV.	Shows no isomerism

Choose the correct answer from the options given below.

(a) A-III, B-II, C-I, D-IV
(b) A-II, B-III, C-I, D-IV
(c) A-I, B-II, C-III, D-IV
(d) A-IV, B-III, C-II, D-I

26. Choose the incorrect statements about factor affecting crystal field splitting (Δ).

(a) The value of principal quantum number (n) increases, then magnitude of Δ increases.
(b) Higher is the oxidation state of metal ion, larger is the value of Δ.
(c) A strong ligand has higher splitting power than a weak ligand.
(d) The value of Δ_t is 9/4 times of Δ_o.

27. Match List-I with List-II.

	List-I (Reaction)		List-II (Reagent and involvement)
A.	HVZ reaction	I.	$ZnCl_2$
B.	Formic acid	II.	Potassium salt of mono carboxylic acid
C.	Kolbe's electrolysis	III.	Replacement of α-H by halogens
D.	Carboxylic acid + alcohol → ester	IV.	$H_2 + CO_2$

Choose the correct answer from the options given below.

(a) A-III, B-IV, C-II, D-I
(b) A-I, B-II, C-IV, D-III
(c) A-I, B-II, C-III, D-IV
(d) A-IV, B-III, C-II, D-I

28. The major product B is formed in the given reaction is

p-toluidine (NH_2, CH_3) $\xrightarrow{(CH_3CO)_2O} A \xrightarrow[CH_3COOH]{Br_2} B.$

(a) $NHCOCH_3$, Br, CH_3
(b) $NHCOCH_3$, Br, CH_3
(c) $NHCOCH_3$, $COCH_3$, CH_3
(d) $NHCOCH_3$, Br, CH_2Br

29. Which of the following vitamin is soluble in water?

(a) Vitamin E (b) Vitamin C
(c) Vitamin A (d) Vitamin D

30. Which of the following statement is not correct for Hofmann bromamide degradation?

(a) It gives tertiary amines as final product.
(b) It gives primary amines as final product.
(c) Product obtained has one carbon less than parent molecule.
(d) Aqueous or alcoholic KOH is used with bromine.

31. Complete the following reaction.

$$\text{Glucose} \xrightarrow[\text{(ii) Hydrolysis, (iii) Heat/HI}]{\text{(i) HCN}} ?$$

(a) Hexanoic acid
(b) n-hexane
(c) Heptanoic acid
(d) Heptane

32. Product of the following reaction,

$$2CH_3—COOAg + I_2 \xrightarrow{CCl_4} ?$$

is

(a) $CH_3—I$
(b) $CH_3—CH_2—I$
(c) $CH_3—\underset{\underset{O}{\|}}{C}—O—\underset{\underset{O}{\|}}{C}—CH_3$
(d) $CH_3—\underset{\underset{O}{\|}}{C}—OCH_3$

33. Complete the following reaction.

Toluene (CH_3) $\xrightarrow[(CH_3CO)_2O]{CrO_3} A \xrightarrow[H_3O^+]{373K} B$

A and B are respectively

(a) CHO, COOH
(b) COOH, H

(c) Ph–$CH(OCOCH_3)_2$, Ph–COOH

(d) Ph–$CH(OCOCH_3)_2$, Ph–CHO

34. Find the product (P) of the following conversion

Phenol (OH on benzene) + $Br_2\,(aq)$ ⟶ Product (P)

(a) 2-bromophenol
(b) 4-bromophenol
(c) 2,4,6-tribromophenol
(d) 2,4-dibromophenol

35. Complete the following reaction,

$$A + B \xrightarrow[\text{Dry ether}]{\text{Na}} CH_3—CH_2—CH_2—\underset{\underset{CH_3}{|}}{CH}—CH_3$$

Identify A and B where each of the compound is made of three carbon atoms.

(a) $CH_3—\underset{\underset{CH_3}{|}}{CH}—Br, CH_3—\underset{\underset{Br}{|}}{CH}—CH_3$

(b) $CH_3—CH_2—CH_2—Br, CH_3—\underset{\underset{Br}{|}}{CH}—CH_3$

(c) $CH_3—CH_2—CH_2—Br, CH_3—CH_2—\underset{\underset{Br}{|}}{CH_2}$

(d) $CH_3—\underset{\underset{Br}{|}}{CH}—CH_3, CH_3—\overset{\overset{CH_3}{|}}{\underset{\underset{Br}{|}}{C}}—Br$

36. Consider the statements given below.

Statement I Conductance of electricity by ions present in the solutions is called ionic conductance.

Statement II The conductivity of electrolytic solution depends on the nature of the electrolyte added.

In the light of the above statements, choose the most appropriate answer from the options given below.

(a) Both Statement I and Statement II are correct.
(b) Statement I is correct but Statement II is incorrect.
(c) Statement I is incorrect but Statement II is correct.
(d) Both Statement I and Statement II are incorrect.

37. A solution containing a group IV cation gives a precipitate on passing H_2S. A solution of this precipitate in dil. HCl produce a white precipitate with NaOH solution and bluish white precipitate with basic potassium ferrocyanide. The cation is

(a) Co^{+2} (b) Ni^{+2}
(c) Zn^{+2} (d) Mn^{+2}

38. Select the correct statement from the following.

A. Weak electrolyte like acetic acid have lower degree of dissociation at higher concentration.
B. For strong electrolytes Λ_m increases slowly with dilution.
C. In electrolytic cell, external source of voltage is used to bring about a chemical reaction.
D. The products of electrolysis depends on the different oxidising and reducing species present in the electrolytic cell and their standard reduction potential.
E. The product of electrolysis may be different for reactive and inert electrodes.

Choose the correct answer from the options given below.

(a) B, C, D only
(b) A, D, E only
(c) A, B, C, D and E
(d) B, C, D and E only

39. Match List-I with List-II.

	List-I (Types of ligands)		List-II (Examples of ligands)
A.	Tetradentate	I.	EDTA ion
B.	Unidentate	II.	Ethane-1, 2-diamine
C.	Didentate	III.	H_2O
D.	Hexadentate	IV.	$N(CH_2CH_2NH_2)_3$

Choose the correct answer from the options given below.

(a) A-IV, B-III, C-II, D-I
(b) A-III, B-IV, C-I, D-II
(c) A-II, B-I, C-III, D-IV
(d) A-IV, B-I, C-III, D-II

40. Given below are two statements, one is labelled as Assertion (A) and the other is labelled as Reason (R).

Assertion (A) Carboxylic acids have higher boiling liquid than aldehydes and ketones.

Reason (R) More extensive association of carboxylic acid molecules is through intermolecular hydrogen bonding.

In the light of the above statements, choose the most appropriate answer from the options given below.

(a) Both (A) and (R) are true and (R) is the correct explanation of (A).
(b) Both (A) and (R) are true but (R) is not the correct explanation of (A).
(c) (A) is true but (R) is false.
(d) (A) is false but (R) is true.

41. 1 mole each of the following solutes are taken in 5 moles of water.

A. NaCl   B. K_2SO_4 C. Na_3PO_4
D. Glucose

Assuming 100% ionisation of the electrolyte, relative decrease in vapour pressure will be in the order.

(a) $A < B < C < D$
(b) $D < C < B < A$
(c) $D < A < B < C$
(d) $A < C < B < D$

42. At 500 K, the half-life period of a gaseous reaction at an initial pressure of 100 kPa is 364s. When the pressure is 50 kPa, the half-life period is 182s. The order of reaction is

(a) one   (b) zero
(c) half   (d) two

43. In the following reaction,

2-bromotoluene (benzene ring with CH_3 and Br) $\xrightarrow[\text{(iii) } KMnO_4/OH^- \text{ (iv) } H^+]{\text{(i) Mg/ether (ii) } H_3O^+}$ A,

End product A is

(a) benzene ring with COOH, OH and CH_3
(b) benzene ring with OH and CH_3
(c) benzene ring with COOH
(d) benzene ring with OH

44. An ester (A) on acidic/hydrolysis gives (B) and (C). (B) gives violet colour and (C) gives blood red colour with neutral $FeCl_3$ solution (A), (B) and (C) are

	A	B	C
(a)	$C_6H_5-COOC_6H_5$	C_6H_5-COOH	C_6H_5-OH
(b)	$C_6H_5-O-\overset{O}{\overset{\|\|}{C}}-CH_3$	C_6H_5-OH	CH_3COOH
(c)	$C_6H_5-O-\overset{O}{\overset{\|\|}{C}}-CH_3$	C_6H_6	CH_3COOH
(d)	$C_6H_5-\overset{O}{\overset{\|\|}{C}}CH_3$	CH_3OH	$C_6H_5-\overset{O}{\overset{\|\|}{C}}OH$

45. Select the incorrect statement regarding oxides of nitrogen.

(a) Dinitrogen oxide is a colourless neutral gas
(b) Dinitrogen pentoxide is a colourless solid, acidic in nature.
(c) Dinitrogen tetroxide is obtained by NO_2. N_2O_4 is a colourless solid/liquid which is basic in nature
(d) Dinitrogen trioxide is a blue solid which is acidic in nature

Response Index

01 ⓐ ⓑ ⓒ ⓓ	14 ⓐ ⓑ ⓒ ⓓ	27 ⓐ ⓑ ⓒ ⓓ	40 ⓐ ⓑ ⓒ ⓓ
02 ⓐ ⓑ ⓒ ⓓ	15 ⓐ ⓑ ⓒ ⓓ	28 ⓐ ⓑ ⓒ ⓓ	41 ⓐ ⓑ ⓒ ⓓ
03 ⓐ ⓑ ⓒ ⓓ	16 ⓐ ⓑ ⓒ ⓓ	29 ⓐ ⓑ ⓒ ⓓ	42 ⓐ ⓑ ⓒ ⓓ
04 ⓐ ⓑ ⓒ ⓓ	17 ⓐ ⓑ ⓒ ⓓ	30 ⓐ ⓑ ⓒ ⓓ	43 ⓐ ⓑ ⓒ ⓓ
05 ⓐ ⓑ ⓒ ⓓ	18 ⓐ ⓑ ⓒ ⓓ	31 ⓐ ⓑ ⓒ ⓓ	44 ⓐ ⓑ ⓒ ⓓ
06 ⓐ ⓑ ⓒ ⓓ	19 ⓐ ⓑ ⓒ ⓓ	32 ⓐ ⓑ ⓒ ⓓ	45 ⓐ ⓑ ⓒ ⓓ
07 ⓐ ⓑ ⓒ ⓓ	20 ⓐ ⓑ ⓒ ⓓ	33 ⓐ ⓑ ⓒ ⓓ	46 ⓐ ⓑ ⓒ ⓓ
08 ⓐ ⓑ ⓒ ⓓ	21 ⓐ ⓑ ⓒ ⓓ	34 ⓐ ⓑ ⓒ ⓓ	47 ⓐ ⓑ ⓒ ⓓ
09 ⓐ ⓑ ⓒ ⓓ	22 ⓐ ⓑ ⓒ ⓓ	35 ⓐ ⓑ ⓒ ⓓ	48 ⓐ ⓑ ⓒ ⓓ
10 ⓐ ⓑ ⓒ ⓓ	23 ⓐ ⓑ ⓒ ⓓ	36 ⓐ ⓑ ⓒ ⓓ	49 ⓐ ⓑ ⓒ ⓓ
11 ⓐ ⓑ ⓒ ⓓ	24 ⓐ ⓑ ⓒ ⓓ	37 ⓐ ⓑ ⓒ ⓓ	50 ⓐ ⓑ ⓒ ⓓ
12 ⓐ ⓑ ⓒ ⓓ	25 ⓐ ⓑ ⓒ ⓓ	38 ⓐ ⓑ ⓒ ⓓ	
13 ⓐ ⓑ ⓒ ⓓ	26 ⓐ ⓑ ⓒ ⓓ	39 ⓐ ⓑ ⓒ ⓓ	

Performance Scanner

> 90% Excellent !	You have mastered the NEET syllabus (12th). The concepts of this entire syllabus are at your fingertips. Maintain this momentum.
76-90% Very Good !	You have a good command over the entire NEET syllabus (12th). Revise it again after a few days to enhance your performance.
60-75% Good !	You have a wide scope to learn for the entire NEET syllabus (12th). Revise it again.
<60% Not Satisfactory!	You have a long way ahead of you to master the NEET syllabus (12th). Revise it thoroughly.

MEDACE

NEET (UG)

SELF ASSESSMENT KIT

Test Booklet No. **3947266**

Test Booklet Code **NSS2**

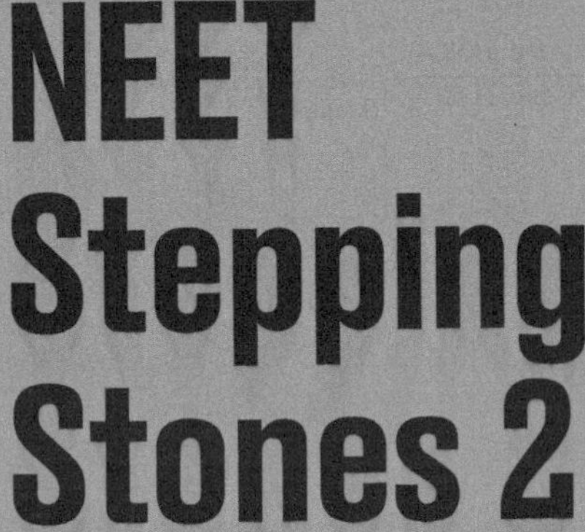

NEET Stepping Stones 2

(Complete Syllabus Test 12th)

Name of the Candidate (In Capitals)

____

____

____

Candidate's Signature _______________

Invigilator's Signature _______________

Facsimile signature stamp of center superintendent_______________

Important Instructions

- The test is of 45 minutes duration and the Test Booklet contains 45 multiple choice questions (four options with a single correct answer) from Chemistry.
- Candidates are advised to read all questions before they start attempting the question paper.
- Each questions carries 4 marks. For each correct response, the candidate will get 4 marks. For each incorrect response, one mark will be deducted from the total scores.
- In the event of candidate marking more than one option then one mark will be deducted. The maximum marks are 180.
- Use **Blue/Black Point Pen** only for writing particular on this page/marking response on Answer Sheet.

Do not open this Booklet until you start attempting the Test

Chemistry (Q.No. 1-45)

1. The osmotic pressure of a solution prepared by dissolving 25 mg of K_2SO_4 in 2 litre of water at 25°C is (assuming that it is completely dissociated)

(a) 5.27×10^{-7} atm

(b) 5.27×10^{-3} atm

(c) 5.27 atm

(d) 5.27×10^{-4} atm

2. Which of the following complex ion is expected to absorb visible light?

(a) $[Ti(en)_2(NH_3)_2]^{4+}$

(b) $[Cr(NH_3)_6]^{3+}$

(c) $[Zn(NH_3)_6]^{2+}$

(d) $[Sc(H_2O)_3(NH_3)_3]^{3+}$

3. The major product Z formed in the given reaction is

p-Toluidine (NH_2, CH_3) $\xrightarrow[0\text{–}5°C]{NaNO_2/HCl} Y \xrightarrow[\Delta]{CuCN/KCN} Z + N_2$

(a) CH_3 / COOH (para-substituted benzene)

(b) CN / CH_3 (para-substituted benzene)

(c) OH (phenol)

(d) CH_3 / CH_3 (1,4-dimethylnaphthalene)

4. $t_{1/4}$ can be taken as the time for concentration of reactant to drop to 3/4 of its initial value. If the rate constant for a first order reaction is k, then $t_{1/4}$ can be written as

(a) $0.10/k$ (b) $0.29/k$

(c) $0.39/k$ (d) $0.82/k$

5. Identify the major product B, formed in the given reaction.

Chlorobenzene $\xrightarrow[\text{Conc. } H_2SO_4]{\text{Conc. } HNO_3} \underset{\text{(Major)}}{A} \xrightarrow[433\text{ K}]{NaOH} B$

(a) Cl, OH, NO_2 (benzene ring: Cl at top, OH ortho, NO_2 para)

(b) OH, NO_2 (ortho-nitrophenol)

(c) OH, NO_2 (para-nitrophenol)

(d) Cl, OH (para-chlorophenol)

6. An aqueous solution of 2% non volatile solute exert a pressure of 1.004 bar at normal boiling point of the solvent. The molecular mass of solute is

(a) 36.38 g mol^{-1}

(b) 41.35 g mol^{-1}

(c) 54.35 g mol^{-1}

(d) 64.35 g mol^{-1}

7. In the reaction sequence,

$CHCl_3 \xrightarrow{\text{Air}/h\nu} [X] \xrightarrow[\text{(Small)}]{C_6H_6/\text{Anhy. } AlCl_3} [Y]$

will be

(a) $C_6H_5-\overset{O}{\overset{\|}{C}}-Cl$

(b) $C_6H_5-\overset{O}{\overset{\|}{C}}-C_6H_5$

(c) $Cl-\overset{O}{\overset{\|}{C}}-Cl$

(d) $C_6H_5-\overset{O}{\overset{\|}{C}}-H$

8. In the reaction sequence,

$$CH_3—CH_2—CH_2—Br \xrightarrow{AgCN} [X] \xrightarrow{H_2O/\bar{O}H} [Y]$$

The compound (Y) is,

(a) $CH_3—CH_2—CH_2—NH_2$
(b) $CH_3—CH_2—NH_2$
(c) $CH_3—(CH_2)_2—CH_2—NH_2$
(d) $CH_3—(CH_2)_3—CH_2—NH_2$

9. The boiling points of 0.01M aqueous solution of sucrose NaCl and $CaCl_2$ would be

(a) highest for sucrose solution
(b) same for all the solutions
(c) highest for $CaCl_2$ solution
(d) highest for NaCl solution

10. The major product A formed in the given reaction is

[1-methylcyclohexyl-$\overset{\oplus}{N}Me_3$] $\xrightarrow[\Delta]{HO^-}$ A (Major)

(a) 1-methylcyclohexene (CH_3)
(b) methylenecyclohexane (CH_2)
(c) 3-methylcyclohexene (CH_3)
(d) cyclohexene with exocyclic CH_2

11. Which of the following compound has the highest boiling point?

(a) $CH_3CH_2CH_2Cl$
(b) $CH_3CH_2CH_2CH_2Cl$
(c) $CH_3CH(CH_3)CH_2Cl$
(d) $(CH_3)_3CCl$

12. Chlorination of toluene in presence of light and heat followed by treatment with aqueous NaOH gives

(a) *o*-cresol
(b) *p*-cresol
(c) mixture of *o*-cresol and *p*-cresol
(d) benzoic acid

13. Consider the following compounds.

(I) o-nitrophenol (OH, NO_2) (II) o-dichlorobenzene (Cl, Cl) (III) o-xylene (CH_3, CH_3)

The correct order of dipole moment

(a) I ≈ II ≈ III (b) I < II < III
(c) I > II > III (d) II < III < I

14. Maxima or minima obtained in the temperature composition curve of a mixture of two liquids indicates

(a) an azeotropic mixture.
(b) micelle formation.
(c) that the liquids are immiscible with one another.
(d) that the liquids are partially miscible at the maxima or minima.

15. Given below are two statements.

Statement I The molecularity of a reaction is a whole number other than zero but generally less than 3.

Statement II The order of a reaction can be whole number or fractional.

In the light of the above statements, choose the correct answer from the options given below.

(a) Both Statement I and Statement II are incorrect.
(b) Statement I is correct but Statement II is incorrect.
(c) Statement I is incorrect but Statement II is correct.
(d) Both Statement I and Statement II are correct.

16. The product X formed by the dehydration of following compound is

[cyclobutyl]$—\underset{CH_3}{CH}—\underset{OH}{CH}—CH_3 \xrightarrow[\Delta]{H_3O^+} X$

(a) [cyclopentyl]$—CH=CH—CH_3$
(b) [cyclopentene ring with CH_3 and CH_3]
(c) [cyclobutyl with CH_3]$—CH=CH_3$
(d) [cyclobutyl with CH_3]$—CH=CH_2$

17. Molarity and molality of a solution of caustic soda are respectively 22.24 M and 94.12 m. The density of a solution is

(a) $1.12\ g\ mL^{-1}$ (b) $5.56\ g\ mL^{-1}$
(c) $55.6\ g\ mL^{-1}$ (d) $0.056\ g\ mL^{-1}$

18. In which of the following compounds, iron has the lowest oxidation number?

(a) $Fe(CO)_5$
(b) Fe_3O_4
(c) $Na_4[Fe(CN)_6]$
(d) $FeSO_4 \cdot (NH_4)_2SO_4 \cdot 6H_2O$

19. The compound that will show maximum osmotic pressure?

(a) 1 M NaCl (b) 1 M $MgCl_2$
(c) 1M $(NH_4)_3PO_4$ (d) 1 M Na_2SO_4

20. Which of the following are arranged in decreasing order of dipole moment?

(a) CH_3Cl, CH_3Br, CH_3F
(b) CH_3Cl, CH_3F, CH_3Br
(c) CH_3Br, CH_3Cl, CH_3F
(d) CH_3Br, CH_3F, CH_3Cl

21. Given below are two statements, one is labelled as Assertion (A) and the other is labelled as Reason (R).

Assertion (A) Alkylbenzene is not prepared by Friedel Crafts alkylation of benzene.

Reason (R) Alkyl halides are less reactive than acyl halides.

In the light of the above statements, choose the correct answer from the options given below.

(a) Both (A) and (R) are true and (R) is the correct explanation of (A).
(b) Both (A) and (R) are true but (R) is not the correct explanation of (A).
(c) (A) is true but (R) is false.
(d) (A) is false but (R) is true.

22. Identify *Z* in the following reaction sequence.

$$CH_2{=}CH_2 \xrightarrow{HBr} X \xrightarrow{Aq.\ NaOH} Y \xrightarrow{Na_2CO_3/\text{Excess } I_2} Z$$

(a) CH_3CH_2I
(b) CH_3CH_2OH
(c) CHI_3
(d) CH_3CHO

23. In the analysis of basic radicals, the group reagent H_2S gas is generally used in the group

(a) I and II groups (b) II and III groups
(c) III and V group (d) II and IV group

24. 3.5 mol of methyl alcohol (CH_3OH) is supplied in 1 kg of water. What is the mole fraction of methyl alcohol in the solution?

(a) 0.100 (b) 0.059
(c) 0.90 (d) 0.080

25. The instantaneous rate of disappearance of the MnO_4^- ion in the following reaction is 9.12×10^{-3} Ms^{-1}.

$$2MnO_4^- + 10I^- + 16H^+ \longrightarrow 2Mn^{2+} + 5I_2 + 8H_2O$$

Then the rate of appearance of I_2 is

(a) $2.28 \times 10^{-5}\ Ms^{-1}$
(b) $5.7 \times 10^{-3}\ Ms^{-1}$
(c) $4.56 \times 10^{-4}\ Ms^{-1}$
(d) $2.28 \times 10^{-2}\ Ms^{-1}$

26. The incorrect statement about collision theory of reaction rate is

(a) collision of molecules is a precondition for any reaction to occur.
(b) all collisions result in the formation of products.
(c) only activated collisions result in the formation of the products.
(d) molecules which have acquired the energy of activation can collide effectively.

27. In which of the following bromides the rate of S_N1 reaction is fastest?

(a) Br / Ph, Ph (b) Br (c) Br / Ph, CH_3 (d) Br / H_3C, CH_2—CH_3

28. Ethylmethyl amine cannot be resolved under normal condition. It is because

(a) the favoured configuration is not chiral.
(b) it isomerises rapidly with chiral isomer triethylamine.
(c) the nitrogen atom rapidly inverts its configuration.
(d) the C—N bond is not stable under conditions used for resolution.

29. The product X, Y and Z in the given reaction sequence is

$C_6H_5CH_2CH_2OH \xrightarrow{X}$ [benzene ring with CH_2COOH] $\xrightarrow{Y}$ Z

(a) X = PCC, Y = NaOH, CaO, $Z = C_6H_5CH_3$
(b) X = PCC, Y = LAH, $Z = C_6H_5CH_2CH_3$
(c) X = Jones reagent, Y = NaOH, CaO, $Z = C_6H_5CH_2CH_3$
(d) X = Jones reagent, Y = NaOH, CaO, Δ, $Z = C_6H_5CH_3$

30. For the reaction,
$CH_3CH_2NH_2 + CHCl_3 + 3KOH \longrightarrow A + B + 3H_2O$
The product A and B formed are respectively.
(a) C_2H_5NC and 3KCl
(b) $CH_3CH_2CONH_2$ and 3KCl
(c) C_2H_5NC and K_2CO_3
(d) C_2H_5CN and 3KCl

31. Which of the following statement is correct regarding the hormone thyroxine?
(a) It is secreted by pancreas.
(b) It is secreted by thyroid.
(c) It decreases blood sugar.
(d) It does not stimulate metabolism.

32. The time for half-life period of a certain reaction, $A \longrightarrow$ products is 1 h. When the initial concentration of the reactant 'A' is 2.0 mol L^{-1}, how much time does it take for its concentration to come from 0.75 to 0.50 mol L^{-1}, if it is a zero-order reaction?
(a) 6 h (b) 3 h
(c) 0.25 h (d) 1.5 h

33. The degree of dissociation (α) of a weak electrolyte, A_xB_y is related to van't Hoff factor (i) by the expression
(a) $\alpha = \frac{i-1}{(x+y-1)}$ (b) $\alpha = \frac{i-1}{x+y+1}$
(c) $\alpha = \frac{x+y-1}{i-1}$ (d) $\alpha = \frac{x+y+1}{i-1}$

34. What will be the unit of constant of proportionality, when conductance (Siemens, S) is directly proportional to the area of the vessel and the concentration of solution in it and is inversely proportional to the length of the vessel,
(a) S m mol^{-1} (b) S^2 m^{-3} mol^{-2}
(c) S m^2 mol^{-1} (d) S^{-2} m mol

35. The product P formed in the given reaction is

$\xrightarrow[H_3O^{\oplus}]{Me_2CuLi} P$

(a) O (b) OH
(c) (d) $\triangleright$—$\overset{O}{\overset{\|}{C}}$—$CH_3$

36. Consider the following statements.
Statement I Potassium ferrocyanide is diamagnetic whereas potassium ferricyanide is paramagnetic.
Statement II Crystal field splitting in ferrocyanide ion is greater than that of ferricyanide ion.
In the light of the above statements, choose the correct answer from the options given below.
(a) Both Statement I and Statement II are correct.
(b) Statement I is correct but Statement II is incorrect.
(c) Statement I is incorrect but Statement II is correct.
(d) Both Statement I and Statement II are incorrect.

37. Consider the reaction given below.
$CH_3CH_2CHO \xrightarrow[\text{(aldol)}]{\text{NaOH, } \Delta} P$. The compound P formed is
(a) $CH_3CH_2CH{=}CHCH_2CHO$
(b) $CH_3CH_2CH{=}\overset{CH_3}{\overset{|}{C}}CHO$

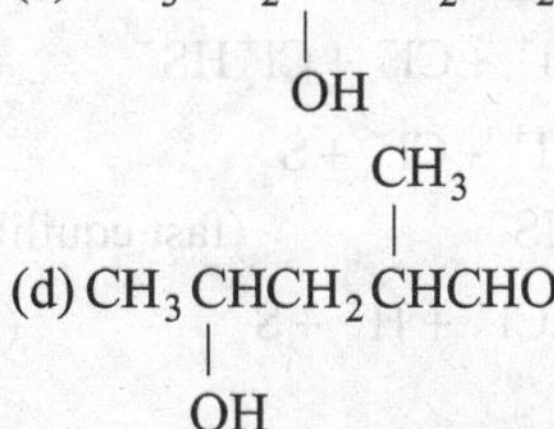

(c) $CH_3CH_2\underset{OH}{\underset{|}{C}H}CH_2CH_2OH$
(d) $CH_3\underset{OH}{\underset{|}{C}H}CH_2\overset{CH_3}{\overset{|}{C}H}CHO$

38. Match List-I with List-II.

	List-I		List-II
A.	$[Fe(CN)_6]^{3-}$	I.	Linear
B.	$[ZnCl_4]^{2-}$	II.	Square planar
C.	$[Ni(CN)_4]^{2-}$	III.	Tetrahedral
D.	$[Ag(CN)_2]^-$	IV.	Octahedral

Choose the correct answer from the options given below.

(a) A-III, B-IV, C-I, D-II
(b) A-IV, B-III, C-II, D-I
(c) A-II, B-IV, C-I, D-III
(d) A-IV, B-II, C-III, D-I

39. Select the incorrect statement about cerium.

(a) Cerium (IV) acts as an oxidising agent.
(b) The +3 oxidation state of cerium is more stable than the +4 oxidation state.
(c) The +4 oxidation state of cerium is not known in solutions.
(d) The common oxidation states of cerium are +2 and +3.

40. One mole for complex compound $[Co(NH_3)_5]Cl_3$ gives 3 moles of ions on dissolution in water. One mole of same complex reacts with two moles of $AgNO_3$ to yield two moles $AgCl(s)$. The complex is

(a) $[Co(NH_3)_4Cl_2]Cl \cdot NH_3$
(b) $[Co(NH_3)_4Cl]Cl \cdot NH_3$
(c) $[Co(NH_3)_5Cl]Cl_2$
(d) $[Co(NH_3)_3Cl_2] \cdot 3NH_3$

41. For $Cl_2(aq) + H_2S(aq) \longrightarrow S(s) + 2H^+(aq) + 2Cl^-(aq)$

The rate equation for this reaction is, Rate $= k[Cl_2][H_2S]$. The mechanism that follows the given rate equation is

A. $Cl_2 + H_2S \longrightarrow H^+ + Cl^- + Cl^+HS^-$ (slow)
$Cl^+ + HS^- \longrightarrow H^+ + Cl^- + S$ (fast)

B. $H_2S \longrightarrow H^+ + HS^-$ (fast equilibrium)
$Cl^+ + HS^- \longrightarrow 2Cl^- + H^+ + S$ (slow)

(a) B only
(b) Both A and B
(c) Neither A and B
(d) A only

42. $2Ph-\overset{O}{\overset{\|}{C}}-CH_3 \xrightarrow[H_2O]{Mg\text{-}Hg} P \xrightarrow[\Delta]{Conc.\ H_2SO_4} Q \xrightarrow[H_2O]{KMnO_4,\ H} R$

The product R in the given reaction is

(a) $CH_3-\underset{O^-}{\overset{Ph}{C}}-\underset{O^-}{\overset{Ph}{C}}-CH_3$
(b) $CH_3-\underset{\|}{\overset{}{C}}(O)-\underset{\|}{C}(O)-CH_3$
(c) $Ph-\underset{\|}{C}(O)-\underset{\|}{C}(O)-Ph$
(d) $CH_3-\underset{Ph}{\overset{Ph}{C}}-\underset{\|}{C}(O)-CH_3$

43. The major product P formed in the given reaction is

2-bromobenzyl bromide ($C_6H_4(Br)CH_2-Br$) $\xrightarrow{NH_3} P$

(a) $C_6H_4(Br)CH_2-NH_2$ (2-bromobenzylamine)
(b) $C_6H_4(Br)NH_2$ (2-bromoaniline)
(c) $C_6H_5CH_2NH_2$
(d) C_6H_5Br

44. Choose the incorrect statement from the following.

(a) Ti^{3+} salts are oxidising agents.
(b) Ga^+ salts are reducing agents.
(c) Pb^{4+} salts are better oxidising agents.
(d) As^{+5} salts are better oxidising agents.

45. Consider the types of isomerism given below.

I. Optical
II. Linkage
III. Ionisation
IV. Coordination
V. Solvate

Type of isomerism that are shown by compound $[Co(NH_3)_5(NO_2)(NO_3)_2]$ are

(a) II and III
(b) I, II and III
(c) I and IV
(d) II and V

Response Index

01 ⓐ ⓑ ⓒ ⓓ	14 ⓐ ⓑ ⓒ ⓓ	27 ⓐ ⓑ ⓒ ⓓ	40 ⓐ ⓑ ⓒ ⓓ
02 ⓐ ⓑ ⓒ ⓓ	15 ⓐ ⓑ ⓒ ⓓ	28 ⓐ ⓑ ⓒ ⓓ	41 ⓐ ⓑ ⓒ ⓓ
03 ⓐ ⓑ ⓒ ⓓ	16 ⓐ ⓑ ⓒ ⓓ	29 ⓐ ⓑ ⓒ ⓓ	42 ⓐ ⓑ ⓒ ⓓ
04 ⓐ ⓑ ⓒ ⓓ	17 ⓐ ⓑ ⓒ ⓓ	30 ⓐ ⓑ ⓒ ⓓ	43 ⓐ ⓑ ⓒ ⓓ
05 ⓐ ⓑ ⓒ ⓓ	18 ⓐ ⓑ ⓒ ⓓ	31 ⓐ ⓑ ⓒ ⓓ	44 ⓐ ⓑ ⓒ ⓓ
06 ⓐ ⓑ ⓒ ⓓ	19 ⓐ ⓑ ⓒ ⓓ	32 ⓐ ⓑ ⓒ ⓓ	45 ⓐ ⓑ ⓒ ⓓ
07 ⓐ ⓑ ⓒ ⓓ	20 ⓐ ⓑ ⓒ ⓓ	33 ⓐ ⓑ ⓒ ⓓ	46 ⓐ ⓑ ⓒ ⓓ
08 ⓐ ⓑ ⓒ ⓓ	21 ⓐ ⓑ ⓒ ⓓ	34 ⓐ ⓑ ⓒ ⓓ	47 ⓐ ⓑ ⓒ ⓓ
09 ⓐ ⓑ ⓒ ⓓ	22 ⓐ ⓑ ⓒ ⓓ	35 ⓐ ⓑ ⓒ ⓓ	48 ⓐ ⓑ ⓒ ⓓ
10 ⓐ ⓑ ⓒ ⓓ	23 ⓐ ⓑ ⓒ ⓓ	36 ⓐ ⓑ ⓒ ⓓ	49 ⓐ ⓑ ⓒ ⓓ
11 ⓐ ⓑ ⓒ ⓓ	24 ⓐ ⓑ ⓒ ⓓ	37 ⓐ ⓑ ⓒ ⓓ	50 ⓐ ⓑ ⓒ ⓓ
12 ⓐ ⓑ ⓒ ⓓ	25 ⓐ ⓑ ⓒ ⓓ	38 ⓐ ⓑ ⓒ ⓓ	
13 ⓐ ⓑ ⓒ ⓓ	26 ⓐ ⓑ ⓒ ⓓ	39 ⓐ ⓑ ⓒ ⓓ	

Performance Scanner

> 90% Excellent !	You have mastered the NEET syllabus (12th). The concepts of this entire syllabus are at your fingertips. Maintain this momentum.
76-90% Very Good !	You have a good command over the entire NEET syllabus (12th). Revise it again after a few days to enhance your performance.
60-75% Good !	You have a wide scope to learn for the entire NEET syllabus (12th). Revise it again.
<60% Not Satisfactory!	You have a long way ahead of you to master the NEET syllabus (12th). Revise it thoroughly.

Space for Rough Work

Test Booklet No. 3947267

Test Booklet Code NSS3

MEDACE
NEET (UG)
SELF ASSESSMENT KIT

NEET Stepping Stones 3

(Based on Class 12th Syllabus)

Name of the Candidate (In Capitals)

____

____

____

Candidate's Signature ____________

Invigilator's Signature ____________

Facsimile signature stamp of center superintendent____________

Important Instructions

- The test is of 45 minutes duration and the Test Booklet contains 45 multiple choice questions (four options with a single correct answer) from Chemistry.
- Candidates are advised to read all questions before they start attempting the question paper.
- Each questions carries 4 marks. For each correct response, the candidate will get 4 marks. For each incorrect response, one mark will be deducted from the total scores.
- In the event of candidate marking more than one option then one mark will be deducted. The maximum marks are 180.
- Use **Blue/Black Point Pen** only for writing particular on this page/marking response on Answer Sheet.

Do not open this Booklet until you start attempting the Test

Chemistry (Q. No. 1-45)

1. A white sodium salt dissolves readily in water to give a solution which is neutral to litmus. When silver nitrate solution is added to given solution, then white precipitate is obtained which does not dissolve in dil. HNO_3. The anion could be

(a) CO_3^{2-} (b) Cl^-
(c) S^{2-} (d) SO_4^{2-}

2. Which of the following compound is stable despite of having more than one —OH group attached with one carbon atom?

(a) $CH_3CH(OH)_2$ (b) $CH_3—C(OH)_3$

(c) $CCl_3—CH(OH)_2$ (d) $CH_3CH(OH)_2$ and $CH_3—C(OH)_3$

3. A 0.1 M solution of glucose ($M_w = 180$ g/mol) and a 0.1 M solution of urea ($M_w = 60$ g/mol) are placed on the two sides of semi permeable membrane to equal heights. In this context, which of the following statement is correct?

(a) Glucose will flow across the membrane into the urea solution.
(b) Urea will flow across the membrane into the glucose solution.
(c) Water will flow across the membrane from the urea solution into the glucose solution.
(d) There will be no net movement across the membrane.

4. A graph showing variation of osmotic pressure (π) *versus* molar concentration (C) of an aqueous solution at temperature T is given below,

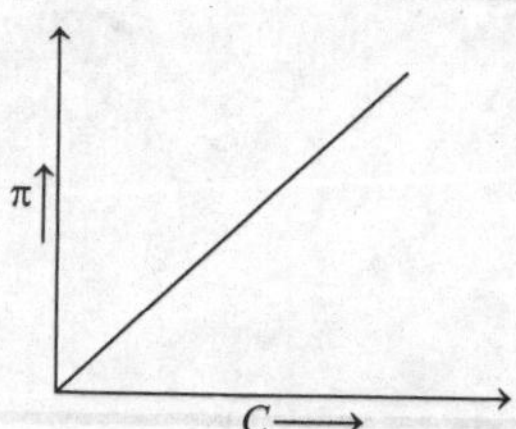

The slope of the line represents

(a) gas constant (R) / absolute temperature (T)
(b) absolute temperature (T) /degree of ionisation of solute (α)
(c) gas constant (R) × absolute temperature (T)
(d) degree of ionisation of solute

5. The percentage dissociation of salt, when 0.95 g KCl solution is dissolved in 100 g water so that the solution freezes at – 0.24°C is (Given K_f of water = 1.86 K kg/mol)

(a) 1% (b) 1.5% (c) 2% (d) 2.5%

6. Boiling point composition diagram of the liquid vapour equilibrium for A and B is shown in the figure. If a binary liquid mixture of A and B is distilled fractionally, which of the following would be correct observation?

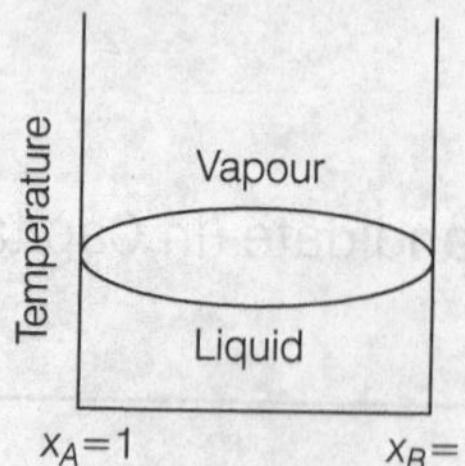

(a) Composition of the residue will approach pure liquid B.
(b) Composition of the distillate will approach pure liquid A only.
(c) Composition of distillate and residue will approach pure liquid A and B respectively.
(d) Neither of the component can be obtained in pure state.

7. What is the standard electrode potential for the reduction of HClO?

$$HClO(aq) + H^+(aq) + 2e^- \longrightarrow Cl^-(aq) + H_2O(l)$$

Given, $Cr^{2+}(aq) \longrightarrow Cr^{3+}(aq) + e^-; E^\circ = 0.41$ V

$$HClO(aq) + H^+(aq) + 2Cr^{2+}(aq) \longrightarrow 2Cr^{3+}(aq) + Cl^-(aq) + H_2O(l); E^\circ = 1.80\text{V}$$

(a) 1.39 (b) 1.54
(c) 1.22 (d) 0.90

8. The resistance of 0.01 N solution of an electrolyte is 210 Ω at 298 K with a cell constant of 0.88 cm^{-1}. The conductivity and equivalent conductivity are

	Conductivity $(\Omega^{-1}cm^{-1})$	Equivalent conductivity $(S\ cm^2\ eq^{-1})$
(a)	3.95×10^{-3}	419
(b)	4.19×10^{-3}	419
(c)	6.28×10^{-3}	419
(d)	5.19×10^{-4}	519

9. $\Lambda_{eq.}$ of 0.10 N solution of CaI_2 is 100.0 S cm^{-2} eq^{-1} at 298 K, G^* of the cell = 0.25 cm^{-1}. How much current will flow, when the potential difference between the electrode is 5V?

(a) 0.55 A (b) 0.45 A
(c) 0.1 A (d) 0.2 A

10. What will be the number of Faraday's required to electrolyse 6.35 g of $Cu^{\oplus}(aq)$ ions from an aqueous solution?

(a) 0.1 F (b) 0.2 F
(c) 0.3 F (d) 0.4 F

11. Which of the following is not an example of pseudo unimolecular reaction?

(a) $CH_3CO_2C_2H_5 + H_2O \xrightarrow{H^+} CH_3CO_2H + C_2H_5OH$

(b) $C_{12}H_{22}O_{11} + H_2O \xrightarrow{H^+} \underset{\text{Glucose}}{C_6H_{12}O_6} + \underset{\text{Fructose}}{C_6H_{12}O_6}$

(c) $CH_3COOCH_3 + H_2O \xrightarrow{OH^-} CH_3COOH + CH_3OH$

(d) $CH_3CO_2C_2H_5 + H_2O \xrightarrow{OH^-} CH_3CO_2H + C_2H_5OH$

12. In the Arrhenius equation for a certain reaction, the value of A and E_a (energy of activation) are $4\times10^{13}\ s^{-1}$ and 98.6 kJ mol^{-1} respectively.

If the reaction is of first order, at what temperature will its life period be 10 minutes ?

(a) 211.35 K (b) 310.96 K
(c) 395.35 K (d) 295.65 K

13. Which of the following statements are correct for first order reaction ?

I. $t_{75\%} = 2t_{1/2}$ II. $t_{87.5\%} = 3t_{1/2}$
III. $t_{96.87\%} = 4t_{1/2}$ IV. $t_{99.9\%} = 9t_{1/2}$

Choose the correct answer from the options given below.

(a) I and II (b) II and III
(c) III and IV (d) I and IV

14. A first order reaction has a rate constant of $15\times10^{-3}\ s^{-1}$. How long will 5.0 g of this reaction take to reduce to 3.0 g?

(a) 30.08 s (b) 24.06 s
(c) 20.05 s (d) 34.07 s

15. Consider the following cell :

Pt, Hg (l)	0.01 M mercurous nitrate solution in 0.1 M NH_3	0.1 M mercurous nitrate solution in 0.1 M HNO_3	Hg(l) 9 Pt

If the emf of the cell is 0.0295 V at 25°C, then th charge on mercurous ion and magnetic moment respectively are

(a) 1, 2 (b) 2, 0
(c) 3, 2 (d) 4, 0

16. Phenol on oxidation gives chloranil. Which of th following oxidant is used in this process?

(a) $K_2S_2O_8$ (b) $KMnO_4$
(c) $KClO_3 + HCl$ (d) H_2SO_4

17. Among the following, which reagent is required to convert propene to 1-propanol?

(a) B_2H_6 followed by H_2O_2/NaOH
(b) Conc. H_2SO_4 followed by hydrolysis
(c) HBr followed by *aq.* KOH
(d) $Hg(OCOCH_3)_2$ followed by $NaBH_4$

18. Find the incorrect statement related to PCl_5 fro the following.

(a) Two axial P— Cl bonds make an angle of 180 with each other.
(b) Axial P— Cl bonds are longer than equatorial P— Cl bonds.
(c) PCl_5 molecule is non-reactive.
(d) The equatorial P— Cl bonds make an angle o 120° with each other.

19. Consider the following reaction,

$K_2Cr_2O_7 + H_2SO_4 \longrightarrow$? (Major product)

(a) $Cr_2(SO_4)_3$ (b) Cr_2O_2
(c) CrO_3 (d) KOH

20. Why is Ce^{4+} in aqueous solution is an oxidising agent?

(a) Due to more electronegativity
(b) Due to more positive charge
(c) Ce^{4+} easily changes into +3 oxidation state
(d) All of the above

21. Which of the following statement is not true for the given reaction?

$$[Cu(H_2O)_4]^{2+} + 4NH_3 \rightleftharpoons [Cu(NH_3)_4]^{2+} + 4H_2O$$

(a) Ligand substitution reaction
(b) NH_3 is relatively strong field ligand while H_2O is a weak field ligand.
(c) During the reaction, there is a change in colour from light blue to dark blue.
(d) $[Cu(NH_3)_4]^{2+}$ has a tetrahedral structure and is paramagnetic.

22. Given below are two statements, one is labelled as Assertion (A) and the other is labelled as Reason (R).

Assertion (A) Property of back donation of e^- density stabilise the metal ligand (CO) bonding.

Reason (R) CO cannot accept electron density from metal.

In the light of the above statements, choose the correct answer from the options given below.

(a) Both (A) and (R) are true and (R) is the correct explanation of (A).
(b) Both (A) and (R) are true but (R) is not the correct explanation of (A).
(c) (A) is true but (R) is false.
(d) (A) is false but (R) is true.

23. The value of spin only magnetic moment for one of the following configuration is 2.82 BM. The correct one is

(a) d^4 (in weak field ligand)
(b) d^2 (in weak field ligand)
(c) d^3 (in weak as well as strong field ligand)
(d) d^5 (in strong field ligand)

24. Choose the correct statements from the following.

A. The chlorofluorocarbon compounds of methane and ethane are collectively called as freons.
B. DDT was the first chlorinated pesticide.
C. In the presence of air chloroform is oxidised to phosgene.
D. Due to liberation of free iodine, triiodomethane was used as antiseptic.
E. Methylene chloride is used as a metal cleaner and finishing solvent.

Choose the correct answer from the options given below.

(a) A, B, C and D
(b) B, C, D and E
(c) A, C, D and E
(d) A, B and D only

25. Which of the following oxide of halogen are used for the estimation of CO?

(a) I_2O_5 (b) I_2O_4
(c) I_2O_7 (d) BrO_3

26. Select the incorrect statement about H_2SO_4.

(a) It is a dehydrating agent .
(b) Sugar converts into carbon in presence of H_2SO_4
(c) Formic acid release carbon monoxide in presence of conc. H_2SO_4.
(d) When H_2SO_4 is strongly heated, then it dissociates into SO_2 and water.

27. Select the incorrect statement.

(a) Oxygen is strongly electronegative in nature as compared to other members of group 16.
(b) Sulphur has a strong tendency for catenation than oxygen.
(c) Oxygen exhibits −1, +2, oxidation state and other elements of this group show −2, +2, −4, +4, −6 and +6 oxidation states.
(d) There is quite large difference between the melting and boiling point of oxygen and sulphur.

28. Choose the correct option for given reaction,

$$CH_4 \xrightarrow{(X)} CH_3I + HI$$

Reagent X is

(a) I_2
(b) $HI + HNO_3/H_2SO_4$
(c) $HI + HIO_3/H_2SO_4$
(d) $HI + HIO_4$ or HNO_3

29. Given below are two statements.

Statement I The reaction of phenol with aqueous sodium hydroxide indicates that phenols are stronger acid than alcohols and water.

Statement II The delocalisation of negative charge makes phenoxide ion more stable and favours the ionisation of phenol.

In the light of the above statements, choose the correct answer from the options given below.

(a) Both Statement I and Statement II are incorrect.
(b) Statement I is correct but Statement II is incorrect.
(c) Statement I is incorrect but Statement II is correct.
(d) Both Statement I and Statement II are correct.

30. Given below are two statements, one is labelled as Assertion (A) and the other is labelled as Reason (R).

Assertion (A) Formaldehyde on reaction with concentrated alkali will undergo disproportionation reaction.

Reason (R) The aldehydes which do not have α-H atom undergo Cannizzaro reaction.

In the light of the above statements, choose the correct answer from the options given below.

(a) Both (A) and (R) are true and (R) is the correct explanation of (A).
(b) Both (A) and (R) are true but (R) is not the correct explanation of (A).
(c) (A) is true but (R) is false.
(d) (A) is false but (R) is true.

31. Consider the following reaction,

$$\text{Cyclohexanone} \xrightarrow{\text{LAH}} A \xrightarrow[\text{H}_2\text{SO}_4]{\text{H}^+} B \xrightarrow[\text{[O]}]{\text{KMnO}_4/\text{H}^+} \text{Final product}$$

The final product formed in the above reaction is

(a) adipic acid
(b) oxalic acid
(c) glutaric acid
(d) succinic acid

32. Which of the following statement is false?

(a) Primary alcohol gives blood red colour in Victor Meyer test.
(b) Tertiary alcohol gives yellow colour with $ZnCl_2/HCl$.
(c) Tertiary alcohol are colourless in Victor Meyer test.
(d) Secondary alcohol gives blue colour on Victor Meyer test.

33. Choose the incorrect statement.

(a) First four carboxylic acids are soluble in water due to intermolecular H-bonding.
(b) Carboxylic acids have high boiling point due to presence of intermolecular H-bonding.
(c) Melting point of carboxylic acids increases with increasing number of C-atoms for first ten members.
(d) Melting point is affected due to alternation effec

34. Which of the following carboxylic acid have low pK$_a$ value?

(a) CF_3COOH (b) $CHCl_2COOH$
(c) NO_2CH_2COOH (d) FCH_2COOH

35. In a reaction,

$$R\text{—}\overset{18}{\text{C}}\text{OOH} + R'\text{—OH} \xrightleftharpoons{\text{H}_2\text{SO}_4} \text{Product } (X)$$

Product (X) is

(a) $R\text{—COOR}'$
(b) $R\text{—CO}\overset{18}{\text{O}}R'$
(c) $RCOOCOOR'$
(d) Both (a) and (b)

36. Match List-I with List-II.

List-I (Reaction)	List-II (Product)
A. $CH_3CH_2OH \xrightarrow[180°C]{H_2SO_4}$	I. Ethane
B. $CH_3CH_2OH \xrightarrow[\text{Red } P]{HI}$	II. Ether
C. $C_2H_5OH \xrightarrow[413\text{ K}]{H_2SO_4}$	III. Acetaldehyde
D. $C_2H_5OH \xrightarrow[\text{[O]}]{KMnO_4}$	IV. Ethene

Choose the correct answer from the options giv below.

(a) A-IV, B-III, C-I, D-II
(b) A-III, B-IV, C-II, D-I
(c) A-IV, B-I, C-II, D-III
(d) A-I, B-II, C-III, D-IV

37. The final product, P formed in the given reactic

$$\text{Phthalimide} \xrightarrow[\text{(iii) 2 NaOH}]{\text{(i) KOH, (ii) } R\text{—}X/\text{DMF}} P$$

(a) $C_6H_5\text{—}NH_2$ (b) $R\text{—}NH_2$
(c) R_2NH (d) R_3N

38. Given below are two statements.

Statement I When benzamide reacts with Br_2 and KOH, aniline is obtained.

Statement II Aniline is obtained by Hofmann's bromamide degradation reaction.

In the light of the above statements, choose the correct answer from the options given below.

(a) Both Statement I and Statement II are incorrect.
(b) Statement I is correct, but Statement II is incorrect.
(c) Statement I is incorrect, but Statement II is correct.
(d) Both Statement I and Statement II are correct.

9. Product *R* of the following reaction.

$$CH_3-CH=CH-CH_3 \xrightarrow[\text{(ii) } NH_3]{\text{(i) HCl}} R$$

(a) $CH_3-CH_2-\underset{\displaystyle NH_2}{\overset{}{CH}}-CH_3$ (NH_2 on the CH)
(b) $CH_3-CH_2-CH_2-CH_3$
(c) $CH_3-\underset{NH_2}{CH}-\underset{NH_2}{CH}-CH_3$
(d) $CH_3-CH_2-\overset{NH_2}{CH}-CH_3$ and $CH_3-CH_2-CH_2-CH_3$

. Consider the following reaction.

$$C_6H_5-CH_2-NH_2 \xrightarrow[\text{(ii) } H_2O\text{, 273 K}]{\text{(i) } HNO_2/HCl}$$

(a) $C_6H_5-CH_2-OH$
(b) $C_6H_5-CH_2-N_2^+Cl^-$
(c) $C_6H_5-CH_2-Cl$
(d) C_6H_5-OH

. During the process of digestion, the proteins present in food materials are hydrolysed to amino acids. The two enzymes involved in the process are

$$\text{Proteins} \xrightarrow{\text{Enzyme }(A)} \text{Polypeptides} \xrightarrow{\text{Enzyme }(B)} \text{Amino acids}$$

(a) invertase and zymase
(b) amylase and maltase
(c) diastase and lipase
(d) pepsin and trypsin

42. Which of the following structure show α-D-glucose configuration?

(a) [Haworth ring: CH_2OH at top; ring O; H, H / H; OH, OH, H, OH; H, H]

(b) [Haworth ring: CH_2OH at top; ring O; H, H / H; OH, OH, H, OH; H, OH]

(c) [Haworth ring: CH_2OH at top; ring O; H, H / OH; OH, H, H, H; H, H]

(d) [Haworth ring: CH_2OH at top; ring O; H, H / OH; OH, OH, OH, H; H, H]

43. Which of the following oxide has N—O—N bond?

(a) N_2O_3 (b) N_2O_4
(c) N_2O (d) N_2O_5

44. Predict major product of the reaction,

$$CH_3-\underset{OH}{\overset{CH_3}{C}}-CH_2-CH_3 \xrightarrow[\text{(ii) Alc. KOH}]{\text{(i) } SOCl_2} \text{Major product}$$

(a) 2-methylbut-1-ene (b) 2-methylbut-2-ene
(c) Pent-1-ene (d) Pent-2-ene

45. In reaction,

$$R-OH + HX \longrightarrow R-X + H_2O$$

Correct order of reactivity of *HX* towards above reaction is

(a) HCl > HBr > HI > HF
(b) HBr > HCl > HI > HF
(c) HI > HCl > HBr > HF
(d) HI > HBr > HCl > HF

Response Index

01	ⓐ	ⓑ	ⓒ	ⓓ
02	ⓐ	ⓑ	ⓒ	ⓓ
03	ⓐ	ⓑ	ⓒ	ⓓ
04	ⓐ	ⓑ	ⓒ	ⓓ
05	ⓐ	ⓑ	ⓒ	ⓓ
06	ⓐ	ⓑ	ⓒ	ⓓ
07	ⓐ	ⓑ	ⓒ	ⓓ
08	ⓐ	ⓑ	ⓒ	ⓓ
09	ⓐ	ⓑ	ⓒ	ⓓ
10	ⓐ	ⓑ	ⓒ	ⓓ
11	ⓐ	ⓑ	ⓒ	ⓓ
12	ⓐ	ⓑ	ⓒ	ⓓ
13	ⓐ	ⓑ	ⓒ	ⓓ
14	ⓐ	ⓑ	ⓒ	ⓓ
15	ⓐ	ⓑ	ⓒ	ⓓ
16	ⓐ	ⓑ	ⓒ	ⓓ
17	ⓐ	ⓑ	ⓒ	ⓓ
18	ⓐ	ⓑ	ⓒ	ⓓ
19	ⓐ	ⓑ	ⓒ	ⓓ
20	ⓐ	ⓑ	ⓒ	ⓓ
21	ⓐ	ⓑ	ⓒ	ⓓ
22	ⓐ	ⓑ	ⓒ	ⓓ
23	ⓐ	ⓑ	ⓒ	ⓓ
24	ⓐ	ⓑ	ⓒ	ⓓ
25	ⓐ	ⓑ	ⓒ	ⓓ
26	ⓐ	ⓑ	ⓒ	ⓓ
27	ⓐ	ⓑ	ⓒ	ⓓ
28	ⓐ	ⓑ	ⓒ	ⓓ
29	ⓐ	ⓑ	ⓒ	ⓓ
30	ⓐ	ⓑ	ⓒ	ⓓ
31	ⓐ	ⓑ	ⓒ	ⓓ
32	ⓐ	ⓑ	ⓒ	ⓓ
33	ⓐ	ⓑ	ⓒ	ⓓ
34	ⓐ	ⓑ	ⓒ	ⓓ
35	ⓐ	ⓑ	ⓒ	ⓓ
36	ⓐ	ⓑ	ⓒ	ⓓ
37	ⓐ	ⓑ	ⓒ	ⓓ
38	ⓐ	ⓑ	ⓒ	ⓓ
39	ⓐ	ⓑ	ⓒ	ⓓ
40	ⓐ	ⓑ	ⓒ	ⓓ
41	ⓐ	ⓑ	ⓒ	ⓓ
42	ⓐ	ⓑ	ⓒ	ⓓ
43	ⓐ	ⓑ	ⓒ	ⓓ
44	ⓐ	ⓑ	ⓒ	ⓓ
45	ⓐ	ⓑ	ⓒ	ⓓ
46	ⓐ	ⓑ	ⓒ	ⓓ
47	ⓐ	ⓑ	ⓒ	ⓓ
48	ⓐ	ⓑ	ⓒ	ⓓ
49	ⓐ	ⓑ	ⓒ	ⓓ
50	ⓐ	ⓑ	ⓒ	ⓓ

Performance Scanner

> 90% Excellent !	You have mastered the NEET syllabus (12th). The concepts of this entire syllabus are at your fingertips. Maintain this momentum.
76-90% Very Good !	You have a good command over the entire NEET syllabus (12th). Revise it again after a few days to enhance your performance.
60-75% Good !	You have a wide scope to learn for the entire NEET syllabus (12th). Revise it again.
<60% Not Satisfactory!	You have a long way ahead of you to master the NEET syllabus (12th). Revise it thoroughly.

Scan for online stepping stones

Space for Rough Work

Test Booklet No. **3947268**

Test Booklet Code **NK01**

MEDACE
NEET (UG)
SELF ASSESSMENT KIT

NEET Knock Offs 1

(NEET Simulator Test)

Name of the Candidate (In Capitals)

____

____

____

Candidate's Signature ______________

Invigilator's Signature ______________

Facsimile signature stamp of center superintendent______________

Important Instructions

- The test is of 45 minutes duration and the Test Booklet contains 45 multiple choice questions (four options with a single correct answer) from Chemistry.
- Candidates are advised to read all questions before they start attempting the question paper.
- Each questions carries 4 marks. For each correct response, the candidate will get 4 marks. For each incorrect response, one mark will be deducted from the total scores.
- In the event of candidate marking more than one option then one mark will be deducted. The maximum marks are 180.
- Use **Blue/Black Point Pen** only for writing particular on this page/marking response on Answer Sheet.

Do not open this Booklet until you start attempting the Test

Chemistry (Q. No. 1-45)

1. 15.7 g of $BaCl_2$ on reaction with 4.3 of H_2SO_4 produces 8.1 g of HCl and some amount of $BaSO_4$. The amount of $BaSO_4$ formed is

(a) 11.9 g (b) 10.8 g
(c) 4.7 g (d) 37.2

2. Molar conductivities of acetic acid at 298 K at the concentration of 0.1 M and 0.001 M are 5.20 and 49.2 S cm^2/mol respectively. The degree of dissociation of acetic acid at these concentration (given) is

$$\Lambda^\circ_{H^+} = 349.8\,\Omega^{-1}\,cm^2/mol,$$

$$\Lambda^\circ_{CH_3COO^-} = 40.9\,\Omega^{-1}\,cm^2/mol$$

	($C = 0.1$ M)	($C = 0.001$ M)
(a)	2.3%	12.5%
(b)	9.5%	12.5%
(c)	1.3%	18.5%
(d)	1.3%	12.5%

3. Which of the following complex form *fac-mer* isomer ?

(a) $[Co(NH_3)_4Cl_2]$
(b) $[Co(en)_2Cl_2]^+$
(c) $[Rh(py)_3Cl_3]$
(d) $[Co(NH_3)_4Cl(NO_2)]$

4. What will be the product of reaction given below.

I. $R—X + AgNO_2 \longrightarrow P$
II. $R—X + KNO_2 \longrightarrow Q$

P and Q are
In this reaction,

	P	Q
(a)	R—NO	$R—NO_2$
(b)	R—ONO	$R—NO_2$
(c)	$R—NO_2$	R—ONO
(d)	$R—NO_2$	R—NO

5. During ozonolysis of $CH_2{=}CH_2$ if hydrolysis is made in absence of Zn the products formed are

(a) HCHO
(b) CH_3CH_2OH
(c) CH_2OHCH_2COOH
(d) HCOOH

6. If water vapour is assumed to be an ideal gas and the molar enthalpy change for vaporisation of one mole of water at 1 bar and 100°C is 41 kJ/mol, the internal energy change when 1 mol of water is vaporised is

(a) 37.9 kJ/mol (b) 75 kJ/mol
(c) 30.2 kJ/mol (d) 89 kJ/mol

7. Emission transitions in the Paschen series to orbit $n = 3$ from orbit n can be represented as

$$v = 3.29 \times 10^{15}\ (\text{Hz}) \left[\frac{1}{(3)^2} - \frac{1}{n^2}\right].$$

The value of n if the transition is observed at 1000 nm (wavelength) is

(a) 3 (b) 2
(c) 7 (d) 6

8. Select the incorrect statement.

(a) Colour of the $K_2Cr_2O_7$ depends on the pH of the solution.
(b) Ce^{4+} is good oxidising agent, whereas Sm^{3+} is a good reducing agent.
(c) Cu^+ ion is not at all stable in aqueous solution.
(d) $La(OH)_3$ is less basic than $Lu(OH)_3$.

9. What mass of zinc is required to produce hydrogen by reaction with HCl which is enough to produce 4 moles of ammonia according to the reaction?

$$Zn + 2HCl \longrightarrow ZnCl_2 + H_2\uparrow$$

$$3H_2 + N_2 \longrightarrow 2NH_3$$

(a) 190 g of Zn (b) 286 g of Zn
(c) 390 g of Zn (d) 398 g of Zn

10. Given below are two statements, one is labelled as Assertion (A) and the other is labelled as Reason (R).

Assertion (A) Reactivity of nucleophilic addition reaction towards carbonyl compound depends upon the nature of attached group with carbonyl group.

Reason (R) Acetaldehyde is more reactive towards nucleophilic addition reaction than acetone.

In the light of the above statements, choose the most appropriate answer from the options given below.

(a) Both (A) and (R) are true and (R) is the correct explanation of (A).
(b) Both (A) and (R) are true but (R) is not the correct explanation of (A).
(c) (A) is true but (R) is false.
(d) (A) is false but (R) is true.

11. Select increasing order of the size of given ions.

(A) Cl^-, (B) P^{3-}, (C) S^{2-}, (D) F^-

(a) (D) < (A) < (C) < (B)
(b) (D) < (A) < (B) < (C)
(c) (B) < (C) < (D) < (A)
(d) (B) < (C) < (A) < (D)

12. Given below are two statements, one is labelled as Assertion (A) and the other is labelled as Reason (R).

Assertion (A) Boric acid is a weak monobasic acid.

Reason (R) Boric acid is not a protonic acid but acts as Lewis acid by accepting electrons from a hydroxyl ion.

In the light of the above statements, choose the most appropriate answer from the options given below.

(a) Both (A) and (R) are true and (R) is the correct explanation of (A).
(b) Both (A) and (R) are true but (R) is not the correct explanation of (A).
(c) (A) is true but (R) is false.
(d) (A) is false but (R) is true.

13. Match List-I with List-II.

List-I (Molecule)	List-II (Oxidation state of the central atom)
A. Br_3O_8	I. +6
B. $S_4O_6^{2-}$	II. +4, +6
C. C_3O_2	III. +5, 0
D. CrO_5	IV. 0, +2

Choose the correct answer from the options given below.

(a) A-II, B-I, C-IV, D-III
(b) A-II, B-III, C-IV, D-I
(c) A-III, B-I, C-II, D-IV
(d) A-III, B-IV, C-II, D-I

14. Select the incorrect set from List-I and List-II.

	List-I		List-II
(a)	$B(OH)_3$ and B_2O	–	Acidic
(b)	$Al(OH)_3$ and Al_2O_3	–	Amphoteric
(c)	$Ln(OH)_3$ and Ln_2O_3	–	Acidic
(d)	$Tl(OH)_3$ and Tl_2O_3	–	Strong basic

15. Which set does not have same bond order and bond length?

(a) N_2^-, O_2^+
(b) F_2, O_2^{2-}
(c) CO, N_2
(d) N_2^{2-}, N_2^+

16. Given below are two statements.

Statement I 2, 6-dimethyl-4-nitrophenol is more acidic than 3, 5-dimethyl-4-nitrophenol.

Statement II 3, 5-dimethyl-4-nitrophenol is more acidic due to steric inhibition of the resonance of —NO_2 group with two methyl groups.

In the light of the above statements, choose the most appropriate answer from the options given below.

(a) Both statement I and Statement II are incorrect.
(b) Statement I is correct but Statement II is incorrect.
(c) Statement I is incorrect but Statement II is correct.
(d) Both Statement I and Statement II are correct.

17. Select the correct statements from the following.

A. Ostwald's theory is related to gases.

B. Order of reaction is the sum of powers of concentration of the reactants in the rate law expression.

C. Maxwell's theory is related to dilute solution.

D. Rate of elementary reactions depends upon the slowest step, i.e. rate determining step of reaction.

E. Transition state theory and absolute reaction rate theory is related to chemical kinetics.

Choose the correct answer from the options given below.

(a) A, B and D (b) B, D and E

(c) B, C and E (d) B, C and D

18. Which of the following statement is correct?

(a) H_3PO_3 is a stronger acid than H_2SO_3.

(b) In aqueous medium, HF is a stronger acid than HCl.

(c) $HClO_4$ is a weaker acid than $HClO_3$.

(d) HNO_3 acid is a stronger acid than HNO_2.

19. What is the final product obtained when *tert*-butyl bromide is treated with *tert*-butoxide?

(a) $CH_3-\overset{CH_3}{\underset{CH_3}{\overset{|}{\underset{|}{C}}}}-\overset{CH_3}{\underset{CH_3}{\overset{|}{\underset{|}{C}}}}-CH_3$

(b) $CH_3-\overset{CH_3}{\underset{CH_2}{\overset{|}{\underset{|}{C}}}}$

(c) $CH_3-\overset{CH_3}{\underset{CH_3}{\overset{|}{\underset{|}{C}}}}-O-CH_3$

(d) $CH_3-\overset{CH_3}{\underset{CH_3}{\overset{|}{\underset{|}{C}}}}-O-\overset{CH_3}{\underset{CH_3}{\overset{|}{\underset{|}{C}}}}-CH_3$

20. When aqueous sodium chloride solution is electrolysed

(a) at cathode H^+ is reduced into H_2 instead of Na^+.

(b) at cathode Na^+ is reduced to Na.

(c) Cl^- oxidised into Cl_2 at cathode.

(d) H^+ oxidised into H_2 at cathode.

21. Which of the following does not show electrical conduction in its physical states?

(a) Graphite (b) Potassium

(c) Diamond (d) Calcium

22. On dissolving 3.24 g of sulphur in 40 g of benzene, it is found that the boiling point of the solution becomes higher than that of benzene by 0.81 K. What is the molecular formula of sulphur? (K_b = 2.53 K kg/mol and atomic mass of sulphur = 32 g/mol)

(a) S_2 (b) S_4

(c) S_8 (d) S_6

23. What will be the resonance energy of N_2O from the following data ?

$$\Delta_f H^\ominus \text{ of } N_2O = 82 \text{ kJ/mol}$$

Standard bond enthalpy of $N\equiv N$, $N=N$, $O=O$ and $N=O$ bonds are 946, 418, 498 and 607 kJ/mol respectively.

(a) – 91 kJ/mol (b) 62 kJ/mol

(c) 82 kJ/mol (d) – 88 kJ/mol

24. Which of the following is a pair of isoelectronic species?

(a) ClO_2, Cl_2^- (b) Cl_2O_3, ICl_2^-

(c) ClO_2^-, ClF_2^+ (d) IF_2^+, I_3^-

25. Which of the following compound shows maximum covalent character?

(a) $FeCl_2$ (b) $SnCl_2$

(c) $AlCl_3$ (d) $MgCl_2$

26. Select the incorrect statement about metals of *d* and *f*-block family.

(a) The highest oxidation state (+8) in compounds is shown by Os and Rh.
(b) In *d*-block elements, Ti and Hf have similar atomic radii.
(c) V_2O_5 catalyst used in formation of SO_3 from SO_2.
(d) Cr^{2+} is reducing agent, while Mn^{3+} is strongly oxidising.

27. For the calomel electrode Hg, Hg_2Cl_2/Cl^- electrode potential measured at different Cl^- ion concentration are plotted against $\log Cl^-$. The variation is correctly represented by the plot.

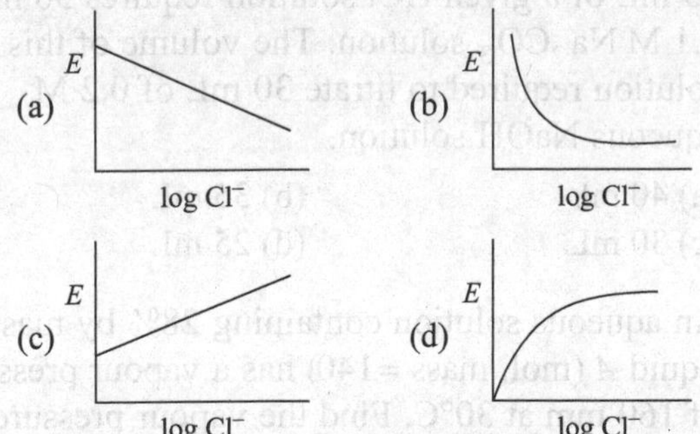

28. If 0.4 g of NaOH is to be dissolved in one litre of the solution, then pOH of the solution is

(a) 2 (b) 3
(c) 1 (d) 4

29. Consider the following reactions.

(i) $2NO_2 + 2OH^- \longrightarrow NO_2^- + NO_3 + H_2O$
(ii) $CH_4 + 2O_2 \longrightarrow CO_2 + 2H_2O$
(iii) $2F_2 + 2OH^- \longrightarrow 2F^- + OF_2 + H_2O$
(iv) $2H_2O_2 \longrightarrow 2H_2O + O_2$
(v) $Cl_2 + 2NaOH \longrightarrow NaCl + NaClO + H_2O$
(vi) $CH_4 + 4Cl_2 \longrightarrow CCl_4 + 4HCl$
(vii) $2NO_2 + H_2O \longrightarrow HNO_3 + HNO_2$

The number of disproportionation reactions are.

(a) 6 (b) 5
(c) 4 (d) 3

30. Given below are two statements.

Statement I Propene reacts with Br_2 at 800 K temperature, to give allyl bromide as a major product formed.

Statement II Allylic free radical is more stable, which gives resonating structures.

In the light of the above statements, choose the most appropriate answer from the options given below.

(a) Both statement I and Statement II are incorrect.
(b) Statement I is correct but Statement II is incorrect.
(c) Statement I is incorrect but Statement II is correct.
(d) Both Statement I and Statement II are correct.

31. An alkane has molecular mass 86. What is molecular formula of the alkane and number of possible structural isomers of this molecular formula?

	Formula	No. of possible isomers (structural)
(a)	C_6H_{14}	3
(b)	C_6H_{14}	4
(c)	C_6H_{14}	5
(d)	C_6H_{14}	6

32. In the following reaction,

$$C_6H_5—C\equiv CH \xrightarrow[CH_3I]{NaNH_2/NH_3} A \xrightarrow{Na/NH_3(l)} B$$

A and *B* are respectively.

(a) 1-phenyl prop-1-yne, *cis*-1-phenyl prop-1-ene
(b) 1-phenyl prop-1-yne, *trans*-1-phenyl prop-1-ene
(c) 1-phenyl prop-1-ene, 1-phenyl propane
(d) 1-phenyl prop-1-ene, 1-amino phenyl propene

33. Which of the following statement is correct ?

(a) If $\Delta_o < p$, low spin state is more stable.
(b) CO is a very weak ligand.
(c) The colour of a complex depends only on the nature of the metal ion.
(d) Tetrahedral complexes have nearly 50% CFSE value than octahedral complexes.

34. Which of the following enzyme catalyse the conversion of glucose to ethanol?

(a) Zymase (b) Amylase
(c) Invertase (d) Maltase

35. Identify the final product $[C]$ obtained in the following sequence of reactions.

$$CH_3CH_2I \xrightarrow{NaCN} A \xrightarrow[\text{Partial hydrolysis}]{OH^-} B \xrightarrow{Br_2/NaOH} C$$

(a) CH_3NH_2
(b) $(CH_3)_2CH—NH_2$
(c) $CH_3CH_2NH_2$
(d) $CH_3CH_2—COONH_4$

36. Select the correct statements about PH_3.

I. When calcium phosphide is boiled with water, then PH_3 is obtained.
II. PH_3 explodes in contact with traces of oxidising agent like HNO_3, Cl_2 and Br_2 vapours.
III. When PH_3 is heated, then it decomposes into P_4 and H_2.
IV. Bond angle at PH_4^+ is higher than PH_3.
V. It is a non toxic, non-flammable gas.

Choose the correct answer from the options given below.

(a) I and II (b) I, II and III
(c) I, III, IV and V (d) I, II, III and IV

37. When excess ammonia is added to $CuSO_4$ solution the deep blue complex obtained is

(a) tetrahedral and paramagnetic
(b) tetrahedral and diamagnetic
(c) square planar and paramagnetic
(d) tetrahedral and ferromagnetic

38. Given below are two statements, one is labelled as Assertion (A) and the other is labelled as Reason (R).

Assertion (A) The multimolecular reactions are quite rare in comparison with bimolecular reaction.

Reason (R) At normal pressure, double collisions are much less frequent than triple ones.

In the light of the above statements, choose the correct answer from the options given below.

(a) Both (A) and (R) are true and (R) is the correct explanation of (A).
(b) Both (A) and (R) are true but (R) is not the correct explanation of (A).
(c) (A) is true but (R) is false.
(d) (A) is false but (R) is true.

39. In the following reaction,

$$CH_3—CH_2—\overset{O}{\overset{\|}{C}}—O—H + R'—\overset{18}{O}—H \xrightarrow{H_2SO_4} A + B$$

A and B are

(a) $CH_3CH_2CO\overset{18}{O}R' + H_2O$
(b) $CH_3—CH_2—COOR' + H_2O^{18}$
(c) $CH_3—CH_2—\overset{O}{\overset{\|}{C}}—H + R'—\overset{18}{O}—O—H$
(d) $CH_3—CH_2—\overset{O}{\overset{\|}{C}}—H + H_2\overset{18}{O}$

40. 25 mL of a given HCl solution requires 30 mL of 0.1 M Na_2CO_3 solution. The volume of this HCl solution required to titrate 30 mL of 0.2 M aqueous NaOH solution.

(a) 40 mL (b) 35 mL
(c) 30 mL (d) 25 mL

41. An aqueous solution containing 28% by mass of liquid A (mol. mass = 140) has a vapour pressure of 160 mm at 30°C. Find the vapour pressure of the pure liquid A.

[The vapour pressure of pure water at 30°C is 150 mmHg.]

(a) 163 mmHg
(b) 393 mmHg
(c) 360 mmHg
(d) 340 mmHg

42. $Cr_2O_7^{2-} + X \xrightarrow{H^+} Cr^{3+}$ + oxidised product of (X)

X in the above reaction cannot be

(a) $C_2O_4^{2-}$ (b) Fe^{2+}
(c) SO_4^{2-} (d) S^{2-}

43. Which of the following bonds are present in tertiary structure of proteins?

I. Ionic or salt-bridge II. Hydrogen bonds
III. van der Waals' interaction IV. Disulphide bonds
V. Dipole-dipole interaction

Choose the correct answer from the options given below.

(a) I, II and V
(b) I and III
(c) I and IV
(d) I, II, III and IV

44. Choose the correct option for the following reaction.

$$\underset{\text{Pentan-2-one}}{CH_3—CH_2—CH_2—COCH_3} \xrightarrow[\Delta]{\text{Conc. } HNO_3} \text{Major products}$$

Major products are

(a) $CH_3CH_2CH_2COOH + CO_2$
(b) $CH_3—CH_2—COOH + CH_3COOH$
(c) $CH_3—CH_2—COOH + CH_3CHO$
(d) $CH_3—CH_2—CH_2—COOH + HCHO$

45. Consider the following reaction.

$$\underset{\text{(An acid)}}{A} \xrightarrow{NH_3/\text{Heat}} B \xrightarrow{Br_2/KOH} C \xrightarrow{CHCl_3/KOH} D \xrightarrow{H_3O^+} HCOOH + E$$

Reduction of (C) forms $(CH_3)_3C—NH_2$, then determine A.

	A	D	E
(a)	CH_3CH_2COOH	$CH_3—CH_2NC$	$CH_3—CH_2—NH_2$
(b)	CH_3CH_2COOH	$CH_3—CH_2—CN$	$CH_3—CH_2—CH_2—NH_2$
(c)	$(CH_3)_3C—COOH$	$(CH_3)_3C—NC$	$(CH_3)_3—CH_2—NH_2$
(d)	$(CH_3)_3C—COOH$	$(CH_3)_3C—NC$	$(CH_3)_3C—NH_2$

Response Index

01 ⓐ ⓑ ⓒ ⓓ	14 ⓐ ⓑ ⓒ ⓓ	27 ⓐ ⓑ ⓒ ⓓ	40 ⓐ ⓑ ⓒ ⓓ
02 ⓐ ⓑ ⓒ ⓓ	15 ⓐ ⓑ ⓒ ⓓ	28 ⓐ ⓑ ⓒ ⓓ	41 ⓐ ⓑ ⓒ ⓓ
03 ⓐ ⓑ ⓒ ⓓ	16 ⓐ ⓑ ⓒ ⓓ	29 ⓐ ⓑ ⓒ ⓓ	42 ⓐ ⓑ ⓒ ⓓ
04 ⓐ ⓑ ⓒ ⓓ	17 ⓐ ⓑ ⓒ ⓓ	30 ⓐ ⓑ ⓒ ⓓ	43 ⓐ ⓑ ⓒ ⓓ
05 ⓐ ⓑ ⓒ ⓓ	18 ⓐ ⓑ ⓒ ⓓ	31 ⓐ ⓑ ⓒ ⓓ	44 ⓐ ⓑ ⓒ ⓓ
06 ⓐ ⓑ ⓒ ⓓ	19 ⓐ ⓑ ⓒ ⓓ	32 ⓐ ⓑ ⓒ ⓓ	45 ⓐ ⓑ ⓒ ⓓ
07 ⓐ ⓑ ⓒ ⓓ	20 ⓐ ⓑ ⓒ ⓓ	33 ⓐ ⓑ ⓒ ⓓ	46 ⓐ ⓑ ⓒ ⓓ
08 ⓐ ⓑ ⓒ ⓓ	21 ⓐ ⓑ ⓒ ⓓ	34 ⓐ ⓑ ⓒ ⓓ	47 ⓐ ⓑ ⓒ ⓓ
09 ⓐ ⓑ ⓒ ⓓ	22 ⓐ ⓑ ⓒ ⓓ	35 ⓐ ⓑ ⓒ ⓓ	48 ⓐ ⓑ ⓒ ⓓ
10 ⓐ ⓑ ⓒ ⓓ	23 ⓐ ⓑ ⓒ ⓓ	36 ⓐ ⓑ ⓒ ⓓ	49 ⓐ ⓑ ⓒ ⓓ
11 ⓐ ⓑ ⓒ ⓓ	24 ⓐ ⓑ ⓒ ⓓ	37 ⓐ ⓑ ⓒ ⓓ	50 ⓐ ⓑ ⓒ ⓓ
12 ⓐ ⓑ ⓒ ⓓ	25 ⓐ ⓑ ⓒ ⓓ	38 ⓐ ⓑ ⓒ ⓓ	
13 ⓐ ⓑ ⓒ ⓓ	26 ⓐ ⓑ ⓒ ⓓ	39 ⓐ ⓑ ⓒ ⓓ	

Performance Scanner

> 90% Excellent !	You have mastered the NEET syllabus (12th). The concepts of this entire syllabus are at your fingertips. Maintain this momentum.
76-90% Very Good !	You have a good command over the entire NEET syllabus (12th). Revise it again after a few days to enhance your performance.
60-75% Good !	You have a wide scope to learn for the entire NEET syllabus (12th). Revise it again.
<60% Not Satisfactory!	You have a long way ahead of you to master the NEET syllabus (12th). Revise it thoroughly.

Space for Rough Work

Test Booklet No. **3947269**

Test Booklet Code **NK02**

MEDACE

NEET (UG)

SELF ASSESSMENT KIT

NEET Knock Offs 2

(NEET Simulator Test)

Name of the Candidate (In Capitals)

____

____

____

Candidate's Signature ____________

Invigilator's Signature ____________

Facsimile signature stamp of center superintendent____________

Important Instructions

- The test is of 45 minutes duration and the Test Booklet contains 45 multiple choice questions (four options with a single correct answer) from Chemistry.
- Candidates are advised to read all questions before they start attempting the question paper.
- Each questions carries 4 marks. For each correct response, the candidate will get 4 marks. For each incorrect response, one mark will be deducted from the total scores.
- In the event of candidate marking more than one option then one mark will be deducted. The maximum marks are 180.
- Use **Blue/Black Point Pen** only for writing particular on this page/marking response on Answer Sheet.

Do not open this Booklet until you start attempting the Test

Chemistry (Q. No. 1-45)

1. Which of the following indicator is used in the titration of acetic acid with sodium hydroxide for quantitative estimation?

(a) Phenolphthalein
(b) Mercury paper
(c) Lichens
(d) Methyl orange

2. Given below are two statements one is labelled as Assertion (A) and the other is labelled as Reason (R).

Assertion (A) In Etard reaction methylbenzene oxidises into benzaldehyde.

Reason (R) Chromyl chloride is an oxidising reagent which oxidises methyl group to benzaldehyde *via* forming a chromyl complex followed by hydrolysis.

In the light of the above statements choose the most appropriate answer from the options given below.

(a) Both (A) and (R) are true and (R) is the correct explanation of (A).
(b) Both (A) and (R) are true but (R) is not the correct explanation of (A).
(c) (A) is true but (R) is false.
(d) (A) is false but (R) is true.

3. Which of the following graph shows a graph plotted between $\log k$ *versus* $\frac{1}{T}$ for calculating activation energy.

(a) 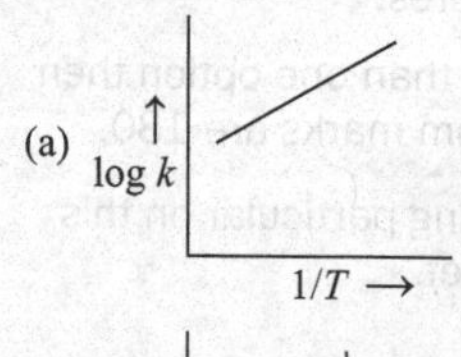

(b) 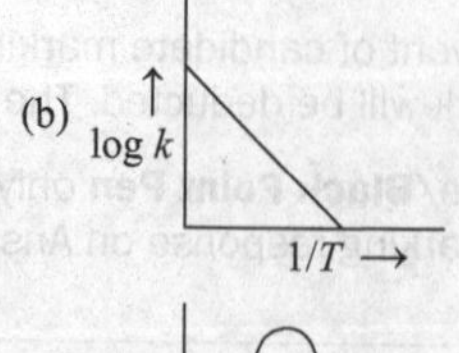

(c) 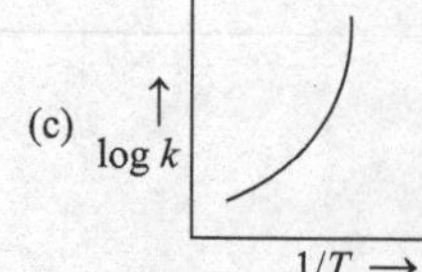

(b) 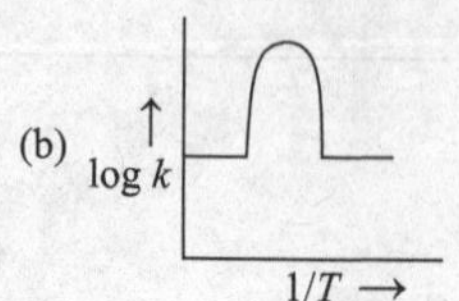

4. Which of the following statement is incorrect about $K_2Cr_2O_7$?

(a) $K_2Cr_2O_7$ is used for volumetric estimation of ferrous salt, iodide and sulphite.
(b) Used in photography for hardening of gelatine film.
(c) Chromic acid mixture used for cleaning glass ware, consists of $K_2Cr_2O_7$ and conc. H_2SO_4.
(d) It is soluble in alcohol and acetone.

5. Which of the following complex does not gives +3 oxidation state of cobalt?

(a) $[Co(en)_2Cl_2]_2SO_4$
(b) $[Co(NH_3)_4Cl_2]SO_4$
(c) $[Co(en)_2F_2]ClO_3$
(d) $[Co(NH_3)_4Cl_2]SO_4$

6. Given below are two statements.

Statement I Aldehydes which do not have an α-hydrogen atom undergoes self oxidation and reduction reaction on heating with alkali solution.

Statement II Due to conc. KOH, one molecule reduces into alcohol while another oxidises into carboxylic acid salt during Cannizzaro reaction.

In the light of the above statements, choose the most appropriate answer from the options given below.

(a) Both Statement I and Statement II are incorrect.
(b) Statement I is correct but Statement II is incorrect.
(c) Statement I is incorrect but Statement II is correct.
(d) Both Statement I and Statement II are correct.

7. The value of rate constant for the decomposition of N_2O_5 is 3.46×10^{-5} at 25°C and 4.87×10^{-3} at 65°C.

$$N_2O_5 \longrightarrow N_2O_4 + \frac{1}{2}O_2$$

The energy of activation for the reaction ($R = 8.314$ J/K/mol) will be

[Use : log 140.75 = 2.148]

(a) 82.58 kJ/mol
(b) 105.62 kJ/mol
(c) 99.68 kJ/mol
(d) 103.58 kJ/mol

8. Select the incorrect match of set from List-I and List-II.

	List-I (Properties)	List-II (Order of element)
(a)	Decreasing non-metallic character	$F > N > C > B > Si$
(b)	Decreasing oxidising power	$F > Cl > O > N$
(c)	Decreasing metallic character	$B > Al > Mg > K$
(d)	Increasing order of size	$Li^+ < Na^+ < F^- < Cl^-$

9. Which of the following salt is used to decolourise the acidified potassium permanganate solution?

(a) Bleaching powder
(b) White vitriol
(c) Mohr's salt
(d) Potash alum

10. Select the incorrect statement about molecular orbital theory.

(a) Atomic orbitals participating in overlap vanish and result in formation of new orbitals called molecular orbitals.
(b) It provides explanation for magnetic behaviour of various chemical species like O_2.
(c) It fails to explain the existence of species like H_2^+ and He_2^+.
(d) According to MOT, resonance has no significant role.

11. Consider the following reaction.

$$CH_3CH_2Cl \xrightarrow{NaCN} X \xrightarrow{Ni/H_2} Y \xrightarrow{\text{Acetic anhydride}} Z$$

The product Z formed in the above reaction is

(a) $CH_3CH_2CH_2CONHCOCH_3$
(b) $CH_3CH_2CONHCH_3$
(c) $CH_3CH_2CH_2NH_2$
(d) $CH_3CH_2CH_2NHCOCH_3$

12. Consider the following compounds.

(i) H_2O (ii) NH_2^- (iii) SF_4
(iv) SeF_4 (v) XeF_2 (vi) I_6^-
(vii) Br_3^-

Which of the following pair do not have same structure?

(a) (i) and (ii) (b) (iii) and (iv)
(c) (v) and (vi) (d) (v) and (vii)

13. Given below are two statements, one is labelled as Assertion (A) and the other is labelled as Reason (R).

Assertion (A) At higher altitude breathing is difficult.

Reason (R) The partial pressure of oxygen decreases at higher altitudes.

In the light of the above statements, choose the most appropriate answer from the options given below.

(a) Both (A) and (R) are true and (R) is the correct explanation of (A).
(b) Both (A) and (R) are true but (R) is not the correct explanation of (A).
(c) (A) is true but (R) is false.
(d) (A) is false but (R) is true.

14. Which of the following statement is incorrect?

(a) According to the Pauli's exclusion principle, no two electrons in an atom can have same values for all the four quantum numbers.
(b) According to Hund's rule, the pairing of electrons in the orbitals of a particular subshell (p, d or f) does not take place until all the orbitals of the sub shell are singly occupied. Morever, the singly occupied orbital must have the electrons with parallel spins.
(c) The half-filled and completely filled degenerate orbitals provide extra stability to the system due to symmetrical arrangement and exchange energy.
(d) According to Aufbau rule, the electrons are added progressively to the various orbitals in their order of decreasing energies, starting with the orbital of highest energy.

15. Which of the following is the de-Broglie wavelength of an electron in the 4th Bohr orbit?

(a) $6\pi a_0$ (b) $2\pi a_0$
(c) $8\pi a_0$ (d) $4\pi a_0$

16. How many moles of AgBr ($K_{sp} = 5 \times 10^{-13}$ mol^2 L^{-2}) will dissolve in a 0.01 M NaBr solution? (NaBr is completely ionised into Na^+ and Br^- ions)
(a) 5×10^{-11} mol
(b) 4.28×10^{-10} mol
(c) 5×10^{-8} mol
(d) 4.28×10^{-11} mol

17. Among the given options, which one of the following has the strong O—O bond is
(a) O_2^+ (b) O_2
(c) O_2^- (d) O_2^{2-}

18. Consider the following reaction.

$$xKMnO_4 + NH_3 \longrightarrow yKNO_3 + MnO_2 + KOH + H_2O$$

The value of $x + y$ is
(a) 10 (b) 13
(c) 14 (d) 11

19. Match List-I with List-II.

	List-I (Reaction)	List-II (Major product)
A.	Cyanohydrin $\xrightarrow{H_3O^+}$	I. 3-hydroxybutanal
B.	2 Ethanal $\xrightarrow[NaOH]{dil.}$	II. Cyclic ketal
C.	Acetone $\xrightarrow[Dry\ HCl]{Glycol}$	III. Trichloromethane
D.	Acetaldehyde $\xrightarrow{NaOCl}$	IV. Lactic acid

Choose the correct answer from the options given below.
(a) A-III, B-I C-II, D-IV
(b) A-I, B-II, C-IV, D-III
(c) A-II, B-III, C-IV, D-I
(d) A-IV, B-I, C-II, D-III

20. The state of hybridisation of C in given compounds respectively are
I. CO II. HCN III. CO_3^{2-}
IV. CaC_2 V. CO_2

Choose the correct answer from the options given below.

	I	II	III	IV	V
(a)	sp	sp^2	sp^2	sp	sp^2
(b)	sp	sp^2	sp	sp	sp^2
(c)	sp	sp	sp^2	sp	sp
(d)	sp	sp	sp	sp	sp

21. Which of the following product is formed when sucrose is heated with conc. HNO_3?
(a) Adipic acid
(b) Citric acid
(c) Oxalic acid
(d) Sucrose nitrate

22. Choose the incorrect statement from the following.
(a) James Watson and Francis Crick gave a double strand helix structure for DNA.
(b) Nucleotides are joined together by hydrogen bond between 5′ and 3′ carbon atoms of pentose sugar.
(c) Nucleoside links with phosphoric acid to give nucleotide.
(d) Adenine forms hydrogen bond with thymine while cytosine forms hydrogen bond with guanine.

23. A mixture of chloroform and diethyl ether shows
(a) postive deviation from Raoult's law.
(b) negative deviation from Raoult's law.
(c) ideal behaviour
(d) separate layers of chloroform and diethyl ether.

24. Correct IUPAC name of following compound is

$$\begin{array}{c} C_2H_5—C=CH_2 \\ | \\ CH_3—CH—C\equiv CH \end{array}$$

(a) 2-ethyl-3-methyl pent-1-en-4-yne
(b) 4-ethyl-3-methyl pent-4-en-yne
(c) 3-methyl-4-ethyl pent-1-en-4-yne
(d) 3-methyl-4-ethyl pent-4-en-1-yne

25. Total number of isomers of organic compound $C_5H_{10}O$ (carbonyl compound) are
(a) 4 (b) 3
(c) 5 (d) 2

26. Given below are two statements, one is labelled as Assertion (A) and the other is labelled as Reason (R).

Assertion (A) HF has highest boiling point among hydrogen halides.

Reason (R) HF has strongest hydrogen bonding among hydrogen halides.

In the light of the above statements, choose the most appropriate answer from the options given below.

(a) Both (A) and (R) are true and (R) is the correct explanation of (A).
(b) Both (A) and (R) are true but (R) is not the correct explanation of (A).
(c) (A) is true but (R) is false.
(d) (A) is false but (R) is true.

27. Which of the following reagents can be used for conversion of cyanide into aldehyde?

I. $SnCl_2 + HCl$ II. DIBAL-H
III. *R*-MgBr/dry ether IV. Dil. H_2SO_4/Hg
V. CO, HCl

Choose the correct answer from the options given below.

(a) I, IV, V
(b) I, II, III
(c) I, II
(d) I, II, III, IV

28. The product *Y* formed in the given reaction is

$\xrightarrow{AlCl_3} Y$ Cl

(a) (b)

(c) (d) Cl Cl Cl

29. Which of the following compound will show geometrical isomerism?

(a) 1, 2-dibromobut-1-ene
(b) 2-butene
(c) 1-propene
(d) Isopropylene

30. The correct IUPAC name of the compound,

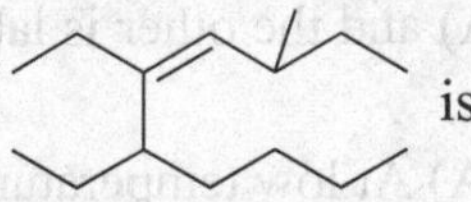

is

(a) 5,6-diethyl-8-methyldee-6-ene
(b) 5-butyl-2-ethyl-3-methyloct-4-ene
(c) 5,6-diethyl-3-methyldec-4-ene
(d) 2,4,5-triethylnon-3-ene.

31. Equivalent weight of FeS_2 (molecular weight = *M*) in the following reaction is

$$FeS_2 + O_2 \longrightarrow Fe_2O_3 + SO_2$$

(a) $\frac{M}{12}$ (b) $\frac{M}{18}$
(c) $\frac{M}{11}$ (d) $\frac{M}{7}$

32. Which type of distillation process is suitable for purification of a substance having boiling point 563 K but it starts decomposing near this temperature?

(a) Distillation
(b) Steam distillation
(c) Fractional distillation
(d) Distillation under reduced pressure

33. The conditions under which, toluene is converted to bromomethyl benzene is

(a) reaction with $Br_2 / FeBr_3$
(b) reaction with Br_2 in sunlight
(c) reaction with Br_2 in dark
(d) reaction with HBr

34. Reaction of benzene with CH_3Cl in the presence of anhydrous $AlCl_3$ forms the following compound is

(a) toluene
(b) chlorobenzene
(c) gammexane
(d) xylene

35. The resistivity of a 0.8 M solution of electrolyte is $5 \times 10^{-3}\ \Omega$ cm. Molar conductivity is

(a) 2.5×10^5 S cm^2 mol^{-1}
(b) 2.1×10^5 S cm^2 mol^{-1}
(c) 1.8×10^4 S cm^2 mol^{-1}
(d) 1.5×10^5 S cm^2 mol^{-1}

36. Given below are two statements, one is labelled as Assertion (A) and the other is labelled as Reason (R).

Assertion (A) At low temperatures, enthalpy change dominates the ΔG value and at high temperature, it is the entropy which dominates the value of ΔG.

Reason (R) The relation of ΔG, ΔH, T and ΔS is $\Delta G = \Delta H - T\Delta S$.

In the light of the above statements, choose the most appropriate answer from the options given below.

(a) Both (A) and (R) are true and (R) is the correct explanation of (A).
(b) Both (A) and (R) are true but (R) is not the correct explanation of (A).
(c) (A) is true but (R) is false.
(d) (A) is false but (R) is true.

37. Consider the following statements about lanthanoids.

I. La^{3+}, Ce^{4+}, Yb^{2+}, Lu^{2+} are diamagnetic in nature.
II. They have fairly high melting points.
III. They are highly dense.
IV. They have fairly high ionisation enthalpies.
V. They can easily form coordination compounds.

Choose the correct answer from the options given below.

(a) I and II
(b) II and III
(c) I, II, III and V
(d) I, II, III and IV

38. A closed container contains 0.6 m^3 of neon gas at 200 K temperature and 1.3×10^5 Pa. The molar heat capacity of neon gas at constant volume is 3.2 cal K^{-1} mol^{-1}. What will be the rise in temperature when 8360 J of heat is supplied to it? Assume the container does not expand on heating.
(Use : $R = 8.31$ $JK^{-1}mol^{-1}$)

(a) 15 K
(b) 13.3 K
(c) 16.8 K
(d) 12 K

39. Consider the following reaction,

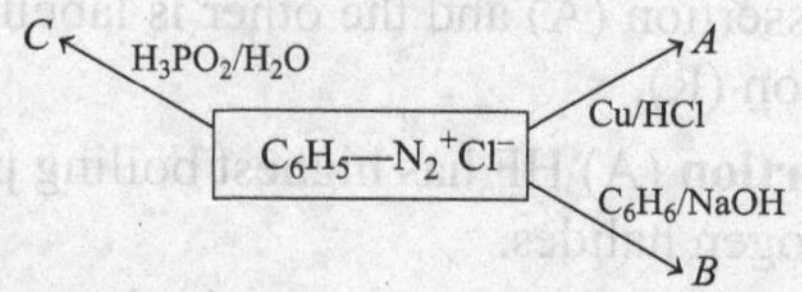

What is A, B and C ?

	A	B	C
(a)	C_6H_5-Cl	Biphenyl	C_6H_6
(b)	C_6H_5-Cl	Benzene	$C_6H_5-C_6H_5$
(c)	C_6H_5-Cl	Chlorobe nzene	C_6H_5-Cl
(d)	C_6H_5-Cl	Benzene	C_6H_5-Cl

40. Select the incorrect option from List-I and List-II.

	List-I	List-II
(a)	$H-F < HCl < HBr < HI$	Acidic nature
(b)	$HClO_4 < HClO_3 < HClO_2 < HClO$	Oxidising power
(c)	$I_2 < Br_2 < Cl_2 < F_2$	Oxidising nature
(d)	$N_2O_5 < N_2O_4 < N_2O_3 < NO < N_2O$	Acidic character

41. Given below are two statements.

Statement I Ethanol reacts with $SOCl_2$ in presence of pyridine to form chloroethane.

Statement II In above case chloroethane is formed through S_N1 mechanism.

In the light of the above statements, choose the most appropriate answer from the options given below.

(a) Both Statement I and Statement II are incorrect.
(b) Statement I is correct but Statement II is incorrect.
(c) Statement I is incorrect but Statement II is correct.
(d) Both Statement I and Statement II are correct.

42. If 100 ml of PH_3 on heating forms P and H_2, then the volume change in the reaction is

(a) a decrease of 50 mL
(b) an increase of 100 mL
(c) an increase of 50 mL
(d) an increase 150 mL

43. Magnetic moments of some complexes are as follows

I. 1.73 BM II. 4.89 BM III. 5.91 BM

Which of the following is the suitable match for complex and above given magnetic moments.

	I	II	III
(a)	$K[MnO_4]$	$K_4[Mn(CN)_6]$	MnO_2
(b)	$[Fe(Cl_6)]^{3-}$	$K_2[MnO_4]$	$MnCl_6$
(c)	$K_4[Mn(CN)_6]$	$[Fe(H_2O)_6]^{2+}$	$K_2[MnCl_4]$
(d)	$K_2(MnCl_4)$	$[Fe(H_2O)_6]^{2+}$	$K_4[Mn(CN)_6]$

44. Complete the following reaction,

$$\text{Propan-1-ol} \xrightarrow[443\text{ K}]{\text{Conc. } H_2SO_4} A$$

The product 'A' is

(a) propene (b) propyne

(c) cyclopropane (d) dipropyl ether

45. Match List-I with List-II.

	List-I		List-II
A.	Spontaneous cell reaction	I.	Hydrogen gas evolved
B.	Electrolysis of NaCl at cathode	II.	$E_{ext} > E_{cell}$
C.	Electrochemical cell behaves as an electrolytic cell when	III.	$PbSO_4$ anode is reduced to Pb
D.	During charging the lead storage battery	IV.	$\Delta G°$ is negative

Choose the correct answer from the options given below.

(a) A-IV, B-II, C-III, D-I

(b) A-IV, B-I, C-II, D-III

(c) A-III, B-IV, C-II, D-I

(d) A-III B-II, C-I, D-IV

Scan to fill up online OMR and get AI based Rank prediction on performance

■ **Response Index**

01	ⓐ ⓑ ⓒ ⓓ	14	ⓐ ⓑ ⓒ ⓓ	27	ⓐ ⓑ ⓒ ⓓ	40	ⓐ ⓑ ⓒ ⓓ
02	ⓐ ⓑ ⓒ ⓓ	15	ⓐ ⓑ ⓒ ⓓ	28	ⓐ ⓑ ⓒ ⓓ	41	ⓐ ⓑ ⓒ ⓓ
03	ⓐ ⓑ ⓒ ⓓ	16	ⓐ ⓑ ⓒ ⓓ	29	ⓐ ⓑ ⓒ ⓓ	42	ⓐ ⓑ ⓒ ⓓ
04	ⓐ ⓑ ⓒ ⓓ	17	ⓐ ⓑ ⓒ ⓓ	30	ⓐ ⓑ ⓒ ⓓ	43	ⓐ ⓑ ⓒ ⓓ
05	ⓐ ⓑ ⓒ ⓓ	18	ⓐ ⓑ ⓒ ⓓ	31	ⓐ ⓑ ⓒ ⓓ	44	ⓐ ⓑ ⓒ ⓓ
06	ⓐ ⓑ ⓒ ⓓ	19	ⓐ ⓑ ⓒ ⓓ	32	ⓐ ⓑ ⓒ ⓓ	45	ⓐ ⓑ ⓒ ⓓ
07	ⓐ ⓑ ⓒ ⓓ	20	ⓐ ⓑ ⓒ ⓓ	33	ⓐ ⓑ ⓒ ⓓ	46	ⓐ ⓑ ⓒ ⓓ
08	ⓐ ⓑ ⓒ ⓓ	21	ⓐ ⓑ ⓒ ⓓ	34	ⓐ ⓑ ⓒ ⓓ	47	ⓐ ⓑ ⓒ ⓓ
09	ⓐ ⓑ ⓒ ⓓ	22	ⓐ ⓑ ⓒ ⓓ	35	ⓐ ⓑ ⓒ ⓓ	48	ⓐ ⓑ ⓒ ⓓ
10	ⓐ ⓑ ⓒ ⓓ	23	ⓐ ⓑ ⓒ ⓓ	36	ⓐ ⓑ ⓒ ⓓ	49	ⓐ ⓑ ⓒ ⓓ
11	ⓐ ⓑ ⓒ ⓓ	24	ⓐ ⓑ ⓒ ⓓ	37	ⓐ ⓑ ⓒ ⓓ	50	ⓐ ⓑ ⓒ ⓓ
12	ⓐ ⓑ ⓒ ⓓ	25	ⓐ ⓑ ⓒ ⓓ	38	ⓐ ⓑ ⓒ ⓓ		
13	ⓐ ⓑ ⓒ ⓓ	26	ⓐ ⓑ ⓒ ⓓ	39	ⓐ ⓑ ⓒ ⓓ		

■ **Performance Scanner**

> 90% Excellent !	You have mastered the NEET syllabus (12th). The concepts of this entire syllabus are at your fingertips. Maintain this momentum.
76-90% Very Good !	You have a good command over the entire NEET syllabus (12th). Revise it again after a few days to enhance your performance.
60-75% Good !	You have a wide scope to learn for the entire NEET syllabus (12th). Revise it again.
<60% Not Satisfactory!	You have a long way ahead of you to master the NEET syllabus (12th). Revise it thoroughly.

Space for Rough Work

Test Booklet No. **3947270**

Test Booklet Code **NK03**

MED ACE

NEET (UG)

SELF ASSESSMENT KIT

NEET Knock Offs 3

(NEET Simulator Test)

Name of the Candidate (In Capitals)

____

____

____

Candidate's Signature ______________

Invigilator's Signature ______________

Facsimile signature stamp of center superintendent____________________

Important Instructions

- The test is of 45 minutes duration and the Test Booklet contains 45 multiple choice questions (four options with a single correct answer) from Chemistry.
- Candidates are advised to read all questions before they start attempting the question paper.
- Each questions carries 4 marks. For each correct response, the candidate will get 4 marks. For each incorrect response, one mark will be deducted from the total scores.
- In the event of candidate marking more than one option then one mark will be deducted. The maximum marks are 180.
- Use **Blue/Black Point Pen** only for writing particular on this page/marking response on Answer Sheet.

Do not open this Booklet until you start attempting the Test

Chemistry (Q.No. 1-45)

1. What will be the uncertainty in the position (Δx) of an electron, if Δv is 0.1% ? Take the velocity of electron $= 2.2\times10^{6}$m/s and mass of electron as 9.108×10^{-31}kg.

(a) 362.4765×10^{-10} m
(b) 203.225×10^{-10} m
(c) 263.4378×10^{-10} m
(d) 169.225×10^{-10} m

2. Aqueous solution of two compounds M_1—O—H and M_2—O—H are prepared in two different beakers. If the electronegativity of $M_1 = 3.4$, $M_2 = 1.2$, O = 3.5 and H = 2.1, then the nature of two solutions will be respectively,

(a) acidic, basic (b) acidic, acidic
(c) basic, acidic (d) basic, basic

3. Enthalpy of neutralisation of acetic acid by NaOH is – 50.6 kJ/mol. What will be the ΔH for ionisation of CH_3COOH ? Given, the heat of neutralisation of a strong acid with a strong base is – 55.9 kJ/mol.

(a) – 5.3 kJ/mol (b) 5.3 kJ/mol
(c) 6.12 kJ/mol (d) – 6.12 kJ/mol

4. Which of the following statement is correct?

(a) An orbital containing an electron having quantum number $n = 2; l = 0, s = +\frac{1}{2}$ is spherical.
(b) All photons have the same energy.
(c) The frequency of X-rays is less than that of radiowaves.
(d) As intensity of light increases, the frequency increases.

5. Given below are two statements.

Statement I Hydroxy ketones are not directly used in Grignard reaction.
Statement II Grignard group reacts with hydroxyl group.

In the light of the above statements, choose the most appropriate answer from the options given below.

(a) Both Statement I and Statement II are incorrect.
(b) Statement I is correct but Statement II is incorrect.
(c) Statement I is incorrect but Statement II is correct.
(d) Both Statement I and Statement II are correct.

6. Which of the following pairs of elements do not have almost similar atomic radii ?

(a) Zr, Hf
(b) Mo, W
(c) Mn, Ni
(d) Nb, Ta

7. Match List-I with List-II.

List-I (Hydrocarbon)	List-II (Types of hydrogen)
A.	I. 15 (1° H) 4 (2° H) 1 (3° H)
B.	II. 17 (1° H) 2 (2° H) 2 (3° H)
C.	III. 12 (1° H) 4 (2° H) 2 (3° H)
D. OH	IV. 15 (1° H) 2 (2° H) 1 (3° H)

Choose the correct answer from the options given below.

(a) A-III, B-I, C-IV, D-II
(b) A-I, B-III, C-IV, D-II
(c) A-IV, B-I, C-III, D-II
(d) A-II, B-I, C-IV, D-III

8. The diagram given below is a vapour pressure-composition diagram for a binary solution of A and B liquids.

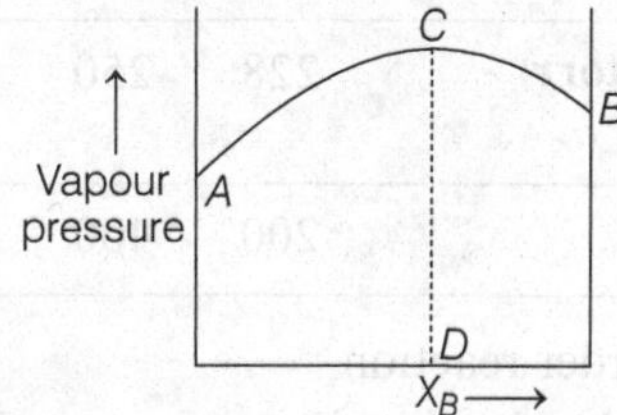

In a solution A—B interactions are

(a) similar to A—A and B—B interactions
(b) greater than A—A and B—B interactions
(c) smaller than A—A and B—B interactions
(d) unpredictable

9. Given below are two statements, one is labelled as Assertion (A) and the other is labelled as Reason (R).

Assertion (A) In $Cr_2O_7^{2-}$ ion, two Cr—O bonds have different bond length than the remaining six Cr—O bonds.

Reason (R) In $Cr_2O_7^{2-}$ ion, all the O—Cr—O bond angle are equal.

In the light of the above statements, choose the correct answer from the options given below.

(a) Both (A) and (R) are true and (R) is the correct explanation of (A).
(b) Both (A) and (R) are true but (R) is not the correct explanation of (A).
(c) (A) is true but (R) is false.
(d) (A) is false but (R) is true.

10. The correct order of decreasing acid strength of the given compounds.

(I) OH (phenol) (II) OH, NO_2 (III) OH, OCH_3

(IV) OH, NO_2 (V) OH, OCH_3

(a) V > IV > III > II > I
(b) IV > V > III > II > I
(c) II > IV > I > III > V
(d) III > IV > I > II > V

11. An ideal monoatomic gas follows the path $ABDC$. The work done during the complete cycle is

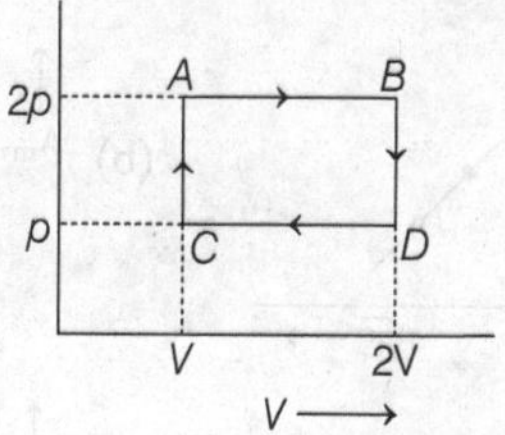

(a) $-pV$ (b) $-2pV$
(c) $-\frac{1}{2}pV$ (d) zero

12. Two samples of HCl of 1.0 M and 0.25 M are mixed. Which of the following set(s) of volume is/are correct in order to prepare 0.75 M HCl solution. [Assume no water is added.]

I. 20 mL, 10 mL II. 100 mL, 50 mL
III. 40 mL, 20 mL IV. 50 mL, 25 mL
V. 60 mL, 30 mL

Choose the correct option for above volume.

(a) I, II and IV
(b) I, II and V
(c) II, III and IV
(d) I, II, III, IV and V

13. Given below are two statements.

Statement I S_N2 reaction is carried out in the presence of polar aprotic solvent.

Statement II Polar aprotic solvent do not contain acidic hydrogen.

In the light of the above statements, choose the most appropriate answer from the options given below.

(a) Both Statement I and Statement II are incorrect.
(b) Statement I is correct but Statement II is incorrect.
(c) Statement I is incorrect but Statement II is correct.
(d) Both Statement I and Statement II are correct.

14. The equilibrium concentration ratio of M to N, if 2.0 mol of M and P were allowed to come to equilibrium at 500 K is

$$M + P \rightleftharpoons N + Q\ ;\ \Delta G° = 490 \text{ cal}$$

(a) 0.522
(b) 0.782
(c) 0.701
(d) 0.799

15. Which of the following curve gives the variation of Λ_m with $\sqrt{C}$ for CH_3COOH?

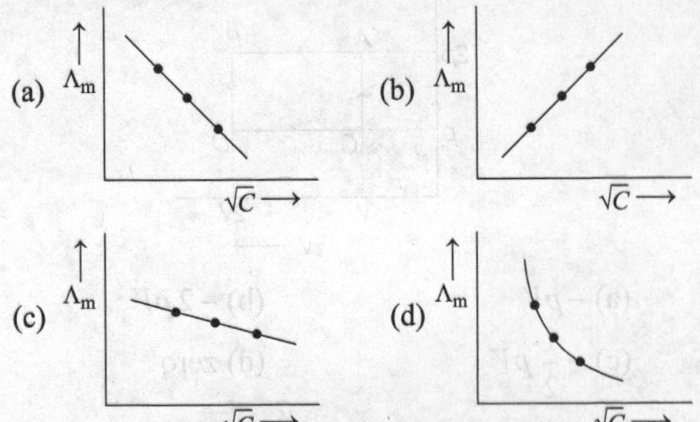

16. Given below are two statements.

Statement I HOF bond angle is higher than HOCl.

Statement II Oxygen is more electronegative than chlorine.

In the light of the above statements, choose the most appropriate answer from the options given below.

(a) Both Statement I and Statement II are incorrect.
(b) Statement I is correct but Statement II is incorrect.
(c) Statement I is incorrect but Statement II is correct.
(d) Both Statement I and Statement II are correct.

17. Consider a reversible reaction,

$$A_2(g)+2B_2(g) \rightleftharpoons 2AB_2(g)$$

The temperature at which the reaction gives equilibrium is 700 K and the equilibrium pressure is in atm. If the value of K_p is 2.66×10^{-6} for the given reversible reaction. Then the value of equilibrium constant (K_C) is

(a) 1.041×10^{-6} (b) 1.529×10^{-3}
(c) 1.426×10^{-3} (d) 1.324×10^{-4}

18. When phenyl acetic acid is heated in presence of hydrazoic acid and conc. H_2SO_4 at 50°C to 55°C, it gives

(a) $C_6H_5NH_2$ (b) $C_6H_5CH{=}NH$
(c) $C_6H_5CH_2NH_2$ (d) $C_6H_5CONH_2$

19. Which of the following condition is correct regarding spontaneous reaction at all temperatures?

(a) $\Delta H > 0$ and $\Delta S < 0$ (b) $\Delta H < 0$ and $\Delta S > 0$
(c) $\Delta H < 0$ and $\Delta S < 0$ (d) $\Delta H > 0$ and $\Delta S = 0$

20. Find the order of the reaction and the rate constant for decomposition of ammonia on a tungsten wire at 856°C. The experimental data are

Total (p) torr pressure	228	250	273	318
Time (t) s	200	400	600	1000

(a) first order reaction
(b) second order reaction
(c) zero order reaction
(d) pseudo first order reaction

21. Match List-I with List-II.

List-I	List-II
A. $p^\circ - p_s$	I. Observed colligative property / Normal colligative property
B. $p^\circ \times \chi_A = p_A$	II. Lowering in vapour pressure
C. Mixture that boils like pure solvent	III. Azeotropic mixture
D. van't Hoff factor	IV. Raoult's law

Choose the correct answer from the options given below.

(a) A-I, B-II, C-III, D-IV
(b) A-IV, B-III, C-II D-I
(c) A-III, B-II, C-IV, D-I
(d) A-II, B-IV, C-III, D-I

22. Given below are two statements, one is labelled as Assertion (A) and the other is labelled as Reason (R).

Assertion (A) But-2-yne give *syn*-addition on reacting with BH_3/THF.

Reason (R) Hydroboration-oxidation of but-2-yne form butan-2-one.

In the light of the above statements, choose the most appropriate answer from the options given below.

(a) Both (A) and (R) are true and (R) is the correct explanation of (A).
(b) Both (A) and (R) are true but (R) is not the correct explanation of (A).
(c) (A) is true but (R) is false.
(d) (A) is false but (R) is true.

23. Given below are two statements, one is labelled as Assertion (A) and the other is labelled as Reason (R).

Assertion (A) Ionisation of *s*-electrons requires more energy than ionisation of *p*-electron of the shell.

Reason (R) *s*-electrons are closer to the nucleus than *p*-electron and hence are more strongly attracted by the nucleus.

In the light of the above statements, choose the most appropriate answer from the options given below.

(a) Both (A) and (R) are true and (R) is the correct explanation of (A).
(b) Both (A) and (R) are true but (R) is not the correct explanation of (A).
(c) (A) is true but (R) is false.
(d) (A) is false but (R) is true.

24. Keto-enol tautomerism is observed in

I. PhCHO II. $PhCOCH_3$
III. PhCOPh IV. $PhCOCH_2COCH_3$

Choose the most appropriate answer from the options given below.

(a) II and IV (b) I and III
(c) I and IV (d) II and III

25. Given below are two statements.

Statement I H_2O_2 gives disproportionation reaction.

Statement II In H_2O_2 oxygen has −1 oxidation number.

In the light of the above statements, choose the most appropriate answer from the options given below.

(a) Both Statement I and Statement II are incorrect.
(b) Statement I is correct but Statement II is incorrect.
(c) Statement I is incorrect but Statement II is correct.
(d) Both Statement I and Statement II are correct.

26. 0.40 g of an organic compound gave 0.3 g of silver bromide by Carius method. The percentage of bromine in the compound is

(a) 41.75% (b) 31.75%
(c) 70.15% (d) 30.15%

27. The solution of $CuSO_4$ in which Cu rod is dipped is diluted to 10 times, the reduction electrode potential will

(a) decrease by 0.0295 V
(b) decrease by 0.0591 V
(c) increase by 0.0295 V
(d) increase by 0.0591 V

28. Consider the following reaction,

$$CH_3-CH=CH_2 + NBS \xrightarrow{h\nu}$$

Correct products formed are

(a) $CH_2(Br)-CH_2-CH_3 + \begin{matrix}CH_2-CO\\|\\CH_2-CO\end{matrix}\!\!>NH$

(b) $CH_2=CH-CH_2-Br + \begin{matrix}CH_2-CO\\|\\CH_2-CO\end{matrix}\!\!>NH$

(c) $CH_2=CH-CH_2Br + \begin{matrix}CH_2-COOH\\|\\CH_2-COOH\end{matrix} + NH_3$

(d) $CH_2(Br)-CH_2-CH_3 + \begin{matrix}CH_2-COOH\\|\\CH_2-COOH\end{matrix} + NH_3$

29. The following conversions are carried out by which enzymes?

$$\text{Proteins} \xrightarrow{\text{Enzyme 'X'}} \text{Polypeptide} \xrightarrow{\text{Enzyme 'Y'}} \text{Amino acids}$$

	X	Y
(a)	Invertase	Pepsin
(b)	Diastase	Trypsin
(c)	Pepsin	Trypsin
(d)	Amylase	Maltase

30. Following data were obtained during the thermal decomposition of sulphuryl chloride at constant volume and 285°C. (log 155 = 0.1909 and log 3.103 = 0.49)

$$SO_2Cl_2(g) \longrightarrow SO_2(g) + Cl_2(g)$$

Time (s)	0	240	600
Pressure (torr)	180	244	302

Determine the order of reaction.

(a) Zero order reaction
(b) First order reaction
(c) Second order reaction
(d) Third order reaction

31. Consider the correct statements regarding diborane.

I. Boron is approximately sp^3-hybridised.
II. B—H—B angle is 180°.
III. There are two terminal B—H bonds for each boron atom.
IV. There are four $2c$—$2e$ bonds and two $3c$—$2e$ bonds.
V. B_2H_6 reacts readily with alkenes to form trialkylboranes.

Choose the correct answer from the options given below.

(a) I, III, IV and V
(b) I, II and III
(c) II, III and V
(d) I, II and IV

32. Osmotic pressure of 0.1 M aqueous solution of $MgCl_2$ at 300 K is 4.92 atm. What will be the percentage ionisation of the salt ?

(a) 59% (b) 49%
(c) 79% (d) 69%

33. The correct order of reactivity of K, Mg, Zn and Cu with water according to the electrochemical series is

(a) K > Mg > Zn > Cu
(b) Mg > Zn > Cu > K
(c) K > Zn > Mg > Cu
(d) Cu > Zn > Mg > K

34. AsF_5 molecule is trigonal bipyramidal. The number of hybrid atomic orbitals used by As atom for bonding are

$s \quad p_x \quad p_y \quad p_z \quad d_{x^2-y^2}, \quad d_{xy}, \quad d_{z^2}$

(a) 5 (b) 6 (c) 4 (d) 3

35. Given that the temperature coefficient for the saponification of ethyl acetate by NaOH is 1.75. When the temperature rises from 25°C to 35°C. The energy of activation will be [log 1.75 = 0.243]

(a) 10.00 kcal/mol
(b) 8.227 kcal/mol
(c) 9.227 kcal/mol
(d) 10.206 kcal/mol

36. Match List-I with List-II.

List-I (Inert gas)	List-II (Property)
A. Helium	I. Ionisation energy is comparable to O_2
B. Argon	II. Provides inert atmosphere in metallurgy
C. Neon	III. Cryogenic
D. Xenon	IV. Advertising sign

Choose the correct answer from the options given below.

(a) A-I, B-II, C-IV, D-III
(b) A-III, B-II, C-IV, D-I
(c) A-IV, B-III, C-II, D-I
(d) A-II, B-I, C-IV, D-III

37. Which of the following species have the same number of lone pair(s) of electrons with their central atom?

I. XeF_5^- II. BrF_5 III. XeF_2
IV. H_3S^+ V. XeO_6^{4-}

Choose the correct answer from the options given below.

(a) IV and V
(b) I and III
(c) I and II
(d) II and IV

38. Consider the following reaction.

(Cyclohexylidene)$=CH—C_6H_5$ $\xrightarrow[Zn/H_2O]{O_3}$ $A + B$ $\xrightarrow[EtOH]{NaOH}$ $H_2O + C$ $\xrightarrow{O_3/Zn+H_2O}$ $D + A$; D $\xrightarrow{H_2/Pt}$ (cyclohexane with OH, OH)

Compound D in the above reaction is

(a) [benzene] (b) [cyclohexanone, O]
(c) [cyclohexane-1,2-dione, O, O] (d) [cyclohexane-1,4-dione, O, O]

39. Consider the following compounds.

$[Co(en)_3][Cr(C_2O_4)_3]$, $[Cu(NH_3)_4][CuCl_4]$, $[Ni(en)_3][Co(NO_2)_6]$

The total possible co-ordination isomers for the following compounds respectively are

(a) 4, 4, 4 (b) 2, 2, 2
(c) 2, 2, 4 (d) 4, 2, 4

40. In this reaction,

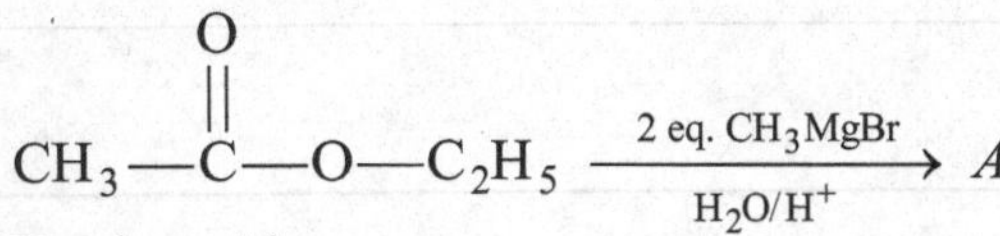

$$CH_3-\overset{\overset{\displaystyle O}{\|}}{C}-O-C_2H_5 \xrightarrow[H_2O/H^+]{2\text{ eq. } CH_3MgBr} A$$

Product A is

(a) methyl propan-2-ol (b) 2-methylpropan-2-ol
(c) *iso*-propyl alcohol (d) butan-2-ol

41. Match List-I with List-II.

List-I (Complex)	List-II (Colour shown)
A. $[Fe(CN)_6]^{4-}$	I. Orange
B. $[Fe(H_2O)_6]^{2+}$	II. Colourless
C. $[Cu(NH_3)_6]^{2+}$	III. Yellow
D. $[Ni(CN)_4]^{2-}$	IV. Pale green

Choose the correct answer from the options given below.

(a) A-III, B-IV, C-I, D-II
(b) A-III, B-II, C-I, D-IV
(c) A-I, B-II, C-III, D-IV
(d) A-IV, B-II, C-III, D-I

42. The correct order of acidity of the following species is CO_2, H_2O, H_2O_2.

(a) $H_2O > CO_2 > H_2O_2$
(b) $H_2O_2 > CO_2 > H_2O$
(c) $CO_2 > H_2O_2 > H_2O$
(d) $CO_2 > H_2O > H_2O_2$

43. 1.8 g of Mg is burnt in a closed vessel which contains 0.8 g of oxygen.

Which of the following statements is not correct? [Atomic weight of Mg = 24.3 g/mol]

(a) 0.05 mole of MgO is formed
(b) 0.8 g of Mg remain unreacted
(c) Oxygen is the limiting reactant
(d) The extent of reactant at the completion of reaction is 0.025 mol

44. What is the pH of the mixture obtained by mixing 50 ml of 0.05 M NH_4OH and 50 ml of 0.05 M CH_3COOH ?

$[K_a = 1.8 \times 10^{-5}$ and $K_b = 1.8 \times 10^{-5}]$

(a) 2 (b) 7
(c) 5 (d) 6

45. Select the incorrect statement.

(a) Amylose is the water soluble and a linear polymer of D(+) glucose unit.
(b) Amylopectin has β-glycosidic linkage.
(c) Cellulose acetate is used in plastics, wrapping films and nail polishes.
(d) Glycogen is the principle reserve of carbohydrate in animals.

Scan to fill up online OMR and get AI based Rank prediction on performance

Response Index

01 ⓐ ⓑ ⓒ ⓓ	14 ⓐ ⓑ ⓒ ⓓ	27 ⓐ ⓑ ⓒ ⓓ	40 ⓐ ⓑ ⓒ ⓓ
02 ⓐ ⓑ ⓒ ⓓ	15 ⓐ ⓑ ⓒ ⓓ	28 ⓐ ⓑ ⓒ ⓓ	41 ⓐ ⓑ ⓒ ⓓ
03 ⓐ ⓑ ⓒ ⓓ	16 ⓐ ⓑ ⓒ ⓓ	29 ⓐ ⓑ ⓒ ⓓ	42 ⓐ ⓑ ⓒ ⓓ
04 ⓐ ⓑ ⓒ ⓓ	17 ⓐ ⓑ ⓒ ⓓ	30 ⓐ ⓑ ⓒ ⓓ	43 ⓐ ⓑ ⓒ ⓓ
05 ⓐ ⓑ ⓒ ⓓ	18 ⓐ ⓑ ⓒ ⓓ	31 ⓐ ⓑ ⓒ ⓓ	44 ⓐ ⓑ ⓒ ⓓ
06 ⓐ ⓑ ⓒ ⓓ	19 ⓐ ⓑ ⓒ ⓓ	32 ⓐ ⓑ ⓒ ⓓ	45 ⓐ ⓑ ⓒ ⓓ
07 ⓐ ⓑ ⓒ ⓓ	20 ⓐ ⓑ ⓒ ⓓ	33 ⓐ ⓑ ⓒ ⓓ	46 ⓐ ⓑ ⓒ ⓓ
08 ⓐ ⓑ ⓒ ⓓ	21 ⓐ ⓑ ⓒ ⓓ	34 ⓐ ⓑ ⓒ ⓓ	47 ⓐ ⓑ ⓒ ⓓ
09 ⓐ ⓑ ⓒ ⓓ	22 ⓐ ⓑ ⓒ ⓓ	35 ⓐ ⓑ ⓒ ⓓ	48 ⓐ ⓑ ⓒ ⓓ
10 ⓐ ⓑ ⓒ ⓓ	23 ⓐ ⓑ ⓒ ⓓ	36 ⓐ ⓑ ⓒ ⓓ	49 ⓐ ⓑ ⓒ ⓓ
11 ⓐ ⓑ ⓒ ⓓ	24 ⓐ ⓑ ⓒ ⓓ	37 ⓐ ⓑ ⓒ ⓓ	50 ⓐ ⓑ ⓒ ⓓ
12 ⓐ ⓑ ⓒ ⓓ	25 ⓐ ⓑ ⓒ ⓓ	38 ⓐ ⓑ ⓒ ⓓ	
13 ⓐ ⓑ ⓒ ⓓ	26 ⓐ ⓑ ⓒ ⓓ	39 ⓐ ⓑ ⓒ ⓓ	

Performance Scanner

> 90% Excellent !	You have mastered the NEET syllabus (12th). The concepts of this entire syllabus are at your fingertips. Maintain this momentum.
76-90% Very Good !	You have a good command over the entire NEET syllabus (12th). Revise it again after a few days to enhance your performance.
60-75% Good !	You have a wide scope to learn for the entire NEET syllabus (12th). Revise it again.
<60% Not Satisfactory!	You have a long way ahead of you to master the NEET syllabus (12th). Revise it thoroughly.

Space for Rough Work

Test Booklet No. **3947271**
Test Booklet Code **NK04**

MEDACE
NEET (UG)
SELF ASSESSMENT KIT

NEET Knock Offs 4

(NEET Simulator Test)

Name of the Candidate (In Capitals)

____

____

____

Candidate's Signature ______________

Invigilator's Signature ______________

Facsimile signature stamp of center superintendent______________

Important Instructions

- The test is of 45 minutes duration and the Test Booklet contains 45 multiple choice questions (four options with a single correct answer) from Chemistry.
- Candidates are advised to read all questions before they start attempting the question paper.
- Each questions carries 4 marks. For each correct response, the candidate will get 4 marks. For each incorrect response, one mark will be deducted from the total scores.
- In the event of candidate marking more than one option then one mark will be deducted. The maximum marks are 180.
- Use **Blue/Black Point Pen** only for writing particular on this page/marking response on Answer Sheet.

Do not open this Booklet until you start attempting the Test

Chemistry (Q.No. 1-45)

1. To make 250 mL of a solution having same concentration of Cl^- as the one containing 3.78 g of NaCl per 100 mL the amount of $BaCl_2$ needed will be

(a) 15.72 g (b) 12.20 g
(c) 10.11 g (d) 16.82 g

2. The decreasing order of second ionisation enthalpy of the element C, N, O, F is

(a) $C > N > O > F$
(b) $N > F > O > C$
(c) $F > O > N > C$
(d) $O > F > N > C$

3. Consider the following reaction;

$$2CrO_4^{2-} \xrightarrow{pH = x} Cr_2O_7^{2-} \xrightarrow{pH = y} 2CrO_4^{2-}$$

Here, x and y can be

(a) 3 and 5 (b) 3 and 8
(c) 8 and 3 (d) 8 and 11

4. Among the given compounds, which will give formic acid on hydrolysis?

(a) CH_3Cl
(b) CH_2Cl_2
(c) $CHCl_3$
(d) CH_3CH_2Cl

5. The kinetic energy of an electron is 4.55×10^{-25}. The mass of electron is 9.1×10^{-31} kg. Then what will be the velocity of the electron.

(a) 10^2 m/s (b) 10^3 m/s
(c) 10^4 m/s (d) 10^5 m/s

6. The correct order of increasing bond strength of the molecule F_2, N_2, O_2 and Cl_2 is

(a) $F_2 < Cl_2 < O_2 < N_2$
(b) $Cl_2 < F_2 < N_2 < O_2$
(c) $F_2 < Cl_2 < N_2 < O_2$
(d) $N_2 < O_2 < Cl_2 < F_2$

7. The structure of tetrathionate ion is

(a) $[O_3S-S-SO_2S]^{2-}$ (b) $O^--SO_2-O^-$
(c) $[O_3S-S-S-SO_3]^{2-}$ (d) $[O_3S-SO_3]^{2-}$

8. Given below are the two statements, one is labelled as Assertion (A) and other is labelled as Reason (R).

Assertion (A) Salt of ClO_3^- and ClO_4^- are well known but that of FO_3^- and FO_4^- are unknown.

Reason (R) F is more electronegative than oxygen while Cl is less electronegative than oxygen.

In the light of the above statements, choose the most appropriate answer from the options given below.

(a) Both (A) and (R) are true and (R) is the correct explanation of (A).
(b) Both (A) and (R) are true but (R) is not the correct explanation of (A).
(c) (A) is true but (R) is false.
(d) (A) is false but (R) is true.

9. Given below are two statements.

Statement I BCl_3 is planar, whereas anhydrous $AlCl_3$ is tetrahedral in shape.

Statement II In BCl_3, B-atom is in sp^2-hybrid state and $AlCl_3$ is in dimer phase.

In the light of the above statements, choose the most appropriate answer from the options given below.

(a) Both Statement I and Statement II are incorrect.
(b) Statement I is correct but Statement II is incorrect.
(c) Statement I is incorrect but Statement II is correct.
(d) Both Statement I and Statement II are correct.

10. Consider the following reaction :

$$C_6H_6 + CH_2{=}O + HCl \longrightarrow A \xrightarrow[-H_2O]{HCl/ZnCl_2} B$$

The product 'B' is
(a) chlorobenzene
(b) biphenyl
(c) dichlorobenzene
(d) benzyl chloride

11. Given below are two statements.
Statement I The boiling point of NH_3 lies between SbH_3 and BiH_3.
Statement II PH_3 has much lower boiling point than NH_3 but it increase from PH_3 to AsH_3 and SbH_3 to BiH_3 due to increase in van der Waals' forces.
In the light of the above statements, choose the most appropriate answer from the options given below.
(a) Both Statement I and Statement II are incorrect.
(b) Statement I is correct but Statement II is incorrect.
(c) Statement I is incorrect but Statement II is correct.
(d) Both Statement I and Statement II are correct.

12. The value of K_C for the reaction,
$2A \rightleftharpoons B + C$ is 2×10^{-3}.
At a given time, the composition of reaction mixture is $[A]=[B]=[C]=3\times10^{-4}$ m. In which direction the reaction will proceed?
(a) Forward direction
(b) Backward direction
(c) In equilibrium
(d) Not predictable

13. A swimmer coming out from a pool is covered with a film of water weighing about 18 g. How much heat must be supplied to evaporate this water at 298 K ? Calculate the internal energy of vaporisation at 100°C $\Delta_{vap}H^{\ominus}$ for water at 373 K = 40.66 kJ/mol.
(a) 30.11 kJ/mol
(b) 37.56 kJ/mol
(c) 29.16 kJ/mol
(d) 51.26 kJ/mol

14. Match List-I with List-II.

List-I (Reaction)	List-II (Product)
A. $HCHO + NH_3$	I. R—CHO
B. R—$CN + LiAlH_4/H_3O^+$	II. $(CH_2)_6N_4$
C. $CCl_3CHO + H_2O$	III. $CH_3CH{=}NH$
D. $CH_3CH{=}O + NH_3$	IV. Chloral hydrate

Choose the correct answer from the options given below.
(a) A-II, B-I, C-IV, D-III
(b) A-I, B-II, C-III, D-IV
(c) A-II, B-III, C-I, D-IV
(d) A-II, B-IV, C-III, D-I

15. The nature of following reaction is

$$CH_4 + Cl_2 \xrightarrow[\text{sunlight}]{\text{Diffused}} CH_3—Cl + HCl$$

(a) electrophilic substitution reaction
(b) nucleophilic substitution reaction
(c) free radical substitution reaction
(d) electrophilic addition reaction

16. The value of IE_1, IE_2, IE_3 and IE_4 of an atom are 7.5 eV, 25.6 eV, 48.6 eV and 170.6 eV respectively. The electronic configuration of the atom will be
(a) $1s^2\ 2s^2\ 2p^6\ 3s^1$
(b) $1s^2\ 2s^2\ 2p^6\ 3s^2\ 3p^1$
(c) $1s^2\ 2s^2\ 2p^6\ 3s^2\ 3p^3$
(d) $1s^2\ 2s^2\ 2p^6\ 3s^2$

17. The correct IUPAC name of [structure] OH is

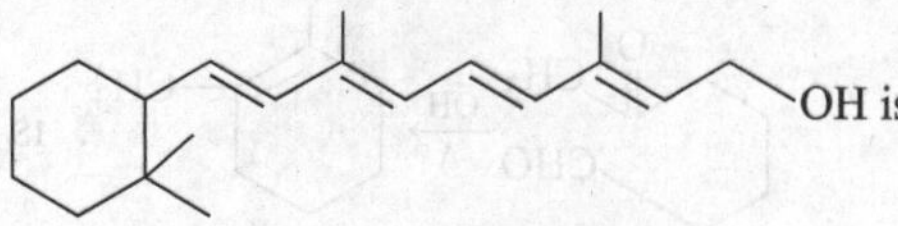

(a) 3,7-dimethyl-9- (2,2-dimethyl cyclohexyl) non-2,4,6,8-tetra-en-1-ol
(b) 2,7-dimethyl-9-(2,2-dimethyl cyclohexyl) non-2,4,6,8-tetra-en-1-ol
(c) 4,7-dimethyl-8 (2,2-dimethyl cyclohexyl) non-2,4,6,8-tetra-en-1-ol
(d) 3,7-dimethyl-9-(6,6-dimethyl cyclohexyl) non-2,4-6-8-tetra-en-1-ol

18. Consider the reactions given below;

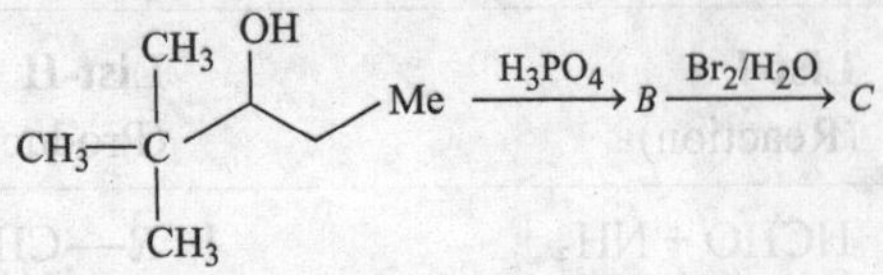

$CH_3-C(CH_3)(CH_3)-CH(OH)-CH_2-Me \xrightarrow{H_3PO_4} B \xrightarrow{Br_2/H_2O} C$

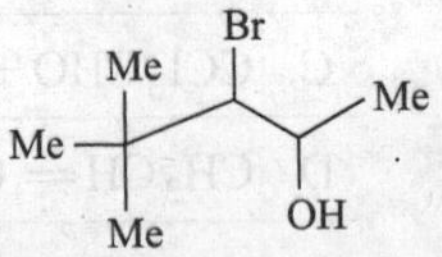

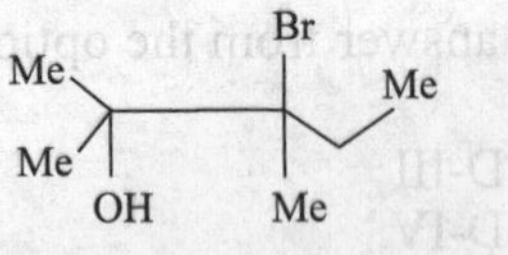

The, compound C is

(a) 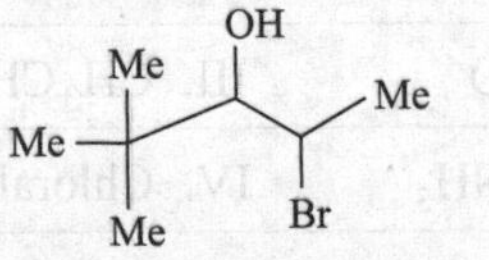 $Me-C(Me)(Me)-C(OH)(Me)-CH(Br)-Me$ (b) $Me-C(Me)(Me)-C(Br)(Me)-CH(OH)-Me$

(c) $(Me)_2C(OH)-C(Br)(Me)-CH_2-Me$ (d) 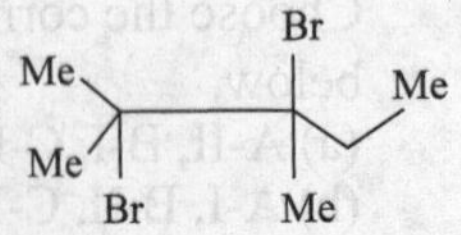 $(Me)_2C(Me)-C(Br)(Me)-...$ [Me, Br, Me substituents]

19. Given below are two statements.

Statement I 1, 2-dibromopropane gives reaction with $NaI + CH_3COCH_3$ while 1, 3-dibromopropane does not.

Statement II In the above reaction I_2 is liberated which gives blue-black colour with starch.

In the light of the above statements, choose the most appropriate answer from the options given below.

(a) Both Statement I and Statement II are incorrect.
(b) Statement I is correct but Statement II is incorrect.
(c) Statement I is incorrect but Statement II is correct.
(d) Both Statement I and Statement II are correct.

20. Given below are two statements, one is labelled as Assertion (A) and the other is labelled as Reason (R).

Assertion (A) The reaction,

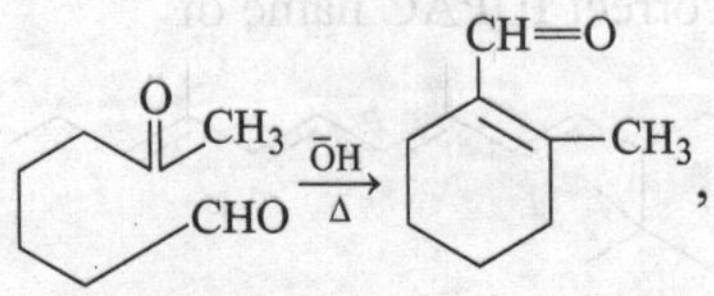

[2-(3-oxobutyl)... cyclohexane with $COCH_3$ and CHO] $\xrightarrow[\Delta]{\overline{O}H}$ [cyclohexene with $CH=O$ and CH_3], is an intramolecular aldol reaction.

Reason (R) CHO is a better acceptor than C=O.

In the light of the above statements, choose the most appropriate answer from options given below.

(a) Both (A) and (R) are true and (R) is the correct explanation of (A).
(b) Both (A) and (R) are true but (R) is not the correct explanation of (A).
(c) (A) is true but (R) is false.
(d) (A) is false but (R) is true.

21. Match List-I with List-II.

	List-I (Hybridisation of the central atom)		List-II (Molecule)
A.	sp^2	I.	XeF_4
B.	sp^3	II.	BF_3
C.	sp^3d	III.	Br_3^-
D.	sp^3d^2	IV.	SO_4^{2-}

Choose the correct answer from the options given below.

(a) A-I, B-II, C-III, D-IV
(b) A-II, B-IV, C-III, D-I
(c) A-IV, B-III, C-II, D-I
(d) A-I, B-III, C-II, D-IV

22. At 298 K, the vapour pressure of water is 23.75 mm Hg. Calculate the vapour pressure at the same temperature over 5% aqueous solution of urea $[CO(NH_2)_2]$.

(a) 20.11 mm Hg
(b) 19.65 mm Hg
(c) 24.12 mm Hg
(d) 25.57 mm Hg

23. The E°_{cell} value of the cell represented below is 3.17 V.

$Mg + 2Ag^+(0.0001\ M) \longrightarrow Mg^{2+}(0.130\ M) + 2Ag$

The E_{cell} of the reaction is

[Given, $\log(0.13 \times 10^8) = 7.11$]

(a) 2.01 V (b) 2.96 V
(c) 3.12 V (d) 3.92 V

24. At a certain temperature, the half-life changes for the electrolytic decomposition of ammonia was found as follows

Pressure (Pa)	6667	13333	26666
Half-life (hours)	3.52	1.92	1.0

The order of reaction will be

(a) 0 (b) 1
(c) 2 (d) 3

25. The reduction potential of following electrode will be Pt, H_2 (4 atm) | H_2SO_4 (0.01 M)

(a) −0.118 V
(b) −0.218 V
(c) +0.118 V
(d) +0.218 V

26. Match List I with List II.

List I (Ion + reagent)	List II (Colour)
A. $Fe^{3+} + [Fe(CN)_6]^{4-}$	I. Cherry red
B. $Fe^{3+} + SCN^-$	II. Pink
C. Ni^{2+} + DMG	III. Blood red
D. $Mn^{2+} + PbO_2 + H^+$	IV. Blue

Choose the correct answer from the options given below

(a) A-I, B-IV, C-II, D-III
(b) A-IV, B-III, C-I, D-II
(c) A-III, B-IV, C-II, D-I
(d) A-III, B-I, C-IV, D-II

27. Calculate the number of atoms and volume of 1 g He gas at STP.

(a) 1236×10^{23} atoms, 2.3 L
(b) 1.506×10^{23} atoms, 5.6 L
(c) 1.506×10^{23} atoms, 2.3 L
(d) 1236×10^{23} atoms, 5.6 L

28. Consider the following reaction ;

$$NH_3 + H_2O \longrightarrow A \xrightarrow{AgCl} B + 2H_2O$$

What is A and B?

(a) N_2O_5, $[Ag(NH_3)_2]Cl$
(b) NO_2, $[Ag(NH_3)_2]Cl$
(c) NH_4OH, $[Ag(NH_3)_2]Cl$
(d) NH_4OH, $[Ag(NH_3)_4]Cl$

29. Given below are two statements.

Statement I Halogens are highly reactive.

Statement II Bond dissociation enthalpy of $X—X$ in halogen is very less.

In the light of the above statements, choose the most appropriate answer from the options given below.

(a) Both Statement I and Statement II are incorrect.
(b) Statement I is correct but Statement II is incorrect.
(c) Statement I is incorrect but Statement II is correct.
(d) Both Statement I and Statement II are correct.

30. Which of the following is the incorrect statement.

(a) Sc^{3+} and Ti^{4+} are colourless due to absence of unpaired electrons.
(b) Cu^{2+} ion shows blue colour in the solution.
(c) Zn^{2+} and Cd^{2+} salts are white because they do not absorb any radiation in visible region.
(d) Fe^{3+} ion impart yellow colour due to *d-d* transition by $3d^6$ electronic configuration.

31. Select the incorrect statement about lanthanoids.

(a) Common oxidation state of lanthanoids is +3, some of the lanthanoid exhibit oxidation state of +2 and +4 also.
(b) Lanthanoids have weaker tendency for complex formation.
(c) Lanthanoids do not form oxo ions.
(d) Lanthanoid compounds are more basic than actinide compounds.

32. The correct IUPAC name of compound $Na_3[Ag(S_2O_3)_2]$ is

(a) sodium thiosulphateargentate (I)
(b) sodium *bis* (thiosulphate) argentate (I)
(c) sodium *bis* (thiosulphate) silver (I)
(d) sodium thiosulphateargentum (I)

33. Given below are two statements.

Statement I Any concentration of NaCl solution can be injected intravenously as NaCl, being a common table salt is harmful chemical.

Statement II 0.9% (mass/volume) NaCl solution is isotonic with the fluid inside the blood cells.

In the light of the above statements, choose the most appropriate answer from the options given below.

(a) Both Statement I and Statement II are correct.
(b) Statement I is correct but Statement II is incorrect.
(c) Statement I is incorrect but Statement II is correct.
(d) Both Statement I and Statement II are incorrect.

34. Consider the following reaction ;

$$CH_3COCH_3 + CH_3COCH_3 \xrightarrow{NaOH} A \xrightarrow{\Delta} B \text{ is}$$

The product '*A*' and '*B*' is

(a) $CH_3-CH(OH)-CH_2-COCH_3$; $CH_3-CH=CH-C(=O)-CH_3$

(b) $CH_3-C(CH_3)(OH)-CH_2-C(=O)-CH_3$; $CH_3-C(CH_3)=CH-C(=O)-CH_3$

(c) $CH_3-C(CH_3)(OH)-CH_2-C(=O)-CH_3$; $CH_3-C(H)(CH_3)-CH(OH)-C(=O)-CH_3$

(d) $CH_3-C(CH_3)_2-C(=O)-CH_3$; $CH_3-C(CH_3)=CH-C(=O)-CH_3$

35. Consider the following reaction,

$$CH_3-CH_2-CH(Br)-CH_3 \xrightarrow{\text{Alc. KOH}} \text{Major product}$$

The major product is

(a) $CH_3-CH_2-CH=CH_2$

(b) $CH_3-CH=CH-CH_3$

(c) $CH_3-C(CH_3)=CH_2$

(d) $CH_3-C\equiv C-CH_3$

36. The product *A* of the following reaction is

$$C_6H_6 + CH_3-CH=CH_2 \xrightarrow[\text{(iii) Dil. } H_2SO_4]{\text{(i) } H_3PO_4/AlCl_3 \text{ (ii) } O_2/\text{Oxidation}} A + CH_3-C(=O)-CH_3$$

(a) acetone (b) cumene
(c) phenol (d) salt of acid

37. Which of the following set of quantum number(s) is not permitted?

(a) $n=3, l=2, m=+1, s=+\frac{1}{2}$

(b) $n=3, l=2, m=+2, s=-\frac{1}{2}$

(c) $n=2, l=1, m=+2, s=-\frac{1}{2}$

(d) $n=3, l=0, m=0, s=+\frac{1}{2}$

38. Consider the following reaction.

$$CH_3-CH=CH_2 + NBS \xrightarrow{h\nu} \text{(Product)}$$

The product obtained is

(a) $CH(Br)=CH-CH_3$ (b) $CH_2(Br)-CH=CH_2$

(c) $CH_2=C(Br)-CH_3$ (d) $CH_2(Br)-CH(Br)-CH_3$

39. Select the correct order of reactivity towards nucleophilic addition reaction.

(a) $HCHO > CH_3CHO > CH_3-COCH_3 > C_6H_5-COCH_3$

(b) $HCHO > CH_3-COCH_3 > CH_3CHO > C_6H_5-COCH_3$

(c) $CH_3CHO > HCHO > CH_3COCH_3 > C_6H_5COCH_3$

(d) $C_6H_5COCH_3 > CH_3CHO > HCHO > CH_3COCH_3$

40. Given below are two statements.

Statement I Partition chromatography is based on continuous differential partitioning of components of a mixture between stationary and mobile phases.

Statement II Paper chromatography is a type of partition chromatography.

In the light of the above statements, choose the most appropriate answer from the options given below.

(a) Both Statement I and Statement II are incorrect.
(b) Statement I is correct but Statement II is incorrect.
(c) Statement I is incorrect but Statement II is correct.
(d) Both Statement I and Statement II are correct.

41. In this reaction,

$$CH_3-CH(CH_3)-O-C_6H_5 \xrightarrow{HI} \text{Product } (P)$$

The product P is

(a) $CH_3—CH(CH_3)—OH$ + iodobenzene (C_6H_5I)

(b) $CH_3—CH(CH_3)—I$ + phenol (C_6H_5OH)

(c) $CH_3—CH(CH_3)—OH$ + 4-iodophenol (OH and I para on benzene ring)

(d) $CH_3—CH{=}CH_2$ + phenol (C_6H_5OH)

42. Select the incorrect statement about carbohydrates.

(a) Sucrose (cane sugar) is hydrolysed and it forms glucose and fructose.

(b) Glucose is reduced in presence of HI and forms *n*-hexane.

(c) Glucose reacts with HCN to form hexanoic acid on hydrolysis.

(d) Gluconic acid is obtained from glucose in presence of Br_2 water.

43. Consider the following reaction

$$H_2C(Br)—CH_2(Br) + KOH \xrightarrow{\text{Alcohol}} A \xrightarrow{NaNH_2} B$$

The product A and B is

(a)	$H_2C{=}CHBr$;	$HC{\equiv}CH$
(b)	$H_2C{=}CH_2$;	$HC{\equiv}CH$
(c)	$H_2C{=}CHBr$;	$H_2C{=}CH_2$
(d)	$H_2C{=}CH_2$;	$HC{\equiv}CBr$

44. In oxidation of alkene,

$$\underset{\text{Alkene}}{R—CH{=}CH—R} \xrightarrow[\text{[Reagent]}]{[O]} \underset{\text{Carboxylic acid}}{2R—COOH}$$

Which of the following reagents is not suitable for above oxidation ?

(a) Hot alkaline $KMnO_4$ followed by acidification

(b) Hot acidic $KMnO_4$ solution

(c) Hot acidic $K_2Cr_2O_7$

(d) Hot Cr_2O_3

45. Match List-I with List-II.

List-I (Property of solution)	List-II (Solution and nature)
A. Minimum boiling azeotropes	I. $CH_3COCH_3 + COCl_3$
B. Maximum boiling azeotropes	II. $C_2H_5OH + H_2O$
C. van't Hoff factor of K_2SO_4	III. $\pi_1 = \pi_2$
D. Isotonic solution	IV. 3

Choose the correct answer from the options given below.

(a) A-I, B-IV, C-I, D-III

(b) A-II, B-I, C-IV, D-III

(c) A-I, B-II, C-IV, D-III

(d) A-II, B-I, C-III, D-IV

Scan to fill up online OMR and get AI based Rank prediction on performance

Response Index

01 ⓐ ⓑ ⓒ ⓓ	14 ⓐ ⓑ ⓒ ⓓ	27 ⓐ ⓑ ⓒ ⓓ	40 ⓐ ⓑ ⓒ ⓓ
02 ⓐ ⓑ ⓒ ⓓ	15 ⓐ ⓑ ⓒ ⓓ	28 ⓐ ⓑ ⓒ ⓓ	41 ⓐ ⓑ ⓒ ⓓ
03 ⓐ ⓑ ⓒ ⓓ	16 ⓐ ⓑ ⓒ ⓓ	29 ⓐ ⓑ ⓒ ⓓ	42 ⓐ ⓑ ⓒ ⓓ
04 ⓐ ⓑ ⓒ ⓓ	17 ⓐ ⓑ ⓒ ⓓ	30 ⓐ ⓑ ⓒ ⓓ	43 ⓐ ⓑ ⓒ ⓓ
05 ⓐ ⓑ ⓒ ⓓ	18 ⓐ ⓑ ⓒ ⓓ	31 ⓐ ⓑ ⓒ ⓓ	44 ⓐ ⓑ ⓒ ⓓ
06 ⓐ ⓑ ⓒ ⓓ	19 ⓐ ⓑ ⓒ ⓓ	32 ⓐ ⓑ ⓒ ⓓ	45 ⓐ ⓑ ⓒ ⓓ
07 ⓐ ⓑ ⓒ ⓓ	20 ⓐ ⓑ ⓒ ⓓ	33 ⓐ ⓑ ⓒ ⓓ	46 ⓐ ⓑ ⓒ ⓓ
08 ⓐ ⓑ ⓒ ⓓ	21 ⓐ ⓑ ⓒ ⓓ	34 ⓐ ⓑ ⓒ ⓓ	47 ⓐ ⓑ ⓒ ⓓ
09 ⓐ ⓑ ⓒ ⓓ	22 ⓐ ⓑ ⓒ ⓓ	35 ⓐ ⓑ ⓒ ⓓ	48 ⓐ ⓑ ⓒ ⓓ
10 ⓐ ⓑ ⓒ ⓓ	23 ⓐ ⓑ ⓒ ⓓ	36 ⓐ ⓑ ⓒ ⓓ	49 ⓐ ⓑ ⓒ ⓓ
11 ⓐ ⓑ ⓒ ⓓ	24 ⓐ ⓑ ⓒ ⓓ	37 ⓐ ⓑ ⓒ ⓓ	50 ⓐ ⓑ ⓒ ⓓ
12 ⓐ ⓑ ⓒ ⓓ	25 ⓐ ⓑ ⓒ ⓓ	38 ⓐ ⓑ ⓒ ⓓ	
13 ⓐ ⓑ ⓒ ⓓ	26 ⓐ ⓑ ⓒ ⓓ	39 ⓐ ⓑ ⓒ ⓓ	

Performance Scanner

> 90% Excellent !	You have mastered the NEET syllabus (12th). The concepts of this entire syllabus are at your fingertips. Maintain this momentum.
76-90% Very Good !	You have a good command over the entire NEET syllabus (12th). Revise it again after a few days to enhance your performance.
60-75% Good !	You have a wide scope to learn for the entire NEET syllabus (12th). Revise it again.
<60% Not Satisfactory!	You have a long way ahead of you to master the NEET syllabus (12th). Revise it thoroughly.

Space for Rough Work

Test Booklet No. **3947272**

Test Booklet Code **NK05**

NEET Knock Offs 5

(NEET Simulator Test)

Name of the Candidate (In Capitals)

____

____

____

Candidate's Signature ____________

Invigilator's Signature ____________

Facsimile signature stamp of center superintendent____________

Important Instructions

- The test is of 45 minutes duration and the Test Booklet contains 45 multiple choice questions (four options with a single correct answer) from Chemistry.
- Candidates are advised to read all questions before they start attempting the question paper.
- Each questions carries 4 marks. For each correct response, the candidate will get 4 marks. For each incorrect response, one mark will be deducted from the total scores.
- In the event of candidate marking more than one option then one mark will be deducted. The maximum marks are 180.
- Use **Blue/Black Point Pen** only for writing particular on this page/marking response on Answer Sheet.

Do not open this Booklet until you start attempting the Test

Chemistry (Q. No. 1-45)

1. Consider the reactions given below.

$$X \xrightarrow{\text{HOH/H}^+} \text{Glucose} + \text{Fructose}$$

$$Y \xrightarrow{\text{HOH/H}^+} \text{Glucose} + \text{Glucose}$$

$$Z \xrightarrow{\text{HOH/H}^+} \text{Glucose} + \text{Galactose}$$

The disaccharide X, Y and Z respectively are

(a) Sucrose, Maltose, Lactose
(b) Sucrose, Lactose, Maltose
(c) Maltose, Lactose, Sucrose
(d) Lactose, Sucrose, Maltose

2. Which among the following compound has highest boiling point?

(a) 0.5 M Na_2SO_4
(b) 0.5 M Glucose
(c) 0.5 M $MgCl_2$
(d) 0.5 M $Al(NO_3)_3$

3. Allyl halide is hydrolysed much more readily than vinyl chloride because

(a) allyl carbocation is unstable
(b) vinyl carbocation is stable
(c) C—Cl bond in vinyl chloride has partial double bond character
(d) due to larger size of Cl-atom

4. The order of reactivity of the following alcohols towards conc. HCl is

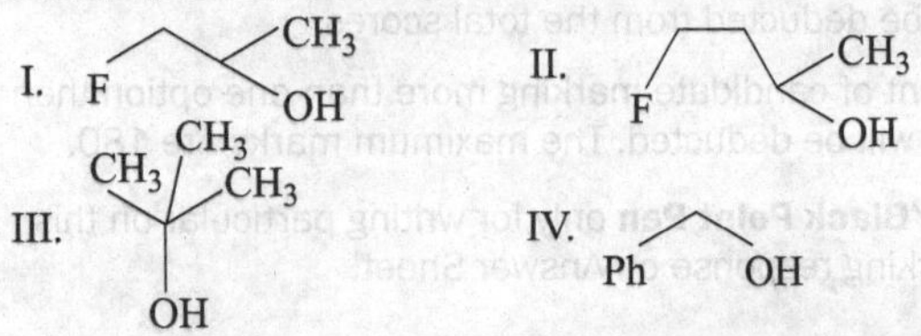

Choose the correct answer from the options given below.

(a) I > II > III > IV
(b) III > IV > II > I
(c) I > III > II > IV
(d) IV > III > I > II

5. Choose the correct statements from the following.

I. In alkaline medium, reaction between aldehyde and Tollen's test is as follows

$$RCHO + 2[Ag(NH_3)_2]^+ + 3\bar{O}H \longrightarrow RCO\bar{O} + 2Ag + 2H_2O + 4NH_3$$

II. Fehling solution A is alkaline sodium potassium tartarate.

III. Fehling solution B is aqueous copper sulphate.

IV. Aromatic aldehydes do not respond to Fehling's test.

V. On heating an aldehyde with Fehling's reagent, a reddish brown precipitate is obtained.

Choose the correct answer from the options given below.

(a) I, IV and V
(b) I, II and III
(c) II, III and IV
(d) III, IV and V

6. At 25°C, the dissociation constant of a base, BOH is 1.0×10^{-16}. The concentration of H^+ ions in 0.01 M aqueous solution of the base will be

(a) 1×10^{-7} mol/L
(b) 1×10^{-5} mol/L
(c) 1×10^{-14} mol/L
(d) 1×10^{-9} mol/L

7. In which of the following species, bond order is different from that of CO?

(a) NO^+ (b) N_2 (c) CN^- (d) NO^-

8. Given below are two statements.

Statement I When concentrated sulphuric acid is added to an inorganic mixture containing chloride, we get colourless pungent smelling gas HCl.

Statement II HCl is a very weak reducing agent, it cannot reduce H_2SO_4 to SO_2 hence, HCl is not oxidised to Cl_2.

In the light of the above statements, choose the most appropriate answer from the options given below.

(a) Both Statement I and Statement II are incorrect.
(b) Statement I is correct but Statement II is incorrect.
(c) Statement I is incorrect but Statement II is correct.
(d) Both Statement I and Statement II are correct.

9. Match List-I with List-II.

List-I (Reaction)	List-II (Product)
A. $C_6H_6 \xrightarrow[\text{Anhyd. } AlCl_3/CuCl]{CO,\ HCl}$	I. $C_6H_5COONa + CHI_3$
B. $CH_3{-}C{\equiv}CH + H_2O \xrightarrow[H_2SO_4]{Hg^{2+}}$	II. C_6H_5COOH
C. $C_6H_5CH_2CH_2CH_3 \xrightarrow{KMnO_4{-}KOH}$	III. $CH_3{-}\overset{\overset{\displaystyle O}{\|}}{C}{-}CH_3$
D. $C_6H_5\overset{\overset{\displaystyle O}{\|}}{C}CH_3 \xrightarrow[I_2]{NaOH}$	IV. C_6H_5CHO

Choose the correct answer from the options given below.

(a) A-III, B-IV, C-II, D-I (b) A-IV, B-III, C-II, D-I
(c) A-I, B-III, C-II, D-IV (d) A-III, B-II, C-IV, D-I

10. Select the correct statements.

I. The magnitude of the equilibrium constant gives an idea of relative amounts of reactant and product.
II. The value of the equilibrium constant is not affected by the addition of catalyst to the reaction.
III. The value of the equilibrium constant for a particular reaction is always constant depending only upon the temperature.
IV. If the equation (having equilibrium constant K) is divided by 2, the equilibrium constant for the new equation is inverse of square root of K.
V. The equilibrium constant for a reaction having positive $\Delta H°$ increases with increase of temperature.

Choose the correct answer from the options given below.

(a) I, II and IV (b) I, III and V
(c) I, II and III (d) I, II, III, IV and V

11. Number of Cl^- and Ca^{2+} ions in 222 g of fused $CaCl_2$ are respectively, where N is Avogadro number.

(a) 2 N, 3 N (b) 4 N, 2 N
(c) 4 N, 3 N (d) 2 N, 2 N

12. The shapes of XeF_4, XeO_2F_2, I_3^- and $SnCl_2$ are

(a) octahedral, square planar, linear and angular
(b) square planar, *see-saw*, linear and angular
(c) square planar, *see-saw*, triangular and bipyramidal angular
(d) octahedral, triangular, *see-saw* and bipyramidal angular

13. Which among the following electron will emit radiation of maximum wavelength?

(a) $n=4,\ l=1,\ m=0$ to $n=3,\ l=2,\ m=-2$
(b) $n=3,\ l=2,\ m=-2$ to $n=3,\ l=1,\ m=-1$
(c) $n=3,\ l=2,\ m=1$ to $n=2,\ l=0,\ m=0$
(d) $n=3,\ l=1,\ m=0$ to $n=2,\ l=1,\ m=1$

14. Select the incorrect statement from the following.

(a) Lower aliphatic amines are soluble in water because they can form hydrogen bonds with water molecules.
(b) The intermolecular association due to hydrogen bonding is less in primary amines than in secondary amines.
(c) Aniline and other arylamines are usually colourless but get coloured on storage.
(d) Amines are soluble in organic solvents like alcohol, ether and benzene.

15. The sample of organic compound is 50% pure. It contains 69% carbon and 4.8% hydrogen, the rest being oxygen. Masses of CO_2 and water produced by the complete combustion of 0.20 g of the sample respectively are

(a) 0.406 g, 0.506 g
(b) 0.516 g, 0.784 g
(c) 0.406 g, 0.0684 g
(d) 0.253 g, 0.0432 g

16. For the redox reaction,

$$Zn + NO_3^- \longrightarrow Zn^{2+} + NH_4^+$$

In basic medium, coefficients of Zn, NO_3^- and OH^- in the balanced equation respectively are

(a) 7, 4, 10
(b) 4, 1, 10
(c) 1, 4, 5
(d) 5, 4, 7

17. Match List-I with List-II.

List-I	List-II
A. $\lambda = h/p$	I. UV radiation
B. Lyman series	II. IR-radiation
C. Paschen series	III. Heisenberg uncertainty principle
D. $\Delta x\, \Delta p \geq h/4\pi$	IV. de-Broglie relationship

Choose the correct answer from the options given below.

(a) A-IV, B-I, C-II, D-III
(b) A-III, B-I, C-II D-IV
(c) A-IV, B-I, C-III, D-II
(d) A-IV, B-III, C-II, D-I

18. Complete the following reaction,

$$\underset{\text{Boric acid}}{4H_3BO_3} \xrightarrow{\Delta} A \xrightarrow{410\text{ K}} B \xrightarrow{\text{Red hot}} C$$

A, B and *C* respectively are

(a) HBO_3, $H_2B_4O_7$ and B_2O_3
(b) HBO_2, $H_2B_4O_7$ and B_2O_3
(c) HBO_2, B_2O_3 and $H_2B_4O_7$
(d) B_2O_3, HBO_2 and $H_2B_4O_7$

19. Which statement is true about a spontaneous cell reaction in galvanic cell?

(a) $E^{\ominus}_{cell} > 0$; $\Delta G^{\ominus} < 0$; $Q < K_C$
(b) $E^{\ominus}_{cell} < 0$; $\Delta G^{\ominus} > 0$; $Q < K_C$
(c) $E^{\ominus}_{cell} > 0$; $\Delta G^{\ominus} > 0$; $Q > K_C$
(d) $E^{\ominus}_{cell} > 0$; $\Delta G^{\ominus} > 0$; $Q < K_C$

20. What will be the standard electrode potential of MnO_4^-/MnO_2. The standard electrode potential of $MnO_4^-/Mn^{2+} = 1.51$ V and $MnO_2/Mn^{2+} = 1.23$ V.

(a) 1.75 V (b) 1.69 V
(c) 1.63 V (d) 1.70 V

21. The density of 0.06 M solution of KI in water is 1.006 g/mL. The molality is

(a) 0.050
(b) 0.060
(c) 0.023
(d) 0.084

22. The bond angles of NH_3, NH_4^+ and $NH_2^{\ominus}$ decreases in the order as

(a) $NH_2^{\ominus}$, NH_3, $NH_4^{\oplus}$
(b) $NH_4^{\oplus}$, NH_3, $NH_2^{\ominus}$
(c) NH_3, $NH_2^{\ominus}$, $NH_4^{\oplus}$
(d) NH_3, $NH_4^{\oplus}$, $NH_2^{\ominus}$

23. Which of the following statement is incorrect?

(a) In starch, D-(+)- glucose units are linked by glycosidic linkage.
(b) In cellulose, D-(+)-glucose units are linked by glycosidic linkage.
(c) Lactose is a reducing sugar.
(d) In lactose two D-(+)-glucose units are linked through glycosidic linkage.

24. Standard enthalpy of vaporisation $\Delta_{vap}H^{\circ}$ for water at 100°C is 20.33 kJ/mol. The internal energy of vaporisation of water at 100°C in kJ/mol is (Assume that water vapour behaves like an ideal gas)

(a) +37.56 (b) −37.56
(c) −17.23 (d) +17.23

25. Consider the following reaction,

$$(CH_3)_2C{=}CH_2 \xrightarrow[373-383\text{K}]{KMnO_4/H^+} A + B\,(g)$$

$$\xrightarrow{CH_3MgX/H_3O^+} C + Mg(X)OH$$

[*B* is one carbon species]

Here, *A* and *C* respectively are

(a) CH_3COCH_3, $(CH_3)_3C{-}OH$
(b) CH_3COCH_3, $CH_3{-}\overset{O}{\overset{\|}{C}}{-}O{-}CH_3$
(c) $CH_3{-}CHO$, $CH_3{-}\underset{OH}{\underset{|}{C}H}{-}CH_3$
(d) $CH_3{-}CHO$, $(CH_3)_3C{-}OH$

26. Complete the following equation.

I. $CH_3{-}CH{=}CH{-}CH_2{-}CH_2{-}CN \xrightarrow[\text{(ii) } H_2O]{\text{(i) AlH}(i\text{-Bu})_2} ?$

II. $CH_3(CH_2)_7{-}\overset{O}{\overset{\|}{C}}{-}OC_2H_5 \xrightarrow[\text{(ii) } H_2O]{\text{(i) DIBAL-H}} ?$

Choose the correct answer from the options given below.

	I	II
(a)	Hex-4-en-1-al	Nonanone
(b)	Hex-2-en-1-al	Nonanal
(c)	Hex-4-en-1-al	Nonanal
(d)	Hex-2-en-1-al	Nonanone

27. Consider the following reaction.

(4-methylacetophenone: benzene ring with $COCH_3$ and CH_3 para) $\xrightarrow[\text{(ii) Dil. } H_2SO_4]{\text{(i) } KMnO_4/KOH}$ Product

Here, product formed is

(a) phthalic acid
(b) terephthalic acid
(c) cinnamic acid
(d) acetic acid

28. According to CFT, $[Mn(H_2O)_6]^{2+}$ and $[Mn(CN)_6]^{4-}$ complexes gives spin, these are

(a) high spin, low spin
(b) low spin, high spin
(c) low spin, low spin
(d) high spin, high spin

29. Which of the following shows optical isomerism?

(a) $[Co(CN)_6]^{3-}$
(b) $[Cu(NH_3)_4]^{2+}$
(c) $[Cr(C_2O_4)_3]^{3-}$
(d) $[Co(en)_2NO_2Cl]$ Br

30. Consider the following.

Benzene $+ CH_3—CH{=}CH_2 \xrightarrow[\text{or } AlCl_3]{\text{(i) } H_3PO_4}$?
(ii) Air (O_2)
(iii) Dil. H_2SO_4

Product formed in above reaction is

(a) phenol and acetone
(b) phenol and acetaldehyde
(c) cumene and acetone
(d) cumene and acetaldehyde

31. The compound which is most reactive towards nucleophilic substitution is

(a) Chlorobenzene (benzene ring with Cl)
(b) Benzene ring with Cl and para-NO_2
(c) Benzene ring with Cl and meta-NO_2
(d) Benzene ring with Cl, ortho-NO_2 and para-NO_2

32. Match List-I with List-II.

	List-I (Reactant + Reagent)		List-II (Product)
A.	$CH_4 + Cl_2 \xrightarrow{h\nu}$	I.	$COCl_2$
B.	$CCl_4 \xrightarrow[\text{Heat}]{Fe/H_2O}$	II.	HCOONa
C.	$NaOH + CCl_3CHO \longrightarrow$	III.	$CHCl_3$
D.	$CHCl_3 + O_2 \longrightarrow$	IV.	CH_3Cl

Choose the correct answer from the options given below.

(a) A-I, B-II, C-III, D-IV
(b) A-IV, B-III, C-II, D-I
(c) A-III, B-II, C-IV, D-I
(d) A-III, B-I, C-II, D-IV

33. $CH_3—C(CH_3)_2—CH(OH)—CH_3 \xrightarrow[\Delta]{H^+}$ Major product (P)

Identify the product (P) from the following.

(a) $CH_3—CH{=}C(CH_3)—CH_2—CH_3$
(b) $CH_2{=}C(CH_2—CH_3)(CH_2—CH_3)$
(c) $CH_3—C(CH_3){=}C(CH_3)—CH_3$
(d) $CH_2{=}C—CH(CH_3)—CH_3$ (with CH_3 on C)

34. The half-life of a first order reaction is 60 minutes. How long will it take to consume 90% of the reactant?

(a) 200 min (b) 250 min (c) 155 min (d) 177 min

35. Given below are two statements.

Statement I Sulphuric acid is weaker acid than perchloric acid.

Statement II The oxidation state of Cl and S in perchloric acid and sulphuric acid respectively are +6 and +7.

In the light of the above statements, choose the most appropriate answer from the options given below.

(a) Both Statement I and Statement II are incorrect.
(b) Statement I is correct but Statement II is incorrect.
(c) Statement I is incorrect but Statement II is correct.
(d) Both Statement I and Statement II are correct.

36. Given below are two statements.

Statement I In Rosenmund reaction, acid chloride is reduced into aldehyde.

Statement II $Pd/BaSO_4$, H_2 in burning xylene is responsible for Rosenmund reduction.

In the light of the above statements, choose the most appropriate answer from the options given below.

(a) Both Statement I and Statement II are incorrect.
(b) Statement I is correct but Statement II is incorrect.
(c) Statement I is incorrect but Statement II is correct.
(d) Both Statement I and Statement II are correct.

37. Which of the following radial distribution graph corresponds to $l = 2$ for H-atom for the least value of n for which $l = 2$ is allowed?

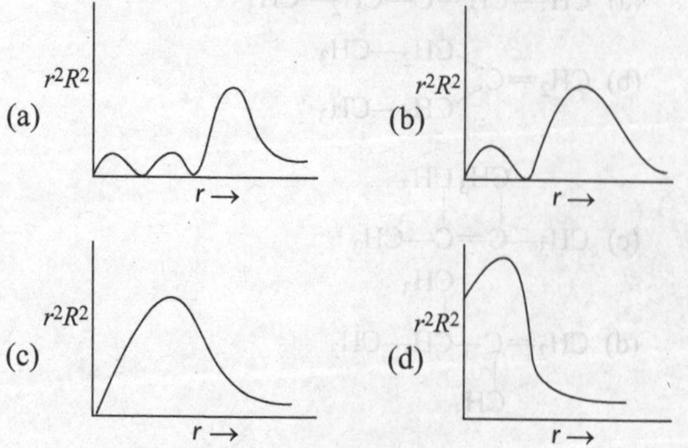

38. For a reaction, $A + B \longrightarrow$ products,

The rate of the reaction at various concentration are given below.

Exp. No.	[A]	[B]	Rate (mol dm^3 s^{-1})
1	0.4	0.4	4
2	0.4	0.8	8
3	1.2	0.8	72

The rate law for the above reaction is

(a) $r = k[A][B]^2$
(b) $r = k[A]^3[B]$
(c) $r = k[A]^2[B]^2$
(d) $r = k[A]^2[B]$

39. Given below are two statements, one is labelled as Assertion (A) and the other is labelled as Reason (R).

Assertion (A) Gabriel's phthalamide reaction is not used for the preparation of aromatic 1° amines.

Reason (R) Aryl halides do not undergo nucleophilic substitution reaction.

In the light of the above statements, choose the most appropriate answer from the options given below.

(a) Both (A) and (R) are true and (R) is the correct explanation of (A).
(b) Both (A) and (R) are true but (R) is not the correct explanation of (A).
(c) (A) is true but (R) is false.
(d) (A) is false but (R) is true.

40. Given below are two statements.

Statement I Chlorination of allylic hydrogen is difficult than vinylic hydrogen.

Statement II Allylic radical is stabilised by resonance.

In the light of the above statements, choose the most appropriate answer from the options given below.

(a) Both Statement I and Statement II are incorrect.
(b) Statement I is correct but Statement II is incorrect.
(c) Statement I is incorrect but Statement II is correct.
(d) Both Statement I and Statement II are correct.

41. Match List-I with List-II.

List-I	List-II
A. $\Delta H = q_p$	I. $\Delta S^\circ = 0$
B. Kirchhoff's equation	II. $\Delta G > 0$
C. $H_2O(l) \longrightarrow H^+(aq) + O\bar{H}(aq)$	III. $\Delta_{total}S^\circ > 0$
D. Spontaneous process	IV. $\Delta H_2 - \Delta H_1 = \Delta C_p(T_2 - T_1)$

Choose the correct answer from the options given below.

(a) A - I, B - IV, C - II, D - III
(b) A - I, B - II, C - III, D - IV
(c) A - II, B - I, C - IV, D - III
(d) A - III, B - II, C - I, D - IV

42. Given below are two statements.

Statement I $(CH_3)_3C^+$ is more stable than $\overset{+}{C}H_3$.

Statement II There are 9α hydrogens in $(CH_3)_3C^+$ due to which its stability increases and zero hyperconjugation forms in CH_3^+ cation.

In the light of the above statements, choose the most appropriate answer from the options given below.

(a) Both Statement I and Statement II are incorrect.
(b) Statement I is correct but Statement II is incorrect.
(c) Statement I is incorrect but Statement II is correct.
(d) Both Statement I and Statement II are correct.

43. Which of the following reagents is suitable to form *trans*-2-butene from but-2-yne?

(a) $Pd/CaCO_3$
(b) Ni/H_2
(c) Na + Liq. $NH_3/2H$
(d) $Pd\text{-}H_2$

44. Match List-I with List-II.

List-I (Solution)	List-II (Type of solution)
A. Ethanol in water	I. Solid in liquid
B. Chloroform mixed with nitrogen gas	II. Liquid in gas
C. Glucose in water	III. Liquid in liquid
D. Amalgam of mercury with sodium	IV. Liquid in solid

Choose the correct answer from the options given below.

(a) A-III, B-II, C-I, D-IV
(b) A-I, B-IV, C-III, D-II
(c) A-IV, B-III, C-I, D-II
(d) A-I, B-II, C-III, D-IV

45. A 5% (*w*/*w*) aqueous solution of cane sugar has a freezing point of 271 K. Freezing point of 5% (*w*/*w*) aqueous solution of glucose will be (Given freezing point of pure water = 273.15 K)

(a) 299.07 K (b) 269.07 K
(c) 369.07 K (d) 294.87 K

Scan to fill up online OMR and get AI based Rank prediction on performance

Response Index

01 ⓐ ⓑ ⓒ ⓓ	14 ⓐ ⓑ ⓒ ⓓ	27 ⓐ ⓑ ⓒ ⓓ	40 ⓐ ⓑ ⓒ ⓓ
02 ⓐ ⓑ ⓒ ⓓ	15 ⓐ ⓑ ⓒ ⓓ	28 ⓐ ⓑ ⓒ ⓓ	41 ⓐ ⓑ ⓒ ⓓ
03 ⓐ ⓑ ⓒ ⓓ	16 ⓐ ⓑ ⓒ ⓓ	29 ⓐ ⓑ ⓒ ⓓ	42 ⓐ ⓑ ⓒ ⓓ
04 ⓐ ⓑ ⓒ ⓓ	17 ⓐ ⓑ ⓒ ⓓ	30 ⓐ ⓑ ⓒ ⓓ	43 ⓐ ⓑ ⓒ ⓓ
05 ⓐ ⓑ ⓒ ⓓ	18 ⓐ ⓑ ⓒ ⓓ	31 ⓐ ⓑ ⓒ ⓓ	44 ⓐ ⓑ ⓒ ⓓ
06 ⓐ ⓑ ⓒ ⓓ	19 ⓐ ⓑ ⓒ ⓓ	32 ⓐ ⓑ ⓒ ⓓ	45 ⓐ ⓑ ⓒ ⓓ
07 ⓐ ⓑ ⓒ ⓓ	20 ⓐ ⓑ ⓒ ⓓ	33 ⓐ ⓑ ⓒ ⓓ	46 ⓐ ⓑ ⓒ ⓓ
08 ⓐ ⓑ ⓒ ⓓ	21 ⓐ ⓑ ⓒ ⓓ	34 ⓐ ⓑ ⓒ ⓓ	47 ⓐ ⓑ ⓒ ⓓ
09 ⓐ ⓑ ⓒ ⓓ	22 ⓐ ⓑ ⓒ ⓓ	35 ⓐ ⓑ ⓒ ⓓ	48 ⓐ ⓑ ⓒ ⓓ
10 ⓐ ⓑ ⓒ ⓓ	23 ⓐ ⓑ ⓒ ⓓ	36 ⓐ ⓑ ⓒ ⓓ	49 ⓐ ⓑ ⓒ ⓓ
11 ⓐ ⓑ ⓒ ⓓ	24 ⓐ ⓑ ⓒ ⓓ	37 ⓐ ⓑ ⓒ ⓓ	50 ⓐ ⓑ ⓒ ⓓ
12 ⓐ ⓑ ⓒ ⓓ	25 ⓐ ⓑ ⓒ ⓓ	38 ⓐ ⓑ ⓒ ⓓ	
13 ⓐ ⓑ ⓒ ⓓ	26 ⓐ ⓑ ⓒ ⓓ	39 ⓐ ⓑ ⓒ ⓓ	

Performance Scanner

> 90% Excellent !	You have mastered the NEET syllabus (12th). The concepts of this entire syllabus are at your fingertips. Maintain this momentum.
76-90% Very Good !	You have a good command over the entire NEET syllabus (12th). Revise it again after a few days to enhance your performance.
60-75% Good !	You have a wide scope to learn for the entire NEET syllabus (12th). Revise it again.
<60% Not Satisfactory!	You have a long way ahead of you to master the NEET syllabus (12th). Revise it thoroughly.

Scan for Online NEET Knock Offs

Test Booklet No. 3947273

Test Booklet Code NC1

NEET Chronicles 1

(2023 Paper)

Name of the Candidate (In Capitals)

____

____

____

Candidate's Signature ____________

Invigilator's Signature ____________

Facsimile signature stamp of center superintendent____________

Important Instructions

- The test is of **45 minutes** duration and the Test Booklet contains **50** multiple-choice questions (four options with a single correct answer) from **Chemistry.** 50 questions in Chemistry are divided into two sections (A and B) as per details given below.
    - **Section A** shall consist of **35 (Thirty-five)** questions (Q. Nos. 1 to 35). All questions are compulsory.
    - **Section B** shall consist of **15 (Fifteen)** questions (Q. Nos. 36 to 50). In Section B, a candidate needs to attempt any 10 (Ten) questions out of 15 (Fifteen).
    Candidates are advised to read all 15 questions of Section B before they start attempting the question paper. In the event of a candidate attempting more than ten questions, **the first ten questions answered by the candidate shall be evaluated.**
- Each question carries 4 marks. For each correct response, the candidate will get 4 marks. For each incorrect response, one mark will be deducted from the total scores.
- Use **Blue/Black Point Pen only** for writing particular on this page/ marking response on Answer Sheet.

Do not open this Booklet until you start attempting the Test

Chemistry (Q. No. 1–50)

1. The relation between n_m, (n_m = the number of permissible values of magnetic quantum number (m)) for a given value of azimuthal quantum number (l), is

(a) $l = 2n_m + 1$ (b) $n_m = 2l^2 + l$

(c) $n_m = l + 2$ (d) $l = \frac{n_m - 1}{2}$

2. Amongst the given options which of the following molecules/ions acts as a Lewis acid?

(a) H_2O (b) BF_3

(c) OH^- (d) NH_3

3. Which of the following statements are not correct?

A. Hydrogen is used to reduce heavy metal oxides to metals.

B. Heavy water is used to study reaction mechanism.

C. Hydrogen is used to make saturated fats from oils.

D. The H—H bond dissociation enthalpy is lowest as compared to a single bond between two atoms of any element.

E. Hydrogen reduces oxides of metals that are more active than iron.

Choose the most appropriate answer from the options given below:

(a) B, D only

(b) D, E only

(c) A, B, C only

(d) B, C, D, E only

4. Which one of the following statements is correct?

(a) All enzymes that utilise ATP in phosphate transfer require Ca as the cofactor.

(b) The bone in human body is an inert and unchanging substance.

(c) Mg plays roles in neuromuscular function and interneuronal transmission.

(d) The daily requirement of Mg and Ca in the human body is estimated to be 0.2-0.3 g.

5. Homoleptic complex from the following complexes is

(a) diamminechloridonitrito-N-platinum (II)

(b) pentaamminecarbonatocobalt (III) chloride

(c) triamminetriaquachromium (III) chloride

(d) potassium trioxalatoaluminate (III)

6. Identify product (A) in the following reaction.

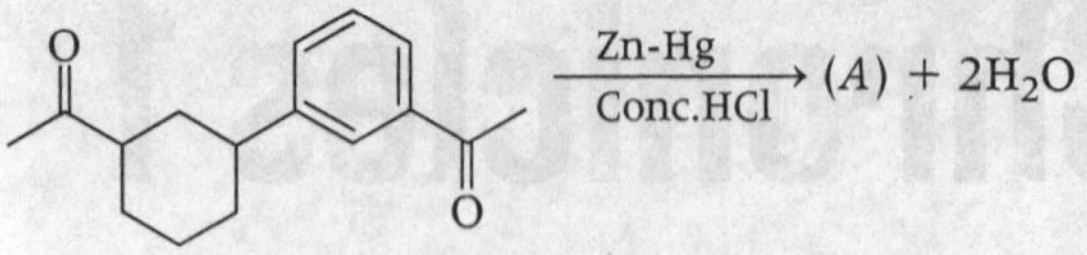

$\xrightarrow[\text{Conc.HCl}]{\text{Zn-Hg}} (A) + 2H_2O$

(a) OH, OH

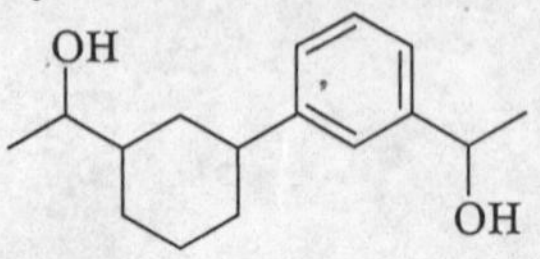

(b) OH, CH_2, CH_2OH

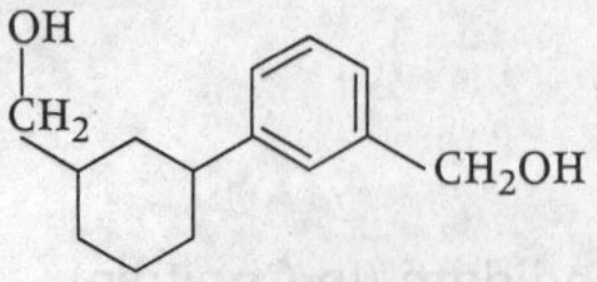

(c) CH_3, CH_3

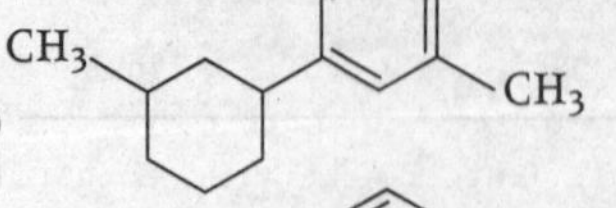

(d)

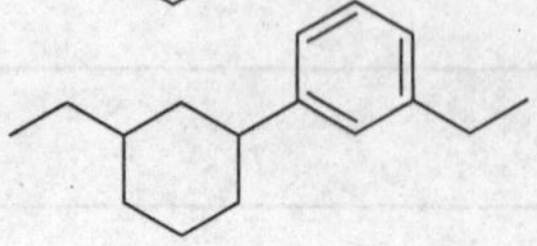

7. Identify the product in the following reaction.

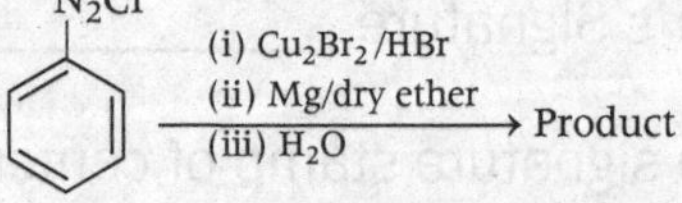

$\overset{+}{N_2}\bar{Cl}$ $\xrightarrow[\text{(iii) } H_2O]{\text{(i) } Cu_2Br_2/HBr \text{ (ii) Mg/dry ether}}$ Product

(a) 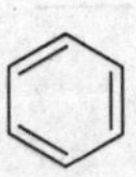 (b) MgBr

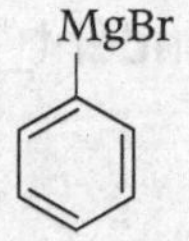

(c) OH, Br (d) OH

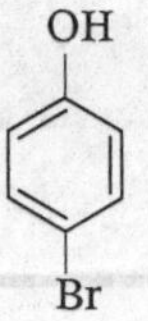

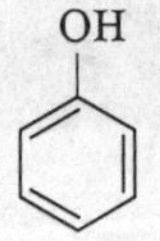

8. The correct order of energies of molecular orbitals of N_2 molecule, is

(a) $\sigma 1s < \sigma^* 1s < \sigma 2s < \sigma^* 2s < \sigma 2p_z < (\pi 2p_x = \pi 2p_y) < (\pi^* 2p_x = \pi^* 2p_y) < \sigma^* 2p_z$

(b) $\sigma 1s < \sigma^* 1s < \sigma 2s < \sigma^* 2s < \sigma 2p_z < \sigma^* 2p_z < (\pi 2p_x = \pi 2p_y) < (\pi^* 2p_x = \pi^* 2p_y)$

(c) $\sigma 1s < \sigma^* 1s < \sigma 2s < \sigma^* 2s < (\pi 2p_x = \pi 2p_y) < (\pi^* 2p_x = \pi^* 2p_y) < \sigma 2p_z < \sigma^* 2p_z$

(d) $\sigma 1s < \sigma^* 1s < \sigma 2s < \sigma^* 2s < (\pi 2p_x = \pi 2p_y) < \sigma 2p_z < (\pi^* 2p_x = \pi^* 2p_y) < \sigma^* 2p_z$

9. For a certain reaction, the rate $= k[A]^2[B]$, when the initial concentration of A is tripled keeping concentration of B constant, the initial rate would

(a) increase by a factor of six
(b) increase by a factor of nine
(c) increase by a factor of three
(d) decrease by a factor of nine

10. Given below are two statements: one is labelled as Assertion (A) and the other is labelled as Reason (R).

Assertion (A) In equation $\Delta_r G = -nFE_{cell}$, the value of $\Delta_r G$ depends on n.

Reason (R) E_{cell} is an intensive property and $\Delta_r G$ is an extensive property.

In the light of the above statements, choose the correct answer from the options given below:

(a) Both (A) and (R) are true and (R) is not the correct explanation of (A).
(b) (A) is true but (R) is false.
(c) (A) is false but (R) is true.
(d) Both (A) and (R) are true and (R) is the correct explanation of (A).

11. The given compound

C_6H_5—CH=CH—CH(X)—CH$_2$CH$_3$

is an example of

(a) aryl halide
(b) allylic halide
(c) vinylic halide
(d) benylic halide

12. Which amongst the following molecules on polymerisation produces neoprene?

(a) $H_2C=C(Cl)-CH=CH_2$
(b) $H_2C=CH-C\equiv CH$
(c) $H_2C=C(CH_3)-CH=CH_2$
(d) $H_2C=CH-CH=CH_2$

13. Consider the following reaction and identify the product (P).

$CH_3-CH(CH_3)-CH(OH)-CH_3 \xrightarrow{HBr}$ Product (P)

3-methylbutan-2-ol

(a) $CH_3CH=CH-CH_3$
(b) $CH_3-CH(CH_3)-CH(Br)-CH_3$
(c) $CH_3-C(CH_3)_2-CH_2Br$
(d) $CH_3-C(Br)(CH_3)-CH_2-CH_3$

14. The conductivity of centimolar solution of KCl at 25°C is 0.0210 ohm^{-1}cm^{-1} and the resistance of the cell containing the solution at 25°C is 60 ohm. The value of cell constant is

(a) 3.28 cm^{-1} (b) 1.26 cm^{-1}
(c) 3.34 cm^{-1} (d) 1.34 cm^{-1}

15. Match List-I with List-II.

List-I	List-II
A. Coke	I. Carbon atoms are sp^3-hybridised.
B. Diamond	II. Used as a dry lubricant.
C. Fullerene	III. Used as a reducing agent.
D. Graphite	IV. Cage like molecules.

Choose the correct answer from the options given below:

(a) A-IV, B-I, C-II, D-III
(b) A-III, B-I, C-IV, D-II
(c) A-III, B-IV, C-I, D-II
(d) A-II, B-IV, C-I, D-III

16. The element expected to form largest ion to achieve the nearest noble gas configuration is

(a) F (b) N
(c) Na (d) O

17. Which of the following reactions will not give primary amine as the product?

(a) $CH_3CN \xrightarrow[\text{(ii) } H_3O^+]{\text{(i) } LiAlH_4} \text{Product}$

(b) $CH_3NC \xrightarrow[\text{(ii) } H_3O^+]{\text{(i) } LiAlH_4} \text{Product}$

(c) $CH_3CONH_2 \xrightarrow[\text{(ii) } H_3O^+]{\text{(i) } LiAlH_4} \text{Product}$

(d) $CH_3CONH_2 \xrightarrow{Br_2/KOH} \text{Product}$

18. The number of σ bonds, π bonds and lone pair of electrons in pyridine, respectively are

(a) 12, 3, 0 (b) 11, 3, 1
(c) 12, 2, 1 (d) 11, 2, 0

19. Given below are two statements.

Statement I A unit formed by the attachment of a base to 1′-position of sugar is known as nucleoside.

Statement II When nucleoside is linked to phosphoric acid at 5′-position of sugar moiety, we get nucleotide.

In the light of the above statements, choose the correct answer from the options given below:

(a) Both Statement I and Statement II are false.
(b) Statement I is true but Statement II is false.
(c) Statement I is false but Statement II is true.
(d) Both Statement I and Statement II are true.

20. Complete the following reaction:

[A] (cyclohexanone) $\xrightarrow{HCN}$ [B] (1-hydroxycyclohexane-1-carbonitrile: OH, CN) $\xrightarrow[\Delta]{\text{conc. } H_2SO_4}$ [C]

is.........

(a) (cyclohexyl)–COOH (b) (cyclohexenyl)–CHO
(c) (cyclohexenyl)–COOH (d) (cyclohexyl)–OH

21. Taking stability as the factor, which one of the following represents correct relationship?

(a) $InI_3 > InI$ (b) $AlCl > AlCl_3$
(c) $TlI > TlI_3$ (d) $TlCl_3 > TlCl$

22. Some tranquilisers are listed below. Which one from the following belongs to barbiturates?

(a) Meprobamate (b) Valium
(c) Veronal (d) Chlordiazepoxide

23. Given below are two statements: one is labelled as Assertion (A) and the other is labelled as Reason (R).

Assertion (A) Helium is used to dilute oxygen in diving apparatus.

Reason (R) Helium has high solubility in O_2.

In the light of the above statements, choose the correct answer from the options given below:

(a) Both (A) and (R) are true and (R) is not the correct explanation of (A).
(b) (A) is true but (R) is false.
(c) (A) is false but (R) is true.
(d) Both (A) and (R) are true and (R) is the correct explanation of (A).

24. The right option for the mass of CO_2 produced by heating 20 g of 20% pure limestone is (Atomic mass of Ca = 40)

$$[CaCO_3 \xrightarrow{1200\text{ K}} CaO + CO_2]$$

(a) 1.76 g (b) 2.64 g
(c) 1.32 g (d) 1.12 g

25. In Lassaigne's extract of an organic compound, both nitrogen and sulphur are present, which gives blood red colour with Fe^{3+} due to formation of

(a) NaSCN
(b) $[Fe(CN)_5NOS]^{4-}$
(c) $[Fe(SCN)]^{2+}$
(d) $Fe_4[Fe(CN)_6]_3 \cdot xH_2O$

26. Given below are two statements: one is labelled as Assertion (A) and the other is labelled as Reason (R).

Assertion (A) A reaction can have zero activation energy.

Reason (R) The minimum extra amount of energy absorbed by reactant molecules so that their energy becomes equal to threshold value, is called activation energy.

In the light of the above statements, choose the correct answer from the options given below:

(a) Both (A) and (R) are true and (R) is not the correct explanation of (A).
(b) (A) is true but (R) is false.
(c) (A) is false but (R) is true.
(d) Both (A) and (R) are true and (R) is the correct explanation of (A).

27. A compound is formed by two elements A and B. The element B forms cubic close packed structure and atoms of A occupy 1/3 of tetrahedral voids. If the formula of the compound is A_xB_y, then the value of $x + y$ is in option

(a) 4 (b) 3
(c) 2 (d) 5

28. The stability of Cu^{2+} is more than Cu^+ salts in aqueous solution due to

(a) enthalpy of atomisation
(b) hydration energy
(c) second ionisation enthalpy
(d) first ionisation enthalpy

29. Select the correct statements from the following:

A. Atoms of all elements are composed of two fundamental particles.
B. The mass of the electrons is 9.10939×10^{-31} kg.
C. All the isotopes of a given element show same chemical properties.
D. Protons and electrons are collectively known as nucleons.
E. Dalton's atomic theory, regarded the atom as an ultimate particle of matter.

Choose the correct answer from the options given below:

(a) C, D and E only
(b) A and E only
(c) B, C and E only
(d) A, B and C only

30. Which amongst the following options is correct graphical representation of Boyle's Law?

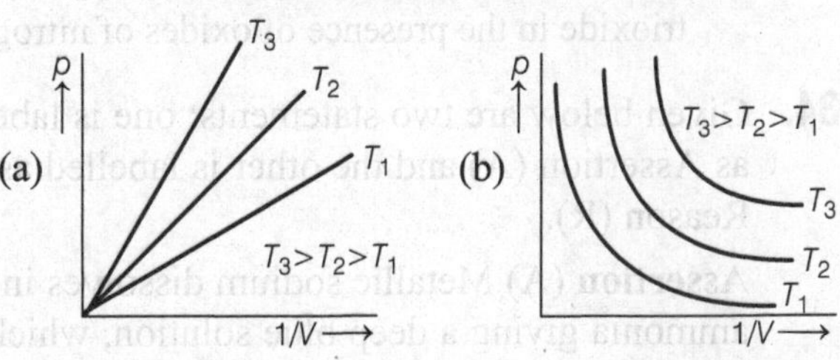

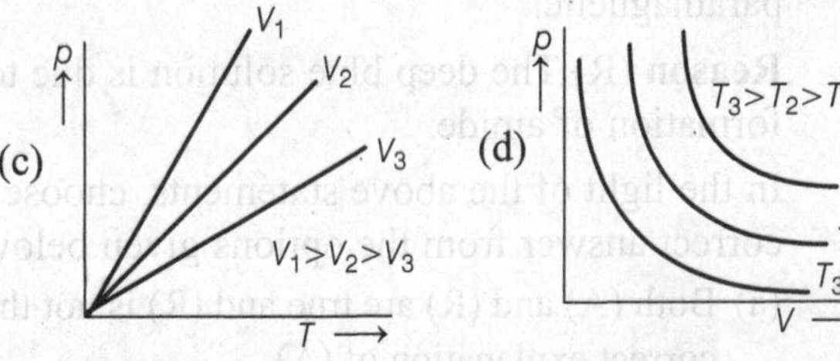

31. Intermolecular forces are forces of attraction and repulsion between interacting particles that will include;

A. dipole-dipole forces
B. dipole-induced dipole forces
C. hydrogen bonding
D. covalent bonding
E. dispersion forces

Choose the most appropriate answer from the options given below.

(a) A, B, C , D are correct.
(b) A, B, C , E are correct.
(c) A, C, D, E are correct.
(d) B, C, D, E are correct.

32. Weight (g) of two moles of the organic compound, which is obtained by heating sodium ethanoate with sodium hydroxide in presence of calcium oxide is

(a) 32 (b) 30
(c) 18 (d) 16

33. Which one is an example of heterogeneous catalysis?

(a) Hydrolysis of sugar catalysed by H^+ ions.
(b) Decomposition of ozone in presence of nitrogen monoxide.
(c) Combination between dinitrogen and dihydrogen to form ammonia in the presence of finely divided iron.
(d) Oxidation of sulphur dioxide into sulphur trioxide in the presence of oxides of nitrogen.

34. Given below are two statements: one is labelled as Assertion (A) and the other is labelled as Reason (R).

Assertion (A) Metallic sodium dissolves in liquid ammonia giving a deep blue solution, which is paramagnetic.

Reason (R) The deep blue solution is due to the formation of amide.

In the light of the above statements, choose the correct answer from the options given below:

(a) Both (A) and (R) are true and (R) is not the correct explanation of (A).
(b) (A) is true but (R) is false.
(c) (A) is false but (R) is true.
(d) Both (A) and (R) are true and (R) is the correct explanation of (A).

35. Amongst the following, the total number of species not having eight electrons around central atom in its outer most shell, is

$$NH_3, AlCl_3, BeCl_2, CCl_4, PCl_5$$

(a) 2 (b) 4 (c) 1 (d) 3

36. Identify the major product obtained in the following reaction

(2-acetylbenzaldehyde) $+ 2[Ag(NH_3)_2]^+ + 3OH^- \xrightarrow{\Delta}$ Major product

(a) (2-acetylbenzyl alcohol: $COCH_3$, CH_2OH)
(b) (2-acetylbenzoate: $COCH_3$, COO^-)
(c) (2-(1-hydroxyethyl)benzoate: $CH(OH)CH_3$, COO^-)
(d) (2-(1-hydroxyethyl)benzyl alcohol: $CH(OH)CH_3$, CH_2OH)

37. Match List-I with List-II.

	List-I (Oxoacids of sulphur)		List-II (Bonds)
A.	Peroxodisulphuric acid	I.	Two S—OH, four S=O, one S—O—S
B.	Sulphuric acid	II.	Two S—OH, one S=O
C.	Pyrosulphuric acid	III.	Two S—OH, four S=O, one S—O—O—S
D.	Sulphurous acid	IV.	Two S—OH, two S=O

Choose the correct answer from the options given below.

(a) A-III, B-IV, C-I, D-II
(b) A-I, B-III, C-IV, D-II
(c) A-III, B-IV, C-II, D-I
(d) A-I, B-III, C-II, D-IV

38. Consider the following compounds/species.

(i) 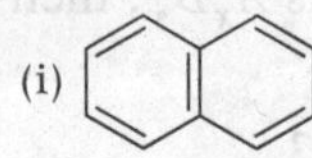

(ii)

(iii)

(iv) 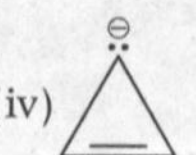

(v) 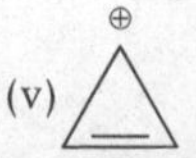

(vi) 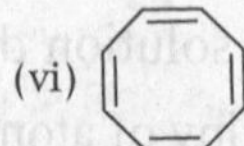

(iv) 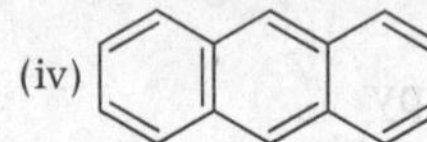

The number of compounds/species which obey Huckel's rule is ....

(a) 6 (b) 2
(c) 5 (d) 4

39. Pumice stone is an example of

(a) gel (b) solid sol
(c) foam (d) sol

40. Which amongst the following options is the correct relation between change in enthalpy and change in internal energy?

(a) $\Delta H = \Delta U + \Delta n_g RT$ (b) $\Delta H - \Delta U = -\Delta nRT$
(c) $\Delta H + \Delta U = \Delta nR$ (d) $\Delta H = \Delta U - \Delta n_g RT$

41. Which amongst the following will be most readily dehydrated under acidic conditions?

(a) [structure: H_3C–CH(OH)–CH(OH)–… with H] (b) [structure with NO_2, H, OH, OH]

(c) [structure with NO_2, OH] (d) [structure with NO_2, HO, H, CH_3]

42. Consider the following reaction.

$$C_6H_5-CH_2-O-C_6H_5 \xrightarrow[\Delta]{HI} A + B$$

Identify products *A* and *B*.

(a) $A = C_6H_5-CH_2OH$ and $B = C_6H_5-I$

(b) $A = C_6H_5-CH_2I$ and $B = C_6H_5-OH$

(c) $A = C_6H_5-CH_2I$ and $B = C_6H_5-I$

(d) $A = C_6H_5-CH_3$ and $B = C_6H_5-OH$

43. On balancing the given redox reaction,

$$a\text{Cr}_2\text{O}_7^{2-} + b\text{SO}_3^{2-}(aq) + c\text{H}^+(aq) \longrightarrow$$

$$2a\text{Cr}^{3+}(aq) + b\text{SO}_4^{2-}(aq) + \frac{c}{2}\text{H}_2\text{O}(l)$$

the coefficients *a*, *b* and *c* are found to be, respectively

(a) 3, 8, 1 (b) 1, 8, 3 (c) 8, 1, 3 (d) 1, 3, 8

44. Which complex compound is most stable?

(a) $[Co(NH_3)_3(NO_3)_3]$

(b) $[CoCl_2(en)_2]NO_3$

(c) $[Co(NH_3)_6]_2(SO_4)_3$

(d) $[Co(NH_3)_4(H_2O)Br](NO_3)_2$

45. What fraction of one edge centred octahedral void lies in one unit cell of fcc?

(a) $\frac{1}{3}$ (b) $\frac{1}{4}$ (c) $\frac{1}{12}$ (d) $\frac{1}{2}$

46. Which of the following statements are incorrect?

A. All the transition metals except scandium form *M*O oxides which are ionic.

B. The highest oxidation number corresponding to the group number in transition metal oxides is attained in Sc_2O_3 to Mn_2O_7.

C. Basic character increases from V_2O_3 to V_2O_4 to V_2O_5.

D. V_2O_4 dissolves in acids to give VO_4^{3-} salts.

E. CrO is basic but Cr_2O_3 is amphoteric.

Choose the correct answer from the options given below:

(a) B and D only (b) C and D only

(c) B and C only (d) A and E only

47. The equilibrium concentrations of the species in the reaction, $A + B \rightleftharpoons C + D$ are 2, 3, 10 and 6 mol L^{-1}, respectively at 300 K, $\Delta G°$ for the reaction is ($R = 2$ cal/ mol K)

(a) –137.26 cal (b) –1381.80 cal

(c) –13.73 cal (d) 1372.60 cal

48. Identify the final product [*D*] obtained in the following sequence of reactions.

$$CH_3CHO \xrightarrow[\text{(ii) } H_3O^+]{\text{(i) } LiAlH_4} [A] \xrightarrow[\Delta]{H_2SO_4} [B] \xrightarrow{HBr} [C] \xrightarrow[\text{Na/dry ether}]{C_6H_5Br} [D]$$

(a) [biphenyl] (b) C_4H_{10}

(c) $HC \equiv C^- Na^+$ (d) [ethylbenzene]

49. Given below are two statements.

Statement I The nutrient deficient water bodies lead to eutrophication.

Statement II Eutrophication leads to decrease in the level of oxygen in the water bodies.

In the light of the above statements, choose the correct answer from the options given below:

(a) Both statement I and statement II are false.

(b) Statement I is true but statement II is false.

(c) Statement I is false but statement II is true.

(d) Both statement I and statement II are true.

50. The reaction that does not take place in a blast furnace between 900 K to 1500 K temperature range during extraction of iron is

(a) $FeO + CO \longrightarrow Fe + CO_2$

(b) $C + CO_2 \longrightarrow 2CO$

(c) $CaO + SiO_2 \longrightarrow CaSiO_3$

(d) $Fe_2O_3 + CO \longrightarrow 2FeO + CO_2$

Response Index

01	a	b	c	d	14	a	b	c	d	27	a	b	c	d	40	a	b	c	d
02	a	b	c	d	15	a	b	c	d	28	a	b	c	d	41	a	b	c	d
03	a	b	c	d	16	a	b	c	d	29	a	b	c	d	42	a	b	c	d
04	a	b	c	d	17	a	b	c	d	30	a	b	c	d	43	a	b	c	d
05	a	b	c	d	18	a	b	c	d	31	a	b	c	d	44	a	b	c	d
06	a	b	c	d	19	a	b	c	d	32	a	b	c	d	45	a	b	c	d
07	a	b	c	d	20	a	b	c	d	33	a	b	c	d	46	a	b	c	d
08	a	b	c	d	21	a	b	c	d	34	a	b	c	d	47	a	b	c	d
09	a	b	c	d	22	a	b	c	d	35	a	b	c	d	48	a	b	c	d
10	a	b	c	d	23	a	b	c	d	36	a	b	c	d	49	a	b	c	d
11	a	b	c	d	24	a	b	c	d	37	a	b	c	d	50	a	b	c	d
12	a	b	c	d	25	a	b	c	d	38	a	b	c	d					
13	a	b	c	d	26	a	b	c	d	39	a	b	c	d					

Performance Scanner

> 90% Excellent !	You have mastered the NEET syllabus (12th). The concepts of this entire syllabus are at your fingertips. Maintain this momentum.
76-90% Very Good !	You have a good command over the entire NEET syllabus (12th). Revise it again after a few days to enhance your performance.
60-75% Good !	You have a wide scope to learn for the entire NEET syllabus (12th). Revise it again.
<60% Not Satisfactory!	You have a long way ahead of you to master the NEET syllabus (12th). Revise it thoroughly.

Test Booklet No. 3947274

Test Booklet Code NC2

NEET Chronicles 2

(2024 Paper)

Name of the Candidate (In Capitals)

____

____

____

Candidate's Signature ______________

Invigilator's Signature ______________

Facsimile signature stamp of center superintendent__________________

Important Instructions

- The test is of **45 minutes** duration and the Test Booklet contains **50** multiple-choice questions (four options with a single correct answer) from **Chemistry**. 50 questions in Chemistry are divided into two sections (A and B) as per details given below.
  - **Section A** shall consist of **35 (Thirty-five)** questions (Q. Nos. 1 to 35). All questions are compulsory.
  - **Section B** shall consist of **15 (Fifteen)** questions (Q. Nos. 36 to 50). In Section B, a candidate needs to attempt any 10 (Ten) questions out of 15 (Fifteen). **Candidates are advised to read all 15 questions of Section B** before they start attempting the question paper. In the event of a candidate attempting more than ten questions, **the first ten questions answered by the candidate shall be evaluated.**
- Each question carries 4 marks. For each correct response, the candidate will get 4 marks. For each incorrect response, one mark will be deducted from the total scores.
- Use **Blue/Black Point Pen only** for writing particular on this page/ marking response on Answer Sheet.

Do not open this Booklet until you start attempting the Test

Chemistry (Q. No. 1-50)

1. 'Spin only' magnetic moment is same for which of the following ions?

A. Ti^{3+} B. Cr^{2+} C. Mn^{2+} D. Fe^{2+} E. Sc^{3+}

Choose the most appropriate answer from the options given below.

(a) B and D (b) A and E
(c) B and C (d) A and D

2. The most stable carbocation among the following is

(a) $H_3C-CH_2-\overset{\oplus}{C}H-CH(CH_3)-CH_3$ (b) $CH_3-\overset{\oplus}{C}H-CH_2-CH(CH_3)-CH_3$

(c) cyclopentyl–$\overset{\oplus}{C}H_2$ (d) 1-methylcyclohexyl cation ($\oplus$ on ring carbon bearing CH_3)

3. Given below are two statements:

Statement I The boiling point of hydrides of group 16 elements follow the order

$$H_2O > H_2Te > H_2Se > H_2S$$

Statement II On the basis of molecular mass, H_2O is expected to have lower boiling point than the other members of the group but due to the presence of extensive H-bonding in H_2O, it has higher boiling point.

In the light of the above statements, choose the correct answer from the options given below.

(a) Both Statement I and Statement II are true.
(b) Both Statement I and Statement II are false.
(c) Statement I is true but Statement II is false.
(d) Statement I is false but Statement II is true.

4. Match List I with List II.

	List I (Compound)		List II (Shape/Geometry)
A.	NH_3	I.	Trigonal pyramidal
B.	BrF_5	II.	Square planar
C.	XeF_4	III.	Octahedral
D.	SF_6	IV.	Square pyramidal

Choose the correct answer from the options given below:

(a) A-I, B-IV, C-II, D-III
(b) A-II, B-IV, C-III, D-I
(c) A-III, B-IV, C-I, D-II
(d) A-II, B-III, C-IV, D-I

5. The highest number of helium atoms is in

(a) 4 moles of helium
(b) 4 u of helium
(c) 4 g of helium
(d) 2.271098 L of helium at STP

6. Identify the correct reagents that would bring about the following transformation.

$$C_6H_{11}-CH_2-CH=CH_2 \longrightarrow C_6H_{11}-CH_2-CH_2-CHO$$

(a) (i) $H_2O/H^{\oplus}$ (ii) CrO_3
(b) (i) BH_3 (ii) $H_2O_2/\overset{\ominus}{O}H$ (iii) PCC
(c) (i) BH_3 (ii) $H_2O_2/\overset{\ominus}{O}H$ (iii) Alk. $KMnO_4$ (iv) $H_3O^{\oplus}$
(d) (i) $H_2O/H^{\oplus}$ (ii) PCC

7. Match List-I with List-II.

	List-I (Process)		List-II (Conditions)
A.	Isothermal process	I.	No heat exchange
B.	Isochoric process	II.	Carried out at constant temperature
C.	Isobaric process	III.	Carried out at constant volume
D.	Adiabatic process	IV.	Carried out at constant pressure

Choose the correct answer from the options given below:

(a) A-IV, B-III, C-II, D-I
(b) A-IV, B-II, C-III, D-I
(c) A-I, B-II, C-III, D-IV
(d) A-II, B-III, C-IV, D-I

8. Which one of the following alcohols reacts instantaneously with Lucas reagent?

(a) $CH_3CH_2CH_2CH_2OH$

(b) $CH_3-CH_2-\underset{\underset{CH_3}{|}}{CH}-OH$

(c) $CH_3-\underset{\underset{CH_3}{|}}{CH}-CH_2OH$

(d) $CH_3-\overset{\overset{CH_3}{|}}{\underset{\underset{CH_3}{|}}{C}}-OH$

9. In which of the following equilibria, K_p and K_C are not equal?

(a) $PCl_5(g) \rightleftharpoons PCl_3(g) + Cl_2(g)$

(b) $H_2(g) + I_2(g) \rightleftharpoons 2HI(g)$

(c) $CO\ (g) + H_2O\ (g) \rightleftharpoons CO_2(g) + H_2(g)$

(d) $2BrCl(g) \rightleftharpoons Br_2(g) + Cl_2(g)$

10. Match List-I with List-II.

	List-I (Quantum number)	List-II (Information provided)
A.	m_l	I. Shape of orbital
B.	m_s	II. Size of orbital
C.	l	III. Orientation of orbital
D.	n	IV. Orientation of spin of electron

Choose the correct answer from the options given below :

(a) A-I, B-III, C-II, D-IV
(b) A-III, B-IV, C-I, D-II
(c) A-III, B-IV, C-II, D-I
(d) A-II, B-I, C-IV, D-III

11. Given below are two statements.

Statement I Aniline does not undergo Friedel-Crafts alkylation reaction.

Statement II Aniline cannot be prepared through Gabriel synthesis.

In the light of the above statements, choose the correct answer from the options given below:

(a) Both statement I and statement II are true.
(b) Both statement I and statement II are false.
(c) Statement I is true but statement II is false.
(d) Statement I is false but Statement II is true.

12. Intramolecular hydrogen bonding is present in

(a) NO_2, OH (ortho)
(b) NO_2, OH (para)
(c) NO_2, HO (meta)
(d) HF

13. On heating, some solid substances change from solid to vapour state without passing through liquid state.

The technique used for the purification of such solid substances based on the above principle is known as

(a) crystallisation
(b) sublimation
(c) distillation
(d) chromatography

14. In which of the following processes entropy increases?

A. A liquid evaporates to vapour.
B. Temperature of a crystalline solid lowered from 130 K to 0 K.
C. $2NaHCO_3(s) \longrightarrow Na_2CO_3(g) + CO_2(g) + H_2O(g)$
D. $Cl_2(g) \longrightarrow 2Cl(g)$

Choose the correct answer from the options given below:

(a) A and C
(b) A, B and D
(c) A, C and D
(d) C and D

15. Among group 16 elements, which one does not show –2 oxidation state?

(a) O
(b) Se
(c) Te
(d) Po

16. Match List-I with List-II.

List-I (Conversion)	List-II (Number of Faraday required)
A. 1 mole of H_2O to O_2	I. 3F
B. 1 mole of MnO_4^- to Mn^{2+}	II. 2F
C. 1.5 mole of Ca from molten $CaCl_2$	III. 1F
D. 1 mole of FeO to Fe_2O_3	IV. 5F

Choose the correct answer from the options given below:

(a) A-II, B-IV, C-I, D-III
(b) A-III, B-IV, C-I, D-II
(c) A-II, B-III, C-I, D-IV
(d) A-III, B-IV, C-II, D-I

17. Arrange the following elements in increasing order of electronegativity:

N, O, F, C, Si

Choose the correct answer from the options given below:

(a) Si < C < N < O < F
(b) Si < C < O < N < F
(c) O < F < N < C < Si
(d) F < O < N < C < Si

18. A compound with a molecular formula of C_6H_{14} has two tertiary carbons. Its IUPAC name is

(a) *n*-hexane
(b) 2-methylpentane
(c) 2,3-dimethylbutane
(d) 2,2-dimethylbutane

19. Fehling's solution '*A*' is

(a) aqueous copper sulphate
(b) alkaline copper sulphate
(c) alkaline solution of sodium potassium tartrate (Rochelle's salt)
(d) aqueous sodium citrate

20. Activation energy of any chemical reaction can be calculated if one knows the value of

(a) rate constant at standard temperature
(b) probability of collision
(c) orientation of reactant molecules during collision
(d) rate constant at two different temperatures

21. Which plot of ln *k* *vs* $1/T$ is consistent with Arrhenius equation?

(a) 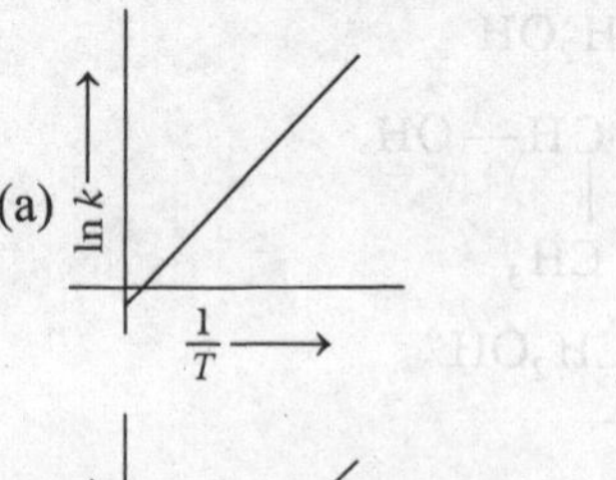

(b) 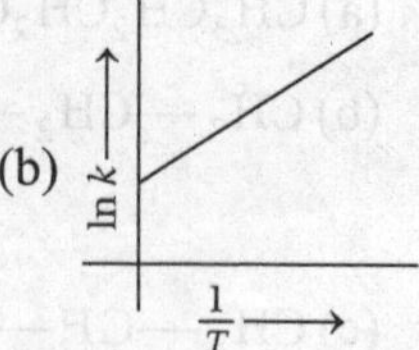

(c) 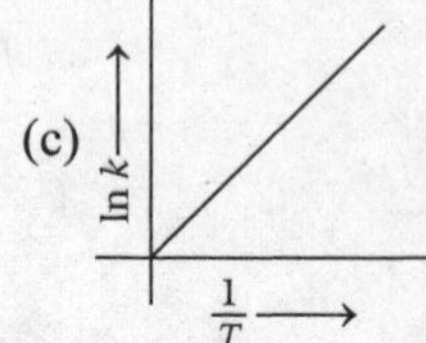

(d) 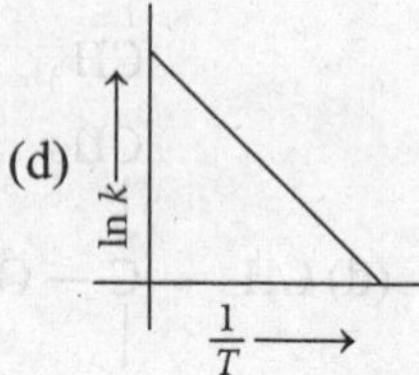

22. Match List-I with List-II.

List-I (Reaction)	List-II (Reagents/Condition)
A. → 2 =O	I. Cl/Anhyd. $AlCl_3$
B. →	II. CrO_3
C. OH → O	III. $KMnO_4/KOH, \Delta$
D. CH_2CH_3 → COOK	IV. (i) O_3 (ii) $Zn\text{-}H_2O$

Choose the correct answer from the options given below:

(a) A-IV, B-I, C-III, D-II
(b) A-III, B-I, C-II, D-IV
(c) A-IV, B-I, C-II, D-III
(d) A-I, B-IV, C-II, D-III

23. The compound that will undergo S_N1 reaction with the fastest rate is

(a) Br (b) Br

(c) 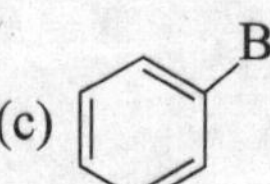

(d) 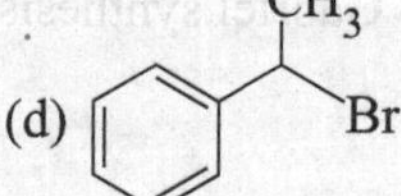

24. Which reaction is not a redox reaction?

(a) $Zn + CuSO_4 \longrightarrow ZnSO_4 + Cu$

(b) $2KClO_3 + I_2 \longrightarrow 2KIO_3 + Cl_2$

(c) $H_2 + Cl_2 \longrightarrow 2HCl$

(d) $BaCl_2 + Na_2SO_4 \longrightarrow BaSO_4 + 2NaCl$

25. Given below are two statements:

Statement I The boiling point of three isomeric pentanes follows the order
n-pentane > isopentane > neopentane

Statement II When branching increases, the molecule attains a shape of sphere. This results in smaller surface area for contact, due to which the intermolecular forces between the spherical molecules are weak, thereby lowering the boiling point.

In the light of the above statements, choose the most appropriate answer from the options given below:

(a) Both Statement I and Statement II are true.
(b) Both Statement I and Statement II are false.
(c) Statement I is true but Statement II is false.
(d) Statement I is false but Statement II is true.

26. Given below are two statements :

Statement I Both $[Co(NH_3)_6]^{3+}$ and $[CoF_6]^{3-}$ complexes are octahedral but differ in their magnetic behaviour.

Statement II $[Co(NH_3)_6]^{3+}$ is diamagnetic whereas $[CoF_6]^{3-}$ is paramagnetic.

In the light of the above statements, choose the correct answer from the options given below:

(a) Both Statement I and Statement II are true.
(b) Both Statement I and Statement II are false.
(c) Statement I is true but Statement II is false.
(d) Statement I is false but Statement II is true.

27. Match List-I with List-II.

List-I (Molecule)	List-II (Number and types of bond(s) between two carbon atoms)
A. Ethane	I. One σ-bond and two π-bonds
B. Ethene	II. two π-bonds
C. Carbon molecule, C_2	III. One σ-bond
D. Ethyne	IV. One σ-bond and one π-bond

Choose the correct answer from the options given below:

(a) A-I, B-IV, C-II, D-III
(b) A-IV, B-III, C-II, D-I
(c) A-III, B-IV, C-II, D-I
(d) A-III, B-IV, C-I, D-II

28. The Henry's law constant (K_H) values of three gases (*A*, *B*, *C*) in water are 145, 2×10^{-5} and 35 kbar, respectively. The solubility of these gases in water follow the order

(a) $B > A > C$ (b) $B > C > A$
(c) $A > C > B$ (d) $A > B > C$

29. The energy of an electron in the ground state ($n = 1$) for He^+ ion is –x J, then that for an electron in $n = 2$ state for Be^{3+} ion in J is

(a) $-x$ (b) $-\frac{x}{9}$
(c) $-4x$ (d) $-\frac{4}{9}x$

30. The E° value for the Mn^{3+} / Mn^{2+} couple is more positive than that of Cr^{3+} / Cr^{2+} or Fe^{3+} / Fe^{2+} due to change of

(a) d^5 to d^4 configuration
(b) d^5 to d^2 configuration
(c) d^4 to d^5 configuration
(d) d^3 to d^5 configuration

31. The reagents with which glucose does not react to give the corresponding tests/products are

A. Tollen's reagent B. Schiff's reagent
C. HCN D. NH_2OH
E. $NaHSO_3$

Choose the correct options from the given below:

(a) B and C (b) A and D
(c) B and E (d) E and D

32. Match List-I with List-II.

List-I (Complex)	List-II (Type of isomerism)
A. $[Co(NH_3)_5(NO_2)]Cl_2$	I. Solvate isomerism
B. $[Co(NH_3)_5(SO_4)]Br$	II. Linkage isomerism
C. $[Co(NH_3)_6][Cr(CN)_6]$	III. Ionisation isomerism
D. $[Co(H_2O)_6]Cl_3$	IV. Coordination isomerism

Choose the correct answer from the options given below:
(a) A-II, B-III, C-IV, D-I
(b) A-I, B-III, C-IV, D-II
(c) A-I, B-IV, C-III, D-II
(d) A-II, B-IV, C-III, D-I

33. Arrange the following elements in increasing order of first ionisation enthalpy:

Li, Be, B, C, N

Choose the correct answer from the options given below:
(a) Li < Be < B < C < N
(b) Li < B < Be < C < N
(c) Li < Be < C < B < N
(d) Li < Be < N < B < C

34. 1 g of sodium hydroxide was treated with 25 mL of 0.75 M HCl solution, the mass of sodium hydroxide left unreacted is equal to
(a) 750 mg (b) 250 mg
(c) zero mg (d) 200 mg

35. For the reaction, $2A \rightleftharpoons B + C, K_C = 4 \times 10^{-3}$. At a given time, the composition of reaction mixture is: $[A] = [B] = [C] = 2 \times 10^{-3}$ M.
Then, which of the following is correct?
(a) Reaction is at equilibrium.
(b) Reaction has a tendency to go in forward direction.
(c) Reaction has a tendency to go in backward direction.
(d) Reaction has gone to completion in forward direction.

36. Given below are certain cations. Using inorganic qualitative analysis, arrange them in increasing group number from 0 to VI.
A. Al^{3+} B. Cu^{2+} C. Ba^{2+} D. Co^{2+} E. Mg^{2+}
Choose the correct answer from the options given below.
(a) B, A, D, C, E (b) B, C, A, D, E
(c) E, C, D, B, A (d) E, A, B, C, D

37. The products *A* and *B* obtained in the following reactions, respectively are

$$3ROH + PCl_3 \longrightarrow 3RCl + A$$
$$ROH + PCl_5 \longrightarrow RCl + HCl + B$$

(a) $POCl_3$ and H_3PO_3 (b) $POCl_3$ and H_3PO_4
(c) H_3PO_4 and $POCl_3$ (d) H_3PO_3 and $POCl_3$

38. Mass in grams of copper deposited by passing 9.6487 A current through a voltmeter containing copper sulphate solution for 100 seconds is (Given : Molar mass of Cu : 63 mol^{-1}, 1 F = 96487 C)
(a) 3.15 g (b) 0.315 g
(c) 31.5 g (d) 0.0315

39. The plot of osmotic pressure (π) *vs* concentration (mol L^{-1}) for a solution gives a straight line with slope 25.73 L bar mol^{-1}. The temperature at which the osmotic pressure measurement is done is (Use $R = 0.083$ L bar $mol^{-1}K^{-1}$)
(a) 37°C (b) 310°C
(c) 25.73°C (d) 12.05°C

40. Identify the major product *C* formed in the following reaction sequence:

$$CH_3—CH_2—CH—I \xrightarrow{NaCN} A \xrightarrow[\text{Partial hydrolysis}]{OH^-} B \xrightarrow[Br_2]{NaOH} C \text{ (major)}$$

(a) propylamine
(b) butylamine
(c) butanamide
(d) α-bromobutanoic acid

41. Identify the correct answer.
(a) Three resonance structures can be drawn for ozone.
(b) BF_3 has non-zero dipole moment.
(c) Dipole moment of NF_3 is greater than that of NH_3.
(d) Three canonical forms can be drawn for CO_3^{2-} ion.

42. Given below are two statements :
Statement I $[Co(NH_3)_6]^{3+}$ is a homoleptic complex whereas $[Co(NH_3)_4Cl_2]^+$ is a heteroleptic complex.
Statement II Complex $[Co(NH_3)_6]^{3+}$ has only one kind of ligands but $[Co(NH_3)_4Cl_2]^+$ has more than one kind of ligands.
In the light of the above statements, choose the correct answer from the options given below.
(a) Both Statement I and Statement II are true.
(b) Both Statement I and Statement II are false.
(c) Statement I is true but Statement II is false.
(d) Statement I is false but Statement II is true.

43. For the given reaction

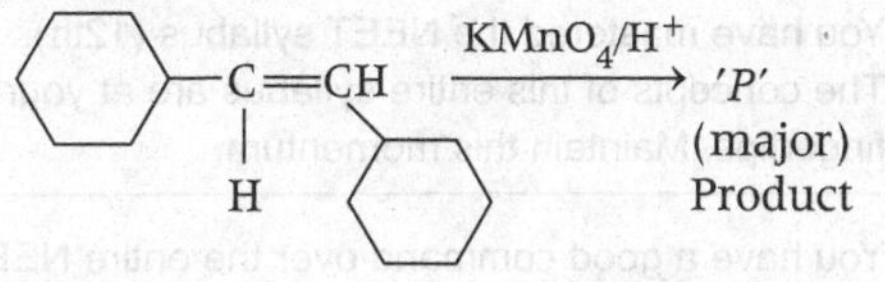

$$\text{C}_6\text{H}_{11}\text{–C(H)=CH–C}_6\text{H}_{11} \xrightarrow{KMnO_4/H^+} \text{'P' (major) Product}$$

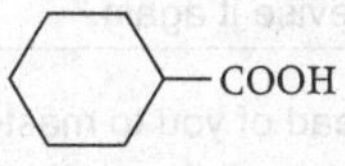

'P' is

(a) 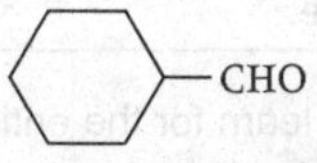 C_6H_{11}–CHO

(b) C_6H_{11}–COOH

(c) C_6H_{11}–CH(OH)–CH(OH)–C_6H_{11}

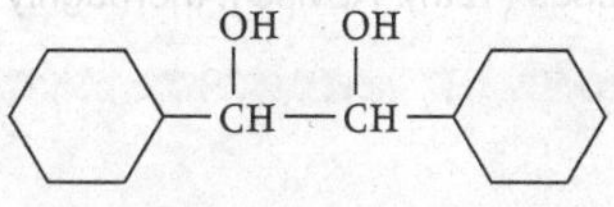

(d) 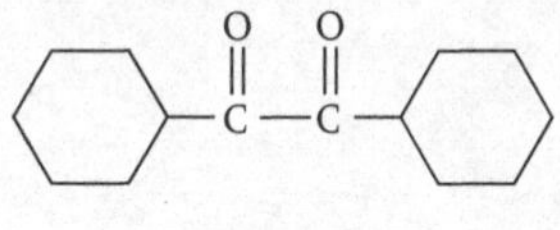 C_6H_{11}–C(=O)–C(=O)–C_6H_{11}

44. The pair of lanthanoid ions which are diamagnetic is

(a) Ce^{4+} and Yb^{2+}
(b) Ce^{3+} and Eu^{2+}
(c) Gd^{3+} and Eu^{3+}
(d) Pm^{3+} and Sm^{3+}

45. Consider the following reaction in a sealed vessel at equilibrium with concentrations of $N_2 = 3.0 \times 10^{-3} M, O_2 = 4.2 \times 10^{-3} M$ and $NO = 2.8 \times 10^{-3}$ M

$$2NO(g) \rightleftharpoons N_2(g) + O_2(g)$$

If 0.1 mol L^{-1} of NO (g) is taken in a closed vessel, what will be degree of dissociation (α) of NO(g) at equilibrium?

(a) 0.00889 (b) 0.0889
(c) 0.8889 (d) 0.717

46. A compound X contains 32% of A, 20% of B and remaining percentage of C. Then, the empirical formula of X is

(Given, atomic masses of $A = 64; B = 40; C = 32$ u)

(a) A_2BC_2 (b) ABC_3
(c) AB_2C_2 (d) ABC_4

47. The work done during reversible isothermal expansion of one mole of hydrogen gas at 25°C from pressure of 20 atmosphere to 10 atmosphere is (Given, $R = 2.0$ cal $K^{-1} mol^{-1}$)

(a) 0 calorie (b) −413.14 calories
(c) 413.14 calories (d) 100 calories

48. During the preparation of Mohr's salt solution (Ferrous ammonium sulphate), which of the following acid is added to prevent hydrolysis of Fe^{2+} ion?

(a) Dilute hydrochloric acid
(b) Concentrated sulphuric acid
(c) Dilute nitric acid
(d) Dilute sulphuric acid

49. The rate of a reaction quadruples when temperature changes from 27°C to 57°C. Calculate the energy of activation.
Given, $R = 8.314$ J $K^{-1} mol^{-1}$, $\log 4 = 0.6021$

(a) 38.04 kJ/mol (b) 380.4 kJ/mol
(c) 3.80 kJ/mol (d) 3804 kJ/mol

50. Major products A and B formed in the following reaction sequence are

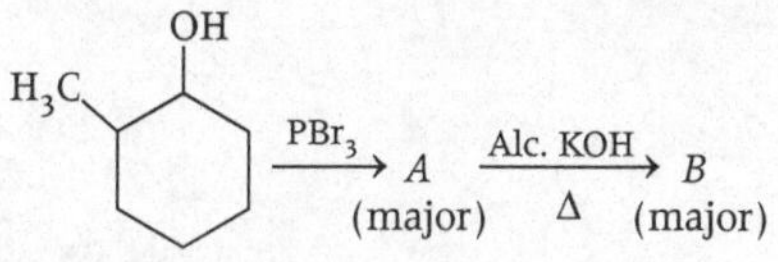

2-methylcyclohexan-1-ol (OH, H_3C) $\xrightarrow{PBr_3}$ A (major) $\xrightarrow[\Delta]{\text{Alc. KOH}}$ B (major)

(a) $A =$ 1-bromo-2-methylcyclohexane (Br, H_3C) ; $B =$ 1-methylcyclohexene (H_3C)

(b) $A =$ 1-bromo-2-methylcyclohexane (Br, H_3C) ; $B =$ 3-methylcyclohexene (H_3C)

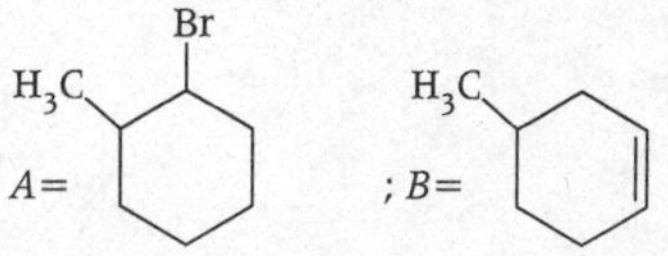

(c) 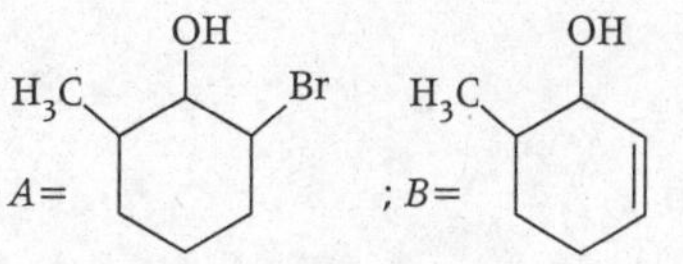 $A =$ 2-bromo-6-methylcyclohexan-1-ol (OH, Br, H_3C) ; $B =$ 6-methylcyclohex-2-en-1-ol (OH, H_3C)

(d) 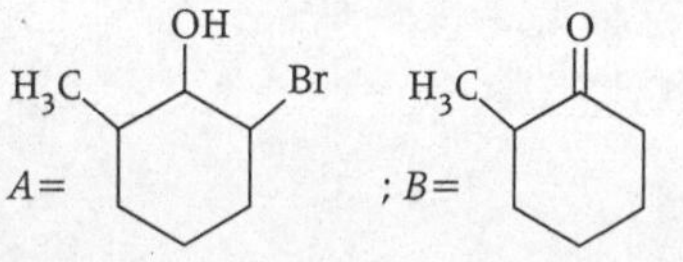 $A =$ 2-bromo-6-methylcyclohexan-1-ol (OH, Br, H_3C) ; $B =$ 2-methylcyclohexanone (O, H_3C)

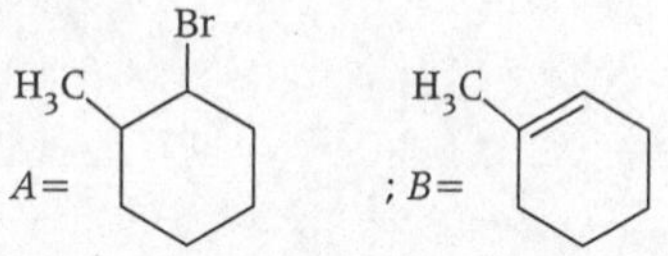

■ Response Index

01	ⓐ	ⓑ	ⓒ	ⓓ	14	ⓐ	ⓑ	ⓒ	ⓓ	27	ⓐ	ⓑ	ⓒ	ⓓ	40	ⓐ	ⓑ	ⓒ	ⓓ
02	ⓐ	ⓑ	ⓒ	ⓓ	15	ⓐ	ⓑ	ⓒ	ⓓ	28	ⓐ	ⓑ	ⓒ	ⓓ	41	ⓐ	ⓑ	ⓒ	ⓓ
03	ⓐ	ⓑ	ⓒ	ⓓ	16	ⓐ	ⓑ	ⓒ	ⓓ	29	ⓐ	ⓑ	ⓒ	ⓓ	42	ⓐ	ⓑ	ⓒ	ⓓ
04	ⓐ	ⓑ	ⓒ	ⓓ	17	ⓐ	ⓑ	ⓒ	ⓓ	30	ⓐ	ⓑ	ⓒ	ⓓ	43	ⓐ	ⓑ	ⓒ	ⓓ
05	ⓐ	ⓑ	ⓒ	ⓓ	18	ⓐ	ⓑ	ⓒ	ⓓ	31	ⓐ	ⓑ	ⓒ	ⓓ	44	ⓐ	ⓑ	ⓒ	ⓓ
06	ⓐ	ⓑ	ⓒ	ⓓ	19	ⓐ	ⓑ	ⓒ	ⓓ	32	ⓐ	ⓑ	ⓒ	ⓓ	45	ⓐ	ⓑ	ⓒ	ⓓ
07	ⓐ	ⓑ	ⓒ	ⓓ	20	ⓐ	ⓑ	ⓒ	ⓓ	33	ⓐ	ⓑ	ⓒ	ⓓ	46	ⓐ	ⓑ	ⓒ	ⓓ
08	ⓐ	ⓑ	ⓒ	ⓓ	21	ⓐ	ⓑ	ⓒ	ⓓ	34	ⓐ	ⓑ	ⓒ	ⓓ	47	ⓐ	ⓑ	ⓒ	ⓓ
09	ⓐ	ⓑ	ⓒ	ⓓ	22	ⓐ	ⓑ	ⓒ	ⓓ	35	ⓐ	ⓑ	ⓒ	ⓓ	48	ⓐ	ⓑ	ⓒ	ⓓ
10	ⓐ	ⓑ	ⓒ	ⓓ	23	ⓐ	ⓑ	ⓒ	ⓓ	36	ⓐ	ⓑ	ⓒ	ⓓ	49	ⓐ	ⓑ	ⓒ	ⓓ
11	ⓐ	ⓑ	ⓒ	ⓓ	24	ⓐ	ⓑ	ⓒ	ⓓ	37	ⓐ	ⓑ	ⓒ	ⓓ	50	ⓐ	ⓑ	ⓒ	ⓓ
12	ⓐ	ⓑ	ⓒ	ⓓ	25	ⓐ	ⓑ	ⓒ	ⓓ	38	ⓐ	ⓑ	ⓒ	ⓓ					
13	ⓐ	ⓑ	ⓒ	ⓓ	26	ⓐ	ⓑ	ⓒ	ⓓ	39	ⓐ	ⓑ	ⓒ	ⓓ					

■ Performance Scanner

> 90% Excellent !	You have mastered the NEET syllabus (12th). The concepts of this entire syllabus are at your fingertips. Maintain this momentum.
76-90% Very Good !	You have a good command over the entire NEET syllabus (12th). Revise it again after a few days to enhance your performance.
60-75% Good !	You have a wide scope to learn for the entire NEET syllabus (12th). Revise it again.
<60% Not Satisfactory!	You have a long way ahead of you to master the NEET syllabus (12th). Revise it thoroughly.

MED+ACE

NEET (UG)

SELF ASSESSMENT KIT

Exactly as per the Latest Pattern of NTA

Released on 25 Jan 2025

CHEMISTRY - XIIth

Hints, Solutions & Mind Maps Booklet

MED ACE

NEET (UG)

SELF ASSESSMENT KIT

Exactly as per the Latest Pattern of NTA

Released on 25 Jan 2025

CHEMISTRY - XIIth

Hints, Solutions & Mind Maps Booklet

Authors

Shalini Singh, Vaishnavi Chaudhary

ARIHANT PRAKASHAN (SERIES), MEERUT

卐 **Administrative & Production Offices**

Regd. Office

'Ramchhaya' 4577/15, Agarwal Road, Darya Ganj, New Delhi -110002
Tele: 011- 47630600, 43518550

卐 **Head Office**

Kalindi, TP Nagar, Meerut (UP) - 250002
Tel: 0121-7156203, 7156204

卐 **Sales & Support Offices**

Agra, Ahmedabad, Bengaluru, Bareilly, Chennai, Delhi, Guwahati, Hyderabad, Jaipur, Jhansi, Kolkata, Lucknow, Nagpur & Pune.

卐 **PRICE** ₹1100.00

卐 **PO No :** TXT-59-T063624-03-25

Published by Arihant Publications (India) Ltd.

For further information about the books published by Arihant, log on to www.arihantbooks.com or e-mail at info@arihantbooks.com

CHEMISTRY XIIth

CONTENT LIST

MED+ACE

NEET (UG)

SELF ASSESSMENT KIT

HINTS & SOLUTIONS

Hints & Explanations

Ch-1 Solutions

Topical Follow Thru

Test-1

1. (a) Mass of solute in solution I

$= \frac{25}{100} \times 300\,g = 75\,g$

Mass of solute in solution II

$= \frac{40}{100} \times 400 = 160\,g$

After mixing both solution

Total mass of solute

$= (75 + 160)\,g = 235\,g$

Total mass of solution

$= (300 + 400)\,g = 700\,g$

Mass % of solute in final solution

$= \frac{235\,g}{700\,g} \times 100 = 33.57\%$

So, mass % of solvent in final solution

$= 100 - 33.57 = 66.43\%$

2. (a) Molarity is inversely proportional to volume of solution and volume is temperature dependent. So, by changing the temperature, molarity also changes.

Hence, both (A) and (R) are true and (R) is the correct explanation of (A).

3. (b) Mass of $C_2H_6O_2 = 40\,g$

Molecular mass of $C_2H_6O_2 = 2 \times 12 + 6 + 16 \times 2$

$= 62\,g/mol$

Mass of water $= 100 - 40 = 60\,g$

Mole fraction of $C_2H_6O_2$

$= \frac{\frac{40}{62}}{\frac{40}{62} + \frac{60}{18}} = \frac{0.645}{0.645 + 3.33}$

$= \frac{0.645}{3.975} = 0.162$

4. (c) On increasing temperature, weight does not change, hence, molality, weight fraction of solute and mole fraction will not change. On the other hand, temperature affects the volume of solution. It means, the expression for concentration that contain volume will change with temperature. Hence, fraction of solute present in 1 L water changes.

5. (a) Molality is the number of moles of solute dissolved in 1000 gram of solvent. So, 1 molal solution contains one mole of solute in 1000 gram of solvent.

6. (b) Statement I is correct but Statement II is incorrect. The correct form of Statement II is in a solution, the component present in largest quantity is called solvent.

7. (b) Statement given in D and E are correct while A, B and C are incorrect. Their correct form are

- Molarity is equal to number of moles of solute dissolved in 1L of solution.
- For sodium carbonate normality is equal to twice of its molarity as valency factor of Na_2CO_3 is 2. So, molarity and normality are not equal.
- Molality is equal to number of moles of solute dissolved in 1 kg of solvent.

8. (a) We know that

$$\text{Molality} = \frac{n_{\text{solute}}}{W_{\text{solvent (in gram)}}} \times 1000$$

Given, $X_{\text{methanol}} = 0.02$

$$\frac{n_{\text{methanol}}}{n_{\text{methanol}} + n_{H_2O}} = 0.02$$

$$\frac{n_{\text{methanol}}}{n_{\text{methanol}} + 55.5} = 0.02$$

$n_{\text{methanol}} - 0.02 n_{\text{methanol}} = 55.5 \times 0.02$

$0.98 n_{\text{methanol}} = 1.11$

$n_{\text{methanol}} = 1.13\,\text{mol}$

So, molality $= 1.13\,m$

9. (c) Given that,

$n_A = n_B = n_C = 0.2\,\text{mol}$

So, mole fraction of

$$A = \frac{n_A}{n_A + n_B + n_C}$$

$$= \frac{0.2}{0.2 + 0.2 + 0.2} = \frac{0.2}{0.6} = \frac{1}{3}$$

Mole fraction of $A = B = C = \frac{1}{3}$

Hence, the sum of mole fraction of A, B and C in an aqueous solution

$= \frac{1}{3} + \frac{1}{3} + \frac{1}{3} = 1$

10. (b) Mass of CH_3COOH dissolved $= 5\,g$

Mole of CH_3COOH dissolved $= \frac{5}{60}$

Volume of ethanol $= 1$ litre $= 1000\,mL$

Mass of ethanol

$= 1000 \times 0.789 = 789\,g$

Molality of solution will be given by

$$m = \frac{\text{Moles of solute}}{\text{Mass of solvent (in kg)}}$$

$$= \frac{\frac{5}{60 \times 789}}{1000} = 0.1056\,\text{molal}$$

11. (d) Both Statement I and Statement II are correct.

12. (c) 40% $FeCl_3$ solution means 100 g of solution contains 40 g $FeCl_3$.

Volume of 100 g solution

$= \frac{100\,g}{1.1\,g/mL} = 90.91\,mL$

Moles of 40 g $FeCl_3 = \frac{40}{162}$

$= 0.247$ moles

Molar concentration of solution

$= \frac{0.247}{90.91} \times 1000 = 2.72$ M

13. (d) Concentration in ppm

$= \frac{2.04}{10^6} \times 10^6$ ppm $= 2.04$ ppm

14. (a) Molality, $m = \frac{w_B}{m_B} \times \frac{1000}{w_A}$

$b = \frac{c}{m_B} \times \frac{1000}{(a-c)}$;

$m_B = \frac{c}{b} \times \frac{1000}{(a-c)}$

15. (b) Weight of nitrogen = 70 g
Weight of oxygen = 140 g and
Weight of carbon dioxide = 44 g.
Moles of N_2 (n_1)

$= \frac{\text{Mass}}{\text{Molecular mass}}$

$= \frac{70}{28} = 2.5$ moles

Similarly, moles of O_2 (n_2) $= \frac{140}{32}$

$= 4.375$ moles

and moles of CO_2 (n_3) $= \frac{44}{44}$

$= 1$ mole

Therefore, mole fraction of nitrogen (N_2)

$= \frac{n_1}{n_1 + n_2 + n_3} = \frac{2.5}{2.5 + 4.375 + 1}$

$= \frac{2.5}{7.875} = 0.317$

Test-2

1. (c) p_0 (vapour pressure of water)

$= 23.8$ mm Hg

p_s(vapour pressure of solution) = ?

$\frac{p_0 - p_s}{p_0} = 0.1$ (mole fraction)

$\frac{23.8 - p_s}{23.8} = 0.1$

$23.8 - p_s = 2.38$

or $p_s = 21.42$ mm of Hg

2. (c) In dilute solutions of non-electrolytes, the solvent and solute molecules are similar in size and molecular attraction.

So, this means the solutions act more, like ideal solutions and follow Raoult's law.

Thus, the determination of correct molecular mass from Raoult's law is applicable to a non-electrolyte in a dilute solution.

3. (b) Chloroform and acetone form a non-ideal solution in which A—B type interactions are more than A—A and B—B type interactions due to H-bonding.

Hence, the solution shows negative deviation from Raoult's law, i.e.

$\Delta V_{mix} = -$ve

$\Delta H = -$ve

Total volume of solution is less than (30 + 50 mL) or < 80 mL.

4. (b) Those solutions show positive deviation in which the partial pressure of each component of solution is greater than the vapour pressure as expected according to Raoult's law.

In solution of methanol and benzene, methanol molecules are held together due to hydrogen bonding.

On adding benzene, the benzene molecules get in between the molecule of methanol thus breaking the hydrogen bonds. As the resulting solution has weak intermolecular attraction, the escaping tendency of methanol and benzene molecules from the solution increases. Consequently, the vapour pressure of the solution is greater than the vapour pressure as expected from Raoult's law.

5. (a) For an ideal solution,

- Raoult's law is obeyed for entire concentration range and temperature.
- The enthalpy change of mixing is zero, $\Delta H_{mix} = 0$
- The volume of mixing is zero, $\Delta V_{mix} = 0$
- But the entropy of mixing is not equal to zero, $\Delta S_{mix} \neq 0$.

6. (b) Due to hydrogen bonding, escaping tendency of both components A and B is lowered showing lower vapour pressure than expected ideally.

Hence, such solution will show negative deviation from Raoult's law.

7. (b) Statement I is correct but Statement II is incorrect because solubility of gas in a liquid is directly proportional to the pressure of gas above the liquid's surface.

8. (c) When a solution shows positive deviation from Raoult's law, the intermolecular forces present are weaker than those present in the ideal solution.

The total vapour pressure of the solution is greater than the total vapour pressure of the ideal solution.

Also, the vapour pressure of each component is greater than that predicted from Raoult's law.

Hence, the azeotropic mixture of two liquids boils at a lower temperature than either of them.

9. (a) Raoult's law is not applicable, if total number of particles of solute changes in the solution due to association or dissociation.

Urea, glucose and sucrose are the non-electrolytes. They cannot dissociate into ions but NaCl dissociates into Na^+ and Cl^- ions.

Hence, option (a) is correct.

10. (c) Ideal solutions obey Raoult's law where the intermolecular interactions between the different components (A—B interactions) are of the same magnitude as the intermolecular interactions found in the pure components (A—A and B—B interactions).

11. (c) The lower the value of K_H at a given pressure, the higher is the solubility of the gas in the liquid. Thus, the correct decreasing order is

formaldehyde > vinyl chloride (1.8×10^{-5} K bar) (0.611 K bar) > carbon dioxide (1.67 K bar)

12. (b) Dalton's law of partial pressure is applicable to non-reacting gases, NH_3 and HCl are reacting gases, So, Dalton's law will not be applicable to them.

13. (b) Since, the ratio of p_A° and p_B° is 1 : 4 and mole fraction is 1 : 4. Therefore, partial pressure of $A(p'_A) = p_A^\circ x_A$ and partial pressure of $B(p'_B) = p_B^\circ x_B$ are related as $p'_B = 16p'_A$

$$p = p'_A + p'_B = p'_A + 16p'_A = 17p'_A$$

The mole fraction of A in the vapour in equilibrium with solution (according to Dalton's law of partial pressure) is

$$x'_A = \frac{p'_A}{p} = \frac{p'_A}{17p'_A} = \frac{1}{17} = 0.06$$

14. (a) Azeotropic mixtures with higher boiling point shows negative deviation. These occurs H-bonding between chloroform and diethyl ether in the solution, hence the escaping tendency of either component becomes less.

```
        Cl
        |           C2H5
  Cl— C —H-----O<
        |           C2H5
        Cl
```

15. (d) For equimolar solution, let us take $x_A = x_B = 0.5$

$p_{\text{benzene}} = 180 \times 0.5 = 90$ torr,

$p_{\text{toluene}} = 100 \times 0.5 = 50$ torr

$p_{\text{total}} = 90 + 50 = 140$ torr

Mole fraction of toluene in vapour phase

$$= \frac{\text{Partial vapour pressure of toluene}}{\text{Total vapour pressure}}$$

$$= \frac{50}{140} = 0.36$$

Test-3

1. (c) $\Delta T_f = K_f \times m \times i$

$i = 2$ (for $NaCl \rightarrow Na^+ + Cl^-$)

where, i is van't Hoff factor

$m = 0.1$ molal

$K_f = 1.86°$ C/molal

$\Delta T_f = 2 \times 1.86 \times 0.1$

$= 0.372°$ C

Therefore, freezing point of solution

$T_f = T_f^\circ - \Delta T_f$

$= 0 - 0.372°$ C

$= -0.372°$ C

2. (b) $\Delta T_b = imK_b$

$= 0.52 \times 1 \times 2 = 1.04°$C

$\Delta T_b = T_b - T_b^\circ$

$\therefore \quad T_b = 100 + 1.04$

$= 101.04°$ C

3. (a) Urea and glucose are non-electrolytes hence, $i = 1$. Water boils at 1 atm pressure, it means boiling point of water is 100°C.

ΔT_b (glucose solution)

$= 100.52 - 100.00 = 0.52°$ C

ΔT_b (glucose solution) $= mK_b i$

$0.52 = 1 \times K_b \times 1$

$\therefore \quad K_b = 0.52°$ C kg mol^{-1}

(Urea solution is 20% by weight of solution, it means 100 g solution (solute + solvent) has 20 g solute and 80 g solvent).

$$\Delta T_b \text{ (urea solution)} = \frac{1000\, K_b w_2 i}{m_2 w_1}$$

$$= \frac{1000 \times 0.52 \times 20 \times 1}{60 \times 80} = 2.17°$$

C

$\therefore$ Boiling point of urea solution $= 100.00 + 2.17° = 102.17°$ C

4. (a) As we know, osmotic pressure is given by

$\pi V = nRT$;

On substituting the given values

$\therefore \quad \pi \times 1 = 0.1 \times 0.082 \times 273$

Hence, $\pi = \frac{0.1}{1} \times 0.082 \times 273$ atm

5. (d) $K_3[Fe(CN)_6]$ on ionisation gives 4 species {$3K^+$ and $1[Fe(CN)_6]^{3-}$} and $Al(NO_3)_3$ also gives 4 species ($1\,Al^{3+}$ and $3NO_3^-$) thus, both will have the same value of van't Hoff factor.

6. (a)

Solute	n	α	$i = [1 + (n-1)\alpha]$
$FeCl_3$	4	0.3	1.9
K_2SO_4	3	0.4	1.8
$SnCl_4$	5	0.2	1.8
KCl	2	0.5	1.5

Thus, 30% ionised $FeCl_3$ will have maximum van't Hoff factor.

7. (b) Dissolution of a non-volatile solute raises the boiling point of a liquid. It is due to decrease in free surface area of vaporisation.

8. (d) If we start with one mole of the compound.

$$A_xB_y \rightleftharpoons xA^{y+} + yB^{x-}$$

After dissociation $1 - \alpha \qquad x\alpha \qquad y\alpha$

$i = n(A_xB_y) + n(A^{y+}) + n(B^{x-})$

$= 1 - \alpha + x\alpha + y\alpha$

$= 1 + \alpha\,(x + y - 1)$

$$\therefore \alpha = \frac{i - 1}{x + y - 1}$$

9. (b) $BaCl_2$ furnishes more ions than KCl and thus shows higher boiling point $T_1 > T_2$.

10. (a) $w_B = 1.25$ g

$w_A = 20$ g

$T_f = 271.9$ K

$\Delta T_f = T_f^\circ - T_f$

$= 273 - 271.9 = 1.1$ K

$K_f = 1.86$ K kg mol^{-1}

$$\therefore \Delta T_f = K_f \cdot \frac{w_B}{M_B} \times \frac{1000}{w_A}$$

$$1.1 = 1.86 \times \frac{1.25}{M_B} \times \frac{1000}{20}$$

$M_B = 105.68 \approx 105.7$ g/mol

11. (a) Both (A) and (R) are true and (R) is the correct explanation of (A).

12. (c) Solution with negative deviation has

$$p_T < p_A x_A + p_B x_B$$

Also, $p_A < p_A x_A$ and $p_B < p_B x_B$

When the vapour pressure decreases the boiling point increases.

13. (c) Vapour pressure is not a colligative property.

14. (d) The only correct statement is (d). The other given statements are incorrect. Their correct form are as follows

(a) Lowering of vapour pressure takes place in both ideal and non-ideal solutions.

(b) Lowering of vapour pressure is the difference between the vapour pressure of pure solvent and vapour pressure of the solvent in the presence of solute.

(c) Solvents with higher boiling points have lower vapour pressure.

15. (c) For urea (NH_2CONH_2) the van't Hoff factor can not be greater than unity because urea is non-ionisable.

16. (c) Mass of glucose = 20 g

No. of moles of glucose = 20/180

Mass of urea = 10 g,

No. of moles of urea = 10/60

Mass of KCl = 1 g,

Moles of KCl $= \frac{1}{74.5}$

Number of ions furnished by one molecule of KCl is 2.

Thus, actual number of particles

$$= \frac{2}{74.5}$$

∴ Total number of particles

$$= \frac{20}{180} + \frac{10}{60} + \frac{2}{74.5}$$

$$= 0.111 + 0.167 + 0.027$$

$$= 0.305$$

Mass of water

$$= 100 - 20 - 10 - 1 = 69 \text{ g}$$

$$\text{Molality} = \frac{0.305}{69} \times 1000 = 4.42$$

$$\Delta T_f = 4.42 \times 1.86 = 8.22$$

$$T_f = T_f^\circ - \Delta T_f$$

$$= 0 - 8.22$$

$$= -8.22^\circ \text{C}$$

17. (d) $\Delta T_f \propto i$ (van't Hoff factor)

i for $C_2H_5OH = 1$,

i for $Ba_3(PO_4)_2 = 5$,

i for $Na_2SO_4 = 3$

i for $Li_3PO_4 = 4$,

i for KCl = 2

Thus, depression in freezing point will be in order

$$C_2H_5OH < KCl < Na_2SO_4 < Li_3PO_4 < Ba_3(PO_4)_2$$

Higher the depression in freezing point, lower will its freezing point.

Hence, freezing point will be in order

$$Ba_3(PO_4)_2 < Li_3PO_4 < Na_2SO_4 < KCl < C_2H_5OH$$

18. (a) $\Delta T_f \propto i$ (van't Hoff factor)

$C_5H_{10}O_5$ and $C_{12}H_{22}O_{11}$ are non-ionisable, thus $i = 1$ for them; for KI, $i = 2$ and for $Al_2(SO_4)_3$, $i = 5$.

Thus, i is maximum for $Al_2(SO_4)_3$, hence depression in freezing point is highest for $Al_2(SO_4)_3$ and also it will have lowest freezing point.

19. (c) All solutes are non-electrolytes.

∴ Osmotic pressure, $p = \frac{wRT}{M \times V}$

$$\therefore \quad p \propto \frac{w}{M}$$

$$M_{\text{glucose}} = 180 \text{ g/mol}$$

$$M_{\text{urea}} = 60 \text{ g/mol},$$

$$M_{\text{sucrose}} = 342 \text{ g/mol}$$

$$p_1 = \frac{50}{180}, \; p_2 = \frac{50}{60}, \; p_3 = \frac{50}{342}$$

∴ The decreasing order of osmotic pressure is,

urea > glucose > sucrose

or $p_2 > p_1 > p_3$.

20. (b) $i = \frac{\text{Normal molecular mass}}{\text{Observed molecular mass}}$

$$= \frac{170}{92.64} = 1.835$$

$$\alpha = \frac{i-1}{n-1}$$

For $AgNO_3$, $n = 2$

$$\therefore \quad \alpha = \frac{1.835 - 1}{2 - 1} = 0.835 = 83.5\%$$

21. (a) Given, osmotic pressure of 0.1 M aqueous solution of $MgCl_2 = 4.92$ atm.

Temperature = 300 K

We know that,

$$\pi = iCRT$$

$$4.92 = i \times 0.1 \times 0.0821 \times 300$$

$$i \simeq 2$$

$$MgCl_2 \rightleftharpoons Mg^{2+} + 2Cl^-$$

$$\therefore \quad n = 3$$

$$\alpha = \frac{i-1}{n-1} = \frac{2-1}{3-1} = \frac{1}{2} = 0.5$$

Percentage of ionisation = 50%

22. (a) Given, $\pi = 16.4$ atm

$R = 0.082 \text{ L atm mol}^{-1} \text{ K}^{-1}$

10% (w/V) means 10 g of glucose is present in 100 mL of solution.

∴ $V = 100 \text{ mL} = 0.1 \text{ L}$

$$\pi = \frac{nRT}{V}$$

$$16.4 = \frac{\frac{10}{180} \times 0.082 \times T}{0.1}$$

$$T = \frac{16.4 \times 0.1}{0.055 \times 0.082}$$

$$= \frac{1.64}{0.0045}$$

$$= 364.4 \text{ K}$$

23. (d) Both Statement I and Statement II are correct.

24. (a) Statement (a) is correct while the other given statements in correct form are as follows

(b) Passage or spontaneous flow of solvent molecules from the solvent to the solution through a semipermeable membrane is called osmosis.

(c) The boiling point of a solution with a non-volatile solute has higher boiling point than pure solvent.

(d) The boiling point of a liquid is the temperature at which its vapour pressure is equal to 1 atm (760 torr/760 mm Hg).

25. (c) Given, $K_f = 1.86° \text{ C kg mol}^{-1}$,
$M_2 = 342 \text{ g}$, $w_1 = 1000 \text{ g}$
Using the formula

$$\Delta T_f = \frac{1000 K_f w_2}{M_2 w_1}$$
$$= \frac{1000 \times 1.86 \times 342}{342 \times 1000}$$
$$= 1.86° \text{ C}$$
$$\therefore T_f = T_f^{\circ} - \Delta T_f$$
$$= 0 - 1.86 = -1.86° \text{ C}$$

Chapter Break Thru

1. (a) The solution that gives more number of ions will show highest boiling point. Hence, the boiling point of 0.1 M $FeCl_3$ is highest.

2. (a) The correct match is
A-II, B-III, C-IV, D-I.
A. For a solution to be ideal, $\Delta S_{mix} > 0$
B. Henry's constant is represented by K_H.
C. Ebullioscopic constant is represented by K_b.
D. Cryoscopic constant is represented by K_f.
Thus, option (a) is correct.

3. (b) $X \rightarrow X_4$ (Tetramerisation)
So, $\alpha = 100\%$ and $n = 4$

$$\alpha = \frac{100}{100} = 1$$

Using, $\alpha = \dfrac{1-i}{1-\dfrac{1}{n}}$

$$1 = \frac{1-i}{1-\dfrac{1}{4}} \Rightarrow i = 0.25$$

4. (c) Incorrect statement is given in option (c). Its correct form is solubility of gases in liquids increases with decrease of temperature.

5. (b) We know that,

$$\frac{p_0 - p_s}{p^{\circ}} = \frac{n}{n+N}$$

Lowering of vapour pressure, i.e. $\left[\dfrac{p_0 - p_s}{p^{\circ}}\right]$ increases. So, number of moles of solute also increases

Also, $\Delta T_f = T_f^{\circ} - T_f$

$$= K_f \times 1000 \times \frac{n}{w}$$

where,
n = number of moles of solute
T_f° = temperature of solvent
T_f = temperature of solution

So, temperature of solution decrease due to increase in number of moles of solute.

Hence, the freezing point of the solution becomes less.

The unit of molal depression constant is K kg mol^{-1} or K m^{-1}.

6. (c) Mole fraction of

$$H_2SO_4 = \frac{n_2}{n_1 + n_2} = 0.14 \quad \ldots\text{(i)}$$

Mole fraction of water

$$= \frac{n_1}{n_1 + n_2} = 0.86 \quad \ldots\text{(ii)}$$

Dividing Eqs. (i) by (ii)

$$\frac{n_2}{n_1} = \frac{0.14}{0.86} \quad \ldots\text{(iii)}$$

Molality is the number of moles of the solute (H_2SO_4) present in 1000 g of H_2O, i.e. $\dfrac{1000}{18}$ moles or 55.55 moles.

Putting $n_1 = 55.55$ in Eq. (iii) we get

$$n_2 = 55.55 \times \frac{0.14}{0.86} = 9.0$$

Hence, molality = 9.0 m

7. (b) Statement given in I, II and V are correct while III and IV are incorrect.
As we know that, $\pi = CRT$
Osmotic pressure

$$= \frac{\text{mass} \times \text{gas constant} \times \text{temperature}}{\text{molar mass} \times \text{volume}}$$

Thus, from the above formula, it is clear that osmotic pressure is directly proportional to temperature and inversely proportional to volume.

8. (a) In osmosis, the solvent molecules flow from pure solvent to the solution. Thus, if the level of solution *A* rises, it means that concentration of *A* is more than *B*.

9. (d) (A) is false but (R) is true. The correct form of (A) is : ΔH_{mix} and ΔV_{mix} both increases for non-ideal solution with positive deviation.

10. (a) At the freezing point liquid and solid remain in equilibrium. If a solution of a non-volatile solute is cooled to a temperature below the freezing point of solution, some of liquid solvent will separate as a solid solvent and thus the concentration of solution will increase.

11. (a) Molecular weight of naphthoic acid $C_{11}H_8O_2 = 172 \text{ g/mol}$
The theoretical value of depressing in freezing point.

$$= K_f \times \text{molality}$$
$$= \frac{1.72 \times 20 \times 1000}{172 \times 50} = 4 \text{ K}$$

van't Hoff factor

$$i = \frac{\text{Observed value of colligative property}}{\text{Theoretical value of colligative property}}$$

$$i = \frac{2}{4} = 0.5$$

12. (b) 1 M $BaCl_2$ ionises to give three (3) ions as a result of which effective molality in solution increases by 3 times. Hence, its freezing point is lowest.

13. (c) Total mass of the solution
$= 1000 + 120 = 1120\,g$

Total volume of the solution
$= \dfrac{\text{mass}}{\text{density}} = \dfrac{1120}{1.15}\,mL$
$= \dfrac{1120}{1.15} \times 10^{-3}\,L = \dfrac{1.12}{1.15}\,L$

Number of moles in urea
$= \dfrac{\text{mass}}{\text{molar mass}} = \dfrac{120}{60} = 2\,mol$

Molarity
$= \dfrac{\text{No. of moles of solute}}{\text{Volume of solution in (L)}}$
$= \dfrac{2\,mol}{\left(\dfrac{1.12}{1.15}\right)L} = \dfrac{2 \times 1.15}{1.12}\,mol\,L^{-1}$
$= 2.05\,M$

14. (b) 5.2 molal solution means 5.2 moles of the solute (CH_3OH) are present in 1000 g of water, i.e. $\dfrac{1000}{18}$ moles = 55.55 moles of water

$\therefore$ Mole fraction of CH_3OH
$= \dfrac{5.2}{5.2 + 55.55} = 0.086$

15. (a) If vapour pressure of a solution is higher than that predicted by Raoult's law, then it exhibits positive deviations. Thus, among the given pairs of solution, acetone and ethanol shows positive deviation. While *n*-hexane and *n*-heptane shows ideal behaviour. Phenol and aniline, HNO_3 and H_2O, CCl_4 and acetone shows negative deviation.

16. (c) Using the law of dilution
$M_1V_1 + M_2V_2 = M_3(V_1 + V_2)$
Substitute the given values in above formula
$0.5 \times 750 + 2 \times 250$
$= M_3(750 + 250)$
or $375 + 500 = 1000M_3$
or $M_3 = \dfrac{875}{1000} = 0.875\,M$

17. (b) We know that, higher the value of Henry's law constant, the lower is the solubility of the gas in the liquid.

From the given plot, the solubility of oxygen is higher than nitrogen and helium, while solubility of nitrogen is higher than helium. Thus, the order of Henry's law constant is as follows

$O_2 < N_2 < He$

Gas	Temperature (in K)	K_H (kbar)
He	293	144.97
N_2	293	76.48
O_2	293	34.86

18. (c) We know that, $\pi = CRT$ where symbols have their usual meaning.
So, if concentration and R is constant then osmotic pressure varies directly with temperature.

19. (d) 29% H_2SO_4 by mass means 29 g H_2SO_4 are present in 100 g of the solution. If d g mL^{-1} is the density of the solution then

volume will be given by $= \dfrac{100\,g}{\text{density}}$

Further, 29 g $H_2SO_4 = \dfrac{29}{98}$ mole

Hence, molarity of the solution
$\dfrac{\dfrac{29}{98}}{\dfrac{100}{d}} \times 1000\,mol\,L^{-1}$
$= 3.60\,mol\,L^{-1}$ (Given)

i.e. $\dfrac{29}{98} \times \dfrac{1}{100} \times 1000\,d = 3.60$

or $d = \dfrac{3.60}{10} \times \dfrac{98}{29} = 1.22\,g\,mL^{-1}$

20. (a) 300 g of 25% solution contain
$NH_4NO_3 = \dfrac{25}{100} \times 300\,g = 75\,g$

150 g of 40% solution contain
$NH_4NO_3 = \dfrac{40}{100} \times 150\,g = 60\,g$

Total solution
$= 300 + 150\,g = 450\,g$

Total solute $= 75 + 60 = 135\,g$

Concentration (mass percent)
$= \dfrac{135}{450} \times 100 = 30\%$

21. (a) By Henry's law,
$p_A = K_H \times \chi_A$
or $\chi_A = \dfrac{p_A}{K_H} = \dfrac{200\,torr}{5.55 \times 10^7\,torr}$
$= 3.6 \times 10^{-6}$

But $\chi_A = \dfrac{n_A}{n_A + n_{H_2O}}$
$\approx \dfrac{n_A}{n_{H_2O}} = \dfrac{n_A}{\dfrac{1000}{18}}$

$\therefore \quad n_A = \chi_A \times \dfrac{1000}{18}$
$= 3.6 \times 10^{-6} \times \dfrac{1000}{18}\,mol$
$= 2.0 \times 10^{-4}\,mol$

22. (c) Vapour pressure of any component in the solution = mole fraction of the component × vapour pressure of that component in the pure state and mole fraction is always less than 1. Thus, the vapour pressure of the given solution is less than the vapour pressure of pure water.

23. (b) Both Statement I is correct but Statement II is incorrect. The corrected form of Statement II is : The molarity of a solution depends upon the density of the solution various molality does not.

24. (a) 12 g urea $= \dfrac{12}{60}\,mol$
$= 0.2\,mol$

68.4 g sucrose $= \dfrac{68.4}{342.2} \simeq 0.2\,mol$

As mole fraction of solute is same in both the solutions. Hence, the lowering of vapour pressure will also be same.

25. (c) The addition of non-volatile solute to the solvent lower the vapour pressure of the solvent. Thus, vapour pressure of pure benzene decreases on addition of naphthalene.

26. (d) Difference between the boiling point of the solution and the boiling point of pure solvent is called elevation in the boiling point.

$$\Delta T_b = K_b \times m$$

Thus, the quantity 'L' is elevation in boiling point.

27. (c) Statement I is incorrect but Statement II is correct. The correct form of Statement I is 0.1 M glucose solution and 0.1 M urea solution have the same depression in freezing point.

28. (c) When the new interaction is weaker than those in the pure constituents, the boiling point of the resultant solution is less than that of constituent. So, among the given options CH_3COCH_3 to CH_3CH_2OH will show lesser boiling point then its constituent.

29. (a) On addition of water, concentration of the solution decrease, i.e. now less solute particles are present on the surface or more solvent molecules are present on the surface. Hence, vapour pressure increases.

30. (b) Using the formula

$$\chi_A = \frac{n_A}{n_A + n_B}$$

and $\chi_B = \dfrac{n_B}{n_A + n_B}$

$$\chi_A = \frac{3}{5} = 0.6, \chi_B = 0.4$$

Substitute the obtained values in the formula given below.

$$p_{\text{total}} = x_A p_A^\circ + x_B p_B^\circ$$

$$184 = 0.6 \times 200 + 0.4 \times p_B^\circ$$

or $0.4 p_B^\circ = 184 - 120$

or $p_B^\circ = \dfrac{64}{0.4} = 160$ torr

31. (a) Isotonic solution have the same molar concentration. Hence, Molar concentration of the substance = Molar concentration of urea.

$$\frac{5.25\,\text{gL}^{-1}}{M} = \frac{1.5\,\text{gL}^{-1}}{60\,\text{g mol}^{-1}}$$

$$\therefore\ M = \frac{5.25 \times 60}{1.5} = 210\,\text{g mol}^{-1}$$

32. (b) CO_2 obeys Henry's law, which governs the solubility of gases in liquids in relation to its pressure. Henry's law states that mole fraction of gas in the solution varies directly with its partial pressure over the surface, i.e. $p \propto x$ (mole fraction). The graph is of the form $y = mx$, a positively straight line passing through the origin.

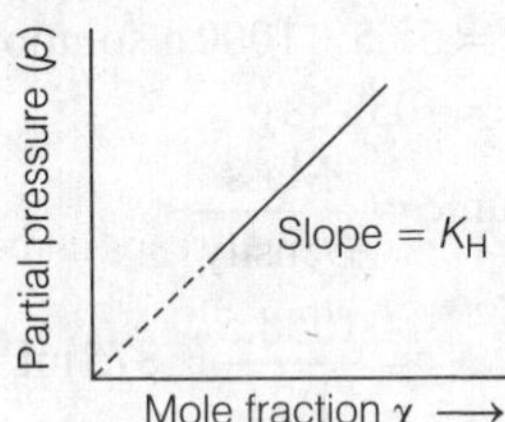

33. (d) Use the formula

$$\Delta T_f = K_f \times m$$

(where, symbols have their usual meaning) to calculate the value of molality. Then use this value of molality in the formula $\Delta T_b = K_b m$ to calculate the value of ΔT_b.

$$0.186 = 1.86 \times m$$

$$m = 0.1\,\text{m}$$

$$\Delta T_b = 0.512 \times 0.1 = 0.0512\,\text{K}$$

Thus, the value of elevation in boiling point is 0.0512 K.

34. (a) For monobasic acid, $n = 2$

$$i = 1 + (n-1)\alpha$$

$$= 1 + (2-1)0.3 = 1.3$$

% increase

$$= \frac{(\Delta T_f)_{\text{obs}} - (\Delta T_f)_{\text{cal}}}{(\Delta T_f)_{\text{cal}}} \times 100$$

$$= \frac{iK_f.m - K_f.m}{K_f.m} \times 100$$

$$= (i-1) \times 100 = 30\%$$

35. (a) $CaCl_2$ lowers the freezing point of water. Hence, formation of snow is reduced.

36. (c) For an ideal solution $\Delta H_{\text{mix}} = 0$ and ΔS_{mix} is always positive. So, ΔG_{mix} is negative. Thus, option (c) is correct.

37. (c) The elevation in boiling point depends upon the van't Hoff factor (i) and molality. So,

$i.m$(glucose)

$$= 1 \times \frac{10}{180} \times \frac{1}{90} \times 1000 = 0.617$$

$i.m$(sucrose)

$$= 1 \times \frac{10}{342} \times \frac{1}{90} \times 1000 = 0.325$$

$i.m$(NaCl)

$$= 2 \times \frac{10}{58.5} \times \frac{1}{90} \times 1000 = 3.799$$

$i.m$($CaCl_2$)

$$= 3 \times \frac{10}{111} \times \frac{1}{90} \times 1000 = 3.003$$

Thus, the concentration of particles is highest in NaCl.

38. (b) $HBr \rightleftharpoons H^+ + Br^-$

$1-\alpha \quad \alpha \quad \alpha$

Total $= 1 + \alpha$

$\therefore\ i = 1 + \alpha = 1 + 0.9 = 1.9$

Now using

$$\Delta T_f = iK_f m$$

$$= 1.9 \times 1.86 \times \frac{8.1}{81} \times \frac{1000}{100}$$

$$\Delta T_f = 3.53^\circ\,\text{C}$$

$$T_f = 0 - 3.53^\circ\,\text{C} = -3.53^\circ\,\text{C}$$

39. (d) We know that osmotic pressure is given by $\pi = iCRT$

$$\pi = iC_1RT,\ \pi_2 = iC_2RT$$

$$\frac{\pi}{\pi_2} = \frac{C_1}{2 \times 0.1} \Rightarrow \frac{\pi}{\pi_2} = \frac{1}{2 \times 0.1}$$

or $\pi_2 = 0.2\pi$

40. (b) Molality, m is directly proportional to p (pressure),

i.e. $m \propto p$

$m = kp$ [k = constant]

$\log m = \log p + \log k$

Comparing with $y = mx + c$, graph equation, we get

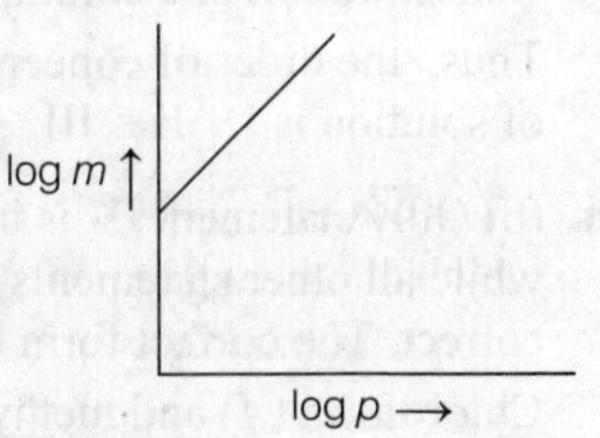

Thus, option (b) is correct.

41. (d) $2C_6H_5OH \rightleftharpoons (C_6H_5OH)_2$

Before asso. 1 mole $\quad 0$

After asso. $1-\alpha \quad \frac{\alpha}{2}$

$$\text{Total} = 1-\alpha+\frac{\alpha}{2} = 1-\frac{\alpha}{2}$$

$$i = 1-\frac{\alpha}{2} \quad \text{or} \quad \frac{\alpha}{2} = 1-i$$

or $\alpha = 2(1-i)$
$= 2(1-0.54)$
$= 0.92$

42. (a) More is the dilution, more will be the dissociation into ions and hence greater is the van't Hoff factor.

43. (c) Only statement IV is incorrect while others are correct.

The value of Henry's law constant (K_H) depends on the gas-solvent system. It is different for different gas solvent systems.

For a given partial pressure of the gas, as the value of K_H increases, the value of the mole fraction decreases and the solubility also decreases.

Hence, higher is the value of K_H, lower is the solubility of gas for a given partial pressure of the gas.

The value of K_H depends upon temperature and with an increase in the temperature, the value of K_H increases.

44. (a) Elevation of boiling point is given by

$\Delta T_b = T_b - T_b^\circ$ or $\Delta T_b = K_b m$

where,

m = molal concentration of the solute in a solution

K_b = molal elevation constant.

$\therefore$ Elevation in boiling point $\propto$ Concentration of a solution.

Thus, the order of concentration of solution is I < II < III.

45. (b) Only statement IV is incorrect, while all other statements are correct. The correct form is :

Chloroform (A) and methyl acetate (B) shows negative deviation from Raoult's law.

As in this case A—B interaction are stronger than those between A—A or B—B interactions. This decreases the escaping tendency of molecules of A or B components and consequently, the vapour pressure decreases resulting in negative deviation from Raoult's law.

46. (b) 1 M NaCl solution

= 1 mol NaCl in 1000 g water

1 mol NaCl = 58.5 g of NaCl

So, total mass of solution

= 58.5 + 1000 g solution

= 1058.58 g

$$\text{Volume} = \frac{\text{Mass}}{\text{Density}}$$

$$= \frac{1058.5}{1.21} \approx 875 \text{ mL}$$

Using formula,

Molarity

$$= \frac{\text{no. of moles of solute}}{\text{Volume of solution (in mL)}} \times 1000$$

$$\text{Molarity} = \frac{1}{875} \times 1000 = 1.143 \text{ M}$$

47. (b) Molar mass of heptane C_7H_{16}

$Mw_A = 100$ g/mol

Molar mass of octane, C_8H_{18}

$Mw_B = 114$ g/mol

Moles of heptane,

$$n_A = \frac{w_A}{Mw_A} = \frac{25}{100} = 0.25 \text{ moles}$$

Moles of octane

$$n_B = \frac{35}{114} = 0.3 \text{ moles}$$

Mole fraction of heptane,

$$x_A = \frac{0.25}{0.25+0.30} = 0.45$$

Mole fraction of octane,

$$x_B = \frac{0.3}{0.25+0.30} = 0.545$$

$$p = p_A^\circ x_A + p_B^\circ x_B$$

$= (105.0 \times 0.45) + (46.0 \times 0.545)$

$= 72.32$ kPa

Hence, option (b) is correct.

48. (d) Both Statement I and Statement II are correct.

49. (b) Osmotic pressure is a colligative property.

As the volume of solution are same,

Osmotic pressure $\propto$ No. of particles

- $NaCl \longrightarrow Na^+ + Cl^-$
  Concentration of particles
  $= 2 \times 2\text{M} = 4\text{ M}$
- Glucose does not dissociate.

$\therefore$ Concentration of particles
$= 1 \times 1\text{M}$
= 1M urea does not dissociate.

$\therefore$ Concentration of urea
$= 1 \times 2 = 2\text{M}$

$\therefore$ Glucose solution have minimum osmotic pressure.

50. (b) Given, $i_X = 2.8$, $i_Y = 1.8$, $i_Z = 3.5$

$\Rightarrow \quad i_Y < i_X < i_Z$

Observed colligative property
$= i \times$ normal colligative property

(a) $T_b = T_b^\circ + \Delta T_b$; $\Delta T_b = K_b im$

That means if value of i increases, then value of ΔT_b increases, i.e. elevation in boiling point follows the order $Y < X < Z$.

(b) $T_f = T_f^\circ - \Delta T_f$

and $\Delta T_f = iK_f m$

That means if value of i increases, value of ΔT_f increases but value of T_f decreases.

$\therefore$ Freezing point of solution follows the order $Z < X < Y$.

(c) $\pi = iRCT$

If value of i increases, then value of π also increases.

$\therefore$ Osmotic pressure follows the order $Y < X < Z$.

(d) $\frac{\Delta p}{p} = i\frac{n_B}{n_A}$

If value of i increases, then value of Δp increases.

Relative lowering in the vapour pressure follows the order $Y < X < Z$. And $\Delta p = p^\circ - p_s$ or $p_s = p^\circ - \Delta p$.

Thus, value of p_s decreases.

So, vapour pressure follows the order as $Z < X < Y$.

Hence, option (b) is correct.

Ch-2 Electrochemistry

Topical Follow Thru

Test - 1

1. (a) EMF = [s.r.p of cathode – s.r.p of anode]

where, s.r.p = Standard reduction potential

If EMF is positive then the reaction is spontaneous.

2. (c) In the electrochemical cell $Zn \mid Zn^{2+} \parallel Cu^{2+} \mid Cu$, the negative electrode (anode) is always written on left side while positive electrode (cathode) on right side. So, here Zn is negative electrode.

3. (a) The correct match is A-III, B-IV, C-I, D-II.

4. (a) In this reaction, zinc acts as an anode and Ag acts as a cathode.

Reduction

$$\overset{0}{Zn}(s) + 2Ag^{+}(aq) \longrightarrow Zn^{2+}(aq) + 2\overset{0}{Ag}(s)$$

Oxidation

5. (a) We know that,

$$\Delta G = -RT \ln K = -nFE^{\circ}_{cell}$$

We know for a spontaneous reaction.

$$\Delta G < 0$$

$\therefore \quad -RT \ln K < 0$

$\therefore \quad \ln K > 1$

and $\quad -nFE^{\circ} < 0$

$\therefore \quad E^{\circ}_{cell} > 0$

6. (d) $E^{\circ} = -3.05$ of Li^{+}/Li is most negative (minimum) and hence Li has maximum tendency to lose electrons or it is the strongest reducing agent.

7. (a) The one with the higher standard reduction potential value is easier to reduce a cell.

Hence, $E^{\circ}_{Zn^{2+}\mid Zn} < E^{\circ}_{Fe^{2+}\mid Fe}$ so, Zn will reduce Fe^{2+}. Zn cannot reduce Mg^{2+} because $E^{\circ}_{Zn^{2+}\mid Zn} > E^{\circ}_{Mg^{2+}\mid Mg}$. One to similar reason Mg and Zn cannot oxidise Fe.

8. (c) $E^{\circ}_{cell} = E^{\circ}_{cathode} - E^{\circ}_{anode}$

$$E^{\circ}_{cell} = 0.33 - (-2.37)$$

$$E^{\circ}_{cell} = 2.7\text{ V}$$

9. (c) Cell reaction is

$$Cu(s) + 2Ag^{+} \longrightarrow Cu^{2+} + 2Ag$$

Two half-cell reaction is

$$Cu \longrightarrow Cu^{2+} + 2e^{-}$$

Oxidation (anode)

$$2Ag^{+} + 2e^{-} \longrightarrow 2Ag$$

Reduction (cathode)

$$E^{\circ}_{cell} = E^{\circ}_{cathode} - E^{\circ}_{anode}$$

$$= 0.80 - 0.34 = +0.46\text{ V}$$

10. (a) Depending on the charges on cations and anions produced on dissociation of the electrolyte in solution, the type of electrolytes respectively are

$NaCl \longrightarrow Na^{+} + Cl^{-}$ (1-1)

$MgCl_2 \longrightarrow Mg^{+2} + 2Cl^{-}$ (2-1)

$CaSO_4 \longrightarrow Ca^{+2} + SO_4^{2-}$ (2-2)

In option (b), $MgCl_2$ is mentioned as weak electrolyte but it is a strong electrolyte. So, option (b) is wrong.

The strength of electrolyte (A) depends on temperature. So, it is constant at the same temperature. Thus, option (c) is wrong.

Option (d) is wrong because molar conductivity depends on the number of moles. So, the electrolytes don't have same molar conductivity.

11. (a) $2H_2O \rightleftharpoons H_3O^{+} + OH^{-}$

$$E^{\circ}_{cell} = \frac{0.0591}{n} \log K$$

$$\log K = \frac{E^{\circ}_{cell} \times n}{0.0591}$$

$$= \frac{-0.8277 \times 1}{0.0591}$$

$$= -14$$

$$K = 10^{-14}$$

12. (b) At equilibrium, $E_{cell} = 0$

K_C = equilibrium constant

$$E_{cell} = E^{\circ}_{cell} - \frac{0.0591}{n} \log K_C$$

$$E^{\circ}_{cell} = \frac{0.0591}{n} \log K_C$$

13. (b) Galvanic cell is a type of electrochemical cell which converts the chemical energy into electrical energy.

14. (a) The purpose of a salt-bridge is not to move electrons from the electrolyte, but maintain charge balance.

The electrons are moving from one half-cell to other and prevent voltage drop.

Once the salt bridge is removed from the cell, the voltage drops to zero.

15. (d) The standard electrode has

- Hydrogen ion concentration of 1 M.
- Operates at room temperature, i.e. 25°C.
- Operate at a pressure of 1 atm.
- It contains a metallic conductor (platinum electrode) which absorb hydrogen.

Hence, option (d) is not true for a standard hydrogen electrode.

Test - 2

1. (a) For a solution to conduct electricity, it requires the solution to have movable ions. A solution of sugar in water does not conduct electricity because the sugar molecules do not dissociate into ions.

Whereas the salts in the other options can dissociate to form ions and helps to conduct electricity.

2. (d) The force of electrostatic attraction are broken down by water. Electrolytes when dissolved in water dissociates completely or partially to form ions. For example,

Sodium chloride, being an ionic compound has electrostatic forces of attraction in a crystal lattice. Thus, when it is dissolved in water, the ion-dipole forces from the water molecules are countered or opposed by the electrostatic forces and thus Na^+ and Cl^- ions are formed.

3. (b) 22.4 L H_2 =1 mole H_2

$= N_A$ molecules of $H_2 = 2\,N_A$ atoms of H

So, charge required to liberate 22.4 litre of H_2

$$= 2 \times N_A \times e = 2\text{F}$$

Hence, charge required to liberate 0.224 litre of H_2

$$= \frac{2\text{F}}{22.4} \times 0.224 = \frac{2\text{F}}{100}$$

$$= 2 \times 965 \text{ C}$$

1F = 96500 C

$$i = \frac{Q}{t} = 2 \times \frac{965}{100} = 19.3 \text{ A}$$

4. (b)

(a) Conductance = Siemens

(b) Conductivity = $\Omega^{-1}\text{m}^{-1}$

(c) Molar conductivity

$= \text{S m}^2 \text{ mol}^{-1}$

(d) Ionic conductivity = S/m

5. (b) 1 Faraday (96500 C) is the electricity which liberated that amount of substance that is equal to equivalent mass. So, liberated amount of Cu is $\frac{63.5}{2}$

$$= 31.75 \text{ g} \approx 32 \text{ g}$$

6. (b) The correct match is A-I, B-II, C-III, D-IV.

7. (c) Statement I is incorrect but statement II is correct. Its correct form is molar conductivity of strong electrolyte decreases with dilution because due to dilution volume of solution increases and ultimately number of ion per unit volume decreases. Hence, conductivity decreases.

8. (a) According to Faraday law, the amount of mass deposited or liberated at an electrode due to the flow of current through an electrolyte is directly proportional to the amount of charge, i.e.

Mass of the substance formed or reacted (m) = electric charge = q.

9. (b) The conduction of electricity depends on the ions involved and here, among all the options C_2H_5OH is a weak electrolyte. It doesn't dissociate 100 % into ions. Hence, C_2H_5OH is a poor conductor of electricity.

10. (c) Specific conductance = S m^{-1}

11. (c) In fused NaCl, chloride ions are oxidised at anode and it is called oxidation.

12. (a) According to Faraday's first law of electrolysis, mass of substance (W) deposited or liberated at any electrode is directly proportional to the quantity of electricity or charge (Q) passed.

$$W = Z \times I \times t\ ; \quad \because (Q = I \times t)$$

Hence, if the duration of the passage of current (I) is doubled then,

$$W = Z \times I \times (2t)$$

$$= 2(Z \times I \times t) = 2W$$

So, the mass liberated (W) will also be doubled.

$$m \propto it$$

13. (b) Faraday's second law

This law states that the amount of different substance deposited at electrodes by passing of the same quantity of electricity are proportional to their chemical equivalent (E).

$$[m = Z \times i \times t]$$

where Z is its electrochemical equivalent, i is current, t is time and m is the mass deposited or liberated.

14. (b) From $m = ZQ$, if $Q = 1$ C

$\Rightarrow m = Z$

Electrochemical equivalent may be defined as "the mass of the ion deposited by passing a current of one ampere for one second (i.e by passing coulomb of electricity)." Its unit is gram per coulomb.

It is represented by Z.

15. (b) Given :

Specific conductance (κ)

$= 0.012 \text{ ohm}^{-1}\text{cm}^{-1}$

Resistance, R = 55 ohm

$$\text{Conductance, } G = \frac{l}{\text{Resistance}}$$

$$\text{Resistance, } R = \rho \frac{l}{A}$$

$$\kappa = G \times G^*$$

$$\kappa = \frac{1}{R} \times G^*$$

$$G^* = \kappa \times R$$

Cell constant G^*

$= 0.012 \text{ ohm}^{-1} \text{ cm}^{-1} \times 55 \text{ ohm}$

Cell constant, $G^* = 0.66 \text{ cm}^{-1}$

Test - 3

1. (c) A primary cells is one in which the electrode reactions occur only once and cannot be reversed by applying electrical energy.

Therefore, primary cells cannot be recharged. A mercury cell is an example of a primary cell, whereas a nickel-cadmium storage cell is an example of a secondary cell.

2. (c) Net cell reaction during discharge :

$$Pb(s) + PbO_2(s) + 2H_2SO_4(aq) \longrightarrow 2PbSO_4(s) + 2H_2O(l)$$

- During discharge, H_2SO_4 is consumed and its density decreases.

  Net cell reaction during recharge :

  $$2PbSO_4(s) + 2H_2O(l) \longrightarrow Pb(s) + PbO(s) + 2H_2SO_4(aq)$$

- The concentration of H_2SO_4 increase as it generated.

3. (a) All statements are true except (a) for a fuel cell. Fuel cells are more efficient, free from pollution and run till reactants are active and used in automobiles too.

4. (d) Lithium has negative reduction potential value. So, it acts as strong reducing agent. Hence, it is used as an electrode in high energy density batteries.

5. (a) At anode,

$$2H_2(g) + 4OH^-(aq) \longrightarrow 4H_2O(l) + 4e^-$$

At cathode,

$$O_2(g) + 2H_2O(l) + 4e^- \longrightarrow 4OH^-(aq)$$

Overall reaction,

$$2H_2(g) + O_2(g) \longrightarrow 2H_2O(l)$$

6. (b) In dry cell, carbon rod is used as cathode and Zn is used as anode.

7. (c) The efficiency of a fuel cell

$$= \frac{\Delta G}{\Delta H}$$

8. (d) Both Statement I and Statement II are correct.

No need for a salt-bridge The sulphuric acid electrolyte allows ions to move freely, so a salt bridge is not required.

No direct contact The solid lead (anode) and lead dioxide (cathode) plates are kept apart by separators, stopping them to be in contact and causing issues.

9. (c) The cell which converts the chemical energy of a fuel directly into electrical energy is called as fuel cell. $H_2 - O_2$ cell is a fuel cell. It is also called as beacon cell.

$$2H_2(g) + O_2(g) \longrightarrow 2H_2O(l)$$

10. (d) Statement given in option (d) is incorrect. It is because mercury cell is a non- rechargeable electrochemical battery, it is a primary cell.

11. (a) When a lead storage battery is discharged then Pb is consumed and $PbSO_4$ is formed. SO_2 is not evolved and water is formed. Thus, statement given in option (a) is incorrect.

12. (d) In a dry cell, in the remaining space between the electrolyte and the graphite cathode, a second paste consisting of ammonium chloride and manganese dioxide is applied. The manganese dioxide acts as a depolariser as it helps to prevent the build-up of hydrogen gas bubbles.

13. (c) In a fuel cell, oxidants used are O_2, H_2O_2 and HNO_3.

14. (d) Both statement I and statement II are correct.

15. (a) Fuel cell is a device that converts energy of combustion of fuels like hydrogen and methane, directly into electrical energy. Electrolytic cell converts electrical energy into chemical energy. Dynamo is an electrical generator that produces direct current with the use of a commutator. Ni- Cd cell is a type of rechargeable battery which consists of cadmium anode and a metal grid containing NiO_2 acting as a cathode.

Chapter Break Thru

1. (a) $NaCl \rightleftharpoons Na^+ + Cl^-$

Molten sodium chlorides conducts electricity due to the presence of free ions.

In order to conduct electricity, a substance must have charge particles such as electrons and ions, that move freely through it. Ions in molten ionic compounds are free to flow and therefore molten sodium chloride can conduct electricity.

2. (c) Among the given options, only statement given in option (c) is correct while other are incorrect. Cathode and anode are (–)ve terminals in both electrolytic and galvanic cell.

3. (a) We know that,

$$M = Z \times I \times t$$

But, $Z = \frac{\text{Equivalent weight}}{96500}$

Put the value of Z in above equation, we get

$$M = \frac{20}{2 \times 96500} \times 25 \times 10^{-3} \times 60$$

$$M = 0.00015544$$

$$\text{No. of moles} = \frac{0.00015544}{20} = 0.000007772$$

$$\text{No. of atoms} = 0.000046811 \times 10^{23} = 4.6811 \times 10^{18} \simeq 4.68 \times 10^{18}$$

4. (b) At cathode,

$$Cu^{2+}(aq) + 2e^- \longrightarrow Cu(s)$$

At anode,

$$4OH^-(aq) \longrightarrow 2H_2O(l) + O_2(g) + 4e^-$$

To deposit 1 mole of copper, we need 2×96500 C.

So, 96500 C will deposit 0.5 moles of copper.

5. (a) For spontaneous reaction, the following condition should be satisfied.

$$\Delta_r G = -nFE < 0$$

So, the cell potential should be positive and $\Delta_r G$ should be negative.

6. (c) Hydrogen can reduce the oxides of less electropositive metals such as Cu, Sn, Fe, Pb etc., but it cannot reduce the oxides of more electropositive metals such as alkali metals, zinc, alkaline earth metals and aluminium.

7. (a) Voltmeter is used to determine EMF. Ammeter measures electric current flowing through a circuit. Spectrometer measures the properties of light over a specific portion of electromagnetic spectrum.
Coulometer measures the amount of electric charge passes through a circuit or electrode.

8. (c) Decreases by $\frac{0.059}{2}$, i.e. 0.0295 V

$$Cu^{2+} + 2e^- \longrightarrow Cu$$

$$E_{cell} = E^\circ_{cell} - \frac{0.0591}{2}\log\frac{1}{[Cu^{2+}]} \quad ...(i)$$

New concentration of Cu^{2+} is $\frac{[Cu^{2+}]}{10}$

$$\therefore E^{(new)}_{cell} = E^\circ_{cell} - \frac{0.0591}{2}\log\frac{10}{[Cu^{2+}]} \quad ...(ii)$$

$$\therefore \Delta E_{cell} = E_{cell} - E^{(new)}_{cell}$$

(i.e. (i) – (ii))

$$\Delta E_{cell} = -\frac{0.0591}{2}\log 10 \quad (\because \log 10 = 1)$$

$$\Delta E_{cell} = -\frac{0.0591}{2} = -0.0295\text{ V}$$

Hence, the electrode potential decreases by 0.0295 V.

9. (b) Electricity required
= No. of gram equivalent × 96500 coulombs
$= 0.5 \times 96500 = 48250$ C

10. (a) $Zn(l) + HgO(s) \longrightarrow Zn(s) + Hg(l)$

The cell potential remain constant during its life as the overall reaction does not involve any ion in solution whose concentration change during its life time. Thus, both (A) and (R) are true and (R) is the correct explanation of (A).

11. (d) A half-cell reaction involves either oxidation or reduction. At the cathode, reduction occurs, so electrons are not released into the external circuit from the cathode. Hence, statement given in option (d) is incorrect.

12. (a) SHE is the correct answer. For any species, standard oxidation potential is the negative of the standard reduction potential (SOP = – SRP). If the SOP equals SRP, then both must be zero. This condition is met only by the standard hydrogen electrode, which is defined to have an SRP of 0 volts by convention.

13. (a) Molar conductivity of H^+ and OH^- are very high as compare to other ions.
Initially conductance of solution sharply decrease due to consumption of free H^+ and after complete neutralisation further slightly increase in conductance due to presence of OH^-.

14. (d) Reduction occurs at cathode and gain of electron is reduction which occurs in option (d) only.

$$Ag \longrightarrow Ag^+ + e^- \text{ (oxidation)}$$

$$2OH^- \longrightarrow H_2O + \frac{1}{2}O_2 + 2e^- \text{ (oxidation)}$$

$$Fe^{+2} \longrightarrow Fe^{3+} + e^- \text{ (oxidation)}$$

$$Cu^{2+} + 2e^- \longrightarrow Cu \text{ (reduction)}$$

15. (b) $\overset{+1}{Na} + e^- \longrightarrow \overset{0}{Na}$, means oxidation number is decreased so, the reaction is reduction.

16. (d) A salt bridge is a device used to connect the oxidation and reduction half-cells of a galvanic cell (a type of electrochemical cell). Strong electrolytes are generally used to make the salt bridges in electrochemical cells. Since, $ZnSO_4$ is not a strong electrolyte, it is not used to make salt bridges.

17. (b) $\frac{w}{\text{eq. wt.}_{Ag}} = \frac{i \cdot t}{96500}$

$$\text{or } w_{Ag} = \frac{107.8 \times 8.46 \times 8 \times 60 \times 60}{96500}$$

$$\text{or } w_{Ag} = 272.18\text{ g}$$

$$\text{Volume of Ag} = \frac{272.18}{10.5} = 25.92\text{ cm}^3$$

$$\therefore \text{Surface area} = \frac{25.92}{0.00254} = 1.02 \times 10^4\text{ cm}^2$$

18. (c) We know that,

$$w_{metal} = \frac{Eit}{96500} = \frac{E \times 3 \times 50 \times 60}{96500}$$

$$E = \frac{96500 \times w_{metal}}{3 \times 50 \times 60} = \frac{96500 \times 1.8}{3 \times 50 \times 60} = 19.3$$

19. (c) Due to nearly same velocities of ions, the saturated solutions of KNO_3 with *agar-agar* is used to make salt-bridge.

20. (b) Reactivity series :
(most reactive)
K > Na > Ca > Mg > Al > Zn > Fe > Ni > Sn > Pb > Cu > Hg > Ag > Au (least reactive)
In the reactivity series, Zn is above to iron. Therefore, Zn can displace iron from its solution as it is more reactive than iron.
Ni is less reactive than Zn. So, it can not displace Zn from its solution. Similarly, Ag is less reactive than Cu and Cu is less reactive than Ni. Hence, option (b) is correct.

21. (d) The correct match is
A-II, B-III, C-I, D-IV.

22. (a) The electrode having higher oxidation potential will be stronger reducing agent than electrode having lower oxidation potential. The electrode having lowest reduction potential will be strongest reducing agent than electrode having higher reducing potential.

Hence, Zn is the strongest reducing agent among the given options.

23. (d) Metal zinc, magnesium and iron will replace Cu from copper sulphate as they are more reactive, according to reactivity series of metal.

Reactivity series
K > Na > Ca > Mg > Al > Zn > Fe > Ni > Pb > Cu > Hg > Ag > Au > Pt

24. (c) On dilution, number of ions decrease in unit volume hence specific conductance decreases. But separation between ions also increases hence equivalent conductance increases.

25. (b) The relation between conductance (*G*), specific conductance (κ) and cell constant $\left(\frac{l}{A}\right)$ is given by

$$G = \kappa \times \left(\frac{A}{l}\right)$$

26. (a) Both (A) and (R) are true and (R) is the correct explanation of (A).

27. (d) $E^\circ_{cell} = E^\circ_{Zn/Zn^{2+}} + E^\circ_{Mg^{2+}/Mg}$

$= -1.608$ (Non- spontaneous)

If E°_{cell} = +ve, then the reaction is possible while if E°_{cell} = –ve, then reaction is not posssible.

28. (a) The correct expression is given in option (a).

$$\Delta G = -2.303\, RT \log K_{eq}$$

or $\Delta G^\circ = -nFE^\circ_{cell}$

29. (d)

- $Br_2 + 2I^- \longrightarrow 2Br^- + I_2$

$E^\circ_{cell} = E^\circ_{Br_2/Br^-} - E^\circ_{I^-/I_2} = 1.63V$ (Spontaneous)

- $Fe + Br_2 \longrightarrow Fe^{2+} + 2Br^-$

$E^\circ_{cell} = E^\circ_{Br_2/Br^-} - E^\circ_{Fe/Fe^{2+}}$

$= 0.65$ V (Spontaneous)

- $Fe + I_2 \longrightarrow Fe^{2+} + 2I^-$

$E^\circ_{cell} = E^\circ_{I_2/I^-} - E^\circ_{Fe/Fe^{2+}} = 0.1$ V (Spontaneous)

- $I_2 + 2Br^- \longrightarrow 2I^- + Br_2$

$E^\circ_{cell} = E^\circ_{Br^-/Br_2} - E^\circ_{I_2/I^-}$

$= -1.63$ V (non-spontaneous)

30. (d) *D* does not react with HCl, so it is not easily oxidised as compared to *A*, *B* and *C*.
C reduced *B* as well as *D* but it is unable to reduce *A*.
Hence, *C* is oxidised easily than *B* and *D*.
So, *A* is oxidised easily as compared to other metals therefore, it has ability to act as reducing agent easily as compared to other metals.
Hence, the correct order of decreasing reducing ability is *A* > *C* > *B* > *D*.

31. (d) Equivalent = no. of moles × (*n*-factor)

$MnO_4^- \longrightarrow Mn^{+2}$; 1F = 96500 C

1 mole × 5 = 5F = 482500 C

$Cr_2O_7^{-2} \longrightarrow Cr^{+3}$;

1 mole × 6 = 6F = 579000 C

$Sn^{+4} \longrightarrow Sn^{+2}$;

1 mole × 2 = 2F = 193000 C

$Al^{+3} \longrightarrow Al$;

1 mole × 3 = 3F = 289500 C

Hence, the correct match is A-III, B-IV, C-I, D-II.

32. (c) $CuCl_2$ can be stored in silver vessel.
Metal with higher standard reduction potential (SRP) (Ag^+ / Ag) cannot reduce metal with lower SRP (Cu^{+2} / Cu).

33. (c) Conductivity, $\kappa = G^* \frac{1}{R}$

where, G^* is the cell constant.

$$G^* = \frac{l}{A}$$

where, *l* is the distance between the electrodes and *A* is the area.

Therefore, $\kappa = \frac{1}{50} \times \frac{2.2}{4.4}$

$= 0.01\,\Omega^{-1}cm^{-1}$

Molar conductivity,

$$\Lambda_m = \kappa \times \frac{1000}{C}$$

$= 0.01 \times \frac{1000}{0.5}$

$= 20\,\Omega^{-1}cm^2mol^{-1}$

$= 0.002\,\Omega^{-1}m^2mol^{-1}$

34. (d) Applying Nernst equation

$$E_{cell} = E^\circ_{cell} - \frac{RT}{nF} \ln \frac{[Cu^{2+}]}{[Ag^+]^2}$$

Doubling (Cu^{2+}) decreases the emf by a small fraction.

35. (b) $NaCl(s) \rightleftharpoons Na^+(aq) + Cl^-(aq)$

$H_2O(l) \rightleftharpoons H^+(aq) + OH^-(aq)$

At cathode, H_2 gas obtained because reduction potential of $Na^+ < H^+$.

Hence, both (A) and (R) are true but (R) is not the correct explanation of (A).

36. (a) The compounds with lower oxidation number and which can not be reduced by one- another can exist together. Thus, $FeCl_2$ and $SnCl_2$ can exist together as Fe^{+2} can not be reduced by Sn^{+2}.

37. (b) Among the given relations only (iii) and (iv) are correct. The correct relations of (i), (ii) and (v) are

- $\alpha = \frac{\Lambda_m}{\Lambda^\circ_m}$
- $\Delta G^\circ = -nFE^\circ$
- $E^\circ_{cell} = \frac{0.0591}{n} \log K_C$

38. (b) Given,
current (*i*) = 1.6 A
The amount of charge flowing across that area

Q = current passed × time (sec)

Q = *it* = 1.6 × 60 = 96 C

Total charge = *n* = number of Cu^{2+} ions = 2

$Q = ne^-$

$n = \frac{Q}{2e^-} = \frac{96}{2\times1.6\times10^{-19}}$

$= 3\times10^{20}$

39. (d) Weak electrolytes have lower degree of dissociation at higher concentrations. The change in Λ_m, with dilution is due to increase in the degree of dissociation and consequently the number of ions in total volume of solution that contain 1 mole of electrolyte. Λ_m increases steeply on dilution, specially near lower concentration. At infinite dilution, electrolyte dissociates completely but at such low concentration, the conductivity of the solution is low that it cannot be measured accurately.

40. (b) On dilution, the specific conductance decreases. It is because the number of ions per mL decrease.

On dilution, the equivalent conductance increases. It is because the degree of ionisation increases with dilution, which increases the number of ions.

41. (d) All the given statements are correct except statement (d) because the amount of the chemical reaction which occur at any electrode during electrolysis by a current is proportional to the quantity of electricity passed through the electrolyte.

42. (b) For a weak electrolyte the conductivity of solution increases very slowly on dilution and goes on increasing upon infinity and graph is not linear. Hence, it can not be measured experimentally. Thus, both (A) and (R) are true but (R) is not the correct explanation of (A).

43. (d) The higher the difference in standard electrode potential between the two metals, the higher the emf of the cell.

Fe and Cu :
$E° = |0.34 - (-0.44)| = 0.78$ V

Pb and Cu :
$E° = |0.34 - (-0.13)| = 0.47$ V

Cu and Au :
$E° = |1.50 - 0.34| = 1.16$ V

Ca and Cu :
$E° = |0.34 - (-2.87)| = 3.21$ V

Hence, Ca and Cu would result in the maximum emf among the given options.

44. (b) In electrolytic cell reduction occur at cathode.

In galvanic cell, (is a type of electrochemical cell), electrical energy is produced due to some chemical reaction occurring at anode and cathode.

Oxidation occurs at anode, while reduction occurs at cathode.

45. (c) $\frac{\text{Weight of Ca}}{\text{Weight of Al}} = \frac{\text{Eq.weight of Ca}}{\text{Eq.weight of Al}}$

$\Rightarrow \frac{40}{w_{Al}} = \frac{\frac{40}{2}}{\frac{27}{3}}$

If current efficiency is 100 %,

$w_{Al} = 18$ kg

But, given efficiency is 50 %.

$\therefore \; w_{Al} = 9$ kg

46. (d) Gram equiv. $= \frac{\text{Weight}}{\text{Molar mass}} \times n_f$

n_f = charge on the ion

Also, gram equiv. $= \frac{\text{Charge passed}}{96500}$

$\frac{24125}{96500} = \frac{7.42\times n_f}{118}$

$n_f = 3.97 = 4$

47. (d) $2H^+ + 2e^- \longrightarrow H_2$

According to Nernst equation,

$E_{H^+/H_2} = E^\circ_{H^+/H_2} - \frac{0.0591}{n}\log\frac{1}{[H^+]^2}$

$= 0 - \frac{0.0591}{2}(-\log[H^+]^2)$

$= -0.0591(-\log[H^+])$

$= -0.0591$ pH

$\{\because -\log[H^+] = pH\}$

48. (d) For a galvanic cell to provide half-cell voltage, the half- cell having higher reduction potential and lower reduction potential should be connected.

In the given half- cell reactions,

$B^+ + e^- \longrightarrow B$; (Lowest $E°$ value)

$A \longrightarrow A^+ + e^-$;

(Highest $E°$ value)

Hence, the cell reaction of cell with largest potential value will be

$A + B^+ \longrightarrow A^+ + B$

$E^\circ_{cell} = 2.1 - (-0.24) = 2.34$

49. (d) The reason for increase in the electrical conduction of a weak electrolyte with increase in temperature are

(i) Increase in the degree of dissociation of electrolytes

(ii) Increase in the number of ions due to an increase in the degree of dissociation.

(iii) Increase in the speed of ions due to increase in kinetic energy.

50. (b) Pure water does not conduct electricity effectively because it is almost non-ionised. In water, only a very small fraction of water molecules dissociate into H^+ and OH^- ions. This means very few charged particles are available to carry an electric current. Therefore, pure water has very low electrical conductance.

Ch-3 Chemical Kinetics

Topical Follow Thru

Test-1

1. (c) The law of mass action states that the rate of a chemical reaction is directly proportional to the product of the molar concentration of the reactants raised to their stoichiometric coefficient.

e.g. For reaction

$aA + bB \rightleftharpoons cC + dD$, the rate of reaction is given as

$$\text{rate} \propto [A]^a [B]^b$$

2. (c) Initial rate $= k[A]^n[B]^m$

$$\text{New rate} = k[2A]^n \left[\frac{1}{2}B\right]^m$$

$$\frac{\text{New rate}}{\text{Initial rate}} = \frac{2^n A^n B^m 2^{-m}}{A^n B^m}$$

$$= 2^n \cdot 2^{-m} = 2^{n-m}$$

3. (d) According to law of mass action, the rate of reaction is directly proportional to the product of the active masses of reactants at the given temperature.

e.g. For the reaction

$$aA + bB \longrightarrow P$$

$$\text{rate} = k[A]^a[B]^b$$

4. (b) As the slowest step is the rate determining step, hence from Eq. (ii) (given in question),

$$r = k[O_3][O]$$

$$\text{From Eq. (i), } K_{eq} = \frac{[O_2][O]}{[O_3]}$$

$$\text{or} \quad [O] = \frac{K_{eq}\,[O_3]}{[O_2]}$$

$$\text{Hence, } r = k\,K_{eq}\frac{[O_3]^2}{[O_2]}$$

$$= k'[O_3]^2[O_2]^{-1}$$

$$[k' = kK_{eq}]$$

5. (d) $2H_2(g) + 2NO(g) \rightleftharpoons N_2(g) + 2H_2O(g)$

$$r_f = k_f[NO]^2[H_2]$$

This means that, for forward reaction the order of reaction w.r.t. [NO] is 2 and that of w.r.t. $[H_2]$ is 1.

$$K_{eq} = \frac{[N_2][H_2O]^2}{[H_2]^2[NO]^2} = \frac{k_f}{k_b}$$

$$\Rightarrow k_f[NO]^2[H_2] = \frac{k_b[N_2][H_2O]^2}{[H_2]}$$

At equilibrium, $r_f = r_b$

$$\Rightarrow \quad r_b = \frac{k_b[N_2][H_2O]^2}{[H_2]}$$

Note In this question, the order of reaction for backward reaction is not given.

6. (b) $N_2 + 3H_2 \rightleftharpoons 2NH_3$

$$-\frac{d[H_2]}{dt} = \frac{3}{2}\frac{d[NH_3]}{dt}$$

$$\text{or} \quad \frac{d[NH_3]}{dt} = -\frac{2}{3}\frac{d[H_2]}{dt}$$

$$= \frac{2}{3} \times \frac{1.8 \times 10^{-2}}{10}$$

$$[NH_3] = 1.2 \times 10^{-3}$$

$$= 12 \times 10^{-4}$$

In 10 min, number of moles of $NH_3 = 12 \times 10^{-3}$

$$\text{then in 0.4 min} = \frac{12 \times 10^{-3} \times 0.4}{10}$$

$$= 4.8 \times 10^{-4}$$

7. (b) Minus signed entities are of reactants and positive signed are of products. Dividing numbers are the coefficients.

So, reaction is

$$B + 3D \longrightarrow 4A + 2C$$

8. (d) For the reaction,

$$xA + yB \longrightarrow zC$$

$$-\frac{1}{x}\frac{d[A]}{dt} = -\frac{1}{y}\frac{d[B]}{dt}$$

$$= \frac{1}{z}\frac{d[C]}{dt} \quad \text{...(i)}$$

$$-\frac{d[A]}{dt} = \frac{-d[B]}{dt} = \frac{3}{2}\frac{d[C]}{dt} \quad \text{...(ii)}$$

$$\frac{1}{x} = 1, \frac{1}{y} = 1, \frac{1}{z} = 1.5 = \frac{3}{2}$$

Multiplying Eq. (ii) by $\frac{2}{3}$, we get

$$x, y, z = 2, 2, 3.$$

9. (d) $2N_2O_5(g) \longrightarrow 4NO_2(g) + O_2(g)$

$$\text{Rate} = -\frac{1}{2}\frac{d[N_2O_5]}{dt}$$

$$= +\frac{1}{4}\frac{d[NO_2]}{dt} = \frac{d[O_2]}{dt}$$

$\therefore$ Rate of decomposition of N_2O_5 to rate of formation of NO_2 is

$$-\frac{1}{2}\frac{d[N_2O_5]}{dt} = \frac{1}{4}\frac{d[NO_2]}{dt}$$

$$\frac{-d\dfrac{[N_2O_5]}{dt}}{\dfrac{d[NO_2]}{dt}} = \frac{2}{4} = 1:2$$

10. (b) $A + B \longrightarrow$ Products

Let $\quad r_1 = k[A]^x[B]^y \quad$ ...(i)

When $B' = 2B, r_2 = 8r_1$

Rate, $8r_1 = k[A]^x[2B]^y \quad$ ...(ii)

By dividing Eqs. (ii) by (i) we get,

$$8 = \frac{[A]^x[2B]^y}{[A]^x[B]^y}$$

$$\Rightarrow \quad 8 = [2]^y \Rightarrow y = 3$$

As concentration of A have no effect, thus $x = 0$

$$\text{Rate} = k[A]^0[B]^3 = k[B]^3$$

11. (a) Out of three states of matter only gases do exert pressure, hence rate of reaction which does not involve gases, is not dependent on pressure.

12. (b) Rate $= k[A]^2[B]$

$$r_1 = k[A_1]^2[B]$$

$$r_2 = k[A_2]^2[B]$$

$$\frac{r_1}{r_2} = \frac{k[A_1]^2[B]}{k[A_2]^2[B]} = \left(\frac{[A_1]}{[A_2]}\right)^2$$

Now given, $[A_2] = 2[A_1]$

$$\frac{r_1}{r_2} = \left(\frac{[A_1]}{2[A_1]}\right)^2 = \frac{1}{4}$$

$$\frac{r_1}{r_2} = \frac{1}{4}$$

$$r_2 = 4r_1$$

13. (d) Rate of disappearance of

$$N_2O_4 = \frac{\Delta[N_2O_4]}{\Delta t} = \frac{0.50 - 0.46}{30}$$

$$= 0.0013 \text{ atm min}^{-1}$$

$$\text{Rate of reaction} = \frac{-d[N_2O_4]}{dt} = \frac{1}{2}\frac{d[NO_2]}{dt}$$

$\therefore$ Rate of appearance of NO_2 = Twice the rate of disappearance of $N_2O_4 = 2 \times 0.0013$ $= 0.0026$ atm min^{-1}

14. (b) $N_2 + 3H_2 \rightleftharpoons 2NH_3$

$$\frac{-\Delta[N_2]}{\Delta t} = -\frac{1}{3}\frac{\Delta[H_2]}{\Delta t} = \frac{1}{2}\frac{\Delta[NH_3]}{\Delta t}$$

$$\frac{-\Delta[H_2]}{\Delta t} = \frac{3}{2} \times \frac{\Delta[NH_3]}{\Delta t}$$

$$= \frac{3}{2} \times 2 \times 10^{-4}$$

$$= 3 \times 10^{-4} \text{ mol L}^{-1} \text{ s}^{-1}$$

15. (c) The stoichiometric coefficient of both SO_2 and SO_3 is same. Hence, the rate of formation of SO_3 is same as the rate of disappearance of SO_2 that is 1.28×10^{-3} mol L^{-1} s^{-1}.

The rate of formation of SO_3 is 1.28×10^{-3} mol L^{-1}s^{-1}.

Test-2

1. (d) Order may or may not be equal to molecularity. It can be greater, lower or equal to molecularity of reaction.

2. (b) Given, $t_{1/2} = 1400$ s

For a first order reaction,

$$t_{1/2} = \frac{0.693}{k} \quad (k = \text{rate constant})$$

$$1400 = \frac{0.693}{k}$$

$$\Rightarrow \quad k = 4.9 \times 10^{-4} \text{ s}^{-1}$$

3. (d) For a zero order reaction, $t_{1/2}$ is given as

$$t_{1/2} = \frac{[A_0]}{2k} \quad \text{or} \quad k = \frac{[A_0]}{2t_{1/2}}$$

Given, $t_{1/2} = 1$ hr, $[A_0] = 2$ mol L^{-1}

$$\therefore \quad k = \frac{2}{2 \times 1} = 1 \text{ mol L}^{-1} \text{ hr}^{-1}$$

Integrated rate law for zero order reaction is $[A] = -kt + [A_0]$

Here, $[A_0] = 0.5$ M

and $[A] = 0.25$ M

$$\Rightarrow \quad 0.25 = -t + 0.5$$

$$[k = 1 \text{ mol}^{-1}\text{L}^{-1}\text{hr}^{-1}]$$

$$\Rightarrow \quad t = 0.25 \text{ hr}$$

4. (b) Given, $t_{50\%} = 2$ h, $t_{75\%} = 4$ h

For 1st order, $t_{75\%} = 2 \times t_{50\%}$

$4 = 2 \times 2$, hence, the reaction is 1st order reaction.

5. (c) $k = \dfrac{2.303}{t} \log \dfrac{a}{a-x}$,

when $a = 100$

$$a - x = \frac{a}{2} = 50$$

$$t_{1/2} = 6.93 \text{ min}$$

$$k = \frac{2.303}{6.93} \times \log \frac{100}{50} = 0.1 \text{ min}^{-1}$$

when $a = 100$,

$(a-x) = 100 - 99 = 1, t = t_{99\%}$

$$t_{99\%} = \frac{2.303}{0.1} \log \frac{100}{1} = \frac{2.303}{0.1} \times 2$$

$$= 46.06 \text{ min}$$

6. (b) From 1st reading

$$\text{rate} = 45.0 \times 10^{-5}$$

$$= k[0.003]^n \quad \ldots\text{(i)}$$

(where, n is order of reaction)

From 2nd reading

$$\text{rate} = 5.0 \times 10^{-5} = k[0.009]^n \ldots\text{(ii)}$$

On dividing Eqs. (i) by (ii),

$$\frac{45.0 \times 10^{-5}}{5.0 \times 10^{-5}} = \frac{k\,[0.003]^n}{k\,[0.009]^n}$$

$$\Rightarrow \quad 9 = \left(\frac{1}{3}\right)^n$$

$$\Rightarrow \quad n = -2$$

7. (c) Inversion of cane sugar is a particular example of pseudo-unimolecular reaction.

8. (a) $a = 100$;

$$a - x = 100 - 87.5 = 12.5$$

$$k = \frac{2.303}{t} \log \frac{a}{a-x}$$

$$= \frac{2.303}{45} \log \frac{100}{12.5} = 0.046$$

$$t_{1/2} = \frac{0.693}{k} = \frac{0.693}{0.046}$$

$$= 15.06 \text{ min} \approx 15 \text{ min}$$

9. (a) $t_{1/2} \propto [A_0]^{1-n}$ given,

$$t_{1/2} = [A_0]^{-3}$$

$$1 - n = -3$$

$$n = 3 + 1$$

$n = 4$, i.e. order of reaction = 4.

10. (b) For zero order reaction, rate of reaction is independent of concentration, i.e. $r = k[\text{Reactant}]^0$. Thus statement given in option (b) is correct while (a), (c) and (d) are incorrect.

11. (b) Statement given in option (b) is incorrect.

It is because molecularity of a reaction never become zero or fractional.

12. (a) Among the given reactions, (a) is an example of pseudo unimolecular reaction.

When in any chemical reaction, one of the reactant is present in large excess, then second-order reaction becomes first-order reaction and is known as pseudo unimolecular reaction, e.g.

$$CH_3COOCH_3 + H_2O \xrightarrow{H^+} CH_3COOH + CH_3OH$$

In this reaction molecularity is 2 but order of reaction is found to be first order experimentally, so it is an example of pseudo unimolecular reaction.

13. (d) Statement given in option (d) is incorrect. It is because, in first order reaction, the reaction rate is directly proportional to the reactant concentration and the unit of first order rate constant is sec^{-1}, i.e. $time^{-1}$.

14. (d) For first order reaction,

$$k = \frac{2.303}{t}\log\frac{a}{a-x}$$

For completion of 75% reaction in 60 min,

$$k = \frac{2.303}{60}\log\frac{100}{(100-75)}$$

or $k = \frac{2.303}{60}\log 4$

$$k = \frac{2.303}{60}\times 0.602$$

For completion of 93.75% reaction, t is given by

$$t = \frac{2.303}{k}\log\frac{100}{(100-93.75)}$$

$$t = \frac{2.303\times 60}{2.303\times 0.602}\log 16$$

$$t = \frac{60}{0.602}\times 1.204$$

$\Rightarrow t = 120\,\text{min}$

15. (b) Statement I is correct but Statement II is incorrect. The correct form of Statement II is, water takes part in a large amount in the acid catalysed hydrolysis of ethyl acetate.

Test-3

1. (b) We know that, $k = Ae^{-E_a/RT}$

$$\log\frac{k}{A} = \frac{-E_a}{2.303RT}$$

$$= \frac{-2.303RT}{2.303RT} = -1$$

$$\log\frac{k}{A} = -1$$

$$\Rightarrow \frac{k}{A} = \text{antilog}(-1) = 0.1$$

2. (a) Temperature coefficient is not the ratio of the rate constant at any two temperatures but at two temperatures differing by 10°C or 10 K.

3. (a) $\log\frac{k_2}{k_1} = \frac{E_a}{2.303R}\left[\frac{T_2 - T_1}{T_1T_2}\right]$

$$\log 2 = \frac{E_a}{2.303\times 2}\left[\frac{300-260}{260\times 300}\right]$$

$$(\because k_2 = 2k_1)$$

$$E_a = 2703.76 \text{ calories}$$

$$\approx 2.7 \text{ kcal}$$

4. (d) Rate of reaction is directly proportional to collision frequency of reactants.

5. (a) From Arrhenius equation

$$\log_e k = \frac{-E_a}{RT} + \log_e A$$

Compare the above equation with straight line equation

$$Y = mx + C$$

$$\text{Slope} = m = \frac{-E_a}{R}$$

So, the graph plotted between $\log k$ *vs* $\frac{1}{T}$ will be in accordance with Arrhenius equation.

6. (d) According to Arrhenius equation, $k = Ae^{-E_a/RT}$

$$\log k = \log A - \frac{E_a}{2.303RT} \quad \ldots(i)$$

For a first order reaction,

$$t_{1/2} = \frac{0.693}{k} = 10\text{ min} = 600\text{ s}$$

$$\therefore \quad k = \frac{0.693}{600} = 1.155\times 10^{-3}\ \text{s}^{-1}$$

Putting value in Eq. (i)

$$\log(1.155\times 10^{-3}) = \log(4\times 10^{13}) - \frac{98.6\times 10^3}{2.303\times 8.314\times T}$$

$$-2.937 = 13.602 - \frac{5149.6}{T}$$

$$13.602 + 2.937 = \frac{5149.6}{T}$$

$$\therefore \quad T = 311.45\text{ K}$$

7. (d) Among the given statements, statements I, II, III and IV are correct, only V is incorrect. Its correct form is as follows. Catalyst does not change the equilibrium constant of a reaction.

8. (a) According to Arrhenius equation, $k = Ae^{-E_a/RT}$

$$\ln k = \ln A - \frac{E_a}{RT}$$

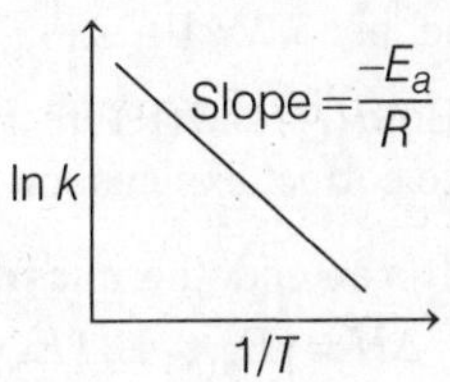

Hence, if $\ln k$ is plotted against $\frac{1}{T}$, slope of the line will be $-E_a/R$.

9. (b) Incorrect statement is (b). Reaction with lower activation energy has higher rate constant.

10. (b) As $2k'' = k'$ so, $k' > k''$, $E_a' < E_a''$ (Greater the rate constant lesser is the activation energy).

11. (b) By using positive catalyst

(i) ΔH does not change

(ii) Activation energy decreases.

Hence, these both conditions are followed in option (b).

12. (b) $\log\frac{k_2}{k_1} = \frac{E_a}{2.303R}\left[\frac{1}{T_1} - \frac{1}{T_2}\right]$

if $\frac{k_2}{k_1} = 2$

$$\log 2 = \frac{E_a}{2.303\times 8.314}\left[\frac{1}{300} - \frac{1}{310}\right]$$

$$E_a = 0.3010\times 2.303 \times 8.314\left(\frac{300\times 310}{10}\right)$$

$$= 53598.5\text{ J}$$

$$= 54\text{ kJ}$$

13. (c) $k = Ae^{-E_a/RT}$

where,

k = rate constant

A = pre-exponential frequency factor

R = gas constant

T = temperature in Kelvin scale.

So, option (c) is correct.

14. (b) When $E_a = 0$, rate constant will be independent of temperature.

So, the rate constant will remains same, i.e. $3.2 \times 10^6 \ s^{-1}$.

15. (a) Both (A) and (R) are true and (R) is the correct explanation of (A).

16. (c) It's an endothermic reaction, so

$$\Delta H = [E_{a(F)}] - [E_{b(F)}]$$

Given, $[E_{a(F)}] = 15 \text{ kcal/mol}$ and

$$\Delta H = 5 \text{ kcal/mol}$$

$$[E_{b(F)}] = 15 - 5 \text{ kcal/mol}$$

For an endothermic reaction, the activation energy for the backward reaction is equal to the difference of the activation energy of the forward reaction and the enthalpy change of the reaction.

The activation energy of the reaction $B \rightarrow A$ is

$15 - 5 = 10 \text{ kcal/mol}$

17. (a) Arrhenius equation is given by

$$k = A_e^{\frac{-E_a}{RT}}$$

Taking log both side we get,

$$\log_e k = \log_e A - \frac{E_a}{RT}$$

$$[\because \log_e C = 1]$$

18. (b) Collision frequency increases when the temperature is increased or heat energy is supplied which increases the kinetic energy of the reacting molecules. This will increase the number of collisions and ultimately the rate of reaction will be enhanced.

19. (d) (A) is false but (R) is true. The correct form of (A) is :

The value of ΔG of a reaction remains unchanged when a catalyst is added to it because ΔG is a state function, i.e. it does not depend on the path taken by reaction to reach the end product. Since, a catalyst only changes the pathway taken by a reaction, it does not alter the value of ΔG.

20. (b) The rate of a reaction is doubled for every 10°C rise in temperature. Thus, the rate of reaction changes by 2^n times, where n is the number of times the temperature increased by 10°C. The value of n when temperature increases from 10°C to 100°C is 9.

So, the increase in reaction rate as a result of the rise in temperature from 10°C to 100°C is $2^9 = 512$ times.

21. (a) The correct match is A-I, B-III, C-IV, D-II.

A. Catalyst alters the rate of reaction by lowering E_a.

B. Energetically favourable reaction are sometimes slow because proper orientation is not always there.

C. Area under the Maxwell Boltzmann curve is constant as the total probability is one.

D. Frequency of succesful collision is increased by increasing the concentration of the reactant as more opportunities for collision increases.

22. (b) The presence of a catalyst increase the reaction rate (in both forward and reverse reactions) by providing an alternative pathway with lower activation energy. Activation energy is the minimum energy barrier which the reagent have to cross for the completion of the reaction. If the activation energy is lowered, the reactants can cross that barrier easily and so, the rate of reaction increases.

23. (d) According to Arrhenius equation

$$k = Ae^{-E_a/RT}$$

If $E_a = 0$ and then $k = A$

In these conditions, the rate constant of the reaction is nearly independent of temperature.

24. (c) When k increase, rate of reaction also increase, $k = \frac{pZ}{e^{E_a/RT}}$

for k to increase p, Z, T should increase and E_a should decrease ($e \approx 2.7$).

25. (d) Both Statement I and Statement II are correct.

Chapter Break Thru

1. (d) For the reaction,

$$BrO_3^- (aq) + 5Br^- (aq) + 6H^+ (aq) \longrightarrow 3Br_2 (l) + 3H_2O(l)$$

$$\text{Rate} = \frac{-1}{5}\frac{d[Br^-]}{dt} = \frac{+1}{3}\frac{d[Br_2]}{dt}$$

$$\text{So, } \frac{d[Br_2]}{dt} = \frac{-3}{5}\frac{d[Br^-]}{dt}$$

Thus, option (d) is correct.

2. (d) Option (d) is incorrect.

For the reaction,

$$4NH_3(g) + 5O_2(g) \longrightarrow 4NO(g) + 6H_2O(g)$$

$$\text{Rate} = -\frac{1}{4}\frac{d[NH_3]}{dt} = -\frac{1}{5}\frac{d[O_2]}{dt}$$

$$= \frac{1}{4}\frac{d[NO]}{dt} = \frac{1}{6}\frac{d[H_2O]}{dt} \quad \ldots(i)$$

Rate of disappearance of NH_3

= Rate of appearance of NO

$= 3.6 \times 10^{-3}$ mol/L/s ...(ii)

Rate of formation of water

$$= \frac{d[H_2O]}{dt}$$

From the rate equation (i),

$$\frac{1}{6}\frac{d[H_2O]}{dt} = \frac{1}{4}\frac{d[NO]}{dt}$$

$$\therefore \frac{d[H_2O]}{dt} = \frac{6}{4} \times 3.6 \times 10^{-3}$$

$$= 5.4 \times 10^{-3} \text{molL}^{-1}\text{s}^{-1}$$

3. (d) Statements (a), (b) and (c) are correct, while (d) is incorrect.

(a) As T decreases, k decreases and thus, rate of reaction decreases.

(b) Rate of reaction
$= k[A]^0 = k =$ constant.
Thus, the rate is uniform in zero order reaction.

(c) As surface area increases, number of molecules will be more to react per unit time and more surface site are available for the reaction.

(d) Average rate is defined for macroscopic rate and instantaneous rate is defined for microscopic time interval.
Thus, option (d) is incorrect.

4. (c) Statement I is incorrect but Statement II is correct.
Order of reaction is equal to the sum of powers of concentration of the reactants in rate law expression. It may or may not be equal to the sum of stoichiometric coefficients.

5. (a) The correct match is
A-II, B-I, C-IV, D-III.
n^{th} order of reaction
$= (\text{mol/L})^{1-n}\ \text{s}^{-1}$
On the basis of nth order formula, we calculate unit of different order of reaction.
A. Zero order reaction
= mol/L/s (II)
B. First order reaction $= \text{s}^{-1}$ (I)
C. Second order reaction
$= \text{mol}^{-1}\ \text{Ls}^{-1}$ (IV)
D. Third order reaction
$= \text{mol}^{-2}\ \text{L}^2\ \text{s}^{-1}$ (III)
Thus, option (a) is correct.

6. (c) Rate $= k\,(\text{Reactant})^n$
If (Reactant) $= a$, rate $= r_1$
If (Reactant) $= 4a$, rate $= 2r_1$

$$r_1 = k[a]^n \quad \text{...(i)}$$
$$2r_1 = k[4a]^n \quad \text{...(ii)}$$

Divide (i), with (ii) equation
$$\frac{1}{2} = \left(\frac{1}{4}\right)^n$$
$$n = \frac{1}{2}$$
So, option (c) is correct.

7. (d) $2\text{NO}(g) + \text{Cl}_2(g) \longrightarrow 2\text{NOCl}(g)$
Let the rate of reaction is
$$r_1 = k[\text{NO}]^\alpha [\text{Cl}_2]^\beta \quad \text{...(i)}$$
(α and β are respective order)
$$r_2 = 2r_1 = k[\text{NO}]^\alpha [2\text{Cl}_2]^\beta \quad \text{...(ii)}$$
$$r_3 = 8r_1 = k[2\text{NO}]^\alpha [2\text{Cl}_2]^\beta \quad \text{...(iii)}$$
Dividing Eqs. (ii) by (i),
$$\frac{r_2}{r_1} = \frac{2r_1}{r_1} = \frac{k[\text{NO}]^\alpha [2\text{Cl}_2]^\beta}{k[\text{NO}]^\alpha [\text{Cl}_2]^\beta}$$
$$(2)^1 = (2)^\beta$$
$$\beta = 1$$
Similarly, divide Eq. (iii) by Eq. (i),
$$\frac{r_3}{r_1} = \frac{8r_1}{r_1} = \frac{k[2\text{NO}]^\alpha [2\text{Cl}_2]^\beta}{k[\text{NO}]^\alpha [\text{Cl}_2]^\beta}$$
$$8 = (2)^\alpha (2)^\beta$$
$$8 = (2)^\alpha (2)^1$$
$$4 = (2)^\alpha$$
$$\alpha = 2$$
Order w.r.t. NO = 2
Order w.r.t. $\text{Cl}_2 = 1$
Overall order $= 2 + 1 = 3$
Hence, option (d) is correct.

8. (b) $\dfrac{-d[\text{MnO}_4^-]}{dt} = 5.36 \times 10^{-3}\ \text{Ms}^{-1}$
$$-\frac{1}{2}\frac{d[\text{MnO}_4^-]}{dt} = +\frac{1}{5}\frac{d[\text{I}_2]}{dt}$$
$$\frac{d[\text{I}_2]}{dt} = \frac{5}{2}\left[\frac{-d[\text{MnO}_4^-]}{dt}\right]$$
$$= \frac{5}{2} \times 5.36 \times 10^{-3}$$
$$= 13.4 \times 10^{-3}\ \text{Ms}^{-1}$$

9. (a) Both (A) and (R) are true and (R) is the correct explanation of (A).

10. (b) The given reaction is
$$2\text{NO}(g) + \text{Cl}_2(g) \rightleftharpoons 2\text{NOCl}(g)$$
$$\text{Rate} = k[\text{NO}]^x [\text{Cl}_2]^y \quad \text{... (i)}$$
[order $= x + y$]
When concentration of Cl_2 is double then rate,
$$2 \times \text{Rate} = k[\text{NO}]^x [2\text{Cl}_2]^y \quad \text{... (ii)}$$
Divide Eqs. (ii) by (i),
$$2 = 2^y \Rightarrow y = 1$$
When concentration of NO is double then rate,
$$4 \times \text{rate} = k[2\text{NO}]^x [\text{Cl}_2]^y \quad \text{...(iii)}$$
Divide Eqs. (iii) by (i),
$$4 = 2^x \Rightarrow x = 2$$
$\therefore$ Order $= 2 + 1 = 3$

11. (b) For first order reaction,
$$t_{1/2} = \frac{0.693}{k} = \frac{0.693}{3.3 \times 10^{-4}}$$
$$= 2100\,\text{s} = 35\,\text{min}$$
From relation,
$$t_{75\%} = 2t_{1/2} = 2 \times 35 = 70\,\text{min}$$

12. (a) For first order,
$$t_{1/2} = \frac{0.693}{k};\ t_{3/4} = t_{75\%}$$
$$t_{3/4} = \frac{2.303}{k}\log\frac{a}{\left(a - \frac{3a}{4}\right)}$$
$$= \frac{2.303}{k}\log 4$$
$$= \frac{2.303}{k} \times 2 \times 0.3010$$
$$= \frac{0.693 \times 2}{k}$$
$$\frac{t_{3/4}}{t_{1/2}} = \frac{0.693 \times 2}{k} \times \frac{k}{0.693}$$
$$\frac{t_{3/4}}{t_{1/2}} = 2$$

13. (d) For the first order reaction,
$$k = \frac{0.693}{t_{1/2}} = \frac{0.693}{60}$$
$$= 11.55 \times 10^{-3}\ \text{min}^{-1}$$
Applying first order kinetics,
$$t = \frac{2.303}{k}\log\frac{a}{a - x}$$
Given, $a = 100, x = 90$
i.e. $(a - x) = 100 - 90 = 10$
Hence, $t = \dfrac{2.303}{11.5 \times 10^{-3}}\log 10$
$$t = 200\,\text{min}$$

14. (c) Rate of reaction decreases with respect to time in first order reaction.
Thus, option (c) is correct.

15. (a) The correct match is A-I, B-III, C-IV, D-II.

A. Order of a complex reaction is determined by rate of a reaction, which is the slowest.

B. Mathematical expression for is known as rate law.

C. Rate of reaction for zero order reaction is equal to rate constant.

$$r = k[A]^0$$
$$\therefore \quad r = k$$

D. Unit of rate of reaction is same as that of rate of reaction.

16. (a) $(CH_3)_2CHN{=}NCH(CH_3)_2 \longrightarrow N_2 + C_6H_{14}$

At $t=0$; p_0 0   0

at $t=t$; $p_0 - x$ x x

$$p_t = p_0 - x + x + x = p_0 + x$$
$$x = p_t - p_0$$
$$a - x = p_0 - (p_t - p_0)$$
$$= 2p_0 - p_t$$
$$k = \frac{2.303}{t}\log\frac{a}{a-x}$$
$$= \frac{2.303}{t}\log\frac{p_0}{2p_0 - p_t}$$

Thus, option (a) is correct.

17. (c)

$SO_2Cl_2(g) \longrightarrow SO_2(g) + Cl_2(g)$

Initial 180   0   0

At time (t) $180 - x$ x x

$$p_{\text{total}} = 180 - x + x + x = 180 + x$$
$$t = 240\,\text{s},\ p_t = 244$$
$$\therefore 180 + x = 244,\ x = 64$$
$$k = \frac{2.303}{240}\log\frac{p}{p-x}$$
$$= \frac{2.303}{240}\log\frac{180}{180-64}$$
$$k = \frac{2.303}{240}\times 0.19$$
$$= 0.00182\,\text{s}^{-1}$$

At $t = 600\,\text{s}$, $p_t = 302$ torr

$180 + x = 302$, $x = 122$ torr

$$k = \frac{2.303}{600}\log\frac{180}{180-122}$$
$$= \frac{2.303}{600}\times 0.49 = 0.00182\,\text{s}^{-1}$$

Thus, option (c) is correct.

18. (d) Only statement (d) is correct, because k_{zero} = mol/L/s and amount of reactant will be changed throughout the reaction.

$t_{1/2}\ \alpha$ initial concentration of the reactant

Thus, option (d) is correct.

19. (b) Given,

Rate constant,

$$k = 2.772\times10^{-3}\,\text{s}^{-1}$$
$$k = \frac{2.303}{t}\log\frac{[A_o]}{[A_t]}$$
$$2.772\times10^{-3} = \frac{2.303}{250}\log\frac{(0.1/2)}{[A_t]}$$
$$\log\left(\frac{0.05}{A_t}\right) = \frac{2.772\times10^{-3}\times250}{2.303}$$
$$\log\left(\frac{0.05}{A_t}\right) = \frac{693\times10^{-3}}{2.303}$$
$$= 300.9\times10^{-3} = 0.3$$
$$\log 0.05 - \log A_t$$
$$= 0.3\ (\log 0.05 = -1.301)$$
$$\log A_t = -1.301 - 0.3$$
$$\log A_t = -1.601$$
$$A_t = \text{antilog}\,(-1.601)$$

20. (c) Given,

Fraction of molecules

$$e^{-E_a/RT} = 3.8\times10^{-16}\%$$
$$e^{-E_a/RT} = \frac{3.8\times10^{-16}}{100}$$
$$\frac{-E_a}{RT} = \ln(3.8\times10^{-18})$$
$$= 2.303\log(3.8\times10^{-18})$$
$$-E_a = 2.303\times(\log 3.8\times10^{-18})$$
$$\times 8.314\times10^{-3}\ \text{kJ mol}^{-1}\text{K}^{-1}$$
$$\times 300\,\text{K}$$
$$-E_a = -100.06\,\text{kJ mol}^{-1}$$
$$E_a \approx 100\,\text{kJ mol}^{-1}$$

21. (d) Both Statement I and Statement II are correct.

22. (b) Given, $E_a = 80 - 40 = 40\,\text{kJ}$

$$k_1 = Ae^{-E_a/RT}$$
$$k_2 = Ae^{-E_a(c)/RT}$$
$$\log\frac{k_2}{k_1} = \frac{E_a - E_a(c)}{2.3\times8.314\times298\ \text{K}}$$
$$= \frac{40\times10^3\ \text{J}}{2.3\times8.314\times298\ \text{K}} = 7.0$$
$$\frac{k_2}{k_1} = 10^7$$

The reaction rate increases by 10^7 times.

Thus, option (b) is correct.

23. (d) The Arrhenius equation is

$$\log\frac{k_2}{k_1} = \frac{E_a}{R\times2.303}\left(\frac{T_2 - T_1}{T_1T_2}\right)$$

Given, $\frac{k_2}{k_1} = 3$, $R = 8.314$ J/K/mol

$$T_1 = 20 + 273 = 293\,\text{K}$$
$$T_2 = 50 + 273 = 323\,\text{K}$$

Substituting the given values in the Arrhenius equation

$$\log 3 = \frac{E_a}{8.314\times2.303}\left(\frac{323-293}{323\times293}\right)$$
$$E_a = \frac{2.303\times8.314\times323\times293\times0.477}{30}$$
$$= 28.8\ \text{kJ/mol}$$

Thus, option (d) is correct.

24. (b) At temperature T(K), rate constant are equal, hence

$$10^{13}\exp\left(\frac{-152300\ \text{J/mol}}{RT}\right)$$
$$= 10^{14}\exp\left(\frac{-157700\ \text{J/mol}}{RT}\right)$$
$$\exp\left(\frac{157700 - 152300}{RT}\right) = 10$$

Taking ln on both sides

$$\Rightarrow \ln_e \exp\left[\frac{157700 - 152300}{RT}\right]$$
$$= \ln 10 = 2.303\log_{10}10$$

or

$$\frac{157700 - 152300}{8.314T} = 2.303$$
$$T = 282.03\,\text{K}$$
$$\approx 282\,\text{K}$$

25. (c) Statements I, IV and V are correct but statements II and III are incorrect.

- The correct Statement of II is given in I part of the question.
- Increasing the temperature of the substances increases the

fraction of molecules, which collide with energies greater than E_a.

26. (a) The number of reacting species (atoms, ions or molecules) taking part in an elementary reaction is called molecularity and it has no major influence on the rate of reaction.

27. (d) Order and molecularity can be same only for elementary reaction and it is different for complex reaction.
However, order is determined experimentally and molecularity is the sum of the stoichiometric coefficient of rate determining elementary step.
Hence, (A) is false but (R) is true.

28. (c) Molecularity of a reaction is always a whole number.

29. (b) Rate = rate constant × [concentration]^n

$$1.02\times10^{-4} = 3.4\times10^{-5}\times[N_2O_5]$$

(unit of rate constant shows that it is a first order reaction)

$$[N_2O_5] = \frac{1.02\times10^{-4}}{3.4\times10^{-5}} = 3\ \text{mol L}^{-1}$$

30. (d) Colliding molecules must have energy greater than activation energy with proper orientation of collision.

31. (a) $k = Ae^{-E_a/RT}$

$$\log k = \left[\frac{-E_a}{R}\right]\frac{1}{T} + \log A$$

Hence, graph of $\log k$ *vs* $\frac{1}{T}$ is linear, indicating the dependence of k with T. Since, slope $= \frac{-E_a}{R}$, the activation energy can be calculated with this plot.
Thus, both (A) and (R) are true and (R) is the correct explanation of (A).

32. (a) I, II, V – represent first order reaction.
III – represents zero order reaction.
IV – represents second order reaction.

33. (c) Conc. is reduced from 0.12 M to 0.06 M in 10 hr.
i.e. $t_{1/2} = 10\,\text{hr}$.
Conc. reduced from 0.12 M to 0.03 M is 20 hr.
So, $t_{3/4} = 20\ \text{hr} = 2\times t_{1/2}$
This is valid condition only for first order reaction.
Hence, order is 1.

34. (d) For a zero order reaction,

$$A \longrightarrow P$$

$$r = -\frac{d[A]}{dt} = k \text{ or } -d[A] = kdt$$

When $t = 0, [A] = [A]_0$
At $t = t, [A] = [A]$

Hence, $\int_{[A]_0}^{[A]} d[A] = \int_{t=0}^{t=t} k\,dt$ or

$[A]_0 - [A] = kt$ or $[A] = [A_0] - kt$
On comparing, $y = mx + c$
slope $(m) = -k$
Thus, plot of $[A]$ *vs* t is linear with negative slope $(-k)$ and intercept $(c) = [A]_0$

35. (a) Half-life gets doubled on doubling initial concentration.
It means, $t_{1/2} \propto [A]$, and we know, $t_{1/2} \propto [A]^{1-n}$ (where, n is order of reaction). Therefore, $n = 0$ (zero order reaction).

36. (b) $k = Ae^{-E_a/RT}$

where, E_a = activation energy, i.e. the minimum amount of energy required by reactant molecules to participate in a reaction.

37. (b) $\Delta H = E_f - E_b$
$\Rightarrow -50 = 349 - E_b$
$\Rightarrow E_b = 399\ \text{kJ/mol}$

38. (d) The rate of a zero-order reaction is independent of the concentration of the reaction. The reaction proceeds at constant rate through out.
For zero order reaction,

$$t_{1/2} = \frac{[A]_0}{2k}$$

Hence, if in a zero order reaction, the concentration of the reactant is doubled, the half-life period is also doubled.
Hence, both statements I and II are correct.

39. (c) Collision theory says that chemical reactions occur by the collisions between atoms and molecules, so, more the number of collisions, faster is the rate of the chemical reactions. It depends on frequency at which reactant molecules collide.

40. (c) $x = 0.1 - 0.08 = 0.02$ M

$$k = \frac{x}{t} = \frac{0.02}{10}$$
$$= 2\times10^{-3}\ \text{M min}^{-1}$$
$$\therefore \quad t_{1/2} = \frac{[A]_0}{2k} = \frac{0.1}{2\times2\times10^{-3}}$$
$$= 25\ \text{min}$$
$$t_{\text{completion}} = 2\times t_{1/2} = 50\ \text{min}$$

41. (c) Given, $t_{1/2} = 15$ minutes
Total time $(t) = 1\ \text{hr} = 60$ min

$$n = \frac{60}{15} = 4$$

From the formula $\frac{N}{N_0} = \left(\frac{1}{2}\right)^n$

$$= \left(\frac{1}{2}\right)^4$$

42. (b) A catalyst lowers the activation energy of the reaction following Arrhenius theory.
$\therefore$ Rate of reaction $\propto \frac{1}{E_a}$

43. (b) $t_{1/2} = \frac{[A]_0}{2k} = \frac{2}{2\times2\times10^{-2}}$
$= 50\,\text{sec}$

44. (d) $k = Ae^{-E_a/RT}$ if $E_a = 0$, then $k = A$ independent of temperature.

45. (b) A straight line plot of $[A]$ *vs* t with negative slope for a reaction is zero order.

46. (c) For a first order reaction

$$k = \frac{2.303}{t}\log\frac{a}{a-x}$$

when $t = t_{1/2}$

$$k = \frac{2.303}{t_{1/2}} \log \frac{a}{a - \frac{a}{2}}$$

or $t_{1/2} = \frac{2.303}{k} \log 2 = \frac{\ln 2}{k}$

47. (d) Rate law equation is given by

$$\frac{dC}{dt} = k[A]^x[B]^y$$

$\therefore \frac{dC}{dt}$ for C at various concentration are

$1.3\times10^{-3} = k(0.1)^x(0.1)^y$ ...(i)

$1.3\times10^{-3} = k(0.1)^x(0.2)^y$ ...(ii)

$2.6\times10^{-3} = k(0.2)^x(0.1)^y$ ...(iii)

Solving for x [divide Eq. (iii) by Eq. (i)]

$$\frac{2.6\times10^{-3}}{1.3\times10^{-3}} = \frac{k(0.2)^x(0.1)^y}{k(0.1)^x(0.1)^y}$$

$$2 = 2^x$$

$\Rightarrow \quad x = 1$

Solving for y [divide Eq. (iii) by Eq. (ii)]

$$\frac{2.6\times10^{-3}}{1.3\times10^{-3}} = \frac{k(0.2)^x(0.1)^y}{k(0.1)^x(0.2)^y}$$

$$2 = (2)^x\left(\frac{0.1}{0.2}\right)^y$$

$$1 = (0.5)^y$$

$$(1)^0 = (0.5)^y$$

$$y = 0$$

Thus, $\frac{dC}{dt} = k[A]^1[B]^0 = k[A]^1$

48. (b) Rate of reaction

$$(r_1) = k[A]^m[B]^n$$

After $A \to 3A \quad B \to 2B$ ...(i)

$$r_2 = k\times[3A]^m\times[2B]^n$$

According to question,

$$r_2 = 72\times r_1$$

$k\times[3A]^m\,[2B]^n = 72r_1$ ...(ii)

On dividing Eqs. (ii) by (i) we get,

$$3^m\times2^n = 72$$

then, $m = 2$ and $n = 3$.

49. (b) For the reaction

$$2NO + Cl_2 \longrightarrow 2NOCl$$

Rate $= k[Cl_2]^m[NO]^n$ ...(i)

where, m and n are order of reaction w.r.t. Cl_2 and NO, respectively.

From the given data,

$1\times10^{-3} = k[0.05]^m[0.05]^n$ ...(ii)

$3\times10^{-3} = k[0.15]^m[0.05]^n$ ...(iii)

$9\times10^{-3} = k[0.05]^m[0.15]^n$ ...(iv)

By Eqs. (ii) and (iii), we get

$$m = 1$$

By Eqs. (ii) and (iv) we get

$$n = 2$$

Hence, the order w.r.t. NO is 2 and w.r.t. Cl_2 is 1.

50. (a) $A + B \longrightarrow$ Product

Rate $= k[A]^1[B]^{-1}$

$\therefore$ Order $= 1 + (-1) = 0$

Ch-4 p-Block Elements-II

Topical Follow Thru

Test-1

1. (b) Statement (b) is incorrect. Since, nitrogen atom has 4 shared electron pairs in N_2O_5, thus the covalency of nitrogen is 4.

2. (d) Among the given statements I and II are correct while rest statements are incorrect.

III. In PCl_5, 3 equatorial and 2 axial bonds are present. These two axial bonds are repelled by equatorial bonds. So, axial bonds are weak and elongated.

IV. The electronegativity of N is 3.0, P is 2.1 and that of hydrogen is 2.1. This difference in electronegativity values makes N—H bond polar in nature.

However, in PH_3, P—H bonds make non-polar bonds because both P and H have almost the same value of electronegativity. Hence, PH_3 does not make hydrogen bonds.

V. Dissolution of NH_3 and PH_3 in water can be explained on the basis of H-bonding. NH_3 forms H-bond with water so it is soluble but PH_3 does not form H-bond with water, so it remains as gas and forms bubble in water.

3. (a) Only statement (a) is correct all the other statements can be corrected as,

(b) On heating it gives pyrophosphoric acid.

(c) Its basicity is three.

(d) It can act only as an oxidising agent and not as reducing agent.

4. (b) Dinitrogen monoxide $(N_2O) = +1$

Dinitrogen trioxide $(N_2O_3) = +3$

Dinitrogen tetraoxide $(N_2O_4) = +4$

Dinitrogen pentaoxide $(N_2O_5) = +5$

The correct match is

A-II, B-III, C-IV, D-I.

5. (d) Reducing character decreases down the group due to the decreases in bond dissociation enthalpy. The order of reducing character is as follows

$$NH_3 < PH_3 < AsH_3 < SbH_3 < BiH_3$$

6. (b) Among the given statements (b) is incorrect while rest are correct.
Its correct form is as follows
α-black phosphorus is formed when red phosphorus is heated in a sealed tube at 803 K.

7. (d) Among the given statements only (d) is the incorrect one.

The hybridisation of ammonia is sp^3.

N (with lone pair), H H H

(sp^3-hybridised)
Trigonal pyramidal structure

8. (a) Among the hydrides of group 15 elements, BiH_3 is the strongest reducing agent. This is because Bi has the largest size which makes Bi—H bond dissociation enthalpy lowest.
Here, both (A) and (R) are true and (R) is the correct explanation of (A).

9. (d) Both statements I and II are correct.
Since, pentavalent metal ion has higher polarising power than trivalent metal ion. Thus, PCl_5 is more covalent than PCl_3.
When PCl_5 is heated, PCl_3 is formed because in PCl_5, three bonds are equatorial and two are axial. When it is heated, the axial bonds are broken and PCl_3 is formed.

10. (a) The correct match is A-IV, B-I, C-II, D-III.

11. (d) Boiling point in (K)

NH_3	PH_3	AsH_3	SbH_3
238.5	185.5	210.6	254.6

Because SbH_3 has a greater molecular weight, the force of attraction between them is stronger. As a result, boiling point rises. Although NH_3 has a strong H-bond, SbH_3 has the greatest boiling point due to its heavier molecular weight. NH_3 has a boiling point 238.5 K and SbH_3 of 254.6 K

$SbH_3 > NH_3 > AsH_3 > PH_3$
(Order of boiling point)

12. (a) PCl_5 form five bonds by using the *d*-orbitals to "expand the octet" and have more places to put bonding pairs of electron. NCl_5 does not exist because there are no *d*-orbital in the second energy level. Therefore, there is no way to arrange five pairs of bonding electron around a nitrogen atom.

13. (a) Unlike NH_3, PH_3 molecules are not associated through hydrogen bonding in liquid state. That is why the boiling point of PH_3 is lower than NH_3.

14. (d)

N_2O_4 : $\ddot{O}=N(-\ddot{O}:)-N(-\ddot{O}:)=\ddot{O}$

NO_2 : $\ddot{O}=\dot{N}-\ddot{O}$

N_2O_5 : O=N(=O)–O–N(=O)=O

N_2O : $\overset{-1}{:\ddot{O}}-\overset{+1}{N}\equiv N:$ and $\ddot{O}=\overset{+}{N}=\overset{-}{N}$

Thus, the correct match is A-III, B-I, C-II, D-IV.

15. (a) Silver reacts with dilute nitric acid to liberate nitric oxide (NO) gas.

$$3Ag + 4HNO_3(\text{dil.}) \longrightarrow 3AgNO_3 + 2H_2O + NO\uparrow$$

16. (b) NO combines with Fe(II) ion to form the brown ring complex in an aqueous medium.

$$\underset{\text{(Brown ring)}}{Fe^{2+}} + NO + 6H_2O \longrightarrow [Fe(H_2O)_5NO]^{+2}$$

17. (d) Tetrabasic acid means acid having 4 replaceable hydrogen atom.
(a) Orthophosphorus acid → H_3PO_3
(b) Orthophosphoric acid → H_3PO_4
(c) Metaphosphoric acid → $(HPO_3)_n$
(d) Pyrophosphoric acid → $H_4P_2O_7$

18. (c) The reaction of heating of ammonium dichromate

$$\underset{\text{(Ammonium dichromate)}}{(NH_4)_2Cr_2O_7} \xrightarrow{\Delta} Cr_2O_3 + N_2 + 4H_2O$$

Ammonium dichromate $[(NH_4)_2Cr_2O_7]$ on heating yields chromic oxide (Cr_2O_3) which is green in colour and water along with the liberation of nitrogen gas.

19. (a) Aluminium forms a protective layer of aluminium oxide on exposure to concentrated nitric acid which now stops the reaction between aluminium and nitric acid.

$$2Al + \underset{\text{(conc.)}}{6HNO_3} \longrightarrow Al_2O_3 + 6NO_2 + 3H_2O$$

20. (b) In the Haber process for the manufacture of NH_3, Fe is used as a catalyst and Mo as a promoter.

21. (b) There is little difference in the strength of these acids because hydrogen in these acids are not all bounded to phosphorus.

22. (b) Bismuth does not show allotropy, other element show allotropy.
Nitrogen → α-nitrogen and β-nitrogen (solid crystalline forms)
Phosphorus → White, red and black forms
Arsenic → Yellow and grey forms
Antimony → Yellow and grey forms

23. (b) Orthophosphorus and pyrophosphorus have same number of P—OH bond in their structure (i.e. two).

So, option (b) is correct.

24. (d) Statements D and E are incorrect. Their correct forms are
- Due to inert pair effect lower oxidation state is more stable.
- Nitrogen belongs to 2nd period and cannot expand its octet.

25. (b) Reaction involved is

$$P_4 + \underset{\text{(Conc.)}}{20HNO_3} \xrightarrow{\Delta} 4H_3PO_4 + 20NO_2 + 4H_2O$$

Test-2

1. (c) The given oxides, SeO_2 and TeO_2 are acidic and amphoteric in nature respectively.

2. (b) The correct order of acidic character is

$$H_2O < H_2S < H_2Se < H_2Te.$$

The acidic character of hydrides depends upon the ability to donate H^+, hence depends upon strength between central atom and hydrogen bond which decreases down the group.

3. (d) Among the given statements only III is incorrect. The correct form is as follows

The covalency of oxygen is 2.

4. (c) (A) is true but (R) is false. Due to the smaller size of oxygen, the electron cloud is distributed over a small region of space, making electron density high which repels the incoming electrons.

5. (b) Among the given statements (b) is incorrect.

The stable form of sulphur is rhombic, which transforms to monoclinic sulphur, when heated above 369 K.

6. (d) Statement (d) is incorrect. The two oxygen-oxygen bond lengths in the ozone molecule are identical to each other, i.e. 128 pm.

7. (a) The complete reaction is as follows

$$H_2SO_4 + 2PCl_5 \longrightarrow SO_2Cl_2 + \underset{(X)}{2POCl_3} + 2HCl$$

Let, the oxidation state of P be y in $POCl_3\,(X)$.

$$y + (-2) + (-3) = 0$$
$$y = +5$$

The oxidation state of P in $POCl_3$ is +5.

8. (d) Both statement I and statement II are correct.

H_2O undergoes extensive H-bonding due to high electronegativity of O-atom and hence exists as a liquid. On the other hand, H_2S does not undergo H-bonding and hence exists as a discrete molecule and as gas.

Fluorine atom is smaller in size, so six F^- ions can surround a sulphur atom. The case is not so with chlorine atom due to its larger size. So, SF_6 is known but SCl_6 is not known due to interionic repulsion between larger Cl^- ions.

9. (a) Among the given statement (a) is correct about peroxodisulphuric acid ($H_2S_2O_8$). Its structure is

($H_2S_2O_8$)
Peroxodisulphuric acid

10. (c) It is beneficial because ozone cuts out the ultraviolet radiation of the sun.

Ozone protects us from harmful UV radiation from the sun.

11. (b) Statement I is corrrect but Statement II is incorrect.

$$\alpha\text{-sulphur} \underset{<369\,K}{\overset{>369\,K}{\rightleftharpoons}} \beta\text{-sulphur}$$

At room temperature α-sulphur (rhombic) is most stable form.

12. (a) Correct order of electron gain enthalpy is

$O < S > Se > Te$ or $S > Se > Te > O$

Generally electron gain enthalpy decreases on moving down the group. But oxygen shows least electron gain enthalpy due to small size of atom.

13. (a) The given oxides can be classified as

Neutral oxides : N_2O, NO, CO,

Amphoteric oxide : TeO_2

Acidic oxides : SeO_2, SO_3, SO_2

Thus, total number of acidic oxides are 3.

14. (d) The correct statement regarding OF_2 is given in A, B and D. Correct statement of C and E is :

- Oxidation state of 'O' is +2.
- Molecular geometry is tetrahedral.

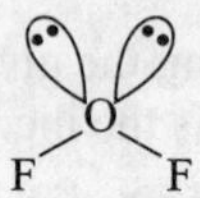

15. (b) The greater the element-element bond strength, the higher is the tendency towards catenation. As the size increase from S to Te, the bond dissociation energy decreases. O—O bond energy is however, smaller than that of S—S because of interelectronic repulsions within the smaller size of oxygen atoms.

Thus, sulphur has a maximum tendency towards catenation.

Test-3

1. (c) In general, higher is the oxidation state, more is the covalent character of the oxide. I_2O_7 and I_2O_9 do not exist. I_2O_4 is ionic in nature. The only covalent oxide of iodine is I_2O_5.

2. (a) The reaction involved is as follows

$$\underset{\text{(Hot, conc.)}}{6NaOH} + 3\overset{0}{Cl_2} \longrightarrow 5Na\overset{+1\,-1}{Cl} + \underset{\text{Sodium chlorate}}{Na\overset{+1\,+5}{ClO_3}} + 3H_2O$$

Thus, oxidation state of Cl changes from 0 to −1 and +5.

3. (d) When Cl_2 reacts with excess of ammonia NH_4Cl is formed and H_2 is released.

The reaction involved is as follows

$$\underset{\text{(Excess)}}{8NH_3} + 3Cl_2 \longrightarrow 6NH_4Cl + N_2\uparrow$$

4. (b) ClF_3 :

Hybridisation = sp^3d

Structure = Bent T-shaped

IF_5 :

Hybridisation = sp^3d^2

Structure = Square pyramidal

IF_7 :

Hybridisation = sp^3d^3

Structure = Pentagonal bipyramidal

I_3^- :

Hybridisation = sp^3d

Structure = Linear

5. (a) The increasing order of oxidising power of oxoacids of chlorine is

$\overset{+7}{HClO_4} < \overset{+5}{HClO_3} < \overset{+3}{HClO_2} < \overset{+1}{HClO}$

It is because with the increase in the oxidation number of halogen atom in oxoacids, oxidising power decreases.

6. (d) Option (d) is not the correct use of chlorine rest all the given statements are the correct uses of chlorine.

Correct statement (d) is :

Helium is used for arc welding.

7. (c) Fluorine does not forms number of stable oxoacids. It form only two stable oxoacids, i.e. OF_2 and O_2F_2.

8. (d) Hydrofluoric acid is one of the most dangerous acid known. It needs to be treated differently then even strong acids like sulphuric and hydrochloric. HF react with many materials, therefore avoid contact with glass, concrete, metals, water, other acids, oxidiser, reducers, alkalis and ceramic.

9. (d)

- Fluorine reacts with water to give the product like hydrogen fluoride, oxygen and ozone.
- As fluorine is the most electronegative halogen in its respective group so its reaction with water is different from other halogens.
- The reaction of fluorine with water is as

$$\underset{\text{(Fluorine)}}{2F_2(g)} + \underset{\text{(Water)}}{2H_2O(l)} \longrightarrow \underset{\text{(Hydrogen fluoride)}}{4HF(aq)} + \underset{\text{(Oxygen)}}{O_2(g)}$$

$$3F_2(g) + 3H_2O(l) \longrightarrow 6HF(aq) + \underset{\text{Ozone}}{O_3(g)}$$

10. (a) The reactivity of halogen decrease with increase in atomic number of halogen. Thus, the correct increasing order of reactivity will be

$I_2 < Br_2 < Cl_2 < F_2$.

11. (a) The stability of oxoacids depends upon the number of resonating structures of its conjugate base.

So, the order of stability is

$HClO_4 > HClO_3 > HClO_2 > HClO$.

12. (a) Fluorine (F_2) is known as super halogen as it is highly reactive. Highly electronegative fluorine forms compounds with almost all other elements (including some noble gases).

13. (b) van der Waals' forces are stronger on going down the groups in halogens. van der Waals' forces depends on mass. When the size and weight of the molecule are larger, then the van der Waals' forces among the molecules are very stronger.

14. (d) The central atom in F_2O is sp^3-hybridised in ClO_2 is sp^2-hybridised, in BrF_3 is sp^3d-hybridised and in IF_5 is sp^3d^2-hybridised.

Then, the correct match is

A-II, B-I, C-IV, D-III.

15. (b) Both (A) and (R) are true but (R) is not the correct explanation of (A).

Test-4

1. (d) Xenon does not form fluorides such as XeF_3 and XeF_5.

All the filled orbitals of Xe have paired electrons. The promotion of 1, 2 or 3 electrons from the $5p$-filled orbitals to the $5d$ vacant orbitals will give rise to 2, 4 and 6 half-filled orbitals. Therefore, Xe can combine with even number of F atoms but not odd.

2. (d) The reaction given in option (d) is incorrect. Correct reaction is :

$$2XeOF_2 + SiO_2 \longrightarrow 2XeO_2F_2 + SiF_4$$

3. (a) The hybridisation of XeF_4 and XeF_6 respectively are sp^3d^2 and sp^3d^3.

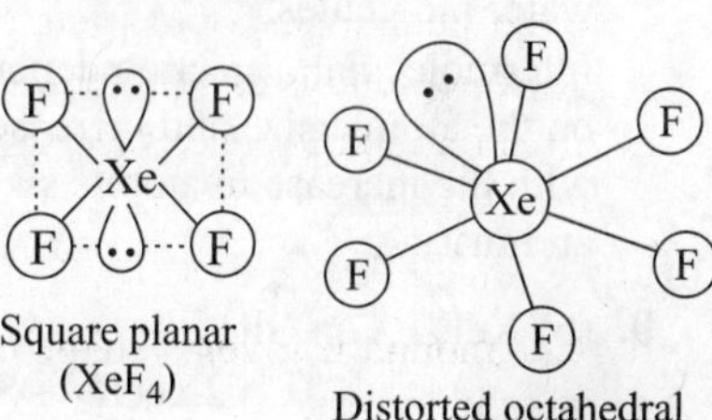

Square planar (XeF_4)

Distorted octahedral (XeF_6)

4. (a) The maximum temperature at which gas can be liquified is called its critical temperature.

The gas which have high boiling point will change into liquid first and so critical temperature of the gas will be more T_C α boiling point and boiling point α molecular weight.

So, Kr liquifies first.

5. (a) Among the given elements, He forms least number of compounds due to small atomic size, high ionisation energy and absence of d-orbitals.

6. (d) The shape of XeF_2 is linear with 3 lone pairs of electrons.

The shape of XeF_4 is square planar with 2 lone pairs of electrons.

The shape of XeF_6 is distorted octahedral with 1 lone pair of electron.

7. (a) The correct order of solubility in water for He, Ne, Ar, Kr, Xe is Xe > Kr > Ar > Ne > He.

Solubility increase with increase in the atomic number on moving down the group due to increase in the intermolecular attraction between inert gas molecules and water molecules.

Intermolecular attraction depend on the atomic size and increase with the increase in atomic size and mass.

8. (b) $XeF_6(X) + SiO_2 \longrightarrow 2XeOF_4 + SiF_4$

So, the compound X is XeF_6. Its hybridisation is sp^3d^3 and geometry is distorted octahedral.

9. (b) Traces of krypton are found in various minerals, the most important. Source of krypton is earth's atmosphere. Air is also the source for the other noble gases, with the exception of helium which is obtained from natural gas and radon which is obtained as a byproduct of the decay of radioactive elements so krypton is not obtained during radioactive disintegration. It is radon formed during radioactive disintegration.

10. (a) Among the given options Rn is not found in atmosphere.

It is radioactive element which is obtained by the disintegration of radium.

$${}_{88}Ra^{226} \longrightarrow {}_{86}Rn^{222} + {}_2He^4$$

11. (b) Partial hydrolysis,

$$XeF_4 + H_2O \longrightarrow XeOF_2 + 2HF$$

Complete hydrolysis,

$$6XeF_4 + 12H_2O \longrightarrow 4Xe + 2XeO_3 + 3O_2 + 24HF$$

Thus, XeF_4 on partial hydrolysis produces $XeOF_2$ while on complete hydrolysis it produces XeO_3.

12. (d) XeF_2 has sp^3d-hybridisation with linear shape.

13. (c) Xenon is an inert gas. Its electronic configuration is [Kr] $4d^{10}5s^25p^6$.

All orbitals that are filled have paired electron when one, two or three electrons are promoted from $5p$ (filled) to $5d$ (empty) orbital, two, four and six half-filled orbitals are formed respectively. Xenon can combine with even number of F atoms to form XeF_2, XeF_4 or XeF_6.

It cannot combine with odd no. of F atoms.

14. (c) Noble gas does not form compound because it posses eight electrons in the valence shell so these are chemically inert but only xenon form compound.

XeF_2, $XeOF_2$, XeF_4, $XeOF_4$, XeF_6, XeO_3

15. (c) Helium is twice as heavy as hydrogen, but its lifting power in is 92% of that of hydrogen.

Helium has the lowest melting and boiling point of any element which makes liquid helium an ideal coolant for many extremely low temperature application such as super conducting magnet and cryogenic research where temperature close to absolute zero are needed.

Chapter Break Thru

1. (a) Sulphur in vapour phase exists as S_2 molecule which has two unpaired electrons in the anti-bonding π^* orbitals. Therefore, it shows paramagnetism.

2. (d) Option (d) is incorrect match because sulphur has three allotropes, i.e. rhombic (α), monoclinic (β) and plastic (γ). Oxygen does not form monoclinic (β) allotropes.

3. (d) Both Statement I and Statement II are correct. Ozone is a powerful oxidising agent which when dissolved in water produces a broad spectrum biocide that destroys all bacteria, viruses etc. Ozone is thermodynamically unstable. Therefore, ozone decomposed into oxygen results in the liberation of heat and increases entropy. During the reaction change in Gibbs free energy is negative.

Therefore, high concentration of ozone can be dangerously explosive.

4. (d) As we move from top to bottom in 16th group atomic size increases, the E—H bond dissociation energy decreases. Hence, E—H bond breaks more easily. Thus, the thermal stability of hydrides of group 16 element decreases down the group. Correct order of thermal stability is

$H_2O > H_2S > H_2Se > H_2Te > H_2Po$.

5. (b) When oxides of non-metal dissolve in water they form acidic solutions. Therefore, nature of non-metal oxides are acidic. e.g. P_4O_{10}, N_2O_5, SO_3.

$$P_4O_{10} + 6H_2O \longrightarrow 4H_3PO_4$$
$$N_2O_5 + H_2O \longrightarrow 2HNO_3$$
$$SO_3 + H_2O \longrightarrow H_2SO_4$$

Amphoteric oxides These oxides react with acid as well as base to produce salts and water. e.g. Al_2O_3, SnO_2.

$$Al_2O_3 + 6HCl \longrightarrow 2AlCl_3 + 3H_2O$$

$$Al_2O_3 + 6NaOH \xrightarrow{3H_2O} 2Na_3[Al(OH)_6]$$

Hence, option (b) is correct.

6. (c) Pt is a noble metal and does not react very easily. All other elements Zn, Ti, Fe are quite reactive. Hence, oxygen does not react with Pt directly.

7. (d) Both Statement I and Statement II are correct.

8. (a) The correct match is A-II, B-III, C-I, D-IV.

A. Marshall's acid ($H_2S_2O_8$) or Peroxodisulphuric acid.

B. Oleum ($H_2S_2O_7$) or Pyrosulphuric acid

C. Caro's acid (H_2SO_5) or Peroxomonosulphuric acid.

D. Dithionic acid ($H_2S_2O_6$)

Hence, option (a) is correct.

9. (d) On moving down the group electron gain enthalpy value decreases. Cl has more negative electron gain enthalpy than F. This is because of small size of F which causes electron- repulsion. So, the order follows

$I < Br < F < Cl \longrightarrow$ Negative electron gain enthalpy.

10. (a) Statements I, II and V are correct while III and IV are incorrect.

- The ionic character of halide decreases on going down the group as $MF > MCl > MBr > MI$. [where, M is a monovalent metal] This is so because polarisation of halide ions increases down the group.
- The Cl_2 is less reactive than ClF. Interhalogen compounds are more reactive than pure halogen molecule as the bonds in the interhalogen compounds are polar and weaker than pure halogen compounds.

Hence, option (a) is correct.

11. (d) Order of acidic character, thermal stability and reducing nature of hydrogen halide are correct but order of boiling point is incorrect because HF shows H-bonding therefore, its boiling point is higher as compare to other halogen halides.

Boiling point increases down the group (except in case of HF). So, correct order of boiling point will be $HCl < HBr < HI < HF$.

12. (b) Among the given analogies (b) is incorrect. Its correct form is as follows

$HOClO_3$: Perchloric acid :: $HOBrO_2$: Bromic acid

(a) Negative electron gain enthalpy of fluorine is less than that of chlorine due to small size of fluorine atom. It has very high inter-electronic repulsion in the relatively small $2p$-orbitals.

Hence, incoming electron experience less attraction from the nucleus. Despite of lower value of its electron gain enthalpy with negative sign, fluorine (F_2) is a stronger oxidising agent than Cl_2.

It is due to

(i) lower enthalpy of dissociation of F—F bond.

(ii) high hydration enthalpy of F^- ion.

(c) **Structure of BrF_3**

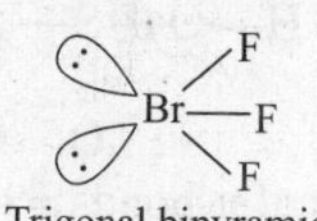

Trigonal bipyramidal

Structure of ClF_5

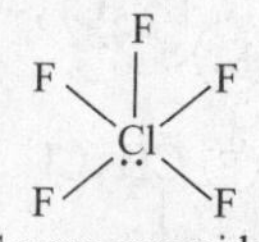

Square pyramidal

(d) ClF_3 is used for the production of UF_6 whereas SO_2 is used in bleaching of wool and silk.

13. (c) Among the given statements only V is incorrect.

Electronegativity of both nitrogen as well as chlorine is 3.0. But only nitrogen forms hydrogen bonding not chlorine because the atomic size of N is less as compared to Cl.

I. AgCl (horn silver) and KCl, $MgCl_2 \cdot 6H_2O$ (carnalite) are source of Cl_2.

II. In Deacon process,

$$4HCl + O_2 \xrightarrow[723\text{ K}]{CuCl_2} 2Cl_2 + 2H_2O$$

III. $Cl_2 + H_2O \longrightarrow 2HCl + [O]$

Coloured matte + [O] $\longrightarrow$ Colourless matte (permanent bleaching action)

IV. $$\underset{\text{(Excess)}}{NH_3 + 3Cl_2} \longrightarrow NCl_3 + 3HCl$$

$$\underset{\text{(Excess)}}{8NH_3} + 3Cl_2 \longrightarrow N_2 + 6NH_4Cl$$

Thus, option (c) is correct.

14. (d) *Syn* gas is not prepared by chlorine. It is a mixture of hydrogen and carbon monoxide in various ratios.

Gases which are prepared by Cl_2 and have poisonous nature are as follow

(a) $$CO + Cl_2 \xrightarrow[\text{Charcoal}]{h\nu} \underset{\text{Phosgene gas}}{COCl_2}$$

(b) $$\underset{\text{Obtained from } Cl_2}{CHCl_3} + HNO_3 \longrightarrow \underset{\text{(Tear gas)}}{CCl_3NO_2} + H_2O$$

(c) $S_8 + 4Cl_2 \longrightarrow 4S_2Cl_2$

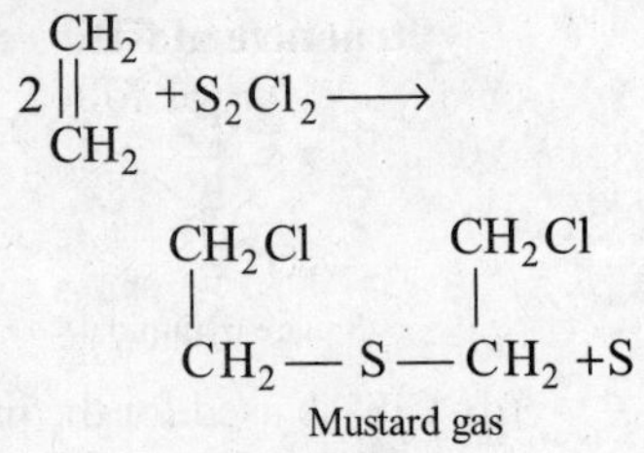

$$2\,\underset{CH_2}{\overset{CH_2}{||}} + S_2Cl_2 \longrightarrow \underset{\text{Mustard gas}}{CH_2Cl{-}CH_2{-}S{-}CH_2{-}CH_2Cl} + S$$

Thus, option (d) is correct.

15. (d) HCl forms insoluble chlorides, i.e. AgCl, $PbCl_2$ and Hg_2Cl_2 with soluble salt of Ag, Pb and Hg. NH_3 on reaction with HCl gives white fumes of NH_4Cl.

16. (a) The acidic strength of oxoacid of the same halogen increase with the increase in oxidation number of the halogen.
Thus, the correct order is

$$\overset{+1}{HOCl} < \overset{+3}{HClO_2} < \overset{+5}{HClO_3} < \overset{+7}{HClO_4}$$

17. (a) According to Le-Chatelier's principle, the contact process must be carried out at low temperature (720 K) and high pressure (2 bar) which gives more yield of SO_3. During the reaction V_2O_5 catalyst is used.
Thus, option (a) is correct.

18. (b) Statement (b) is correct, whereas (a), (c), (d) statements are incorrect because when mercury comes in contact with ozone, it loses its meniscus and sticks to the glass tube due to formation of mercurous oxide.

19. (a) Inert gases are sparingly soluble in water and their solubility increases with increase in atomic number.

20. (b) The correct match is
A-II, B-III, C-I, D-IV.

A. $XeOF_2 \rightarrow$ Trigonal bipyramidal arrangement and has T-shape (sp^3d)

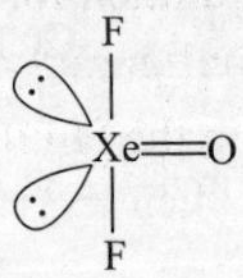

F, Xe=O, F (structure with two lone pairs)

B. $XeOF_4 \rightarrow$ Square pyramidal (sp^3d^2)

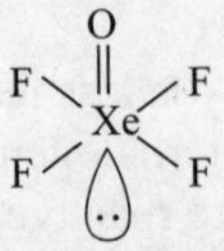

O, F, F, Xe, F, F (structure with one lone pair)

C. $XeO_3 \rightarrow$ Pyramidal (sp^3)

Xe, O, O, O (structure with one lone pair)

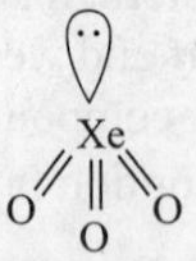

D. $XeF_4 \rightarrow$ Square planar (sp^3d^2)

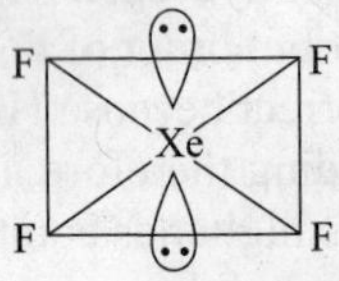

F, F, Xe, F, F (structure with two lone pairs)

21. (b) Among the given statements, only statement (b) is incorrect. Radon is a radioactive element. Hence, is not found in atmosphere.

22. (a) Both (A) and (R) are true and (R) is the correct explanation of (A).
O_2 molecules are held together by weak van der Waals' forces because of small size and high electronegativity of oxygen. This van der Waals' forces of attraction can be easily overcome by collisions of the molecules at room temperature therefore, O_2 exists as a gas at room temperature.
In contrast, sulphur shows catenation and forms stronger S—S bonds. Due to catenation, sulphur forms octa-atomic S_8 molecules having 8 membered puckered ring structure.
Because of its bigger size, the force of attraction holding S_8 molecules are much stronger. Hence, sulphur is a solid at room temperature.

23. (d) Correct order is (d).

H_2SO_6, H—O—S(=O)(=O)—S(=O)(=O)—OH,

Number of π-bonds = 4.

H_2SO_5, H—O—S(=O)(=O)—O—O—H,

Number of π-bonds = 2

H_2SO_4, H—O—S(=O)(=O)—O—H,

Number of π-bonds = 2

24. (a)

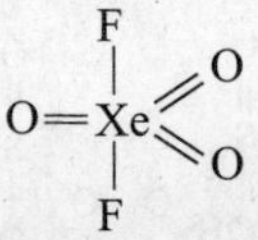

XeO_3F_2: O=Xe(=O)(=O) with F above and F below

So, bond pairs = 5, π-bonds = 3 and lone pairs = 0.

25. (a) Oxygen family is also known as chalcogen family. O, Se, S, Te and Po are chalcogen family member.

26. (a) At room temperature, water is liquid and has boiling point 373 K because of hydrogen bonding. But H_2S is a gas and it has no hydrogen bonding. So, boiling point of H_2S is less than 300 K (boiling point of H_2S is –60°C).

27. (a) H_2O does not have reducing property. This is because 0 is stable in +2 state while other elements (S, Se and Te) generally favour positive states hence they act as reducing agents.

28. (a) The *X* and *Y* are respectively N_2O and NO_2.
Thus, the oxidation state of N in *X* and *Y* are respectively.

$$4Zn + \underset{\text{(dil.)}}{10HNO_3} \longrightarrow 4Zn(NO_3)_2 + 5H_2O + \underset{(X)}{\overset{+1}{N_2O}}$$

$$Zn + \underset{\text{(conc.)}}{4HNO_3} \longrightarrow Zn(NO_3)_2 + 2H_2O + \underset{(Y)}{\overset{+4}{2NO_2}}$$

29. (b) Among the given statements only (II) is incorrect as nitrogen show catenation properties less than phosphorus due to unavailability of *d*-orbital.

30. (a) Among the 15 group elements nitrogen does not show any allotropy due to its weak N—N single bond.

31. (a) Nitrous acid undergo disproportionation reaction in acidic medium giving nitric acid (X), nitric oxide (Y) and H_2O. During this reaction the oxidation state of N changes from +3 to +5 and +2.

$$3\overset{+3}{HNO_2} \longrightarrow \underset{(X)}{\overset{+5}{HNO_3}} + \underset{(Y)}{2\overset{+2}{NO}} + H_2O$$

32. (a) Both (A) and (R) are true and (R) is the correct explanation of (A).
As the electronegativity decreases and atomic size increases on moving down the group therefore, there is a gradual decreases in the force of repulsion between the shared pair of electron around the central atom. Thus, bond angle decreases as we move down the group.

33. (c) Statement I is incorrect while statement II is correct.
PCl_5 has no lone-pair on the central atom but has empty d-orbital in valence shell. So, that it can accept a pair of electrons (from a Lewis base). Hence, PCl_5 act as a Lewis acid.
BiH_3 is a strongest reducing agent among group-15 hydrides. It is because as we move down the group, the M—H bond can break more easily to evolve H_2 gas which acts as the reducing.

34. (a) Very pure nitrogen can be produced by thermal decomposition of $Ba(N_3)_2$. The reaction involved is as follows

$$Ba(N_3)_2 \xrightarrow[\text{decomposition}]{\text{Thermal}} Ba + 3N_2$$

35. (a) $2NO + N_2O_4 \xrightarrow{250\text{ K}} \underset{(A)}{2N_2O_3}$

$$2Pb(NO_3)_2 \xrightarrow{673\text{ K}} \underset{(B)}{4NO_2} + 2PbO + O_2$$

$$2HNO_3 + P_2O_5 \longrightarrow 2HPO_3 + \underset{(C)}{N_2O_5}$$

36. (b) N_2O_4 and N_2O_3 have N—N bond.

N_2O $:\ddot{N}{=}N{=}\ddot{O} \longleftrightarrow N{\equiv}\overset{+}{N}{-}\ddot{O}:^-$

N_2O_4 $O_2N{-}NO_2 \longleftrightarrow$ (resonance structure)

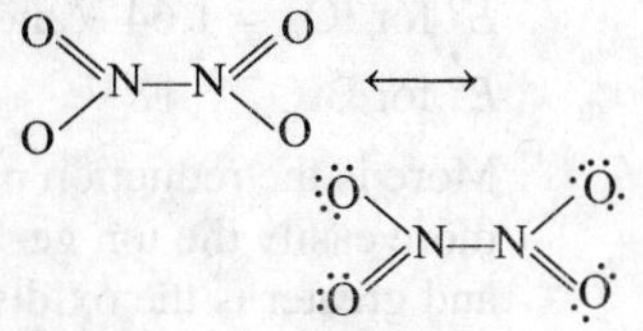

N_2O_3 $O{=}N{-}NO_2 \longleftrightarrow$ (resonance structure)

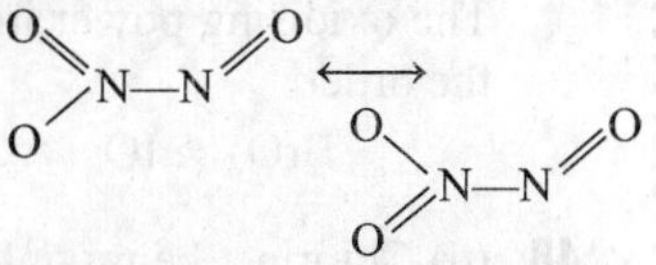

37. (a) Recovery of NH_3 from Solvay process is

$$\underset{\text{Ammonium chloride}}{2NH_4Cl} + \underset{\text{Calcium hydroxide}}{Ca(OH)_2} \longrightarrow 2NH_3 + \underset{\text{Calcium chloride}}{CaCl_2} + H_2O$$

So, by-product is $CaCl_2$ and H_2O.

38. (a) The reaction involved is as follows

$$\underset{(A)}{XeF_6} + H_2O \longrightarrow XeOF_4 + 2HF$$

Thus, the compound (A) is XeF_6. It has one lone pair.

39. (d) Among the given statements only III is correct while rest are incorrect.
PCl_5 have axial bonds which are weaker than equatorial bonds, because the axial bond are longer than equatorial one as they experience more repulsion.

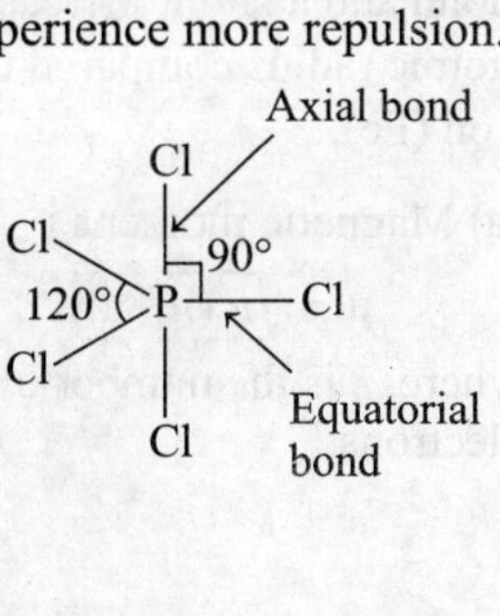

Axial bond; 90°; 120°; Equatorial bond

40. (a) The structure of given compounds are as follow

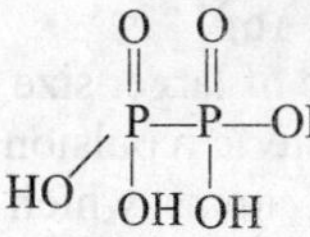

($H_4P_2O_6$) 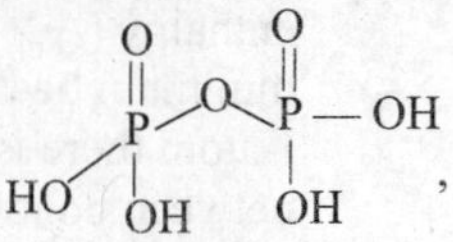 ($H_4P_2O_7$) 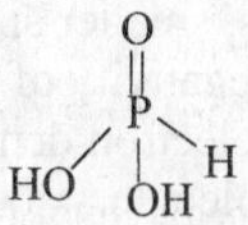 (H_3PO_3)

41. (d) HO—P(=O)(H)—O—P(=O)(H)—OH

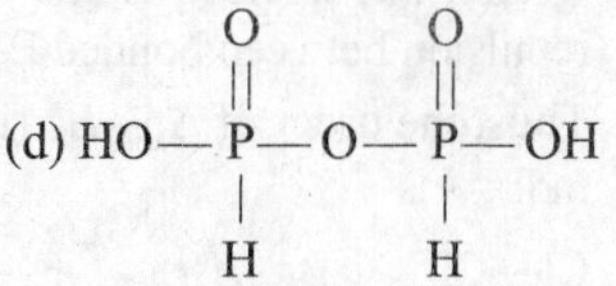

($H_4P_2O_5$)

Due to presence of P—H bond in $H_4P_2O_5$, it acts as a reducing agent and hence reduces $AgNO_3$ to metallic Ag which forms silver mirror.

42. (b) $Br_2 + 5F_2$ (excess) $\longrightarrow 2BrF_5$
Due to highly reactive nature of Br F_5, it absorbs moisture from surrounding results into the formation of $HBrO_3$.

43. (b) The reaction will take place as follows

$$P_4 + \underset{\text{(Thionyl chloride)}}{10SO_2Cl_2} \longrightarrow \underset{(A)}{4PCl_5} + 10SO_2$$

$$\underset{(A)}{PCl_5} + H_2O \longrightarrow POCl_3 + 2HCl$$

$$POCl_3 + 3H_2O \longrightarrow \underset{\substack{\text{Phosphoric acid}\\(B)}}{H_3PO_4} + 3HCl$$

44. (b) The structure of perchloric acid is

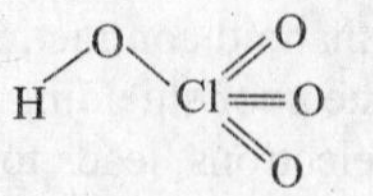

H—O—Cl(=O)₃

Thus, the number of Cl=O bond is 3.

45. (b) Statement (b) is correct.
$1s^2$ configuration for helium and ns^2np^6 configuration for all other elements in the family contributing to lack of chemical reactivity.

46. (d) Among halogens (F_2, Cl_2, Br_2 and I_2), bond dissociation enthalpy ($\Delta_{diss}H°$) of I_2 is minimum because of larger size of I-atom there is a steric repulsion between bonded I-atoms, which makes I—I bond weakest. Whereas, smaller size and highest electronegativity of F-atom cause highest electron density on F-atom of F_2 molecule.

As a result, F—F bond becomes weaker due to electrostatic repulsion between bonded F-atoms. Thus, the order of $\Delta_{diss}H°$ (in kJ mol^{-1}) is

Cl—Cl > Br—Br > F—F > I—I
(24.26) (192.3) (158.8) (151.1)
Electrostatic repulsion (F—F); Steric repulsion (I—I)

47. (d) The oxidising power of perhalates can be explained on the basis of electrode potential data for the reaction.

$$XO_4^- + 2H^+ + 2e^- \longrightarrow XO_3^- + H_2O$$

$E°$ for $ClO_4^- = 1.23$ V,
$E°$ for $IO_4^- = 1.64$ V and
$E°$ for $BrO_4^- = 1.8$ V.

More is the reduction potential, more easily the ion get reduced and greater is the oxidising power. The oxidising power increase in the order

$$BrO_4^- > IO_4^- > ClO_4^-$$

48. (d) Chlorine, being only a slightly stronger oxidising agent than bromine cannot oxidise it to +7 oxidation state as is required for the formation of the compound $BrCl_7$.

49. (a) Correct match is A-I, B-III, C-IV, D-II.

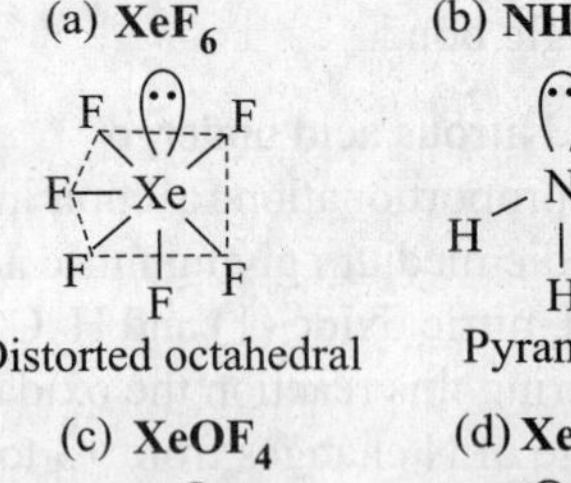

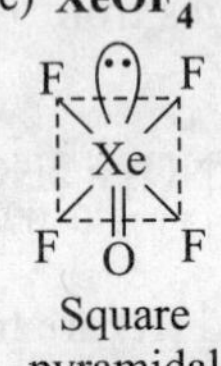

50. (c) Due to interelectronic repulsions in the relatively small F atom, its negative electron gain enthalpy is lower than that of Cl.

Ch-5 *d* and *f*-Block Elements

Topical Follow Thru

Test-1

1. (d) Statement given in option (d) is incorrect while all other statements are correct. The correct form of statement (d) is
Most of the transition elements show variable oxidation state.

2. (c) The anomaly in first ionisation enthalpy arises primarily due to lanthanoid contraction in Hf.

Lanthanoid contraction is caused by the poor shielding of 4*f*-electrons, leads to a smaller than expected atomic size for Hf. This increased effective nuclear charge makes it harder to remove an electron from Hf, resulting in a higher ionisation enthalpy.

3. (d) As electrons are added to the 3*d*-orbitals, they start to occupy the same orbitals with opposite spins. This leads to increased electron- electron repulsion within the 3*d*-subshell. While the effective nuclear charge increases, the 3*d*-electrons are not very effective at shielding each other from the nucleus's pull.

In the case of cobalt (Co), the increase in electron-electron repulsion due to the addition of another electron to the 3*d*-subshell slightly outweighs the increased nuclear charge. This results in a small expansion of the electron cloud and a slight increase in atomic radius compared to iron (Fe).

4. (a) Magnetic moment

$$\mu = \sqrt{n(n+2)}$$

where, n is the number of unpaired electrons. Cu^{+2} there is only 1 unpaired electron so its magnetic moment is the least.

S. No.	Ion	Electronic configuration	Number of unpaired electron
(i)	Cu^{+2}	d^9	1
(ii)	Ni^{+2}	d^8	2
(iii)	Co^{+2}	d^7	3
(iv)	Fe^{+2}	d^6	4

5. (d) Statements (a), (b) and (c) about *d*-block elements are correct but statement (d) is incorrect because yttrium ($Z = 39$) is the first element of second transition series whereas hafnium is second element of third transition series.

6. (d)
A. Transition series – III transition series elements.
B. Transition series – II transition series elements.
C. Transition series – I transition series elements.
Middle of each series have higher atomisation enthalpy due to presence of stronger interatomic interaction.
In general, greater the number of valence electrons, stronger is the resultant bonding.

7. (b) Among the given options, Hg has the lowest melting and boiling point as there is no unpaired electron. Hg is therefore liquid at room temperature with melting point 234 K.

8. (d) Statements (a), (b) and (c) are correct but statement (d) is incorrect because the filling of $4f$ before $5d$-orbital results in regular decrease in atomic radii called lanthanoid contraction, which compensates for the expected increase in atomic size or moving down the group, with increasing atomic number.
So, option (d) is correct answer.

9. (d) Statements (a), (b) and (c) are correct about interstitial compounds but statement (d) is incorrect because interstitial compounds are chemically inert due to occupying of voids by small elements.

10. (d) Cuprous ion is colourless while cupric ion is coloured because cuprous ion has completely filled *d*-orbital while cupric ion has incompletely filled *d*-orbital with unpaired electrons.
Hence, it shows colour due to *d-d* transition.

11. (c) Ionic radii $\propto \dfrac{1}{\text{Atomic no.}}$
Also, ionic radius decrease from left to right in a period.

12. (a) Use the formula $\mu = \sqrt{n(n+2)}$ where *n* is the number of unpaired electron.
For Cr^{3+}, number of unpaired electrons = 3, $\mu = \sqrt{15}$ B.M.
For Co^{3+}, number of unpaired electrons = 4, $\mu = \sqrt{24}$ B.M.
For Fe^{+3}, number of unpaired electrons = 5, $\mu = \sqrt{35}$ B.M.
For Ni^{2+} number of unpaired electrons = 2, $\mu = \sqrt{8}$ B.M.
So, the correct match is A-IV, B-III, C-II, B-I.

13. (c) Incorrect statement about interstitial compounds is given in option (c). Its correct form is, they are chemically inert.

14. (c) Cr^{3+} has d^3-electronic configuration whereas other metals show $V^{3+}(d^2)$, $Ti^{3+}(d^1)$ and $Fe^{2+}(d^6)$ electronic configuration

$Cr^{3+}(d^3)$ | 1 | 1 | 1 | | |

n (unpaired electron) = 3

$$\mu_{ob} = \sqrt{n(n+2)}\ \text{BM}$$
$$\mu_{ob} = \sqrt{3(3+2)}$$
$$= \sqrt{15} = 3.87\,\text{BM}$$

15. (b) Statement I is correct but Statement II is incorrect. The correct form of Statement II is, in $Ni(CO)_4$ and $Fe(CO)_5$ the oxidation state of nickel and iron is zero.

Test-2

1. (b) The reaction is as follows
$$K_2Cr_2O_7 \xrightarrow{\Delta} K_2CrO_4 + Cr_2O_3 + O_2$$
Green colour compound $\Rightarrow Cr_2O_3$.

2. (c) Basic character decreases with increase in atomic number. Oxides of transition metals in low oxidation state, i.e. +2 and +3 are generally basic except Cr_2O_3. Hence, the correct order is
TiO > VO > CrO > FeO.

3. (d) The given reaction is represented as
$$2MnO_4^- + H_2O + I^{\ominus} \longrightarrow 2MnO_2 + 2OH^- + IO_3^-$$
The oxidation state of Mn in MnO_4^- is
$\Rightarrow (x-8) = -1 \Rightarrow x = +7$
The oxidation state of M in MnO_2 is
$\Rightarrow (x-4) = 0 \Rightarrow x = +4$
Hence, the change in oxidation state of manganese is $+4-7=-3$

4. (c) $2KMnO_4 + 16HCl \longrightarrow 2KCl + 2MnCl_2 + 8H_2O + 5Cl_2(g)$ (greenish-yellow gas)
HCl is mild reducing agent and oxidised to free chlorine which is greenish yellow colour gas with pungent and suffocation odour.

5. (b) On heating pyrollusite with KOH, potassium manganate is formed.
$$\underset{\text{Pyrollusite}}{MnO_2} + KOH \xrightarrow{\text{Air}} K_2MnO_4$$

6. (c) The colour of $K_2Cr_2O_7$ changes from red orange to lemon yellow due to formation of K_2CrO_4.
$$\underset{\text{Potassium dichromate}}{K_2Cr_2O_7} + 2KOH \longrightarrow \underset{\text{Potassium chromate}}{2K_2CrO_4} + H_2O$$

7. (a) In $K_2Cr_2O_7$,
Cr has +6 oxidation state.
Let the oxidation state of Cr be *x*, then
$$2(1) + 2(x) + 7(-2) = 0$$
$$2 + 2x - 14 = 0$$
$$x = +6$$

8. (b) The reaction of I^- with MnO_4^- in alkaline medium takes place as follows
$$I^- + 2MnO_4^- + H_2O \longrightarrow 2MnO_2 + IO_3^- + 2\bar{O}H$$
Thus, the product formed is IO_3^-.

9. (c) The reaction of $KMnO_4$ with oxalic acid in acidic medium takes place as follows

$$2MnO_4^- + 16H^+ + 5C_2O_4^{2-} \longrightarrow 2Mn^{2+} + 8H_2O + 10CO_2$$

Thus, from the reaction it is clear that oxidation number of Mn changes from +7 to +2.

10. (a) The reaction takes place as

$$2MnO_2 + 4KOH + O_2 \longrightarrow \underset{\text{(Green)}}{2K_2MnO_4} + 2H_2O$$

11. (a) $KMnO_4 \longrightarrow K^+ + MnO_4^-$

In MnO_4^-, Mn has +7 oxidation state having no electron in *d*-orbitals. It is considered that higher the oxidation state of metal, greater is the tendency to occur $L \rightarrow M$ charge transfer, because ligand is able to donate the electron into the vacant *d*-orbital of metal. Since, charge transfer is laporte as well as spin allowed, therefore, it shows colour.

12. (b) In the reaction given, products *A, B, C* are

$$MnO_4^- + 1e^- \xrightarrow[\text{medium}]{\text{Alkaline}} \underset{[A]}{MnO_4^{2-}}, x = 1$$

$$MnO_4^- + 5e^- \xrightarrow[\text{medium}]{\text{Acidic}} \underset{[B]}{Mn^{2+}}, y = 5$$

$$MnO_4^- + 3e^- \xrightarrow[\text{medium}]{\text{Neutral}} \underset{[C]}{MnO_2}, z = 3$$

13. (d) Except (d), all other statements are correct.

Potassium dichromate is indeed a powerful oxidising agent in acidic medium. It readily oxidises all the other species. However, the reaction with hydrogen peroxide (H_2O_2) is different. Potassium dichromate actually reduces hydrogen peroxide to oxygen gas (O_2) in acidic medium, while the dichromate itself gets reduced to Cr^{3+} ions. This is the basis for the "dichromate volcano" demonstration.

14. (d) Both Statement I and Statement II are correct.

15. (c) Statement given in option (c) is incorrect. Its correct form is : potassium dichromate is used as primary standard in volumetric analysis.

Test-3

1. (c) Among the given options, statement in option (c) is incorrect. Its correct form is, +4 oxidation state of Ce is less stable than Ce^{+3} because $E^\circ_{Ce^{4+}/Ce^{3+}} = 1.74$ Volt, indicating more fovourable +3 oxidation state.

2. (a) $Ho = [Xe]\,4f^{11}\,6s^2$

$Ho^{3+} = [Xe]\,4f^{10}$

So, number of e^- present in $4f$-orbital is 10.

3. (b) $_{63}Eu \Rightarrow [Xe]\,4f^7\,5d^0\,6s^2$

$Eu^{2+} \Rightarrow [Xe]\,4f^7$

$_{58}Ce \Rightarrow [Xe]\,4f^1\,5d^1\,6s^2$

$Ce^{3+} \Rightarrow [Xe]\,4f^1$

4. (c) Due to lanthanoid contraction, the ionic radii of Ln^{+3} decreases from La^{+3} to Lu^{+3}. Thus, the lowest value (0.85 Å) is the ionic radius of Lu^{+3}.

5. (b) Statements I and IV are incorrect.

Their correct forms are

- $La(OH)_3$ is the most basic among lanthanoids hydroxides.
- Most common oxidation state of lanthanoids is + 3.

6. (b) Statements given in I, II and V are correct while III and IV are incorrect. The correct form of statements is :

- CeO_2 is insoluble in water and moderately soluble in strong mineral acids.
- Ce have +4 oxidation state in CeO_2.

7. (a) Stability of Gd^{3+} ion is due to half-filled $4f$-subshell.

$Gd = 4f^7\,5d^1\,6s^2$; $Gd^{+3} = 4f^7$

8. (d) Across the lanthanoid series the size of the cations decreases thereby decreasing ionic character and increasing covalent character of hydroxides of lanthanoids. Thus, the basicity of hydroxides decreases.

9. (a) Due to lanthanoid contraction order will be

$Yb^{3+} < Pm^{3+} < Ce^{3+} < La^{3+}$.

10. (c) Np and Pu show maximum oxidation state +7 by forming oxygenated ions $[NpO_6]^{-5}$ involving $5f$, $6d$ and $7s$-electrons.

11. (d) Promethium (Pm) is the only element among lanthanoids which is radioactive in nature. Promethium is relatively unstable in itself and there are other more stable isotopes that it can decay to. Thus, answer is option (d).

12. (d) Yb^{3+} has one unpaired electron. Therefore, it show paramagnetic nature while La^{3+}, Ce^{4+} and Lu^{3+} do not have unpaired electron. Therefore, these ion show diamagnetic nature.

13. (d) Both Statement I and Statement II are correct.

14. (c) Statement given in option (c) is incorrect. Its correct form is : Eu^{2+} is a strong reducing agent.

15. (a) No and Lr have completely filled *f*-orbital while others have half-filled or partially filled *f*-orbital.

Chapter Break Thru

1. (b) The electronic configuration of Mn is given by $= [Ar]\,3d^5\,4s^2$

So, the electronic configuration of Mn^{2+} will be given by $= [Ar]\,3d^5$

Mn^{2+} has 5 unpaired e^-.

2. (a) Fe, Co, Ni with the increase in the *d*-electron, screening effect increase, this counter balances the increased nuclear charge due to increase in atomic number.

As a result atomic radii remain practically same after chromium.

3. (a) Spin only magnetic moment depends upon the number of unpaired electrons. It is given by

$$\mu = \sqrt{n(n+2)}$$

For Mn^{2+} electronic configuration is $= [Ar]\,3d^5\,4s^0$

$$\mu = \sqrt{5(5+2)} = \sqrt{35}\text{ BM}$$

For Cr^{2+} electronic configuration is $= [Ar]\,3d^4\,4s^0$

$$\mu = \sqrt{4(4+2)} = \sqrt{24}\text{ BM}$$

For Ti^{2+} electronic configuration is $= [Ar]\,3d^2\,4s^0$ BM

$$\mu = \sqrt{2(2+2)} = \sqrt{8}$$

So, the correct increasing order is

$Ti^{2+} < Cr^{2+} < Mn^{2+}$

4. (c) The correct order of melting points is Cr < V < Ti > Mn. The melting point of transition elements first increase to a maximum and then decreases as atomic number increases. Mn, however has low melting point, due to stable configuration and weak intermetallic bonding.

5. (a) Among the given oxides, MnO is ionic in nature. MnO is ionic due to lower oxidation state.

6. (d) The paramagnetic character in 3*d*-series element first increase from Sc to Mn as the number of unpaired electron increase and than decrease with decrease in the number of unpaired electron from Fe to Cu.

7. (a) 5*f*-orbitals can participate in bonding to a far greater extent. Hence, actinoids exhibit more number of oxidation states than the lanthanoids.

8. (a) Among the given statements, statement given in (a) is incorrect while all other are correct. Correct form of statement (a) is, 5*f*-orbitals extend in space beyond 6*s* and 6*p*-orbital whereas 4*f*-orbitals are buried deep inside the atom. Hence, 5*f*-orbitals are poorly shielded than 4*f*-orbitals.

9. (b) Lanthanoid contraction is caused due to the imperfect shielding on outer electron by 4*f*-electron from the nuclear charge.

10. (a) Statement given in option (a) is incorrect. It is because colourless compounds do not possess any unpaired electrons. Hence, they are diamagnetic in nature.

11. (a) Both (A) and (R) are true and (R) is the correct explanation of (A).

12. (a) The reaction of $K_2Cr_2O_7$ with NaOH on heating is as follows

$$K_2Cr_2O_7 + 2NaOH \longrightarrow K_2CrO_4 + Na_2CrO_4 + H_2O$$

Thus, CrO_4^{2-} is obtained on following reaction.

13. (a) Among the given oxides, MnO_2 is an amphoteric oxide due to intermediate oxidation state of +4.

14. (d) The electronic configuration of given elements are as follows

$_{63}Eu = [Xe]\,4f^7\,6s^2$

$_{64}Gd = [Xe]\,4f^7\,5d^1\,6s^2$

$_{65}Tb = [Xe]\,4f^9\,6s^2$

15. (c) $E^\circ_{M^{2+}/M}$ value for copper is positive because the sum of the first and second ionisation enthalpy for copper is very large due to exceptionally high $\Delta_i H_{(II)}$ enthalpy. This is not compensated by hydration enthalpy $\Delta_{hyd} H$ of Cu^{2+} ion.

16. (a)

A. $_{62}Sm = 4f^6\,6s^2$

B. $_{63}Eu = [Xe]\,4f^7\,6s^2$

C. $_{65}Tb = [Xe]\,4f^9\,6s^2$

D. $_{64}Gd = [Xe]\,4f^7\,5d^1\,6s^2$

E. $_{61}Pm = [Xe]\,4f^5\,6s^2$

17. (a) Elements or ions containing unpaired electron are paramagnetic in nature.

$_{28}Ni = [Ar]\,3d^8\,4s^2$

$Ni^{2+} = [Ar]\,3d^8\,4s^0$

Since, Ni^{2+} have 2 unpaired electrons in 3*d*-subshell therefore it is paramagnetic.

18. (b) Statement I is correct but Statement II is incorrect. Correct form of Statement II is :

MnO_4^{2-} ion is paramagnetic due to the presence of one unpaired electron whereas, MnO_4^- ion is diamagnetic due to presence of paired electrons.

19. (c) Y, La = 180 pm, 187 pm

Sc, Ti = 164 pm, 132 pm

Zr, Hf ≈ 160 pm

Nb, Ta ≈ 146 pm

Usual increase in size on moving down the group from second to third transition elements is cancelled by the decrease in size due to lanthanoid contraction.

As a result of lanthanoid contraction the second and third rows of transition elements resembles each other more closely than do the first and second row.

20. (c) The atomic weight of Co, Ni and Fe are 58.90, 58.60, 55.85 respectively.

Therefore, Co > Ni > Fe is the correct sequence of atomic weight.

21. (d) The first ionisation energies of Ti, V, Cr and Mn are 656, 650, 653 and 717 kJ/mole respectively.

I.E. increases in a period from left to right.

Hence, manganese has maximum first ionisation potential.

22. (b) Those metals which show higher oxidation state, show acidic nature while lower oxidation state show basic character.

$\overset{(+6)}{CrO_3}$ and $\overset{(+7)}{Mn_2O_7}$ are acidic oxides further both oxides gives acid on dissolving water.

$\overset{+2}{NiO}$, $\overset{+2}{CaO}$ and $\overset{+2}{FeO}$ are basic.

Hence, option (b) is correct.

23. (d) All statements are correct.

I. [Dichromate structure: O–Cr–O–Cr–O bridged; 179 pm, 126°, 163 pm; charge 2−] Tetrahedral structure

II. $2Cr_2O_7^{2-} + H_2O \rightleftharpoons 2HCrO_4^{2-} + 2n^+$ (Orange-red) ⟶ Yellow

III. [Chromate ion structure: Cr bonded to O^-, O^-, O, O] (Tetrahedral) (Chromate ion)

IV. $2HCrO_4^- \xrightarrow{\text{Alkali}} Cr_2O_7^{2-}$

V. Nessler's reagent is formed as follows

$HgI_2 + 2KI \longrightarrow K_2[HgI_4] \longrightarrow 2K^+ + [HgI_4]^{2-}$

Thus, option (d) is correct.

24. (b) Both (A) and (R) are true but (R) is not the correct explanation of (A). Correct explanation is :
The electronic configurations of europium (II) and cerium (II) are
$Eu^{2+} = [Xe]4f^7$,
$Ce^{2+} = [Xe]4f^2$.
In Eu^{2+}, f-subshell is half-filled and thus more stable.

25. (d) Pt because it is a noble metal and does not react with air, water and acid at room temperature.

26. (a) Configuration given in option (a) represents the correct configuration of Cr.
This configuration is more stable because of symmetrical distribution of e^- and exchange energy.

$d^5s^1 =$ [↿ ↿ ↿ ↿ ↿] (d^5) [↿] (s^1)

27. (b) Brass is an alloy of copper and zinc, in proportions that can be varied to achieve different mechanical and electrical properties.

28. (c) Brass contains Cu, Zn and German silver contains Cu, Zn and Ni.

29. (b) Both (A) and (R) are true but (R) is not the correct explanation of (A). Correct explanation is :
Due to larger surface area and variable valencies to form intermediate absorbed complex easily, transition metals are used as catalysts.

30. (d) Oxide of Zn is amphoteric as it can react with both acid and base.

$ZnO + 2HCl \longrightarrow ZnCl_2 + H_2O$

$ZnO + 2NaOH \longrightarrow Na_2ZnO_2 + H_2O$

31. (a) The correct match is
A-III, B-I, C-II, D-IV.

A. $I^- + 2MnO_4^- + H_2O \xrightarrow{\text{Neutral medium}} IO_3^- + MnO_2$

B. $2MnO_4^- + 3Mn^{2+} + 2H_2O \longrightarrow 5MnO_2 + 4H^+$

C. $SO_3^{2-} + 2MnO_4^- + 6H^+ \longrightarrow 2Mn^{2+} + 5SO_4^{2-} + 3H_2O$

D. $10I^- + 2MnO_4^- + 16H^+ \longrightarrow 2Mn^{2+} + 5I_2 + 8H_2O$

32. (c) $TiCl_4$ with $Al(CH_3)_3$ or $Al(C_2H_5)_3$ is used as Zeigler-Natta catalyst in the polymerisation of ethylene.
So, statement (c) is incorrect.

33. (a) 58 (Ce)$\rightarrow$4 f-series lanthanoids
63 (Eu) $\rightarrow$ 4 f-series lanthanoids
71 (Lu) $\rightarrow$ 4 f-series lanthanoids
91 (Pa) $\rightarrow$ 5 f-series actinoids
99 (Es) $\rightarrow$ 5 f-series actinoids
103 (Lr) $\rightarrow$ 5 f series actinoids
Therefore, I and II set of elements belongs to same periods.
Thus, option (a) is correct.

34. (d) Both Statement I and Statement II are correct. Highest oxidation state of the transition metal are found in their compound with fluorine and oxygen.
The common oxidation state of Ti are +3 and +4.

35. (c) $Cr_2O_7^{2-} + 3H_2S + 8H^+ \longrightarrow 2Cr^{3+} + 3S + 7H_2O$ (A)

$Cr_2O_7^{2-} + 6I^- + 14H^+ \longrightarrow 2Cr^{3+} + 3I_2 + 7H_2O$ (B)

Hence, option (c) is correct.

36. (d) In this reaction, final product C is $K_2Cr_2O_7$ (potassium dichromate).

$4Fe_2Cr_2O_4 + 16NaOH + 7O_2 \longrightarrow 8Na_2CrO_4 + 2Fe_2O_3 + 8H_2O$ (Na_2CrO_4 = (A))

$2Na_2CrO_4 + H_2SO_4 \longrightarrow Na_2Cr_2O_7 + Na_2SO_4 + H_2O$ (Na_2CrO_4 = (A), $Na_2Cr_2O_7$ = (B))

$Na_2Cr_2O_7 \xrightarrow{2KCl} K_2Cr_2O_7 + 2NaCl$ ($Na_2Cr_2O_7$ = (B), $K_2Cr_2O_7$ = (C) (Potassium dichromate))

Thus, option (d) is correct.

37. (a) The electronic configuration of Co^{2+} is $[Ar]4s^0 3d^7$.
Hence, there are 3 unpaired electrons in Co^{2+}. Now the electronic configuration of Cr^{3+} is $[Ar]3d^3$.
Hence, there are 3 unpaired electrons in Cr^{3+}. We know magnetic moment, $\mu = \sqrt{n(n+2)}$.
where, n is number of unpaired electrons.
So, when $n = 3$,

$\mu = \sqrt{3(3+2)} = \sqrt{15}$

Hence, option (a) is correct answer.

38. (d) The characteristic electronic configuration of transition element is given by $(n-1)s^2p^6d^{1-10}\ ns^{1-2}$.

39. (b) $V = 1s^2 2s^2 2p^6 3s^2 3p^6 3d^3 4s^2$
$Cr = 1s^2 2s^2 2p^6 3s^2 3p^6 3d^5 4s^1$
$Mn = 1s^2 2s^2 2p^6 3s^2 3p^6 3d^5 4s^2$
$Fe = 1s^2 2s^2 2p^6 3s^2 3p^6 3d^6 4s^2$
In second ionisation enthalpy Cr^+ ($3d^5$) has exact half-filled d-subshell which is highly stable.

Hence, chromium has the highest second ionisation energy.

40. (c) Incorrect statement about chromium is given in option (c). It is because it has 5 electrons in 3*d*-orbital.

41. (d) Fe^{3+} is easily hydrolysed than Fe^{2+} due to more positive charge.

42. (a) Manganese is stronger oxidising agent in +7 oxidation state. e.g. $KMnO_4$.

43. (b) In the given reaction Mo is used as a catalytic promoter.

44. (c)

$$\underset{\substack{\text{Sulphide}\\(Z)}}{Ln_2S_3} \xleftarrow[\Delta]{S} Ln \xrightarrow{H_2SO_4} \text{Sulphate} + \underset{\text{liberated}}{H_2(X)\text{ gas}}$$

$$Ln \xrightarrow{\text{With C, 2773K}} \underset{\text{carbide}}{LnC_2\ (Y)}$$

Hence, option (c) is correct.

45. (a) Cu^+ in aqueous solution undergo disproportionation.

$$2Cu^+(aq) \longrightarrow Cu^{2+}(aq) + Cu(s)$$

The $E°$ value for disproportionation is favourable.

46. (d) All the given statements are correct.

47. (b) Statements I, II, IV and V are correct while statement III is incorrect.

I. Manganese exhibits +7 oxidation state in its oxide. (Mn_2O_7)

II. Ru and Os form RuO_4 and OsO_4 oxide in +8 oxidation state.

III. Sc does not show +4 oxidation state.

Sc have two oxidation states +2 and +3 which is due to 4*s* and 3*d*-electrons.

IV Cr in +6 oxidation state show oxidising nature.

V. Mn is in (+7) state, it has no unpaired electron. So, charge transfer from ligand to metal occurs and shows intence pink colour.

48. (d) The correct match is A-II, B-I, C-IV, D-III.

49. (b) Highest magnetic moment depends upon number of unpaired electron since

$Cr^{2+} = 3d^4 4s^0$, $Mn^{2+} = 3d^5 4s^0$,
$Cu^{2+} = 3d^9 4s^0$, $Co^{2+} = 3d^7 4s^0$,
$Ni^{2+} = 3d^6 4s^0$

So, Mn^{2+} contain maximum number of unpaired electron, i.e. 5.

50. (a) Due to poor shielding of 4*f*-orbitals, nucleus will exert a strong attraction causes lanthanoid contraction.

Ch-6 Coordination Compounds

Topical Follow Thru

Test-1

1. (d) $\underset{\text{Cation}}{K_3}\underset{\text{Anion}}{[Fe(CN)_6]}$

Oxidation state of Fe in anion = +3

Thus, it is potassium hexacyanoferrate (III).

2. (a) en, $\begin{matrix} CH_2-NH_2 \\ | \\ CH_2-NH_2 \end{matrix}$ is bidentate ligand, $C_2O_4^{2-}$ is also a bidentate ligand. Hence, coordination number of the element *E* in the given complex comes out to be 6.

3. (d) $[Ni(H_2O)_4(NH_3)_2]^{2+}$ and $[Ni(H_2O)_3(NH_3)_3]^{2+}$ show geometrical isomerism.

4. (c)

(Structures of two mirror-image forms of Co with two en and two Cl ligands, separated by a mirror line)

Mirror

cis-$[Co(en)_2Cl_2]$

5. (c) $[Cr(SCN)_2(NH_3)_4]^+$ show linkage, geometrical and optical isomerism.

6. (b) The given ligand is tetradentate as it contains four donor atoms. It can bind through two nitrogen and two oxygen atom to central metal ion.

It can act as Lewis base.

7. (c) Octahedral complexes of formula $[Ma_4b_2]$ in which the two ligands *a* and *b* may be oriented *cis* or *trans* to each other.

e.g.

(Structures: *cis* — Co with Cl, Cl, H_3N, H_3N, NH_3, NH_3; *trans* — Co with Cl above and below, H_3N, NH_3, H_3N, NH_3; each in brackets with charge +)

cis   *trans*

Geometrical isomers (*cis* and *trans*) of $[Co(NH_3)_4Cl_2]^+$.

8. (a) The correct match is A-II, B-III, C-IV, D-I

Let the oxidation state of Cr in all cases is '*x*'.

(A). Oxidation state of Cr in $[Cr(H_2O)_6]Cl_3$

$$x + (0 \times 6) + (-1 \times 3) = 0$$

(B) Oxidation state of Cr in $[Cr(C_6H_6)_2]$.

$x + (2 \times 0) = 0$ or $x = 0$

(C) Oxidation state of Cr in $K_2[Cr(CN)_2(O)_2(O_2)(NH_3)]$.

$1 \times 2 + x + (-1 \times 2) + (-2 \times 2) + (-2) + 0 = 0$

or $2 + x - 2 - 4 - 2 = 0$

or $x - 6 = 0$

Hence, $x = +6$

(D) Oxidation of Mn in $[Mn(CN)_6]^{5-}$ be x.

$x + (6 \times (-1)) + 5 = 0$

$x = +1$

9. (d) E.C. of $Co^{3+} = [Ar] 4s^0 3d^3$, therefore it can accomodate total 6 ligands.

As, $CoCl_3 \cdot xNH_3 + AgNO_3(aq) \longrightarrow 2$ moles of AgCl

$\therefore$ 2 chloride ions in $CoCl_3 \cdot xNH_3$ are primary/ionisable valency (present outside the square bracket) $[CoCl(NH_3)_x]Cl_2$.

Now, as total number of ligands that can bond to cobalt are 6, out of which one is Cl.

$\therefore \quad x = 5$

Thus, $[Co(Cl)(NH_3)_5]Cl_2$, might be the complex.

10. (a) Both Statements I and II are incorrect.

The coordination number of a central metal atom in a complex is determined by the number of ligands around a metal ion bonded by sigma bonds only.

11. (c) Here, more than one atom function as donor site as oxygen in first one and nitrogen in second, so they show linkage isomerism.

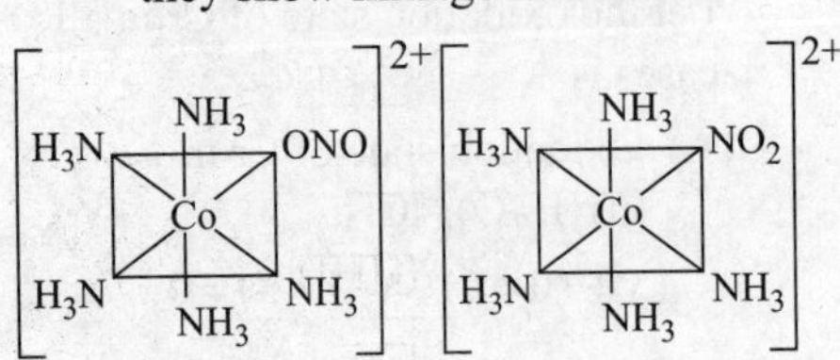

12. (b) $[Co(en)_2Cl_2]^+$ have three optical isomers which are

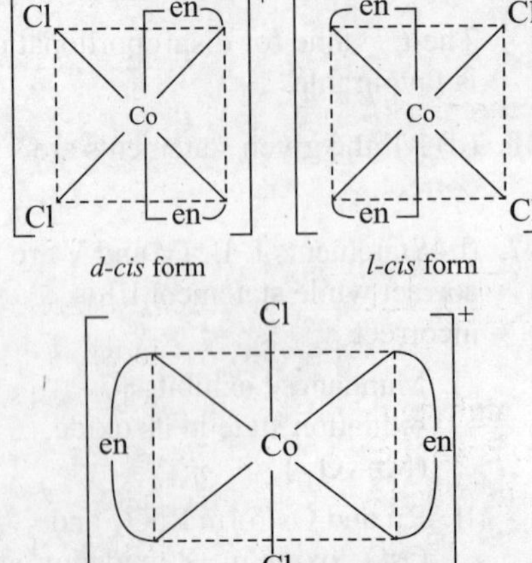

13. (a) $[Co(NH_3)_3Cl_3]$ does not have optical isomers. It is because its formula is MA_3B_3 which does not show optical isomerism.

14. (b) Dimethyl glyoxime

N—OH, CH_3, CH_3, HO—N   Donor sites (2)

Glycinato

$CH_2 \langle^{NH_2}_{COO^-}$ Donor sites (2)

Diethylenetriamine

H, H, N̈, N̈, N̈, H, H, H   Donor sites (3)

EDTA : Hexadentate No. of donor sites (6)

15. (a) Let the oxidation state of Co be x

$[Co(NH_3)_4ClNO_2]$

$x + 4(0) + 1(-1) + 1(-1) = 0$

$x - 2 = 0$

$\Rightarrow \quad x = +2$

Test-2

1. (a) In $[Cu(NH_3)_4]^{2+}$ and $[Ni(NH_3)_4]^{2+}$, the central atoms have dsp^2 hybridisation.

2. (a) $K_3[Cr(ox)_3]$ the oxidation state of Cr in $K_3[Cr(C_2O_4)_3]$ is $x = +3$.

$Cr \rightarrow 3d^5 4s^1$ (ground state electronic configuration)

$Cr^{3+} \rightarrow 3d^3 4s^0$ (Excited state)

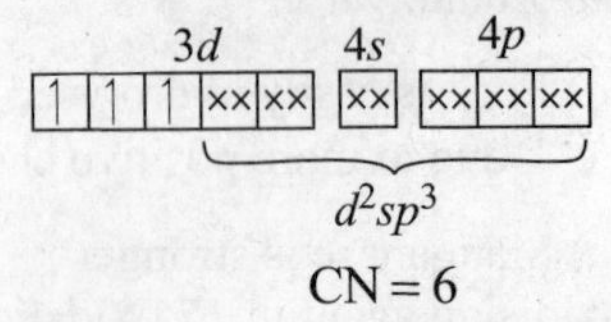

CN = 6

$\therefore$ Oxalate is weak field ligand

$\therefore$ 3 unpaired electron in d-orbital.

3. (b) Electronic configuration of Co^{2+} : [Ar] $3d^7$ and CN^- is a strong field ligand which can pair electron of central atom.

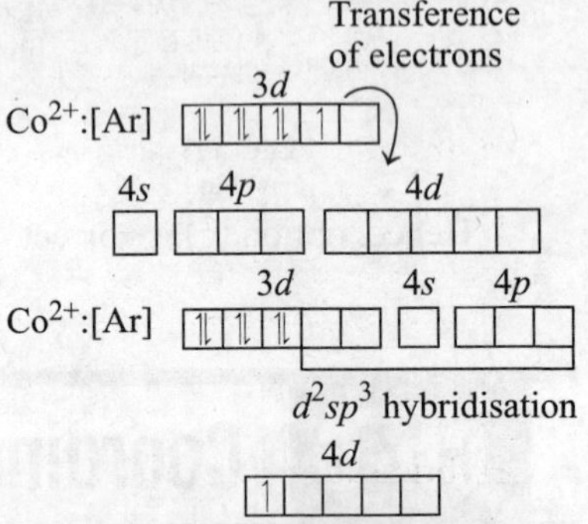

So, spin only magnetic moment

$(\mu) = \sqrt{n(n+2)}$ BM

$= \sqrt{1(1+2)}$ BM

$= \sqrt{3}$ BM

where, n = number of unpaired electrons

$\mu = \sqrt{3}$ BM

$= 1.73$ BM

Nearest integer = 2

4. (d) Both Statement I and Statement II are correct.

Only paramagnetic substance or complex response to external magnetic field.

$[Fe(H_2O)_6]^{3+}$; Electronic configuration of

$Fe^{3+} = [Ar] 3d^5 4s^0$

All electrons are unpaired (No pairing as H_2O is a weak field ligand)

$\therefore [Fe(H_2O)_6]^{3+}$

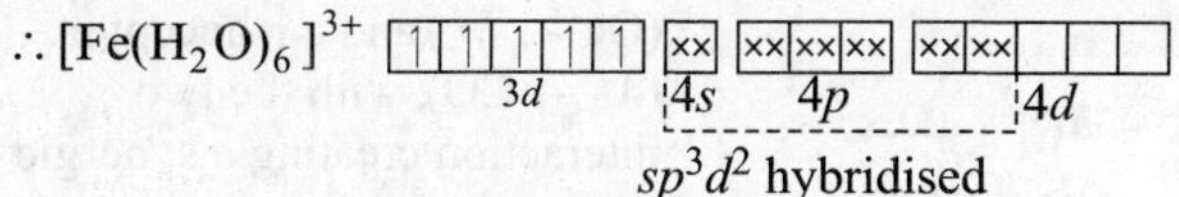

Unpaired electrons $(n) = 5$

Magnetic nature = Paramagnetic (so this complex response to external magnetic field)

$[MnCl_6]^{3-}$

$Mn^{3+} \Rightarrow [Ar]$ 3d: ↿ ↿ ↿ ↿ □ | 4s: xx | 4p: xx xx xx | 4d: xx xx □ □ □

sp^3d^2

Cl is a weak field ligand, so Mn^{3+} forms high spin complex or outer orbital complex. Hence, it will be sp^3d^2 hybridised. It is paramagnetic as Mn^{+3} has 4 unpaired electrons.

5. (b) The correct match is A-I, B-III, C-IV, D-II.

$[CoF_6]$, Co^{+3} = 3d: ⇅ ↿ ↿ ↿ ↿ | 4s: xx | 4p: xx xx xx | 4d: xx xx □ □ □

Hybridisation $\Rightarrow sp^3d^2$

$[NiCl_4]^{2-}$, Ni^{2+} = 3d: ⇅ ⇅ ⇅ ↿ ↿ | 4s: xx | 4p: xx xx xx

Hybridisation $\Rightarrow sp^3$

$[Ni(CN)_4]^{2-}$, Ni^{2+} = 3d: ⇅ ⇅ ⇅ ⇅ xx | 4s: xx | 4p: xx xx □

Hybridisation $\Rightarrow dsp^2$

$[Co(CN)_6]^{3-}$, Co^{3+} = 3d: ⇅ ⇅ ⇅ xx xx | 4s: xx | 4p: xx xx xx

Hybridisation $\Rightarrow d^2sp^3$

6. (a) Among the given statements I, II, III and IV are correct. While V is incorrect.

I. In presence of weak field ligand like Cl^-, both octahedral Mn(II) and tetrahedral Ni(II) complexes can be high spin, like

$\overset{II}{[MnCl_6]^{4}} \Rightarrow Mn^{2+}$: 3d: ↿ ↿ ↿ ↿ ↿ | 4s: xx | 4p: xx xx xx | 4d: xx xx □ □ □
(d^5)

sp^3d^2 (octahedral complex)
[outer orbital, high spin

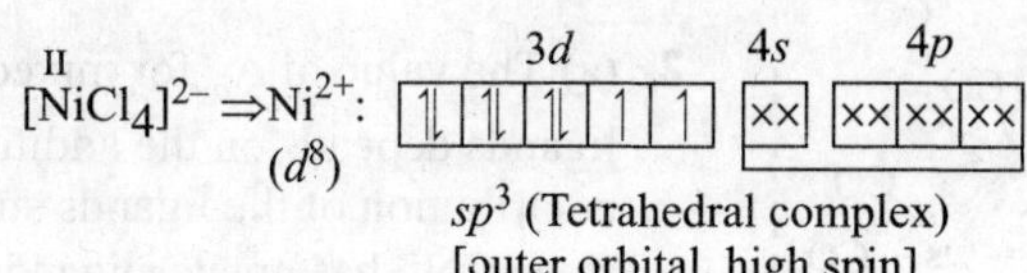

II. In presence of strong field ligand like CN^-, Ni^{2+} can form low spin square planar complex.

$\overset{II}{[Ni(CN)_4]^{2-}} \Rightarrow Ni^{2+}$: ⇅ ⇅ ⇅ ⇅ xx | xx | xx xx □

dsp^2 (Square planar complex)
[Inner orbital, low spin]

III. With strong field ligands like —CN^-, Mn(II) octahedral complexes can be low spin.

$[Mn(CN)_6]^{4-} \Rightarrow Mn^{2+}$: ⇅ ⇅ ↿ xx xx | xx | xx xx xx
(d^5)

d^2sp^3 (octahedral complex)
[Inner orbital, low spin

IV. Aqueous solution of Mn^{2+} is pink in colour.

V. Tetrahedral Ni(II) complex are usually high spin.

7. (c) The correct order is IV < I < III < II.
In general, the weak field ligand have maximum wavelength of absorption.

8. (d) All the given transition metals have same oxidation states.

$[Cr(H_2O)_6]^{3+} \rightarrow 3d$ series

$[Mo(H_2O)_6]^{3+} \rightarrow 4d$ series

$[Os(H_2O)_6]^{3+} \rightarrow 5d$ series

For the same oxidation state,
CFSE increasing order will be $3d < 4d < 5d$.
So, $[Os(H_2O)_6]^{3+}$ has maximum CFSE (Δ_o).

9. (a) Among the given statements I and III are correct, while II, IV and V are incorrect.

II. It does not give quantitative interpretation of magnetic data.

IV. It does not give a quantitative interpretation of the thermodynamic or kinetic stabilities of coordination compounds.

V. It does not make exact predictions regarding the tetrahedral and square planar structure of 4-coordinate complexes.

10. (b) The correct order of the spin only magnetic moment of metal ions in the given low-spin complexes is

$$V^{2+} > Cr^{2+} > Ru^{3+} > Fe^{2+}.$$

Complex	Oxidation state	Configuration	Orbital splitting	No. of unpaired electrons
$V[(CN)_6]^{4-}$	V^{2+}	$t_{2g}^3e_g^0$	e_g □□ ; t_{2g} ↿↿↿	3
$[Cr(NH_3)_6]^{2+}$	Cr^{2+}	$t_{2g}^4e_g^0$	e_g □□ ; t_{2g} ⇅↿↿	2
$[Ru(NH_3)_6]^{3+}$	Ru^{3+}	$t_{2g}^5e_g^0$	e_g □□ ; t_{2g} ⇅⇅↿	1
$[Fe(CN)_6]^{4-}$	Fe^{2+}	$t_{2g}^6e_g^0$	e_g □□ ; t_{2g} ⇅⇅⇅	0

11. (a) Both A and R are true and R is the correct explanation of A.

12. (a)

(a) $[Co(CN)_6]^{3-}$	d^2sp^3	0	0
(b) $[Fe(CN)_6]^{3-}$	d^2sp^3	1	$\sqrt{3}$ BM
(c) $[Mn(CN)_6]^{3-}$	d^2sp^3	2	$\sqrt{8}$ BM
(d) $[Cr(CN)_6]^{3-}$	d^2sp^3	3	$\sqrt{15}$ BM

Therefore, least paramagnetic is in (a).

13. (b) In $[Co(NH_3)_6]^{3+}$ oxidation state of Co = + 3 and its coordination number is six.
The electronic configuration of
$_{27}Co = 1s^2, 2s^2, 2p^6, 3s^2 3p^6 3d^7, 4s^2$
$Co^{3+} = 1s^2 2s^2 2p^6, 3s^2 3p^6 3d^6$
Thus, $[Co(NH_3)_6]^{3+}$ forms inner orbital complex but diamagnetic in behaviour (due to absence of an unpaired electron).
$[Fe(CN)_6]^{4-}, d^2sp^3$, diamagnetic
$[Fe(NO_2)_6]^{4-}, d^2sp^3$, diamagnetic
$[Cr(NH_3)_6]^{3+} \rightarrow d^2sp^3$ hybridisation (inner) and paramagnetic.

14. (c) $3d < 4d < 5d$ $(Z_{eff}) \Rightarrow$ Stability
$[Co(H_2O)_6]^{+3} < [Rh(H_2O)_6]^{+3}$

15. (a) $[Ag(CN)_2]^-$ is linear (sp) with no unpaired electron, (Ag^+), hence magnetic moment = 0.
$[Cu(CN)_4]^{3-}$ is tetrahedral (sp^3) with no unpaired electron (Cu^+) hence magnetic moment = 0.
$[Cu(CN)_6]^{4-}$ is octahedral (sp^3d^2) with one unpaired electron, hence magnetic moment $= \sqrt{1(1+2)}$
$= 1.73$ BM.
$[Cu(NH_3)_4]^{2+}$ is square planar (dsp^2) with one unpaired electron, hence magnetic moment
$= \sqrt{1(1+2)} = 1.73$ BM.
Thus, the correct match is
A-II, B-IV, C-III, D-I.

Test-3

1. (c) $Au + 4H^+ + NO_3^- + 4Cl^- \longrightarrow AuCl_4^- + NO + 2H_2O$
$3Pt + 16H^+ + 4NO_3^- + 18Cl^- \longrightarrow 3PtCl_6^{2-} + 4NO + 8H_2O$

2. (a) $(CH_3)_4Sn$ is a σ-bonded organometallic compound.

3. (b) The pigment responsibile for photosynthesis, i.e. chlorophyll is a coordination compound of magnesium.

4. (a) The complex formed is $[Ag(S_2O_3)_2]^{3-}$ ion.

5. (c) Among the given statements only (c) is incorrect as cyanocobalamine is the coordination compound of cobalt (Co).

6. (b) $[Mn_2(CO)_{10}]$ displays one Mn—Mn bond, ten terminal CO and zero bridging. Its structure is as follows

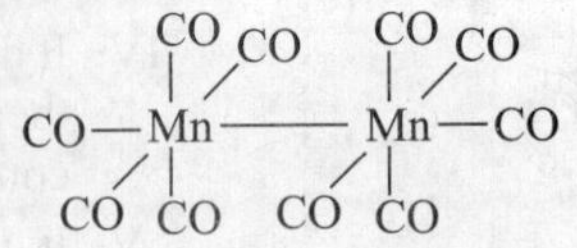

$(CO)_5Mn$—$Mn(CO)_5$

7. (a) Compounds having atleast one carbon metal (M—C) bond are known as organometallic compounds.

8. (a) Only $(Co_2(CO)_8)$ has bridging CO bonds.

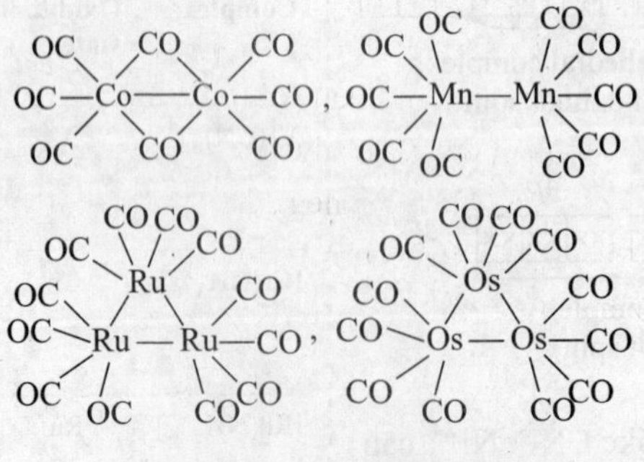

$(OC)_3Co(\mu\text{-}CO)_2Co(CO)_3$, $(OC)_5Mn$—$Mn(CO)_5$

$Ru_3(CO)_{12}$, $Os_3(CO)_{12}$

9. (d) The (M — C) π-bond is formed by the donation of a pair of electrons from a filled d-orbital of metal to the vacant antibonding, π-orbital of carbonyl ligand. Thus, CO acts as a σ-donor (OC → M) and a π-acceptor (M → CO), with the two interaction creating a synergic effect which strengthens the bond between CO and the metal.
So, all the given five complexes have CO ligands and all will exhibit synergic bonding.

10. (a) Here, A and B respectively are D-penicillamine and desferrioxime B.

11. (d) The correct match is A-IV, B-III, C-I, D-II.

12. (c) $[Co(CO)_5NH_3]^{2+}$ is the organometallic compound which has σ and π-bonds present.

13. (c) $Al(OC_2H_5)_3$ contain bonding through O and thus, it doesn't have metal-carbon bond.

14. (d) Wilkinson's catalyst is used as homogeneous catalyst in the hydrogenation of alkenes.

15. (b) Among the given options, *cis*-platin, i.e. *cis*-$[PtCl_2(NH_3)_2]$ is used as an anti-cancer agent.

Chapter Break Thru

1. (b) The compound which has same composition but give different ions in solution, show ionisation isomerism.
So, $[Co(NH_3)_5Br]SO_4$ is an ionisation isomer.
$[Co(NH_3)_5Br]SO_4 \rightleftharpoons [Co(NH_3)_5Br]^{2+} + SO_4^{2-}$
$[Co(NH_3)_5SO_4]Br \rightleftharpoons [Co(NH_3)SO_4]^+ + Br^-$

2. (a) The value of Δ_o for mixed ligands depends on the additive contribution of the ligands strength since CN^- has greater ligand strength than H_2O. The strength increase as the number of CN^- ions increase.

3. (b) If $\Delta_o < P$, the fourth electron will go to higher energy e_g orbital because pairing energy (P) is higher.

So, the electronic configuration for d^4 will be $t_{2g}^3 e_g^1$.

4. (a) $[MA_3B_3]$ type of compound exist as facial and meridional isomer.

5. (a) Complexes *cis*-$[Cr(ox)_2Cl_2]^{-3}$, $[Co(en)_3]^{+3}$, *cis*-$[Pt(en)_2Cl_2]^{+2}$, *cis*-$[Co(en)_2Cl_2]^{-1}$ show optical isomerism as they doesn't possess plane of symmetry.

6. (b) $[Co(NH_3)_3(NO_2)_3]$ exists in following two isomeric form. *cis* and *fac* or facial isomer and *trans* or *mer* or meridional isomer.

7. (b) The number of unpaired electron in I, II, III, IV are 0, 1, 3 and 4 respectively.

8. (c) Organometallic compounds are those compounds in which carbon atom is directly linked to metal. But in sodium ethoxide as oxygen is attached to sodium metal so it is not an organometallic compound.

9. (c) Stability of complex increases with increase in charge on the central metal ion and with increase in basic strength of ligand.

In $[Fe(CN)_6]^{3-}$, oxidation state of Fe is +3 and CN^- is stronger ligand than OH^-, Cl^- and H_2O

10. (b) The magnetic moment is given by

$$\mu = \sqrt{n(n+2)}$$

where, n = number of unpaired electrons.

$$1.73 = \sqrt{n(n+2)}$$
$$n = 1$$

11. (b) CO ligand is bonded to the central metal atom through σ and π-bonding.

Hence, option (b) is correct.

12. (d) $[Ni(CO)_4] \rightarrow$ diamagnetic, sp^3 hybridisation, number of unpaired electron = 0

$[NiCl_4]^{2-} \rightarrow$ paramagnetic, sp^3 hybridisation, number of unpaired electron = 2

13. (c) (A) is true but (R) is false. $[FeF_6]^{3-}$ is a high spin complex since F^- is a weak ligand.

14. (c) $[Co(en)_2Br_2]Cl_2$

C.N. of Co = 2 × Number of bidentate ligand + 1 × Number of monodentate ligand

$$= 2 \times 2 + 1 \times 2 = 6$$

So, the coordination number of Co is 6.

15. (b) In TiF_6^{2-}, titanium is in +4 state. In Cu_2Cl_2, the copper is in +1 state. Thus, in both cases, transition from one *d*-orbital to other is not possible.

$Ti \rightarrow 3d^2 4s^2$; $Ti^{4+} \rightarrow 3d^0 4s^0$

$Cu \rightarrow 3d^{10} 4s^1$; $Cu^+ \rightarrow 3d^{10} 4s^0$

16. (c) Only those transition metal complexes are expected to absorb visible light, in which *d*-subshell is incomplete and excitation of an electron from a lower energy orbital to higher energy orbital is possible.

- In $[Sc(H_2O)_2(NH_3)_4]^{3+}$, Sc is present in $Sc^{3+} = [Ar]\,3d^0, 4s^0$
  Since, in this complex excitation of the electron is not possible, it will not absorb visible light.
- $[Ti(en)_2(NH_3)_2]^{4+}$, Ti is present as Ti^{4+}
  $Ti^{4+} = [Ar]\,3d^0, 4s^0$
  Hence, it will not absorb visible light.
- In $[Cr(NH_3)_6]^{3+}$, Cr is present as Cr^{3+}
  $Cr^{3+} = [Ar]\,3d^3, 4s^0$
  Since, this complex has three unpaired electrons excitation of electrons is possible and thus, it is expected that this complex will absorb visible light.
- In $[Zn(CN)_4]^{2-}$, Zn is present as Zn^{2+}
  $Zn^{2+} = [Ar]\,3d^{10}, 4s^0$
  Hence, this complex will not absorb visible light.

The correct option is (c).

17. (c) (A) is true but (R) is false.

Correct form of (R) is :

$H_2N—NH_2$ does not act as chelating ligand.

The coordination by hydrazine leads to a three membered highly unstable strained ring and thus, it does not act as chelating agent.

18. (b) The reaction,

$$2Na + 2CH_3CH_2OH \longrightarrow 2CH_3CH_2ONa + H_2\uparrow$$

There is no direct bonding between metal atom and the carbon atom in CH_3CH_2ONa.

19. (b) $[Cr(en)_3]^{2+}$

Let the oxidation number of Cr to be x.

$\Rightarrow \quad x + 3(0) = +2$

$\Rightarrow \quad x = +2$

$Cr^{+2} = [Ar]\,3d^4$

$(d)^4$

Cr^{2+} = | 1 | 1 | 1 | 1 | |

Unpaired electron = 4

Hence, option (b) is incorrect.

20. (d) $[Co(NH_3)_5(CO_3)]ClO_4$

Oxidation number (x),

$\Rightarrow x + 5(0) + 1(-2) + (-1) = 0$

$x = +3$

Coordination number = 6, i.e. $(5NH_3)(1CO_3^{2-})$

$Co^{+3} \Rightarrow [Ar]\,3d^6$

$3d^6$

Co^{3+} = | ⇅ | 1 | 1 | 1 | 1 |

Thus, option (d) is correct.

21. (d) Both Statement I and Statement II are correct.

22. (d) *trans*-$[CoCl_2(en)_2]^+$ is optically inactive because it has plane of symmetry.

$$\left[\begin{array}{c} Cl \\ en \;\; Co \;\; en \\ Cl \end{array}\right]^+$$

23. (d) In square planar complex

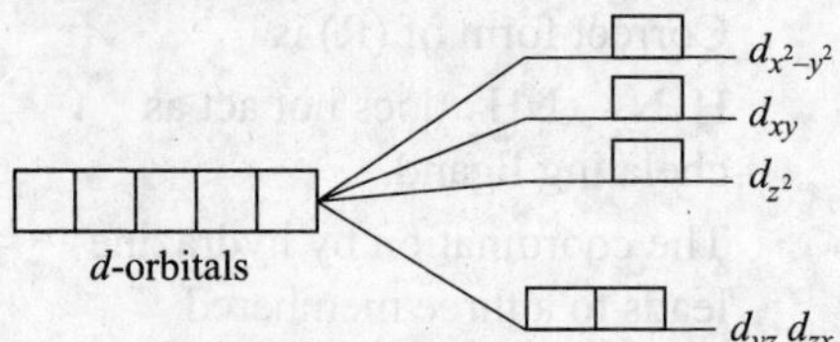

So, energy order is
$d_{x^2-y^2} > d_{xy} > d_{z^2} > d_{zx} = d_{yz}$

24. (d) $[MA_3B_3]$ form *facial* and *meridional* isomer.

Facial (cis) (*fac*) *Meridional* (*mer*) or *trans*

25. (c) $Na_2[Ni(EDTA)]$
Correct IUPAC name Disodium ethylenediamminetetraacetato nickel(II)
Hence, option (c) is correct.

26. (b) Among the given statements II and IV are incorrect while other are correct.
II. The formula of Wilkinson catalyst is $[(Ph_3P)_3RhCl]$.
IV. Carboxypeptidase-A is an enzyme and contain zinc.

27. (a) C_2H_4 is neutral and Cl is uninegative ligand thus in $[Pt(C_2H_4)Cl_3]^-$,
$x + 3(-1) = -1 \Rightarrow x = +2$

28. (c) The correct order of ligands in spectrochemical series is
$$CN^- > en > NCS^- > Cl^-$$
Thus, CN^- causes the highest CFSE, Δ_o as a ligand.

29. (d) In $Fe(CO)_5$, Fe is dsp^3 hybridised and thus trigonal bipyramidal in shape.

$Fe(CO)_5$
Trigonal bipyramidal

30. (d) The overlap of a lone pair on the C atom with the empty hybrid metal orbital forms a metal-to-carbon σ bond. The transition metal atom in a metal carbonyl has filled non-bonding *d*-orbitals which are of proper symmetry to overlap with the anti-bonding orbitals of CO. The electronic charge is transferred from the filled non-bonding orbitals of the metals to π^* orbitals of the ligand CO. This reduces the bond order of CO. The π back-bonding thus strengthens the M—C bond order as it weakens the C—O bond order.

31. (c) Among the given compounds $LiAlH[(CH_3)_3CO]_3$ has no metal carbon bond.

32. (b) In a metal carbonyl, the metal carbon bond possesses both the σ- and π-character. A σ-bond between metal and carbon atom is formed when a vacant hybrid orbital of the metal atom overlaps with an orbital of C atom of carbon monoxide containing a lone pair of electrons. Formation of π-bond is caused when a filled orbital of the metal atom overlaps with a vacant antibonding π^* orbital of C atom of CO. This overlaps is also called back donation of electrons by metal atom to carbon.

33. (c) Ethylene diamminetetraacetate $(EDTA)^{4-}$ ion is used for the removal of the toxic effect of lead metal in body in chelate therapy treatment because it forms complex with lead.

34. (c) (A) is true but (R) is false.
Correct (R) is :
The ligands having vacant π-type orbitals have a tendency to receive back donated π-electrons, thus these are called π-acid ligands or π-acceptor ligands, e.g. CO and CN have lone pair as well as π-electrons or π-orbitals which take part in the formation of π-bond with central metal atom as observed in case of carbonyls.

35. (b) Zeigler-Natta catalyst is an organometallic compound containing titanium. It is $TiCl_4$ and $(C_2H_5)_3Al$. It is used in the preparation of polyethylene.
$$\underset{\text{Ethylene}}{nCH_2 = CH_2} \xrightarrow[TiCl_4 + (C_2H_5)_3Al]{330\text{-}350\text{ K, 1-2 atm}} \underset{\text{Polyethylene}}{(-CH_2-CH_2-)_n}$$

36. (a)

Metal complex	Configuration of central metal atom	Magnetic behaviour
$K_3[Cu(CN)_4]$	$Cu^+ (3d^{10}4s^0)$	Diamagnetic (All electrons paired)
$K_2[Cu(CN)_4]$	$Cu^{2+} (3d^9 4s^0)$	Paramagnetic (1 unpaired electron)
$K_3[Fe(CN)_6]$	$Fe^{3+} (3d^5 4s^0)$	Paramagnetic (1 unpaired electron)
$K_4[FeCl_6]$	$Fe^{2+} (3d^6 4s^0)$	Paramagnetic (4 unpaired electron)

37. (a) As the number of unpaired electrons increase, magnetic moment of complex also increases.
(a) $[FeF_6]^{3-}$ is a high-spin complex. So, pairing of electrons will not occur.
$[FeF_6]^{3-}$ = 1 1 1 1 1
Number of unpaired $e^- = 5$
(b) $[Fe(CN)_6]^{3-}$ is a low-spin complex. So, pairing of electrons occur in *d*-orbital.
$[Fe(CN)_6]^{3-}$ = 1l 1l 1 xx xx
Number of unpaired $e^- = 1$
(c) $[MnCl_6]^{3-}$ is a high spin complex. So, pairing of electrons will not occur.
$[MnCl_6]^{3-}$ = 1 1 1 1
Number of unpaired $e^- = 4$

(d) $[Mn(CN)_6]^{3-}$ is a low-spin complex. So, pairing of electrons take place.

$[Mn(CN)_6]^{3-}$ = ⇅⇅↑ | ×× ×× | ××

Number of unpaired $e^- = 0$

38. (a) $\underbrace{[Cr(NH_3)_6]}_{\text{Coordinate sphere}}\ \underbrace{Cl_3}_{\text{Ionisable}} \rightleftharpoons$

$[Cr(NH_3)_6]^{3+} + 3Cl^- \xrightarrow{AgNO_3} \underset{\text{White precipitate}}{AgCl\downarrow}$

In $[Cr(NH_3)_6]^{3+}$, Cr exists as Cr^{3+} ion. Hence, it forms an inner orbital complex.

Thus, among the given statements only III is incorrect.

39. (a) Among the given complexes only $[V(NH_3)_6]^{3+}$ will be most likely to absorb visible light.

$V^+(20) = 1s^2 2s^2 2p^6 3s^2 3p^6 3d^2 4s^0$

Two unpaired e^-.

$[Sc(H_2O)_6]^{3+}$, $[Ti(NH_3)_6]^{4+}$, $[Zn(NH_3)_6]^{2+}$ and $[Co(NH_3)_6]^{3+}$ have no unpaired electron present.

Hence, $[V(NH_3)_6]^{3+}$ will most likely absorb visible light due to presence of highest number of unpaired electron.

40. (b) In $[Co(NH_3)_6]Cl_2$ oxidation state of Co is +2

E.C of Co^{2+}:[Ar] $4s^0 3d^7$

⇅⇅↑↑↑

As NH_3 act as strong field ligand with Co^{+3} thus, pairing will took place.

$[Co(NH_3)_6]^{2+}$

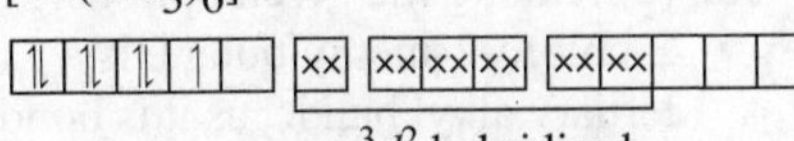

sp^3d^2 hybridised

Thus, there is only one unpaired electron is present in $[Co(NH_3)_6]^{2+}$. In $[Co(NH_3)_6]Cl_3$ oxidation state of Co is +3.

E.C of Co^{3+}:[Ar] $4s^0 3d^6$

⇅↑↑↑↑

As NH_3 act as strong field ligand, thus pairing will took place.

$[Co(NH_3)_6]^{3+}$

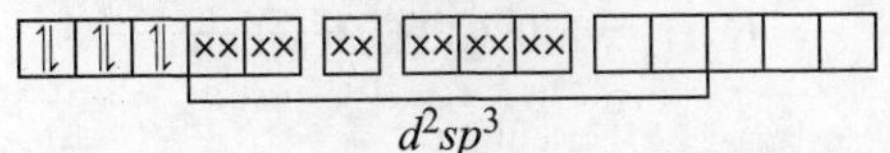

d^2sp^3

It has zero unpaired.

Thus, the value of $x + y = 1$

41. (b) Among the given options, $[Cr(C_2O_4)_3]^{3-}$ show optical isomerism as its mirror image is not superimposable.

42. (b) The correct match is A-II, B-I, C-IV, D-III

43. (c)

Complex	Isomerism shown
$[Co(en)_3]^{3+}$	Optical only
$[Ni(NH_3)_5Br]^+$	No geometrical isomer
$[Co(NH_3)_2(en)_2]^{3+}$	*cis* and *trans*
$[Cr(NH_3)_4(en)]^{3+}$	No geometrical isomer

44. (b) $\underset{x}{[Ag(NH_3)_2]^{+1}}\ \underset{y}{[Ag(CN)_2]^{-1}}$

$x + 0 \times 1 = +1 \Rightarrow x = +1$

$y + (-1 \times 2) = -1 \Rightarrow y = +2 - 1 = +1$

∴ The sum of oxidation states of two silver ions in $[Ag(NH_3)_2][Ag(CN)_2]$ complex is 2.

45. (a) Here, bpy is a bidentate ligand. So, coordination number of cobalt is 6 (i.e. two from bpy and four from Cl ligand).

46. (c) The IUPAC name for the complex $[Co(NO_2)(NH_3)_5]Cl_2$ is pentaammine nitrito-N-cobalt (III) chloride.

47. (c) Linkage isomerism arises in a coordination compound containing ambidentate ligand. Thus, among the given pairs $[Pd(PPh_3)(NCS)_2]$ and $[Pd(PPh_3)_2(SCN)_2]^2$.

48. (b) Among given complexes III, IV and V will display geometrical isomerism.

Pt^{2+} complexes with coordination number equals to 4 are square planar.

In $[Pt(NH_3)_2Cl(NO_2)]$ two NH_3 ligands could arrange in *cis* or *trans* positions.

∴ There are two geometrical isomers.

cis *trans*

$[Pt(NH_3)_4ClBr]^{2+}$: Two geometrical isomers coordination number = 6

∴ Octahedral geometry

Cl and Br can be *cis* or *trans*

∴ 2 geometrical isomers

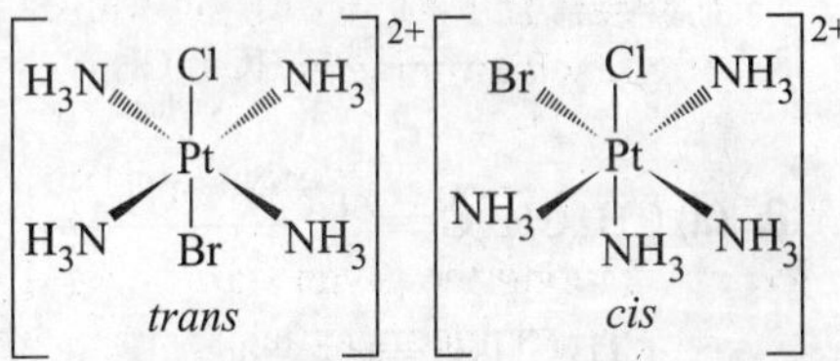

$[Co(H_2O)(Cl)(en)_2]Cl$ show geometrical isomerism.

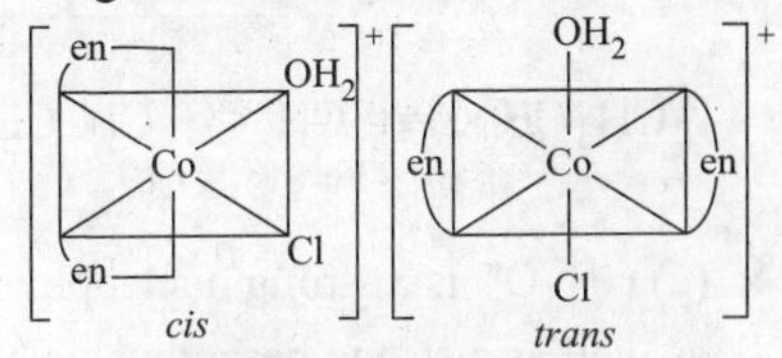

Geometrical isomers

49. (a) Among the given complexes, (a) is homoleptic complex. Homoleptic complex are those complexes which contain only one type of ligand.

50. (c) *cis*-platin, oxaliplatin and carboplatin among the given compounds can be considered to be anti-cancer.

cis-platin

Oxaliplatin Carboplatin

Ch-7 Haloalkanes and Haloarenes

Topical Follow Thru

Test-1

1. (a) The peroxide effect is only applicable in case of HBr, not observed with HI. Therefore, only Markownikoff's addition occurs i.e.

$$CH_3 - CH = CH_2 \xrightarrow[\text{Markownikoff's addition}]{\text{HI/Peroxide}} \underset{(P)}{CH_3CHICH_3}$$

2. (c)

$$\text{Br}\text{CH}_2\text{CH}_2\text{Br} \text{ (1, 2-dibromoethane)} \xrightarrow[-\text{KBr}, -H_2O]{\text{KOH (alc.)}} CH_2{=}CH{-}Br \xrightarrow{NaNH_2} \underset{\text{Acetylene}}{HC{\equiv}CH}$$

3. (a) $\underset{\text{1-butyne}}{CH_3CH_2C{\equiv}CH} \xrightarrow{NaNH_2 \text{ in liq. } NH_3} \underset{\text{Sodium-1-butynide}}{CH_3CH_2C \equiv C^- Na^+}$

$$\xrightarrow[S_N2]{BrCH_2CH_2CH_2CH_3} \underset{\text{3-octyne}}{CH_3CH_2C{\equiv}CCH_2CH_2CH_2CH_3}$$

4. (c) CH_3O^- is a strong nucleophile as well as a strong base, thus it can either bring about substitution or elimination. The CH_3- group at β-carbon causes steric hindrance to nucleophilic substitution (S_N2), therefore, elimination (E_2) occurs preferentially to form 2-methylpropene.

$$CH_3-\overset{CH_3}{\underset{H}{C}}-CH_2-Br \xrightarrow[E_2/(-HBr)]{CH_3O^-/CH_3OH} \underset{\text{2-methylpropene}}{CH_3-\overset{CH_3}{C}{=}CH_2}$$

5. (c) The reactivity of S_N1 reactions depends upon the stability of the intermediate carbocations. Since, the stability of the carbocations derived from (*A*), (*B*) and (*C*) follows the order

Allylic carbocation > 2° carbocation > 1° carbocation

Allylic carbocation is more stable than other two carbocation due to conjugation. 2° carbocation is more stable than 1° carbocation due to hyperconjugation.

Therefore, S_N1 reactivity of these three bromide follows the order $B > C > A$, i.e. option (c) is correct.

6. (c) The order of reactivity in S_N2 reactions is 1° > 2° > 3°.

Further, amongst 1° alkyl halides, unsubstituted alkyl halides are more reactive than substituted alkyl halides. Thus, the overall decreasing reactivity in S_N2 reactions is I > III > II > IV.

7. (a) A mixture containing two enantiomers in equimolar amount have zero optical rotation, as the rotation due to one isomer is cancelled by the rotation due to other isomer. Such a mixture is known as racemic mixture. All those compounds which follow S_N1 mechanism during nucleophilic substitution reaction form racemic mixture.

Order of reactivity of alkyl halides towards S_N1 reaction follows as tertiary halide > secondary halide > primary halide > CH_3X.

Thus, in $CH_3-\underset{C_3H_7}{CH}-Cl$

Cl atom is attached to a chiral carbon. So, it will give a racemic product. Hence, option (a) is correct.

8. (c) $CH_3-CHBr_2 + 4Na + Br_2CHCH_3 \xrightarrow[-4NaBr]{\text{Ether}} \underset{\text{But-2-ene}}{CH_3-CH{=}CH-CH_3}$

Thus, the product formed is but-2-ene.

9. (b) Dipole moment decreases with decrease in charge separation and electronegativity difference. Greater the value of electronegativity, higher will be the dipole moment. So, CH_3F should have greater dipole moment but due to smaller size of fluorine, the dipole moment of CH_3Cl surpass that of CH_3F. Hence, the order of dipole moment is

$CH_3Cl > CH_3F > CH_3Br$.

10. (b) The given reaction is S_N2, hence yield with 1°-alkyl halide will be maximum, i.e. $CH_3CH_2CH_2Cl$.

11. (a) The reaction is as follows

$$CH_2{=}CH-CH_2-CH{=}CH_2 \xrightarrow{NBS} \underset{(A)}{CH_2{=}CH\underset{Br}{CH}CH{=}CH_2}$$

12. (a) Among the given options, 2-chloro-2-methylbutane is a tertiary alkyl halide, as it is bonded to a tertiary carbon.

$$CH_3-\overset{Cl}{\underset{CH_3}{C}}-CH_2-CH_3$$

13. (d) Statement given in option (a) and (b) are incorrect. It is because the product formed by reaction of C_2H_5Br with alc. KOH will form C_2H_4 while C_2H_5Br when treated with metallic sodium gives butane. Their reaction are as follows

$$C_2H_5Br + \text{Alc. KOH} \longrightarrow C_2H_4 + H_2O + KBr$$

$$C_2H_5\,Br + 2Na + Br\,C_2H_5 \longrightarrow \underset{\text{Butane}}{C_2H_5—C_2H_5} + 2NaBr$$

14. (d) The reaction of 2-methyl propene with HBr takes place as follows

$$CH_3—\underset{CH_3}{\underset{|}{CH}}=CH_2 + HBr \longrightarrow \underset{\text{2-bromo-2-methylpropane}}{CH_3—\overset{Br}{\overset{|}{\underset{CH_3}{\underset{|}{C}}}}—CH_3}$$

Thus, the major product formed is 2-bromo-2-methylpropane.

15. (c) The equation of Wurtz reaction is as follows

$$CH_3\,Br + 2Na + Br—CH_3 \longrightarrow CH_3—CH_3$$

Thus, sodium, i.e. Na metal is used in Wurtz synthesis.

Test-2

1. (d)

Toluene ($C_6H_5CH_3$) $\xrightarrow[\text{(Nuclear chlorination)}]{Cl_2/FeCl_3}$ p-chlorotoluene (Major) (Y) + o-chlorotoluene (Minor)

Toluene $\xrightarrow{Cl_2/h\nu}$ $C_6H_5CCl_3$ Trichloromethyl-benzene (X)

2. (d) (A) is false but (R) is true. The correct form of (A) is

In S_N1 reaction, reactivity depends upon the stability of carbocations. $C_6H_5—\overset{+}{C}H—C_6H_5$ carbocation is more stable as compared to $C_6H_5\overset{+}{C}H_2$ due to resonance with two phenyl groups. Therefore, $C_6H_5CHClC_6H_5$ gets hydrolysed more easily than $C_6H_5CH_2Cl$.

3. (a) Both Statements I and II are incorrect. Their corrected form are as follows

I. The presence of nitro group facilitates nucleophilic substitution reaction in aryl halides.

II. The intermediate carbonium ion is stabilised due to presence of the nitro group. C—X bond polarity increases and the bond cleavage becomes more easy.

4. (a) Raschig process is the commercial method for the preparation of chlorobenzene from benzene.

$$2\,\underset{\text{Benzene}}{C_6H_6} + 2HCl + O_2 \xrightarrow[500\text{ K}]{CuCl_2} 2\,\underset{\text{Chlorobenzene}}{C_6H_5Cl} + 2H_2O$$

In Dow's process, firstly sodium phenoxide is obtained by the reaction of chlorobenzene with NaOH at 623 K and 200 atm, which on acid hydrolysis forms phenol.

$$\underset{\text{Chlorobenzene}}{C_6H_5Cl} + NaOH \xrightarrow[200\text{ atm},\,-HCl]{623\text{ K}} \underset{\text{Sodium phenoxide}}{C_6H_5\overset{\ominus}{O}\overset{\oplus}{Na}} \xrightarrow[-NaCl]{HCl} \underset{\text{Phenol}}{C_6H_5OH}$$

5. (a) The Wurtz-Fittig reaction is the reaction of an aryl halide with an alkyl halide and sodium metal to give substituted aromatic compound.

Thus, Wurtz-Fittig reaction is

$$C_6H_5I + 2Na + CH_3I \longrightarrow C_6H_5CH_3 + 2NaI$$

6. (b) The complete reaction is as follows

$$C_6H_5CH_2CH_3 \xrightarrow[H_2SO_4]{HNO_3} \underset{(A)}{p\text{-}NO_2C_6H_4CH_2CH_3} \xrightarrow[\Delta]{Br_2} \underset{(B)}{p\text{-}NO_2C_6H_4CH(Br)CH_3}$$

7. (c) In chlorobenzene, the C of C—Cl bond is sp^2-hybridised, whereas the C of C—Cl bond in chloromethane in sp^3-hybridised. Thus, there is more s-character in the carbon of the C—Cl bond in chlorobenzene and as a result holds the electron pair of C—Cl bond more tightly.

8. (a) Both (A) and (R) are true and (R) is the correct explanation of (A).

9. (a) When a primary aromatic amine, dissolved or suspended in cold aqueous mineral acid and treated with sodium nitrite, a diazonium salt is formed.

When this freshly prepared diazonium salt is mixed with cuprous chloride, then diazonium group is replaced by —Cl. Then, chlorobenzene is formed which is X in this reaction.

$$C_6H_5NH_2 \xrightarrow[273\text{-}278\text{ K}]{NaNO_2+HCl} C_6H_5\overset{+}{N_2}\overset{-}{Cl} \xrightarrow{Cu_2Cl_2} \underset{(X)}{C_6H_5Cl} + N_2$$

10. (c) Reaction (c) is incorrect because iodobenzene reacts with Cu in sealed tube to form biphenyl. This reaction is named as "Ullmann reaction".

$$2\,C_6H_5I \xrightarrow[-CuI_2]{Cu\ (Sealed\ tube)} C_6H_5{-}C_6H_5$$

(Biphenyl)

11. (d) ***Step* I** $CH_3{-}\underset{CH_3}{\underset{|}{CH}}{-}CH_2{-}Br + AlCl_3 \longrightarrow AlCl_3^- Br^+ + CH_3{-}\underset{CH_3}{\underset{|}{CH}}{-}CH_2^{\oplus}$

$$\xrightarrow{H\text{-shifting}} CH_3{-}\overset{CH_3}{\overset{|}{\underset{\oplus}{C}}}{-}CH_3$$

Attacking species

Step II Chlorobenzene (Cl, H) + $\overset{\oplus}{C}H_3{-}\underset{CH_3}{\underset{|}{C}}{-}CH_3 \longrightarrow$ (arenium ion with Cl, H and $H_3C{-}\underset{CH_3}{\underset{|}{C}}{-}CH_3$) $\xrightarrow{-H^+}$ p-Cl-C$_6$H$_4$-$\underset{CH_3}{\underset{|}{C}}(CH_3){-}CH_3$

Now, the H^+ ion release with $AlCl_3^- Br^+$

$$H^+ + AlCl_3^- Br^+ \longrightarrow HBr + AlCl_3$$

12. (a) The presence of $-NO_2$ group on the ring, facilitates the substitution of F by $-OCH_3$ group (through nucleophilic attack).

$$\text{p-}F{-}C_6H_4{-}NO_2 \xrightarrow{NaOCH_3} \text{p-}OCH_3{-}C_6H_4{-}NO_2$$

Thus, option (a) is correct.

13. (c) Melting point of molecule depends on packing efficiency. If a molecule is symmetrical, then close packing is possible due to better crystal fitting which results in strong intermolecular attractive force. Thus, more energy is required to break the bond, which results in increased melting point.

Thus, *para*-dichlorobenzene has high melting point than *meta* and *ortho*. Moreover, *ortho* dichlorobenzene is more closely packed than *meta*. Thus, the order for melting point is I > III > II.

14. (c) Reactions (a), (b) and (d) are correct match while reaction (c) is not a correct match.

$C_2H_5Cl + NaI \longrightarrow C_2H_5I + NaCl$
$\Rightarrow$ Finkelstein reaction

15. (b) The mechanism of the given reaction is as follows

$$\underset{\text{Benzene}}{C_6H_6} \xrightarrow{Cl_2,\ Fe} \underset{\text{Chlorobenzene}}{C_6H_5Cl} + HCl$$

Test-3

1. (c) Statement I is incorrect while Statement II is correct.

$CHCl_3$ should be stored in closed, dark coloured bottles completely filled so that air is kept out.

2. (a) On heating, C—I bond in CHI_3 breaks whereas C—Cl bond in $CHCl_3$ does not break. This is because the bond strength of C—I bond is less than C—Cl bond. Thus, $AgNO_3$ gives precipitate of AgI with iodoform.

3. (d)

$$3\,C_6H_6 + CHCl_3 \xrightarrow{AlCl_3} (C_6H_5)_3C{-}H + 3HCl$$

Triphenyl methane
(Friedel -Crafts reaction)
(*X*)

4. (b) Ethyl alcohol retards the oxidation of $CHCl_3$ to phosgene as well as it converts any phosgene formed to harmless diethyl carbonate.

The reaction involve is as follows

$$\underset{\text{Phosgene}}{COCl_2} + 2C_2H_5OH \longrightarrow \underset{\text{Diethyl carbonate}}{(C_2H_5)_2CO_3} + 2HCl$$

5. (a) Alc. KOH can be used to distinguish between $CHCl_3$ and CCl_4.

$$CHCl_3 + RNH_2 + 3\ KOH(alc.) \longrightarrow \underset{\text{Isocyanide}}{RN{\equiv}C} + 3KCl + 3H_2O$$

This reaction is known as carbylamine reaction.

$$CCl_4 + RNH_2 + KOH\ (alc.) \longrightarrow \text{No isocyanide formation}$$

6. (d) Benzene hexachloride (BHC) is used as an insecticide.

7. (b) $CHCl_3 + CH_3COCH_3 \longrightarrow \underset{\text{Chloretone}}{(CH_3)_2C(OH)CCl_3}$

Chloretone is used as a hypnotic drug.

8. (d) Chloroform is tested before use, for the presence of extremely poisonous gas phosgene. This gas may be formed on storage of the chemical for long period of time. If $CHCl_3$ sample contains phosgene ($COCl_2$), then it will give a white ppt. when treated with $AgNO_3$ solution in the cold.

9. (c) Statements I, II and III are correct while statements IV and V are incorrect. Their correct form are as follows

IV. Freon is manufactured from tetrachloromethane by Swarts reaction.

V. Freons are extremely stable and unreactive.

10. (b) When chloroform is treated with concentrated nitric acid, its hydrogen is replaced by nitro group which leads to formation of chloropicrin.

$$CHCl_3 + HONO_2 \longrightarrow \underset{\text{Chloropicrin}}{Cl_3CNO_2} + H_2O$$

11. (a) Freons are chlorofluorocarbons and are responsible for depletion of ozone layer.

12. (d) Reaction of $CHCl_3$ with NaOH forms sodium formate.

$$CHCl_3 + 4NaOH \rightarrow HCOONa + 3NaCl + 2H_2O$$

13. (a) Primary amines react with chloroform in the presence of base then converts into isocyanide.

Thus, it is used to test the presence of primary amines.

14. (d) Since, the compound on heating produces CO_2 and no water, thus the compound does not contain any hydrogen atom hence it is CCl_4.

15. (a) Both (A) and (R) are true and (R) is the correct explanation of (A).

Chapter Break Thru

1. (b) Tertiary alcohol readily reacts with conc. HCl even in absence of $ZnCl_2$ and form *tert*-butyl chloride.

Complete reaction is as follows

$$CH_3-C(OH)(CH_3)-CH_3 \xrightarrow[\text{Room temp.}]{\text{Conc. HCl}} \underset{(P)}{CH_3-C(CH_3)(Cl)-CH_3}$$

2-chloro-2-methylpropane

2. (c) $\overset{1}{CH_3}(H)\overset{2}{C}=\overset{3}{C}(CH_3)-\overset{4}{C}H(Br)-\overset{5}{CH_3}$

4-bromo-3-methylpent-2-ene

3. (b) Reaction of alkene in presence of peroxide (H_2O_2) followed by Kharasch effect gives haloalkane.

$$CH_3-CH_2-C(C_2H_5)=CH-CH_3 + HBr \xrightarrow{\text{Peroxide } (H_2O_2),\ \text{Kharasch effect}} CH_3-CH_2-C(C_2H_5)(H)-CH(Br)-CH_3$$

2-bromo-3-ethylpentane

4. (d) Reactions given in I, III, IV and V are correct while II is incorrect. Dehydrohalogenation takes place on heating alkyl dihalide with zinc dust.

$$\text{1,2-dichlorocyclohexane} \xrightarrow[\Delta]{\text{Zn dust}} \text{cyclohexene} + ZnCl_2$$

5. (c) As the stability of intermediate increases, reactivity towards S_N1 increases. I is an alkyl halide having 3α-H while II has resonance stabilised carbocation having 4α-H and III have 5α-H. Due to the formation of stable carbocation II is highly reactive. Thus, the correct order is : II > III > I.

6. (a) Complete reaction is as follows

$$2CH_3COOH + Ag_2CO_3 \xrightarrow{-H_2CO_3} \underset{(A)}{2CH_3COO^-Ag^+}$$

$$CH_3COO^-Ag^+ + Br_2 \xrightarrow{CCl_4} AgBr + \underset{(B)}{CH_3Br} + CO_2$$

7. (a) Among isomeric alkyl halides, the boiling point decreases with increase in branching in the alkyl group because of which molecules attain spherical shape with less surface area. As a result, interparticle force becomes weaker resulting in lower boiling point.

Correct order is

$$CH_3-CH_2-CH_2-CH_2-Cl > CH_3-CH(Cl)-CH_2-CH_3 > CH_3-CH(CH_3)-CH_2-Cl > (CH_3)_3C-Cl$$

8. (b) Only statement (b) is incorrect. Its correct statement is : Order of reactivity toward S_N1 reaction is $3° > 2° > 1° > R-X$.

9. (c) Statements (a), (b) and (d) are correct but statement (c) is incorrect because stronger nucleophile favours S_N2 reaction, whereas weaker nucleophile favours S_N1 reaction.

10. (b) Statement I is correct but Statement II is incorrect. The corrected form of Statement II is In S_N1 mechanism carbocation are formed as intermediate.

11. (d) In *neo*-pentyl bromide there is no formation of secondary carbocation on cleavage of C—Br bond.

12. (a) A good leaving group is the conjugate base of a strong acid and a weak base.

During the substitution reaction, C— I bond in (butyl iodide) is easily dissociated whereas C—F bond in (butyl fluoride) does not easily dissociate as it has more bond strength and hence does not give substitution reaction.

So, correct order towards nucleophilic substitution (S_N2) is as follows

butyl–F < butyl–Cl < butyl–Br < butyl–I

13. (c) (A) is true but (R) is false because vinyl halide is a chemical compound in which the halogen group is attached to one of the carbons present in the alkene group. Vinyl group is an electron withdrawing group in vinyl bromide. The carbon atom to which the halogen group is attached will be having sp^2-hybridisation.

Due to the presence of double bonds it can undergo delocalisation. It will be having resonance structure and hence, the vinyl halide is less reactive.

Therefore, it will be difficult to carry out the $S_N 1$ reaction.

14. (b) Generally, density of halogen derivative increases with increase in number of halogens and atomic mass of the halogen atom.

Therefore, correct order of density is IV < II < I < III.

15. (a) The correct match is

A-III, B-IV, C-I, D-II.

A. Allylic substrate, strong $\ddot{Nu}$, protic solvent → $S_N 2$ reaction and bimolecular.

B. Allylic substrate, weak $\ddot{Nu}$, polar solvent, $S_N 1$ and unimolecular.

C. (S=O) group is EWG and will stabilise carbanion formed in the first step, OPh is a poor leaving group. So, denatured product is obtained. These are necessary condition for E_1 CB.

D. Both are 1° alkyl bromide so, react with same rate with alc. KOH towards E_1 reaction.

Thus, option (a) is correct.

16. (b) Statement I is correct but Statement II is incorrect. The correct form of statement II is Alkyl halide on reaction with $LiAlH_4$ gives alkane.

$$R—Cl \xrightarrow{LiAlH_4} R—H$$

where, R = an alkyl group.

17. (b) Complete reaction is as follows

Chlorobenzene $\xrightarrow[Cu_2O]{NH_3}$ Aniline (X) $\xrightarrow[HCl]{NaNO_2}$

Diazonium chloride salt (Y) ($N_2^+Cl^-$) $\xrightarrow[-KCl, -N_2]{KI}$ Iodobenzene (Z)

18. (a) Complete reaction is as follows

$$CHI_3 + 6Ag + I_3CH \xrightarrow[-6AgI]{Heat} CH{\equiv}CH + 6AgI$$

Iodoform; Ethyne

Thus, option (a) is correct.

19. (b)

$C_6H_5CH_2OH$ (Phenyl methanol) (A) $\xrightarrow[S_N1 \text{ mechanism}]{SOCl_2, \text{ Pyridine}}$ $C_6H_5CH_2Cl$ $\xrightarrow{KCN \text{ (Nucleophilic substitution)}}$ $C_6H_5CH_2CN$ (B) $\xrightarrow{H_3O^+ \text{ Complete hydrolysis of cyanide}}$ $C_6H_5CH_2COOH$ (2-phenyl ethanoic acid) (C)

Hence, option (b) is correct.

20. (a) If EWG group is attached with benzene ring, then —C—Cl bond gets weaker.

Thus, reactivity towards nucleophilic substitution reaction increases.

—NO_2 is a EWG and if more number of EWG is present, reactivity toward nucleophilic substitution reaction increases.

Thus, the correct increasing order will be

Chlorobenzene < 4-nitrochlorobenzene < 2,4-dinitrochlorobenzene < 2,4,6-trinitrochlorobenzene

21. (d)

$$CH_3O—CH{=}CH_2 \xrightarrow{H^+} CH_3\ddot{O}—\overset{+}{C}H—CH_3 \longleftrightarrow CH_3\overset{+}{O}{=}CH—CH_3 \xrightarrow{Br^-} CH_3O—CH(Br)—CH_3$$

More stable carbocation is formed in this manner due to stabilisation with lone pair of electrons of oxygen of —OCH_3 group.

22. (a) $CH_2=CH—CH_3 + Cl_2 \xrightarrow{600\ K} CH_2=CH—CH_2—Cl + HCl$

$CH_2=CH—CH_3$ + NBS (N-bromosuccinimide) $\xrightarrow{h\nu}$ $CH_2=CH—CH_2—Br$ + Succinimide

$$CH_2=CH—CH_3 + SO_2Cl_2 \xrightarrow{h\nu} CH_2=CH—CH_2—Cl + SO_2 + HCl$$

23. (b)

Toluene $\xrightarrow[-3\ HCl]{3Cl_2, \Delta}$ $C_6H_5CCl_3$ (A) $\xrightarrow{Br_2/Fe}$ m-bromo-benzotrichloride (B) $\xrightarrow{Zn/HCl \text{ (Hydrogenolysis)}}$ m-bromotoluene (C)

24. (b) As the 3° radicals are more stable than 2° and 1°, thus

1-(2-chloropropan-2-yl)-3-methylcyclopentane [$C(Cl)(CH_3)_2$ on cyclopentane ring bearing CH_3]

is the major monochlorination isomer formed in the given reaction.

25. (b) In CH_2Cl_2, there are 2C—H bonds and 2C—Cl bonds. Here, the resultant of 2C—H dipole bonds are reduced by the 2C—Cl dipole bond. This result in non-zero dipole moment of CH_2Cl_2.

(μ=1.60D)

Similarly, the net dipole moment of $CHCl_3$ is non-zero.

(μ=1.08D)

26. (b) In $CH_2=CHCl$ (vinyl chloride) C—Cl bond is shortest due to resonance of lone pair of —Cl (chlorine atom).

Due to resonance C—Cl bond acquire partial double bond character.

Hence, vinyl chloride have least C—Cl bond length.

Cl: ← lone pair involved in resonance

HC=CH_2

27. (a) Magnitude of van der Waals' forces goes on decreasing with branching. Hence, the order of the boiling points is

$CH_3CH_2CH_2CH_2Br$ > $CH_3CH_2-CH(CH_3)-Br$ > $CH_3-C(CH_3)_2-Br$

28. (d)

Nitrobenzene $\xrightarrow[\text{(Bromination)}]{Br_2/Fe}$ m-bromonitrobenzene (P) $\xrightarrow[\text{(Reduction)}]{Sn/HCl}$ m-bromoaniline (Q)

—NO_2 group is a deactivating and m-directing group so it directs the incoming of Br^- ion to the *m*-position thereby leading to the formation of *m*-bromonitrobenzene. Upon reduction with Sn/HCl, the $-NO_2$ group reduces to —NH_2, i.e. the final product is *m*-bromoaniline.

29. (d) II is most reactive as it produces an aromatic carbocation while IV is less reactive as it produces a non-resonance stabilised carbocation. III is least reactive than I as former involve an anti-aromatic carbocation.

30. (c) Grignard reagent is formed by reacting magnesium with ethyl iodide.

$$\underset{\text{Ethyl iodide}}{C_2H_5I} + Mg \xrightarrow{\text{Dry ether}} \underset{\text{Ethyl magnesium iodide}}{C_2H_5MgI}$$

31. (a) The general formula for alkyl halides is $C_nH_{2n+1}X$.

32. (a) CCl_4 is symmetrical so, $\mu = 0$.

In CH_2Cl_2, only the polarity vectors of 2 'Cl' atoms add up and in CH_3Cl only one 'Cl' contribute.

Hence, the order of dipole moment is $CH_3Cl > CH_2Cl_2 > CHCl_3 > CCl_4$.

33. (c) The given reaction will proceed by free radical mechanism.

$Ph_2CH-C_6H_4-CH_3 \xrightarrow{\text{Excess } Cl_2/hv}$ $(C_6H_5)_2C(Cl)-C_6H_4-CCl_3$

34. (d)

Toluene $\xrightarrow[\text{Halogenation}]{Cl_2/FeCl_3}$ $CH_3-C_6H_4-Cl$ *p*-chlorotoluene (Major product) (*X*) + o-chlorotoluene (Minor product) (*X*)

Toluene $\xrightarrow[\text{(Side chain halogenation)}]{Cl_2/hv}$ $C_6H_5-CCl_3$ Trichloromethylbenzene (Major product) (*Y*)

35. (c) Electron-withdrawing group increase and electron-donating group decrease the reactivity towards nucleophilic substitution. The more the number of electron-withdrawing group the higher will be the reactivity. Hence, the correct order is IV > III > II > I.

36. (a) Among the given statements only I, IV and V are incorrect while II and III are correct.

I. Grignard reagents ($R-Mg-X$) are readily decomposed by water to produce alkanes. That is why, they should be prepared under anhydrous conditions. Instead, ether is used as a solvent during the preparation of Grignard reagent.

IV. Partial double bond character of a bond increases the strength of the bond and hence, decreases the stability. Thus, phenol will not react with a mixture of NaBr and H_2SO_4 because it is resonance stabilised.

V. Water molecules have enough strong H-bonding (intermolecular) which is difficult to be broken by alkyl halides, though they are also polar in nature. Therefore, alkyl halides do not dissolve in water and form separate layers.

37. (a) Both (A) and (R) are true and (R) is the correct explanation of (A).

Reactions of arenes with iodine are reversible in nature. So, aryl iodides are prepared in the presence of an oxidising agent such as HNO_3, HIO_4 etc, in order to oxidise the HI formed during iodination.

$$C_6H_6 + I_2 \underset{}{\overset{HIO_3}{\rightleftharpoons}} C_6H_5I + HI$$

$$5HI + HIO_3 \longrightarrow 3I_2 + 3H_2O$$

38. (a) 3-bromoanisole $\xrightarrow{NaNH_2}$ (A) (m-anisidine) Direct substitution + Distabilised by $-I$ effect of the $-OCH_3$ group. (not formed) Cine substitution

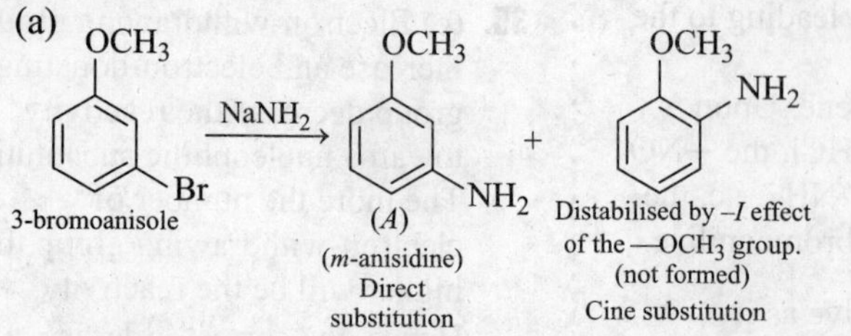

If nucleophile occupies same position of the leaving group, product is called direct substitution product. If nucleophile occupies adjacent position of the leaving group, product is called cine substitution product. Intermediate is benzyne.

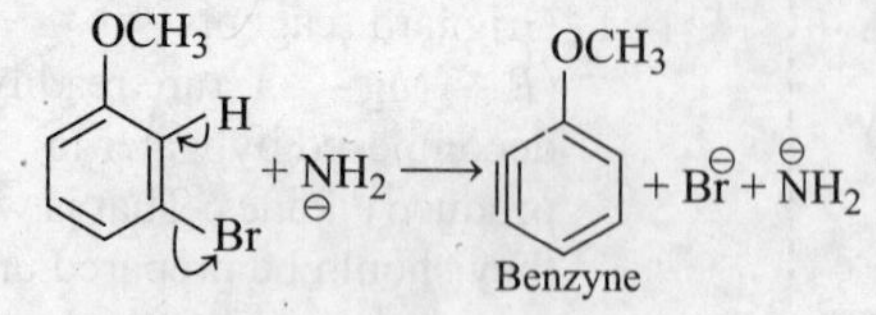

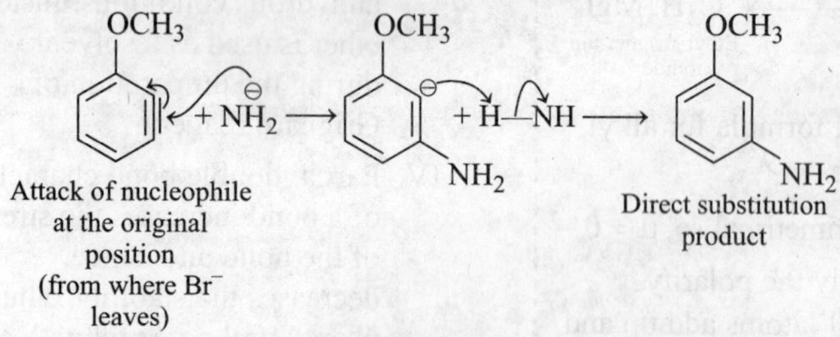

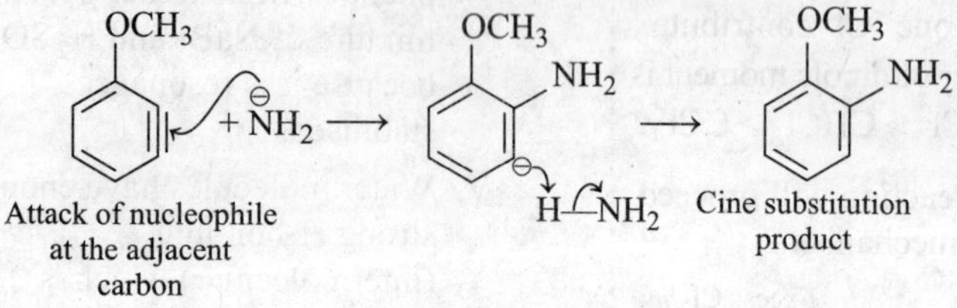

$+ \overset{\ominus}{N}H_2 \longrightarrow$ Benzyne $+ \overset{\ominus}{Br} + \overset{\ominus}{N}H_2$

Attack of nucleophile at the original position (from where Br^- leaves) $+ \overset{\ominus}{N}H_2 \longrightarrow + H-NH \longrightarrow$ Direct substitution product

Attack of nucleophile at the adjacent carbon $+ \overset{\ominus}{N}H_2 \longrightarrow$ $H-NH_2$ $\longrightarrow$ Cine substitution product

39. (b) The complete reaction is as follows

$$CH_3-\underset{}{CH}(Cl)-Cl + 2KOH(aq) \xrightarrow{-2KCl} CH_3-CH(OH)_2 \xrightarrow{-H_2O} CH_3CHO$$

(1, 1-dichloroethane) (Unstable) Acetaldehyde

40. (a)

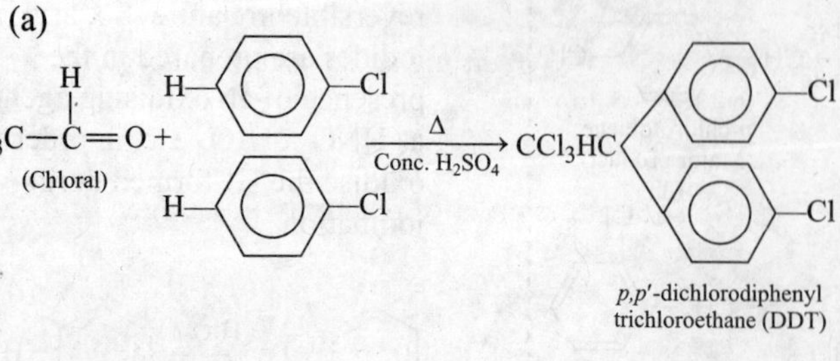

$$Cl_3C-\overset{H}{C}=O + 2\,H-C_6H_4-Cl \xrightarrow[\text{Conc. } H_2SO_4]{\Delta} CCl_3HC(C_6H_4Cl)_2$$

(Chloral) p,p'-dichlorodiphenyl trichloroethane (DDT)

41. (d) When chlorobenzene is treated with NaOH at 623 K temperature and 300 atm pressure, sodium phenoxide is formed by nucleophilic substitution.

$$C_6H_5Cl + NaOH \xrightarrow[300\ atm]{623\ K} C_6H_5\ddot{O}Na^+$$

Chlorobenzene Sodium phenoxide

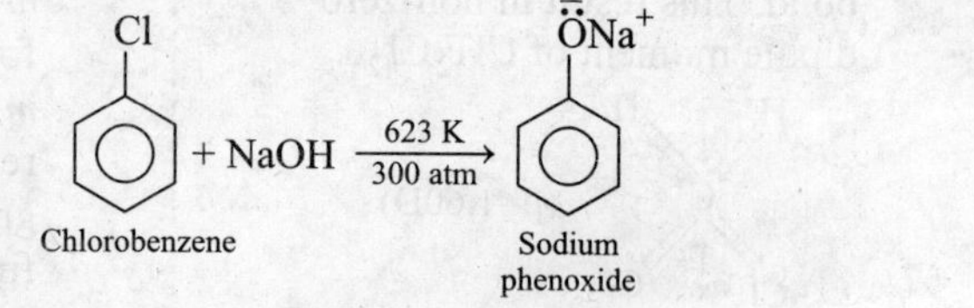

(Dow's process)

Nucleophilic substitution is not preferred in aromatic compounds. So, to do such reactions high temperature and pressure are required.

42. (a) Primary alkyl halides favour substitution whereas secondary and tertiary alkyl halides favour elimination.

43. (c) $CH_3-CH_2-CH_2-Br + 2Na$ (n-propyl bromide)

$+ Br-CH_2-CH_2-CH_3 \xrightarrow{\text{Dry ether}} CH_3-(CH_2)_4-CH_3$ (n-propyl bromide) (n-hexane)

This is the Wurtz reaction in which n-propyl bromide reacts with sodium in presence of dry ether giving n-hexane.

In this reaction, two n-propyl groups join together to give pure n-hexane.

44. (c) Electrophile will attack at *ortho* and *para*-position with respect to better electron donating group (EDG).

EDG : OH $> -CH_3$

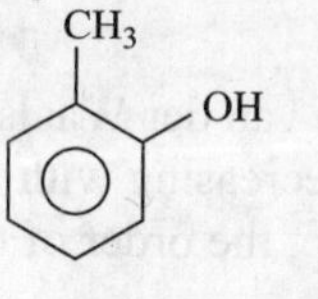

para-position with respect to $-OH$ $(+R)$ group and it will be *meta*-position with respect to CH_3 (methyl group).

45. (c) The mechanism of the given reaction is

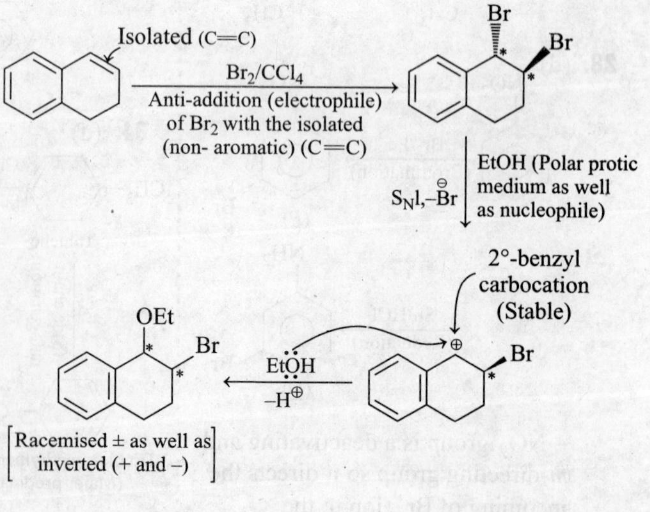

Isolated (C=C) $\xrightarrow{Br_2/CCl_4}$ Anti-addition (electrophile) of Br_2 with the isolated (non- aromatic) (C=C)

$S_N1, -\overset{\ominus}{Br}$ EtOH (Polar protic medium as well as nucleophile)

2°-benzyl carbocation (Stable) $\xrightarrow[-H^\oplus]{Et\ddot{O}H}$ Racemised ± as well as inverted (+ and −)

46. (c) Statements I, II, III and IV are correct while V is incorrect.

The full form of DDT is *p, p'*-dichlorodiphenyltrichloroethane.

47. (c) A nucleophilic aromatic substitution is a substitution reaction in organic chemistry in which the nucleophile displace a good leaving group, such as a halide, on an aromatic ring. Thus, among the given options, reaction of NaOH with dinitrochlorobenzene represents nucleophilic aromatic substitution reaction.

48. (d) Incorrect statement regarding benzyl chloride is given in option (d). It is because benzyl chloride is more reactive than vinyl chloride.

49. (c) Among the given options, *p*-methoxy benzyl carbocation generated from *p*-methoxy benzyl bromide is more stable due to $+R$ effect of ethoxy group so it will react easily.

$\overset{\oplus}{C}H_2$ (on benzene ring, para) OCH_3

50. (d) Complete reaction sequence is as follows

$$C_6H_6 \xrightarrow{Cl_2/\text{Anhy. } AlCl_3} C_6H_5Cl \xrightarrow{\text{Conc. } HNO_3} o\text{-}ClC_6H_4NO_2 + p\text{-}ClC_6H_4NO_2$$

Ch-8 Alcohols, Phenols and Ethers

Topical Follow Thru

Test-1

1. (b) Solubility of alcohols in water decreases with increase in molecular masses.

Among the given statements, the correct form, of other options are as follows

(a) Lower members are soluble in water as they form H-bonding with water molecules.

(c) Higher members are colourless and tasteless; lower members have a pleasant smell and burning taste.

(d) The boiling point of alcohols increases with increase in number of C-atoms.

2. (d) Both Statement I and Statement II are correct.

Due to the repulsion between two lone pairs on oxygen atom, the bond angle is slightly less than the tetrahedral bond angle (109°28′).

3. (c) The correct match is A-IV, B-III, C-I, D-II.

4. (a) Both (A) and (R) are true and (R) is the correct explanation of (A).

Oxygen has two unshared pairs of electrons on it. Because of this, it acts as a Lewis base.

5. (b) Mixing of $CuSO_4$ (to give the colour) and pyridine (a foul smelling solid) to make the commercial alcohol unfit for drinking is known as denaturation of alcohol.

6. (c) Boiling points of alcohols increase with increase in the number of carbon atoms and decrease with increase of branching in carbon chain.

$$(CH_3)_3C{-}OH < CH_3{-}CH(CH_3){-}CH_2OH < CH_3CH_2CH_2CH_2OH$$

7. (b) Whenever an alkyl halide reacts with alcoholic potash, β-elimination of the halide occurs, leading to the formation of an alkene.

8. (c) Statements (a), (b) and (d) are correct whereas statement (c) is incorrect.

Corrected form of statement (c) is as follows

In the presence of strong acids, alcohols act as Bronsted bases because they can accept a proton from strong acids to form protonated alcohols.

9. (a) The correct order of reactivity of halogen acids on alcohols is

$$HI > HBr > HCl.$$

This order is due to the bond strengths of hydrogen halides.

HI is most reactive as it has the weakest H—I bond. HBr is less reactive than HI but more reactive than HCl due to its weaker HBr bond compared to HCl.

10. (b) The boiling point of alcohols increases with increase in the number of carbon atoms (increase in van der Waals' forces). In alcohols, the boiling point decreases with increase of branching in carbon chain (because of decrease in van der Waals' forces with decrease in surface area).

Hence, Statement I is correct but statement II is incorrect.

11. (b) The complete reaction proceeds as follows

Butan-2-ol $\xrightarrow[-H_2O\ \text{(dehydration)}]{\text{Conc. } H_2SO_4/\Delta}$ but-2-ene (trans) + but-2-ene (cis) + but-1-ene

12. (b) The complete reaction proceeds as follows

4,4-diethylcyclohexa-2,5-dien-1-one $\xrightarrow{H^+}$ protonated carbonyl → carbocation $\xrightarrow{\text{Ethyl group shift}}$ carbocation $\xrightarrow{-H^+}$ 3,4-diethylphenol

13. (c) $C_2H_5OH \xrightarrow{H_2SO_4,\ 110°C} \underset{\text{Ethyl hydrogen sulphate}}{C_2H_5HSO_4} + H_2O$

$C_2H_5OH \xrightarrow{H_2SO_4,\ 140°C} \underset{\text{Diethyl ether}}{C_2H_5-O-C_2H_5} + H_2O$

$C_2H_5OH \xrightarrow{H_2SO_4,\ 170°C} \underset{\text{Ethene}}{C_2H_4} + H_2O$

Thus, among the given options, only acetylene will not be formed.

14. (d) Both Statement I and Statement II are correct.

15. (d) Statement given in option (d) is incorrect. It is because oxidation of alcohols involves the formation of carbon-oxygen double bond with cleavage of O—H and C—H bonds both.

Test-2

1. (c) Statements (a), (b) and (d) are correct, whereas statement (c) is incorrect.

Corrected form of statement (c) is as follows

The reactions of phenol with metals and sodium hydroxide indicate its acidic nature.

2. (c) Substituted phenols react with *aq*. NaOH to form sodium phenoxides which on reaction with CH_3I undergoes S_N2 reaction to give 2-methoxy-1-methyl benzene.

o-Cresol $\xrightarrow[\text{Acid-base reaction},\ -H_2O]{\text{(i) NaOH } (aq.)}$ sodium o-cresolate ($\overset{\ominus}{O}\overset{\oplus}{Na}$) $\xrightarrow[S_N2\text{ reaction},\ -NaI]{\text{(ii) } \overset{\delta+}{CH_3}-\overset{\delta-}{I}}$ 2-methoxy-1-methyl benzene

3. (b) Statement I is correct but Statement II is incorrect.

In case of phenol, the polarisation of bromine molecule takes place even in the absence of Lewis acid. In phenol the —OH group has the highly activating effect when attached to the benzene ring.

4. (a) On reaction with conc. HNO_3 and conc. H_2SO_4, phenol is converted to 2,4,6-trinitrophenol. The product is commonly known as picric acid.

Reaction is as follows

Phenol $\xrightarrow[\text{Conc. } H_2SO_4]{\text{Conc. } HNO_3}$ 2,4,6-trinitrophenol

5. (a) Both (A) and (R) are true and (R) is the correct explanation of (A).

6. (b)

	List-I (Reactant)	List-II (Product)
A.	Phenol + Zn ⟶	II. Benzene
B.	Phenol $\xrightarrow[H_2SO_4]{Na_2Cr_2O_7}$	IV. Benzoquinone
C.	Phenol $\xrightarrow{\text{(i) } CHCl_3 + aq.\ NaOH,\ \text{(ii) NaOH},\ \text{(iii) } H^{\oplus}}$	III. Salicylaldehyde
D.	2 Phenol + 2Na ⟶	I. Sodium phenoxide

Hence, the correct match is A-II, B-IV, C-III, D-I.

7. (d) Both Statement I and Statement II are correct.

In phenol, carbon of C—O bond is more electronegative than the carbon of C—O bond in methanol. Hence, C—O bond in phenol is less polar than in methanol.

8. (d) Acidic nature of phenol depends on the ability to donate H^+ ions. Presence of electron withdrawing group increases the acidic nature.

Hence, correct order of acidic nature is

4-nitrophenol > 2-nitrophenol > phenol > 4-methylphenol

9. (b) Picric acid (2,4,6-trinitrophenol) is more acidic than the given compounds due to the presence of three strong electron withdrawing groups ($—NO_2$ group) at *ortho* and *para*-positions.

It is due to the effective delocalisation of negative charge in phenoxide ion.

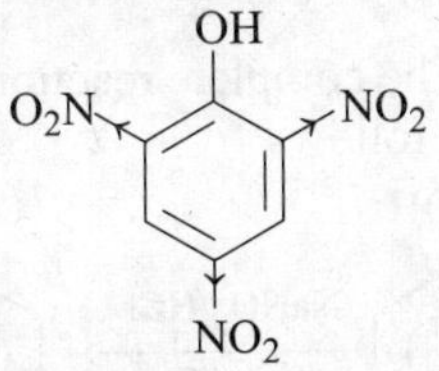

10. (c) When phenol reacts with CH_3I in presence of NaOH, it gives methoxybenzene due to formation of phenoxide ion, which is a better nucleophile than phenol.

The reaction takes place as follows

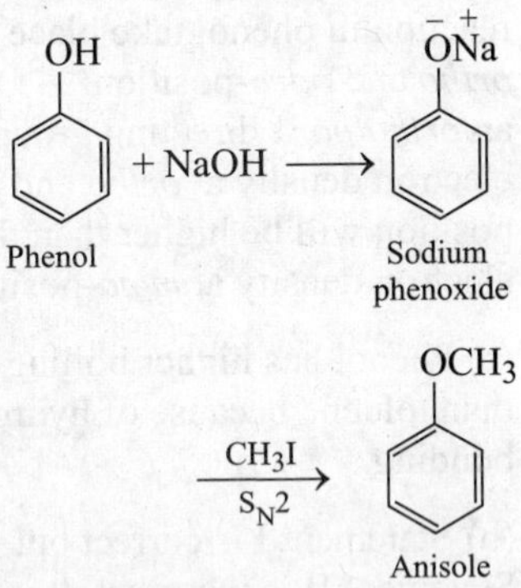

Phenol + NaOH ⟶ Sodium phenoxide $\xrightarrow[S_N2]{CH_3I}$ Anisole

Thus, (A) is true but (R) is false.

11. (a) The complete reaction sequence is as follows

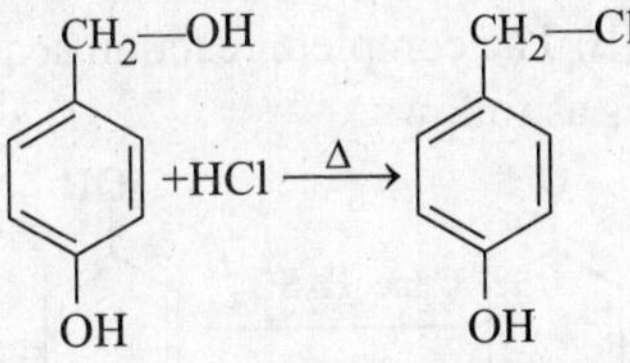

$$HO-C_6H_4-CH_2-OH + HCl \xrightarrow{\Delta} HO-C_6H_4-CH_2-Cl$$

Substitution reaction easily takes place at sp^3-carbon.

12. (a) The Riemer-Tiemann reaction is a chemical reaction used for the orthoformylation of phenols with the simplest example being the conversion of phenol to salicylaldehyde.

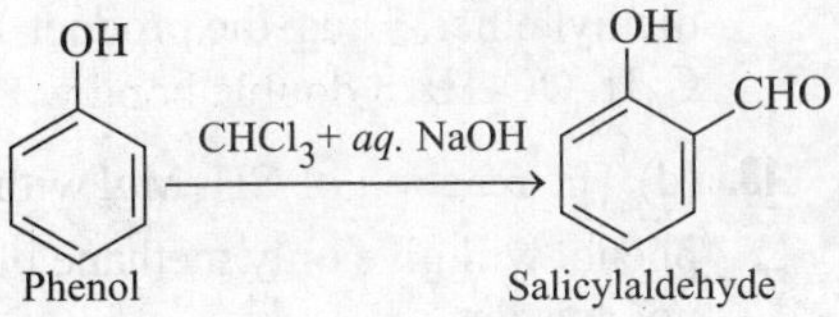

Phenol $\xrightarrow{CHCl_3 + aq.\ NaOH}$ Salicylaldehyde

13. (b) Statement I is correct but Statement II is incorrect. It is because phenol is more acidic than alcohol and H_2O.

14. (b) Phenol is manufactured from the hydrocarbon, cumene (*iso*-propylbenzene). When cumene is oxidised in the presence of air it form cumene hydroperoxide. It is converted to phenol and acetone by treating it with dilute acid. Acetone (as a by-product of this reaction) is also obtained in large quantity by this method.

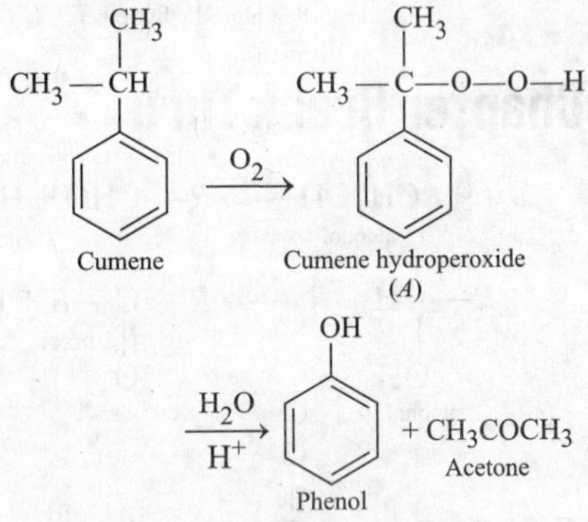

$$C_6H_5-CH(CH_3)_2 \xrightarrow{O_2} C_6H_5-C(CH_3)_2-O-O-H$$

Cumene ⟶ Cumene hydroperoxide (*A*)

$$\xrightarrow[H^+]{H_2O} C_6H_5OH + CH_3COCH_3$$

Phenol + Acetone

15. (a) Both (A) and (R) are true and (R) is the correct explanation of (A).

Test-3

1. (c) Statements (a), (b) and (d) are correct whereas statement (c) is incorrect. Corrected form of statement (c) is as follows

An etheral oxygen can be present in an open chain or as part of a cyclic system.

2. (d) Both Statement I and Statement II are correct. Ethers are the least reactive among all the functional groups. That's why, the cleavage of C—O bond in ethers takes place under drastic conditions with excess of hydrogen halides.

Reactions involved are as follows

$$R—O—R + HX \longrightarrow RX + ROH$$
$$ROH + HX \longrightarrow RX + H_2O$$

3. (c) (cyclohexane with H_3C, CH_3 and OC_2H_5)

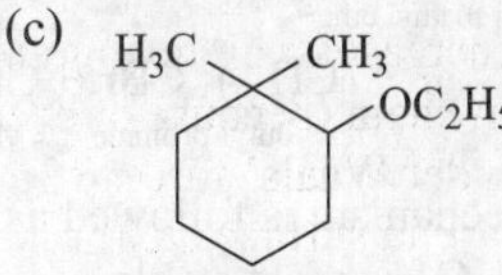

IUPAC name is 2-ethoxy-1, 1-dimethyl cyclohexane.

4. (b) $CH_3—CH(CH_3)—CH_2OCH_2CH_3 + HI \longrightarrow CH_3—CH(CH_3)—CH_2—OH + CH_3—CH_2—I$

5. (d) The dehydration of secondary and tertiary alcohols taking place to give ethers is unsuccessful as elimination competes over substitution and as a consequence alkenes are easily formed.

Thus, (A) is false but (R) is true.

6. (d) Complete reaction is as follows

$$CH_3CH_2CH_2OC(CH_3)_3 \xrightarrow[\Delta]{HI} CH_3CH_2CH_2OH + (CH_3)_3C—I$$

Propanol + 2-iodo-2-methylpropane (*B*)

$$CH_3CH_2CH_2OH \xrightarrow[\Delta]{Excess\ HI} CH_3CH_2CH_2I$$

Iodopropane (*A*)

7. (d) Both Statement I and Statement II are correct.

8. (a) The product is 1-methoxy-1 methyl cyclohexane.

Reaction involved is as follows

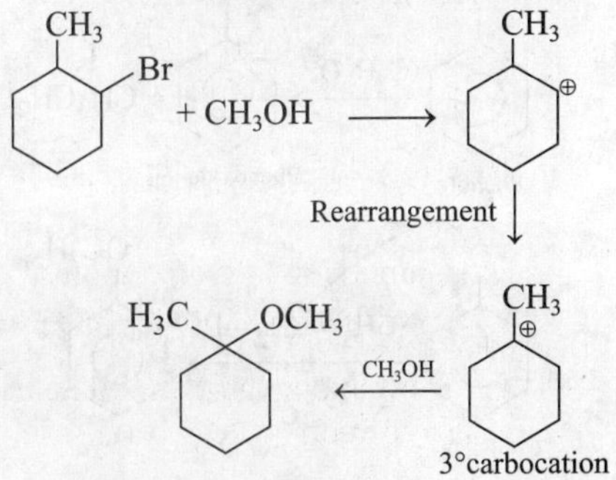

1-bromo-2-methylcyclohexane (CH₃, Br) + CH_3OH ⟶ 2° carbocation $\xrightarrow{Rearrangement}$ 3°carbocation $\xrightarrow{CH_3OH}$ 1-methoxy-1-methylcyclohexane (H_3C, OCH_3)

9. (c) Ethers are readily reacted by halogen acids at 373 K to form an alcohol and an alkyl halide.

$$\underset{\textit{tert}\text{-butyl methyl ether}}{(CH_3)_3COCH_3} + HBr \longrightarrow \underset{\textit{tert}\text{-butyl bromide}}{(CH_3)_3CBr} + \underset{\text{Methanol}}{CH_3OH}$$

S_N1 mechanism is followed as $(CH_3)_3C^+$ is most stable carbocation and Br^- is attached to it.

Thus, (A) is true but (R) is false.

10. (c) The reaction of alkyl halides with sodium alkoxide or sodium phenoxide to form ethers is called Williamson synthesis. Here, in this reaction alkyl halide should be primary and alkoxide may be bulkier to form the required ether as shown below.

$$CH_3-C(CH_3)_2-\overset{-}{O}\overset{+}{Na} + CH_3CH_2Cl \xrightarrow{-NaCl} CH_3-C(CH_3)_2-O-CH_2-CH_3$$

11. (c) 2° alkyl halides tend to undergo elimination. Thus, bromocyclopentane on treatment with sodium ethoxide gives cyclopentene rather than cyclopentyl ethyl ether.

12. (a) The given reaction is represented as

$$\underset{\text{Phenol}}{C_6H_5OH} \xrightarrow{C_2H_5O^-} \underset{\text{Phenoxide ion}}{C_6H_5O^-} + CH_3CH_2OH$$

$$C_6H_5O^- + CH_3-CH_2-I \longrightarrow \underset{(Y)}{C_6H_5OC_2H_5}$$

The stronger nucleophile, i.e. $C_6H_5O^-$ will attack C_2H_5I to form diethyl ether. Thus, the product Y is $C_6H_5OC_2H_5$.

13. (d) The reaction of CH_3MgI with phenol will give only methane but not anisole.

$$C_6H_5OH + CH_3MgI \longrightarrow CH_4 + C_6H_5OMgI$$

14. (b) Both (A) and (R) are true but (R) is not the correct explanation of (A).

Due to $+R$-effect, methoxy group increases electron density at *o*- and *p*-position.

15. (c) Reaction of diethyl ether with excess of Cl_2 in presence of sunlight takes place as follows

$$CH_3CH_2OCH_2CH_3 \xrightarrow{Cl_2/h\nu} \underset{\text{Perchlorodiethyl ether}}{CCl_3CCl_2-O-CCl_2CCl_3}$$

Chapter Break Thru

1. (a) $\underset{1^\circ\text{ alcohol}}{RCH_2OH} \xrightarrow{Cu} R-CHO + H_2$

$$\underset{2^\circ\text{ alcohol}}{R-CH(OH)-R} \xrightarrow{Cu} R-\overset{O}{\overset{\|}{C}}-R + H_2$$

2. (b) $\underset{\text{Acetophenone}}{C_6H_5-\overset{O}{\overset{\|}{C}}-CH_3} \xrightarrow[\text{(ii) }H^+]{\text{(i) LiAlH}_4} \underset{2^\circ\text{ alcohol}}{C_6H_5-CH(OH)-CH_3}$

While the remaining reactions (a), (c) and (d) will produce 3° alcohol, 1° alcohol and bromoform respectively.

3. (c) Phenol forms a coloured complex with $FeCl_3$, indicating the presence of the hydroxyl group attached to the aromatic ring.

4. (c) X = Hydroboration oxidation, Y = Oxymercuration and demercuration, Z = Hydration reaction.

5. (b) Phenol is a stronger acid than ethanol because phenoxide ion is resonance stabilised. When a group having $+M$ effect is at *p*-position then (like halide group) it decreases the acidity of phenols. So, (A) and (R) are true but (R) is not the correct explanation of (A).

6. (c) In anisole, OCH_3 group is *o*, *p*-directing.
So, on nitration it gives a mixture of *o*- and *p*-nitroanisole.

7. (c) The complete reaction sequence is as follows

$$C_6H_5OH \xrightarrow[(0-5^\circ C)]{NaNO_2/HCl} \underset{p\text{-nitrosophenol}}{p\text{-}HOC_6H_4N{=}O}$$

Thus, the major product formed is given in option (c).

8. (d) Electrophilic substitution reaction in phenol take place at *ortho* and *para*-position. —OH is an *ortho*/*para* directing group. The electron density at *ortho* and *para* position will be higher than the electron density at *meta*-position.

9. (c) Phenol has higher boiling point than toluene because of hydrogen bonding.

10. (b) Statement I is correct but Statement II is incorrect. It is because the primary alcohols react very slowly and their turbidity comes after long time.

11. (b) The complete reaction sequence is as follows

$$C_6H_5OH \xrightarrow{\text{Conc. }H_2SO_4} \underset{(X)}{p\text{-}HOC_6H_4SO_3H} \xrightarrow{Br_2/H_2O} \underset{(Y)}{2,4,6\text{-}Br_3C_6H_2OH} + SO_3$$

Thus, the product *Y* is 2,4,6-tribromophenol.

12. (d) Acidic strength order is *p*-nitrophenol > *m*-nitrophenol > phenol > ethanol.

The stronger the acid, greater will be the ionisation and lower will be the value of pK_a.

So, the correct match is A-II, B-I, C-IV, D-III.

13. (c) Kolbe's reaction takes place as follows

Phenol $\xrightarrow{CO_2+NaOH}$ Salicylic acid

Phenol on reaction with CO_2 and NaOH yields salicylic acid.

14. (a) Both (A) and (R) are true and (R) is the correct explanation of (A).

15. (b) The reaction is as follows

Phenol $\xrightarrow[\text{Basic medium}]{C_6H_5N_2^+Cl^-}$ p-hydroxyazobenzene ($N{=}N{-}C_6H_5$)

16. (c) Picric acid is phenolic while others are non-phenolic as they don't contain phenol functional group.

Picric acid (OH, O_2N, NO_2, NO_2)

Phthalic acid (COOH, COOH)

Benzyl alcohol (CH_2OH)

Phenyl acetic acid (COOH)

17. (a) Due to steric hindrance, I^- ion attacks the smaller alkyl group giving ethyl iodide and *iso*-butyl alcohol.

$$CH_3-\underset{CH_3}{\overset{|}{C}H}-CH_2OCH_2CH_3 \xrightarrow{HI} CH_3-\underset{CH_3}{\overset{|}{C}H}-CH_2OH + CH_3CH_2I$$

18. (b) Both (A) and (R) are true but (R) is not the correct explanation of (A). CH_3OH is a nucleophile because it can donate a pair of electrons.

19. (c) The correct match is A-III, B-I, C-II, D-IV.

Phenol $\xrightarrow{Zn,\ \Delta}$ Benzene

Phenol $\xrightarrow[HCl]{CHCl_3-NaOH}$ Salicylaldehyde

Phenol $\xrightarrow[HCl]{CO_2+NaOH}$ Salicylic acid

Phenol $\xrightarrow{Conc.\ HNO_3}$ Picric acid

20. (a) Commercial preparation of methanol takes place by reduction of CO in presence of ZnO-Cr_2O_3.

$$CO + H_2 \xrightarrow[573\text{ K, }200\text{ atm}]{ZnO\text{-}Cr_2O_3} \underset{\text{Methanol}}{CH_3OH}$$

21. (d) Among the given compounds, compound given in option (d) will lose a molecule of water. The reaction is as follows

$$C_2H_5OH \xrightarrow[170°C]{Conc.\ H_2SO_4} C_2H_4 + H_2O$$

22. (a) The reaction between an alcohol and an acid with the elimination of water molecule is called esterification.

$$\underset{\text{Acetic acid}}{CH_3COOH} + \underset{\text{Methanol}}{CH_3OH} \xrightarrow{\text{Esterification}} \underset{\text{Methyl ethanoate}}{CH_3COOCH_3} + H_2O$$

23. (d) Lucas reagent is a solution of anhydrous zinc chloride in concentrated hydrochloric acid. The Lucas test in alcohols is a test of difference between primary, secondary and tertiary alcohols.

Tertiary alcohols react immediately with Lucas reagent.

Secondary alcohols react very slowly.

Primary alcohol don't react appreciably with Lucas reagent at room temperature.

So, ethyl alcohol do not react with Lucas reagent at room temperature.

Benzyl alcohol gives positive Lucas test.

24. (a) Due to presence of intermolecular hydrogen bonding, the boiling point of alcohol is comparatively higher than corresponding alkane.

25. (d)

Phenol $\xrightarrow{Dil.\ HNO_3}$ *X* = *o*-nitrophenol + *Y* = *p*-nitrophenol

Phenol $\xrightarrow{Conc.\ HNO_3+H_2SO_4}$ *Z* = 2,4,6-trinitrophenol

Acidity is directly proportional to stability of conjugate base so order of acidity is

2,4,6-trinitrophenol (*Z*) > *p*-nitrophenol (*Y*) > *o*-nitrophenol (*X*)

26. (c) $ZnCl_2$ + conc. HCl is Lucas reagent.

1° alcohol gives Lucas test with in 30 min.

2° alcohol gives Lucas test with in 5 min.

3° alcohol gives Lucas test with in 1 min.

$$CH_3-\overset{2}{C}(\overset{1}{C}H_3)(\overset{3}{C}H_3)-OH$$

2-hydroxy-2-methyl propane

So, among the given option (c) produces turbidity immediately.

27. (b) During S_N1 reaction carbocation is formed as the intermediate and rate of dehydration depend upon stability of carbocation. So, the correct order is III > IV > II > I.

28. (a) Both (A) and (R) are true and (R) is the correct explanation of (A).

29. (d) Alcohols can be produced by oxidation of alkenes.

The reaction involved is as follows

$$R-CH=CH_2 \xrightarrow{C_6H_5COOH} R-CH\underset{O}{-}CH_2 \xrightarrow{HOH/H^{\oplus}} R-CHOH-CH_2OH$$

30. (b) In acidic medium cleavage occur by S_N1 mechanism. The reaction involved is as follows

(1-methyl-1,2-epoxycyclohexane) $\xrightarrow{H^+}$ (protonated epoxide, $\overset{\oplus}{O}H$) ; (tertiary carbocation with CH_3, OH) $\xrightarrow{Br^-}$ (1-bromo-1-methylcyclohexan-2-ol: CH_3, Br, OH)

31. (c) 1° alkyl halides on treatment with an alkoxide ion tend to undergo substitution to form ethers. Thus, sodium *tert*-butoxide and ethyl bromide is the right choice of reagents, i.e.

$$(CH_3)_3CO^-Na^+ + CH_3CH_2Br \rightarrow (CH_3)_3C-O-CH_2CH_3 + NaBr$$

32. (a) The phenol (C_6H_5-OH) can not be converted to benzyl alcohol because the oxidation of phenol can't give benzyl alcohol ($C_6H_5-CH_2-OH$).

33. (d) Propanal can be converted to 1-propanol by using $NaBH_4$.

$$CH_3-CH_2-CHO \xrightarrow{NaBH_4} \underset{\text{1-propanol}}{CH_3-CH_2-CH_2OH}$$

34. (b) When excess ethanol is heated with sulphuric acid at temperature 413 K (140°C) we get diethyl ether. But when excess sulphuric acid is used at 443 K (170°C) it behave like a dehydrating agent and we get ethene.

$$C_2H_5-OH\,(\text{excess}) \xrightarrow[140°C]{\text{Conc. } H_2SO_4} C_2H_5-O-C_2H_5$$

$$C_2H_5-OH \xrightarrow[170°C]{\text{Conc. } H_2SO_4\,(\text{excess})} C_2H_4$$

35. (b) Phenol and benzoic acid can be distinguished by aqueous $NaHCO_3$.

Phenol are very weak acids. They do not react with weak bases such as sodium hydrogen carbonate.

Benzoic acid is a strong acid. It reacts with sodium hydrogen carbonate to give effervescence of carbon dioxide gas.

$$C_6H_5OH + NaHCO_3 \longrightarrow \text{No reaction}$$

$$PhCOOH + NaHCO_3 \rightarrow PhCOONa + H_2O + CO_2\uparrow$$

36. (b) A. $CH_3-\underset{OH}{CH}-CH_3 \xrightarrow{[O]} CH_3-\overset{O}{\overset{\|}{C}}-CH_3$

B. $CH_3-CH_2-OH \xrightarrow[180°C]{\text{Conc. } H_2SO_4} \underset{\text{(Ethylene)}}{CH_2=CH_2} + H_2O$

C. $CH_3OH \xrightarrow{I_2 + NaOH}$ No reaction

D. $CH_3CH_2OH \xrightarrow{Na} CH_3-CH_2-\overset{-}{O}Na^+ + \frac{1}{2}H_2$

E. $R-CH=CH_2 \xrightarrow{H_2SO_4} RCH(OH)CH_3$

So, the total number of correct statements are four.

37. (c)

$$\underset{(A)}{CH_3CHO} \xleftarrow[\Delta]{Cu} CH_3-CH_2-OH \xrightarrow[\Delta]{Al_2O_3} \underset{(B)}{CH_2=CH_2}$$

So, the compounds *A* and *B* respectively are alkanal and alkene.

38. (a) Both (A) and (R) are true and (R) is the correct explanation of (A).

39. (c)

Phenol $\xrightarrow[273\text{ K}]{Br_2/CS_2}$ o-bromophenol + p-bromophenol

Phenol $\xrightarrow{Br_2/FeBr_3}$ o-bromophenol + p-bromophenol

$$C_6H_5OH \xrightarrow{Br_2\ water} \text{2,4,6-tribromophenol} + 3HBr$$

40. (c)

$$\underset{\text{Benzaldehyde}}{C_6H_5CHO} + \underset{\text{Methyl magnesium iodide}}{CH_3MgI} \xrightarrow{H_2O} C_6H_5-HC(OMgI)-CH_3 \xrightarrow{H^+, H_2O} \underset{\text{1-phenylethanol}}{C_6H_5-HC(OH)-CH_3}$$

41. (d) The given reaction is a Riemer-Tiemann reaction. In this reaction the electrophile involved is dichlorocarbene ($:CCl_2$).

42. (a)

4-methylphenol $\xrightarrow{Br_2, H_2O}$ 2,6-dibromo-4-methylphenol [A]

4-methylphenol $\xrightarrow{Br_2/CS_2}$ 3-bromo-4-methylphenol (Minor) + 2-bromo-4-methylphenol (Major) [B]

43. (c) Statement given in option (c) is not a characteristic of alcohol.

44. (c) The reaction of dehydration of 2-methyl butanol with conc. H_2SO_4 is as follows

$$H_3C-CH_2-CH(CH_3)-CH_2-OH \xrightarrow{\text{Conc. } H_2SO_4} CH_3-CH_2-CH(CH_3)-CH_2^{\oplus}$$

$$\xrightarrow{\text{(1, 2-H shift)}} CH_3-CH_2-\overset{+}{C}(CH_3)-CH_3 \xrightarrow{-H^+} \overset{4}{C}H_3-\overset{3}{C}H=\overset{2}{C}(CH_3)-\overset{1}{C}H_3$$

2-methyl but-2-ene (major)

45. (b) Tertiary alcohol readily reacts with HCl

$$(CH_3)_3C-OH \xrightarrow{H^+} (CH_3)_3C^+$$

Presence of 3° alkyl group increases electron density on 3° carbon atom due to $+I$ effect.

After the removal of —OH group 3° carbonium ion is formed which is most stable.

46. (c) (A) is true but (R) is false. It is because the $+I$-effect of the additional alkyl group increase the electron density in O—H bond thereby making its cleavage difficult.

47. (b)

1-cyclohexylethanol $\xrightarrow[-H_2O]{H^{\oplus}}$ secondary carbocation $\xrightarrow{\text{Rearrangement}}$ tertiary carbocation $\xrightarrow[-H^+]{\Delta}$ ethylidenecyclohexane

48. (b)

$$CH_3-CH=CH-C_6H_4-OH \xrightarrow{HBr} \underset{(P)}{CH_3-CH_2-CH(Br)-C_6H_4-OH}$$

49. (c) The reaction of acid with alcohol is known as esterification.

$$R-\overset{O}{\overset{\|}{C}}-OH + H-O-R' \longrightarrow R-\overset{O}{\overset{\|}{C}}-O-R' + H_2O$$

The reaction involves breaking of O—H bond in alcohol and C—O bond in carboxylic acid.

50. (a) Phenol is more acidic among the given compounds. The resonance stabilisation of the phenoxide ion makes phenol more acidic.

Ch-9 Aldehydes, Ketones and Carboxylic Acids

Topical Follow Thru

Test-1

1. (d) $>C=O \rightleftharpoons >\overset{+}{C}-\overset{-}{O} \xrightarrow{H^+} >\overset{+}{C}-OH$

Due to protonation, electrophilic nature of carbonyl carbon is increased hence, nucleophilic attack is increased. Thus, statement (d) is incorrect.

2. (a) Both (A) and (R) are true and (R) is the correct explanation of (A).

In carbonyl group ($>\overset{\delta+}{C}=\overset{\delta-}{O}$), the more electronegative oxygen atom attracts π-electrons towards itself and acquires –ve charge and thus acts as a nucleophilic centre whereas the less electronegative carbon atom acquires positive charge and thus it can be easily attacked by nucleophiles (bases) or acts as an electrophilic centre.

3. (a) The dehydrogenation of secondary alcohols give ketones. Aldehydes are obtained by the dehydrogenation of primary alcohol.

4. (d) Both Statement I and Statement II are correct.

Benzaldehyde is less reactive than propanal towards nucleophilic addition reactions due to resonance.

Benzaldehyde can be obtained by the given reaction as

$$\underset{\text{Toluene}}{C_6H_5CH_3} \xrightarrow{Cl_2,\ h\nu} \underset{\text{Benzal chloride}}{C_6H_5CHCl_2} \xrightarrow[373\text{ K}]{2H_2O} \underset{\text{Benzaldehyde}}{C_6H_5CHO}$$

5. (a) The reaction of benzaldehyde with acetophenone takes place as follows

$$C_6H_5CHO + CH_3COC_6H_5 \xrightarrow[-H_2O]{NaOH} \underset{\text{Benzal acetophenone}}{C_6H_5-CH=CH-\overset{O}{\overset{\|}{C}}-C_6H_5}$$

Thus, among the given option, product given in option (a) is the correct answer.

6. (b) When *m*-chlorobenzaldehyde is treated with 50% alkali, it undergoes oxidation to give an acid salt as well as reduction to give an alcohol. This reaction is called Cannizzaro's reaction and the products formed are shown below.

$$m\text{-}ClC_6H_4CHO \xrightarrow{50\%\ KOH} \underset{m\text{-chlorobenzyl alcohol}}{m\text{-}ClC_6H_4CH_2OH} + \underset{m\text{-chlorobenzoate}}{m\text{-}ClC_6H_4COO^-K^+}$$

7. (a) Both (A) and (R) are true and (R) is the correct explanation of (A).

8. (a) Addition of water to ethyne in the presence of H_2SO_4 and $HgSO_4$ gives acetaldehyde.

$$\underset{\text{Ethyne}}{CH\equiv CH} + H_2O \xrightarrow[H_2SO_4]{HgSO_4} \underset{\text{Acetaldehyde}}{CH_3CHO}$$

9. (a) Aldol condensation is shown by the molecules having α-carbon atom.

$$CH_3-\overset{O}{\underset{}{\overset{\|}{C}}}H + CH_3CHO \xrightarrow[NaOH]{Dil.} CH_3-\underset{OH}{\underset{|}{CH}}-CH_2CHO$$

10. (b) Carbonyl compounds having α-H atom undergo Aldol condensation in presence of dilute base, (e.g. NaOH, $Ba(OH)_2$ etc.) to form a class of compounds known as aldol (a syrupy liquid).

So, (b) is the correct option.

11. (c) Reaction of formaldehyde with KOH to give methanol and potassium formate is Cannizzaro's reaction.

$$\underset{\text{Formaldehyde}}{HCHO + HCHO} \xrightarrow{KOH} \underset{\text{Methanol}}{CH_3OH} + \underset{\text{Potassium formate}}{HCOOK}$$

In Cannizzaro's reaction, the one substance is oxidised and other is reduced.

12. (a) In the Stephen's reduction, alkyl cyanide is reduced to aldehyde by $SnCl_2/HCl$.

$$R-C\equiv N + 2H \xrightarrow{SnCl_2/HCl} RCH=NH\cdot HCl \xrightarrow{H_2O} \underset{\text{Aldehyde}}{RCHO} + NH_4Cl$$

13. (c) Reaction of acetaldehyde with PCl_5 gives ethylidene chloride.

$$CH_3-CHO + PCl_5 \longrightarrow \underset{\text{Ethylidene chloride or } gem\text{-dihalide}}{CH_3-\underset{Cl}{\underset{|}{CH}}-Cl} + POCl_3$$

14. (b) The product formed in the given reaction is a secondary alcohol.

$$CH_3-\underset{H}{\underset{|}{C}}=O + CH_3MgBr \longrightarrow \underset{(B)}{(CH_3)_2C(H)OMgBr} \xrightarrow{H_2O} \underset{(2°\text{ alcohol})\ (A)}{CH_3-\overset{CH_3}{\overset{|}{\underset{H}{\underset{|}{C}}}}-OH}$$

15. (b) In ozonolysis, alkene converted into carbonyl compounds.

$$CH_3-CH_2-CH_2-CH=CH_2 \text{ (Pent-1-ene)} \xrightarrow{\text{(i) } O_3,\ \text{(ii) } H_2O/Zn} CH_3-CH_2-CH_2-\underset{\text{Ozonide}}{CH(O-O)(O)CH_2} \xrightarrow{Zn-H_2O} \underset{\text{Butanal}}{CH_3-CH_2-CH_2-CHO} + \underset{\text{Methanal}}{CH_2O} + ZnO + H_2O$$

Test-2

1. (b) Ketones are formed when secondary alcohols are oxidised and dehydrogenated.

2. (c) Alkyne will be converted into aldehyde followed by oxidation with Grignard reagent which yields alcohol and then acetone will be formed.

$$HC\equiv CH \longrightarrow \underset{(A)}{CH_3CHO} \xrightarrow[H_2O]{CH_3MgX} \underset{(B)}{CH_3CH(OH)CH_3} \xrightarrow{[O]} \underset{\text{Acetone } (C)}{CH_3COCH_3}$$

3. (a) Acetophenone is prepared in the laboratory from benzene by a substitution reaction.

$$C_6H_6 + CH_3COCl \xrightarrow{AlCl_3} C_6H_5COCH_3 + HCl$$

4. (a) Alkene ends with two methyl groups each side can be oxidised with ozone to form ketones.

(a) $(CH_3)_2C=C(CH_3)_2 \xrightarrow[Zn/H_2O]{O_3} 2CH_3-CO-CH_3$

(b) $CH_3-CH=CH_2 \xrightarrow[Zn/H_2O]{O_3} \underset{\text{Acetaldehyde}}{CH_3CHO} + \underset{\text{Formaldehyde}}{HCHO}$

(c) $C_6H_5CH=CH_2 \xrightarrow[Zn/H_2O]{O_3} \underset{\text{Benzaldehyde}}{C_6H_5CHO} + \underset{\text{Formaldehyde}}{HCHO}$

(d) $CH_3-CH=CH-CH_3 \xrightarrow[Zn/H_2O]{O_3} \underset{\text{Acetaldehyde}}{2CH_3CHO}$

5. (a) Fehling's solution can be used to distinguish aldehyde and ketone functional groups. The compounds to be tested is added to the Fehling's solution and the mixture is heated. Aldehydes are oxidised, giving a positive result, but ketones do not react, unless they are α-hydroxy ketones.

6. (d) Statements (a), (b) and (c) are correct while statement (d) is incorrect. Its correct form is as follows

Due to possessing CH_3 group, it undergoes, iodoform reaction with iodine and alkali.

7. (b) The reaction is as follows

$$\underset{\text{Propyne}}{CH_3-C\equiv CH} + H_2O \xrightarrow[Hg^{2+}]{H_2SO_4} \underset{\text{Acetone}}{CH_3-\overset{O}{\overset{||}{C}}-CH_3}$$

8. (d) Both Statement I and Statement II are correct.

9. (c) The complete reaction is shown below.

$$(H)(H_3C)C=C(CH_3)-C(=O)-CH_3 \xrightarrow{NaOCl} (H)(H_3C)C=C(CH_3)-C(=O)-ONa + CHCl_3\downarrow$$

This reaction is an example of haloform reaction.

10. (b) The solubility decreases due to the increase in bulkiness as due to this steric hindrance around the carbonyl group increases. So, the water molecules can not interact with the carbonyl group easily and less tendency of formation of hydrogen bond.

Hence, both (A) and (R) are true but (R) is not the correct explanation of (A).

11. (d) Acetophenone can be prepared by Friedel-Craft's acylation. Acetyl chloride reacts with benzene in the presence of anhydrous aluminium chloride to form acetophenone.

$$\underset{\text{Benzene}}{C_6H_6} + \underset{\text{Acetyl chloride}}{CH_3-\overset{O}{\overset{||}{C}}-Cl} \xrightarrow[AlCl_3]{\text{Anhyd.}} \underset{\text{Acetophenone}}{C_6H_5-\overset{O}{\overset{||}{C}}-CH_3} + HCl$$

12. (c) The most appropriate reagent for the conversion of 2-pentanone to acetic acid is alkaline $KMnO_4$, Δ.

$$CH_3COCH_2CH_2CH_3 \xrightarrow[\Delta]{\text{Alkaline } KMnO_4} CH_3COOH + HOOCCH_2CH_3$$

$-\overset{O}{\overset{||}{C}}-$ will remain toward smaller part of compound (Popoff rule).

13. (b) Both Zn(Hg), HCl and NH_2NH_2, OH^- can reduce $-\overset{O}{\overset{||}{C}}-$ group to $-CH_2-$ group but HCl will also bring about dehydration of alcohol to form alkene. Hence, the appropriate reagent for the conversion is NH_2NH_2, OH^-.

14. (c) Statement given in III and IV are incorrect while all other are correct.

Acetophenone undergoes electrophilic substitution at *meta*-position and also gives iodoform test.

15. (b) The product formed in the given reaction are as

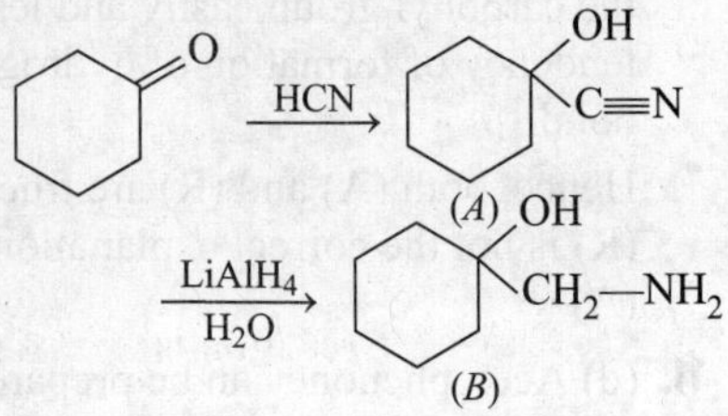

Cyclohexanone $\xrightarrow{HCN}$ (A) 1-hydroxycyclohexane carbonitrile (OH, $C\equiv N$) $\xrightarrow[H_2O]{LiAlH_4}$ (B) 1-(aminomethyl)cyclohexanol (OH, CH_2-NH_2)

Test-3

1. (b) Reagents that are used for the conversion of ethanoic acid to ethanoic anhydride are mineral acids such as H_2SO_4 or P_2O_5.

Reaction is as follows

$$2CH_3COOH \xrightarrow[P_2O_5, \Delta]{} (CH_3CO)_2O$$

2. (c) The presence of electron withdrawing group on the benzene ring of aromatic carboxylic acid increases its acidity, while electron donating group decreases its acidity. Therefore, the correct increasing order of acidity is,

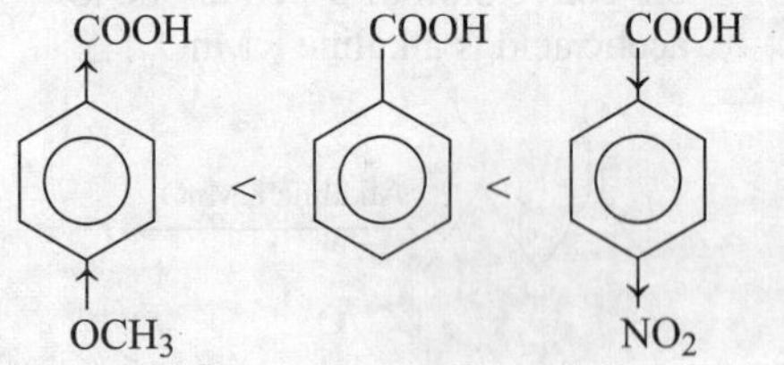

4-methoxybenzoic acid (COOH, OCH_3) ($pK_a = 4.46$) < benzoic acid (COOH) ($pK_a = 4.19$) < 4-nitrobenzoic acid (COOH, NO_2) ($pK_a = 3.14$)

3. (b) The reaction is as follows

Benzoic acid (COOH) $\xrightarrow[\text{Conc. } H_2SO_4]{\text{Conc. } HNO_3}$ m-nitrobenzoic acid (COOH, NO_2)

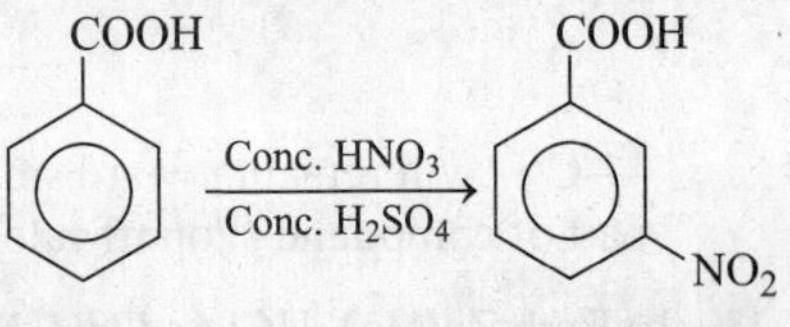

4. (d) Both Statement I and Statement II are correct.

5. (b) The product formed in the given reaction is as follows

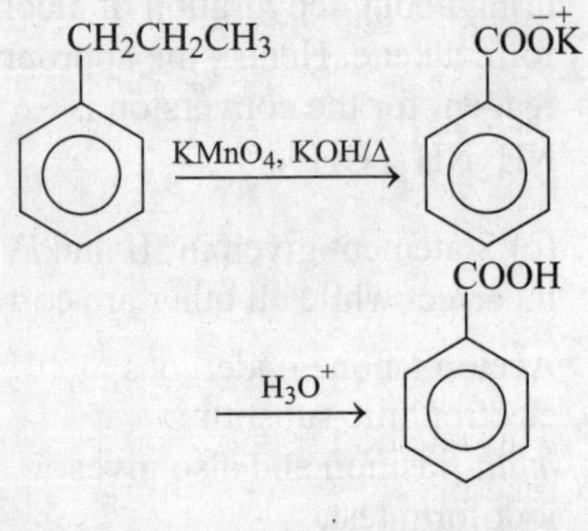

Propylbenzene ($CH_2CH_2CH_3$) $\xrightarrow{KMnO_4, KOH/\Delta}$ $C_6H_5COO^-K^+$ $\xrightarrow{H_3O^+}$ C_6H_5COOH

6. (a) Statement (a) is incorrect. Its correct form is as follows

The conjugate base of carboxylic acid, a carboxylate ion is stabilised by two equivalent resonance structures in which the negative charge is at the more electronegative oxygen atom. Its resonance structures are shown below.

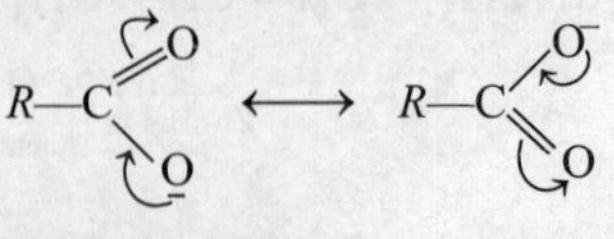

$$R-C(=O)O^- \longleftrightarrow R-C(O^-)=O$$

Rest other statements are correct.

7. (c) Formic acid cannot be prepared by Grignard reagent because it is a step up process, i.e. used to synthesise carboxylic acids having one carbon atom more than that present in reactant. As formic acid (HCOOH) contain one carbon atom, so, it cannot be synthesised by this method.

8. (b) The reaction is as follows

Benzoic acid (COOH) $\xrightarrow[\text{Bromination}]{Br_2/FeBr_3}$ *m*-bromobenzoic acid (COOH, Br) + HBr

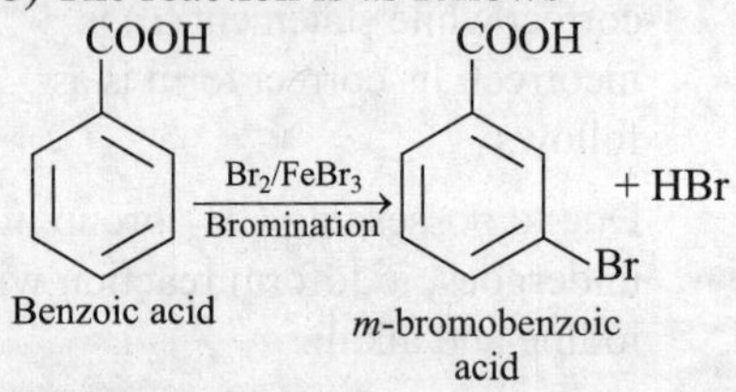

9. (a) Both (A) and (R) are true and (R) is the correct explanation of (A).

10. (d) HVZ reaction is given by carboxylic acid which has atleast one α-hydrogen. Thus, 2-methylpropanoic acid will give HVZ reaction.

11. (c) The correct option is (c). Esters are derived from carboxylic acids and alcohols.

The correct reaction is as follows

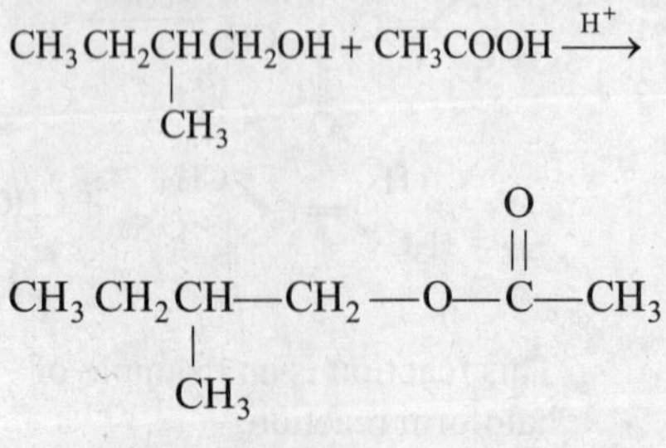

$$CH_3CH_2CH(CH_3)CH_2OH + CH_3COOH \xrightarrow{H^+} CH_3CH_2CH(CH_3)-CH_2-O-\overset{O}{\overset{\|}{C}}-CH_3$$

12. (a) Grignard reagent reacts with CO_2 to form salts of carboxylic acid which in turn give corresponding carboxylic acid after acidification with mineral acid.

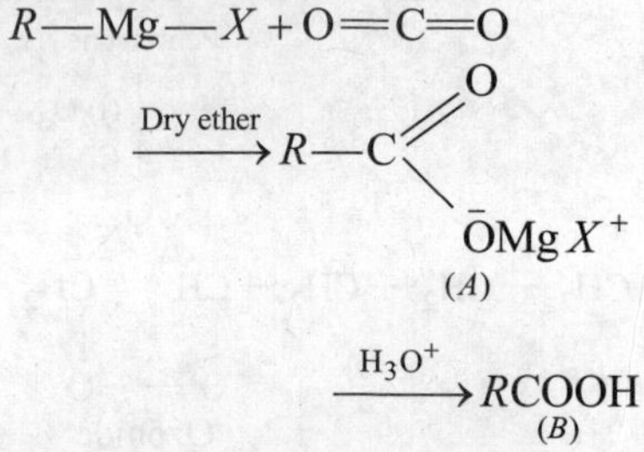

$$R-Mg-X + O=C=O \xrightarrow{\text{Dry ether}} \underset{(A)}{R-C(=O)\bar{O}MgX^+} \xrightarrow{H_3O^+} \underset{(B)}{RCOOH}$$

13. (a) Statement given in option (c) is incorrect. Its correct form is, nitriles are hydrolysed to amides and then to acids in the presence of H^+ or OH^- as a catalyst.

14. (d) Complete reaction is as follows

$$CH_3-\overset{O}{\overset{\|}{C}}-\overset{O}{\overset{\|}{C}}-H + OH^- \longrightarrow CH_3-\overset{O^-}{\overset{|}{C}}(=O)-\underset{OH}{\underset{|}{C}}-H \xrightarrow[\text{rearangement}]{\text{Intramolecular}} CH_3-\underset{O^-}{\underset{|}{\overset{H}{\overset{|}{C}}}}-\overset{O}{\overset{\|}{C}}-OH \xrightarrow[OH^-]{H_2O, \Delta} CH_3-\underset{OH}{\underset{|}{CH}}-\overset{O}{\overset{\|}{C}}-OH$$

α-hydroxy propanoic acid

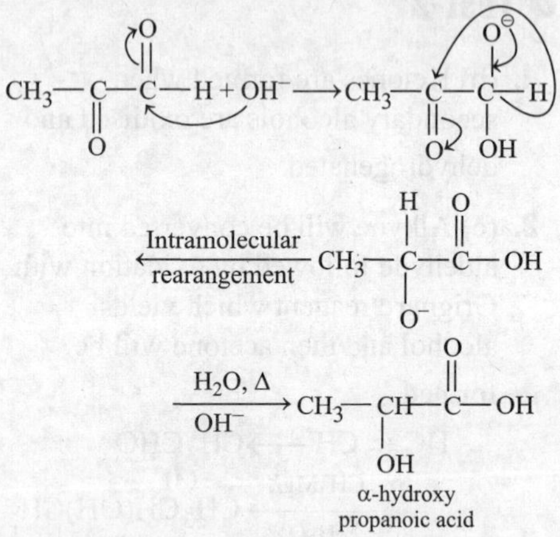

15. (d) Both Statement I and Statement II are correct.

pK_a value of 4-nitrobenzoic acid is lower than benzoic acid because of the presence of strong electron withdrawing group (i.e. NO_2). Thus, NO_2 stabilises the carboxylate anion and easily releases proton.

Chapter Break Thru

1. (b) Selenium dioxide is a selective oxidising agent which oxidises an active methyl center to ketone. Hence, correct option is (b) as the α-carbon on the left acidic hydrogen is active.

2. (d) Statement (d) is incorrect because π-electron cloud of carbonyl group is slightly shifted toward oxygen atom instead of carbon atom.

3. (b) Reagents CrO_3/H_2SO_4 or H_2CrO_4, (Jone's reagent) $(C_5H_5N)_2CrO_3/CH_2Cl_2$ (PCC) or $(CH_3COO)_4Pb$ used for oxidation of alcohol into aldehyde or ketone.

4. (c) Alkenes react with CO and H_2 in the presence of $[HCo(CO)_4]$ catalyst at high temperature and high pressure to form aldehyde. (Oxo process)

$$\underset{\text{Ethene}}{CH_2=CH_2} + CO + H_2 \xrightarrow{[HCo(CO)_4]} \underset{\text{Propanal}}{CH_3-CH_2-CHO}$$

5. (a) In Etard reaction, toluene converts into benzaldehyde.

$$\underset{\text{Toluene}}{C_6H_5CH_3} \xrightarrow[(CH_3CO)_2O]{\text{(i) } CrO_3\ [O]} C_6H_5CH(OCOCH_3)_2 \xrightarrow{\text{(ii) } H_3O^+\ 373\text{ K}} \underset{\text{Benzaldehyde}}{C_6H_5CHO} + \underset{\text{Acetic acid}}{2CH_3COOH}$$

6. (a) Nucleophilic addition reaction depends upon the group attached around the carbonyl. If EWG attached with $>C=O$ then electron deficiency at carbon atom increases and more attraction towards nucleophile, results in increasing reactivity.

While EDG decrease the positive charge on carbon atom.

Thus, reactivity decreases. So, the correct order is as follows

$$(C_6H_5)(CH_3)C=O < (C_6H_5)(H)C=O < (CH_3)(H)C=O < (H)(H)C=O$$

(Benzaldehyde is less reactive than aliphatic aldehyde, due to resonance)

7. (b) Complete reaction is as follows

$$R(H)C=O + H_2N-NH-\overset{O}{\overset{\|}{C}}-NH_2 \xrightarrow{-H_2O} \underset{\text{Semicarbazone}}{R(H)C=N-NH-\overset{O}{\overset{\|}{C}}-NH_2}$$

8. (b) $CH_3-\underset{O}{\underset{\|}{C}}-\underset{H}{\underset{|}{CH}}-\underset{H}{\underset{|}{CH}}-\underset{O}{\underset{\|}{C}}-CH_3 \xrightarrow[{[O]}]{SeO_2} \underset{\text{Hex-3-ene-2, 5-dione}}{CH_3-\underset{O}{\underset{\|}{C}}-CH=CH-\underset{O}{\underset{\|}{C}}-CH_3} + H_2O$

9. (d) Statements (a), (b) and (c) are correct but statement (d) is incorrect because HI in the presence of red phosphorus acts as reducing agent which reduces aldehyde and ketone to alkane.

$$\underset{\text{Ethanal}}{CH_3CHO} \xrightarrow[425\text{ K}]{\text{Red P/HI}} \underset{\text{Ethane}}{CH_3CH_3} + H_2O$$

10. (c) (A) is true but (R) is false. Correct form of (R) is : Carboxylate ion is relative more stable due to stabilising by two equivalent structures and electron charge in the carboxylate ion is more dispersed in comparison to the phenoxide ion.

11. (a) The correct match is
A-IV, B-II, C-I, D-III.

A. $\underset{\text{Semicarbazide}}{H_2N-NH-\overset{O}{\overset{\|}{C}}-NH_2} + >C=O \longrightarrow \underset{\text{Semicarbazone}}{>C=N-NH-\overset{O}{\overset{\|}{C}}-NH_2}$

B. $\underset{\text{2, 4-dinitrophenyl hydrazine}}{H_2N-NH-C_6H_3(NO_2)_2} + >C=O \longrightarrow \underset{\text{2, 4-dinitrophenyl hydrazone}}{>C=N-NH-C_6H_3(NO_2)_2}$

C. $\underset{\text{Hydrazine}}{H_2N-NH_2} + >C=O \longrightarrow \underset{\text{Hydrazone}}{>C=N-NH_2}$

D. $\underset{\text{Hydroxyl amine}}{H_2N-OH} + >C=O \longrightarrow \underset{\text{Oxime}}{>C=N-OH}$

12. (b) Complete reaction is as follows

$$C_6H_5CH=CH_2 \xrightarrow{KMnO_4/KOH} \underset{(A)}{C_6H_5\overset{-}{CO}\overset{+}{OK}} \xrightarrow{H_3O^+} \underset{(B)}{C_6H_5COOH}$$

13. (b) Complete reaction is as follows

$$\underset{\text{Acetic acid}}{CH_3-COOH} + Cl_2 \xrightarrow[\text{Hell-Volhard-Zelinsky reaction}]{PCl_3} \underset{(A)}{\underset{Cl}{\underset{|}{CH_2}}-COOH} \xrightarrow[\text{Substitution reaction}]{Aq.\ KOH} \underset{\alpha\text{-hydroxy acid } (B)}{\underset{OH}{\underset{|}{CH_2}}-COOH}$$

14. (b) Acidity increases as the electronegativity of the C-atom directly attached to —COOH group increases or the hybridisation of the C-atom directly attached to —COOH group changes from $sp^3 \rightarrow sp^2 \rightarrow sp$. Hence, the acidic strength decreases in the order

$HC\equiv C-COOH > C_6H_5COOH > CH_2=CH-COOH > CH_3COOH$

15. (d) Both Statement I and Statement II are correct.

Fatty acids that are essential to human beings are made up of carboxylic acids. For example, omega-6 and omega-3-fatty acids.

16. (d) (a)

$$\underset{\text{Toluene}}{C_6H_5CH_3} \xrightarrow[H_3O^+]{CrO_2Cl_2, CS_2} \underset{\text{Benzaldehyde}}{C_6H_5CHO}$$

This reaction is known as Etard reaction.

(b)

$$C_6H_5COCl + H_2 \xrightarrow[\text{(Boiling xylene)}]{Pd/BaSO_4} C_6H_5CHO + HCl$$

Benzoyl chloride → Benzaldehyde

This reaction is called Rosenmund reaction.

(c)

$$C_6H_6 + CO + HCl \xrightarrow{\text{Anhy. } AlCl_3} C_6H_5CHO + HCl$$

Benzene → Benzaldehyde

The above reaction is known as Gattermann-Koch aldehyde synthesis.

(d)

$$C_6H_5COOH + Zn/Hg \xrightarrow{\text{Conc. HCl}} \text{No reaction}$$

Benzoic acid

Thus, benzaldehyde is not obtained from the reaction given in option (d).

17. (c) Statements I, II, and IV are correct statements but statements III and V are incorrect. Their correct form are as follows

- Aldehydes are more reactive towards nucleophilic addition reactions than ketones.
- Aldehydes are easily oxidised to carboxylic acids containing the same number of carbon atoms.

18. (b) The correct match is A-IV, B-III, C-II, D-I.

A. $$CH_3-\underset{\underset{O}{\|}}{C}-CH_3 \xrightarrow[\text{Conc. HCl (Clemmensen reduction)}]{Zn\text{-}Hg} CH_3CH_2CH_3$$

B. $$CH_3-\underset{\underset{O}{\|}}{C}-H \xrightarrow{\text{(i) HCN}} CH_3-\underset{\underset{CN}{|}}{CH}-OH \xrightarrow{\text{(ii) } H_2O/H^+} CH_3-\underset{\underset{COOH}{|}}{CH}-OH$$

C. $$CH_3-\underset{\underset{O}{\|}}{C}-H \xrightarrow[\text{Haloform reaction}]{NaOI} CHI_3 + HCO\overset{-}{O}\overset{+}{N}a$$

D. $$CH_3CHO \xrightarrow[\text{Dil. NaOH}]{CH_2O} \underset{\underset{CH_2-CHO}{|}}{CH_2}-OH$$

19. (b) When benzene is treated with benzoyl chloride in the presence of anhydrous aluminium chloride, it gives benzophenone.

$$C_6H_6 + C_6H_5COCl \xrightarrow{\text{Anhy. } AlCl_3} C_6H_5-\underset{\underset{}{}}{\overset{\overset{O}{\|}}{C}}-C_6H_5$$

Benzene + Benzoyl chloride → Benzophenone

20. (a) As the carbon chain increases in length, solubility of aldehydes and ketones in water decreases, Hence, HCHO will be most soluble having one carbon atom.

21. (d) Anhydrides are more reactive for nucleophilic substitution than esters because $RCOO^-$ is a better leaving group than RO^-.
Hence, (A) is false but (R) is true.

22. (c) Aromatic aldehyde does not give Fehling's test. Thus, among the given options, benzaldehyde is not oxidised by Fehling's solution.

23. (a) The carboxylic acids like alcohols evolve hydrogen with electropositive metals and form salts with alkalies similar to phenols. However, unlike phenols they react with weaker bases such as sodium and hydrogen carbonates to evolve CO_2.

The reactions are,

$$2RCOOH + 2Na \longrightarrow 2RCOO^-Na^+ + \underset{(A)}{H_2}\uparrow$$

$$RCOOH + NaHCO_3 \longrightarrow RCOO^-Na^+ + H_2O + \underset{(B)}{CO_2}\uparrow$$

Here, $(A) = H_2$ and $(B) = CO_2$.

24. (d) Both Statement I and Statement II are correct.

25. (c) Statements (a), (b) and (d) are correct statements but statement (c) is incorrect because aliphatic carboxylic acids upto C_9 are colourless liquids at room temperature.

26. (a) The major product of the given reaction is benzoic acid (C_6H_5COOH). On vigorous oxidation of alkyl benzene with acidic or alkaline $KMnO_4$, aromatic acids are obtained. During oxidation of alkyl benzene, the aromatic nucleus remains intact and the entire chain is oxidised to —COOH group irrespective of the length of carbon chain.

$$C_6H_5CH_2CH_3 \xrightarrow{\text{Alk. } KMnO_4} C_6H_5CO\overset{-}{O}\overset{+}{K} \xrightarrow{H_3O^+} C_6H_5COOH$$

Ethyl benzene → Potassium benzoate → Benzoic acid

27. (d) Alkaline $KMnO_4$ converts complete carbon chain (that is directly attached to benzene nucleus) to —COOH group. Br_2 in the presence of halogen carrier causes bromination by electrophilic substitution reaction and ethyl alcohol in acidic medium results in esterification.

$$C_6H_5CH_2CH_3 \xrightarrow[KOH]{KMnO_4} C_6H_5COOH \xrightarrow{Br_2/FeCl_3}$$

(m-directing) (B)

$$m\text{-}BrC_6H_4COOH\ (C) \xrightarrow[H^+]{C_2H_5OH} m\text{-}BrC_6H_4COOC_2H_5\ (D)$$

28. (b) Benzyl chloride gives benzoic acid on oxidation.

$$\underset{\text{Benzyl chloride}}{C_6H_5CH_2Cl} + 2KOH + 2[O] \longrightarrow C_6H_5COOK + KCl + H_2O$$

29. (b) On reduction of benzaldehyde, it gives benzyl alcohol.

$$C_6H_5CHO \xrightarrow{2H} C_6H_5CH_2OH$$

30. (a) Reduction of aldehydes to hydrocarbon take place in the presence of Zn amalgam and HCl. It is known as Clemmensen reduction.

31. (d) Both Statement I and Statement II are correct.

- Cyclohexanone is a synthetic organic liquid used primarily as an intermediate in the production of nylon.
- Methyl ethyl ketone is used as an effective plastic welding agent. It can dissolve the surface where it is applied.

32. (a) Both (A) and (R) are true and (R) is the correct explanation of (A).

33. (b) Benzaldehyde can be prepared by oxidation of toluene by CrO_2Cl_2.

34. (c)

$$\underset{\text{Acetone}}{2CH_3-\overset{CH_3}{\overset{|}{C}}=O} \xrightarrow{Mg/C_6H_6} CH_3-\overset{CH_3}{\overset{|}{C}}(O)-\overset{CH_3}{\overset{|}{C}}(O)-CH_3\ (\text{O–Mg–O bridge})$$

$$\xrightarrow{H_2O} \underset{\text{Pinacol (P)}}{CH_3-\overset{CH_3}{\overset{|}{\underset{OH}{\underset{|}{C}}}}-\overset{CH_3}{\overset{|}{\underset{OH}{\underset{|}{C}}}}-CH_3}$$

35. (c) When Cl_2 or Br_2 is reacted with carboxylic acid in the presence of red phosphorus then, α-hydrogen of carboxylic acid is replaced by Cl_2 or Br_2.

$$\underset{\text{Acetic acid}}{CH_3COOH} \xrightarrow{Br_2} \underset{\alpha\text{-bromoacetic acid}}{CH_2BrCOOH}$$

This reaction is known as Hell-Volhard Zelinsky reaction.

36. (d) Cannizzaro reaction involves self oxidation and self reduction. So, in this reaction, benzaldehyde will change into benzyl alcohol.

$$\underset{\text{Benzaldehyde}}{C_6H_5CHO} \xrightarrow{OH^-} \underset{\text{Benzyl alcohol}}{C_6H_5CH_2OH} + \underset{\text{Benzoate ion}}{C_6H_5COO^-}$$

37. (a) The pK_a value indicates the strength of an acid. A lower pK_a value indicates a stronger acid, i.e. the lower value indicates the acid more fully dissociates in water. Formic acid with lower pK_a value of 3.77 is the strongest acid.

38. (c) Carbonyl compound having α-H gives aldol condensation. So, among the given option, CH_3CH_2CHO will undergo aldol condensation.

39. (b) In the Rosenmund's reduction, $BaSO_4$ taken with catalyst Pd acts as catalytic poison by reducing the activity of palladium due to its low surface area meaning it decrease the reducing power of palladium in order to prevent over-reduction of the acid.

40. (b) Among the given options, aldehyde and ketone react easily with Grignard reagent.

$$\underset{\text{Aldehyde}}{R-\underset{H}{\underset{|}{C}}=O} + \underset{\text{Grignard reagent}}{R-Mg-X} \longrightarrow R-\overset{R}{\overset{|}{\underset{H}{\underset{|}{C}}}}-OMgX$$

$$\underset{\text{Ketone}}{R-\underset{R}{\underset{|}{C}}=O} + R-Mg-X \longrightarrow R-\overset{R}{\overset{|}{\underset{H}{\underset{|}{C}}}}-O-MgX$$

41. (b) The correct match is
A-I, B-II, C-IV, D-III.

42. (d) Statement given in option (d) is incorrect. While all other statements are correct.

Methyl salicylate occurs in natural essential oils like winter green.

43. (c) (A) is true but (R) is false.

Due to resonance, electrophilicity of carbonyl carbon is reduced in carboxylic acids than in aldehydes and ketones.

44. (b) Mixed ketones are the complex ketones in which both the groups are not same, i.e. one is alkyl and another is aromatic.

Acetophenone

45. (a) $CH_3COOH \xrightarrow[Cl_2]{\text{Red P}} Cl{-}CH_2COOH$

Thus, reaction given in option (a) is not correctly matched.

46. (b) Both (A) and (R) are true but (R) is not the correct explanation of (A).

Benzoate ion is more resonance stabilised than phenoxide ion.

47. (b) Wolff-Kishner reduction doesn't convert $>CO$ to —CHOH but converts it to $>CH_2$.

Thus, reaction (b) is not matched correctly.

48. (a) Action of hydrazine on aldehydes and ketones gives compound of the general structure.

$$>C{=}O + H_2N{-}NH_2 \xrightarrow{-H_2O} >C{=}N{-}NH_2$$

49. (a) The Rosenmund reduction is a hydrogenation process where molecular hydrogen reacts with acyl chloride in the presence of palladium and barium sulphate catalyst. Barium sulphate reduce the activity of palladium due to its low surface area, therefore preventing over reduction.

50. (a) **Wolff-Kishner reduction**

Hydrazine (NH_2-NH_2) followed by reaction with strong base like KOH reduces carbonyl group into alkyl group.

$$\underset{\text{Carbonyl group}}{>C{=}O} + NH_2{-}NH_2 \xrightarrow[\text{reduction}]{\text{Wolff-Kishner}}$$

$$>C{=}N{-}NH_2 \xrightarrow{KOH} \underset{\text{Alkyl group}}{>CH_2}$$

Ch-10 Amines

Topical Follow Thru

Test-1

1. (c) The complete given reaction is as follows

$$C_2H_5NH_2 + CH_3{-}C(=O){-}O{-}C(=O){-}CH_3 \longrightarrow CH_3{-}C(O^-)(NH^+HC_2H_5){-}O{-}C(=O)CH_3$$

$$\longrightarrow \underset{\substack{\text{Acetic acid} \\ (B)}}{CH_3COOH} + \underset{\substack{(A) \\ \text{N-ethylacetamide}}}{CH_3{-}C(=O){-}NHC_2H_5}$$

Thus, option (c) is correct.

2. (c) The reaction sequence involved is as follows

$$CH_3-CH_2-NH_2 \xrightarrow[{[O]}]{KMnO_4}$$

$$CH_3-CH{=}NH \xrightarrow{H_3O^+} \underset{\text{Acetaldehyde}}{CH_3-CHO}$$

3. (b) The reagent 'X' can be Fe +HCl. Reduction with iron scrap is preferred because $FeCl_2$ formed gets hydrolysed to release HCl during the reaction.

4. (a) Basicity of amines increase with increase in number of —CH_3 group (or any group which cause $+I$ effect) due to increase in electron density on N atom.

As a rule, the basicity of 3° amine should be more than that of 2° amine, but actually it is found to be lesser than 2°-amines. This is due to steric hindrance of bulkier alkyl group, which decrease the availability of lone pair of electron on the N atom of the amino group.

Hence, the correct order of basicity is $(CH_3)_2NH > (CH_3)_3N > CH_3NH_2$.

5. (a) Only primary amines give Schiff base with aldehyde. The complete reaction is as follows

$$R{-}NH_2 + R{-}\underset{H}{C}{=}O \xrightarrow{H^+} \underset{\text{Schiff base}}{R{-}N{=}CH{-}R} + H_2O$$

6. (c) Among the given compounds, only (c) is an aliphatic primary amines.

7. (b) The reaction sequence involved is as follows

$$\underset{\text{Acetamide}}{CH_3CONH_2} + Br_2 + 4NaOH \longrightarrow \underset{\text{Methylamine}}{CH_3NH_2} + Na_2CO_3 + 2NaBr + 2H_2O$$

Thus, the reagent will be NaOH and Br_2.

8. (c) The Gabriel synthesis is a chemical reaction that converts primary alkyl halides into primary amines.

Benzyl halide and allyl halide both are primary halides, hence, they can be used in Gabriel synthesis.

$$\underset{\substack{(1°) \\ \text{Benzyl halide}}}{C_6H_5{-}CH_2{-}X} \qquad \underset{\substack{(1°) \\ \text{Allyl halide}}}{CH_2{=}CH{-}CH_2{-}X}$$

9. (c) The correct IUPAC name is

$$CH_3{-}C_6H_{10}{-}N(CH_3){-}CH_3$$

N,N-dimethyl-4-methyl cyclohexanamine

10. (d) Hydrazoic acid N_3H, dissociates into N_3^- and H^+. Due to the formation of hydrogen ion, it is an acid.

However, in N_2H_4, nitrogen easily donates its lone pair, so it is a base.

NH_2OH is basic because it has hydroxyl ions.

The compound trimethylamine, $(CH_3)_3N$, is a weak base when dissolved in water.

11. (b) The complete reaction is as follows

$\overset{\oplus}{NMe_3}$ (on cyclohexane) $\xrightarrow{\bar{O}H}$ (A) (Major)

Elimination reaction will be take place.

12. (b) Among the given compounds only II and III are used to distinguish amines. Primary and secondary amines react with Hinsberg reagent (benzene sulphonyl chloride) and tosyl chloride (*p*-toluene sulphonyl chloride) to form N-substituted amides soluble and insoluble in alkali respectively. While tertiary does not react.

13. (a) Complete reaction is as follows

$$\underset{\text{Methyl amine}}{CH_3—NH_2} + \underset{\text{Chloroform}}{CHCl_3} + 3KOH \xrightarrow{\text{Heat}} \underset{\text{(Methyl isocyanide)}}{CH_3—N \overset{\rightarrow}{\equiv} C} + 3KCl + 3H_2O$$

This reaction is named as carbylamine reaction.

Thus, option (a) is correct.

14. (b) $CH_3—CH_2—COOH \xrightarrow{\text{(i) } NH_3\text{, Heat}} CH_3—CH_2—CONH_2 \xrightarrow{\text{(ii) } Br_2/NaOH} \underset{(A)}{CH_3—CH_2—NH_2} \xrightarrow[\text{HCl}]{\text{(i) } NaNO_2} CH_3CH_2—OH \xrightarrow[\text{Oxidation}]{\text{(ii) } K_2Cr_2O_7/H^+} CH_3COOH$

Thus, option (b) is correct.

15. (b) $\underset{\text{Methanamine}}{CH_3—NH_2} \xrightarrow{\text{(i) } NaNO_2/HCl} \underset{\text{Methanol}}{CH_3OH} \xrightarrow{\text{(ii) } PCl_5} \underset{\text{Chloromethane}}{CH_3Cl} \xrightarrow[C_2H_5OH]{\text{(iii) KCN}} CH_3—CN \xrightarrow{\text{(iv) } H_2/Pt} \underset{\text{Ethanamine}}{CH_3CH_2—NH_2}$

Thus, option (b) is correct.

Test-2

1. (d) Reaction of aniline with excess of bromine water is as follows

$$\underset{\text{Aniline}}{C_6H_5NH_2} + \underset{\text{(Excess)}}{3Br_2(aq)} \longrightarrow \underset{\text{(2,4,6-tribromoaniline)}}{C_6H_2Br_3NH_2} + 3HBr$$

2. (c) Reaction given in option (c) is correctly matched with its name.

Reaction given in option (a) is Gattermann-Koch reaction.

Reaction given in option (b) is Chlorination.

Reaction given in option (c) is Hofmann Bromamide.

Reaction given in option (d) is Sandmeyer reaction.

3. (b) The correct order of basicity of given compounds is as follows

Pyridine (II) > Aniline (III) > Pyrrole (I)

Pyrrole is least basic because lone pair is involved in aromaticity and are not available for donation. The lone pair in aniline is involved in resonance. N-atom in pyridine is sp^2-hybridised and its lone pair is not involved anyhow.

Thus, the conclusion that follows is II is more basic than I and III.

4. (b) Statements given in I, II and V are correct while III and IV are incorrect. Their correct form are as follows

p-nitroaniline is a weaker base than aniline.

Aniline is a stronger base than *o*-methoxyaniline.

5. (c) In the given resonating structures, structure II is not an acceptable canonical structure because the nitrogen has ten valence electrons which is not possible.

6. (b) The complete reaction sequence is as follows

$$p\text{-toluidine} \xrightarrow{Br_2\text{ (excess)}} \underset{(X)}{\text{2,6-dibromo-4-methylaniline}} \xrightarrow[\text{(ii)}H_3PO_2]{\text{(i)}NaNO_2/HCl} \underset{(Y)}{\text{3,5-dibromotoluene}}$$

7. (c) (A) is true but (R) is false.

$$\underset{\text{Aniline}}{C_6H_5NH_2} + CH_3COCl \xrightarrow[\text{(Pyridine)}]{-HCl} C_6H_5NHCOCH_3 \xrightarrow[CH_3COOH]{Br_2} p\text{-}BrC_6H_4NHCOCH_3 \xrightarrow{H_3O^+} \underset{\substack{p\text{-bromoaniline} \\ \text{(major product)}}}{p\text{-}BrC_6H_4NH_2}$$

Addition of CH_3COCl controls the activating power of NH_2, hence the desired product is obtained.

8. (b) The complete reaction sequence is as follows

$$\underset{\text{Aniline}}{C_6H_5NH_2} \xrightarrow[\text{HCl, 278K}]{NaNO_2} \underset{\text{Benzenediazonium chloride }(A)}{C_6H_5N_2^+Cl^-} \xrightarrow[\Delta]{CuCN} \underset{\text{Benzonitrile }(B)}{C_6H_5CN}$$

9. (d) Both Statement I and Statement II are correct.

10. (c) The complete reaction sequence is as follows

$$p\text{-}CH_3C_6H_4NH_2 \xrightarrow[\text{(Acetylation)}]{(CH_3CO)_2O} p\text{-}CH_3C_6H_4NHCOCH_3\ (A) \xrightarrow{Br_2/CH_3COOH} (B) \xrightarrow[\text{(Hydrolysis)}]{H^+/H_2O} (C)$$

(A) NHCOCH$_3$, CH$_3$; (B) NHCOCH$_3$, Br, CH$_3$; (C) NH$_2$, Br, CH$_3$

11. (b) Both (A) and (R) are true but (R) is not the correct explanation of (A). It is because NH_2 group being *o*, *p*-directing directs the SO_3H group to the less hindered *p*-position, hence forms *p*-amino sulphonic acid.

12. (a) Peroxytrifluoroacetic acid oxidise the amino group directly to the nitro-group.

$$C_6H_5-NH_2 \xrightarrow{CF_3CO_3H} C_6H_5-NO_2\ (86\%)$$

Thus, the missing reagent is CF_3CO_3H

13. (a) The complete reaction involved is as follows

$$C_6H_5-NH_2 + CHCl_3 + 3KOH \longrightarrow \underset{\text{Phenyl isocyanide}}{C_6H_5NC} + 3KCl + 3H_2O$$

Thus, the compound *Y* is phenyl isocyanide.

14. (b) The correct IUPAC name is 4-ethyl-2-methyl phenylamine.

15. (b)

(i) $C_6H_5CONH_2 \xrightarrow[\text{Hofmann Bromamide reaction}]{Br_2+NaOH} C_6H_5NH_2$

(ii) Phthalimide N^-K^+ + chlorobenzene $\xrightarrow{S_N2}$ No reaction

S_N2 never take place at sp^2 carbon

(iii) $C_6H_5NO_2 \xrightarrow[\text{Reduction}]{H_2,\ Pd/C} C_6H_5NH_2$

(iv) $C_6H_5NHCOCH_3 \xrightarrow[\text{(b) Alkaline hydrolysis}]{\text{(a) } HNO_3, H_2SO_4,\ 288\text{ K}} p\text{-}NO_2C_6H_4NH_2 + CH_3COOH$

(v) $C_6H_5N_2^+Cl^- \xrightarrow{H_2O} C_6H_5OH$

Thus, among the given transformations, three reactions will give aromatic amines.

Test-3

1. (b) Statement I is correct but statement II is incorrect because primary aromatic amines form arene diazonium salts which are stable for a short time in solution at low temperature.

2. (c)

$C_6H_5N_2^+Cl^- \xrightarrow[\text{displacement of Cl by I}]{KI} C_6H_5I$ (Iodobenzene) (*B*)

$C_6H_5N_2^+Cl^- \xrightarrow{HBF_4} C_6H_5N_2^+BF_4^- \xrightarrow{NaNO_2/Cu} C_6H_5NO_2$ Nitrobenzene (*A*)

3. (b) When diazonium chloride solution mix with ice cold alkaline solution of β-napthol, then orange dye is obtained.

$$C_6H_5N_2^+Cl^- + \beta\text{-naphthol} \xrightarrow[\text{pH (9-10)}]{\text{NaOH, Basic solution}} C_6H_5-N{=}N-(\text{2-hydroxynaphthyl})$$

Orange dye

4. (d)

$$Ar-NH_2 \xrightarrow[NaNO_2]{HBF_4} \overset{+}{N_2}\overset{-}{BF_4}\ (\text{Arene diazonium fluoroborate } (A)) \xrightarrow{\text{Heat}} ArF + N_2 + BF_3\ (B)$$

5. (a) An azo coupling is a reaction between a diazonium compound $CR—N_2^+$ and another aromatic compound that produces an azo compound. Reaction (a) is azo coupling reaction in which azo dye is formed.

6. (b) The complete reaction sequence is as follows

$$C_6H_5NO_2 \xrightarrow{Sn/HCl} \underset{\text{Aniline }(X)}{C_6H_5NH_2} \xrightarrow{C_6H_5COCl} \underset{\text{Benzanilide }(Y)}{C_6H_5NHCOC_6H_5} + HCl$$

Thus, the compound Y is benzanilide (Y).

7. (a) The complete reaction sequence is as follows

2,4-dinitroaniline $\xrightarrow{NaNO_2/HCl}$ 2,4-dinitrobenzenediazonium chloride (A) $\xrightarrow{\text{anisole}}$ p-methoxy-2,4-dinitroazobenzene (B)

Thus, option (a) is correct.

8. (b) (A) $R—CN \xrightarrow[\text{Partial hydrolysis}]{H_2O/OH^-} \underset{\text{Amide}}{RCONH_2}$

(B) $R—NC \xrightarrow[\text{Hydrolysed only in acidic medium}]{H_2O/H^+} \underset{1^\circ \text{ amine}}{R—NH_2} + HCOOH$

Thus, option (b) is correct.

9. (c) The given reaction is known as Sandmeyer reaction. It is a method to synthesise variety of organic compound by substituting amino group of aromatic amines.

$$C_6H_5N_2Cl \xrightarrow{Cu_2Cl_2/HCl} \underset{(X)}{C_6H_5Cl} + \underset{(Y)}{N_2}$$

10. (b)

Nitrobenzene $\xrightarrow[6[H]]{Sn + HCl}$ Aniline $\xrightarrow{NaNO_2+HCl}$ $C_6H_5N_2^+Cl^-$ $\xrightarrow[-N_2,\ -KCl]{CuCN/KCN}$ C_6H_5CN $\xrightarrow{H_3O^+}$ Benzoic acid (COOH)

11. (d)

(i) $\underset{\text{Nitroethane}}{CH_3CH_2NO_2} \xrightarrow{LiAlH_4, \text{ Ether}} \underset{\text{Ethanamine}}{CH_3CH_2NH_2}$

(ii) $\underset{\text{Nitrobenzene}}{C_6H_5NO_2} \xrightarrow{LiAlH_4, \text{ Ether}} \underset{\text{Azobenzene}}{C_6H_5N{=}NC_6H_5}$

12. (a) Nitration in naphthalene produce 1-nitronaphthalene (A) and 2-nitronaphthalene (B) depending upon the reaction temperature. At room temperature, kinetically controlled product (KCP) is formed, while at high temperature, thermodynamically controlled product (TCP) is formed.

The σ-complex corresponding to C-1 attack is more stable than the σ-complex corresponding to C-2 attack, thus, A will form at a faster rate than B.

Hence, at room temperature A will be the product.

(Naphthalene) $\xrightarrow[\text{(Room temperature)}]{HNO_3,\ H_2SO_4}$ 1-nitronaphthalene [A] (Major) + 2-nitronaphthalene [B] (Minor)

13. (a) Both Statement I and Statement II are incorrect. Their correct forms are

I. Azo dye is prepared by the coupling of phenol and diazonium chloride.

II. p-hydroxyazobenzene is an orange colour dye.

14. (b) The reaction takes place as,

(m-dinitrobenzene) $\xrightarrow[\text{(ii) Partial reduction}]{\text{(i) } (NH_4)_2S}$ m-nitroaniline $\xrightarrow[\text{[Diazotisation followed by Sandmeyer reaction]}]{\text{(i) } NaNO_2/HCl \text{ (ii) } CuCl/HCl}$ (m-nitrochlorobenzene) (P)

15. (d) The correct match is

A-II, B-III, C-IV, D-I.

A. $ArN_2^+Cl^-$ reacts with H_2O to form Ar—OH.

B. $ArN_2^+Cl^-$ reacts with H_3PO_2 in presence of Cu^+ to form Ar—H alongwith N_2 and H_3PO_3.

C. $ArN_2^+Cl^-$ reacts with CH_3CH_2OH to form Ar—H

D. $ArN_2^+Cl^-$ reacts with C_6H_6 to form Ar—C_6H_5.

Thus, option (d) is correct.

Chapter Break Thru

1. (b) The number of isomeric amines obtained from $C_4H_{11}N$ are four. These are

$CH_3CH_2CH_2CH_2NH_2$, $(CH_3)_2CHCH_2NH_2$

$CH_3CH(NH_2)CH_2CH_3$, $(CH_3)_3CNH_2$

2. (b) Among the given species, Hinsberg's reagent ($C_6H_5SO_2Cl$) will react with primary and secondary amines only which are (i), (iii), (iv) and (v).

3. (a) Correct order of basic nature of aromatic amine is

aniline > m-nitroaniline > p-nitroaniline > o-nitroaniline

If the substituent has electron withdrawing inductive (–*I*) as well as resonance – *R* effect. Then, all the substituted aniline are weaker bases than aniline with *ortho* isomer being the weakest base.

The *m*-isomer in this case relatively stronger base because *R*-effect does not operate at *m*-position.

Due to *ortho* effect, *ortho* substituted aniline are weaker base among the compounds.

4. (a) Both (A) and (R) are true and (R) is the correct explanation of (A).

5. (a) 1° amines react with $C_6H_5SO_2Cl$ to give N-alkylbenzene sulphonamide which dissolves in *aq.* KOH due to presence of an acidic hydrogen on N-atom.

$$\underset{1°\text{ amine}}{R—NH_2} + C_6H_5SO_2Cl \longrightarrow R—\underset{H}{\underset{|}{N}}—SO_2C_6H_5 \xrightarrow[-H_2O]{KOH} \underset{\text{Soluble in alkali}}{[R—\bar{N}—SO_2C_6H_5]K^+}$$

6. (c)

$$\underset{(+)\text{ or }(-)}{CH_3—\overset{*}{C}H(C_6H_5)—NH_2} \xrightarrow{HONO} \underset{\text{(unstable)}}{H_3C—CH(C_6H_5)—\overset{+}{N}{\equiv}N} \xrightarrow{-N_2} CH_3—\overset{+}{C}H—C_6H_5 \xrightarrow[-H^+]{H_2O} CH_3—\overset{*}{C}H(OH)—C_6H_5$$

Since, carbocations are planar species, nucleophilic attack by H_2O gives a racemic mixture of alcohol.

7. (a) NMe_2 group is an electron donating group.

Under the highly acidic condition — NMe_2 group will get protonated and will get converted into —$\overset{+}{N}HMe_2$, which is a very strong electron withdrawing group. Hence, it will deactivate the ring through –*I* and –*R*-effect and it will behave as *meta*-directing group. Therefore, N, N-dimethyl aniline on nitration with conc. H_2SO_4 and HNO_3 mixture will give *m*-nitro-N, N-dimethyl aniline as the major product. The reaction scheme is as follows

$$\underset{\text{(N, N-dimethyl aniline)}}{C_6H_5N(Me)_2} \xrightarrow{H^+} C_6H_5\overset{\oplus}{N}H(Me)_2 \xrightarrow{NO_2^+} \underset{(m\text{-nitro-N, N-dimethylaniline})}{m\text{-}NO_2C_6H_4N(Me)_2}$$

8. (d) Statement given in option (d) is correct while remaining statements are incorrect.

$$C_6H_5NH_2 \xrightarrow{HNO_2 \,|\, H_2SO_4} \underset{51\%}{p\text{-nitroaniline}} + \underset{47\%}{m\text{-nitroaniline}} + \underset{2\%}{o\text{-nitroaniline}}$$

9. (c) In Hinsberg test, a primary amine (RNH_2) forms a white precipitate (*A*) with benzene sulphonyl chloride ($C_6H_5SO_2Cl$) known as Hinsberg reagent. The precipitate (*A*) gets dissolved in *aq.* KOH.

$$C_6H_5SO_2Cl + RNH_2 \xrightarrow{-HCl} \underset{\substack{\text{N-alkyl benzene sulphonamide}\\(A)}}{RNHSO_2C_6H_5} \xrightarrow{Aq.\ KOH} [R—\overset{\ominus}{N}SO_2C_6H_5]K^+(aq) + H_2O \xrightarrow{H^+} \underset{\text{(White solid ppt.)}}{RNHSO_2C_6H_5}$$

10. (c) Aniline on protonation gives anilinium ion which is *meta* directing. So, considerable amount of *meta* product is formed.

$$C_6H_5NH_2 \xrightarrow[+H_2SO_4]{\text{Conc. }HNO_3} \underset{\text{(Anilinium ion)}}{C_6H_5\overset{+}{N}H_3} \text{ (Very high } -I\text{ effect)}$$

11. (d) Both Statement I and Statement II are correct.

12. (c) The complete reaction sequence is as follows

$$C_6H_5NH_2 \xrightarrow[\text{Acetylation}]{CH_3—\overset{O}{\overset{\|}{C}}—Cl} \underset{(A)}{C_6H_5NH—\overset{O}{\overset{\|}{C}}—CH_3} \xrightarrow[H_2O]{Br_2} \underset{(B)}{p\text{-}BrC_6H_4NH_2}$$

13. (d) $LiAlH_4$ can reduce nitroalkanes/ arenes (i), imine (ii), alkyl/arylnitrile, (iii), acid amide (iv), (v) : and alkyl-azide (vi) into respective 1° amines.

14. (a) Both A and R are true and R is the correct explanation of A.

15. (c) The end product of the synthetic sequence is *iso*-indolin-1-one. The first step is Hofmann bromamide degradation, in which an amide is treated with bromine and aqueous or alcoholic sodium hydroxide to form a primary amine containing one carbon atom less.

The second step is intramolecular acyl transfer reaction.

$$o\text{-}(CH_2CONH_2)C_6H_4COOCH_3 \xrightarrow[\text{Hofmann degradation}]{Br_2/NaOH} o\text{-}(CH_2\ddot{N}H_2)C_6H_4\overset{O}{\overset{\|}{C}}—OCH_3 \xrightarrow{\text{Cyclisation}} \text{iso-indolin-1-one (C=O, NH ring)}$$

16. (d) Electron releasing groups increase the basic strength of amines, whereas electron withdrawing groups decrease the basic strength of N–bases. Therefore, the order of basic strength will be III > II > IV > I. Since, in I, —NH group is placed between two electrons withdrawing groups, it is less basic among the given compounds.

17. (b) The complete reaction sequence is as follows

$$\text{CH}_3\text{CH}_2\text{CH}_2\text{C}\equiv\text{N} \xrightarrow[\text{(ii) H}_3\text{O}^+]{\text{(i) LiAlH}_4\text{ (excess)}} \text{CH}_3\text{CH}_2\text{CH}_2\text{CH}_2\text{NH}_2$$

Thus, the product formed is given in option (b).

18. (b) The reaction of acetamide in presence of P_2O_5 is as follows

$$\underset{\text{Acetamide}}{\text{CH}_3\text{CONH}_2} \xrightarrow{\text{P}_2\text{O}_5} \underset{\text{Acetonitrile}}{\text{CH}_3-\text{C}\equiv\text{N}} + \text{H}_2\text{O}$$

Thus, the product formed is acetonitrile.

19. (d)

Aniline (X) $\xrightarrow{\text{Br}_2}$ 2,4,6-tribromoaniline (Y) $\xrightarrow[\text{HCl}]{\text{NaNO}_2}$ 2,4,6-tribromobenzenediazonium chloride (Z) $\xrightarrow[\text{C}_2\text{H}_5\text{OH}]{\text{Boiling}}$ Tribromobenzene

Thus, the compound X is aniline.

20. (d) The complete reaction sequence involved is as follows

4-Hydroxybenzaldehyde $\xrightarrow[\text{Bromination}]{\text{Br}_2}$ 3,5-dibromo-4-hydroxybenzaldehyde (A) $\xrightarrow{\text{NH}_2\text{OH}}$ oxime, HC=N—OH (B) $\xrightarrow{\text{P}_2\text{O}_5}$ 3,5-dibromo-4-hydroxybenzonitrile, CN (C)

21. (a) Gabriel phthalimide is firstly treated with alcoholic KOH to form potassium phthalimide which on further reaction with ethyl iodide gives N-ethyl phthalimide. The product N-ethyl phthalimide proceeds with alkaline hydrolysis to form primary amine, i.e. ethylamine. This reaction is known as Gabriel phthalimide synthesis.

22. (b) The correct reaction sequence involved is as follows

p-Toluidine $\xrightarrow[\text{HCl}]{\text{NaNO}_2/}$ p-methylbenzenediazonium chloride ($\overset{\oplus}{\text{N}}_2\overset{\ominus}{\text{Cl}}$) + phenol $\xrightarrow{\text{Mild Basic}}$ CH_3–C_6H_4–N=N–C_6H_4–OH

23. (d) Statements given in A, B, C and E are correct while D is incorrect. It is because in methyl amine, only one electron releasing group is present but in dimethyl amine, two electron releasing groups are present which increase the basicity higher in dimethyl amine.

24. (b) The complete reaction sequence is as follows.

Aniline (X) $\xrightarrow[\text{0-5°C}]{\text{NaNO}_2\text{-HCl}}$ Benzenediazonium chloride ($\overset{\oplus}{\text{N}}_2\overset{\ominus}{\text{Cl}}$) (A) $\xrightarrow{\text{CuCN}}$ Benzonitrile, CN (B) $\xrightarrow[\text{HCl}]{\text{H}_2\text{O}}$ Benzoic acid, COOH (C)

Thus, the reactant X is aniline.

25. (c) Hinsberg's test helps to distinguish between primary, secondary and tertiary amine both aliphatic and aromatic.

Thus, option (c) is incorrect, whereas statements (a), (b) and (d) are correct.

26. (c) The correct match is A-III, B-II, C-I, D-IV.

A. Aniline $\xrightarrow[\Delta]{\text{H}_2\text{SO}_4}$ $\overset{+}{\text{NH}_3}$–C_6H_4–SO_3^- (Zwitter ion)

B. Aniline $\xrightarrow[\text{H}_2\text{SO}_4]{\text{HNO}_3\text{, 293 K}}$ o-nitroaniline + m-nitroaniline + p-nitroaniline

C. Aniline $\xrightarrow{\text{HNO}_3 \; \text{CH}_3\text{COCl/H}_3\text{O}^+}$ p-nitroaniline

D. Aniline $\xrightarrow{\text{Br}_2 \; \text{CH}_3\text{COCl/H}_2\text{O}}$ p-bromoaniline

27. (d) Among the given compounds, compound given in option (d) will not give Hofmann bromamide reaction because this reaction is given by primary amides only.

28. (c) The given reaction proceeds as follows

$$\text{C}_6\text{H}_5\text{NH}_2 \xrightarrow[\text{0 - 5°C}]{\text{NaNO}_2/\text{HCl}} \underset{(X)}{\text{C}_6\text{H}_5\text{N}_2^+\text{Cl}^-} \xrightarrow[\text{H}_2\text{O}]{\text{HNO}_2} \underset{(Y)}{\text{C}_6\text{H}_5\text{NO}_2} + \text{N}_2 + \text{HCl}$$

Thus, the compounds X and Y are $C_6H_5N_2^+Cl^-$ and $C_6H_5NO_2$ respectively.

29. (b) The complete reaction sequence is as follows

p-nitroaniline $\xrightarrow{HNO_2}$ p-nitrobenzenediazonium chloride ($N_2^+Cl^-$) $\xrightarrow{KI}$ p-iodonitrobenzene $\xrightarrow{Fe/H^+}$ p-iodoaniline $\xrightarrow{HNO_2}$ p-iododiazonium chloride $\xrightarrow[Warm]{H_2O}$ p-iodophenol

30. (b) The complete reaction sequence is as follows

Cyclopentyl–$C(=O)–NH_2$ $\xrightarrow[-H_2O]{P_2O_5/\Delta}$ Cyclopentyl–$C\equiv N$ (*A*)

31. (b)

$$R-CH_2-X \xrightarrow[NH_3]{Ag_2O+H_2O} R-CH_2-NH_2 \xrightarrow[-H_2SO_4]{[O]\ K_2Cr_2O_7} R-COOH \xrightarrow[Heat]{NH_3} R-\underset{\underset{O}{\|}}{C}-NH_2 \xrightarrow{Br_2\ NaOH} R-NH_2\ (P)$$

Thus, option (b) is correct.

32. (d) The correct match is I-Q, II-S, III-P, IV-R.

Aniline $\xrightarrow[(ii)\ H_2O,\ warm]{(i)\ NaNO_2+HCl}$ Phenol

Phenol $\xrightarrow[(ii)\ OH^-]{(i)\ C_6H_5N_2Cl}$ p-hydroxyazobenzene

Phenol $\xrightarrow[(ii)\ H^+]{(i)\ CHCl_3+Aq.\ NaOH}$ Salicylaldehyde (o-hydroxybenzaldehyde, CHO)

Phenol $\xrightarrow[(iii)\ H^+]{(i)\ NaOH,\ (ii)\ CO_2}$ Salicylic acid (o-hydroxybenzoic acid, COOH)

33. (c) (1) Amino group of aniline is acetylated with acetic anhydride/pyridine to form *P*.

(2) *P* is then brominated with bromine/acetic acid. As the $NHCOCH_3$ is *ortho/para* directing group (since lone pair on N activates the ring). Bromine enters in *para*-position (*para* product is major) and forms *Q*.

(3) The final step is acid hydrolysis in which $-NHCOCH_3$ group is hydrolysed to $-NH_2$ group.

So, the product *R* formed is *p*-bromoaniline.

Aniline $\xrightarrow[Pyridine]{CH_3COCl}$ Acetanilide (*P*) $\xrightarrow[CH_3COOH]{Br_2}$ p-bromoacetanilide (*Q*) $\xrightarrow{H^+/OH^-}$ p-bromoaniline (*R*)

34. (b) The reaction sequence involved is as follows

$$\underset{\text{Ethyl amine}}{C_2H_5NH_2} + CHCl_3 + 3KOH \longrightarrow \underset{\substack{\text{Ethyl isocyanide}\\ \text{(Unpleasant smell)}}}{C_2H_5N\equiv C} + 3KCl + 3H_2O$$

35. (b) Hofmann-Bromamide degradation reaction is given as

$$RCONH_2 + 4NaOH + Br_2 \longrightarrow RNH_2 + Na_2CO_3 + 2NaBr + 2H_2O$$

Hence, four moles of NaOH and one mole of Br_2 are used.

36. (c) Only 1° amine give Hofmann's mustard oil reaction, which are

$CH_3CH_2CH_2NH_2$; $CH_3CH_2CH(NH_2)CH_3$; $Ph-C(CH_3)_2-NH_2$; $C_6H_5-CH_2-NH_2$

37. (d)

$C_6H_5-N=N-C_6H_4-NH_2$

(Yellow colour)
p-aminoazobenzene

38. (a) Only 1° amines (aliphatic or aromatic) give carbylamine reaction, i.e. (A), (C) and (E) will respond to carbylamine reaction.

39. (b)

3, 4, 5-tribromoaniline $\xrightarrow[NaNO_2-HCl/0-5°C]{\text{Diazotisation}}$ 3,4,5-tribromobenzenediazonium chloride ($N_2^{\oplus}Cl^{\ominus}$) $\xrightarrow{H_3PO_2}$ 1, 2, 3-tribromobenzene

40. (c) Statement I is incorrect but Statement II is correct. The correct form of statement I is that Hofmann bromamide degradation reaction is used for the preparation of primary amines.

41. (d) When the given amine compound is treated with $NaNO_2$ and HCl at 0°C-5°C, unstable diazonium chloride will form, which will readily breaks down into unstable 1° carbocation.

Hence, readily bond migration (ring expansion) will occur to generate more stable 2° carbocation which will be readily attacked by the nucleophile, water to form (d) as the major product.

The reaction scheme with possible mechanism is shown below

(Aliphatic 1°-amine) $\xrightarrow[\text{(Diazotisation)}]{NaNO_2, HCl}$ $\overset{\oplus}{N_2}\overset{\ominus}{Cl}$ $\xrightarrow{-N_2}$ carbocation $\rightarrow$ rearranged carbocation $\xrightarrow{H_2\ddot{O}}$ $\xrightarrow{-H^+}$ OH (d)

42. (c) NH_2 + CH_3Cl → $N(CH_3)_2$ $\xrightarrow{CH_3Cl}$ $N^+(CH_3)_3$ Quaternary ammonium salt; $NHCH_3$ $\xrightarrow{CH_3Cl}$

43. (b) The complete reaction sequence involved is as follows

Benzene $\xrightarrow[\text{333K (Nitration)}]{HNO_3/H_2SO_4}$ NO_2 $\xrightarrow[\text{(Chlorination)}]{Cl_2/Fe}$ NO_2, Cl $\xrightarrow[\text{(Reduction)}]{Sn/HCl}$ NH_2, Cl (3-chloroaniline)

Thus, the correct sequence of reaction is nitration, chlorination and reduction.

44. (c)

Benzene $+3HNO_3$ $\xrightarrow{\text{Fuming}}$ Sym – trinitrobenzene $+3H_2O$

Thus, the product formed when benzene is nitrated by fuming nitric acid is *sym*-trinitrobenzene.

45. (a) $\underset{\text{Nitromethane}}{CH_3NO_2} + 3Cl_2 + 3NaOH \longrightarrow$

$\underset{\text{(Chloropicrin)}}{CCl_3—NO_2} + 3NaCl + 3H_2O$

46. (a) It is a Balz-Schiemann reaction. It is a chemical reaction in which primary aromatic amine is converted into aryl fluoride *via* diazonium tetrafluoroborate intermediate.

NH_2 $\xrightarrow[HNO_2]{HBF_4}$ $[\overset{+}{N_2}BF_4^-]$ $\xrightarrow{\Delta}$ F

Benzene diazonium tetrafluoroborate into fluorobenzene

47. (c) $CH_3—N \rightleftarrows C + 4[H] \xrightarrow{\text{Reduction}} CH_3—\ddot{N}H—CH_3$ 2° amine

48. (b) The complete reaction sequence is as follows.

NH_2 $\xrightarrow{NaNO_2+HCl}$ $\overset{+}{N_2}Cl^-$ $\xrightarrow{Cu_2Cl_2}$ Cl $\xrightarrow[H^+]{\text{NaOH, 623K, 300 atm}}$ OH (*A*)

49. (c) (A) is true but (R) is false. The correct form of (R) is :

The reaction can be used to prepare 1°, 2°, 3° amines and finally quaternary ammonium salts.

50. (b) Only primary aromatic amines can undergo diazotisation.

NH_2 $\xrightarrow{NaNO_2+HCl}$ $\overset{+}{N_2}Cl$

Ch-11 Biomolecules

Topical Follow Thru

Test-1

1. (d) Statement given in option (d) is incorrect. Its correct form is polysaccharides are not sweet in taste, hence they are called as non-sugars.

2. (b) Glucose gets oxidised to six carbon carboxylic acid (gluconic acid) on reaction with a mild oxidising agent like bromine water.

CHO–$(CHOH)_4$–CH_2OH $\xrightarrow{Br_2\text{ water}}$ COOH–$(CHOH)_4$–CH_2OH (Gluconic acid *X*)

This the compound *X* is gluconic acid.

3. (d) Statements (a), (b) and (c) are correct while (d) is incorrect.

When starch is hydrolysed then, glucose is obtained.

$\underset{\text{Starch}}{(C_6H_{10}O_5)_n} + nH_2O \xrightarrow[\text{393 K, 2-3 bar}]{H^+} \underset{\text{Glucose}}{n\,C_6H_{12}O_6}$

4. (b) The correct match is A-III, B-IV, C-II, D-I.

A. Glucose form pyranose ring containing 6-atoms.
B. Fructose form furanose ring containing 5 atoms.
C. C_1-carbon of glucose chain is called an anomeric carbon which gives different orientation of hydroxyl group.
D. Glucose and galactose are stereoisomers of each other.

Thus, option (b) is correct.

5. (c) Statement I is incorrect but statement II is correct because glucose does not contain any free aldehydic group in its cyclic form, hence does not give a positive result in 2,4-DNP test.

6. (a) In sucrose, the two monosaccharide units are joined together by $\alpha-1, 2$ glycosidic bond. Since, sucrose does not have hemiacetal carbon. Therefore, it is a non-reducing sugar and does not show any reducing test of aldehyde.

7. (a) Glucose is reduced to sorbitol, a hexahydric alcohol on reaction with hydrogen in the presence of Ni catalyst or on reaction with sodium amalgam in aqueous solution.

$$\underset{\text{(Glucose)}}{HOCH_2\cdot(CHOH)_4\cdot CHO} \xrightarrow{Ni/H_2} \underset{\text{Sorbitol}}{HOCH_2\cdot(CHOH)_4\cdot CH_2OH}$$

Hence, option (a) is correct.

8. (c)

β-D-fructofuranose: ring O; C2 bearing OH and CH_2OH; C3 bearing HO and H; C4 bearing OH and H; C5 bearing H and $HOH_2\overset{6}{C}$

β-D-fructofuranose

Thus, option (c) is correct.

9. (c) (A) is true but (R) is false. The correct form of (R) is :

Reaction of glucose with Fehling's solution gives cuprous oxide (Cu_2O) and gluconic acid.

10. (d) Statement given in option (d) is incorrect. Its correct form is sucrose is a non-reducing sugar and does not show Tollen's test as it does not contain any free aldehyde group.

11. (b)

$$\begin{array}{c} O\!\!=\!C\!-\!H \\ H-\!\!\!-\!OH \\ HO-\!\!\!-\!H \\ H-\!\!\!-\!OH \\ H-\!\!\!-\!OH \\ CH_2OH \end{array}$$

D-glucose

—OH group is present on left hand side of carbon number 3.

12. (c) Each of these two forms can be synthesised and isolated as pure compounds.

The alpha (α) anomer of D-glucose has a specific rotation of +112 degree in water.

The beta (β) anomer of D-glucose has a specific rotation of +19 degree (18.7 actually but rounding upto 19) and when either anomer is dissolved in water, the value of the specific rotation change over time eventually reaching the same value of +52°. The specific rotation of α-D-glucose decreases from +112° to 52°. The specific rotation of β-D-glucose increases from +19° to +52°. This behaviour is called mutarotation.

13. (d) Both Statement I and Statement II are correct.

14. (a) Glucose and fructose form same osazone. The two compounds differ only at carbon number 1 and 2 and both of them get involved in osazone formation and thus the osazone formed is identical for both.

$$\underset{\text{(Fructose)}}{\begin{array}{c} CH_2OH \\ | \\ C=O \\ | \\ (CH_2OH)_3 \\ | \\ CH_2OH \end{array}} \xrightarrow{3PhNHNH_2} \underset{\text{(Osazone)}}{\begin{array}{c} CH=N-NHPh \\ | \\ C=N-NHPh \\ | \\ (CHOH)_3 \\ | \\ CH_2OH \end{array}} \xleftarrow{3PhNHNH_2} \underset{\text{(Glucose)}}{\begin{array}{c} CH=O \\ | \\ CHOH \\ | \\ (CHOH)_3 \\ | \\ CH_2OH \end{array}}$$

15. (c) (a) is D-glucose.
(b) is L-glucose.
(c) is L-galactose.
(d) is L-mannose.

Thus, option (c) is correct.

16. (a) The given structure is lactose. It is composed of β-D-galactose (left) and β-D-glycosidic linkage between the C_1 of galactose and C_4 of β-D-glucose unit. It is a non-reducing sugar.

17. (d)

$$\underset{\text{Starch}}{(C_6H_{10}O_5)_n} \xrightarrow[\text{Diastase}]{+H_2O} \underset{\text{Maltose}}{nC_{12}H_{22}O_{11}} \xrightarrow{\Delta} \underset{\text{Glucose}}{C_6H_{12}O_6}$$

Thus, option (d) is correct.

18. (c) Among the given options, inulin is a carbohydrate, which is stored in over 36,000 plant species while leucine is an amino acid. Albumin is a family of globular proteins and maltase is an enzyme.

19. (d) (A) is false but (R) is true. In maltose, two α-D-glucose units are joined by $C_1 - C_4\,\alpha$-(1, 4)-glycosidic linkage.

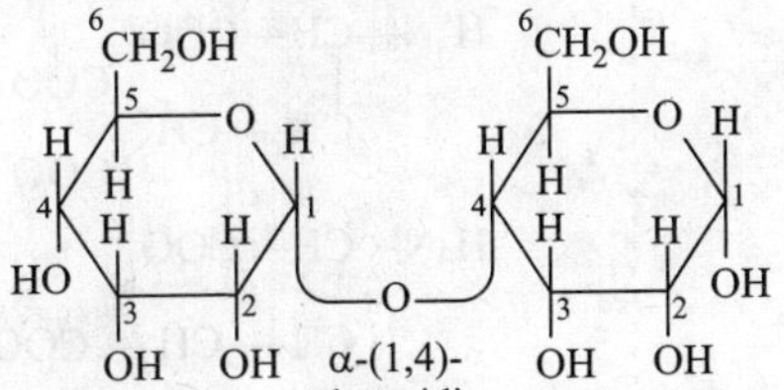

$^6CH_2OH$ ... α-D-glucose — α-(1,4)-glucosidic bond (Maltose) — α-D-glucose

20. (c) The structure of A matches with structure (c), as

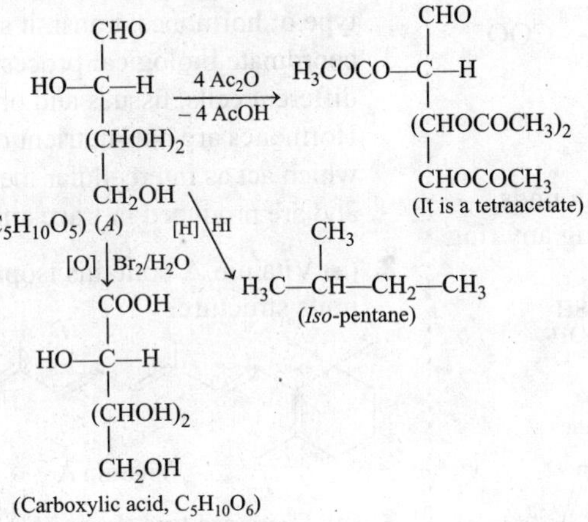

$$\underset{(C_5H_{10}O_5)\,(A)}{CHO-C(H)(OH)-(CHOH)_2-CH_2OH} \xrightarrow[-4\,AcOH]{4\,Ac_2O} H_3COCO-C-H(CHOCOCH_3)_2\,CHOCOCH_3 \text{ (It is a tetraacetate)}$$

$A \xrightarrow{[H]\,HI} H_3C-CH(CH_3)-CH_2-CH_3$ (*Iso*-pentane)

$A \xrightarrow{[O]\,Br_2/H_2O}$ COOH–C(HO)(H)–$(CHOH)_2$–CH_2OH (Carboxylic acid, $C_5H_{10}O_6$)

21. (b) D-(+)-sucrose (invert sugar) is an equimolar mixture of D-(+)-glucose and D-(–)-fructose. It is called invert sugar due to the fact that on hydrolysis, there is a change in the sign of rotation from positive to negative.

22. (b) Lactose (milk sugar) is composed of β-D-galactose and β-D-glucose through C_1 (of β-D-galactose) and C_4 (of β-D-glucose) glycosidic linkage.

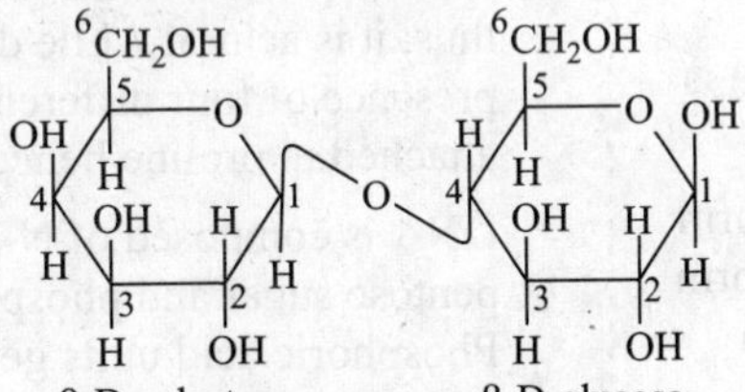

β-D-galactose — β-D-glucose
Lactose

23. (b) Complete reaction is as follows
When the D-aldopentose is treated with a series of reagents (i) KCN, HCN ; (ii) H_2, Pd/$BaSO_4$; (iii) H^+ / H_2O, a mixture (B) of epimeric hexoses is formed which are D-glucose and D-mannose. This reaction is known as Fisher-Kiliani reaction.

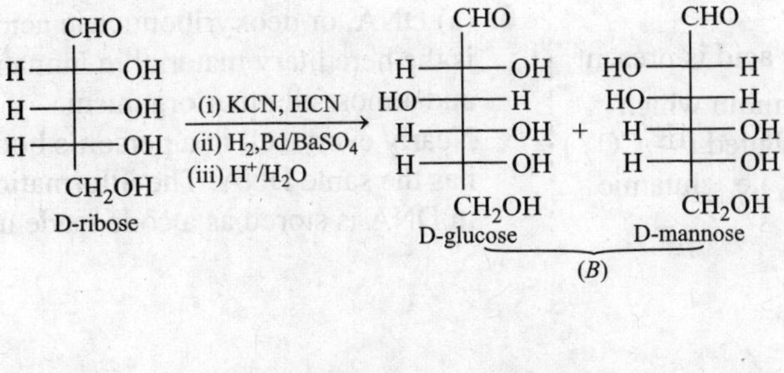

D-ribose $\xrightarrow[\text{(ii) } H_2,Pd/BaSO_4 \quad \text{(iii) } H^+/H_2O]{\text{(i) KCN, HCN}}$ D-glucose + D-mannose (B)

On the other hand, when the D-ribose is treated with a series of reagents- (i) Br_2 / H_2O, (ii) $Ca(OH)_2$, (iii) H_2O_2 / $Fe_2(SO_4)_3$, a erythrose (A) is formed. This reaction is known as Ruff's reaction.

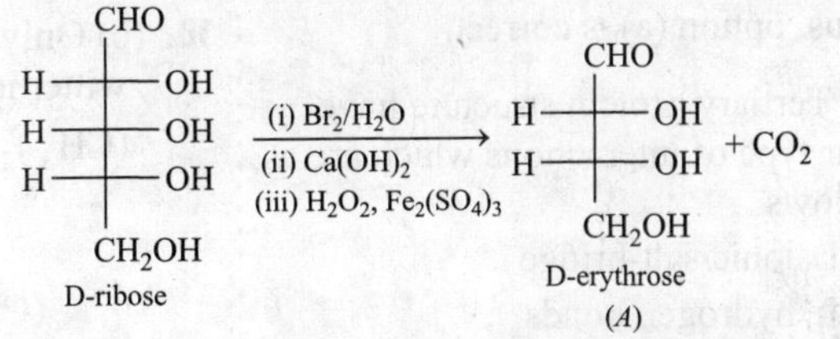

D-ribose $\xrightarrow[\text{(ii) } Ca(OH)_2 \quad \text{(iii) } H_2O_2, Fe_2(SO_4)_3]{\text{(i) } Br_2/H_2O}$ D-erythrose (A) + CO_2

24. (d) Statement given in option (d) is incorrect. Its correct form is the two cyclic hemiacetals of glucose differ in the configuration of the hydroxyl group at C_1 called anomeric carbon.

25. (b) Complete reaction is as follows

Glucose $\xrightarrow[\text{(Excess)}]{C_6H_5NHNH_2}$ CH=NNHPh–CH=NNHPh–$(CHOH)_3$–CH_2OH (A) $\xrightarrow[\text{Heat}]{H_3O^{\oplus}}$ CHO–CH=O–$(CHOH)_3$–CH_2OH (B) $\xrightarrow{Zn/AcOH}$ CH_2OH–CH=O–$(CHOH)_3$–CH_2OH Fructose (C)

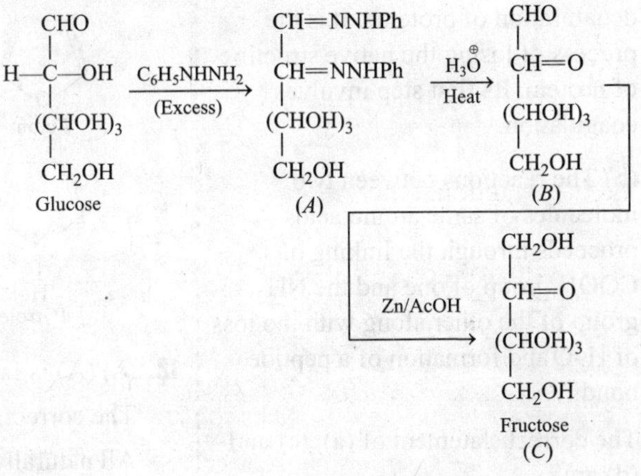

Test-2

1. (b) Statement I is correct but statement II is incorrect because glycine and alanine are synthesised in the body and are known as non-essential amino acids.

2. (d) Tyrosinase is a copper containing oxidase which is widely distributed in plants, animals tissues (including human). It oxidises tyrosine to melanin in mammal and causes the cut surfaces of many fruits and vegetables to darken.

Carbonic anhydrase and lactic dehydrogenase contain zinc as a necessary metal co-factor. While, tryptophanase does not require copper for its activity, it is involved in the metabolism of tryptophan.

3. (c) Among the given options, antigen is not considered as classification of proteins because antigens are polysaccharides that are present on RBC's surface.

4. (a) α-amino acid except glycine are chiral molecule and exhibit optical activity due to presence of L-amino acid group.

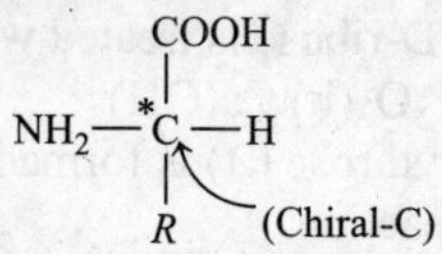

$$NH_2-\overset{*}{C}(COOH)(R)-H \quad \text{(Chiral-C)}$$

Thus, option (a) is correct.

5. (d) Tertiary protein structure have four type of interactions which are as follows

I. ionic/salt-bridge
II. hydrogen bonds
III. van der Waals' interactions
IV. disulphide (S—S) bonds.

Thus, option (d) is correct.

6. (c) Statements (a), (b) and (d) are correct while (c) is incorrect about denaturation of proteins. It is the process of losing the native structure of protein. Its first step involves coagulation.

7. (b) The reactions between two molecules of same amino acids proceeds through the linking of COOH group of one and the NH_2 group of the other along with the loss of H_2O and formation of a peptide bond.

The correct statement of (a), (c) and (d) are

- Proteins are made up of amino acids, which are linked together in chains by peptide bonds.
- Dipeptides consist of only 2 amino acids.
- Glycylalanine is a dipeptide.

8. (b) Nitrogenase is used in nitrogen fixation, not in alcohol production. Lipase breaks down fats and oils in detergent.

Pectinase clarifies fruit juices.

Amylase removes starch from textiles.

9. (a) Sulphur containing amino acids are

(II) Cysteine $HS-CH_2-CH(NH_2)-COOH$ and

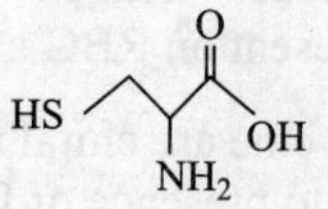

(IV) Methionine

$$CH_3-S-CH_2-CH_2-CH(NH_2)-\overset{O}{\overset{\|}{C}}-OH$$

10. (b) Only compound (b) exists in zwitter ion state.

$$(CH_3)_2\cdot CH\cdot CH(NH_2)-COOH \rightleftharpoons (CH_3)_2-CH\cdot CH(NH_3^+)-COO^-$$

(Zwitter ion)

11. (d) Among the given compounds, cysteine does not containing any ring in its structure.

Furan, 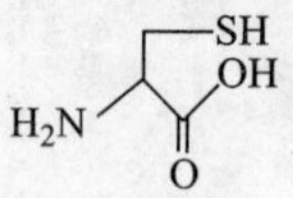 Cysteine, 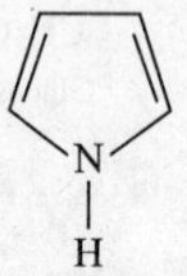 Pyrrole,  Thiophene

12. (d) (A) is false but (R) is true.

The correct form of (A) is :

All naturally occurring α-amino acids except glycine are optically active.

13. (b) Statement given in option (b) is incorrect. It is because :

All proteins are not found in *l*-form but they may be present in the form of *d* or *l*. Rest all the other given statements are correct.

14. (a) Secondary structure involves α-helical and β-pleated sheet like structures. α-helix is formed when the chain of α-amino acid coils as a right handed screw, whereas in β-pleated sheet the chains are held together by a large number of H-bonds.

15. (a) γ-carboxyglutamic acid is present in the protein, prothrombin which readily gets decarboxylated ($-CO_2$) to another amino acid, i.e. glutamic acid (*A*).

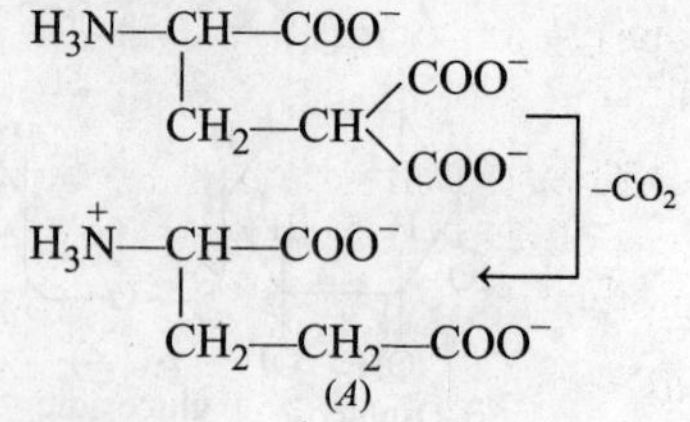

$$H_3N-CH(COO^-)-CH_2-CH(COO^-)_2 \xrightarrow{-CO_2} H_3\overset{+}{N}-CH(COO^-)-CH_2-CH_2-COO^- \; (A)$$

Test-3

1. (a) Messenger protein, such as some type of hormones, transmit signals to coordinate biological process between different cells, tissues and organs. Hormones are non-nutrient chemical which act as intercellular messengers and are produced in trace amounts.

2. (a) Vitamin A contains isoprene unit in its structure.

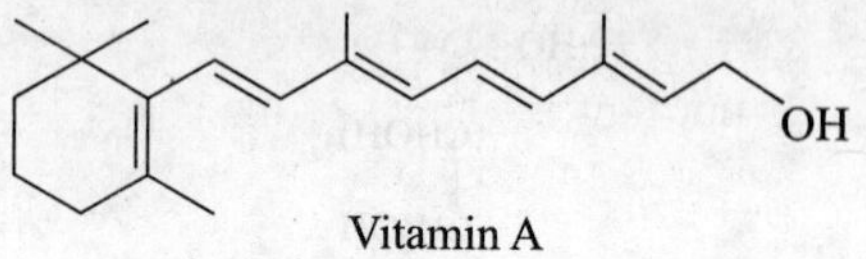

Vitamin A

3. (a) There are two types of nucleobase : Purine and pyrimidine. Purine nucleobase contains adenine and guanine, while pyrimidine nucleobase contains uracil, thymine and cytosine bases respectively. Glycine in its Zwitter ion form bears no chiral centres and can superimposed on its mirror image, thus, it is achiral while due to presence of four different groups attached in proline hence it is chiral.

DNA is composed of N-bases, pentose sugar and phosphoric acid. Phosphoric acid units get attached with sugar through glycosidic bonds.

4. (c) First hormone to have actually been isolated and synthesized was the adrenaline hormone identified by japanese American chemist Jokichi Takemine in 1901.

5. (d) The correct match is A-III, B-I, C-IV, D-II.

6. (a) DNA, or deoxyribonucleic acid, is the hereditary material in humans and almost all other organism. Nearly every cell in a person's body has the same DNA. The information in DNA is stored as a code made up four chemical bases : adenine (A), guanine (G), cytosine (C) and thymine (T).

7. (c) The correct statement about DNA is given in option (c), i.e. Phosphate of one unit connects to the pentose of another unit.

8. (d) The correct match is A-II, B-III, C-I, D-IV.

A. ***r*-RNA** (Ribosomal RNA) forms the site for protein synthesis and helps the binding of *m*-RNA to the ribosomes.

B. ***m*-RNA** (Messenger RNA) carries the genetic information from DNA to the ribosomes, where protein is being synthesised.

C. ***t*-RNA** (Transfer RNA) acts as a carrier of amino acids, that is, it carries amino acids from different parts of cytoplasm to the ribosomes, during protein synthesis.

D. ***Sn*-RNA** Catalyses splicing of pre *m*-RNA.

9. (d) Testesterone, estradiol, progesterone are steroid hormones, while peptide hormone is non-steroid hormone. Thus, option (d) is correct.

10. (c) RNA and DNA are nucleic acids which on complete hydrolysis yield a pentose sugar, phosphoric acid and nitrogen containing heterocyclic compounds called bases.

11. (a) Vitamin-A (cartenoids), soluble in oils and fats but insoluble in water.
Thus, option (a) is correct.

12. (a) Among the given vitamins, vitamin A, D, E, K and B_{12} are stored in liver and adipose tissue.

13. (a) The tripeptide hormone present in most of the living cell is glutathione. Three amino acid p.esent in glutathione are glutamic acid, cysteine and glycine. Glutathione is required for the action of both enzymes and insulin.

14. (a) The backbone of nucleic acid molecule consists of an alternating sugar and phosphate groups one linked by phosphate ester bond which can be shown as,

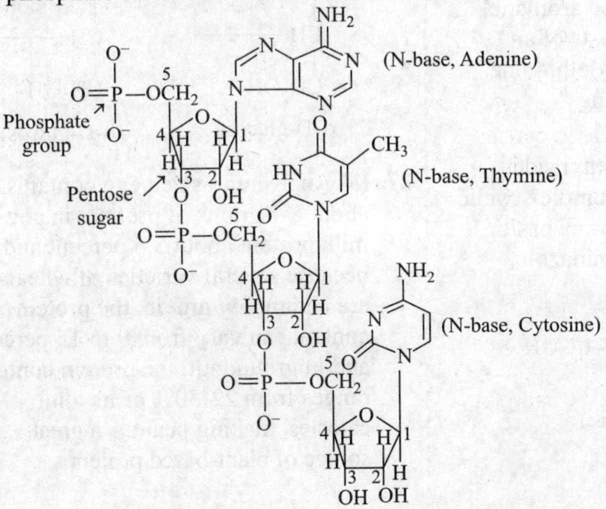

Phosphate group
Pentose sugar
(N-base, Adenine)
(N-base, Thymine)
(N-base, Cytosine)

15. (c) One strand of DNA : ATCGTATG
Complementary strand : TAGCATAC

Base pairing rules :

- Adenine (A) pairs with Thymine (T) in DNA (or Uracil (U) in RNA).
- Cytosine (C) pairs with guanine (G).

Chapter Break Thru

1. (a) In all the three structures (I, II and III), the configuration of OH at the penultimate carbon (C_2 in I and C_5 in II and III) is towards right and hence all have D-configuration.

2. (c) The given observation of glucose is due to presence of a ring structure. CH_3OH can attack the anomeric carbon in 2 way leading to two configurations.

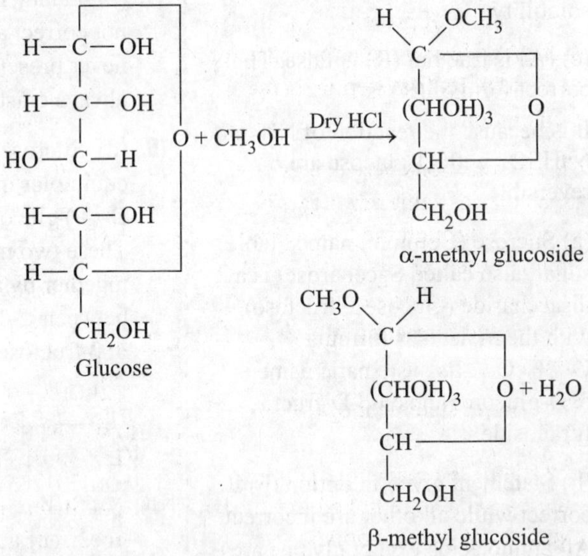

Glucose $+ CH_3OH \xrightarrow{\text{Dry HCl}}$ α-methyl glucoside + β-methyl glucoside $+ H_2O$

3. (b) All amino acids have amine and a carboxyl group. They also have a functional group which is unique to each of them. Depending on the polarity of the functional group, the amino acid can be rendered optically inactive or active. The simplest of all amino acids, glycine which has H as a functional group lacks optical activity, as the saturated alpha carbon is unsubstituted. Others among the 20 amino acids have D or L, stereoisomers. So, the correct answer is 'glycine'.

4. (d) Protein is a body building substance not energy giving substances.
Thus, providing energy for metabolism is not a function of protein.

5. (b) Blood sugar, or glucose, is the main carbohydrates found in blood. The human body contains approximately 5 litres of blood. This amounts to 4 grams of sugar in the blood.

6. (c) The formula of maltose is $C_{12}H_{22}O_{11}$. Thus, it contains 11 oxygen atom in it.

7. (b) Sugar relative sweetness

Sucrose — 100
Glucose — 74
Lactose — 16
Fructose — 173

Thus, fructose is the sweetest sugar.

8. (c) Insulin hormone maintains the blood sugar level in the human body. It is secreted by pancreas.

9. (b) Due to complete occurrence of Zwitter ionic structure at isoelectric point, an amino acid has minimum solubility.

10. (c) (A) is true but (R) is false. The correct form of (R) is :

It is because the reaction of NH_3 and $NaHSO_3$ with D-glucose are reversible.

11. (a) Sucrose (Common name : table sugar, also called Saccharose) is a disaccharide (glucose + fructose) with the molecular formula $C_{12}H_{22}O_{11}$. Its systematic name is α-D-glucopyranosyl-β-D-fructo furanoside.

12. (b) Statement given in option (b) is correct while all other are incorrect. All amino acids except glycine are optically active.

13. (a) All carbohydrates give Molisch's test, i.e. produce a violet colouration with an alcoholic solution of α-naphthol and conc. H_2SO_4. Thus, sugars will be detected by Molisch's test.

14. (c) Ribose is a pentose sugar hence it contains 5 carbon atoms. Thus, statement (c) is incorrect.

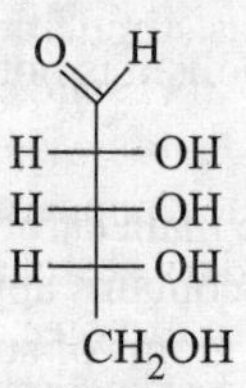

O H
H—OH
H—OH
H—OH
CH_2OH
Ribose

15. (c) Among the given amino acids, tyrosine contains aromatic ring.

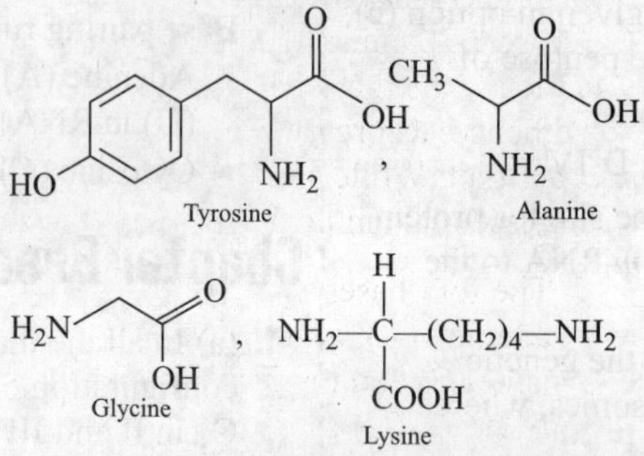

Tyrosine, Alanine, Glycine, Lysine

16. (c) (A) is true but (R) is false. It is because vitamin D is fat soluble and water insoluble vitamin.

17. (c) Statement given in option (c) is not correct about glucose. Glucose is never present in furanose form. It always exist in the pyranose form.

18. (d) Sucrose on hydrolysis gives equimolar mixture of D-(+)-glucose and D-(−)-fructose. These two monosaccharides are held together by a glycosidic linkage between C-1 of α-glucose and C-2 of β-fructose.

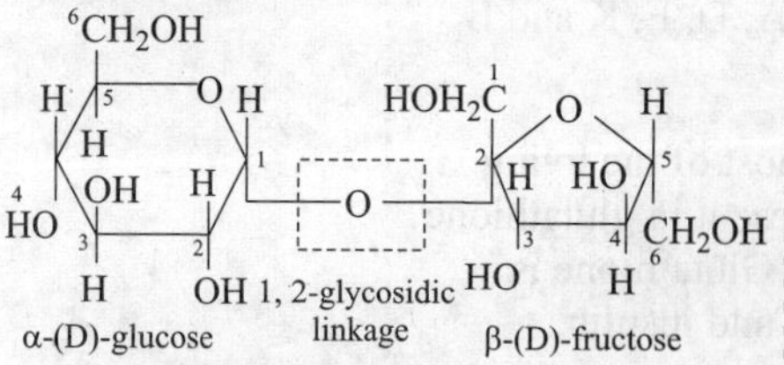

α-(D)-glucose — 1, 2-glycosidic linkage — β-(D)-fructose

Hence, both Statement I and Statement II are correct.

19. (d) Amino acids can be aromatic only if their side consists of an aromatic compound. Methionine has a sulphur containing straight chain.

Isoleucine has an isobutyl side group. Proline has a complex cyclic side chain. Histidine has a basic aromatic side group imidazole.

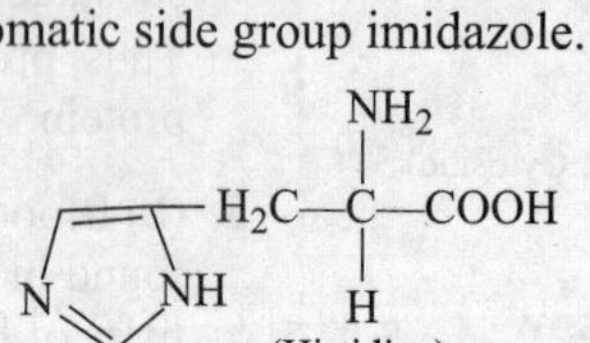

(Histidine)

20. (d) The amino acids, that can be synthesised in the body are called non-essential amino acids. Thus, among the given amino acids, alanine is non-essential amino acid.

21. (d) Among the given options α-helix structure is present in protein.

22. (c) The correct match is
A-IV, B-III, C-I, D-II.

23. (a) Glucose and mannose are epimers because they both differ in configuration at C-2 and the isomer which differ at C_2 position known as epimers of each other.

24. (b) 2-amino pyridine is not present in nucleic acid and as cytosine, adenine, thymine and guanine are four main bases found in nucleic acid. Adenine and Guanine are purine while thymine and cytosine are pyrimidines. They together form triple bonded histones of DNA. 2-amino pyridine is an organic compound with the formula $H_2NC_5H_4N$. It is one of three isomeric amino pyridines.

25. (a) The enzyme ptyalin, also known as amylase is present in saliva and is responsible for breaking down starch into simple sugars such as dextrin and maltose which are further broken down in the intestine.

26. (c) The two configurations of glucose are

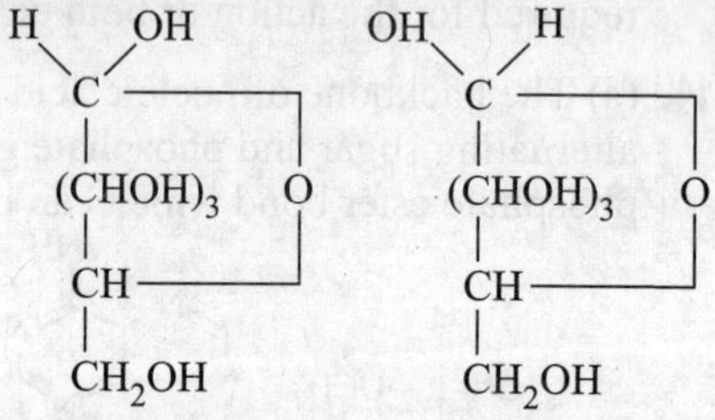

α-D-glucose, β-D-glucose

27. (a) An average-sized egg contains about 6-7 grams of protein, in cow milk protein about 3.5 percent and because several varieties of wheat are commonly grown, the protein content can vary from 9 to 15 percent and in groundnut, the protein content ranges from 22-30% of its total calories, making peanuts a great source of plant-based protein.

28. (c) Aldohexose is a monosaccharide whose molecular structure contains both an aldehyde (an aldose) and six carbon (a hexose). Molecular structure of D-glucose is most common aldohexose.

29. (a) D-glucose on oxidation with Ag_2O gives D-gluconic acid or glycoric acid in which oxidation of only —CHO group occur.

30. (d) Deficiency of vitamin K causes haemmorrhage and increased time of blood clotting.

31. (a) Glucose is a monosaccharide having chemical composition $C_6H_{12}O_6$. Thus, statement given in option (a) is incorrect.

32. (d) Due to insolubility of protein in benzene, protein can be easily removed from benzene.

33. (d) Both Statement I and Statement II are correct.

34. (a) Isoelectric point of amino acid

$$= \frac{pK_{a_1} + pK_{a_2}}{2} = \frac{4.6 + 19.4}{2} = \frac{24}{2} = 12$$

35. (d) Statement given in D is not true regarding lactose while all other statements are correct. The molecule of (+)-lactose is composed of D-(+) glucose unit and D- (+)-galactose unit. The units are joined by the β-glycosidic linkage (at C-4 of glucose and C-1 of galactose.) The structure is shown below.

Glycosidic linkage

β-D-glucose

β-D-galactose

Due to reducing functional group present at C-1 of glucose unit, lactose is a reducing sugar. It also undergoes mutarotation.

36 (a) Among the given amino acids, methionine $[CH_3SCH_2CH_2CH(NH_2)\ COOH]$ is an essential amino acid because it cannot be synthesised by our body and hence, its presence is necessary in our diet. While all other are non-essential amino acids.

37. (d) The four bases present in DNA are adenine (A), guanine (G), cytosine (C) and thymine (T). In RNA, uracil (U) is present in place of thymine (T). Structure of all these, bases are given below :

Adenine (A)

Guanine (G)

Cytosine (C)

Thymine (T)

Uracil (U)

Hence, the given structure (d), i.e. uracil is absent in DNA and present in RNA.

38. (c)

Letter code	Amino acid
G	Glycine
V	Valine
W	Tryptophan
H	Histidine
A	Alanine

Thus, W is the letter code of tryptophan. The structure of tryptophan is as follows:

Thus, 4 amino acids are correctly represented by their one letter code.

39 (d) Amino acids which can be synthesised in the body are called non-essential amino acids, e.g. alanine, glycine, proline etc. Amino acids which cannot be synthesised in the body are called essential amino acids, e.g. lysine, valine, leucine, phenylalanine etc.

40. (d) Both Statement I and Statement II are correct.

41. (d) Maltose is composed of two α-D-glucopyranose units in which C-1 of one glucose is linked to C-4 of another glucose unit.

42. (d) Upon heating, the proteins get coagulated. This process is called denaturation of proteins. During this process, the secondary and tertiary structures get destroyed but primary structure remains intact.

43. (b) The triplet of nucleotides having a specific sequence of bases is known as codon.

Each codon (a sequence of three nucleotides in *m*-RNA) corresponds to a specific amino acid.

More than one codon can specify same amino acid. Specificity of a codon is determined by first two bases, the third base of codon is not very important as it is less specific but it still dictates the specific amino acid coded for.

Every *t*-RNA is specific for particular amino acid and has only one amino acid attachment site.

44. (c) Estrogens produce wide ranging actions such as stimulation of growth and activities of female secondary sex organs, development of growing ovarian follicles, appearance of female secondary sex characters (e.g. high pitch of voice, etc.), mammary gland development.

45. (b) The helical structure of protein is stabilised by hydrogen bonds between amide group of the same peptide chain. These bonds are formed by —NH— group of one unit and oxygen of carbonyl group of the third unit. This H-bonding is responsible for holding helix in a position.

46. (b) Hormone that causes glycogenolysis and gluconeogenesis is glucagon.

47. (a) Statements given in options I, II, III and V are correct while IV is incorrect. Its correct form is fructose is not oxidised by Br_2 water instead glucose is oxidised with bromine water and produces gluconic acid.

48. (a) Glucose gives silver mirror with ammoniacal silver nitrate due to the presence of —CHO group (aldehyde group) in the structure of glucose.

$$\underset{\text{Glucose}}{CH_2OH(CHOH)_4CHO} + Ag_2O \xrightarrow{NH_3} \underset{\text{Ammonium salt of gluconic acid}}{CH_2OH(CHOH)_4 - COO^-NH_4^+} + \underset{\text{Silver mirror}}{2Ag\downarrow}$$

49. (a) Abnormally low level of thyroxine leads to hypothyroidism which is characterised by lethargicness and obesity.

50. (d) Glucose and fructose both give positive Tollen's test, form same osazone, on reaction with phenyl hydrazine and form *n*-hexane on reaction with P/HI (reduction) but with conc. HNO_3 both give different products.

$$\text{Glucose} \xrightarrow{\text{Conc. } HNO_3} \underset{\text{Saccharic acid}}{COOH-(CHOH)_4-COOH}$$

$$\text{Fructose} \xrightarrow{\text{Conc. } HNO_3} \underset{\text{Tartaric acid}}{HOOC-(CHOH)_2-COOH} + \underset{\text{Glycolic acid}}{HOCH_2-COOH}$$

Ch-12 Principles Related to Practical Chemistry

Topical Follow Thru

Test-1

1. (c) Oxalic acid is used as a primary reagent for standardising NaOH.

2. (d) $KMnO_4$ itself works as an indicator. So, titration between oxalic acid and $KMnO_4$ does not need any indicator.

3. (a) Structure of phenolphthalein in acidic and basic medium is given below.

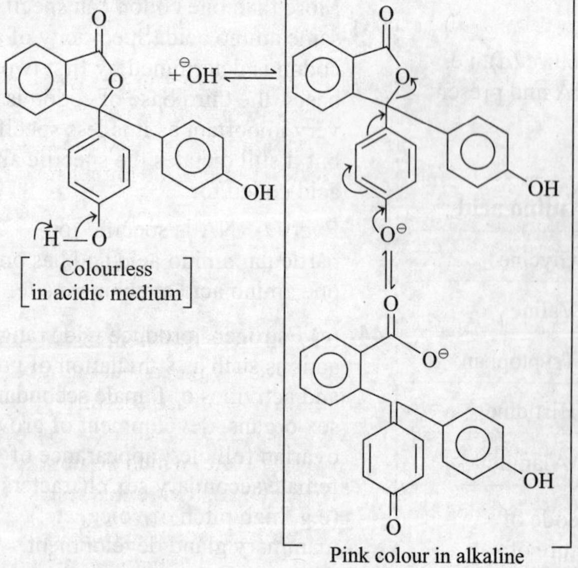

Colourless in acidic medium

Pink colour in alkaline

The negative ion in its structure is responsible for the pink colour in alkaline medium.

4. (c) Hydrophilic, i.e. lyophilic sols are reversible sols.

5. (b) $AuCl_3$ is reduced by formaldehyde to form colloidal gold sol.

6. (d) $Fe(OH)_3$ sol is prepared by shaking $FeCl_3$ with boiling water.

7. (d) In the given titration, phenolphthalein detects the end point when NaOH is completely neutralised and half of Na_2CO_3 is neutralised which occurs when pH reaches a certain threshold, indicating halfway point of the reaction.

8. (c) $AuCl_3$ is reduced by $SnCl_2$ to form colloidal sol of gold. There is no peptisation involved.

9. (a) The sol of egg albumin can be prepared by shaking white part of the egg with cold water.

10. (d) Colloidal particles do not settle down but keep on moving within the sol.

11. (d) Sulphur dissolved in CS_2 forms a true solution and hence will not scatter light.

12. (b) As $KMnO_4$ attacks rubber, therefore, burette with rubber pinch cock is not suitable in $KMnO_4$ titrations.

13. (d) Among the given indicators, potassium dichromate ($K_2Cr_2O_7$) is an oxidising agent and not an indicator.

14. (d) Change in colour of an indicator during titration does not indicate that the reaction is an exothermic reaction.

15. (c) Statement (c) is not correct because colloidal particles can pass through filter paper but not through animal membranes.

Test-2

1. (c) Co^{2+} ion is precipitated by H_2S in presence of NH_4OH which is a reagent of group IV in cationic analysis.

2. (c) The brown ring test for NO_2^- and NO_3^- is due to formation of $[Fe(H_2O)_5NO]^{+2}$. Hence, (A) is true but (R) is false.

3. (d) Nessler's reagent $K_2[HgI_4]$ is used to detect NH_4^+ in alkaline medium.

4. (a) $2NaCl + Pb(NO_3)_2 \longrightarrow \underset{\text{White ppt.}}{PbCl_2} + 2NaNO_3$

$2NaCl + Ba(NO_3)_2 \longrightarrow \underset{\text{Soluble}}{BaCl_2} + 2NaNO_3$

5. (d) In this test, a blue residue is due to formation of $Al_2O_3 \cdot CoO$, also known as thenard's blue. So, Al^{3+} is responsible for blue coloured residue.

6. (c) In chromyl chloride test, $K_2Cr_2O_7$ is used to detect chloride ions.

$$4NaCl + K_2Cr_2O_7 + 6H_2SO_4 \longrightarrow 2KHSO_4 + \underset{\text{Chromyl chloride}}{2CrO_2Cl_2} + 4NaHSO_4 + 3H_2O$$

7. (a) With F^-, no precipitate is obtained because of low lattice energy of AgF, so it remains in ionised state.

8. (a) Among the given options, $AgNO_3$ will give black ppt. when H_2S gas is passed through it.

$$2AgNO_3 + H_2S \longrightarrow \underset{\text{Black ppt.}}{Ag_2S} + 2HNO_3$$

9. (c) AgCl $\longrightarrow$ most soluble in NH_4OH due to the formation of a complex.

$$AgCl + NH_4OH \longrightarrow \underset{\text{Highly stable complex}}{[Ag(NH_3)_2]^+}$$

10. (c) The group I acidic radicals are detected by dilute H_2SO_4. Thus, sulphite on reacting with dilute H_2SO_4 gives colourless SO_2 gas.

(i) When baryta water $[Ba(OH)_2]$ is treated with this gas, it gives turbidity due to formation of barium sulphite.

$$Ba(OH)_2 + SO_2 \longrightarrow BaSO_3\downarrow + H_2O$$

(ii) $K_2Cr_2O_7 + H_2SO_4 + 3SO_2 \longrightarrow K_2SO_4 + \underset{\text{(Green)}}{Cr_2(SO_4)_3} + H_2O$

When SO_2 is treated with acidified $K_2Cr_2O_7$, the solution turns green due to formation of chromic sulphate. Hence, the reaction confirms the presence of SO_3^{2-} ions.

11. (b) $Ba(OH)_2$ is not highly basic and bond is not easily broken.

12. (a) A solution of a salt in dilute sulphuric acid impart deep blue colours with starch iodine solution, it confirms the presence of NO_2^-.

$$NO_2^- + I_2 \longrightarrow NO + I^-$$

13. (a) The sulphides of all metals (Cu, Zn and Cd will be precipitated if the solution is aqueous and neutral, i.e. it does not contain any acid.

14. (d) The following metal ions will respond to flame test

Sr^{2+}, Ba^{2+}, Ca^{2+}, Cu^{2+}, Na^+, K^+ and Bi^{3+}.

Hence, option (d) is correct.

15. (c) The reaction involved are

$$\underset{\text{(Dry)}}{KNO_3} + H_2SO_4 \xrightarrow{\Delta} KHSO_4 + HNO_3$$

$$4HNO_3 \longrightarrow 2H_2O + 4NO_2\uparrow + O_2$$

Test-3

1. (d) During the fusion of sulphanilic acid with sodium metal, NaCN, NaCNS and Na_2S all are formed.

2. (d) A mixture of phenol and benzoic acid can be separated by using $NaHCO_3$ as phenol does not react with $NaHCO_3$ while benzoic acid does.

3. (c) Benzaldehyde forms a crystalline soluble addition compound with $NaHSO_3$ but acetophenone does not because of steric hindrance.

4. (d) Statement given in option (d) is not correct. Its correct form is *o*-nitroacetanilide is yellow coloured while *p*-nitroacetanilide is colourless.

5. (c) Primary aromatic amino ($—NH_2$) group can be test by azo dye test while $—NO_2$ group by Mulliken's test.

6. (c) Brady's reagent, i.e. 2, 4-dinitrophenyl hydrazine is used for detection of aldehydes or ketones.

7. (c) Benzoic acid is, soluble in hot water but not naphthalene and hence can be separated by crystallisation.

8. (b) The Lassaigne's extract for the presence of halogens, it first boiled with dil. HNO_3. This is done to decompose NaCN and Na_2S to HCN and H_2S respectively.

9. (d) Aniline ($C_6H_5NH_2$) is a colourless oily liquid which is insoluble in water and steam, volatile and is, thus, purified by steam distillation.

10. (d) (A) is false but (R) is true. The correct form of (A) is : Potassium is not used in Lassaigne's test because of its higher reactivity.

11. (c) $Fe^{+3} + 3NaSCN \longrightarrow \underset{\text{(Blood red colouration)}}{Fe(SCN)_3} + 3Na^+$

12. (c) Positive Beilstein test does not necessarily mean that halogen is definitely present because certain compound such as urea, thiourea, pyridine etc. which do not contain halogen, also give this test.

Therefore, positive Beilstein test shows that halogen may be present.

13. (d) Among the given compounds, 4-methyl-1-pentanol does not react with Lucas reagent at room temperature because it is the primary alcohol and 1°—OH do not react with Lucas reagent at room temperature, it requires high temperature.

14. (a) Both (A) and (R) are true and (R) is the correct explanation of (A).

Due to presence of sulphur, sodium thiocyanate is produced which produced blood red coloured precipitate with Fe^{3+} ion.

$$Na + C + S + N \xrightarrow{\Delta} NaSCN$$

$$Fe^{3+} + 3NaSCN \longrightarrow Fe(SCN)_3 + 3Na^+$$

15. (c) The boiling point of benzene (353 K) and aniline (453 K) differ by about 100 K and hence can be separated by simple distillation.

Chapter Break Thru

1. (c) The presence of P in organic compound can be identified by using oxidising agent sodium peroxide. In this test, a yellow ppt. is formed indicating the presence of P.

2. (c) Methyl orange shows yellow colour in basic medium and red colour in acidic medium. Since, the original solution is basic, so the initial colour is yellow and after titrated with acid, the final colour is pinkish red.

3. (b) Naphthylamine and sulphanilic acid in acetic acid is used for the detection of NO_2^-.

4. (b) Reagent for group II is an acidic solution of H_2S.

Group II cations are Cu^{2+}, Bi^{3+}, Cd^{2+}, Hg^{2+}, As^{3+}, Sb^{3+} and Sn^{4+}. Hence, only Cu^{2+} will be precipitated.

5. (c) AgCl and Cu_2Cl_2 are not dissolved in water while $ZnCl_2$ and $CuCl_2$ are dissolved but $ZnCl_2$ is colourless and $CuCl_2$ is coloured.

6. (c) Absolute alcohol is prepared from rectified spirit by azeotropic distillation because alcohol and water form a constant boiling mixture (azeotrope).

7. (a) Since, given compound '*X*' burns with sooty flame therefore, it must be aromatic compound. Again when it reacts with Brady's reagent (acidic 2,4-dinitrophenyl hydrazine solution), it yields orange precipitate.

Therefore, it must be aldehyde or ketone. But ketone does not perform Tollen's reagent test therefore, it must be a ketone. Hence '*X*' is acetophenone.

8. (d) The correct match is A-IV, B-I, C-II, D-III.

9. (d) $Na_4[Fe(CN)_5NO] + S^{2-} \longrightarrow Na_4[Fe(CN)_5NOS]$
Sodium thionitroprusside (violet)

10. (c) Small amount of zinc dust is added to reaction mixture during preparation of acetanilide because zinc in reaction mixture prevents oxidation of aniline.

11. (b)

COOH, OH, NH_2 (each with Cl at meta position)
(*A*) (*B*) (*C*)

$NaHCO_3$

Soluble: COO^-Na^+ (Cl) | Insoluble: OH (Cl), NH_2 (Cl)

Dil. NaOH

Soluble: NH_2 (Cl) | Insoluble: O^-Na^+ (Cl)

12. (b) Statement I is correct but Statement II is incorrect because essential oil are insoluble in water but are volatile in steam.

13. (c) $PbSO_4$ and $PbCl_2$ are insoluble in cold water. Hence, the reagent $Pb(NO_3)_2$ is used to remove SO_4^{2-} and Cl^-.

14. (a) In steam distillation, the mixture begins to boil when the sum of the vapour pressure of the organic liquid and that of water become equal to that of the atmosphere.

15. (b) Sr^{2+} gives bright red colour to the flame.

The colour is due to the excitation of electrons by the thermal energy, which is then followed by de-excitation of electron to ground state along with liberation of light in the visible range.

16. (b) $Cu(NH_3)_4(NO_3)_2 + 4CH_3COOH \longrightarrow Cu(NO_3)_2 + 4CH_3COONH_4$

$$2Cu(NO_3)_2 + K_4[Fe(CN)_6] \longrightarrow Cu_2Fe(CN)_6 + 4KNO_3$$
Chocolate ppt.

17. (a) Ethyl bromide does not provide free Br^- ions to react with $AgNO_3$ due to its covalent nature.

18. (d) Both Statement I and Statement II are correct.

19. (a)

Ion	Colour in Flame
Cu^{2+}	Blue-green
Sr^{2+}	Red
Ba^{2+}	Apple-green
Ca^{2+}	Orange-red

20. (a) SO_3^{2-}, S^{2-} and SO_4^{2-} salts from comparatively stronger acids (than H_2CO_3) in solution, hence, evolve CO_2 with Na_2CO_3 solution and give effervescence.

While CO_3^{-2} does not react with Na_2CO_3 solution.

21. (c) Calcium oxalate will not dissolve in acetic acid (weak acid) but only in strong acid.

22. (b) In presence of NH_4OH, dissociation of H_2S is remarkably high to increase the solubility product of IV group sulphides.

$$H_2S \longrightarrow 2H^+ + S^{2-}$$
$$NH_4OH \longrightarrow \overset{+}{NH_4} + \overset{-}{OH}$$
$$OH + H^+ \longrightarrow H_2O$$

23. (c) When ammonium hydroxide is added to the solution of copper sulphate dropwise then a pale blue precipitate of copper hydroxide is obtained. But when ammonium hydroxide is added in excess the precipitate dissolve and gives a deep blue solution of tetraammine copper sulphate.

$$\underset{\text{(Dropwise)}}{2NH_4OH + CuSO_4} \longrightarrow (NH_4)_2SO_4 + \underset{\text{(Pale blue)}}{Cu(OH)_2 \text{ (ppt.)}}$$

$$\underset{\text{(Excess)}}{4NH_4OH + CuSO_4} \longrightarrow \underset{\text{(Deep blue)}}{[Cu(NH_3)_4]SO_4} + 4H_2O$$

24. (d) CuS, PbS, CdS substance are soluble in concentrated HNO_3.

While $BaSO_4$ is insoluble because H^+ ions of the acid cannot remove SO_4^{2-} ions from $BaSO_4$.

25. (c) Element in highest oxidation state can oxidise iodide to liberate I_2 which is volumetrically measured by iodometric titration using hypo solution ($Na_2S_2O_3$)

$$2I^- \longrightarrow I_2$$

$Pb^{+2} \longrightarrow$ Lowest oxidation state cannot oxidise iodide to I_2.

However, Ag^+ can also be reduced to Ag by iodine in the presence of a reducing agent.

26. (d) Cobalt sulphide does not ppt. in second group.

27. (d) $Ni^{2+} + 2dmg^- \longrightarrow [Ni(dmg)_2]$

Rose red/Bright red precipitate

28. (b) The brown ring complex formed is $[Fe(H_2O)_5NO]^{2+}$.

In this complex, H_2O is a neutral ligand and NO is +1 charged ligand.

$$[Fe(H_2O)_5(NO)]^{2+}$$
$$x + (0 \times 5) + (+1 \times 1) = +2$$
$$x = +1$$

29. (d) Zinc salt solution on passing H_2S in the presence of NH_4OH gives a white ppt. of ZnS.

30. (a) **Carbylamine Test** Identification of primary amines.

Lucas Test Differentiation between 1°, 2° and 3° alcohols.

Tollen's Test Identification of aldehydes.

Phthalein Dye Test Identification of phenols.

SPT1 Syllabus Part Thru

1. (d) Osmotic pressure of cane sugar $= 4.32$ atm

$T = 37°C = 310 K$

$R = 0.0821$ L atm mol^{-1} K^{-1}

According to van't Hoff equation for osmotic pressure

$\pi = iCRT$

$C = \frac{4.32}{0.0821 \times 310}$ $(\because i = 1)$

$= 0.170$

2. (a) The correct match is A-IV, B-III, C-II, D-I.

3. (a) Paramagnetic character is based upon the presence of unpaired electrons in *d*-subshell.

- In $[Zn(H_2O)_6]^{2+}$, Zn is present as $Zn^{2+} = 1s^2 2s^2 2p^6 3s^2 3p^6 3d^{10}$

  3d: ⥮ ⥮ ⥮ ⥮ ⥮ No unpaired electron

- In $[Cr(H_2O)_6]^{3+}$, Cr is present as Cr^{3+} (Oxidation number $= +3$) $Cr^{3+} = 1s^2 2s^2 2p^6 3s^2 3p^6 3d^3$

  3d: 1 1 1 _ _ 3 unpaired electrons

- In $[Fe(H_2O)_6]^{2+}$, Fe is present as $Fe^{2+} = 1s^2 2s^2 2p^6 3s^2 3p^6 3d^6$

  3d: ⥮ 1 1 1 1 4 unpaired electrons

- In $[Cu(H_2O)_6]^{2+}$, Cu is present as $Cu^{2+} = 1s^2 2s^2 2p^6 3s^2 3p^6 3d^9$

  3d: ⥮ ⥮ ⥮ ⥮ 1 1 unpaired electron

  So, paramagnetic character is negligible in $[Zn(H_2O)_6]^{2+}$

4. (b) Statement I is correct but Statement II is incorrect. The correct form of Statement II is $[Ni(CO)_4]$ with sp^3 hybridisation has tetrahedral geometry while $[Ni(CN)_4]^{2-}$ with dsp^2 hybridisation will have square planar geometry.

5. (c) $3MnO_4^{2-} + 2H_2O \longrightarrow 2MnO_4^- + MnO_2 + 4OH^-$

The reaction can go to completion by removing OH^- ions by adding CO_2 as it reacts with OH^- ions to form CO_3^{2-} ions.

$4OH^- + 2CO_2 \longrightarrow 2CO_3^{2-} + 2H_2O$

6. (c) Rate of reaction is given by

$r_1 = k[P]^2[Q]$

When the volume is reduced to half, concentration becomes double.

$\therefore r_2 = k[2P]^2[2Q] = 8k[P]^2[Q] = 8r_1$

So, the rate of reaction increases by eight times.

7. (b) Statement I is correct but Statement II is incorrect. The correct form of Statement II is activation energy for both forward and backward reaction is lowered to same extent.

8. (a) The statements given in I, II, III and IV are correct while statement V is incorrect. Its correct form is: The dissociation constant of hydrides of group 16 elements increases down the group.

9. (c) (A) is true but (R) is false. The correct form of (R) is:

Fe has atomic number 26. So, its electronic configuration is [Ar] $3d^6 4s^2$. Fe^{2+} has electronic configuration.

[Ar]$3d^6$ 3d: ⥮ 1 1 1 1 4s: _

So, it has four unpaired electrons, that's why it is paramagnetic.

10. (c) Given, $\Delta T_b = 0.208$ K

$K_b = 0.52$ K kg mol^{-1}

$K_f = 1.86$ K kg mol^{-1}, $\Delta T_f = ?$

Using formula,

$\Delta T_b = K_b m$ (where, m = molality)

$\Rightarrow m = \frac{0.208}{0.52} = 0.4$ m

Substitute this value of molality in equation

$\Delta T_f = K_f m$

$= 1.86 \times 0.4$ K

$= 0.744$ K

11. (c) When the central atom of an oxide of *p*-block element has its highest group oxidation state $[(ON)_{max}]$, it cannot be oxidised further, i.e., it will not act as a reducing agent.

$\overset{+4}{SO_2}$	$\overset{+4}{NO_2}$	$\overset{+4}{CO_2}$	$\overset{+4}{ClO_2}$
Group 16 $[(ON)_{max} = +6]$	Group 15 $[(ON)_{max} = +5]$	Group 14 $[(ON)_{max} = +4]$	Group 17 $[(ON)_{max} = +7]$
		↓ Cannot act as a reducing agent	

12. (c) Given, $I = 2$ A

The reaction involved in reduction of Fe^{3+} is

$3Fe^{3+} + 3e^- \longrightarrow 3Fe^{2+}$

Charge required $= 3 \times 96500$

$= 289500$ C

Also, we know that

charge = current × time

So, time $= \frac{289500}{6}$

$= 48250$ s or 13.40 hrs

13. (a)

	Ion/ Complex	Central metal ion	Configuration of metal ion	Hybridisation of metal ion involved	No. of unpaired electrons	Magnetic behaviour
1.	$[Mn(CN)_6]^{3-}$	Mn^{3+}	d^4	d^2sp^3 (Inner orbital complex)	2	Paramagnetic
2.	$[Fe(CN)_6]^{3-}$	Fe^{3+}	d^5	d^2sp^3 (Inner orbital complex)	1	Paramagnetic
3.	$[Co(C_2O_4)_3]^{3-}$	Co^{3+}	d^6	d^2sp^3 (Inner orbital complex)	0	Diamagnetic
4.	$[MnCl_6]^{3-}$	Mn^{3+}	d^4	sp^3d^2 (Outer orbital complex)	4	Paramagnetic
5.	$[Fe(CN)_6]^{4-}$	Fe^{2+}	d^6	d^2sp^3 (Inner orbital complex)	0	Diamagnetic

Thus, the number of diamagnetic compounds are two i.e. $[Co(C_2O_4)_3]^{3-}$ and $[Fe(CN)_6]^{4-}$.

14. (b)

I. $[\mathbf{Fe(CN)_6}]^{4-}$

Atomic number of Fe = 26

Ground state configuration of $Fe = [Ar]\,3d^6\,4s^2$

$Fe^{2+} = [Ar]\,3d^6$

Since, cyanide is a strong field ligand, therefore, all the electrons will be paired.

Number of unpaired electrons in $[Fe(CN)_6]^{4-} = 0$

II. $[\mathbf{Fe(H_2O)_6}]^{2+}$

Atomic number of Fe = 26

Ground state configuration of $Fe = [Ar]\,3d^6\,4s^2$

$Fe^{2+} = [Ar]\,3d^6$

As H_2O is a weak field ligand, it will not cause pairing.

Number of unpaired electrons in $[Fe(H_2O)_6]^{2+} = 4$

III. $[\mathbf{Co(H_2O)_6}]^{2+}$

Atomic number of Co = 27

Ground state configuration of $Co = [Ar]\,3d^7\,4s^2$

$Co^{2+} = [Ar]\,3d^7$

H_2O will not cause pairing as it is a weak ligand.

Number of unpaired electrons in $[Co(H_2O)_6]^{2+} = 3$

So, the number of unpaired electrons are 0, 4 and 3 respectively.

15. (d) Given, (concentration) $a = 1.0$ M, $a - x = 0.25$ M, $t = 40$ min

For a first order reaction,

$$k = \frac{2.303}{t}\log\frac{a}{a-x}$$

$$= \frac{2.303}{40}\log\frac{1}{0.25}$$

$$= \frac{2.303}{40}\log 4$$

$$= \frac{2.303 \times 2 \times 0.3010}{40}$$

$$= 0.03466\ \text{min}^{-1}$$

Now, Initial rate $= k[A]$

$= 0.03466\,(0.4)$

$= 0.013864\ \text{mol L}^{-1}\ \text{min}^{-1}$

$= 1.386 \times 10^{-2}\ \text{mol L}^{-1}\ \text{min}^{-1}$.

16. (b) When a minimum boiling azeotrope is formed, the resulting solution will have greater vapour pressure than that corresponding to an ideal solution. So, it has minimum boiling point.

Interactions between $A - A$ or $B - B$ are stronger than $A - B$ interactions.

$\therefore \Delta V > 0, \Delta H_{mix} > 0$

$\therefore$Only statement (b) is correct.

17. (b) For the first order reaction,

$C_2H_5I(g) \longrightarrow C_2H_4(g) + HI(g)$

Using formula,

$$\log\frac{k_2}{k_1} = \frac{E_a}{2.303R}\left[\frac{T_2 - T_1}{T_1T_2}\right]$$

$$\log\frac{4x}{x} = \frac{E_a}{2.303 \times 8.3}\left[\frac{900 - 800}{900 \times 800}\right]$$

$$\log 4 = \frac{E_a \times 100}{2.303 \times 8.3 \times 900 \times 800}$$

$\Rightarrow E_a = 82576.36\ \text{J mol}^{-1}$

or $E_a \approx 82.57\ \text{kJ mol}^{-1}$

18. (b) Partial pressure of dichloromethane $(p_A) = 571$ mm Hg

Partial pressure of chloroform $(p_B) = 124.8$ mm Hg

According to Dalton's law of partial pressure

$p_{total} = p_A + p_B$

$= (571 + 124.8)$ mm Hg

$= 695.8$ mm Hg

19. (a) Both Statement I and Statement II are incorrect.

- Hydrides of group 16 elements shows volatility in the order $H_2S > H_2Se > H_2Te > H_2O$
- Electronegativity of group 16 element decreases down the group O > S > Se > Te > Po.

20. (c) Given, $k = 0.001 \text{ Ms}^{-1}$

$$t = 10 \text{ min}$$
$$[A] = 1 \text{ M}$$
$$[A]_t = [A]_o - kt$$
$$= 1 - 0.001 \times 10 \times 60$$
$$= 0.4 \text{ M}$$
$$[B]_t = 0.001 \times 10 \times 60$$
$$= 0.6 \text{ M}$$

21. (a) Both (A) and (R) are true and (R) is the correct explanation of (A).

22. (d) We know that, $\Delta T_b = K_b m$

$$m = \frac{\Delta T_b}{K_b}$$
$$= \frac{0.128}{0.512} = 0.25 \text{ mol/kg}$$

Now, $K_f = 1.86 \text{ °C kg mol}^{-1}$

$$m = 0.25 \text{ mol kg}^{-1}$$
$$\therefore \quad \Delta T_f = K_f \times m$$
$$\Delta T_f = 1.86 \times 0.25 = 0.465 \text{° C}$$

$\therefore$ Freezing point of solution

$$\Rightarrow \quad T_f = T° - \Delta T_f$$
$$= 0 - 0.465 = -0.465 \text{° C}$$

23. (b) First order rate constant is given as $k = \frac{2.303}{t} \log \frac{[A_0]}{[A_t]}$

40% completed, then

$$[A_0] = 100$$
$$[A_t] = 100 - 40 = 60$$
$$k = \frac{2.303}{t} \log \frac{100}{60}$$
$$k = \frac{2.303}{t} (\log 10 - \log 6)$$
$$k = \frac{2.303}{t} (1 - 0.8)$$
$$k = \frac{2.303 \times 0.2}{t}$$
$$t = \frac{0.46}{k}$$

24. (d) Incorrect order is given in option (d). The correct order of negative $\text{p}K_a$ value is

$$\underset{(-10.0)}{\text{HI}} > \underset{(-9.5)}{\text{HBr}} > \underset{(-7.0)}{\text{HCl}} > \underset{(3.2)}{\text{HF}}$$

25. (b) Down the group the electronegativity decreases and the size increases. Thus, it becomes easy to lose H^+ ion. This causes the increase in acidic strength down the group.

Thus, the correct order is

$$\text{HF} < \text{HCl} < \text{HBr} < \text{HI}.$$

26. (a)

$$6XeF_4 + 12H_2O \longrightarrow 4Xe + 2XeO_3 + 24HF + 3O_2$$

27. (a) Statement given in option (a) is incorrect.

For zero order reaction, $t_{1/2} \propto A_0$

28. (b) Among the given species, Cr^{2+} and Fe^{2+} show 4.90 BM as it contains four unpaired electrons.

$$\mu = \sqrt{n(n+2)} = \sqrt{4(4+2)}$$
$$= \sqrt{24} = 4.90 \text{ BM}$$

29. (b) $\Delta T_f = K_f \times \frac{w_1 \times 1000}{w_2 \times m_1}$

w_1 = weight of solute = 2 g

w_2 = weight of solvent = 20.4 g

m_1 = molar mass of solute = 500 g/mol

$K_f = 8.1 \text{ K kg mol}^{-1}$

Now, $\Delta T_f = 8.1 \times \frac{2 \times 1000}{20.4 \times 500}$

$$\Delta T_f = 1.59 \text{ K}$$

30. (a) Statement given in option (a) is incorrect. Its correct form is if an external opposite potential is applied in galvanic cell, and increased slowly then the reaction continues to take place till the opposing voltage reaches the value of 1.1 V.

31. (a) Both (A) and (R) are true and (R) is the correct explanation of (A).

32. (a) Among the given options, $KMnO_4$ is not oxidised by O_3, because $KMnO_4$ produces MnO_4^- ion in which Mn exhibits +7 oxidation state which is maximum for Mn.

So, it cannot be further oxidised. Hence, the correct option is (a).

33. (d) The correct match is A-III, B-IV, C-I, D-II.

34. (a) Pressure, $p = 4$ bar

Mole fraction, $\chi = 0.04$

$$p = K_H \times \chi \quad \text{(Henry law)}$$
$$4 = K_H \times 0.04 \quad \text{...(i)}$$

Pressure tripled

$$p = K_H \times \chi$$
$$12 = K_H \times \chi \quad \text{...(ii)}$$

From Eqs. (i) and (ii)

$$\frac{1}{3} = \frac{0.04}{\chi}$$
$$\chi = 0.12$$

35. (a) Given current, $i = 20$ A

Time, $t = 3.216$ min or 193 seconds (app.)

Weight of aluminium $W_{Al} = ?$

Atomic weight of aluminium $= 27$ g/mol (M)

We know that,

$$AlCl_3 \longrightarrow Al^{3+} + 3Cl^-, n = 3$$

At cathode, reduction

$$Al^{3+} + 3e^- \longrightarrow Al$$

Formula, $W_{Al} = \frac{\varepsilon \times i \times t}{96500}$

where, $\varepsilon = \frac{\text{Mol. wt.}}{n\text{-factor}}$

$$W_{Al} = \frac{27}{3} \times \frac{20 \times 193}{96500} \Rightarrow W_{Al} = 0.36 \text{ g}$$

Mass of Al deposited will be 0.36 g.

36. (b) Two solutions are isotonic when they have the same osmotic pressure. It is only possible when they have same molar concentration at the same temperature.

A 50% solution of cane-sugar means 100 g of solution contains 50 g of cane-sugar.

For dilute solution 100 g is approximately equal to 100 mL.

Molarity of cane-sugar (M_1)

$$= \frac{\text{Number of mole of cane-sugar}}{\text{Volume (in L)}}$$

$$= \frac{50}{342\,\text{g/mol} \times 100\,\text{mL}} \times 1000\,\text{mL}$$

$$= 1.462\,\text{M} \quad \ldots\text{(i)}$$

Now, 10% solution of substance A means 100 g of the solution contains 10 g of substance A.

Molarity of $A(M_2)$

$$= \frac{10}{M'\,\text{g/mol} \times 100\,\text{mL}} \times 1000$$

$$= \frac{100}{M'}\,\text{M} \quad \ldots\text{(ii)}$$

We get,

$$1.462 = \frac{100}{M'}$$

$$M' = \frac{100}{1.462} = 68.399\,\text{g/mol}$$

Hence, molecular weight of A is 68.399 g/mol ≈ 68.4

37. (a) Both (A) and (R) are true and (R) is the correct explanation of (A).

38. (b) 10 g Cd should with 90 g Hg.

Wt. of Cd required with 4.5 g of Hg at cathode

$$= \frac{10}{90} \times 4.5 = 0.5$$

$$\Rightarrow Cd^{2+} + 2e^- \longrightarrow Cd$$

Using $W_{Cd} = \frac{\varepsilon \times i \times t}{96500}$

where, $\varepsilon = \frac{112}{2}$

$$\therefore\ 0.5 = \frac{56 \times 8 \times t}{96500}$$

$$t = 107.7\,\text{sec}$$

39. (b) The correct match is

A-IV, B-III, C-II, D-I.

40. (a) Given, resistance of 0.2 M solution of NaCl = 200 ohm.

Resistance of 0.04 mol/L NaCl = 516 ohm

Conductivity of 0.04 mol/L NaCl = ?

Conductivity of 0.2 mol/L NaCl = $2.58\ \text{Sm}^{-1}$

Cell constant = Conductivity × Resistance

$$\Rightarrow \kappa \times R = 2.58 \times 200 = 516\ \text{m}^{-1}$$

Conductivity of 0.4 M KCl solution

$$= \frac{\text{Cell constant}}{\text{Resistance}} = \frac{516}{516} = 1\ \text{Sm}^{-1}$$

41. (d) Cuprous ion (Cu^+) is colourless while cupric ion (Cu^{2+}) is coloured because cuprous ion has a completely filled d-orbital i.e. $3d^{10}4s^0$ configuration and cuprous ion has an incompletely filled d-orbitals due to $3d^9 4s^0$ configuration. So, this one unpaired electron makes d-d transition possible and impart colour.

42. (d) Among the given orders w.r.t property, only (d) is incorrect.

(a) Basic character of metal oxides decreases with increase in oxidation number.

$$\overset{+2}{M}O, \overset{+3}{M_2}O_3, \overset{+4}{M}O_2, \overset{+5}{M_2}O_5$$

(Decreasing basic character)

(b) Manganese (Mn) has maximum number of oxidation state.

Sc have only single oxidate state, i.e. +3.

V has 4 oxidation states (*viz*, +2 to +5).

Cr has 5 oxidation states (*viz*, +2 to +6).

Mn has 6 oxidation states (+2 to +7).

Sc, V, Cr, Mn (Increasing number of oxidation states)

(c) Magnetic moment = $\sqrt{n(n+2)}$

(n = number of unpaired electron)

Magnetic moment ∝ unpaired electron

Configuration	Unpaired electron	Magnetic moment
d^5	5	5.92
d^3	3	3.87
d^1	1	1.73
d^4	4	4.90

So, the correct order of magnetic moment is

$$d^5 > d^4 > d^3 > d^1$$

(d) $Mn^{2+} \rightarrow 3d^5$

$Fe^{2+} \rightarrow 3d^6$

$Cr^{2+} \rightarrow 3d^4$

$Co^{2+} \rightarrow 3d^7$

Mn^{2+} is most stable as d-subshell is half-filled.

Cr^{2+} has higher tendency on losing electron as compared to Fe^{2+}. So, Fe^{2+} is more stable than Cr^{2+}. Co^{2+} is least stable as it contains 3 unpaired electrons and has least exchange energy.

So, the correct order of decreasing stability is

$$Mn^{2+} > Fe^{2+} > Cr^{2+} > Co^{2+}$$

43. (b) Being hygroscopic or deliquescent sodium dichromate, ($Na_2Cr_2O_7$) cannot be used in volumetric analysis. The rest of the statements are true.

44. (b) Among the given options, Eu and Yb will show highest third ionisation enthalpy. It is because Eu^{2+} and Yb^{2+} has half filled and completely filled f-orbital which is stable.

Thus, to break stability high energy is required. Eu and Yb has highest third ionisation energy.

45. (d) Both Statement I and Statement II are correct.

SPT2 Syllabus Part Thru

1. (d) The complete reaction is as follows

$$H_2N-C(CH_3)_2-CH_2CH_2-C(=O)OCH_3 \xrightarrow[\Delta]{H_2/Ni} \ldots \xrightarrow{-H^+} (X)$$

(X)

2. (b) The complete reaction is as follows

$$CH_3CH_2-CH=O + CH_3CH_2-\underset{H}{CH}-CHO$$

Propanal (electrophile)

(Active hydrogen)

Butanal (Nucleophile)

$$\overset{5}{C}H_3-\overset{4}{C}H_2-\overset{3}{C}H(OH)-\overset{2}{C}H(CH_2CH_3)-\overset{1}{C}HO$$

2-ethyl-3-hydroxypentanal

3. (c) (A) is true but (R) is false. Correct form of (R) is : The amino acid which are not synthesized in body are called essential amino acids.

4. (c) The complete reaction is as follows

$$m\text{-cresol} \xrightarrow[-3HBr]{3Br_2/H_2O} \text{2,4,6-tribromo-3-methylphenol}$$

m-cresol

m-cresol has two *o*- and one *p*-position free w.r.t OH group and hence gives tribromo derivative on treatment with Br_2/H_2O.

5. (d) The reaction occurs as shown below :

Step I : $CH_3-CH_2-\ddot{O}-H + H^+ \rightarrow CH_3-CH_2-\overset{+}{O}(H)-H$

Step II : $CH_3CH_2-\ddot{O}(H): + CH_3-CH_2-\overset{+}{O}H_2 \rightarrow CH_3CH_2-\overset{+}{O}(H)-CH_2CH_3$

Step III : $CH_3CH_2-\overset{+}{O}(H)-CH_2CH_3 \rightarrow CH_3CH_2-O-CH_2CH_3 + H^+$

The above mentioned reaction mechanism follows S_N2 mechanism.

This S_N2 mechanism works best for making symmetrical ethers from primary alcohols.

6. (a) Vitamin B complex is water soluble while other (D, E, A) are fat soluble.

7. (b) The complete reaction is as follows :

$$\underset{\text{Ethanol}}{CH_3CH_2OH} \xrightarrow{\text{Alk. }KMnO_4} \underset{\text{Acetic acid }(X)}{CH_3-\overset{O}{\overset{\|}{C}}-OH} \xrightarrow[H^+]{CH_3OH} \underset{\substack{\text{Methyl acetate }(Y)\\ \text{(Sweet smell)}}}{CH_3-\overset{O}{\overset{\|}{C}}-OCH_3}$$

8. (b) The complete reaction which involves the preparation of 3-ethyl-3-pentanol is,

$$\underset{\text{3 – pentanone}}{(CH_3CH_2)_2C=O} + CH_3CH_2MgBr \xrightarrow{\text{Dry ether}} (CH_3CH_2)_3C-OMgBr \xrightarrow{H_3O^+} \underset{\text{3-ethyl-3-pentanol}}{(CH_3CH_2)_3C-OH}$$

9. (b) The correct sequence is I < II < III.

Solubility in H_2O decreases as the extent of H-bonding decreases, i.e. solubility in water decreases as the size of the hydrocarbon part increases.

Thus, the solubility increases in the order I < II < III.

10. (a) As the size of hydrocarbon part (R) of the alcohol increases, the tetrahedral intermediate (I) formed during esterification becomes more and more crowded and hence, the rate of esterification decreases accordingly. Thus, the smallest alcohol, i.e. CH_3OH reacts at the fastest rate.

11. (b) The complete reaction is

$$\text{3-methylphenol} \xrightarrow[\text{(ii) } H_3O^+]{\text{(i) } CHCl_3/NaOH/\Delta} \underset{(X)}{\text{Me, OH, CHO substituted benzene}}$$

Reimer-Tiemann Reaction

$$\xrightarrow{Br_2/Fe} \underset{(Y)}{\text{Me, OH, Br, CHO substituted benzene}}$$

12. (c) Statement I is correct but Statement II is incorrect. The correct form of statement II is :

Carbocation of $C_6H_5CH(C_6H_5)Br$ is more stable than $C_6H_5CH(CH_3)Br$ because its carbocation is stabilised by two phenyl groups.

13. (a) Both (A) and (R) are true and (R) is the correct explanation of (A).

Picric acid (OH with O_2N, NO_2, NO_2)

The presence of 3 electron withdrawing $—NO_2$ groups in picric acid activate the phenolate ion and thus, H^+ can be easily removed.

Hence, picric acid is a stronger acid than phenol.

14. (a) $LiAlH_4$ reduces both ketones and esters (or lactones) to alcohols but $NaBH_4$ reduces only ketones to alcohols.

Lactone (keto) $\xrightarrow[CH_3OH]{NaBH_4}$ (X) (lactone with OH)

Lactone (keto) $\xrightarrow{LiAlH_4}$ (Y) (triol: OH, OH, OH)

15. (a) Aldehydes other than formaldehyde react with Grignard reagent followed by acid hydrolysis to give 2° alcohols, i.e. C_2H_5CHO.

The complete reaction is given by

$$C_2H_5CHO \xrightarrow{RMgX} \left[C_2H_5—\underset{}{\overset{OMgX}{CH}}—R \right] \xrightarrow{H_3O^+} \underset{2° \text{ Alcohol}}{C_2H_5—\overset{OH}{CH}—R}$$

16. (c)

(a) $C_6H_5COCH_3$ ← Acetophenone

2,4-DNP reacts with both aldehydes and ketones.

Here, acetophenone containing ketone group, gives 2, 4-DNP test and forms its derivative 2, 4-dinitrophenyl-hydrazone.

$$\underset{\text{Acetophenone}}{C_6H_5COCH_3} + H_2N—NH—C_6H_3(NO_2)_2 \xrightarrow{-H_2O} \underset{\text{2, 4-DNP derivative}}{C_6H_5C(CH_3)=N—NH—C_6H_3(NO_2)_2}$$

So, the statement (a) is correct.

(b) Acetophenone does not give Tollen's test as there is no H-atom which is attached to the carbonyl carbon.

So, this statement (b) is correct.

(c) Acetophenone react with aqueous sodium hydroxide (NaOH) and iodine (I_2), a yellow precipitate of iodoform is form. So, the statement (c) is not correct.

(d)

$$C_6H_5COCH_3 \xrightarrow[H^+]{KMnO_4} \underset{(C_7H_6O_2)}{C_6H_5COOH}$$

So, this statement (d) is correct.

Hence, among the given statements, (c) statement is not correct about acetophenone.

17. (b) H_3PO_2 serves both as an acid as well as reducing agent. In other words, the diazonium salt initially formed is reduced to give benzene.

$$C_6H_5NH_2 \xrightarrow{H_3PO_2/NaNO_2} C_6H_5N_2^+HPO_2^- \xrightarrow{+H_2O} C_6H_6 + N_2 + H_3PO_3$$

Aniline, Benzenediazonium hypophosphite, Benzene

18. (b) In lactose, C_1 of β-galactose is connected to C_4 of β-glucose.

Hence, option (b) is correct.

19. (a) The complete reaction is as follows

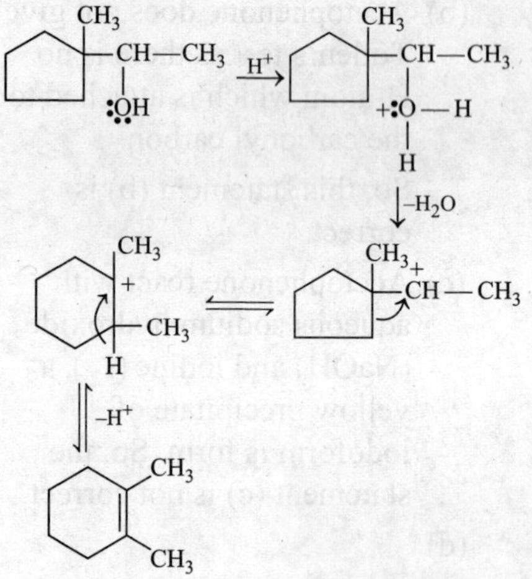

Hence, option (a) is correct.

20. (c) (A) is true but (R) is false.

The correct form of (R) is :

COOH is the principal functional group while CN is the substituent group.

21. (a) During osazone formation, the reaction occurs at C_1 and C_2 of a simple monosaccharide while rest of the molecule remains intact. Since, glucose and fructose differ from each other only in the arrangement of atom at C_1 and C_2, therefore they give the same osazone.

22. (d) Acute chloroform intoxication can cause depression of the central nervous system and may lead to death from respiratory arrest.

23. (c) Iodoform test is carried out in hot alkaline medium. Under these conditions, esters get hydrolysed to give the corresponding alcohol.

Now, ethyl acetate gives ethyl alcohol which respond to iodoform test to give yellow ppt of CHI_3, while methyl acetate will give methanol which does not give iodoform test.

$$CH_3COOC_2H_5 \xrightarrow[\Delta]{I_2/NaOH} CH_3COONa + C_2H_5OH \xrightarrow{I_2 \; NaOH} CHI_3 \text{ (Yellow ppt.)}$$

$$CH_3COOCH_3 \xrightarrow[\Delta]{I_2/NaOH} CH_3COONa + CH_3OH \xrightarrow{I_2/NaOH} \text{(No reaction)}$$

24. (b) The phosphorus present in the organic compound is oxidised to phosphate by the oxidising agent sodium peroxide.

25. (a) The intermediate product (*L*) is

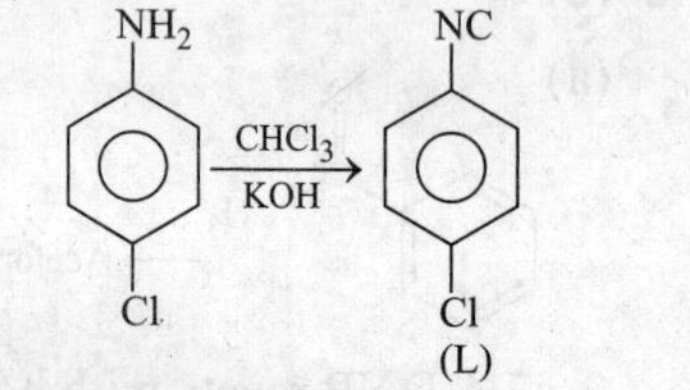

$$\text{4-chloroaniline} \xrightarrow[KOH]{CHCl_3} \text{(L)}$$

Now, at 300 K (*L*) is heated in presence of HCl.

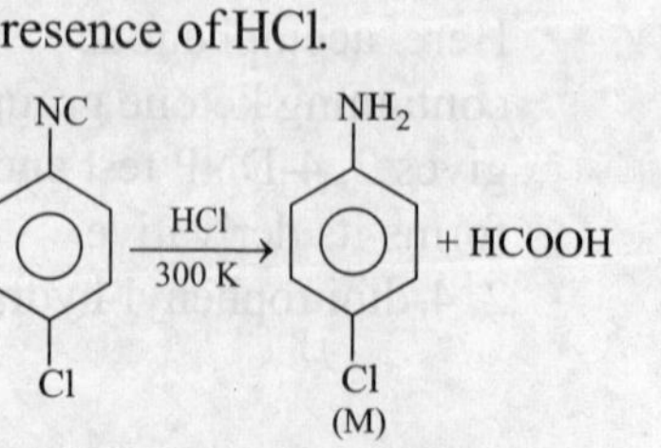

$$\text{(L)} \xrightarrow[300\,K]{HCl} \text{(M)} + HCOOH$$

26. (c) The complete reaction sequence is as follows

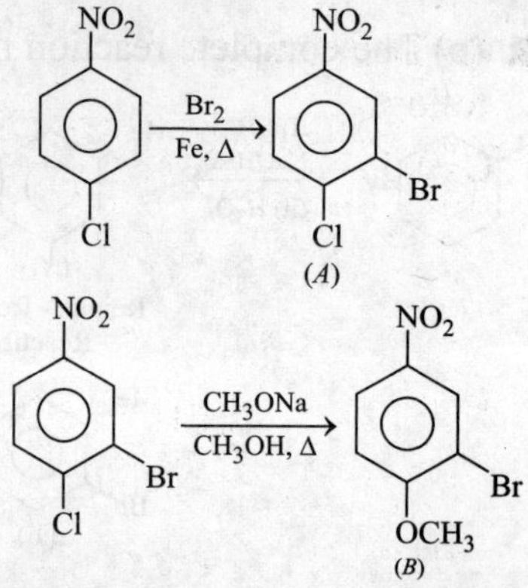

$$\text{(A)} \xrightarrow[Fe, \Delta]{Br_2} \text{(A)}$$

$$\text{(A)} \xrightarrow[CH_3OH, \Delta]{CH_3ONa} \text{(B)}$$

Hence, option (c) is correct.

27. (d) The complete reaction is as follows

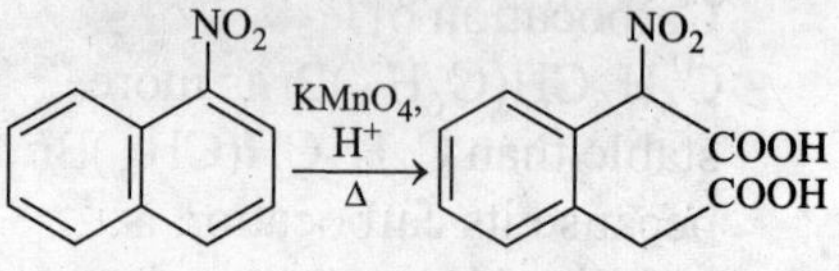

$$\xrightarrow[\Delta]{KMnO_4, H^+}$$

Hence, option (d) is correct.

28. (d) Statement (d) is incorrect. Its correct form is :

The hydrogen bonding plays important role in secondary structure of amino acids.

Hence, option (d) is correct.

29. (d) The complete reaction is as follows

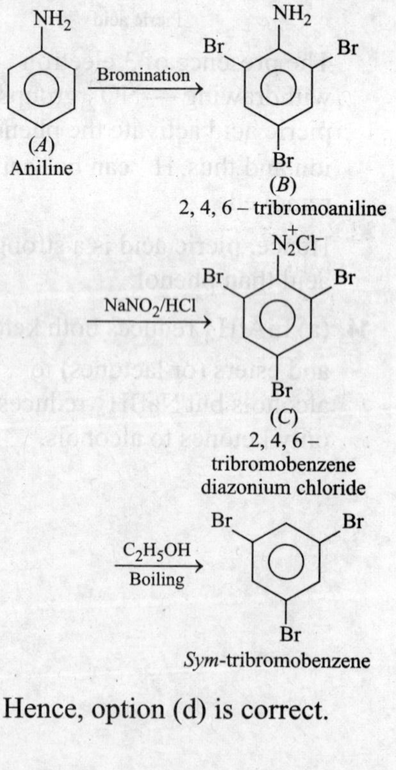

$$\text{Aniline (A)} \xrightarrow{\text{Bromination}} \text{(B) 2, 4, 6 – tribromoaniline} \xrightarrow{NaNO_2/HCl} \text{(C) 2, 4, 6 – tribromobenzene diazonium chloride} \xrightarrow[\text{Boiling}]{C_2H_5OH} \textit{Sym}\text{-tribromobenzene}$$

Hence, option (d) is correct.

30. (b) The complete reaction is as follows

$C_2H_5I \xrightarrow[-HI]{KOH\ (alc)} \underset{\text{Ethene}\ (A)}{CH_2=CH_2} \xrightarrow{Br_2} \underset{\text{(Dibromoethane)}\ B}{BrCH_2-CH_2Br}$

$\xrightarrow[-KBr]{2KCN} \underset{\text{Butane-1, 4-dinitrile}\ (C)}{NCCH_2-CH_2CN}$

31. (d) In Williamson's synthesis, ethers are prepared and nucleophilic substitution is involved.

Di-*tert*-butyl ether cannot be prepared due to the tendency of the *tert*-butyl group to undergo elimination rather than nucleophilic substitution.

Tert-butyl bromide $(CH_3)_3C-Br$ + Sodium *tert*-butoxide $Na^+\ {}^-O-C(CH_3)_3$ $\xrightarrow{\text{Elimination } (-NaBr)}$ *Iso*-butylene $(CH_3)_2C=CH_2$ + $(CH_3)_3COH$ *Tert*-butyl alcohol

32. (d) The complete reaction is as follows

$CH_3-CH_2-CH_2-Br \xrightarrow{KOH\ (alc)} \underset{(X)}{CH_3CH=CH_2} \xrightarrow{HBr} \underset{(Y)}{CH_3-CH(Br)-CH_3} \xrightarrow{KOH(aq)} \underset{\text{Propan-2-ol}\ (Z)}{CH_3-CH(OH)-CH_3}$

Hence, option (d) is correct.

33. (b) The complete reaction is as follows

p-Chloroanisole $\xrightarrow{NaNH_2}$ benzyne (with OCH_3) $\xrightarrow{Liq.\ NH_3}$ m-anisidine (OCH_3, H_2N)

Hence, option (b) is correct.

34. (b) The complete reaction is as follows

Cyclohexanone + cyclohexanone $\xrightarrow{Dil.\ NaOH}$ 2-(1-hydroxycyclohexyl)cyclohexanone $\xrightarrow[HCl]{Zn/Hg}$ 1-cyclohexylcyclohexanol

Hence, option (b) is correct.

35. (b) The complete reaction is as follows

$CH_3C\equiv CCH_2CH_3 \xrightarrow[H_3O^+/H_2O_2]{O_3} CH_3COOH + CH_3CH_2COOH$

Hence, option (b) is correct.

36. (a) The correct match is A-III, B-IV, C-I, D-II.

A. $CH_3CH_2CH_2Cl \xrightarrow[\text{Acetone}]{NaI} CH_3CH_2CH_2I$

⇒ Finkelstein reaction

B. $CH_3CH_2Cl \xrightarrow[\Delta]{Hg_2F_2} CH_3CH_2F$

⇒ Swarts reaction

C. $RCOOAg \xrightarrow[CCl_4]{Br_2} RBr$

⇒ Hunsdiecker reaction

D. $C_6H_5Br \xrightarrow[\Delta]{Na} C_6H_5C_6H_5$

⇒ Fittig reaction

37. (d) Both Statement I and Statement II are correct.

38. (b) $S^{2-} + K_2Cr_2O_7 \longrightarrow \underset{\text{(Green solution)}}{Cr_2(SO_4)_3} + 2K^+$

$S^{2-} + Pb(OAc)_2 \longrightarrow \underset{\text{(Black ppt.)}}{PbS\downarrow}$

39. (b) Benzoyl chloride is prepared from benzoic acid by $SOCl_2$.

$\underset{\text{Benzoic acid}}{C_6H_5COOH} + SOCl_2 \longrightarrow \underset{\text{Benzoyl chloride}}{C_6H_5COCl} + SO_2 + HCl$

40. (d) Phenol (OH) ⇌ cyclohexa-2,4-dienone (O)

Tautomerism is a process where a single chemical compound exhibits more than one interconvertible structure that generally differs in terms of relative positions of hydrogen atoms. Hence, only structure present in option (d) is the correct tautomer of phenol.

41. (d) The complete reaction is as follows

$$p\text{-}CH_3C_6H_4NO_2 \xrightarrow[\text{(ii) } CS_2]{\text{(i) } CrO_2Cl_2} \left[O_2N\text{-}C_6H_4\text{-}CH(OCrCl_2HO)(OCrCl_2OH) \right] (X) \xrightarrow{H_3O^+} p\text{-}OHC\text{-}C_6H_4NO_2 \; (Y)$$

42. (c) Ethyl amine undergoes oxidation in the presence of $KMnO_4$ to form an aldehyde.

$$\underset{\text{Ethylamine}}{CH_3—CH_2—NH_2} \xrightarrow[\text{[O]}]{KMnO_4} \underset{\text{Acetaldehyde}}{CH_3—CHO}$$

43. (b) Among the following given statements, A, B and D are correct whereas C and E are incorrect. Correct form of C and E are

- Benzene diazonium fluoroborate is water insoluble and stable at room temperature.
- The azo products are often coloured and are used as dyes.

44. (a) The complete reaction is as follows

$$F\text{-}C_6H_4\text{-}NO_2 \xrightarrow[\text{Nucleophilic substitution}]{(CH_3)_2NH \mid DMF, \Delta} \underset{(X)}{(CH_3)_2N\text{-}C_6H_4\text{-}NO_2} \xrightarrow[\text{Reduction}]{H_2/Ni} \underset{(Y)}{(CH_3)_2N\text{-}C_6H_4\text{-}NH_2}$$

45. (b) The free aldehyde group can be produced at the C1 carbon of the second α-D-glucose unit in solution and it shows reducing properties.

Hence, it is a reducing sugar.

NSS1 NEET Stepping Stones

1. (c) According to Kohlrausch law,

$$\Lambda^{\circ}_{m\,\{Al_2(SO_4)_3\}} = 2\Lambda^{\circ}_{Al^{3+}} + 3\Lambda^{\circ}_{SO_4^{2-}}$$

$$858 = 2\Lambda^{\circ}_{Al^{3+}} + (3 \times 160)$$

or $\quad 2\Lambda^{\circ}_{Al^{3+}} = 858 - (3 \times 160)$

$$= 378 \text{ S cm}^2\text{/mol}$$

or $\Lambda^{\circ}_{Al^{3+}} = \frac{378}{2} = 189 \text{ S cm}^2\text{/mol}$

Thus, option (c) is correct.

2. (d) Both Statement I and Statement II are correct. *ortho*-nitrophenol is more acidic than *ortho*-methoxy phenol due to electron withdrawing nature of NO_2 group.

3. (b) $t_{1/2} \propto (C_0)^{1-n}$

or $t_{1/2} = k\,(C_0)^{1-n}$

k = constant

$\therefore \log t_{1/2} = \log k + (1-n)\log C_0$

Compare above equation with straight line equation

$$y = mx + c$$

Thus, plot of $\log t_{1/2}$ *vs* $\log C_0$ will be linear with slope $= 1 - n$.

But, as graph is parallel to $\log C_0$ axis slope = 0, i.e. $1 - n = 0$.

So, order of reaction $(n) = 1$

Hence, $t_{1/2} = \frac{2.303}{k}\log 2$

4. (c) Statements (a), (b) and (d) are correct, but statement (c) is incorrect because S_8 molecule has paired electron, therefore it is diamagnetic.

Only S_2 in vapour state of sulphur is paramagnetic due to presence of two unpaired electrons.

5. (a) Pyrophosphoric acid ($H_4P_2O_7$) contains one P—O—P bond.

$$HO\text{-}P(=O)(OH)\text{-}O\text{-}P(=O)(OH)\text{-}OH$$

2P=O bond

4P—OH bond

1 P—O—P bond

Hence, option (a) is correct.

6. (d) Observed molar mass of phenol $(M_o) = \dfrac{K_f \times w_B \text{ (g)}}{w_A \text{ (kg)} \times \Delta T_f}$

$$= \frac{14 \times 75.2}{1 \times 7} = 150.4 \text{ g/mol}$$

Actual molar mass of C_6H_5OH (phenol)

$$M_x = 94 \text{ g/mol}$$

$\Rightarrow$ van't Hoff factor $(i) = \dfrac{M_x}{M_o}$

$$= \frac{94 \text{ g / mol}}{150.4 \text{ g / mol}}$$

$$= 0.625$$

$\Rightarrow$ Now, $\alpha_{\text{asso}} = \dfrac{1-i}{1-\dfrac{1}{m}}$

Here, for dimerisation of phenol, $m = 2$

$$\alpha_{\text{asso}} = \frac{1-0.625}{1-\dfrac{1}{2}}$$

$$= 0.75 = 75\%$$

7. (d) Both Statement I and Statement II are correct.

8. (a) The correct match is A-III, B-I, C-IV, D-II.

Conductivity $(\kappa) = \dfrac{1}{\rho} \times \dfrac{l}{a}$

$$= \Omega^{-1} \times \text{cm}^{-1} = \text{S cm}^{-1}$$

Molar conductance $(\Lambda_m) = \dfrac{\kappa \times 1000}{M}$

$$= \frac{\text{S cm}^{-1} \times 1000 \text{ (cm}^3 \text{ / dm}^3)}{(\text{mol / dm}^3)}$$

$$= \text{S cm}^2 \text{ mol}^{-1}$$

$$= \text{ohm}^{-1} \text{ cm}^2 \text{ mol}^{-1}$$

Equivalent conductance $(\Lambda_{eq}) = \dfrac{\kappa \times 1000}{N}$

$$= \Omega^{-1} \text{ cm}^2 \text{ equivalent}^{-1}$$

Cell constant $(Z^*) = \dfrac{l}{a} = \text{cm}^{-1}$

Thus, option (a) is correct.

9. (c) Correct IUPAC name of $[Co(NH_3)_4(NO_2)Cl]NO_3$ is tetraamminechloridonitrito (N) cobalt(III) nitrate

Thus, option (c) is correct.

10. (c) Tollen's reagent, Fehling solution and Benedict's solution are very weak oxidising agents. These can oxidise only aldehydes but not ketones.

So, these reagents may be used to distinguish between aldehyde and ketone. Thus, statement (c) is incorrect.

Hence, option (c) is correct answer.

11. (b) Colour of a compound is a property of unpaired *d*-electrons.

Ion	Cu^{2+}	Ti^{4+}	Co^{2+}	Fe^{2+}	V^{3+}
Outer electronic configuration	$3d^9$	$3d^0$	$3d^7$	$3d^6$	$3d^2$
No. of unpaired electrons	1	0	3	4	2

Since, Cu^{2+}, Co^{2+}, Fe^{2+} and V^{3+} contain unpaired electrons, these are coloured ions.

12. (b) $CH_3—NO_2 \xrightarrow{Zn/NH_4Cl} \underset{\text{N-methyl hydroxyl amine}}{CH_3—NHOH} + ZnO$

13. (b) PbO_2 readily dissolves in acid forming Pb(II) salts with the liberation of oxygen.

$$\overset{(IV)}{PbO_2} + 2HNO_3 \longrightarrow \overset{(II)}{Pb(NO_3)_2} + H_2O + \frac{1}{2}O_2$$

14. (a) Both (A) and (R) are true and (R) is the correct explanation of (A).

15. (b)

$$\underset{\text{Benzene}}{C_6H_6} + \frac{9}{2}O_2 \xrightarrow[-2CO_2,\ -H_2O]{V_2O_5,\ 725\text{ K}} \begin{matrix} CH—COOH \\ \| \\ CH—COOH \end{matrix} \xrightarrow[-H_2O]{\Delta} \underset{\text{Maleic anhydride (Final product)}}{[P]}$$

16. (b) $E^{\ominus}_{Ag^+/Ag}$ is larger than $E^{\ominus}_{Fe^{3+}/Fe^{2+}}$.

Hence, reduction will occur at silver electrode than cell is

$$Fe^{2+} | Fe^{3+} || Ag^+ | Ag$$

Overall reaction is

$$Fe^{2+} + Ag^+ \longrightarrow Fe^{3+} + Ag$$

$\Rightarrow$ According to Nernst Eq.

$$E_{\text{cell}} = E^{\ominus}_{\text{cell}} + \frac{0.059}{1} \log \frac{[Fe^{2+}][Ag^+]}{[Fe^{3+}][Ag]}$$

$[Fe^{3+}] = [Fe^{2+}]$ and $[Ag] = 1$

So, $E_{\text{cell}} = (0.80 - 0.77) + \dfrac{0.059}{1} \log [Ag^+]$

$$\Rightarrow \log [Ag^+] = \frac{-0.03}{0.059} \approx -0.508$$

17. (a) In given, $E_a = 209.5$ kJ/mol

$$= 209500 \text{ J/mol}$$

$T = 581$ K, $R = 8.314$ J/K/mol

Now, the fraction of molecules of reactant having energy equal to or greater than activation energy is given as $x = e^{-E_a/RT}$

$$\ln x = -\frac{E_a}{RT}$$

$$\log x = \frac{-E_a}{2.303RT}$$

$$= \frac{209500}{2.303 \times 8.314 \times 581}$$

$$= -18.83$$

$$x = 1.48 \times 10^{-19}$$

18. (d) Both Statement I and Statement II are correct because $Cu^+(g)$ ion has stable electronic configuration (d^{10}).

19. (c) $K_4[Fe(CN)_6] \rightleftharpoons 4K^+ + [Fe(CN)_6]^{4-}$

Since, one molecule dissociated into five particles

$n = 5$

Degree of dissociation, $\alpha = 50\%$ or 0.5

$i = 1 + \alpha(n-1) = 1 + 0.5(5-1) = 3$

The osmotic pressure, $\pi = i \times CRT$

Here, $C = \frac{1}{10}$ mol/L

$R = 0.082$ L-atm K^{-1} mol^{-1}

$T = 300$ K

$\pi = 3 \times \frac{1}{10} \times 0.082 \times 300 = 7.38$ atm.

20. (c) The given reaction is represented as

1-Methylnaphthalene (CH_3) $\xrightarrow{Cl_2/h\nu}$ 1-($CHCl_2$)naphthalene [P] $\xrightarrow[373\ K]{H_2O}$ 1-naphthaldehyde (CHO)

21. (c) Ti^{3+} (d^1) has one unpaired electron and shows *d-d* transition hence, it is coloured but Ti^{4+} does not contain unpaired electron.

Thus, it does not show *d-d* transition and hence, colourless. Hence, option (c) is correct.

22. (d) Both Statement I and Statement II are correct.

$$\underset{\text{Ethene}}{CH_2{=}CH_2} + CO + H_2 \xrightarrow[\text{Oxo reaction}]{[Co(CO)_4]_2} \underset{\text{Propanal}}{CH_3CH_2CHO}$$

23. (d) Among the given options, the achiral amino acid is glycine, H_2NCH_2COOH. It does not have any chiral centre.

24. (b) Alkenes react with carbon monoxide and hydrogen in the presence of octacarbonyl dicobalt as catalyst and at high temperature, pressure to yield aldehyde. This process is called oxo process.

$$\underset{\text{Ethene}}{CH_2{=}CH_2} + CO + H_2 \xrightarrow[\text{High temp.}]{[Co(CO)_4]_2} \underset{\text{Propanal } (A)}{CH_3{-}CH_2{-}CHO} \xrightarrow{Ni/H_2} \underset{\text{Propanol } (B)}{CH_3{-}CH_2{-}CH_2{-}OH}$$

Thus, option (b) is correct.

25. (a) The correct match is A-III, B-II, C-I, D-IV.

A.	$[CoCl_2(en)_2]^+$	–	Optically active as well as geometrical active
B.	$[Cr(ox)_3]^{3-}$	–	Optical isomerism only
C.	$[RhCl_3(py)_3]$	–	Geometrical active
D.	$[ZnCl_3(NH_3)]$	–	It cannot show isomerism

Hence, option (a) is correct.

26. (d) All statements are true regarding the crystal field splitting (Δ) except (d). As the value of Δ_t is 4/9 times of Δ_o.

27. (a) The correct match is A-III, B-IV, C-II, D-I.

A. HVZ reaction, α-H of carboxylic acid is replaced by halogen and form α-halo acid.

$$\underset{\text{Carboxylic acid}}{R{-}CH_2{-}COOH} \xrightarrow[\text{Red P}]{Br_2} \underset{\alpha\text{-bromocarboxylic acid}}{R{-}CH(Br){-}COOH} + HBr$$

B. Reaction of H_2 and CO_2 at high temperature gives formic acid.

$$CO_2 + H_2 \xrightarrow{\Delta} \underset{\text{Formic acid}}{HCOOH}$$

C. In Kolbe's electrolysis reaction potassium salt of carboxylic acid is electrolysed and forms alkane at anode, H_2 gas at cathode.

D. Carboxylic acid and alcohol reacts with each other to form ester in presence of dehydrating reagent like $ZnCl_2$.

Thus, option (a) is correct.

28. (b)

p-Toluidine (NH_2, CH_3) $\xrightarrow[-AcOH]{(CH_3CO)_2O}$ N-(4-methylphenyl)acetamide ($N(H){-}C(=O){-}CH_3$, CH_3) (A) $\xrightarrow[AcOH]{Br_2}$ 2-bromo-4-methylacetanilide ($NHCOCH_3$, Br, CH_3) (B)

29. (b) Vitamin C is water soluble vitamins, whereas Vitamins A, D and E are fat soluble.

$RCONH_2 + Br_2 + 4KOH \longrightarrow RNH_2 + 2KBr + K_2CO_3 + 2H_2O$
(1° amine)

31. (c) When glucose reacts with HCN/H_2O and further heated with HI, then heptanoic acid is obtained.

CHO–$(CHOH)_4$–CH_2OH (Glucose) $\xrightarrow{HCN}$ CH(OH)(CN)–$(CHOH)_4$–CH_2OH (Cyanohydrin)

$\xrightarrow{Hydrolysis}$ CH(OH)(COOH)–$(CHOH)_4$–CH_2OH $\xrightarrow{HI/Heat}$ CH_3—$(CH_2)_5COOH$ (Heptanoic acid)

Thus, option (c) is correct.

32. (d) If silver salt of an acid is used in excess amount, then it forms ester on treating with I_2 in presence of CCl_4. This reaction is called Birnbaum Simonini reaction.

CH_3—C(=O)—O—Ag + I—I + Ag—O—C(=O)—CH_3 $\xrightarrow{CCl_4}$ $2AgI + CH_3$—C(=O)—$OCH_3 + CO_2$
Methyl acetate (ester)

33. (d) Methyl benzene (toluene) is oxidised by $CrO_3/(CH_3CO)_2O$ and forms benzaldehyde with $H_3O^+/373$ K. The complete reaction is as follows

(Toluene) $\xrightarrow[(CH_3CO)_2O]{CrO_3}$ $C_6H_5CH(OCOCH_3)_2$ (Benzylidene diacetate) (A) $\xrightarrow[H_3O^+]{373K}$ C_6H_5CHO + 2 CH_3COOH
Benzaldehyde (B)

34. (c) When phenol is treated with aqueous Br_2, then it forms a white precipitate of 2,4,6-tribromophenol.

Phenol + $3Br_2$ $\xrightarrow{H_2O}$ 2, 4, 6-tribromophenol (White ppt.) (P)

35. (b) Wurtz reaction proceeds in presence of Na and dry ether.

CH_3—CH_2—CH_2—Br (1-bromopropane) + 2Na + Br—$CH(CH_3)_2$ (2-bromopropane) $\xrightarrow{\text{Dry ether}}$ CH_3—CH_2—CH_2—$CH(CH_3)_2$ (2-methylpentane)

36. (a) Both Statement I and Statement II are correct.

37. (c)

$Zn^{+2} + H_2S \longrightarrow ZnS \xrightarrow{\text{Dil. HCl}} ZnCl_2$

$ZnCl_2 \longrightarrow Zn(OH)_2$ (White ppt.)

$ZnCl_2 \xrightarrow{K_4[Fe(CN)_6]} Zn_2[Fe(CN)_6]$ (Bluish white ppt.)

Thus, the cation is Zn^{2+}.

38. (c) All the given statements are correct.

39. (a) The correct match is A-IV, B-III, C-II, D-I.

40. (a) Both (A) and (R) are true and (R) is the correct explanation of (A).

41. (c) Relative decrease in vapour pressure × mole fraction of water = 5 mol

Solute	Mole in solution from 1 mole solute	Mole fraction of solute
A(NaCl)	2	$\frac{2}{7} = 0.29$
$B(K_2SO_4)$	3	$\frac{3}{8} = 0.38$
$C(Na_3PO_4)$	4	$\frac{4}{9} = 0.44$
D(Glucose)	1	$\frac{1}{6} = 0.17$

Hence, $D < A < B < C$.

42. (b) $p_1 = 100\,\text{kPa}, (t_{1/2})_1 = 364$ s

$p_2 = 50\,\text{kPa}, (t_{1/2})_2 = 182$ s

$$(t_{1/2})_1 = \frac{1}{k(p_1)^{n-1}} \quad \text{...(i)}$$

and $$(t_{1/2})_2 = \frac{1}{k(p_2)^{n-1}} \quad \text{...(ii)}$$

Divide (i) and (ii),

$$\frac{(t_{1/2})_1}{(t_{1/2})_2} = \frac{(p_2)^{n-1}}{(p_1)^{n-1}}$$

Now substitute given values in above equations

$$\frac{364}{182} = \left(\frac{50}{100}\right)^{n-1}$$

$$(2)^{-1} = \left(\frac{1}{2}\right)^{n-1}$$

$$n - 1 = -1$$

$$n = 0$$

The order of the reaction is zero.

43. (c)

o-Bromotoluene $\xrightarrow{Mg/ether}$ o-$CH_3C_6H_4MgBr$ $\xrightarrow{H_3O^+}$ Toluene $\xrightarrow[H^+]{KMnO_4/OH^-}$ C_6H_5COOH (A)

44. (b)

B. Gives violet colour with neutral $FeCl_3$, thus it is phenol.

C. Gives blood red colour with neutral $FeCl_3$, thus it is CH_3COOH.

$$C_6H_5-O-\overset{O}{\overset{\|}{C}}-CH_3 \ (A) \xrightarrow[\text{Hydrolysis}]{H_3O^+} C_6H_5-OH \ (B) + CH_3COOH \ (C)$$

45. (c) Statement given in (c) is incorrect. Its correct form is dinitrogen tetroxide is obtained by NO_2.

$$2NO_2 \underset{\text{Heat}}{\overset{\text{Cool}}{\rightleftharpoons}} N_2O_4$$

This N_2O_4 is a colourless solid/liquid which is acidic in nature.

NSS2 NEET Stepping Stones

1. (b) K_2SO_4 dissolved $= 25$ mg $= 0.025$ g

Volume of solution $= 2$ L, $T = 25°C = 298$ K

Molar mass of K_2SO_4

$= 2 \times 39 + 32 + 4 \times 16$

$= 174 \text{ g mol}^{-1}$

As, K_2SO_4 dissolve completely

$K_2SO_4 \longrightarrow 2K^+ + SO_4^{2-}$, i.e. ions produced $= 3$

$\therefore \quad i = 3$

$\pi = iCRT$

$= i\frac{n}{V}RT = \frac{i}{M} \times \frac{w}{V} \times RT$

$3 \times \frac{0.025}{174} \times \frac{1}{2} \times 0.0821 \times 298$

$\pi = 5.27 \times 10^{-3}$ atm

2. (b) $d^0(Ti^{4+}, Sc^{3+})$ and $d^{10}(Zn^{2+})$ species will not absorb visible light and are colourless whereas, $d^3(Cr^{3+})$ can undergo *d-d* transition on absorption of visible light of a particular wavelength and will be coloured.

3. (b) The complete reaction will take place as follows

$$p\text{-}CH_3C_6H_4NH_2 \xrightarrow[0\text{–}5°C]{NaNO_2/HCl} p\text{-}CH_3C_6H_4\overset{+}{N_2}Cl^- \ (Y) \xrightarrow[\Delta]{CuCN/KCN} p\text{-}CH_3C_6H_4CN \ (Z) + N_2$$

Thus, the compound (Z) is $p\text{-}CH_3C_6H_4CN$ (4-methylbenzonitrile).

4. (b) $k = \frac{2.303}{t}\log\frac{a}{a-x}$

$= \frac{2.303}{t_{1/4}}\log\frac{a}{3a} = \frac{2.303}{t_{1/4}}\log\frac{4}{3}$

$k = \frac{2.303 \times 0.125}{t_{1/4}} = \frac{0.29}{t_{1/4}}$

$t_{1/4} = \frac{0.29}{k}$

5. (c) The complete reaction sequence is as follows

$$C_6H_5Cl \xrightarrow[\text{Conc. } H_2SO_4]{\text{Conc. } HNO_3} p\text{-}ClC_6H_4NO_2 \ (A) \xrightarrow[433\text{ K}]{NaOH} p\text{-}HOC_6H_4NO_2 \ (B)$$

6. (b) Vapour pressure of pure water at boiling point $(p°)$ $= 1$ atm $= 1.013$ bar

Vapour pressure of solvent $(p_s) = 1.004$ bar

Mass of solute $(w_2) = 2$ g

Mass of solution $= 100$ g

Mass of solvent $(W_1) = 98$ g

Applying Raoult's law of dilute solution (being 2%)

$$\frac{p° - p_s}{p°} = \frac{n_2}{n_1} = \frac{w_2/M_2}{w_1/M_1}$$

$$= \frac{w_2}{M_2} \times \frac{M_1}{w_1}$$

$$\Rightarrow \frac{(1.013 - 1.004)}{1.013} = \frac{2}{M_2} \times \frac{18}{98}$$

$$M_2 = 41.35 \text{ g mol}^{-1}$$

7. (a) The complete reaction is as follows

$$CHCl_3 \xrightarrow{\text{Air}/h\nu} \underset{[X]}{Cl-\overset{O}{\overset{\|}{C}}-Cl} \xrightarrow{C_6H_6,\ \text{Anhyd. }AlCl_3} \underset{[Y]}{C_6H_5-\overset{O}{\overset{\|}{C}}-Cl}$$

8. (a) $CH_3-CH_2-CH_2-Br \xrightarrow{AgCN} \underset{[X]}{CH_3-CH_2-CH_2-\overset{+}{N}\equiv\overset{-}{C}} \xrightarrow{H_2O/\bar{O}H/\Delta} \underset{[Y]}{CH_3-CH_2-CH_2-NH_2} + HCOOH$

9. (c) Sucrose $\longrightarrow$ no dissociation

$NaCl \longrightarrow Na^+ + Cl^-$

$CaCl_2 \longrightarrow Ca^{2+} + 2Cl^-$

Elevation in boiling point is directly proportional to the number of particles.

Hence, ΔT_b will be maximum for $CaCl_2$ and so highest will be the boiling point.

10. (b) Hofmann elimination take place because of poor leaving group $-\overset{+}{N}Me_3$, reaction proceed through stable carbanion in transition state. In Hofmann elimination least substituted alkene is major product.

[Structure: cyclohexane bearing $-CH_2-\overset{\oplus}{N}Me_3$ with $\overset{\delta\ominus}{OH}$ abstracting H ($\delta\ominus$ on CH_2) $\xrightarrow{\Delta}$ methylenecyclohexane ($=CH_2$)]

Stable carbanion

11. (b) Molecules having higher molecular weight and less branching have higher boiling point. Thus, among the given options, $CH_3CH_2CH_2CH_2Cl$ will have highest boiling point.

12. (d) Chlorination of toluene in presence of light and heat is as follows.

$$C_6H_5CH_3 \xrightarrow[-3HCl]{3Cl_2,\ h\nu,\ \Delta} C_6H_5CCl_3 \xrightarrow[-NaCl]{\text{Aq. NaOH}} C_6H_5C(OH)_3 \xrightarrow{-H_2O} \underset{\text{Benzoic acid}}{C_6H_5COOH}$$

13. (d) In I : H-bonding between —OH and —NO_2 group decreases bond angle. Thus, dipole moment (μ) is increased.

In II, repulsion between two Cl-atoms increases bond angle thus μ is decreased. In III, No strain thus μ remains unchanged.

Thus, II < III < I.

14. (a) An azeotropic mixture boil at a particular temperature without changing its composition.

15. (d) Both Statement I and Statement II are correct.

16. (b)

[Structure: cyclopentyl–$CH(OH)$–CH_3 with CH_3 on ring carbon $\xrightarrow{H^+}$ cyclopentyl–$CH(\overset{+}{O}H_2)$–CH_3 $\xrightarrow{-H_2O}$ 2° carbocation $\overset{+}{C}H-CH_3$ $\rightleftharpoons$ ring expansion to cyclohexyl cation with CH_3, CH_3, H $\underset{}{\xrightarrow{-H^+}}$ 1,2-dimethylcyclohexene (X)]

17. (a)

$$d = M\left(\frac{1}{m} + \frac{\text{Molar mass of solute}}{1000}\right)$$

$$d = 2.224\left(\frac{1}{94.12} + \frac{40}{1000}\right)$$

$$= 1.12 \text{ g mL}^{-1}$$

18. (a) In metal carbonyls, the oxidation number of metal is always zero. Thus, $Fe(CO)_5$ has lowest oxidation number.

19. (c) 1 M NaCl,

$NaCl \longrightarrow Na^+ + Cl^-$

1 M $MgCl_2$,

$MgCl_2 \longrightarrow Mg^{2+} + 2Cl^-$

1 M $(NH_4)_3PO_4$,

$(NH_4)_3PO_4 \longrightarrow 3NH_4^+ + PO_4^{3-}$

$(NH_4)_3PO_4$ dissociates to give maximum number of particles. Hence, its osmotic pressure will be maximum.

20. (b) Dipole moment decreases with decrease in electronegativity of halogen. Fluorides have lower dipole moment than chlorides because of smaller C—F bond length which outweighs the effect of greater electronegativity.

21. (b) Both (A) and (R) are true but (R) is not the correct explanation of (A).

22. (c) The complete reaction is

$$CH_2=CH_2 \xrightarrow{HBr} \underset{(X)}{CH_3CH_2Br} \xrightarrow{\text{Aq. NaOH}} \underset{(Y)}{CH_3CH_2OH} \xrightarrow[\text{(Iodoform reaction)}]{Na_2CO_3/\text{Excess } I_2} \underset{(Z)}{CHI_3}$$

23. (d) In the analysis of basic radicals, the group reagent H_2S gas is generally used in the group II and IV groups.

24. (b) Molality

$$= \frac{\text{Moles of (solute) } CH_3OH}{1 \text{ kg of } H_2O} = \frac{3.5 \text{ mol}}{1 \text{ kg}}$$

Thus, $m_{CH_3OH} = 3.5$ m

$$n_{H_2O} = \frac{1000}{18} = 55.56$$

$\therefore$ Total moles $= 3.5 + 55.56 = 59.06$ mol

$$\therefore \chi_{CH_3OH} = \frac{\text{Moles of } CH_3OH}{\text{Total moles}} = \frac{3.5}{59.05} = 0.059$$

25. (d) Rate of disappearance of MnO_4^- is given by

$$-\frac{d[MnO_4^-]}{dt} = 9.12\times10^{-3}\ Ms^{-1}$$

$$-\frac{1}{2}\frac{d[MnO_4^-]}{dt} = +\frac{1}{5}\frac{d[I_2]}{d}$$

$$\frac{d[I_2]}{dt} = \frac{5}{2}\left[-\frac{d[MnO_4^-]}{dt}\right]$$

$$\frac{d[I_2]}{dt} = \frac{5}{2}\times9.12\times10^{-3} = 2.28\times10^{-2}\ Ms^{-1}$$

26. (b) All collisions are not effective and does not result in the formation of products.

27. (a) S_N1 rate depends on the stability of carbocation formed as an intermediate. The carbocations formed by given bromides will be

(a) Ph–CH(Br)–Ph → Ph–$\overset{\oplus}{C}$H–Ph

(b) 4-biphenylyl–CH$_2$Br → biphenyl carbocation ($\oplus$)

(c) Ph–CH(Br)–CH$_3$ → Ph–$\overset{\oplus}{C}$H–CH$_3$

(d) CH$_3$–CH(Br)–CH$_2$–CH$_3$ → CH$_3$–$\overset{\oplus}{C}$H–CH$_2$CH$_3$

The carbocation Ph–$\overset{\oplus}{C}$H–Ph is most stable as it can be resonance stabilised by two phenyl rings.

$\therefore$ The S_N1 will be faster in Ph–CH(Br)–Ph

28. (c) The N-atom of ethyl methylamine undergoes fast inversion so it cannot be resolved under normal condition.

29. (d) C$_6$H$_5$–CH$_2$–CH$_2$–OH $\xrightarrow[\text{(Oxidation)}]{\text{Jones reagent (X)}}$ C$_6$H$_5$–CH$_2$COOH $\xrightarrow[\text{(Decarboxylation reaction)}]{\text{NaOH, CaO-}\Delta\ (Y)}$ C$_6$H$_5$–CH$_3$ (Z) Toluene

30. (a) The given reaction is a carbylamine reaction. So, the product formed is C_2H_5NC and KCl.

$$CH_3CH_2NH_2 + CHCl_3 + 3KOH \longrightarrow C_2H_5NC + KCl + 3H_2O$$

31. (b) The hormone thyroxine is secreted from thyroid gland, which stimulates the rate of oxidation metabolism and regulates general growth and development.

32. (c) Half-life for a zero-order reaction is given by

$t_{1/2} = \frac{[A_0]}{2k}$ [Where, $[A_0]$ = intial concentration of reactant]

$$\Rightarrow k_0 = \frac{[A_0]}{2t_{1/2}} = \frac{2.0\ mol\ L^{-1}}{2\times1\ h} = 1.0\ mol\ L^{-1}h^{-1}$$

Rate constant for a zero-order reaction is given by

$$k = \frac{1}{t}[(A_0)-(A)]$$

$$\Rightarrow t = \frac{1}{k}[(A_0)-(A)]$$

$$\Rightarrow t = \frac{0.75-0.50\ mol\ L^{-1}}{1\ mol\ L^{-1}\ h^{-1}} = 0.25\,h$$

33. (a) vant't Hoff factor (i) is related to degree of dissociation (α) as

$$\alpha = \frac{i-1}{n-1}$$

Thus, the degree of dissociation of A_xB_y is given by $\left(\frac{i-1}{x+y-1}\right)$

34. (c) $c \propto a$ and $c \propto$ molarity

$$c \propto \frac{a}{l}\times\text{molarity} = k\times\frac{a}{l}\times\text{molarity}$$

$$\therefore \text{Unit of } k = S\times\frac{m}{m^2}\times\frac{(m^3)}{mol} = S\ m^2\ mol^{-1}$$

35. (a) Me$_2$$\overset{\ominus}{Cu}\overset{\oplus}{Li}$ + CH$_2$=CH–CO–CH$_3$ → Me–CH$_2$–CH=C(O$^{\ominus}$Li$^{\oplus}$)–CH$_3$ $\xrightarrow{H^{\oplus}/H_2O}$ Me–CH$_2$–CH=C(OH)–CH$_3$ $\rightleftharpoons$ Me–CH$_2$–CH$_2$–CO–CH$_3$

36. (b) $K_4[Fe(CN)_6]$ and $K_3[Fe(CN)_6]$ both are low spin complex due to strong ligand field and have 0, 1 unpaired electron respectively. That's why $K_4[Fe(CN)_6]$ is diamagnetic and $K_3[Fe(CN)_6]$ is paramagnetic crystal field splitting in ferrocyanide is less than ferricyanide ion because higher the oxidation state of metal, greater the field splitting.

37. (b) The complete reaction sequence is as follows

$$CH_3CH_2CHO + CH_3CH_2CHO \xrightarrow{\text{NaOH, }\Delta\text{ (aldol)}}$$

CH$_3$CH$_2$–CH(OH)–CH(CHO)–CH$_3$ $\xrightarrow{\Delta}$ CH$_3$CH$_2$–CH=C(CHO)–CH$_3$

38. (b) The correct match is A-IV, B-III, C-II, D-I.

S.No.	Complex structure	Electronic configuration	Hybridisation	Geometry
A.	$[Fe(CN)_6]^{3-}$	$Fe^{3+} = 3d^5$	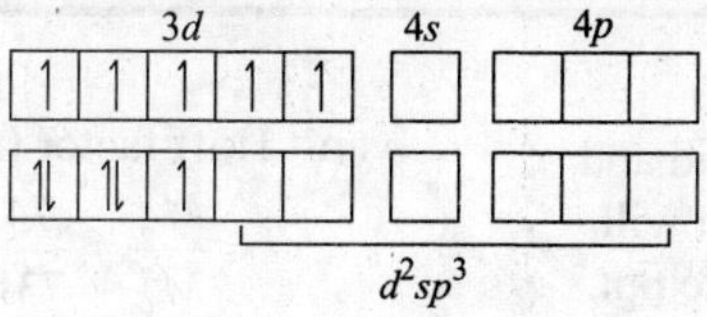 3d: 1 1 1 1 1; 4s; 4p → 3d: 11 11 1 _ _, 4s, 4p; d^2sp^3	Octahedral
B.	$[ZnCl_4]^{2-}$	$Zn^{2+} = 3d^{10}$	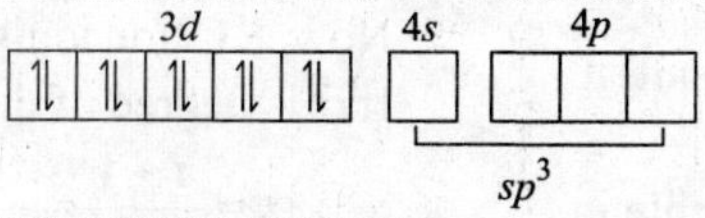 3d: 11 11 11 11 11; 4s; 4p; sp^3	Tetrahedral
C.	$[Ni(CN)_4]^{2-}$	$Ni = 3d^8$	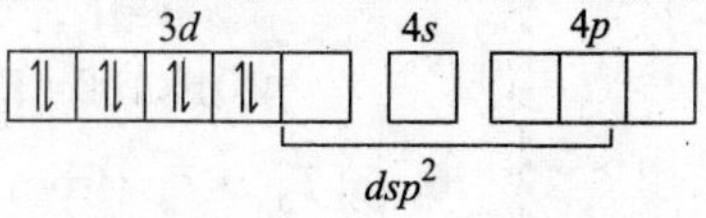 3d: 11 11 11 11 _; 4s; 4p; dsp^2	Square planar
D.	$[Ag(CN)_2]^-$	$Ag^+ = 4d^{10}$	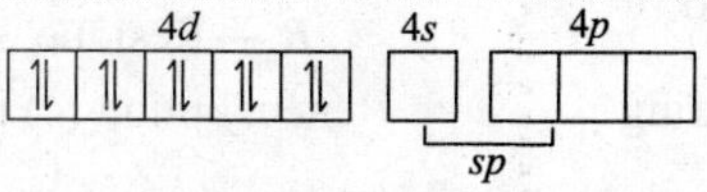 4d: 11 11 11 11 11; 4s; 4p; sp	Linear

39. (c) Incorrect statement about cerium is given in option (c). Its correct form is : Ce^{4+} is oxidising agent and is known in solution.

$$Ce^{4+} + Fe^{2+} \longrightarrow Ce^{3+} + Fe^{3+}$$

40. (c) According to question, the reaction involved is as follows

$$[Co(NH_3)_5Cl]Cl_2 \xrightarrow{H_2O} [Co(NH_3)_5Cl]^+ + 2Cl^-$$

$$2AgNO_3 + 2Cl^- \longrightarrow 2AgCl + 2NO_3^-$$

41. (d) Slowest step is the rate determining step.

Thus, in case (A) rate law is given as rate $= k[Cl_2][H_2S]$

While for the reaction given in case (II), rate law is given as rate $= k[H_2S][Cl_2][H^+]^{-1}$.

Hence, only mechanism (A) is consistent with the given rate law.

42. (c) The complete reaction sequence is as follows

$$2Ph{-}\overset{\overset{O}{\|}}{C}{-}CH_3 \xrightarrow[H_2O]{Mg\text{-}Hg} \underset{(P)}{Ph{-}\underset{CH_3}{\overset{OH}{C}}{-}\underset{CH_3}{\overset{OH}{C}}{-}Ph} \xrightarrow[\Delta]{Conc.\ H_2SO_4}$$

$$\underset{(Q)}{Ph{-}\underset{CH_2}{\overset{}{C}}{-}\underset{CH_2}{C}{-}Ph} \xrightarrow[H_2O]{KMnO_4,\ H^+} \underset{(R)}{Ph{-}\underset{O}{\underset{\|}{C}}{-}\underset{O}{\underset{\|}{C}}{-}Ph}$$

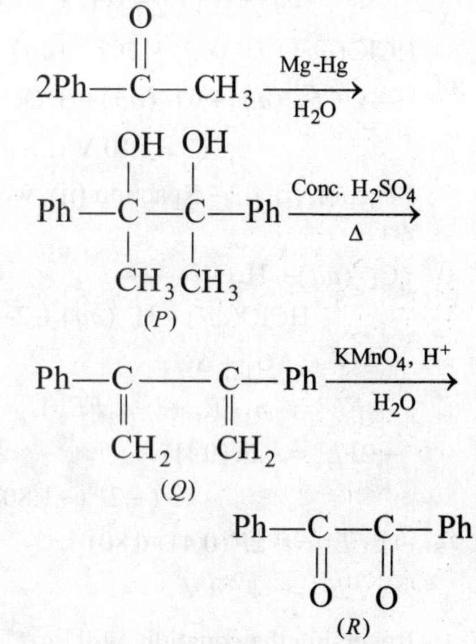

43. (a) The complete reaction sequence is as follows

$$\text{(2-bromobenzyl bromide, } C_6H_4(Br)CH_2{-}Br) \xrightarrow{NH_3} C_6H_4(Br)CH_2{-}NH_2$$

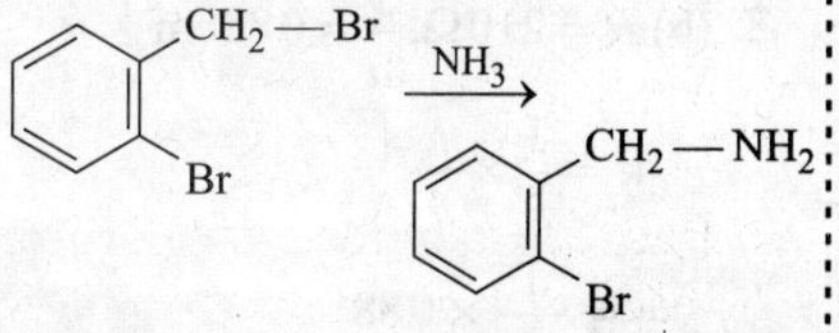

44. (d)

(a) Tl is more stable in +1 oxidation state, than +3 oxidation state, therefore Tl^{3+} salts are oxidising agents.

(b) $Ga^+ - 2e^- \longrightarrow Ga^{3+}$ (More stable)

$\therefore Ga^+$ is a reducing agent.

(c) $Pb^{4+} + 2e^- \longrightarrow Pb^{2+}$ (More stable)

Pb^{4+} is an oxidising agent.

(d) $As^{5+} + 2e^- \longrightarrow As^{3+}$ (Less stable)

Thus, As^{5+} cannot be reduced so As^{5+} salts are not a good oxidising agent. An oxidising agent is defined as substance whose oxidation number decreases while reducing agents are defined as substance whose oxidation number increases.

45. (a) The given compound $[Co(NH_3)_5(NO_2)(NO_3)_2]$ exhibits linkage and ionisation isomerism. While it does not show coordination isomerism because their complex has only one metal ion and for coordination isomerism two different metal ions are required in the complex. Optical isomerism is shown by the compounds that are non-superimposable mirror images of each other.

NSS3 NEET Stepping Stones

1. (b) NaCl is a salt of strong acid and strong base, hence dissolution will give neutral solution. As white ppt. is obtained by the addition of $AgNO_3$ to the solution of Na salt, it can be AgCl.

Moreover, AgCl is also insoluble in HNO_3. Hence the anion is Cl^-.

2. (c) Chloral hydrate, i.e.

$CCl_3—CH(OH)_2$ is stable due to intramolecular hydrogen bonding.

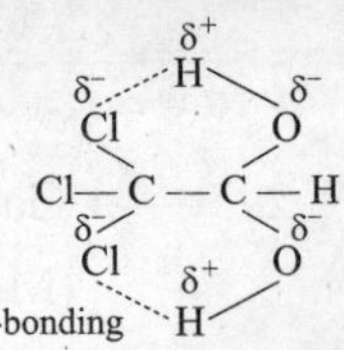

3. (d) 0.1 M glucose and 0.1 urea, since both the solution have same concentration, there will be no net movement of water molecules across the membrane.

4. (c) Graph of concentration *versus* temperature doesn't represent (a), (b) and (d).

We know that, $\pi = CRT$

Comparing with $y = mx + C$

Slope RT, i.e.

gas constant × absolute temperature

5. (a) Mass of KCl $(w_B) = 0.95$ g

Mass of water $(w_A) = 100$ g

$\Delta T_f = 0-(-0.24) = 0.24°C = 0.24$ K

Molar mass of KCl (M_0) is given as

$$M_0 = K_f \times \frac{w_B \times 1000}{w_A \times \Delta T_f}$$

$$M_0 = \frac{1.86 \text{ K kg / mol} \times 0.95 \text{ g} \times 1000 \text{ g}}{100 \text{ kg} \times 0.24 \text{ K}}$$

$= 73.62$ g/mol

Normal molar mass of KCl

$M_n = 39 + 35.5 = 74.5$ g/mol

van't Hoff factor (i) is given by

$$i = \frac{M_n}{M_0} = \frac{74.5}{73.62} = 1.01$$

Now, KCl ion ionises in K^+ and Cl^-.

If α is degree of dissociation

$$\alpha = \frac{i-1}{m-1} = \frac{1.01-1}{2-1} = 0.01$$

$0.01 \times 100 = 1\%$

6. (c) $T_B^\circ > T_A^\circ$ (from diagram)

$B \rightarrow$ Residue, $A \rightarrow$ Distillate

Hence, option (c) is correct.

7. (a) $Cr^{2+}(aq) \longrightarrow$

$Cr^{3+}(aq) + e^-$; $E° = 0.41$ V ...(i)

$HClO(aq) + H^+(aq) + 2Cr^{2+}(aq)$

$\longrightarrow 2Cr^{3+}(aq) + Cl^-(aq) + H_2O(l)$;

$E° = 1.80$ V ...(ii)

Reaction (i) × 2 − Reaction (ii), we get

$Cl^-(aq) + H_2O(l) \longrightarrow$

$HClO(aq) + H^+(aq) + 2e^-$

$$\Delta G° = \Delta G_1 + \Delta G_2$$

$$-nFE° = -n_1FE_1 + (-n_2FE_2)$$

$$-2FE° = -2F(0.41) + (-2F(-1.80))$$

$$-2FE° = -2F(0.41-1.80)$$

$$E° = -1.39 \text{ V}$$

Reversing the equation, will reverse E°_{value}

$$E° = 1.39 \text{ V}$$

8. (b) $R = 210\,\Omega$, $\frac{l}{a} = 0.88 \text{ cm}^{-1}$

$$\kappa = \frac{1}{R} \times \frac{l}{a}$$

$$= \frac{1}{210} \times 0.88$$

$= 4.19 \times 10^{-3}\ \Omega^{-1}\text{cm}^{-1}$ or S cm^{-1}

(equivalent conductivity)

$$\Lambda_{eq} = \frac{\kappa \times 1000}{N}$$

$$= \frac{4.19 \times 10^{-3} \times 1000}{0.01}$$

$= 419$ S cm^2 eq^{-1}

9. (d) $\Lambda_{eq} = \frac{\kappa \times 1000}{N}$

and $\kappa = \frac{\Lambda_{eq} \times N}{1000}$

$$= \frac{100 \times 0.1}{1000} = 0.01 \text{ S cm}^{-1}$$

G (conductance)

$$= \frac{\kappa}{G^* \text{ (cell constant)}}$$

$$= \frac{0.01}{0.25} = 0.04\ \Omega^{-1} \text{ or S}$$

$$R = \frac{1}{G} = \frac{1}{0.04} = 25\,\Omega$$

Current in Ampere

$$= \frac{\text{Potential difference}}{\text{Resistance } (\Omega)}$$

$$= \frac{5}{25} = 0.2 \text{ A}$$

10. (a) Reduction of $Cu^\oplus$ at cathode

$Cu^\oplus + e^- \longrightarrow Cu$

$e^- = 1F = 1$ mole of Cu

$= 63.5$ g of Cu

$\therefore$ 6.35 g of Cu will be deposited

$$= \frac{1 \text{ F} \times 6.35 \text{ g}}{63.5 \text{ g}} = 0.1\text{F}$$

Hence, option (a) is correct.

11. (c) Those reactions in which more than one species is involved in the rate determining step, but the order of reaction is 1, such reactions are called pseudo first order reactions in which solvent molecules or a catalyst act as one of the reacting species.

Thus, all given reaction proceeds with solvents except (c) first molecular reaction.

The reaction involves the hydrolysis of methyl acetate in the presence of base which is second order reaction, because in basic medium, the amount of NaOH influences the rate of reaction.

12. (b) $k = Ae^{-E_a/RT}$

$$= 4 \times 10^{13}\, e^{-98.6\times10^3\ \text{J}/(8.314\times T)}$$

For first order, $k = \dfrac{0.693}{600}\ \text{s}^{-1}$

$$\Rightarrow \frac{0.693}{600} = 4\times10^{13}\, e^{-(98.6\times10^3)/8.314\times T}$$

Taking log on both sides

$$\log\frac{0.693}{600} = \log 4\times10^{13} - \frac{98.6\times10^3}{8.314\times2.303\times T}$$

$$T = 310.96\ \text{K}$$

13. (a) $\dfrac{t_{x\%}}{t_{1/2}} = \dfrac{\log\left(\dfrac{100}{100-x}\right)}{0.3}$

In case of $t_{75\%}$,

$$\frac{t_{75\%}}{t_{1/2}} = \frac{\log\left(\dfrac{100}{100-75}\right)}{0.3}$$

$$t_{75\%} = \frac{t_{1/2}\times\log\left(\dfrac{100}{25}\right)}{0.3}$$

$$= \frac{t_{1/2}\times(\log 100 - \log 25)}{0.3}$$

$$= \frac{t_{1/2}(0.6)}{0.3} = 2t_{1/2}$$

In case of $t_{87.5\%}$

$$\frac{t_{87.5\%}}{t_{1/2}} = \frac{\log\left(\dfrac{100}{100-87.5}\right)}{0.3}$$

$$t_{87.5\%} = \frac{t_{1/2}\times(\log 100 - \log 12.5)}{0.3}$$

$$= \frac{t_{1/2}(0.9)}{0.3}$$

$$= 3t_{1/2}$$

Similarly, in case of $t_{96.8\%}$,

$$t_{96.8\%} = 5t_{1/2}$$

and in case of $t_{99.9\%}$,

$$t_{99.9\%} = 10t_{1/2}$$

Thus, option (a) is correct.

14. (d) Applying first order kinetic equation,

$$t = \frac{2.303}{k}\log\frac{a}{(a-x)}$$

$$k = 15\times10^{-3}\ \text{s}^{-1},\ a = 5\ \text{g},$$

$$a - x = 3\ \text{g}$$

$$t = \frac{2.303}{15\times10^{-3}}\log\frac{5}{3} = 34.07\ \text{s}$$

15. (b) The given cell is an electrolytic concentration cell.

$$E_{\text{cell}} = E^{\circ}_{\text{cell}} - \frac{0.059}{n_{\text{cell}}}\log\frac{(C)_{\text{anode}}}{(C)_{\text{cathode}}}$$

$$0.0295 = 0 - \frac{0.059}{n_{\text{cell}}}\log\frac{0.01}{0.1}$$

$$n_{\text{cell}} = -\frac{0.059}{0.0295}\times(-1) = +2$$

Thus, charge on mercurous ion is + 2. In mercurous ion Hg is present as $Hg^+—Hg^+$.

Therefore, in Hg^+ the unpaired electron is zero. So, the magnetic moment in mercurous ion will be zero.

16. (c) Phenol on oxidation with $K_2S_2O_8$ yields quinol and with $KMnO_4$, *meso*-tartaric acid is produced.

Phenol on oxidation with $KClO_3$ and HCl give chloranil.

$$\text{Phenol} \xrightarrow[\text{HCl}]{KClO_3\,+} \text{Chloranil}$$

17. (a) Anti to Markovnikov's hydration occurs by hydroboration-oxidation of alkenes and results in formation of 1-propanol.

$$CH_3CH{=}CH_2 \xrightarrow[\text{(ii) } H_2O_2/OH^-]{\text{(i) } B_2H_6} \underset{\text{1-propanol}}{CH_3CH_2CH_2OH}$$

Other three hydration will lead to Markovnikov's hydration, i.e.

$$CH_3CH{=}CH_2 \longrightarrow \underset{\text{2-propanol}}{CH_3CHOHCH_3}$$

18. (c) In gaseous and liquid phase, the structure of PCl_5 is trigonal bipyramidal and its hybridisation is sp^3d.

Cl, Axial bond, 90°, Cl, P, 120°, Equatorial bond, Cl

Due to presence of longer and weaker axial bonds, PCl_5 is a reactive molecule.

19. (a) $K_2Cr_2O_7$ act as strong oxidising agent. When it is treated with acid H_2SO_4 then $Cr_2(SO_4)_3$ formed.

$$K_2Cr_2O_7 + 4H_2SO_4 \longrightarrow K_2SO_4 + Cr_2(SO_4)_3 + 4H_2O + 3[O]$$

20. (c) The most stable state of Ce is + 3. Thus, Ce^{4+} is good oxidising agent because it can readily change to the most stable + 3 oxidation state by gaining one electron.

21. (d) In $[Cu(NH_3)_4]^{2+}$, Cu^{2+} is dsp^2- hybridised. Hence, structure is square planar.

In Cu^+ state, one e^- is unpaired. Thus, it is paramagnetic.

22. (c) (A) is true but (R) is false but ability of CO to accept electron density back into its empty π-orbitals is known as π acidity and such ligand are called π acceptor.

Back donation of electron density stabilise the metal-ligand (CO) bonding.

23. (b)

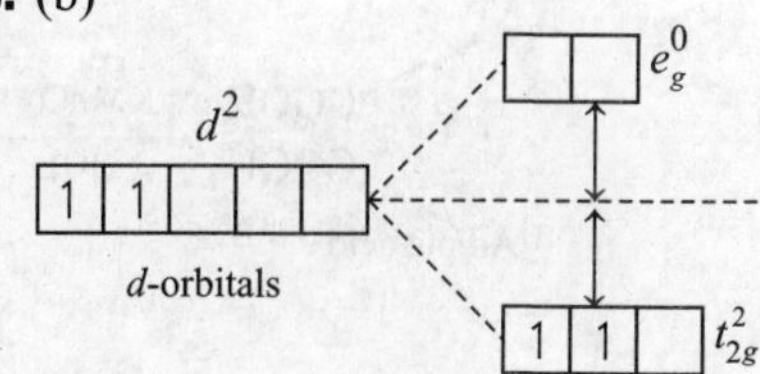

$\mu = \sqrt{n(n+2)}$ BM (n = unpaired e^-)

$= \sqrt{2(2+2)}$

$= 2.82$ BM

24. (c) Statements given in A, C, D and E are correct. While B is incorrect. Its correct form is

DDT was the first chlorinated insecticide.

25. (a) I_2O_5 is very good oxidising agent and it is used for the estimation of carbon monoxide.

$$5CO + I_2O_5 \longrightarrow 5CO_2 + I_2$$

$$I_2 + 2Na_2S_2O_3 \longrightarrow 2NaI + Na_2S_4O_6$$

26. (d) Statement (d) is incorrect. On strong heating H_2SO_4 dissociates into SO_3 and H_2O.

$$H_2SO_4 \rightleftharpoons H_2O + SO_3$$

27. (c) Statements (a), (b) and (d) are correct but statement (c) is incorrect because oxygen is electronegative element therefore, it shows -1 oxidation state (generally) and $+2$ oxidation state in OF_2.

Electronegativity decreases down the group thus, stability of -2 oxidation state decreases.

Therefore, other elements except S do not show negative oxidation state and exhibit $+2$, $+4$ and $+6$ oxidation states generally.

28. (d) The iodination of alkanes is reversible and is done by heating with conc. HNO_3, HIO_4 or HIO_3.

The function of using such reagent is to oxidise HI formed during the reaction to iodine.

Hence, reaction shifts the equilibrium in the forward direction.

$$CH_4 + I_2 \xrightleftharpoons{\text{Heat}} CH_3I + HI$$

$$5HI + HIO_3 / HIO_4 \longrightarrow 3I_2 + 3H_2O$$

29. (d) Both Statement I and Statement II are correct.

30. (a) Both (A) and (R) are true and (R) is the correct explanation of (A).

31. (a) The complete reaction sequence is as follows

Cyclohexanone $\xrightarrow[\text{[H]}]{\text{LAH}}$ Cyclohexanol (A) $\xrightarrow[-H_2O]{H^+, \text{ Conc. } H_2SO_4}$ Cyclohexene (B) $\xrightarrow[\text{[O]}]{KMnO_4/H^+}$ Adipic acid (HOOC–$(CH_2)_4$–COOH)

32. (b) All statements except (b) are true.

$$3°\text{alcohol} \xrightarrow[HCl]{ZnCl_2} \text{Milky colour}$$

Tertiary alcohol gives milky colour with Lucas reagent.

$$\underset{1°}{R-CH_2-OH} \xrightarrow[\text{(ii) } AgNO_3 \text{ (iii) } HNO_2 \text{ (iv) KOH}]{\text{(i) } P/I_2} \text{Blood red colour}$$

$$\underset{2°}{R_2CH-OH} \xrightarrow[\text{(ii) } AgNO_3 \text{ (iii) } HNO_3 \text{ (iv) KOH}]{\text{(i) } P/I_2} \text{Blue colour}$$

$$\underset{3°}{R_3C-OH} \xrightarrow[\text{(ii) } AgNO_3 \text{ (iii) } HNO_3 \text{ (iv) KOH}]{\text{(i) } P/I_2} \text{Colourless}$$

33. (c) Statement (c) is incorrect because in first ten members of homologous series an alternation effect is observed, in which, even number of C-atoms fit better in crystal lattice of carboxylic acids have higher melting point (terminal groups are on opposite side).

In odd number of C-atoms, they fit poorly in crystal lattice and have lower melting point (terminal groups are on same side).

34. (a) Carboxylic acids that have lower value of pK_a are more acidic.

Acidic nature is affected by the presence of EWG.

Correct order of acidity is as follows

$CF_3COOH > CHCl_2COOH >$
$NO_2CH_2COOH > FCH_2COOH$

35. (a) In esterification reaction,

—OH is removed from carboxylic acid and H^+ ion remove from alcohol and form final product ester.

$$R-\underset{\parallel}{\overset{}{C}}(=O)-\overset{18}{O}-H + R'-OH \longrightarrow R-C(=O)-O-R' + H_2\overset{18}{O}$$

36. (c) The correct match is A-IV, B-I, C-II, D-III.

A. $CH_3CH_2OH \xrightarrow[180°C]{H_2SO_4} CH_2=CH_2 + H_2O$ Ethene (IV)

B. $CH_3CH_2OH \xrightarrow[\text{Red P reduction}]{HI} CH_3-CH_3 + H_2O$ Ethane (I)

C. $C_2H_5OH \xrightarrow[413\text{ K}]{H_2SO_4} C_2H_5OC_2H_5$ Diethyl ether (II)

D. $C_2H_5OH \xrightarrow[\text{[O]}]{KMnO_4} CH_3CHO$ Acetaldehyde (III)

37. (b)

Phthalimide (NH) $\xrightarrow[-H_2O]{KOH}$ Potassium phthalimide (NK) $\xrightarrow[DMF]{R—X}$ N-alkylphthalimide (NR) + KX

N-alkylphthalimide (NR) $\xrightarrow[\text{hydrolysis}]{\text{2NaOH, Alkaline}}$ Sodium phthalate ($C—\overset{-\ +}{ONa}$, $C—\overset{-\ +}{ONa}$) + $R—NH_2$ (1° amine) (P)

Primary aromatic amines cannot be prepared by this.

38. (d) Both Statement I and Statement II are correct. Due to Hofmann bromamide degradation reaction one C decreases in the product.

$$C_6H_5—\underset{\underset{O}{\|}}{C}—NH_2 + Br_2 + 4KOH \xrightarrow{343\text{ K}} C_6H_5—NH_2 + 2KBr + K_2CO_3 + 2H_2O$$

Benzamide → Aniline

39. (a) $CH_3—CH{=}CH—CH_3 + HCl \longrightarrow$

$$CH_3—CH_2—\underset{\underset{Cl}{|}}{CH}—CH_3 \xrightarrow{NH_3} CH_3—CH_2—\underset{\underset{NH_2}{|}}{CH}—CH_3$$

40. (a) $C_6H_5—CH_2—NH_2 \xrightarrow{\text{(i) } HNO_2/HCl}$

$$C_6H_5—CH_2—\overset{+}{N_2}Cl^- \xrightarrow[-HCl]{\text{(ii) } H_2O, 278\text{ K}} C_6H_5—CH_2—OH$$

Benzylic alcohol

41. (d) Pepsin (enzyme *A*) converts protein into polypeptides. These polypeptides are further converted to amino acids by action of trypsin (enzyme *B*).

42. (b)

α-D(+)-glucose (ring structure: CH_2OH; H, H; OH, OH; H, OH; H, OH)

Glucose has many isomers β-D glucose is also an isomer of glucose.

43. (d) N_2O_5 has one N—O—N bond

N_2O_5: O=N(–O⁻)–O–N(=O)–O⁻, N–O–N angle 112°, Planar

Structure of other given nitrogen compounds are as follows

(a) N_2O_3: $^-O—\overset{+}{N}(=O)—N{=}O$

(b) N_2O_4: $(O^-)(O{=})\overset{+}{N}—\overset{+}{N}(=O)(O^-)$

(c) N_2O: $N^-{=}N^+{=}O$

44. (b) $CH_3—\underset{\underset{OH}{|}}{\overset{\overset{CH_3}{|}}{C}}—CH_2—CH_3 \xrightarrow[\text{substitution reaction } —SO_2, —HCl]{\text{(i) } SOCl_2\text{, Nucleophilic}}$

2-methyl butane 2-ol

$$CH_3—\underset{\underset{Cl}{|}}{\overset{\overset{CH_3}{|}}{C}}—\underset{\underset{H}{|}}{CH}—CH_3 \xrightarrow{\text{(ii) Alc. KOH}} CH_3—\underset{\underset{OH}{|}}{\overset{\overset{CH_3}{|}}{C}}—\underset{\underset{H}{|}}{CH}—CH_3$$

$$\xrightarrow[\text{(Accordingly to Saytzeff rule)}]{\text{Elimination reaction}} CH_3—\overset{\overset{CH_3}{|}}{C}{=}CH—CH_3$$

2-methyl but-2-ene

45. (d) Correct order of reactivity of H*X* is HI > HBr > HCl > HF.

It is because of the fact that the bond dissociation energy of HI is less than that of HBr, which is less than that of HCl and HF.

NK01 NEET Knock Offs

1. (a) According to law of conservation of mass,

Mass of reactants = Mass of products

$15.7 + 4.3 = 8.1 + \text{Mass of } BaSO_4$

$\therefore \text{Mass of } BaSO_4 = 11.9 \text{ g}$

2. (d) Degree of dissociation is given by

$$\alpha = \frac{\Lambda_c}{\Lambda_m^\circ}$$

Further, we name to calculate $\Lambda^\circ_{m(CH_3COOH)}$

$$\Lambda^\circ_{(CH_3COOH)} = \Lambda^\circ_{(CH_3COO^-)} + \Lambda^\circ_{(H^+)}$$

$$= 40.9 + 349.8$$

$$= 390.7 \ \Omega^{-1} \text{ cm}^2/\text{mol}$$

Degree of dissociation at $C = 0.1$ M

$$\alpha = \frac{\Lambda_m}{\Lambda_m^\circ} = \frac{5.20}{390.7} = 0.013 \text{ or } 1.3\%$$

Degree of dissociation at $C = 0.001$ M

$$\alpha = \frac{\Lambda_m}{\Lambda_m^\circ} = \frac{49.2}{390.7}$$

$$= 0.125 \text{ or } 12.5\%$$

3. (c) Complex (*c*) gives *fac-mer* isomer.

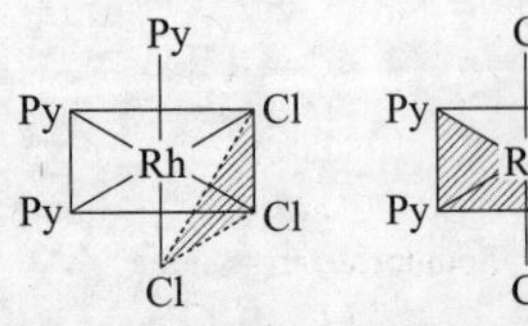

facial or *fac* isomer   meridional or *mer* isomer

4. (c) Ag—O bond is covalent in nature, the lone pair of nitrogen attacks on carbon and nitroalkane is obtained.

$$R{-}X + Ag\ddot{N}O_2 \longrightarrow \underset{(P)}{R{-}NO_2} + AgX$$

K—O bond is ionic in nature ($K^+ \bar{O}NO$). Therefore, $\bar{O}NO$ nucleophile attacks on carbon atom and alkyl nitrite is obtained.

$$R{-}X + K{-}\ddot{O}{-}N{=}O \longrightarrow K{-}X + \underset{(Q)}{R{-}O{-}N{=}O}$$

5. (d)

$$CH_2{=}CH_2 \xrightarrow{O_3} \text{(ozonide)} \xrightarrow{H_2O} HCOOH + HCOOH$$

Reductive hydrolysis of ozonide with Zn dust gives carbonyl compound whereas oxidative hydrolysis yields carboxylic acid.

6. (a) $H_2O(l) \longrightarrow H_2O(g)$

$\Delta H = 41$ kJ/mol

$\Delta H = \Delta U + \Delta n_g RT$

or $\Delta U = \Delta H - \Delta n_g RT$

$\Delta n_g = 1 - 0 = 1, R = 8.314,$

$T = 373$ K

$\Delta U = 41 - (1 \times 8.314 \times 373 \times 10^{-3})$

$= 37.9$ kJ/mol

7. (c) $v = \frac{c}{\lambda} = 3.29 \times 10^{15} \left[\frac{1}{(3)^2} - \frac{1}{(n)^2}\right]$

$$\frac{3 \times 10^8}{1000 \times 10^{-9}} = 3.29 \times 10^{15} \left(\frac{1}{9} - \frac{1}{n^2}\right)$$

$$\left(\frac{1}{9} - \frac{1}{n^2}\right) = 0.0912$$

$$\Rightarrow \frac{1}{n^2} = \frac{1}{9} - 0.0912$$

$$\frac{1}{n^2} = 0.0200$$

$$\Rightarrow n = 7$$

8. (d) Statements (a), (b) and (c) are correct.

- In acidic medium, $K_2Cr_2O_7$ exists as $Cr_2O_7^{2-}$ hence produces orange colour. In basic medium, it exists as CrO_4^{2-} ion and produces yellow colour.
- Ce^{4+} tends to go over to +3 state by undergoing reduction, hence it acts as oxidising agent, whereas Sm^{3+} tends to go over +3 state by oxidation. So, it is a reducing agent.
- Cu^+ ion is less stable than Cu^{2+} in aqueous solution, hence it gives disproportionation reaction.
- Statement (d) is incorrect, because $La(OH)_3$ is stronger base than $Lu(OH)_3$ because ionisation energy increases from La to Lu and basic strength decreases.

9. (c) The given reactions are

$$Zn + 2HCl \longrightarrow ZnCl_2 + H_2 \uparrow$$

$$3H_2 + N_2 \longrightarrow 2NH_3$$

From the equation, it is clear that 2 moles of NH_3 requires 3 moles of H_2 and 1 mole of H_2 requires 1 mole of Zn.

3 moles of H_2 require 3 moles of Zn.

Thus, 2 moles of NH_3 requires 3 moles of Zn $= 3 \times 65$ g of Zn

$\therefore$ 4 moles of NH_3 require

$$= \frac{3 \times 65}{2} \times 4 = 390 \text{ g of Zn}$$

10. (b) Both (A) and (R) are true but (R) is not the correct explanation of (A).

Reactivity of carbonyl groups depends upon the nature of attached group towards nucleophilc addition reaction because nucleophile are strongly attracted by greater positive charge on carbonyl C-atom.

Acetaldehyde is more reactive towards nucleophilic addition reaction in compare to acetone due to less positive inductive effect.

11. (a) As we increases the negative charge for isoelectronic ions, the size of anions also increases.

$Cl^{\ominus}$ ($18\,e^-$) has larger size than F^- ($10\,e^-$).

Correct increasing order of ionic size is

$$\underset{(10\,e^-)}{F^-} < \underbrace{Cl^- < S^{2-} < P^{3-}}_{(18\,e^-)}$$

So, the correct order is D < A < C < B.

12. (a) Boric acid is a weak monobasic acid. It is not a protonic acid but it accepts electron so, acts as Lewis acid.

$$B(OH)_3 + 2HOH \longrightarrow [B(OH)_4]^- + H_3O^+$$

13. (b) The correct match is A-II, B-III, C-IV, D-I.

A. $O{=}\overset{+6}{Br}(=O)_2{-}\overset{+4}{Br}(=O)_2{-}\overset{+6}{Br}(=O)_2{=}O$ (Br_3O_8)

B. $^-O{-}\overset{+5}{S}(=O)_2{-}\overset{(0)}{S}{-}\overset{(0)}{S}{-}\overset{+5}{S}(=O)_2{-}O^-$ $(S_4O_6^{2-})$

C. $\overset{(0)}{O}{=}\overset{+2}{C}{=}\overset{(0)}{C}{=}\overset{+2}{C}{=}\overset{(0)}{O}$ (C_3O_2)

D. $\overset{+6}{Cr}$ with one $\overset{-2}{O}$ (double bond) and two peroxo groups ($\overset{-1}{O}-\overset{-1}{O}$) (Cr = +6)

Thus, option (b) is correct.

14. (c) Down the group, basic character of hydroxide and oxide increases.

Thus, $Ln(OH)_3$ and Ln_2O_3 are basic.

So, the incorrect match is given in option (c).

15. (d) N_2^{2-} and N_2^+ have 16 and 13 electrons respectively, therefore bond order will be changed.

Thus, bond length will also be changed.

Bond order,

$$N_2^{2-}(B.O.) = \frac{10-6}{2} = 2$$

$$N_2^{+}(B.O.) = \frac{9-4}{2} = 2.5$$

So, both have different bond length.

$$N_2^- (B.O.) = \frac{10-5}{2} = 2.5$$

$$O_2^+ (B.O.) = \frac{10-5}{2} = 2.5$$

Thus, both have same bond order and bond length.

$$F_2 (B.O.) = \frac{10-8}{2} = 1$$

$$O_2^{2-} (B.O.) = \frac{10-8}{2} = 1$$

Thus, both have same bond order and bond length.

$$CO (B.O.) = \frac{10-4}{2} = 3$$

$$N_2(B.O.) = \frac{10-4}{2} = 3$$

Thus, both have same bond order and bond length.

Therefore, option (d) is correct.

16. (d) Both Statement I and Statement II are correct.

17. (b) Statements (B), (D) and (E) are correct while (A) and (C) statements are incorrect.

Corrected form are as follows

A. Ostwarld's theory is related to dilute solutions that relates the degree of ionisation with concentration.

C. Maxwell's theory is related to gases.

18. (d) Option (d) is correct because HNO_3 is stronger acid than HNO_2 due to easily releasing protons.

The other statements in the correct form are

- H_2SO_3 is a stronger acid than H_3PO_3 due to greater electronegativity of S atom and higher oxidation state.
- HF is a weaker acid than HCl due to higher dissociation energy of H—F bond and molecular association due to H-bonding.
- $HClO_4$ is a stronger acid than $HClO_3$ due to higher oxidation state.

19. (b) Alkene is obtained as the final product.

$$CH_3{-}\underset{CH_3}{\overset{CH_3}{C}}{-}Br$$

3°alkyl bromide

$$+ Na^+O^-{-}\underset{CH_3}{\overset{CH_3}{C}}{-}CH_3 \xrightarrow[(E2)]{-NaBr}$$

Sodium *tert*-butoxide

$$CH_3{-}\underset{CH_3}{C}{=}CH_2$$

2-methylpropene

tert-butyl bromide gives elimination reaction (E2) in presence of *tert*-butoxide (act as base).

In this reaction, ether product will not be obtained.

Therefore, option (b) is correct.

20. (a) When aqueous solution of NaCl is electrolysed, there is a competition between the following reduction reactions at cathode.

$Na^+ + e^- \longrightarrow Na;\quad E^\circ_{cell} = -2.71\,V$

$H^+ + e^- \longrightarrow \frac{1}{2}H_2;\quad E^\circ_{cell} = 0.00\,V$

The reaction with higher value of E° is preferred and therefore, the second reaction occurs at cathode, i.e. H^+ is reduced instead of Na^+.

21. (c) Graphite, potassium and calcium all three are electrical conductor except diamond which is an insulator of electric current.

22. (c) The given values are

$w_B = 3.24\,g,\ w_A = 40\,g$

$\Delta T_b = 0.81\,K,$

$K_b = 2.53\,K\,kg/mol$

Using formula,

$$M_B = \frac{K_b \times 1000 \times w_B}{\Delta T_b \times w_A}$$

On substituting all the values, we get

$$M_B = \frac{2.53 \times 1000 \times 3.24}{0.81 \times 40}$$

$= 253\,g/mol$

Let the molecular formula of sulphur $= S_x$

Atomic mass of sulphur $= 32\,g/mol$

Molecular mass $= 32 \times x\,g/mol$

$32x = 253$

$x = \frac{253}{32} = 7.91 \simeq 8$

Molecular formula of sulphur $= S_8$

23. (d) $N{\equiv}N + \frac{1}{2}(O{=}O)(g) \longrightarrow \overset{-}{N}{=}\overset{+}{N}{=}O(g)$

$\Delta H^\ominus$ = (Energy required to break the bonds) – (Energy released in forming the bonds)

$= \Delta_{N\equiv N}H^\ominus + \frac{1}{2}\Delta_{O=O}H^\ominus - (\Delta_{N=N}H^\ominus + \Delta_{N=O}H^\ominus)$

$= \left(946 + \frac{1}{2} \times 498\right) - (418 + 607)$

$= (1195 - 1025)$

$= 170\,kJ/mol$

Observed value of $\Delta H^\ominus$ of N_2O $= 82\,kJ/mol$

Resonance energy

= (Observed value of ΔH_f°) – (Expected value of ΔH_f°)

$= 82 - 170 = -88\,kJ/mol.$

24. (c) Number of electrons in ClO_2^- $= 17 + 16 + 1 = 34$ electrons

Number of electrons in ClF_2^+ $= 17 + 18 - 1 = 34$ electrons

Hence, ClO_2^- and ClF_2^+ are isoelectronic species.

25. (c) According to Fajans' rule, the polarising power and covalent character depends on greater charge on ions and size of the ions (smaller size of cation and larger size of anion).

(i) Here, all anions are same i.e. Cl^- anion, hence the covalent character will be decided by polarising power of cation.

$Fe^{2+},\ Sn^{2+},\ \underset{\substack{\uparrow \\ \text{Maximum charge}}}{Al^{3+}},\ Mg^{2+}$

Out of the above ions Al^{3+} has maximum charge and polarising power, hence maximum covalent character.

26. (b) Ti and Hf do not have similar atomic radii, but Zr and Hf have similar radii due to lanthanoid contraction.

Thus, statement (b) is incorrect while the other given statements are correct.

27. (c) The half-cell reaction of the calomel electrode is

$2Hg(l) + 2Cl^-(aq) \longrightarrow Hg_2Cl_2(s) + 2e^-$

$$E = E^\circ - \frac{0.0591}{2}\log\frac{1}{[Cl^-]^2}$$

$E = E^\circ + 0.0591 \log [Cl^-]$

Thus, plot of E *vs* $\log Cl^-$ is linear with a positive slope (i.e. E increase linearly with $\log [Cl^-]$).

28. (a) Moles of NaOH

$$= \frac{\text{Mass of NaOH}}{\text{Molecular mass of NaOH}}$$

$= \frac{0.4}{40} = 0.01\,mol$

$[OH^-] = [NaOH] = \frac{0.01}{1} = 10^{-2}$

$pOH = -\log[OH^-]$

$= -\log[10^{-2}] = 2$

29. (c) Reactions in which the same substance is oxidised as well as reduced are called disproportionation reactions. Hence, reactions (i), (iv), (v) and (vii) are disproportionation reaction.

30. (d) Both Statement I and Statement II are correct.

$$\underset{\text{(Propene)}}{CH_2{=}CH{-}CH_3} + Br_2 \xrightarrow{800\,K} \underset{\text{(Allyl bromide)}}{\underset{\displaystyle Br}{\underset{|}{CH_2}}{-}CH{=}CH_2} + HBr$$

(i) $Br_2 \xrightarrow{800\,K} 2\dot{B}r$

(ii) $CH_2=CH-CH_2-H \xrightarrow{800\ K} CH_2=CH-\dot{C}H_2$

$\xrightarrow{+HBr}$ $[CH_2=CH-\dot{C}H_2 \longleftrightarrow$ (I) Allylic free radical

$\dot{C}H_2-CH=CH_2]$ (II) Resonance stabilised

(iii) $\dot{C}H_2-CH=CH_2 + Br_2 \longrightarrow \underset{Br}{CH_2}-CH=CH_2$ (Allyl bromide)

31. (c) The molecular formula of an alkane is C_nH_{2n+2}.
Let, the molecular formula of the given alkane be C_xH_{2x+2}.
Molecular mass would be
$=12\times x+1\times(2x+2)=14x+2$
But molecular mass = 86
$\Rightarrow \quad 14x+2=86$
$\Rightarrow \quad x=6$
So, alkane is C_6H_{14}.
Possible structural isomers of C_6H_{14} are

I. $CH_3-CH_2-CH_2-CH_2-CH_2-CH_3$ (Hexane)

II. $CH_3-CH_2-CH_2-\underset{CH_3}{CH}-CH_3$ (2-methylpentane)

III. $CH_3-CH_2-\underset{CH_3}{CH}-CH_2-CH_3$ 3-methylpentane

IV. $CH_3-CH_2-\underset{CH_3}{\overset{CH_3}{C}}-CH_3$ (2, 2-dimethylbutane)

V. $CH_3-\underset{CH_3}{CH}-\underset{CH_3}{CH}-CH_3$ (2, 3-dimethylbutane)

32. (b) Option (b) is correct, final product *trans*-alkene is obtained.

$C_6H_5-C\equiv CH \xrightarrow[NH_3]{NaNH_2} C_6H_5-C\equiv\overset{+}{C}-\overset{-}{N}a \xrightarrow[-NaI]{CH_3-I} C_6H_5-C\equiv C-CH_3$ 1-phenyl prop-1-yne (*A*)

$\xrightarrow{Na/NH_3\,(l)}$ Birch reduction (*trans* addition of hydrogen)

$\overset{C_6H_5}{H}>C=C<\overset{H}{CH_3}$ *trans*-1-phenyl prop-1-ene (*B*)

33. (d) If $P<\Delta_o$ low spin state is more stable. Hence, (a) is incorrect.
CO is very strong ligand. Thus, statement (b) is also incorrect.
The colour of complex depends on number of unpaired electrons or transition electrons. So, statement (c) is incorrect.
CFSE of tetrahedral species is $\frac{4}{9}\Delta_o$ So, that is approximately 50%. Hence, option (d) is correct.

34. (a) $\underset{\text{Glucose}}{C_6H_{12}O_6} \xrightarrow{\text{Zymase}} \underset{\text{Ethanol}}{2C_2H_5OH} + 2CO_2$

35. (c) $CH_3CH_2I \xrightarrow{NaCN} \underset{(A)}{CH_3CH_2CN} \xrightarrow{\overset{-}{O}H} \underset{(B)}{CH_3CH_2CONH_2} \xrightarrow{Br_2/NaOH} \underset{(C)}{CH_3CH_2NH_2}$

36. (d) All statements about PH_3 are correct except (V).
I. $\underset{\text{Calcium phosphide}}{Ca_3P_2} + 6H_2O \longrightarrow 2PH_3 + 3Ca(OH)_2$
II. PH_3 explodes in contact with traces of oxidising agent like HNO_3, Cl_2 and Br_2 vapours.
III. $4PH_3 \xrightarrow{\Delta} P_4 + 6H_2$
IV. PH_4^+ is tetrahedral, while PH_3 is pyramidal thus, bond angle of PH_4^+ is greater than PH_3.
V. PH_3 is a highly toxic and flammable gas.

37. (c) $CuSO_4 + 4NH_3 \longrightarrow CuSO_4.4NH_3$
or $[Cu(NH_3)_4]SO_4$
Coordination number = 4
$[Cu(NH_3)_4]^{2+}$ shows hybridisation = dsp^2
Thus, it is a square planar complex having one unpaired electron present in orbitals. So, it is paramagnetic in nature.
Hence, option (c) is correct.

38. (c) The multimolecular reactions are quite rare in comparison with bimolecular reactions because at normal pressure, triple collisions are much less frequent than double ones.
Thus, (A) is true but (R) is false.

39. (a) When carboxylic acid reacts with R'—OH, then ester compound is obtained in which OH^- part is removed from carboxylic acid and H (of OH) is removed from alcohol in presence of acidic medium.

$CH_3-CH_2-\overset{O}{\overset{\|}{C}}-OH + R'-\overset{18}{O}-H \underset{H_2SO_4}{\overset{\text{Esterification reaction}}{\rightleftharpoons}} CH_3-CH_2-\underset{O}{\underset{\|}{C}}-\overset{18}{O}-R' + H_2O$

40. (d) The reaction of HCl with Na_2CO_3 is as follows,
$2HCl + Na_2CO_3 \longrightarrow 2NaCl + H_2O + CO_2$
As we know that
M_{eq} of HCl = M_{eq} of Na_2CO_3
$$\frac{25}{1000}\times 1\times M_{HCl} = \frac{30}{1000}\times 0.1\times 2$$
$$M_{HCl} = \frac{6}{25}M$$
Now, the reaction of HCl with NaOH is as follows
$NaOH + HCl \longrightarrow NaCl + H_2O$

Also, M_{eq} of HCl = M_{eq} of NaOH

$$\frac{6}{25}\times 1\times\frac{V}{1000}=\frac{30}{1000}\times 0.2\times 1$$

$$V=25\text{ mL}$$

41. (c) For two miscible liquids,

p_{total} = Mole fraction of $A\times p_A^\circ$ + Mole fraction of $B\times p_B^\circ$

Number of moles of

$$A=\frac{28}{140}=0.2\text{ moles}$$

Liquid B is water, its mass is

$$(100-28)=72\text{ g}$$

Number of moles of

$$B=\frac{72}{18}=4.0\text{ moles}$$

Total number of moles

$$=0.2+4.0=4.2\text{ moles}$$

Given, $p_{total}=160$ mmHg

$$p_B^\circ=150\text{ mmHg}$$

$$\text{So, }160=\frac{0.2}{4.2}\times p_A^\circ+\frac{4.0}{4.2}\times 150$$

$$p_A^\circ=\frac{17.15\times 4.2}{0.2}$$

$$=360\text{ mmHg}$$

42. (c) SO_4^{2-} cannot be oxidised, since the oxidation state of +6 of S is highest.

$\therefore X$ in the above reaction cannot be SO_4^{2-}.

43. (d) Each amino acid sequence has a specific native state.

It may be noted that the relative stability of the tertiary structure depends upon the interactions between various parts of the protein molecules through the substituent present in the side chain of the constituent of amino acid.

These chains have four types of interactions as follows

I. ionic or salt-bridge

II. hydrogen bonds

III. van der Waals' interaction

IV. disulphide (S—S) bonds.

44. (b) In case of asymmetrical ketone, the point of cleavage is such that keto group stay with smaller alkyl group preferentially (Popoff's rule).

Oxidative cleavage

$$CH_3—CH_2—CH_2—\underset{\underset{O}{\|}}{C}—CH_3\xrightarrow[\Delta]{\text{Conc. }HNO_3}CH_3—CH_2—COOH+CH_3COOH$$

(Major product)

45. (d)

$$\underset{(A)}{(CH_3)_3C—COOH}\xrightarrow[\text{Heat}]{NH_3}\underset{(B)}{(CH_3)_3C—CONH_2}$$

$(B)\xrightarrow{Br_2/KOH}$ (Hofmann Bromamide reaction) $\underset{(C)}{(CH_3)_3C—NH_2}$

$(C)\xrightarrow[\text{(Carbylamine reaction)}]{CHCl_3/KOH}\underset{(D)}{(CH_3)_3C—NC}$

$(D)\xrightarrow[H_3O^+]{\text{Hydrolysis}}\underset{(E)}{(CH_3)_3C—NH_2}+HCOOH$

Hence, option (d) is correct.

NK02 NEET Knock Offs

1. (a) NaOH is a strong base, hence indicator used is phenolphthalein for acid-base titration.

2. (a) Chromyl chloride oxidises methyl group to a chromium complex which on hydrolysis gives corresponding benzaldehyde.

Toluene $\xrightarrow[CS_2]{CrO_2Cl_2}$ $C_6H_5CH(OCrOHCl_2)_2$ (Chromium complex) $\xrightarrow{H_3O^+}$ C_6H_5CHO (Benzaldehyde)

Thus, both (A) and (R) are true and (R) is the correct explanation of (A).

3. (b) According to Arrhenius equation, $k=Ae^{-E_a/RT}$

$$\log k=\log A-\frac{E_a}{2.303\times R}\times\frac{1}{T}$$

Compare it with, $y=c+mx$, equation of straight line.

The value of $\log k$ should increase uniformly with T or decrease with $\frac{1}{T}$.

Hence, the answer is (b).

4. (d) The incorrect statement is given in option (d) because $K_2Cr_2O_7$ is insoluble in alcohol and acetone.

5. (d) $[Co(en)_2Cl_2]_2SO_4$

$$2x+4(0)+4(-1)-2=0$$
$$x=+3$$

$[Co(en)_2F_2]ClO_3$

$$x+2(0)+2(-1)-1=0$$
$$x=+3$$

$[Co(NH_3)_3Cl_3]$

$$x+3(0)+(-3)=0$$
$$x=+3$$

$[Co(NH_3)_4Cl_2]SO_4$

$$x+4(0)+2(-1)-2=0$$
$$x=+4$$

Hence, only in option (d) the oxidation state of Co is not +3 while in other case it is +3.

6. (d) Both Statement I and Statement II are correct.

Aldehydes which do not have α-H atom undergoes self oxidation and reduction (disproportionation) reaction on heating with conc. alkali. This reaction is known as Cannizzaro reaction.

In this reaction, one molecule of aldehyde is reduced to alcohol, while another molecule is oxidised to salt of carboxylic acid.

$$2R\text{—}CHO \xrightarrow{\text{Conc. KOH}} R\text{—}COO^- + RCH_2OH$$

Oxidised product

Reduced product

7. (d) We know that ,

$$\log \frac{k_2}{k_1} = \frac{E_a}{2.303\,R}\left[\frac{T_2 - T_1}{T_1T_2}\right]$$

$$\Rightarrow \log \frac{4.87 \times 10^{-3}}{3.46 \times 10^{-5}} = \frac{E_a}{2.303 \times 8.314} \times \left(\frac{338-298}{338 \times 298}\right)$$

$$\Rightarrow \log 140.75 = \frac{E_a}{19.15}\left(\frac{40}{338 \times 298}\right)$$

$$E_a = \frac{\log 140.75 \times 19.15 \times 338 \times 298}{40}$$

$$= \frac{2.148 \times 19.15 \times 338 \times 298}{40}$$

$= 103580.03$ J/mol

$= 103.58$ kJ/mol

8. (c) Sets (a), (b) and (d) are correct but (c) is incorrect. It is because across a period metallic character decreases as we move from left to right.

However,within a group the metallic character increases from top to bottom. Therefore, K is expected to be most metallic and B is the least metallic.

Thus, the correct decreasing order of metallic character is

K > Mg > Al > B.

9. (c) Mohr's salt is $[FeSO_4 \cdot (NH_4)_2SO_4 \cdot 6H_2O]$

$$\underset{\text{Purple}}{2K\overset{+7}{Mn}O_4} + 8H_2SO_4 + \underset{\text{From Mohr's salt}}{10\,FeSO_4} \longrightarrow K_2SO_4 + \underset{\text{Colourless}}{2\overset{+2}{Mn}SO_4} + 5Fe_2(SO_4)_3$$

So, Mohr's salt decolourises $KMnO_4$ by reducing Mn^{7+} ions to Mn^{2+}.

10. (c) Statements (a), (b) and (d) are correct but statement (c) is incorrect, because MOT gives proper explanation about existence of species like He_2^+ and H_2^+.

11. (d) $CH_3CH_2Cl \xrightarrow{\text{NaCN}} \underset{(X)}{CH_3CH_2CN} \xrightarrow{\text{Ni/H}_2} \underset{(Y)}{CH_3CH_2CH_2NH_2} \xrightarrow[\text{anhydride}]{\text{Acetic}} \underset{(Z)}{CH_3CH_2CH_2NHCOCH_3}$

12. (c) (a) H_2O and NH_2^- have 2 lone pairs and 2 bond pairs. So, both are bent.

(b) SF_4, SeF_4 both have 4 bond pairs and 1 lone pair thus, they exhibit *see-saw* structure.

(d) XeF_2, Br_3^- both have 2 bond pairs and 3 lone pairs. So, both exhibits linear structure.

(c) XeF_2 have 2 bond pairs and 3 lone pairs while I_6^- has 5 bond pairs and one lone pair.

13. (a) Both (A) and (R) are true and (R) is the correct explanation of (A).

14. (d) Statements (a), (b) and (c) are correct but statement (d) is incorrect.

Aufbau principle states that the electrons are added progressively to the various orbitals in their order of increasing energies, starting with the orbital of lowest energy.

15. (c) The de-Broglie wavelength of an electron,

$$\lambda = \frac{h}{p} \text{ or } \frac{h}{mv}$$

But, from the Bohr's postulate of quantisation of angular momentum of electrons,

$$l = mvr = \frac{nh}{2\pi}$$

$$\therefore \quad mv = \frac{nh}{2\pi r}$$

Upon substitution,

$$\lambda = \frac{h}{\left(\frac{nh}{2\pi r}\right)} = \frac{2\pi r}{n}$$

where, r = radius of orbits in Bohr model.

$$r = \frac{n^2 a_0}{z}$$

$$\therefore \quad \lambda = \frac{2\pi \times n^2 \times a_0}{n \times z}$$

$$= \frac{2\pi n a_0}{z} = 8\pi a_0$$

[$z = 1$ for hydrogen, $n = 4$ (given)]

$\therefore \lambda = 8\pi a_0$

16. (a) NaBr is completely ionised as,

$$NaBr \longrightarrow Na^+ + Br^-$$

Concentration of Br^- ion in solution is 0.01 M or $[Br^-] = 0.01$ mol/L

The expression of K_{sp} of AgBr

$$K_{sp} = [Ag^+][Br^-]$$

$K_{sp} = 5\times10^{-13}\ mol^2\ L^{-2}$.

$[Ag^+][Br^-] = 5\times10^{-13}\ mol^2\ L^{-2}$

or $[Ag^+] = \frac{5\times10^{-13}}{[Br^-]}$

$= \frac{5\times10^{-13}\ mol^2\ L^{-2}}{0.01\ mol\ L^{-1}}$

$= 5\times10^{-11}$ mol/L

Moles of AgBr

$= 5\times10^{-11}$ mol

17. (a) Bond order ∝ bond strength

Bond order of O_2^+ is 2.5

Bond order of O_2 is 2

Bond order of O_2^- is 1.5

Bond order of O_2^{2-} is 1

Thus, O_2^+ has the strongest O—O bond among the given options.

18. (d) The balanced reaction is as follows

$$8KMnO_4 + 3NH_3 \longrightarrow 8MnO_2 + 3KNO_3 + 5KOH + 2H_2O$$

∴ x and y are respectively 8 and 3. Thus value of $x + y = 11$.

19. (d) The correct match is

A-IV, B-I, C-II, D-III.

A. $CH_3-CH(OH)-C\equiv N$ (Cyanohydrin) $\xrightarrow{H_2O/H^+}$ $CH_3-CH(OH)-COOH$ (Lactic acid)

B. $2CH_3CHO$ (Ethanal) $\xrightarrow[\text{Aldol condensation}]{\text{Dil. NaOH}}$ $CH_3-CH(OH)-CH_2-CHO$ (3-hydroxybutanal)

C. $(CH_3)_2C=O$ (Acetone) + $HO-CH_2-CH_2-OH$ (Glycol) $\xrightarrow{\text{Dry HCl}}$ $(CH_3)_2C(O-CH_2)_2$ (Cyclic ketal) $+ H_2O$

D. CH_3CHO (Acetaldehyde) + NaOCl or $(NaOH + Cl_2)$ $\longrightarrow$ $CHCl_3$ (Trichloromethane) $+ HCO\overset{-}{O}\overset{+}{Na}$

Hence, option (d) is correct.

20. (c) $:C\equiv\ddot{O}\rightarrow$ *sp*-hybridised

$H-C\equiv\ddot{N}\rightarrow$ *sp*-hybridised

CO_3^{2-} (C bonded to :O: by double bond and to two $^-$:O:) $\rightarrow$ sp^2-hybridised

$[C\equiv C]^{2-}\ Ca^{2+}$ → *sp*-hybridised

$\ddot{O}=C=\ddot{O}$ → *sp*-hybridised

21. (c) Oxalic acid is formed.

$$C_{12}H_{22}O_{11}\ (\text{Sucrose}) + 36\ HNO_3 \longrightarrow 6\ (COOH)_2\ (\text{Oxalic acid}) + 23\ H_2O + 36NO_2$$

22. (b) Incorrect statement is given in option (b) while all other are correct. Nucleotides are joined together by phosphodiester linkage between 5′ and 3′ carbon atoms of pentose sugar.

23. (b) Intermolecular force of attraction between chloroform and diethyl ether are stronger than the forces among themselves. Hence, mixture of chloroform and diethyl ether shows negative deviation. So, total vapour pressure of the mixture is less than ideal condition.

24. (a) $C_2H_5-\overset{2}{C}(=\overset{1}{C}H_2)-\overset{3}{C}H(CH_3)-\overset{4}{C}\equiv\overset{5}{C}H$

IUPAC name : 2-ethyl-3-methyl-pent-1-en-4-yne

25. (c) Isomers of $C_5H_{10}O$ (Carbonyl compound) are

I. $CH_3-CH_2-CH_2-C(=O)-CH_3$

II. $CH_3-CH_2-C(=O)-CH_2-CH_3$

III. $CH_3-CH_2-CH_2-CH_2-CHO$

IV. $CH_3-CH(CH_3)-CH_2-CHO$

V. $CH_3-C(CH_3)_2-CHO$

26. (a) Both (A) and (R) are true and (R) is the correct explanation of (A).

HF has highest boiling point among hydrogen halides because it has strongest hydrogen bonding. Here, the hydrogen bond exists between hydrogen of one molecule and fluorine atom of another molecule as shown below.

$$\ldots\overset{\delta+}{H}-\overset{\delta-}{F}\ldots\overset{\delta+}{H}-\overset{\delta-}{F}\ldots\overset{\delta+}{H}-\overset{\delta-}{F}$$

27. (c) $R-C\equiv N \xrightarrow[\text{(ii) } H_2O]{\text{(i) } SnCl_2 + HCl} R-CHO$ (Aldehyde)

$R-C\equiv N \xrightarrow[\text{(ii) } H_2O]{\text{(i) DIBAL–H (Di-}isobutyl\text{ aluminium hydride}} R-CHO$ (Aldehyde)

28. (b) The product formed in the given reaction sequence is a *tert*-butylbenzene.

$\xrightarrow[-AlCl_4^-]{AlCl_3}$ Cl, H, + 1° carbocation (less stable)

$\longrightarrow$ ⊕ 3° carbocation (more stable) $\xrightarrow{-H^+}$

tert-butylbenzene

29. (a) Among the given options, 1, 2-dibromobut-1-ene will show possess geometrical isomerism.

$H_3C—CH_2—C(Br)=C(Br)—H$ *cis*

$H_3C—CH_2—C(Br)=C(H)(Br)$ *trans*

30. (c)

5,6-diethyl-3-methyldec-4-ene

31. (c) Calculate total change in oxidation number (O.N.) of one molecule of FeS_2.

O.N increase by 1

$\overset{+2}{Fe}\overset{-1}{S_2} + O_2 \longrightarrow \overset{+3}{Fe_2}O_3 + \overset{+4}{S}O_2$

Oxidation number increase by 5 × 2

Total increase in ON $=10+1=11$

$\therefore$ Equivalent wt. = Molecular weight/11

32. (d) For the given substance, distillation under reduced pressure should be used.

33. (b)

Toluene (CH_3) $+ Br_2 \xrightarrow{h\nu}$ Benzylbromide or Bromomethyl benzene (CH_2Br) $+ HBr$

34. (a) This is Friedel-Crafts alkylation.

Benzene $+ CH_3Cl \xrightarrow{\text{Anhyd. } AlCl_3}$ Toluene (CH_3)

35. (a) Here, the resistivity,

$\rho = 5\times10^{-3}\ \Omega\text{ cm}$

$$\kappa = \frac{1}{\rho} = \frac{1}{5\times10^{-3}\ (\Omega\text{cm})}$$

$$= \frac{1}{5}\times 10^3\ \text{S cm}^{-1}$$

$$= 0.2\times10^3\text{S cm}^{-1}$$

Now, molar conductivity is given by

$$\Lambda_m = \frac{1000\times\kappa}{M}$$

$$= 10^3\times\frac{1}{5}\times10^3\times\frac{1}{0.8}$$

$$= 2.5\times10^5\ \text{S cm}^2\text{ mol}^{-1}$$

36. (a) Both (A) and (R) are true and (R) is the correct explanation of (A).

$$\Delta G = \Delta H - T\Delta S$$

At low temperature, $T\Delta S$ is small. Hence, ΔH dominates.

At high temperature, $T\Delta S$ is large, i.e. ΔS dominates the value of ΔG.

37. (c) I, II, III and V statements about lanthanoids are correct, while IV is incorrect. Its correct form is lanthanoids have low ionisation enthalpy.

38. (b) Number of moles of neon gas

$$= \frac{pV}{RT}$$

$$= \frac{1.3\times10^5\times0.6}{8.31\times200} = 46.9 \simeq 47\text{ mol}$$

Now, $\Delta q = nC_V\Delta T$

$$\text{or } \Delta T = \frac{\Delta q}{nC_V} = \frac{\frac{8360}{4.18}}{47\times3.2}$$

$$= \frac{2000}{150.4}\quad [\because 1\text{ cal} = 4.18\text{ J}]$$

$$= 13.29\text{ K} \simeq 13.3\text{ K}$$

39. (a) Complete reactions are as follows,

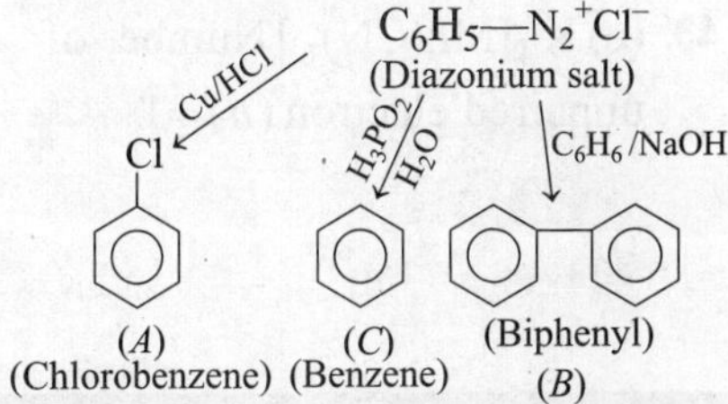

40. (d) The acidic character of non-metal oxides increases with the increase in the oxidation state of the non-metal. So, the correct order of acidic nature is,

$$\overset{+1}{N_2O} < \overset{+2}{NO} < \overset{+3}{N_2O_3} < \overset{+4}{N_2O_4} < \overset{+5}{N_2O_5}$$

Acidic character increases →

So, option (d) is incorrect.

41. (d) Both Statement I and Statement II are correct.

CH_3CH_2OH (Ethanol) $+ SOCl_2$ (Thionyl chloride) $\xrightarrow{\text{Pyridine}}$

$CH_3CH_2—Cl$ (1-chloroethane) $+ SO_2\uparrow + HCl\uparrow$

Mechanism $CH_3-CH_2-\ddot{O}H + S^{\delta+}(=O^{\delta-})(Cl)(Cl) \longrightarrow$

$CH_3CH_2-\overset{+}{O}(H)-S(-O^-)(Cl)-Cl$

$\longrightarrow CH_3-CH_2-\overset{\oplus}{O}(H)-S(=O)-Cl \xrightarrow{-H^+}$

$CH_3-CH_2-Cl + SO_2\uparrow + HCl\uparrow$

Chloroethane

This mechanism involves nucleophilic substitution (S_N1) as carbocation is formed as an intermediate in this mechanism.

42. (c) $2PH_3 \longrightarrow 2P + 3H_2$

2 mol, 100 mL → 3 mol, 150 mL

$\therefore$ There is an increase of $150 - 100 = 50$ mL.

43. (c) $K_4[Mn(CN)_6]$ Number of unpaired electron $(n) = 1$

$$\mu = \sqrt{n(n+2)}$$
$$= \sqrt{1(1+2)} = 1.73 \text{ BM}$$

$[Fe(H_2O)_6]^{2+}$ $n = 4$ electrons (unpaired)

$$\mu = \sqrt{4(4+2)} = \sqrt{24} = 4.89 \text{ BM}$$

$K_2[MnCl_4]$ $n = 5$ electrons (unpaired)

$$\mu = \sqrt{5(5+2)} = 5.91 \text{ BM}$$

44. (a) Alcohol undergoes dehydration in presence of conc. H_2SO_4 at 443 K.

$CH_3-CH_2-CH_2-OH$ (Propanol) $\xrightarrow[\text{Conc. } H_2SO_4]{443 \text{ K}} CH_2=CH-CH_3$ (Propene)

Mechanism

Step I $H_2SO_4 \rightleftharpoons H^+ + HSO_4^-$

Step II

$CH_3-CH_2-CH_2-\ddot{\underset{..}{O}}H + H^+$

$\longrightarrow CH_3-CH_2-CH_2-\overset{+}{O}H_2$

$\xrightarrow{-H_2O} CH_3-CH_2-\overset{+}{C}H_2$

$\xrightarrow{-H^+} CH_3-CH=CH_2$

Propene

45. (b) The correct match is A-IV, B-I, C-II, D-III.

A.	Spontaneous cell eaction	$\Delta G°$ is negative
B.	Electrolysis of NaCl at cathode	Hydrogen gas evolved
C.	Electrochemical cell behaves as an electrolytic cell when	$E_{ext} > E_{cell}$
D.	During charging the lead storage battery	$PbSO_4$ anode is reduced to Pb.

NK03 NEET Knock Offs

1. (c) Given, $\Delta v = 0.1\%$ of the velocity of the electron

$$= \frac{0.1}{100} \times 2.2 \times 10^6$$
$$= 2.2 \times 10^3 \text{ m/s}$$

From Heisenberg uncertainty principle

$$\Delta x . m \Delta v = \frac{h}{4\pi}$$

or

$$\Delta x = \frac{6.636 \times 10^{-34} \text{ Js}}{4 \times 3.14 \times 9.108 \times 10^{-31} \text{ kg} \times 2.2 \times 10^3 \text{ m/s}}$$
$$= 0.02634378 \times 10^{-6} \text{ m}$$
$$= 263.4378 \times 10^{-10} \text{ m}$$

Since, Δx is much larger than the atomic diameter ($\approx 10^{-10}$ m), the uncertainty principle is applicable in this case.

2. (a) The electronegativity difference between M_1 and O is 0.1 (3.5 and 3.4), which indicates M_1—O bond will be covalent. Since, O—H bond having more ionic character thus, bond will break and H^+ ion will release due to which acidic solution is formed.

Whereas, difference between electronegativity of M_2 and O bond is 2.3 (3.5 and 1.2).

Thus, M_2—OH bond will break.

Hence, solution will be basic in nature.

So, option (a) is correct.

3. (b) The neutralisation of a strong acid by a strong base is represented by

$$H^{\oplus}(aq) + OH^{\ominus}(aq) \longrightarrow H_2O(l); \quad \Delta H_1 = -55.9 \text{ kJ/mol} \quad \text{...(i)}$$

Given, $CH_3COOH + OH^- \longrightarrow CH_3COO^- + H_2O$; $\Delta H_2 = -50.6$ kJ mol ...(ii)

We have to calculate

$CH_3COOH \longrightarrow CH_3COO^- + H^+$; $\Delta H = ?$

Substract Eq. (i) from Eq. (ii) we get,

$$\Delta H = \Delta H_2 - \Delta H_1 = -50.6 - (-55.9) = 5.3 \text{ kJ/mol}$$

4. (a) $l = 0$ or s-orbital; the shape of s-orbital is spherical.

Thus, option (a) is correct.

Rest of the statements are incorrect. Their correct form are as follows

- Photons have different energies. The energy of photons depends on its frequency or wavelength.
- The frequency of X-rays is more than that of radiowaves.

5. (d) Both Statement I and Statement II are correct.

6. (c) All the pairs have approximately similar radii due to the consequence of lanthanoid contraction except option (c).

Size of Zr = Size of Hf
Size of Nb = Size of Ta
Size of Mo = Size of W
Size of Mn ≠ Size of Ni

7. (a) The correct match is A-III, B-I, C-IV, D-II.

A. 12 (1°H), 4 (2°H), 2 (3°H)

B. 15 (1°H), 4 (2°H), 1 (3°H)

C. 15 (1°H), 2 (2°H), 1 (3°H)

D. 17 (1°H), 2 (2°H), 2 (3°H)

Thus, option (a) is correct.

8. (c) The given figure is showing positive deviation from Raoult's law, $p_A > p_A^\circ x_A$.

Thus, A—B attractive force are weaker than A—A and B—B attractive forces.

9. (c) (A) is true but (R) is false because Cr—O—Cr bond in the middle is different from other O—Cr—O bond angles.

10. (c) Phenols are acidic in nature due to resonance stabilisation of phenoxide ion. Presence of electron withdrawing groups (such as $-NO_2$, $-X$, $-NR_3^+$, $-CHO$, $-COX$, $-COOR$, $-CN$) in the ring stabilise phenoxide ion and increases the acidic nature of phenols. On the other hand, presence of electron releasing group (such as $-CH_3$, $-OR$) in the ring destabilise the phenoxide ion and decreases the acidic nature of phenols.

Further, *meta*-isomer is less acidic than *p*-and *o*-isomers because it is stabilised by inductive effect only. So, the correct order is

II > IV > I > III > V.

11. (a) Net work done during the complete cycle is equal to area under the cycle is –ve if the cycle is clockwise, i.e. work is done by the gas and + ve, when cycle is anticlockwise, i.e. work is done on the gas

$$W = -p \times V = -(2p - p) \times (2V - V) = -pV$$

12. (d) $M_1V_1 + M_2V_2 = M_3V_3$ $[\because (V_3 = V_1 + V_2)]$

$M_1 = 1.0$ M, $M_2 = 0.25$ M

Let V_1 and V_2 are required.

$$(1.0 \times V_1 + 0.25 \times V_2) = 0.75\,(V_1 + V_2)$$
$$0.25V_1 = 0.5V_2$$
$$V_1 : V_2 = 2:1$$

Therefore, all (I, II, III, IV and V) are correct.

13. (d) Both Statement I and Statement II are correct. S_N2 reaction is carried out in the presence of polar aprotic solvent and this solvent does not contain acidic hydrogen.

14. (b) Since ΔG° is given, hence, the equilibrium constant under given condition

$M = P$ and $N = Q$

$$\because \quad -\Delta G^\circ = 2.303\,RT \log K$$
$$\log K = \frac{-\Delta G^\circ}{2.303\,RT}$$
$$\log K = \frac{-490}{2.303 \times 2 \times 500}$$
$$\log K = -0.213,\ K = 0.612$$

Also, at equilibrium

$$M = P,\ N = Q$$
$$K = \frac{[A][Q]}{[A][M]} = \frac{[N]^2}{[M]^2}$$

so, $\frac{[N]}{[M]} = \sqrt{K} = \sqrt{0.613} \approx 0.782$

15. (d) In weak electrolyte like CH_3COOH, degree of ionisation increases with dilution as follows

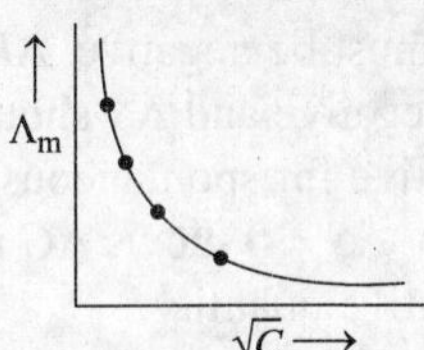

16. (c) In HOCl, oxygen is more electronegative than Cl. Hence, it will contain more s-character in hybrid orbital.

Hence, bond angle will be more than expected.

So, bond angle of HOCl is greater than HOF.

So, statement I is incorrect while statement II is correct.

17. (b) We know

$$K_p = K_C (RT)^{\Delta n} \quad \ldots(i)$$

For the reaction,

$$\Delta n = 2-(1+2)$$
$$\Delta n = -1$$

Put the value of Δn in Eq. (i)

$$K_p = K_C (RT)^{-1}$$

Given values,

$$K_p = 2.66 \times 10^{-6}$$
$$R = 0.0821 \text{ L atm/mol.K}$$
$$T = 700 \text{ K}$$
$$2.66 \times 10^{-6} = K_C \times (0.0821 \times 700)^{-1}$$
$$K_C = \frac{2.66 \times 10^{-6}}{(0.0821 \times 700)^{-1}}$$
$$K_C = 152.87 \times 10^{-5}$$
$$= 1.529 \times 10^{-3}$$

18. (c) The reaction take place as follows

$$\text{Phenyl acetic acid } (C_6H_5CH_2COOH) + \underset{\text{Hydrazoic acid}}{N_3H} \xrightarrow[\text{Heat}]{\text{Conc. } H_2SO_4} \underset{\text{Benzylamine}}{C_6H_5CH_2NH_2} + N_2 + CO_2$$

19. (b) According to Gibbs-Helmholtz reaction for spontaneity,

$$\Delta G = \Delta H - T\Delta S$$

ΔG must be negative, ΔH should be negative and ΔS should be positive for spontaneous reaction. Also, $\Delta S = 0$ shows ΔG is a negative quantity.

20. (c) Change of pressure

Δp	22	45	90
Δt	200	400	800
$\frac{\Delta p}{\Delta t}$	0.11	0.1125	0.1125

Since, the rate of change of pressure remains constant therefore, it is zero order of reaction.

The rate constant,

$$k = \frac{0.11 + 0.1125 + 0.1125}{3}$$
$$= 0.1117 \text{ torr/s}$$

21. (d) The correct match is

A-II, B-IV, C-III, D-I.

A. $p^\circ - p_s$	Lowering in vapour pressure
B. $p^\circ \times \chi_A = p_A$	Raoult's law
C. Mixture that boils like pure solvent	Azeotropic mixture
D. van't Hoff factor	Observed colligative property / Normal colligative property

Thus, option (d) is correct.

22. (b) Both (A) and (R) are true but (R) is not the correct explanation of (A).

$$3CH_3-C\equiv C-CH_3 \xrightarrow[\textit{Syn-addition}]{BH_3+THF} \left(CH_3-\underset{H}{C}=\overset{CH_3}{C}-\right)_3 B$$

$$\xrightarrow{H_2O_2/OH^-} CH_3-CH=\underset{OH}{\overset{CH_3}{C}} \xrightleftharpoons{\text{Tautomerise}} \underset{\text{Butan-2-one}}{CH_3-CH_2-\overset{O}{\overset{\|}{C}}-CH_3}$$

23. (a) Both (A) and (R) are true and (R) is the correct explanation of (A).

24. (a) Molecules II and IV show tautomerism because they have acidic H-atom (α-hydrogen) due to which they undergo proton-transfer equilibrium.

In I and III, molecules do not have α-H atom. So, they do not show tautomerism.

25. (d) H_2O_2 gives disproportionation reaction (reduction and oxidation both takes place simultaneously).

$$\overset{+1-1}{2H_2O_2} \longrightarrow \overset{+1-2}{2H_2O} + \overset{(0)}{O_2}$$

Thus, both Statement I and Statement II are correct.

26. (b) Mass of the compound $= 0.40$ g

Now, 188 g of AgBr contains Br $= 80$ g

$\therefore$ 0.3 g of AgBr contains Br

$$= \frac{80}{188} \times 0.3$$
$$= 0.127 \text{ g}$$

The percentage of Br in the organic compound

$$= \frac{0.127}{0.40} \times 100 = 31.75\%$$

27. (a) $Cu^{2+} + 2e^- \longrightarrow Cu(s)$

By using Nernst equation initially

$$E_{(Cu^{2+}/Cu)\text{ initial}} = E^\ominus_{Cu^{2+}/Cu} - \frac{0.059}{2} \log \frac{1}{[Cu^{2+}_{\text{initial}}]}$$

Given, final concentration of Cu^{2+} is $\frac{1}{10}$ of $[Cu^{2+}]$

Using Nernst equation after dilution

$$E_{(Cu^{2+}/Cu)\text{ final}} = E^\ominus_{Cu^{2+}/Cu} - \frac{0.059}{2} \log \frac{1}{[Cu^{2+}]_{\text{final}}}$$

$$\Delta E_{\text{cell}} = E_{(Cu^{2+}/Cu)\text{ final}} - E_{(Cu^{2+}/Cu)\text{ initial}}$$

$$= \frac{0.059}{2} \log \frac{1}{10} = \frac{0.059}{2} \times (-1)$$

$$= -0.0295 \text{ V}$$

Reduction potential of the electrode decreases by 0.0295 V.

28. (b) The allylic substitution can be carried out by treating the alkene with N-bromosuccinimide (NBS)

$$CH_2{=}CH{-}CH_3 + \begin{matrix} CH_2{-}CO \\ | \\ CH_2{-}CO \end{matrix}\!\!>N{-}Br \xrightarrow{h\nu} \underset{\text{Allyl bromide}}{\begin{matrix} CH_2{=}CH \\ | \\ CH_2{-}Br \end{matrix}} + \begin{matrix} CH_2{-}CO \\ | \\ CH_2{-}CO \end{matrix}\!\!>NH$$

29. (c) The given process can be carried out by enzymes pepsin and trypsin as follows

$$\text{Proteins} \xrightarrow{\text{Pepsin}} \text{Polypeptide}$$

$$\xrightarrow{\text{Trypsin}} \text{Amino acids}$$

This process involves digestion in which proteins of food material are hydrolysed to make amino acid.

30. (b)

$$SO_2Cl_2(g) \longrightarrow SO_2(g) + Cl_2(g)$$

Initial : 180   0   0

At time t : $180 - x$ x x

$$p_{\text{total}} = 180 - x + x + x = 180 + x$$

I. At $t = 240\,\text{s}$, $p_t = 244$ torr

$$\therefore \quad 180 + x = 244 \text{ torr}$$

$$x = 64$$

$$k = \frac{2.303}{240}\log\frac{a}{a-x}$$

$$= \frac{2.303}{240}\log\frac{180}{180-64}$$

$$= \frac{2.303}{240}\times 0.1909$$

$$= 0.0018\ \text{s}^{-1}$$

II. At $t = 600\,\text{s}$, $p_t = 302$ torr

$$180 + x = 302$$

$$x = 122$$

$$k = \frac{2.303}{600}\log\frac{180}{180-122}$$

$$= \frac{2.303}{600}\times 0.4918$$

$$= 0.0018\ \text{s}^{-1}$$

Since, value of k remains constant throughout the reaction.

Hence, the given reaction is of first order.

31. (a) Statements I, III, IV and V are correct but statement II is incorrect.

Each boron atom (B) is linked with four hydrogen atoms. This make tetrahedral geometry.

Hence, each boron atom is sp^3-hybridised and the B—H—B bond angle is 120°.

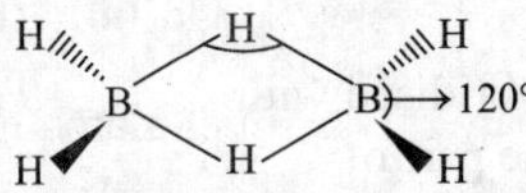

32. (b) We know that,

$$\pi = i\,CRT$$

$$4.92 = i \times 0.1 \times 0.0821 \times 300$$

$$i = 1.99$$

Degree of ionisation

$$\alpha = \frac{i-1}{n-1}$$

$$MgCl_2 \rightleftharpoons Mg^{2+} + 2Cl^-$$

$\therefore$ No. of ions dissociate $(n) = 3$

$$= \frac{1.99-1}{3-1}$$

$$= \frac{0.99}{2} = 0.49$$

Percentage of ionisation,

$$= 0.49 \times 100$$

$$(\alpha) = 49\%$$

33. (a) According to electrochemical series, correct order of reactivity is K > Mg > Zn > Cu.

34. (a) As in AsF_5 is sp^3d hybridised and geometry of the molecule is trigonal bipyramidal.

$$\begin{matrix} & F & \\ & | & \diagup F \\ F{-} & As & \\ & | & \diagdown F \\ & F & \end{matrix}$$

Here, two axial As—F bonds are formed by contribution of d_{z^2} orbital of 4d subshell of the central atom (As). Thus, 5 orbitals are used.

i.e. s, p_x, p_y, p_z and d_{z^2}

35. (d) Given,

$$\frac{k_2}{k_1} = 1.75, T_1 = 298\text{ K}, T_2 = 308\text{ K}$$

Since, temperature coefficient is the ratio of rate constant at 35°C and 25°C

$$2.303\log\frac{k_2}{k_1} = \frac{E_a}{R}\left(\frac{T_2 - T_1}{T_1T_2}\right)$$

$$2.303\log 1.75 = \frac{E_a}{1.987}\times\left(\frac{308-298}{308\times 298}\right)$$

$$E_a = \frac{2.303\times 0.243\times 308 \times 298\times 1.987}{10}$$

$$= 10.206\ \text{kcal/mol}$$

36. (b) The correct match is A-III, B-II, C-IV, D-I.

A. Helium	—	Cryogenic
B. Argon	—	Provides inert atmosphere in metallurgy
C. Neon	—	Advertising sign
D. Xenon	—	Ionisation energy is comparable to O_2

37. (d)

I. $\ddot{X}eF_5^-$ ⇒ The central atom (Xe) is sp^3d^3-hybridised with pentagonal bipyramidal geometry and Xe has two lone pairs of electrons on it.

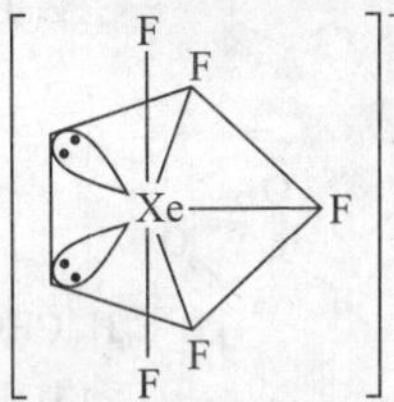

II. $\dot{B}rF_5$ ⇒ The central atom (Br) is sp^3d^2-hybridised with octahedral geometry and Br has one lone pair of electrons on it.

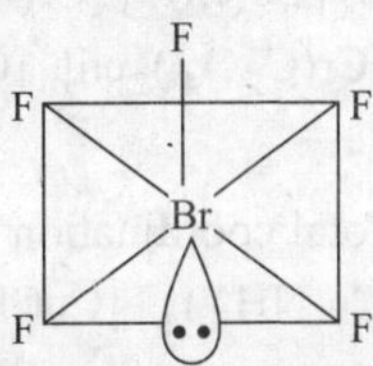

III. $:\ddot{X}eF_2$ ⇒ The central atom (Xe) is sp^3d-hybridised with trigonal bipyramidal geometry and Xe has three lone pairs of electrons on it.

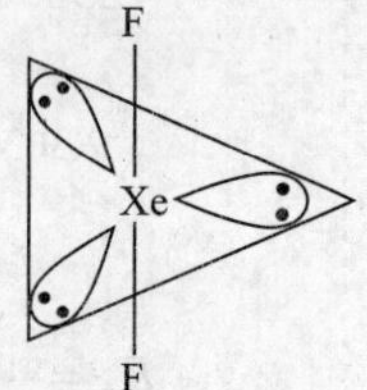

IV. $H_3\ddot{S}^+ \Rightarrow$ The central atom(s) is sp^3-hybridised with tetrahedral geometry and S has one lone pair of electrons on it.

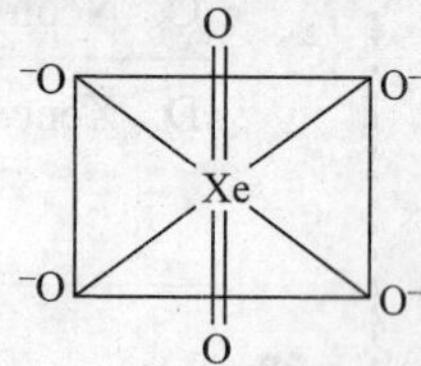

V. $XeO_6^{4-} \Rightarrow$ The central atom (Xe) is sp^3d^2-hybridised with octahedral geometry and Xe does not have lone pair of electrons on it.

So, in II and IV, their central atoms contain same number of lone pair of electrons (1 pair).

38. (c)

Cyclohexylidene–$CH-C_6H_5$ $\xrightarrow[Zn/H_2O]{O_3}$ C_6H_5CHO (A) + cyclohexanone (B)

(B) $\xrightarrow{EtOH \mid Dil.\ NaOH}$ 2-benzylidenecyclohexanone (C) + H_2O

(C) $\xrightarrow{O_3/Zn+H_2O}$ cyclohexane-1,2-dione (D) + C_6H_5CHO (A)

(D) $\xrightarrow{H_2/Pt}$ cyclohexane-1,2-diol

39. (d) $[Co(en)_3][Cr(C_2O_4)_3]$, $[Co(C_2O_4)(en)_2][Cr(C_2O_4)_2en]$, $[Cr(C_2O_4)(en)_2][Co(C_2O_4)_2en]$, $[Cr(en)_3][Co(C_2O_4)_3]$

Total coordination isomers = 4

$[Cu(NH_3)_4][CuCl_4]$, $[CuCl(NH_3)_3][CuCl_3(NH_3)_3]$

Total coordination isomers = 2

$[Ni(en)_3][Co(NO_2)_6]$, $[Ni(NO_2)_2(en)_2]$ $[Co(NO_2)_4(en)]$, $[Co(NO_2)_2(en)_2][Ni(NO_2)_4(en)]$, $[Co(en)_3][(Ni(NO_2)_2]$

Total coordination isomers = 4.

Thus, option (d) is correct.

40. (b) In the given reaction, 2-methylpropan-2-ol is obtained.

$$CH_3-\overset{O}{\overset{\|}{C}}-OC_2H_5 \xrightarrow{CH_3MgBr} CH_3-\underset{CH_3}{\underset{|}{\overset{OMgBr}{\overset{|}{C}}}}-OC_2H_5$$

$$\xrightarrow{-C_2H_5OMgBr} CH_3-\overset{O}{\overset{\|}{C}}-CH_3 \xrightarrow{CH_3MgBr} CH_3-\underset{CH_3}{\underset{|}{\overset{OMgBr}{\overset{|}{C}}}}-CH_3$$

$$\xrightarrow{H_2O/H^+} CH_3-\underset{CH_3}{\underset{|}{\overset{OH}{\overset{|}{C}}}}-CH_3$$

2-methylpropan-2-ol (tertiary alcohol) (A)

41. (a) The correct match is A-III, B-IV, C-I, D-II.

Complex ion	Oxidation Number	Colour shown
A. $[Fe(CN)_6]^{4-}$	(+2)	Diamagnetic (Yellow)
B. $[Fe(H_2O)_6]^{2+}$	(+2)	Paramagnetic (Pale green)
C. $[Cu(NH_3)_6]^+$	(+2)	Paramagnetic (Orange)
D. $[Ni(CN)_4]^{2-}$	(+2)	Diamagnetic (Colourless)

42. (c) The correct order of acidic nature is

$$CO_2 > H_2O_2 > H_2O$$

CO_2 is an acidic oxide, H_2O is neutral and H_2O_2 is more acidic than H_2O because it gives two H^+ ions/molecules whereas, H_2O gives one H^+ ion/molecule.

43. (b) $2Mg + O_2 \longrightarrow 2MgO$

$$n_{max}(Mg) = \frac{1.8/24.3}{2} = 0.037\, mol$$

$$n_{max}(O_2) = \frac{0.8/32}{1} = 0.025\, mol$$

Since, $n_{max}(Mg) > n_{max}(O_2)$, the limiting reagent is O_2

$$n_{MgO} = 2 \times n_{max}(O_2)$$
$$= 2 \times 0.025$$
$$= 0.05\, mol$$

In the combustion reaction whole O_2 will be used

Mass of Mg consumed

$$= [2 \times n_{max}(O_2)] \times 24.3\, g$$
$$= 1.215\, g$$

Mass of Mg remains unreacted

$$= (1.8 - 1.215)\, g$$
$$= 0.585\, g$$

Thus, statement (b) is incorrect.

44. (b) The reaction involved is

$$NH_4OH + CH_3COOH \rightleftharpoons CH_3COO^-NH_4^+ + H_2O$$

Before hydrolysis	2.5	2.5	0	0
After hydrolysis	0	0	2.5	2.5

In this case, pH is decided on the basis of hydrolysis of salt.

$$[CH_3COONH_4] = \frac{2.5}{100} = 2.5 \times 10^{-2}\, M$$

$\Rightarrow$ $K_a = 1.8 \times 10^{-5}$

$\therefore$ $pK_a = -\log[K_a] = 4.7 = pK_b$

$[\because K_a = K_b = 1.8 \times 10^{-5}]$

$\therefore$ $pH = 7 + \frac{1}{2}[pK_a - pK_b]$

$$= 7 + \frac{1}{2}[4.7 - 4.7] = 7 + 0 = 7$$

45. (b) Statements (a), (c) and (d) are correct, but statement (b) is incorrect, because in amylopectin α-glycosidic linkage is present.

NK04 NEET Knock Offs

1. (d) $N_{NaCl} = \frac{\text{Given mass} \times 1000}{\text{Equivalent mass} \times \text{Volume}}$

$$N_{NaCl} = \frac{3.78 \times 1000}{58.5 \times 100} = 0.646$$

Let w g of $BaCl_2$ is dissolved in 250 mL, then

$$N_{BaCl_2} = \frac{w}{\frac{208}{2} \times \frac{250}{1000}} = 0.0384\, w$$

$\therefore$ Conc. of Cl^- in both is same.

$$N_{NaCl} = N_{BaCl_2}$$
$$0.646 = 0.0384\, w$$

So, $w = 16.82\, g$

2. (d) Second ionisation enthalpies of C, N, O and F correspond to the ionisation enthalpies of C^+, N^+, O^+ and F^+ are respectively;

$$C^+ = 1s^2\, 2s^2\, 2p_x^1$$
$$N^+ = 1s^2\, 2s^2\, 2p_x^1\, 2p_y^1$$
$$O^+ = 1s^2\, 2s^2\, 2p_x^1\, 2py^1\, 2p_z^1$$
$$F^+ = 1s^2\, 2s^2\, 2p_x^2\, 2p_y^1\, 2p_z^1$$

All these ions have second shell as the outermost shell. The nuclear charge decreases in the order.

$$F^+ > O^+ > N^+ > C^+$$

Therefore, the expected order of ionisation enthalpies is

$$F^+ > O^+ > N^+ > C^+$$

O^+ has stable configuration, because it has exactly half-filled *p*-subshell. Hence, would have higher ionisation enthalpy than that of F^+.

Therefore, the decreasing order of second ionisation enthalpies of C, N, O and F is $O > F > N > C$.

3. (b) In alkaline medium ($pH > 7$), chromate ions are present, while in acidic medium ($pH < 7$), dichromate ions are present.

$$\therefore\ \underset{\text{Chromate ion}}{2CrO_4^{2-}} \xrightarrow[pH=3]{H^+} \underset{\text{Dichromate ion}}{Cr_2O_7^{2-}} \xrightarrow[pH=8]{OH^-} \underset{\text{Chromate ion}}{2CrO_4^{2-}}$$

4. (c)

$$\underset{\text{Chloroform}}{CHCl_3} + \underset{\text{Potassium hydroxide}}{3KOH} \xrightarrow{-3KCl} H-\overset{OH}{\underset{OH}{C}}-OH \xrightarrow[-H_2O]{KOH} HCO\overset{-+}{OK}$$

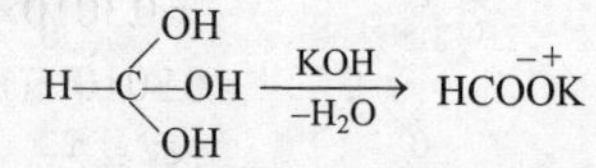

$$\xrightarrow{\text{Dil. HCl}} \underset{\text{Formic acid}}{HCOOH} + KCl$$

5. (b) Kinetic energy $= \frac{1}{2}mv^2$

$= 4.55 \times 10^{-25}$ J

$= 4.55 \times 10^{-25}$ kg m^2 s^{-2}

$\Rightarrow \quad v^2 = \frac{2 \times KE}{m}$

$\Rightarrow v^2 = \frac{2 \times 4.55 \times 10^{-25} \text{ kg m}^2 \text{ s}^{-2}}{(9.1 \times 10^{-31} \text{ kg})}$

$\Rightarrow \quad v^2 = 10^6 \text{ m}^2 \text{ s}^{-2}$

Velocity $v = (10^6 \text{ m}^2\text{s}^{-2})^{1/2}$

$= 10^3$ m/s

6. (a) We know that,

Bond order $\propto$ Bond strength

Bond order of O_2 is 2.

Bond order of N_2 is 3.

Bond order of F_2 and Cl_2 is 1.

The bond strength of F_2 is smaller than Cl_2 because the presence of 3 lone pairs around each small size F-atom cause repulsive interactions, whereas Cl has larger size. Thus, less repulsion occurs.

Therefore, the correct order of bond strength is $F_2 < Cl_2 < O_2 < N_2$.

7. (c) The correct structure of tetrathionate ion is

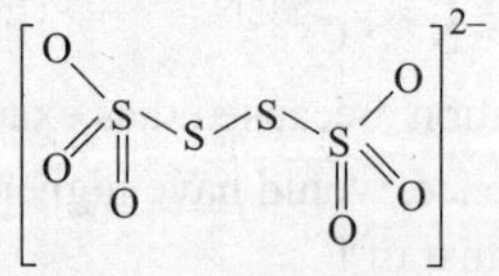

$$\left[O_2S(O)-S-S-S(O)O_2 \right]^{2-}$$

8. (b) Both (A) and (R) are true but (R) is not the correct explanation of (A). The correct reason is that F cannot show positive oxidation state of + 5 and + 7 as it is most electronegative. Hence, FO_3^- and FO_4^- are unknown.

9. (d) In BCl_3 molecule, B-atom is in sp^2-hybridised state. The three sp^2-hybrid orbitals are used to form three sigma bonds with three Cl-atom and give trigonal planar structure.

Anhydrous $AlCl_3$ exists in the form of dimer Al_2Cl_6. In Al_2Cl_6, each Al-atom is surrounded by 4 bond pairs. As a result it assumes tetrahedral shape.

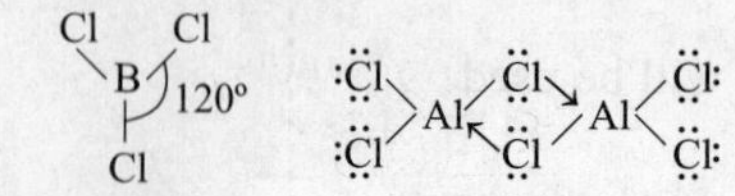

(Trigonal) Planar structure of BCl_3 (Cl–B–Cl 120°)

Dimer of Al_2Cl_6 (Tetrahedral)

Hence, both Statement I and Statement II are correct.

10. (d) The reaction takes place as follows :

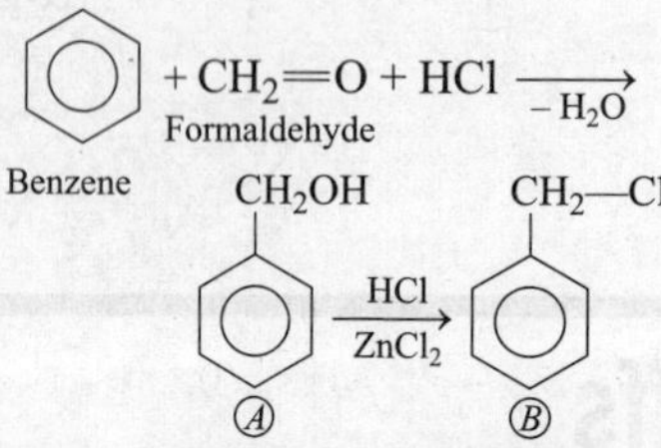

$$\underset{\text{Benzene}}{C_6H_6} + \underset{\text{Formaldehyde}}{CH_2{=}O} + HCl \xrightarrow{-H_2O} \underset{\text{Benzyl alcohol (A)}}{C_6H_5CH_2OH} \xrightarrow[ZnCl_2]{HCl} \underset{\text{Benzyl chloride (B)}}{C_6H_5CH_2{-}Cl}$$

Thus, option (d) is correct.

11. (c) Statement I is incorrect but Statement II is correct. Its correct form is :

The boiling point of NH_3 is less than SbH_3 and BiH_3. The order of boiling point is

$PH_3 > AsH_3 < NH_3 < SbH_3 < BiH_3$.

12. (b) For the reaction

$$2A \rightleftharpoons B + C$$

$K_C = 2.0 \times 10^{-3}$ given,

The reaction quotient,

$$Q_C = \frac{[B][C]}{[A]^2}$$

Substituting the values of A, B and C we get,

$$Q_C = \frac{[3 \times 10^{-4}][3 \times 10^{-4}]}{[3 \times 10^{-4}]^2} = 1$$

Since, $Q_C > K_C$, therefore, reaction will proceed in the backward direction.

13. (b) The process of evaporation is

$$\underset{18g}{H_2O\,(l)} \underset{}{\overset{\text{Vaporisation}}{\rightleftharpoons}} \underset{18\,g}{H_2O\,(g)}$$

Number of moles in 18 g H_2O (l) is

$= \frac{18 \text{ g}}{18 \text{ g/mol}} = 1 \text{ mol}$

$\Delta_{vap}U^\ominus = \Delta_{vap}H^\ominus - p\Delta V$

$= \Delta H^\ominus - \Delta_{n_g} RT$

$= 40.66$ kJ/mol $- (1) \times 8.314$ J/K/mol $\times 373$ K $\times 10^{-3}$ kJ

$\Delta_{vap}U^\ominus = 40.66$ kJ/mol-3.10 kJ/mol

$= 37.56$ kJ/mol

14. (a) The correct match is

A-II, B-I, C-IV, D-III.

A. $6HCHO + 4NH_3 \longrightarrow (CH_2)_6N_4 + 6H_2O$

B. $R{-}CN \xrightarrow[H_3O^+]{LiAlH_4} R{-}CHO$

C. $CCl_3CHO + H_2O \longrightarrow \underset{\text{Chloral hydrate}}{CCl_3CH(OH)_2}$

D. $CH_3CHO + NH_3 \longrightarrow CH_3CH{=}NH + H_2O$

15. (c) Chlorination of alkane in the presence of diffused sunlight involves the attack of chlorine free radicals

$$\underset{\text{Methane}}{CH_4} + Cl_2 \xrightarrow[\text{Sunlight}]{\text{Diffused}} \underset{\text{1-chloro methane}}{CH_3{-}Cl} + HCl$$

16. (b) There is a high jump from IE_3 to IE_4.

Therefore, it is difficult to remove the 4th valence electron.

So, electronic configuration of element must have three valence electrons.

17. (a)

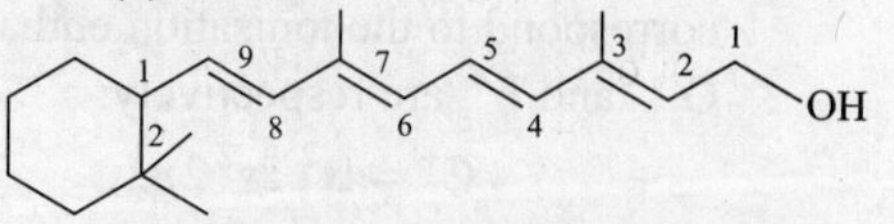

3, 7-dimethyl-9- (2, 2-dimethyl cyclohexyl) non-2, 4, 6, 8-tetra-en-1-ol

18. (c) Complete reaction is given as

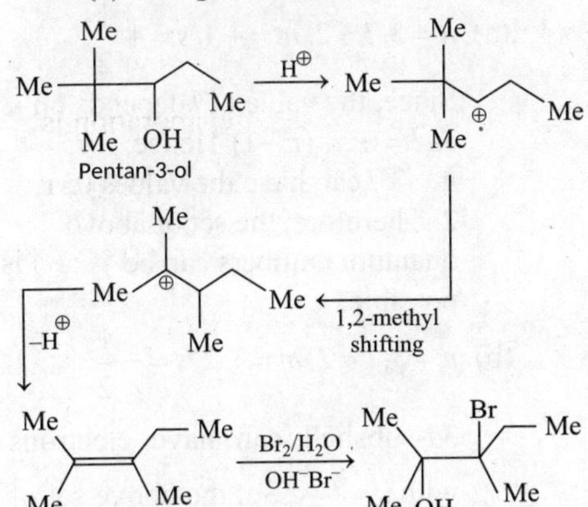

19. (d) Both Statement I and Statement II are correct.

Br, Br, CH_3 $\xrightarrow[\text{NaI}+CH_3COCH_3]{I^{\ominus}}$ CH_3 (alkene) $+ 2Br^- + I_2$

1, 2-dibromopropane (*Vicinal*-dibromide)

Br, Br $\xrightarrow[\text{NaI}+CH_3COCH_3]{I^{\ominus}}$ X

I_2 is liberated which gives blue-black colour with starch.

20. (d) (A) is false but (R) is true. This is because the product formed in the question is incorrect. The correct reaction is as follows

O, CH_3, C—H, O $\xrightarrow[\Delta]{OH^-}$ a, b, C=O, CH_3

α, β-unsaturated ketone

Hence, option (c) is correct.

21. (b) The correct match is

A-II, B-IV, C-III, D-I.

$$H = \frac{1}{2}(V + M - C + A)$$

$$BF_3 : H(B) = \frac{1}{2}(3+3-0+0) = 3(sp^2)$$

$$SO_4^{2-} : H(S) = \frac{1}{2}(6+0-0+2) = 4(sp^3)$$

Br_3^- or $[BrBr_2]^-$: H(Br)

$$= \frac{1}{2}(7+2-0+1) = 5(sp^3d)$$

$$XeF_4 : H(Xe) = \frac{1}{2}(8+4-0+0)$$

$$= 6(sp^3d^2)$$

22. (c) By applying Raoult's law,

$$\frac{p^\circ - p_S}{p^\circ} = \frac{n_2}{n_1}$$

$$\frac{w_2/M_2}{w_1/M_1} = \frac{p^\circ - p_S}{p^\circ}$$

$$\frac{w_2 \times M_1}{w_1 \times M_2} = \frac{p^\circ - p_S}{p^\circ}$$

where, w_1 = mass of solvent (water),

w_2 = mass of solute (urea)

M_1 = molar mass of water,

M_2 = molar mass of urea.

$$\frac{23.75 - p_S}{23.75} = \frac{5}{60} \times \frac{18}{95}$$

$$23.75 - p_S = \frac{5}{60} \times \frac{18}{95} \times 23.75$$

or $23.75 - p_S = 0.375$

$$p_S = 24.125 \text{ mm}$$

$$= 24.12 \text{ mm Hg}$$

23. (b) The cell is represented as,

$$\text{Mg}|\text{Mg}^{2+}(0.130 \text{ M})||$$

$$\text{Ag}^+(0.0001 \text{ M})|\text{Ag}$$

Reaction at anode,

$$\text{Mg} \longrightarrow \text{Mg}^{2+}(0.130 \text{ M}) + 2e^-$$

Reaction at cathode,

$$2\text{Ag}^+(0.0001 \text{ M}) + 2e^- \longrightarrow 2\text{Ag}(s)$$

Cell reaction is

$$\text{Mg}(s) + 2\text{Ag}^+(0.0001 \text{ M}) \longrightarrow \text{Mg}^{2+}(0.130 \text{ M}) + 2\text{Ag}(s)$$

From Nernst equation,

$$E_{\text{cell}} = E^\circ_{\text{cell}} - \frac{0.059}{2} \log \frac{[\text{Mg}^{2+}]}{[\text{Ag}^+]^2}$$

$$= 3.17 - \frac{0.059}{2} \log \frac{(0.130)}{(0.0001)^2}$$

$$= 3.17 - 0.209 \text{ V} = 2.96 \text{ V}$$

24. (c) $\frac{(t_{1/2})_1}{(t_{1/2})_2} = \left(\frac{a_2}{a_1}\right)^{n-1}$

(where, n is order of reaction)

From the given data

$$\frac{3.52}{1.92} = \left(\frac{13333}{6667}\right)^{n-1}$$

($a \propto$ initial pressure)

$$= (2)^{n-1}$$

Taking log on both sides

$$\log \frac{3.52}{1.92} = (n-1)\log 2$$

$$= 0.3010 \times (n-1)$$

$$0.2632 = 0.3010 \times (n-1)$$

$$n = 1.87 \approx 2$$

Similar calculations are made between first and third observation, n comes equal to $1.908 \approx 2$.

Thus, the reaction is of second order.

25. (c) Half-cell reaction (n factor of $H_2SO_4 = 2$)

$$H_2(4 \text{ atm}) \rightarrow 2H^+ (0.01 \text{ M or } 0.02 \text{ N}) + 2e^-$$

$$E_{H_2/2H^+} = E^{\ominus}_{H_2/2H^+} - \frac{0.059}{2} \log \frac{[H^+]^2}{p_{H_2}}$$

$$= 0 - \frac{0.059}{2} \log \frac{(0.02)^2}{4 \text{ atm}}$$

$$= -\frac{0.059}{2} \log \frac{0.02 \times 0.02}{4}$$

$$= -\frac{0.059}{2} \log 10^{-4}$$

$$= -\frac{0.059}{2} \times (-4 \log 10)$$

$$= 0.059 \times 2 = 0.118 \text{ V}$$

$$E^\circ_{2H^+/H_2} = 0.118 \text{ V}$$

26. (b) The correct match is

A-IV, B-III, C-I, D-II.

- $4Fe^{3+} + 3[Fe(CN)_6]^{4-} \longrightarrow Fe_4[Fe(CN)_6]_3$ Prussian blue
- $Fe^{3+} + 3SCN^- \longrightarrow [Fe(SCN)_3]$ Blood red
- $Ni^{2+} + 2DMG \longrightarrow Ni(DMG)_2]$ Cherry red
- $2Mn^{2+} + 5PbO_2 + 4H^+ \xrightarrow{H^+} 2MnO_4^- + 5Pb^{2+} + 2H_2O$ Pink

27. (b) 4 g He has 6.023×10^{23} atoms

1 g He has $\frac{6.023 \times 10^{23}}{4}$ atoms

$$= 1.506 \times 10^{23} \text{ atoms}$$

Also, 4 g He has volume at STP = 22.4 L

1 g He has volume at STP

$$= \frac{22.4}{4} = 5.6 \text{ L}$$

Hence, option (b) is correct.

28. (c) Ammonia dissolves in water and forms a basic solution. On adding this solution to AgCl soluble complex is formed.

$$\underset{\text{Ammonia}}{NH_3} + H_2O \longrightarrow \underset{\text{Basic (A)}}{NH_4OH}$$

$$\underset{\text{Silver chloride}}{AgCl} + \underset{\text{Ammonium hydroxide}}{2NH_4OH} \longrightarrow \underset{(B)}{[Ag(NH_3)_2]Cl} + 2H_2O$$

29. (d) Both Statement I and Statement II are correct.

$X—X$ bond dissociation enthalpy is very less in the case of halogens making them, highly reactive. High electronegativity is another reason for high reactivity of halogen molecule.

30. (d) Statement (d) is incorrect.

- Sc^{3+} and Ti^{4+} do not have unpaired electrons. Therefore, these metal ion can not give *d-d* transition. Hence, these are colourless.
- Cu^{2+} has one unpaired electron so, it shows blue colour.
- Zn^{2+} and Cd^{2+} have d^{10} electronic configuration. Thus, can not absorb any radiation through *d-d* transition in visible region.
- Fe^{3+} has $3d^5$ configuration so, yellow colour is produced.

31. (d) Statement (d) is incorrect, whereas all other statements are correct.

The basic strength of hydroxide decreases from $La(OH)_3$ to $Lu(OH)_3$ due to lanthanoid contraction but lanthanoid compounds are less basic than actinide compounds.

32. (b) $Na_3[Ag(S_2O_3)_2]$

$$x + 3 - 2 \times 2 = 0 \Rightarrow x = +1$$

The correct IUPAC name is sodium *bis* (thiosulphate) argentate (I).

33. (c) Statement I is incorrect but Statement II is correct because only 0.9% NaCl solution can be injected intravenously because it is isotonic with the fluid inside the blood cells, otherwise they will shrinked or swell. Hence, option (c) is correct.

34. (b) When 2 moles of acetone reacts in presence of NaOH, then self aldol condensation takes place.

$$\underset{\text{Propanone}}{CH_3—\overset{O}{\overset{\|}{C}}—CH_3} + \underset{\text{Propanone}}{CH_2(H)—\overset{O}{\overset{\|}{C}}—CH_3} \xrightarrow{NaOH} \underset{\text{4-hydroxy 4-methyl pent-2-one } (A)}{CH_3—\overset{CH_3}{\overset{|}{\underset{OH}{\underset{|}{C}}}}—CH_2—\overset{O}{\overset{\|}{C}}—CH_3}$$

$$\xrightarrow[-H_2O]{\Delta} \underset{\text{4-methyl pent-3-en-2-one } (B)}{CH_3—\overset{CH_3}{\overset{|}{C}}=CH—\overset{O}{\overset{\|}{C}}—CH_3}$$

35. (b) When 2-bromobutane reacts with alc. KOH, then β-elimination takes place.

According to Saytzeff rule, more substituted alkene, i.e. but-2-ene is major product.

$$\underset{\text{2-bromobutane}}{CH_3—CH_2—\underset{Br}{\underset{|}{CH}}—CH_3} \xrightarrow[\text{Heat}]{\text{Alc. KOH}} \underset{\text{But-2-ene (major) 80\%}}{CH_3—CH=CH—CH_3} + \underset{\text{But-1-ene (minor) 20\%}}{CH_3—CH_2—CH=CH_2}$$

36. (c)

$$\underset{\text{(Benzene)}}{C_6H_6} + \underset{\text{(Propene)}}{CH_3—CH=CH_2} \xrightarrow[/AlCl_3]{H_3PO_4} \underset{\text{(Cumene)}}{C_6H_5—CH(CH_3)_2} \xrightarrow[\cdot O_2]{\text{Oxidation, Air}} \underset{\text{Cumene hydroperoxide}}{C_6H_5—C(CH_3)_2—OOH} \xrightarrow[H^+]{\text{Dil.}H_2SO_4} \underset{\text{(Phenol) } (A)}{C_6H_5OH} + \underset{\text{(Acetone)}}{CH_3COCH_3}$$

37. (c)

(a) $n = 3, l = 2, m = +1, s = +\frac{1}{2}$

Since, the value of l depends on n as $l = 0 \ldots (n-1)$. Hence, for $n = 3$, l can have the values 0, 1, 2. Therefore, the set of above quantum numbers can be possible.

(b) $n = 3, l = 2, m = +2, s = -\frac{1}{2}$

3*d*-subshell can have electrons with $s = -\frac{1}{2}$. So, the above set of quantum numbers can be possible.

(c) $n = 2, l = 1, m = +2, s = -\frac{1}{2}$ as $m = -l \ldots\ldots\ldots 0 \ldots\ldots\ldots +l$.

2*p*-subshell does not exist with $m = +2$ value.

Thus, the above set of quantum numbers is not possible.

(d) $n = 3, l = 0, m = 0, s = +\frac{1}{2}$

3*s*-subshell can have electrons with $s = +\frac{1}{2}$ spin. Thus, the set of above quantum number can be possible.

Hence, option (c) is correct.

38. (b) The allylic substitution is carried out by treating the alkene with N-bromo succinimide (NBS).

$$\underset{\uparrow \text{(Allylic–C)}}{CH_2=CH—CH_3} + \underset{\text{(NBS)}}{(CH_2CO)_2N—Br} \xrightarrow{h\nu} \underset{\text{3-bromopropene}}{CH_2=CH—CH_2—Br} + \underset{\text{(Succinimide)}}{(CH_2CO)_2N—H}$$

39. (a) In nucleophilic addition reaction,

$$\overset{\delta^+}{>C}=\overset{\delta^-}{O} + Nu^{\ominus} \longrightarrow >C\begin{smallmatrix}Nu\\O^-\end{smallmatrix} \xrightarrow{E^{\oplus}} >C\begin{smallmatrix}Nu\\OE\end{smallmatrix}$$

Nucleophile attacks on positively charged carbonyl carbon atom. When positive charge increases at carbon atom, then attraction towards nucleophilic addition reaction increases.

$$\underset{H}{\overset{H}{>}}C{=}O > \underset{H}{\overset{CH_3}{>}}C{=}O > \underset{CH_3}{\overset{CH_3}{>}}C{=}O > \underset{C_6H_5}{\overset{CH_3}{>}}C{=}O$$

Positive charge at C-atom decreases →

Reactivity towards nucleophillic addition reaction decreases →

40. (d) Both Statement I and Statement II are correct.

41. (b) The reactions takes place as follows

$$CH_3{-}\underset{CH_3}{CH}{-}\ddot{O}{-}C_6H_5 \xrightarrow{HI} CH_3{-}\underset{CH_3}{CH}{-}\overset{+}{\underset{H}{O}}{-}C_6H_5$$

I^- attack, on more stable carbocation

$$C_6H_5OH \text{ (Phenol)} + CH_3{-}\underset{CH_3}{CH}{-}I \text{ (2-iodopropane)}$$

Here, 2° carbocation is more stable than phenyl cation.

Thus, isopropyl iodide and phenol is obtained.

42 (c) Statement (c) is incorrect because glucose reacts with HCN and form heptanoic acid on hydrolysis.

$$\underset{\text{Glucose}}{CHO{-}(CHOH)_4{-}CH_2OH} \xrightarrow{HCN} \underset{\text{Cyanohydrin}}{CH(OH)(CN){-}(CHOH)_4{-}CH_2OH} \xrightarrow{H_3O^+} CH(OH)(COOH){-}(CHOH)_4{-}CH_2OH \xrightarrow{\text{HI, Heat Reduction}} \underset{\text{Heptanoic acid}}{CH_3(CH_2)_5COOH}$$

43. (a) *Vicinal*-dihalides on treatment with alcoholic KOH undergo dehydrohalogenation. One molecule of hydrogen halide is eliminated to form alkenyl halide which on treatment with sodamide gives alkyne. The given reaction is as follows

$$\underset{Br\quad Br}{H_2C{-}CH_2} + KOH \xrightarrow[-KBr,\ -H_2O]{\text{Alcohol}} \underset{\text{(Bromoethene)}}{\underset{(A)}{H_2C{=}CH{-}Br}} \xrightarrow[-NaBr,\ -NH_3]{NaNH_2} \underset{(B)}{\underset{\text{Ethyne)}}{HC{\equiv}CH}}$$

Thus, the correct option is (a).

44. (d) $R{-}CH{=}CH{-}R \xrightarrow[\text{Reagent}]{[O]} 2R{-}COOH$ (Oxidative cleavage)

Following reagent can be used during oxidative cleavage of alkene.

(a) Hot alkaline $KMnO_4$ solution followed by acidification.
(b) Hot acidic $KMnO_4$ solution.
(c) Hot acidic $K_2Cr_2O_7$ solution.
(d) But hot Cr_2O_3 cannot be used where Cr is present in + 3 oxidation state.

45. (b) The correct match is A-II, B-I, C-IV, D-III.

A. Positive deviated non-ideal solution gives minimum boiling azeotropes, i.e. $C_2H_5OH + H_2O$.
B. Negative deviated non-ideal solution gives maximum boiling azeotropes, i.e. $CH_3COCH_3 + COCl_3$.
C. van't Hoff factor $K_2SO_4 \longrightarrow 2K^+ + SO_4^{2-}$ $i = 3$ (due to ionic nature)
D. Isotonic solutions have equal osmotic pressure. So, $\pi_1 = \pi_2$

Hence, option (b) is correct.

NK05 NEET Knock Offs

1. (a) The given reactions are

$$\underset{(X)}{\text{Sucrose}} \xrightarrow{HOH/H^+} \text{Glucose} + \text{Fructose}$$

$$\underset{(Y)}{\text{Maltose}} \xrightarrow{HOH/H^+} \text{Glucose} + \text{Glucose}$$

$$\underset{(Z)}{\text{Lactose}} \xrightarrow{HOH/H^+} \text{Glucose} + \text{Galactose}$$

Thus, X, Y and Z are sucrose, maltose and lactose.

2. (d) Elevation in boiling point

$\Delta T_b = i \times K_b \times m$

∴ Greater is the value of van't Hoff factor, greater will be the boiling point.

In Na_2SO_4, three ions are produced $2Na^+$ and $1SO_4^{2-}$.

∴ $i = 3$

In $Al(NO_3)_3$, four ions are produced. So, $i = 4$

In $C_6H_{12}O_6$, no dissociation takes place,

So, $i = 1$

In $MgCl_2$, three ions are produced $1Mg^+$ and $2Cl^-$

So, $i = 3$

Thus, 0.5 M $Al(NO_3)_3$ has highest boiling point.

3. (c) $\underset{\text{3-chloroprop-1-ene}}{CH_2{=}CH{-}CH_2Cl} \xrightarrow{H_2O} \underset{\text{Allyl carbocation}}{CH_2{=}CH{-}\overset{+}{CH_2}} + Cl^-$

Allyl carbocation being highly stabilised by resonance thus, formed at faster rate.

Hence, allyl chloride undergoes hydrolysis easily. Whereas C—Cl bond in vinyl chloride has partial double bond character due to resonance, hence it is difficult to break. Thus, rate of hydrolysis is less.

$$CH_2{=}CH{-}\ddot{Cl}: \longleftrightarrow \overset{\ominus}{C}H_2{-}CH{=}\overset{\oplus}{Cl} \equiv [\overset{\delta-}{CH_2}{\cdots}CH{\cdots}\overset{\delta+}{Cl}]$$

4. (b) When alcohol reacts with conc. HCl, then carbocation intermediate is obtained. Rate of reactivity depends on stability of carbocation.

(IV) Ph–CH₂–OH $\xrightarrow{H^+, Cl^-}$ Ph–$\overset{\oplus}{C}H_2$ Benzylic carbocation (Resonance stabilised) stable

(III) $(CH_3)_3C$–OH $\xrightarrow{H^+, Cl^-}$ $(CH_3)_3\overset{\oplus}{C}$ 3° carbocation

(I) $\xrightarrow{H^+, Cl^-}$ 2° carbocation

(II) $\xrightarrow{H^+, Cl^-}$ 2° carbocation

In (I) carbocation, stability of carbocation is less than (II) due to smaller chain than II. *Tert*-butyl carbocation is more stable than benzylic carbocation.

Hence, the order of reactivity

III > IV > II > I.

5. (a) Statements given in option I, IV and V are correct while II and III are incorrect. The correct form of II and III are

- Fehling solution *A* is aqueous copper sulphate.
- Fehling solution *B* is alkaline sodium potassium tartarate (Rochelle salt).

6. (b)

$$BOH(s) \rightleftharpoons B^+(aq) + OH^-(aq)$$

Initial conc. C 0   0

Eq. conc. $C-x$ x x

$$K_C = \frac{[B^+][OH^-]}{[BOH]}$$

$$= \frac{x^2}{C-x} = \frac{x^2}{C} \quad [\because C >> x]$$

$$x = \sqrt{K_C \cdot C}$$

$$= \sqrt{10^{-16} \times 10^{-2}}$$

$$= 10^{-9} \text{ mol L}^{-1}$$

$$[H^+] = \frac{K_w}{[OH^-]} = \frac{10^{-14}}{10^{-9}}$$

$$= 10^{-5} \text{ mol/L}$$

7. (d) Species that have same number of electrons have same bond order.

So, among the given options, NO^- bond order is different from CO because CO have 14 electrons while NO^- have 16 electrons and rest of other species have 14 electrons.

8. (d) Both Statement I and Statement II are correct. In reaction I, pungent smelling gas (HCl) is produced because stronger acid displaces a weaker acid from its salt.

$$NaCl + H_2SO_4 \longrightarrow NaHSO_4 + \underset{\text{Weaker acid}}{HCl}$$

$$HCl + H_2SO_4 \longrightarrow HSO_3Cl + H_2O$$

HCl is weaker reducing agent it cannot reduce H_2SO_4 to SO_2 and hence, HCl is not oxidised to Cl_2.

9. (b) The correct match is

A-IV, B-III, C-II, D-I.

A. Benzene $\xrightarrow[\text{Anhyd. AlCl}_3\text{, CuCl}]{\text{CO, HCl}}$ Benzaldehyde (CHO)

This reaction is Gattermann Koch reaction.

B. $\underset{\text{Propyne}}{CH_3-C\equiv CH} + H_2O \xrightarrow[\substack{H_2SO_4 \\ \text{(Hydration of alkene)}}]{Hg^{2+}}$ $\underset{\text{Unstable}}{CH_3-\underset{OH}{C}=CH_2}$ $\xrightarrow[\text{Tautomerisation}]{\text{enol} \to \text{keto}}$ $\underset{\text{Acetone}}{CH_3-\underset{O}{\overset{\|}{C}}-CH_3}$

C. Propyl benzene (C_6H_5–CH_2–CH_2–CH_3) $\xrightarrow[\text{Oxidation of alkyl benzene}]{KMnO_4-KOH}$ $C_6H_5\overset{-}{CO}\overset{+}{OK}$ $\xrightarrow{H_3O^+}$ C_6H_5COOH Benzoic acid

D. C_6H_5–$\underset{O}{\overset{\|}{C}}$–$CH_3$ $\xrightarrow[\text{Haloform reaction}]{NaOH + I_2}$ $C_6H_5COO^-Na^+$ + CHI_3 Iodoform

Thus, option (b) is correct.

10. (d) All the given statements are correct.

11. (b) Molar mass of $CaCl_2$

$$= 40 + 35.5 \times 2 = 111 \text{ g}$$

$$\underset{1 \text{ mol}}{CaCl_2} \longrightarrow \underset{1 \text{ mol}}{Ca^{2+}} + \underset{2 \text{ mol}}{2Cl^-}$$

111 g of $CaCl_2 \longrightarrow$ 1 mole of Ca^{2+}

222 g of $CaCl_2 \longrightarrow$ 2 moles of Ca^{2+}

Therefore, number of Ca^{2+} ion

$$= 2 \times N = 2 \times 6.023 \times 10^{23}$$

111 g of $CaCl_2 \longrightarrow$ 2 moles of Cl^-

222 g of $CaCl_2 \longrightarrow \frac{2}{111} \times 222$

$$= 4 \text{ moles of } Cl^-$$

Thus, number of Cl^- ions $= 4N$

$$= 4 \times 6.023 \times 10^{23}$$

12. (b) The formula to calculate hybridisation is

$$H=\frac{1}{2}(V+X-C+A)$$

where,

H = number of hybrid orbitals.

V = number of valence electrons in central atom.

X = number of monovalent atoms surrounding central atom.

C = cation's positive charge.

A = negative charge on anion.

Hybrid orbitals of Xe in XeF_4

$$=\frac{8+4+0}{2}=6$$

(sp^3d^2-hybridisation)

Lone pair = 6 − bond pair

$$=6-4=2$$

So, XeF_4 has 4 bond pairs + 2 lone pairs = Square planar

$$Xe(XeO_2F_2)=\frac{8+2+0}{2}$$

$$=5\ (sp^3d)$$

So, XeO_2F_2 has 4 bond pairs + 1 lone pair = *See-saw*

$$\text{Central I }(I_3^-)=\frac{7+2+1}{2}$$

$$=5\ (sp^3d)$$

Lone pair = 5 − 2 = 3

So, I_3^- has 2 bond pairs + 3 lone pairs = Linear structure

$$Sn(SnCl_2)=\frac{4+2+0}{2}=3(sp^2)$$

Lone pair = 3 − 2 = 1

So, $SnCl_2$ have 2 bond pairs +1 Lone pair = Angular

13. (a) For λ_{max}, $E_{radiation}$ = minimum

$$=13.6Z^2\left(\frac{1}{n_1^2}-\frac{1}{n_2^2}\right)$$

i.e. $\left(\frac{1}{n_1^2}-\frac{1}{n_2^2}\right)$ has to be minimum.

This is independent of quantum numbers l, m and s.

Therefore, $n_1=3$ and $n_2=4$ for minimum E (radiation).

Thus, option (a) is correct.

14. (b) Statement given in option (b) is incorrect. Its correct form is the intermolecular association due to hydrogen bonding is more in primary amines than in secondary amines as there are two hydrogen atoms available for hydrogen bond formation in it.

15. (d) Mass of sample of 0.20 g

% purity = 50%

∴ Mass of pure organic compound

$$=\frac{50}{100}\times 0.20=0.10\text{ g}$$

For CO_2, 0.10 g of pure organic compound will contain

$$=\frac{69\times 0.10}{100}=0.069\text{ g of C}$$

Molecular mass of CO_2 = 44 g

$$12\text{ g C}=44\text{ g of }CO_2$$

$$\frac{44\times 0.069}{12}=0.253\text{ g of }CO_2$$

Similarly for H_2O,

$$\frac{4.8\times 0.10}{100}=0.0048\text{ g of H}$$

0.048 g of H will produce

$$=\frac{18\times 0.0048}{2}=0.0432\text{ g of }H_2O$$

16. (b) The balanced chemical reaction is

$$4Zn+NO_3^-+7H_2O\longrightarrow 4Zn^{2+}+NH_4^++10\ OH^-$$

17. (a) The correct match is

A-IV, B-I, C-II, D-III.

A. de-Broglie equation, $\lambda=h/p$

B. The spectral lines for atomic hydrogen Lyman series lies in UV spectral region.

C. Paschen series lies in IR spectral region.

D. Heisenberg uncertainty principle, $\Delta x\cdot\Delta p\geq h/4\pi$

18. (b) Orthoboric acid above 370 K leads to partial removal of water to yield metaboric acid, HBO_2 which on further heating yields first tetraboric acid, $H_2B_4O_7$ and finally boric oxide B_2O_3, which is the principle oxide of boron.

$$\underset{\text{Boric acid}}{4H_3BO_3}\xrightarrow[-4H_2O]{\text{Heat}}\underset{\substack{\text{Metaboric acid}\\(A)}}{4HBO_2}\xrightarrow[-H_2O]{410\text{ K}}\underset{\substack{\text{Tetraboric acid}\\(B)}}{H_2B_4O_7}\xrightarrow[-H_2O]{\text{Red hot}}\underset{(C)}{2B_2O_3}$$

19. (a) For a spontaneous cell reaction

$$E^\ominus_{cell}>0;\Delta G^\circ<0;Q<K_C$$

In these conditions, reaction moves in the forward direction.

20. (d) Given,

$$MnO_4^-+8H^++5e^-\longrightarrow Mn^{2+}+4H_2O;\Delta G_1^\circ\quad\ldots(i)$$

$$MnO_2+4H^++2e^-\longrightarrow Mn^{2+}+2H_2O;\Delta G_2^\circ\quad\ldots(ii)$$

Subtracting Eq. (ii) from Eq. (i) gives the required equation, i.e.

$$MnO_4^-+4H^++3e^-\longrightarrow MnO_2+2H_2O;\ \Delta G_3^\circ$$

$$\therefore\quad \Delta G_3^\circ=\Delta G_1^\circ-\Delta G_2^\circ$$

$$-n_3FE_3^\circ=-n_1FE_1^\circ-(-n_2FE_2^\circ)$$

$$E_3^\circ=\frac{n_1E_1^\circ-n_2E_2^\circ}{n_3}$$

$$=\frac{(5\times 1.51)\text{ V}-(2\times 1.23)\text{ V}}{3}$$

$$E_3^\circ=1.70\text{ V}$$

21. (b) Molar mass (M_B) of KI

$$= 39 + 127 = 166 \text{ g/mol}$$

$$m = \frac{1000\, M}{1000\, d - M M_B}$$

$$= \frac{1000 \times 0.06}{1000 \times 1.006 - 0.06 \times 166}$$

$$= \frac{60}{1006 - 9.96}$$

$$= 0.060 \text{ molal}$$

22. (b)

I. NH_4^+, sp^3-hybridised with no lone pair. So, shape of molecule is tetrahedral and bond angle is 109° 28′.

II. NH_3 is sp^3-hybridised with one lone pair. So, $lp-bp$ and $bp-bp$ repulsion decreases the bond angle to 107°.

III. NH_2^- is sp^3-hybridised with two lone pairs. Here, $lp-lp$, $lp-bp$ and $bp-bp$ repulsion decreases the bond angle to 104.5° and angular or V shape is the structure.

Thus, correct order of bond angle is $NH_4^+ > NH_3 > NH_2^-$.

23. (d) Lactose is a reducing sugar. In lactose, D-glucose and D-galactose units are linked through β-glycosidic linkage between C-1 of galactose and C-4 of glucose unit.

24. (d) $H_2O(l) \xrightarrow{100°C} H_2O(g)$

$$\Delta_{vap}H° = \Delta_{vap}U° + \Delta n_g RT$$

For above reaction,

$$\Delta n_g = 1 - 0 = 1$$

$$\Delta H = \Delta U + \Delta n_g RT$$

$$\therefore \quad 20.33 = \Delta_{vap}U° + 1 \times 8.314 \times 10^{-3} \times 373$$

$$\Delta_{vap}U° = 20.33 - 3.1 \text{ kJ/mol}$$

$$\Delta_{vap}U° = +17.23 \text{ kJ/mol}$$

25. (a) In presence of high concentration of $KMnO_4$ or acidic medium at higher temperature, the carbon-carbon multiple bonds is completely cleaved and final product formed ketones or carboxylic acids. This reaction is known as oxidative cleavage.

$$\underset{\text{2-methylpropene}}{(CH_3)_2C{=}CH_2} \xrightarrow[373-383\text{K}]{KMnO_4/H^+} \underset{(A)}{(CH_3)_2C{=}O} + \underset{(B)}{CO_2}$$

$$(A) \xrightarrow[H_2O]{CH_3MgX} CH_3-\overset{CH_3}{\underset{CH_3}{C}}-\overset{-}{O}\overset{+}{Mg}X$$

$$\xrightarrow{H_3O^+} \underset{(3° \text{ alcohol}) \; (C)}{CH_3-\overset{CH_3}{\underset{CH_3}{C}}-OH} + Mg(X)(OH)$$

26. (c)

I. $\overset{6}{C}H_3-\overset{5}{C}H{=}\overset{4}{C}H-\overset{3}{C}H_2-\overset{2}{C}H_2-\overset{1}{C}N$

$\downarrow$ AlH(i-Bu)$_2$, H_2O

$\overset{6}{C}H_3-\overset{5}{C}H{=}\overset{4}{C}H-\overset{3}{C}H_2-\overset{2}{C}H_2-\overset{1}{C}HO$

Hex-4-en-1-al

II. $\underset{\text{Ester}}{CH_3(CH_2)_7-\overset{O}{\overset{\|}{C}}-OC_2H_5} \xrightarrow[H_2O]{\text{DIBAL-H}} \underset{\text{Nonanal}}{CH_3(CH_2)_7-\overset{O}{\overset{\|}{C}}-H}$

27. (b)

4-methylacetophenone (CH_3–C_6H_4–$COCH_3$) $\xrightarrow[-CO_2]{KMnO_4/KOH}$ $\overset{-}{COO}\overset{+}{K}$–$C_6H_4$–$\overset{-}{COO}\overset{+}{K}$ $\xrightarrow{\text{Dil. } H_2SO_4}$ HOOC–C_6H_4–COOH (Terephthalic acid)

28. (a) Mn in +2 state has the configuration $3d^5$. In presence of H_2O as ligand, (weak field) the distribution of these five electrons is t_{2g}^3, e_g^2, it means all the electrons remain unpaired.

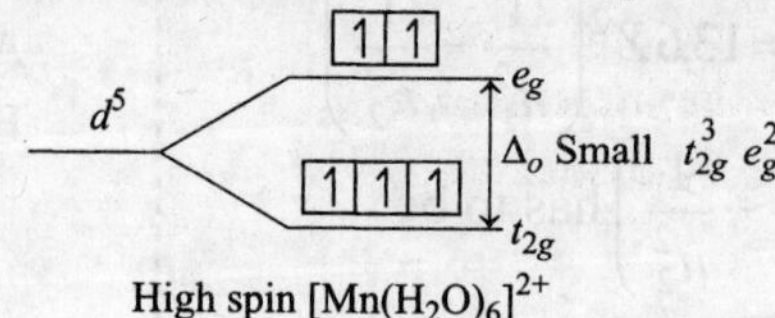

High spin $[Mn(H_2O)_6]^{2+}$

While cyanide ion (CN^-) is a strong field ligand, therefore, all five electrons enter into t_{2g} orbitals and two e_g orbitals remain empty.

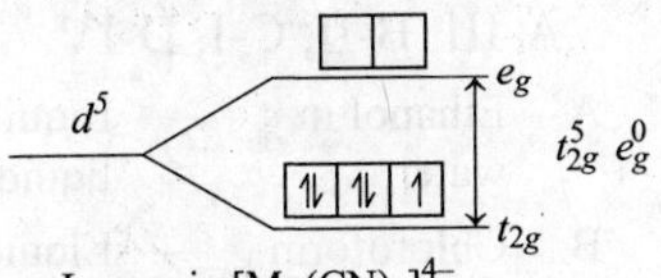

d^5 → $t_{2g}^5 e_g^0$

Low spin $[Mn(CN)_6]^{4-}$

29. (c)

$\left[Cr(C_2O_4)_3 \right]^{3-}$

Mirror

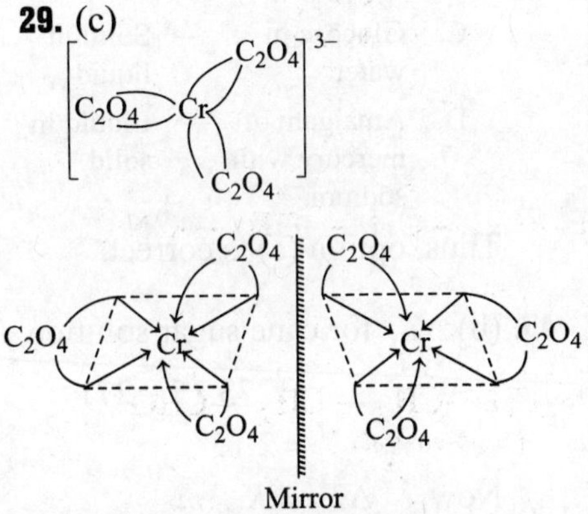

Their mirror image is not superimposable, hence, optical isomerism is possible.

30. (a) In this reaction,

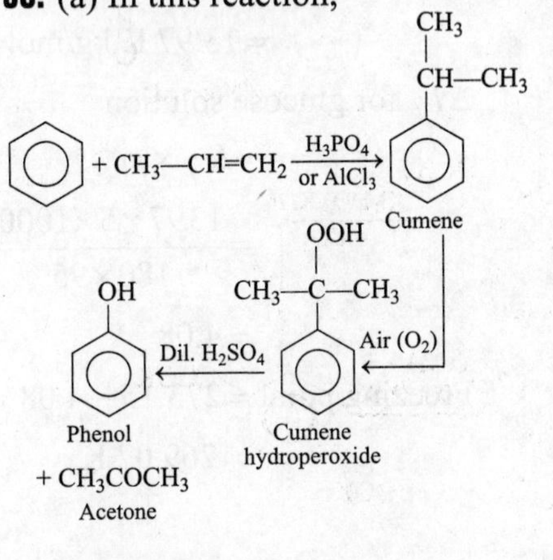

Benzene $+ CH_3—CH=CH_2 \xrightarrow[\text{or } AlCl_3]{H_3PO_4}$ Cumene $\xrightarrow{\text{Air } (O_2)}$ Cumene hydroperoxide $\xrightarrow{\text{Dil. } H_2SO_4}$ Phenol $+ CH_3COCH_3$ (Acetone)

31. (d) The presence of electron withdrawing group like NO_2 at *ortho* and *para* position withdraws the electron density from the ring and hence, stabilises the intermediate carbanion by dispersal of negative charge, thus, increase the rate of nucleophilic substitution. Therefore, option (d) is correct.

32. (b) The correct match is

A-IV, B-III, C-II, D-I.

A. $CH_4 + Cl_2 \xrightarrow[-HCl]{} CH_3Cl$

B. $CCl_4 \xrightarrow[\text{Heat}]{Fe/H_2O} CHCl_3$

C. $NaOH + CCl_3CHO \longrightarrow HCO\overset{-}{O}\overset{+}{N}a + CHCl_3$

D. $2CHCl_3 + O_2 \xrightarrow{\text{Sunlight}} 2COCl_2 + 2HCl$

33. (c) The complete reaction is as follows

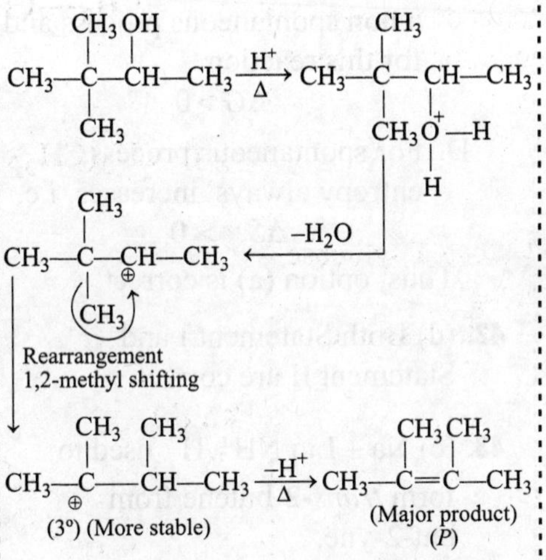

$CH_3—C(CH_3)_2—CH(OH)—CH_3 \xrightarrow[\Delta]{H^+} CH_3—C(CH_3)_2—CH(\overset{+}{O}H_2)—CH_3 \xrightarrow{-H_2O} CH_3—C(CH_3)_2—\overset{\oplus}{C}H—CH_3$

Rearrangement 1,2-methyl shifting

$CH_3—\overset{\oplus}{C}(CH_3)—CH(CH_3)—CH_3$ (3°) (More stable) $\xrightarrow[\Delta]{-H^+} CH_3—C(CH_3)=C(CH_3)—CH_3$ (Major product) (*P*)

Thus, option (c) is correct.

34. (a) For the first order reaction,

$$k = \frac{0.693}{t_{1/2}} = \frac{0.693}{60}$$

$$= 11.55 \times 10^{-3} \text{ min}^{-1}$$

Applying first order kinetics equation

$$t = \frac{2.303}{k} \log \frac{a}{a-x}$$

Given $a = 100$, $x = 90$, i.e. $(a-x) = (100-90) = 10$

Hence, $t = \frac{2.303}{11.55 \times 10^{-3}} \log 10$

≈ 200 min.

35. (b) The oxidation state of Cl in perchloric acid ($HClO_4$) is +7, whereas that of S in H_2SO_4 is +6.

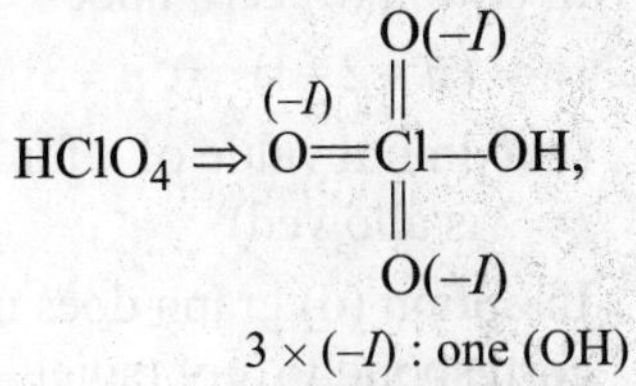

$HClO_4 \Rightarrow O=Cl(=O)(=O)—OH$, each O(−*I*)

$3 \times (-I)$: one (OH)

Acid strength α-*I*

∝ Polarity of OH graph

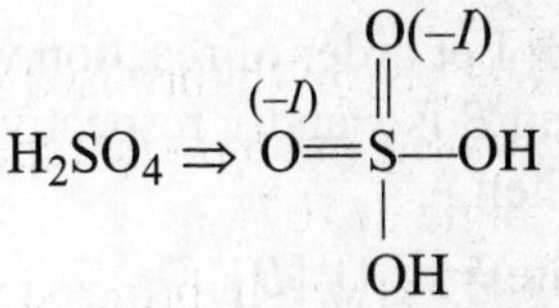

$H_2SO_4 \Rightarrow O=S(=O)(OH)—OH$, each O(−*I*)

$2 \times (-I)$ = two (OH)

$1 \times (-I)$ = one (OH)

Greater the number of (O) with the central atom, more readily is the cleavage of the O—H bond hence stronger the acid.

So, Statement I is correct but Statement II is incorrect.

36. (d) Both Statement I and Statement II are correct.

Aldehydes are prepared from acid chloride by reaction with H_2 in the presence of Pd catalyst supported on barium sulphate. The catalyst poisoned by addition of $BaSO_4$ or sulphur or quinoline. This reaction is called Rosenmund reaction.

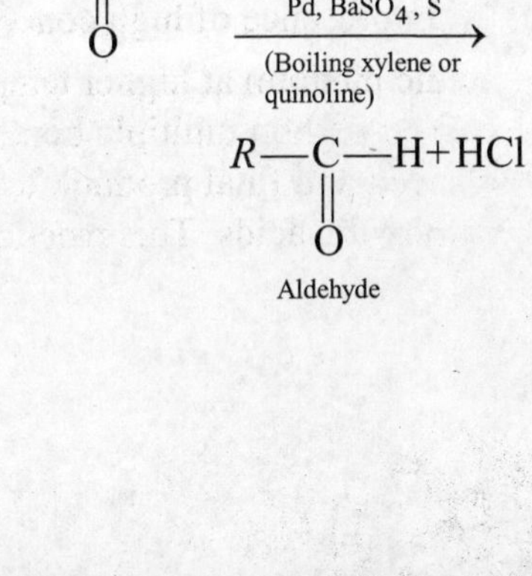

$$R—\underset{\underset{O}{\|}}{C}—Cl + H_2 \xrightarrow[\text{(Boiling xylene or quinoline)}]{Pd, BaSO_4, S} R—\underset{\underset{O}{\|}}{C}—H + HCl$$

Aldehyde

37. (c) Option (c) represents the distribution of $l=2$ for H-atom.

In option (a) → Two nodes

$n=5$ (High value of n)

In option (b) → $(n-2-1)=1$, $n=4$

In option (c) zero node

$(n-2-1)=0$, $n=3$

(maximum value of n for which $l=2$ is allowed)

In option (d) graph does not correspond to any radial distribution curve.

38. (d) Let order of reaction wrt A and B is x and y respectively. Then

rate $= k[A]^x[B]^y$

$4 = k[0.4]^x[0.4]^y$ ...(i)

$8 = k[0.4]^x[0.8]^y$ ...(ii)

$72 = k[1.2]^x[0.8]^y$ ...(iii)

On comparing Eqs. (i) and (ii) we get

$$\frac{8}{4}=\left[\frac{0.8}{0.4}\right]^y$$

$(2)^1=(2)^y \Rightarrow y=1$

Similarly, on comparing Eqs. (ii) and (iii) we get

$$\frac{72}{8}=\left(\frac{1.2}{0.4}\right)^x$$

$9=(3)^x=3^2 \Rightarrow x=2$

$\therefore$ Rate law, $r=k[A]^2[B]$.

39. (a) Both (A) and (R) are true and (R) is the correct explanation of (A).

40. (c) Statement I is incorrect but Statement II is correct because chlorination of allylic hydrogen is easier than vinylic hydrogen.

41. (a) The correct match is A-I, B-IV, C-II, D-III.

A. At constant pressure

$\Delta H = q_p$

$\Delta S^\ominus = 0$

B. Kirchhoff's equation

$\Delta H_2 - \Delta H_1 = \Delta C_p(T_2 - T_1)$

or $\Delta H = \Delta C_p(T_2 - T_1)$

C. Dissolution of H^+ in water is a non spontaneous process and for this reaction

$\Delta G > 0$

D. For spontaneous process, entropy always increases, i.e.

$\Delta S^\circ > 0$

Thus, option (a) is correct.

42. (d) Both Statement I and Statement II are correct.

43. (c) Na + Liq NH_3/H_2 used to form *trans*-2-butene from but-2-yne.

$CH_3—C≡C—CH_3$ (But-2-yne) $\xrightarrow[\text{(Birch reduction)}]{\text{Na + liq. } NH_3 + (2H)}$ $CH_3(H)C=C(H)CH_3$ (*trans*-2-butene)

Pd/$CaCO_3$, Pd-H_2 and Ni-H_2 reduce it into *cis*-2-butene

Thus, option (c) is correct.

44. (a) The correct match is A-III, B-II, C-I, D-IV.

A.	Ethanol in water.	—	Liquid in liquid
B.	Chloroform mixed with nitrogen gas.	—	Liquid in gas
C.	Glucose in water.	—	Solid in liquid
D.	Amalgam of mercury with sodium.	—	Liquid in solid

Thus, option (a) is correct.

45. (b) ΔT_f for cane sugar solution

$= 273.15 - 271$

$= 2.15°$

Now, $\Delta T_f = K_f . m$

or $K_f = \Delta T_f \times \frac{1}{m}$

$= \frac{2.15 \times 342 \times 95}{5 \times 1000}$

$= 13.97$ K kg/mol

ΔT_f for glucose solution

$= K_f \times m$

$= \frac{13.97 \times 5 \times 1000}{180 \times 95}$

$= 4.08$

Freezing point $= 273.15 - 4.08$

$= 269.07$ K

NC1 NEET Chronicles

1. (d) We know that, $n_m = 2l + 1$

$\therefore \quad 2l = n_m - 1$

and $\quad l = \dfrac{n_m - 1}{2}$

2. (b) Among the given option BF_3 molecule acts as a Lewis acid. As it is an electron deficient molecule and has vacant orbital to accept the electron pair.

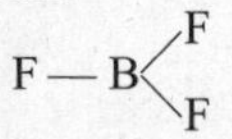

F—B(F)(F)

BF_3 has six electrons around central atom B that means its octet is not complete.

3. (b) Among the given statements, D and E are not correct because H—H bond dissociation enthalpy is not the lowest because bond formed between hydrogen atom is due to overlapping of 1*s*-1*s* orbital. So, it has smaller bond length and higher, bond enthalpy. There are also many other bond which are less stable then H—H and thus have less bond dissociation enthalpy.

Next, hydrogen does not reduces oxides of metals that are more active than iron. It can reduces oxides of elements like copper, mercury, silver, gold etc. as these metals are less reactive than hydrogen.

4. (d) Among the given options. Only option (d) is correct while other options are incorrect. The correct form of other statements are as follows.

(a) All enzymes that utilise ATP in phosphate transfer require Mg as the co-factor.

(b) The bone in human body is not inert and unchanging substance. It changes throughout the life.

(c) Ca plays roles in neuromuscular function and interneuronal transmission.

5. (d) Among the given option potassium trioxalatoaluminate (III) is an example of homoleptic complex while all other are examples of hetroleptic complex. Complexes in which a metal is bound to only one kind of donor groups are known as **homoleptic complexes**. Complexes in which a metal is bonded to more than one kind of donor groups are known as hetreroleptic complexes.

6. (d) The final reaction is as follows

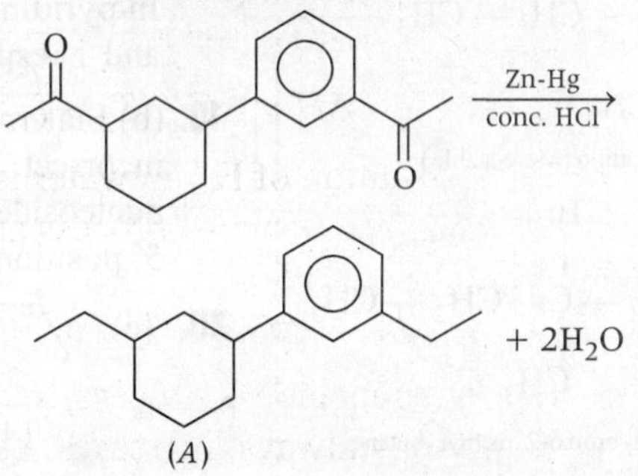

$\xrightarrow[\text{conc. HCl}]{\text{Zn-Hg}}$ + $2H_2O$

(*A*)

This reaction is an example of Clemmensen reduction reaction.

7. (a)

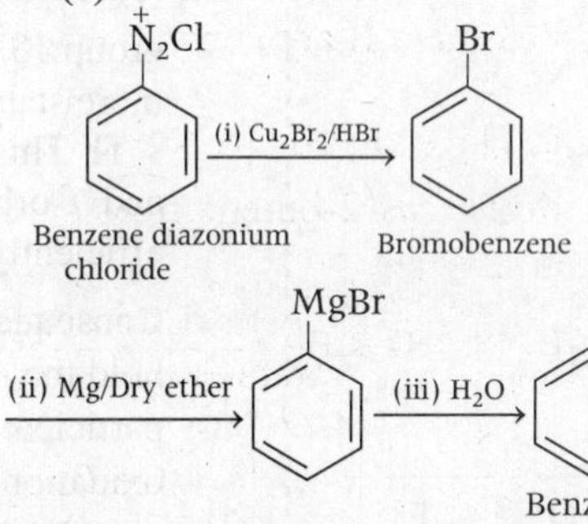

$\overset{+}{N_2}Cl$ $\xrightarrow{\text{(i) } Cu_2Br_2/HBr}$ Br

Benzene diazonium chloride — Bromobenzene

$\xrightarrow{\text{(ii) Mg/Dry ether}}$ MgBr $\xrightarrow{\text{(iii) } H_2O}$ Benzene

8. (d) The correct order of energies of molecular orbitals of N_2 molecule is,

$$\sigma 1s < \sigma^* 1s < \sigma 2s < \sigma^* 2s < (\pi 2p_x = \pi 2p_y) < \sigma 2p_z < (\pi^* 2p_x = \pi^* 2p_y) < \sigma^* 2p_z$$

N_2 has total of 14 electrons. Thus, electrons can be filled as

$$\sigma 1s^2 < \sigma^* 1s^2 < \sigma 2s^2 < \sigma^* 2s^2 < (\pi 2p_x^2 = \pi 2p_y^2) < \sigma 2p_z^2$$

9. (b) Given, rate

$$(r) = k[A]^2 [B] \quad \ldots\text{(i)}$$

$$r_1 = k[3A]^2 [B] \quad \ldots\text{(ii)}$$

Dividing Eqs. (i) by (ii), we get

$$\frac{r}{r_1} = \frac{k\,[A]^2\,[B]}{k\,[3A]^2\,[B]}$$

$$\frac{r}{r_1} = \frac{1}{9} \Rightarrow r_1 = 9r$$

The initial rate would increase by a factor of nine.

10. (d) Both (A) and (R) are true and (R) is the correct explanation of (A).

The given relation i.e. is correct. Thus, according to this relation $\Delta_r G$ depends on *n*.

Also as ΔG depends on *n* i.e. number of mole, thus it is an extensive property and E_{cell} is independent of the amount of substance thus, it is an intensive property. As extensive properties are dependent on the amount of the substances.

11. (b) The given compound

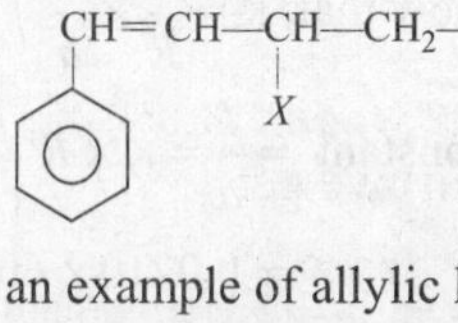

C_6H_5—CH=CH—CH(X)—CH_2—CH_3

is an example of allylic halides. As in this the halogen is bonded to the sp^3-hybridised carbon atom next to the carbon-carbon double bond, which is called as allylic halides.

Benzylic halides In these halides, the halogen atom is bonded to the sp^3-hybridised carbon atom next to an aromatic ring.

Vinylic halide In these halides, the halogen atom is bonded to the sp^2-hybridised carbon of one of the carbon atoms of a double bond.

Aryl halide In these halides, the halogen atom is bonded to the sp^2-hybridised carbon atom of an aromatic ring.

12. (a) Chloroprene [$CH_2-C(Cl)-CH=CH_2$] is the monomer of neoprene.

$$x\,CH_2=C(Cl)-CH=CH_2 \xrightarrow{\text{Polymerisation}} [-CH_2-C(Cl)=CH-CH_2-]_n$$

Chloroprene → Neoprene

13. (d) $CH_3-CH(CH_3)-CH(OH)-CH_3 \xrightarrow{H^+} CH_3-CH(CH_3)-\overset{+}{C}H-CH_3$

3-methylbutan-2-ol → 2° carbocation (Less stable)

$\xrightarrow{\text{Hydride shift}} CH_3-\overset{+}{C}(CH_3)-CH_2-CH_3 \xrightarrow{Br^-}$

3° carbocation (More stable)

$CH_3-C(Br)(CH_3)-CH_2-CH_3$

2-bromo-2-methyl butane

14. (b) Given, conductivity $(\kappa) = 0.0210\,\Omega^{-1}cm^{-1}$

Resistance = $60\,\Omega$

Cell constant = ?

We know that, $\kappa = \frac{1}{R} \times \frac{l}{a}$

Cell constant $= \frac{l}{a} = \kappa \times R$

$= 0.0210 \times 60 = 1.26\ cm^{-1}$

15. (b) The correct match is A-III, B-I, C-IV, D-II.

16. (b)

Given elements	Na	N	O	F
Formed ions to attain by nearest nobel gas configuration	Na^+ ($10e^-$)	N^{3-} ($10e^-$)	O^{2-} ($10e^-$)	F^- ($10e^-$)

Thus, all are isoelectronic species. In case of isoelectronic species, more is the negative charge on the ion, lesser is the effective nuclear charge, more will be the radius.

Hence, N^{3-} has the largest radius among the above ions.

17. (b) Among the given reactions, primary amine will not form in case of 2nd reaction.

- $CH_3NC \xrightarrow[H_2O]{LiAlH_4} CH_3-NH-CH_3$ (2° amine)
- $CH_3-CN \xrightarrow[H_2O]{LiAlH_4} CH_3CH_2NH_2$ (Primary amine)
- $CH_3-C(=O)NH_2 \xrightarrow[H_2O]{LiAlH_4} CH_3CH_2NH_2$ (Primary amine)
- $CH_3CONH_2 \xrightarrow{Br_2/NaOH} CH_3NH_2$ (Primary amine)

18. (b)

In pyridine the number of σ, π and lone pair are 11, 3 and 1 respectively.

19. (b) Statement I is correct while Statement II is incorrect. The correct form of statement II is — When nucleoside is linked to phosphoric acid at 5′-position of sugar moiety, we get nucleoside.

20. (c) Cyclohexanone [A] $\xrightarrow{HCN}$ 1-hydroxycyclohexanecarbonitrile (OH, CN) [B] $\xrightarrow[\Delta]{\text{conc. } H_2SO_4}$ cyclohex-1-enecarboxylic acid (COOH) [C]

21. (c) Among the given relation $TlI > TlI_3$ is correct. As in group 13 element +1 oxidation state becomes more and more stable as we go down the group, i.e. Al < Ga < In < Tl. This is because of the presence of intervening *d* and *f*-orbitals which do not shield the nucleus efficiently.

Consequently effective nuclear charge increases, that hold the *ns* electron tightly, so that they do not participate in bonding (inert pair effect). Thus, in Tl +1 oxidation state is more predominant whereas the +3 is strongly oxidising in nature.

22. (c) Among the given tranquilizers, veronal belongs to barbiturates.

23. (b) (A) is true while (R) is false. This is because at normal temperature and pressure helium is practically insoluble in oxygen. However, under extreme conditions very small amount of helium dissolve in oxygen.

24. (a) Given reaction, $CaCO_3 \xrightarrow{\Delta} CaO + CO_2$

Molar mass = 100 g/mol

20 g CO_2 of 20% pure limestone on heating gives $\frac{20\times 20}{100} = 4$ g

$$\text{Mole} = \frac{4}{100} = 0.004$$

Mass of CO_2 produces

$= \text{Mole} \times \text{Molecular mass of } CO_2$

$= 0.004 \times 44 = 1.76$ g

25. (c) If the compound contains sulphur and nitrogen both, sodium sulphocyanide is formed in Lassaigne's extract, which gives blood red colouration of $Fe(SCN)_3$ with $FeCl_3$.

$$Fe^{3+} + SCN^- \longrightarrow \underset{\text{Blood red}}{[Fe(SCN)]^{2+}}$$

26. (c) (A) is false but (R) is true.

When a reaction have zero activation energy, the initial energy of the reactant will be equal to the activation energy of the reaction.

That means every collision results into a chemical reaction which is not possible.

Mathematically,

If $E_a = 0$, the according to Arrhenius equation

$$k = Ae^{-E_a/RT}$$

$$= Ae^0 = A$$

27. (d) The element B forms cubic close packed structure = 4

Atom A occupy $\frac{1}{3}$ tetrahedral voids

$= \frac{1}{3} \times 8$

[∵ Tetrahedral voids = 2 of atom occupy by B]

∴ The formula of the compound is $A_{\frac{8}{3}}B_4$ or A_2B_3

∴ The value of $x + y = 2 + 3 = 5$.

28. (b) In aqueous solution, copper (I) undergoes disproportionation reaction.

$$2Cu^+(aq) \longrightarrow Cu^{2+} + Cu(s)$$

The highest stability of Cu^{2+} ion in aqueous solution is due to negative enthalpy of hydration.

29. (c) Among the given statements (B), (C) and (E) are correct while remaining are incorrect. The correct form of (A) and (D) are as follows

(A) Atoms of all elements are composed of three fundamental particles i.e. electrons, protons and neutrons.

(D) Protons and neutrons are collectively known as nucleons.

30. (a) According to Boyle's law, at constant temperature, the pressure of a fixed amount of a gas varies inversely with its volume.

$$p \propto \frac{1}{V}$$

or $$p = (nRT)\frac{1}{V}$$

Compare it with straight line equation, $y = mx + C$

we will get, $y = p$, $x = \frac{1}{V}$ with $C = 0$

and slope $(m) = T$

Thus, from the given options we can clearly see that, the correct option is given in option (a),

i.e. p vs $1/V$ is a straight line with $T_3 > T_2 > T_1$.

31. (b) Among the given options covalent bonding is not an intermolecular force. It is the bond which is formed by mutual sharing of electrons between the combining atoms of the same or different element.

Whereas dipole-dipole forces, dipole-induced dipole forces, hydrogen bonds and dispersion forces are intermolecular forces.

32. (a) $\underset{\text{Sodium ethanoate}}{CH_3-\overset{\overset{}{}}{\underset{\underset{O}{\|}}{C}}-\overset{-\ +}{ONa}} + NaOH \xrightarrow[\text{Decarboxylation}]{CaO,\ \Delta} CH_4 + Na_2CO_3$

The product formed in above reaction is CH_4. Thus, weight of two moles of CH_4 is 2×12 i.e. 32.

33. (c) Among the given cases, option (c) is an example of heterogeneous catalysis as in this case the reactant and the catalyst are present in different phase.

Whereas all other are example of homogeneous catalysis as in respective reaction the reactants and the catalyst are present in same phase.

(a) $\underset{\text{Sugar solution}}{C_{12}H_{22}O_{11}(aq)} + H_2O(l) \xrightarrow{H_2SO_4(l)} \underset{\text{Glucose}}{C_6H_{12}O_6(aq)} + \underset{\text{Fructose}}{C_6H_{12}O_6(aq)}$

(b) $NO(g) + O_3(g) \longrightarrow O_2(g) + NO_2(g)$

$NO_2(g) + O(g) \longrightarrow NO(g) + O_2(g)$

[These reactions are involve in ozone depletion through nitrous oxide.]

(c) $N_2(g) + 3H_2(g) \xrightarrow{Fe(s),\ Mo(s)} 2NH_3(g)$

(d) $2SO_2(g) + O_2(g) \xrightarrow{NO(g)} 2SO_3(g)$

34. (b) (A) is true but (R) is false.

(A) is correct because all alkali metals gives deep blue solution by giving electrons.

When sodium metal dissolved in liquid ammonia following reaction takes place.

$$Na + (x+y)NH_3 \longrightarrow \underset{\text{Ammoniated cations}}{[Na(NH_3)_x]^+} + \underset{\text{Ammoniated electrons}}{2[e^-(NH_3)_y]^-}$$

Thus, the correct (R) statement is:

The ammoniated electrons are responsible for the blue colour of the solution as they absorb the energy from visible region of light and, thus impart blue colour to the solution.

35. (d)

Given species	NH_3	$AlCl_3$	$BeCl_2$	CCl_4	PCl_5
Number of electrons central atom	8	6	4	8	10

Thus, among the given species $AlCl_3$, $BeCl_2$, PCl_5 does not have eight electrons around the central atom.

36. (b) The complete given reaction is as follows

$$+ 2[Ag(NH_3)_2] + 3\,\bar{O}H \xrightarrow[H_2O]{\Delta}$$
[Tollen's reagent]

$H_2O + NH_3 +$ (Major) $+ Ag\downarrow$ Silver

Tollen's reagent oxidises only the aldehyde group in the above reaction not the ketonic group.

37. (a) The correct match is A-III, B-IV, C-I, D-II.
Structure of given oxoacids of sulphur are as follows

Peroxodisulphuric acid [Two S—OH, four S=O one S—O—S bonds.]

Sulphuric acid [Two S—OH, two S=O bonds.]

Pyrosulphuric - acid [Two S—OH, four S=O bond, one S—O—S bonds]

Sulphrous acid [Two S—OH, one S=O bond.]

38. (d) Among the given species that follows Huckel rule are given as

Benzene [No. of π e^-=6]

Cyclopentadienyl [No. of π e^-=6]

Cyclopropenyl cation [No. of π e^-=2]

Anthracene [No. of π e^- =14]

Whereas all other are non-aromatic and does not follows Huckel rule, as (iii), (iv) and (vi) have 4, 4 and 8 π electrons respectively.

39. (b) Pumice stone is an example of solid sol. In this dispersion phase is gas and dispersion medium is solid.

40. (a) Among the given option the correct relation between change in enthalpy (ΔH) and change in internal energy (ΔU) is, $\Delta H = \Delta U + \Delta n_g RT$

41. (a) Among the given alcohols, will most readily dehydrated under acidic conditions to give ( ) 1, 3 butadiene as a product, in which double bonds are present in conjugation.

42. (b) Benzyl phenyl ether on heating with HI gives benzyl iodide (*A*) and phenol (*B*). The complete reaction is as follows

$$C_6H_5-CH_2-O-C_6H_5 \xrightarrow[\Delta]{HI} C_6H_5-CH_2I + C_6H_5OH$$

Benzyl phenyl ether; (*A*) Benzyliodide; (*B*) Phenol

43. (d) The value of *a*, *b* and *c* is 1, 3, 8 the complete balanced equation is as follows.

$$Cr_2O_7^{2-} + 3SO_3^{2-}(aq) + 8H^+(aq) \longrightarrow 2Cr^{3+}(aq) + 3SO_4^{2-}(aq) + \frac{8}{2}H_2O(l)$$

44. (b) Among the given complex $[Co(Cl_2)(en)_2]NO_3$ is most stable because it is a chelating complex.
It coordinates with central metal atom to form a ring compound.
Due to this reason, there is more force of attraction between the central metal ion and the chelating agent therefore it is more stable.

45. (b) As we know that, octahedral voids are present at the centre of edge length of the cube. Also, if any atom is present at the edge length then it divide into 1/ 4 parts.

Thus, fraction of one edge centred octahedral void lies in one unit cell of fcc is 1/ 4.

46. (b) Among the given statements C and D statements are incorrect. Their correct forms are as follows

(C) Basic character decreases from V_2O_3 to V_2O_4 to V_2O_5.

In general, the oxides in lower oxidation states of metals are basic and in their higher oxidation states they are acidic.

(D) V_2O_4 dissolves in acids to give VO_2^+ salts.

47. (b) According to given, general equation

$$A + B \rightleftharpoons C + D$$

$$\text{Equilibrium constant } (K_{eq}) = \frac{(10)(6)}{(2)(3)} = \frac{60}{6}$$

$$K_{eq} = 10$$

We know that,

$$\Delta G^\circ = -2.303\, RT \log K_{eq}$$

$$\therefore \quad \Delta G^\circ = -2.303 \times 2 \times 300 \times \log(10)$$

$$= -1381.8 \text{ cal}$$

48. (d)

$$\underset{\text{Ethanal}}{CH_3C\overset{O}{\overset{\|}{C}}-H} \xrightarrow[\text{(ii) } H_3O^+]{\text{(i) LiAlH}_4} CH_3-CH_2OH \xrightarrow[\Delta]{H_2SO_4}$$

$$\underset{\substack{\text{Ethene}\\(B)}}{CH_2=CH_2} \xrightarrow{HBr} \underset{\substack{[C]\\\text{Bromoethane}}}{CH_3CH_2Br} \xrightarrow[\text{Na/Dry ether}]{C_6H_5Br} \underset{\substack{\text{Ethyl benzene}\\[D]}}{C_6H_5CH_2CH_3}$$

49. (c) Statement I is false but statement II is true. The correct statement I is : The nutrient rich water bodies lead to eutrophication.

The process in which nutrient enriched water bodies support a dense population, which kills animals life by depriving it of oxygen and results in subsequent loss of biodiversity is known as eutrophication.

50. (d) Among the given reaction, $Fe_2O_3 + CO \longrightarrow 2FeO + CO_2$ reaction does not occur between 900 K to 1500 K temperature range in the blast furnace during extraction of iron. This reaction occur in temperature range of about 500-800 K (i.e. reduction zone).

NC2 NEET Chronicles

1. (a) Spin only magnetic moment is given by,

$$\mu_s = \sqrt{n(n+2)}$$

where, n = number of unpaired electrons

A. $Ti^{3+} \longrightarrow 3d^1, n=1$

$\mu_s = \sqrt{1(1+2)} = \sqrt{3}$

B. $Cr^{2+} \longrightarrow 3d^4, n=4$

$\mu_s = \sqrt{4(4+1)} = \sqrt{20}$

C. $Mn^{2+} \longrightarrow 3d^5, n=5$

$\mu_s = \sqrt{5(5+1)} = \sqrt{30}$

D. $Fe^{2+} \longrightarrow 3d^6, n=4$

$\mu_s = \sqrt{4(4+1)} = \sqrt{20}$

E. $Sc^{3+} \longrightarrow 3d^0, \mu_s = 0$

Hence, B and D have same value of magnetic moment.

2. (d) The stability of carbocation is depending on number of α-hydrogen.

The more the number of alpha hydrogen atoms, more is the stability of the carbocation.

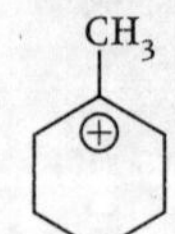

has 7 α-hydrogen, which is highest among all given structures.

3. (a) Both statement I and statement II are true.

4. (a) The correct match is
A-I, B-IV, C-II, D-III.

A. $NH_3 \longrightarrow sp^3$ hybridised with 1 lone pair $\longrightarrow$ trigonal pyramidal.

B. $BrF_5 \longrightarrow sp^3d^2$ hybridised with 1 lone pair $\longrightarrow$ square pyramidal

C. $XeF_4 \longrightarrow sp^3d^2$ hybridised with 2 lone pairs $\longrightarrow$ square planar

D. $SF_6 \longrightarrow sp^3d^2$ hybridised with zero lone pair $\longrightarrow$ octahedral

5. (a) In 4 moles of He, number of He atom $= 4 \times N_A$

In 4u of He, number of He atom = 1

In 4g of He, number of He atom $= N_A$

In 2.271098 L of He, number of He atom $= \frac{2.27}{22.7} \times N_A = 0.1 N_A$

Hence, option (a) is correct.

6. (b) The complete reaction is as follows,

$$C_6H_{11}\text{—}CH_2\text{—}CH{=}CH_2 \xrightarrow[H_2O_2/\bar{O}H]{BH_3} C_6H_{11}\text{—}CH_2\text{—}CH_2\text{—}CH_2OH \xrightarrow{\text{PCC}} C_6H_{11}\text{—}CH_2\text{—}CH_2\text{—}CHO$$

PCC (oxidation of 1° alcohol into aldehyde)

7. (d) The correct match is
A-II, B-III, C-IV, D-I.

8. (d) The reactivity order of alcohols toward Lucas reagent is 3° alcohols > 2° alcohols > 1° alcohol.

(a) $CH_3\text{—}CH_2\text{—}CH_2\text{—}CH_2\text{—}OH$
(1° alcohol)

(b) $CH_3\text{—}CH_2\text{—}CH(CH_3)\text{—}OH$
(2° alcohol)

(c) $CH_3\text{—}CH(CH_3)\text{—}CH_2\text{—}OH$
(1° alcohol)

(d) $CH_3\text{—}C(CH_3)_2\text{—}OH$
(3° alcohol)

Hence, option (d) is correct.

9. (a) In

$$PCl_5(g) \rightleftharpoons PCl_3(g) + Cl_2(g)$$

$$K_p = K_C (RT)^{\Delta n_g}$$

when $\Delta n_g = 0$ then $K_p = K_C$
$\Delta n_g \neq 0$ then $K_p \neq K_C$

In $PCl_5(g)$,
$\Delta n_g \neq 0$
$\therefore K_p \neq K_C$

Rest all options has $\Delta n_g = 0$.
So, $K_p = K_C$ for them.

10. (b) The correct match is
A-III, B-IV, C-I, D-II.

11. (a) Both statement I and statement II are true.

12. (a) Intramolecular hydrogen bonding is present in *o*-nitrophenol.

(Structure of *o*-nitrophenol: N(=O)→O, O---H–O, Intramolecular H-bond)

13. (b) The process of changing the state directly from solid to vapour is called as sublimation.

Hence, option (b) is correct.

14. (c) The statement given in A, C, D are correct in regard to increase in entropy.

A. When liquid evaporates to vapour, randomness increases, so entropy increases.

C. $\Delta n_g = 2 - 0 = 2$
$\Delta n_g = +ve \longrightarrow \Delta S = +ve$
$\Rightarrow$ Entropy increases.

D. $\Delta n_g = 2 - 1 = 1$
$\Delta n_g = +ve \longrightarrow \Delta S = +ve$
$\Rightarrow$ Entropy increases.

Statement given in B is incorrect, because, when temperature decreases, entropy decreases.

15. (d) Among the given elements, only Po does not show −2 oxidation state due to its highly metallic nature.

16. (a) The correct match is
A-II, B-IV, C-I, D-III.

A. $2H_2O \longrightarrow O_2 + 4H^+ + 4e^-$

2 mol H_2O require 4F charge
1 mol H_2O will require 2F charge.

B. $8H^+ + MnO_4^- + 5e^- \longrightarrow Mn^{2+} + 4H_2O$

1 mole of MnO_4^- will require 5F charge.

C. $CaCl_2 + 2e^- \longrightarrow Ca + 2Cl^{-1}$

1 mole of Ca will require 2F charge.

1.5 moles of Ca will require 3F charge.

D. $FeO + H_2O \longrightarrow Fe_2O_3 + 2H^+ + 2e^-$

2 moles of FeO will require 2F charge.

1 mole of FeO will require 1 F charge.

17. (a) Electronegativity increases in period from left to right. The electronegativity values of given elements are,

$Si = 1.8, \quad C = 2.5, \quad N = 3.0,$
$O = 3.5, \quad F = 4$

Hence, the correct sequence is

$Si < C < N < O < F.$

18. (c) The correct IUPAC name and structure is,

$$\overset{}{CH_3}-\overset{3°}{CH}-\overset{3°}{CH}-CH_3$$
$$\quad\;\; | \qquad\; |$$
$$\quad CH_3 \quad CH_3$$

2, 3-dimethylbutane

[2 tertiary (3°) carbon]

19. (a) Fehling reagent comprises of two solutions.

Fehling $A \rightarrow$ Aqueous solution of $CuSO_4$.

Fehling $B \rightarrow$ Alkaline sodium potassium tartrate (Rochelle's salt).

20. (d) Formula for calculating activation energy is given by

$$\log_{10}\left(\frac{k_2}{k_1}\right) = \frac{E_a}{2.303R}\left[\frac{1}{T_1} - \frac{1}{T_2}\right]$$

Here, k_1 is rate constant at T_1

k_2 is rate constant at T_2.

Hence, rate constant at two different temperatures should be known to calculate the activation energy of any chemical reaction.

21. (d) According to Arrhenius equation,

$$k = A.e^{-E_a/RT}$$

$$\ln k = \ln A - \frac{E_a}{RT}$$

$$\ln k = \frac{-E_a}{R}\left(\frac{1}{T}\right) + \ln A$$

Compare it with $y = mx + c$

$\ln k \rightarrow y$ and $1/T \rightarrow x$

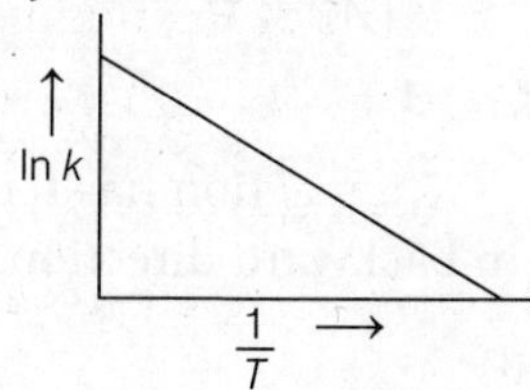

Hence, option (d) match the correct graph.

22. (c) The correct match is

A-IV, B-I, C-II, D-III.

A. [cyclohexylidene-cyclohexane] $\xrightarrow[\text{(ii) Zn}-H_2O]{\text{(i) } O_3}$ 2 [cyclohexanone]

Reduction ozonolysis

B. [benzene] $\xrightarrow{C_6H_5COCl\,/\,\text{Anhy. } AlCl_3}$ [benzophenone]

Friedel-Craft acylation

C. [cyclohexanol] $\xrightarrow{CrO_3}$ [cyclohexanone]

D. [ethylbenzene, CH_2-CH_3] $\xrightarrow[\text{KOH, } \Delta]{KMnO_4}$ [potassium benzoate, COOK]

23. (d) Reactivity toward $S_N1 \propto$ stability of carbocation, and stability of carbocation depends on number of α-hydrogen.

(a) [cyclohexylmethyl bromide] $\downarrow -Br^{\ominus}$ (1α-hydrogen)

(b) [bromocyclohexane] $\downarrow -Br^{\ominus}$ (4α-hydrogen)

(c) [bromobenzene] $\downarrow$ No S_N1

(d) [1-bromoethylbenzene, CH_3, Br] $\downarrow -Br^{\ominus}$ [benzylic carbocation, CH_3]

(Resonance + 4α-hydrogen)

Hence, (d) is correct option.

24. (d) $\underset{+2\;-1}{BaCl_2} + \underset{+1\;+6\;-2}{Na_2SO_4} \longrightarrow \underset{+2\;+6\;-2}{BaSO_4} + \underset{+1\;-1}{2NaCl}$

As there is no change in oxidation state of any element, hence it is not a redox reaction.

25. (a) Both statement I and statement II are true.

26. (a) Both statement I and statement II are true.

27. (c) The correct match is

A-III, B-IV, C-II, D-I.

Molecule	Structure	(Type of bonds between two carbon atoms)
A. Ethane	H_3C-CH_3	1σ
B. Ethene	$H_2C=CH_2$	1 σ, 1 π
C. C_2	C=C	2π (as per MOT)
D. Ethyne	H—C≡C—H	1 σ, 2π

28. (b) The relation between solubility and Henry's law constant is

$$\text{Solubility} \propto \frac{1}{K_H}$$

if K_H decreases then solubility increases.

K_H for gas B is lowest (2×10^{-5} k bar) and A has highest (145 k bar).

Hence, the order of solubility is given by

$$B > C > A.$$

29. (a) $E \propto \frac{Z^2}{n^2} \Rightarrow \frac{E_1}{E_2} = \frac{Z_1^2}{n_1^2} \times \frac{n_2^2}{Z_2^2}$

$He^+ \longrightarrow n_1 = 1$ and $Z_1 = 2$

$Be^{3+} \longrightarrow n_2 = 2$ and $Z_2 = 4$

$$\frac{E_1}{E_2} = \frac{2^2}{1^2} \times \frac{2^2}{4^2} = 1 \Rightarrow E_1 = E_2$$

Hence, it will be same as $-x$J for Be^{3+} ion.

30. (c) $E° = +ve$ for Mn^{3+} / Mn^{2+}

$Mn = 25 \longrightarrow 3d^5 4s^2$

$Mn^{2+} \longrightarrow 3d^5$

$Mn^{3+} \longrightarrow 3d^4$

Mn^{2+} has half-filled ($3d^5$) stable configuration.

Thus, Mn^{3+} has very high tendency to gain an electron due to this it has high +ve value of electrode potential (E°) while in other case, they does not gain electron easily. Hence, the reason is change of d^4 to d^5-configuration.

31. (c) Glucose does not react with Schiff's reagent and $NaHSO_3$.

Glucose + Tollen's reagent ⟶ Silver mirror

Glucose + HCN ⟶ Cyanohydin formation

Glucose + NH_2OH ⟶ Oxime formation

32. (a) The correct match is

A-II, B-III, C-IV, D-I.

33. (b) First ionisation enthalpy is the energy required to remove the first most loosely bound electron from an isolated atom in its ground state.

The electronic configuration is,

$Li \rightarrow 2s^1$, $Be \rightarrow 2s^2$, $B \rightarrow 2s^2, 2p^1$

$C \rightarrow 2s^2 2p^2$, $N \rightarrow 2s^2 2p^3$

The correct increasing order is,

Li < B < Be < C < N

34. (b) $NaOH + HCl \longrightarrow NaCl + H_2O$

Given, mass of NaOH = 1g

Mole of NaOH $= \frac{1}{40}$ mol = 0.025 mol

Mole of HCl $= \frac{0.75 \times 25}{1000} = 0.01875$ mol

Now, finding the limiting reagent (LR) value

$$= \frac{\text{Given amount}}{\text{Stiochiometry coefficient}}$$

NaOH : HCl

$$\frac{0.025}{1} > \frac{0.01875}{1}$$

So, limiting reagent (LR) will be HCl

Unreacted moles of NaOH

$= 0.025 - 0.01875 = 0.00625$ mol

Unreacted mass $= 0.00625 \times 40$ g

$= 0.25$ g $= 250$ mg

35. (c) For the given reaction,

$$2A \rightleftharpoons B + C,\ K_C = 4 \times 10^{-3}$$

At a given time

$[A] = [B] = [C] = 2 \times 10^{-3}$ M

$$Q_C = \frac{[B][C]}{[A]^2}$$

$$\Rightarrow \quad Q_C = 1$$

As $Q_C > K_C$, reaction has tendency to go in backward direction.

36. (a)

Basic radical	Group number
(B) Cu^{2+}	II
(A) Al^{3+}	III
(D) Co^{2+}	IV
(C) Ba^{2+}	V
(E) Mg^{2+}	VI

Group number increases ↓

Hence, the correct order is B, A, D, C, E.

37. (d) The reaction involves are,

$3R—OH + PCl_3 \longrightarrow 3RCl + H_3PO_3\,(A)$

$R—OH + PCl_5 \longrightarrow R—Cl + HCl + POCl_3\,(B)$

Hence, products *A* and *B* are

$A = H_3PO_3$;

$B = POCl_3$

38. (b) Given, current (i) = 9.6487 A

1F = 96487 C and t = 100 s

$$w = \frac{E(it)}{96487}$$

$$w = \frac{\frac{63}{2} \times 9.6487 \times 100}{96487}$$

$w = 0.315$ g of Cu

39. (a) Osmotic pressure is given by,

$\pi = CRT$

Plot is of between osmotic pressure and concentration, i.e. π *vs* C.

On comparing with $y = mx + C$

Slope $m = RT$

$25.73 = 0.083 \times T$

$T = 310$ K $= 37°$C

40. (a) The complete reaction is as follow,

$CH_3—CH_2—CH_2I \xrightarrow[S_N2]{NaCN} CH_3CH_2—CH_2CN$ (Product *A*)

$\xrightarrow[\text{Partial hydrolysis}]{\overline{O}H}$ $CH_3CH_2CH_2—C(=O)—NH_2$ (Product *B*)

$\xrightarrow[Br_2]{NaOH}$ $CH_3—CH_2—CH_2—NH_2$ Propylamine (*C*)

41. (d) Three canonical form can be drawn for CO_3^{2-} ion.

$CO_3^{2-} \longleftrightarrow O^-—C(=O)—O^- \longleftrightarrow O=C(—O^-)—O^- \longleftrightarrow O^-—C(—O^-)=O$

Canonical structure

$\longleftrightarrow [O \cdots C \cdots O (O)]^{2-}$

Resonance hybrid

Other corrected forms are

(a) Ozone has only two resonating structure.

(b) BF_3 has zero dipole moment.

(c) Dipole moment of NH_3 is greater than NF_3.

42. (a) Both Statement I and Statement II are true.

43. (b) The complete reaction is as follows,

$C_6H_5—C(H)=CH—C_6H_5 \xrightarrow{KMnO_4/H^+} 2\,C_6H_5—COOH$ (Major) product

44. (a) $Ce^{4+} = [Xe]\,4f^0\,5d^0$

$Yb^{2+} = [Xe]\,4f^{14}5d^0$

Both ions does not contain any unpaired electrons.

Hence, they are diamagnetic.

45. (d) $\underset{(2.8\times10^{-3}M)}{2NO(g)} \rightleftharpoons \underset{(3\times10^{-3}M)}{N_2(g)} + \underset{(4.2\times10^{-3}M)}{O_2(g)}$

$$K_C = \frac{[N_2][O_2]}{[NO]^2}$$

$$= \frac{3\times10^{-3}\times4.2\times10^{-3}}{(2.8\times10^{-3})^2} = 1.60 \quad ....(i)$$

$$\underset{t=t_{eq}\ (C-C\alpha)}{2NO(g)} \rightleftharpoons \underset{\frac{C\alpha}{2}}{N_2(g)} + \underset{\frac{C\alpha}{2}}{O_2(g)}$$

$$K_C = \frac{(C\alpha)^2}{4C^2(1-\alpha)^2}$$

$$\left(\frac{\alpha}{1-\alpha}\right)^2 = 4\times1.6 \text{ [from Eq.(i) } K_C = 1.60]$$

$$\frac{\alpha}{1-\alpha} = 2\times1.26 \Rightarrow \alpha = 0.717$$

46. (b)

Element	%	mole	Simple ratio
A	32	$\frac{32}{64}=\frac{1}{2}$	1
B	20	$\frac{20}{40}=\frac{1}{2}$	1
C	46	$\frac{48}{32}=\frac{3}{2}$	3

Empirical formula = ABC_3

47. (b) In reversible isothermal process, work done is,

$$W = -2.303nRT\log_{10}\left(\frac{p_1}{p_2}\right)$$

$$= -2.303\times1\times2\times298\log_{10}\left(\frac{20}{10}\right)$$

$$= -413.14 \text{ calories}$$

48. (d) Dilute H_2SO_4 do not act as oxidising agent which prevent oxidation of Fe^{2+} into Fe^{3+} while concentrated H_2SO_4 will oxidise Fe^{2+} into Fe^{3+}.

49. (a) Given, rate is quadruples, i.e. $r_2 = 4r_1$

We know, $\frac{r_2}{r_1} = 4 = \frac{k_2}{k_1}$

Now, $\log_{10}\left(\frac{k_2}{k_1}\right) = \frac{E_a}{2.303R}\left[\frac{1}{T_1} - \frac{1}{T_2}\right]$

[where, $T_1 = 27°C = 300$ K, $T_2 = 57°C = 330$K]

$$\log_{10}(4) = \frac{E_a\times1000}{2.303\times8.314}\left(\frac{1}{300} - \frac{1}{330}\right)$$

$$E_a = 38.04 \text{ kJ/mol}$$

50. (a) The complete reaction is as follow,

OH, H_3C (cyclohexanol) $\xrightarrow{PBr_3}$ Br, H_3C (cyclohexyl bromide) (Major product A) $\xrightarrow[\Delta]{\text{Alc. KOH}}$ H_3C (cyclohexene) (Major product B)

CHEMISTRY-XIIth

MIND MAP

MEDACE

Test 1

Syllabus

- Different Methods for Expressing the Concentration of Solution : Molarity, Molality, Mole Fraction, Percentage (by Volume and Mass Both).

NCERT Page 1 to 5

For deeper insight **Scan the QR Code**

Chapter 01

Solute and Solvent

A solution is a homogeneous mixture of two or more than two components, whose composition can be varied with certain limits.

Solute (lesser quantity) + Solvent (excess quantity) → Solution (Solute, Solvent)

Types of Solutions

1. On the basis of quantity of components.

(i) **Saturated solution** It is the solution containing the maximum possible quantity of solute dissolved in a solvent at a certain temperature.

(ii) **Unsaturated solution** It is the solution in which more amount of solute can be dissolved at a given temperature. It can be further divided into two types,

(a) **Dilute solution** It is the solution containing lower quantity of solute.

(b) **Concentrated solution** It is the solution containing higher quantity of solute but still lower than the quantity of a saturated solution.

2. On the basis of physical states of components.

Types of solution	Solute	Solvent	Examples
Gaseous solutions	Gas	Gas	Mixture of nitrogen and oxygen gases.
	Liquid	Gas	Chloroform mixed with nitrogen gas.
	Solid	Gas	Camphor in nitrogen gas.
Liquid solutions	Gas	Liquid	Oxygen dissolved in water.
	Liquid	Liquid	Ethanol dissolved in water.
	Solid	Liquid	Glucose dissolved in water.
Solid solutions	Gas	Solid	Solution of hydrogen in palladium.
	Liquid	Solid	Amalgam of mercury with sodium.
	Solid	Solid	Copper dissolved in gold.

3. On the basis of number of compounds.

Solutions
- **Binary** (2 components)
- **Ternary** (3 components)
- **Quaternary** (4 components)

Expressing Concentration of Solutions

The relative amount of a solute present in a solution. The concentration of the solution may be expressed in any of the following ways

- **Mass Percentage (*w/w*)**
The mass of a component present in 100 g of the solution.
Mass % of a component

$$= \frac{\text{Mass of the component in the solution}}{\text{Total mass of the solution}} \times 100$$

e.g. 10% *w/w* solution of NaCl in water means that 10 g of NaCl is dissolved in 90 g of water resulting in a 100 g solution.

- **Volume Percentage (*V/V*)**
The volume of a component present in 100 parts by volume of the solution.
Volume % of a component

$$= \frac{\text{Volume of the component}}{\text{Total volume of solution}} \times 100$$

- **Mass by Volume Percentage (*w/V*)**
The mass of solute dissolved in 100 mL of the solution.
e.g. A 10% solution of sodium chloride (*w/V*) means that 10 g of sodium chloride is dissolved in 100 mL of solution. This unit is commonly used in medicine and pharmacy.

- **Mole Fraction (χ)**
The number of moles of one component divided by the total number of moles of all the components present in the solution.
e.g. In a binary solution containing two components *A* and *B*.

$$\text{Mole fraction of } A(\chi_A) = \frac{n_A}{n_A + n_B}$$

$$\text{Mole fraction of } B(\chi_B) = \frac{n_B}{n_A + n_B}$$

n_A = no. of moles of *A*, (Solute)
n_B = no. of moles of *B*, (Solvent)
Sum of mole fraction of solute and solvent is always unity. So,

$$\chi_A + \chi_B = 1$$

- **Molality (*m*)**
The number of moles of solute present in per kilogram (kg) of the solvent.

$$\text{Molality } (m) = \frac{\text{No. of moles of solute}}{\text{Mass of solvent (in kg)}}$$

- When molality of a solution is one, it is called one molal solution.
- Its unit is mol/kg.

- **Parts per million (ppm)**
The number of parts of the component dissolved in one millionth part of the total number of all components of the solution.

$$\text{ppm} = \frac{\text{Number of parts of the component}}{\text{Total number of parts of all components of the solution}} \times 10^6$$

Concentration in ppm can be expressed as mass to mass, volume to volume and mass to volume. The concentration of pollutants in water or atmosphere is often expressed in terms of $\mu g\ mL^{-1}$ or ppm.

- **Parts per billion (ppb)**
The amount of solute, which is dissolved in 10^9 parts of a solution.

$$\text{ppb} = \frac{\text{Number of parts of the component}}{\text{Total number of parts of all components of the solution}} \times 10^9$$

- **Molarity (*M*)**
The number of moles of solute present in 1 L of solution.

$$\text{Molarity } (M) = \frac{\text{Number of moles of solute}}{\text{Volume of solution (in L)}}$$

$$M = \frac{\text{Mass of solute (in g)}}{\text{Molar mass of solute (g/mol)} \times \text{Volume of solution (in L)}}$$

- When molarity of a solution is one, it is called one molar solution.
- Its unit is mol/L.

- **Normality (*N*)**
The number of gram equivalents of substance dissolved in per litre of the solution.

$$\text{Normality } (N) = \frac{\text{Number of gram-equivalent of solute}}{\text{Volume of solution (in L)}}$$

$$= \frac{\text{Mass of solute (in g)}}{\text{Equivalent weight (g/equiv)} \times \text{Volume (in L)}}$$

Unit = equivalents per litre.

- **Formality (*F*)**
The number of gram formula present in a litre of solution for an ionic solid.

$$\text{Formality } (F) = \frac{\text{Mass of solute}}{\text{Formula mass} \times \text{Volume (in L)}}$$

Calculation of Normality/Molarity on Dilution

- If a solution is diluted from V_1 to V_2, the normality of that solution changes according to the equation,

$$\underset{\text{Before dilution}}{N_1V_1} = \underset{\text{After dilution}}{N_2V_2}$$

- Similarly, in terms of molarities, it can be given by the equation,

$$\underset{\text{Before dilution}}{M_1V_1} = \underset{\text{After dilution}}{M_2V_2}$$

Calculation of Normality/Molarity on Mixing

- If two solutions of the same solute are mixed then normality of the final solution is given by
$N_1V_1 + N_2V_2 = N_3V_3$ [where, $V_3 = V_1 + V_2$]
Similarly, in terms of molarities
$M_1V_1 + M_2V_2 = M_3V_3$
- If n_1 moles of reactant 1 react with n_2 moles of reactant 2 then
$n_2N_1V_1 = n_1N_2V_2$
- Similarly in terms of molarity
$n_2M_1V_1 = n_1M_2V_2$

Inter-Relation Between Different Concentration of Solution

- Relation between molality and weight percentage of solute (χ)

$$= \frac{1000 \times \text{weight \% of solute } (\chi)}{(100-\chi) \times \text{molecular weight of solute}}$$

- Relation between molality (*m*) and mole fraction of the solute (χ)

$$\chi = \frac{mM_1}{1 + mM_1}$$

where, M_1 = molecular mass of the solvent

- Relation between molality (*m*) and molarity (*M*)
- Molality $(m) = \frac{M}{d - MM_2}$
(If *d* in kg/L and M_2 in kg/mol)

$$= \frac{M}{1000d - MM_2} \times 1000$$

(If *d* in g/L and M_2 in g/mol)

- Molarity $(M) = \frac{m \times d}{1 + \frac{m \times M_2}{1000}}$

where, M_2 = molar mass of the solute
d = density of the solution.

Test 2

Syllabus
- The Vapour Pressure of Solutions and Raoult's Law-Ideal and Non-Ideal Solutions, Vapour Pressure-Composition, Plots For Ideal and Non-Ideal Solutions.

NCERT Page 5 to 15

For deeper insight **Scan the QR Code**

Solubility

The maximum amount of a substance that can be dissolved in a specified amount of solvent at a specified temperature.

Solubility of a Solid in a Liquid

- Every solid does not dissolve in a given liquid, e.g. NaCl and sugar dissolve readily in water while naphthalene and anthracene do not.
- The following factors affect the solubility of a solid in a liquid.
- **Nature of Solute and Solvent**
- Like dissolves like.
- Ionic solute dissolves in polar solvent, whereas covalent solute dissolves in non-polar solvents.
- **Effect of Temperature**
- Dissolution can be exothermic or endothermic.
- For exothermic → ($\Delta_{sol}H < 0$)
- For endothermic → ($\Delta_{sol}H > 0$)
- **Effect of pressure** It does not have any significant effect on solubility.

Solubility of a Gas in a Liquid

All gases are soluble in water as well as in other liquids to a greater or smaller extent. The solubility of gases in liquids depends upon following factors.

- **Nature of the Gas**
- The gases which can be easily liquified are more soluble in common solvents. e.g. CO_2 is more soluble than H_2 and O_2 in water.
- Different gases dissolve to a different extent in the same solvent.
- Same gas has different solubilities in different solvents.
- **Nature of the Solvent**
- The gases which are capable of forming ions in aqueous solutions are much more soluble in water than in other solvents.
- e.g. Gases like NH_3 and HCl are highly soluble in water but not in organic solvents in which they do not ionise.
- **Temperature**
  The solubility of most gases in liquids decreases with increase of temperature. When dissolved, the gas molecules are present in liquid phase and the process of dissolution can be considered similar to condensation and heat is evolved in this process.
- **Pressure**
  The solubility of gas in liquid is also influenced by pressure. The relation between the solubility and pressure is given by Henry's Law.

Henry's Law

- Henry proposed a quantitative relation between pressure and solubility of a gas in a solvent which is known as Henry's law. It states that, "The solubility of a gas in a liquid at constant temperature is directly proportional to the partial pressure of the gas present above the surface of liquid or solution."
- **Alternatively** The partial pressure of the gas in vapour phase is proportional to the mole fraction of the gas in the solution.

$$p \propto \chi \text{ or } p = K_H\chi$$

- Here, p=partial pressure of the gas in vapour phase, χ=mole fraction of the gas in the solution and K_H=Henry's law constant.
- The graph between the partial pressure and the mole fraction of the gas is a straight line.

- Different gases have different K_H values at same temperature. It can be understood from the following examples.

Henry's Law Constant for O_2 and N_2 in Water

Temperature (K)	K_H(kbar) for O_2	K_H(kbar) for N_2
293	34.86	76.48
303	46.82	88.84

- K_H is a function of nature of the gas. Greater the value of K_H, lower is the solubility of the gas in the liquid at the same pressure.
- K_H increases with increase of temperature implying that solubility of gases decreases with increase of temperature at the same pressure.

Applications of Henry's Law

- **In production of carbonated beverages.** To increase the solubility of CO_2 in soft drinks and soda water, the bottle is sealed under high pressure.
- **In deep sea diving.** Compressed air cylinder is used by scuba divers to get more oxygen in the blood but N_2 dissolved causes a disease called decompression sickness. Hence, air diluted with helium is used.
- **For climbers or people living at high altitude.** The partial pressure of O_2 is less at high altitudes than that at the ground level. Concentration of O_2 in the blood and tissues is so low that they feel weak and are unable to think properly, a disease called anoxia.

Limitations of Henry's Law

Although, Henry's law is an important law for solubility of gases but it is applied only, when
- pressure is not in excess.
- temperature is not at the lowest.
- gases are feebly soluble in solvent.
- the atomic state of gases is similar in both the liquid and gaseous states.

Vapour Pressure of Liquid Solutions

- Liquid solutions are the solutions in which liquid is the solvent. The solute can be a gas, liquid or a solid.
- The most important property of liquid-liquid solution is the vapour pressure. Total pressure exerted by the vapour above the liquid surface in equilibrium with the liquid at a given temperature is called **vapour pressure**.
- Vapour pressure doesn't depend upon the amount of liquid so it is an intensive property.

Vapour Pressure of Liquid-Liquid Solutions

- The vapour pressure of liquid in liquid solutions can be explained by using Raoult's law.
  This law states that "the partial pressure of any volatile constituent of a solution at a constant temperature is equal to the vapour pressure of pure constituent multiplied by the mole fraction of that constituent in the solution".

$$p_A = p^\circ_A\chi_A \qquad \left[p_A = \text{partial pressure of liquid } A\right.$$
$$p_B = p^\circ_B\chi_B \qquad \left.p_B = \text{partial pressure of liquid } B\right]$$

$$p_{Total} = p^\circ_A + (p^\circ_B - p^\circ_A)\chi_B$$

Following conclusions can be drawn from the equation
- Total vapour pressure over the solution can be related to the mole fraction of any one component.
- It varies linearly with the mole fraction of component B.
- Depending on the vapour pressure of the pure components A and B. Total vapour pressure over the solution decreases or increases with the increase of the mole fraction of component.

Relationship of vapour pressure and mole fraction of an ideal solution at constant temperature.

Ideal Solutions

- These are the solutions in which solute-solute and solvent-solvent interactions are almost similar to solute-solvent interactions ($A—B$=$A—A$ or $B—B$ interactions).
  Such solutions satisfy the following requirements.
- They obey Raoult's law for entire range of concentration at a given temperature.
- $\Delta_{mix}H = 0$
- $\Delta_{mix}V = 0$
- Examples of Ideal solution are n-hexane and n-heptane, bromoethane and chloroethane, benzene and toluene.

Non-Ideal Solutions

- These are the solutions in which solute-solvent interactions are different from solute-solute and solvent-solvent interactions.
- These solutions do not obey Raoult's law.
- Such solution satisfy the following requirements for the entire range of concentrations
- $\Delta_{mix}H \neq 0$
- $\Delta_{mix}V \neq 0$

Non-Ideal solutions show the following two types of deviations from ideal behaviour.

- **Non-ideal Solutions Showing Positive Deviations**
  When total vapour pressure for any solution is more than what is expected according to Raoult's law then it exhibits positive deviation ($A—B < A—A$ or $B—B$ interactions).

  For example,
  - Acetone + Carbon disulphide
  - Acetone + Benzene
  - Carbon tetrachloride + Methanol
  - Ethanol + Water

- **Non-ideal Solution Showing Negative Deviations**
  When total vapour pressure for any solution is less than that expected from Raoult's law then it exhibits negative deviation ($A—B > A—A$ or $B—B$ interactions).

  For example,
  - Chloroform + Benzene
  - Acetone + Aniline
  - Nitric acid + Water
  - Acetic acid + Pyridine

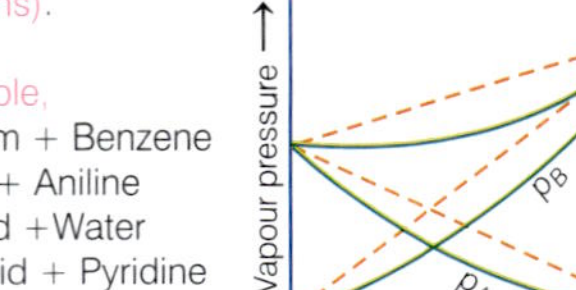

Test 3

Syllabus

- Colligative Properties of Dilute Solutions-Relative Lowering of Vapour Pressure, Depression of Freezing Point, Elevation of Boiling Point and Osmotic Pressure, Determination of Molecular Mass Using Colligative Properties, Abnormal Value of Molar Mass, van't Hoff Factor and its Significance.

NCERT Page 15 to 25

For deeper insight **Scan the QR Code**

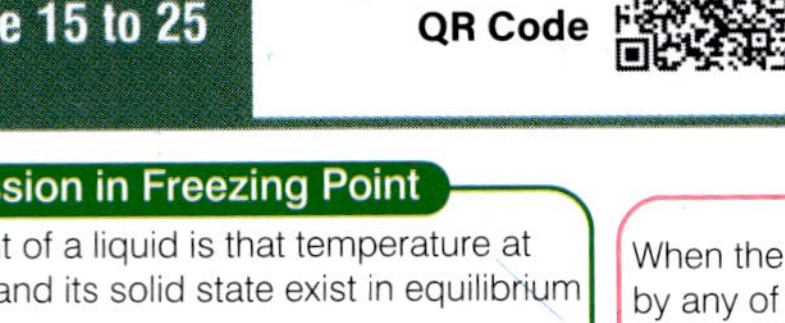

Colligative Properties

- The properties of a dilute solution, which depends only upon the number of particles present in a solution and their concentration are called **colligative properties**. (colligative : from Latin : co means together, ligare means to bind).
- They depend on the fraction of solute and solvent particles but not on the chemical nature of solute, i.e. these are proportional to the number of solute particles in the solution.

There are following four types of colligative properties.

Colligative Properties:
- Relative lowering of vapour pressure
- Elevation of boiling point
- Depression of freezing point
- Osmosis and osmotic pressure

For applying the formulae of colligative properties following conditions should be satisfied

- The solution should be very dilute.
- The solute should be non-volatile.
- The solute should not dissociate or associate in the solution.

Relative Lowering of Vapour Pressure

- When a non-volatile solute is mixed with a volatile solvent, the vapour pressure of solution (p) becomes less than the vapour pressure of pure solvent p_1°. It is called lowering of vapour pressure.
- The lowering of vapour pressure $= p_1^\circ - p = \Delta p$
- The ratio of the lowering of vapour pressure and the vapour pressure of pure solvent is defined as the relative lowering of vapour pressure.

$$\frac{p_1^\circ - p_1}{p_1^\circ} = \text{Relative lowering of vapour pressure}$$

- According to Raoult's law,

$$\frac{p_1^\circ - p_1}{p_1^\circ} = \chi_2 = \frac{n_2}{n_1 + n_2}$$

- Here, n_A and n_B are the number of moles of solvent and solute respectively, present in the solution.
- For a dilute solution $n_2 <<< n_1$

$$\frac{p_1^\circ - p_1}{p_1^\circ} = \frac{n_2}{n_1}$$

Elevation of Boiling Point

- The boiling point of a liquid is that temperature at which its vapour pressure becomes equal to the atmospheric pressure.
- When a non-volatile solute is dissolved in a pure solvent, its vapour pressure is decreased and boiling point increases.
- The difference in boiling points of the solution and pure solvent is called **elevation of boiling point** (ΔT_b).
- If T°_b is the boiling point of pure solvent and T_b is the boiling point of the solution then, $T_b > T^\circ_b$ and the elevation in boiling point, $\Delta T_b = T_b - T^\circ_b$.

1.013 bar or 1 atm
Boiling point of solvent solution
Solvent
Solution
T_b°
ΔT_b
T_b
Vapour pressure →
Temperature/K ⟶

- The vapour pressure curve for solution lies below the curve for solvent. The diagram shows that ΔT_b denotes the elevation in boiling point of a solvent in solution.
- The elevation in the boiling point (ΔT_b) of a solution is proportional to the molal concentration of the solute in a solution, i.e. $\Delta T_b \propto m$ or $\Delta T_b = K_b m$.
- Here, m (molality) is the number of moles of solute dissolved in 1 kg of solvent and is called **boiling point elevation constant** or **molal elevation constant (Ebullioscopic constant)**. If $m = 1$ then $\Delta T_b = K_b$

$$\Delta T_b = \frac{K_b \times 1000 \times w_2}{M_2 \times w_1}$$

- where, w_2 is mass of solute, M_2 is molar mass of solute and w_1 is mass of solvent.
- **Molal elevation constant** is the elevation in boiling point for 1 molal solution, i.e. a solution containing 1 gram mole of solute dissolved in 1000 g of the solvent.
- The unit of K_b is K kg mol^{-1}.
- The values of K_b which depends upon the nature of the solvent, can be calculated by using

$$K_b = \frac{R \times M_1 \times (T_b)^2}{1000 \times \Delta_{vap}H}$$

- Here, R = gas constant
  M_1 = molar mass of solvent
  T_b = boiling point of pure solvent in Kelvin
  $\Delta_{vap}H$ = enthalpy for vaporisation.

Depression in Freezing Point

- The freezing point of a liquid is that temperature at which the liquid and its solid state exist in equilibrium with each other.
- It is the temperature at which the liquid and solid states of a substance have the same vapour pressure.
- When a non-volatile solute is dissolved in a pure solvent the vapour pressure of the solvent is decreased and freezing point also decreases.
- If T°_f is the freezing point of pure solvent and T_f is the freezing point of its solution then, $T_f < T^\circ_f$. The difference in the freezing point of pure solvent and solution is called **depression in freezing point (ΔT_f)**.

$$\Delta T_f = T^\circ_f - T_f$$

- Graph showing ΔT_f, depression of the freezing point of a solvent in a solution.

Liquid solvent
Solution
Frozen solvent
T_f
ΔT_f
T_f°
Vapour pressure →
Temperature/K ⟶

- Depression in freezing point of a solution is proportional to the molal concentration of the solution, i.e. $\Delta T_f \propto m$ or $\Delta T_f = K_f m$
- where, K_f is called freezing point depression constant, molal depression constant or cryoscopic constant. If $m = 1$ then $\Delta T_f = K_f$.
- Molal freezing point depression constant is defined as the depression in freezing point for 1 molal solution, i.e. a solution containing 1 gram mole of solute dissolved in 1000 g of solvent.
- The unit of K_f is K kg mol^{-1}.
- The value of K_f that depends upon the nature of the solvent, can be calculated by using

$$K_f = \frac{R \times M_1 \times T_f^2}{1000 \times \Delta_{fus}H}$$

- Here, R = gas constant, M_1 = molar mass of the solvent, $\Delta_{fus}H$ = enthalpy for fusion and T_f = freezing point of pure solvent.

Osmosis and Osmotic Pressure

- **Osmosis** The phenomenon of the flow of solvent through a semipermeable membrane from pure solvent to the solution.
- **Reverse Osmosis** The process of movement of solvent through a semipermeable membrane from the solution to the pure solvent by applying excess pressure on the solution side.
- **Osmotic Pressure (π)** It is the excess pressure that must be applied to a solution to prevent osmosis, i.e. to stop the passage of solvent molecules through a semipermeable membrane into the solution.

$$\pi = CRT = \frac{n}{V}RT$$

Abnormal Molar Mass

When the molecular mass of a substance determined by any of the colligative properties comes out to be different than the expected value. Then the substance shows abnormal molecular mass.

van't Hoff factor (i) It is the ratio of the experimental value of the colligative property to the calculated value of the colligative property.

$$i = \frac{\text{Normal (calculated) molar mass}}{\text{Observed/abnormal molar mass}}$$

$$= \frac{\text{Observed colligative property}}{\text{Calculated colligative property}}$$

$$= \frac{\text{actual number of particles in solution}}{\text{number of particles taken}}$$

$$= \frac{\text{Total number of moles of particles after association/dissociation}}{\text{Number of moles of particle before association/dissociation}}$$

van't Hoff Factor (i)

van't Hoff factor can be applied in case of dissociation and association as follows

van't Hoff factor:
- $i = 1$
  - Neither association nor dissociation takes place
  - e.g. Glucose, urea.
- When $i > 1$
  - Dissociation will occur
  - e.g. NaCl, $AlCl_3$.
- When $i < 1$
  - Association will occur
  - e.g. CH_3COOH and PhCOOH in benzene.

Relationship Between van't Hoff Factor (i) and Colligative Properties

Relation between van't Hoff factor and different colligative properties are as follows

- With osmotic pressure,

$$\pi = \frac{n_2}{V} RTi = \frac{w_2}{m_2 V} RTi$$

- With relative lowering of vapour pressure,

$$\frac{p_1^\circ - p_1}{p_1^\circ} = i\frac{w_2 m_1}{m_2 w_1}$$

- With elevation in boiling point,

$$\Delta T_b = i \times K_b \times m$$

- With depression in freezing point,

$$\Delta T_f = i \times K_f \times m$$

All the symbols have their usual meaning.

Test 1

Syllabus

- Electrochemical Cells-Electrolytic and Galvanic Cells, Different Types of Electrodes, Electrode Potential Including Standard Electrode Potential, Half-Cell and Cell Reactions, EMF of Galvanic Cell and Its Measurement, Nernst Equation and Its Application, Relationship Between Cell Potential and Gibb's Energy Change.

NCERT Page 31 to 40

For deeper insight **Scan the QR Code**

Chapter 02

Electrochemistry

It is the branch of chemistry that deals with the study of production of electricity from energy released during spontaneous chemical reactions and the use of electrical energy to bring about non-spontaneous chemical transformation.

Electrochemical Cells

- It is a device that produces electricity as a result of chemical reaction. In other words, in this device the Gibbs energy of the spontaneous redox reaction is converted into electrical energy.
- They are also called as voltaic cell.
- The change of chemical energy to electrical energy causes lowering of free energy which appears as electrical energy and is measured in terms of emf.

Representation of Electrochemical Cell

The following conventions are used in representing an electrochemical cell.

- The electrode on which oxidation takes place is written on the left hand side. While the electrode on which reduction takes place is written on the right hand side.
- The electrode on the left hand side is written by writing the symbol of the metal (or the gas) first followed by the symbol of the ion with its concentration in brackets.
- The electrode on the right hand side is represented by writing the electrolyte first (anion) and then the metal or solid phase.
- Single vertical lines represent the base boundaries of the electrodes. Double vertical line represents the salt-bridge. C_1 and C_2 (or a_1 and a_2) represents the concentrations that are written within the brackets after the cation.

Terms Related with Electrochemical Cell

- **Electrode potential** The potential difference developed between the electrode and the electrolyte due to charge on metal.
- **Standard electrode potential** Electrode potential when concentration of all species in half-cell is unity.
- **Cell potential or EMF of cell** Electromotive force (EMF) is the potential difference, when no current is drawn from the system. It is measured in volts (V).

$$E^\circ_{cell} = E^\circ_{cathode} - E^\circ_{anode} \text{ or } E^\circ_{right} - E^\circ_{left}$$

- **Standard hydrogen electrode** It is a reference electrode against which the electrode potentials of all electrodes are measured.

Daniell Cell

- In this cell, anode is made up of Zn-rod which is placed in zinc sulphate solution (oxidation half-cell).
- Similarly, a Cu-rod is placed in copper sulphate solution taken in another beaker (reduction half-cell).
- In general, electrochemical cell involves the chemical reactions that takes place in two vessels each of which is called half-cell or redox couples.
- The two electrodes are connected by a wire and the two solutions are connected by a salt-bridge.

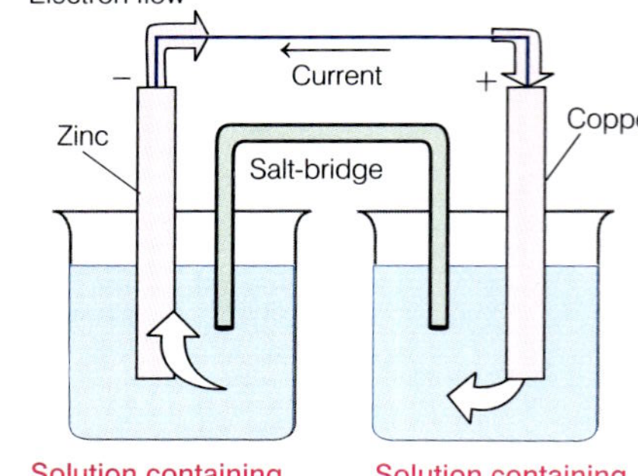

- When the Zn and Cu electrodes are joined by wire, following reactions takes places.
- At cathode, $Cu^{2+} + 2e^- \longrightarrow Cu(s)$ (Reduction half reaction)
- At anode, $Zn(s) \longrightarrow Zn^{2+} + 2e^-$ (Oxidation half reaction)
- Net reaction,

$$Zn(s) + Cu^{2+}(aq) \longrightarrow Zn^{2+}(aq) + Cu(s)$$

Function of Daniell cell when external voltage is applied.

- When $E_{ext} < 1.1$ V
  - (i) Electrons flow from Zn rod to Cu rod. Hence, current flows from Cu to Zn.
  - (ii) Zn dissolves at anode and copper deposits at cathode.
- When $E_{ext} = 1.1$ V
  - (i) No flow of electrons or current
  - (ii) No chemical reaction
- When $E_{ext} > 1.1$ V
  - (i) Electrons flow from Cu to Zn and current flows from Zn to Cu.
  - (ii) Zinc is deposited at the zinc electrode and copper dissolves at copper electrode.

Salt-Bridge

It is a U-shaped glass tube which contains *agar-agar* paste with, NH_4NO_3, KNO_3 or KCl as conducting electrolytes.

The significance of salt-bridge are

- It connects the solutions of two half-cells and complete the cell circuits.
- It keeps the solutions in two half-cells electrically neutral.
- It prevents the transference or diffusion of the solutions from one half-cell to the other.
- It prevents liquid-liquid junction potential. i.e. the potential difference that arise between two solutions when in contact with each other.

Comparison Between Galvanic Cell and Electrolytic Cell

Basis of Comparison	Galvanic/ Voltaic cell	Electrolytic cell
Charge of the anode	Negative	Positive
Charge of the cathode	Positive	Negative
The electrolyte solution(s)	Two different electrodes with two different electrolytes are usually set up in two separate beakers.	Both the electrodes are suspended in electrolyte solution in the same beaker.
Energy changes	Chemical energy converted to electrical energy.	Electrical energy is converted to chemical energy.
Spontaneity	It is based upon the reaction which is spontaneous.	The redox reaction is non-spontaneous and takes place only when electrical energy is supplied.
Applications	Electroplating and batteries	Electrolysis, e.g. NaCl

- If the concentration of all the reacting species is unity then $E_{cell} = E^\circ_{cell}$.

$$\Delta_r G^\circ = -nFE^\circ_{cell} \quad \text{or} \quad \Delta_r G^\circ = -RT \ln K$$

- E_{cell} is an intensive property, while $\Delta_r G$ is an extensive property.

Electrochemical Series

- A series of half-cells arranged in increasing order of standard electrode potential.

⟶ Increasing strength of oxidising agent.

$Li^+ < K^+ < Ca^{2+} < Na^+ < Mg^{2+} < Al^{3+} < H_2O < Zn^{2+} < Cr^{3+} < Fe^{2+} < Ni^{2+} < Sn^{2+} < Pb^{2+} < H^+ < Cu^{2+} < Cu^+ < Ag^+ < Hg^{2+} < Br_2 < Cl_2 < Au^{3+} < Co^{3+} < F_2$

⟵ Increasing strength of reducing agent.

- Positive E° means the redox couple is a weaker reducing agent than H^+/H_2.
- Negative E° means the redox couple is stronger reducing agent than H^+/H_2.
- This series helps in comparing the relative oxidising and reducing power, relative activities of metals and to predict spontaneity of the redox reactions.

Nernst Equation

The relationship between electrode potential and concentration of solution is given by Nernst equation.

For a general electrochemical reaction,

$$aA + bB \xrightarrow{ne^-} cC + dD$$

$$E_{cell} = E^\circ_{cell} - \frac{2.303\,RT}{nF} \log Q$$

where, n = total number of electrons gained or lost, 1F = 96500 C, T = temperature, R = gas constant and Q = reaction quotient of overall reaction.

Equilibrium Constant from Nernst Equation

At equilibrium, $E_{cell} = 0$

(i) $E^\circ_{cell} = \frac{2.303\,RT}{nF} \log K_C$

where, K_C = equilibrium constant.

(ii) At, $T = 298$ K, $E^\circ_{cell} = \frac{0.0591}{n} \log K_C$

Electrochemical Cell and Gibbs Energy of Reaction

- The reversible work done by a galvanic cell is equal to decrease in its Gibbs energy. So, if the emf of the cell is E and nF is the amount of charge passed and $\Delta_r G$ is the Gibbs energy then,

$$\Delta_r G = -nFE_{cell}$$

Test 2

Syllabus
- Electrolytic and Metallic Conduction, Conductance in Electrolytic Solution, Molar Conductivities and their Variation with Concentration, Kohlrausch's Law and its Applications.

NCERT Page 41 to 54

For deeper insight Scan the QR Code

Conductors and Insulators

- Substances which allow electric current to flow through them are known as **conductors**, e.g. metals like Fe, Ag, Cu.
- The substances which do not allow the passage of electricity through them are called **insulators**, e.g. wood, rubber.

Types of Conductors

Electronic conductors or Metallic conductors	Electrolytic conductors
Passage of current by movement of electrons in the metallic lattice, e.g. Cu, Ag, etc.	Passage of current by ions in molten state or in aqueous solution of electrolytes, e.g. NaCl (*aq*) or NaCl (fused).
Passage of current brings only physical changes.	Passage of current brings physical as well as chemical changes.
It generally shows no transfer of matter.	It involves transfer of matter in the form of ions.
It depends upon nature and structure of metal, number of valence electron per atom, density of metal and temperature (inverse relation).	It depends upon nature of electrolyte, size of ions produced and their solvation, nature of solvent and its viscosity and temperature (direct relation).
The conducting power of metals is usually high.	The conducting power of electrolytic conductors is relatively low.

Resistance (*R*)

- The hinderance provided by the medium in the flow of current is called **resistance**.
- From Ohm's law, $V \propto I$

$$V = RI \quad \text{(where, } R = \text{resistance)}$$

- Unit of resistance is Ω (ohm).

Resistivity or Specific Resistance (ρ)

- Resistance provided by unit volume of the medium is called, **resistivity**.
- For any medium, Resistance $\propto$ length

Also, resistance $\propto \dfrac{1}{\text{area}}$

$$R \propto \frac{\text{length}}{\text{area}} \qquad R = \rho \frac{l}{a}$$

where, ρ is called resistivity or specific resistance
If l = 1cm, a = 1 cm^2, then $R = \rho$, its unit is ohm– cm.

Conductance of Electrolytic Solution

Property	Formula	Units	Definition	Effect of dilution
Conductance (*G*)	$\frac{1}{R} = \frac{A}{\rho l} = \frac{\kappa A}{l}$	ohm^{-1} = (S)Simens	Reciprocal of resistance	Increases as larger number of ions are produced
Specific conductance (κ) or conductivity	$\frac{l}{\rho} = G\frac{l}{A}$	ohm^{-1} cm^{-1} = Sm^{-1}	Conductance of 1 cm^3 of the conductor	Decreases as number of ions per cm^3 decrease.
Equivalent conductivity (Λ_{eq})	$\kappa \times V = K\frac{1000}{N}$ N = Normality	Ω^{-1} cm^2 eq^{-1} = Sm^2 eq^{-1}	Conductance of a solution containing 1g equivalent of an electrolyte dissolved in *V* cm^3 of the solution.	Increases with dilution due to large increase in volume.
Molar conductivity (Λ_m)	$\kappa V = \kappa \times \frac{1000}{M}$	Ω^{-1} cm^2 mol^{-1} = Sm^2 mol^{-1}	It is conductance of that volume of solution containing one mole of electrolyte.	Increases with dilution due to large increase in volume.

Kohlrausch's Law

- It is also called as **law of independent migration of ions**.
- It states that limiting molar conductivity (Λ_m°) of an electrolyte is the sum of the individual contribution of cation and anion as

$$\Lambda_m^\circ(AB_2) = \Lambda_m^\circ(A^{2+}) + 2\Lambda_m^\circ(B^-)$$
$$\Lambda_m^\circ(\text{NaCl}) = \Lambda_m^\circ(\text{Na}^+) + \Lambda_m^\circ(\text{Cl}^-)$$

- The molar conductivity of weak electrolytes at infinite dilution can be calculated using this law.
- It is helpful for the calculation of α and K_a as

$$\alpha = \frac{\Lambda_m}{\Lambda_m^\circ} \text{ and } K_a = \frac{C\alpha^2}{(1-\alpha)}$$

Cell Constant (G^*)

- It is the ratio of distance between electrode (l) and total surface area (a) of the electrodes.

$$G^* = \frac{l}{a}$$

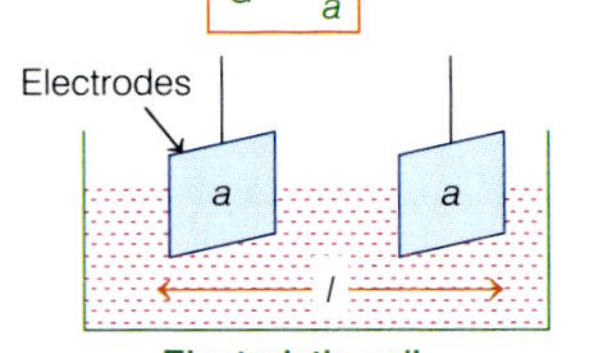

Electrolytic cell

- Unit of cell constant = m^{-1} or cm^{-1}
- The cell constant is a function of the electrode areas, the distance between the electrodes and the electrical field pattern between the electrodes.

$$\text{Cell constant} = \frac{\text{Resistance}}{\text{Resistivity}}$$

Factors Affecting Conductivity

The conductivity of electrolytes can be affected by the following factors.

(i) **Interionic attraction** If interionic attraction between solute molecules is higher than conductivity becomes lower.

(ii) **Polarity of solvent** If solvent is more polar than its ionisation and conductivity will be greater.

(iii) **Viscosity of medium** On increasing viscosity of medium, conductivity decreases.

(iv) **Temperature** On increasing the temperature of electrolytic solution, conductivity increases.

(v) **Concentration of the solution** All types of conductivities are affected by changing the concentration.

(a) **Effect of concentration on specific conductivity** Conductivity always decreases with decrease in concentration (i.e. with dilution) of both the strong and weak electrolytes. This is due to the fact that the number of ions that carry current in a unit volume of solution always decreases with decrease in concentration.

(b) **Effect of concentration on molar and equivalent conductivity** On decreasing the concentration of electrolytic solution, molar conductivity and equivalent conductivity increases. It is because on progressively decreasing the concentration the dissociation of electrolytes goes on increasing. Thus, the number of ions goes on increasing.

Λ_m (S cm^2 mol^{-1}): 400, 200; $C^{1/2}$ (mol/L)$^{1/2}$: 0, 0.2, 0.4; CH$_3$COOH; KCl

Electrolysis

It is defined as a process of decomposition of an electrolyte by the passage of electricity through aqueous solution or molten state.
The analysis is done in mainly two ways.

(i) Qualitative electrolysis
Study of possible products formed at cathode and anode during electrolysis.

(ii) Quantitative electrolysis
Study of amount/moles/volume of the products formed at cathode and anode during electrolysis.

Products of Electrolysis

Electrolyte	Reactions involved: At cathode	Reactions involved: At anode	Products: Cathode	Products: Anode
Molten NaCl	$\text{Na}^+(aq) + e^- \longrightarrow \text{Na}(s)$	$\text{Cl}^-(l) \longrightarrow \frac{1}{2}\text{Cl}_2(g) + e^-$	Na (s)	Cl$_2$ gas
Aq. NaCl	$\text{H}_2\text{O}(l) + e^- \longrightarrow \frac{1}{2}\text{H}_2(g) + \text{OH}^-(aq)$	$\text{Cl}^-(aq) \longrightarrow \frac{1}{2}\text{Cl}_2(g) + e^-$	H$_2$ gas	Cl$_2$ gas
Dil. H$_2$SO$_4$	$\text{H}^+(aq) + e^- \longrightarrow \frac{1}{2}\text{H}_2(g)$	$2\text{H}_2\text{O}(l) \rightarrow \text{O}_2(g) + 4\text{H}^+(aq) + 4e^-$	H$_2$ gas	O$_2$ gas
Conc. H$_2$SO$_4$	$\text{H}^+(aq) + e^- \longrightarrow \frac{1}{2}\text{H}_2(g)$	$2\text{SO}_4^{2-}(aq) \longrightarrow \text{S}_2\text{O}_8^{2-} + 2e^-$	H$_2$ gas	S$_2$O$_8^{2-}$

Faraday's Law of Electrolysis

- **Faraday's First Law**
- It states that the amount of chemical reaction occurring at any electrode by passing current is directly proportional to the quantity of electricity passed through the electrolyte.

$$W = Zit$$

$$\text{where, } Z = \frac{\text{Equivalent wt. of element}}{96500}$$

- The amount of electricity means the quantity of charge (*Q*) in coulombs. If *i* is current in amperes (*A*) and *t* is the time in seconds, then $Q = it$.
- If *W* is the amount of substance liberated or deposited, then $W \propto Q$; $W = ZQ$
- where, *Z* is electrochemical equivalent of a substance.
- **Faraday's Second Law**
- When the same quantity of electricity is passed through different electrolytes the amount of different substances formed are directly proportional to their chemical equivalent weights.

$$\frac{w_1}{E_1} = \frac{w_2}{E_2} = \frac{w_2}{E_3}$$

Test 3

Syllabus

- Dry Cell and Lead Accumulator, Fuel Cells.

NCERT Page 54 to 58

For deeper insight **Scan the QR Code**

Primary Batteries

In these type of batteries, redox reactions occur only once and the battery becomes dead after sometime. They cannot be recharged or used again, e.g. dry cell like leclanche cell, mercury cell.

Leclanche Cell

It is called dry cell as it has constituents in dry powdered or paste form and not in solution form.

The cell consists of

At anode Zinc metal container.

At cathode Inert graphite rod surrounded by powdered manganese dioxide and carbon.

Electrolyte Moist paste of NH_4Cl and $ZnCl_2$.

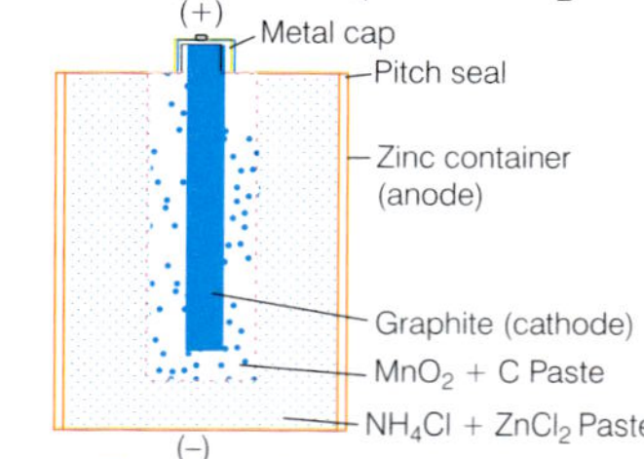

The dry cell

Reactions Involved

At anode, $Zn(s) \longrightarrow Zn^{2+} + 2e^-$

At cathode, $MnO_2 + NH_4^+ + e^- \longrightarrow MnO(OH) + NH_3$

- In the reaction at cathode, manganese is reduced from the + 4 oxidation state to the + 3 state. Ammonia produced in the reaction forms a complex with Zn^{2+} to given $[Zn(NH_3)_4]^{2+}$.
- The cell has a potential of nearly 1.5 V.

Mercury Cell

These cells are suitable for low current devices like hearing aids, watches etc.

(Zn-Hg) Anode, Anode cap, Gasket, Separator, Cathode (HgO), Cell can

The cell consists of

At anode Zinc and mercury amalgam

At cathode Paste of carbon and HgO

Electrolyte Paste of KOH and ZnO.

Reactions Involved

At anode,

$Zn(Hg) + 2OH^- \longrightarrow ZnO(s) + H_2O + 2e^-$

At cathode,

$HgO + H_2O + 2e^- \longrightarrow Hg(l) + 2OH^-$

Net reaction, $Zn(Hg) + HgO(s) \longrightarrow ZnO(s) + Hg(l)$

Net reaction does not involve any ion, i.e. hence, cell potential is independent of concentration. The cell potential is approximately 1.35V.

Batteries

- A cell or a battery (arrangement of one or more cells connected in series) is basically a galvanic cell.
- It is used where the chemical energy of redox reaction is converted into electrical energy.
- The voltage provided by the battery is the sum of the individual cell voltage. These batteries can be classified as primary and secondary batteries.

Secondary Batteries

- It is a chemical device in which energy may be stored in the form of chemical energy and it may be drawn out when required.
- It can be recharged by passing an electric current through them.
- It can be used over and over again.
- It acts as an accumulator or storage cell.
- It shows reversible reactions.

Nickel-Cadmium Batteries

Nickel-cadmium or 'Ni-Cad' batteries are rechargeable storage batteries. They have longer life but are more expensive.

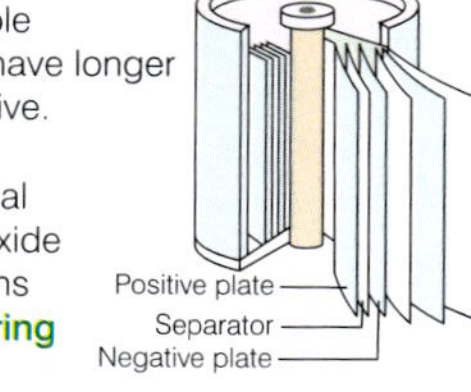

The cell consists of

At anode Cadmium metal

At cathode Nickel (IV) oxide

Electrolyte KOH solutions

Reactions involved during discharge

At anode, $Cd(s) + 2OH^-(aq) \longrightarrow Cd(OH)_2(s) + 2e^-$

At cathode,

$NiO_2(s) + 2H_2O + 2e^- \longrightarrow Ni(OH)_2(s) + 2OH^-(aq)$

Net reaction,

$Cd(s) + NiO_2(s) + 2H_2O \xrightarrow{\text{Discharging}} Cd(OH)_2(s) + Ni(OH)_2(s)$

When cell is recharging, the reactions are reversed.

Corrosion

- It is the oxidative deterioration of a metal, such as conversion of iron to rust $[Fe_2O_3 \cdot xH_2O]$, tarnishing of silver (due to formation of Ag_2O), development of a green coating on copper and bronze.
- It is basically an electrochemical phenomenon. A metal is oxidised by loss of electrons to oxygen and forms metal oxide.

At anode, $2Fe(s) \longrightarrow 2Fe^{2+}(aq) + 4e^-$

At cathode, $O_2(g) + 4H^+(aq) + 4e^- \longrightarrow 2H_2O(l)$

Overall reaction,

$2Fe(s) + O_2(g) + 4H^+(aq) \longrightarrow 2Fe^{2+}(aq) + 2H_2O(l)$

Prevention The metal surface is coated with paint and grease which keeps it out of contact with air, moisture etc.

Lead-Storage Batteries

A typical 12-V battery consists of six cells connected in series, each cell providing a potential of about 2 V.

The cell consists of

At anode Lead

At cathode Grid of lead packed with lead dioxide.

Electrolyte 38% solution of H_2SO_4

Discharge of battery When the cell gets discharged, (providing current), it acts as an electrochemical cell.

The reactions involved are

At anode, $Pb(s) + SO_4^{2-}(aq) \longrightarrow PbSO_4(s) + 2e^-$

At cathode,

$PbO_2(s) + 4H(aq) + SO_4^{2-}(aq) + 2e^- \longrightarrow PbSO_4(s) + 2H_2O(l)$

Net reaction,

$Pb(s) + PbO_2(s) + 2H_2SO_4(aq) \rightarrow 2PbSO_4(s) + 2H_2O(l)$

Anode, Cathode, 38% sulphuric acid solution, Positive plates (lead grids filled with PbO_2), Negative plates (lead grids filled with spongy lead)

Sulphuric acid is consumed during discharging and when the concentration of H_2SO_4 falls to 1.20 g L^{-1} it requires recharging.

Hydrogen Fuel Cell Car

H_2 Tank, Fuel Cell, Battery, Power control unit, Hydrogen fuel, Water H_2O, Oxygen O_2, Motor

Fuel Cells

- A fuel cell is a galvanic cell in which energy produced during the combustion of fuels like CH_4, H_2 etc., is converted directly into electrical energy.
- Reactants are not contained within the cell but instead are continuously supplied from an external reservoir.
- Electrodes are made of porous carbon impregnated with metallic catalysts (Pt or Pd).
- Electrolyte Concentrated KOH or NaOH

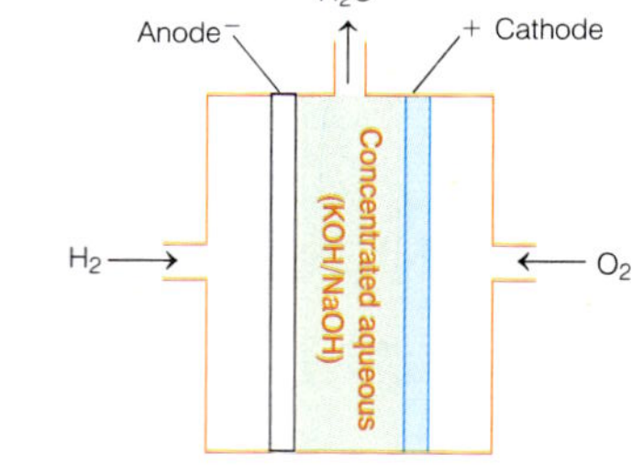

- Reactions involved
- At anode,
  $2H_2(g) + 4OH^-(aq) \longrightarrow 4H_2O(l) + 4e^-$
- At cathode,
  $O_2(g) + 2H_2O(l) + 4e^- \longrightarrow 4OH^-(aq)$
- Net reaction,
  $2H_2(g) + O_2(g) \longrightarrow 2H_2O(l)$
- Catalyst used in the cell increase the rate of electrode reactions.

Advantages

- Fuel cells are pollution free cell, light in weight and have high reliability.
- Efficiency of fuel cell is very high (about 70%).
- Due to continuous supply of gaseous materials, there cells never become dead.

Disadvantages

- It is very difficult to handle gaseous fuels.
- Catalyst used are very costly.
- Electrode preparation is very difficult and time taking.

Uses

- The primary use of this kind of cells is in space craft, where by-product (H_2O) can be used for other purposes as well.
- These cells are also used in other vehicles like electric cars, submarines etc.

Test 1

Syllabus
- Rate of a Chemical Reaction, Factors Affecting the Rate of Reactions, Concentration, Temperature, Pressure and Catalyst, Elementary and Complex Reactions.

NCERT Page 61 to 68

For deeper insight **Scan the QR Code**

Chapter 03

Chemical Kinetics

- The branch of chemistry that deals with the study of rate of reactions, factors affecting the rate of reaction and mechanism of the reaction is called as **chemical kinetics**.
- The feasibility of a reaction can be predicted with the help of thermodynamic principle but it does not deal with the rate at which chemical reaction occurs.
- The word kinetic is derived from Greek word kinesis which means movement. So, chemical kinetics explains the movement of reacting particles.

Chemical Reactions

When one or more substances undergo a change which result in the formation of a new product, it is called chemical reactions.

Types of Chemical Reactions

Depending upon reaction rates or speeds, chemical reactions can be classified in the following ways.

(i) **Instantaneous or fast reactions** These reactions proceed at very fast speed. So, it is practically impossible to measure the speed of such reactions. e.g. Neutralisation reactions, precipitation reactions etc.

(ii) **Extremely slow reactions** These type of reactions proceed at very low speed. So, it is also very difficult to measure the speed of these reactions. e.g. Rusting of iron, etc.

(iii) **Moderately slow reactions** These type of reactions proceed with a measurable speed at room temperature. Thus, these reactions are utilised in the study of chemical kinetics. e.g. Inversion of cane sugar, decomposition of ammonium nitrate etc.

Depending upon number of steps, chemical reactions are classified in the following ways

(i) **Elementary reactions** The reactions taking place in one step are called elementary reactions.

(ii) **Complex reactions** The reactions which do not take place in one step are called complex reactions. In these reactions, all the atoms, ions or molecules as represented in the balanced chemical equation may not come together to collide simultaneously. Such reactions occur in a sequence of a number of steps.

e.g. $4HBr + O_2 \longrightarrow 2H_2O + 2Br_2$

Step I $HBr + O_2 \xrightarrow{\text{Slow}} HOOBr$

Step II $HOOBr + HBr \xrightarrow{\text{Fast}} 2HOBr$

Step III $[HOBr + HBr \xrightarrow{\text{Fast}} H_2O + Br_2] \times 2$

$4HBr + O_2 \longrightarrow 2H_2O + 2Br_2$

Rate of Reaction

- It is the change in concentration of any one of the reactants or products per unit time.
- **Average Rate** It is the rate measured over a long time interval.

$$r_{av} = \frac{-\Delta R}{\Delta t} = \frac{\Delta P}{\Delta t}$$

- **Instantaneous Rate** It is the rate measured over a long time interval.

$$r_{ins} = \frac{-d[R]}{dt} = \frac{d[P]}{dt}$$

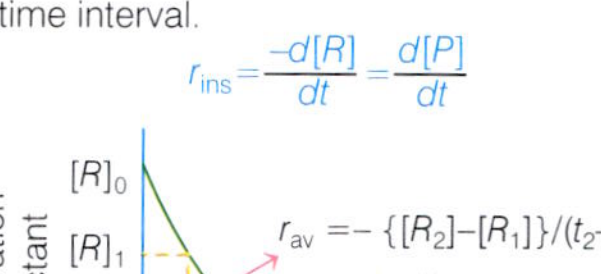
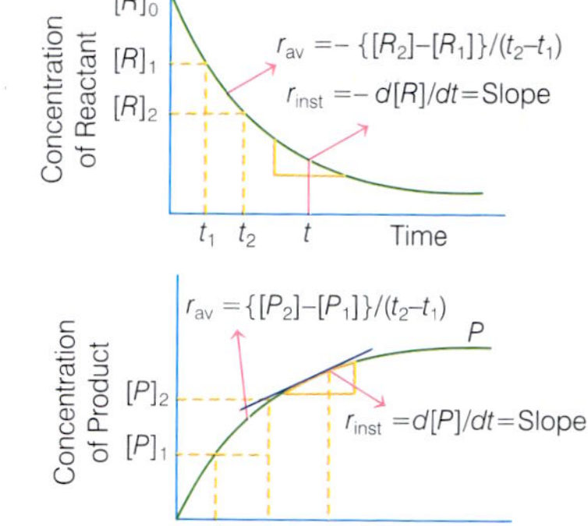

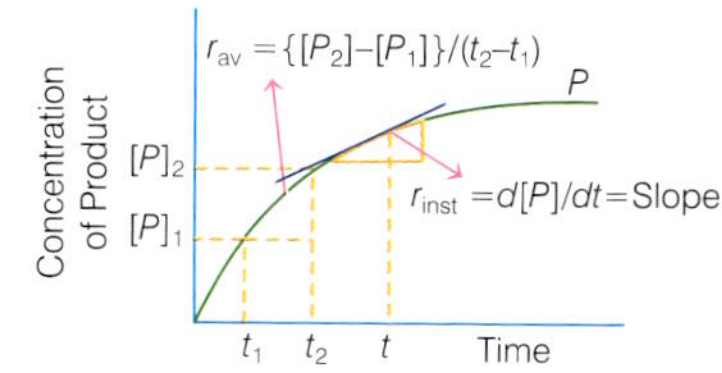

- The negative sign indicates that the concentration of reactants decreases with time.
- The positive sign indicates that the concentration of products increases with time.
- The concentration change may be positive or negative but the rate of reaction is always positive.

Factors Affecting Rate of Reaction

- **Concentration of Reactants** Increase in concentration increases rate of reaction.
- **Catalyst** It increases the speed of reaction by lowering the energy barrier, i.e. a new path is followed with lower activation energy.
- **Surface Area** Greater the surface area faster is the reaction.
- **Temperature** Generally, the rate of reaction becomes almost double for every 10°C rise in temperature.
- Temperature coefficient $= \frac{k_T + 10}{k_T}$
- Rate constant at temperature $(T + 10°)$
- **Physical State of Reactants** Reactions involving gaseous reactants are faster generally.

Calculating the Rate of Reaction

- The rate of a reaction can be calculated by recording the amount of a reactant or a product at regular time intervals during a single reaction (continuous monitoring) or by determining the initial rate of several reactions and finding an average.
- There are several methods of continuous monitoring.
- Monitoring by gas collection-use a syringe to measure the volume of gas evolved.
- Mass loss-set up the system on a balance so the decrease in mass of reactant can be measured.
- Colorimetry - concentration change is monitored by measuring the amount of light absorbed by a sample.
- A graph can be plotted using the variable measured against time. The gradient of the graph is equal to the rate, i.e. y/x=concentration change/time=rate.

Rate of Reaction in the form of Stoichiometry

- The rate of a reaction can be expressed in terms of each reactant and product.
- For a general reaction,

$$aA + bB \longrightarrow cC + dD$$

- The rate expression may be expressed as

$$\text{Rate} = -\frac{d[A]}{a\,dt} = -\frac{d[B]}{b\,dt} = +\frac{d[C]}{c\,dt} = +\frac{d[D]}{d\,dt}$$

- Stoichiometric coefficient does not involve in the expression of disappearance rate of reactant and formation rate of product.
- Stoichiometric coefficient must be involved in the expression of rate of a reaction.
- During this change, concentration is divided by stoichiometric coefficient to maintain uniformity. The instantaneous rate expression for the given reaction is,

(i) $2NO(g) + O_2(g) \longrightarrow 2NO_2(g)$

$$\text{Rate} = \frac{-d[NO]}{2dt} = \frac{-d[O_2]}{dt} = \frac{d[NO_2]}{2dt}$$

(ii) $N_2 + 3H_2(g) \longrightarrow 2NH_3$

$$\text{Rate} = \frac{-d[N_2]}{dt} = \frac{-d[H_2]}{dt} = \frac{d[NH_3]}{2dt}$$

- For a gaseous reaction at constant temperature, concentration is directly proportional to the partial pressure of a species.
- Hence, rate can also be expressed as rate of change in partial pressure of the reactant or the product.

Rate Constant (k)

It is equal to the rate of reaction when concentration of each of the reactant is unity.

Characteristics of Rate Constant

- It is a characteristic constant for a reaction at a given temperature. For a reaction, higher value of k indicates higher rate of reaction.
- It is independent of concentration of reactants and time taken in reaction. Different reactions have different value of k. Value of rate constant depends upon temperature and catalyst.
- It increases with increase in temperature for endothermic reaction as well as exothermic reaction. Positive catalyst increases the rate constant while negative catalyst decreases the rate constant.
- Quantitative dependence of temperature and catalyst can be given by Arrhenius equation.

Unit

The dimension of rate are concentration/ time and the SI units for concentration are mol m^{-3}, mol dm^{-3} or mol L^{-1} and second(s) for time. For gaseous reactions concentrations are expressed in terms of pressure with unit of atmosphere. Thus, the rate has the unit of atm per second.

Differences Between Rate of Reaction and Rate Constant

Rate of reaction	Rate constant
It is the speed with which reactants are converted into products.	It is the proportionality constant in the rate law.
It is measured as the rate of decrease in the concentration of reactants or increase in the products with time.	It is equal to the rate of reaction when the concentration of reactants is unity.
It depends upon the initial concentration of reactants or product.	It is independent of the initial concentration of reactants or product.
Its unit is mol L^{-1} $time^{-1}$	Its unit depend upon the order of reaction $(conc.)^{1-n}$ $time^{-1}$ or $(mol/L)^{1-n}$ $time^{-1}$.

Test 2

Syllabus

- Order and Molecularity of Reaction, Rate Law, Rate Constant and its Units. Differential and Integral Forms of Zero and First Order Reaction, their Characteristics and Half-lives.

NCERT Page 68 to 78

For deeper insight **Scan the QR Code**

Chapter 03

Order of a Reaction

- It is the sum of the powers of the concentration terms in the rate law.
  For a given reaction,
  $$aA + bB \longrightarrow \text{Product}$$
  $$\text{Rate} = k[A]^m\,[B]^n$$
  $\therefore$ Order of reaction $= m+n$
- It can be a whole number or a fractional number and can only be determined experimentally.
- It can change with change in conditions such as temperature, pressure etc.
- It is applicable to elementary as well as complex reactions.

Characteristic of Order of Reaction

- It is an experimentally determined quantity. It cannot be calculated by balanced form of reaction.
- It may be zero or fractional but infinite and imaginary values of order of reaction are not possible.
- For elementary reaction (simple single step reaction) order and molecularity remain same.
- For complex multiple step reactions, order of reaction is meant for the reaction and not for its individual steps.
- If a reactant is taken in excess in a complex reaction then order with respect to it, becomes zero.
- Order is decided by reaction mechanism. Slowest step is used to write experimental rate expression, called rate determining step.

Integrated Rate Equations

- **For Zero Order**
  Rate $= k$, or $k = \frac{1}{t}\{[A]_0 - [A]\}$
  where, k = rate constant, t = time
  $[A]_0$ = initial reactant concentration
  $[A]$ = final reactant concentration at time (t)
- **For First Order**
  Rate $= k[A]$, $k = \dfrac{2.303}{t}\log\dfrac{[A]_0}{[A]}$
- For gas phase reaction,
  $$k = \frac{2.303}{t}\log\frac{p_i}{2p_i - p_t}$$
  where, p_i = initial pressure
- **For n^{th} order**, $k = \dfrac{1}{t(n-1)}\left[\dfrac{1}{[A]^{n-1}} - \dfrac{1}{[A]_0^{n-1}}\right]$
  where, k = rate constant
  $[A]_0$ = initial concentration of reactant
  n = order of reaction
  x = concentration of reactant decomposed at time t.

Zero Order Reaction

- The reaction in which rate of reaction is directly proportional to the zero power of product of concentrations of reactants is called as zero order reaction.
- The rate is independent of concentration, the plot of rate *versus* concentration will be a straight line parallel to the concentration axis.
- Unit of rate constant is mol $L^{-1}\,s^{-1}$.
- e.g. $2NH_3(g) \xrightarrow[\Delta]{Pt} N_2(g) + 3H_2(g)$

First Order Reaction

- A reaction is said to be of first order if its rate is determined by the change of one concentration term only. It means rate is directly proportional to the concentration of one reactant raised to first order.
- The rate directly depends upon the concentration, so the plot of rate *vs* concentration will be a straight line passing through the origin.
- Unit of rate constant is s^{-1}.
- e.g. All natural and artificial radioactive decay of unstable nuclei.

Pseudo First Order Reaction

- A reaction which is not truly of first order but under certain conditions becomes a reaction of first order, e.g. hydrolysis of ester.
  $$\underset{\text{Ester}}{CH_3COOCH_2CH_3} + \underset{\text{Water}}{H_2O} \xrightleftharpoons{H^+(aq)} \underset{\text{Acid}}{CH_3COOH} + \underset{\text{Alcohol}}{CH_3CH_2OH}$$
  Rate $= k[CH_3COOCH_2CH_3]$
- The concentration of water does not get altered much during the course of the reaction. So, the reaction behave as first order reaction. Such reactions are called pseudo first order reaction.

Half-life Period

- It is the period of time in which the concentration of the reactant is reduced to half of its initial concentration.
- General expression for $t_{1/2}$ for different order are as follows
- For zero order reaction, $t_{1/2} = \dfrac{[A]_0}{2k}$
- For first order reactions, $t_{1/2} = \dfrac{0.693}{k}$
- For second order reaction, $t_{1/2} = \dfrac{1}{k[A]_0}$ when $n \geq 2$
- Amount of substance left after n half-lives $= \dfrac{[A]_0}{2^n}$

Plots for Different Order Reaction

For zero order | **For first order**

(i) Plot of rate of reaction *vs* concentration

Rate ↑ / Conc. ⟶ (zero order); Rate ↑ / Conc. ⟶ (first order)

(ii) Plot from integrated rate equations

$[A]$ ↑ / t ⟶ (zero order); $\log[A]$ ↑ / t ⟶ (first order), Intercept $= \log[A_0]$, Slope $= \dfrac{-k}{2.303}$

(iii) Plot of half-life *vs* concentration

$t_{1/2}$ ↑ / $[A]_0$ ⟶ (zero order); $t_{1/2}$ ↑ / $[A]_0$ ⟶ (first order)

Characteristics of Molecularity of a Reaction

- It cannot be zero, fractional or more than three.
- In case of complex reactions, the atoms, molecules or ion participating in rate determining step decide the molecularity. Among several steps, the slowest step is the rate determining step then molecularity is two.
- It does not provide the information about mechanism of the reaction.

Differences Between Molecularity and Order of a Reaction

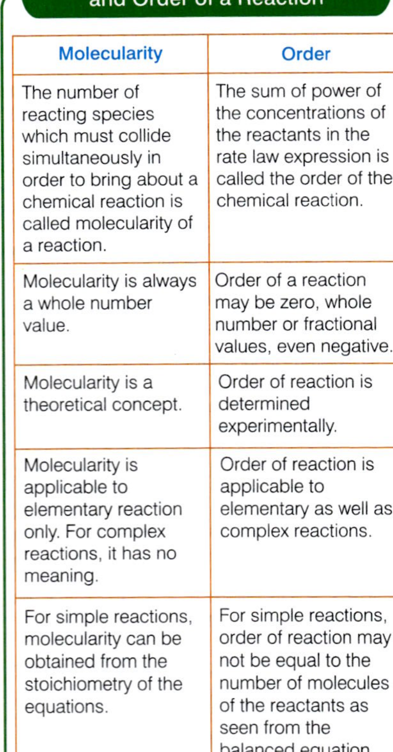

Molecularity	Order
The number of reacting species which must collide simultaneously in order to bring about a chemical reaction is called molecularity of a reaction.	The sum of power of the concentrations of the reactants in the rate law expression is called the order of the chemical reaction.
Molecularity is always a whole number value.	Order of a reaction may be zero, whole number or fractional values, even negative.
Molecularity is a theoretical concept.	Order of reaction is determined experimentally.
Molecularity is applicable to elementary reaction only. For complex reactions, it has no meaning.	Order of reaction is applicable to elementary as well as complex reactions.
For simple reactions, molecularity can be obtained from the stoichiometry of the equations.	For simple reactions, order of reaction may not be equal to the number of molecules of the reactants as seen from the balanced equation.

Molecularity

- It can be defined as the number of reacting species (atoms, ions or molecules) taking part in an elementary reaction which must collide simultaneously in order to bring about a chemical reaction is called molecularity.
- If one reactant is involved, the reaction is called **unimolecular reactions**.
- Reaction involving simultaneous collision between two species are called **bimolecular reactions**.
- Reaction involving simultaneous collision between three reacting species are called **trimolecular reactions**.

Test 3

Syllabus

- Arrhenius Theory, Activation Energy and its Calculation, Collision Theory of Bimolecular Gaseous Reaction, The Effect of Temperature On the Rate of Reactions.

NCERT Page 78 to 83

For deeper insight **Scan the QR Code**

Collision Theory

- Reactant molecules are assumed to be hard spheres.
- Reaction occurs due to collision of reactant molecules.
- Only effective collisions (having threshold energy and proper orientation) give product.
- Threshold energy = Activation energy + Potential energy of reactant.
- **Collision frequency** It is the number of collisions that take place per unit time per unit volume of the reaction mixture.
- Rate $= PZ_{AB}\, e^{-E_a/RT}$

  where, P = probability or steric factor

  Z_{AB} = collision frequency

Factors Affecting Effective Collision

1. For a collision to be effective, the reacting species must

- **Possess at least a certain minimum energy, i.e. threshold energy** which is defined as the minimum amount of energy which the colliding molecules must possess so as to make the chemical reaction to take place.
- **Have proper orientation towards each other at the time of collision** If colliding molecules have improper orientations, they do not react even though they may possess sufficient energy.

  The average kinetic energy of a collection of molecules is proportional to the absolute temperature. At high temperatures, more molecules possess sufficient energy to react.

  Reaction, $NO + N_2O \longrightarrow NO_2 + N_2$

2. The minimum additional energy required by the molecule to attain threshold energy is called **activation energy**, which is required by the species during collision as a result of interchange of energies.

$$E_a = E_{(\text{threshold energy})} - E_{(\text{reactants})}$$

- The fraction of collisions f with an energy equal to or greater than the activation energy E_a is given as,

$$f = e^{-E_a/RT}$$

where, $e^{-E_a/RT}$ is called **Boltzmann factor.**

- The fraction of collisions having proper orientation for conversion of reactants to products is called the **probability or steric factor**, P.
- Thus, in collision theory activation energy and proper orientation of the molecules together determine the criteria for an effective collision and hence rate of a chemical reaction.
- This theory explains the results of a number of reactions but it does not give satisfactory explanation in some cases as it consider atoms/molecules to be hard sphere and ignores their structural aspect.

Transition State Theory

- For a reaction to occur, some covalent bonds must break so that others can be formed. This can occur only if the molecules collide with enough kinetic energy to overcome the potential energy stabilisation of the bond.

  The process of conversion of reactant into product is shown.

(i) Exothermic reaction

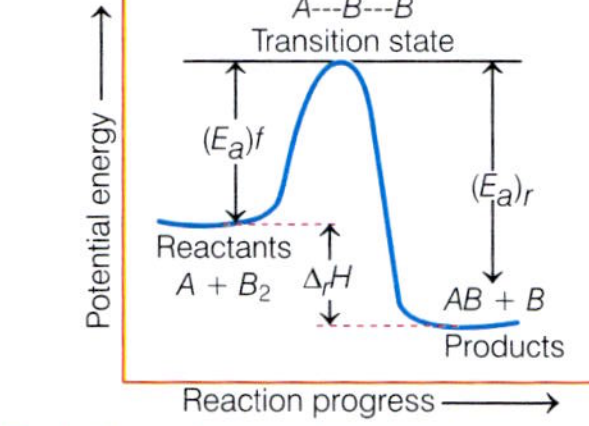

(ii) Endothermic reaction

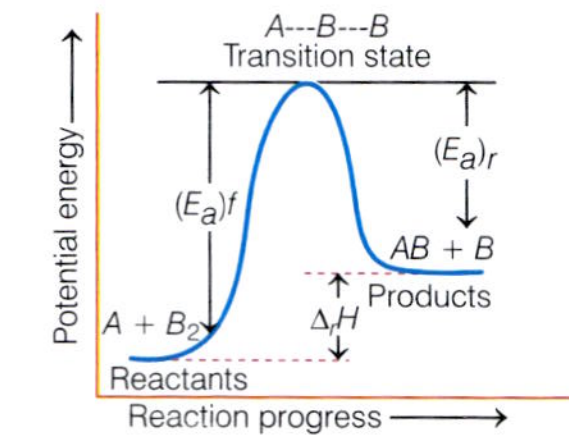

- Potential energy profile for the reaction $A+B_2 \rightarrow AB+B$ showing the energy barrier between the reactants and products.

Arrhenius Equation

- Reactant molecules collide with each other.
- These collisions form an intermediate unstable complex.
- Relation between energy required to form this intermediate and rate constant is given as,

ln k ↑ — Slope $= \frac{-E_a}{R}$ — 1/T

where, A = pre-exponential factor,
E_a = activation energy,
R = gas constant and
T = temperature (K).

- The plot between ln k and $\frac{1}{T}$ gives a straight line with slope $= \frac{-E_a}{R}$ and intercept ln A.

Activation Energy

- It is the energy required by the reactant molecules for effective collision to form products.
- Reaction favours the direction where activation energy is lesser.

Threshold energy; E_{th}; Energy; B; Activation energy for reverse reaction $(E_{a_1} + \Delta E) = E_{a_2}$; E_a; Activation energy for forward reaction; Heat of reaction; A Reactants; ΔE; C Products; Progress of reaction

- Activation energy can never be zero. If $E_a = 0$, then according to Arrhenius equation the value of k will become equal to A · A is energy of collision between molecules which leads to a chemical reaction. This can never be true.

Important Points Related to Arrhenius Equation

- The temperature dependence on the rate of a chemical reaction can be accurately explained by this equation.

If T increases ⇒ E_a/RT decreases ⇒ $-E_a/RT$ increases ⇒ $e^{-E_a/RT}$ increases ⇒ k increases ⇒ Reaction speeds up

- When $T \rightarrow \infty$, $k = Ae^{\circ}$ or rate constant becomes equal to Arrhenius or frequency factor.
- Larger the activation energy, smaller is the value of rate constant (k).

If E_a increases ⇒ E_a/RT increases ⇒ $-E_a/RT$ decreases ⇒ $e^{-E_a/RT}$ decreases ⇒ k decreases

Effect of Temperature On Rate of Reactions

Most of the chemical reactions are accelerated by increase in temperature. It has been found that for a chemical reaction with rise in temperature by 10°, the rate constant is nearly doubled. The effect of temperature is usually expressed in terms of temperature coefficient. Mathematically,

Calculation of Activation Energy

Two methods for the calculation of activation energy are given below.

(i) Graphical Method

$$\ln k = \ln A - \frac{E_a}{RT}$$

$$\log_{10} k = \log_{10} A - \frac{E_a}{2.303RT}$$

Comparing it with $y = c + mx$

The plot between $\log_{10} k$ and $(1/T)$ is a straight line and is given by

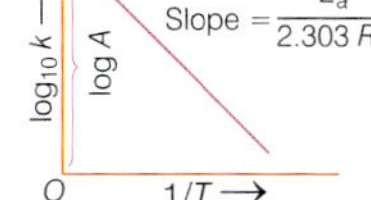

Plot of $\log_{10} k$ vs $1/T$

$$\text{Slope} = -\frac{E_a}{2.303R} \text{ (slope has negative value)}$$

The intercept of the line will give the value of log A.

(ii) Experimental Method

At temperature T_1 and T_2 rate constant are k_1 and k_2 respectively,

$$\log_{10} k_2 = \log_{10} A - \frac{E_a}{2.303RT_2}$$

and

$$\log_{10} k_1 = \log_{10} A - \frac{E_a}{2.303RT_1}$$

$$\therefore \log_{10}\left(\frac{k_2}{k_1}\right) = \frac{E_a}{2.303R}\left[\frac{1}{T_1} - \frac{1}{T_2}\right] \text{ [Here, } T_2 > T_1]$$

This relation is used when rate constant at two different temperature are given.

$$\text{Temperature cofficient } (n) = \frac{\text{rate constant at } (T+10)^\circ}{\text{rate constant at } T^\circ}$$

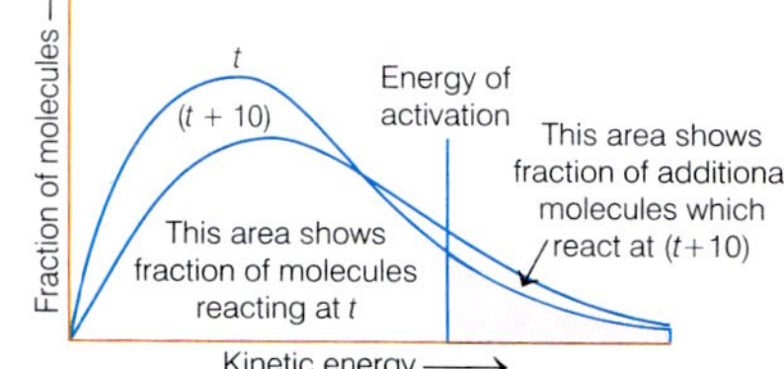

Distribution curve showing temperature dependence of rate of a reaction

Syllabus

- General Introduction, Electronic Configuration, General Trends in Physical and Chemical Properties of Elements Across the Periods and Down the Groups, Unique Behaviour of 1st Element.

NCERT Page 165 to 180

For deeper insight **Scan the QR Code**

Introduction

- Group 15 of the periodic table contains five elements namely, **nitrogen** (N), **phosphorus** (P), **arsenic** (As), **antimony** (Sb) and **bismuth** (Bi).
- They are commonly known as pnictogens (pnicogen) meaning choking.
- The first two elements, N and P are non-metals, arsenic and antimony are metalloids, whereas the last element bismuth is a metal.

Occurrence

- Molecular nitrogen constitutes about 78% by volume of atmosphere.
- In combined state, it is found as nitrates ($NaNO_3$ Chile saltpetre, KNO_3 Indian saltpetre) as proteins and amino acids in plants and animals.
- Phosphorus is found as phosphates. The rest elements occur as sulphides or oxides.
- Moscovium is a synthetic radioactive element. It is because its half-life is very short and also present in very little amount.

Electronic Configuration

- The general electronic configuration of 15 group element in ns^2np^3.
- The *s*-orbital in these elements is completely filled and *p*-orbitals are half-filled, making their electronic configuration extra stable.

Element	Atomic number	Electronic configuration
Nitrogen (N)	7	$[He]2s^2 2p^3$
Phosphorus (P)	15	$[Ne]3s^2 3p^3$
Arsenic (As)	33	$[Ar]3d^{10} 4s^2 4p^3$
Antimony (Sb)	51	$[Kr]4d^{10} 5s^2 5p^3$
Bismuth (Bi)	83	$[Xe]4f^{14} 5d^{10} 6s^2 6p^3$

Allotropes of Phosphorus

(i) White Phosphorus

- Catches fire in air.

$P_4 + 5O_2 \longrightarrow P_4O_{10}$ (White fumes)

(ii) Red Phosphorus Polymeric chains of P_4.

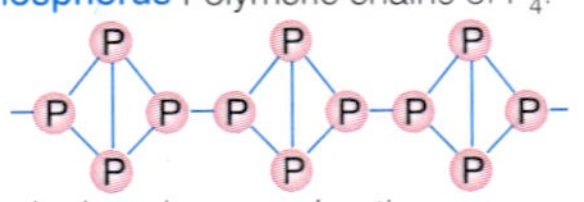

- Gives black phosphorus on heating.

(iii) Black Phosphorus

- Exists as α and β-forms.
- Sublimes in air.

General and Physical Properties

- **Physical Appearance**
- Nitrogen is gaseous in nature and exist as a diatomic molecule (N≡N).
- Phosphorus exist as tetraatomic molecule in the gaseous state, whereas in solid state, it exists in different allotropic forms. Arsenic, antimony and bismuth are solids.
- **Atomic/Ionic Radii**
- It increases with increase in size down the group. There is a considerable increase in covalent radius form N to P.
- However, from As to Bi only a small increase in covalent radius is observed. This is due to the presence of completely filled *d* and /or *f*-orbitals in heavier members.

  N<P<As<Sb<Bi
- **Ionisation Enthalpy**
- It decreases down the group due to gradual increase in atomic size. Because of the extra stable half-filled *p*-orbitals electronic configuration and smaller size, $IE_{15} > IE_{14}$.
- The order of successive ionisation enthalpies of this group as expected is $\Delta_i H_1 < \Delta_i H_2 < \Delta_i H_3$.
- **Electronegativity**

  It decreases down the group with increasing atomic size. But amongst the heavier elements, the difference is not that much noticeable.
- **Melting and Boiling Points**
- These elements do not show a regular trend of melting and boiling points.
- In this group, the melting point first increases from N to As and afterwards decreases. While boiling point first increases from N to Sb and then decreases. But Bi has low boiling point as compared to Sb.
- We can write these order as;

  N<P<As>Sb>Bi (melting point)

  N<P<As<Sb>Bi (boiling point)
- **Allotropy**
- All the members of group 15 (except Bi) show the phenomenon of allotropy. Nitrogen exists in two solid and one gaseous allotropic forms.
- Phosphorus exists in several allotropic forms such as white, red, scarlet, violet and black phosphorus.
- Arsenic exists in three allotropic forms. i.e. grey, yellow and black. Similarly, antimony (Sb) exists as metallic, α-or yellow and black or β-antimony.
- **Metallic Character**

  It increases on moving down the group as, nitrogen and phosphorus are distinctly non-metals, succeeding two members are amphoteric in nature, i.e. As and Sb have metallic as well as non-metallic character while, the last element Bi is a metal.

Chemical Properties

- Common oxidation state are – 3, + 3 and + 5.
- +5 state is not stable down the group due to inert pair effect.
- Stability of +3 O.S increases down the group due to increase in size.
- **Reactivity Towards Hydrogen**
- All the elements of Group 15 form hydrides of the type EH_3 where E = N,P, As, Sb or Bi. The hydrides show regular gradation in their properties.
- The stability of hydrides decreases from NH_3 to BiH_3 which can be observed from their bond dissociation enthalpy. Consequently, the reducing character of the hydrides increases.
- Ammonia is only a mild reducing agent while BiH_3 is the strongest reducing agent amongst all the hydrides.
- Basicity also decreases in the order

  $NH_3 > PH_3 > AsH_3 > SbH_3 > BiH_3$.
- **Reactivity Towards Oxygen**
- All these elements form two types of oxides: E_2O_3 and E_2O_5. The oxide in the higher oxidation state of the element is more acidic than that of lower oxidation state.
- Their acidic character decreases down the group.
- The oxides of the type E_2O_3 of nitrogen and phosphorus are purely acidic, arsenic and antimony are amphoteric while bismuth is predominantly basic.
- **Reactivity Towards Halogens**
- These elements react to form two series of halides: EX_3 and EX_5. Nitrogen does not form pentahalide due to non-availability of the *d*-orbitals in its valence shell. Pentahalides are more covalent than trihalides.
- All the trihalides of these elements except those of nitrogen are stable.
- In case of nitrogen, only NF_3 is known to be stable. Trihalides except BiF_3 are predominantly covalent in nature.
- **Reactivity Towards Metals**
- All these elements react with metals to form their binary compounds exhibiting –3 oxidation state, such as, Ca_3N_2 (calcium nitride) Ca_3P_2 (calcium phosphide), Na_3As_2 (sodium arsenide), Zn_3Sb_2 (zinc antimonide) and Mg_3Bi_2 (magnesium bismuthide).

Anomalous Behaviour of Nitrogen

- Nitrogen, shows many properties that are quite different from other members of the group. This is because of its small size, high electronegativity, high ionisation energy, non-availability of *d*-orbital and capacity of $p\pi-p\pi$ multiple bond formation. These properties are as follows
- It is found in a gaseous state while other members are found in solid state.
- It exists in diatomic form while other elements like phosphorus, arsenic and antimony exist as tetra-atomic molecules (P_4, As_4, Sb_4).
- It forms trinegative ion, i.e.N^{3-}, while other members do not form.
- It is chemically inert under ordinary conditions due to high bond dissociation energy. While other members are quite reactive because of the presence of single bond in their molecules.
- It does not show pentacovalency due to non-availability of *d*-orbitals while it is shown by all other elements.
- The hydride of nitrogen (NH_3) is highly basic in nature while the hydrides of other elements are slightly basic. Moreover, only hydrides of nitrogen shows H-bonding while other members do not.
- It forms oxides of five types (i.e.N_2O, NO, N_2O_3, N_2O_4 and N_2O_5) while other members of this family form oxides of only two types (i.e. tri and pentaoxides).
- Except NF_3, other halides of nitrogen i.e. NCl_3, NBr_3 and NI_3 are unstable while the halides of other elements are fairly stable.
- It does not form complexes due to the non-availability of *d*-orbitals while other members have a tendency of complex formation, e.g. $[PCl_6]^-$, $[AsCl_6]^-$, etc.

Oxoacids of Phosphorus

- $H_3\overset{+1}{P}O_2$, (Hypophosphorus or phosphinic acid)
- $H_3\overset{+3}{P}O_3$, (*Ortho*-phosphorus acid, phosphonic acid)
- $H_4\overset{+3}{P_2}O_5$, (Pyrophosphorus acid)
- $H_4\overset{+4}{P_2}O_6$, (Hypophosphoric acid)
- $H_3\overset{+5}{P}O_4$, (*Ortho*-phosphoric acid)
- $H_4\overset{+5}{P_2}O_7$, (Pyrophosphoric acid)
- $(H\overset{+5}{P}O_3)_n$, (*Meta*-phosphoric acid) Exist in polymeric form only

Test 2

Syllabus

• General Introduction, Electronic Configuration, General Trends in Physical and Chemical Properties of Elements Across the Periods and Down the Groups, Unique Behaviour of 1st Element.

NCERT Page 180 to 191

For deeper insight **Scan the QR Code**

Introduction

- Group 16 of the periodic table contains five elements namely, **oxygen** (O), **sulphur** (S), **selenium** (Se), **tellurium** (Te) and **polonium** (Po).
- The first four elements are non-metals while the last element, polonium is a **radioactive metal**. These non-metallic elements are commonly referred to as **chalcogens** (meaning ore forming) because many metal ores occur as oxides, sulphides etc. They are also known as members of **oxygen family**.

Occurrence

- Oxygen is the most abundant element in the earth's crust. Sulphur is the seventeenth in abundance and in the earth's crust occurs as sulphide (HgS, PbS etc.) in natural gas and oil as disulphide ion.
- Selenium and tellurium are comparatively rare on earth's crust occur in sulphide ores in the form of selenides and telluride.

Electronic Configuration of Elements of Group 16

The general electronic configuration of all the elements of this groups is $ns^2\,np^4$.

Element	Atomic Number	Electronic Configuration
Oxygen (O)	8	$[He]2s^2 2p^4$
Sulphur (S)	16	$[Ne]3s^2 3p^4$
Selenium (Se)	34	$[Ar]3d^{10} 4s^2 4p^4$
Tellurium (Te)	52	$[Kr]4d^{10} 5s^2 5p^4$
Polonium (Po)	84	$[Xe]4f^{14} 5d^{10} 6s^2 6p^4$

General and Physical Properties

- **Physical state**

Oxygen occurs as diatomic molecule O_2 and is therefore, a gas while sulphur occurs as polyatomic molecule S_8 and therefore, is a solid. All other elements also exist as solids.

(i) Atomic radii

- It increase gradually on moving down the group, i.e. from O to Po. This occurs due to an increase in the number of electronic shells.
- Group 16 elements have shorter atomic radii than those of corresponding elements of nitrogen family but larger than those of halogens due to the increase in effective nuclear charge from left to right in a period. $O < S < Se < Te < Po$

Allotropes of Group 16 Elements

- Allotropes are the different forms of the same element, where the atoms combine in different ways, so at the same temperature and pressure they can exist in different form. Oxygen exists in two allotropic forms O_2 and O_3 (ozone).
- Sulphur occurs as rhombic (α) sulphur, monoclinic (β) sulphur.
- Selenium exists in two forms, i.e. red form and grey form which is metallic in nature.
- Tellurium also exists in two forms, i.e. non-metallic and metallic (more stable) form. While allotropes of polonium are α and β-forms.

• Allotropes of S.

(i) Rhombic S (α-sulphur)

- Yellow in colour.
- Insoluble in water.
- Readily soluble in CS_2.
- Is octahedral in shape.

(ii) Monoclinic S (β-sulphur)

- Prepared by melting α-sulphur.
- Soluble in CS_2.
- Is needle shaped crystal.
- Both forms have an S_8 ring which has a crown shape.
- In cyclo-S_6, the ring adopts the chair form.

(ii) Metallic and non-metallic character Down the group metallic character increases due to decrease in Ionisation enthalpy.The first four elements are non-metals but the non-metallic character is stronger in oxygen and sulphur.
It is weaker in selenium and tellurium. The last element, polonium is distinctly a metal however, it is radioactive and is only short-lived.

(iii) Melting and boiling point

- Both increases down the group.
- Melting point and Boiling point of O are much lesser than S.

(iv) Ionisation enthalpy

- Decreases down the group due to combined effect of the increased atomic size and shielding effect.
- Lower than those of group 15 elements.

(v) Electronegativity

- O has the highest electronegativity in its groups.
- It decreases down the group.

(vi) Electron affinity

- It decreases as the atomic size increases. However, electron affinity of O is lesser as compared to S. This is because of the small size and high charge density of O atom.

Chemical Properties

- Generally -2 and $+2$ oxidation state are shown by almost all elements.
- S, Se and Te also exhibit $+4$ and $+6$ oxidation state.
- Stability of $+6$ state decreases down the group.
- Stability of $+4$ state increases down the group.

Trends in Reactivity

(i) With Hydrogen

Properties of hydride	Order	Reason
Bond angle	$H_2O > H_2S > H_2Se > H_2Te$	As bond pair-bond pair repulsion decreases.
Covalent character	$H_2O < H_2S < H_2Se > H_2Te$	Difference in electronegativity of M—H decreases.
Thermal stability	$H_2O > H_2S > H_2Se > H_2Te$	Due to increase in size of central atom strength of M—H bond decreases.
Reducing character	$H_2S < H_2Se < H_2Te$	Due to strength of M—H bond decreases.
Acidic character	$H_2O < H_2S < H_2Se < H_2Te$	Due to strength of M—H bond decreases

(ii) With Halogens

- Stability : $F^- > Cl^- > Br^- > I^-$
- In case of hexahalides, only fluorides are stable, $SF_6 > SeF_6 > TeF_6$
- They have octahedral structure.
- SF_6 is exceptionally stable for steric reasons.
- Ease of hydrolysis : $TeF_6 > SeF_6 > SF_6$

Halides	X	Oxidation numbers
S_2X_2	F, Cl, Br, I	+1
SX_2	F, Cl	+2
SX_4	F	+4
SX_6	F	+6
Se_2X_2	Cl, Br	+1
SeX_2, TeX_2	Cl, Br	+2
SeX_4, TeX_4	F, Cl, Br	+4
TeX_4	I	+4
SeX_6, TeX_6	F	+6

- Some important characteristic of 16th group halides are as follows
- For same elements the stability of the halides decreases in the order $F > Cl > Br > I$.

- SF_6 is thermodynamically inert, non-toxic gas. Inertness of SF_6 is due to the presence of sterically protected sulphur atom.
- SF_6 is used as a gaseous insulator in high voltage generators.

(ii) With Oxygens

- Acidic nature decreases down the group for both MO_2 and MO_3 types.
- Reducing property $SO_2 > SeO_2 > TeO_2$
- Some important characteristics of oxides of group 16 elements are given below.
- O_3 and SO_2 are gases but SeO_2 is solid. On moving from SO_2 to TeO_2, reducing property decreases.
- TeO_2 acts as an oxidising agent. MO_3 type oxide are formed by sulphur, selenium and tellurium but tendency to form MO_3 type of oxides decreases down the group due to inert pair effect.
- These oxides are acidic in nature, i.e. form acids with water and this nature decreases down the group due to decrease in electronegativity and increase of metallic character.
  Hence, order of acidic nature of oxides is $SO_3 > SeO_3 > TeO_3$

Anomalous Behaviour of Oxygen

Oxygen, the first member of 16th group, differs in some important ways from other group members. This is due to its

- small size,
- high electronegativity and
- non-availability of d-orbitals for bonding.

The main points of difference between oxygen and other members of 16th group are given below.

- Oxygen exists as O_2, (diatomic) gas while all other members are solid.
- Oxygen is paramagnetic while others are not (S_2, is also paramagnetic).
- Compounds of oxygen are ionic and polar covalent due to its high electronegativity.
- Oxygen exhibit -2 oxidation state while other members show $+6$ oxidation states.
- Oxygen form $p\pi$-$p\pi$ bonds while sulphur forms $d\pi$-$p\pi$ bonds.
- Only hydride of oxygen is non-poisonous, i.e. H_2O while other hydrides are poisonous gases.

Test 3

Syllabus

- General Introduction, Electronic Configuration, General Trends in Physical and Chemical Properties of Elements Across the Periods and Down the Groups, Unique Behaviour of 1st Element.

NCERT Page 192 to 202

For deeper insight **Scan the QR Code**

Chapter 04

Introduction

This group consists of five elements namely **fluorine** (F), **chlorine** (Cl), **bromine** (Br), **iodine** (I) and **astatine** (At). These elements are also called as halogen (means sea salts), i.e. their salts are abundantly present in sea water.

Occurrence

Fluorine and chlorine are fairly abundant while bromine and iodine are less. Fluorine is mainly present as insoluble fluorides [Fluorspar CaF_2, cryolite Na_3AlF_6 and fluorapatite $3Ca_3(PO_4)_2 \cdot CaF_2$] and small quantities are present in soil, river water plants etc. Iodine occurs as iodate. Chlorine is most abundant among halogen and its commercial source is NaCl (common salt).

Electronic Configuration

- The general electronic configuration of halogens is $ns^2 np^5$ (where, $n = 1, 3, 4, \ldots$).
- Due to the presence of 7 electrons in their valence shell, these elements have a high tendency to gain one electron and achieve nearest noble gas configuration.

Element	Atomic number	Electronic configuration
Fluorine (F)	9	$[He]2s^2 2p^5$
Chlorine (Cl)	17	$[Ne]3s^2 3p^5$
Bromine (Br)	35	$[Ar]3d^{10} 4s^2 4p^5$
Iodine (I)	53	$[Kr]4d^{10} 5s^2 5p^5$
Astatine (At)	85	$[Xe]4f^{14} 5d^{10} 6s^2 6p^5$

General and Physical Properties

- **Physical state** On moving down the group, the tendency to form condensed molecules increases. Thus, fluorine and chlorine are gases at ordinary temperature, bromine is a highly fuming liquid while iodine is a volatile solid.
- **Atomic and Ionic radii** Halogens have small atomic radii than the elements of group 16 due to high effective nuclear charge. On moving down the group, it increases as the number of shells increases by one.
  F < < Cl < Br < I
- **Melting and boiling points** On moving down the group from F to At, there is an increase in melting and boiling points.
- **Ionisation energy** These all have high ionisation energy, i.e. have a little tendency to lose electrons. On moving down the group this tendency of ionisation energy decreases. F > Cl > Br > I
- **Electronegativity** Halogens have the high values of electronegativities and it decreases on moving down from F to I. F > Cl > Br > I
- **Electron gain enthalpy** These elements have maximum electron gain enthalpies in their respective periods because they have only one electron less than noble gas configuration, i.e. On moving down the group the magnitude of electron gain enthalpy (i.e., electron affinity) usually decreases. But electron affinity of fluorine is unexpectedly lower than Cl. This is because of the smaller size of F. Cl > F > Br > I
- **Electron affinity** Halogens have seven electrons in their valence shell, they have a very strong tendency of gaining an electron to acquire a stable noble gas configuration. Therefore, they have very high negative electron affinities. In fact, their electron affinities are the highest in their respective periods. The order follows as Cl > F > Br > I.
  The smaller electron affinity of fluorine than that of chlorine is a consequence of the small size of fluorine and high charge density.
- **Colours** All these halogens are coloured. F_2 is yellow, Cl_2 is greenish yellow, Br_2 is reddish brown and I_2 is violet. The colour is because of absorption of energy from visible light by halogen molecules for excitation of outer electron from the highest occupied π^* molecular orbital to the lowest unoccupied σ^* molecular orbital.
- **Solubility** Halogens being non-polar in molecular form are readily soluble in organic solvents like hexane. However, they're not as much soluble in polar solvents like water. Their solubility in water decreases down the group as $F_2 > Cl_2 > Br_2 > I_2$.
  Fluorine reacts with water violently. Chlorine and bromine are fairly soluble, while iodine is least soluble.

	F_2	Cl_2	Br_2	I_2
Melting point/K	54.4	172.0	265.8	386.6
Boiling point/K	84.9	239.0	332.5	458.2
Density/g cm^{-3}	1.5(8.5)[c]	1.66(203)[c]	3.19(273)[c]	4.94 (293)[d]
Distance X-X/pm	143	199	228	266
Bond dissociation enthalpy/(kJ mol^{-1})	158.8	242.6	192.8	151.1
$E^\ominus/V^\ominus$	2.87	1.36	1.09	0.54

Chemical Properties

Trends in Reactivity

(i) Towards Hydrogen

- H—F > H—Cl > H—Br > H—I (Bond dissociation enthalpy)
- HI > HBr > HCl > HF (Acidic strength)
- HI > HBr > HCl > HF (Reducing character)
- HF > HI > HBr > HCl (Boiling point)
- HF > HCl > HBr > HI (Thermal stability)
- HI > HBr > HCl > HF (Bond length)
- They all react with hydrogen to give hydrogen halides but affinity for hydrogen decreases from fluorine to iodine.
- Hydrogen halides dissolve in water to form hydrohalic acids.

(ii) Towards Oxygen

- Stability of oxides formed by halogens.
  I > Cl > Br
- F forms OF_2 and O_2F_2.
- Cl oxides are good oxidising agents.

Structure of Oxides of Chlorine

Name	Formula	Oxidation state of chlorine	Hybridisation of chlorine	Structure
Chlorine monoxide	Cl_2O	+1	sp^3	
Chlorine dioxide	ClO_2	+3	sp^2	
Chlorine hexoxide	Cl_2O_6	+5	sp^3	
Chlorine heptoxide	Cl_2O_7	+7	sp^3	

(ii) Towards Metals

- Halogens react with metals to form metal halides.
- Ionic character $MF > MCl > MBr > MI$
- Covalent character $\propto$ oxidation state of metals

(iv) Towards Halogens

- Different halogens react with water in different manners. These reactions represent relative oxidising power of halogens. Fluorine oxidises water to give oxygen gas.

$$F_2 + 2H_2O \longrightarrow 4H^+ F^- + O_2$$

- Chlorine and bromine form hydrohalic acid and hypohalous acid, upon reactions with water.

$$X_2 + H_2O \longrightarrow 4H + HOX \quad \text{(Here, X=Cl, Br)}$$

- Whereas iodine does not give reaction with water spontaneously.

$$I_2 + H_2O \longrightarrow \text{No reaction}$$

Anomalous Behaviour of Fluorine

Fluorine, because of its small size, high charge density, non-availability of *d*-orbitals and low bond dissociation energy differs from the rest of the halogens in following ways

- Fluorine shows only −1 oxidation state due to its maximum electronegativity, whereas the other halogens can show negative as well as positive oxidation state, i.e. between −1 and +7.
- Maximum covalency of fluorine is one as there is no *d*-orbital in its valence shell. Other members can have maximum covalency of 7 because of vacant *d*-orbitals.
- Fluorine because of its low bond dissociation energy is very reactive. However, in Cl_2 and Br_2, X—X bond is stronger.
- HF has a high tendency to form H-bond, thus, it is a liquid (b.p. 19°C) while HCl, HBr and HI due to lack of such a tendency, are gases under ordinary conditions.
- Hydrofluoric acid being a dibasic acid (H_2F_2) forms two series of salt such as $NaHF_2$ and Na_2F_2 while HCl, HBr and HI are monobasic in nature.
- Mostly fluorides are ionic and contain F^- ion while other halides have frequently molecular lattices.
- Fluorine when combines with sulphur, forms SF_6 while no other halogen forms the hexahalide with sulphur.

Some Properties of Interhalogen Compounds

When two different halogens react with each other, interhalogen compounds are formed.

Type	Formula	Physical state and colour	Structure
XX'_1	ClF	Colourless gas	—
	BrF	Pale brown gas	—
	IF[(x)]	Detected spectroscopically	—
	BrCl[(y)]	Gas	
	ICl	Ruby red solid (α-form)	—
		Brown-red solid (β-form)	—
	IBr	Black solid	—
XX'_3	ClF_3	Colourless gas	Bent T-shaped
	BrF_3	Yellow-green liquid	Bent T-shaped
	IF_3	Yellow powder	Bent T-shaped
	ICl_3[(z)]	Orange solid	Bent T-shaped
XX'_5	IF_5	Colourless gas but solid below 77 K	Square pyramidal
	BrF_5	Colourless liquid	Square pyramidal
	ClF_5	Colourless liquid	Square pyramidal
XX'_7	IF_7	Colourless gas	Pentagonal bipyramidal

Test 4

Syllabus

- General Introduction, Electronic Configuration, General Trends in Physical and Chemical Properties of Elements Across the Periods and Down the Groups, Unique Behaviour of 1st Element.

NCERT Page 202 to 205

For deeper insight **Scan the QR Code**

Chapter 04

Introduction

- This group of periodic table contains six elements collectively known as noble gases.
- These are **helium** (He), **neon** (Ne), **argon** (Ar), **krypton** (Kr), **xenon** (Xe) and **radon** (Rn).
- They are also known as inert gases as they have stable configuration due to which they are inert in nature at normal condition.

Occurrence

- All these gases except radon (Rn) are present in atmosphere. Rn results from disintegration of radium (is itself radioactive).
- The total abundance of these elements in dry air (except Rn) is ~1% by volume, out of which Ar is the major component.

Isolation of Elements

- Helium is commercially obtained from natural gas. Natural gas contains hydrocarbons (such as methane), CO_2, H_2S and He as main constituents.
- The hydrocarbon and other impurities are liquefied at about 120K and helium is pumped out.
- Ar, Ne, Kr and Xe are prepared by fractional distillation of liquid air. It gives O_2, N_2 and mixture of the noble gases.
- The separation depends upon the boiling points of the noble gases and to enhance the separation charcoal is used.

Electronic Configuration

The general electronic configuration of this group is $ns^2\,np^6$ or $ns^2\,np_x^2,\,np_y^2,\,np_z^2$ (except helium for which it is $1s^2$).

Element	Atomic Number	Electronic Configuration
Helium (He)	2	$1s^2$
Neon (Ne)	10	$[He]2s^22p^6$
Argon (Ar)	18	$[Ne]3s^23p^6$
Krypton (Kr)	36	$[Ar]3d^{10}4s^24p^6$
Xenon (Xe)	54	$[Kr]4d^{10}5s^25p^6$
Radon (Rn)	86	$[Xe]4f^{14}5d^{10}6s^26p^6$

General and Physical Properties

- **Atomic and ionic radii** The atomic radii of 18th group elements correspond to the van der Waals' radii and increases on moving down the group.
  He < Ne < Ar < Kr < Xe
- **Boiling points** They have low boiling points in comparison to other elements. It increases with increase in atomic sizes, i.e. increases down the group. It is because they are monoatomic and have no interatomic forces except weak dispersion forces. Therefore they are liquified at very low temperatures and have very low boiling points. Helium has the lowest boiling point of any known substance.
  He < Ne < Ar < Kr < Xe
- **Ionisation energy** Noble gases have stable ns^2np^6 (fully-filled) electronic configuration. Thus, have no tendency to add or lose electron. Therefore, their ionisation energy is very high. It decreases on moving down the group. He > Ne > Ar > Kr > Xe
- **Solubility** They are slightly soluble in water and their solubility generally increases on moving down the group.
- **Adsorption** Except He, all the noble gases are adsorbed by coconut charcoal. This ease of adsorption increases on moving down the group.
- **Conductivity** They have high electrical conductivity at low pressures.
- **Spectra** All of them give characteristic spectra, by which they can be identified.
- **Liquefaction** Due to the presence of weak van der Waals' forces of attraction, it is difficult to liquify noble gases. Ease of liquefaction increases down the group from He to Rn due to increase in intermolecular forces.
- **Heat of vaporisation and polarisability** They possess very low values of heat of vaporisation. This is due to the presence of very weak van der Waals' forces of attraction between their monoatomic molecules. However, this value increases with atomic number. This shows that there is an increase in polarisability of the larger electronic clouds of the elements with higher atomic number. In other words, the polarisability increases down the group as,
  He < Ne < Ar < Kr < Xe

Clathrates of Noble Gas

- Noble gases form a number of compounds in which the gases are entrapped in the cavities of crystal lattices of some organic and inorganic compounds. Such compounds are called **clathrates** or **cage compounds** or **host-guest compounds**.
  e.g. $Xe{\cdot}6H_2O$, quinol clathrate.
- The organic or inorganic compound with cavities is called **host** and the gas entrapped in them is called **guest**. He and Ne do not form such compound because of small size. Only Ar, Kr and Xe form clathrates.

Chemical Properties

- Least reactive due to filled valence shell, high I.E and positive electrons gain enthalpy.
- Only few compounds of Kr are known.

Compounds of Group 18 Elements

(i) Xenon-Fluorine Compounds

$$Xe\,(g) + F_2\,(g) \xrightarrow{673K,\ 1bar} XeF_2\,(s)$$
(Xenon in excess)

$$Xe\,(g) + 2F_2\,(g) \xrightarrow{873K,\ 7bar} XeF_4\,(s)$$
(1 : 5 ratio)

$$Xe\,(g) + 3F_2\,(g) \xrightarrow{573K,\ 60\text{-}70bar} XeF_6\,(s)$$
(1 : 20 ratio)

(ii) Xenon-Oxygen Compounds

With water

$$6XeF_4 \xrightarrow{12H_2O} 4Xe + 2XeO_3 + 24HF + 3O_2$$

$$XeF_6 \xrightarrow{H_2O} XeOF_4 + 2HF$$

$$XeF_6 \xrightarrow{2H_2O} XeO_2F_2 + 4HF$$

With F donor and acceptors

$$XeF_2 \xrightarrow{PF_5} [XeF]^+[PF_6]^-$$

$$XeF_6 \xrightarrow{MF} [XeF_7]^-M^+ \quad [M = Na, K, Rb \text{ or } Cs]$$

$$XeF_4 \xrightarrow{SbF_5} [XeF_3]^+[SbF_6]^-$$

Structures

Compounds of xenon	Hybridisation	Geometry
XeF_2	sp^3d	Linear
XeF_4	sp^3d^2	Square planar
XeF_6	sp^3d^3	Distorted octahedral
XeO_3	sp^3	Pyramidal
XeO_4	sp^3	Tetrahedral
$XeOF_4$	sp^3d^2	Square pyramidal

Uses of Noble Gases

There are many uses of noble gases. Some of the uses are summarised in the table given below.

Noble gas	Uses	Reasons
Helium	1. Filling balloons for meteorological observations	Non-flammable, 93% lifting power as compared to flammable H_2
	2. He/O_2 mixture use for deep-sea breathing, instead of N_2/O_2 mixture	Low solubility in blood, prevents nitrogen narcosis and "bends"
	3. Diluent use for gaseous anaesthetics	Non-flammable, non-reactive
	4. He/O_2 mixtures use for respiratory patients	Low density, flows easily through restricted passages
	5. Heat transfer medium for nuclear reactions	Transfers heat readily, does not become radioactive, chemically inert
	6. (Liquid He) To maintain very low temperature in research (cryogenics)	Extremely low boiling point
Neon	Neon signs	Even at low Ne pressure, moderate electric current causes bright orange-red glow, can be modified by coloured glass or mixing with Ar or Hg vapour.
Argon	1. Inert atmosphere for welding	Chemically inert
	2. Filling incandescent light bulbs	Inert, prevents vaporisation of tungsten and blackening of bulbs
Krypton	Airport runway and approach lights	Gives longer life to incandescent lights than Ar but more expensive
Xenon	Xe and Kr mixture in high intensity, short exposure photographic flash tubes	Both have fast response to electric current
Radon	Radiotherapy of cancerous-tissues	Radioactive

Test 1

Syllabus

- **Transition Elements** : General Introduction, Electronic Configuration, Occurrence and Characteristics, General Trends in Properties of the First Row Transition Elements, Physical Properties, Ionisation Enthalpy, Oxidation States, Atomic Radii, Colour, Catalytic Behaviour, Magnetic Properties, Complex Formation, Interstitial Compounds, Alloy Formation.

NCERT Page 89 to 105

For deeper insight **Scan the QR Code**

Chapter 05

Transition Elements (*d*-Block)

- The *d*-block occupies the large middle section of the periodic table flanked between *s*- and *p*-blocks in the periodic table.
- The *d*-orbitals of the penultimate energy level of atoms receive electrons giving rise to four rows of transition metals, i.e. 3*d*, 4*d*, 5*d* and 6*d*.
- Except $_{30}Zn$, $_{48}Cd$, $_{80}Hg$ and $_{112}Cn$, *d*-block elements are known as transition elements.
- Their general electronic configurations is $(n-1)\,d^{1-10}\,ns^{1-2}$ [n = 4, 5, 6 and 7].
- **Exceptional Configuration**
- Due to more stable half-filled configuration Cr from 3*d* series and Mo from 4*d* series shows $3d^5\,4s^1$ and $4d^5\,5s^1$ electronic configuration instead of $3d^4\,4s^2$ and $4d^4\,5s^2$ respectively.
- Due to more stable fully filled configuration of Cu from 3*d* series and Ag from 4*d* series shows $3d^{10}\,4s^1$ and $4d^{10}\,5s^1$ electronic configuration instead of $3d^9\,4s^2$ and $4d^9\,5s^2$.

	Expected configuration	Observed configuration
Cr	$[Ar]3d^44s^2$	$[Ar]3d^54s^1$
Cu	$[Ar]3d^94s^2$	$[Ar]3d^{10}4s^1$

Physical Properties of *d*-Block Elements

- Generally, *d*-block elements are very hard and have low volatility (Zn, Cd and Hg are exceptions).
- Have higher **melting and boiling points** due to involvement of *d*-electrons in metallic bonding.
- Sc < Ti < V < Cr > Mn < Fe > Co > Ni > Cu > Zn
- **Atomic Radius**
  Shows progressive decrease along the period, due to increased effective nuclear charge but this decrease in atomic radii become small after midway.
- Sc > Ti > V > Cr > Mn > Fe ≈ Co ≈ Ni ≤ Cu < Zn
- Among 3*d*, 4*d* and 5*d* series , order of radii is 3*d* < 4*d* ≈ 5 *d* due to lanthanide contraction.
- **Density**
  In 3*d* series, it increases from left to right, Cu being an exception.
- **Ionisation Enthalpy**
  Increases from left to right due to increase in nuclear charge, although the increase is not regular.
- **Oxidation States**
  Shows variable oxidation states due to involvement of *ns* and (*n*-1)*d* electrons in bonding.
- Highest oxidation states is possible for elements in middle of the series.
- Stability of higher oxidation states increases down the group with some halides and oxygen.

Magnetic Properties

- Magnetic moment increases with the increasing number of unpaired electrons.
- When magnetic field is applied to substances, mainly two types of magnetic behaviour are observed diamagnetism and paramagnetism. Magnetic moment, $\mu = \sqrt{n(n+2)}$BM where, n = number of unpaired electrons.

Magnetic Moment of 1st Transition Elements

Ion	Configuration	Unpaired electron(s)	Magnetic moment
Sc^{3+}	$3d^0$	0	0
Ti^{3+}	$3d^1$	1	1.73
Ti^{2+}	$3d^2$	2	2.84
V^{2+}	$3d^3$	3	3.87
Cr^{2+}	$3d^4$	4	4.90
Mn^{2+}	$3d^5$	5	5.92
Fe^{2+}	$3d^6$	4	4.90
Co^{2+}	$3d^7$	3	3.87
Ni^{2+}	$3d^8$	2	2.84
Cu^{2+}	$3d^9$	1	1.73
Zn^{2+}	$3d^{10}$	0	0

Catalytic Properties

- Many transition metals (like Fe, Co, Ni, Pt, Mo etc.) and their compounds are used as catalysts due to their ability to show variable oxidation states, available vacant *d*-orbitals and large surface area available for adsorption.
- Catalyst at a solid surface involve the formation of bonds between reactant molecules and atoms of the surface of catalyst. This has the effect of increasing the concentration of the reactants at the catalyst surface and also weakening of the bonds in the reacting molecules (the activation energy is lowered). Also because transition metal ions can change their oxidation states, they become more effective as catalysts.

Transition Metals and the Compounds as Catalyst

Fe/Mo	Promoter Fe used in Haber-Bosch process of NH_3.
$TiCl_4$	Used as Ziegler-Natta catalyst in production of polyethene.
Ni	Hydrogenation process.
Pt	Ostwald process form HNO_3 from NH_3
V_2O_5	Used in contact process.
$CuCl_2$	Deacon's process for making Cl_2 from HCl.

Formation of Interstitial Compounds

- Transition metals can trap some small atoms like hydrogen, boron, carbon, nitrogen, etc., in vacant spaces in their crystal lattice to form interstitial compounds.
- Carbon and nitrogen always occupy octahedral holes; hydrogen is smaller and occupies tetrahedral holes.
- As only transition metals form such compounds, the *d*-electrons are, therefore, presumably involved in the bonding.
- The structure of the metal often changes during the formation of such compounds. The composition of these compounds is generally non-stoichiometric.

Characteristics of interstitial compounds

- They have high melting points, higher than those of pure metals.
- They are chemically inert.
- They are less malleable and ductile.
- Interstitial compounds are neither ionic nor covalent.
- They are very hard and retain metallic conductivity.

Alloy Formation

- An alloy is a blend of metals prepared by mixing the components. They are homogeneous solid solutions in which the atoms of one metal are distributed randomly among the atoms of the other. Because of similar radii and other characteristics of transition metals, alloys are readily formed by these metals.
- Alloys are generally harder, have higher melting points and more resistant to corrosion than the individual metals. Metals such as Cr, V, Mo, W and Mn are used in the production of alloy steels and stainless steels. Alloys containing mercury as one of the constituent elements are called amalgams.
- Alloys of transition metals with non transition metals such as brass (copper-zinc) and bronze (copper-tin) etc., are of considerable industrial importance.

Some Important Alloys of Transition Metals

Rolled gold	Cu + Al
Invar	Fe + Ni
Alnico	Fe + Al + Ni + Co
Stainless steel	Fe + Ni + Cr
German silver	Ni + Cu + Zn
20 carat gold	Au + Cu
24 carat gold	100% Au

Formation of Complex Compounds

- Transition metal ions form a large number of complexes in which the central metal ion is linked to a number of ligands. This is because of the following characteristic properties of transition metals.
- They have high nuclear charge and small size, i.e. charge/size ratio (charge density) is large.
- They have empty *d*-orbitals to accept the lone pairs of electrons donated by the ligands.
- Thus, in complex metal ions behave as Lewis acids and ligands behave as Lewis bases.
- Complexes can be linear (*sp*-hybridisation), square planar dsp^2-hybridisation), tetrahedral (sp^3-hybridisation), octahedral (d^2sp^3-hybridisation) or trigonal bipyramidal sp^3d-hybridisation).

Formation of Coloured Ions

- Many ionic and covalent compounds of transition elements (and also inner transition elements) are coloured.
  Colour in *d*-block element complexes arises due to transition of electron from one *d*-orbital to another. This transition is called ***d-d** transition**.
- The colour of a transition metal complex is dependent on how big the energy difference is between the two *d*-levels. This in turn depends on the nature of the ligand, and the type of the complex formed. The colour which we see is the colour of the transmitted wavelength.
- $[Ni(NH_3)_6]^{2+} \rightarrow$ Blue • $[Ni(H_2O)_6]^{2+} \rightarrow$ Green
- $[Ni(NO_2)_6]^{2-} \rightarrow$ Brown-red

Applications of *d* -Block Elements

- TiO_2 in pigment industry. MnO_2 in dry batteries. V_2O_5 is used as catalyst in contact process of H_2SO_4. $TiCl_4$ with $Al(CH_3)_3$ is used as Ziegler catalyst. Fe is used as a catalyst in Haber's process.
- $PdCl_2$ is used as a catalyst in Wacker process.
- Nickel is used in polymerisation reactions.
- AgBr is used in photographic industry.
- Cu is used in alloy formation like bronze (Cu+Sn) and brass (Cu+Zn).
- Cu, Ag and Au are used for making coins and ornaments.Steel, titanium nitride, titanium carbide etc. are used for making artificial joint replacement of bones.
- Tungsten is used in making electrical fibres.

Test 2

Syllabus
- Preparation, Properties and Uses of $K_2Cr_2O_7$ and $KMnO_4$

NCERT Page 105 to 108

For deeper insight **Scan the QR Code**

Oxides and Oxoanions of Metals

- These oxides are generally formed by the reaction of metals with oxygen at higher temperatures. All the metals except Sc form MO oxides which are ionic.
- On moving along a period from Sc to Zn basic nature decreases and acidic nature increases.

Sc_2O_3	TiO_2	V_2O_5	Cr_2O_3	MnO_2	Fe_2O_3	Co_2O_3	NiO	CuO	ZnO
A	A	A	A	A	B	B	B	B	A

- *A* : Amphoteric
- *B* : Basic
- This behaviour differs when oxidation states are different. With increase in the oxidation state of a given transition metal, covalent character of its compound increases and thus acidic character also increases.

	MnO	Mn_3O_4	Mn_2O_3	MnO_2	MnO_3	Mn_2O_7
Nature of oxide	Basic	Amphoteric			Weakly acidic	Strongly acidic

- The basic and amphoteric oxides dissolve in non-oxidising acids and form hexaaqua ions $[M(H_2O)_6]^{n+}$.

Characteristics of Oxides and Some Ions of V and Cr

O.S.	Oxide/ Hydroxide	Behavior	Ion	Name of ion	Colour of ion
+2	VO	Basic	V^{2+}	Vanadium (II) (Vanadous)	Violet
+3	V_2O_3	Basic	V^{3+}	Vanadium (III) (vanadic)	Green
+4	VO_2	Amphoteric	VO^{2+} $V_4O_9^{2-}$	Oxovandium (IV) (vanadyl) Hypovanadate (vandite)	Blue brown
+5	V_2O_5	Amphoteric	VO_2^+ VO_4^{3-}	Dioxovanadium (V) Orthovandate (V)	Yellow Colourless
+2	CrO $Cr(OH)_2$	Basic	Cr^{2+}	Chromium (II) (chromous)	Light blue
+3	Cr_2O_3 $Cr(OH)_3$	Amphoteric	Cr^{3+} $Cr(OH)_4^-$	Chromium (III) (chromic) Chromite	Violet Geen
+6	CrO_3 $CrO_2(OH)_2$ $H_2Cr_2O_7$	Acidic	CrO_4^{2-} $Cr_2O_7^{2-}$	Chromate Dichromate	Yellow Orange

Potassium Dichromate ($K_2Cr_2O_7$)

- **Prepared from Chromite Ore ($FeCr_2O_4$)**

$$4FeCr_2O_4+8Na_2CO_3+7O_2 \longrightarrow 8Na_2CrO_4+2Fe_2O_3+8CO_2$$
$$2Na_2CrO_4+H_2SO_4 \longrightarrow Na_2Cr_2O_7+Na_2SO_4+H_2O$$
$$Na_2Cr_2O_7+2KCl \longrightarrow K_2Cr_2O_7+2NaCl$$

The chromates and dichromates are interconvertible in aqueous solution depending upon pH of the solution.

$$2CrO_4^{2-} + 2H^+ \longrightarrow \underset{\text{(Orange)}}{Cr_2O_7^{2-}} + H_2O$$
$$Cr_2O_7^{2-} + 2OH^- \longrightarrow \underset{\text{(Yellow)}}{2CrO_4^{2-}} + H_2O$$

(Structure of $Cr_2O_7^{2-}$) [Cr–O–Cr angle 126°, bond lengths 179 pm and 163 pm]

Reason for inter conversion In dichromate solution, the orange-red $Cr_2O_7^{2-}$ ions are invariably in equilibrium with yellow CrO_4^{2-} ions.

$$\underset{\text{Orange red}}{Cr_2O_7^{2-}} + H_2O \rightleftharpoons \underset{\text{Yellow}}{2CrO_4^{2-}} + 2H^+$$

Thus, on the basis of Le-Chatelier's principle

- When the conc. of OH^- is increased, then forward reaction proceeds faster resulting in more yellow coloured CrO_4^- ion.
- Similarly when acid is added concentration of H^+ ions is increased resulting in faster backward reaction.

Hence, organic solution is visible due to more orange-red coloured $Cr_2O_7^{2-}$ ions.

- **Oxidising Properties**

$$Cr_2O_7^{2-} + 14H^+ + 6e^- \longrightarrow 2Cr^{3+} + 7H_2O$$
$$6Fe^{2+} \longrightarrow 6Fe^{3+} + 6e^-$$
$$6I^- \longrightarrow 3I_2 + 6e^-$$

The full equation is obtained by adding the half reaction for potassium dichromate to the half reaction for the reducing agent for e.g.

e.g. $Cr_2O_7^{2-} + 14H^+ + 6I^- \longrightarrow 2Cr^{3+} + 7H_2O + 3I_2$

- **Chromyl Chloride Test**

$$K_2Cr_2O_7+4NaCl+6H_2SO_4 \longrightarrow \underset{\text{Chromyl chloride}}{2CrO_2Cl_2}+2KHSO_4+3H_2O+4NaHSO_4$$

- $K_2Cr_2O_7$ when heated with conc. H_2SO_4 and soluble chloride (like NaCl, KCl) gives deep red vapour of CrO_2Cl_2. This test is called as **chromyl-chloride test**. It is used to identify Cl^- in inorganic salt-analysis. But AgCl, $PbCl_2$, $SnCl_4$, HgCl or $HgCl_2$ does not show chromyl chloride test.

Potassium Permanganate ($KMnO_4$)

- **Prepared from the Pyrolusite Ore** (MnO_2)

$$2MnO_2 + 4KOH + O_2 \longrightarrow 2K_2MnO_4 + 2H_2O$$
$$3MnO_4^{2-} + 4H^+ \longrightarrow 2MnO_4^- + MnO_2 + 2H_2O$$

- **Commercial method**

$$MnO_2 \xrightarrow[\text{Oxidised with air or } KNO_3]{\text{Fused with KOH}} \underset{\text{Manganate ion}}{MnO_4^{2-}}$$
$$MnO_4^{2-} \xrightarrow[\text{in alkaline solution}]{\text{Electrolytic oxidation}} \underset{\text{Permanganate ion}}{MnO_4^-}$$

Thus, both manganate and permanganate ions are tetrahedral the bonding takes place by overlap of *p*-orbital of oxygen with *d*-orbitals of manganese. The given manganate is paramagnetic but the permanganate is diamagnetic.

Physical Properties

- It exists as deep purple black prisms with a greenish lustre which becomes dull in air due to reduction.
- It is moderately soluble in water at room temperature and more soluble in hot water.

Uses

- In volumetric analysis, it is used as standard solution for the estimation of Fe^{2+}, I^- etc.
- In organic reactions, it is used as an oxidising agent. For preparation of many azo compounds.
- It is used in preparation of chrome alum.

$$K_2Cr_2O_7 + H_2SO_4 + 3SO_2 \xrightarrow{\Delta} K_2SO_4 + Cr_2(SO_4)_3$$

Crystallises as $\downarrow + H_2O$

$KCr(SO_4)_2 \cdot 12H_2O$ Chrome alum

- In calico printing and dyeing. It is deep purple compound used for leather tanning.
- In photography.
- In hardening of gelatin film.

Chemical Properties

(i) **Effect of heat** When heated to 513 K, it readily decompose to give potassium manganate, manganese (IV) oxide and oxygen.

$$2KMnO_4 \xrightarrow{513K} K_2MnO_4 + MnO_2 + O_2$$

(ii) **Effect of Conc. H_2SO_4**

- With cold conc. H_2SO_4, it gives a green oily compound Mn_2O_7 which is highly explosive in nature.

$$\underset{\text{(Cold conc.)}}{2KMnO_4 + 2H_2SO_4} \longrightarrow \underset{\text{(Green)}}{Mn_2O_7} + 2KHSO_4 + H_2O$$
$$2Mn_2O_7 \xrightarrow{\Delta} 4MnO_2 + 3O_2$$

- With warm conc. H_2SO_4

$$\underset{\text{(Warm conc.)}}{4KMnO_4 + 6H_2SO_4} \longrightarrow 2K_2SO_4 + 4MnSO_4 + 6H_2O + 5O_2$$

(iii) **Stability in acidic medium** Permanganate solutions are intrinsically unstable in acidic solution and decompose slowly. Decomposition is catalysed by sunlight, so $KMnO_4$ solution should be stored in dark bottles and they must be standardised at the moment of its use in volumetric analysis.

$$4MnO_4^- + 4H^+ \longrightarrow 4MnO_2 + 3O_2 + 2H_2O$$

(iv) **Oxidising property** $KMnO_4$ is a good oxidising agent. The actual oxidising action depends upon the use of the $KMnO_4$ in (A) neutral (B) alkaline or (C) acidic medium.

- Some oxidising properties of $KMnO_4$ in the neutral or faintly alkaline medium.
- $S_2O_3^{2-}$ is oxidised to SO_4^{2-}.

$$8MnO_4^- + 3S_2O_3^{2-} + H_2O \longrightarrow 8MnO_2 + 6SO_4^{2-} + 2OH^-$$

- Mn^{2+} is oxidised to MnO_2.

$$2MnO_4^- + 3Mn^{2+} + 2H_2O \longrightarrow 5MnO_2 + 4H^+$$

- **In acidic medium** It acts as a strong oxidising agent.

$$\underset{\text{(Purple)}}{MnO_4^-} + 5Fe^{2+} + 8H^+ \longrightarrow \underset{\text{(Colourless or extremely light pink)}}{Mn^{2+}} + 4H_2O + 5Fe^{3+}$$

- $2MnO_4^- + 10I^- + 16H^+ \longrightarrow 2Mn^{2+} + 8H_2O + 10I_2$

- It oxidise oxalates or oxalic acid to CO_2.
- $2MnO_4^- + 5C_2O_4^{2-} + 16H^+ \longrightarrow 2Mn^{2+} + 8H_2O + 10CO_2$

Test 3

Syllabus

- Inner-Transition Elements
  Lanthanoids : Electronic Configuration, Oxidation States and Lanthanoid Contraction.
  Actinoids : Electronic Configuration and Oxidation States.

NCERT Page 108 to 114

For deeper insight **Scan the QR Code**

Chapter 05

The Inner-Transition Elements (*f*-Block Elements)

- The elements in which differentiating electron enters in $(n-2)f$ subshell are called *f*-**block elements**. They are also called **inner-transition elements**.
- In periodic table they are placed inside the transition elements.
  These elements are divided into two series : (i) 4*f*-series or lanthanoids (ii) 5*f*-series or actinoids

General Characteristics of Lanthanoids

Some of the general characteristics of lanthanoids are discussed below.

- The general electronic configuration of these elements is $[Xe]\ 4f^{1-14}\ 5d^{0-1}6s^2$.
- **Physical state** All are silvery white soft metals having tensile strength and are good conductor of heat and electricity. The hardness increases with increasing atomic number, samarium being steel hard. They have typical metallic structure.
- They have higher density values which increases with increase in atomic number. They have high melting point with no regularity.
- **Atomic and ionic size** In the lanthanoid series with increasing atomic number, there is a progressive decrease in the size from lanthanum (La) to lutetium (Lu). This contraction in size is known as **lanthanoid contraction**. In these elements, the added electron enters in the diffused *f*- orbitals and therefore experiences considerable pull by the nucleus leading to contract the size of atom.
- **Oxidation states** Most common +3, Ce shows +4. Pr, Nd, Tb, and Dy and also show + 4 but only in oxides. Some elements (La, Eu, Yb, Sm) show +2 as well.
- **Colour** They have unpaired electrons in their 4*f*-orbitals. Thus, ions absorbs visible light by undergoing *f*-*f* transition and hence, exhibit colour.
- **Complex formation** Do not have much tendency to form complexes due to low charge density and large size.

4*f*-Series or Lanthanoides

Fourteen elements of the first row (4*f*-series) from lanthanum ($Z=57$) to lutetium ($Z=71$) which follow lanthanum ($Z=57$) in the periodic table are called **lanthanides** or **lanthanones**. These elements are characterised by successive filling of 4*f*-orbitals in their electronic configuration.

Chemical Reaction of Lanthanoids

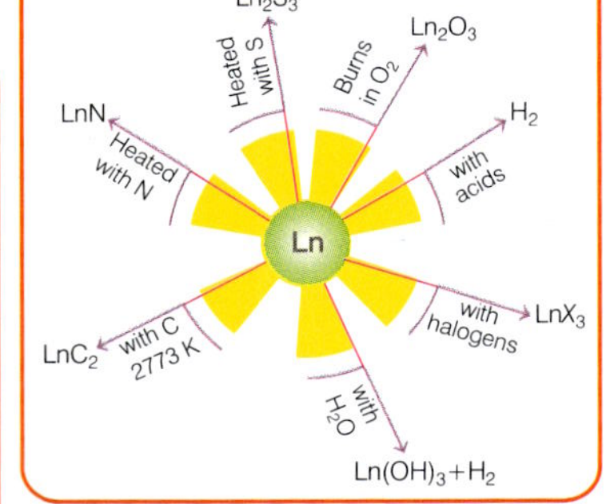

Consequences of Lanthanoid Contraction

- Due to lanthanide contraction, the normal increase in size from Sc→ Y→ La disappears after the lanthanide and the pairs of elements such as Zr and Hf, Nb and Ta, Mo and W etc., have nearly same size. The properties of these elements are very similar.
- The similarities in properties within these pair make their separation very difficult. Due to this contraction, their ability to form complexes varies slightly. This slight variation is utilised to separate lanthanides by ion-exchange method.
- Due to lanthanide contraction, the elements of 5*d* and 4*d*-transition series resemble each other much more closely than to that of 4*d* and 3*d* series.
- Covalent character of hydroxides of lanthanides increases as the size decreases, from La^{3+} to Lu^{3+} but basic strength decreases, i.e. $La(OH)_3$ is most basic whereas $Lu(OH)_3$ is least basic.
- Tendency to form stable complexes from La^{3+} and Lu^{3+} increases as the size decreases in that order.

5*f*-Series or Actinoids

- In 5*f*-series elements, the differentiating electron occupies 5*f*-orbital, thus these elements are said to belong to 5*f*-series. These are also called **actinoids** because of their close resemblance in properties with actinium.
- This series includes 14-elements from Th to Lr following actinium in the seventh period of the periodic table. Most of them are radioactive and therefore have the greatest importance in the study of **nuclear chemistry**.
- Elements with atomic numbers greater than 92 (atomic number of uranium) are called the **transuranium elements**. All these elements are man-made, i.e. they are produced in the laboratory through artificial nuclear reactions.

General Characteristics of Actinoids

- The general electronic configuration of actinoids is
  $[Rn]\ 5f^{1-14}\ 6d^{0-1}\ 7s^2$.
- **Physical state** They are silvery white in appearance and display a variety of structures. Generally actinoids have high density (except thorium and americium)
- **Ionic size** Gradual decrease along the series due to actinoid contraction.
- It is due to poor shielding effect of the 5*f*-electrons which results in increase in effective nuclear charge (which causes contraction in size of the electron cloud).
- Actinoids and many of their compounds are paramagnetic.
- **Oxidation state** The most stable oxidation state is +3. Also, shows different oxidation states like +2, +3, +4, +5, +6 and +7.
- **General properties**
- Highly reactive metals.
- Irregularities in metallic radii.
- Ionisation enthalpies are lower than that for the lanthanoids.
- Reacts with boiling water to form oxides and hydrides.
- Do not react with alkalies.
- Reacts with HCl easily but only few reacts with nitric acid due to formation of protective oxide layer.

Comparative Study of Lanthanoids and Actinoids

Lanthanoids	Actinoids
These exhibit mainly +3 oxidation state. In addition to +3 oxidation state, the lower oxidation state of +2 and higher oxidation state of +4 are noticed.	These also exhibit +3 oxidation state. In addition to +3 states, higher oxidation state of +3 to +7 are also noticed.
They show lanthanoids contraction.	They show actinoid contraction.
These are separated by ion exchange behaviour.	They also show ion exchange behaviour.
Most ions of lanthanoids elements are colourless.	Most ions of actinoids are coloured.
They possess lesser tendency for complexation.	They possess greater tendency for complexation.
They do not give oxocations.	They give oxocations, e.g. UO_2^{2+} etc.
Their compounds are less basic in nature.	Their compounds are more basic in nature.
These are non-radioactive (only promethium shows radioactivity)	All these are radioactive.
They are referred to as rare earth metals.	Elements beyond $_{92}U$ are referred to as transuranium elements.
Their magnetic nature can be easily explained.	Their magnetic nature can not be easily explained.
Their chemical and physical nature has been studied thoroughly.	Chemical and physical nature of these elements beyond $_{92}U$ has not been studied considerably.

Uses of *f*-Block Elements

Lanthanoids

- Form alloys like mischmetal and pyrophoric alloys.
- Used in making magnetic and electronic devices.
- Oxides are used in glass industry and their mixed oxides are used as catalysts in petroleum cracking.
- Recently used in lasers.

Actinoids

- These are used for the synthesis of transuranic elements.
- Thorium is used in the manufacture of fine rods for atomic reactors.
- ThO_2 is used for making incandescent gas mantles.
- **Uranium** is used in the production of nuclear energy.
- Uranium oxides are used in textile and ceramic industry.
- Plutonium is used as a fuel in atomic reactors and also used in nuclear bombs.

Important Points Regarding *f*-Block Elements

- Actinoid ions are generally coloured because of the *f*-*f* electronic transition (charge transfer). But those ion having , $5f^0$, $5f^7$ and $5f^{14}$ electronic configuration are colourless.
- Europium and yetterbium dissolve in liquid ammonia at 195K forming blue coloured solutions which give spectra characteristics of M^{2+} and ammoniated electrons.
- U^{3+} in aqueous solution evolves hydrogen on standing, aqueous solution of Np^{3+} and Pu^{3+} are stable but are easily oxidised to Np^{4+} and Pu^{4+}. All the other trivalent ions upto No^{3+} are stable.
- U^{4+} and Np^{+} are stable to water, but are slowly oxidised by air to UO_2^{2+} and NpO_2^{2+}.
- Carbonyls are not formed by lanthanoides due to non-availability of *d*-electron for π-bonding. However, an unstable $Nd(CO)_6$ has been prepared. Ce and Tb give CeF_4 and TbF_4 instead of CeF_3 and TbF_3 respectively.

Test 1

Syllabus

- Introduction to Coordination Compounds, Werner's Theory, Ligands, Coordination Number, Denticity, Chelation, IUPAC Nomenclature of Mononuclear Coordination Compounds, Isomerism.

NCERT Page 118 to 128

For deeper insight **Scan the QR Code**

Chapter 06

Addition Compounds

When solution having two or more stable compounds, combine in a simple molecular (stoichiometric) proportions, they form a new compound called **addition** or **molecular compounds**.

These addition compounds can be divided into two types

(i) Double salts or lattice compounds
The addition compounds which dissociate and lose their identity in solution are called **double salts**.
e.g. Mohr's salt→ $FeSO_4.(NH_4)_2 SO_4{\cdot}6H_2O$
Potash alum → $KAl(SO_4)_2{\cdot}12H_2O$
Carnallite → $KCl.MgCl_2{\cdot}6H_2O$

(ii) Coordination or complex compounds
The addition compounds which do not dissociate and retain their identity in solution are called **complex** or **coordination compounds**.
e.g. $K_2[PtCl_6]$, $K_4[Fe(CN)_6]$

Werner's Theory

Postulates

Metals show two types of linkages

(i) Primary valency (ii) Secondary valency

- Primary valency (Oxidation number) is ionisable, secondary valency (coordination number) is non-ionisable.
- Primary valency is satisfied by negative ions and secondary valency is satisfied by ligands.

Colour	Formula	Solution conductivity corresponds to
Yellow	$[Co(NH_3)_6]^{3+}\ 3Cl^-$	1:3 electrolyte
Purple	$[CoCl(NH_3)_5]^{2+}2Cl^-$	1:2 electrolyte
Green	$[CoCl_2(NH_3)_4]^+Cl^-$	1:1 electrolyte
Violet	$[CoCl_2(NH_3)_4]^+Cl^-$	1:1 electrolyte

Limitations • It could not explain.

- Why only certain elements possess complex forming property.
- Why bonds in coordination compounds have directional nature. Magnetic and optical property in complexes.

Important Terms Regarding Coordination Compounds

Complex Ion or Coordination Entity

It is a metal ion with a Lewis base attached to it through coordinate bonds, e.g. $[Fe(CN)_6]^{4-}$.

Complex ion can be represented as

Coordination sphere → $[Fe(CN)_6]^{4-}$ (Charge on complex ion; Central metal ion; Ligand; Coordination number)

Different types of complex ions are as follows

- Complex ion which bears positive charge is called **cationic complex ion**, e.g. $[Co(NH_3)_6]^{3+}$.
- Complex ion which bears negative charge is called **anionic complex ion**, e.g. $[Ag(CN)_2]^-$.
- Complex ion which has no charge is called **neutral complex ion**, e.g. $[Ni(CO)_4]$.
- **Central metal atom/ion** The atom (or ion) to which a fixed number of groups or ions are bonded in a definite geometrical arrangement, is called central metal ion. e.g. In $[Fe(CN)_6]^{3-}$, Fe^{3+} is a central metal ion.
- **Ligands** ions or molecules bound to central atom.
- **Unidentate** Ligand bound to metal ion through a single donor e.g. NH_3, Cl^-, OH^-.
- **Didentate** When ligand can bind through two donor atoms. e.g. $C_2O_4^{2-}$ and en($NH_2CH_2CH_2NH_2$).
- **Polydentate** When several donor atoms are present in a ligand e.g EDTA.
- **Ambidentate** When ligand has two donor atoms but either of the two binds to the metal in a complex. e.g. NO_2^-, SCN^-.
- **Chelate ligands** When a didentate or polydentate ligand uses its two or more donor atoms to bind to a single metal atom. Chelate complexes are generally more stable.
- **Homoleptic complexes** Complexes in which a metal is bound to only one kind of donor groups, e.g. $[Co(NH_3)_6]^{3+}$.
- **Heteroleptic complexes** Complexes in which a metal is bound to more than one kind of donor groups, e.g. $[Co(NH_3)_4Cl_2]^+$.
- **Coordination sphere** The central atom/ion and the ligands attached are enclosed in square brackets and are collectively called as coordination sphere. It represents single entity in coordination compounds. The ionisable groups are written outside the bracket and are called counter ions. e.g. In the complex $K_4[Fe(CN)_6]$ the coordination sphere is $[Fe(CN)_6]$ and K^+ is the counter ion.
- **Coordination polyhedron** It is the spatial arrangement of the ligand atoms which are directly attached to the central atom/ion is called coordination polyhedron e.g. $[Co(NH_3)_6]^{2+}$ is octahedral, $Ni(CO)_4$ is tetrahedral and $[PtCl_4]^{2-}$ is square planar.
- **Coordination number** It is the number of ligands to which a central metal ion is directly bonded.e.g. In $[Ni(NH_3)_4]^{2+}$, here coordination number of Ni is 4.
- **In case of polydentate ligands,** C.N. = number of ligand × denticity of ligand. For example, in $[Fe(C_2O_4)_3]^{3-}$ coordination number of Fe is 6.

Nomenclature

- Coordination compounds contain two parts : cation and anion. Cations are named before anions. e.g. In $K_4[Fe(CN)_6]$, K^+ is a cation, it is named before the anion $[Fe(CN)_6]^{4-}$. Hence, IUPAC name of compound is potassium hexacyanoferrate (II).
  If more than one type of ligands are present then they are written in alphabetical order.
- Names of anionic ligands ending with 'ide' changes to 'o', 'ite' changes to 'o', 'ate' changes to 'o'.
- Positive ligands end with 'ium' and neutral ligands like H_2O, NH_3 are given names such as aqua, ammine respectively. In latest trend **e** is simply replaced by **o**.
- Oxidation state of the metal is indicated by roman numeral in parenthesis.
- Prefixes mono, di, tri etc are used to indicate the number of the individual ligands.
- When the names of the ligands include a numerical prefix then the terms *bis*, *tris*, *tetrakis* are used, the ligands to which they refers are placed in parenthesis.

Isomerism

- **Stereoisomerism** (i) Geometrical-*cis* and *trans* (ii) Optical-*dextro* and *laevo*
- **Structural Isomerism**
- **Linkage isomerism** shown by complexes having ambidentate ligands. Such as —SCN and —NO_2 e.g. $[Co(NH_3)_5(ONO)]Cl_2$ and $[Co(NH_3)_5(NO_2)]Cl_2$
- **Coordination isomerism** arises from interchange of ligands between cationic and anionic entities of different metal ions. e.g $[Cr(NH_3)_6][Co(CN)_6]$, $[Co(NH_3)_6][Cr(CN)_6]$
- **Ionisation isomerism** occurs when counter ion is itself a potential ligand and displaces ligand in the coordination sphere. e.g. $[Co(NH_3)_5(SO_4)]Br$ and $[Co(NH_3)_5Br]SO_4$
- **Solvate isomerism** Exchange of solvent molecules inside the sphere with counter ions. If solvent is water, it is called hydrate isomerism. e.g $[Cr(H_2O)_6]Cl_3$ (Violet) and $[Cr(H_2O)_5Cl]Cl_2\cdot H_2O$ (Grey -green).

- **Geometrical Isomerism**
- arises in heteroleptic complexes
- possible in coordination number 4 and 6.
- For coordination number = 4;

– MA_2B_2 type

cis   trans

– *MABXL* type

cis   cis   trans

- For coordination number = 6:

– MA_2B_4 type

trans   cis

- Other forms will be said to be identical.

– MA_2B_2 type [B is didentate ligand]

trans   cis

- **Facial isomers (*Fac*)** If three donor atoms of same ligand occupy adjacent positions at the corners of an octahedral face. e.g.

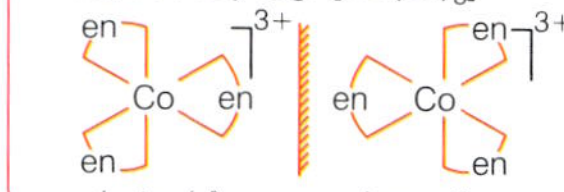

- **Meridional (*Mer*)** When the positions of donor atoms of same ligand are around the meridian of octahedron.

mer–

- **Optical isomerism** mirror images of a compound which can not be superimposed on one another.
- molecules which can not be superimposed are chiral.
- can either be *dextro* (rotates left to right) or *laevo* (rotates right to left)
- represented by *d*- and *l* respectively e.g. $[Co(en)_3]^{3+}$

dextro (*d*)   laevo (*l*)

- Pt and Pd with coordination number 4 are always square planar.
- Complex with coordination number 4 having bidentate ligand are always square planar. Square planar complex with *AA* type bidentate ligand do not gives geometrical isomerism.

Test 2

Syllabus

- Bonding-Valence Bond Approach, Basic Idea of Crystal Field Theory, Colour and Magnetic Properties.

NCERT Page 128 to 135

For deeper insight **Scan the QR Code**

Valence Bond Theory (VBT)

- It describes bonding in terms of hybridised orbitals of central metal atom or ion.
- Central metal atom makes available a number of vacant orbitals equal to its coordination number. The vacant hybrid orbitals form coordinate bond with ligands.
- Some $(n-1)$-orbitals are vacant and therefore, central metal ion provides number of empty orbitals equal to its coordination number for formation of complex.
- Atomic orbitals present on central metal ion hybridise to form hybrid orbitals. There is interaction of hybrid orbitals of metal ion and orbitals of ligands.
- Ligands donate its lone pairs of electrons, to form bond with metal ion. It describes the geometrical structure of complex ion.
- If $(n-1)$ d-orbitals are involved in hybridisation, then inner orbital or low spin or spin paired complex are formed. Involvement of nd-orbitals results in outer orbital or high spin or spin free complex.
- Octahedral, square planar and tetrahedral complexes are formed as a result of d^2sp^3, dsp^2 and sp^3 hybridisation respectively of the central metal atom or ion. It helps to predict the geometry, hybridisation, magnetic properties of a complex.

Coordination number	Hybridisation	Geometry	Examples
4	sp^3	Tetrahedral	$[NiCl_4]^{2-}$
4	dsp^2	square planar	$[Ni(CN)_4]^{2-}$
5	sp^3d	Trigonal bipyramidal	$Fe(CO)_5$
6	sp^3d^2	Octahedral	$[CoF_6]^{3-}$
6	d^2sp^3	Octahedral	$[Co(NH_3)_6]^{3+}$

- In octahedral complex, two types of hybridisation is possible, i.e. d^2sp^3 and sp^3d^2. In d^2sp^3 hybrids, the principal quantum number of d-orbitals is one less than the principal quantum number of the s and p-orbital.
- While in sp^3d^2 hybridisation all the hybrids, i.e. s, p and d have same value of principal quantum number.

Magnetic Properties

- Complexes can be paramagnetic or diamagnetic.
- Spin-only magnetic moment can be calculated by using the formula $\mu_s = \sqrt{n(n+2)}$, where n = number of unpaired electrons.
- **Limitations** Could not explain colour and spectra of complexes. Does not distinguish between weak and strong ligands.
- It does not give quantitative interpretation of the thermodynamic or kinetic stabilities of coordination compounds.
- It does not explain why some complexes are inner orbital complex and some complexes are outer orbital.

Applications of VBT

- **In Formation of Complex with Coordination Number 4** Coordination compounds which have C.N. = 4 can have tetrahedral or square planar geometry. It depends upon the orbitals available for hybridisation.

1. In Tetrahedral Complexes

Complexes which involve one s and three p-orbitals for bonding, i.e. sp^3, are said to be tetrahedral complexes. e.g. $[NiCl_4]^{2-}$, $[Ni(CO)_4]$, $[CuCl_4]^{2-}$, $[Zn(NH_3)_4]^{2+}$ etc.

- **$[NiCl_4]^{2-}$**

Electronic configuration of Ni(Z = 28) = [Ar] $3d^84s^2$.
Due to presence of $4Cl^-$, oxidation state of Ni is +2
Therefore, electronic configuration of Ni^{2+} is $[Ar]3d^84s^0$.

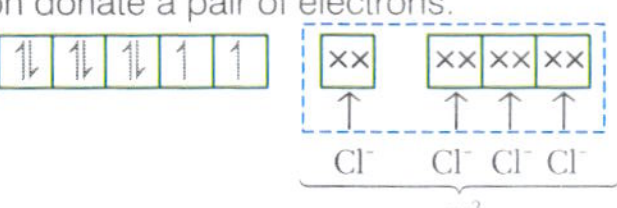

Due to presence of two unpaired electrons, $[Ni(Cl)_4]^{2-}$ is paramagnetic in nature.

2. In Square Planar Complexes

- Complexes which involves one d, one s and two p-orbitals for bonding, i.e. dsp^2 are said to be square planar complexes. e.g. $[Ni(CN)_4]^{2-}$, $[Pt(CN)_4]^{2-}$, $[Cu(NH_3)_4]^{2+}$ etc.
- **$[Ni(CN)_4]^{2-}$**

Ni is present in +2 oxidation state due to four CN^- ligands.

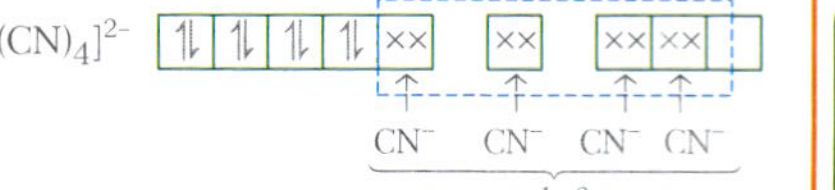

All the electrons in $[Ni(CN)_4]^{2-}$ complex are paired. Therefore, it is diamagnetic.

Inner and Outer Orbital Complex

- Inner orbital complexes involve two inner d-orbitals, one s and three p-orbitals for bonding. These are formed by strong field ligands hence are low spin complex.
e.g. $[Co(NH_3)_6]^{3+}$, $[Fe(CN)_6]^{4-}$, $[Cr(NH_3)_6]^{3+}$, $[Fe(CN)_6]^{3-}$ $[Co(ox)_3]^{3-}$.
- Outer orbital complex involves one s, three p and two outer d-orbitals for bonding. These are formed by weak field ligands.
Hence, are high spin complex,
$[CoF_6]^{3-}$, $[Fe(H_2O)_6]^{3+}$, $[Co(H_2O)_6]^{2+}$.

Limitations

- It involves a number of assumptions.
- It describes bonding in coordination compounds only qualitatively.
- It does not offer any explanation for the optical absorption spectra of complexes or in other words. It could not give any satisfactory explanation for the colour of the complexes.
- It does not describe the detailed magnetic properties of coordination compounds.
- It does not give a quantitative interpretation of the thermodynamic or kinetic stabilities of coordination compounds.
- It does not make exact predictions regarding the tetrahedral and square planar structures of 4-coordinate complexes.
- It does not distinguish between weak and strong ligands, i.e. It can not explain why some complexes are low spin and others are high spin.

Jahn-Teller Distortion

- If the d-orbitals are asymmetrically filled, they will repel some ligand in the complex more than the others. This results in distortion of octahedral complexes.
- Distortion caused by asymmetric filling of t_{2g} is too small to measure. Asymmetric filling of e_g orbitals causes a significant distortion.

Colour of Complexes

- Compounds are colourless in absence of ligands.
- Colour of complexes is due to d-d transition.
- With increase in splitting, wavelength of light absorbed is decreased.

• Limitations of CFT

- Could not explain why anionic ligands are weak field ligand even though they are stronger point charges.

Crystal Field Theory

Considers metal-ligand bonding to be ionic and interactions between metal and ligand to be purely electrostatic.

- **Postulates**
- Ligands are point charges in case of anions and dipoles in case of neutral molecules.
- Degeneracy of d-orbitals (same energy) is lifted in presence of ligands and splitting occurs.

CFSE for tetrahedral complexes, $\Delta_t = \frac{4}{9}\Delta_o$
Δ_o = CFSE of octahedral complexes.

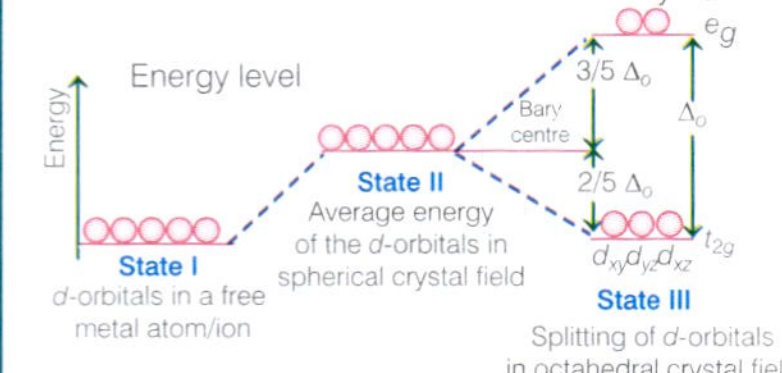

Splitting of octahedral complex

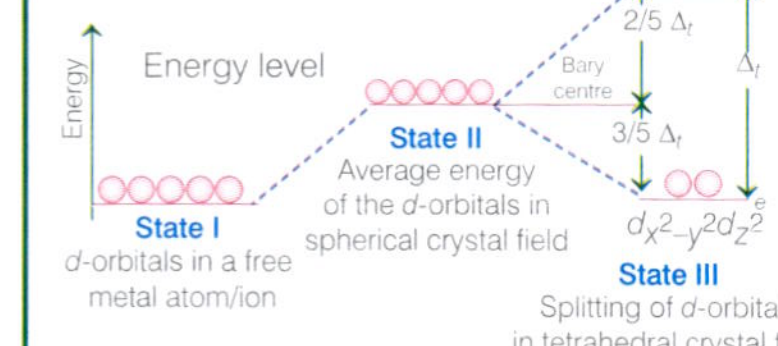

Splitting of tetrahedral complex

- **Spectrochemical series**
$I^- < Br^- < SCN^- < Cl^- < S^{2-} < F^- < OH^- < C_2O_4^{2-} < H_2O < NCS^- < edta^{4-} < NH_3 < en < CN^- < CO$
- For strong field ligands, $\Delta_o > P$, hence pairing occurs and low spin complex forms.
- For weak field ligands, $P > \Delta_o$, hence no pairing occurs and high spin complex forms.

- Did not take into account the covalent nature of metal-ligand bond.
- Some complexes like CrO_4^{2-}, $Cr_2O_7^{2-}$, MnO_4^- etc., have configuration of metal ion but have intense colour. Here, colour is due to charge transfer spectra and not due to d-d transition.
- Crystal field theory was explained by **ligand field theory** (LFT).

Test 3

Syllabus
- Importance of Coordination Compounds. (In Qualitative Analysis, Extraction of Metals and in Biological Systems)

NCERT Page 135 to 137

For deeper insight Scan the QR Code

Organometallic Compounds

- These are the compounds which contain metal-carbon bond.
- Some examples of organometallic compounds are $[Pt(C_2H_4)Cl_3]^-$, $Ni(CO)_4$, $[Fe(C_5H_5)_2]$, (also known as ferrocene).

Bonding in Metal Carbonyls

- The homoleptic carbonyls, i.e. the compounds containing carbonyl ligands only, are formed by most of the transition metals. These carbonyls have simple and well defined structures.
- In these compounds CO act as donor ligand and donates lone pairs of electrons of carbonyl carbon into vacant orbital of metal forming σ-bond.
- It also behaves as an acceptor ligands and forms π-bond by back donation of electrons from filled d-orbital of metal to vacant antibonding (π^*)-orbital of CO.
- This back-bonding stabilises the metal-ligands interaction. It is also called synergic bonding.

Example of synergic bonding interactions in a carbonyl complex.

- Synergic back-bonding increases with increasing electron density on central metal atom/ion.

Classification of OMC

- **Ionic Organometallic Compounds**
- Most of the alkali and alkaline earth metals bond together to form organometallic compound.
- Soluble in polar solvents.
- Short life periods.
- **Covalent bonded organometallic compound**
  These are the compounds in which carbon atom of the organic ligand is bonded to the metal by a 2c-2e covalent bond.
- **Organometallic compounds containing π-ligands.**
  The organometallic compounds of alkene, alkynes and other carbon containing compounds have electrons in their π molecular orbitals.

Structures of Homoleptic Metal Carbonyl

$Ni(CO)_4$ Tetrahedral

$Fe(CO)_5$ Trigonal bipyramidal

$Cr(CO)_6$ Octahedral

$[Mn_2(CO)_{10}]$

$[Co_2(CO)_8]$

Chemical Properties

- The stability of organometallic compounds depends on the properties of the central metal and the type of organic ligands attached.
- All organometallic compounds are potential reducing agents with increased reducing power linked to highly electropositive metal atoms. This is because the metal atom readily gives up electrons to the carbon atom. A highly electropositive metal atom leads to a partial negative charge on the organic group, leading to carbanion or nucleophilic character.

$$-\overset{|}{\underset{|}{C}}{:}\; M^+ \longleftrightarrow \overset{\delta+}{M^+}\overset{\delta-}{-}\overset{|}{\underset{|}{C}}-$$

Ionic   Polarised

- Due to the high reactivity of organometallic compounds with oxygen and water, they are typically handled under inert conditions. When in contact with water, the organic group is immediately liberated, often violently.

Importance and Applications of Coordination Compounds

- **In Medicinal Chemistry**
  The platinum complex *cis*$[Pt(NH_3)_2Cl_2]$ commonly known as ***cis*-platin** is used in the treatment of cancer. It has the ability to block the uncontrolled division of cancerous cells that results in growth of tumours.
- EDTA complex of calcium, $[Ca(EDTA)]^{2-}$ is used to treat a person suffering from lead poisoning.
  $Pb^{2+} + [Ca(EDTA)]^{2-} \longrightarrow [Pb(EDTA)]^{2-} + Ca^{2+}$
- EDTA complex of lead is more stable than $[Ca(EDTA)]^{2-}$ complex. Thus, lead complex is excreted from the body and Ca^{2+} remains as the body nutrient.
- **In Quantitative and Qualitative Analysis**
- Traces of Ni^{2+} salt can be detected by dimethyl glyoxime when cherry red precipitate of nickel-dimethyl glyoxime (chelate) is formed.

$$Ni^{2+} + 2\;\; \begin{matrix} HO-N=C-CH_3 \\ | \\ HO-N=C-CH_3 \end{matrix} \xrightarrow[\text{Alcohol}]{NH_4OH/}$$

Nickel-dimethyl glyoximate (chelate) (red ppt.)

- In qualitative analysis of group I, there is formation of white precipitate of AgCl, Hg_2Cl_2 and $PbCl_2$. $PbCl_2$ is soluble in hot water.
- In group II, Cd^{2+} can be precipitated as CdS in presence of Cu^{2+}.
- By treating the solution of Cu^{2+} and Cd^{2+} with an excess of CN^-, Cu^{2+} forms a stable complex in a redox reaction.
  $2Cu^{2+} + 10CN^- \longrightarrow 2[Cu(CN)_4]^{3-} + C_2N_2$
  while Cd^{2+} forms less stable complex
  $Cd^{2+} + 4CN^- \rightleftharpoons \underset{\text{(Unstable)}}{[Cd(CN)_4]^{2-}}$
- When H_2S gas is passed, $[Cd(CN)_4]^{2-}$ is precipitated as CdS without affecting $[Cu(CN)_4]^{3-}$ complex.
- **In Extraction of Metals**
  Nickel can be extracted by Mond's process which involves formation of carbonyl complex of nickel.
  $Ni(s) + 4CO(g) \longrightarrow [Ni(CO)_4](g)$
  Silver (Ag) and gold (Au) can be extracted by ion formation of cyanide complex.

$4Au(s) + 8CN^-(aq) + O_2(g) + 2H_2O(l) \longrightarrow 4OH^-(aq) + 4[Au(CN)_2]^-(aq)$

$2[Au(CN)_2]^-(aq) + Zn(s) \longrightarrow [Zn(CN)_4]^{2-}(aq) + 2Au(s)$

- **In Purification of Water**
- It can be done through complex formation. It involves chelation with sodium salt of EDTA.
- The formation constant of $[Ca(EDTA)]^{2-}$ and $[Mg(EDTA)]^{2-}$ are very large. Hence, on treating water with sodium salt of EDTA, concentration of Ca^{2+} and Mg^{2+} can be reduced to the point that these ions will not precipitate with soap or detergent.
  Ca^{2+} $(EDTA)^{4-} \rightleftharpoons [Ca(EDTA)]^{2-}$
  $Mg^{2+} + (EDTA)^{4-} \rightleftharpoons [Mg(EDTA)]^{2-}$
- **In Photography**
  The photographic "fixing" process removes unreacted AgBr which forms soluble complex with sodium thiosulphate.
  $AgBr(s) + 2S_2O_3^{2-} \longrightarrow [Ag(S_2O_3)_2]^{3-} + Br^-$
- **In Biological Processes**
- Many important biological substances are coordination compounds, e.g. Haemoglobin is a protein that carries O_2 in blood. It contains iron (II) ions bound to large porphyrin rings.
- Chlorophyll is necessary for photosynthesis in plants. It contains magnesium ions bound to porphyrin rings. Vitamin B_{12} is a large complex of cobalt.
- **In Purification of Metals**
  It can be achieved through formation and subsequent decomposition of their coordination compounds.
  e.g. Impure nickel is converted to $[Ni(CO)_4]$ which is decomposed to yield pure nickel.
- **In Industries as Catalysts**
  They are used as catalysts for many industrial processes. e.g. Rh complex, $[(PH_3P)_3RhCl]$ a Wilkinson catalyst is used for hydrogenation of alkenes and alkynes.
- **In Electroplating**
- Articles can be electroplated with Ag and Au much more smoothly and evenly from solutions of the complexes, $[Ag(CN_2)]^-$ and $[Au(CN)_2]^-$ than from a solution of simple metal ions. It describes bonding in terms of hybridised orbitals of central metal atom or ion.
- Central metal atom makes available a number of vacant orbitals equal to its coordination number. The vacant hybrid orbitals form coordinate bond with ligands.

Test 1

Syllabus

- **Haloalkanes** : General Methods of Preparation, Properties and Reactions, Nature of C—X Bond, Mechanism of Substitution Reactions.

NCERT
Page 159 to 165
Page 167 to 181

For deeper insight **Scan the QR Code**

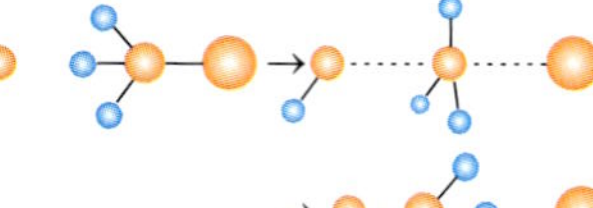

Chapter 07

Haloalkanes

The replacement of hydrogen atom(s) attached to a sp^3 hybridised carbon atom of an alkyl group by a halogen atom(s) forms an alkyl halide or haloalkanes.

Classification

Haloalkanes can be classified as follows

1. On the Basis of Number of Halogen Atoms These may be classified as mono, di, or polyhalogen (tri, tetra etc.) compounds depending upon whether they contain one, two or more halogen atoms in their structures. For example,

C_2H_5X (Monohaloalkane) $\quad CH_2X$—CH_2X (Dihaloalkane) $\quad CH_2X$—CHX—CH_2X (Trihaloalkane)

2. On the Basis of Types of Hybridisation The monohalo compounds may be further classified according to the type of hybridisation of the carbon atom bonded to the halogen atom.

(i) Compounds Containing sp^3 C—X Bond (X = F, Cl, Br, I) Compounds containing sp^3 C—X bond may be classified as primary (1°), secondary (2°) or tertiary (3°) according to the nature of carbon to which halogen is attached.

These are of following types

- **Alkyl halides or haloalkanes** (R—X) In alkyl halides, the halogen atom is bonded to an alkyl group (R). They form a homologous series represented by $C_nH_{2n+1}X$. (where, X = F, Cl, Br, I)

R—CH_2—X Primary (1°) $\quad R''$—CHR'—X Secondary (2°) $\quad R''$—$C(R')(R''')$—X Tertiary (3°)

- **Allylic halides** In these compounds the halogen atom is bonded to a sp^3-hybridised carbon atom adjacent to carbon-carbon double bond (C=C), i.e. to an allylic carbon.

CH_2X Allylic carbon

(ii) Compounds Containing sp^2 C—X Bond (Vinylic halides) In these halides, the halogen atom bonded to a sp^2-hybridised carbon atom of a carbon carbon double bond, i.e. to a vinylic carbon. e.g.

Vinyl halide $\quad CH_2=CH$—Cl Vinyl chloride

Nomenclature

- The common name of alkyl halides are derived by naming the alkyl group followed by the name of halide.
- In the IUPAC system of nomenclature, alkyl halides are named as halosubstituted hydrocarbons.
- For monohalogen substituted derivatives of benzene, common and IUPAC names are same.
- For dihalogen derivatives, the prefixes o-,m-,p- are used in common system, and in IUPAC system, 1, 2; 1, 3 and 1, 4 are used.
- When two halogen atoms are attached to the same C-atom, these are called **geminal halide** or ***gem*-dihalides**. These are also called alkylidene dihalides or simply alkylidene halides.
- When the two halogen atoms are attached in adjacent C-atoms, they are called **vicinal dihalides** or simply ***vic*-dihalides**. These are also called as **alkylene dihalides**.

Nature of C—X Bond

- Carbon-halogen bond of alkyl halide is polarised, due to higher electronegativity of halogen than that of carbon.
- A partial positive charge is present on carbon atom and a partial negative charge is present on halogen atom. $\;\overset{\delta^+}{C}$—$\overset{\delta^-}{X}$
- The size of halogen atom increases on moving down the group. Consequently the carbon halogen bond length also increases from C—F to C—I.
- The sequence of bond enthalpy of C—X bond is CH_3—F > CH_3—Cl > CH_3—Br > CH_3—I.
- Bond enthalpy is inversely proportional to bond length. In other words, higher the bond length lower will be the bond enthalpy.

Physical Properties

- Poorly soluble in water.
- Have higher boiling points than those of hydrocarbons of comparable molecular mass. BP decrease with increase in branching.
- Density higher than water.
- Dipole moment and solubility decrease with increase in mass.

Preparation

Finkelstein reaction For converting alkyl chlorides and bromides to iodides.
R—X + NaI ⟶ R—I + NaX

Swart's reaction For converting alkyl chlorides and bromides to fluorides.
$H_3CBr + AgF \longrightarrow H_3C$—F + AgBr

(Halogen exchange method → R—X)

Free radical halogenation of alkanes
$CH_3CH_2CH_2CH_3 \xrightarrow[\Delta]{Cl_2,\ UV\text{-}light} CH_3CH_2CH_2CH_2Cl + CH_3CH_2CH(Cl)CH_3$

Addition of halogens
$H_2C=CH_2 + Br_2 \xrightarrow{CCl_4} BrCH_2$—$CH_2Br$

Addition of HX to alkenes
>C=C< + HX ⟶ >C(H)—C(X)<

From alcohols
- $3ROH + PCl_3 \longrightarrow 3R$—Cl + H_3PO_3
- $ROH + PCl_5 \longrightarrow R$—Cl + $POCl_3$ + HCl
- $ROH + HCl \xrightarrow{ZnCl_2} R$—Cl + H_2O
- $ROH \xrightarrow{Red\ P/Cl_2} R$—Cl
- R—OH + $SOCl_2 \longrightarrow R$—Cl + $SO_2\uparrow$ + HCl

Borodine-Hunsdiecker reaction
$RCOO^-Ag^+ + Br_2 \xrightarrow{CCl_4/Reflux} R$—Br + $CO_2\uparrow$ + AgBr

Chemical Reactions

The reactions of haloalkanes may be divided into the following categories.
- Nucleophilic substitution
- Elimination reactions
- Reaction with metals

Nucleophilic Substitution Reactions

X group is replaced by other nucleophiles like CN^-, NO_2^-, OH^-, NH_2^-, etc.

S_N1 Reactions

- It is a two step reaction.
- Involves the formation of carbocation intermediate in step - I.
- Involves the inversion of configuration as well as retention, so give racemic mixture if reactant is optically active.

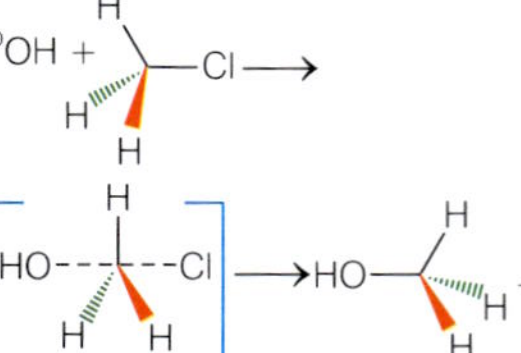

$(CH_3)_3CBr \xrightleftharpoons{Step\ I} (CH_3)_2\overset{\oplus}{C}CH_3 + Br^{\ominus}$

$(CH_3)_2\overset{\oplus}{C}CH_3 + {}^-OH \xrightarrow{Step\ II} (CH_3)_3COH$

- Rate ∝ [substrate], hence it is a first order reaction.
- Formation of carbocation is the rate determining step.
- Second step is the attack of nucleophile on the intermediate i.e. carbocation.
- Most favourable substrate is a 3° alkyl halide.
- 1° alkyl halide is least favourable.
- Solvent conditions of a polar protic solvent favours this type of reaction.

S_N2 Reactions

- It is one step reaction.
- Involves the formation of transition state.

${}^{\ominus}OH$ + CH_3—Cl ⟶ [HO- - -C- - -Cl] ⟶ HO—CH_3 + $Cl^{\ominus}$

- The above reaction can be represented diagrammatically as shown.

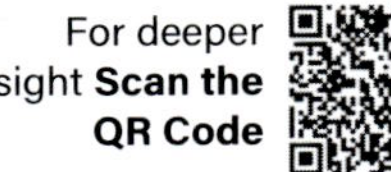

Red ball represents the incoming hydroxide ion and blue ball represents the outgoing halide ion

- Favoured by less hindered alkyl halide and non-polar solvent.
- Results in inversion of configuration if reactant is optically active.
- Rate ∝ [substrate] [nucleophile], hence it is a second order reaction.
- Most favoured substrate is a 1° alkyl halide.
- It is favoured in non-polar or polar aprotic solvents like dimethyl sulphide (DMS) and dimethyl sulphoxide (DMSO) etc.
- Less hindered the transition state, faster will be the reaction.

For S_N2 reaction →

Tertiary halide, Secondary halide, Primary halide, CH_3X

← For S_N1 reaction

Nucleophilic Substitution of Alkyl halides

The general reaction is
R—X + $Nu^- \longrightarrow R$—Nu + X^-

R—X with:
- NaOH (KOH) ⟶ ROH (Alcohol) + HO^-
- H_2O ⟶ ROH (Alcohol) + H_2O
- $NaOR'$ ⟶ ROR' (Ether) + $R'O^-$
- NaI ⟶ R—I (Alkyl iodide) + I^-
- NH_3 ⟶ RNH_2 (Primary amine) + NH_3
- $R'NH_2$ ⟶ $RNHR'$ (Secondary amine) + $R'NH_2$
- $R'R''NH$ ⟶ $RNR'R''$ (Tertiary amine) + $R'R''NH$
- KCN ⟶ RCN (Nitrile) + $\bar{C}\equiv N$:
- AgCN ⟶ RNC (Isonitrile) + AgCN:
- KNO_2 ⟶ R—O—N=O (Alkyl nitrite) + O=N—O
- $AgNO_2$ ⟶ R—NO_2 (Nitroalkane) + Ag—Ö—N=O
- $R'COOAg$ ⟶ $R'COOR$ (Ester) + $R'COO^-$
- $LiAlH_4$ ⟶ RH (Hydrocarbon) + H
- R'—M^+ ⟶ RR' (Alkane) + R'^-

Elimination Reaction

Haloalkanes with β-hydrogen undergo dehydrohalogenation to give an alkene. These are two types
- E1 reaction
- E2 reaction

Reaction with Metals

- Grignard reagent
$RMgX + H$—$G \longrightarrow RH + Mg(X)(G)$ $\quad (G = \bar{O}H, R\bar{O}, \bar{N}H_2)$
- Wurtz reaction
$2R$—X + 2Na $\xrightarrow{Ether} R$—R + 2NaX
- R—$X \xrightarrow{R'_2CuLi} R$—$R'$
- R—$X \xrightarrow{Li} R$—Li

Test 2

Syllabus

- **Haloarenes :** General Methods of Preparation, Properties and Reactions, Nature of C — X bond, Mechanism of Substitution Reactions.

NCERT Page 166, Page 181 to 186

For deeper insight Scan the QR Code

Chapter 07

Haloarenes

The replacement of a hydrogen atom(s) of an aromatic hydrocarbon by a halogen atom (F, Cl, Br and I) results in the formation of haloarene (aryl halide).

Classification

Haloarenes may be classified as follows

1. On the Basis of Number of Halogen Atoms The halogen derivatives of hydrocarbons may be classified as mono, di, or polyhalogen (tri, tetra etc.) compounds depending upon whether they contain one, two or more halogen atoms in their structures. For examples,

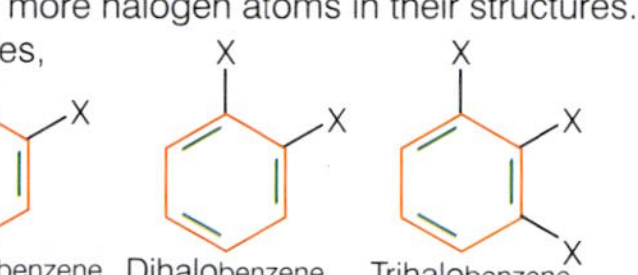

2. On the Basis of Types of Hybridisation The monohalo compounds may be further classified according to the type of hybridisation of the carbon atom bonded to the halogen atom.

(i) Compounds Containing sp^3 C—X Bond (X = F, Cl, Br, I) These compounds may be primary (1°), secondary (2°) or tertiary (3°).

- **Benzylic halide** In these compounds the halogen atom is bonded to a sp^3-hybridised carbon atom next to an aromatic ring.

(CH_2X (1°); $CH(R)X$ (2°); $C(R)(R)X$ (3°))

- **Allylic halides** These are the compounds in which the halogen atom is bonded to a sp^3-hybridised carbon atom adjacent to carbon-carbon double bond (C=C), i.e to an allylic carbon. (Allylic carbon)

(ii) Compounds Containing sp^2 C—X Bond

- **Vinylic halides** These are the compounds in which the halogen atom is bonded to a sp^2-hybridised carbon atom of a carbon-carbon double bond (C=C).
- **Aryl halides** These are the compounds in which the halogen atom is directly bonded to the sp^2-hybridised carbon atom of an aromatic ring.

Nomenclature

For dihalogen derivative, the prefix *o*-, *m*- and *p*- are used in common system. In IUPAC system, the numerals 1, 2-, 1, 3- and 1, 4- are used.

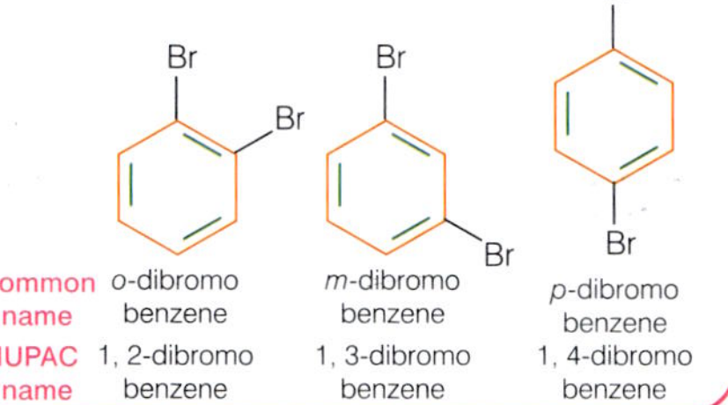

Common name	*o*-dibromo benzene	*m*-dibromo benzene	*p*-dibromo benzene
IUPAC name	1, 2-dibromo benzene	1, 3-dibromo benzene	1, 4-dibromo benzene

Preparations

(i) From Hydrocarbons by Electrophilic Substitution

Acyl chlorides and bromides can be prepared by electrophilic substitution of arenes with chlorine and bromine respectively in the presence of Lewis acid catalyst like iron or Iron (III) chloride.

$$C_6H_5CH_3 + X_2 \xrightarrow[\text{Dark}]{\text{Fe}} o\text{-}XC_6H_4CH_3 + p\text{-}XC_6H_4CH_3$$

(ii) From Amines by Sandmeyer's Reaction

- When a primary aromatic amine, dissolved or suspended in cold aqueous mineral acid is treated with sodium nitrite a diazonium salt is formed.
- Mixing the solution of freshly prepared diazonium salt with cuprous chloride or cuprous bromide results in the replacement of the diazonium group by —Cl or —Br.

$$C_6H_5NH_2 \xrightarrow[273\text{-}278K]{NaNO_2 + HX} C_6H_5\overset{+}{N_2}\bar{X} \text{ (Benzene diazonium halide)}$$

$$C_6H_5\overset{+}{N_2}\bar{X} \xrightarrow{Cu_2X_2} C_6H_5X \text{ (Aryl halide)} + N_2 \quad (X\text{=Cl, Br})$$

- Replacement of the diazonium group by iodine does not require the presence of cuprous halide and is done simply by shaking the diazonium salt with potassium iodide.

$$C_6H_5\overset{+}{N_2}\bar{X} \xrightarrow{KI} C_6H_5I + N_2$$

Physical Properties

- They are heavier than water.
- These are though polar but immiscible with water due to their incapability to form H-bond.
- The boiling point of haloarenes are nearly same as that of haloalkanes with same number of carbon atoms.
- Order of boiling point : ArI > ArBr > ArCl > Ar F
- B.P of isomers dihalobenzenes → nearly same.
- M. P. of isomers dihalobenzenes → *p* > *o* > *m*

Chemical Reactions

The reactions of haloarenes may be divided into the following categories.

- Nucleophilic substitution
- Electrophilic substitution
- Reaction with metals

Nucleophilic Substiution Reaction

Aryl halides are extremely less reactive towards nucleophilic substitution reactions due to the following reasons.

- **Resonance Effect** The C—X bond in halobenzene has a partial double bond character due to involvement of halogen electrons in resonance with benzene ring.
- **Difference in hybridisation of carbon atom in C—X bond** The C—X bond in aryl halides is less polar as compared to that in alkyl halides as sp^2 hybridised carbon is more electronegative than sp^3 hybridised carbon.
- **Instability of phenyl cation** In case of haloarenes, the phenyl cation formed as a result of self ionisation will not be stabilised by resonance and therefore S_N1 mechanism is ruled out.

Because of the possible repulsion, it is less likely for the electron rich nucleophile to approach electron rich arenes.

- ArX — With OH (300°C, NaOH) → C_6H_5OH
- ArX — With CN (CuCN/200°C) → C_6H_5CN
- ArX — With NH_3 (*Aq*. NH_3,200°C) → $C_6H_5NH_2$

Electrophillic Substitution Reaction

- $-I$ effect of halogen atom withdraws electrons from the benzene ring. Due to this, electron density of benzene ring decreases. Hence, haloarenes are less reactive than benzene towards electrophilic substitution reaction, i.e. haloarenes are deactivating.
- $+M$ effect of halogen increases electron density at *ortho*- and *para*-position rather than *meta*-position. That is why haloarenes are *o*, *p*-directing.
- **Mechanism**

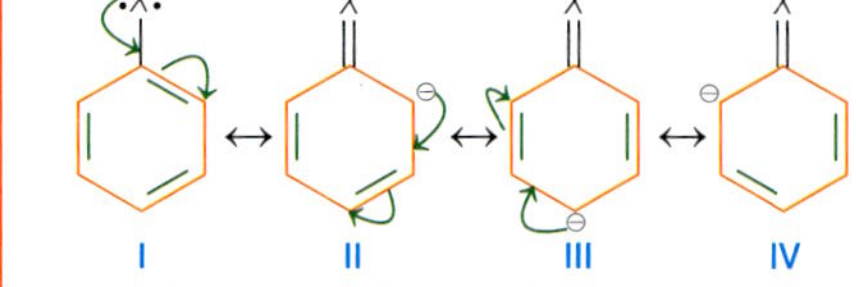

- Some of the electrophilic substitution reactions are

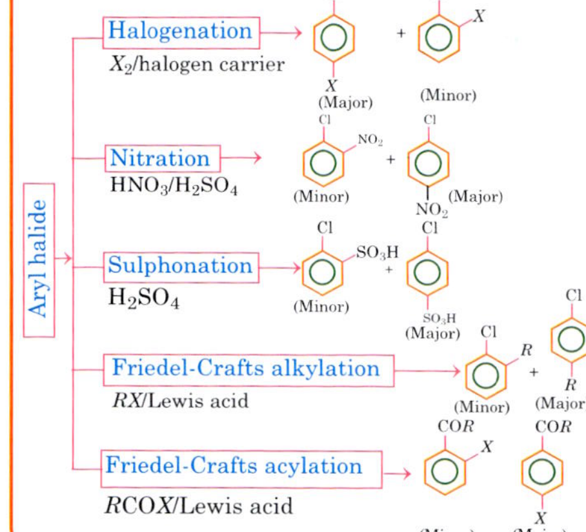

Reaction with Metals

- **Wurtz Fittig reactions**

$$C_6H_5X + Na + RX \xrightarrow{\text{Dry ether}} C_6H_5R \text{ (Toluene)} + NaX$$

- **Fittig reaction**

$$2C_6H_5X + 2Na \xrightarrow{\text{Dry ether}} C_6H_5\text{—}C_6H_5 \text{ (Diphenyl)} + 2NaX$$

Test 3

Syllabus
- Uses, Environmental Effects of Chloroform, Iodoform, Freons and DDT.

NCERT Page 187 to 188

For deeper insight **Scan the QR Code**

Polyhalogen Compounds

Carbon compounds having more than one halogen atom are usually referred to as **polyhalogen compounds**. Many of these compounds are useful in industry and agriculture.

Dichloromethane (Methylene Chloride, CH_2Cl_2)

It is a colourless, sweet smelling, volatile liquid having low boiling point of 313 K and specific gravity of 1.37. It is prepared industrially by the direct chlorination of methane in the presence of diffused sunlight.

$$\underset{\text{Methane}}{CH_4} + 2Cl_2 \xrightarrow{h\nu} \underset{\text{Methylene chloride}}{CH_2Cl_2} + 2HCl$$

- **Uses**

 It is used in the following ways
- As a paint remover.
- As a propellant in aerosols.
- As a metal cleaning and finishing solvent.
- As a refrigerant and dewaxing agent.
- As a process solvent in the manufacture of drugs.
- **Harmful Effects** (Physiological Effects)

 Some of the important harmful effects of methylene chloride are as follows
- It affects the human central nervous system.
- Exposure to low levels of methylene chloride in air can lead to slightly impaired hearing and vision.
- Exposure to high levels of methylene chloride can cause dizziness, nausea, tingling and numbness in the fingers and toes.
- Direct contact with skin in humans causes intense burning and mild redness of the skin.
- Direct contact with eyes can burn the cornea.

Trichloromethane (Chloroform, $CHCl_3$)

- It is commonly known as chloroform. It is a colourless liquid with sweet odour. It is non-flammable but its vapour burns with green flame. In industry, $CHCl_3$ is produced by heating a mixture of chlorine and either chloromethane or methane.
- CH_3CH_2OH on reaction with moist bleaching powder is converted into $CHCl_3$.

$$CaOCl_2 + H_2O \longrightarrow Ca(OH)_2 + Cl_2$$
$$Cl_2 + H_2O \longrightarrow 2HCl + \underset{\text{(Oxidising agent)}}{[O]}$$
$$CH_3CH_2OH + [O] \longrightarrow CH_3CHO + H_2O$$
$$CH_3CHO + 3Cl_2 \longrightarrow \underset{\text{Chloral}}{CCl_3CHO} + 3HCl$$
$$\underset{\text{Chloral}}{2CCl_3CHO} + Ca(OH)_2 \longrightarrow \underset{\text{Chloroform}}{2CHCl_3} + (HCOO)_2Ca$$

- It can also be prepared by the partial reduction of carbon tetrachloride. $CCl_4 \xrightarrow{Fe/H_2O} CHCl_3$

Structures of Polyhalogen Compound

Dichloromethane, Trichloromethane, Tetrachloromethane, Triiodomethane

Some of the Important Reactions of Chloroform

(i) Oxidation Chloroform is slowly oxidised by air in the presence of light to an extremely poisonous gas carbonyl chloride also called phosgene. It is therefore stored in dark coloured bottles. These bottles are completely filled with chloroform upto the brim and are properly stopped to keep air out.

$$\underset{\text{Chloroform}}{2CHCl_3} + O_2 \xrightarrow{\text{Sunlight}} \underset{\text{Phosgene}}{2COCl_2} + 2HCl$$

(ii) Reduction Partial reduction of chloroform is carried out with zinc and hydrochloric acid that converts chloroform to methylene chloride. However, when zinc dust and water is used then it is completely reduced to methane.

$$\underset{\text{Methane}}{CH_4} \xleftarrow[-HCl,\ 6[H]]{Zn/H_2O} \underset{\text{Chloroform}}{CHCl_3} \xrightarrow[2[H]^+]{Zn/HCl\text{-}C_2H_5OH} \underset{\text{Methylene chloride}}{CH_2Cl_2}$$

(iii) Halogenation When chlorine is passed through chloroform in the presence of sunlight, it forms carbon tetrachloride.

$$\underset{\text{Chloroform}}{CHCl_3} + Cl_2 \xrightarrow{h\nu} \underset{\text{Tetrachloromethane}}{CCl_4}$$

- **Uses**

 It is used in following ways
- As a solvent for fats, alkaloids, iodine and other substances.
- As a laboratory reagent.
- In the preparation of chloropicrin, chloretone, etc.
- **Harmful Effects**
- Chloroform affects the central nervous system. Inhaling it, 900 ppm (in air), for a short time can cause dizziness, fatigue and headache.
- Chronic exposure to chloroform damages liver and kidney due to the formation of phosgene gas inside the body.
- Skin develops sore if immersed directly into the chloroform.

Tetrachloromethane (Carbon Tetrachloride, CCl_4)

It is a colourless oily liquid with sweet smell. Its boiling point is 350 K. It is formed from chloroform as follows

$$CHCl_3 + Cl_2 \xrightarrow{\text{Sunlight}} CCl_4 + 2HCl$$

- **Uses**

 It is used in following ways
- In large quantities, in the manufacture of refrigerants and propellants for aerosol cans.
- As a feed stock in the synthesis of chlorofluorocarbons (freons).
- As a cleaning fluid, as a degreasing agent and as a spot remover.
- As fire extinguisher, under the name of pyrene.
- Used as general solvent.
- **Harmful Effects (Physiological Effects)**
- Its harmful effects are as follows
- Exposure to CCl_4 causes liver cancer in humans.
- The most common effects are dizziness, light headedness, nausea and vomiting which can cause permanent damage to nerve cells. In several cases, these effects can lead to stupor coma, unconsciousness or even death.
- Exposure of CCl_4 vapours can make heartbeat irregular or even can stop it.
- When brought in contact with eyes, it may cause irritation in eyes.
- It is also harmful to environment. When it is released in air, it rises in the atmosphere and depletes the ozone layer.
- Depletion of ozone layer increases the human exposure to UV rays which causes skin cancer, eye diseases and disorders and possible disruption of the immune system.

Triiodomethane (Iodoform, CHI_3)

It is yellow coloured crystalline solid with characteristic unpleasant odour.
- **Uses**
- As an antiseptic due to the liberation of free iodine.

$$\underset{\text{Triiodomethane}}{CHI_3} \xrightarrow[\text{Heat}]{\text{Air, moisture}} \underset{\text{Iodine}}{I_2}\uparrow + CO_2 + H_2O$$

- In the pharmaceutical industry.
- **Harmful Effect**
- Causes irritation in skin and eye.
- It can damage or harm the central nervous system, heart, kidney and liver.

Freons

- Chlorofluorocarbon compounds (CFC) of methane and ethane are collectively known as freons.
- They are extremely stable, unreactive, non-toxic, non-corrosive and easily liquefiable gases.
- Freon-12 (dichlorodifluoromethane, CCl_2F_2) is the most common freons in industrial use.
- It is manufactured from tetrachloromethane by Swarts reaction.

$$CCl_4 + 2AgF_2 \longrightarrow CCl_2F_2 + 2AgCl$$

- **Uses**

 It is used in following ways
- As refrigerants in refrigerators and air conditioners.
- As propellants for aerosols and foams to spray out deodorants, cleansers, shaving creams, hair sprays and insecticides.
- **Harmful Effects**

 Most freon makes its way into the atmosphere where it undergoes photochemical decomposition and initiates radical chain reactions for depletion of the ozone layer.

DDT (*p,p'*-dichlorodiphenyl trichloroethane)

- It was the first chlorinated organic insecticides.
- **Paul Muller** was awarded the Nobel prize in medicine and physiology in 1948 for this discovery.

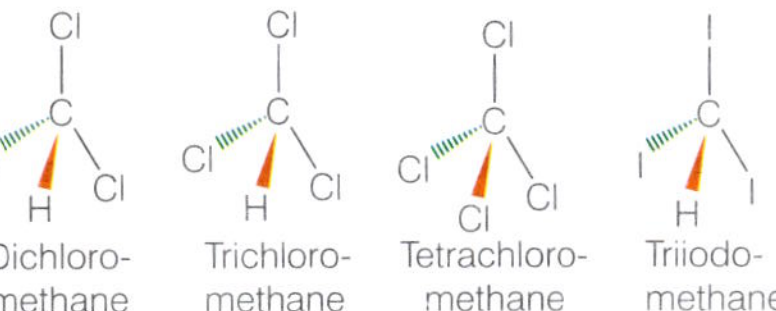

(DDT)

- Its IUPAC name is 2, 2- *bis* (4-chlorophenyl)–1, 1, 1- trichloroethane.
- It is formed, when chlorobenzene reacts with CCl_3CHO (chloral) in presence of conc. H_2SO_4.
- It is a white powder, insoluble in water but soluble in oil.
- **Uses**
- It is a powerful insecticide.
- It is popularly very effective against anopheles mosquitoes (causes malaria) and lices that carry typhus.
- **Harmful Effects**
- DDT is a non-biodegradable and extremely stable compound. It acts as water pollutant and kills aquatic animals thus imbalancing the water ecosystem. When higher animals (including humans) feed on dead fishes killed by DDT, it enters in their food chains.
- DDT gets stored in fatty tissues of animal and increases in amount over the time. If ingestion continues at a steady rate, DDT builds up within the animal over time.

Test 1

Syllabus

- **Alcohols :** General Methods of Preparation, Properties, Reaction and Uses, Identification of Primary, Secondary and Tertiary Alcohols, Mechanism of Dehydration.

NCERT
Page 193 to 196
Page 198 to 201
Page 203 to 210
Page 214

For deeper insight **Scan the QR Code**

Chapter 08

Alcohols

It contains one or more hydroxyl (—OH) group(s) directly attached to carbon atom(s) of an aliphatic system (*R*OH).

Structure

- The structure of an alcohol resembles the structure of water with an alkyl group replacing one of the hydrogen atoms of water.
- Both have sp^3-hybridised oxygen atoms but the C—O—H bond angle in methanol (108.9°) is considerably larger than the H—O—H bond angle in water (104.5°) because the methyl group is much larger than a hydrogen atom.

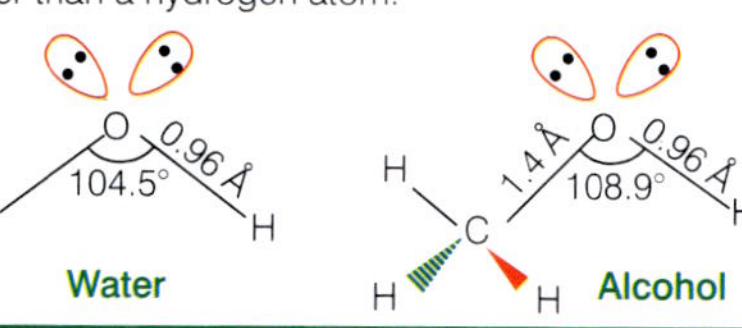

Nomenclature

For the simpler alcohols, the common name consists of the name of the alkyl group followed by the word 'alcohol'. e.g. CH_3CH_2OH ethyl alcohol.
IUPAC nomenclature for alcohol can be done by following rules

- Select the longest continuous carbon chain that contains the —OH group as the parent chain.
- Each name is derived by replacing the terminal '–e' of the corresponding alkane name by '–ol'.
- Indicate the position of —OH group by a number in the parent chain, generally using the lowest possible number for this purpose.
- Indicate the position of other groups by the number in the parent chain.
- For naming of polyhydric alcohol 'e' is retained.

Examples

- **Compounds**: CH_3OH, $CH_3CH(OH)—CH_3$
- **Common name**: Methyl alcohol, *Iso*-propyl alcohol
- **IUPAC name**: Methanol, Propan-2-ol
- **Compound**: $CH_3—C(CH_3)_2—OH$
- **Common name**: *Tert*-butyl alcohol
- **IUPAC name**: 2-methyl propan-2-ol

Classification

- **Monohydric alcohols**
  - A class of alcohol that have one hydroxyl group.
  - 1° alcohols, e.g. CH_3CH_2OH(Ethyl alcohol)
  - 2° alcohols, e.g. $(CH_3)_2—CH—OH$ (1-methyl ethanol)
  - 3° alcohols, e.g. $(CH_3)_3—C—OH$ (*tert*-butyl alcohol)
- **Dihydric alcohol**
  - A class of alcohol having two hydroxyl groups in each molecule. e.g. $CH_2OH—CH_2OH$
- **Trihydric alcohol**
  - A class of alcohol having three hydroxyl groups in each molecule. e.g. $CH_2OH—CHOH—CH_2OH$
- **Polyhydric alcohol**
  - They have more than three —OH groups.

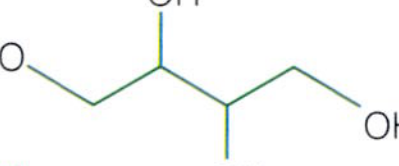

- **Vinylic alcohol**
  - The —OH group is bonded to a carbon-carbon double bond.
  - When—OH group is attached to vinylic C atom.

  Vinylic carbon $CH_2{=}CH—OH$
- **Allylic alcohol**
  - The —OH group is attached to sp^3 hybridised carbon next to the carbon-carbon double bond. i.e. to allylic carbon.

  Allylic carbon $CH_2{=}CH—CH_2—OH$
- **Benzylic alcohol**
  - The —OH group is attached to a sp^3 hybridised carbon atom next to an aromatic ring.

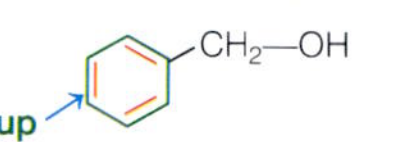

Physical Properties

- Lower members are colourless, volatile liquids with a characteristic smell and burning taste.
- Higher members are odourless and tasteless. Alcohol with more than 12 carbon atoms are colourless crystalline solids or liquids.
- Boiling point ∝ number of C-atoms
- Boiling point ∝ (1°>2°>3°)
- Alcohols have higher boiling point than those of hydrocarbons of comparable molecular masses due to H-bonding.
- They are soluble in water due to intermolecular H-bonding.
- Solubility ∝ branching.

Preparations

- **From Alkenes**

(i) By Acid Catalysed Hydration

$$CH_2{=}CH_2 \xrightarrow[\Delta]{H_2O/H^+} CH_3—CH_2—OH$$

$$CH_3—CH{=}CH_2 \xrightarrow[\Delta]{H_2O/H^+} CH_3CH(OH)CH_3$$

Markownikoff's rule is followed.

(ii) By Hydroboration-Oxidation

$$CH_3CH{=}CH_2 + (H—BH_2)_2 \longrightarrow CH_3—CH(H)—CH_2(BH_2)$$

$$\xrightarrow{CH_3—CH=CH_2} (CH_3—CH_2—CH_2)_2BH \xrightarrow{CH_3—CH=CH_2} (CH_3—CH_2—CH_2)_3B$$

$$\xrightarrow{H_2O,\ 3H_2O_2,\ ^-OH} 3CH_3—CH_2—CH_2—OH + B(OH)_3$$

Propan-1-ol

Anti-Markownikoff's rule is followed.

- **Action of Grignard's Reagent (G.R) with Carbonyl Compounds**

(a) G.R + HCHO or Ethylene oxide $\xrightarrow{H_3O^+}$ 1°alcohol

(b) G.R + Any aldehyde $\xrightarrow{H_3O^+}$ 2°alcohol

(c) G.R + Any ketone $\xrightarrow{H_3O^+}$ 3°alcohol

- **From Carbonyl Compounds**

(i) By Reduction of Carbonyl Compound

$$CH_3CHO \xrightarrow{Pd} CH_3CH_2OH\ (1°)$$

$$CH_3COCH_3 \xrightarrow{NaBH_4} CH_3—CH(OH)—CH_3\ (2°)$$

(ii) By Reduction of Carboxylic Acids and Esters

$$R—COOH \xrightarrow[(b)\ H_2O]{(a)\ LiAlH_4} RCH_2OH$$

$$R—COOH \xrightarrow[H^+]{R'OH} RCOOR' \xrightarrow[Catalyst]{H_2} RCH_2OH + R'OH$$

Chemical Reactions

- **Cleavage of O — H bond**
  - Ease of reaction depends on stability of alkoxide ion.
  - Alcohols can act as nucleophiles as well as electrophiles.
  - Acidity : Phenols > Water > 1° alcohol > 2° alcohol > 3° alcohol
  - EWG increases while EDG decreases acidity.
- **Cleavage of C — OH bond**
  - Ease of reaction depends on stability of carbocations. Order of reactivity with HX is 3° > 2° > 1° > CH_3OH.
- **Reaction with Hydrogen Halides**

$$R—OH + HX \longrightarrow R—X + H_2O$$

- **Reaction with Phosphorus Trihalides**

$$3ROH + PX_3 \longrightarrow 3RX + H_3PO_3 \quad [X = Br, I]$$

- **Dehydration**

$$—\underset{H}{C}—\underset{OH}{C}— \xrightarrow[Heat]{H^+} >C{=}C< + H_2O$$

- Ethanol undergoes dehydration by heating it with concentrated H_2SO_4 at 443 K.

$$C_2H_5OH \xrightarrow[443K]{H_2SO_4} CH_2{=}CH_2 + H_2O$$

- Secondary and tertiary alcohols are dehydrated under milder conditions.

$$CH_3—CH(OH)—CH_3 \xrightarrow[440K]{85\%\ H_3PO_4} CH_3—CH{=}CH_2 + H_2O$$

$$H_3C—C(CH_3)_2—OH \xrightarrow[358K]{20\%\ H_3PO_4} CH_3—C({=}CH_2)—CH_3 + H_2O$$

Distinguishing Test for Alcohols

Alcohol	Dichromate (Oxidation) test	Victor Meyer test	Lucas test
1°	Acid (Orange solution becomes green)	Blood red colour	No turbidity
2°	Ketone (Orange solution becomes green)	Blue colour	Turbidity in 5 minutes
3°	No reaction	Colourless	Turbidity immediately

Some Commercially Important Alcohols

- **Methanol** It is a colourless liquid and boils at 337K. It is also known as 'wood spirit' as it was produced by destructive distillation of wood.

$$CO + 2H_2 \xrightarrow[200\text{-}300\ atm\ 373\text{-}676\ K]{ZnO—Cr_2O_3} CH_3OH$$

It is used as a solvent in paints, varnishes and for manufacturing formaldehyde, dyes, medicines and perfumes.

- **Ethanol** It is obtained by fermentation.

$$C_{12}H_{22}O_{11} + H_2O \xrightarrow{Invertase} \underset{Glucose}{C_6H_{12}O_6} + \underset{Fructose}{C_6H_{12}O_6}$$

It is used in making wines.

Test 2

Syllabus

- **Phenols :** General Methods of Preparation, Properties, Acidic Nature, Electrophilic Substitution Reaction, Halogenation, Nitration, Sulphonation, Reimer-Tiemann Reaction.

NCERT
Page 195 to 199
Page 201 to 204
Page 206 to 208
Page 210 to 213

For deeper insight **Scan the QR Code**

Chapter 08

Phenols

- These are aromatic organic compounds containing –OH group directly attached to carbon atom.
- These are generally named as the derivatives of the simplest member of the family.

Classification

- **On the basis of number of —OH groups** These are classified as mono-,di-, tri- or polyhydric compounds depending on whether they contains one, two, three or more hydroxyl group respectively.

Monohydric (phenol) | Dihydric (benzene-1,2-diol) | Trihydric (benzene-1,2,4-triol)

- **Compound containing C_{sp^2} — OH bond**
They contain —OH group bonded to a carbon-carbon double bond.
e.g. (phenol), (2-methylphenol)

Nomenclature

- Phenol is an accepted IUPAC as well as common name.
- In its substituted compound the positions of the substituents are indicated by the prefix 1,2 (*ortho*), 1,3 (*meta*) and 1,4 (*para*). e.g.

IUPAC name	3-methylphenol	2-bromophenol
Common name	*m*-cresol	*o*-bromophenol
IUPAC name	4-nitrophenol	2, 4, 6-trinitrophenol
Common name	*p*-nitrophenol	Picric acid

Preparations

- **From Haloarenes**

$$C_6H_5Cl + NaOH \xrightarrow[350^\circ C]{300\ atm} C_6H_5O^-Na^+ \xrightarrow{HCl} C_6H_5OH$$

- **From Cumene**

$$\text{Cumene} + O_2 \longrightarrow \text{Cumene hydroperoxide} \xrightarrow[H^+]{H_2O} C_6H_5OH + CH_3-\overset{O}{\overset{\|}{C}}-CH_3$$

- **From Diazonium Salt**

$$C_6H_5NH_2 \xrightarrow[HCl]{NaNO_2} C_6H_5N_2^+Cl^- \xrightarrow[Warm]{H_2O} C_6H_5OH + N_2 + HCl$$

- **From Grignard's Reagent**

$$C_6H_5Br + Mg \xrightarrow{ROR} C_6H_5MgBr \xrightarrow[H_2O/H^+]{O_2} C_6H_5OH$$

- **From Benzene Sulphonic Acid**

$$C_6H_5SO_3H \xrightarrow{NaOH} C_6H_5SO_3Na \xrightarrow{NaOH} C_6H_5O^-Na^+ \xrightarrow{HCl} C_6H_5OH$$

- **From Benzene** Phenol can also be prepared by oxidation of benzene with V_2O_5 at 315°C.

$$2\,\text{Benzene} + O_2 \xrightarrow[315^\circ C]{V_2O_5} 2\,\text{Phenol}$$

Physical Properties

- These are colourless liquids or solids with red tint and have carbolic odour. Phenols are highly toxic.
- Due to stronger intermolecular H-bonding their boiling point are higher than corresponding alcohols.

Reactions of Phenols

- **Electrophilic Aromatic Substitution**

Phenol $\xrightarrow{\text{Conc. } HNO_3}$ 2,4,6-trinitrophenol (O_2N, NO_2, NO_2)

Phenol $\xrightarrow[25^\circ C]{\text{Conc. } H_2SO_4}$ o-hydroxybenzenesulphonic acid (SO_3H)

Phenol $\xrightarrow[100^\circ C]{\text{Conc. } H_2SO_4}$ p-hydroxybenzenesulphonic acid (SO_3H)

Phenol $\xrightarrow{NaOH}$ ONa (sodium phenoxide) $\xrightarrow[(ii)\ H^+]{(i)\ CO_2}$ salicylic acid (OH, COOH)

Phenol $\xrightarrow{Zn}$ ZnO + benzene

Phenol $\xrightarrow[H_2SO_4]{Na_2Cr_2O_7}$ benzoquinone (O, O)

Phenol $\xrightarrow{3Br_2}$ 2,4,6-tribromophenol + 3HBr

Phenol $\xrightarrow[273K]{Br_2 \text{ in } CS_2}$ o-bromophenol + p-bromophenol

Phenol $\xrightarrow[25^\circ C]{\text{Dil. } HNO_3}$ o-nitrophenol + p-nitrophenol

Phenol $\xrightarrow[aq.\ NaOH]{CHCl_3+}$ [O^-Na^+, $CHCl_2$] $\xrightarrow{NaOH}$ O^-Na^+, CHO $\xrightarrow{H^+}$ OH, CHO (salicylaldehyde)

- **Based On the Cleavage of O—H Bond**
- **Reaction with Metals**
Phenols react with active metals such as sodium, potassium and aluminium to yield corresponding phenoxide and hydrogen.

$$2C_6H_5OH + 2Na \longrightarrow 2C_6H_5ONa + H_2$$

- They are more miscible with water as compare to alcohols.
- They have high dipole moments and are acidic in nature.
- The solubility of phenols in water is due to their ability to form hydrogen bonds with water molecules.
- Solubility decreases with increase in size of alkyl/aryl groups.

- **Acidity of Phenols**
– The acidic nature of phenols can be explained by resonating structures.
– Due to resonance, the oxygen atom acquires a partial positive charge and partial double bond character with sp^2 hybridised carbon of the ring.
– It weakens the O—H bond and thus, the release of proton is facilitated.

- **Esterification**
– Phenols react with carboxylic acids, acid chlorides and acid anhydride to form ester.

$$Ar—OH + R'—COOH \overset{H^+}{\rightleftharpoons} ArOCOR' + H_2O$$

$$Ar—OH + (R'CO)_2O \overset{H^+}{\rightleftharpoons} ArOCOR' + R'COOH$$

$$Ar—OH + R'COCl \xrightarrow{Pyridine} ArOCOR' + HCl$$

Note Reaction involving cleavage of C—O bond in phenols takes place only with zinc.

Test 3

Syllabus
- General Methods of Preparation, Structure, Properties, Reactions and Uses.

NCERT Page 215 to 220

For deeper insight Scan the QR Code

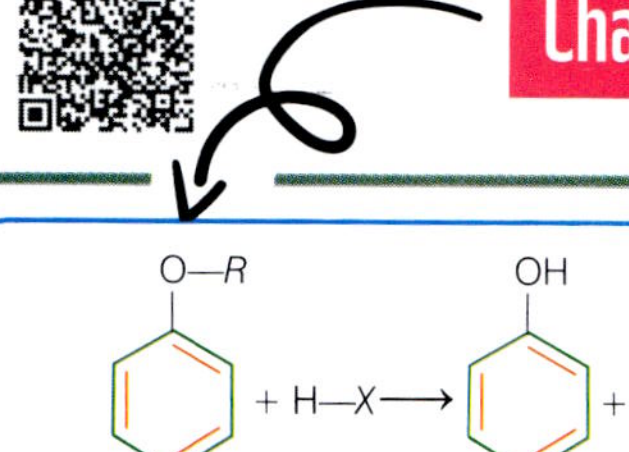

Chapter 08

Ethers

- These are the class of organic compounds that contains oxygen atom bonded to two alkyl or aryl groups.
- They have the general formula $R - \ddot{O} - R'$ where, R and R' may be same or different.

Classification

- **On the Basis of Type of Attached Groups**
- **Aliphatic Ethers**

Both attached groups (R and R') are alkyl groups. They have the general formula as $C_nH_{2n+2}O$.

e.g. $CH_3CH_2OCH_2CH_3$ (Diethyl ether); $CH_3 - O - C(CH_3)_2 - CH_3$ (Methyl *tert*-butyl ether)

- **Aromatic Ethers**

Either one or both the attached groups (R and R') is/are aryl groups.

e.g.

Diphenyl ether; $C_6H_5 - O - C_2H_5$ Ethyl phenyl ether

Aromatic ethers are further classified as

(i) Phenolic Ethers

One of the group is aryl and other is alkyl.

e.g. $CH_3 - O - C_6H_5$ Phenolic ether

(ii) Diaryl Ethers

Both the groups are aryl.

e.g. $C_6H_5 - O - C_6H_5$ Diphenyl ether

- **On the Basis of Symmetry**

(i) Simple or Symmetrical Ethers

Both alkyl or aryl groups bonded to O-atom are same.

e.g. $CH_3 - O - CH_3$ (Dimethyl ether); $C_6H_5 - O - C_6H_5$ (Diphenyl ether)

(ii) Mixed or Unsymmetrical Ethers

Both alkyl or aryl groups bonded to O-atom are different.

e.g. $CH_3 - O - CH_2CH_3$ (Ethyl methyl ether); $C_6H_5 - O - CH_2C_6H_5$ (Benzyl phenyl ether)

Structure

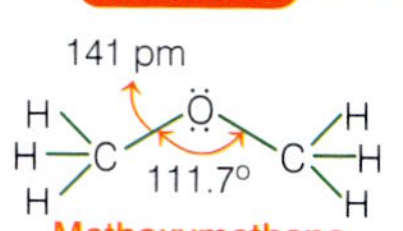

- Bond angle is higher than tetrahedral angle due to high % s character in C — O bonds.
- The bulkier R group result in the greater forces of repulsion and thus the R–O–R bond angle is 110°.

Nomenclature

- In IUPAC system, ethers are called as alkoxyalkanes.
- Ethereal oxygen is taken alongwith smaller alkyl group, which is regarded as substituent on large alkyl group as parent hydrocarbon.

e.g. $CH_3 - O - CH(CH_3)_2$; $CH_3 - O - C(CH_3)_2 - CH_3$

IUPAC name: 2-methoxypropane; 2-methoxy-2-methylpropane

$CH_3O - CH(OCH_3) - CH_3$; $CH_3 - CH(OH) - CH_2CH_2OCH_3$

IUPAC name: 1,1-dimethoxyethane; 4-methoxybutan-2-ol

Physical Properties

- C—O bonds are slightly polar due to bent structure.
- Boiling point are lower than isomeric alcohols.
- Solubility ∝ 1/Molecular mass (soluble upto three carbon atoms due to H-bonding).
- Ethers upto three carbon atoms are soluble in water due to the formation of intermolecular hydrogen bonds between water and ethereal oxygen.

$R_2\overset{\delta^-}{O}\cdots\overset{\delta^+}{H}-\overset{\delta^-}{O}-\overset{\delta^+}{H}\cdots\overset{\delta^-}{O}R_2$

- The large difference in boiling point of alcohol and ether is due to the presence of H-bonding in alcohol.
- As molecular mass increases, solubility of ethers in water decreases.

Preparations

- **Dehydration of Alcohols**
  - They undergo dehydration in the presence of protic acid.
  - Formation of reaction product, alkene or ether depends on the reaction conditions.

$$CH_3CH_2OH \xrightarrow[443\,K]{H_2SO_4} CH_2{=}CH_2$$
$$CH_3CH_2OH \xrightarrow[413\,K]{H_2SO_4} C_2H_5OC_2H_5$$

  - This reaction involves S_N2 attack of a alcohol molecule on protonated alcohol. Symmetrical ethers are formed.
- **Williamson Synthesis**

$$R - ONa + R' - X \longrightarrow R - O - R' + NaX$$
$$CH_3CH_2ONa + CH_3Br \longrightarrow CH_3CH_2 - O - CH_3 + NaBr$$
$$C_6H_5 - ONa + CH_3Br \longrightarrow C_6H_5 - O - CH_3 + NaBr$$

  - This reaction is S_N2. Suitable for mixed ethers. $R - X$ should be 1° and alkoxide should be 2° or 3°.

$$(CH_3)_3C - O^-Na^+ + CH_3CH_2Br \longrightarrow CH_3 - C(CH_3)_2 - O - CH_2CH_3 + NaBr$$

Chemical Reactions

- **Cleavage of C—O Bond in Ethers**
  - These are the least reactive of the functional groups.
  - The cleavage of C—O bond in ethers takes place under drastic condition with excess of hydrogen halides.

$$R - O - R + HX \longrightarrow RX + R - OH$$
$$R - OH + HX \longrightarrow R - X + H_2O$$

  - Alkyl/aryl ethers are cleaved at the alkyl-oxygen bond due to the more stable aryl-oxygen bond.

$$C_6H_5 - O - R + H - X \longrightarrow C_6H_5OH + R - X$$
$$R - O - R' + HX \longrightarrow RX + R' - OH$$

- Order of reactivity of hydrogen halide is HI > HBr > HCl.

- **Electrophilic Substitution**
  - The alkoxy group (—OR is *ortho*, *para*-directing and activates the aromatic ring towards electrophilic substitution.

(i) Halogenation

- Phenyl alkyl ethers undergo halogenation in the benzene ring.

$$\text{Anisole} \xrightarrow{Br_2 \text{ in ethanoic acid}} p\text{-bromoanisole} + o\text{-bromoanisole}$$

(ii) Friedel-Crafts Reaction

- The alkyl and acyl groups are introduced at *ortho* and *para*-positions by reaction with alkyl halide and acyl halide in the presence of Lewis acid.

$$C_6H_5OCH_3 + CH_3Cl \xrightarrow[CS_2]{\text{Anhy. } AlCl_3} o\text{-}CH_3C_6H_4OCH_3 + p\text{-}CH_3C_6H_4OCH_3$$

(iii) Nitration

- Anisole reacts with a mixture of concentrated sulphuric and nitric acids to yield a mixture of *ortho* and *para*-nitroanisole.

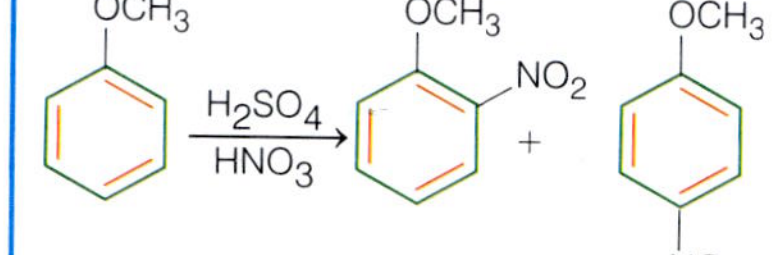

$$C_6H_5OCH_3 \xrightarrow[HNO_3]{H_2SO_4} o\text{-}NO_2C_6H_4OCH_3 + p\text{-}NO_2C_6H_4OCH_3$$

Test 1

Syllabus

- General Methods of Preparation, Properties, Reaction and Uses, Nature of Carbonyl Group, Nucleophilic Addition to $>C=O$ Group, Nucleophilic Addition Reaction, Grignard Reagent, Oxidation, Reduction, Aldol Condensation, Cannizzaro Reaction.

NCERT Page 227 to 232, Page 234 to 243

For deeper insight **Scan the QR Code**

Chapter 09

Aldehyde

- An aldehyde is a carbonyl group ($>C=O$) containing organic compound in which the carbonyl carbon atom has atleast one hydrogen atom directly attached to it.
- The remaining group attached to the carbonyl carbon atom can be hydrogen, an alkyl group, cycloalkyl group, or an aryl group (Ar). $Ar/R-C(=O)-H$

Structure

- Carbonyl carbon atom in aldehydes are sp^2-hybridised. It is attached to three atoms which lie in same plane while the π-electron cloud lies above and below the plane.
- The bond angle formed between the bond pairs is about 120° as expected of a trigonal coplanar.

Orbital diagram for the formation of carbonyl group

Nomenclature

- The common names of most aldehydes are derived from the common names of the corresponding carboxylic acids by replacing the ending '(–)ic' of acid with aldehyde. In IUPAC system, naming of aldehyde is done by replacing the terminal 'e' of the alkanes with suffix 'al'.
- Position of carbonyl carbon in aldehydes is always C-1.

e.g. $H-CO-H$ (Methanal); CH_3-CO-H (Ethanal); $CH_3-CH(CH_3)-CHO$ (2-methylpropanal)

Physical Properties

- Methanal is a gas while ethanal is a volatile liquid. Rest of the aldehydes containing upto eleven carbon atoms are colourless liquids and higher members are solids. Aldehydes are soluble in water. Carbonyl group readily forms H-bond with water.
- Solubility decreases with increase in length of alkyl chain. Therefore, carbonyl compounds upto four carbon atoms are soluble and higher members are insoluble. Higher carbonyl compounds are soluble in organic solvents like ether, benzene, $CHCl_3$ etc.
- Boiling points of aldehydes are lower than alcohols due to absence of intermolecular hydrogen bonding but higher than non-polar compounds such as hydrocarbons due to dipole-dipole interaction.

Preparations

- **Reduction of Acid Chlorides (Rosenmund's Reduction)**

$$CH_3COCl + H_2 \xrightarrow{Pd\text{-}BaSO_4} CH_3CHO + HCl$$

- **From esters**
  - Di-*iso*-butyl aluminium hydride (DIBAL-H) reduces esters into aldehydes.

$$CH_3CH_2COOCH_3 \xrightarrow[H_2O]{DIBAL\text{-}H} CH_3CH_2CHO$$

- **Reduction of Nitriles (Stephen Reduction)**

$$R-C\equiv N \xrightarrow[H_3O^+,\Delta]{SnCl_2/HCl} R-CHO$$

- **Oxidation of Alcohols**
  - 1° Alcohol $\xrightarrow{\text{Mild oxidising agent}}$ Aldehydes
  - Mild Oxidising agents used are CrO_3-Pyridine (Collin's Reagent) Pyridinium Chlorochromate (PCC)—$C_5H_5NHCrO_3Cl/CH_2Cl_2$ pyridinium dichromate (PDC).
- **From Hydrocarbon**

(i) By Using Chromyl Chloride (Etard Reaction)

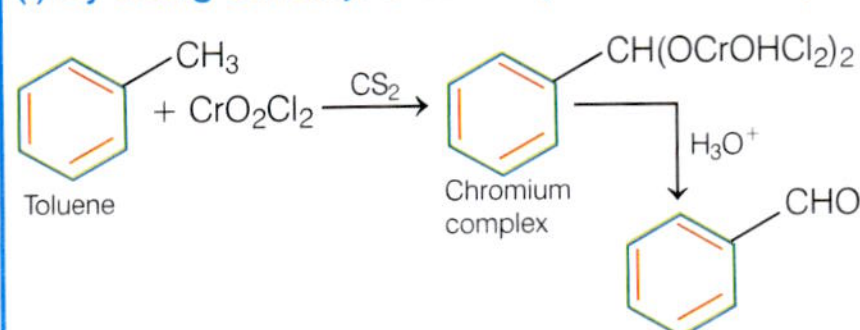

(ii) Use of Chromic Oxide (CrO_3)

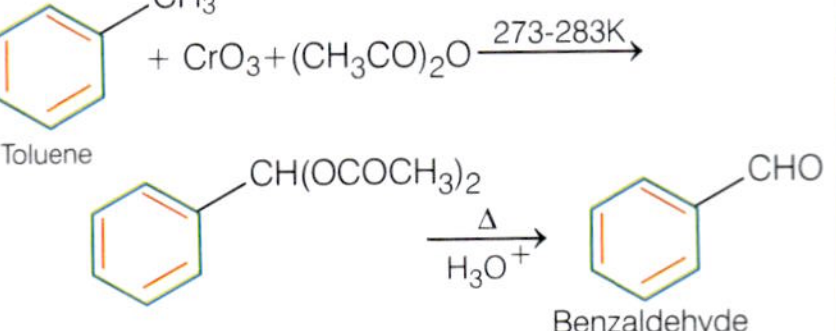

(iii) By Side Chain Chlorination

Toluene ($C_6H_5CH_3$) $\xrightarrow{Cl_2/h\nu}$ $C_6H_5CHCl_2$ $\xrightarrow[373K]{H_2O}$ C_6H_5CHO (Benzaldehyde)

(iv) By Gatterman-Koch Reaction

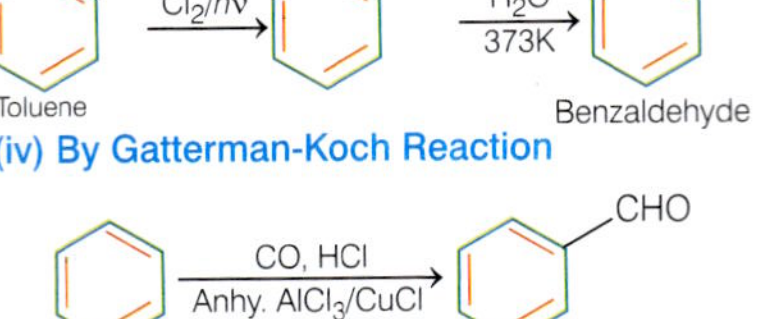

Chemical Reactions

Aldehydes carry partial +ve charge on C-atom of $(>\overset{\delta^+}{C}=\overset{\delta^-}{O})$ group. Hence, they undergo nucleophilic addition reactions.

Planar → Slow, Step I → Tetrahedral Intermediate → H^+, fast, Step 2 → Addition Product

Nucleophilic attack on carbonyl carbon

Nucleophilic Addition Reactions

(i) Addition with HCN

$$>\overset{\delta^+}{C}=\overset{\delta^-}{O} + \bar{C}N \overset{H^+}{\rightleftharpoons} >C(OH)(CN)$$

Cyanohydrin

(ii) Addition with $NaHSO_3$

$$>C=O + NaHSO_3 \rightleftharpoons >C(OH)(OSO_2Na)$$

Bisulphite addition product

(iii) Addition of alcohols

$$>C=O + \underset{\text{(2 equivalent)}}{H\text{-}OCH_3, H\text{-}OCH_3} \overset{H^+}{\rightleftharpoons} >C(OCH_3)_2 + H_2O$$

Acetal or Ketal

(iv) Addition of Grignard's reagent

$$HCHO + R'MgX \xrightarrow[H_2O]{H^+} R'CH_2OH \text{ (1° alcohol)}$$

$$R-CHO + R'MgX \xrightarrow[H_2O]{H^+} R-CH(OH)-R' \text{ (2° alcohol)}$$

Oxidation

- Aldehydes are easily oxidised to carboxylic acids on treatment with common oxidising agents like HNO_3, $KMnO_4$ and $K_2Cr_2O_7$.
- Mild oxidising agents like Tollen's and Fehling's reagent also oxidise aldehydes.
- **Haloform reaction** Acetaldehyde are oxidised by sodium hypohalite to give haloform.

Reduction

Reduction of Hydrocarbon

$>C=O$ to $-CH_2-$ group

$$>C=O \xrightarrow[\Delta]{Zn\text{-}Hg/HCl} >CH_2 + H_2O \text{ (Clemmensen's reduction)}$$

$$>C=O \xrightarrow[-H_2O]{NH_2NH_2} >C=NNH_2 \xrightarrow[\text{Heat}]{\text{KOH/Ethylene glycol}} >CH_2 + N_2$$

(Wolff-Kishner reduction)

Aldol Condensation

Aldehydes having at least one α-hydrogen undergo a reaction in the presence of dilute alkali as catalyst to form β-hydroxy aldehydes (aldol). This is known as **aldol reaction**.

$$\underset{\text{Ethanal}}{2CH_3-CHO} \overset{\text{Dil.NaOH}}{\rightleftharpoons} \underset{\text{3-hydroxybutanal (Aldol)}}{CH_3-CH(OH)-CH_2-CHO}$$

$$\xrightarrow[-H_2O]{\Delta} \underset{\text{But-2-enal}}{CH_3-CH=CH-CHO}$$

(Aldol condensation product)

Cannizzaro Reaction

- Aldehydes which do not have an α-hydrogen atom, undergo self oxidation and reduction (disproportionation) reaction on heating with concentrated alkali. In this reaction, one molecule of the aldehyde is reduced to alcohol while another is oxidised to carboxylic acid salt.

$$\underset{\text{Formaldehyde}}{HCHO + HCHO} + \text{Conc. KOH} \xrightarrow{\Delta} \underset{\text{Methanol}}{H-C(H)_2-OH} + \underset{\text{Potassium formate}}{H-C(=O)-OK}$$

Uses of Aldehydes

- 40% fomaldehyde in water (formalin) is used as a preservative for biological specimens.
- Benzaldehyde is used in preparation of flavoring agents, perfumes, drugs and dyes.

Test 2

Syllabus

- General Methods of Preparation, Properties, Reaction and Uses, Reduction, Aldol Condensation, Haloform Reaction, Chemical Tests to Distinguish Between Aldehydes and Ketones.

NCERT
Page 227 to 231
Page 233 to 243

For deeper insight **Scan the QR Code**

Chapter 09

Ketones

The compounds which are having carbonyl compounds bonded to two carbon atoms. $Ar/R-\overset{O}{\overset{\|}{C}}-R'$

Structure and Nomenclature

- Organic compounds containing carbon-oxygen double bond, i.e. $>C=O$ group are called carbonyl compounds. General formula of ketones $= C_nH_{2n+1}COC_nH_{2n+1}$
- The common names of ketones are derived by naming two alkyl or aryl groups bonded to the carbonyl group.
- IUPAC name of ketones = Alkanone

Preparation of Aldehydes and Ketones

Oxidation of Alcohols

$2°\text{ alcohol} \longrightarrow R_2CO$

Catalytic Dehydrogenation of Alcohols

$R_2CH_2OH \xrightarrow[\Delta]{Cu} R_2CO$

Ozonolysis of Alkenes

$RCH = CHR' \xrightarrow[Zn/H_2O]{O_3} RCHO + R'CHO$

$R_2C = CR'_2 \xrightarrow[Zn/H_2O]{O_3} R_2CO + R'_2CO$

Hydrolysis of Ethylacetoacetate (EAA)

$CH_3COCH_2COOC_2H_5 \xrightarrow[\Delta]{H_2O/H^+} CH_3COCH_3 + CO_2\uparrow + H_2O$

Hydration of Alkyne

$\underset{\text{Ethyne}}{CH\equiv CH} \xrightarrow[HgSO_4]{H_2O/H^+} \underset{\text{Ethanal}}{CH_3CHO}$

$\underset{\text{Propyne}}{CH_3C\equiv CH} \xrightarrow[HgSO_4]{H_2O/H^+} \underset{\text{Propanone}}{CH_3COCH_3}$

Physical Properties

- **Physical State** Generally they are colourless liquids.
- **Boiling Points** Have higher boiling points than hydrocarbons and ethers of comparable molecular mass due to dipole-dipole interactions.
- **Solubility decreases with increase in molecular mass.** Lower ketones are soluble in water.
- Aromatic ketones are less soluble than corresponding aliphatic aldehydes and ketones due to large hydrocarbon part in benzene ring.

Preparation of Ketones

- **From Grignard Reagents**

$CH_3MgX + RC\equiv N \xrightarrow{H_2O/H^+} R-\underset{CH_3}{\underset{|}{C}}=O + NH_3 + MgXOH$

$\triangleright\!-MgBr + HC\equiv N \longrightarrow H-\underset{\triangle}{\underset{|}{C}}=O$

- **Hydrolysis of *Gem*-dihalides**

$CH_3-\underset{Cl}{\overset{Cl}{C}}-CH_3 \xrightarrow{aq.\ KOH} CH_3-\underset{OH}{\overset{OH}{C}}-CH_3 \xrightarrow{-H_2O} CH_3-\overset{O}{\overset{\|}{C}}-CH_3$

- **Wacker's Process**
- Alkenes are oxidised to ketones.

$CH_3CH_2=CH_2 \xrightarrow[CuCl,\ H_2O]{PdCl_2} CH_3-CO-CH_3$

- **From Acyl Chloride**

$2R-Mg-X + CdCl_2 \longrightarrow R_2Cd + 2Mg(X)Cl$

$2R'-\underset{O}{\underset{\|}{C}}-Cl + R_2Cd \longrightarrow 2R'-\underset{O}{\underset{\|}{C}}-R + CdCl_2$

- **From Nitriles**
- Treating a nitrile with Grignard reagent followed by hydrolysis yields a ketone.

$CH_3-CH_2-C\equiv N + C_6H_5MgBr \xrightarrow{Ether}$

$CH_3CH_2-\overset{NMgBr}{\overset{\|}{C}}-C_6H_5 \xrightarrow{H_3O^+} C_2H_5-\overset{O}{\overset{\|}{C}}-C_6H_5$

Propiophenone (1-phenylpropanone)

- **From Benzene or Substituted Benzenes**

$C_6H_6 + Ar/R-\overset{O}{\overset{\|}{C}}-Cl \xrightarrow[AlCl_3]{Anhyd.} C_6H_5-\overset{O}{\overset{\|}{C}}-Ar/R$

Distinction Test

Test	Aldehydes	Ketones
Tollen's test	Silver mirror	No change
Fehling's test (only aliphatic)	Red precipitate	No change
Benedict test (only aliphatic)	Red precipitate	No change
Schiff's test	Pink colour	No change

Chemical Reactions of Ketones

Nucleophilic Addition Reactions

With HCN $\longrightarrow R-\overset{O}{\overset{\|}{C}}-R \xrightarrow{HCN} (CN)(OH)C(R)(R)$

With NH_3 and its Derivatives $\longrightarrow R-\overset{O}{\overset{\|}{C}}-R \xrightarrow{NH_3}$ Schiff's base

With RMgX $\longrightarrow R-\overset{O}{\overset{\|}{C}}-R \xrightarrow[H_2O]{RMgX}$ Alcohols

Addition of Alcohols

$R-\overset{O}{\overset{\|}{C}}-R \xrightarrow{ROH}$ Hemiacetal or hemiketal $\xrightarrow[-H_2O]{ROH}$ Acetal or ketal.

Oxidation $\longrightarrow R_2CO \xrightarrow[Strong]{[O]} RCOOH$

Reduction $\longrightarrow$

$R_2CO \xrightarrow{NaBH_4/LiAlH_4} R_2CHOH$

$R_2CO \xrightarrow[NH_2+NH_2/KOH]{Zn/Hg,\ HCl} RCH_2R$

Haloform Reaction

$RCOCH_3 \xrightarrow[NaOX]{} RCOONa + CHX_3$

Reaction at α-CH_3 group.

Aldol Condensation

$2R_2CO \xrightarrow{NaOH\ (dil.)} \beta$-hydroxy ketone $\xrightarrow{\Delta}$ α,β-unsaturated ketone

Cannizzaro Reaction

$RCOR \xrightarrow{NaOH}$ No reaction

(Ketones do not undergo Cannizzaro reaction.)

Important Points Regarding Chemical Reactions

- When I_2 is used as the halogen in the above reaction, yellow ppt. iodoform are formed and the test is called iodoform test.
- Iodoform reaction is carried out with sodium hypoiodite which is used for detection of CH_3CO group or $CH_3CH(OH)$ group which produces CH_3CO group on oxidation.

Cross Aldol Condensation

- Different carbonyl compounds having acidic hydrogen at -α position are condensed to give, α, β-unsaturated compounds. Then, reaction is called cross-aldol condensation.

$\underset{\text{Acetaldehyde}}{CH_3-\overset{H}{\overset{|}{C}}=O} + \underset{\text{Acetone}}{HCH_2-\overset{O}{\overset{\|}{C}}-CH_3} \xrightarrow{OH^-} CH_3-\overset{H}{\underset{OH}{C}}-CH_2-\overset{}{\underset{O}{\underset{\|}{C}}}-CH_3$

- There are four products possible by cross-aldol condensation if both the reactants have α-hydrogen.

e.g. $CH_3CHO + CH_3CH_2CHO \xrightarrow[\Delta]{NaOH}$

$CH_3-CH=CH-CHO$ But-2-enal (From two molecules of ethanal) $+ CH_3CH_2CH=\underset{CH_3}{\underset{|}{C}}CHO$ 2-methylpent-2-enal (From two molecules of Propanal)

Simple or Self aldol products

$CH_3-CH=\underset{CH_3}{\underset{|}{C}}-CHO$ 2-methylbut-2-enal $+ CH_3CH_2CH=CHCHO$ Pent-2-enal

(From one molecule of ethanal and one molecule of propanal)

Cross aldol products

Uses of Ketones

- Used as solvent in explosive manufacturing.
- Acetone is used in cosmetics and as a nail paint remover.
- Acetophenone is used in flavouring agents.
- Used in drug testing.

- If two or more carbonyl groups are present in the molecule, there can be intramolecular aldol reaction thus formation of rings is preferred as Six membered> Five membered, Four membered
- Clemmensen reduction is used for selective reduction of ketones which contain phenolic or carboxylic groups as these groups are sensitive to base. While Wolff-Kishner reduction is preferred for compounds sensitive to acid.

Syllabus

- General Method of Preparation, Properties, Reactions, Uses, Acidic Strength and Factors Affecting it.

NCERT Page 244 to 254

For deeper insight **Scan the QR Code**

Introduction

- The carbonyl compounds in which carbonyl group is bonded to oxygen are known as carboxylic acids.
- The general formula of aliphatic carboxylic acids is R — COOH (aliphatic class).

Classification

Depending upon the number of carboxylic groups present in molecules, these are classified as monocarboxylic acid, dicarboxylic acid or tricarboxylic acids.

- **Monocarboxylic acids**

HCOOH (Formic acid); C_6H_5—COOH (Benzoic acid)

- **Dicarboxylic acid**

COOH—COOH (Oxalic acid); $CH_2(COOH)_2$ (Malonic acid); $C_6H_4(COOH)_2$ (Phthalic acid)

- **Tricarboxylic acid**

HOOC—CH_2—C(OH)(COOH)—CH_2—COOH (Citric acid)

Structure and Nomenclature

- **Structure**

$$-C(=O)-\ddot{O}-H \longleftrightarrow -C^+(-O^-)-\ddot{O}-H \longleftrightarrow -C(-O^-)=\overset{+}{O}-H$$

- The bonds to the carboxyl carbon lie in one plane and are separated by about 120°.
- The carboxylic carbon is less electrophilic than carbonyl carbon because of the possible resonance structure.
- **Common name** Suffix – ic acid at the end e.g. acetic acid
  IUPAC name Suffix – oic acid is added in the name of corresponding alkane.

Names of Some Carboxylic Acids with their Common and IUPAC Names

Molecular formulae	Common name	IUPAC name
$CH_3(CH_2)_4COOH$	Caproic acid	Hexanoic acid
$CH_3(CH_2)_8COOH$	Capric acid	Decanoic acid
$H_2C(COOH)_2$	Malonic acid	Propanedioic acid
CH_2COOH—CH_2COOH	Succinic acid	Butanedioic acid
CHCOOH=CHCOOH	Maleic acid	But-2-enedioic acid
CH_2COOH—CHCOOH—CH_2COOH	Carballylic acid	Propane-1,2,3-tricarboxylic acid

Acidic Strength

- Carboxylic acids are acidic in nature but they are weaker acids than mineral acids.
- They are stronger acids than phenols because the carboxylate ion is more estabilised with resonance as compared to phenoxide ion.
- Electron withdrawing groups increase the acidity of carboxylic acids by stabilising the conjugate base.
- Electron donating groups decrease the acidity by destabilising the conjugate base.
- Dissociate in water to give hydronium ion.

$$R-C(=O)-OH + H_2O \rightleftharpoons H_3O^+ + \left[R-C(=O)-O^- \longleftrightarrow R-C(-O^-)=O\right]$$

- Hydroxyl group of acids is more acidic than the hydroxyl group of alcohols.
  Acidity Order :
  Carboxylic Acids > Phenols > Alcohols
- More is the electronegativity of the atom attached to the carboxyl group, more will be acidity.

Physical Properties

- Lower acids and derivatives are colourless liquids. Exists as dimer in vapour phase.
- Boiling point of carboxylic acids are higher than aldehydes, ketones and alcohols of comparable molecular masses due to intermolecular H-bonding.
- **Boiling point order** Carboxylic acids > Alcohols > Aldehydes > Ketones > Hydrocarbons
- Solubility ∝ 1/Number of C atoms ∝ Intermolecular H-bonding

Preparation

From Hydrocarbons

$$2RCH_3 + 3O_2 \xrightarrow[\text{stearate}]{\text{Manganese}} 2RCOOH + 2H_2O$$

Oxidation of Alcohols

$$2RCH_2OH + 3O_2 \xrightarrow{[O]} RCHO \xrightarrow{[O]} R-COOH$$

Hydrolysis of Esters

$$R-C(=O)-O-R' \xrightarrow{H_2O/H^+} R-C(=O)-OH + R'OH$$

Ozonolysis of Alkenes

$$CH_2=CH_2 + O_3 \xrightarrow[AgO]{HgO_2} HCOOH + H_2O$$ (Formic acid)

From Grignard's Reagent

$$RMgX + O=C=O \longrightarrow R-C(=O)-O^-MgX^+ \xrightarrow{H_3O^+} R-C(=O)-OH + Mg(OH)X$$

From Nitriles and Amides

$$R-CN \xrightarrow[H_2O]{H^+ \text{ or } ^-OH} R-C(=O)-NH_2 \xrightarrow[\Delta]{H^+ \text{ or } ^-OH} RCOOH$$

From Alkyl Benzene

$$C_6H_5CH_3 \xrightarrow[\Delta]{KMnO_4\text{-}KOH} C_6H_5COOK \xrightarrow{H_3O^+} C_6H_5COOH$$

Uses

- Higher fatty acids are used in manufacture of soaps.
- Organic acids are used for preparation of many drugs such as aspirin, phenacetin etc.
- Acetic acid is used as coagulant in manufacture of rubber. It is also used in dye stuffs, perfumes, rayon etc.
- Tannic acid is yellow or light brown powder, is highly soluble in water. It is used for staining wood and dyeing cotton.
- Salicylic acid is used in acne creams to reduce acne. It is also used as food preservatives.
- Citric acid is a natural preservative. It is used in foods and soft drinks. Oxalic acid is used in bleaching and cleansing solutions.
- Acetic acid is used in foods such as 2-3% solution of CH_3COOH in water known as vinegar.

Chemical Reactions

- **Reactions Involving Cleavage of —OH Group**

$R-C(=O)-OH$:
- $\xrightarrow[P_2O_5]{+RCOOH/\Delta} (RCO)_2O$ Anhydride
- $\xrightarrow[-H_2O]{ROH/H^+} RCOOR'$ Ester
- $\xrightarrow{PCl_3 \text{ or } PCl_5 \text{ or } SOCl_2 \text{ in pyridine}} RCOCl$ Acid chloride
- $\xrightarrow[-H_2O_2]{NH_3,\Delta} RCONH_2$ Amide

- **Reactions Involving Proton of —OH Group**

$R-C(=O)-OH$:
- $\xrightarrow{Na} 2RCOONa + H_2$
- $\xrightarrow{NaHCO_3} 2RCOONa + CO_2 + H_2O$

- **Reaction Involving >C=O Group**

$$R-C(=O)-OH \xrightarrow[\text{(ii) } H_3O^+ \text{(Reduction)}]{\text{(i) } LiAlH_4/\text{ether or } B_2H_6} RCH_2OH$$

$$R-COONa \xrightarrow[\Delta]{\text{NaOH and CaO}} R-H + Na_2CO_3$$

- **Substitution Reaction in Hydrocarbon Part**

$$RCH_2COOH \xrightarrow{\text{(i) } X_2/\text{Red phosphorus}} R-CH(X)-COOH$$

$$C_6H_5COOH \xrightarrow{\text{Conc. } HNO_3 + \text{Conc. } H_2SO_4} m\text{-}NO_2C_6H_4COOH$$

$$C_6H_5COOH \xrightarrow{Br_2/FeBr_3} m\text{-}BrC_6H_4COOH$$ (*m*-bromobenzoic acid)

Important Points Regarding Chemical Reactions

- Benzoic acids are *meta*-directing in nature as they remove electrons through resonance.
- The *meta* carbons are more e⁻-dense, hence more attractive to an attacking electrophile.

No positive charge on *meta* carbons

- Due to the *meta*-directing nature, benzoic acids do not undergo Friedal Craft alkylation or Friedal-Craft acylation reactions.

Test 1

Syllabus

- **Aliphatic Amines**: Nomenclature, Classification, Structure, Basic Character, General Methods of Preparation, Properties, Reactions and Uses.

NCERT Page 259 to 266, Page 268

For deeper insight **Scan the QR Code**

Introduction

Aliphatic amines are derived by replacing one or more H-atom(s) of NH_3 by alkyl group(s).

Classification

- Aliphatic amines are classified as primary, secondary and tertiary depending upon the number of hydrogen atoms replaced by alkyl groups in ammonia molecule.

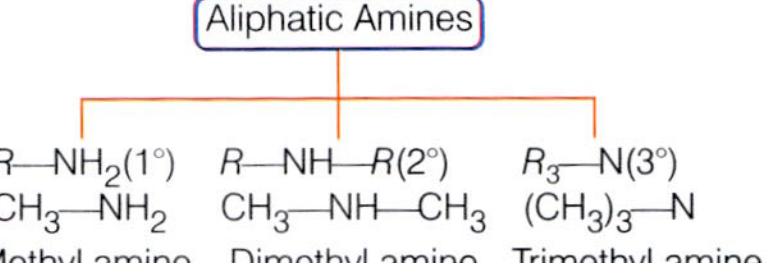

- Amines are said to be simple when all the alkyl or aryl groups are same and mixed when they are different.

Structure

- The nitrogen atom in amines is sp^3-hybridised. The three alkyl groups are at the corners of a tetrahedron and their shape is trigonal pyramidal.
- Each of the three sp^3-hybridised orbitals of nitrogen overlap with orbitals of hydrogen or carbon depending upon the composition of the amines.
- The bond angle becomes lesser than 109.5° due to the bond pair-lone pair repulsion.

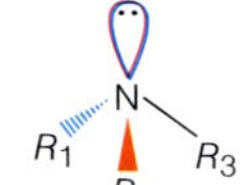

Pyramidal shape

Nomenclature

- In common system, aliphatic amines are named as **alkylamines** as one word.
- In systematic IUPAC nomenclature, they are named as alkanamines by adding the suffix "amine" to the name of the chain to which NH_2 group is attached with replacement of the final '–e'.
- In case, more than one amino group is present at different positions in the parent chains, their positions are specified by giving numbers to the carbon atoms bearing —NH_2 groups and suitable prefix such as di, tri etc., is attached to the amine. To name 2° and 3° amines. Locant N is used to designate substituent attached to N-atom.

Preparation of Primary Amines

Primary Amines

- $RCN \xrightarrow{H_2/Ni \text{ or } Na(Hg)/C_2H_5OH}$ Primary amines **[Reduction]**
- $RNO_2 \xrightarrow{Sn/HCl \text{ or } Fe+HCl}$ Primary amines **[Reduction]**
- $RCONH_2 \xrightarrow{\text{(i) } LiAlH_4 \text{ (ii) } H_2O}$ Primary amines **[Reduction]**
- Phthalimide $\xrightarrow{\text{(i) KOH (ii) } RX \text{ (iii) } H_2O/OH^-}$ Primary amines [Gabriel phthalimide reaction]
- $RCONH_2 \xrightarrow{Br_2,\ NaOH\,(aq)}$ Primary amines **[Hofmann Bromamide degradation reaction]**
- $R\text{—}N{\equiv}C \xrightarrow{H_2O,\ H^+}$ Primary amines **[Hydrolysis]**
- $R\text{—}CO\text{—}H \xrightarrow{\text{(i) } NH_3 \text{ (ii) } H_2/Ni}$ Primary amines

[Reductive amination of carbonyl compounds]

Preparation of Secondary Amines

- Primary amines + RX (excess)

$$\longrightarrow RNH_2 + RX \xrightarrow[\Delta]{NaOH} R_2NH$$

- Reduction
  - (i) of isonitriles

$$R\text{—}N{\equiv}C \xrightarrow{H_2/Pt} RNHCH_3$$

  - (ii) of N-substituted amides

$$RCONHR' \xrightarrow{LiAlH_4} RCH_2\text{—}NH\text{—}R'$$

- Reductive amination of carbonyl compounds

$$RCHO \xrightarrow[-H_2O]{R'NH_2} [R\text{—}CH{=}NR'] \xrightarrow{H_2/Ni} \underset{2^\circ \text{ amine}}{RCH_2\text{—}NH\text{—}R'}$$

Preparation of Tertiary Amines

$$3RX + \text{Alc.}NH_3 \xrightarrow{\Delta} R_3N^+HX^- \xrightarrow{NaOH} R_3N + NaX$$

$$RCONR'_2 \xrightarrow[\text{Ether}]{LiAlH_4} \underset{3^\circ \text{ amine}}{RCH_2\text{—}NR'\text{—}R'}$$

Physical Properties

- **Boiling point** Amines are more polar than alkanes but less polar than alcohols.
- Lower amines are gases or low-boiling liquids, with a characteristic ammonia like smell.
- Their boiling point are higher in comparison to non-polar compounds of same molecular weight due to intermolecular H-bonding.
- However, tertiary amines are exceptions of this due to absence of H-bonding.
- These are miscible with water due to inter-molecular H-bonding with H_2O molecules also.

Preparation of Mixture of Amines

- Hofmann's Ammonolysis Method

$$\longrightarrow RI \text{ (excess)} \xrightarrow[-HI]{NH_3/\Delta} 1^\circ + 2^\circ + 3^\circ + \text{Quaternary amine}$$

- Reaction of Alcohols with Ammonia ROH (Excess)

$$+ NH_3 \xrightarrow[\Delta]{Al_2O_3} 1^\circ + 2^\circ + 3^\circ + \text{Quaternary amine}$$

- Leukart Reaction

$$RCOMe + HCOONH_4 \xrightarrow{\Delta} RCH(NH_2)Me + H_2O + CO_2\uparrow$$

Chemical Properties of Aliphatic Amines

- Oxidation with $KMnO_4$
  - 1° → $RCHO$ or $R_2C{=}O$
  - 2° → $R_2N\text{—}NR_2$
  - 3° → No effect
- Oxidation with H_2SO_5
  - 1° → Aldoxime or Ketoxime or nitroso alkane
  - 2° → R_2NOH
  - 3° → R_3NO
- With carbonyl compounds
  - 1° → Schiff's base
  - 2° → Enamines
  - 3° → No reaction

Basicity of Aliphatic Amines

- Basic nature of amines depends upon the ease of formation of the cation by accepting a proton from the acid.
- These are stronger bases than water but weaker bases than —OH^-, —OCH_3^- and —CH_3^-

$$R\text{—}\ddot{N}H_2 + H\text{—}OH \rightleftharpoons \underset{\text{Ammonium ion}}{R\text{—}\overset{+}{N}H_3} + OH^-$$

$$K_b = \frac{[R\text{—}\overset{+}{N}H_3][OH]^-}{[R\text{—}NH_2]}$$

$$pK_b = -\log K_b$$

- Larger the K_b, smaller the pK_b, stronger the base.
- Due to electron releasing nature of alkyl group in alkanamines, the 'R' group pushes electrons towards nitrogen. Thus, makes the lone pair more available for sharing with the proton of acid.
- The alkyl groups stabilises the ammonium ion due to $+I$ effect with the increase in alkyl substitution the basic nature increases. Thus, the basic nature of aliphatic amines increases with increase in the number of alkyl groups.
- In gaseous phase the order is

$$\underset{3^\circ}{(CH_3)_3\text{—}N} > \underset{2^\circ}{(CH_3)_2\text{—}NH} > \underset{1^\circ}{CH_3\text{—}NH_2} > NH_3$$

- In aqueous solution the order is

$$\underset{2^\circ}{(CH_3)_2\text{—}NH} > \underset{1^\circ}{CH_3\text{—}NH_2} > \underset{3^\circ}{(CH_3)_3\text{—}N} > NH_3$$

Reactions

- With HNO_2
  - 1° → N_2 gas
  - 2° → Yellow oily liquid
  - 3° → Water soluble salt
- $CHCl_3$/3KOH → Isocyanides
- Mineral acids → Salts
- Aqueous solution → Hydroxide
- Acylation $RCOCl$ or $(RCO)_2O$
  - 1° amine → N-substituted amides
  - 2° amine → N,N-disubstituted amides
  - 3° amine → No reaction (as no replaceable H is seen on N of tertiary amine)
- Grignard's reagent → Alkane
- Hofmann elimination → 3° amine + alkene

Syllabus

- **Aromatic Amines**: Nomenclature, Classification, Basic Character, General Methods of Preparation, Properties, Reactions and Uses. Identification of Primary, Secondary and Tertiary Amines.

NCERT Page 266 to 273

For deeper insight **Scan the QR Code**

Introduction

Aromatic amines are derived by replacing one or more H-atom(s) of NH_3 molecules by aryl group(s).

Classification

Aromatic amines are also classified as 1°, 2° and 3° depending upon the number of hydrogen atoms replaced by aryl groups from ammonia molecule.

Nomenclature

In common system of nomenclature, they are named as derivatives of aniline while in IUPAC system, the names are obtained by replacing the terminal 'e' from the name of the corresponding arene by the suffix 'amine'.

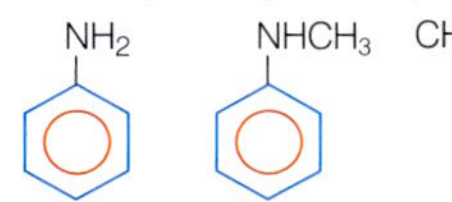

Methods of Preparation

Some of the important methods for the preparation of aniline are given below.

- **Hofmann's Bromamide Degradation Reaction**
  Aromatic amides react with an aqueous solution of KOH and Br_2 to give aromatic primary amine.

$$Ar-\overset{O}{\overset{\|}{C}}-NH_2 \xrightarrow{Br_2 + KOH} Ar-NH_2 + K_2CO_3 + 2KBr + 2H_2O$$

  This reaction involves intramolecular phenyl migration, the rate of which is increased by the presence of electron releasing substituent.

- **Reduction of Nitro Compounds**
  Nitro arenes can be reduced to amines by passing hydrogen gas in the presence of finely divided Ni, Pd or Pt and also by reduction with metals in acidic medium.

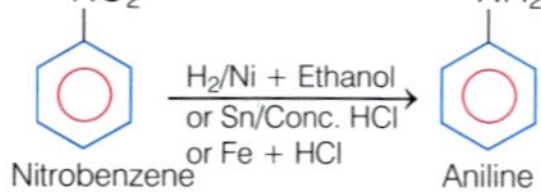

- Reduction with iron scrap and hydrochloric acid is preferred because $FeCl_2$ formed gets hydrolysed to release HCl during the reaction. Thus, only a small amount of HCl is required to initiate the reaction.

Physical Properties

- **Physical state** They are colourless liquids or solids, but due to air oxidation, they turn brown.
- **Solubility** They are slightly soluble or insoluble in water (polar solvent) having larger hydrocarbon part which decreases their ability to form H-bonds with water. But highly soluble in benzene and other organic solvents.
- **Boiling point** They have high boiling point due to intermolecular H-bonding. N,N-dimethyl aniline has lower boiling point due to lack of H-bonding. *para*-substituted aniline, being the most symmetric, has the highest melting point. Thus, *p*-toluidine is solid at room temperature while *o*-and *m*-toluidines are liquids.

Distinguishing Test for Amines

- **Hinsberg Test**
  $C_6H_5SO_2Cl$ + 1° + 2° + 3° amines
  - Clear solution $\xrightarrow{KOH}$ Soluble salt [For 1° amine]
  - ppt. $\xrightarrow{KOH}$ No reaction [For 2° amine]
  - No reaction [For 3° amine]
- **Liebermann's Nitroso Test**
  HONO + 1° + 2° + 3° amines
  - $R-OH + N_2\uparrow + H_2O$ [For 1° amine]
  - $R_2NNO + H_2O$ [For 2° amine]
  - $R_3N^+HNO_2^-$ [Soluble in water](yellow oily liquid)
- **Carbylamine Test** Given by both aliphatic and aromatic amines but secondary and tertiary amines do not show this reaction.
- **Azo Dye Test** Only primary aromatic amines will give orange coloured azo dyes.

Chemical Properties of Aromatic Amines

Aromatic Amines (Mainly Aniline)

- Salt formation, HCl or H_2SO_4 → $Ar\overset{+}{N}H_3Cl^-$
- Alkylation (with RX) → Secondary and tertiary amines
- Acids and acid derivatives → N-arylamide
- With aldehydes → Imines (Schiff's bases)
- Benzoylation → Schotten Baumann Reaction → Benzanilide
- With HNO_2 → Depending upon the degree of aromatic amine taking part benzene diazonium chloride or nitroso compounds.
- Oxidation
  - (i) $K_2Cr_2O_7/H_2SO_4$ → *p*-benzoquinone
  - (ii) CF_3COOOH → Nitrobenzene
  - (iii) H_2SO_5 (Caro's acid) → Nitrosobenzene + Nitrobenzene
- Carbylamine Reaction → phenyl carbylamine
- Hofmann Mustard oil Reaction → N,N′ diphenylthiourea (which gives phenylisothiocyanate with conc. HCl)
- Electrophilic Substitution Reactions → Halogenation, Nitration, Sulphonation

- **Ammonolysis of Aryl Chlorides** Aryl chlorides react with ammonia to form aromatic amines.
  e.g. Chlorobenzene $+ 2NH_3 \xrightarrow[\text{Under pressure}]{CuCl_2/210°C}$ Aniline
- This method can be carried out conveniently under ordinary conditions if a strong electron withdrawing group (e.g. NO_2) is present at *ortho* or *para*-position to —Cl.
  (p-nitrochlorobenzene) $+2NH_3 \xrightarrow[\text{Under pressure}]{CuCl_2/200°C}$ (p-nitroaniline)

- **Reduction of Azo Compounds**
  These azo compounds on catalytic hydrogenation give amines. The equation of complete reaction is given below.

$$Ar-N=N-Ar \xrightarrow[Ni,\ \Delta]{H_2} Ar-\underset{H}{N}-\underset{H}{N}-Ar \xrightarrow[Ni,\ \Delta]{H_2} 2ArNH_2$$

- **Schmidt Reaction**
  Benzoic acid on reduction with hydrogen acid gives aniline as shown below.

$$C_6H_5COOH + N_3H \xrightarrow{\text{Conc. } H_2SO_4} C_6H_5NH_2 + CO_2 + N_2\uparrow$$

Basicity of Aromatic Amines

- Factors that increase the ability of nitrogen atom in an amine to share its electron pair, increases the basicity of amine and *vice-versa*.
- Generally, aromatic amines are less basic than ammonia and aliphatic amines. It is because; in arylamines, the $-NH_2$ group is attached directly to the benzene ring. The unshared electron pair on nitrogen atom is in conjugation with benzene ring and thus making it less available for protonation.
- Also, anilinium ion is less resonance stabilised than aniline.

(resonance stabilised aniline decreases basic character compared to aliphatic amines)

- Greater the number of resonating structures, greater is the stability. Thus, aniline is more stable than anilinium ion.
- Hence, the proton acceptability or the basic nature of aniline or other aromatic amines would be less than that of ammonia.
- **Effect of Substituent Group on Basicity of Aromatic Amines**
- Electron-releasing groups like ($-NH_2$, $-OCH_3$, $-CH_3$) increases the basic nature of aromatic amines.
- Electron-withdrawing groups like ($-NO_2$, $-SO_3H$, $-COOH$, $-X$) decreases the basic nature of aromatic amines.

Uses of Amines

- Amines are the important constituents of proteins, enzymes, many harmones. Thus, these play an important role in human life.
- Lower members of the aliphatic amines such as ethylamine, diethylamine etc., are used as reagents in the synthesis of organic compounds and also as solvents both in the laboratory and industry.
- Quaternary ammonium salts derived from long chain tertiary amines are used as detergents.
- Aniline and other aromatic amines used in the manufacture of dyes and drugs.
- Aniline is used to synthesise diazonium salts which have synthetic importance.

Test 3

Syllabus

- **Diazonium Salts**: General Methods of Preparation, Properties, Reactions and Uses.
- Importance in Synthetic Organic Chemistry.

NCERT Page 274 to 277

For deeper insight **Scan the QR Code**

Chapter 10

Diazonium Salt

- They have the general formula $ArN_2^+X^-$.
- All benzene diazonium salts contain benzene diazonium ion that has following structure.

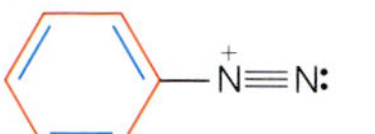

- Primary aromatic amines form arenediazonium salts which are stable for a short time in solution at low temperature (273-278K).
- Presence of electron releasing group like $-NR_2$, $-OR$ at *ortho*/*para* position in the benzene ring stabilises the benzene diazonium ion.
- Aromatic diazonium salts are more stable than aliphatic diazonium salts (RN_2) and the stability is attributed to resonance.

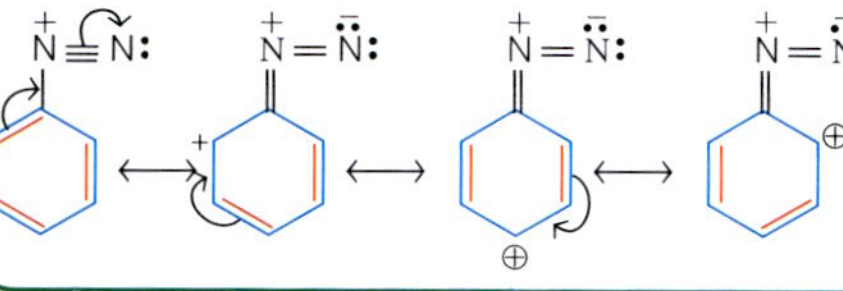

Methods of Preparation

- Diazonium salts can be prepared by diazotisation of aniline. Primary aromatic amines when reacts with HNO_2 forms diazonium salt at low temperature (0-5°C).
- Due to its instability, the diazonium salt is not generally stored and is used immediately after its preparation.

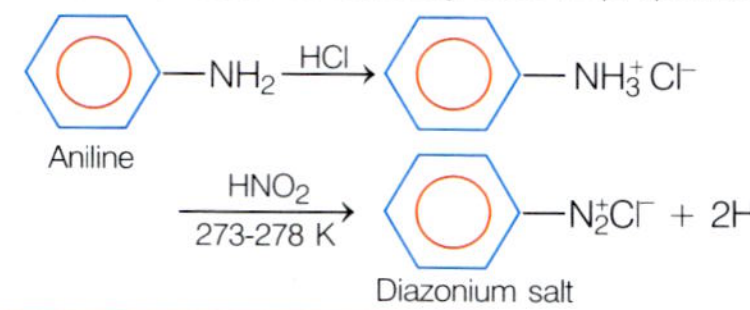

Physical Properties

- Dry diazonium salts are crystalline solids.
- They are water soluble due to their ionic nature.
- In aqueous solution, they are good conductors of electricity.
- Higher boiling points than hydrocarbons of comparable molecular masses due to intermolecular H-bonding.
- Boiling points are lower than those of alcohols and carboxylic acids.
- Order of boiling points of isomeric amines is $1° > 2° > 3°$.

Chemical Reactions

- The reactions of diazonium salts can be broadly divided into following two categories.

I. Reactions Involving Displacement of Nitrogen

II. Reactions *via* Retention of Diazo Group.

Replacement by Halide or Cyanide Ion

- In the presence of Cu(I) ion, the halide (Cl^- and Br^-) cyanide (CN^-) nucleophiles can be introduced in benzene ring. This reaction is called **Sandmeyer reaction**.

$$C_6H_5N_2^+Cl^- \xrightarrow{Cu_2Cl_2,\ HCl} C_6H_5Cl + N_2\uparrow$$

$$C_6H_5N_2^+Cl^- \xrightarrow{Cu_2Br_2,\ HBr} C_6H_5Br + N_2\uparrow$$

$$C_6H_5N_2^+Cl^- \xrightarrow{CuCN,\ HCN} C_6H_5CN + N_2\uparrow$$

- The nucleophiles such as Cl^- or Br^- can also be introduced in the benzene ring by treating the diazonium salt solution with corresponding halogen acid in the presence of copper powder. This reaction is known as **Gattermann reaction**.

$$CH_3C_6H_4N_2^+Br^- \xrightarrow[HBr]{Cu,\ \Delta} CH_3C_6H_4Br + N_2\uparrow + CuBr$$

Bromotoluene

$$CH_3C_6H_4N_2^+Cl^- \xrightarrow[HCl]{Cu,\ \Delta} CH_3C_6H_4Cl + N_2\uparrow + CuCl$$

Chlorotoluene

Replacement by Iodide Ion

- Iodine is not easily introduced into the benzene ring directly but when the diazonium salt solution is treated with potassium iodide, iodobenzene is formed.

$$C_6H_5N_2^+Cl^- + KI \longrightarrow C_6H_5I + KCl + N_2\uparrow$$

Iodobenzene

Replacement by Hydrogen

- Certain mild reducing agents like hypophosphorus acid (phosphinic acid) or ethanol reduce diazonium salts to arenes and themselves get oxidised to phosphorus acid and ethanal, respectively.

$$ArN_2^+Cl^- + H_3PO_2 + H_2O \rightarrow ArH + N_2 + H_3PO_3 + HCl$$

$$ArN_2^+Cl^- + CH_3CH_2OH \rightarrow ArH + N_2 + CH_3CHO + HCl$$

Replacement by Fluoride Ion

- When arenediazonium chloride is treated with fluoroboric acid, arenediazonium fluoroborate is precipitated which on heating decomposes to yield aryl fluoride or fluorobenzene.

$$C_6H_5N_2^+Cl^- + HBF_4 \longrightarrow C_6H_5N_2^+BF_4^- \xrightarrow{\Delta} C_6H_5F + BF_3 + N_2\uparrow$$

Diazonium salt — Fluorobenzene

Replacement by Hydroxyl Group

- If the temperature of the diazonium salt solution is raised to 283 K, then the salt gets hydrolysed to phenol. $ArN_2^+Cl^- + H_2O \rightarrow ArOH + N_2 + HCl$

Replacement by $-NO_2$ Group

- When diazonium fluoroborate is heated with aqueous sodium nitrite solution in the presence of copper then nitrobenzene is formed.

$$C_6H_5N_2^+Cl^- + HBF_4 \longrightarrow C_6H_5N_2^+BF_4^- \xrightarrow[Cu,\ \Delta]{NaNO_2} C_6H_5NO_2 + N_2 + NaBr$$

Fluoroboric acid

Reactions *via* Retention of Diazo Group

- Benzene diazonium salts react with highly reactive electron rich compounds such as phenols and amines to form bright coloured azo compounds which are used as dyes. This reaction is called **coupling reaction**.
- The azo products obtained have an extended conjugate system having both the aromatic rings joined. In general, through the $-N{=}N-$ bond.

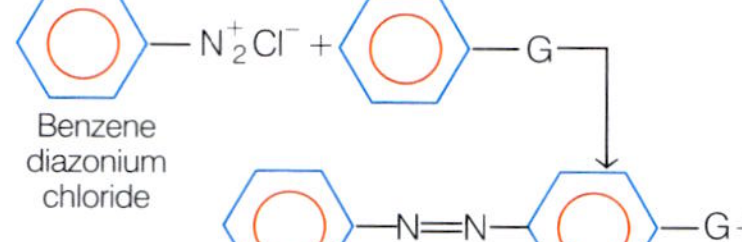

(G is strong electron-releasing group: $-OH, -NR_2, -NHR, -NH_2$ etc.)

Coupling with Phenols

- Coupling with phenols occurs in the basic medium (pH 9-10) at 273-298 K.

$$C_6H_5N^{\oplus}{\equiv}N\,Cl^{\ominus} + C_6H_5OH \xrightarrow[OH^-]{\text{Weakly alkaline}} C_6H_5{-}N{=}N{-}C_6H_4{-}OH$$

Benzene diazonium salt + Phenol → *p*-hydroxyazobenzene (orange dye)

Coupling with Amines

- Coupling with amines occur in the acidic medium (pH 4.5) at 273-298 K.

$$C_6H_5N_2^+Cl^- + C_6H_5NH_2 \xrightarrow[OH^-]{H^+} C_6H_5{-}N{=}N{-}C_6H_4{-}NH_2$$

p-aminoazobenzene (yellow dye)

Important Point Related to Coupling Reactions

- Coupling with benzene substrates occur preferentially at the less sterically hindered *p*-position to the hydroxy or amino group but if this position is blocked, then o-coupling occurs

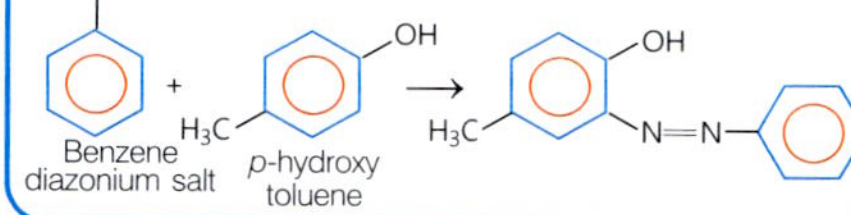

Importance of Diazonium Salts in Synthetic Organic Chemistry

- Diazonium salts are commonly used chemicals in synthetic organic chemistry.
- Diazonium salts are very good intermediates for the introduction of —F, —Cl, —Br, —I, —CN etc. groups into the aromatic ring.
- Now these salts are widely employed in the pigment and dye industries, primarily in producing coloured fabrics.
- It is used in making of azo dye which come in various colours as red, blue, brown and yellow.

Test 1

Syllabus
- General Introduction and Importance of Carbohydrates
- **Carbohydrates** : Classification, Aldoses and Ketoses, Monosaccharides (Glucose and Fructose) and Constituents Monosaccharide of Oligosaccharides (Sucrose, Lactose, Maltose).

NCERT Page 281 to 290

For deeper insight **Scan the QR Code**

Chapter 11

Introduction

A living system is composed of non-living atoms and molecules but has ability to grow, sustain and reproduce itself. Living systems are made up of a number of complex organic compounds called biomolecules like carbohydrates, proteins, nucleic acids etc.

Carbohydrates

- Saccharides or carbohydrates occur naturally in the animal and plant kingdom. Sugars, starch and cellulose are the best known members of this class.
- Chemical analysis of sugar and other carbohydrates shows that they are composed of only the carbon, hydrogen and oxygen and they appear to be the hydrates of carbon. Their general formula is $C_x(H_2O)_y$.
- All the compounds which fit into this formula may not be classified as carbohydrates. e.g. Acetic acid (CH_3COOH). Similarly, rhamnose ($C_6H_{12}O_5$) is a carbohydrate but does not fit in the formula.
- Chemically, the carbohydrates may be defined as optically active polyhydroxy aldehydes or ketones or the compounds which produce such units on hydrolysis.

Classification of Carbohydrates

Depending upon their behaviour on hydrolysis these are classified into three categories.
(i) Monosaccharides
(ii) Oligosaccharides
(iii) Polysaccharides

On the basis of sweetness in taste carbohydrates are divided into two simple types which are as follows

(i) Sugars
They taste sweet on our tongue. This class includes monosaccharides and disaccharides.

(ii) Non-sugars
They are not sweet in taste and include mainly polysaccharides.

On the basis of reducing activity carbohydrate can be classified as follows

(i) Reducing carbohydrates
They contain free functional group (aldehyde or ketone) and reduce Fehling's solution and Tollen's reagent. These include all the monosaccharides (aldose and ketose).

(ii) Non-reducing carbohydrates
They have bonded functional groups and cannot reduce Fehling's solution or Tollen's reagent. These include oligosaccharides and polysaccharides.

Monosaccharides

- Smallest unit which can not be hydrolysed further to given simpler unit of polyhydroxy aldehyde or ketone.
- Monosaccharides are further classified on the basis of number of carbon atoms and the functional group present in them.
- For example, glucose, fructose, ribose etc.
- If a monosaccharide contains an aldehyde functional group present in them it is called as an aldose and if it contains keto group, it is called as a ketose.

Different Types of Monosaccharides

Carbon atoms	General term	Aldehyde	Ketone
3	Triose	Aldotriose	Ketotriose
4	Tetrose	Aldotetrose	Ketotetrose
5	Pentose	Aldopentose	Ketopentose
6	Hexose	Aldohexose	Ketohexose
7	Heptose	Aldoheptose	Ketoheptose

Glucose

- Its molecular formula is $C_6H_{12}O_6$.

CHO — $(CHOH)_4$ — CH_2OH
Open chain structure

- **Preparation**

(i) Sucrose $\xrightarrow{H_2O/H^+}$ Glucose + Fructose

(ii) Starch or cellulose $\xrightarrow[393K,\ 2\text{-}3\ atm]{H_2O/H^+}$ Glucose

- **Cyclic Structure**

α-D-(+)-glucopyranose   β-D-(+)-glucopyranose

- **Reactions**

Glucose
- HNO_3 → Saccharic acid $\xleftarrow{[O]}$ Gluconic acid
- HI/Δ → n-hexane
- Br_2 water → Gluconic acid (Test for aldehydic group)
- HCN → Cyanohydrin
- NH_2OH → Oxime
- Acetic anhydride → Glucose pentaacetate (confirms presence of five — OH group)

Disaccharides

- Yields two units of monosaccharides on hydrolysis.
- Joined together by glycosidic linkage (— O —).
- **Sucrose**

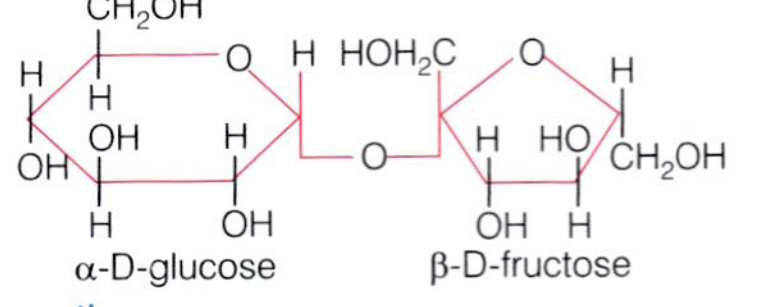

- **Properties**
- It is a non-reducing sugar.
- It is dextrorotatory but after hydrolysis gives dextrorotatory glucose and laevorotatory fructose.
- α-D-glucose + β-D-fructose $\xrightarrow{-H_2O}$ $(C_{12}H_{22}O_{11})$ Sucrose

Fructose

- **Preparation**
- Sucrose $\xrightarrow{H_2O/H^+}$ Glucose + Fructose
- **Cyclic Structure**
- Obtained by addition of — OH at C-5 to >C=O group.
- Five membered ring called furanose exists in two forms.

CH_2OH — C=O — $(CHOH)_3$ — CH_2OH
D-(–)-fructose

α-D(–)-fructofuranose   β-D(–)-fructofuranose

- **Reactions**

Fructose
- Red P/HI → n-hexane
- HCN → Fructose cyanohydrin
- NH_2OH → Fructose oxime
- Tollen's reagent → Gluconic acid
- Br_2 water → No reaction

Polysaccharides

Carbohydrates which yield a large number of monosaccharide units on hydrolysis are called polysaccharides. Some common examples are starch, cellulose, glycogen, gums, etc. Polysaccharides are not sweet in taste, hence they are also called non-sugars.

Maltose

It is composed of two α-D-glucose units in which C1 of one glucose is linked to C4 of another glucose unit.

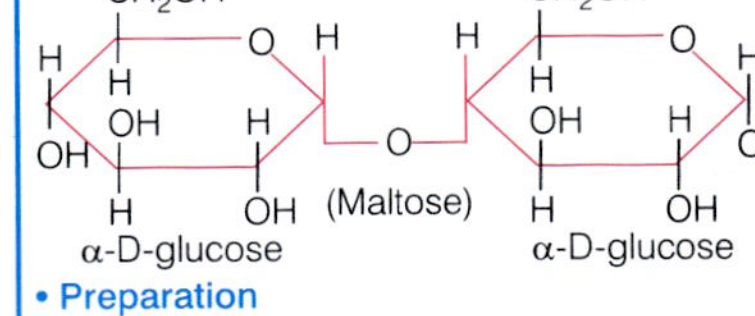

- **Preparation**

Starch $\xrightarrow[Maltase]{H_2O}$ $(C_{12}H_{22}O_{11})$ [Maltose]

- **Properties**
- It is a dimer of α-D-glucose.
- One glucose unit is non-reducing while another is reducing sugar.
- It is a reducing sugar.

- **Reactions**

Maltose
- H_2O/H^+ → D-glucose
- Tollen's reagent → Positive test
- Fehling's solution → Positive test

Lactose

It is composed of β-D-galactose and β-D-glucose.

β-D-galactose   β-D-glucose   (Lactose)

- **Preparation**

β-D-galactose + β-D-glucose ⇌ Lactose (Reducing)

- **Properties**
- Occurs in milk.
- It is a reducing sugar that can undergo mutarotation.

- **Reactions**

Lactose
- H_2O/H^+ or lactose → D-glucose + D-galactose (Equimolar)
- Tollen's reagent → Positive test
- Fehling's solution → Positive test

Importance of Carbohydrates

- They are used as storage molecules as starch in plants and glycogen in animals.
- Cell wall of bacteria and plants is made up of cellulose.
- They provide raw materials for many important industries like textiles, papers, lacquers and breweries.
- They form a major portion of our food.

Test 2

Syllabus

- **Proteins** : Elementary Idea of α-Amino Acids, Peptide Bond, Polypeptides, Primary, Secondary, Tertiary and Quaternary Structure, Denaturation of Proteins, Enzymes.

NCERT Page 290 to 295

For deeper insight **Scan the QR Code**

Chapter 11

Proteins

- These are the most abundant biomolecules that occur in every living organism. Chief sources of proteins are milk, cheese, pulses, peanuts, fish, meat, etc. The word protein is derived from Greek word, "proteios" which means primary. All proteins are polymers of α-amino acids.
- All proteins are made up of several amino acid units linked together into a long chain, through peptide bonds.
- On hydrolysis of protein, it forms smaller units called peptides which on further hydrolysis produce monomer units, which are α-amino acids.

$$\text{Proteins} \xrightarrow{\text{Hydrolysis}} \text{Peptides} \xrightarrow{\text{Hydrolysis}} \alpha\text{-amino acid}$$

Amino Acids

- They contain an acidic carboxyl group (—COOH) and a basic amino group (—NH_2). Depending upon the relative position of these two groups, amino acids are classified as α, β, γ, δ etc.
- Hydrolysis of proteins gives only α-amino acid. In this type, both —COOH and —NH_2 groups are attached to the same carbon atom as represented below.

$$R-\underset{NH_2}{\overset{H}{C}}-\overset{O}{\overset{\|}{C}}OH$$

α-carbon; Carboxyl group; Alkyl chain; Amino group

α-amino acids

Classification of Amino Acids

On the basis of relative number of amino (—NH_2) and carboxyl (—COOH) groups present, amino acids are classified in following three types.

(i) Acidic amino acids They contain more number of carboxylic (—COOH) groups than amino (—NH_2) groups. e.g. Asp, Glu etc.

(ii) Basic amino acids They contain more number of amino (—NH_2) groups than carboxyl (—COOH) groups. e.g. Lys, Arg, His etc.

(iii) Neutral amino acids They contain equal number of amino (—NH_2) groups and carboxyl (—COOH) groups, e.g. Gly, Ala, Val etc.

On the basis of requirement in human diet, amino acids are classified into following two types.

(i) Essential amino acids These are the amino acids that are not synthesised in human body and must be obtained from our diet. e.g. Val, Leu, Lys etc.

(ii) Non-essential amino acids These are the amino acids that can be synthesised in our body and hence are not essentially required in our diet, e.g. Gly, Ala, Ser etc.

Types of Proteins

Proteins are classified into two types on the basis of their molecular shape.

(i) Fibrous proteins These are elongated thread like molecules held together by hydrogen and disulphide bonds. These proteins are insoluble in water (due to hydrophobic part) and are highly resistant to digestive enzymes. They form protective covering of body. e.g. Keratin, myosin etc.

(ii) Globular proteins These are spherical in shape, having highly coiled chains and are soluble in water. e.g. Myoglobin, albumin, enzymes, antibodies.

If a protein on hydrolysis give a non-protein portion (prosthetic group) it is called **conjugated protein**. e.g. Nucleoproteins (nucleic acid + protein), phosphoproteins (phosphate group+protein).

If a smaller is formed by partial hydrolysis of larger protein with acid, alkalies or enzymes, it is called **derived protein**. e.g. Protease, peptones etc.

Peptide Bond

- Amino acids may be joined together by an amide linkage called as peptide linkage ($-\overset{O}{\overset{\|}{C}}NH-$) or **peptide bond**.
- Each amino acid unit in a peptide is called a **residue**.
- In this linkage, an amino group from one residue forms an amide bond with the carboxyl of a second residue; the amino group of the second, forms an amide bond with the carboxyl of a third, and so on.

$$H_2N-\underset{H}{\overset{R}{C}}-CO\boxed{OH+H}-\underset{H}{N}-\underset{H}{\overset{R}{C}}-COOH$$

$$\downarrow$$

$$H_2N-\underset{H}{\overset{R}{C}}-\overset{O}{\overset{\|}{C}}-\boxed{\overset{H}{N}-\overset{R}{C}}-COOH$$

Peptide bond

Dipeptide molecule

- The molecule derived from two amino acids containing a single peptide linkage is called a **dipeptide**.
- Peptide derived from three amino acids is called **tripeptide**.
- While peptides having more than 10 amino acid residues are called **polypeptides**.

Structure of Proteins

On the basis of different configuration or conformations, there are mainly four types of structure of protein. These are as follows

(i) Primary Structure

It refers to the number and linear sequence of amino acids held together by peptide bonds.

(ii) Secondary Structure

They are found to exist in two different types of structures, i.e. α-helix and β-pleated sheet structure.

– **α-helix**

Twisting of chain due to H- bonds between all NH_2 and COOH groups.

– **β-pleated Sheet**

Polypeptide chains stretched and laid side by side. Held together by intermolecular H-bonds.

(iii) Tertiary Structure

– Represents overall folding of secondary structure of proteins.

– The main forces which stabilise the 2° and 3° structures of proteins are hydrogen bonds, disulphide linkages, van der Waals' and electrostatic force of attraction.

(a) Hydrogen bond Present between oxygen atom of —COOH group of one amino acid and hydrogen atom of —NH_2 group of another amino acid. e.g. All types of protein.

(b) Electrostatic bond Present between —COO^- group of one amino acid and —NH_3^+ of another amino acid, e.g. aspartic acid, glutamic acid.

(c) Disulphide bond Formed between the —SH group of sulphur containing amino acid. e.g. Cysteine and methionine.

(d) Hydrophobic bond No true bond formed between hydrophobic alkyl chains of amino acids. e.g. All types of protein.

(iv) Quaternary Structure

Denaturation of Proteins

- When a protein in its native form, is subjected to physical change like change in temperature or chemical change like change in pH, the hydrogen bonds are disturbed.
- The loss in biological activity of proteins due to unfolding of globules and uncoiling of helix is called **denaturation of proteins**.
- During the denaturation, primary structure remains intact but secondary and tertiary structures are destroyed.
- e.g. The coagulation of egg white on boiling, curdling of milk caused by bacteria due to formation of lactic acid etc.

Important Test Related to Proteins

Proteins can be easily characterised by colour reactions. Their presence can be detected by the following tests.

(i) Ninhydrin test Protein when treated with a pyridine solution of ninhydrin, it result in formation of intense purple coloured complex.

(ii) Biuret test When an alkaline solution of proteins is treated with a drop of aqueous copper sulphate, it gives reddish-violet colour indicating the presence of peptide linkage.

(iii) Nitroprusside test When sodium nitroprusside is added to proteins containing —SH group, a violet colour is observed.

(iv) Millon's test Protein with Millon's reagent gives white precipitate that on heating gives red precipitate.

Enzymes

- **Properties**
  - Are biological catalysts that catalyse biochemical reactions.
  - Generally are globular proteins.
  - Increases rate of reactions.
  - Are highly substrate specific.
- **Mechanism**
  - Reduces the activation energy of reaction.
  - Mechanism is known as lock and key model.

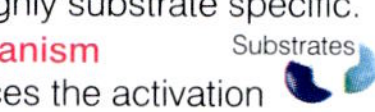
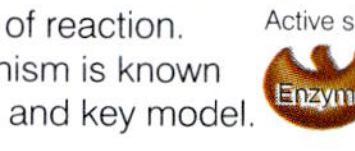
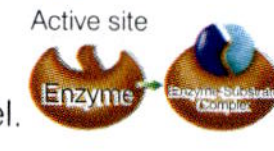

Classification of Enzymes

S. No.	Main class	Some subclasses	Types of reaction catalysed
1.	Hydrolases	Lipases	Hydrolysis of an ester group
		Nucleases	Hydrolysis of a phosphate group
		Proteases	Hydrolysis of an amide group
2.	Isomerases	Epimerases	Isomerisation of stereogenic centre
3.	Ligases	Carboxylases	Addition of CO_2
		Synthetases	Formation of new bond
4.	Lyases	Decarboxylases Dehydrases	Loss of CO_2 Loss of H_2O
5.	Oxidoreductases	Dehydrogenases	Introduction of double bond by removal of H_2
		Oxidases	Oxidation
		Reductases	Reduction
6.	Transferases	Kinases	Transfer of a phosphate group
		Transaminases	Transfer of an amino group

Test 3

Syllabus
- **Vitamins :** Classification and Functions
- **Nucleic Acids :** Chemical Constitution of DNA and RNA, Biological Functions of Nucleic Acids, Hormones (General Introduction).

NCERT Page 295 to 301

For deeper insight **Scan the QR Code**

Chapter 11

Vitamins

- These are the organic molecules which function in trace amounts in the body. They are required for the proper functioning of the cell, normal growth and reproduction and their absence causes specific deficiency diseases. Plants can synthesise all vitamins whereas only a few are synthesised in animals.
- These are generally regarded as organic compounds required in the diet in small amounts to perform specific biological functions for normal maintenance of optimum growth and health of the organism. The term "Vitamine" was coined from the word vital + amine.

Physiological Functions

- The daily dose of any vitamin for any individual is not a fixed quantity and varies according to the size, age and rate of metabolism of the individual. A lack of one or more vitamins leads to characteristic deficiency symptoms in human.
- Multiple deficiencies caused by lack of more than one vitamin are common and this condition is known as avitaminosis.

Classification of Vitamins

Depending upon their solubility, all the known vitamins can be classified into following two groups.

(i) Water-soluble vitamins These include vitamins B and C. These vitamins must be supplied regularly in diet because they are regularly excreted through urine and cannot be stored (except vitamin B_{12}) in our body. Fruits and vegetables are a good source of water soluble vitamins. These vitamins are destroyed by prolonged heating (cooking).

(ii) Fat-soluble vitamins These vitamins are soluble in fat and oils but insoluble in water. These include vitamins A, D, E and K. These vitamins are non-polar, hydrophobic (water insoluble), fairly stable and are not destroyed by heat. These are stored in liver and adipose tissues.

Water Soluble Vitamins

Vitamins	Name	Sources	Causes
B_1	Thiamine	Pulses, nuts	Beri-Beri
B_2	Riboflavin	Eggs, Green veggies	Cheilosis
B_6	Pyridoxine	Rice bran, fish	Convulsions
C	Ascorbic acid	Citrus fruits, chillies	Scurvy (bleeding gums)

Fat Soluble Vitamins

Vitamins	Name	Sources	Causes
A	Retinol	Milk, butter	Xerophthalmia (hardening of cornea of eye) Night blindness
D	Ergocalciferol / Cholecalciferol	Milk, fish, liver oil	Rickets and osteomalacia
E	Tocopherol	Wheat germ oil, almonds	Increased fragility of RBCs, Muscle degeneration
K	Phylloquinone	Green leafy vegetables	Haemorrhages (Increased blood clotting time)

Importance of Vitamins

- Many though not all, coenzymes are vitamins, small organic molecules that must be obtained in the diet are required in trace amounts for proper growth.
- Vitamins have diverse biochemical functions. Vitamin A acts as a regulator of cell and tissue growth and differentiation. Vitamin D provides a hormone-like function, regulating mineral metabolism for bones and other organs. The B complex vitamins function as enzyme cofactors (coenzymes) or the precursors for them.

Nucleic Acids

- The nucleus of a living cell is responsible for the transmission of inherent characters also called heredity. The particles in nucleus of the cell, responsible for heredity are called chromosomes which are made up of proteins and another type of biomolecules called nucleic acids.
- The nucleic acids are the chemical carriers of a cell's genetic information. The chemical composition of nucleic acids acts as coded information. This information when expressed, determines the nature of the cell, controls cell growth (and division) and directs biosynthesis of proteins (including enzymes) required for cellular functions.

Nucleic acids are of two types
(i) **DNA**-Deoxyribonucleic acid
(ii) **RNA**-Ribonucleic acid

Structure of Nucleic Acids

- **Primary structure** Nucleotides are joined together by phosphodiester linkages between 5′ and 3′ carbon atom of pentose sugar.
- **Secondary structure** Two strands of polynucleotides coil around each other in the form of double helix.

Chemical Composition of Nucleic Acids

Nucleic acids are bipolymers made up of nucleotides joined together to form a long chain. Hence, these are also called **polynucleotides**. Each nucleotide is composed of an aldopentose sugar linked to a heterocyclic nitrogenous base and further to a phosphate group. Combined form of sugar and base is called **nucleoside** and that of nucleoside and phosphate group is called **nucleotide**.

(i) Pentose sugar The sugar component in RNA is β-D- ribose and the sugar in DNA is β-D-2-deoxyribose.
The prefix -deoxy means that oxygen is missing from the position of ribose.

(ii) Phosphoric acid It is present as a phosphate (PO_4^{3-}) group in the nucleotide. It plays an important role of linking two nucleotides. The linkage is called phosphodiester linkage.

β-D-ribose β-D-2-deoxyribose

(iii) Nitrogenous bases These are the heterocyclic compounds of nitrogen. These are further divided into two groups.

(a) Purines These are bicyclic groups containing N-atoms in each of the cycles.
The examples are adenine (A) and guanine (G)

Adenine (A) Guanine (G)

(b) Pyrimidines These are single cyclic bases. The examples are cytosine (C), thymine (T) and uracil (U).

Cytosine (C) Thymine (T) Uracil (U)

DNA Fingerprinting

- A British geneticist, Alec Jeffreys developed the technique of fingerprinting.
- DNA is the master molecule of all the life forms. It constitute the blueprints of every living organism through which character are passed from one generation to other generation.
- Every living organism differs only due to nucleotide sequences of chromosome. The nucleotides form codes; this coded genetic information can be profiled to produce most authentic identity card of any organism. This identification at genetic level is called DNA fingerprinting or DNA profiling.

Uses

- In forensic laboratories for identification of criminals.
- To determine paternity of an individual.
- To identify the dead bodies in any accident by comparing the DNA's of parents or children.
- To identify racial groups and to rewrite biological evolution.

Har Gobind Khorana shared the Nobel Prize for Medicine and Physiology in 1968 with **Marshall Nirenberg** and **Robert Holley** for cracking the genetic code.

Hormones

Act as intercellular messengers and are governed by endocrine glands.

- **Steroidal Hormones**

(i) Sex Hormones
- Includes androgens (testosterone), estrogens (estrone, estradiol) and progesterone.
- Androgens are generally secreted in testes. Estrogens in ovary and progesterone in corpus luteum.

(ii) Corticoids
e.g. Glucocorticoids, found in adrenal cortex.

- **Peptide Hormones**

(i) Insulin Secreted in pancreas and helpful in blood sugar control.
(ii) Glucagon Secreted in pancreas and increases blood glucose
(iii) Endorphins Secreted in pituitary gland and relieves pain

- **Amino Acid Derived Hormones**

(i) Epinephrine
- Secreted in adrenal medulla.
- Regulates CNS, increases pulse rate.

(ii) Thyroxine Secreted in thyroid gland and controls metabolism.

Test 1

Chapter 12

Syllabus

- The Chemistry Involved in the Titrimetric Exercise-Acids, Bases and Use of Indicators, Oxalic Acids *vs* $KMnO_4$, Mohr's Salt *vs* $KMnO_4$. **Chemical Principles Involved in the Following Experiments:** Enthalpy of Solution of $CuSO_4$. Enthalpy of Neutralisation of Strong Acid and Strong Base. Preparation of Lyophilic and Lyophobic Sols. Kinetic Study of the Reaction of Iodide Ions with Hydrogen Peroxide at Room Temperature.

For deeper insight **Scan the QR Code**

Chemistry Involved in Titration

Titration is a common method of a quantitative chemical analysis. It is used to determine the unknown concentration of a known compound (analyte). It is also called as **volumetric analysis**.

Terminologies Related to Titration

(i) **Titrant** It is a substance (as a reagent solution of precisely known concentration) that is added in titration.

(ii) **Titration volume** During the process of titration, the volume of titrant reacted.

(iii) **Standard solution** It is a solution that contain a precisely known concentration of an element or substance. These are of two types

(a) **Primary standard solution** If concentration of a substance can be known simply by dissolving its known amount in a given volume of solution. Then the solutions formed are primary standard solutions, e.g. oxalic acid, potassium dichromate.

(b) **Secondary standard solution** When concentration of solution can be determined by standardisation against primary standard solution. Such solutions are called secondary standard solution, i.e. H_2SO_4, HNO_3 etc.

(iv) **Equivalence point and End point** It is the volume of added titrant at which the number of moles of titrant is equal to the number of moles of analyte. It indicates the theoretical completion of reaction.

Acid-Base Titration

- Involves reaction between an acid and a base.
- Uses an acid-base indicator for making the end point.
- The analysis can be done by neutralisation method may be grouped in two general classes.
  - Determination of acid or base or their anhydride in a sample by titrating with a standard solution of base or acid.
  - Determination of salts of weak acids or bases by titrating with a standard solution of a strong base or acid.

Acid-Base Indicator

Indicators	pH range	Colour in acid solution	Colour in alkaline solution
Methyl orange	3.1-4.5	Red	Yellow
Methyl red	4.2-6.3	Red	Yellow
Phenol red	6.4-8.2	Yellow	Red
Phenolphthalein	8.0-9.8	Colourless	Pink

Redox Titration

- Based on reduction-oxidation.
- Titrants used are $K_2Cr_2O_7$.
- Titrant acts as self-indicator. e.g. Oxalic acid *versus* $KMnO_4$. Mn reduces itself from +7 to +2 in MnO_4 acidic medium. Colour change from colourless to pink marks the end point.

$$\text{Equivalent weight} = \frac{\text{molecular weight}}{\text{total change in ON}} = \frac{\text{molecular weight}}{\text{number of electrons gained or lost}}$$

Titration of Oxalic Acid *vs* $KMnO_4$

- It is a redox titration in which the concentration of oxalic acid (reducing agent) is determined by titrating it with a standard solution of an oxidising agent, $KMnO_4$.
- Such reactions are accompanied by the change in valency of ions. In these titrations, oxidation and reduction takes place simultaneously, while one substance is being oxidised, the other one is being reduced.

$$\underset{\text{Oxidising agent}}{2KMnO_4} + 3H_2SO_4 \longrightarrow K_2SO_4 + 2MnSO_4 + 3H_2O + 5[O]; \left(E_{KMnO_4} = \frac{M}{5}\right)$$

$$\underset{\text{Reducing agent}}{5\begin{vmatrix}COOH\\COOH\end{vmatrix}} + 5[O] \rightarrow 5H_2O + 10CO_2\uparrow; \left(E_{H_2C_2O_4} = \frac{M}{2}\right)$$

- $KMnO_4$ acts as a self indicator for end point detection. This titration is carried out in the presence of HCl or H_2SO_4 but not in the presence of conc. HNO_3 because it is a strong oxidising agent and hence, interfere with oxidising action of $KMnO_4$. In $KMnO_4$ *versus* oxalic acid titration, the oxalic acid solution is heated with dil. H_2SO_4 up to 70-80°C.

Titration of Mohr's Salt *vs* $KMnO_4$

- The titration of Mohr's salt $(FeSO_4 \cdot (NH_4)_2SO_4 \cdot 6H_2O)_n$ *versus* $KMnO_4$ (acts as an oxidising agent) is also a redox titration.
- In this titration, the active constituent of ferrous ammonium sulphate (Mohr's salt) is ferrous sulphate, which is oxidised to ferric sulphate by acidified potassium permanganate as follows

$$2KMnO_4 + 3H_2SO_4 \longrightarrow K_2SO_4 + 2MnSO_4 + 3H_2O + 5[O]; \left(E_{KMnO_4} = \frac{M}{5}\right)$$

$$[2FeSO_4 + H_2SO_4 + [O] \longrightarrow Fe_2(SO_4)_3 + H_2O] \times 5$$

$$2KMnO_4 + 8H_2SO_4 + 10FeSO_4 \longrightarrow K_2SO_4 + 2MnSO_4 + 5Fe_2(SO_4)_3 + 8H_2O \quad \left(E_{FeSO_4} = \frac{M}{1}\right)$$

$KMnO_4$ acts as self indicator for end point detection. This titration is carried out at room temperature because Mohr's salt is oxidised by air on heating. Sulphuric acid should be present in excess otherwise a brown precipitate due to the formation of MnO_2 will be formed.

- **Back Titration**

It is sometimes necessary to add an excess of the standard titrant and then, determine the excess amount by back titration with a second titrant. Back titrations are useful in case of precipitation reactions or when the reaction between the analyte and titrant is very slow or when the analyte is insoluble solid.

Chemical Principles Involved in Experiments

- **Enthalpy of Solution of $CuSO_4$**
- **Principle** The enthalpy of solution of $CuSO_4$ can be determined by dissolving a known amount of salt in a measured volume of water in a calorimeter. The rise of fall in temperature is recorded as ΔH. It can be calculated as

$$\Delta H = \frac{(W - w) \times \Delta T \times M}{m}$$

where, W = water equivalent of calorimeter
w = mass of water taken
M = molar mass of solute
m = mass of solute, $\Delta T = T_{final} - T_{initial}$

- The dissolution of solute in a solvent is exothermic or endothermic depending upon the nature of solute. If heat is absorbed, enthalpy change comes with **positive sign** and if heat is evolved, enthalpy change comes with negative sign

$$\Delta H_{solution} = \Delta H_{ionisation} + \Delta H_{hydration}$$

- **Preparation of Lyophilic and Lyophobic Sols**
- **Principle** The main concern in the preparation of colloidal solutions is that the dispersed particles must be within the size range of 1mμ–300mμ. Lyophilic sols are easily prepared as colloidal materials like starch, gelatin, acacia etc., when added to water, they swell up and spontaneously break into particulates of matter of colloidal range. However, lyophobic sols, need special techniques of preparation. There are basically two methods.

(i) **Dispersion method** Coarser of aggregates are break down into particles of colloidal size.

(ii) **Condensation method** Molecules are grouped into layer aggregates of colloidal size.

- **Enthalpy of Neutralisation of Strong Acid and Strong Base**
- **Principle** Basically, enthalpy or heat of neutralisation is the amount of heat liberated when 1 g equivalent of a base is neutralised completely by acid. In case of strong acid and strong base, the heat released is maximum and its value is 13.7 kcal. e.g. in case of NaOH (strong base) and HCl (strong acid). It can be represented as follows

$$HCl + NaOH \longrightarrow H_2O + 13.7 \text{ kcal}$$

As both of these are strong, they get dissociated completely and the reaction is precisely.

$$H^+ + OH^- \longrightarrow H_2O + 13.7 \text{ kcal}$$

- **Kinetic Study of Reaction of Iodide Ions with Hydrogen Peroxide at Room Temperature**
- **Principle** The rate of reaction between H_2O_2 and I^- ions can be studied by considering different concentrations of iodide ions. In the presence of an acid, this reaction occurs as follows $2H_3O^+ + 2I^- + H_2O_2 \longrightarrow 4H_2O + I_2$

$$2I^- + H_2O_2 + 2H^+ \longrightarrow I_2 + 2H_2O$$

To maintain this reaction, a known volume of sodium thiosulphate solution and starch solution is added to the reaction mixture. Iodine liberated here, reacts readily with sodium thiosulphate solution and get reduced to I^- ions. $I_2 + 2S_2O_3^{2-} \longrightarrow S_6O_6^{2-} + 2I^-$

When thiosulphate gets completely consumed, the liberated iodine reacts with starch solution to give blue coloured complex.

I_2 + Starch $\longrightarrow$ Blue coloured complex.

Important Facts of $KMnO_4$ Titrations

- Potassium permanganate acts as a strong oxidising agent in acidic medium.
- Equivalent mass of $KMnO_4$ is 1/5th of its molecular mass in acidic medium.
- It is not a primary standard.
- $KMnO_4$ acts as a self indicator.
- Never use burette having a rubber stop-cock as $KMnO_4$ attacks rubber.
- Read the upper meniscus while taking burette reading as $KMnO_4$ solution is dark in colour.
- Standardise $KMnO_4$ solution by titrating against Mohr's salt or oxalic acid solution.

Test 2

Syllabus

- The Chemistry Involved in the Preparation of Mohr's Salt, Potash Alum.
- Chemical Principles Involved in Qualitative Salt Analysis.
- **Cations :** Pb^{2+}, Cu^{2+}, Al^{3+}, Fe^{3+}, Zn^{2+}, Ni^{2+}, Ca^{2+}, Ba^{2+}, Mg^{2+}, NH_4^+
- **Anions :** CO_3^{2-}, S^{2-}, SO_4^{2-}, NO_3^-, NO_2^-, Cl^-, Br^-, I^- (Insoluble Salts Excluded)

For deeper insight **Scan the QR Code**

Chapter 12

Salt Analysis

Qualitative salt analysis is a method of analytical chemistry that seeks to find the elemental composition of inorganic compounds.

- **Dry Tests** Physical observation e.g. odour, colour, density. Effect of heating, solubility, flame test, charcoal cavity test, borax bead test.
- **Wet Tests** For confirmation of analysis of dry tests. It is used for analysis of acid and basic radicals In the analysis of inorganic salt mixture, first acid radicals are analysed and then basic radicals.

Physical Observation of Salt or Mixture

In physical examination of colour, smell, density etc., of the salt or mixture are observed.

Observation	Inference
A. colour of the subsatnce	
(i) Blue whose aqueous solution is also blue	Hydrated salts of Cu^{2+} (except CO_3^{2-} and Cl^-)
(ii) Colourless substance	Transition metal ions absent (except some salts of Mn^{2+})
(iii) Green whose aqueous solution is also green	Salts of Ni^{2+}
B. Odour of the substance	
(i) Ammonical smell	NH_4^+ salts
(ii) Vinegar like smell	Acetates
(iii) Like smell form rotten eggs	S^{2-} salts

Charcoal Cavity Test

In this test, salt is fused with anhydrous Na_2CO_3. The fusion reactions may be represented as given below :

$$CuCl_2 + Na_2CO_3 \xrightarrow{\Delta} CuCO_3 + 2NaCl$$
$$CuCO_3 \xrightarrow{\Delta} CuO + CO_2\uparrow$$
$$CuO + C \longrightarrow Cu + CO\uparrow$$

The conclusions can be made through the following table

S.No.	Sample bead	Crust	Inference
(i)	Greyish white soft bead which marks paper.	Brown which turns yellow on cooling	Pb^{2+}
(ii)	White-brown bead	Orange which turns yellow on cooling	Bi^{3+}
(iii)	Smell of ammonia	Red	NH_4^+
(iv)	—	Black precipitate	Fe^{3+}, Co^{2+}, Mn^{2+}

Analysis of Acid Radicals

- **Group I Anions**
- Group reagent : Dil. H_2SO_4
- Test for CO_3^{2-}
- $Na_2CO_3 + 2HCl \longrightarrow 2NaCl + H_2O + CO_2\uparrow$
- $Ca(OH)_2 + CO_2 \longrightarrow CaCO_3\downarrow + H_2O$
- Test for NO_2^-
- $2NaNO_2 + H_2SO_4 \longrightarrow Na_2SO_4 + 2HNO_2$
- $3HNO_2 \longrightarrow HNO_3 + 2NO\uparrow + H_2O$
- $2NO + O_2 \longrightarrow \underset{\text{Brown fumes}}{2NO_2\uparrow}$
- $2KI + 2NO_2 \longrightarrow 2KNO_2 + I_2$
- I_2 + Starch ⟶ Blue colour
- Test for S^{2-}
- $Na_2S + H_2SO_4 \longrightarrow \underset{\text{(Rotten egg smell)}}{H_2S} + Na_2SO_4$
- $(CH_3COO)_2Pb + H_2S \longrightarrow \underset{\text{(Black)}}{PbS}\downarrow + 2CH_3COOH$
- **Group II Anions**
- Group reagent: Conc. H_2SO_4
- Test for Cl^-
- $HCl + NH_4OH \longrightarrow \underset{\text{White fumes}}{NH_4Cl}\uparrow + H_2O$
- Chromyl Chloride Test
- $4NaCl + K_2Cr_2O_7 + \underset{\text{(Conc.)}}{3H_2SO_4} \longrightarrow \underset{\text{Chromyl chloride (orange yellow gas)}}{2CrO_2Cl_2} + 2Na_2SO_4 + K_2SO_4 + 3H_2O$

$CrO_2Cl_2 + 4NaOH \rightarrow \underset{\text{(Yellow)}}{Na_2CrO_4} + 2NaCl + 2H_2O$

- Test for Br^-
- $NaBr + AgNO_3 \longrightarrow \underset{\text{(Pale yellow)}}{AgBr}\downarrow + NaNO_3$
- Test for I^-
- $H_2SO_4 + 2HI \longrightarrow \underset{\text{(Violet vapours)}}{I_2}\uparrow + SO_2 + 2H_2O$
- Test for NO_3^-
- $NaNO_3 + \underset{\text{Conc.}}{H_2SO_4} \longrightarrow NaHSO_4 + HNO_3$
- $4HNO_3 \xrightarrow{\Delta} \underset{\text{(Brown)}}{4NO_2}\uparrow + O_2\uparrow + 2H_2O$
- **Group III Anions**
- Test for SO_4^{2-}
- $Na_2SO_4 + BaCl_2 \longrightarrow \underset{\text{White}}{BaSO_4}\downarrow + 2NaCl$
- Lead acetate + $Na_2SO_4 \longrightarrow \underset{\text{White}}{PbSO_4}\downarrow + 2CH_3COO^-Na^+$

Analysis of Basic Radicals

- **Group Zero Cations (NH_4^+)**
- Group reagent : NaOH(dil.)
- $NH_4Cl + NaOH \xrightarrow{\Delta} NH_3(g) + NaCl$
  - NH_3 + NaOH, Nessler's reagent ⟶ Iodide of Milon's base (Brown ppt.)
  - NH_3 + HCl ⟶ NH_4Cl (White fumes)

- **Group I Cations (Pb^{2+})**
- Group reagent : Dil. HCl
- Tests of Pb^{2+}
- $\underset{\text{(Cold O.S)}}{Pb^{2+}} + \underset{\text{From HCl}}{2Cl^-} \longrightarrow \underset{\text{White ppt.}}{PbCl_2}\downarrow$
- $\underset{\text{(Soluble in hot water)}}{PbCl_2} + K_2CrO_4 \longrightarrow \underset{\text{Yellow ppt.}}{PbCrO_4}\downarrow + 2KCl$
- $PbCl_2 + H_2SO_4 \longrightarrow \underset{\text{White ppt.}}{PbSO_4}\downarrow + 2HCl$

- **Group II Cations (Cu^{2+})**
- Group reagent, ⟶ H_2S + Dil. HCl
- Test for Cu^{2+}
- $Cu^{2+} + H_2S \xrightarrow{\text{Dil.HCl}} \underset{\text{Black ppt.}}{CuS}\downarrow$
- $3CuS + 8HNO_3 \longrightarrow \underset{\text{Soluble blue}}{3Cu(NO_3)_2}$
- $Cu(NO_3)_2 + 2CH_3COOH \rightarrow (CH_3COO)_2Cu + 2HNO_3$
  - $(CH_3COO)_2Cu \xrightarrow{K_4Fe(CN)_6} \underset{\text{Chocolate brown ppt.}}{Cu_2[(Fe(CN)_6]}$

- **Group III Cations (Al^{3+}, Fe^{3+})**
- Group reagent : $NH_4OH + NH_4Cl$ Precipitates as hydroxides.
- Test for Al^{3+}
- $Al(OH)_3 + NaOH \xrightarrow{\Delta} NaAlO_2 + 2H_2O$
- $NaAlO_2 + NH_4Cl + H_2O \longrightarrow \underset{\text{White gelatinous}}{Al(OH)_3} + NaCl + NH_3$
- Test for Fe^{3+}
- $Fe(OH)_3 + 3HCl \longrightarrow FeCl_3 + 3H_2O$
- $4FeCl_3 + 3K_4[Fe(CN)_6] \longrightarrow \underset{\text{(Dark blue colour)}}{Fe_4[Fe(CN)_6]_3}$

- **Group IV Cations (Zn^{2+}, Ni^{2+})**
- Group reagent : H_2S in NH_4OH
- Precipitates as sulphides.
- Test for Ni^{2+}
- $3NiS + 6HCl + 2HNO_3 \longrightarrow 3NiCl_2 + 2NO + 3S + H_2O$

$NiCl_2$ + 2DMG ⟶ Dimethylglyoximate complex (Cherry red ppt.)

- Test for Zn^{2+}
- $ZnS + 2HCl \longrightarrow ZnCl_2 + H_2S$
- $ZnCl_2 + 2NaOH \longrightarrow \underset{\text{White}}{Zn(OH)_2}\downarrow + 2NaCl$
- $ZnCl_2 + K_4[Fe(CN)_6] \longrightarrow \underset{\text{Bluish white ppt.}}{Zn_2[Fe(CN)_6]}\downarrow$

- **Group V Cations (Ca^{2+}, Ba^{2+})**
- Group reagent : $(NH_4)_2CO_3 + NH_4OH$
- Test for Ba^{2+}
- $BaCO_3 + 2CH_3COOH \xrightarrow{\Delta} CO_2 + H_2O + (CH_3COO)_2Ba$
  - $(CH_3COO)_2Ba \xrightarrow{K_2CrO_4} 2CH_3COOK + \underset{\text{Yellow ppt.}}{BaCrO_4}$
- Test for Ca^{2+}
- $CaCO_3 + 2CH_3COOH \xrightarrow{\Delta} CO_2 + H_2O + (CH_3COO)_2Ca$
  - $(CH_3COO)_2Ca \xrightarrow{(NH_4)_2C_2O_4} 2CH_3COONH_4 + \underset{\text{White ppt.}}{CaC_2O_4}\downarrow$
  - $CaC_2O_4 \xrightarrow{H^+ \,|\, KMnO_4\text{(Pink)}} 10CO_2 + 5CaCl_2 + \underset{\text{(Colourless)}}{2MnCl_2}$

- **Group VI Cations (Mg^{2+})**
- Group reagent : $NH_4OH + Na_2HPO_4$
- $MgCl_2$ + Group reagent $\xrightarrow[-2NaCl]{\Delta}$ $\underset{\text{White ppt.}}{Mg(NH_4)PO_4}$

Chemistry Involved in Preparation of Inorganic Compounds

- **Mohr's Salt** $(NH_4)_2SO_4 + FeSO_4{\cdot}7H_2O \longrightarrow FeSO_4(NH_4)_2SO_4{\cdot}6H_2O + H_2O$
- Dil. H_2SO_4 is added to prevent hydrolysis of salt.
- To prevent oxidation of Fe^{2+} to Fe^{3+}, water is boiled beforehand.

- **Potash Alum**
- Preparation
- $K_2SO_4 + Al_2(SO_4)_3 + 24H_2O \longrightarrow K_2SO_4 \cdot Al_2(SO_4)_3 \cdot 24H_2O$
- H_2SO_4 is added to prevent hydrolysis.

Test 3

Syllabus

- Detection of Extra Elements (Nitrogen, Sulphur, Halogen) in Organic Compound, Detection of the Following Functional Groups, Hydroxyl (Alcoholic and Phenolic), Carbonyl (Aldehyde and Ketones), Carboxyl and Amino Groups, Organic Compounds : Preparation of Acetanilide, *p*-Nitroacetanilide, Aniline Yellow, Iodoform.

For deeper insight **Scan the QR Code**

Qualitative Analysis of Organic Compounds

The elements present in organic compounds are carbon and hydrogen. In addition to these they may also contain oxygen, nitrogen, sulphur, halogens and phosphorus.

Detection of Nitrogen

Lassaigne's extract is boiled with $FeSO_4$. A few drops of $FeCl_3$ followed by acidification with HCl gives bluish green or Prussian blue colour of ferriferrocyanide.

$2NaCN + FeSO_4 \longrightarrow Na_2SO_4 + Fe(CN)_2 \xrightarrow{4NaCN} Na_4[Fe(CN)_6]$

$12NaCl + Fe_4[(Fe(CN)_6]_3 \cdot xH_2O \xleftarrow{FeCl_3} Na_4[Fe(CN)_6]$

(Prussian blue)

Detection of Halogen

- Lassaigne's extract, acidified with HNO_3 is added with $AgNO_3$ solution. The resultant solution when dissolved in NH_4OH helps in detection of halogen.

$NaX + AgNO_3 \longrightarrow AgX\downarrow + NaNO_3$

$NH_4NO_3 + AgX \longrightarrow [Ag(NH_3)_2] + 2H_2O$

- If $X = Cl^-$ ppt. AgCl is white and is soluble.
- If $X = Br^-$ ppt. AgBr is dull yellow and partially soluble.
- If $X = I^-$ ppt. AgI is yellow and insoluble.

Detection of Sulphur

- Presence of sulphur can de detected using following reagents.

– $Na_2S + (CH_3COO)_2Pb \longrightarrow PbS\downarrow + 2CH_3COO^-Na^+$ (Lead acetate; Black ppt.)

– $Na + C + N + S \longrightarrow NaSCN \xrightarrow[FeCl_3]{With} [Fe(SCN)]^{2+} + 3NaCl$ (Sodium sulphocyanide; Ferric sulphocyanide (Blood red))

Detection of Phosphorus

The solution is boiled with nitric acid and then treated with ammonium molybdate. A yellow colouration or precipitate indicates the presence of phosphorus.

Test for Carbonyl Group

- **Sodium Bisulphite Test** Both aldehydes and ketones give water soluble crystalline bisulphite products.

$\underset{R/H}{\overset{R}{>}}C{=}O + NaHSO_3 \longrightarrow \underset{R/H}{\overset{R}{>}}C\underset{SO_3^-Na^+}{\overset{OH}{<}}$

Crystalline addition product

- **2, 4-DNP Hydrazine Test** Formation of yellow-orange ppt. indicates presence of carbonyl group.

$>C{=}O + H_2NHN{-}C_6H_3(NO_2){-}NO_2 \longrightarrow >C{=}N{\cdot}HN{-}C_6H_3(NO_2){-}NO_2\downarrow + H_2O$

2,4-DNP — Yellow or orange red coloured derivative

Detection of Functional Groups Present in Organic Compound

- Elemental detection shows the presence or absence of different elements. On the basis of the present element, corresponding functional group test is carried out.
- Organic compounds are classified into different classes based on the presence of functional groups.

Test for Alcoholic (— OH) Group

- **Sodium Test** H_2 gas evolves.

$2ROH + 2Na \longrightarrow 2RO^-Na^+ + H_2\uparrow$

- **Ceric Ammonium Nitrate Test**

$ROH + (NH_4)_2Ce(NO_3)_6 \longrightarrow$ Cerium complex + $2NH_4NO_3$ (Red colour)

Distinction Between Alcohols

- **Lucas Test** Lucas reagent : $[ZnCl_2 + HCl]$
- Organic compound + Lucas reagent → Solution
- If turbidity appears in solution immediately-3° alcohol. If turbidity appears after 4-5 min-2° alcohol. If clear solution -1° alcohol.
- **Victor Meyer's Test**
- Only 1° and 2° alcohols give this test.
- $RCH_2OH \xrightarrow{P/I_2} RCH_2I \xrightarrow{AgNO_2} RCH_2NO_2 \xrightarrow{HONO} R{-}\overset{NOH}{\overset{\|}{C}}{-}NO_2$ (1° alcohol)

Blood red colour $\xleftarrow{NaOH}$ Nitrolic acid

Test for Phenolic (— OH) Group

- **Litmus Test**
- Converts blue litmus paper to red.
- Phenols are weak acids.
- Do not give effervescence with Na_2CO_3 solution.
- **Ferric Chloride Test**
- Phenol + Ferric chloride (Few drops) $\longrightarrow [Fe(OPh)_6]^{3-}$ (Violet)
- **Liebermann's Nitroso Test**
- Phenol $\xrightarrow{HNO_2}$ *p*-nitrosophenol $\xrightarrow[H^+]{Phenol}$ Indophenol ion $\xrightarrow{NaOH}$ Indophenol(Blue)

Test for — COOH Group

- **$NaHCO_3$ Test** Gives brisk effervescence

$RCOOH + NaHCO_3 \longrightarrow RCOO^-Na^+ + H_2O + CO_2\uparrow$

- **Ester Test** Compounds containing — COOH group gives fruity smelling esters with alcohols.

$RCOOH + C_2H_5OH \xrightarrow[\Delta]{Conc.\ H_2SO_4} RCOOC_2H_5 + H_2O$ (Fruity smell)

Test for — NH_2 Group

- **Azo-dye Test**
- For confirming presence of primary aromatic amines.
- Aniline $\xrightarrow[0°-10°C]{NaNO_2/HCl}$ Diazonium salt $\xrightarrow{\beta\text{-naphthol}}$ Azo–dye (Red or Orange)
- **Carbylamine Test**
- Formation of a highly toxic isocyanide.
- Only given by primary amines.

$RNH_2 + CHCl_3 + 3KOH \text{ (alc.)} \xrightarrow{-3H_2O} R{-}N \equiv C + 3KCl + 3H_2O$

Test for Ester Group ($R{-}\overset{O}{\overset{\|}{C}}{-}OR$)

Esters react with hydroxyl amine (NH_2OH) to give hydroxamic acid, which complexes with Fe(III) to give a purple or deep red colour.

$R\overset{O}{\overset{\|}{C}}OR' + NH_2OH \longrightarrow R\overset{O}{\overset{\|}{C}}NHOH + R'OH$ (Ester; Hydroxamic acid)

$3R\overset{O}{\overset{\|}{C}}OR' + FeCl_3 \longrightarrow \left[R{-}C{\overset{O}{\underset{NH-O}{<}}}Fe\right] + 3HCl$ (Ferric chloride; Hydroxamic acid Purple or deep red colour)

Test for Amide Group ($-\overset{O}{\overset{\|}{C}}-NH_2$)

Amides are decomposed by alkali solution liberating NH_3 which yields white fumes with HCl.

$(R{-}\overset{O}{\overset{\|}{C}}{-}NH_2) + NaOH \xrightarrow{\Delta} R{-}\overset{O}{\overset{\|}{C}}{-}ONa + NH_3\uparrow$

$NH_3 + HCl \longrightarrow NH_4Cl$ (White fumes)

Distinguishing 1°,2° and 3° Amines

- **Nitrous Acid Test**
- 1° amine $\xrightarrow{HNO_2}$ $N_2\uparrow + ROH + H_2O$
- 2° amine $\xrightarrow{HNO_2}$ $R_2N = NO$ (Oily compound)
- 3° amine $\xrightarrow{HNO_2}$ salt formation (Soluble).
- **Hinsberg Test**
- 1° amine $\xrightarrow{\text{Hinsberg reagent}}$ N–alkylbenzene sulphonamide (Soluble in NaOH)
- 2° amine $\xrightarrow{\text{Hinsberg reagent}}$ N,N–dialkylbenzene sulphonamide (Insoluble in NaOH)

Distinction Between Aldehydes and Ketones

- **Tollen's Test**

$RCHO + 2Ag[NH_3]^+_2OH^- \longrightarrow 2Ag\downarrow + RCOO^-NH_4^+ + 3NH_3\uparrow + H_2O$ (Tollen's reagent; Silver mirror)

- Formation of silver mirror confirms the presence of aldehydic group.
- Only aldehydes give this test
- **Fehling Test**
- Fehling solution is made by mixing Fehling *A* and Fehling *B* and is a blue coloured complex of Cu^{2+}.
- $RCHO + 2CuO \longrightarrow RCOOH + Cu_2O\downarrow$ (Red ppt.)
- Only aliphatic aldehydes give this test
- Benzaldehyde is confirmed by malachite green test. Reducing sugar shows both the tests given above.

Preparation of Organic Compounds

- **Acetanilide** $C_6H_5{-}NHCOCH_3$
- **Preparation**
- Ph — NH_2 + Acetic anhydride ⟶ Acetanilide
- **Properties**
- — $NHCOCH_3$ group is *p*-directing in nature.

- ***p*-nitroacetanilide**
- *p*-nitro derivative of acetanilide
- It is used as an intermediate in production of some dyes
- It is prepared by nitration of acetanilide at low temperature below 10°C.

Acetanilide $\xrightarrow[Conc.\ HNO_3]{Conc.\ H_2SO_4}$ *p*-nitroacetanilide (Major)

- **Iodoform CHI_3**
- Detects carbonyl compounds with α-methyl group.
- $NaOCl + KI \xrightarrow{Oxidation} NaOI + KCl$
- $CH_3COCH_3 \xrightarrow{KOI} Cl_3COCH_3 \xrightarrow{NaOH} CHI_3\downarrow$

- **Aniline Yellow**

$C_6H_5{-}N{=}N{-}C_6H_4{-}NH_2$

- Formed by coupling reaction between diazonium chloride and aniline.
- $Ph{-}NH_2 \xrightarrow{HNO_2} Ph{-}\overset{+}{N}{\equiv}NCl^- \xrightarrow{Aniline}$ Aniline yellow

MEDACE

OMR SHEET

ROLL No.

1	1	1	1	1	1	1	1	1	1
2	2	2	2	2	2	2	2	2	2
3	3	3	3	3	3	3	3	3	3
4	4	4	4	4	4	4	4	4	4
5	5	5	5	5	5	5	5	5	5
6	6	6	6	6	6	6	6	6	6
7	7	7	7	7	7	7	7	7	7
8	8	8	8	8	8	8	8	8	8
9	9	9	9	9	9	9	9	9	9
0	0	0	0	0	0	0	0	0	0

TEST BOOKLET No.

1	1	1	1	1	1	1
2	2	2	2	2	2	2
3	3	3	3	3	3	3
4	4	4	4	4	4	4
5	5	5	5	5	5	5
6	6	6	6	6	6	6
7	7	7	7	7	7	7
8	8	8	8	8	8	8
9	9	9	9	9	9	9
0	0	0	0	0	0	0

TEST BOOKLET Code

Q No.	Response				Q No.	Response			
001	a	b	c	d	051	a	b	c	d
002	a	b	c	d	052	a	b	c	d
003	a	b	c	d	053	a	b	c	d
004	a	b	c	d	054	a	b	c	d
005	a	b	c	d	055	a	b	c	d
006	a	b	c	d	056	a	b	c	d
007	a	b	c	d	057	a	b	c	d
008	a	b	c	d	058	a	b	c	d
009	a	b	c	d	059	a	b	c	d
010	a	b	c	d	060	a	b	c	d
011	a	b	c	d	061	a	b	c	d
012	a	b	c	d	062	a	b	c	d
013	a	b	c	d	063	a	b	c	d
014	a	b	c	d	064	a	b	c	d
015	a	b	c	d	065	a	b	c	d
016	a	b	c	d	066	a	b	c	d
017	a	b	c	d	067	a	b	c	d
018	a	b	c	d	068	a	b	c	d
019	a	b	c	d	069	a	b	c	d
020	a	b	c	d	070	a	b	c	d
021	a	b	c	d	071	a	b	c	d
022	a	b	c	d	072	a	b	c	d
023	a	b	c	d	073	a	b	c	d
024	a	b	c	d	074	a	b	c	d
025	a	b	c	d	075	a	b	c	d
026	a	b	c	d	076	a	b	c	d
027	a	b	c	d	077	a	b	c	d
028	a	b	c	d	078	a	b	c	d
029	a	b	c	d	079	a	b	c	d
030	a	b	c	d	080	a	b	c	d
031	a	b	c	d	081	a	b	c	d
032	a	b	c	d	082	a	b	c	d
033	a	b	c	d	083	a	b	c	d
034	a	b	c	d	084	a	b	c	d
035	a	b	c	d	085	a	b	c	d
036	a	b	c	d	086	a	b	c	d
037	a	b	c	d	087	a	b	c	d
038	a	b	c	d	088	a	b	c	d
039	a	b	c	d	089	a	b	c	d
040	a	b	c	d	090	a	b	c	d
041	a	b	c	d	091	a	b	c	d
042	a	b	c	d	092	a	b	c	d
043	a	b	c	d	093	a	b	c	d
044	a	b	c	d	094	a	b	c	d
045	a	b	c	d	095	a	b	c	d
046	a	b	c	d	096	a	b	c	d
047	a	b	c	d	097	a	b	c	d
048	a	b	c	d	098	a	b	c	d
049	a	b	c	d	099	a	b	c	d
050	a	b	c	d	100	a	b	c	d

DECLARATION BY THE CANDIDATE

I declare that particulars and signature on this OMR Answer sheet are mine and are Name as in Attendance Sheet. I fruther declare that particulars filled in and Signature as well as the circles darkened on this ORIGINALCOPY is same as in OFFICE COPY.

Signature with time (in running handwriting)

CANDIDATE's NAME (in running handwriting)

MOTHER's NAME (in running handwriting)

FATHER's NAME (in running handwriting)

CANDIDATE LEFT HAND IMPRESSION

SIGNATURE OF INVIGILATOR'S WITH TIME

1

2

OMR SHEET

ROLL No.

1	1	1	1	1	1	1	1	1	1
2	2	2	2	2	2	2	2	2	2
3	3	3	3	3	3	3	3	3	3
4	4	4	4	4	4	4	4	4	4
5	5	5	5	5	5	5	5	5	5
6	6	6	6	6	6	6	6	6	6
7	7	7	7	7	7	7	7	7	7
8	8	8	8	8	8	8	8	8	8
9	9	9	9	9	9	9	9	9	9
0	0	0	0	0	0	0	0	0	0

TEST BOOKLET No.

1	1	1	1	1	1	1
2	2	2	2	2	2	2
3	3	3	3	3	3	3
4	4	4	4	4	4	4
5	5	5	5	5	5	5
6	6	6	6	6	6	6
7	7	7	7	7	7	7
8	8	8	8	8	8	8
9	9	9	9	9	9	9
0	0	0	0	0	0	0

TEST BOOKLET Code

Q No.	Response				Q No.	Response			
001	a	b	c	d	051	a	b	c	d
002	a	b	c	d	052	a	b	c	d
003	a	b	c	d	053	a	b	c	d
004	a	b	c	d	054	a	b	c	d
005	a	b	c	d	055	a	b	c	d
006	a	b	c	d	056	a	b	c	d
007	a	b	c	d	057	a	b	c	d
008	a	b	c	d	058	a	b	c	d
009	a	b	c	d	059	a	b	c	d
010	a	b	c	d	060	a	b	c	d
011	a	b	c	d	061	a	b	c	d
012	a	b	c	d	062	a	b	c	d
013	a	b	c	d	063	a	b	c	d
014	a	b	c	d	064	a	b	c	d
015	a	b	c	d	065	a	b	c	d
016	a	b	c	d	066	a	b	c	d
017	a	b	c	d	067	a	b	c	d
018	a	b	c	d	068	a	b	c	d
019	a	b	c	d	069	a	b	c	d
020	a	b	c	d	070	a	b	c	d
021	a	b	c	d	071	a	b	c	d
022	a	b	c	d	072	a	b	c	d
023	a	b	c	d	073	a	b	c	d
024	a	b	c	d	074	a	b	c	d
025	a	b	c	d	075	a	b	c	d
026	a	b	c	d	076	a	b	c	d
027	a	b	c	d	077	a	b	c	d
028	a	b	c	d	078	a	b	c	d
029	a	b	c	d	079	a	b	c	d
030	a	b	c	d	080	a	b	c	d
031	a	b	c	d	081	a	b	c	d
032	a	b	c	d	082	a	b	c	d
033	a	b	c	d	083	a	b	c	d
034	a	b	c	d	084	a	b	c	d
035	a	b	c	d	085	a	b	c	d
036	a	b	c	d	086	a	b	c	d
037	a	b	c	d	087	a	b	c	d
038	a	b	c	d	088	a	b	c	d
039	a	b	c	d	089	a	b	c	d
040	a	b	c	d	090	a	b	c	d
041	a	b	c	d	091	a	b	c	d
042	a	b	c	d	092	a	b	c	d
043	a	b	c	d	093	a	b	c	d
044	a	b	c	d	094	a	b	c	d
045	a	b	c	d	095	a	b	c	d
046	a	b	c	d	096	a	b	c	d
047	a	b	c	d	097	a	b	c	d
048	a	b	c	d	098	a	b	c	d
049	a	b	c	d	099	a	b	c	d
050	a	b	c	d	100	a	b	c	d

DECLARATION BY THE CANDIDATE

I declare that particulars and signature on this OMR Answer sheet are mine and are Name as in Attendance Sheet. I fruther declare that particulars filled in and Signature as well as the circles darkened on this ORIGINALCOPY is same as in OFFICE COPY.

Signature with time (in running handwriting)

CANDIDATE's NAME (in running handwriting)

MOTHER's NAME (in running handwriting)

FATHER's NAME (in running handwriting)

CANDIDATE LEFT HAND IMPRESSION

SIGNATURE OF INVIGILATOR'S WITH TIME

1

2

MEDACE

OMR SHEET

ROLL No.

1	1	1	1	1	1	1	1	1	1
2	2	2	2	2	2	2	2	2	2
3	3	3	3	3	3	3	3	3	3
4	4	4	4	4	4	4	4	4	4
5	5	5	5	5	5	5	5	5	5
6	6	6	6	6	6	6	6	6	6
7	7	7	7	7	7	7	7	7	7
8	8	8	8	8	8	8	8	8	8
9	9	9	9	9	9	9	9	9	9
0	0	0	0	0	0	0	0	0	0

TEST BOOKLET No.

1	1	1	1	1	1	1
2	2	2	2	2	2	2
3	3	3	3	3	3	3
4	4	4	4	4	4	4
5	5	5	5	5	5	5
6	6	6	6	6	6	6
7	7	7	7	7	7	7
8	8	8	8	8	8	8
9	9	9	9	9	9	9
0	0	0	0	0	0	0

TEST BOOKLET Code

Q No.	Response				Q No.	Response			
001	a	b	c	d	051	a	b	c	d
002	a	b	c	d	052	a	b	c	d
003	a	b	c	d	053	a	b	c	d
004	a	b	c	d	054	a	b	c	d
005	a	b	c	d	055	a	b	c	d
006	a	b	c	d	056	a	b	c	d
007	a	b	c	d	057	a	b	c	d
008	a	b	c	d	058	a	b	c	d
009	a	b	c	d	059	a	b	c	d
010	a	b	c	d	060	a	b	c	d
011	a	b	c	d	061	a	b	c	d
012	a	b	c	d	062	a	b	c	d
013	a	b	c	d	063	a	b	c	d
014	a	b	c	d	064	a	b	c	d
015	a	b	c	d	065	a	b	c	d
016	a	b	c	d	066	a	b	c	d
017	a	b	c	d	067	a	b	c	d
018	a	b	c	d	068	a	b	c	d
019	a	b	c	d	069	a	b	c	d
020	a	b	c	d	070	a	b	c	d
021	a	b	c	d	071	a	b	c	d
022	a	b	c	d	072	a	b	c	d
023	a	b	c	d	073	a	b	c	d
024	a	b	c	d	074	a	b	c	d
025	a	b	c	d	075	a	b	c	d
026	a	b	c	d	076	a	b	c	d
027	a	b	c	d	077	a	b	c	d
028	a	b	c	d	078	a	b	c	d
029	a	b	c	d	079	a	b	c	d
030	a	b	c	d	080	a	b	c	d
031	a	b	c	d	081	a	b	c	d
032	a	b	c	d	082	a	b	c	d
033	a	b	c	d	083	a	b	c	d
034	a	b	c	d	084	a	b	c	d
035	a	b	c	d	085	a	b	c	d
036	a	b	c	d	086	a	b	c	d
037	a	b	c	d	087	a	b	c	d
038	a	b	c	d	088	a	b	c	d
039	a	b	c	d	089	a	b	c	d
040	a	b	c	d	090	a	b	c	d
041	a	b	c	d	091	a	b	c	d
042	a	b	c	d	092	a	b	c	d
043	a	b	c	d	093	a	b	c	d
044	a	b	c	d	094	a	b	c	d
045	a	b	c	d	095	a	b	c	d
046	a	b	c	d	096	a	b	c	d
047	a	b	c	d	097	a	b	c	d
048	a	b	c	d	098	a	b	c	d
049	a	b	c	d	099	a	b	c	d
050	a	b	c	d	100	a	b	c	d

DECLARATION BY THE CANDIDATE

I declare that particulars and signature on this OMR Answer sheet are mine and are Name as in Attendance Sheet. I fruther declare that particulars filled in and Signature as well as the circles darkened on this ORIGINALCOPY is same as in OFFICE COPY.

Signature with time (in running handwriting)

CANDIDATE's NAME (in running handwriting)

MOTHER's NAME (in running handwriting)

FATHER's NAME (in running handwriting)

CANDIDATE LEFT HAND IMPRESSION

SIGNATURE OF INVIGILATOR'S WITH TIME

1

2

MEDACE

OMR SHEET

ROLL No.

TEST BOOKLET No.

TEST BOOKLET Code

DECLARATION BY THE CANDIDATE

I declare that particulars and signature on this OMR Answer sheet are mine and are Name as in Attendance Sheet. I fruther declare that particulars filled in and Signature as well as the circles darkened on this ORIGINALCOPY is same as in OFFICE COPY.

Signature with time (in running handwriting)

CANDIDATE's NAME (in running handwriting)

Q No.	Response			
001	a	b	c	d
002	a	b	c	d
003	a	b	c	d
004	a	b	c	d
005	a	b	c	d
006	a	b	c	d
007	a	b	c	d
008	a	b	c	d
009	a	b	c	d
010	a	b	c	d
011	a	b	c	d
012	a	b	c	d
013	a	b	c	d
014	a	b	c	d
015	a	b	c	d
016	a	b	c	d
017	a	b	c	d
018	a	b	c	d
019	a	b	c	d
020	a	b	c	d
021	a	b	c	d
022	a	b	c	d
023	a	b	c	d
024	a	b	c	d
025	a	b	c	d
026	a	b	c	d
027	a	b	c	d
028	a	b	c	d
029	a	b	c	d
030	a	b	c	d
031	a	b	c	d
032	a	b	c	d
033	a	b	c	d
034	a	b	c	d
035	a	b	c	d
036	a	b	c	d
037	a	b	c	d
038	a	b	c	d
039	a	b	c	d
040	a	b	c	d
041	a	b	c	d
042	a	b	c	d
043	a	b	c	d
044	a	b	c	d
045	a	b	c	d
046	a	b	c	d
047	a	b	c	d
048	a	b	c	d
049	a	b	c	d
050	a	b	c	d

Q No.	Response			
051	a	b	c	d
052	a	b	c	d
053	a	b	c	d
054	a	b	c	d
055	a	b	c	d
056	a	b	c	d
057	a	b	c	d
058	a	b	c	d
059	a	b	c	d
060	a	b	c	d
061	a	b	c	d
062	a	b	c	d
063	a	b	c	d
064	a	b	c	d
065	a	b	c	d
066	a	b	c	d
067	a	b	c	d
068	a	b	c	d
069	a	b	c	d
070	a	b	c	d
071	a	b	c	d
072	a	b	c	d
073	a	b	c	d
074	a	b	c	d
075	a	b	c	d
076	a	b	c	d
077	a	b	c	d
078	a	b	c	d
079	a	b	c	d
080	a	b	c	d
081	a	b	c	d
082	a	b	c	d
083	a	b	c	d
084	a	b	c	d
085	a	b	c	d
086	a	b	c	d
087	a	b	c	d
088	a	b	c	d
089	a	b	c	d
090	a	b	c	d
091	a	b	c	d
092	a	b	c	d
093	a	b	c	d
094	a	b	c	d
095	a	b	c	d
096	a	b	c	d
097	a	b	c	d
098	a	b	c	d
099	a	b	c	d
100	a	b	c	d

MOTHER's NAME (in running handwriting)

FATHER's NAME (in running handwriting)

CANDIDATE LEFT HAND IMPRESSION

SIGNATURE OF INVIGILATOR'S WITH TIME

1

2

OMR SHEET

ROLL No.

1	1	1	1	1	1	1	1	1	1
2	2	2	2	2	2	2	2	2	2
3	3	3	3	3	3	3	3	3	3
4	4	4	4	4	4	4	4	4	4
5	5	5	5	5	5	5	5	5	5
6	6	6	6	6	6	6	6	6	6
7	7	7	7	7	7	7	7	7	7
8	8	8	8	8	8	8	8	8	8
9	9	9	9	9	9	9	9	9	9
0	0	0	0	0	0	0	0	0	0

TEST BOOKLET No.

1	1	1	1	1	1	1
2	2	2	2	2	2	2
3	3	3	3	3	3	3
4	4	4	4	4	4	4
5	5	5	5	5	5	5
6	6	6	6	6	6	6
7	7	7	7	7	7	7
8	8	8	8	8	8	8
9	9	9	9	9	9	9
0	0	0	0	0	0	0

TEST BOOKLET Code

Q No.	Response				Q No.	Response			
001	a	b	c	d	051	a	b	c	d
002	a	b	c	d	052	a	b	c	d
003	a	b	c	d	053	a	b	c	d
004	a	b	c	d	054	a	b	c	d
005	a	b	c	d	055	a	b	c	d
006	a	b	c	d	056	a	b	c	d
007	a	b	c	d	057	a	b	c	d
008	a	b	c	d	058	a	b	c	d
009	a	b	c	d	059	a	b	c	d
010	a	b	c	d	060	a	b	c	d
011	a	b	c	d	061	a	b	c	d
012	a	b	c	d	062	a	b	c	d
013	a	b	c	d	063	a	b	c	d
014	a	b	c	d	064	a	b	c	d
015	a	b	c	d	065	a	b	c	d
016	a	b	c	d	066	a	b	c	d
017	a	b	c	d	067	a	b	c	d
018	a	b	c	d	068	a	b	c	d
019	a	b	c	d	069	a	b	c	d
020	a	b	c	d	070	a	b	c	d
021	a	b	c	d	071	a	b	c	d
022	a	b	c	d	072	a	b	c	d
023	a	b	c	d	073	a	b	c	d
024	a	b	c	d	074	a	b	c	d
025	a	b	c	d	075	a	b	c	d
026	a	b	c	d	076	a	b	c	d
027	a	b	c	d	077	a	b	c	d
028	a	b	c	d	078	a	b	c	d
029	a	b	c	d	079	a	b	c	d
030	a	b	c	d	080	a	b	c	d
031	a	b	c	d	081	a	b	c	d
032	a	b	c	d	082	a	b	c	d
033	a	b	c	d	083	a	b	c	d
034	a	b	c	d	084	a	b	c	d
035	a	b	c	d	085	a	b	c	d
036	a	b	c	d	086	a	b	c	d
037	a	b	c	d	087	a	b	c	d
038	a	b	c	d	088	a	b	c	d
039	a	b	c	d	089	a	b	c	d
040	a	b	c	d	090	a	b	c	d
041	a	b	c	d	091	a	b	c	d
042	a	b	c	d	092	a	b	c	d
043	a	b	c	d	093	a	b	c	d
044	a	b	c	d	094	a	b	c	d
045	a	b	c	d	095	a	b	c	d
046	a	b	c	d	096	a	b	c	d
047	a	b	c	d	097	a	b	c	d
048	a	b	c	d	098	a	b	c	d
049	a	b	c	d	099	a	b	c	d
050	a	b	c	d	100	a	b	c	d

DECLARATION BY THE CANDIDATE

I declare that particulars and signature on this OMR Answer sheet are mine and are Name as in Attendance Sheet. I fruther declare that particulars filled in and Signature as well as the circles darkened on this ORIGINALCOPY is same as in OFFICE COPY.

Signature with time (in running handwriting)

CANDIDATE's NAME (in running handwriting)

MOTHER's NAME (in running handwriting)

FATHER's NAME (in running handwriting)

CANDIDATE LEFT HAND IMPRESSION

SIGNATURE OF INVIGILATOR'S WITH TIME

1

2

MEDACE

OMR SHEET

ROLL No.

1	1	1	1	1	1	1	1	1	1
2	2	2	2	2	2	2	2	2	2
3	3	3	3	3	3	3	3	3	3
4	4	4	4	4	4	4	4	4	4
5	5	5	5	5	5	5	5	5	5
6	6	6	6	6	6	6	6	6	6
7	7	7	7	7	7	7	7	7	7
8	8	8	8	8	8	8	8	8	8
9	9	9	9	9	9	9	9	9	9
0	0	0	0	0	0	0	0	0	0

TEST BOOKLET No.

1	1	1	1	1	1	1
2	2	2	2	2	2	2
3	3	3	3	3	3	3
4	4	4	4	4	4	4
5	5	5	5	5	5	5
6	6	6	6	6	6	6
7	7	7	7	7	7	7
8	8	8	8	8	8	8
9	9	9	9	9	9	9
0	0	0	0	0	0	0

TEST BOOKLET Code

Q No.	Response				Q No.	Response			
001	a	b	c	d	051	a	b	c	d
002	a	b	c	d	052	a	b	c	d
003	a	b	c	d	053	a	b	c	d
004	a	b	c	d	054	a	b	c	d
005	a	b	c	d	055	a	b	c	d
006	a	b	c	d	056	a	b	c	d
007	a	b	c	d	057	a	b	c	d
008	a	b	c	d	058	a	b	c	d
009	a	b	c	d	059	a	b	c	d
010	a	b	c	d	060	a	b	c	d
011	a	b	c	d	061	a	b	c	d
012	a	b	c	d	062	a	b	c	d
013	a	b	c	d	063	a	b	c	d
014	a	b	c	d	064	a	b	c	d
015	a	b	c	d	065	a	b	c	d
016	a	b	c	d	066	a	b	c	d
017	a	b	c	d	067	a	b	c	d
018	a	b	c	d	068	a	b	c	d
019	a	b	c	d	069	a	b	c	d
020	a	b	c	d	070	a	b	c	d
021	a	b	c	d	071	a	b	c	d
022	a	b	c	d	072	a	b	c	d
023	a	b	c	d	073	a	b	c	d
024	a	b	c	d	074	a	b	c	d
025	a	b	c	d	075	a	b	c	d
026	a	b	c	d	076	a	b	c	d
027	a	b	c	d	077	a	b	c	d
028	a	b	c	d	078	a	b	c	d
029	a	b	c	d	079	a	b	c	d
030	a	b	c	d	080	a	b	c	d
031	a	b	c	d	081	a	b	c	d
032	a	b	c	d	082	a	b	c	d
033	a	b	c	d	083	a	b	c	d
034	a	b	c	d	084	a	b	c	d
035	a	b	c	d	085	a	b	c	d
036	a	b	c	d	086	a	b	c	d
037	a	b	c	d	087	a	b	c	d
038	a	b	c	d	088	a	b	c	d
039	a	b	c	d	089	a	b	c	d
040	a	b	c	d	090	a	b	c	d
041	a	b	c	d	091	a	b	c	d
042	a	b	c	d	092	a	b	c	d
043	a	b	c	d	093	a	b	c	d
044	a	b	c	d	094	a	b	c	d
045	a	b	c	d	095	a	b	c	d
046	a	b	c	d	096	a	b	c	d
047	a	b	c	d	097	a	b	c	d
048	a	b	c	d	098	a	b	c	d
049	a	b	c	d	099	a	b	c	d
050	a	b	c	d	100	a	b	c	d

DECLARATION BY THE CANDIDATE

I declare that particulars and signature on this OMR Answer sheet are mine and are Name as in Attendance Sheet. I fruther declare that particulars filled in and Signature as well as the circles darkened on this ORIGINALCOPY is same as in OFFICE COPY.

Signature with time (in running handwriting)

CANDIDATE's NAME (in running handwriting)

MOTHER's NAME (in running handwriting)

FATHER's NAME (in running handwriting)

CANDIDATE LEFT HAND IMPRESSION

SIGNATURE OF INVIGILATOR'S WITH TIME

1

2

MEDACE

OMR SHEET

ROLL No.

1	1	1	1	1	1	1	1	1	1
2	2	2	2	2	2	2	2	2	2
3	3	3	3	3	3	3	3	3	3
4	4	4	4	4	4	4	4	4	4
5	5	5	5	5	5	5	5	5	5
6	6	6	6	6	6	6	6	6	6
7	7	7	7	7	7	7	7	7	7
8	8	8	8	8	8	8	8	8	8
9	9	9	9	9	9	9	9	9	9
0	0	0	0	0	0	0	0	0	0

TEST BOOKLET No.

1	1	1	1	1	1	1
2	2	2	2	2	2	2
3	3	3	3	3	3	3
4	4	4	4	4	4	4
5	5	5	5	5	5	5
6	6	6	6	6	6	6
7	7	7	7	7	7	7
8	8	8	8	8	8	8
9	9	9	9	9	9	9
0	0	0	0	0	0	0

TEST BOOKLET Code

Q No.	Response			
001	a	b	c	d
002	a	b	c	d
003	a	b	c	d
004	a	b	c	d
005	a	b	c	d
006	a	b	c	d
007	a	b	c	d
008	a	b	c	d
009	a	b	c	d
010	a	b	c	d
011	a	b	c	d
012	a	b	c	d
013	a	b	c	d
014	a	b	c	d
015	a	b	c	d
016	a	b	c	d
017	a	b	c	d
018	a	b	c	d
019	a	b	c	d
020	a	b	c	d
021	a	b	c	d
022	a	b	c	d
023	a	b	c	d
024	a	b	c	d
025	a	b	c	d
026	a	b	c	d
027	a	b	c	d
028	a	b	c	d
029	a	b	c	d
030	a	b	c	d
031	a	b	c	d
032	a	b	c	d
033	a	b	c	d
034	a	b	c	d
035	a	b	c	d
036	a	b	c	d
037	a	b	c	d
038	a	b	c	d
039	a	b	c	d
040	a	b	c	d
041	a	b	c	d
042	a	b	c	d
043	a	b	c	d
044	a	b	c	d
045	a	b	c	d
046	a	b	c	d
047	a	b	c	d
048	a	b	c	d
049	a	b	c	d
050	a	b	c	d

Q No.	Response			
051	a	b	c	d
052	a	b	c	d
053	a	b	c	d
054	a	b	c	d
055	a	b	c	d
056	a	b	c	d
057	a	b	c	d
058	a	b	c	d
059	a	b	c	d
060	a	b	c	d
061	a	b	c	d
062	a	b	c	d
063	a	b	c	d
064	a	b	c	d
065	a	b	c	d
066	a	b	c	d
067	a	b	c	d
068	a	b	c	d
069	a	b	c	d
070	a	b	c	d
071	a	b	c	d
072	a	b	c	d
073	a	b	c	d
074	a	b	c	d
075	a	b	c	d
076	a	b	c	d
077	a	b	c	d
078	a	b	c	d
079	a	b	c	d
080	a	b	c	d
081	a	b	c	d
082	a	b	c	d
083	a	b	c	d
084	a	b	c	d
085	a	b	c	d
086	a	b	c	d
087	a	b	c	d
088	a	b	c	d
089	a	b	c	d
090	a	b	c	d
091	a	b	c	d
092	a	b	c	d
093	a	b	c	d
094	a	b	c	d
095	a	b	c	d
096	a	b	c	d
097	a	b	c	d
098	a	b	c	d
099	a	b	c	d
100	a	b	c	d

DECLARATION BY THE CANDIDATE

I declare that particulars and signature on this OMR Answer sheet are mine and are Name as in Attendance Sheet. I fruther declare that particulars filled in and Signature as well as the circles darkened on this ORIGINALCOPY is same as in OFFICE COPY.

Signature with time (in running handwriting)

CANDIDATE's NAME (in running handwriting)

MOTHER's NAME (in running handwriting)

FATHER's NAME (in running handwriting)

CANDIDATE LEFT HAND IMPRESSION

SIGNATURE OF INVIGILATOR'S WITH TIME

1

2

MEDACE

OMR SHEET

ROLL No.

1	1	1	1	1	1	1	1	1	1
2	2	2	2	2	2	2	2	2	2
3	3	3	3	3	3	3	3	3	3
4	4	4	4	4	4	4	4	4	4
5	5	5	5	5	5	5	5	5	5
6	6	6	6	6	6	6	6	6	6
7	7	7	7	7	7	7	7	7	7
8	8	8	8	8	8	8	8	8	8
9	9	9	9	9	9	9	9	9	9
0	0	0	0	0	0	0	0	0	0

TEST BOOKLET No.

1	1	1	1	1	1	1
2	2	2	2	2	2	2
3	3	3	3	3	3	3
4	4	4	4	4	4	4
5	5	5	5	5	5	5
6	6	6	6	6	6	6
7	7	7	7	7	7	7
8	8	8	8	8	8	8
9	9	9	9	9	9	9
0	0	0	0	0	0	0

TEST BOOKLET Code

Q No.	Response				Q No.	Response			
001	a	b	c	d	051	a	b	c	d
002	a	b	c	d	052	a	b	c	d
003	a	b	c	d	053	a	b	c	d
004	a	b	c	d	054	a	b	c	d
005	a	b	c	d	055	a	b	c	d
006	a	b	c	d	056	a	b	c	d
007	a	b	c	d	057	a	b	c	d
008	a	b	c	d	058	a	b	c	d
009	a	b	c	d	059	a	b	c	d
010	a	b	c	d	060	a	b	c	d
011	a	b	c	d	061	a	b	c	d
012	a	b	c	d	062	a	b	c	d
013	a	b	c	d	063	a	b	c	d
014	a	b	c	d	064	a	b	c	d
015	a	b	c	d	065	a	b	c	d
016	a	b	c	d	066	a	b	c	d
017	a	b	c	d	067	a	b	c	d
018	a	b	c	d	068	a	b	c	d
019	a	b	c	d	069	a	b	c	d
020	a	b	c	d	070	a	b	c	d
021	a	b	c	d	071	a	b	c	d
022	a	b	c	d	072	a	b	c	d
023	a	b	c	d	073	a	b	c	d
024	a	b	c	d	074	a	b	c	d
025	a	b	c	d	075	a	b	c	d
026	a	b	c	d	076	a	b	c	d
027	a	b	c	d	077	a	b	c	d
028	a	b	c	d	078	a	b	c	d
029	a	b	c	d	079	a	b	c	d
030	a	b	c	d	080	a	b	c	d
031	a	b	c	d	081	a	b	c	d
032	a	b	c	d	082	a	b	c	d
033	a	b	c	d	083	a	b	c	d
034	a	b	c	d	084	a	b	c	d
035	a	b	c	d	085	a	b	c	d
036	a	b	c	d	086	a	b	c	d
037	a	b	c	d	087	a	b	c	d
038	a	b	c	d	088	a	b	c	d
039	a	b	c	d	089	a	b	c	d
040	a	b	c	d	090	a	b	c	d
041	a	b	c	d	091	a	b	c	d
042	a	b	c	d	092	a	b	c	d
043	a	b	c	d	093	a	b	c	d
044	a	b	c	d	094	a	b	c	d
045	a	b	c	d	095	a	b	c	d
046	a	b	c	d	096	a	b	c	d
047	a	b	c	d	097	a	b	c	d
048	a	b	c	d	098	a	b	c	d
049	a	b	c	d	099	a	b	c	d
050	a	b	c	d	100	a	b	c	d

DECLARATION BY THE CANDIDATE

I declare that particulars and signature on this OMR Answer sheet are mine and are Name as in Attendance Sheet. I fruther declare that particulars filled in and Signature as well as the circles darkened on this ORIGINALCOPY is same as in OFFICE COPY.

Signature with time (in running handwriting)

CANDIDATE's NAME (in running handwriting)

MOTHER's NAME (in running handwriting)

FATHER's NAME (in running handwriting)

CANDIDATE LEFT HAND IMPRESSION

SIGNATURE OF INVIGILATOR'S WITH TIME

1

2

MEDACE

OMR SHEET

ROLL No.

1	1	1	1	1	1	1	1	1	1
2	2	2	2	2	2	2	2	2	2
3	3	3	3	3	3	3	3	3	3
4	4	4	4	4	4	4	4	4	4
5	5	5	5	5	5	5	5	5	5
6	6	6	6	6	6	6	6	6	6
7	7	7	7	7	7	7	7	7	7
8	8	8	8	8	8	8	8	8	8
9	9	9	9	9	9	9	9	9	9
0	0	0	0	0	0	0	0	0	0

TEST BOOKLET No.

1	1	1	1	1	1	1
2	2	2	2	2	2	2
3	3	3	3	3	3	3
4	4	4	4	4	4	4
5	5	5	5	5	5	5
6	6	6	6	6	6	6
7	7	7	7	7	7	7
8	8	8	8	8	8	8
9	9	9	9	9	9	9
0	0	0	0	0	0	0

TEST BOOKLET Code

Q No.	Response				Q No.	Response			
001	a	b	c	d	051	a	b	c	d
002	a	b	c	d	052	a	b	c	d
003	a	b	c	d	053	a	b	c	d
004	a	b	c	d	054	a	b	c	d
005	a	b	c	d	055	a	b	c	d
006	a	b	c	d	056	a	b	c	d
007	a	b	c	d	057	a	b	c	d
008	a	b	c	d	058	a	b	c	d
009	a	b	c	d	059	a	b	c	d
010	a	b	c	d	060	a	b	c	d
011	a	b	c	d	061	a	b	c	d
012	a	b	c	d	062	a	b	c	d
013	a	b	c	d	063	a	b	c	d
014	a	b	c	d	064	a	b	c	d
015	a	b	c	d	065	a	b	c	d
016	a	b	c	d	066	a	b	c	d
017	a	b	c	d	067	a	b	c	d
018	a	b	c	d	068	a	b	c	d
019	a	b	c	d	069	a	b	c	d
020	a	b	c	d	070	a	b	c	d
021	a	b	c	d	071	a	b	c	d
022	a	b	c	d	072	a	b	c	d
023	a	b	c	d	073	a	b	c	d
024	a	b	c	d	074	a	b	c	d
025	a	b	c	d	075	a	b	c	d
026	a	b	c	d	076	a	b	c	d
027	a	b	c	d	077	a	b	c	d
028	a	b	c	d	078	a	b	c	d
029	a	b	c	d	079	a	b	c	d
030	a	b	c	d	080	a	b	c	d
031	a	b	c	d	081	a	b	c	d
032	a	b	c	d	082	a	b	c	d
033	a	b	c	d	083	a	b	c	d
034	a	b	c	d	084	a	b	c	d
035	a	b	c	d	085	a	b	c	d
036	a	b	c	d	086	a	b	c	d
037	a	b	c	d	087	a	b	c	d
038	a	b	c	d	088	a	b	c	d
039	a	b	c	d	089	a	b	c	d
040	a	b	c	d	090	a	b	c	d
041	a	b	c	d	091	a	b	c	d
042	a	b	c	d	092	a	b	c	d
043	a	b	c	d	093	a	b	c	d
044	a	b	c	d	094	a	b	c	d
045	a	b	c	d	095	a	b	c	d
046	a	b	c	d	096	a	b	c	d
047	a	b	c	d	097	a	b	c	d
048	a	b	c	d	098	a	b	c	d
049	a	b	c	d	099	a	b	c	d
050	a	b	c	d	100	a	b	c	d

DECLARATION BY THE CANDIDATE

I declare that particulars and signature on this OMR Answer sheet are mine and are Name as in Attendance Sheet. I fruther declare that particulars filled in and Signature as well as the circles darkened on this ORIGINALCOPY is same as in OFFICE COPY.

Signature with time (in running handwriting)

CANDIDATE's NAME (in running handwriting)

MOTHER's NAME (in running handwriting)

FATHER's NAME (in running handwriting)

CANDIDATE LEFT HAND IMPRESSION

SIGNATURE OF INVIGILATOR'S WITH TIME

1

2

OMR SHEET

ROLL No.

1	1	1	1	1	1	1	1	1	1
2	2	2	2	2	2	2	2	2	2
3	3	3	3	3	3	3	3	3	3
4	4	4	4	4	4	4	4	4	4
5	5	5	5	5	5	5	5	5	5
6	6	6	6	6	6	6	6	6	6
7	7	7	7	7	7	7	7	7	7
8	8	8	8	8	8	8	8	8	8
9	9	9	9	9	9	9	9	9	9
0	0	0	0	0	0	0	0	0	0

TEST BOOKLET No.

1	1	1	1	1	1	1
2	2	2	2	2	2	2
3	3	3	3	3	3	3
4	4	4	4	4	4	4
5	5	5	5	5	5	5
6	6	6	6	6	6	6
7	7	7	7	7	7	7
8	8	8	8	8	8	8
9	9	9	9	9	9	9
0	0	0	0	0	0	0

TEST BOOKLET Code

Q No.	Response				Q No.	Response			
001	a	b	c	d	051	a	b	c	d
002	a	b	c	d	052	a	b	c	d
003	a	b	c	d	053	a	b	c	d
004	a	b	c	d	054	a	b	c	d
005	a	b	c	d	055	a	b	c	d
006	a	b	c	d	056	a	b	c	d
007	a	b	c	d	057	a	b	c	d
008	a	b	c	d	058	a	b	c	d
009	a	b	c	d	059	a	b	c	d
010	a	b	c	d	060	a	b	c	d
011	a	b	c	d	061	a	b	c	d
012	a	b	c	d	062	a	b	c	d
013	a	b	c	d	063	a	b	c	d
014	a	b	c	d	064	a	b	c	d
015	a	b	c	d	065	a	b	c	d
016	a	b	c	d	066	a	b	c	d
017	a	b	c	d	067	a	b	c	d
018	a	b	c	d	068	a	b	c	d
019	a	b	c	d	069	a	b	c	d
020	a	b	c	d	070	a	b	c	d
021	a	b	c	d	071	a	b	c	d
022	a	b	c	d	072	a	b	c	d
023	a	b	c	d	073	a	b	c	d
024	a	b	c	d	074	a	b	c	d
025	a	b	c	d	075	a	b	c	d
026	a	b	c	d	076	a	b	c	d
027	a	b	c	d	077	a	b	c	d
028	a	b	c	d	078	a	b	c	d
029	a	b	c	d	079	a	b	c	d
030	a	b	c	d	080	a	b	c	d
031	a	b	c	d	081	a	b	c	d
032	a	b	c	d	082	a	b	c	d
033	a	b	c	d	083	a	b	c	d
034	a	b	c	d	084	a	b	c	d
035	a	b	c	d	085	a	b	c	d
036	a	b	c	d	086	a	b	c	d
037	a	b	c	d	087	a	b	c	d
038	a	b	c	d	088	a	b	c	d
039	a	b	c	d	089	a	b	c	d
040	a	b	c	d	090	a	b	c	d
041	a	b	c	d	091	a	b	c	d
042	a	b	c	d	092	a	b	c	d
043	a	b	c	d	093	a	b	c	d
044	a	b	c	d	094	a	b	c	d
045	a	b	c	d	095	a	b	c	d
046	a	b	c	d	096	a	b	c	d
047	a	b	c	d	097	a	b	c	d
048	a	b	c	d	098	a	b	c	d
049	a	b	c	d	099	a	b	c	d
050	a	b	c	d	100	a	b	c	d

DECLARATION BY THE CANDIDATE

I declare that particulars and signature on this OMR Answer sheet are mine and are Name as in Attendance Sheet. I fruther declare that particulars filled in and Signature as well as the circles darkened on this ORIGINALCOPY is same as in OFFICE COPY.

Signature with time (in running handwriting)

CANDIDATE's NAME (in running handwriting)

MOTHER's NAME (in running handwriting)

FATHER's NAME (in running handwriting)

CANDIDATE LEFT HAND IMPRESSION

SIGNATURE OF INVIGILATOR'S WITH TIME

1

2

OMR SHEET

ROLL No.

1	1	1	1	1	1	1	1	1	1
2	2	2	2	2	2	2	2	2	2
3	3	3	3	3	3	3	3	3	3
4	4	4	4	4	4	4	4	4	4
5	5	5	5	5	5	5	5	5	5
6	6	6	6	6	6	6	6	6	6
7	7	7	7	7	7	7	7	7	7
8	8	8	8	8	8	8	8	8	8
9	9	9	9	9	9	9	9	9	9
0	0	0	0	0	0	0	0	0	0

TEST BOOKLET No.

1	1	1	1	1	1	1
2	2	2	2	2	2	2
3	3	3	3	3	3	3
4	4	4	4	4	4	4
5	5	5	5	5	5	5
6	6	6	6	6	6	6
7	7	7	7	7	7	7
8	8	8	8	8	8	8
9	9	9	9	9	9	9
0	0	0	0	0	0	0

TEST BOOKLET Code

Q No.	Response				Q No.	Response			
001	a	b	c	d	051	a	b	c	d
002	a	b	c	d	052	a	b	c	d
003	a	b	c	d	053	a	b	c	d
004	a	b	c	d	054	a	b	c	d
005	a	b	c	d	055	a	b	c	d
006	a	b	c	d	056	a	b	c	d
007	a	b	c	d	057	a	b	c	d
008	a	b	c	d	058	a	b	c	d
009	a	b	c	d	059	a	b	c	d
010	a	b	c	d	060	a	b	c	d
011	a	b	c	d	061	a	b	c	d
012	a	b	c	d	062	a	b	c	d
013	a	b	c	d	063	a	b	c	d
014	a	b	c	d	064	a	b	c	d
015	a	b	c	d	065	a	b	c	d
016	a	b	c	d	066	a	b	c	d
017	a	b	c	d	067	a	b	c	d
018	a	b	c	d	068	a	b	c	d
019	a	b	c	d	069	a	b	c	d
020	a	b	c	d	070	a	b	c	d
021	a	b	c	d	071	a	b	c	d
022	a	b	c	d	072	a	b	c	d
023	a	b	c	d	073	a	b	c	d
024	a	b	c	d	074	a	b	c	d
025	a	b	c	d	075	a	b	c	d
026	a	b	c	d	076	a	b	c	d
027	a	b	c	d	077	a	b	c	d
028	a	b	c	d	078	a	b	c	d
029	a	b	c	d	079	a	b	c	d
030	a	b	c	d	080	a	b	c	d
031	a	b	c	d	081	a	b	c	d
032	a	b	c	d	082	a	b	c	d
033	a	b	c	d	083	a	b	c	d
034	a	b	c	d	084	a	b	c	d
035	a	b	c	d	085	a	b	c	d
036	a	b	c	d	086	a	b	c	d
037	a	b	c	d	087	a	b	c	d
038	a	b	c	d	088	a	b	c	d
039	a	b	c	d	089	a	b	c	d
040	a	b	c	d	090	a	b	c	d
041	a	b	c	d	091	a	b	c	d
042	a	b	c	d	092	a	b	c	d
043	a	b	c	d	093	a	b	c	d
044	a	b	c	d	094	a	b	c	d
045	a	b	c	d	095	a	b	c	d
046	a	b	c	d	096	a	b	c	d
047	a	b	c	d	097	a	b	c	d
048	a	b	c	d	098	a	b	c	d
049	a	b	c	d	099	a	b	c	d
050	a	b	c	d	100	a	b	c	d

DECLARATION BY THE CANDIDATE

I declare that particulars and signature on this OMR Answer sheet are mine and are Name as in Attendance Sheet. I fruther declare that particulars filled in and Signature as well as the circles darkened on this ORIGINALCOPY is same as in OFFICE COPY.

Signature with time (in running handwriting)

CANDIDATE's NAME (in running handwriting)

MOTHER's NAME (in running handwriting)

FATHER's NAME (in running handwriting)

CANDIDATE LEFT HAND IMPRESSION

SIGNATURE OF INVIGILATOR'S WITH TIME

1

2

MEDACE

OMR SHEET

ROLL No.

1	1	1	1	1	1	1	1	1	1
2	2	2	2	2	2	2	2	2	2
3	3	3	3	3	3	3	3	3	3
4	4	4	4	4	4	4	4	4	4
5	5	5	5	5	5	5	5	5	5
6	6	6	6	6	6	6	6	6	6
7	7	7	7	7	7	7	7	7	7
8	8	8	8	8	8	8	8	8	8
9	9	9	9	9	9	9	9	9	9
0	0	0	0	0	0	0	0	0	0

TEST BOOKLET No.

1	1	1	1	1	1	1
2	2	2	2	2	2	2
3	3	3	3	3	3	3
4	4	4	4	4	4	4
5	5	5	5	5	5	5
6	6	6	6	6	6	6
7	7	7	7	7	7	7
8	8	8	8	8	8	8
9	9	9	9	9	9	9
0	0	0	0	0	0	0

TEST BOOKLET Code

Q No.	Response				Q No.	Response			
001	a	b	c	d	051	a	b	c	d
002	a	b	c	d	052	a	b	c	d
003	a	b	c	d	053	a	b	c	d
004	a	b	c	d	054	a	b	c	d
005	a	b	c	d	055	a	b	c	d
006	a	b	c	d	056	a	b	c	d
007	a	b	c	d	057	a	b	c	d
008	a	b	c	d	058	a	b	c	d
009	a	b	c	d	059	a	b	c	d
010	a	b	c	d	060	a	b	c	d
011	a	b	c	d	061	a	b	c	d
012	a	b	c	d	062	a	b	c	d
013	a	b	c	d	063	a	b	c	d
014	a	b	c	d	064	a	b	c	d
015	a	b	c	d	065	a	b	c	d
016	a	b	c	d	066	a	b	c	d
017	a	b	c	d	067	a	b	c	d
018	a	b	c	d	068	a	b	c	d
019	a	b	c	d	069	a	b	c	d
020	a	b	c	d	070	a	b	c	d
021	a	b	c	d	071	a	b	c	d
022	a	b	c	d	072	a	b	c	d
023	a	b	c	d	073	a	b	c	d
024	a	b	c	d	074	a	b	c	d
025	a	b	c	d	075	a	b	c	d
026	a	b	c	d	076	a	b	c	d
027	a	b	c	d	077	a	b	c	d
028	a	b	c	d	078	a	b	c	d
029	a	b	c	d	079	a	b	c	d
030	a	b	c	d	080	a	b	c	d
031	a	b	c	d	081	a	b	c	d
032	a	b	c	d	082	a	b	c	d
033	a	b	c	d	083	a	b	c	d
034	a	b	c	d	084	a	b	c	d
035	a	b	c	d	085	a	b	c	d
036	a	b	c	d	086	a	b	c	d
037	a	b	c	d	087	a	b	c	d
038	a	b	c	d	088	a	b	c	d
039	a	b	c	d	089	a	b	c	d
040	a	b	c	d	090	a	b	c	d
041	a	b	c	d	091	a	b	c	d
042	a	b	c	d	092	a	b	c	d
043	a	b	c	d	093	a	b	c	d
044	a	b	c	d	094	a	b	c	d
045	a	b	c	d	095	a	b	c	d
046	a	b	c	d	096	a	b	c	d
047	a	b	c	d	097	a	b	c	d
048	a	b	c	d	098	a	b	c	d
049	a	b	c	d	099	a	b	c	d
050	a	b	c	d	100	a	b	c	d

DECLARATION BY THE CANDIDATE

I declare that particulars and signature on this OMR Answer sheet are mine and are Name as in Attendance Sheet. I fruther declare that particulars filled in and Signature as well as the circles darkened on this ORIGINALCOPY is same as in OFFICE COPY.

Signature with time (in running handwriting)

CANDIDATE's NAME (in running handwriting)

MOTHER's NAME (in running handwriting)

FATHER's NAME (in running handwriting)

CANDIDATE LEFT HAND IMPRESSION

SIGNATURE OF INVIGILATOR'S WITH TIME

1

2

OMR SHEET

ROLL No.

1	1	1	1	1	1	1	1	1	1
2	2	2	2	2	2	2	2	2	2
3	3	3	3	3	3	3	3	3	3
4	4	4	4	4	4	4	4	4	4
5	5	5	5	5	5	5	5	5	5
6	6	6	6	6	6	6	6	6	6
7	7	7	7	7	7	7	7	7	7
8	8	8	8	8	8	8	8	8	8
9	9	9	9	9	9	9	9	9	9
0	0	0	0	0	0	0	0	0	0

TEST BOOKLET No.

1	1	1	1	1	1	1
2	2	2	2	2	2	2
3	3	3	3	3	3	3
4	4	4	4	4	4	4
5	5	5	5	5	5	5
6	6	6	6	6	6	6
7	7	7	7	7	7	7
8	8	8	8	8	8	8
9	9	9	9	9	9	9
0	0	0	0	0	0	0

TEST BOOKLET Code

Q No.	Response				Q No.	Response			
001	a	b	c	d	051	a	b	c	d
002	a	b	c	d	052	a	b	c	d
003	a	b	c	d	053	a	b	c	d
004	a	b	c	d	054	a	b	c	d
005	a	b	c	d	055	a	b	c	d
006	a	b	c	d	056	a	b	c	d
007	a	b	c	d	057	a	b	c	d
008	a	b	c	d	058	a	b	c	d
009	a	b	c	d	059	a	b	c	d
010	a	b	c	d	060	a	b	c	d
011	a	b	c	d	061	a	b	c	d
012	a	b	c	d	062	a	b	c	d
013	a	b	c	d	063	a	b	c	d
014	a	b	c	d	064	a	b	c	d
015	a	b	c	d	065	a	b	c	d
016	a	b	c	d	066	a	b	c	d
017	a	b	c	d	067	a	b	c	d
018	a	b	c	d	068	a	b	c	d
019	a	b	c	d	069	a	b	c	d
020	a	b	c	d	070	a	b	c	d
021	a	b	c	d	071	a	b	c	d
022	a	b	c	d	072	a	b	c	d
023	a	b	c	d	073	a	b	c	d
024	a	b	c	d	074	a	b	c	d
025	a	b	c	d	075	a	b	c	d
026	a	b	c	d	076	a	b	c	d
027	a	b	c	d	077	a	b	c	d
028	a	b	c	d	078	a	b	c	d
029	a	b	c	d	079	a	b	c	d
030	a	b	c	d	080	a	b	c	d
031	a	b	c	d	081	a	b	c	d
032	a	b	c	d	082	a	b	c	d
033	a	b	c	d	083	a	b	c	d
034	a	b	c	d	084	a	b	c	d
035	a	b	c	d	085	a	b	c	d
036	a	b	c	d	086	a	b	c	d
037	a	b	c	d	087	a	b	c	d
038	a	b	c	d	088	a	b	c	d
039	a	b	c	d	089	a	b	c	d
040	a	b	c	d	090	a	b	c	d
041	a	b	c	d	091	a	b	c	d
042	a	b	c	d	092	a	b	c	d
043	a	b	c	d	093	a	b	c	d
044	a	b	c	d	094	a	b	c	d
045	a	b	c	d	095	a	b	c	d
046	a	b	c	d	096	a	b	c	d
047	a	b	c	d	097	a	b	c	d
048	a	b	c	d	098	a	b	c	d
049	a	b	c	d	099	a	b	c	d
050	a	b	c	d	100	a	b	c	d

DECLARATION BY THE CANDIDATE

I declare that particulars and signature on this OMR Answer sheet are mine and are Name as in Attendance Sheet. I fruther declare that particulars filled in and Signature as well as the circles darkened on this ORIGINALCOPY is same as in OFFICE COPY.

Signature with time (in running handwriting)

CANDIDATE's NAME (in running handwriting)

MOTHER's NAME (in running handwriting)

FATHER's NAME (in running handwriting)

CANDIDATE LEFT HAND IMPRESSION

SIGNATURE OF INVIGILATOR'S WITH TIME

1

2

OMR SHEET

ROLL No.

1	1	1	1	1	1	1	1	1	1
2	2	2	2	2	2	2	2	2	2
3	3	3	3	3	3	3	3	3	3
4	4	4	4	4	4	4	4	4	4
5	5	5	5	5	5	5	5	5	5
6	6	6	6	6	6	6	6	6	6
7	7	7	7	7	7	7	7	7	7
8	8	8	8	8	8	8	8	8	8
9	9	9	9	9	9	9	9	9	9
0	0	0	0	0	0	0	0	0	0

TEST BOOKLET No.

1	1	1	1	1	1	1
2	2	2	2	2	2	2
3	3	3	3	3	3	3
4	4	4	4	4	4	4
5	5	5	5	5	5	5
6	6	6	6	6	6	6
7	7	7	7	7	7	7
8	8	8	8	8	8	8
9	9	9	9	9	9	9
0	0	0	0	0	0	0

TEST BOOKLET Code

Q No.	Response				Q No.	Response			
001	a	b	c	d	051	a	b	c	d
002	a	b	c	d	052	a	b	c	d
003	a	b	c	d	053	a	b	c	d
004	a	b	c	d	054	a	b	c	d
005	a	b	c	d	055	a	b	c	d
006	a	b	c	d	056	a	b	c	d
007	a	b	c	d	057	a	b	c	d
008	a	b	c	d	058	a	b	c	d
009	a	b	c	d	059	a	b	c	d
010	a	b	c	d	060	a	b	c	d
011	a	b	c	d	061	a	b	c	d
012	a	b	c	d	062	a	b	c	d
013	a	b	c	d	063	a	b	c	d
014	a	b	c	d	064	a	b	c	d
015	a	b	c	d	065	a	b	c	d
016	a	b	c	d	066	a	b	c	d
017	a	b	c	d	067	a	b	c	d
018	a	b	c	d	068	a	b	c	d
019	a	b	c	d	069	a	b	c	d
020	a	b	c	d	070	a	b	c	d
021	a	b	c	d	071	a	b	c	d
022	a	b	c	d	072	a	b	c	d
023	a	b	c	d	073	a	b	c	d
024	a	b	c	d	074	a	b	c	d
025	a	b	c	d	075	a	b	c	d
026	a	b	c	d	076	a	b	c	d
027	a	b	c	d	077	a	b	c	d
028	a	b	c	d	078	a	b	c	d
029	a	b	c	d	079	a	b	c	d
030	a	b	c	d	080	a	b	c	d
031	a	b	c	d	081	a	b	c	d
032	a	b	c	d	082	a	b	c	d
033	a	b	c	d	083	a	b	c	d
034	a	b	c	d	084	a	b	c	d
035	a	b	c	d	085	a	b	c	d
036	a	b	c	d	086	a	b	c	d
037	a	b	c	d	087	a	b	c	d
038	a	b	c	d	088	a	b	c	d
039	a	b	c	d	089	a	b	c	d
040	a	b	c	d	090	a	b	c	d
041	a	b	c	d	091	a	b	c	d
042	a	b	c	d	092	a	b	c	d
043	a	b	c	d	093	a	b	c	d
044	a	b	c	d	094	a	b	c	d
045	a	b	c	d	095	a	b	c	d
046	a	b	c	d	096	a	b	c	d
047	a	b	c	d	097	a	b	c	d
048	a	b	c	d	098	a	b	c	d
049	a	b	c	d	099	a	b	c	d
050	a	b	c	d	100	a	b	c	d

DECLARATION BY THE CANDIDATE

I declare that particulars and signature on this OMR Answer sheet are mine and are Name as in Attendance Sheet. I fruther declare that particulars filled in and Signature as well as the circles darkened on this ORIGINALCOPY is same as in OFFICE COPY.

Signature with time (in running handwriting)

CANDIDATE's NAME (in running handwriting)

MOTHER's NAME (in running handwriting)

FATHER's NAME (in running handwriting)

CANDIDATE LEFT HAND IMPRESSION

SIGNATURE OF INVIGILATOR'S WITH TIME

1

2

MEDACE

OMR SHEET

ROLL No.

1	1	1	1	1	1	1	1	1	1
2	2	2	2	2	2	2	2	2	2
3	3	3	3	3	3	3	3	3	3
4	4	4	4	4	4	4	4	4	4
5	5	5	5	5	5	5	5	5	5
6	6	6	6	6	6	6	6	6	6
7	7	7	7	7	7	7	7	7	7
8	8	8	8	8	8	8	8	8	8
9	9	9	9	9	9	9	9	9	9
0	0	0	0	0	0	0	0	0	0

TEST BOOKLET No.

1	1	1	1	1	1	1
2	2	2	2	2	2	2
3	3	3	3	3	3	3
4	4	4	4	4	4	4
5	5	5	5	5	5	5
6	6	6	6	6	6	6
7	7	7	7	7	7	7
8	8	8	8	8	8	8
9	9	9	9	9	9	9
0	0	0	0	0	0	0

TEST BOOKLET Code

Q No.	Response				Q No.	Response			
001	a	b	c	d	051	a	b	c	d
002	a	b	c	d	052	a	b	c	d
003	a	b	c	d	053	a	b	c	d
004	a	b	c	d	054	a	b	c	d
005	a	b	c	d	055	a	b	c	d
006	a	b	c	d	056	a	b	c	d
007	a	b	c	d	057	a	b	c	d
008	a	b	c	d	058	a	b	c	d
009	a	b	c	d	059	a	b	c	d
010	a	b	c	d	060	a	b	c	d
011	a	b	c	d	061	a	b	c	d
012	a	b	c	d	062	a	b	c	d
013	a	b	c	d	063	a	b	c	d
014	a	b	c	d	064	a	b	c	d
015	a	b	c	d	065	a	b	c	d
016	a	b	c	d	066	a	b	c	d
017	a	b	c	d	067	a	b	c	d
018	a	b	c	d	068	a	b	c	d
019	a	b	c	d	069	a	b	c	d
020	a	b	c	d	070	a	b	c	d
021	a	b	c	d	071	a	b	c	d
022	a	b	c	d	072	a	b	c	d
023	a	b	c	d	073	a	b	c	d
024	a	b	c	d	074	a	b	c	d
025	a	b	c	d	075	a	b	c	d
026	a	b	c	d	076	a	b	c	d
027	a	b	c	d	077	a	b	c	d
028	a	b	c	d	078	a	b	c	d
029	a	b	c	d	079	a	b	c	d
030	a	b	c	d	080	a	b	c	d
031	a	b	c	d	081	a	b	c	d
032	a	b	c	d	082	a	b	c	d
033	a	b	c	d	083	a	b	c	d
034	a	b	c	d	084	a	b	c	d
035	a	b	c	d	085	a	b	c	d
036	a	b	c	d	086	a	b	c	d
037	a	b	c	d	087	a	b	c	d
038	a	b	c	d	088	a	b	c	d
039	a	b	c	d	089	a	b	c	d
040	a	b	c	d	090	a	b	c	d
041	a	b	c	d	091	a	b	c	d
042	a	b	c	d	092	a	b	c	d
043	a	b	c	d	093	a	b	c	d
044	a	b	c	d	094	a	b	c	d
045	a	b	c	d	095	a	b	c	d
046	a	b	c	d	096	a	b	c	d
047	a	b	c	d	097	a	b	c	d
048	a	b	c	d	098	a	b	c	d
049	a	b	c	d	099	a	b	c	d
050	a	b	c	d	100	a	b	c	d

DECLARATION BY THE CANDIDATE

I declare that particulars and signature on this OMR Answer sheet are mine and are Name as in Attendance Sheet. I fruther declare that particulars filled in and Signature as well as the circles darkened on this ORIGINALCOPY is same as in OFFICE COPY.

Signature with time (in running handwriting)

CANDIDATE's NAME (in running handwriting)

MOTHER's NAME (in running handwriting)

FATHER's NAME (in running handwriting)

CANDIDATE LEFT HAND IMPRESSION

SIGNATURE OF INVIGILATOR'S WITH TIME

1

2

OMR SHEET

ROLL No.

1	1	1	1	1	1	1	1	1	1
2	2	2	2	2	2	2	2	2	2
3	3	3	3	3	3	3	3	3	3
4	4	4	4	4	4	4	4	4	4
5	5	5	5	5	5	5	5	5	5
6	6	6	6	6	6	6	6	6	6
7	7	7	7	7	7	7	7	7	7
8	8	8	8	8	8	8	8	8	8
9	9	9	9	9	9	9	9	9	9
0	0	0	0	0	0	0	0	0	0

TEST BOOKLET No.

1	1	1	1	1	1	1
2	2	2	2	2	2	2
3	3	3	3	3	3	3
4	4	4	4	4	4	4
5	5	5	5	5	5	5
6	6	6	6	6	6	6
7	7	7	7	7	7	7
8	8	8	8	8	8	8
9	9	9	9	9	9	9
0	0	0	0	0	0	0

TEST BOOKLET Code

Q No.	Response				Q No.	Response			
001	a	b	c	d	051	a	b	c	d
002	a	b	c	d	052	a	b	c	d
003	a	b	c	d	053	a	b	c	d
004	a	b	c	d	054	a	b	c	d
005	a	b	c	d	055	a	b	c	d
006	a	b	c	d	056	a	b	c	d
007	a	b	c	d	057	a	b	c	d
008	a	b	c	d	058	a	b	c	d
009	a	b	c	d	059	a	b	c	d
010	a	b	c	d	060	a	b	c	d
011	a	b	c	d	061	a	b	c	d
012	a	b	c	d	062	a	b	c	d
013	a	b	c	d	063	a	b	c	d
014	a	b	c	d	064	a	b	c	d
015	a	b	c	d	065	a	b	c	d
016	a	b	c	d	066	a	b	c	d
017	a	b	c	d	067	a	b	c	d
018	a	b	c	d	068	a	b	c	d
019	a	b	c	d	069	a	b	c	d
020	a	b	c	d	070	a	b	c	d
021	a	b	c	d	071	a	b	c	d
022	a	b	c	d	072	a	b	c	d
023	a	b	c	d	073	a	b	c	d
024	a	b	c	d	074	a	b	c	d
025	a	b	c	d	075	a	b	c	d
026	a	b	c	d	076	a	b	c	d
027	a	b	c	d	077	a	b	c	d
028	a	b	c	d	078	a	b	c	d
029	a	b	c	d	079	a	b	c	d
030	a	b	c	d	080	a	b	c	d
031	a	b	c	d	081	a	b	c	d
032	a	b	c	d	082	a	b	c	d
033	a	b	c	d	083	a	b	c	d
034	a	b	c	d	084	a	b	c	d
035	a	b	c	d	085	a	b	c	d
036	a	b	c	d	086	a	b	c	d
037	a	b	c	d	087	a	b	c	d
038	a	b	c	d	088	a	b	c	d
039	a	b	c	d	089	a	b	c	d
040	a	b	c	d	090	a	b	c	d
041	a	b	c	d	091	a	b	c	d
042	a	b	c	d	092	a	b	c	d
043	a	b	c	d	093	a	b	c	d
044	a	b	c	d	094	a	b	c	d
045	a	b	c	d	095	a	b	c	d
046	a	b	c	d	096	a	b	c	d
047	a	b	c	d	097	a	b	c	d
048	a	b	c	d	098	a	b	c	d
049	a	b	c	d	099	a	b	c	d
050	a	b	c	d	100	a	b	c	d

DECLARATION BY THE CANDIDATE

I declare that particulars and signature on this OMR Answer sheet are mine and are Name as in Attendance Sheet. I fruther declare that particulars filled in and Signature as well as the circles darkened on this ORIGINALCOPY is same as in OFFICE COPY.

Signature with time (in running handwriting)

CANDIDATE's NAME (in running handwriting)

MOTHER's NAME (in running handwriting)

FATHER's NAME (in running handwriting)

CANDIDATE LEFT HAND IMPRESSION

SIGNATURE OF INVIGILATOR'S WITH TIME

1

2

MEDACE

OMR SHEET

ROLL No.

1	1	1	1	1	1	1	1	1	1
2	2	2	2	2	2	2	2	2	2
3	3	3	3	3	3	3	3	3	3
4	4	4	4	4	4	4	4	4	4
5	5	5	5	5	5	5	5	5	5
6	6	6	6	6	6	6	6	6	6
7	7	7	7	7	7	7	7	7	7
8	8	8	8	8	8	8	8	8	8
9	9	9	9	9	9	9	9	9	9
0	0	0	0	0	0	0	0	0	0

TEST BOOKLET No.

1	1	1	1	1	1	1
2	2	2	2	2	2	2
3	3	3	3	3	3	3
4	4	4	4	4	4	4
5	5	5	5	5	5	5
6	6	6	6	6	6	6
7	7	7	7	7	7	7
8	8	8	8	8	8	8
9	9	9	9	9	9	9
0	0	0	0	0	0	0

TEST BOOKLET Code

Q No.	Response				Q No.	Response			
001	a	b	c	d	051	a	b	c	d
002	a	b	c	d	052	a	b	c	d
003	a	b	c	d	053	a	b	c	d
004	a	b	c	d	054	a	b	c	d
005	a	b	c	d	055	a	b	c	d
006	a	b	c	d	056	a	b	c	d
007	a	b	c	d	057	a	b	c	d
008	a	b	c	d	058	a	b	c	d
009	a	b	c	d	059	a	b	c	d
010	a	b	c	d	060	a	b	c	d
011	a	b	c	d	061	a	b	c	d
012	a	b	c	d	062	a	b	c	d
013	a	b	c	d	063	a	b	c	d
014	a	b	c	d	064	a	b	c	d
015	a	b	c	d	065	a	b	c	d
016	a	b	c	d	066	a	b	c	d
017	a	b	c	d	067	a	b	c	d
018	a	b	c	d	068	a	b	c	d
019	a	b	c	d	069	a	b	c	d
020	a	b	c	d	070	a	b	c	d
021	a	b	c	d	071	a	b	c	d
022	a	b	c	d	072	a	b	c	d
023	a	b	c	d	073	a	b	c	d
024	a	b	c	d	074	a	b	c	d
025	a	b	c	d	075	a	b	c	d
026	a	b	c	d	076	a	b	c	d
027	a	b	c	d	077	a	b	c	d
028	a	b	c	d	078	a	b	c	d
029	a	b	c	d	079	a	b	c	d
030	a	b	c	d	080	a	b	c	d
031	a	b	c	d	081	a	b	c	d
032	a	b	c	d	082	a	b	c	d
033	a	b	c	d	083	a	b	c	d
034	a	b	c	d	084	a	b	c	d
035	a	b	c	d	085	a	b	c	d
036	a	b	c	d	086	a	b	c	d
037	a	b	c	d	087	a	b	c	d
038	a	b	c	d	088	a	b	c	d
039	a	b	c	d	089	a	b	c	d
040	a	b	c	d	090	a	b	c	d
041	a	b	c	d	091	a	b	c	d
042	a	b	c	d	092	a	b	c	d
043	a	b	c	d	093	a	b	c	d
044	a	b	c	d	094	a	b	c	d
045	a	b	c	d	095	a	b	c	d
046	a	b	c	d	096	a	b	c	d
047	a	b	c	d	097	a	b	c	d
048	a	b	c	d	098	a	b	c	d
049	a	b	c	d	099	a	b	c	d
050	a	b	c	d	100	a	b	c	d

DECLARATION BY THE CANDIDATE

I declare that particulars and signature on this OMR Answer sheet are mine and are Name as in Attendance Sheet. I fruther declare that particulars filled in and Signature as well as the circles darkened on this ORIGINALCOPY is same as in OFFICE COPY.

Signature with time (in running handwriting)

CANDIDATE's NAME (in running handwriting)

MOTHER's NAME (in running handwriting)

FATHER's NAME (in running handwriting)

CANDIDATE LEFT HAND IMPRESSION

SIGNATURE OF INVIGILATOR'S WITH TIME

1

2

MEDACE

OMR SHEET

ROLL No.

1	1	1	1	1	1	1	1	1	1
2	2	2	2	2	2	2	2	2	2
3	3	3	3	3	3	3	3	3	3
4	4	4	4	4	4	4	4	4	4
5	5	5	5	5	5	5	5	5	5
6	6	6	6	6	6	6	6	6	6
7	7	7	7	7	7	7	7	7	7
8	8	8	8	8	8	8	8	8	8
9	9	9	9	9	9	9	9	9	9
0	0	0	0	0	0	0	0	0	0

TEST BOOKLET No.

1	1	1	1	1	1	1
2	2	2	2	2	2	2
3	3	3	3	3	3	3
4	4	4	4	4	4	4
5	5	5	5	5	5	5
6	6	6	6	6	6	6
7	7	7	7	7	7	7
8	8	8	8	8	8	8
9	9	9	9	9	9	9
0	0	0	0	0	0	0

TEST BOOKLET Code

DECLARATION BY THE CANDIDATE

I declare that particulars and signature on this OMR Answer sheet are mine and are Name as in Attendance Sheet. I fruther declare that particulars filled in and Signature as well as the circles darkened on this ORIGINALCOPY is same as in OFFICE COPY.

Signature with time (in running handwriting)

CANDIDATE's NAME (in running handwriting)

Q No.	Response				Q No.	Response			
001	a	b	c	d	051	a	b	c	d
002	a	b	c	d	052	a	b	c	d
003	a	b	c	d	053	a	b	c	d
004	a	b	c	d	054	a	b	c	d
005	a	b	c	d	055	a	b	c	d
006	a	b	c	d	056	a	b	c	d
007	a	b	c	d	057	a	b	c	d
008	a	b	c	d	058	a	b	c	d
009	a	b	c	d	059	a	b	c	d
010	a	b	c	d	060	a	b	c	d
011	a	b	c	d	061	a	b	c	d
012	a	b	c	d	062	a	b	c	d
013	a	b	c	d	063	a	b	c	d
014	a	b	c	d	064	a	b	c	d
015	a	b	c	d	065	a	b	c	d
016	a	b	c	d	066	a	b	c	d
017	a	b	c	d	067	a	b	c	d
018	a	b	c	d	068	a	b	c	d
019	a	b	c	d	069	a	b	c	d
020	a	b	c	d	070	a	b	c	d
021	a	b	c	d	071	a	b	c	d
022	a	b	c	d	072	a	b	c	d
023	a	b	c	d	073	a	b	c	d
024	a	b	c	d	074	a	b	c	d
025	a	b	c	d	075	a	b	c	d
026	a	b	c	d	076	a	b	c	d
027	a	b	c	d	077	a	b	c	d
028	a	b	c	d	078	a	b	c	d
029	a	b	c	d	079	a	b	c	d
030	a	b	c	d	080	a	b	c	d
031	a	b	c	d	081	a	b	c	d
032	a	b	c	d	082	a	b	c	d
033	a	b	c	d	083	a	b	c	d
034	a	b	c	d	084	a	b	c	d
035	a	b	c	d	085	a	b	c	d
036	a	b	c	d	086	a	b	c	d
037	a	b	c	d	087	a	b	c	d
038	a	b	c	d	088	a	b	c	d
039	a	b	c	d	089	a	b	c	d
040	a	b	c	d	090	a	b	c	d
041	a	b	c	d	091	a	b	c	d
042	a	b	c	d	092	a	b	c	d
043	a	b	c	d	093	a	b	c	d
044	a	b	c	d	094	a	b	c	d
045	a	b	c	d	095	a	b	c	d
046	a	b	c	d	096	a	b	c	d
047	a	b	c	d	097	a	b	c	d
048	a	b	c	d	098	a	b	c	d
049	a	b	c	d	099	a	b	c	d
050	a	b	c	d	100	a	b	c	d

MOTHER's NAME (in running handwriting)

FATHER's NAME (in running handwriting)

CANDIDATE LEFT HAND IMPRESSION

SIGNATURE OF INVIGILATOR'S WITH TIME

1

2

MEDACE

OMR SHEET

ROLL No.

1	1	1	1	1	1	1	1	1	1
2	2	2	2	2	2	2	2	2	2
3	3	3	3	3	3	3	3	3	3
4	4	4	4	4	4	4	4	4	4
5	5	5	5	5	5	5	5	5	5
6	6	6	6	6	6	6	6	6	6
7	7	7	7	7	7	7	7	7	7
8	8	8	8	8	8	8	8	8	8
9	9	9	9	9	9	9	9	9	9
0	0	0	0	0	0	0	0	0	0

TEST BOOKLET No.

1	1	1	1	1	1	1
2	2	2	2	2	2	2
3	3	3	3	3	3	3
4	4	4	4	4	4	4
5	5	5	5	5	5	5
6	6	6	6	6	6	6
7	7	7	7	7	7	7
8	8	8	8	8	8	8
9	9	9	9	9	9	9
0	0	0	0	0	0	0

TEST BOOKLET Code

DECLARATION BY THE CANDIDATE

I declare that particulars and signature on this OMR Answer sheet are mine and are Name as in Attendance Sheet. I fruther declare that particulars filled in and Signature as well as the circles darkened on this ORIGINALCOPY is same as in OFFICE COPY.

Signature with time (in running handwriting)

CANDIDATE's NAME (in running handwriting)

Q No.	Response				Q No.	Response			
001	a	b	c	d	051	a	b	c	d
002	a	b	c	d	052	a	b	c	d
003	a	b	c	d	053	a	b	c	d
004	a	b	c	d	054	a	b	c	d
005	a	b	c	d	055	a	b	c	d
006	a	b	c	d	056	a	b	c	d
007	a	b	c	d	057	a	b	c	d
008	a	b	c	d	058	a	b	c	d
009	a	b	c	d	059	a	b	c	d
010	a	b	c	d	060	a	b	c	d
011	a	b	c	d	061	a	b	c	d
012	a	b	c	d	062	a	b	c	d
013	a	b	c	d	063	a	b	c	d
014	a	b	c	d	064	a	b	c	d
015	a	b	c	d	065	a	b	c	d
016	a	b	c	d	066	a	b	c	d
017	a	b	c	d	067	a	b	c	d
018	a	b	c	d	068	a	b	c	d
019	a	b	c	d	069	a	b	c	d
020	a	b	c	d	070	a	b	c	d
021	a	b	c	d	071	a	b	c	d
022	a	b	c	d	072	a	b	c	d
023	a	b	c	d	073	a	b	c	d
024	a	b	c	d	074	a	b	c	d
025	a	b	c	d	075	a	b	c	d
026	a	b	c	d	076	a	b	c	d
027	a	b	c	d	077	a	b	c	d
028	a	b	c	d	078	a	b	c	d
029	a	b	c	d	079	a	b	c	d
030	a	b	c	d	080	a	b	c	d
031	a	b	c	d	081	a	b	c	d
032	a	b	c	d	082	a	b	c	d
033	a	b	c	d	083	a	b	c	d
034	a	b	c	d	084	a	b	c	d
035	a	b	c	d	085	a	b	c	d
036	a	b	c	d	086	a	b	c	d
037	a	b	c	d	087	a	b	c	d
038	a	b	c	d	088	a	b	c	d
039	a	b	c	d	089	a	b	c	d
040	a	b	c	d	090	a	b	c	d
041	a	b	c	d	091	a	b	c	d
042	a	b	c	d	092	a	b	c	d
043	a	b	c	d	093	a	b	c	d
044	a	b	c	d	094	a	b	c	d
045	a	b	c	d	095	a	b	c	d
046	a	b	c	d	096	a	b	c	d
047	a	b	c	d	097	a	b	c	d
048	a	b	c	d	098	a	b	c	d
049	a	b	c	d	099	a	b	c	d
050	a	b	c	d	100	a	b	c	d

MOTHER's NAME (in running handwriting)	FATHER's NAME (in running handwriting)

CANDIDATE LEFT HAND IMPRESSION	SIGNATURE OF INVIGILATOR'S WITH TIME
	1
	2

MEDACE

OMR SHEET

ROLL No.

1	1	1	1	1	1	1	1	1	1
2	2	2	2	2	2	2	2	2	2
3	3	3	3	3	3	3	3	3	3
4	4	4	4	4	4	4	4	4	4
5	5	5	5	5	5	5	5	5	5
6	6	6	6	6	6	6	6	6	6
7	7	7	7	7	7	7	7	7	7
8	8	8	8	8	8	8	8	8	8
9	9	9	9	9	9	9	9	9	9
0	0	0	0	0	0	0	0	0	0

TEST BOOKLET No.

1	1	1	1	1	1	1
2	2	2	2	2	2	2
3	3	3	3	3	3	3
4	4	4	4	4	4	4
5	5	5	5	5	5	5
6	6	6	6	6	6	6
7	7	7	7	7	7	7
8	8	8	8	8	8	8
9	9	9	9	9	9	9
0	0	0	0	0	0	0

TEST BOOKLET Code

Q No.	Response				Q No.	Response			
001	a	b	c	d	051	a	b	c	d
002	a	b	c	d	052	a	b	c	d
003	a	b	c	d	053	a	b	c	d
004	a	b	c	d	054	a	b	c	d
005	a	b	c	d	055	a	b	c	d
006	a	b	c	d	056	a	b	c	d
007	a	b	c	d	057	a	b	c	d
008	a	b	c	d	058	a	b	c	d
009	a	b	c	d	059	a	b	c	d
010	a	b	c	d	060	a	b	c	d
011	a	b	c	d	061	a	b	c	d
012	a	b	c	d	062	a	b	c	d
013	a	b	c	d	063	a	b	c	d
014	a	b	c	d	064	a	b	c	d
015	a	b	c	d	065	a	b	c	d
016	a	b	c	d	066	a	b	c	d
017	a	b	c	d	067	a	b	c	d
018	a	b	c	d	068	a	b	c	d
019	a	b	c	d	069	a	b	c	d
020	a	b	c	d	070	a	b	c	d
021	a	b	c	d	071	a	b	c	d
022	a	b	c	d	072	a	b	c	d
023	a	b	c	d	073	a	b	c	d
024	a	b	c	d	074	a	b	c	d
025	a	b	c	d	075	a	b	c	d
026	a	b	c	d	076	a	b	c	d
027	a	b	c	d	077	a	b	c	d
028	a	b	c	d	078	a	b	c	d
029	a	b	c	d	079	a	b	c	d
030	a	b	c	d	080	a	b	c	d
031	a	b	c	d	081	a	b	c	d
032	a	b	c	d	082	a	b	c	d
033	a	b	c	d	083	a	b	c	d
034	a	b	c	d	084	a	b	c	d
035	a	b	c	d	085	a	b	c	d
036	a	b	c	d	086	a	b	c	d
037	a	b	c	d	087	a	b	c	d
038	a	b	c	d	088	a	b	c	d
039	a	b	c	d	089	a	b	c	d
040	a	b	c	d	090	a	b	c	d
041	a	b	c	d	091	a	b	c	d
042	a	b	c	d	092	a	b	c	d
043	a	b	c	d	093	a	b	c	d
044	a	b	c	d	094	a	b	c	d
045	a	b	c	d	095	a	b	c	d
046	a	b	c	d	096	a	b	c	d
047	a	b	c	d	097	a	b	c	d
048	a	b	c	d	098	a	b	c	d
049	a	b	c	d	099	a	b	c	d
050	a	b	c	d	100	a	b	c	d

DECLARATION BY THE CANDIDATE

I declare that particulars and signature on this OMR Answer sheet are mine and are Name as in Attendance Sheet. I fruther declare that particulars filled in and Signature as well as the circles darkened on this ORIGINALCOPY is same as in OFFICE COPY.

Signature with time (in running handwriting)

CANDIDATE's NAME (in running handwriting)

MOTHER's NAME (in running handwriting)

FATHER's NAME (in running handwriting)

CANDIDATE LEFT HAND IMPRESSION

SIGNATURE OF INVIGILATOR'S WITH TIME

1

2